DICTIONARY OF BIBLICAL THEOLOGY

Dictionary of
BIBLICAL
THEOLOGY

UPDATED SECOND EDITION

EDITED UNDER THE DIRECTION OF
Xavier Léon-Dufour

Translated under the direction of P. Joseph Cahill S.J.
Revisions and new articles translated by E. M. Stewart.

The Word Among Us Press
9639 Doctor Perry Road
Ijamsville, Maryland 21754

www.wau.org

Originally published under the title *Vocabulaire de theologie biblique*, © 1962, 1968
Les Editions du Cerf, Paris

English translation © 1967, 1973, 1988 Geoffrey Chapman, a Cassell imprint

English edition first published 1967
Second edition, revised and enlarged 1973
First English paperback edition 1982
Reprinted with revisions 1988
Reprinted 1992, 1995, 2000

Published by arrangement with HarperSanFrancisco Publishers, Inc.
All rights reserved.

ISBN 0-932085-09-1

Made and printed in the U.S.A.

FOREWORD TO THE SECOND EDITION

It is now six years since the English edition of this work, now known as the Dictionary of Biblical Theology, *was first published. The French edition was first published in 1962. The welcome it received was beyond all expectations. 70,000 copies of the French edition have circulated throughout Christian circles. In the British Commonwealth alone, 10,000 copies of the English version have sold. And it can be said without exaggeration that its readership will soon be worldwide since it has already appeared in Arabic, Chinese, Croatian, Dutch, German, Greek, Hungarian, Italian, Japanese, Polish, Portuguese, Russian, Spanish, and Vietnamese; translations into Czech, Korean, Tamil and Ukrainian are nearly complete.*

A new edition seemed desirable as far as possible to take into account the suggestions received since the Dictionary *first appeared. Most of the articles have been revised and corrected by their respective authors. Forty new articles have been added, which complete the first edition on certain, sometimes important, topics:*

> *Aaron, Abel, Adultery, Anathema, Anguish, Apparitions of Christ, Ashes, Burial, City, Conscience, Cupidity, Deception/Disappointment, Dove, Dreams, Farewell Speeches, Head, Heresy, Jesus Christ, Joshua, Magic, Melchizedek, Noah, Oath, Old Age, Perfume, Pilgrimage, Predestine, Providence, Responsibility, Rights/Laws, Run, Salt, Schism, Sexuality, Sign, Tenderness, Virtues & Vices, Violence, Widows, Yahweh.*

Fuller and more detailed cross-references have been added at the end of each article, in order to help the reader looking for extended information to find without difficulty the extra information on the theme that interests him. To make the book still more easy to use, those words to which no article has been devoted but which can be associated with one or other article have been inserted in the course of the book, in their place alphabetically. This enabled us to do away with the Analytic Table *that appeared at the back of the book in the first edition. To give an example of this system: we find in sequence:* Aaron *(an article with its own cross-references),* Abandonment *and* Abba *(references to various articles),* Abel *(an article with its own cross-references), and so on. This list has been worked out methodically over the course of many months by Mlle Jacqueline Thevenet under the direction of Père Xavier Léon-Dufour.*

The reader will not, of course, find every word with a theological connotation or association, nor even all the synonyms of the words dealt with in the articles, in the alphabetical sequence. On the other hand, he will find there certain traditional terms connected with biblical language, such as decalogue, deposit . . . , *some words related to the words dealt with in the articles, such as* devil, road . . . , *some current expressions that one would expect to find treated, such as* eschatology, parousia . . . , *and, finally, words that for reasons of economy have been grouped together under one entry, such as* healing, temptation, evil. *More often than not precise directions enable the reader to find the exact place in the article to which he is referred, but of course there is nothing to stop him from reading further.*

FOREWORD TO THE SECOND EDITION

An Index *has been set at the end of the book, drawn up by Père Marc-François Lacan, so that the reader is able to regroup the themes, which appear in alphabetical order throughout the book. There is a note at the head of this index that explains how it has been compiled and how it is to be used.*

We had hoped to offer readers of the first edition a separate booklet to spare them the expense of buying the new edition. But this idea had to be abandoned in their own interests. The fact is that the changes to the original articles are so numerous and so widespread that they could not possibly have been reproduced in the proposed booklet. Moreover, the subdivisions of the articles have been so greatly altered that the cross-references would have been difficult to use with the first edition. It seemed more reasonable not to involve the reader in something that would have been temporary and not very useful.

We are well aware that this new edition is neither final nor perfect; but we do hope that it represents a considerable advance on the preceding one, and we wish it as widespread and fruitful a success.

FOREWORD TO THE FIRST EDITION

The edition of Missel Biblique *was supplemented by a short Biblical Dictionary drawn up by Father Xavier Léon-Dufour in 1945. The preparation of this lexicon brought home to its compiler the necessity of a more profound work which would direct the clergy and the laity in reading the Bible and would lead them to a better understanding and more effective presentation of the Word of God. Based on a technical structure, major theological themes would be therein presented in a form easily understood. The double purpose, scientific and pastoral, made the proposed enterprise difficult. Only in January, 1958, on the occasion of a meeting of exegetes from in and around Lyons, was this project able to receive serious consideration. Meanwhile, similar works had appeared, Protestant as well as Catholic. Nonetheless, none of these works corresponded exactly to the book we had in mind which was to be a series of syntheses for pastoral use. For this reason the present work was proposed.*

The committee which assumed responsibility for this enterprise sought the help of all French-speaking professors of Sacred Scripture. The topics were finally divided among seventy collaborators. These men agreed to contribute to a project which would not be a simple collection of juxtaposed monographs but rather a truly communal piece of work. Through every stage of editing there were endless exchanges between the committee and the contributors. Prior to the final printing the articles were subjected to reconsiderations terminating in modifications of various degrees and, sometimes, in profound alterations. The two signatures affixed to the end of a third of the articles are visible evidence of this close collaboration demanded by the initial decision which had determined the goal of this work. Overall coordination had been assured by Father Xavier Léon-Dufour, secretary of the committee. Assisted especially by the Reverend Pierre Grelot, Father Léon-Dufour carried out the last revision and sought to achieve a total coherence within the book. To achieve a greater good, individual collaborators accepted their task, agreed to submit to discussion the finished investigations, to modify personal perspectives, and even to put aside personal views. For all of this we extend sincere thanks. The present work, therefore, is truly the result of team effort to accomplish a work of the Church, with all the mutual understanding and sacrifice involved in such large scale cooperation.

To the list of collaborators it would be necessary to add the names of our advisors in the fields of liturgical and pastoral theology, the names of those who assisted in the literary refinement of the articles, in checking references, and in proofreading. We mention here, however, only the memory of two deceased men, Father Victor Fontoynont, S.J., who first suggested this work, and Canon Albert Gelin, P.S.S., who was one of the original members of our committee.

*
* *

This work has been conceived within the perspective of biblical theology. Its

FOREWORD

title justifies the choice of words discussed and the method of presentation. We have eliminated everything which would give the book the appearance of an encyclopedia. The reader will not find here articles of an archeological type with detailed names of places, persons, etc. Nor will the reader find purely historical articles—dates of books, details of institutions, etc.—or general exegetical explanations such as questions of method, critical theories, etc. However, insofar as information of this type can contribute directly to the theological understanding of the Bible, that information is noted in passing or even at times becomes the subject of a particular paragraph. Likewise, certain presuppositions necessary by way of background are presented in the second part of the Introduction: each of the sacred books is there located in time and in the world of thought.

In an area of such broad dimensions one could give extensive treatment to the major themes of revelation. As much as possible, these themes have been related to information pertinent to the history of religions; in a certain number of cases liturgical or doctrinal implications have been indicated. The essentials, however, are found in the thematic outlines generally developed in historical order. Actually the Dictionary of Biblical Theology *is less concerned with semantic analysis of important and recurring Scriptural terms than with doctrinal investigation of themes often expressed by means of a variety of words. The semantic groundwork is always supposed, sometimes even moderately explained. But primarily we have attempted to guide the reader through the maze of ideas emerging from texts by opening avenues of approach. Title words are given in accord with this aim. We will not speak of the "deliberation" or "decree" of God but of His "plan," in order to conform to present usage. Articles devoted to "laughter" or to "pride" suppose a confrontation between biblical categories and modern thought patterns. For example, several Hebrew and Greek terms are signified by our one English word* pride. *Assuming the reader's viewpoint is a risk, namely that of leaving the concrete data of Scripture and entering the area of the lecture or the homily. We hope we have overcome this danger through a constant concern for objectivity and exactness.*

Despite the effort of the book to synthesize, there is present the evident analytical structure common to every dictionary. To alleviate slightly this disadvantage, the Introduction tries to express precisely the large and central dimensions of the Bible by a preliminary presentation of biblical language, a consideration to open the way to a biblical theology. In addition, at the end of each individual article, the reader is referred to other articles. This will allow the reader to follow through major themes. Numerous asterisks (*) run through the text as incessant reminders not to rely on mere common sense to determine the meaning and scope of the terms. We have not given a bibliography for each word. A bibliography limited to works in French would have been often too narrow and too rapidly outmoded.

The authors have not tried to furnish exhaustive biblical references; for this there are Concordances which are indispensable working tools. But an objectivity of this type, completely material, would have been unrealistic in the present project. As we have noted, this book intends to be synthetic. Surely the exegete correctly fears syntheses, for he knows the totality in the light of the limited data over which he has control. At the end of his study he would often prefer to reserve judgment, content to present whatever analyses he has made. But his reader cannot completely dispense with syntheses: despite precautions the reader will fabricate his own synthesis, regrouping in his own way materials which have a purely objective meaning. In place of these highly dangerous syntheses is it not preferable to have the modestly presented synthesis of the specialist? We have, therefore, attempted this venture hoping, in the interest of those who will use this book, to avoid the impression of being swallowed up in the dust of scattered details or the temptation to assemble details in artificial constructs.

The future will prove whether the Dictionary of Biblical Theology *satisfies both the often divergent needs of the scholar and the simple faithful. Its authors would hope, thanks to the dialogue which the book can open between exegete, on the one hand, and theologian and pastor of souls, on the other, that the book may gradually become less imperfect.*

SIGLA & ABBREVIATIONS

BOOKS OF THE BIBLE

Ac	Acts of the Apostles	2 K	2 Kings
Am	Amos	Lm	Lamentations
Ap	Apocalypse	Lv	Leviticus
Ba	Baruch	Lk	Luke
1 Ch	1 Chronicles	1 M	1 Maccabees
2 Ch	2 Chronicles	2 M	2 Maccabees
Col	Colossians	Ml	Malachi
1 Co	1 Corinthians	Mk	Mark
2 Co	2 Corinthians	Mt	Matthew
Dn	Daniel	Mi	Micah
Dt	Deuteronomy	Na	Nahum
E	Ephesians	Ne	Nehemiah
Es	Esther	Nm	Numbers
Ex	Exodus	Ob	Obadiah
Ez	Ezekiel	1 P	1 Peter
Ezr	Ezra	2 P	2 Peter
G	Galatians	Phm	Philemon
Gn	Genesis	Ph	Philippians
Ha	Habakkuk	Pr	Proverbs
Hg	Haggai	Ps	Psalms
He	Hebrews	Qo	Qoheleth (Ecclesiastes)
Ho	Hosea	R	Romans
Is	Isaiah	Rt	Ruth
Jm	James	1 S	1 Samuel
Jr	Jeremiah	2 S	2 Samuel
Jb	Job	Si	Ben Sira (Ecclesiasticus)
Jl	Joel	Ct	Song of Songs
Jn	John	1 Th	1 Thessalonians
1 Jn	1 John	2 Th	2 Thessalonians
2 Jn	2 John	1 Tm	1 Timothy
3 Jn	3 John	2 Tm	2 Timothy
Jon	Jonah	Tt	Titus
Js	Joshua	Tb	Tobit
Jude	Jude	Ws	Wisdom of Solomon
Jg	Judges	Ze	Zechariah
Jdt	Judith	Zp	Zephaniah
1 K	1 Kings		

TRANSCRIPTIONS

OTHER ABBREVIATIONS

From the Hebrew:

'	Aleph	NT	New Testament
ḥ	Heth	OT	Old Testament
'	Ayin	LXX	Septuagint (Greek Version)
ṣ	Tsahde	Sym	Symmachus (2nd cent Greek)
s	Sin and Samekh	Vulg.	Vulgate (Latin Version)
š	Shin	art.	article
ṭ	Teth	hb.	Hebrew
t	Taw	gr.	Greek
y	Yodh	i.e.	that is
		lat.	Latin

From the Greek:

h	rough breathing	f	and the following verse
ē	Eta	ff	and the two following verses
ô, ō	Omega	p	parallel passages
y	Upsilon	cf	confer
		vg	for example
		comp	compare
		v	verse
		vv	verses

CROSS REFERENCES

* = compare the indicated title or article
→ = compare the indicated titles or articles

EXAMPLES OF THE REFERENCES

1 Co 2,7	1 Corinthians, Chapter 2, Verse 7
1 Co 2,7f	1 Corinthians, Chapter 2, Verses 7 and 8
1 Co 2,7ff	1 Corinthians, Chapter 2, Verses 7, 8, and 9
1 Co 2,7-10	1 Corinthians, Chapter 2, Verses 7 to 10 inclusive
1 Co 2,7...	1 Corinthians, Chapter 2, Verses 7 and following
1 Co 2,7—3,4	1 Corinthians, Chapter 2, Verse 7 to Chapter 3, Verse 4 inclusive
1 Co 2,7.15	1 Corinthians, Chapter 2, Verse 7 and Verse 15
1 Co 2,7; 4,6	1 Corinthians, Chapter 2, Verse 7 and Chapter 4, Verse 6
Ps 55,23=1 P 5,7	The text of the psalm is cited by Peter

N.B.—In the *Introduction*, the reader will find the explanation or the designation for certain terms or of certain extra-biblical works: such as The Book of Henoch, Book of Jubilees, Psalms of Solomon, Midrash, Targums, etc.

LIST OF CONTRIBUTORS

†François Amiot, P.S.S.
Jean-Louis d'Aragon, S.J. (Montréal).
Jean Audusseau, S.M.M. (Marseille).
Charles Augrain, P.S.S. (Angers).
†Paul Auvray, P.O.
André Barucq, S.D.B. (Lyons).
Evode Beaucamp, O.F.M. (Montréal).
Paul Beauchamp, S.J. (Paris).
Gilles Becquet, F.M.C. (Loris, Loiret).
Pierre Benoit, O.P. (Jerusalem).
Marie-Emile Boismard, O.P. (Jerusalem).
†Pierre-Emile Bonnard.
Jean Brière, P.S.S. (Angers).
Jean-Baptiste Brunon, P.S.S. (Tulle).
Jules Cambier, S.D.B. (Louvain-la-Neuve).
Jean Cantinat, C.M. (Paris).
Henri Cazelles, P.S.S. (Paris).
Jean Corbon (Beirut).
André Darrieutort (Dax).
Jean Delorme (Lyons).
†Msgr. Albert Descamps.
Raymond Deville, P.S.S. (Paris).
Marcel Didier (Namur).
François Dreyfus, O.P. (Jerusalem).
†Jean Duplacy.
Jacques Dupont, O.S.B. (Ottignies, Belgium).
Jean-Marie Fenasse, O.M.I. (Brussels).
André Feuillet, P.S.S. (Paris).
René Feuillet, P.S.S. (Paris).
†Jean de Fraine, S.J.
Pierre-Marie Galopin, O.S.B. (Tournay).
†Augustin George, S.M.
Jean Giblet (Louvain).
Félix Gils, C.S.Sp. (Chevilly, Val-de-Marne).
Raymond Girard, P.S.S. (Lyons).
Pierre Grelot (Paris).

Jacques Guillet, S.J. (Paris).
Edgar Haulotte, S.J. (Paris).
Charles Hauret (Strasbourg).
Edmond Jacquemin, O.C.R. (Scourmont).
Michel Join-Lambert, P.O. (Strasbourg).
Marc-François Lacan, O.S.B. (Hautecombe).
Paul Lamarche, S.J. (Paris).
Xavier Léon-Dufour, S.J. (Paris).
Colomban Lesquivit, O.S.B. (Benet Lake, Wisconsin, U.S.A.).
Stanislas Lyonnet, S.J. (Rome).
†Donatien Mollat, S.J.
René Motte, O.M.I. (Solignac).
†Armand Négrier, P.S.S.
Joseph Pierron, M.E.P. (Paris).
Ignace de la Potterie, S.J. (Rome).
Maurice Prat, S.A.M. (Paris).
Jean Radermakers, S.J. (Brussels).
Marie-Léon Ramlot, O.P. (Toulouse).
Henri Renard (Lille).
Bernard Renaud (Strasbourg).
André Ridouard (Poitiers).
†Béda Rigaux, O.F.M.
Léon Roy, O.S.B. (Fontgombault).
Pierre Sandevoir (Paris).
Daniel Sesboüé (Le Mans).
Ceslas Spicq, O.P. (Fribourg, Switzerland).
Paul de Surgy (Brest).
Ladislas Szabó, S.J. (Beirut).
Paul Ternant, P.B. (Jerusalem).
Charles Thomas, P.S.S. (Angers).
Albert Vanhoye, S.J. (Rome).
Jules de Vaulx (Nancy).
André-Alphonse Viard, O.P. (Rome).
Claude Wiéner (Bobigny, Seine-St-Denis).

AUTHORS OF ARTICLES

(upper-case initials at end of articles)

AAV	André-Alphonse Viard		*JCan*	Jean Cantinat
AB	André Barucq		*JCo*	Jean Corbon
ADa	André Darrieutort		*JDel*	Jean Delorme
ADes	Albert Descamps		*JDt*	Jacques Dupont
AF	André Feuillet		*JDu*	Jean Duplacy
AG	Augustin George		*JdF*	Jean de Fraine
AN	Armand Négrier		*JG*	Jacques Guillet
AR	André Ridouard		*JGi*	Jean Giblet
AV	Albert Vanhoye		*JLA*	Jean-Louis d'Aragon
			JMF	Jean-Marie Fenasse
BRe	Bernard Renaud		*JP*	Joseph Pierron
BRi	Béda Rigaux		*JR*	Jean Radermakers
			JdV	Jules de Vaulx
CA	Charles Augrain			
CH	Charles Hauret		*LR*	Léon Roy
CL	Colomban Lesquivit		*LS*	Ladislas Szabó
CS	Ceslas Spicq			
CT	Charles Thomas		*MD*	Marcel Didier
CW	Claude Wiéner		*MEB*	Marie-Emile Boismard
			MFL	Marc-François Lacan
DM	Donatien Mollat		*MJL*	Michel Join-Lambert
DS	Daniel Sesboüé		*MLR*	Marie-Léon Ramlot
			MP	Maurice Prat
EB	Evode Beaucamp			
EH	Edgar Haulotte		*PA*	Paul Auvray
EJ	Edmond Jacquemin		*PBe*	Pierre Benoit
			PBp	Paul Beauchamp
FA	François Amiot		*PEB*	Pierre-Emile Bonnard
FD	François Dreyfus		*PG*	Pierre Grelot
FG	Félix Gils		*PL*	Paul Lamarche
			PMG	Pierre-Marie Galopin
GB	Gilles Becquet		*PS*	Pierre Sandevoir
			PdS	Paul de Surgy
HC	Henri Cazelles		*PT*	Paul Ternant
HR	Henri Renard			
			RD	Raymond Deville
IdlP	Ignace de la Potterie		*RF*	René Feuillet
			RG	Raymond Girard
			RM	René Motte
JA	Jean Audusseau			
JB	Jean Brière		*SL*	Stanislas Lyonnet
JBB	Jean-Baptiste Brunon			
JCa	Jules Cambier		*XLD*	Xavier Léon-Dufour

LIST OF TRANSLATORS

Glicerio S. Abad, S.P. (Philippines).
Henry J. Bourguignon, S.J. (Ann Arbor).
Patrick J. Boyle, S.J. (Cincinnati).
Joseph A. Bracken, S.J. (Freiburg).
Donald F. Brezine, S.J. (Cleveland).
John R. Crowley, S.J. (Munster).
John J. Kilgallen, S.J. (Vienna).
John P. Langan, S.J. (Chicago).
Arthur F. McGovern, S.J. (Paris).

Patrick H. McNamara, S.J. (San Francisco).
Maurice J. Moore, S.J. (Munster).
Robert C. O'Connor, S.J. (Drongen).
Thomas M. Spittler, S.J. (Cleveland).
Edward M. Stewart (Cotton College).
Joseph R. Sweeney, S.J. (Brussels).
Eugene C. Ulrich, S.J. (Cambridge).
W. Jared Wicks, S.J. (Munster).
William J. Young, S.J. (North Aurora).

TRANSLATORS OF ARTICLES

(lower-case initials at end of articles)

afmcg	Arthur F. McGovern	jrc	John R. Crowley
dfb	Donald F. Brezine	jrs	Joseph R. Sweeney
ecu	Eugene C. Ulrich	mjm	Maurice J. Moore
ems	Edward M. Stewart	phmcn	Patrick H. McNamara
gsa	Glicerio S. Abad	pjb	Patrick J. Boyle
hjb	Henry J. Bourguignon	rco'c	Robert C. O'Connor
jab	Joseph A. Bracken	tms	Thomas M. Spittler
jjk	John J. Kilgallen	wjw	W. Jared Wicks
jpl	John P. Langan	wjy	William J. Young

INTRODUCTION

I

BIBLICAL THEOLOGY AND THE DICTIONARY

The earlier outlines of this work did not foresee the word *theology* in the title; they envisaged only a "biblical dictionary" whose articles would emphasize the doctrinal and spiritual import of biblical words. But the initial work on these articles quickly made it clear that there exists a profound unity in the language of the Bible. Throughout the diversity of historical periods, environments, and events there is a true community of spirit and of expression among all the sacred authors. The unity of the Bible, an essential fact of faith, is verified on the concrete level of language. So was born the definitive title: *Dictionary of Biblical Theology*.

I. BIBLICAL THEOLOGY

Sacred Scripture is the Word of God to man; theology seeks to be the word of man about God. When theology limits its study to the immediate content of the inspired books, eager to listen to them in their own terms, to penetrate into their language—in brief, to become the precise echo of the Word of God—then theology is biblical in the strict sense of the term.

Such theology can be alert to differing points in the Bible, can gather together syntheses, more or less elaborated, more or less conscious, which mark the principal moments in the development of revelation. Yahwistic history and Deuteronomic history, the Sacerdotal tradition, the Wisdom tradition, the synoptic gospels, the Pauline doctrine and that in the epistle to the Hebrews, the apocalyptic fresco of John and the fourth gospel—all are so many "theologies" which can be explained in themselves. But likewise, from a much broader point of view we can consider the Bible as a whole. We can try to grasp the organic continuity and coherence which manifest the profound unity of these diverse theologies: this is biblical theology.

1. *The basis of unity.* Only faith declares with certitude the unity of the Bible and at the same time recognizes the boundaries of the Bible. Why have certain maxims of Wisdom folklore entered the canonical collection of Proverbs when some books of great religious value and comparable to the most beautiful of canonical writings —one thinks of the Parables of Henoch and the Psalms of Solomon—remained outside the Canon? Only faith supplies the criterion here. It is faith which transforms the various books of the Old and New Testament into an organic unit. Even for the man who may not share its vantage point, faith is presupposed as the point of departure for Biblical theology.

The unity of the Bible is not bookish; unity comes from the person who is its very center. The books of the Jewish Canon are for the Christian literally only the "Old" Testament; they announce and prepare the way for Him who has come and has completed them all: Jesus Christ. The books of the New Testament, completely dependent upon the appearance of Jesus Christ in history, are orientated to His return at the end of time. The OT, then, is Jesus Christ in preparation and in prefiguration; the NT, Jesus Christ who has come and is coming. This is that basic truth precisely formulated by Jesus Himself: "I have come, not to abolish the Law and the prophets, but to fulfill them." The fathers of the Church did not weary of reflecting on this fundamental principal and of using it to draw from the Bible itself very expressive figures of speech, comparing, for example, the NT to wine into which the water of the OT has been transformed. The articles in the *Dictionary* endeavor to participate in this profound movement of Christian thought which passes from figures* to fulfillment* until finally the newness* of the gospel appears. The consequences of such a principle are multiple. A biblical theology cannot, for example, isolate the teaching of Genesis on marriage* from that of Jesus and Paul on virginity*. The prototype of humanity is not the old Adam*; and not in the old Adam is the reason why men are brothers*, but rather in the new Adam, Jesus Christ.

Finally, the unity of the Bible is not only that of a center which polarizes men's experiences and orients their history. The unity is one of a life everywhere present, of a constantly dynamic spirit. Biblical theology is merely the echo of the Word of God as it was received by a people in the different stages of its existence, ultimately becoming the very substance of its thought. For the Word*, before being a teaching, is an event and a call. The Word is God Himself who has come to speak to His people, God who comes unceasingly, God who will come in His own day* to restore everything and to complete His plan* of salvation in Christ Jesus. This event, in which an intimate bond between God and men is sealed, the biblical authors describe by means of different terms: covenant*, election*, presence* of God, etc. Terminology is not as important as the acknowledgment of the event itself, which gives to all the authors a kind of mental affinity, an identical structure of thought and of faith. This structure becomes evident, for example, when the sacred writers react to materials furnished by neighboring cultures and religions. If they incorporate and purify them, it is always to put them at the service of the unique revelation, proceeding by diverse methods but always in the same general spirit. Whether it is a question of the imagery arising from the Babylonian myths on creation, or the Mesopotamian tradition of the flood*, or the symbolism of the storm* from Canaanite mythology, or the Persian concepts of angelology*, or the folklore which portrays satyrs and malevolent beasts*—all, in some way, is refined and refashioned as a consequence of faith in God the Creator whose plan of salvation develops in our history. This unity of spirit throughout the Bible animates the traditions and religious concepts and makes possible a biblical theology; that is, a synthetic understanding of the unique Word of God in all its aspects.

2. *Light upon the universe and on God.* The unity of the Bible is as simple as God, as vast as His Creation. Hence God alone can comprehend it in a simple glance. Employing the term *theological,* our book presupposes the unity of the divine work and the synthesis of the divine comprehension. In presenting this synthesis in the analytic form of a dictionary, we do not wish to discourage the reader from trying to understand the unity of the Bible, but only to avoid forcing on him

an abstract system, necessarily arbitrary in some places. With this affirmed, the reader is invited to page from one article to another, to compare and group them in order to draw from comparisons a real understanding of the faith.

Furthermore, this method is basic in dealing with the Bible. By successively assuming the perspectives of the Books of Samuel and Chronicles, the reader acquires a more nuanced knowledge of David in his own times and in the memory of Israel. Similarly, the mystery of Jesus becomes more profound when the reader approaches it through the varied viewpoints of the four evangelists. In this fashion, the *Dictionary* gives the reader a better understanding of the mystery of the covenant because of an approach through the varied expressions of past history: people* of God, kingdom*, Church*; an approach through its guiding figures. Abraham*, Moses*, David*, Elijah*, John* the Baptist, Peter*, or Mary*; through its institutions: the ark*, the altar*, the temple*, the Law*; through those who defended the covenant: the prophets*, the priests*, the apostles*; through its fulfillment despite its enemies: the world*, the Antichrist*, Satan*, the beast*. Likewise, the man of prayer appears here in his various postures: adoration*, praise*, silence*, kneeling, thanksgiving*, blessing*—so numerous are the reactions of man in the presence of the God who comes to him.

We must go still further and discover (is this not the task of theology?) the presence of God in every place and in every age. For the personality of Yahweh, the Lord of history, has repercussions on His entire work. Without doubt it is important to locate certain anthropological ideas, taken over by the Bible, which depend on a precise cultural milieu and have only a relative value, and which are subject to scientific criticism. Such an idea is, for instance, the synthetic conception of man, not solely a human composite divisible into "parts," body and soul, but a personal being expressing himself fully in variegated aspects: spirit*, soul*' body*, flesh*. These aspects, of which we should not be oblivious, remain secondary insofar as they pertain to a simple and basic study of man. The Bible does not of itself analyze this microcosm which stirred the admiration of the Greek philosophers. "The Bible, theological as it is, considers man only as he stands before God, whose image he is," through Christ who has restored that image* (art. *man*).

Likewise, beginning with the events, institutions, and persons of which the Bible speaks, we see delineated a theology of history, an understanding of the ways* in which God accomplishes His work. To grasp this doctrinal aspect, we must understand that in the eyes of the Semites time is not an empty setting which human actions are later to fill up. For the Semite centuries are made up of generations* throbbing with the life of the Creator. But once this ordinary image derived from the culture of the biblical milieu is acknowledged, we must consider differentiating factors and arrive at that which is peculiar to the biblical concept of time*. Contrary to the contemporary mythological beliefs of their neighbors, time was not conceived as the repetition in our own world of the primordial time of the gods. If, in worship*, revelation assumes the cycle of festival periods consecrated by usage, it gives them a new meaning by placing them between two terms: the beginning and the end of human history, creation* and the day* of the Lord. This history itself, then, will fall into a rhythm of years, of weeks*, of days, of hours*. But all these elements of our calendar are removed from the sterility of repetition by the presence* of the Lord, by the memory* of His arrival among us, by the hope* for His return. As a consequence of such an end, the struggle of the two cities, Jerusalem* and Babylon*, the confrontation of good and evil, the battle against the enemy*, is no longer a catastrophic war*, but the prelude to an unending peace* guaranteed at the moment by the existence of the Church in which the Spirit lives.

Through these acts God ultimately unveils His own heart and reveals man to himself. If man should speak of the wrath* and hatred of God who condemns sins, he learns to recognize, even in the punishments* which he undergoes, the love* which teaches* and seeks to give him life. Likewise will man attempt to model his behavior on that which he sees in God. Gentleness, humility, obedience, patience, simplicity, mercy, but also power and pride—all these "virtues" gain their true meaning and their efficacious consistency through the living presence of God and of His Son Jesus Christ in the power of the Holy Spirit. So too, in biblical theology, will all human events acquire their full significance: joy and suffering, solace and sadness, peaceful victory and persecution, life and death—all must be placed in the salvific plan the Word of God reveals to us. Everything then assumes a meaning and a value in the death and resurrection of Jesus Christ, our Lord.

II. DICTIONARY

The intellectual and religious structure which dominates the entire intelligible content of the Bible extends to the point of creating for itself a community of verbal expression, so that we can speak of a biblical language. Certainly, in the books of the Bible, as in those of strictly human origin, words change in the course of time. But the scope of inspiration is such that it reaches beyond the ideas to the words themselves which express those ideas. We can recognize a Gospel *koine*; that is, an "ordinary language" in which a new revelation has been expressed. But this *koine* depends closely on the language of the Septuagint, the Greek translation of the Bible. The Septuagint, in its turn, "translates" and adapts the Hebrew text of the OT. Does not such continuity mean that there was, at least for properly theological ideas, a truly technical language? This fact alone would justify the format of a dictionary given to our sketches of biblical theology. There is no question here of pure semantics, but of an expressive language of images and symbols. Obviously, to people of our own age, the question arises as to the value the biblical language has for us who live in a completely different intellectual climate. Should the mystery of heaven be announced today in the same imagery which the NT uses, the imagery of paradise* and of superposed celestial spheres, that of the banquet and the wedding? Can we still speak of the wrath* of God? What does the "ascent" of Jesus into heaven and His sitting "at the right hand of God" mean? Will not the agreement, rather easily reached on the content of "biblical theology," be shattered when we seek to establish a precise terminology for this theology? Is it not necessary to "demythologize" the language to attain the essence of revelation? Is not the alliance of a *dictionary* and *theology* merely the prolongation of an unfortunate illusion? Without pretending to resolve here the general problem of "demythologizing" a language, we would only point out on two deeper levels in what sense language mediates truth.

1. *Imagery and languages.* In the face of divine revelation, the human spirit reacts with two inverse movements. On the one hand, a man attempts to describe as simply as possible the revealing event; on the other hand, he tries to express in more and more precise formulas the dogmatic content of revelation. These two relations, the existential description of the event and the essential formulation of its intelligible content, are each conditioned by the cultural environment in which

they arose; and each is exposed to some distortions. But the danger we encounter is different in the two instances: the description of the event could be reduced to a purely literal statement, devoid of all divine meaning, which would drain faith of all spiritual commitment. Doctrinal formulation, in being detached from the event which gave it existence, would degrade the mystery by abstract speculation. The language of revelation supposes this twofold mode of expression, abstract formulation and imaginative description. Nevertheless, although the language of revelation at times uses "formulas," vg, creedal cult formulas (Dt) or definitions of faith (He), it appears more generally as an existential description which evokes within the context of imagery the mystery of the covenant such as it was lived by the people of God. The primary problem is not "demythologizing" the language in an attempt to adjust the content to the tenor of modern attitudes. The problem is rather to find ways of access which permit a sensible understanding of this language.

At a lower level of expression lies the simple metaphor. Thus, Isaiah describes the tree shaking in the wind...If the metaphor can enrich the vocabulary of revelation, it cannot immediately and of itself translate this revelation. Detached from the original experience which brought it into being, changeable at will, with more or less felicity according to the taste and imagination of the person utilizing it, the metaphor is, in expressing revelation, an interchangeable garment. Nonetheless, this garment holds a position in biblical language which we can hardly envisage. It is through the metaphor that the original image preserves for the Semite a power of suggestion which is always vital. What Frenchman, speaking of the "office" *(bureau)* where he works, still has in mind "rough serge" *(bure)*, which in the old days covered the desks? For a Semite, on the other hand, the *kābôd*, the glory*, while gradually assuming the meaning of "radiant splendor," still has a background of weight and wealth—a fact which causes Paul to speak of "weight of glory" awaiting the chosen in heaven.

Together with this permanence of the image and bound up with a cultural phenomenon, there is a life in the image, a life animated by the spirit which preserves the true meaning of it throughout the variety of expressions. This fact is particularly evident in the Septuagint translation. Sometimes this translation retains a Greek word of a clearly different meaning in an attempt to preserve thereby the full meaning of the Hebrew word. Thus the Septuagint expresses the Hebrew *kābôd* by the Greek *doxa* which, contrary to the real signification of weight, means an "opinion," the snap judgment. Sometimes it avoids a word pertaining to cult which would entail confusion. Thus, to translate *berākāh*, blessing*, the Septuagint chooses in preference to *euphēmia* the word *eulogia* which, if it no more expresses the nuance of the *berākāh* than does *euphēmia*, has the advantage of being neutral and flexible. Finally, sometimes the Septuagint uses a Greek word to cut through the ambiguity of the Hebrew. The Greek *diathēkē* used to signify "the act by which one disposes of his goods (will) or states the conditions which he intends to impose." While thus translating the Hebrew term *berīth*, which properly means a pact or contract, the Septuagint accentuates "the transcendence of God and the condescension which is at the origin of the people of Israel and of its law" (art. *covenant*). Such a mastery of language thus points out that the word matters less than the mind which uses the word and by the word opens up the desired horizon. But this control is also an admission of impotence, for no human language is capable of giving an account of the experience of God; God is necessarily beyond images and metaphors. In preserving the imagery and fully realizing its limitations, the language of the Bible risks remaining a mode of concrete expression rooted in human experience while attempting to express through the material images themselves realities of the spiritual order. Thus the early figures of beatitude* or of reward* all express an earthly happiness in which man, body and soul, participates. When the hope* of Israel becomes more spiritual, these figures of speech, instead of disappearing, remain; they are then less direct expressions of the experience of happiness which awaits man than symbols of an elevated hope, of an expectation of God impossible to translate into fitting words. At this point, image and metaphor become the normal supports of revelation without having by themselves a "revealing" value. But because of their history in the language, because of mental associations these figures evoke, reactions which they arouse, such figures mediate the divine Word. We could not, therefore, simply disregard the figures.

2. *Symbol and experience.* Contrary to the metaphor which can be transposed equally well into all areas of expression, the biblical symbol remains in a constant relation to the revelation which generated the symbols. The articles of the *Dictionary* strive to point out how elements of the world, events lived by the people, the very customs themselves, become part of the dialogue between God and man; in fact God is already speaking to man through creation and history, which He controls.

Thus, the Bible knows not two kinds of heaven, one material, the other spiritual. But in the visible sky the Bible discovers the mystery of God and of His work (art. *heaven*). Certainly the original heaven and earth are destined to disappear. But while they remain, the sky and the impression which it produces on man remain indispensable for expressing at one and the same time the transcendence and nearness of the God of the heavens or for expressing the idea that in "ascending into heaven" Jesus has been glorified. In Babylonian mythology the sea*, untamed and terrifying, personified the chaotic powers of disorder reduced to impotency by the god Marduk. In the Bible the sea is nothing more than a subdued creature, though it retains signs of hostile forces which God must conquer to accomplish His plans. Under this aspect the sea reminds us of death's dominion which threatens men. The same can be said for most of the world's realities: earth, stars, light, day, night, water, fire, wind, storms, darkness, stones, rocks, mountains, deserts...Always in direct harmony with the sovereignty of God the Creator, they have a rich symbolic meaning in God's revelation.

However, the real value of the biblical symbol depends on its relationship with the events of salvation. Thus night* is a symbol common to most religions, "an ambivalent reality, powerful as death and indispensable as the time in which worlds begin." The Bible knows this symbolism but is not content with it. The Bible absorbs the symbolism into an historical perspective which alone bestows on it its peculiar significance. In the Bible the paschal night is the principal experience in which Israel understood the mysterious meaning of night. Among many other symbols (like those of the cloud* or the day*) let us recall here the symbol of the desert*. The people had to cross the desolate regions of Sinai. But this experience did not bestow on the desert any value in itself, nor did it consecrate a sort of mysticism of flight into the desert. Certainly the attitude of Christ and the teaching of the NT show that the Christian does lead his life, after a fashion, in the desert. But this portrayal henceforth is related not to man's external behavior but to his sacramental life. Thus the desert symbol is not destroyed but becomes a tool to explain the nature of the Christian life.

Put in the language of revelation, events lived by the people of God are not some simple metaphors which we may now pass over as if they acted merely as a springboard. The events possess a mediatory value. It is by reference to the captivity* in Egypt or to the Babylonian exile* that the Christian understands his condition as a sinner ransomed from slavery*. The baptized are those rescued from the flood*. The spiritually circumcised*, these are the Jews* in spirit; they are crucified to the world and to their lusts; they are nourished on the true manna*; they are the true offspring of Abraham. In the symbols used in the language of revelation the history is in a certain sense past. That is why this symbolic language today goes back to and echoes the original history.

Finally, the human dimension itself plays a role in this type of language since the Son of God has made that dimension His own. Activities of the farmer—from planting to harvesting—portray the history of the kingdom of God. Actions of man —eating, working, resting, sleeping—recall realities of the world of God. Marriage, motherhood, birth, sickness, and death are so many analogies setting the human spirit on the path that leads to the invisible mysteries. The symbol is the privileged means of expressing the encounter of man with the God who comes to him. And when the symbol has led man to the mystery, it is absorbed with him in silence.

III. THE WORD MADE FLESH

The Son of God came to live with us and thus bestowed on the symbolic language of revelation its ultimate and complete justification. The Word made flesh is in Himself revelation in act. By word and deed He brings about a perfect fusion : each of His words is a deed; each of His actions speaks to us and calls us. As St. Augustine says, "Because Christ is in person the Word of God, the very actions of the Word are for us language (*etiam factum Verbi, verbum nobis est*)." In Him the most humble earthly realities, as well as the glorious events in the history of His predecessors, take on a meaning. The activity of the Word of God made flesh reveals the meaning of all earthly reality and events. By a procedure contrary to that which the imagination of man follows when it transforms realities into metaphors, Jesus Christ makes evident the figurative value of all the realities which precede Him and announce Him. Since the time of Christ, earth's realities are seen as symbols of this unique reality who is the Word made flesh. Neither bread nor water, road nor door, human life nor light, are permanent "realities," of ultimate value. Their essential reason for existing is to speak symbolically to us of Jesus Christ.

XLD jjk

II

THE LITERARY HISTORY OF THE BIBLE

Though a dictionary of biblical theology does not have to present the critical problems posed by the sacred books, it cannot bypass them completely. In the effort to understand the doctrinal themes of Scripture in their historical development and to trace the divine pedagogy, a dictionary cannot be content with assembling texts and references in a purely logical order. Each inspired text has a living context. Text and context cannot be separated without distortion, for the growth of revelation has taken place within the rhythm of history. Everything which puts us in a position to understand better the literary development of the Bible allows us at the same time a better perception of God's ways. For God has spoken to our fathers "in diverse times and varying manners," before finally speaking to us in His Son (He 1,1f). It is important to understand these "times" and these "manners" if we wish to come to a correct evaluation of the content of His Word. For this reason, before turning to the analytical articles devoted to the individual topics, it will be good to recall briefly how the collection of the sacred books came into being.

THE OLD TESTAMENT

It is not easy to retrace the literary history of the OT. In today's Bibles the books are grouped logically in large categories, without concern for the dates of their composition. In a great number of cases the dates themselves cause a problem for the critics. Hence we can only propose some probable hypotheses. To omit the hypotheses would be an indolent solution and, moreover, an attitude impossible to defend. We must know how to make a choice among hypotheses. All the theories advanced by critics of the last hundred years are not equally compatible with the theological study of the Bible. Some theories suppose a conception of the religious evolution of Israel which proceeds from rationalistic assumptions and which objective textual study in no way imposes. In other cases, it is necessary to make a distinction between perfectly objective critical observations and their tendentious exploitation. In raising these questions, the believer is not in an inferior position. Reading the Bible "from within," in fundamental agreement with the spirit of its testimony, the believer knows that the development of religious ideas among the people of God, if it has been subjected to the pressure of varied historical factors, has also been guided above all by the Word of God which has always served as its norm. This does not prevent the sacred books from having had a history, often complex. In the documentary framework bequeathed to the Church by ancient Judaism, the entire Pentateuch was considered as a literary composition of Moses. All the psalms came from David, the sapiential books from Solomon, the sixty-six chapters of Isaiah from one prophet of the eighth century. We know now that this was a simplification with which we can no longer be satisfied. We should, of course, do justice to the elements of truth in the traditional views and at the same time profit from present studies. In this way we greatly enrich our own concrete knowledge of the texts; for not only do we restore each text to its actual historical setting, but we bring out otherwise indiscernible mutual interrelations.

I. THE ORIGINS OF THE SACRED LITERATURE

Biblical literature has its roots in oral tradition. This fact is important to note, for, in its written form, this literature has been able to take shape only in a relatively late period, after the establishment of the Davidic monarchy. All the previous centuries—those of the patriarchs, of Moses, of Israel's settlement in Canaan, of the judges and of the kingship of Saul—belong to the period of oral tradition. This does not mean that there had not been some written documents at that time or literary works in well-defined forms. For example, there is agreement in acknowledging the antiquity of legislative documents such as the Covenant Code (Ex 20,22 —23,33) and the Decalogue (Ex 20 and Dt 5); of poems such as the song of Deborah (Jg 5) and the apologue of Jotham (Jg 9,7-15). But around these fragments which the Israelite scribes have preserved, oral tradition remained the essential method of transmitting through the ages the recollections, the customs, the rites, the faith of ancient times. Throughout many centuries the people of God had lived on this treasure bequeathed by their ancestors—a treasure, moreover, which was enriched in each generation without yet having been clothed in its final literary form. The religious testimony of the patriarchs, of Moses, of the ancient messengers of God, was thus found preserved faithfully and in a vital way. But it is impossible for us to grasp this oral material as directly as we can the testimony of Isaiah or Jeremiah.

When David, and especially Solomon, had given the scribal institution an official position in the administration of the kingdom, the time had come when all these traditional materials were able to be crystallized into large groups, at the same time that historiography was being born. Let us note well that the collectors of these materials were not preoccupied only with putting in writing the cultural heritage of the previous centuries and with retracing the origins of the Israelite nation. The literature of Israel arose in the shadow of the sanctuary. From the beginning its essential aim had been to foster the faith of God's people. As historiography, it sought to call to mind the sacred history. Although analysis of the Pentateuch remains partially hypothetical, we can discern the hand of an editor or a group of editors, traditionally called the Yahwist, in an early collection of oral materials which was supposed to relate this sacred history from its beginnings to the settlement of Israel in Canaan. Its spirit and its interests are found in various accounts in Joshua and in Judges, in one of the accounts of Saul's kingdom which the First Book of Samuel has preserved (vg 1 S 9,1—10,16), in the history of David and his succession (2 S 2—1 K 2). This body of material could have been formed at Jerusalem from the tenth century, although it might be necessary to reckon with some possible enlargements during the following century. In using the units or elements of this total composite, one should not forget the double testimony contained therein: that of antiquity whose scribes had gathered their heritage with the care essential for faithful transmission; and the testimony of the scribes themselves who were unable to work out their synthesis without submitting the synthesis to their own theological reflection. The scribes felt that the history of the plan of God developed in stages, from the patriarchal promises and the covenant on Sinai to the decisive choice of the Davidic lineage (2 S 7) and the temple of Jerusalem (1 K 8); the people of God, descended from the federation of the twelve tribes, ultimately had taken the form of a centralized nation which the anointed of Yahweh governed.

It is noteworthy that in a considerably later age the same heritage should have been utilized in a slightly different spirit by other collectors of traditions; those of the collection called the Elohist where we can sense the influence of the first prophets, Elijah and Elisha. Very likely in this instance it is in the sanctuaries of the north (perhaps Shechem?) where the sacred writers must have collected and fixed in writing the materials transmitted to them by Israelite antiquity. Quite similar doctrinal preoccupations are found in the biographies of Elijah and Elisha and in one version of the history of Saul which shows little liking for the kingly institution (1 S 8; 10,17-25; 12). Consequently, probably in the reign of Hezekiah (the end of the eighth century), Yahwistic and Elohistic traditions were gathered together in a compilation, the materials of which are now distributed throughout many books, from Genesis to the First Book of Kings. This schematic survey of the process which generated the first collection of sacred literature admits in details a certain amount of fluidity and uncertainty. But the outline at least allows us a slight glimpse of the ways in which recollections of the formation of God's people and their settlement in the land have come down to us.

On the fringe of collected traditions and of the legal or poetic materials of which they are the vehicle, it is also necessary to allow for the living tradition which kept going on. Even without codification in written texts, the unwritten law and the rituals, products of a Mosaic tradition which had been developed over the years, governed Israel's existence. Likewise the lyricism of worship, begun at an early period (cf Nm 10,34-36), had its materials accumulated from the time of David who was himself a poet (cf 2 S 1,17-27); and it found in the temple of Jerusalem a favorable environment for its literary development. Finally, to the very early popular or folk wisdom was grafted in the time of Solomon (cf I K 5,9-14) a sophisticated literary wisdom. This literary wisdom enabled an international culture to develop in Israel and also harmonized the culture with Yahwism. Many elements go back to this period—material in the Psalter and in the collections of Proverbs which are considered to be the oldest (Pr 10,1—22,16; 25—29). Before the period of the literary prophets, the various forms into which we divide the inspired literature are already authoritatively represented. Behind these forms we discover the activity of the principal media which transmitted the biblical tradition: the priests who were the depositaries of the law and of the historiography which constitutes the setting and framework of the law; the prophets, spokesmen of God; the scribes, masters of wisdom. Though revelation is still only in its beginning stage it has established some very solid doctrinal principles which following ages will only deepen.

II. THE AGE OF PROPHETS

The prophetic movement in Israel is very ancient. However, before the eighth century, we possess only a small number of genuine oracles (2 S 7,1-17; 1 K 11,17) or related fragments (Gn 49; Nm 23—24; Dt 33). Disciples of Elijah and Elisha have preserved the memory of their deeds, not the exact words of their discourses, so that we know the discourses only through the later recensions. From the eighth century, the disciples of the prophets, and sometimes the prophets themselves, collected their discourses, their prophecies, and certain biographical stories (notably that of their calling). Historical allusions which run through these texts often allow us to date them with sufficient precision. It is thus possible to determine the history of this literature which is intensely involved in the world of action. The literary prophets known by name range from the eighth century to the fifth century. They are: in the eighth century, in Israel, Amos and Hosea; in Judah, Isaiah and Micah. In the last quarter of the seventh century, Zephaniah, Nahum (612), Habakkuk, and especially Jeremiah, whose ministry extended from 625 until after 587. In the sixth century, Ezekiel (593 to 571), Haggai and Zechariah (between 520 and 515). In the fifth century, Malachi (about 450), Obadiah, and probably Joel.

This jejune enumeration, however, does not give a sufficient idea of the complexity of the prophetic books. Actually, authoritative collections of which we have just spoken grew in the course of time, thanks to the contributions of disciples, their successors and inspired glossators. Even the collection of Jeremiah, in the composition of which Baruch certainly had a great part (cf Jr 36), contains some later fragments (Jr 50—51); similarly that of Amos (9,11-15), Micah (7,8-20), even of Ezekiel (Ez 38—39?). The second part of Zechariah (Ze 9—14) seems to be an anonymous addition from the time of Alexander the Great (around 330). As for the Book of Isaiah, we see in it so many different hands and historical contexts that it is, in its present state, a genuine summation of prophetic teaching. Besides glosses touching minor points, several clearly defined collections stand out in detail: the Message of Consolation to the exiled (Is 40—55), written between 545 and 538; the oracles against Babylon (13—14), virtually contemporaneous; the small apocalypse (34—35), which may date from the first journeys back to Palestine; chapters 56—66, which have for a background the last quarter of the sixth century; the great apocalypse (24—27), the date of which is variously estimated (between 485 and the third century). It is understood that the attention here given to the exact origin of fragments gathered under some familiar names has not for its purpose simply the settling of problems of literary authenticity. With full regard for the inspiration of the texts, and as a consequence of the concrete problems which the anonymous prophets had to face, our consideration aims at a better appreciation of doctrinal value.

If the prophets personally are trustees of the Word of God and have the responsibility of its transmission to their contemporaries, it is still not necessary to represent them as isolated individuals. On the one hand the people of God lived out their drama around them; on the other hand literary currents that existed before the prophets developed and flourished because of the prophetic movement. We spoke earlier of the old redactions of the Mosaic law, center of common law, and of the first collections of traditional material. In the eighth and seventh centuries, the revision of this legislation ended in the Deuteronomic Code (Dt 12—28) and probably has for its point of departure the juridical tradition of the northern sanctuaries which it accepts and adapts to the needs of the times. But this revised product does present some undeniable affinities of spirit with Hosea and Jeremiah. Furthermore, this revisal becomes the center of an entire religious literature which orchestrates its own themes: priestly discourses of Dt 1—11; works of sacred history which recapture the period from the conquest to the exile (Joshua, Judges, 1—2 Samuel, 1—2 Kings) and unite into one whole materials borrowed from ancient sources. With these works we come to the end of the monarchy and the period of exile.

But at this same time, the Jerusalem priesthood is likewise taking pains to give a literary form to its customs, its rites, its law. The Holiness Code (Lv 17—26), which is a counterpart of the Deuteronomic Code and shows notable kinship with Ezekiel, could have been edited about the end of the seventh century. Around it finally clustered the bulk of religious legislation collected in Ex, Lv and Nm within the framework of a *sacred priestly history* based on traditions already used by Yahwistic and Elohistic scribes. Paralleling this work, the wisdom tradition cultivated by scribes of the court is enriched with new maxims in which the moral doctrine of the prophets is easily recognizable. The ritual lyricism also bears the traces of prophetic influence. At the time of the exile when the deported Jews gather the literary inheritance of past centuries so that not only the nation may survive but the religion which is tied to it, what they had in their hands was already a complete Bible. In fact, further development of the inspired literature will come into contact with this Bible and will thoroughly bear its imprint.

III. THE AGE OF THE SCRIBES

Until the exile the prophetic movement was represented by men of action. During the first two centuries of Jewish restoration this movement begins to fade into the background. At this point we are in the age of the scribes. Priest or layman, they put their talents to the service of the Word of God. The ancient tradition, in written or oral form, continually furnishes the vital atmosphere in which their works are rooted. But their interests, their habits of mind, their methods of composition, are marked by a notable dependence on their predecessors. The Persian period (520-330) and the beginning of the Greek period (330-175) remain obscure to the historian who seeks a detailed reconstruction. But from the literary point of view both periods are rich.

The work of the priestly scribes must be mentioned first. Organizing into one single body all the legal materials and their accompanying traditions, scribes give the Torah its definitive form preserved in our Pentateuch. Some suspect that this fixing of the Law should have a connection with the activity of Ezra (447, 427, or 397). Likewise, the collection of the earlier prophets, from Joshua to Kings, will change no more. That of the Latter Prophets (Is, Jr, Ez and smaller collections) will be subject to only minor additions, sometimes simple editorial glosses. But new literary forms now begin to flourish. The didactic tale, basically constructed as a religious object lesson which can be drawn out of the story, was of common occurrence in Israel; for example, the books of Jonah and Ruth (fifth century) which developed from traditions impossible to verify. In a similar spirit, but using more solid historical sources, the Chronicler (undoubtedly in the third century) reworks the complete narrative account of Israelite history to the time of Nehemiah and Ezra (1—2 Ch, Ne, Ezr): within the narrative, theology is always present and imposes a definite manner of factual presentation.

After the exile, however, it is especially wisdom literature which experiences a growing success. Directed to a consideration of life on the practical level, gradually it enlarges its field of investigations to include difficult doctrinal problems: the problem of existence and the problem of evil. On these issues older books provide principles of solution which are traditional. But wisdom literature sometimes both criticizes and goes beyond the traditional solutions. The collection of Proverbs, with quite a new type of editorial preface (Pr 1—11), is the starting point of this trend (fifth century). It is followed by the Book of Job (fifth or fourth century), Ecclesiastes (fourth or third century), the didactic story of Tobit (third century), the Book of Ben Sira (edited about 180). It is not surprising to note the influence of the same current in the Psalter where many late fragments discuss problems of wisdom (Ps 37; 73; 112, for example) or praise the divine law which is for man the source of true wisdom (Ps 1; 19; 119). This occurred because the schools of chanters who gave final form to the collection lived in an ambiance where the principal elements were the temple worship and reflection on Scripture. Old or new, the canonical psalms echo all the currents of sacred literature, all the historical experience of Israel, all the aspects of the Jewish spirit which the psalms reflect perfectly. All the essential elements of divine revelation come together in the psalms, the starting point of inspired prayer.

IV. THE CONCLUSION OF THE OT

With the crisis of the Maccabean period, the OT reaches its final turning point. Prophecy is here heard one final time, but in a new form: the apocalypse. Indeed, it is this literary form which the author of the Book of Daniel (about 165) uses to deliver his message of consolation to the persecuted Jews. To the eschatological visions which interpret the promises (Dn 2; 7—12), the author adds several didactic narratives which support the lessons of the visions (1; 3—5; 13—14). Furthermore, Judaism of the period has a taste for stories of this type: Esther is a typical deliverance of the people of God; Judith exalts a religious and warlike resistance which could be a reflection of the Maccabean revolt. The persecution of Antiochus Epiphanes, then the holy war which followed, are known also through sources slightly later than the events, namely the two books of Maccabees which in different ways are influenced by Greek historiography. If to these books is added the Book of Baruch, which puts together varied pieces, and the Wisdom of Solomon, written in Greek at Alexandria in the first century before Christ, we arrive at the end of the writings acknowledged as inspired by Alexandrian Judaism and subsequently by the apostolic Church.

Hereafter it is on the periphery of the Bible that the religious literature of the Jews will develop—evidence of the doctrinal progress which still takes place in a living tradition, though often warped by one or other spirit of the sects with which the authors or compilers are associated. The artificial grouping of the Apocrypha manifests differing affinities—to Essene thought (Henoch, The Book of Jubilees, The Testament of the Twelve Patriarchs, The Assumption of Moses), or to Pharisaism (The Psalms of Solomon, The Fourth Book of Ezra, The Apocalypse of Baruch). Works of strictly Essene provenance are now accessible to us because of the Qumrân manuscripts (Rules of the sect, The Damascus Document, commentaries on Scripture). Alexandrian Judaism, besides its Greek translation of the Bible (Septuagint), possesses an entire literature which is dominated by the work of the philosopher Philo. Finally, rabbinical compilations, written from the second century under the aegis of the learned Pharisees, have inherited a tradition of a much more ancient origin. (The Mishna, a compilation of jurisprudence; its commentaries form the Talmuds; the Midrashim, explanations of scriptural texts; the Targums, or Aramaic interpretations of the same texts.) If these works no longer interest us as sacred texts, they do represent at the very least the living context in which the NT was born.

INTRODUCTION

THE NEW TESTAMENT

Jesus has written nothing. It is to the minds of His disciples that He entrusted both His teachings and the remembrance of the events which brought our salvation. At the origin of the canonical NT literature, the existence of this oral tradition must never be forgotten—a tradition not at all consigned to the confused initiative of an anonymous community, but initially structured by the witness of those to whom Jesus had committed the transmission of His message. All the writings of the apostolic age derive, in some manner, from this witness. The literary development of the NT took place in a much shorter period of time than was the case with the OT: two thirds of a century perhaps. Nevertheless, a notable variety, not corresponding exactly to the logical divisions of our Bibles, is there evident.

I. THE SYNOPTIC GOSPELS AND THE ACTS OF THE APOSTLES

The most ancient Christian documents which we possess are the apostolic epistles. But these epistles presume the existence of a prior evangelical tradition, the one which ultimately took shape in the first three gospels, on the one hand, in the Johannine gospel, on the other. A tradition attested to from the second century asserts that the first gospel collection was composed by Matthew "in the Hebrew language" (practically speaking, Aramaic). But we no longer have this work. We can only surmise its presence as the background of the three Synoptics. Moreover, since the Christian community of Jerusalem very early had been bilingual (Ac 6), it is under the twofold form of Aramaic and Greek that the gospel materials had to be therein transmitted. The discourses of the Acts (2,22-39; 3,12-26; 4,9-12; 5,29-32; 10,34-43; 13,16-41) furnish a primitive account of the apostolic preaching which documents for us an important point: the general framework in which the materials were grouped to present the person of Jesus, author of our salvation.

This schematic outline governs the development of the gospel of Mark. Echoing the preaching of Peter, the Markan Gospel could have been redacted between 65 and 70, with a much more ancient document as its basis. The work of Luke must have been published in the following decade. It goes quite a bit beyond the limits of that of Mark since it comprises two books. On the one hand, the gospel portrays the Lord according to the memories of His witnesses, whereas the Acts of the Apostles shows how the message of salvation spreads from Jerusalem to the pagan world and to Rome, its capital. These two books form a whole in which the intent to teach theologically is still more perceptible than in the gospel of Mark. The canonical gospel of Matthew undoubtedly has a close relationship with the primitive document attributed by the ancient tradition to the same author. But this gospel is, at the very least, an amplified recasting of the early document, and parallels the work of Luke with regard to dating and didactic intent.

The manner in which the gospels have taken form invites study on two different levels: that of their final editing, in which factual presentation, selection, and expression of Jesus' words are governed by the doctrinal perspective proper to each author; and the level of the apostolic tradition from which the material, often in fixed literary form before its collection, was taken. Right at the first level, theological reflection is present because the apostolic testimony is not a disinterested description of the past. Adapting its formulation to the spiritual needs of the

Christian community and fulfilling an essential function in the life of the Church, the testimony aims above all to nourish faith and to focus on the mystery of salvation revealed in the words and deeds of Jesus—the mystery fulfilled in His life, His death, and His resurrection.

II. THE APOSTOLIC EPISTLES

The gospel tradition, oral or partially written, existed before the other writings transmitted to us from the era of the apostles: the epistles. The epistles are not treatises in abstract and systematic theology. They are incidental writings, deeply involved in the pastoral activity of the apostles and of their immediate disciples.

A first group consists of the Pauline epistles for which the Acts of the Apostles supplies a valuable historical background. The epistles map out the apostolate of St. Paul on pagan soil. In the course of the second missionary journey we have the epistles to the Thessalonians (51). During the following voyage: the epistle to the Philippians (about 56; according to others, about 61-63); the epistle to the Galatians and the epistles to the Corinthians (57), the epistle to the Romans (57-58). During the Roman captivity (61-63). the epistles to the Colossians, to Philemon, and to the Ephesians. There are still the "pastoral" epistles whose background the Acts does not give. The final missionary activity of Paul is reflected in 1 Tm and Tt. But 2 Tm supposes a new captivity, preparatory to martyrdom. These last three documents, moreover, pose a delicate literary problem: they suppose at least the use of a secretary who has left the mark of his own style on the letters while at the same time depending on Pauline thought. The case of the epistle to the Hebrews is different. If ancient tradition has always attached it to the Pauline *corpus*, its editor was a man of literary individuality and of an originality of thought which contrasts sharply with that of Paul and which manifests its Alexandrian origins. The document should still be before 70, for it appears not to know the destruction of Jerusalem and the end of the temple worship.

The group of Catholic epistles is of a much more irregular nature. For the first epistle of Peter, the editor himself is indicated: Silvanus or Silas, an old companion of Paul (1 P 5,12). Its background is the persecution of Nero in which Peter met death. The epistle of James is connected with "the brother of the Lord" who presided, after the year 44, over the destinies of the Jerusalem community. The epistle has the characteristics of a group of collected homilies. The epistle of Jude is already struggling against the influence of false teachers who are corrupting the Christian faith, and it probably has as its background the years 70-90. The second epistle of Peter makes use of that of Jude, and its editor considers the apostolic period from some distance. The testimony of Peter, therefore, permeates the letter in an indirect way; that is, through the composition of a disciple.

III. THE JOHANNINE WRITINGS

Finally it is necessary to group together those writings which are connected with the tradition about the apostle John. Of this group the Apocalypse appears to be the oldest work, but it could have gone through several editings and each time been enriched; one after 70, another about 95, during the persecution of Domitian. It depends upon a literary type initiated by the Book of Daniel and repeated occasionally in the other writings of the NT: in the gospels (Mk 13 p) and Pauline epistles (1 Th 5; 2 Th 1; 1 Co 15). If the second and third epistles of John are only short notes, the first epistle has the character of a homiletic collection in which the theological reappears in the fourth gospel which must have been preached before being put into book form. Ancient testimony (second and third centuries) places its date at the end of the first century. It is not surprising then that the words of Jesus and the recollections of His life are not there transmitted in unpolished form but in a highly articulated elaboration in which the writer's theology is incorporated into the data about which he writes. His long meditation on the message and mystery of Christ has permitted him to highlight the profound significance of the facts he reports and the hidden reverberations of the words he reproduces. Obvious language and style differences in all the writings coming from the Johannine tradition indicate that their final editing must have been the work of John's disciples.

Thus does the NT gather the apostolic testimony so that the Church may benefit from it in every age. Bearers of the revelation received from Christ and understood through the Holy Spirit, the apostles first of all entrusted it to the living memory of the Christian communities. This legacy was transmitted faithfully in the churches through the channels of the liturgy, preaching, catechesis, where both form and content were rapidly stereotyped. The Church of following centuries preserved this general structure while evolving its essential data. But already, apart from this, from the end of the apostolic age, inspired writings had come to fix forever the guiding lines of the testimony, thus making the living tradition a norm from which it would never deviate.

PG jjk

A

AARON

1. It is only slowly, over the course of the centuries, that the *picture of the ancestor* of the priestly class (Lv 1,5), of the "house of Aaron" (Ps 118,3), takes shape. According to the ancient traditions Aaron, the "levite" (Ex 4,14), brother of Miriam (15,20), is Moses'* spokesman (4,14-17) in his dealings with the Israelites (4,27-31) or even with Pharaoh (5, 1-5). He supports his brother in the battle against the Amelekites (17,10-13) and accompanies him up Mt. Sinai (19,24), where he is allowed "to see* God" (24,10-11). His memory is not free from faults: a considerable share of the responsibility in the affair of the golden calf must be laid on his shoulders (Ex 32; cf Ac 7,40) and he revolted against Moses (Nb 12,1-15).

Later, according to the priestly tradition and probably reflecting the struggles between the priestly* castes in the period of the second temple, Aaron becomes the specialist in religious matters, the eponym of the caste of the "sons of Aaron" (Ex 28,1; cf Lk 1,5). He is pictured as having been anointed* like the High Priest (Ex 29,1-30), and he wears the same clothes and is the origin of his gestures (39,1-31). God confirms this privilege by a judgment (Nb 16) and by the miracle of the flowering rod (17,6-26), which from then on is kept in the ark (He 9,4). From that time on he is associated with his brother Moses whenever God gives His orders (Ex 9,8-10; 12,1...) or when the people express their discontent (Ex 16,2; Nb 16,3). He also shares in Moses' unbelief* at Meriba (Nb 20,1-21) and experiences the same fate, dying before the entry into the Promised Land (20,22-29). Aaron remains for ever *the* High Priest (Si 45,6-22), the admirable intercessor turning away the divine wrath (Wi 18,20-25). Finally amongst the Essenes in Jesus' time it is not only a Messiah*-King, son of David, that is expected, but above all the Messiah of Aaron, the sovereign Messiah-Priest.

2. In the whole of the NT it is only the *Epistle to the Hebrews* that speaks of Aaron, concentrating on two aspects of this remarkable figure. Christ did not take upon Himself the function of the merciful High Priest, but was "like Aaron called by God" (He 5,2-5; cf Ex 28,1; Nb 18,1). On the other hand the priesthood of Aaron, passed on by inheritance, does not foreshadow that of Christ, unlike the priesthood of Melchizedek whose genealogy cannot be traced (He 7,3.15-21). Finally the priesthood of Aaron cannot claim the perfection* which is a mark of Christ's priesthood (7,11.23-27).

→Anointing III 3—Calling I—Messiah OT II 2 —Priesthood OT I 3.4; NT I 3.

XLD ems

ABANDON→Confidence — Deception / Disappointment III — Faith — Providence — Sadness NT 1—Sleep I 1.

ABBA→Adoration II 3—Fathers & Father V 1, VI—God NT IV—Grace V—Heart II 2 b— Mission NT III 2—Prayer IV 2, V 2 d—Son of God NT I 1—Spirit of God NT V 5.

ABEL

1. *Abel, the just.* The story of Cain and Abel is the beginning of the theme of the just* man suffering*, set by the narrator in the very first generation. It has an exemplary value and presents in concrete terms one of the general characteristics of the human condition, a characteristic that is present throughout the ages. The latent opposition between human brothers, in spite of their common origin (Ac 17,26), leads to fratricidal quarrels. Unlike the sacrifice* of Cain, that of Abel is pleasing to God (Gn 4,4f). The reason for this is less the nature of the offering than the interior dispositions of the man offering it. In contrast with the wicked man, who is rejected, Abel represents the just man, in whom God finds

1

pleasure. But the wicked man lies in wait for the just in order to kill him (Ps 10,9-11). This is a universal law and the blood* of the just that has been shed since the beginning of the ages cries from the earth to God and demands justice (Gn 4,10).

2. *The figure of Jesus.* This law of a harsh world will find its supreme application in the case of Jesus. He, the Holy and the Just (Ac 3,14), will be put to death by the people of His own religion. This is the ultimate crime. And so "the blood of every holy man that has been shed on earth, from the blood of Abel the Holy to the blood of Zechariah...murdered between the sanctuary and the altar...will recoil on this generation" (Mt 23,35f). This gloomy outlook does not only concern the special case of the chief Jews, who are responsible for the death of Jesus; it extends to the whole world, since everywhere there are cases of innocent people being put to death: this bloodshed calls for blood vengeance* (Ap 16,16; 18,24). Nevertheless, while there is this voice crying for revenge, there is another blood, more eloquent than that of Abel: the purifying blood of Jesus (He 12,24). This invites God to pardon*: "Father, forgive them, for they know not what they do" (Lk 23,34). The situation created by the murder of Abel, the just man, is therefore reversed in Jesus, *the* suffering just man. But Abel, unlike Cain, who stands in our eyes for the dramatic lack of charity in the human heart (1 Jn 3,12), remains the model of interior righteousness, of the faith that leads to justice; and this is why, although dead, he still speaks (He 11,4).

→Blood OT 1—Brother OT 1—Hatred I 1.2—Vengeance 1—Violence II.

PG ems

ABIDE

Forever on the move, Israel, nomadic and then exiled, never really discovered what it meant "to abide." It did not even have a word that expressed the idea precisely, but was forced merely to describe what it saw: a man sitting (Gn 25,27), the conqueror standing, the sole survivor of the battle (Js 7,12), or again, its tents pitched continuously in the same fields (Gn 16,12; 25,18). It is only the Greek translators who express our familiar ideas of house, stability, permanence.

This people, forever on the march, dreamed nonetheless of resting* from the fatigue of the desert*: they wished to be settled and live in peace in the land which God had promised them (cf Gn 49,9.15; Dt 33,12.20). In the evening of each great stage of its history, Israel dreams of pitching its tents "permanently" (Dt 12,8ff). And in the morning of new departures she takes courage again by listening to the prophets foretelling a place where she would sink roots (Am 9,15), a tent that would not be uprooted (Is 33,20), or even a lasting home and a firmly established city (2 S 7,9ff; cf Is 54, 2). But always Yahweh, her shepherd*, "destroyed her abodes" (cf Am 5,15; Jr 12,14) to punish her and bring her back again to the desert, or, on the other hand, to set her on the march toward greener pastures (Ps 23; Jr 50, 19; Ez 34,23-31). To have their abode is thus an ideal always desired but never attained. This ideal would find its fulfillment only in God.

I. THE TRANSITORY AND THE PERMANENT

1. *"The shape of this world passes away" (1 Co 7,31; 2 Co 4,18).* Man, the eternal traveler, is not able to dwell permanently here below, he does not endure: like all flesh*, comparable to grass, his life is short, he fades away and dies (Is 40,8; Jb 14,2). At any rate the world in which man lives appears more permanent (2 P 3.4). The earth is solid on its foundations (Ps 104,5), and God assured Noah of permanent consistency in the laws of nature (Gn 8,22). But this promise holds good only as long "as the earth will last," for "the heavens will be shaken" (He 12,26f). And Christ has warned His own: "heaven* and earth will pass away, but my words will not pass away" (Mt 24,35 p).

Even the Sinai covenant, though based on the Law and on the words of God, was declared transitory: the Hebrews, unfaithful to Yahweh, disobedient to the Law, could not remain permanently in the promised land (Dt 8,19f; 28,30.36). In a word, they "would not abide by their agreement" (He 8,9.13). This covenant, moreover, was but a passing type of the new covenant (Jr 31,31; Mt 26,28 p; G 4,21-31).

Even among the realities of the new economy, certain elements will pass away, such as charisms* of prophecy* and of knowledge or the gift of tongues*; but "faith, hope and charity remain, all three" (Co 13,8-13). This world is thus not a "lasting city"; one must leave it (He 13,13f). The Christian himself knows that "his earthly abode" is only a "tent" from which he will have to dislodge himself to reside with the Lord (2 Cor 5,1-8).

2. *God alone abides*; indeed, He, who is, who was, and will come (Ap 4,8; 11,17), "He is the living God who lasts forever" (Dn 6,27; Ps 102, 27f). Seated in the inaccessible heavens, the holy and eternal abode, He laughs at threats (Ps 2,4; 9,8; Is 57,15). He is the steadfast rock* on which one must lean. His word* (Is 40,8; 1 P 1,23ff), His plan* (Is 14,24), His promise* (R 4,16), His kingdom (Dn 4,31), His justice* (Ps 111,3), His love* (Ps 136) remain forever. He it is who gives firmness to anything permanent on the earth in the physical order as well as in the moral order (Ps 119,89ff; 112,3.6).

The just* man is, therefore, like a planted tree that remains standing until the day of judgment (Ps 1,3ff), or like a man who built his house on stone (Mt 7,24f p), that is on Christ, the only unshakable cornerstone* (Is 28,16; 1 C 3,10-14; E 2,20ff). In order to subsist, man must indeed rely on the strength of God, that is, he must believe (Is 7,9) and persevere in faith* (Jn 8,31; 15,5ff; 2 Tm 3,14; 2 Jn 9) in Him who is "the same yesterday, today and forever" (He 13,8).

II. GOD LIVES IN US AND WE IN HIM

1. *By His presence*, God allows men to abide.* He has built on Zion a temple* where His name* resides and which is filled by His glory* (Dt 12, 5-14; 1 K 8,11; Mt 23,21). This dwelling place, however, is provisional. Indeed, it will be profaned by sin: then the glory of Yahweh will leave it and the people will be led out into exile* (Ez 8,1—11,12).

2. *"The Word was made flesh and dwelt among us" (Jn 1,14).* He, "Emmanuel" (Mt 1,23; Is 7,14), whose kingdom will have no end (Lk 1,33), is "to remain forever" (Jn 12,34), because the Father dwells in Him and He in the Father (14,10). Yet His sensible presence is to cease; He is to leave His own (13,33), because He must make ready for them the many mansions of His Father's house (14,2f).

3. *That the Holy Spirit* may be given to us and abide in us (Jn 14,17),* the return of Christ to His Father was necessary (16,7). Having thus received the anointing* of Christ (1 Jn 2, 27f), the Christian abides in Him if he "eats His flesh*" (Jn 6,27-56), if he lives as He lived (1 Jn 2,6)—in His love (Jn 15,9), without sinning (1 Jn 3,6), and keeping His word (Jn 14, 15-23; 1 Jn 3,24). By this fact the Father, like Christ and the Spirit, abides in him (Jn 14,23). A union as intimate and fruitful as that of the vinestock and the vine* is forged between God and the Christian (Jn 15,4-7). The union allows the Christian to abide, that is, to bear fruit* (15,16) and to live eternally (Jn 6,56ff).

Thus it is that Christ, "in whom dwells all the fullness* of the divinity" (Col 1,19; 2,9), inaugurates the kingdom which lasts forever (He 12,27f) and builds the firm city (He 11,10) of which He Himself is the only foundation (Is 28,16; 1 Co 3,11; 1 P 2,4).

→Communion NT 2 b—Heaven III, IV—Hospitality 2—House—Paraclete 1—Presence of God—Stone 2—Temple OT.

JdV jrc

ABNEGATION→Cross II—Death NT III.

ABRAHAM

As ancestor of the chosen people, Abraham occupies a privileged place in salvation history. His calling* does not simply institute the initial phase of the plan* of God; the call determines the fundamental orientations of God's plan.

I. THE CALLING OF ABRAHAM

Instead of a simple chonology of Abraham, Genesis offers a religious narrative in which there are traces of three streams of tradition: the Yahwist insists on divine blessings and promises; the Elohist, on the thoroughly tested faith of the patriarch; the priestly tradition, on the covenant and circumcision. In this light the figure of Abraham appears as that of a man whom God has drawn to Himself and then tested with the idea of making him the extraordinarily blessed father of a people beyond count.

1. *Abraham, chosen by God.* The life of Abraham develops totally under the free initiative of God. God intervenes first; He chooses

Abraham out of a family that "served other gods" (Js 24,2), "causes him to leave" Ur (Gn 11,30-31), and leads him by His own ways* into an unknown country (He 11,8). This initiative is a loving initiative. From the beginning, God manifests toward Abraham a startling generosity. His promises* outline a marvelous future. The endlessly recurring phrase is: "I will give." God will give to Abraham land (Gn 12,7; 13,15ff; 15,18; 17,8); He will bless him, will make him prolific (12,2; 16,10; 22,17). Indeed circumstances appear to contradict these prospects, for Abraham is a nomad and Sarah is no longer of childbearing age. For all of this the gratuity of the divine promises stands out all the more. Abraham's future depends completely on the power and goodness of God. Abraham in himself thus recapitulates the people of God elected* with no prior merit. What is demanded of him above all is an attentive and fearless faith, an unhesitating acceptance of God's plan.

2. *Abraham tested.* This faith had to be purified and strengthened by trial*. God tried Abraham by asking him to sacrifice Isaac, exactly him on whom the promise rested (Gn 22,1f). Abraham "did not refuse his son, his only son" (22,12,16). (It is known that infant sacrifice was practiced in the Canaanite cults). But it is God who preserves Isaac and who Himself assumes the care of "providing a lamb for the burnt-offering" (22,8.13f). Thus was made clear the depth of Abraham's "fear* of God" (22,12). On the other hand, on the same occasion God was disclosing that His plan was not directed toward death but to life. "He does not rejoice in the destruction of the living" (Ws 1,13; cf Dt 12,31; Jr 7,31). Death one day will be overcome; the "sacrifice of Isaac" will then appear as a prophetic scene (He 11,19; 2,14-17; cf R 8,32).

3. *Abraham, blessed father.* The obedience of Abraham ended in the confirmation of the promise (Gn 22,16ff), the attainment of which he saw in rough draft: "Yahweh blesses Abraham in all things" (Gn 24,1). "No one was equal to him in glory" (Si 44,19). It is not a question of an individual's welfare: the calling of Abraham is to be a father*. His glory* is in his offspring. According to the priestly tradition, the change of name* (*Abram* becoming *Abraham*) substantiates this orientation because the new name is translated "father of multitudes" (Gn 17,5). The destiny of Abraham

is to have great consequences; since God is not concealing His intentions, the patriarch already makes it his business to intercede for the condemned cities (18,16-33). Paternity will enlarge still further his influence. Its radiation will touch all men: "Through your offspring will all nations* be blessed" (22,18). Meditating on this prophecy, Jewish tradition will recognize therein a profound meaning: "God solemnly promised him to bless all the nations in his posterity" (Si 44,21; cf Gn 22,18 LXX).

Thus if the destinies of sinful humanity were outlined in the sinner, the destinies of saved humanity are sketched in the believer.

II. THE DESCENDANTS OF ABRAHAM

1. *God's faithfulness.* In the case of Abraham the promises pointed also to his descendants (Gn 13,15; 17,7f), as defined by the divine choice. God does not establish His Covenant with Ishmael nor later with Esau but with Isaac and Jacob (17,15-22; 21,8-14; 27; cf R 9). God renews His promises to them (Gn 26, 3ff; 28,13f), and they transmit them as an inheritance (28,4; 48,15f; 50,24). While the sons of Abraham were oppressed in Egypt, God bent His ear to their groanings, for He "remembered His covenant with Abraham, Isaac and Jacob" (Ex 2,23ff; cf Dt 1,8). "He remembered His sacred word to Abraham, His servant. In joy He brought His people out" (Ps 105,42f). Later He consoles the exiles by calling them the "race of Abraham, my friend" (Is 41,8).

When the existence of Israel is threatened in times of adversity, it is by recalling the call of Abraham that the prophets restore confidence: "Look to the rock from which you have been cut, the trench from which you have come. Look to Abraham your father..." (Is 51,1f; cf Is 29,22; Ne 9,7f). And to obtain the favors of God, the best prayer consists in making use of Abraham's name: "Be mindful of Abraham ..." (Ex 32,13; Dt 9,27; 1 K 18,36); "grant... to Abraham your grace" (Mi 7,20).

2. *Sonship in the flesh.* But there is a bad way of depending on the patriarch. It is not at all sufficient to be his corporal offspring to be legitimate heirs; it is rather necessary to adhere to him spiritually. False confidence* is that which is not accompanied with a profound docility toward God. Ezekiel tells this to his contemporaries (Ez 33,24-29). When he announces the judgment of God, John the Bap-

tist attacks the same illusion more vigorously: "Do not imagine that you can say to yourselves, 'We have Abraham for our father.' For I tell you, God can produce offspring for Abraham out of the stones you see here" (Mt 3,9). It is no use for the self-centered rich man of the parable to cry out "Father Abraham." He gets nothing from his ancestor. Through his sin, an abyss stretches between them (Lk 16, 24ff). The fourth gospel offers the same evidence: Jesus unmasks the homicidal plans of the Jews and puts before their eyes the fact that their being the children of Abraham has not prevented them from becoming in fact sons of the devil (Jn 8,37-44). Sonship in the flesh is nothing without faithfulness*.

3. *Faith and works.* That this faithfulness be authentic, another deviation should be avoided. Through the course of ages, tradition has celebrated the merits of Abraham—his obedience* (Ne 9,8; Si 44,20), his heroism (1 M 2,52; Ws 10,5-6). Pursuing this course certain Jewish groups finally over-estimated this aspect: they put all their confidence in human works*, the perfect observance of the Law; and they forgot that what is essential is to rely on God.

This haughty pretense is already opposed in the parable of the Pharisee and the Publican (Lk 18,9-14), and is completely dismantled by Paul. Paul relies on Gn 15,6: "Abraham believed in God who took it to him as justice," to prove that it is faith* and not works which constitutes the basis of salvation (G 3,6; R 4.3). Man should not glorify himself, for all comes to him from God "by an unmerited title" (R 3,27; 4,1-4). No work precedes the favor of God; all works are the result of it. Be assured that this fruit will not be wanting (G 5,6; cf 1 Co 15,10), as it did not fail in the life of Abraham; this is what James remarked in regard to the same text (Jm 2,20-24; cf He 11, 8-19).

4. *Genuine posterity.* What is, therefore, definitively, the true offspring of Abraham? It is Jesus Christ, the son of Abraham (Mt 1,1), who is however greater than Abraham (Jn 8,53): among the descendants of the patriarch, He is even the only one to whom the inheritance* of the promise comes in its plenitude. He is the offspring above all others (G 3,16). It is truly toward the coming of Jesus that Abraham, from the time of his calling, labored, and his joy* was to see that day* through the blessings of his own life (Jn 8,56; cf Lk 1,54f.73).

Far from being a restriction, this concentration of the promise in one single descendant is the condition of a true universalism, which is also defined according to God's plan (G 4,21-31; R 9—11). All those who believe in Christ, circumcised or uncircumcised, Israelites or gentiles, can have a part in the blessings* of Abraham (G 3,14). Their faith* makes of them the spiritual offspring of Him who has believed and is from that time "the father of all believers" (R 4,11f). "All of you make only one in Christ Jesus. But if you belong to Christ, you are then the offspring of Abraham, inheritors according to the promise" (G 3,28f).

Such is the crown of biblical revelation, brought to term by the Spirit of God. It is also the last word on this "grand recompense" (Gn 15,1) announced to the patriarch: his fatherhood extends to all the elect of heaven. The definitive home of believers is the "bosom of Abraham" (Lk 16,22), where the liturgy of the dead longs for souls to arrive.

→Blessing III 2, IV o—Circumcision OT 2; NT 1—Election OT I 2.3 a b; NT III—Faith O—Fathers & Father I 2, II 1.2—Generation —Hebrew—Hope OT I—Inheritance OT 12— Justice B I OT—Justification I—Love I OT I—Mediator I 1—Melchizedek 1—Peter 3 a— People A II 1; B II 1; C II—Promises II 1— Trial/Temptation OT I 1.

RF & AV jjk

ABSENCE→Farewell Speeches—Hell NT III— Presence of God—Silence 1.

ABSTINENCE→Fasting—Wine I 2.

ABUNDANCE→Blessing—Fullness—Wealth.

ABYSS→Beasts & Beast 3 a—Creation OT II 2 —Hell—Sea—Water I, II 2.

ACCLAMATION→Amen 1—Blessing II 3—Confession NT 1—Praise.

ACCOMPLISH→Fulfil.

ACCUSE→Satan—Trial.

ACTIONS→Arm & Hand—Fruit—Grace V— Heart I 1—Work—Works.

ADAM

I. ADAM AND THE SONS OF ADAM

1. *The meaning of the words.* Contrary to what translations of the Bible insinuate, the word *Adam* is extremely widely used and offers a great variety of meanings. When a Jew pronounces this word, he is far from thinking primarily about the first man: outside of the creation narrative in which the expression is ambiguous, *Adam* designates the first man for certain only in four passages (Gn 4,1.25; 5, 1.3ff; Tb 8,6). Ordinarily, and rightly so, the term is understood as man in general (Jb 14,1), as the nations (Is 6,12), as anyone in general (Qo 2,12; cf Ze 13,5), as person (1 K 8,46; Ps 105,14), as human being (Ho 11,4; Ps 94,11). Clearly the collective sense dominates.

The same holds true for the expression *son of Adam*, which never looks to a descendant of the individual Adam, but is found as parallel to man (Jb 25,6; Ps 8.5) and designates a person (Jr 49,18.33; vg Ezekiel) or a group (Pr 8,31; Ps 45,3; 1 K 8,39.42). Used in contrast to God, the expression emphasizes, like the term *flesh**, the perishable and feeble condition of humanity: "from the height of heaven, Yahweh looks down. He sees all the sons of Adam" (Ps 33,13: cf Gn 11,5; Ps 36,8; Jr 32,19). The "sons of Adam" then are human beings as found in their earthly condition. It is what the popular etymology of the word indicates, which says it is delivered from *adamah*, earth; Adam is the earthy one, made from the dust of the earth.

This semantic fact has theological import: we cannot be content to see in the first Adam one individual among others. This is what the striking movement from the singular to the plural implies in the word of God, the Creator; "Let us make *Adam* to our likeness...and *they* shall rule..." (Gn 1,26). What therefore was the intention of the narrator of these first chapters of Genesis?

2. *Concerning the narrative of creation and the sin of Adam.* The first three chapters of Genesis constitute, as it were, a preface to the whole of the Pentateuch. But they are not of a single provenance; they were written at two intervals by two successive editors, the Yahwist (Gn 2-3), and the priestly (Gn 1). On the other hand, it is quite surprising to discover that they have left no trace in the literature up to the second century before Christ; it is only then that, as the source of the death of man, Ecclesiasticus denounces woman (Si 25, 24); and Wisdom, the devil (Ws 2,24). Nonetheless, these same narratives sum up a general experience, slowly thought out from before the second century, certain elements of which we can find in the prophetic and sapiental tradition.

a) *Belief in the universality of sin** is therein affirmed more and more; it is in some sort the Adamite condition: the psalmist bewails, "my mother has conceived me in sin" (Ps 51,7). Elsewhere the sin of man is described as that of a being, a marvelous being placed, like an angel, in the garden by God and fallen by a sin of pride* (Ez 28,13-19; cf Gn 2,10-15; 3,22f).

b) *The faith in God the creator and redeemer is no less alive.* This God is a potter who fashions man (Jr 1,5; Is 45,9; cf Gn 2,7); it is He who causes him to return to dust (Ps 90,3; Gn 3,19). "What then is man that you should remember him, a son of Adam whose care you undertake? A little less than a God have you made him, crowning him with glory and splendor; you have put him in charge over the works of your hands, everything was subjected by You beneath his feet" (Ps 8,5ff; cf Gn 1,26ff; 2,19f). After the sin, God does not appear only as the magnificent Lord (Ez 28, 13f; Gn 2,10-14) who dethrones the haughty and sends them back to their modest beginnings (Ez 28,16-19; Gn 3,23f); He is also the patient God, who slowly teaches His child (Ho 11,3f; Ez 16; cf Gn 2,8—3,21). Likewise, the prophets have announced an end-time similar to the ancient paradise* (Ho 2,20; Is 11, 6-9); death will be destroyed (Is 25,8; Dn 12,2; cf Gn 3,15), and even a mysterious Son* of Man, of a heavenly nature, will appear as conqueror upon the clouds (Dn 7,13f).

3. *Adam our ancestor.* In the development of the tradition just outlined, we can see, in large lines, the teachings of the creation* narratives. In a first effort to reflect on the human condition, the Yahwist, convinced that the ancestor included in himself all his descendants, announces to every man how, created good by God, the man* who sinned should one day be redeemed. The priestly narrative (Gn 1) reveals that man is created to the image* of God; then, with the help of the genealogies (Gn 5; 10), it shows that all men form a unity* beyond Israel: the human race.

II. THE NEW ADAM

1. *Toward a theology of the new Adam.* The NT says that all descend from one man alone (Ac 17,26), or that the first parents are the prototypes of conjugal unity (Mt 19,4f p; 1 Tm 2, 13f) which would be restored in the new humanity. The newness of its message resides in the presentation of Jesus Christ as the new Adam. Attention had been drawn by the apocrypha to the recapitulation of all sinners in Adam; especially, Jesus Himself was presented as the Son* of Man, eager to show at one and the same time that He was indeed of the human race and that He must fulfill the glorious prophecy of Daniel. The synoptics make a more or less explicit comparison between Jesus and Adam. Mark describes how Jesus dwelt among the animals (Mk 1,13); Matthew recalls Gen 5,1 in the "book of the generation of Jesus Christ" (Mt 1,1); and for Luke the one who had just triumphed over temptation is "son of Adam, son of God" (Lk 3,38), the real Adam, who had resisted the tempter. Undoubtedly we can also recognize behind a Pauline hymn (Ph 2,6-11) a contrast planned between Adam, who sought to make himself equal to the divine condition, and Jesus, who did not jealously retain it. To these insinuations we can join some explicit comparisons.

2. *The second and true Adam.* In 1 Co 15, 45-49, Paul strongly opposes the two types according to which we are constituted; the first man, Adam, had been made a living soul, belonging to earth, with spiritual operations; "the second Adam is a spirit who gives life," for He belongs to heaven, is spiritual. To the picture of the origins corresponds that of the end of time, but an abyss separates the second creation from the first, the spiritual from the carnal, the heavenly from the earthly.

In R 5,12-21, Paul explicitly says that Adam was "the figure* of Him who should come." Trusting in the conviction that the act of the first Adam had a universal effect—death* (cf 1 Co 15,21f)—he affirms likewise the redeeming action of Christ, the second Adam. But he clearly notes the differences: from Adam, disobedience, condemnation, death; from Jesus Christ, obedience, justification, and life. Also, by Adam sin* entered the world; by Christ, its source, grace* has superabounded. Finally, the fruitful union of Adam and Eve prefigured the union of Christ and the Church; this in its turn becomes the mystery which founds Christian marriage* (E 5,25-33; cf 1 Co 6,16).

3. *The Christian and the two Adams.* Son of Adam by his birth and reborn in Christ by his faith, the Christian preserves a lasting relationship with the first and second Adam, though this relationship is of a different nature and scope. He is faithful to the true meaning of the account of the beginnings and does not use the sin of the first man as an excuse to free himself from blame but realizes that Adam is himself, with his weakness, his sin, and it is his duty to put off from himself the old man, according to the words of Paul (E 4,22f; Col 3, 9f). And this in order "to put on Jesus Christ, the new man"; thus his entire destiny is written in the drama of the two Adams. Or better, he finds in Christ the man* unexcelled, according to the commentary made by He 2,5-9 on Psalm 8,3ff. He who was temporarily beneath the angels, to merit the salvation of all men, has received the glory* promised to the true Adam.

→Abraham I 3—Brother OT 1; NT o.2—Conscience 2 c—Creation OT II 1.2; NT II 2—Earth OT I 2—Fathers and Father I 2, III 1—Generation—Image II, IV, V—Jesus Christ II 1 d—Man—New III 3a—Paradise 2a—Responsibility 1—Sin I—Son of Man OT I; NT II—Woman OT 1.

MJL & XLD jjk

ADMIRATION→Adoration—Blessing I, II 3, III 5—Eucharist IV 2—Miracle—Praise II 2—Thanksgiving—Works OT I 1.2.

ADONAI→Lord OT—Name OT 4—Yahweh 3.

ADOPTION→Child III—Fathers & Father III 3. 4, V 2, VI—Fruitfulness II 3—Son of God I; NT II—Sterility.

ADORATION

Ezekiel before the glory* of Yahweh (Ez 1,28), Saul before the vision of the risen Christ (Ac 9,4), are found prostrated on the ground, as if dead. The holiness* and the grandeur of God* have something of the overwhelming for a creature; this plunges him deep into his own nothingness.

If it is exceptional that man is found thus

to encounter God directly, it is normal that, in the universe and all through life, he recognize the presence* and the action of God, His glory and His holiness. Adoration is the expression both spontaneous and conscious, imposed and willed, of the complex reaction of man seized by the proximity of God; man is in a state of awareness sharpened by his own insignificance or his own sin*; a state of silent confusion (Jb 42,1-6), veneration, trembling (Ps 5,8) and thankfulness (Gn 24,48), jubilant homage (Ps 95,1-6) in all his being.

Because it invades in fact his whole being, this reaction of faith translates itself into external acts; and it is hardly true adoration unless the body* expresses in some way the sovereignty of the Lord* over His creation* and the homage of the creature, rapt and acquiescent. But the sinful creature continually tries to escape the divine embrace, and to reduce his adhesion to external forms; thus the only adoration which pleases God is that which comes from the heart*.

I. ACTS OF ADORATION

These acts are reduced to two, prostration and kissing. Each in worship* takes on its own consecrated form, but they always join together the spontaneous movement of the creature before God, torn between fear* of panic and the fascination of wonder.

1. *Prostration*, before becoming a spontaneous gesture, is an attitude forcibly imposed by a more powerful adversary, such as that of Sisera falling mortally stricken by Jael (Jg 5,27), or that to which Babylon submitted the captive Israelites (Is 51,23). To avoid being constrained to this by violence, the weak man often prefers on his own initiative to lower himself before the stronger and implore his grace* (1 K 1,13). The Assyrian bas-reliefs like to show the vassals of the king on their knees, their heads touching the earth. To the Lord* Yahweh, "who is raised above all" (1 Ch 29,11), belongs the adoration of all peoples (Ps 99,1-5) and of the whole earth (96,9).

2. *The kiss* unites with respect the need of contact and adherence, the nuance of love* (Ex 18,7; 1 S 10,1...). The pagans kissed their idols* (1 K 19,18); but the kiss of one adoring who, not being able to reach his god, places his hand before his mouth (*ad os = adorare*,

cf Jb 31,26ff), is a gesture well suited to show at one and the same time his own desire to touch God and the distance which separates him from God. The classical gesture of the "orantes" of the catacombs (perpetuated in the Christian liturgy) with arms extended, hands showing by their position the offering, the supplication, or the salutation, no longer involves the kiss but does reflect its profound meaning.

3. *All the gestures of worship*, not only the ritual prostration before Yahweh (Dt 26,10; Ps 22,28ff) and before the ark* (Ps 99,5), but the totality of the actions performed before the altar* (2 K 18,22) or in the "house* of Yahweh" (2 S 12,20), among others the sacrifices* (Gn 22,5; 2 K 17,36), that is to say, all the gestures belonging to the service* of God, can be gathered together under the formula "to adore Yahweh" (1 S 1,3; 2 S 15,32). This is so because adoration has become the most fitting expression, and also the most varied, for homage to God before whom the angels prostrate themselves (Ne 9,6) and before whom false gods cease any longer to exist (Zp 2,11).

II. YOU SHALL ADORE THE LORD YOUR GOD

1. *Yahweh alone has the right to adoration.* If the OT is familiar with prostration before men, stripped of equivocations (Gn 23,7.12; 2 S 24,20; 2 K 2,15; 4,37) and often provoked by the more or less clear sense of the divine majesty (1 S 28,14.20; Gn 18,2; 19,1; Nm 22,31; Js 5,14), it forbids rigorously every gesture of adoration capable of giving any value whatsoever to any possible rival of Yahweh: idols*, stars* (Dt 4,19), strange gods (Ex 34,14; Nm 25, 2). There is no doubt that the systematic proscription of all determined idolaters rooted in Israel the profound sense of true adoration, and gave its pure religious value to the proud refusal of Mordecai (Es 3,2.5), and to that of the three Jewish youths before the statue of Nebuchadnezzar (Dn 3,18). All this is contained in the answer that Jesus gives the Tempter: "You shall adore the Lord your God and worship Him alone" (Mt 4,10f).

2. *Jesus Christ is Lord.* The adoration reserved to God alone, was "a scandal to the Jews" (1 C 1,23), proclaimed as due to Jesus* crucified, acknowledged as Christ and Lord* (Ac 2,36). "At His name*, every knee bends,

in heaven, on earth and below the earth" (Ph 2,9ff; Ap 15,4). This worship* has for its object the risen and exalted Christ (Mt 28,9.17; Lk 24,52), but faith* already recognized the Son* of God and adores Him (Mt 14,33; Jn 9,38) in the man still destined to death, and even in the newborn man (Mt 2,2.11; cf Is 49,7).

The adoration of the Lord Jesus takes nothing away from the firmness of Christians, alert to refuse to the angels* (Ap 19,10; 22,9) and to the apostles (Ac 10,25f; 14,11-18) even the external gestures of adoration. But, to confess* their adoration of a Messiah*, a God made Man and Savior, they are led to defy openly the worship of the Caesars, represented by the beast* of the Apocalypse (Ap 13,4-15; 14,9ff), and to brave the imperial power.

3. *Adoration in spirit and in truth.* The novelty of Christian adoration is not merely in the new personage which it contemplates: God in three persons; this God, "who is Spirit*," transforms adoration and brings it to its perfection: from this time those born of the Spirit (Jn 3,8) can adore "in spirit and truth" (4,24). This attitude does not mean a purely interior procedure without gestures or outward forms. It comes from a consecration of the whole being, mind, soul and body (1 Th 5,23). Radically sanctified in this way, the true adorers no longer need Jerusalem* or Gerazim (Jn 4,20-23), or a national religion. All is theirs, because they are Christ's and Christ is God's (1 Co 3,22f).

Adoration in spirit actually takes place in the only temple* agreeable to the Father, the body* of Christ risen (Jn 2,19-22). The "spiritual ones" (Jn 3,8) join their adoration to the only adoration in which the Father* finds complacence (Mt 3,17): they repeat the cry of the well-beloved Son*: "Abba, Father" (G 4,4-9). Finally, in heaven, there will no longer be a temple: instead there will be God and the Lamb (Ap 21,22). Adoration will continue night and day (4,8), giving honour and glory to Him who lives for ever and ever (4,10; 15,3f).

→Blasphemy—Creation OT IV—Fear of God I—Idols I—Knee—Perfume 2—Prayer—Serve II 1—Silence 2—Worship.

JdV & JG jjk

ADULTERY

Although the Ten Commandments and later the prophets condemn adultery absolutely, the faithfulness* demanded of the two spouses in their marriage* will only be fully revealed by Christ. But the total fidelity demanded of the woman* in the OT can symbolize what God expects of His people; consequently the prophets condemn unfaithfulness to the covenant as a spiritual adultery.

1. *Marriage and adultery.* Although adultery is forbidden (Ex 20,14; Dt 5,18; Jr 7,9; Ml 3,5), the Law's definition of it is restricted. It is the act by which the possession of a woman by her husband or fiancé is violated (Lv 20,10; Dt 22, 22ff). The woman is regarded as the man's chattel (Ex 20,17) rather than as a person with whom he forms but one in the fidelity of a mutual love* (Gn 2,23f). This degradation of the woman is connected with the appearance of polygamy, which is associated with one of Cain's descendants who is remarkable for his violence (Gn 4,19-24). Polygamy will be tolerated for a long time (Dt 21,15; cf 17,17; Lv 18,18); and yet the wise men point out the gravity of adultery (Pr 6,24-29; Si 23,22-28) and urge men to reserve their love for the wife of their youth (Pr 5,15-19; Ml 2,14f). Moreover, they condemn relations with prostitutes, although this does not make a man an adulterer (Pr 23,27; Si 9,3.6).

Jesus, whose mercy saves the adulterous woman, condemns her sin (Jn 8,1-11), but at the same time reveals the full scope of conjugal fidelity (Mt 5,27f.31f; 19,9 p). It binds men as well as women (Mk 10,11); it binds them indissolubly (Mt 19,6) and inwardly (5, 28); to remarry after divorce is to commit adultery; to desire to be united with any other than one's husband or wife is to commit adultery in one's heart. To avoid this sin, which excludes a person from the kingdom (1 Co 6,9), Paul warns that it is necessary to look for the source of faithfulness in love (R 13,9f). In this way it will be possible to avoid defiling the sanctity of marriage (He 13,4).

2. *Covenant and adultery.* The covenant*, which is meant to unite men with God by a bond of faithful love, is pictured by the prophets as an indissoluble marriage (Ho 2,21f; Is 54,5f) (cf Spouse*); and so the infidelity of the people is branded as infidelity and prostitution (Ho 2,4), for the people give themselves up to

the worship of idols like a prostitute surrendering herself to her lovers, for the sake of gain (Ho 2,7; 4,10; Jr 5,7; 13,27; Ez 23,43ff; Is 57,3).

Jesus takes up the image in order to condemn lack of faith; He calls those who are slow to believe and ask for signs, and the unfaithful ones who are ashamed of Him and His Gospel, "an adulterous generation" (Mt 12,39; 16,4; Mk 8,38). These condemnations emphasize the absolute fidelity which is both the result and the prerequisite of love.

→Covenant OT II 2—Desire II—Marriage OT II 3; NT I 1—Pardon I—Sexuality III—Spouse OT—Woman OT 3.

MFL ems

ADVENT→Day of the Lord—Fulfil NT 1—Visitation—Watch I.

ADVERSARY→Antichrist—Satan.

ADVICE→Plan of God—Wisdom.

AFFLICTION→Console—Joy NT I 2, II 2—Persecution — Poor — Sadness — Suffering — Widows o.

AFTERLIFE→Death—Resurrection—Soul II 2.3.

AGAPE→Eucharist II 3—Love O—Meal III.

AGE→Time OT III 2; NT II 2, III 1—World NT.

AGONY→Anguish—Death NT II 1—Sadness NT 1—Suffering NT II—Watch II 1.

AGRICULTURE→Earth OT I, II 3—Fruit—Harvest—Sowing I—Vine—Vintage—Work.

AID→Grace V — Providence 1 — Salvation — Strength II—Woman OT 1.

ALIEN→Stranger.

ALLEGORY→Figure NT III—Parable I 3.

ALLELUIA→Praise II 2.

ALLIANCE→Covenant.

ALMSGIVING

OT

1. *The meaning of the word.* Hebrew does not have any special term to signify almsgiving. Our English word comes from the Greek *eleemosyne*, which in the LXX means either God's mercy* (Ps 24,5; Is 59,16) or (rarely) "justice," the loyal response of men to God (Dt 6,25), or finally the mercy of man for his fellow-man (Gn 47,29). This last is genuine only if it is carried over into actions among which the material aid to those who are in need plays a prominent role. The Greek word of itself comes to be limited to the precise meaning of "almsgiving" in the NT and some of the late books of the OT: Dn, Tb, Si. These three books, however, admit again the *eleemosyne* of God for man (Dn 9,16; Tb 3,2; Si 16,14; 17,29): for the entire Bible, almsgiving, a charitable deed of one man for another, is primarily an imitation of the actions of God who has first given proof of His goodness toward man.

2. *The duty of almsgiving.* If the word is late, the idea of almsgiving is as old as the biblical religion which demands from the very beginning love* for our brothers* and the poor*. Thus some codified forms of almsgiving, certainly old, are found in the Law*: the obligation to leave a part of the crops for the gleaning and the picking (Lv 19,9; 23,22; Dt 24,20f; Rt 2), the tri-annual tithe for the profit of those who have no land: Levites, foreigners, orphans, and widows (Dt 14,28f; cf Tb 1,8). The poor man exists and his cry ought to be answered with generosity (Dt 15,11; Pr 3,27f; 14,21) and tact (Si 18,15ff).

3. *Almsgiving and religious life.* This almsgiving must not be pure philanthropy but a religious gesture. Often tied in with special liturgical celebrations (2 S 6,19; Ne 8,10ff; 2 Ch 30,21-26; 35,7ff), generosity toward the poor is part of the normal course of feasts* (Dt 16, 11.14; Tb 2,1f). Moreover this gesture assumes its value from the fact that it attains God Himself (Pr 19,17) and gives a right to His reward* (Ez 18,7; cf 16,49; Pr 21,13; 28,27) and to pardon* for sins (Dn 4,24; Si 3,30). It is equivalent to a sacrifice* offered to God (Si 35,2). In depriving himself of his goods, man makes a treasury for himself (Si 29,12). "Happy is he who thinks of the poor and the weak" (Ps 41,1-4; cf Pr 14,21). Old Tobit thus warmly

exhorts his son: "Do not ever turn your face away from a poor man, and God will never turn His away from you... If you have much, give more; if you have little, give less, but do not hesitate to give alms... When you give alms, do not have any regrets in your eyes..." (Tb 4,7-11.15f).

NT

With the coming of Christ, almsgiving preserves its worth but is situated in a new economy which confers on it a new meaning.

1. *The practice of almsgiving.* It is admired by believers especially when practiced by strangers*, those "fearing God," who also manifest their sympathy for the faith (Lk 7,5; Ac 9,36; 10,2). Besides, Jesus reckoned it along with fasting* and prayer* as one of the three pillars of the spiritual life (Mt 6,1-18).

But in recommending it Jesus requires that it be done with perfect disinterestedness, without any ostentation (Mt 6,1-4), "without expecting anything in return" (Lk 6,35; 14,14), even without measure (Lk 6,30). No one should be satisfied because he has achieved a regulated "tariff," however elevated: for the traditional tithe John the Baptist seems to substitute a half-portion (Lk 3,11) which Zaccheus indeed realizes (Lk 19,8); but what Christ expects of His followers is that they should not remain deaf to any call (Mt 5,42 p), since the poor* are always with us (Mt 26,11); and, if they have nothing left of their own (cf Ac 2,44), they still have the duty of sharing the gifts of Christ (Ac 3,6) and to work* to provide for those who are in need (E 4,28).

2 *Almsgiving and Christ.* If almsgiving is so basic a duty, it is because its meaning is found in the faith in Christ, and this in a more or less profound way.

a) If Jesus holds with the Jewish tradition that almsgiving is the source of heavenly reward* (Mt 6,2.4), that it constitutes a treasure in heaven (Lk 12,21.33f), thanks to the friends* that are made by doing this (Lk 16,9), this is not by reason of a calculated interest: it is because through our less fortunate brothers* we reach Jesus in person: "This that you have done to one of these little ones..." (Mt 25,31-46).

b) If the disciple must give all in alms (Lk 11,41; 12,33; 18,22), it is primarily in order that he may follow* Jesus without looking sullenly upon his goods (Mt 19,21f p); finally it is to be liberal as Jesus Himself who, "rich as He was, made Himself poor for you so as to enrich you by His poverty" (2 Co 8,9).

c) Finally, in order to show that Christian almsgiving is governed by laws different from those of mere philanthropy, Jesus did not hesitate to defend against Judas the gratuitous gesture of the woman who had just "lost" the value of three hundred days of work in pouring out her precious perfume: "The poor you will always have with you, but me you will not always have" (Mt 26,11 p). "The poor" pertain to the ordinary economy of things (Dt 15,11) which is normal to our sinful humanity; Jesus Himself signifies the Messianic supernatural economy; and the former finds its true meaning only through the latter: the poor are helped in a Christian manner only in reference to the love of God manifested in the passion and death of Jesus Christ.

3. *Almsgiving in the Church.* Even if certain gratuitous gestures remain necessary so as to prevent the confusing of the gospel of the kingdom with the extinction of poverty, it still remains that, in order to reach the "Spouse who has been taken away from us" (Mt 9,15), we must help our neighbor*; "How does the love of God abide in him who closes his heart to his brother in need" (1 Jn 3,17; cf 2,15)? How can one celebrate the sacrament of eucharistic communion* without sharing his goods fraternally (1 Co 11,20ff)?

Almsgiving can have a scope even more vast and signify the union of churches. This is what Paul means when he attaches a holy name to begging, to the collection which he makes in favor of the mother Church of Jerusalem: it is a "service" (2 Co 8,4; 9,1.12f), a "rite" (9,12). In order to mend the breach which began to widen between the gentile Church and the Jewish Church, Paul takes care to explain through substantial almsgiving the union that exists between these two divisions of the same body* of Christ (cf Ac 11,29; G 2,10; R 15,26f; 1 Co 16,1-4); with what ardor does he utter a true "sermon on charity" in the address to the Corinthians (2 Co 8—9)! We must aim at establishing equality between brothers (8,13) in imitating the liberality of Christ (8,9); in order that God be glorified (9,1-14), we must "sow* abundantly"; for "God loves the joyful giver" (9,6f).

11

CW pjb

ALTAR

In every religion the altar is the center of sacrificial worship* (hb. *zabah* = to sacrifice, root of *mizbeah* = altar). The altar is the sign of the divine presence*; Moses supposes such a belief when he throws half of the blood of the victims upon the altar and the other half on the people who in this way enter into communion with God (Ex 24,6ff); Paul says also: "Are not those who eat the victims partakers of the altar" (1 Co 10,18)? In the perfect sacrifice* the sign gives way to the reality: Christ is at one time priest, victim, and altar.

1. *From the memorial to the place of worship.* In the beginning if a man built an altar, it was in order to respond to God who had just visited him; it is this which the oft-repeated formula, found in the deeds of the patriarchs, means: "He built an altar to Yahweh and he called upon His name*" (Gn 12,7f; 13,18; 26,25). Besides being a place where sacrifices are offered, the altar was a memorial of divine favor; the symbolic names which these altars received are a witness* of this (Gn 33,20; 35, 1-7; Jg 6,24). However it was also the place of libations and sacrifices. If, at the beginning, more or less suitable rocks* were deemed satisfactory (Jg 6,20; 13,19f), a person quickly took care to build an altar of beaten earth or of the rough stones* which were coarse but better adapted to its end (Ex 20,24ff).

For the descendants of the patriarchs, the place of worship tended to have more value than the memory of the theophanies which had given them birth; so it frequently became a place of pilgrimage*. This primacy of place over memorial was already manifest in the fact that the ancient places of Canaanite worship, Bethel (Gn 35,7) or Schechem (33,19) and later Gilgal (Js 4,20) or Jerusalem (Jg 19,10), would often be chosen. In fact, when they enter Canaan, the chosen people are in the presence of pagan altars which the law demands be torn down without mercy (Ex 34,13; Dt 7,5; Nm 33,52); hence Gideon (Jg 6,25-32) or Jehu (2 K 10,27) thus destroy the altars of Baal. But ordinarily the chosen people are satisfied to

"baptize" the high places with their material offering (1 K 3,4).

At this stage the altar can contribute to the degradation of religion in a twofold manner: by forgetting that the altar is only a sign to attain the living God, and by making the worship of Yahweh like the worship of idols*. In fact, Solomon inaugurates a period of tolerance for the idols introduced by his foreign wives (1 K 11,7f). Ahab will do likewise (1 K 16,32); Ahaz and Manasseh will bring some pagan-style altars into the temple itself (2 K 16,10-16; 21,5). For their part, the prophets will reprimand the multiplication of altars (Am 2,8; Ho 8,11; Jr 3,6).

2. *The altar of the one temple in Jerusalem.* A solution to the problem was brought forward by centralizing the worship at Jerusalem (2 K 23,8f; cf 1 K 8,63f). The altar of holocausts from this time crystalizes the religious life of Israel, and numerous psalms testify to the place it holds in the hearts of the faithful (Ps 26,6; 43,4; 84,4; 118,27). When Ezekiel describes the future temple, the altar is the object of minute descriptions (Ez 43,13-17), and the priestly legislation which concerns it is referred to Moses (Ex 27,1-8; Lv 1—7). The horns of the altar, already mentioned long ago as a place of refuge (1 K 1,50f; 2,28), take on great importance: they will be frequently sprinkled with blood* for the rite of expiation* (Lv 16,18; Ex 30,10). These rites clearly indicate that the altar symbolizes the presence of Yahweh.

At the same time the priestly* functions are stated precisely: the priests become exclusively the ministers of the altar, whereas the levites are charged with the material cares (Nm 3,6-10). The Chronicler, who emphasizes this use (1 Ch 6,48f), writes the history of the kingdom in accord with these prescriptions (2 Ch 26, 16-20; 29,18-36; 35,7-18). Finally, as a sign of veneration for the altar, the first caravan of repatriates from the exile are anxious to reconstruct at once the altar of holocausts (Ezr 3,3ff), and Judas Maccabeus will manifest the same piety later (1 M 4,44-59).

3. *From sign to the reality.* For Jesus the altar remains holy*, but it is by reason of that which it signifies. Jesus recalls this signification which was effaced by the casuistry of the Pharisees (Mt 23,18ff) and neglected in practice: to approach the altar to sacrifice is to draw near to God: this cannot be done with anger in one's heart (5,23f).

Christ does not only give the true meaning to ancient worship, but He puts an end to it. In the new temple which is His body (Jn 2,21), there is no altar but He (He 13,10). For it is the altar which sanctifies the victim (Mt 23,19); thus when He, the perfect victim, is offered, it is He Himself who sanctifies Himself (Jn 17,19); He is at the same time priest and altar. Furthermore, to partake of the body and blood of the Lord is to partake at the altar which is the Lord; it is to share His table (1 Co 10, 16-21).

Thus the Apocalypse speaks of the heavenly altar under which the martyrs are kept (Ap 6,9), a golden altar whose flame causes abundant and fragrant smoke to rise to God, to which are united the prayers of the saints (8,3). This flame is also a symbol which stands for Christ and perfects the symbolism of the Lamb*. It is the one altar of the only sacrifice whose fragrance is pleasing to God; it is the celestial altar on which the offerings of the Church are presented to God, united to the only and perfect offering of Christ (He 10,14). Our altars of stone are only images of this altar, which the *Pontifical* expresses when it says: "the altar is Christ."

→Blood OT 3—Mountain II 2—Perfume 2—Pilgrimage OT 1—Sacrifice OT I 1; NT II 1 —Stone 1—Temple—Worship OT I.

DS pjb

AMEN

Far from being always and exactly rendered by the usual translation, "So be it!" which expresses a simple wish and not a certitude, the term *Amen* means above all: certainly, truly, surely, or simply yes. Actually this adverb comes from a Hebrew root which implies firmness, solidity, sureness (cf faith*). To say Amen is to proclaim that one holds for true what has just been said, with a view to ratifying a proposition or to uniting oneself to a prayer.

1. *Commitment and acclamation.* When it confirms a word, *Amen* can have a weak meaning which would equal our "So be it!" (Jr 28,6). But most often it is a word* which commits: by it one testifies to his own agreement with someone (1 K 1,36), one accepts a mission (Jr 11,15), one assumes the responsi-

bility of an oath and the judgment of God which will follow (Nm 5,22). More solemn yet is the collective commitment taken during the liturgical renewal of the covenant (Dt 27,15-26; Ne 5,13).

In the liturgy the word can also assume another value; if man commits himself before God, it is because one has confidence in His word and one entrusts oneself to the power and goodness of that word; this total adhesion is at the same time a blessing* from Him to whom one submits oneself (Ne 8,6); it is a prayer sure of being heard (Tb 8,8; Jdt 15,10). *Amen* then is a liturgical acclamation, and under this aspect it finds a place after the doxologies (1 Ch 16,36); it frequently has this meaning in the NT (R 1,25; G 1,5; 2 P 3,18; He 13,21). As an acclamation by which the assembly unites itself to him who prays in its name, the Amen supposes that, to adhere to the words being heard, one understands their meaning (1 Co 14,16). As adherence and acclamation, the Amen finally concludes the canticles of the elect in the liturgy of heaven (Ap 5,14; 19,4), where it is united to the Alleluia.

2. *The Amen of God and the Amen of the Christian.* God who has so liberally committed Himself remains faithful to His promises*. He is the God* of truth*. This is the meaning of the title God-Amen (Is 65,16).

The Amen of God is Jesus Christ. In fact, by Him God realizes His promises in their fullness and manifests that there is not in Him Yes and No, but only Yes (2 Co 1,19f). In this text, Paul substitutes for the Hebrew *Amen* a Greek word, *Naï*, which means *Yes*. When Jesus prefaces what He is going to say with the word Amen (Mt 5,18; 18,3...), doubled in John's Gospel (Jn 1,51; 5,19), He is acting in a way that was unheard of among the Jews. No doubt He is using the liturgical formula, but in adopting it for His own special use He is probably transposing the prophetic announcement: "it is Yahweh who speaks." He is not only stressing that He is the messenger of the God of truth, but also that His words are true. The statement introduced in this way has a pre-history, which remains unexpressed and of which the Amen is the conclusion. And what else could this be except the dialogue between the Father and the Son? For Jesus is not only He who speaks the truth in speaking the words of God; He is the Word* itself of the true God, the Amen transcending all others, the witness* faithful and true (Ap 3,14).

Thus it is in uniting oneself to Christ that the Christian ought to respond to God if he wishes to be faithful*; the only efficacious Amen is that which is pronounced by Christ to the glory of God (2 Co 1,20). The Church pronounces this Amen in union with the elect in heaven (Ap 7,12) and no one can pronounce it unless the grace of the Lord Jesus is with him; thus the desire which terminates the Bible and which a final Amen seals is that this grace be with us all (Ap 22,21).

→Faith O—Faithfulness—Praise III—Promises —Truth OT—Unbelief O.

CT jjk

ANATHEMA

The semitic root of the word *herem*, anathema, means "to set aside," "to remove from profane use." Its use in the Bible indicates essentially a consecration to God.

OT

In the oldest texts the custom of the anathema, which Israel has in common with its neighbors, like Moab, is not the simple massacre of the conquered enemy, but one of the religious rules of the holy* war*. In order to obtain victory, Israel, waging Yahweh's wars, vows the booty to the anathema, that is, it renounces the right to make any profit out of it and makes a vow to consecrate it to Yahweh (Nb 21,2f; Js 6). This consecration entails the total destruction of the booty, both living beings and material objects. If it is not carried out, punishment is to be expected (1 S 15); and it is the same if it is violated by sacrilege, which leads to defeat (Js 7).

In fact, its application seems to have been rather rare; the majority of Canaanite towns were occupied by Israel (Js 24,13; Jg 1,27-35), like Gezer (Js 16,10; 1 K 9,16) or Jerusalem (Jg 1,21; 2 S 5,6f). Some of these towns even concluded alliances, like Gabaon (Js 9) and Sichem (Gn 34).

The deuteronomic historians knew that the anathema had not been applied at the time of the conquest (Jg 3,1-6; 1 K 9,21). Nevertheless, they made a general law out of it in a reaction against the corrupting influence of the Canaanite religion on Israel and to reaffirm the sanctity of the chosen people (Dt 7,1-6). This is the reason for the very systematic presentation of the history of the conquest: they have transferred into the past religious reaction, at a time when the exclusive sovereignty of Yahweh over the holy land* and its inhabitants was at stake.

The evolution of the word *herem* seems to have led to a separation of its two elements: on the one hand, the destruction and the punishment that follow infidelity toward Yahweh in particular (Dt 13,13-18; Jr 25,9); on the other hand, in the priestly literature, the consecration of a human being or of an object to God, without any possibility of it being bought back (Lv 27,28f; Nb 18,14).

NT

In the NT the question of a holy war no longer arises, nor does the idea of vowing enemies* to the anathema. But the word continues in use, meaning a curse* (and, in Lk 21, 5, referring to the votive offerings in the temple of Jerusalem).

When used by the Jews in oath* formulas (Mk 14,71 p; Ac 23,12), it means the curse pronounced against oneself in the event of committing perjury.

In the writings of Paul it is a form of curse expressing the judgment of God against the unfaithful (G 1,8f; 1 Co 16,22). It is impossible for a Christian to pronounce this word against Jesus (1 Co 12,3). When the apostle says that he would rather be anathema if this would lead to his fellow Jews winning salvation, he makes it clear that this would mean for him separation from Christ (R 9,3). This paradoxical formula, then, stands for the ultimate curse.

→Apostles II 1—Curse—Holy OT III 2—Pure OT I 1—War OT II.

PS ems

ANGELS

The name of angel is not a name that indicates nature but function: hb. *mal'ak*, gr. *angelos*, means "messenger." The angels are "spirits destined to serve, sent on missions for the good of those who should inherit salvation" (He 1,14). Angels escape our ordinary perception and make up a mysterious world. Never did their existence cause a problem in the

Bible; but beyond this point, the teaching on angels manifests a certain development, and the manner in which they are spoken of and in which they are represented supposes a continuous recourse to the wealth of religious symbolism.

OT

1. *The angels of Yahweh and the angel of Yahweh.* Taking up a characteristic common in the oriental mythologies, but adapting it to the revelation of the one God, the OT often represents God as an oriental sovereign (1 K 22,19; Is 6,1ff). The members of His court are also His servants* (Jb 4,18); they are likewise called the holy* ones (Jb 5,1; 15,15; Ps 89,6; Dn 4,10); or the sons* of God (Ps 29,1; 89,7; Dt 32,8). Among them, the cherubim (whose name is of Mesopotamian origin) support His throne (Ps 80,2; 99,1), draw His chariot (Ez 10,1), serve as His mounts (Ps 18,11), or protect the entrance of His domain to keep out the profane (Gn 3,24); the seraphim (the "fiery ones") sing His glory (Is 6,3), and it is one of them who purifies the lips of Isaiah during his inaugural vision (Is 6,7). The cherubim are found in the iconography of the temple in which they shelter the ark with their wings (1 K 6,23-29; Ex 25,18f). A whole heavenly army (1 K 22,19; Ps 148,2; Ne 9,6) thus extol the glory* of God; this army is at His disposal to govern the world and to carry out His orders (Ps 103,20); it establishes a link between heaven and earth (Gn 28,12).

Nevertheless, besides these enigmatic messengers, the ancient biblical narratives know an angel of Yahweh (Gn 16,7; 22,11; Ex 3,2; Jg 2,1) who is not different from Yahweh Himself and manifests himself here below in visible form (Gn 16,13; Ex 3,2): living in light inaccessible (1 Tm 6,16), God* cannot allow creatures to see His face* (Ex 33,20); men perceive only a mysterious reflection of it. The angel of Yahweh of the old texts serves therefore to hand down a theology still archaic, which, by the title "Angel of the Lord," leaves traces even in the NT (Mt 1,20.24; 2,13.19; Lk 1,11; 2,9) and also in patristic writings. However, in accord with the progression of revelation, God's role has more and more devolved upon the angels, His ordinary messengers.

2. *Development of the doctrine of angels.* Originally, to the angels was attributed without discrimination tasks both good and bad (cf Jb 1,12). God sent His good angel to protect Israel (Ex 23,20); but for a mission* of death, He sent angels of evil (Ps 78,49), such as the exterminator (Ex 12,23; cf 2 S 24,16f; 2 K 19,35). Even the Satan* of the Book of Job still took part in the divine court (Jb 1,6-12; 2,1-10). However, after the exile, angelic tasks were henceforth more specialized, and the angels acquired a moral quality as was fitting their role: good angels on one side, Satan and the evil spirits* on the other; between them there was constant opposition (Ze 3,1f). This conception of a spiritual world which was divided was indirectly influenced by Mesopotamia and Persia: to be able better to face the Irano-Babylonian syncretism, Jewish thought developed its earlier doctrine; without departing from its rigorous monotheism, it sometimes made use of a borrowed symbolism and systematized its representation of the angelic world. Thus it is that the Book of Tobit cites the seven angels who stand before the face of God (Tb 12,15; cf Ap 8,2)—a structure similar to the angelology of Persia. But the role attributed to the angels has not changed. They watch over men (Tb 3,17; Ps 91,11; Dn 3,49f) and present their prayers to God (Tb 12,12); they preside over the destinies of nations (Dn 10,13-21). Since Ezekiel, they explain to the prophets the meaning of their visions (Ez 40,3f; Ze 1,8f); this finally becomes a literary trait characteristic of apocalypses (Dn 1,5-19; 9,21ff). They receive names* corresponding to their functions: Raphael, "God heals" (Tb 3,17; 12,15); Gabriel "Hero of God" (Dn 8,16; 9,21); Michael, "Who is like God?" (Dn 10,13.21; 12,1). It is to the last, the leader of all, that the Jewish community is entrusted (Dn 10,13.21; 12,1). These facts are more amplified in the apocryphal literature (Book of Henoch) and in rabbinical literature, which tried to organize them into more or less coherent systems. Thus the doctrine of the OT on the existence of the angelic world and its presence in the world of men is constantly affirmed. But the mode of presentation and the classifications which OT teaching used have necessarily a symbolic character which makes understanding a delicate question.

NT

The NT resorts to the same conventional language, which it draws both from the sacred books and from contemporary Jewish tradition. So the NT enumerates the archangels (1 Th 4,16; Jude 9), the cherubim (He 9,5), the thrones, dominations, principalities, and powers (Col 1,16), to which elsewhere are added the virtues (E 1,21). This hierarchy, the degrees of which vary in expression, does not have the character of a fixed teaching, but of a secondary element, and one with rather fluctuating outlines. But as in the OT, the essential of the thought is from elsewhere, reorganized here around the revelation of Jesus Christ.

1. *The angels and Christ.* The angelic world occupies a place in the thought of Jesus. The evangelists sometimes talk of His intimate dealings with the angels (Mt 4,11; Lk 22,43); Jesus mentions the angels as real and active beings. While watching over men, they see the face of the Father (Mt 18,10 p). Their life escapes subjection to earthly condition (cf Mt 22,30 p). Although they do not know the date of the last judgment, which is known to the Father alone (Mt 24, 36 p), they will be its executors (Mt 13,39.49; 24,31). From now on, they share in the joy of God when sinners are converted (Lk 15,10). All these traits are in conformity with the traditional tenets.

Jesus, moreover, clarifies their situation in relation to the Son* of Man, that mysterious figure who defines Him, notably in His future glory*: the angels will accompany Him at the day of His parousia (Mt 25,31); they will rise from and descend upon Him (Jn 1,51), as earlier upon Jacob's ladder (Gn 28,10...); He will send them forth to gather the elect (Mt 24,31 p) and to reject the damned from the kingdom (Mt 13,41f). From the time of the passion, they are at His service, and He can demand their intervention (Mt 26,53).

Primitive Christian thought is only elaborating the words of Jesus when it assures us that the angels are inferior to Him. Humbled below them by His incarnation (He 2,7), He merited nonetheless their adoration by His status as Son* of God (He 1,6f; cf Ps 97,7). Since His resurrection, it is clear that God made them subject to Him (E 1,20f), they who have been created by Him, in Him, and for Him (Col 1,16). They now acknowledge His dominion (Ap 5,11f; 7,11f), and they will form His escort on the last day* (2 Th 1,7; Ap 14, 14-16; cf 1 Th 4,16). Thus the angelic world is subordinated to Christ, the mystery it has contemplated (1 Tm 3,16; cf 1 P 1,12).

2. *Angels and men.* In this perspective, the angels continue to accomplish for men the tasks which the OT already attributed to them. When a supernatural communication comes from heaven to earth, they remain its mysterious messengers: Gabriel transmits the twofold annunciation (Lk 1,19.26); a celestial army intervenes on the night of the nativity (Lk 2,9-14); again, angels announce the resurrection (Mt 28,5ff p) and make the apostles understand the meaning of the ascension (Ac 1,10f). Helpers of Christ in the work of salvation (He 1,14), they guarantee the protection of men (Mt 18,10; Ac 12,15), they present to God the prayers of the saints (Ap 5,8; 8,3), they lead the souls of the just to paradise (Lk 16,22: *"In Paradisum deducant te Angeli"*). To protect the Church, they continue with Michael, their leader, the fight against Satan which has existed from the beginning (Ap 12,1-9).

An intimate bond thus links the earthly world with the celestial world; above, the angels celebrate a perpetual liturgy (Ap 4,8-11) to which is united here below the liturgy of the Church (cf *Gloria*, Preface, *Sanctus*). Supernatural presences surround us; the seer of the Apocalypse concretizes these presences in the conventional language sanctified by usage. This demands on our part a reverence (cf Js 5,13ff; Dn 10,9; Tb 12,16) which is not to be confused with adoration (Ap 22,8f). Beyond these explicit statements in the Bible, the critic may ask what is the meaning of these representations, largely borrowed from the surrounding pagan world, which introduce peripheral elements into the biblical message. The problem is not easy to resolve. One point is sure. Whatever may be the nature and structure of the spiritual universe that surrounds God and carries out His designs, it is through this submission to Christ, the mediator of salvation, that it is incorporated into the divine plan of creation and salvation. This is how it enters the sphere of our faith.

→Apparitions of Christ 1—Evil Spirits OT 1.3 —Heaven IV—Mediator I 3, II 3—Satan I 1— Son of God OT O—Stars 2.4.

PMG & PG jjk

ANGUISH

Unlike fear, which is caused by beings of this world, and unlike care*, which means a particular concern or an excessive preoccupation with a precise task or an actual mission, anguish betrays a feeling of uneasiness springing from the depths of one's being, a feeling of uncertainty in the face of death or with regard to the future in general. In the Bible, at least in its Greek translation, this feeling appears in accounts that include one or the other of the following words. The people under siege are in *agonia* over the outcome of the battle (2 M 3,14ff; cf 15,19; Lk 22,44). A man's heart fails where the situation seems to be impossible (*aporeo, aporia*; Ho 13,8; 2 M 8,20; Ws 11,5; Lk 21,25). The term *synechomai* conveys the idea of blockade, of being cut off (1 S 23,8; 2 S 20,3); one is seized, overwhelmed, stifled, overcome by fear (Lk 8,37) or by sickness (Mt 4,24; Lk 4,38); moreover, one is oppressed, plunged in distress (*stenochoria*: Dt 28,53; 2 Co 4,8; 6,4.12...).

1.   The Covenant* of Yahweh with His *people* ensures the presence of the Lord of the promises; but this depends on man's faithful observance of the *Law*, so much so that such an assurance is constantly in danger of disappearing in the face of reality.

Jacob arrives at the gate of Jabbok and sees himself in an impossible situation (*eporeito*: Gn 32,8). But he has behind him the repeated covenants of Yahweh with his father (22,16ff) and with himself (28,14). However, before his meeting with his brother Esau he is faced with a situation that causes him anguish. He struggles with the angel of the Lord and, when he has been thrown to the ground, obtains from him the certainty that God is with him (32,23-33).

Lying under a castor-oil tree Elijah is in despair: he would rather die (1 K 19,3f). Being sure (wrongly) of the general apostasy of the people, is he not right to consider his life a failure? But, like Jesus later in Gethsemani, he is strengthened by the Angel of the Lord and can continue on his way until the meeting with Yahweh, which sets him back on the right path (19,5-18).

The whole people is plunged into darkness: are they not in anguish (*stenochoria*: Is 8,22f; *aporia*: 5,30; 24,19)? Jeremiah too is overwhelmed and his heart fails him, when the people suffer from the famine (*aporia*: Jr 8, 18.21): on this occasion it is in his capacity as an upholder of the covenant. But when he alone is concerned, his reaction is different: although, when persecuted, he is driven to curse the day of his birth (15,10; 20,14), he finds a solution in recourse to the one who can avenge him and protect him (11,20; 20,12).

In the case of Job (according to the Greek text only: *synechomai*), obsession with the idea of individual salvation is apparent. "Overcome by fear," he weeps (Jb 3,24); "whatever I fear comes true, whatever I dread befalls me" (3,25); he speaks because his soul has become embittered (10,1; cf 7,11). "The fear of the Lord has seized (him)" (31,23). And finally, without even using these words, the Just One in his anguish cries to God, who can save him from his impossible situation (*thlipsis*) (Ps 22; 31; 35; 38; 57; 69; 88; 102...).

In all these cases the individual occupies a central place, for death lies in wait for him; there is a certain ambiguity in his anguish because God's cause is associated with his own. Moses* too at first sees death as the only solution to his problem (Nb 11,11-15 [E]); but in what follows, if he is in anguish, it is quite simply because of the people's apostasy. When he asks God to strike him from the Book* of life at the same time as the people are struck from it, he shows his solidarity with his sinful brethren, while at the same time remaining certain of the conquering love of God (Ex 32,31f).

2.   If such anguish can be felt in the heart of every man, its motif changes with the coming of *Jesus*. He has taken upon Himself not only the anxiety in the face of death but also the terrible feeling of ambiguity, of uncertainty. In the Garden of Olives He is overcome by grief, by fear, by distress and by fright (Mk 14,33f). His own anguish sums up the anguish of the just of all time (Ps 42,6.12; 43,5...): He utters cries and sheds tears: He prays to the One who can save Him from death (He 5,7) and finally brings His will slowly into harmony with His Father's (Mk 14,36). The Angel comes once again and strengthens the one who fights until He sweats blood and who "stands up" after this, victorious and ready to face His destiny (Lk 22,41-45).

In experiencing the depths of human anguish, Jesus becomes "for all who obey Him the source of eternal salvation" (He 5,9); He creates a new and irreversible epoch. The action on which the believer relies to assure himself of the quality of the present time, in which he lives, did indeed take place in the past (7,27); but it stands outside time and dominates the fluctuations of history (Ap 1,5). In the person of Jesus anguish is not suppressed but set in its place, for from now on hope is certainty and death is fruitful.

3. In the heart of the *believer* anguish can be experienced at two levels of depth and extent. See how Paul faces the prospect of death: "Despairing of staying alive, (he) learns in this way not to put his confidence in (himself), but in God, who raises the dead" (2 Co 1,9; 5,4). In fact he knows that "nothing can separate (him) from Christ's love, not even tribulation or anguish" (R 8,35.39). This anguish is accepted in the radical certainty that, in Christ, death has been overcome (1 Co 15,54f). Death* even takes on a meaning and a redemptive value, when it is united to Jesus' agony: "Death is at work in us, but life in you" (2 Co 4,12).

But anguish can appear again at a deeper level. In this case it does not simply concern the death of a man nor his personal salvation, for he knows that this has been won by faith (R 5,1-5; 8,24). It arises over the question of other people's liberty, with regard to the salvation of others. This is what Paul means when he wishes, like Moses, to be anathema* on behalf of his fellow-Jews (9,3); he wants to suffer, to suffer together (*synpaschein*) with Christ (8,17). In fact the world is groaning until the end (8,18-23); and now hope* is seen under another of its aspects; it is not only certainty, but also expectation and constancy, thanks to the Spirit (8,24ff). And so we see the Apostle overwhelmed (*synecho*) by the love of Christ (2 Co 5,14), just as Jesus was overwhelmed (*synechomai*) at the prospect of His sacrifice (Lk 12,50). We see Him in the grip of distress and anguish (*stenochoria*: 2 Co 6,4), yet without being crushed or in despair (*aporia*: 4,8). The agony of Christ lasts until the end of the world.

If, then, the Christian can in faith overcome the anguish that seizes him at the prospect of death and with regard to his salvation, he can at the same time live through an indescribable anguish by being in communion with all the members of Christ's Body. Certainty and uncertainty are not on the same plane and do not refer to the same object.

→Cares 2—Death NT III 4—Fear of God I, III—Jesus Christ I 3—Suffering.

XLD ems

ANIMALS

The animal world constitutes that part of visible creation closest to man. This affinity, which can at times escape us, was particularly sensed by the Hebrews, who lived more than we in permanent contact with animals. This is why the Bible uses, for purposes of illustrative description, animal characteristics to express certain human attitudes: the enemy is called a dog (vg Ps 22,17); invading troops become a cloud of locusts (vg Is 33,4); sometimes God, sometimes the enemy is described as a lion (it is necessary to see behind the ambivalence of certain symbols the ambiguity of this animal world in which we take part, capable of the best as of the worst); often the people are compared to a flock (vg the parable of Nathan: 2 S 12,1-4; Jr 23,1-8; Ez 34; Jn 10,1-16); the lamb* even serves to represent Christ (Jn 1,29; Ap 5,6...) and the dove, the Holy Spirit* (Mt 3,16 p).

But besides these casual observations one must follow the efforts of these men in the biblical stories, as they faced the power of the animal world and gradually realized their superiority.

What is more, in speaking of this animal world in which they participate and onto which they project more or less consciously their own situation, the sacred writers reveal in the end the drama of mankind and of all creation, the longing for redemption.

I. ANIMALS AND MAN IN CREATION

1. *Animals superior to man?* The worship of animals, although it may assume the meaning and diverse aspects of zoolatry, shows with what sacred respect certain primitive religions, as that of the Egyptians, considered those non-human beings. To the temptation of divinizing animals or adoring their image, Israel sometimes succumbed (Ex 32; 1 K 12,28-32). However, the law of Moses, the warnings of the prophets, the counsels of Wisdom, turned the Hebrews from this degrading path (vg Ws 15, 18f; cf R 1,23). As for idolatrous enemies, far from being preserved by the animals they adored, they will be punished by them (Ws 15—16; Ez 39,4.17-20; Ap 19,17f.21).

2. *The bond between the animal and man.* The resemblance of man to the animal, especially their common origin from dust and their

common way of ending in the grave, is at times brutally expressed (Qo 3,19ff; Ps 49,13). More often and more unobtrusively these two creatures, alike under the common denomination of "living beings," are united by a fraternal bond. Sometimes it is man who helps the animal: Noah* saved from the waters one pair of each living species; sometimes it is the animal which aids man: the clairvoyant she-ass saves Balaam (Nm 22,22-35); ravens feed Elijah (1 K 17,6); a great fish saves the stubborn Jonah and guides him back onto the right path (Jon 2). By their perfection the animals lead Job to recognize the omnipotence of the Creator (Jb 38,39—39,30; 40,15—41,26). Finally they remind men that God does not cease to extend His benefits to all living things (vg Ps 104,27; 147,9; Mt 6,26).

Animals are so close to man that they take part in the covenant concluded between God and Noah (Gn 9,9ff); and they themselves become subjects of the Mosaic law! The sabbath holds for both ox and slave (Ex 23,12; Dt 5,14). A human attitude toward them is prescribed (Ex 23,5; Dt 22,6f; 25,4; cf 1 Co 9,9; 1 Tm 5,18). As for animals who harm others, they will be punished (Gn 9,5; Lv 20,15f); in certain cases they will even be stoned (Ex 21,28-32). Finally they are associated with the penitence of men (Jon 3,7), and with their punishment (Ex 11,5).

3. *Superiority of man over animal.* Nevertheless from the stories of creation certain very clear characteristics indicate the sharp awareness of the superiority of man over the animal. Affirming his domination, Adam names* the animals (Gn 2,20). No one of the animals, moreover, can be for man "a help which would be equal to him" (Gn 2,18-23), and bestiality is severely punished (Ex 22,18; Dt 27,21; Lv 18,23). Moreover, the animal can be killed by man and serve for his nourishment (Gn 9,2f). Finally, the superiority of man is affirmed with a lyricism which resounds like the victory chant of triumphant awareness (Gn 1,26-30; Ps 8,6-9). Inversely, in order to punish the unreasonableness of Nebuchadnezzar, "there shall be given to him the heart of a beast*" (Dn 4,13), human bestiality symbolizing the revolt against the spirit, ultimately against God.

Nevertheless, from the belief in the superiority of animals there remains perhaps a residual element in the imagination of the sacred writers who do not hesitate to speak of fabulous animals. These, whatever be the origin of the portrayals, indicate something beyond nature, whether in the domain of the superhuman (Dn 7; Ap 9,3-11) which is close to the demonic (Ap 12; 13; 16,13f; 20,1ff), or in the domain of the divine (Ez 1,4-24; Ap 4,6ff).

II. ANIMALS AND MAN
IN THE REDEMPTION

1. *The revolt and submission of the animals.* The existence of wild animals brings about and symbolizes the revolt of nature against man, and the disorder which was introduced into the world. This situation is the result of man's sin. Before the disobedience of Adam, all the animals, domestic or wild, seem submissive to him who had given them their names. But because of sin all creation, including the animal world, is a slave of corruption (cf R 8,19-22). However, by anticipation or by Messianic grace, in certain privileged cases, conquered animals regain a docility reminiscent of paradise* (Dn 6,17-25; 14,31-42; Ps 91,13; Mk 1,13; 16,18; Ac 28,3-6). At the end of time, when the world will be entirely purified of its sins, fierce animals will disappear (Lv 26,6; Ez 34,25) or will become tame (Ho 2,20; Is 11,5ff; 65,25). In the reunified universe nature will no longer know revolt. And what there is of the animal in man (cf Jm 3,2-8) will also be entirely overcome and transformed (1 Co 15,44ff).

2. *Beyond the division of clean and unclean.* Long standing and mysterious as it may be, the division of animals into pure* and impure (cf Lv 11; Dt 14) has brought into and popularized in Judaism the division of humanity into two parts: the clean Israelites and the unclean pagans. Between these two worlds the impossibility of eating at the same table and thus of having familiar contact was, if not created, at least re-enforced by the food prescriptions concerning unclean animals. With this in mind one comprehends more easily the vision of Peter at Joppa (Ac 10), in which the abolition of the division "clean-unclean" among animals signified that this same division no longer exists among men. Behind this animal symbol, the unity of men and the catholicity of the Church were at stake.

3. *Animals and divine worship.* Not only do all the animals associated with the universe (Ps 148,7.10) or with Israel (Is 43,20) sing the praises of the Creator and Savior, not only had they become subjects of the Mosaic law and

participants in the penitence of men, but more, they were judged worthy ordinarily to compose the matter of the sacrifices* and thus to prefigure the divine victim of the new covenant (Gn 22,13; Ex 13,12f). Still it would have been necessary that, through the symbol constituted by these animal victims, the Israelites commit themselves with all their being and aspire to the perfection of the reality to come (Ps 40,7ff; 51,18f; He 10,1-18). Only the sacrifice of the servant Jesus, like a lamb which one leads to the slaughter (Is 53,7), could win eternal redemption (He 9,12).

Thus the whole drama of salvation is found portrayed and at times even lived because of and through the animals of the Bible: revolt; idolatry; distinction of clean and unclean; obedience to the Mosaic law; penitence; offerings and sacrifices; participation in the salvation of the ark of Noah; eschatological submission. Disfigured by the demoniacal serpent, menaced by the satanic dragon, creation is saved and will finally be transformed because of the sacrifice of Him who is the Lamb* of God.

→Beast & Beasts—Creation OT II 1—Man I i b—Pure OT I 1.

PL jjk

ANOINTING

For the Hebrews, oil* penetrates deeply into the body (Ps 109,18) and it gives the body strength, health, joy, and beauty. On the religious level, it is understandable that anointings of oil were considered as signs of rejoicing or of respect; they were also utilized as rites of healing or consecration.

I. ANOINTING, SIGN OF JOY OR OF HONOR

1. Oil, especially perfumed oil, being a *symbol of joy* (Pr 27,9; cf Qo 9,8), was used particularly in festivals (Am 6,6). To have to deprive oneself of all anointing was a misfortune (Dt 28, 40; Mi 6,15); this privation, joined to fasting*, was a sign of mourning (Dn 10,3; cf 2 S 12,20). Jesus prescribed, however, that one who fasts should anoint his head as for a banquet (Mt 6,17), in order that his penance be not displayed before men.

The image of anointing served to express the joy* of the people of Israel, assembled at Jerusalem for the great festivals (Ps 133,2), or the consolation* brought to the afflicted of Zion after the exile (Is 61,3); it also played a part in the description of the Messianic banquet: "On this mountain they will drink joy, they will drink wine: they will be anointed with perfumed oil upon this mountain" (Is 25,6f LXX). It is especially in this context of Messianic joy that there recurs the formula "oil of gladness" (Is 61,3; Ps 45,8; He 1,9).

2. To pour oil upon a guest was a *mark of honor*. The expression appears in the psalms to represent the abundance of divine favors: "You spread the table before me in the sight of my foes; you anoint my head with oil" (Ps 23,5; cf 92,11). The gospels on two occasions mention that a woman rendered Jesus this mark of honor. The first was the sinful woman at the house of Simon the Pharisee; seeing that the latter, though Jesus was his guest, had not poured oil upon His head, the woman anointed with perfume the feet of Jesus (Lk 7,38.46). On the eve of the entry into Jerusalem, Mary, the sister of Lazarus, repeated this testimony of respect by anointing Jesus with a spikenard of great price, to the scandal of the disciples (Mt 26,6-13 p; Jn 12,1-8). But Jesus approved Mary, and at the same time gave her action a new and prophetic significance by reference to the custom (Mk 16,1) of anointing dead bodies with aromatic spices: the woman's deed became an anticipation and a sign of the rite of burial which would be performed on the body of Jesus after His death on the cross (Jn 19,40).

II. THE ANOINTING OF THE SICK AND THE POSSESSED

1. In view of the *healing of the sick*, oil was again utilized, e.g. in the care of wounds (Is 1,6), as in the case of the good Samaritan (Lk 10,34); according to Lv 14,10-32, anointings of oil were performed upon healed lepers as rites of purification. When the disciples were sent by Christ to preach the kingdom of God, they were given the power to cast out unclean spirits and to heal every sickness and infirmity (Mt 10,1; Lk 9,1f); having set out on the mission*, they performed anointings of oil on many of the sick and healed them miraculously (Mk 6,13). These anointings performed by the apostles, probably at the instruction of Jesus,

are at the origin of the rite of anointing the sick in the Church. The epistle of James prescribed that the presbyters anoint the sick with oil in the name of the Lord: "the prayer of faith will save the sick man, and the Lord will raise him up. And if he be in sins, they shall be forgiven him" (Jm 5,15). Since sickness is a consequence of sin, the anointing made "in the name of the Lord" brings into reality the "salvation*" of the sick man: it makes him share in the victory* of Christ over sin and death, whether by healing, or by an increase of strength for the purpose of facing death.

2. *The expulsion of the evil spirits* is, in Mk 6,13, linked closely with healing the sick: both of these thaumaturgical powers were a sign of the advent of the kingdom. Moreover, several churches eventually performed upon the catechumens rites of anointing as exorcisms before baptism*.

III. ANOINTING-CONSECRATION

The anointings spoken of in the OT are, in the greater number of cases, rites of consecration.

1. *Certain objects for worship* were consecrated by means of anointings—in particular the altar* (Ex 29,36f; 30,26-29; Lv 8,10f), which acquired by this fact "an eminent sanctity." An analogous and very old rite, probably Canaanite, had been practiced by Jacob: after his nocturnal vision, he erected a commemorative stele, and poured some oil on top of it to mark the spot of the divine presence*: whence the name Bethel, "house of God" (Gn 28,18; cf 31,13; 35,14).

2. *The royal anointing* held a unique place among the rites of consecration. It was applied by man of God, prophet or priest. Saul (1 S 10,1) and David (1 S 16,13) were anointed by Samuel; Jehu, by a prophet who had been sent by Elisha (2 K 9,6). The kings of Judah were consecrated in the temple and anointed by a priest: Solomon received the anointing of Zadoq (1 K 1,39); Joash, of the high priest Jehoiado (2 K 11,12). The significance of this rite was to indicate by an exterior sign that these men had been elected* by God to become His instruments in the government of the people. Through the anointing, the king became a sharer in the spirit* of God as can be seen in the instance of David: "Samuel took

the horn of oil and anointed him in the midst of his brothers. The spirit of Yahweh seized David from that day forward" (1 S 16,13). If the anointing qualified the king for his function and manifested exteriorly that he had been elected by God to be His servant*, it is understandable that the name of anointed of Yahweh, which was used of the king of Israel in the first place, could be applied metaphorically to a pagan king, Cyrus (Is 45,1), for it is he who puts an end to the captivity of Babylon and permits the chosen people to return to Israel.

But the theme of royal anointing was to receive all its importance from its application to the *Messiah**. Ps 2, which speaks of Yahweh and His Anointed (2,2), was interpreted in Jewish and Christian tradition in the messianic sense (Ac 4,25ff). For the first Christians this title still had a royal significance: it only received its true meaning from the time when Jesus had been enthroned at the right hand of God and had received from Him the anointing with the oil of gladness (He 1,8f; cf Ps 45, 7f). By this royal anointing He became Lord and "Christ" (Messiah) in the full sense of the word and by right (Ac 2,36; cf Ph 2,11). With regard to this title of "Anointed," later Christian tradition was to speak of a three-fold anointing of Christ, as king, priest and prophet.

3. *The priests*, and most especially the high priest, are also anointed (cf priesthood*). At the command of Yahweh (Ex 29,7), Moses confers the anointing on Aaron* (Lv 8,12), and in the prescriptions intended for the High Priest, the latter is called several times "the priest consecrated by anointing" (vg Lv 4,5; 16,32). In addition, anointing is conferred on simple priests, "sons of Aaron" (vg Ex 28,41; 40,15; Nm 3,3). These different texts belong, however, to the priestly code, after the exile. Thus it is probable that under the monarchy, only the king was anointed; at the time of the second temple, the high priest, having become head of the people, received the anointing for his office, as also, shortly afterwards, all the priests. Around the first century, the Qumrân community awaited not only a Messiah (a king), but also an "anointed" descended from Levi, a Messiah-priest.

4. *The prophets** were not anointed with oil; the anointing of the prophets designates metaphorically their investiture: Elijah received the order to anoint Elisha (1 K 19,19), but at the

moment of the latter's call, the Tishbite did nothing but throw his cloak around him and communicate to him his spirit (1 K 19,19; 2 K 2,9-15). It is to explain this prophetic mission that the author of Is 61 wrote: "the Spirit of the Lord Yahweh is upon me, for He has anointed me. He has sent me to bring the good news to the poor" (Is 61,1).

5. *The anointing of Christ.* The NT mentions only a single anointing of Jesus during His earthly life (for the royal anointing at His heavenly enthronement, cf He 1,9), when He received baptism: "He was anointed with the Holy Spirit and with power" (Ac 10,38). In applying to Himself the text of Is 61,1 at the beginning of His ministry (Lk 4,18-21), Jesus Himself explains this anointing as a prophetic unction to announce the message. But the apostolic community, inspired by the words of Jesus (Mk 10,38; Lk 12,50), went on to interpret baptism in the perspective of the death of Christ (Ac 4,27; cf R 6,3f): the mission received at the outset of the public life was still only a mission of preaching, that of the Servant-Prophet (Is 42,1-7); but it had to be completed on Calvary (cf 1 Jn 5,6) in the sacrifice of the suffering Servant.

6. *The Christian* himself also receives an anointing (2 Co 1,21; 1 Jn 2,20.27); in these passages, however, there is no question of a sacramental rite (baptism or confirmation), but of a participation in the prophetic anointing of Jesus, a spiritual anointing through faith. Before receiving the seal* of the Spirit* at the moment of baptism, the catechumen had been "anointed" by God (2 Co 1,21; cf E 4,30). God effected the penetration in him of the teaching of the gospel*; He stirred up in his heart faith in the word of truth (cf E 1,13). This is why John calls this word coming from Christ an "oil of anointing" (*chrisma*): it is interiorized by faith under the action of the Spirit (Jn 14,26; 16,13); the "oil of anointing dwells in us" (1 Jn 2,27); it gives us the sense of truth (v 20f); it teaches us concerning all things (v 27). John can therefore say that the Christian has no more need of being taught: the expectation of the prophets in the new covenant is realized (Jr 31,34; cf Is 11,9). This doctrine of interior unction is important in Christian tradition and spirituality. Clement of Alexandria has Christ address this invitation and promise to the pagans: "I shall anoint you with the ointment of faith"; and St. Bernard considers as a dis-

tinctive trait of the sons of God that "the anointing teaches them all things."

→Burial 2—David 2—King OT I 1.2—Messiah —Oil 2—Paraclete 2—Perfume—Priesthood OT I 4—Sickness/Healing NT II 1—Spirit of God OT I 2.3.

IdlP pmcm

ANTICHRIST

The term *Antichrist* (literally "against Christ") appears exclusively in 1 Jn 2,18.22; 4,3; 2 Jn 7. But the same or an analogous reality is envisaged in diverse apocalyptic passages of the NT: Mk 13,14 p; 2 Th 2,3-12; Ap 13,4-18. And as it is registered in a dualistic framework witnessed to by the OT, it is in the OT that it is first necessary to observe the early revelation of it, imperfect, but already suggestive.

OT

From the time of the OT, one sees the action of God here below clashing with adverse forces which wear, according to the situation, quite diverse apparel.

1. The religious symbolism of the ancient East has provided for revelation a poetic delineation of creation* in the form of a struggle between God the Creator and the forces of chaos; monstrous beasts* personify the untamed power of the sea* (Is 51,9f; Ps 74,13f; 89,10ff). The same mythical language, purified of all traces of polytheism, serves to recall the "last times" by the description of a combat of Yahweh with the serpent (Is 27,1). One finds it again, quite probably, as the background of an original drama; indeed, in Genesis, the adversary of the plan of God takes the mythical form of a serpent (Gn 3). Thus, by means of symbols, the profile of Satan* is drawn at the two extremities of the plan of salvation; he is the adversary of God above all others.

2. However, in the framework of history, Satan acts here below through the mediation of human powers. The enemies* of the people of God are the adversaries of God Himself when they put up some obstacle to His providential plan. Thus Egypt* at the moment of exodus; so again the potentates of Ashur and Babylon*, the oppressors of Israel, and the worshipers of

false gods whose spiritual domination they try to extend here below; thus finally all the pagan kings whose sacrilegious excesses inclined them to make themselves equal to God (Ez 28,2ff; Is 14,13). History admits therefore a continuous engagement between Yahweh and these historic forces, while waiting for the meeting in which "Gog, king of Magog," will be defeated forever (Ez 38—39); after this will come the eschatological salvation.

3. The action of Antiochus Epiphanes, enemy of Israel at the same time as he was persecutor of the true adorers of God, allows the book of Daniel to achieve the synthesis between the two preceding portrayals. He is the ungodly one who pretends to take tthe place of God (Dn 11,36) and who installs in His holy place the abomination of desolation (9,27). He is also the eleventh horn of the fourth beast who has the appearance of Satan (7,8). Thus his judgment and destruction are a prelude to the establishment of the kingdom of God (7,11-27; 11,40—12,2).

NT

This is the eschatological view adopted by the NT teaching, but with this difference, that God's reign is inaugurated in the person of Christ. The anti-God of the OT becomes the anti-Christ, who is already at work through his supporters before he reveals himself in the eschatological battle when he will be finally conquered.

1. In the synoptic apocalypse, the "great distress" announced by Jesus as prelude to the coming in glory of the Son of Man implies the appearing of "false Christ," whose seduction will lead men to apostasy (Mk 13,5f.21f; Mt 24,11 p); and it has for a symptom "the abomination of desolation" set up in the holy place (Mk 13,14 p).

2. In 2 Th 2,3-12, the adversary of the last times, the lost being, the godless one, takes on the appearance of a genuine anti-God, analogous to those of the OT (Dn 2,4); he is an Antichrist who imitates the characteristics of the Lord, with his coming, his own moment of time, fixed by God, his power which is above nature and which works deceptive prodigies to the perdition of mankind (2,8-10). Thus this is the work Satan will accomplish here below (2,9). But the mystery of godlessness*, of which he will be the outstanding artisan, is

already under way (2,7); this is why so many lose their way and attach themselves to falsehood instead of believing in the truth* (2,11f). If the godless one does not yet manifest himself in person, it is because something, or someone, "holds him back" (2,7)—an enigmatic allusion which Paul does not explain. In any event, the revelation of the impious one will be a prelude to the parousia of Jesus, who will annihilate him through the manifestation of His coming (2,8; cf 1,7-10).

3. The Apocalypse is written from a similar eschatological viewpoint and uses the symbolism of the two monstrous beasts*. The first is a political power: it blasphemes God, seeks self-adoration, and persecutes the true believers (Ap 13,1-10). The second is a religious reality: it acts against the Lamb (that is, Christ), performs deceptive prodigies, and seduces men to make them adore the first beast (13,11-18). So does the work of Satan proceed here on earth; he is the ancient dragon, who has transmitted his powers to the first beast (13,2). This stately symbolic presentation, entirely concerned with the "last times," was nonetheless related by its ambiguous words to the present situation in which the Church of Jesus was in conflict, persecuted by the pagan empire of Rome.

4. In the letters of St. John, it is mainly a present reality which is described under the name of Antichrist: whoever denies that Jesus is the Christ, denying thus the Father and the Son (1 Jn 2,22), whoever does not confess Jesus come in the flesh (1 Jn 4,3; 2 Jn 7), that one is the deceiver, the Antichrist. John clearly alludes to heretics and apostates, among whom the apostasy announced by Jesus and predicted by Paul is taking place. The eschatology is therefore present reality; but the current drama of faith must be understood in relation to a much larger horizon, that which the Apocalypse fully describes.

The teaching about the Antichrist remains very mysterious. It is understood only in relation to the world-wide war* in which God and His Christ stand face to face with Satan and his earthly agents. By the twofold means of temporal persecution and religious seduction, there is the attempt to thwart the plan of salvation. It would be erroneous to wish to put proper names on each of the symbols which may bring to mind a particular existence; but whoever acts like them in some measure shares in the same mystery of the Antichrist. But this enterprise will continue on without respite during the whole course of history, setting men at the heart of a battle in which no human means is capable of victory. But where men will fail, the Lamb will conquer (Ap 17,14), and His witnesses will share His victory (Ap 3,21).

→Babel/Babylon 6—Beasts & Beast 3 b. 4—Calamity 2—Day of the Lord NT I 2—Error NT—Godless Man NT 2—Lie II 2 b—Satan III—War NT III—World NT I 2, III 2.

BRi & PG jjk

APOSTLES

In the NT, many persons receive the title of apostle: the twelve disciples chosen by Jesus to found His Church (Mt 10,2; Ap 21,14), as well as Paul, outstanding apostle of the gentiles (R 11,13), are well known. But it was Paul's habit from very early times to give Silvanus, Timothy (1 Th 2,7) and Barnabas (1 Co 9,6) the same title as himself: besides Peter and the twelve there are "James and the apostles" (1 Co 15,5ff; cf G 1,19), not to speak at all of the charism of the apostolate (1 Co 12,28; E 4,11), nor of the "false apostles" and of the "super-apostles" whom Paul denounces (2 Co 11,5.13; 12,11). So broad a use of this title raises a problem: what relation is there between these diverse "apostles"? To resolve this problem, failing a NT definition of the apostolate which is applicable to all, it is necessary to situate the different persons who bear this title, after having collected the information about the term and about the office in its specifically non-Christian aspects.

The substantive *apostolos* has not the same sense in literary Greek that we give it (except for Herodotus and Josephus who seem to reflect popular language), but the verb from which it is derived (*apostellô*), "to send," expresses well its content; the idea is specified by the analogies of the OT and the Jewish customs. The OT knew its use for ambassadors who should be respected as the king who sends them (2 S 10); the prophets* undertake missions* of the same type (cf Is 6,8; Jr 1,7; Is 61,1ff), although they never receive the title of apostle. But rabbinic Judaism, after the year 70 A.D., was familiar with the institution of official envoys (*selîhîn*), the use of which seems much earlier according to the texts themselves

of the NT. Paul "asks for some letters for the synagogues of Damascus" with a view to persecuting the faithful of Jesus (Ac 9,2 p): this is a delegated official fortified with official letters (cf Ac 28,21f). The Church took over the custom when, from Antioch and from Jerusalem, she sent Barnabas and Silas with their letters (Ac 15,22), or made Barnabas and Paul her delegates (Ac 11,30; 13,3; 14,26; 15,2); Paul himself sends out two brothers who are the *apostoloi* of the Churches (2 Co 8,23). According to the word of Jesus, which has antecedents in Jewish literature, the apostle represent Him who sent him: "The servant is no greater than his master, nor the *apostolos* any greater than He who sent him" (Jn 13,16).

Thus, to judge by that age's use of the term, the apostle is not first of all a missionary, or a man of the Spirit, nor ever a witness*: he is an emissary, a delegate, a plenipotentiary, an ambassador.

I. THE TWELVE AND THE APOSTOLATE

Before giving rise to a proper title, the apostolate was a function. It is actually at the end of a slow evolution that the title of Apostle was used in the privileged sense and restricted to the circle of the twelve (Mt 10,2) and later attributed to our Lord (Lk 6,13). But if this title of honor belongs to the twelve alone, it is clear that others with them exercise a function which can be qualified as "apostolic."

1. *The twelve apostles.* From the beginning of His public life, Jesus wanted to multiply His presence and to diffuse His message through men who would be other Christs. He calls the first four disciples to be fishers of men (Mt 4, 18-22 p); He chooses twelve of them to be "with Him" and, like Him, preach the gospel and drive out demons (Mk 3,14 p); He sends them on a mission* to speak in His name (Mk 6,6-13 p), armed with His own authority: "Who hears you, hears me, and who hears me, hears Him who sent me" (Mt 10,40 p); they learn to distribute the bread multiplied in the desert (Mt 14,19 p), they receive a special authority over the community which they had to direct (Mt 16,18; 18,18). In a word, they constituted the foundations of the new Israel* whose judges they will be on the last day (Mt 19,27 p); this is what the number* 12 in the apostolic college means. It is to them that the

risen one, always present with them to the end of the ages, gives the task of making disciples for Him and of baptizing all the nations (Mt 28,18ff). From that time, the choice of a twelfth apostle as a replacement for Judas appeared indispensable, so that the image of the new Israel might be found in the nascent Church (Ac 1,15-26). They must be the witnesses* of Christ, that is to say, they must testify that the risen Christ is the same Jesus with whom they lived (1,8.21); this unique witnessing confers on their apostolate (understood here in the strongest meaning of the word) a singular character. The twelve are forever the foundation of the Church: "the walls of the house rest on twelve foundation-stones, each one bearing the name of one of the twelve apostles of the Lamb" (Ap 21,14).

2. *The apostolate of the newborn Church.* Though the twelve are above all others the apostles—and in this sense the Church is "apostolic"—the apostolate of the Church, understood in a larger sense, does not limit itself to the activity of the twelve. Just as Jesus, *"apostolos* from God" (He 3,1), wished to institute a privileged group which would multiply His presence and His word, so the twelve communicate to others not the privilege that makes them for ever the witnesses of the Risen Lord, for that cannot be transferred, but the exercise of their apostolic mission. Already in the OT Moses had transmitted to Joshua the fullness of his powers (Nm 27,18); in the same way Jesus desired that the pastoral charge confided to the twelve continue through the course of ages: while preserving completely a special unity with them, the presence of the risen one will go infinitely beyond their circle.

From the time of the public life, however, Jesus had Himself opened the way to this extension of the apostolic mission. Besides the predominant tradition which narrates the mission of the twelve, Luke has retained another tradition, according to which Jesus "again selected seventy-two [disciples] others and sent them on ahead of Him" (Lk 10,1). Here we have the same object of the sending as for the twelve, the same official character: "Who hears you, hears me; who refuses you refuses me and who refuses me refuses Him who sent me" (Lk 10,16; cf Mt 10,40 p). In Jesus' mind, therefore, the apostolic mission is not limited to that of the twelve.

The twelve themselves act in this spirit. From the choice of Matthias, they know that a good number of disciples could fulfill the necessary requirements (Ac 1,21ff); he is not properly an apostle, but a twelfth witness whom God selects. Besides there is Barnabas, an apostle of the same fame as Paul (14,4.14); and if the seven helpers chosen by the twelve are not called apostles (6,1-6), they are able to found a new Church: thus Philip at Samaria, although his powers are limited by those of the twelve (8,14-25). The apostolate, the official representative of the risen one in the Church, remains forever founded on the "apostolic" college of the twelve; but it is exercised by all men on whom they confer authority.

II. PAUL, APOSTLE OF THE GENTILES

The existence of Paul confirms, in its own way, what Jesus had hinted at on earth in sending out the seventy-two in addition to the twelve. From heaven the risen one sends forth Paul in addition to the twelve; through this apostolic mission, the nature of the apostolate will be able to be made more precise.

1. *The ambassador of Christ.* When Paul insistently repeats that he was "called" to be an apostle (R 1,1; G 1,15) in an apocalyptic vision of the risen one (G 1,16; 1 Co 9,1; 15,8; cf Ac 9,5.27), he makes clear that a particular calling* was at the basis of his mission*. An apostle, he is one "sent," not by men (even if they were apostles themselves!) but by Jesus personally. He recalls especially this fact when he vindicates his apostolic authority: "we are an ambassador of Christ; it is as if God were exhorting through us" (2 Co 5,20); "the Word which we have made you hear is not the Word of man but the Word of God" (1 Th 2,13). Happy those who have "received him as an angel of God, as Christ Jesus" (G 4,14). For the apostles are the "co-workers of God" (1 Co 3,9; 1 Th 3,2). Further, through them is accomplished the ministry of eschatological glory* (2 Co 3,7-11). And in order that the ambassador should not turn to his own profit this divine power and this glory, the apostle is a man despised by the world; behold him persecuted, delivered to death so that life may be given to men (2 Co 4,7—6,10; 1 Co 4,9-13).

Concretely, the apostolic authority is exercised in connection with doctrine, ministry, and jurisdiction. Often Paul appeals to his doctrinal authority, because he believes himself able to hurl an anathema upon anyone who would announce a gospel* different from his (G 1,8f). Paul knows himself capable of delegating his own powers to others, as when he ordains Timothy by imposing* hands upon him (1 Tm 4,14; 2 Tm 1,6), a gesture which Timothy could perform in his turn (1 Tm 5,22). Finally this authority is exercised by a real jurisdiction over the Churches which Paul has founded and which are entrusted to him: he judges and imposes sanctions (1 Co 5,3ff; 1 Tm 1,20), he regulates everything at the time of his visitations (1 Co 11,34; 2 Co 10,13-16; 2 Th 3,4), he knows how to exact obedience from the community (R 15,18; 1 Co 14,37; 2 Co 13,3), with the aim of maintaining communion* (1 Co 5,4). This authority is not tyrannical (2 Co 1,24), it is a service (1 Co 9,19), that of a shepherd* (Ac 20,28; 1 P 5,2-5) who knows how to renounce his rights in times of need (1 Co 9,12); far from being a weight upon the faithful, he cherishes them as a father, as a mother (1 Th 2,7-12), and offers them the example* of faith (1 Th 1,6; 2 Th 3,9; 1 Co 4,16).

2. *The unique case of Paul*. In this ideal description of the apostolate, Paul would readily know what he expected of his collaborators; of Timothy (cf 1 Th 3,2) and of Silvanus, whom he called, it seems, apostles (2,5ff); or again of Sosthenes and of Apollos (1 Co 4,9). However, Paul was given a place apart in the apostolate of the Church: he is the apostle of the pagan nations: he has a special understanding of the mystery Christ. This unique role in the Christian economy is a personal one and belongs to the charismatic* order: it cannot be handed on.

a) *The apostle of the gentiles*. Paul has not been the first to bring the gospel to the pagans: Philip had already evangelized the Samaritans (Ac 8) and the Holy Spirit had descended upon the pagans of Caesarea (Ac 10). But God desired that at the birth of His Church an apostle be more specially charged with the evangelization of the gentiles, alongside that of the Jews. This is what Paul labored to bring to Peter's knowledge. Not that he wanted in this to be an envoy of Peter: he remained the envoy of Christ, directly; but he felt obliged to refer this matter to the leader of the twelve, so that he might not "run in vain" and lead to a division of the Church (G 1—2).

b) *The mystery of Christ* for Paul is "Christ among the nations" (Col 1,27); already Peter

had understood in a vision that no forbidden habits of eating should any longer separate the Jews from the gentiles (Ac 10,10—11,18). But Paul had, by the grace of God, a special knowledge* of this mystery* (E 3,4) and had been charged with transmitting it to men; he suffers persecution, endures sufferings, is a prisoner, to fulfill this mystery (Col 1,24-29; E 3,1-21).

Such was the special and incommunicable grace of Paul; but the role of ambassador of Christ, and even, in a certain measure, the spiritual understanding which he had of his apostolate, can be given to all the apostles by the Lord of the Spirit (1 Co 2,6-16).

The apostolate of the faithful is not the object of explicit teaching in the NT, but it finds its basis in some facts. While being preeminently the function of the twelve and of Paul, the apostolate was exercised from the beginning by the whole Church: for example, the churches of Antioch and Rome were existing when the leaders of the Church arrived there. In a broad sense, the apostolate was the doing of every disciple* of Christ, "light of the world and salt of the earth" (Mt 5,13f). At his own level, he should participate in the apostolate of the Church, imitate Paul, the twelve, and the first apostles in their apostolic zeal*.

→Authority NT II—Build III 2—Calling III— Charisms II 2.4—Church III 2—Disciple NT —Election NT II 1—Farewell NT 2—Fruitfulness III 3—Gospel—Mediator II 2—Ministry—Mission NT II, III—Nations NT II— Peter—Power V 3—Preach—Priesthood NT III —Revelation NT I 2, II 2, III 2—Sign NT II 2— Teach NT II—Tradition NT I 2.3; II 2.

XLD jjk

APPARITIONS OF CHRIST

1. *In the Bible, apparitions* form one of the methods of God's revelation*. Through them, beings who are naturally invisible to men make themselves present in a visible fashion. In the OT God* appears in person ("theophany"), manifests His glory* or makes His presence felt through His angels. To a lesser degree the apparitions of angels or dreams* can be included with these apparitions. The NT reports apparitions of the Angel of the Lord or of angels on the occasions of Jesus' birth (Mt 1— 2; Lk 1,11.26; 2,9) or of His resurrection (Mt 28,2ff; Mk 16,5; Lk 24,4; Jn 20,12), in order to

show that in these great moments of Christ's existence heaven is present on earth. To this extent the NT carries on the OT approach.

But it takes a decisive step forward, when it refrains from reporting theophanies, for this term cannot be applied to the Transfiguration* (Mt 17,1-9 p) nor even to the walking on the water (14, 22-27 p), although on these occasions the mysterious nature of Jesus shines through. In fact a radical change has taken place, expressed by John in this way: "No one has ever seen God; it is the only Son, who is nearest the Father's heart, who has made Him known" (Jn 1,18). But how? Simply by His existence: "To have seen me is to have seen the Father" (14,9; cf 12,45); God has appeared in Christ. In this way the great mystery has become clear (ephanerothe) (1 Tm 3,16), "when the kindness and the love of God our savior for mankind were revealed (epephane)" (Tt 3,4). We are only waiting for "the Appearing of (His) glory" (2,13), at the parousia. This final appearance will be like lightning (Lk 17,24). Then it will no longer be the appearance of the witness* seen by Stephen "standing at the right hand of God" (Ac 7,55) but of the judge "seated at the right hand of the Power" (Mt 26,64 p). Revealed at last, Christ will reveal us "in all (our) glory with him" (Col 3,4), "when he appears a second time, . . .to reward with salvation those who are waiting for him" (He 9,28) and gives them "the crown of unfading glory" (1 P 5,4). "When it is revealed we shall be like him because we shall see him as he really is" (1 Jn 3,2).

The apparitions of the risen Jesus find their place between the theophanies of the OT and the parousia of the future, for they give a glimpse of the previous existence of Jesus of Nazareth and at the same time anticipate His return.

2. *The various apparitions of Christ.* The oldest list is given by Paul in the year 55, following a tradition that he had received long before that and had then handed on to the Corinthians (toward A.D. 50) (1 Co 15,3ff). According to this ancient confession of faith, Christ appeared to Cephas, to the Twelve, to more than five hundred of the brethren, to James, to all the apostles and last of all to Paul. The Gospels only refer to the first two appearances: the appearance to Simon (Lk 24,34) and to the Eleven (Mt 28,16-20; Mk 16,14-18; Jn 20,19-29) together with several other disciples (Lk 24,33-50). On the other hand they do tell of appearances to individuals: to Mary and to the Women (Jn 20,11-18; Mt 28,9-10; Mk 16, 9-11), to the disciples on the road to Emmaus (Lk 24,13-35; Mk 16,12f) and to the Seven at the lakeside (Jn 21,1-23). These different apparitions can be reduced to two types, depending upon whether they are meant for the apostolic college or for the disciples in general. On the other hand we have the official apparitions, which have a bearing on the mission* on which the Church* is founded: and on the other hand we have the private apparitions, in which the center of interest in the story is the recognition of the one who appears.

3. *Neither apocalypse nor chronicle.* The Gospel accounts cannot be classed in the apocalyptic genre: there is no insistence on glory*, no revelation of secrets, nothing extraordinary about the setting of the narration, but simply the familiar presence and the mission. Such a new approach to the description suggests a unique original experience, capable of transforming what the apocalyptic language, which was, however, anxious to speak of heavenly things, was trying to express.

Nor did the narrators intend to produce a biographical chronicle of the apparitions of the risen Christ. It is impossible to arrange the accounts in such a way that they agree from the point of view of time and space. Any attempt that makes the appearances in Jerusalem on Easter day (Lk, Jn) and on the eighth day (Jn), then in Galilee (Mt, Jn), and then again in Jerusalem for the Ascension (Lk) follow one another results in an unacceptable harmony, for it overlooks certain definite literary factors. According to Lk 24,49 the disciples are told to stay in Jerusalem until the day of Pentecost; so this excludes any possible appearance in Galilee. On the other hand Mt and Mk state that Galilee is the place fixed for their meeting. It is impossible to harmonize these topographies. And it is the same with the chronology: the "many days" of which Ac 1,3 speaks contradicts Lk 24, which clearly places the Ascension on Easter day; it also contradicts Jn 20, which speaks of the gift of the Spirit on Easter day itself, not to mention the account of a later appearance on the shores of Lake Tiberias (Jn 21). The account of Lk, with his concentration on Jerusalem and the duration of one day, and that of Jn, with his distribution of the apparitions over a period of one week, can be seen to be artificial literary constructions.

27

Nor again was it the intention of the evangelists to hand on to us something of the nature of photographic souvenirs: the details (such as closed doors, the touching of the body...) must not be considered independently of the mystery, seen as a whole, for they simply present one aspect of this.

4. *Initiative, recognition, mission.* These are the three aspects that each of the accounts have in common, and they allow us to get some positive idea of the authors' intentions.

a) When they show Jesus appearing among people who are not expecting it, the evangelists (except Lk 24,34) prove that there is no question of subjective invention on the part of interested parties, the result of a too vivid faith or of uncontrolled imagination. This idea that it is the risen Christ who takes the *initiative* (and that is really what the verb *ophthe*, "he allowed himself to be seen," in the list of 1 Co 15 is trying to say), shows that the accounts of the apparitions are describing experiences that the disciples really lived through. This aspect of the accounts corresponds with the approach of the early preaching: God intervened to raise up Jesus and allowed Him to show Himself alive after his death. Faith* is a consequence of this encounter.

b) *Recognition* is the second characteristic. The disciples discover the identity of the one who confronts them; it is Jesus of Nazareth, whose life and death are known to them. The one who was dead is living. In Him the prophecies have been fulfilled. In a way there is nothing more for them to "see*" in the future, for everything is given to them in the risen Christ. This recognition takes place in stages: in the man who comes to them the disciples first see an ordinary person, a traveller (Lk 24, 15f; Jn 21,4f) or a gardener (Jn 20,15); then they recognize the Lord. This recognition is not forced, for according to the theme of unbelief* that is part of the tradition as a whole (Mt 28,17; Mk 16,11.13f; Lk 24,37.41; Jn 20, 25-29), they could have refused to believe. And finally the fact that the Master usually appears to a group of people makes it possible for them to check the reality of what they have seen.

In their attempt to fit this fundamental fact into a literary composition the narrators have tried to stress two aspects at the same time. The risen Christ is not subject to the normal conditions of earthly life; like God in the OT theophanies (Gn 18,2; Nb 12,5; Js 5.13; 1 Ch 21,15f; Ze 2,7; 3,5; Dn 8,15; 12,5...), He appears and disappears at will. On the other hand He is not a ghost; hence, the insistence on physical contacts. To avoid any errors, these two aspects must be considered together. The body* of the risen Christ is a real body, but, to use St. Paul's apparently paradoxical expression, it is a "spiritual body" (1 Co 15,44-49), for it is a body transformed by the Spirit (cf R 1,4).

c) In the words that are spoken a third aspect characteristic of these accounts can be seen. When they recognize the Master, the disciples anticipate the vision that will be the prerogative of heaven. When they hear the Word*, they are brought back to earthly conditions. In this way they hear the promise of a presence* that will continue for all time (Mt 28,20) and the invitation to carry on Jesus' work with a *mission** properly so called (28,19; Mk 16,15-18; Lk 24,48f; Jn 20,22f; cf Mt 28,10; Jn 20,17). The presence of Jesus is not something static, but dynamic, missionary.

These three aspects must remain in a dynamic relation with one another. The present is constantly renewed by the initiative of the risen Christ; the disciple is invited to take hold of the past in the person of Jesus of Nazareth, who then invites him to build the future, which is the Church.

5. *The appearance to Paul* has a place of its own (G 1,12-17; Ac 9,3-19 p). Paul puts it on the same level as the other appearances: like the disciples he has seen the living Master. And so he distinguishes the Damascus episode from the simple visions (*horama*) that he is to have after this (Ac 16,9; 18,9; 23,11; 27,23). This appearance is interpreted as a mission entrusted to Paul (G 1,16), not through any human intermediary (1,1; cf Ac 9,6; 22,15), but directly (Ac 26,16ff). It has made him an apostle* (1 Co 9,1), but for all that it has not made him one of the Twelve. They recognized in the figure of the risen Christ the Jesus of Nazareth with whom they had lived (cf Ac 2,21f) and on the word of Christ they built the Church. Paul for his part did not recognize Jesus except through the Church that he was persecuting; and that indicates two things. The apparition with which he was favored is not part of the origin of the Church; it is directed not toward the prepaschal Jesus but toward the already existing Church. For these reasons, and also because Luke puts it after the Ascension, it is presented

in an apocalyptic style, in accordance with Paul's own language (*apokalypsai*: G 1,15): the light, the voice, the glory, all give the scene quite a different style compared with the familiar apparitions meant for the Eleven. In spite of these differences, Paul ranks this apparition among those that were the mark of the forty days.

6. *The event and language.* Two conditions must be observed if we are to find a correct interpretation of the language used by the evangelists to report the paschal experience. At the outset there is an event that must be described as eschatological. Since the resurrection of Jesus is not a return to earthly life but entry into the life where there is no more death (R 6,9), the apparitions are events that fall outside the framework of the life that we live and the categories that we use to express ourselves: in itself it is indescribable. On the other hand it is a case of a real experience on the part of the disciples, which took place in our historical time and depends on historical knowledge.

Therefore, there are two extremes to be avoided. Since the resurrection is not a myth, the language of the apparitions cannot be "demythologized:" this would inevitably reduce the presence of Christ to that of some hero surviving in the memory of his admirers. To avoid such an extreme and in order not to make a purely subjective experience out of the apparitions, there is no need to go to the other extreme and suppose it necessary to maintain that the objectivity belongs exclusively to the sensible order, the order of space and time. To compare the contact established by the risen Christ with His disciples with the situation of the risen Lazarus, once again united with his family and friends, would be to overlook the unique character of Jesus' resurrection. It is not enough to make some adjustments to the notion that we have of a reanimated body*: such a comparison would lead to undue importance being attached to the material details of the accounts.

The fact is that the experience of the disciples, which was not purely subjective, and which was repeated and shared by a number of them, has been handed down by means of the language of the time and through the medium of religious tradition, especially with the help of their faith in the collective resurrection* at the end of time. If we want to avoid the mistake of seeing contact with the risen Christ as if it were similar to the sort of contact we can

have with a man here below, we have only to recall the threefold dimension evident in the accounts. Through the initiative of the risen Christ the disciples are preserved from the illusion that could lead them to doubt the genuineness of their meeting with the Living One. When they "see" Him, they relate this experience to the past through which they have lived. When they listen to Him, their minds are directed to the future. It is in the relationship between these three dimensions that the secret of the presence of Christ living today lies.

7. *"Happy are those who have not seen and yet believe"* (Jn 20,29). When John describes the unbelief of Thomas he has future believers in mind. Their situation cannot in fact be compared in every way with that of the first witnesses. Of course the Gospels do suggest that the disciples too should not have needed these experiences: the announcement should have been enough for them (Mk 16,13); and if they had understood the Scriptures, that too should have led the disciples to faith in the resurrection (Jn 20,9). In one sense the apparitions are the answer to the needs of a faith that is still imperfect.

However, in another sense they were necessary and have a unique importance, which the evangelists have pointed out in their description of the apparitions of the forty days. Those who had lived with Jesus of Nazareth were to be the unique and privileged witnesses of Jesus* the Christ. It was essential to give a firm historical foundation to the beginning of the Christian faith and Church. And so it can be said that the disciples saw the living Master in an historical experience: it was no doubt in the course of a community meal, of a walk, of a fishing expedition...Suddenly they were in contact with the living Christ. In allowing them to recognize Jesus, God gave them the faith: and so faith is in a certain sense the consequence of seeing.

It is not the same for the believers who are not privileged witnesses. For their part they have not seen *what* the disciples saw, but they know *that* they saw it. The believers only know the meaning of the apparitions through the preaching of the Church, the Body of Christ, in their day.

The threefold dimension of the presence of the risen Christ is still there, but at a different level. The initiative still comes from God, and more precisely from the risen Christ, but today He speaks through the day-to-day preaching*.

Jesus of Nazareth allows Himself to be recognized, but it is through the historical experience of the first witnesses. The Master still sends men on a mission, but this time in direct continuity with the apostolic mission. The risen Christ is, then, still present today (Mt 28,20), but through the mediation of the living Church, His Body; and He still allows men to recognize Him "at the breaking of bread" (Lk 24,35).

→Ascension II 3—Body of Christ I 3—Faith NT II 1—Farewell Speeches NT 1—Glory IV 2—Meal III—Mission NT II 1—Passover III 1 —Presence of God NT I—Resurrection NT I 2—Revelation NT I 2 a—See NT I 2, II— Transfiguration 3—Unbelief II 2.

XLD ems

ARK OF THE COVENANT

The presence* of God in Israel is manifested in various ways. The ark is one of the visible signs of this in two ways:—in a coffer, approximately 125×75×75 cm [five feet long, three feet wide, and three feet high], are enclosed the ten words written by the finger of God on stone (Dt 10,1-5);—this coffer, covered over with a plate of gold, the "propitiatory," and mounted with the cherubim, is the throne or footstool of Yahweh (Ps 132,7; 1 Ch 28,2). Thus Yahweh, "seated upon the Cherubim" (1 S 4,4; Ps 80,2), protects His Word under His feet.

The ark, sheltered under the tent, is like a mobile sanctuary, which accompanies Israel from the beginning, at the departure from Sinai, to the construction of the temple* in which it was secured. From then on the temple came into the foreground and the ark lost its importance; it is no longer spoken of in the texts; it disappears undoubtedly at the same time as the temple at the period of the exile. It seems that in the second temple, the propitiatory was the substitute for the ark in worship.

By the ark, the God of the covenant manifested that He is present in the midst of His people—to guide and protect them—to make known His Word and hear their prayer.

I. GOD PRESENT BY HIS ACTION

The ark makes concrete the active presence of God during the exodus and the conquest of the promised land. The most ancient mention (Nm 10,33) shows Yahweh Himself guiding the travels of His people in the desert; the transporting of the ark is accompanied by a martial chant (Nm 10,35; 1 S 4,5): it is the emblem of the holy war*, witnessing to the part which Yahweh, the "valiant warrior" (Ex 15,3), Himself took in accomplishing the promise: passage of the Jordan, the capture of Jericho, the struggle against the Philistines. At the sanctuary of Shiloh, there appeared in connection with the ark the expression *Yahweh-Sabaoth** (1 S 1,3; 4,4; 2 S 6,2). From this martial history, the ark preserved a sacred character, at the same time formidable and beneficent. People identified it with God, giving it His name* (Nm 10,35; 1 S 47). It is the "glory of Israel" (1 S 4,22; cf Lm 2,1), the Power of the Strong One of Jacob (Ps 132,8; 78,61), the presence of the Holy God among His people; demand of holiness* in him who would approach it (1 S 6,19f; 2 S 6,1-11; the priestly ritual), it manifests the liberty of God, who did not allow Himself to be annexed by the people, though He continued to act in their favor (1 S 4—6).

The history of the ark achieved its heights and termination when David, amidst the joy of the people, caused it to be borne solemnly into Jerusalem (2 S 6,12-19; cf Ps 24,7-10), where it found its place of repose (Ps 132), and where finally Solomon installed it in the temple (1 K 8). Up till then the movable ark was in some way at the disposition of the tribes; after the prophecy of Nathan (2 S 7), the covenant* passed through the family of David which fashioned the unity of the people: Jerusalem and the temple came to inherit the characteristics proper to the ark.

II. GOD PRESENT BY HIS WORD

The ark is at the same time the place of the Word* of God. First, because it contains the two tables of the Law*, it perpetuates in Israel the "witness*" which God gave of Himself, the revelation which He made of His will (Ex 31,18), and the response which Israel had given to this Word (Dt 31,26-27). Ark of the covenant, ark of witness—these expressions designate the ark in relation to the clauses of the covenant* engraved on the tablets for the two parties.

The ark in a certain way continues the Sinai encounter. During the desert marches, when he wishes to consult Yahweh, to obtain from Him a statement for the people (Ex 25,22), or inversely to pray in favor of the people (Nm 14),

Moses enters the tent; and over the ark Yahweh speaks to him and "converses with him as with His neighbor" (Ex 33,7-11; 34,34; Nm 12,4-8). Later, Amos will claim that his teaching comes from the ark as from a new Sinai (Am 1,2). And it is while he is praying in front of the ark that Isaiah receives his calling as a prophet (Is 6).

Similarly it is "before" the ark that the faithful come to encounter God, either to hear His Word like Samuel (1 S 3), or to consult Him through His intermediaries, the priests, guardians and interpreters of the Law* (Dt 31,10ff; 33,10), or to pray to Him like Hannah (1 S 1,9) or David (2 S 7,18). This is a type of "devotion" to the ark which itself also will pass to the temple (prayers of Solomon, 1 K 8,30; of Hezekiah, 2 K 19,14).

III. THE ARK IN THE HOPE OF ISRAEL AND THE NT

Jeremiah, after 587, called upon the people not to regret the disappearance of the ark; for the new Jerusalem*, having become the center of the nations*, will itself be the Throne of Yahweh (Jr 3,16-17), and under the regime of the new covenant the law will be inscribed in their hearts (31,31-34). Ezekiel used the imagery of the ark, the movable home of Yahweh, to show that the "glory*" leaves the defiled temple to rejoin the exiles: God henceforth will be present in the remnant*, the sacred community (Ez 9—11). Judaism hoped, it seems, for a reappearance of the ark at the end of time (2 M 2,4-8), and this is represented in the Apocalypse (Ap 11,19). The NT shows that the ark has found its fulfillment* in Christ, Word of God living among men (Jn 1,14; Col 2,9), acting for their salvation (1 Th 2,13), making Himself their guide (Jn 8,12), and becoming the true propitiatory (R 3,25; cf 1 Jn 2,2; 4,10).

→Covenant OT I 3—Glory III 2—Manna 1—Pilgrimage OT 1—Presence of God OT II, III 1—Power I 1—Temple OT—Witness OT II 2—Worship OT I; NT III 2.

JB jjk

ARM & HAND

The arm and the hand are normally the organs and the signs of action, expression, relation. The arm symbolism often suggests also power*; the hand suggests ability and capability.

1. *The arm and the hand of God.* The hand of God made heaven and earth (Is 66,2). Like the potter's hand, it gives shape (Jb 10,8; Jr 18,6; cf Gn 2,7). Thus, God reveals the power of His arm [cf "His arm" in the general sense (Is 53,1)] in creation (Jr 32,17) and in history (Dt 4,34; Lk 1,51). Often He acts "with arm outstretched and with a strong hand." His "arm of holiness" (Is 52,10), His "good hand" (Ezr 7,9), the "shadow* of His hand" (Is 49,2), His uplifted hand in oath (Dt 32,40), recall His powerful protection (cf Jn 10,29). In God's hand security is found (Ws 3,1; cf Ps 31,6= Lk 23,46); and when the hand of God "is upon" a prophet*, it takes possession of him and communicates to him, as it were, the Spirit of vision (Ez 1,3...). God's hand is not "too short" to save (Is 50,2). It can, however, make itself heavy (Ps 32,4), and strike (Is 5,25; cf He 10,31) when the persistent love which it attested (cf Is 65,2=R 10,21) has been despised. Like God's hand, the hand of Christ is all-powerful (Mk 6,2; cf Jn 10,28); it possesses everything (Jn 3,35); it is willing to relieve (Mt 8,3).

2. *The arm and the hand of man.* Compared with that of God, the "arm of flesh*" is powerless (2 Ch 32,8; cf Is 40,12; Pr 30,4). However, the arm is also in man an instrument and symbol of vigorous action (Ps 18,35). The gesture of the hand expresses the movement of the soul: joy (2 K 11,12), distress (Jr 2,37), blessing* (Gn 48,14), oath (Gn 14,22), and, above all, prayer* and adoration* (Ps 28,2; 1 Tm 2,8; Jb 31,27); finally, the hands of the suppliant should be pure (Ps 24,4; Jm 4,8; cf Is 1,15). If the hand of God "is with" someone (cf Lk 1,66), it is in order that it might protect him or endow the action of this man with divine power (Ac 11,21; 5,12). Thus the apostles, by imposing* their hands, can communicate the Spirit of God Himself (Ac 19,6; cf 1 Tm 4,14).

Today also, the hand of a bishop or a priest, like that of Christ and of the apostles, passes on life—especially in the sacramental actions.

→Imposition of Hands—Power—Right Hand —Spirit of God OT II 2—Strength I 1.

AR pjb

ARROGANCE

1. *Arrogance and its effects.* "Odious to the Lord and to men" (Si 10,7), haughtiness is

also laughable in man "who is dust and ashes" (Si 10,7). It has several more or less serious forms. There is the vain man who lays claim to honors (Lk 14,7; Mt 23,6f); who aspires to greatness, sometimes in the spiritual order (R 12, 16,3); who is jealous of others (G 5,26); the insolent man with a haughty look (Pr 6,17; 21,24); the arrogant rich man who shows off his luxury (Am 6,8) and whom his riches render presumptuous (Jm 4,16; 1 Jn 2,16); the ostentatious hypocrite* who does everything in order to be seen and whose heart is corrupted (Mt 23,5.25-28); the pharisee* who is confident in his pretended justice and scorns others (Lk 18, 9-14).

Finally, at the top there is the proud man who rejects all dependence and aspires to be equal to God (Gn 3,5; cf Ph 2,6; Jn 5,18); he does not like reprimands (Pr 15,12) and holds humility* in horror (Si 13,20); he sins boldly (Nm 15,30f) and laughs* at the servants of God and His promises (Ps 119,51; 2 P 3,3f).

God curses the arrogant man and holds him in horror (Ps 119,21; Lk 16,15); one whom pride contaminates (Mk 7,22) is closed to grace* (1 P 5,5) and to faith* (Jn 5,44); blinded by his fault (Mt 23,24; Jn 9,39ff), he cannot find wisdom (Pr 14,6) who calls him to conversion (Pr 1,22-28). Whoever associates with him becomes like to him (Si 13,1); thus, blessed is he who shuns him (Ps 1,1).

2. *The arrogance of the pagans, oppressors of Israel.* Where arrogant men, ignorant of the true God, are in power, the weak are reduced to servitude. Israel had experience of this in Egypt, where the Pharaoh tried to stand in the way of their liberation by God (Ex 5,2). Israel will be constantly threatened with enslavement at the hands of the pagans whose haughty power* "challenges the living God" (1 S 17,26). From the giant Goliath to the persecutor Antiochus (1 S 17,4; 2 M 9,4-10), not to mention Sennacherib (2 K 18,33ff). it is the same arrogance which is expressed in the intolerable utterance of Holofernes: "Who is God, if not Nebuchadnezzar" (Jdt 6,2).

The type of that domineering arrogance of nations which today are called totalitarian is Babylon*, which was named "sovereign of the kingdoms" (cf. Is 13,19) and which boasted of being "everlasting," saying in its heart: "I and I alone!" (Is 47,5-10). Here is collective arrogance whose symbol is the tower of Babel standing uncompleted on the threshold of biblical history: its builders aspired to make a name* for themselves in reaching for the sky (Gn 11,4).

3. *The arrogance of the ungodly men, oppressors of the poor.* In Israel itself, haughtinesss could produce fruits of oppression and impiety. The Law prescribed kindness toward the weak (Ex 22,21-27) and called upon the king not to grow haughty whether in amassing too much silver and gold, or in raising himself above his brothers (Dt 17,17.20). In order to enrich himself, the haughty man does not hesitate to crush the poor* whose blood pays for the luxury of the rich (Am 8,4-8; Jr 22,13ff). But the contempt for the poor is contempt for God and His justice. Haughty men are godless* men, similar to the pagans. Those whom they persecute (Ps 10,2ff) and look on with contempt (Ps 123,4) appeal to God in the psalms, emphasizing the arrogance of their persecutors (Ps 73, 6-9) whose heart is insensible (Ps 119,70). To the Pharisees who have in their hearts haughtiness and love of money, Jesus recalls that no man can serve two masters: one who is attached to riches cannot help but scorn God (Lk 16,13ff).

4. *The punishment of the arrogant.* God mocks the haughty (Pr 3,34) and the powerful ones who pretend to throw off His yoke (Ps 2,2ff). Let them heed the terrible satire of the tyrant who rots without burial on the field of battle, where he caused the massacre of his people, he who aspired to set his throne above the stars, like unto the most high (Is 14,3-20; Ez 28,17ff; 31). Empires, like their tyrants, will be hurled down. They are occasionally instruments of God for chastising His people; but God punishes them afterwards for the haughtiness with which they accomplished their mission*; such is the case of Assyria (Is 10,12) and of Babylon, suddenly overthrown by an inevitable, unforseeable blow (Is 47,9.11).

The people of God and the holy city of Jerusalem, where pride is extensive (Jr 13,9; Ez 7,10), will be punished also on the day* of Yahweh. "On that day, the haughtiness of man will be brought low, his arrogance humiliated: Yahweh will be exalted, He alone!" (Is 2,6-22). Yahweh will pay back with interest what is due to the haughty (Ps 31,24). Those who have mocked the just (Ws 5,4; cf Lk 16,14), will pass away like smoke (Ws 5,8-14). Their loftiness is but a prelude to their ruin (Pr 16,18; Tb 4,13): "He who exalts himself will be humbled" (Mt 23,12).

5. *The conqueror of the haughty: the Savior of the humble.* How does "the Lord scatter the proud-hearted" (Lk 1,51)? How does He triumph over Satan*, the old serpent who enticed man to haughtiness (Gn 3,5), the devil who wishes to seduce the entire world into adoring him as its god (Ap 12,9; 13,5; 2 Co 4,4)? By means of a humble virgin (Lk 1,48) and her newborn, Christ the Lord, who took a manger as His crib (Lk 2,11f; cf Ps 8,3).

He whom the haughtiness of Herod had wished to slay (Mt 2,13) begins His mission by rejecting the glory of the world*, which Satan offers Him, and any Messianism* which pride would falsify (Mt 4,3-10). He is reproached for making Himself equal to God (Jn 5,18); yet, far from taking advantage of this equality, He does not seek His own glory (Jn 8,50), but only the lifting up on the cross* (Jn 12,31ff); Ph 2,6ff). If He asks His Father to glorify Him, it is that the Father might be glorified in Him (Jn 12,28; 17,1).

Along this road the disciples, and especially the shepherds of His Church, will have to follow* Him (Lk 22,26f; 1 P 5,3; Tt 1,7). In His name* will they triumph over the dominion of the demon (Lk 10,18ff); but the powers of pride will be overthrown only on the day* of the Lord, by the manifestation of His glory* (2 Th 1,7f). Then the godless one who made himself equal to God will be destroyed by the breath of the Lord (2 Th 2,4.8); then the great Babylon, symbol of the deified state, will be overthrown at a blow (Ap 18,10.21). Then, too, the humble, and they alone, will appear like unto God whose children they are (Mt 18,3f; 1 Jn 3,2).

→Babel / Babylon 1—Humility—Pride—Power III—Wealth II.

MFL pmcm

ASCENSION

It is of faith that the risen Christ has entered into His glory. But we have here a mystery which transcends sense experience and cannot be confined, for instance, within that single scene on the Mount of Olives, where the apostles saw their master leave them to return to God. In fact, the sacred texts treat of the meaning, the moment, and the manner of Christ's celestial exaltation with a variety the richness of which is instructive. We are going to try in the light of these texts to grasp the pro-found reality of the mystery through the origin of its literary expression.

I. THE PASSAGE BETWEEN HEAVEN AND EARTH

According to a spontaneous and universal belief taken up by the Bible, heaven* is so considered the home of the divinity that the term serves as a metaphor signifying God*. The earth*, His footstool (Is 66,1), is the home of men (Ps 115,16; Qo 5,1). In order to visit these men, God "descends" from heaven (Gn 11,5; Ex 19,11ff; Mi 1,3; Ps 144,5) and "reascends" there (Gn 17,22). The cloud* is His vehicle (Nm 11,25; Ps 18,10; Is 19,1). The Spirit* whom He sends must also descend (Is 32,15; Mt 3,16; 1 P 1,12); in the same manner the Word* descends and returns to Him, once His work is accomplished (Is 55,10f; Ws 18,15). The angels* themselves, who inhabit heaven with God (1 K 22,19; Jb 1,6; Tb 12,15; Mt 18,10), descend to accomplish their missions (Dn 4,10; Mt 28,2; Lk 22,43) and afterwards return (Jg 13,20; Tb 12,20); this ascent and descent establish the connection between heaven and earth (Gn 28,12; Jn 1,51).

For men the passage is of itself impossible. To speak about ascending to heaven is equivalent to expressing the search for the inaccessible (Dt 30,12; Ps 139,8; Pr 30,4; Ba 3,29), when this is not the presumption of senseless pride (Gn 11,4; Is 14,14; Jr 51,53; Jb 20,6; Mt 11,23). It is already a great deal that prayers ascend to heaven (Tb 12,12; Si 35,16f; Ac 10,4) and that God gives to men a rendezvous upon mountains* where He descends while they mount; such mountains are Sinai (Ex 19,20) or Mount Zion (Is 2,3 and 4,5). By way of exception some chosen ones, as Henoch (Gn 5,24; Si 44, 16; 49,14) or Elijah (2 K 2,11; Si 48,9-12; 1 M 2,58), have had the privilege of being raised up to heaven by divine power. In Dn 7,13 it is toward the Ancient of Days that the Son* of Man comes, and this also suggests an ascent although its starting point is mysterious and the clouds of heaven are here, perhaps, not a vehicle, but only the ornament of the divine dwelling place.

II. THE ASCENT OF CHRIST TO HEAVEN

According to biblical cosmology, Jesus, glorified at the right* hand of God through the resurrection* (Ac 2,34; R 8,34; E 1,20f; 1 P 3,22; cf Mk 12,35ff p; 14,62 p); where He is enthroned as king* (Ap 1,5; 3,21; 5,6; 7,17), had to "ascend" to heaven. In fact, His ascension appears in the first affirmations of the faith, less as a phenomenon considered in itself but rather as the indispensable expression of the heavenly exaltation of Christ (cf Ac 2,34; Mk 16,19; 1 P 3,22). But with the progress of revelation and the development of the faith, the ascension has taken on an historical and theological individuality which is more and more marked.

1. *Descent and re-ascent.* The pre-existence of Christ, being implicit at the dawn of faith, has gone on to become more explicit, His pre-existence as announced in the Scriptures helping toward perceiving His ontological pre-existence. Before coming to live upon earth, Jesus was with God as son, word, wisdom. Hence His heavenly exaltation has not been merely the triumph of a man elevated to the ranks of the divine, as a primitive Christology suggested (Ac 2,22-36; 10,36-42), but the return to the heavenly world whence He had come. It is John who has expressed most clearly this descent from heaven (Jn 6,33.38.41f.50f.58) and has related the re-ascent to the ascension (Jn 3,13; 6,62). R 10,6f cannot be appealed to here because the motion which follows the descent of the incarnation is the re-ascent from the kingdom of the dead rather than the ascent into heaven. On the other hand, E 4,9f exposes a wider journey where the descent into the lower regions of the earth (or in the earth?) is followed by a re-ascent which leads Christ beyond all the heavens. It is again this same journey which the hymn of Ph 2,6-11 supposes.

2. *Triumph of a cosmic order.* Another motif was a necessary contribution to specify the ascension as a glorifying stage distinct from the resurrection* and from the celestial enthronement: the care to express in a better way the cosmic supremacy of Christ. When the heresy of the Colossians had threatened to lower Christ to an inferior rank among the hierarchies of the angels, Paul repeats in a most categorical way what he had already said about His triumph over the heavenly powers (1 Co 15,24), affirming that this triumph has been already accomplished through the cross* (Col 2,15), and that Christ now reigns in heaven over these powers whoever they may be (E 1,20f); then it is that he exploits Ps 68,19 to point out that the

ascent of Christ above all the heavens has been to take possession of the universe which He "fills" (E 4,10), as well as "recaptiulates" (E 1,10), with the title of head. It is the same cosmic horizon which appeared in the hymn of 1 Tm 3,16: the lifting up into glory comes there after the manifestation to the angels and to the world. The epistle to the Hebrews recounts in its turn the ascent of Christ in view of its perspective of a celestial world where there are found the realities of salvation and toward which men journey. In order to sit there at the right hand of God (He 1,3; 8,1; 10,12f; 12,2) above the angels (1,4-13; 2,7ff), the high priest has gone up first, passing through the heavens (4,14) and penetrating behind the veil (6,19f) into the sanctuary where He intercedes in the presence of God (9,24).

3. *The time of the ascension.* Distinguished from the departure out of the tomb by its cosmic manifestation, the ascent of Christ to heaven had still further to be detached from the emergence from the tomb because of the pedagogical necessity of narrating in time to men an event which transcends time, and also to take into account a period of time for the apparitions. Certainly nothing prevents, and in fact everything demands, that Jesus, manifesting Himself to His disciples, should come for this purpose from the world of glory* which He had entered from the moment of His resurrection; otherwise it is hard to see where He was during the interval of these manifestations and it is His already-glorified state that He shows them. In fact, Mt also seems to perceive this situation: he does not speak of the ascension, but implies, through the declaration of Jesus as to the power which has been given to Him in heaven and upon earth (Mt 28,18), that the accession of the heavenly throne is already accomplished at the time of the apparition on the mountain of Galilee. John teaches the same thing in a different manner: if Jesus had to inform the disciples through Mary Magdalen that He ascends to His Father (Jn 20,17), it follows that He will have already ascended and returned when He appeared to them the same evening (20,19). The delay of some hours between the resurrection and the ascension is entirely pedagogical and permits Jesus to impress on Mary Magdalen that He is entering into a new state where the contacts of old (comp 20,17 and 11,2; 12,3) will be spiritualized (6,58 and 62).

In the other texts the time of the ascension is distinguished even more so from that of the resurrection: Lk 24,50f, coming after vv 13,33. 36.44, gives the impression that the ascension is placed in the evening of Easter Sunday after the diverse discourses of Jesus with His disciples. At the end of Mk 16,19, which depends in good part on Lk, the ascension is related after successive manifestations, and it is difficult to see if these appearances occupied a single day or several days. Finally, from Ac 1,3-11 it is at the end of forty days of apparitions and discourses that Jesus left His own to ascend to heaven. The ascension, as related by these three texts, endeavors manifestly to put an end to the period of the apparitions; it does not wish to describe the first entry of Christ into His glory after a changeable and inexplicable delay, but rather to describe the last departure which puts an end to His temporal manifestation. The very incertitude of the delay is better explained by reason of its contingent dating; in Acts the number* 40 is, without doubt, chosen in view of the 50 days of pentecost*: if Jesus ascends to heaven definitively, it is to send His Spirit who henceforth will replace Him among His disciples.

The diversified teaching of the sacred texts, in short, invites one to recognize in this mystery two connected but distinct aspects: on the one hand, the celestial glorification of Christ which coincided with His resurrection; on the other hand, His final departure after a period of apparitions—a departure and return to God which the apostles witnessed on the Mount of Olives and which, more particularly, the liturgical feast of the ascension commemorates.

4. *Manner of the ascension.* Ac 1,9 is the only canonical text which describes, however so little, Jesus' ascent into heaven; and its extreme caution confirms the idea that it does not pretend to describe the first entry of Christ into glory. Such a sober presentation owes nothing either to the deification of pagan heroes, as Romulus and Mithras, or to the biblical precedent of Elijah*. Making use of the stereotyped cloud of the theophanies and the angelic speech which explains the scene, the text is unwilling to furnish for the mystery a realistic description of doubtful taste, such as certain apocryphal inventions, and limits itself to the essential facts which bring out the basic meaning of the scene. It is not that this scene, localized in a very precise manner upon the Mount of Olives, is not an historical event, or that Jesus was not able to give to His disciples a certain sense experience of His return to God. The purpose of this

account is certainly not to describe the triumph which is produced in fact at the instant of the resurrection; but its purpose is only to point out that after a certain period of familiar companionship with His disciples, the risen one withdrew His visible presence* from the world, not to manifest it again until the end of time.

III. THE ASCENSION, PRELUDE OF THE PAROUSIA

"He who has been taken up from you, this same Jesus, will come in the same manner in which you have seen Him departing toward heaven" (Ac 1,11). Besides explaining the purpose of the ascension account, this angelic discourse establishes a profound bond between the ascent of Christ to heaven and His return at the end of time. While the latter is awaited, the stay of Christ in heaven—in itself definitive in relation to the person of Christ—remains a transitory stage in the general economy of salvation: He resides in heaven hidden from men until His final manifestation (Col 3,1-4) at the time of the universal restoration (Ac 3,21); 1 Th 1,10). Then He will come as He departed (Ac 1,11), descending from heaven (1 Th 4,16; 2 Th 1,7) upon the clouds (Ap 1,7; cf 14,14ff), while His elect ascend to meet Him, likewise upon the clouds (1 Th 4,17), as the two witnesses of the Apocalypse (Ap 11,12). It is still the same cosmological presentation inherent in our human imagination and yet reduced to a minimum.

The profound meaning which evolves from these themes is that Christ, triumphant over death, has initiated a new manner of life with God. He has gone there first to prepare a place for His elect, then He will return and lead them there so that they might always be with Him (Jn 14,2f).

IV. CHRISTIAN SPIRITUALITY OF THE ASCENSION

While awaiting the day of this final manifestation, Christians must remain united to their glorified Lord through faith and the sacraments. At this very moment arisen and even seated in heaven with Him (E 2,6), they seek "the things that are above;" for their real life* is "hidden with Christ in God" (Col 3,1ff). Their city is in heaven (Ph 3,20). The heavenly mansion which awaits them and with which they desire to be clothed (2 Co 5,1ff) is none other than this same glorious Christ Himself (Ph 3,21), the "heavenly Man" (1 Co 15,45-49).

From this springs forth an entire spirituality of the ascension which is the basis of hope*, for it makes the Christian life from this time in the reality of the new world where Christ reigns. Nonetheless, he is not so much uprooted from the old world which still possesses him, but on the contrary he has a mission and power to live there in a new way which elevates this world toward the transformation of glory to which God calls it.

→Cloud 4—Elijah OT 4; NT 2—Glory IV 2—Mountain III 1—Resurrection NT I 2.

PBe pjb

ASHES

The original meaning of ashes is a much debated question, in spite of their widespread use in most ancient religions. They are often associated with dust (the Septuagint translates "dust" by "ashes" on more than one occasion) and symbolize both the sin and the weakness of man.

1. In the first place the heart* of the *sinner** is compared with dust: Isaiah calls the idolator "a man who hankers after ashes" (Is 44,20), and the Wise Man says of him. "Ashes, his heart, meaner than dirt his hope" (Ws 15,10). This is why the wages of sin can only be ashes: the proud will see themselves reduced to "ashes on the ground (Ez 28,18), and the wicked will be trodden under foot by the just like ashes" (Ml 3,21). Moreover, the sinner, who does not become hardened in his pride (Si 10,9) and who realizes his fault, confesses precisely that he is only "dust and ashes" (Gn 18,27; Si 17,32). And to prove to himself and others that he is convinced of this, he sits amidst ashes (Jb 42,6; Jn 3,6; Mt 11,21 p) and covers his head with them (Jdt 4,11-15; 9,1; Ez 27,30).

2. But this same symbol of repentance is also used to express the sadness* of man crushed by *misfortune*, no doubt because a connection between misfortune and sin is taken for granted. When she is scorned Tamar covers herself with ashes (2 S 13,19); and so do the Jews when threatened by death (Es 4,1-4; cf 1 M 3,47; 4,39). In this way man wants to show the state

to which he has been reduced (Jb 30,19) and even goes so far as to eat ashes (Ps 102,10; Lm 3,16). But it is especially on the occasion of a bereavement that he feels nothingness and then he expresses it by covering himself with dust and ashes: "Wrap yourself in sackcloth, daughter of my people, roll in ashes; mourn..." (Jr 6,26).

Thus to cover oneself with ashes is to act in mime a sort of public confession (cf the liturgy of Ash Wednesday). Using the language of this lifeless matter that returns to dust, man admits himself sinful and weak, and in this way forestalls God's judgment and attracts His mercy. To anyone admitting his nothingness like this is addressed the promise of the Messiah, as he comes to triumph over sin and death, "to comfort all who mourn, and to give them for ashes a garland" (Is 61,3).

→Repentance/Conversion OT I 2—Sin III 3.

GB ems

AUTHORITY

OT

I. "ALL AUTHORITY COMES FROM GOD"

This principle, which Paul formulated (R 13, 1), is constantly supposed in the OT: but the whole exercise of this authority appears there as subordinated to the imperative demands of the divine will.

1. *Aspects of earthly authority.* In the creation that God has made, all power proceeds from Him: of man over nature (Gn 1,28), of husband over his wife (Gn 3,16), of parents over their children (Lv 19,3). When the more complex structures of human society are considered, those who govern hold their responsibility for the common good and for their subjects from God: Yahweh orders Hagar to render obedience to her mistress (Gn 16,9); it is He who confers on Hazael the government of Damascus (1 K 19,15; 2 K 8,9-13) and on Nebuchadnezzar of the entire Orient (Jr 27,6). If this is true among the pagans themselves (cf Si 10,4), all the more should it be true among the people of God. But here the problem posed by earthly authority assumes a special character which merits separate study.

2. *Conditions for the exercise of authority.* The authority entrusted by God is not absolute; it is limited by moral obligations. The law* regulates its exercise in stating precisely the rights* of slaves* (Ex 21,1-6.26f; Dt 15,12-18; Si 33,30...). As for children, the father's authority over them must have for its end their good education* (Pr 23,13f; Si 7,22f; 30,1 ...). It is in matters of political authority that man is more likely to exceed the bounds of his power. Intoxicated with power*, he attributes its merit to himself, just like the victorious Assyrians (Is 10,7-11.13f); he deifies himself (Ez 28,2-5) and elevates himself against the sovereign master (Is 14,13f), even so far as to offend Him blasphemously (Dn 11,36). At this point, he is similar to the satanic beasts* which Daniel saw rising up from the sea and to whom God gave power for a time (Dn 7,3-8.19-25). But an authority perverted in such a way is given over to the divine judgment* which will not fail to destroy it on a fixed day (Dn 7,11f. 26): having joined its cause to evil powers, it will in the end fall with them.

II. AUTHORITY AMONG THE PEOPLE OF GOD

Man has not, then, respected the order and the conditions of its exercise, which belong to earthly authority. In order to restore them, God inaugurates in the history of His people a plan of salvation* in which earthly authority is going to take on a new meaning within the perspective of the redemption.

1. *The two powers.* At the head of His people, God places some authorized agents. These are not primarily political personages but religious mediators* who have a mission* to make Israel "a priestly kingdom and a holy nation" (Ex 19, 6). Moses*, the prophets*, and the priests* are the recipients of a power essentially spiritual which they exercise visibly by divine delegation. Nevertheless, Israel is still a national community, a state structured into a political organization. This state is theocratic because the power, whatever the form may be, is exercised in the name of God: power of the ancients who assist Moses (Ex 18.21ff; Nm 11, 24f), of the charismatic leaders as Joshua and the judges, and finally some of the kings*.

The covenant supposes an intimate association between the two powers, and the subordination of the political to the spiritual, in conformity with the national calling. However, in practice this leads to some inevitable conflicts: of Saul with Samuel (1 S 13,7-15; 15), of Ahab with Elijah (1 K 21,17-24), and of so many kings with their contemporary prophets. Among the people of God human authority is dogged by the same abuse as everywhere else. This is another reason why it is subjected to the divine judgment: the political power of the Israelite royalty will end by foundering in the tragedy of the exile.

2. *In relation to pagan empires.* When Judaism was reformed after the exile, its structure was along the lines of the original theocracy. Here the distinction between the spiritual power and the political power was all the more evident since the latter was in the hands of foreign empires in which the Jews were now subjects. In this new situation the people of God adopted, according to the requirements of the situation, two attitudes. The first was open acceptance: it is from God that Cyrus and his successors have received the empire (Is 45,1ff); since they favor the restoration of the holy worship, they must be served loyally and prayed for (Jr 29,7; Ba 1,10f). The second attitude was an appeal to the divine vengeance* and, in the end, to revolt when the pagan nation turns persecutor (Jdt; 1 M 2,15-28). But the restoration of the monarchy in the Maccabean period brought back again a doubtful conconcentration of the powers which rapidly sank into the worst decadence. In the year 63, when Rome intervened, the people of God found themselves back under the yoke of the detested pagans.

NT

I. JESUS

1. *Jesus, recipient of authority.* During His public life Jesus appears as the recipient of a singular authority (*exousia*): He preaches with authority (Mk 1,22 p), He has the power to remit sins (Mt 9,6ff), and He is Lord of the Sabbath (Mk 2,28p). He has all the spiritual power of a divine envoy before whom the Jews pose the essential question: by what authority does he do these things (Mt 21,23 p)? Jesus does not respond directly to this question (Mt 21,27 p). But the signs that He accomplishes sharpen their thoughts to an answer: He has power (*exousia*) over sickness (Mt 8,8f p), over the elements (Mk 4,41 p), and over demons

(Mt 12,28 p). His authority, then, extends even to political things; in this domain, the power which He refused to take from Satan* (Lk 4,5ff) He has received in reality from God. And yet He does not take advantage of this power among men. At the time when the leaders of this world manifest it to them by exercising dominion, He displays Himself among His own as one who serves (Lk 22,25ff). He is master and Lord (Jn 13,13); but He has come to serve* and to give His life (Mk 10,42ff p). And it is because He takes on the condition of slave* that all knees* will eventually bend before Him (Ph 2,5-11). That is why, after His resurrection, He will tell His followers that from then on "all power (*exousia*) has been given Him in heaven and on earth" (Mt 28,18).

2. *Jesus before earthly authorities.* The attitude of Jesus toward earthly authorities is all the more meaningful. Before the Jewish authorities, He claims His title of Son of Man* (Mt 26, 63f p), the basis of a power which Scripture asserts (Dn 7,14). Before the political authority, His position is different. He recognizes the proper competence of Caesar (Mt 22,21 p); but this does not close His eyes to the injustice perpetrated by the representatives of authority (Mt 20,25; Lk 13,32). When He stands before Pilate, He does not discuss his power, the divine origin of which He knows; but He stresses the injustice of which He is the victim (Jn 19,11), and He claims for Himself once again the kingdom which is not of this world (Jn 18,36). If, then, the spiritual and the temporal, each in its own way, have their origin from Him, nevertheless He sanctifies their clear distinction and lets it be known that, for the time being, the temporal in its order retains its true standing: and this is the state of affairs that will last until His return in glory. The two powers were mixed in theocratic Israel; there will be none of this intermingling in the Church.

II. THE APOSTLES

1. *The recipients of Jesus' authority.* In sending His disciples* on a mission*, Jesus delegated His own authority ("he who hears you hears me," Lk 10,16f) and entrusted His powers (cf Mk 3,14f p; Lk 10,19) to them. However, He also taught them that the exercise of these powers was in reality a service* (Lk 22,26 p; Jn 13,14f). Later on the apostles* make effective use of their prerogatives, for example by excluding unworthy members from the community (1 Co 5,4f). Nevertheless, far from making the weight of their authority felt, above all they are engrossed in serving Christ and men (1 Th 2,6-10). This authority is still spiritual even though it is exercised in a visible way: it concerns the government of the Church exclusively. There is an important innovation there: contrary to the cities of antiquity, the distinction between the spiritual and the temporal is now effective.

2. *The exercise of human authority.* The apostolic writings confirm the doctrine of the OT as to the validity of human authority and the conditions of its exercise, but they give it a new foundation. The wife must be subject to her husband as the Church is to Christ; but in return the husband must love his wife as Christ has loved the Church (E 5,22-33). Children must obey their parents (Col 3,20f; E 6,1ff) because all paternity receives its name from God (E 3,15); but parents must take care in rearing them not to irritate them (E 6,4; Col 3, 21). Slaves* must obey even hard and unreasonable masters (1 P 2,18) as Christ Himself (Col 3,22; E 6,5...); but masters must bear in mind that they also have a master in heaven (E 6,9) and remember to treat their slaves as brothers* (Phm 16). It is not enough to say that this social morality safeguards a proper conception of authority in society; it provides as a foundation and an ideal the service of others performed in charity.

3. *The relations of the Church with human authorities.* The apostles, recipients of Jesus' authority, are faced with human authority with which they must enter into relationship. Among these, the Jewish authorities are not like other authorities: they have a power of a spiritual order and take their origin from a divine institution; thus the apostles treat them with respect (Ac 4,9; 23,1-5), insofar as their opposition to Christ is not open. But these authorities incurred a grave responsibility in refusing to acknowledge Christ and in having condemned Him (Ac 3,13ff; 13,27f). They make it worse by opposing the preaching of the gospel; the apostles, therefore, ignore their prohibitions, thinking that they ought to obey God rather than men (Ac 5,29). By refusing the authority of Christ, the Jewish leaders lost their spiritual power.

The relations with political authority pose a different problem. Before the Roman empire Paul professes complete loyalty; he claims his title to Roman citizenship (Ac 16,37; 22,25...)

and appeals to Caesar to obtain justice (Ac 25, 12). He proclaims that all authority comes from God, and that it is given in view of the common good; thus submission to the civil powers is a matter of conscience because they are the ministers of divine justice (R 13,1-7). Kings and subjects with authority must be prayed for (1 Tm 2,2). This same doctrine is found in the first epistle of Peter (1 P 2,13-17). This supposes that the civil authorities are themselves submissive before the law of God. But nowhere can one find that the spiritual authorities of the Church claim a direct power over political affairs.

If, on the contrary, political authority rebels in its turn against God and His Christ just as the Syrian empire, persecutor of the Jews, did formerly, then the Christian prophets solemnly announce judgment and defeat. This the Apocalypse did before the Rome of Nero and Domitian (Ap 17,1—19,10). In the totalitarian empire which pretends to be the incarnation of divine authority, the political power is nothing more than a satanic caricature before which no believer should bow his head.

→Apostles—Charisms II 4—Church III 2 b c —Conscience 2 b—Desert NT II—Fathers & Father I 1, III 2.3, V 3—Fear of God III—King—Law C I—Listen 1 a—Lord—Ministry II 1.3—Mission—Oath NT 1—Obedience—Pardon II 3—Peter 2.3—Power—Rights OT 1 —Seal 1— Shepherd & Flock—Teaching—Tradition OT II 2; NT II 1—Watchfulness 2 —Word of God NT I 1.

FA & PG pjb

B

BABEL/BABYLON

Contrary to Egypt*, which in its status as a biblical symbol has an ambiguous meaning, Babylon always represents an evil power although God can on occasion utilize it in order to achieve His ends.

1. *The sign of Babel.* Even before Israel entered into direct relationship with the great Mesopotamian city*, it was present on the horizon of sacred history. For Babel is the Hebrew name for Babylon, and the famous tower of which Gn 11,1-9 speaks is none other than the tower of various levels (or *ziggurat*) of its great temple. The outstanding sign of Babylonian idolatry*, this tower is also presented as the symbol of human pride*. Biblical tradition attaches the confusion of tongues* to the sign of Babel: this is the way that God has chastised men for their proud idolatry.

2. *The scourge of God.* Still, from the beginning of the seventh century, Babylon plays a more direct role in sacred history. At that time the Chaldeans, who conquered it, dreamed of carrying the rule of the Middle East to Nineveh. She is a formidable power, which "makes strength* its God" (Ha 1,11); but God intends to make this power part of His plan. To this Babylon contributes by executing His judgment* against Nineveh (Na 2,2—3,19). She is the scourge of God for Israel and the neighboring kingdoms: Yahweh delivered them all up to the hands of Nebuchadnezzar, her king, for whom they must carry the yoke (Jr 27, 1—28,17). She is the cup* of gold with which Yahweh inebriates His people (Jr 25,15-29; 51, 7). She is the hammer of which He makes use to pound the whole earth (Jr 50,23; 51,20ff). She will above all execute the judgment of Yahweh against Judah (Jr 21,3-7): her land will be the place of exile* where God will gather together the remnant of His people (Jr 29,1-20). This is the hard reality which the Books of Kings describe (2 K 24—25); but "by the rivers of Babylon," where the chants give place to tears (Ps 137), the exiled Jews experience purifying suffering which prepares for future restorations.

3. *The city of evil.* This providential role of Babylon does not prevent it from being in unequalled fashion the city of evil. She is surely called to be united one day to the people of God (Ps 87,4) as the other nations and as Nineveh herself (Is 19,24; cf Jon). But just

like Nineveh, she is satisfied with her own power (Is 47,7f.10; cf 9,7-14). She stands before Yahweh with pride and insolence (Jr 50,29-32; cf Is 14,13f). She has multiplied her crimes: sorcery (Is 47,12), idolatry (Is 46,1; Jr 51,44-52), cruelties of all kinds. She has truly become the temple of evil (Ze 5,5-11), the "city of nothingness" (Is 24,10).

4. *The exit from Babylon.* If the exile was a just chastisement for guilty Israel, it is now for the little remnant, converted by the ordeal, an intolerable captivity* and even a dangerous sojourn. Once the 70 years predicted (a conventional number*: Jr 25,11; 29,10; 2 Ch 36,21) have passed, the year of forgiveness is going to come (Is 61,2; cf Lv 25,10). This so long awaited liberation is for the people of God "good news" (Is 40,9; 52,7ff). The exiled are invited to leave the evil city: "Go forth from Babylon!" (Is 48,20; Jr 50,8). "Get out! Do not touch anything impure!" (Is 52,11). They are going to set forth toward Jerusalem, as in a new exodus*. This is a moment the mere recall of which, in the following centuries, will fill the hearts with joy (Ps 126,1f). It is an important date which Matthew makes a stepping stone toward the Messianic era (Mt 1,11f).

5. *The judgment of Babylon.* As sacred history takes a new turn, Babylon, the scourge of God, experiences in its turn the divine judgments. Judgment has been drawn up against the city of evil. The sentence is joyfully announced by the prophets (Is 21,1-10; Jr 51,11f). They intone ironic lamentations over Babylon (Is 47). They describe in advance her dreadful ruin (Is 13; Jr 50,21-28; 51,27-43). It will be the day* of Yahweh against her (Is 13,6...), the vengeance* of Yahweh against her gods (Jr 51,44-57). The triumphal march of Cyrus is the precursor of this event (Is 41,1-5; 45,1-6); the armies of Xerxes will execute it in 485 so that a stone upon a stone will not remain in Babylon (cf perhaps Is 24,7-18; 25,1-5). Nevertheless, Babylon will continue to live in the memory of the Jews as the type of pagan city doomed to perdition, and her king Nebuchadnezzar, as the type of proud and sacrilegious tyrant (Dn 2—4; Jdt 1,1-12).

6. *Permanence of the mystery of Babel.* The historic city of Babylon fell long before the advent of the NT. But through her the people of God became aware of a mystery of iniquity which is constantly at work here below: Babylon and Jerusalem*, facing one another, are the two cities between which men are divided; in Christian language it is the city of God against the city of Satan*. The primitive Church very quickly realized that she herself was drawn into this drama of the two cities. Babylon at every instant continues to be arrayed opposite the new Jerusalem (G 4,26; Ap 21). At the beginning of Nero's persecution, Babylon takes the concrete form of imperial Rome (1 P 5,13). The Apocalypse describes her under the guise of the famous prostitute, seated upon a scarlet beast*, drunk with the blood of saints (Ap 17). She went her way in company with the dragon, who is Satan*, and the beast, who is the Antichrist*. Thus the people of God are invited to flee (Ap 18,4), for His judgment is approaching; she, the great Babylon (Ap 18,1-8), is going to fall; and the nations, enemies of God, will bewail her whereas the heavens will resound with jubilation (Ap 18,9—19,10). Such is the fate finally reserved for the city of evil; every historic disaster which comes upon earthly empires in opposition to God and His Church is an actualization of this divine judgment. The oracles against Babylon which are preserved in the OT find their eschatological realization in this perspective: they remain suspended menacingly over the sinful nations* which from century to century incarnate the mystery of Babylon.

→Antichrist OT 2—Arrogance 2—Captivity—City — Exile — Nations — Pentecost II 2 d — People C III—Persecution I 3—Power III o —Tongue 2—War OT III 2.

JA & PG pjb

BAPTISM

The name of baptism is derived from the verb *baptein/bantizein*, which signifies "to immerse, to wash." Baptism is, then, an immersion or a washing. The symbolism of water* as a sign of purification and of life is too frequent in the history of religions for its existence in the pagan mysteries to be surprising. But the similarities with the Christian sacrament are purely external and have no bearing upon the deeper realities. Analogies are to be sought primarily in the OT, the Jewish beliefs, and the baptism of John.

I. OT AND JUDAISM

1. *The purifying role of water is very evident in the OT*. It appeared in many events of sacred history which will be looked on later as a prefiguration of baptism: the deluge, for example (cf 1 P 3,20f), or the passage through the Red Sea* (cf 1 Co 10,1f). In numerous cases of impurity the Law imposes ritual ablutions which purify* and make one fit for worship (Nm 19,2-10; Dt 23,10f). The prophets proclaim a pouring forth of water which cleanses from sin (Ze 13,1). Ezekiel associates this eschatological purification with the gift of the Spirit of God (Ez 36,24-28; cf Ps 51,9.12f).

2. *Post-exile Judaism* multiplies ritual ablutions. They become extreme minutiae and do not escape the formalism among the Pharisees contemporaneous with the gospel (Mk 7,1-5 p). These practices symbolized the cleansing of the heart and achieved it when they were joined with some sentiments of repentance. At the time of the NT the rabbis baptize proselytes of pagan origin who are joined to the Jewish people (cf Mt 23,15). It even appears that some people consider this baptism just as necessary as circumcision*.

According to Josephus, the ritual baths are common among the Essenes, as well as in the communities of Damascus and Qumrân. However, this bath is not a rite of initiation; one is admitted only after a long period of trial which manifests the sincerity of his conversion. It is a daily occurrence, and expresses one's endeavor toward a pure life and his longing for purifying grace. They submerged themselves in the water, whereas the penitents who will present themselves to John will receive the baptism from his hands, and that only once.

II. THE BAPTISM OF JOHN

The baptism of John can perhaps be compared to the baptism of the proselytes. The latter introduced a man into the people of Israel; the baptism of John realizes a sort of aggregation to the true posterity of Abraham* (Mt 3,8 p), to the remnant of Israel*, who henceforth are rescued from the wrath* of God (Mt 3,7.10 p) and are awaiting the Messiah* who is coming. It is offered to the whole Jewish people and not only to sinners and proselytes. It is a unique baptism given in the desert in view of repentance and pardon (Mk 1,4 p). It implies a confession of sins and an effort at a definitive conversion which the rite must express (Mt 3,6ff). John insists upon moral purity; he asks neither the publican nor the soldier to give up his way of life (Lk 3,10-14).

The baptism of John set up only a provisional economy: it is a baptism of water which is preparatory to the Messianic baptism in the Holy Spirit and fire* (Mt 3,11 p; Ac 1,5; 11,16; 19,3f), the supreme purification (cf Ps 51) which will inaugurate the new world and in which the perspective at this time seems to be confused with that of judgment*. In fact, the gift of the Spirit who is sent by the glorified Messiah is going to be distinguished from the judgment (Lk 3,16f p).

III. THE BAPTISM OF JESUS

1. In presenting Himself to receive the baptism of John, Jesus submits to the will of His Father (Mt 3,14f) and humbly places Himself among sinners. He is the Lamb* of God who thus takes upon Himself the sins of the world (Jn 1,29.36). The baptism of Jesus in the Jordan announces and prepares for His baptism "in death" (Lk 12,50; Mk 10,38), which indeed frames His public life between two baptisms. This is what John the Evangelist means when he reports that water and blood* flowed from the pierced side of Jesus (Jn 19,34f) and when he says that the Spirit, the water and the blood are intimately connected (1 Jn 5,6-8).

2. The baptism of Jesus by John is crowned by the descent of the Holy Spirit* in the form of a dove* and by the proclamation of His divine sonship by the heavenly Father. The descent of the Spirit upon Jesus is an investiture which fulfills the prophecies (Is 11,2; 42,1; 61,1); at the same time it is the announcement of Pentecost* which will initiate the baptism in the Spirit for the Church (Ac 1,5; 11,16) and for all those who enter in there (E 5,25-32; Tt 3,5ff). The recognition of Jesus as Son* announces the adoptive sonship of believers. This adoptive sonship is a participation in that sonship of Jesus and a result of the gift of the Spirit (G 4,6). In fact, the "baptism in death" must lead Jesus to His resurrection*; at that time, in receiving the plenitude of the Spirit, His glorified humanity will be constituted "the living Spirit" (1 Co 15, 45) who communicates the Spirit to those that believe in Him.

IV. CHRISTIAN BAPTISM

1. *Baptism of water and the Spirit.* John the Baptist announced baptism in the Spirit and fire (Mt 3,11 p). The Spirit is the promised Messianic gift. The fire* is the judgment* which begins to see its fulfillment in the coming of Jesus (Jn 3,18-21; 5,22-25; 9,39). Both are begun in the baptism of Jesus which is a prelude to that of His faithful. Paul sees Christian baptism foretold in the passage of the Red Sea which delivers Israel from servitude (1 Co 10,1f). Its effective realization begins at Pentecost which is, as it were, the baptism of the Church in the Spirit and fire. Immediately after this Peter preaches to the crowd attracted by the extraordinary event, telling them that they must receive baptism in a spirit of repentance, in order to obtain the forgiveness of sins and the gift of the Holy Spirit. And this is what in fact happens at once (Ac 2,38-41). Peter's action presupposes an order given by Christ, such as the one announced in Jn 3,3ff and expressly formulated after the resurrection (Mt 28,19; Mk 16,16). Usually baptism means a total immersion (cf Ac 8,38) or, if that is not possible, at least a sprinkling of water over the head, as we read in the *Didache*, 7,3. The imposition of hands* follows baptism and this confers the full gift of the Holy Spirit (Ac 8.15ff; 19,6).

St. Paul develops and completes the doctrine of baptism that evolved from the teaching of our Lord (Mk 10,38) and the practice of the Church (R 6,3). Baptism conferred in the name of Christ (1 C 1,13) unites a man with the death, burial and resurrection of our Lord (R 6,3ff; Col 2,12). The immersion represents the death and burial of Christ, and the coming out of the water symbolizes the resurrection* in union with Him. Baptism kills the body* in so far as it is an instrument of sin (R 6,9) and confers a share in the life of God in Christ (6,11).

Death to sin and the gift of life are inseparable; the washing with pure water is at the same time a sprinkling with the blood* of Christ, more eloquent than that of Abel (He 12,24; 1 P 1,2), an effective participation in the merits acquired by Christ on Calvary as rights for all, a union with His resurrection and, in principle, with His glorification (E 2,5f). Baptism is, then, a paschal sacrament, a communion with the Pasch of Christ; the baptized dies to sin and lives for God in Christ (R 6,11), he lives the very life* of Christ (G 2,20; Ph 1,21). The transformation thus realized is radical; it is a stripping and death of the old man and a reclothing

of the new man* (R 6,6; Col 3,9; E 4,24), a new creation* in the image* of God (G 6,15).

A similar but more summary doctrine can be found in 1 P 3,18-21, which sees in Noah's* crossing over the flood-waters the foreshadowing of the passage of the Christian through the waters of baptism, a passage that leads to freedom, thanks to the resurrection of Christ.

2. *The baptized persons and the divine Persons.* Baptism in the name of Jesus Christ or of the Lord Jesus (Ac 2,38; 8,16; 10,48; 19,5; 1 Co 6,11) shows that the baptized person belongs to Christ, that he is inwardly associated with Him (G 3,27; R 13,14). All who receive baptism are also united among themselves in the unity of Christ (G 3,28) and of His glorified Body (1 Co 12,13; E 4,4f); from this moment on they form only one spirit with Christ (1 Co 6,17).

It seems clear that baptism in the name of Christ supposes the use of a form in which Christ alone was mentioned. The trinitarian formula that prevailed later (cf *Didache* 7,1.3) comes from Mt 28,19. It expresses in an excellent way the fact that the baptized person, united to the Son, is united at the same time to the two other Persons. In fact the believer receives baptism in the name of the Lord Jesus and through the Spirit of God (1 Co 6,11); he becomes the temple* of the Spirit (1 Co 6,19), the adopted child of the Father (G 4,5f), the brother and co-heir of Christ, living intimately with His life and destined to share His glory (R 8,2.9.17.30; E 2,6).

3. *Conversion and baptismal faith.* Baptism supposes that a man has heard the preaching of the Gospel and confessed* his faith* in Jesus Christ: and the essential article of this faith, which sums up and contains the others, is the resurrection* of Christ (R 10,9). However, the object of faith can be known implicitly when the Spirit is given before baptism (Ac 10,44-48), and it seems that the faith of the father* of the family can be valid for all his household: this is the case with Cornelius and the jailer at Philippi (Ac 10,47; 16,33). But faith in Christ does not only mean that the mind accepts the messianic message; it involves a total conversion*, a complete abandonment to Christ, who transforms the whole of a man's life. It normally leads to a request for baptism, which is its sacrament and in the reception of which it finds its perfection. Paul never separates the two, and when he speaks of justification* by faith it is only in contrast with

the alleged justification by the works* of the Law, to which the judaizers appealed. He always takes it for granted that the profession of faith is crowned by the reception of baptism (G 3,26f). By faith a man responds to the divine call that has become clear to him through the preaching of the apostles (R 10,14f), and this response is, moreover, the work of grace* (E 2,8). At baptism the Spirit takes possession of the believer, incorporates him into the body of the Church and gives him the certainty that he has entered the Kingdom* of God.

It is quite clear that the sacrament does not act in any magic way. The total conversion that it calls for must be the start of a new life in a spirit of unshakable faithfulness.

4. *The loyalty required of the baptized person.* There are other ways in which the depth of the spiritual transformation brought about at baptism is stressed. For the catechumen it means a new birth* in water and the Spirit (Jn 3,5), a bath of regeneration and of renewal in the Holy Spirit (Tt 3,5), a seal* impressed on the soul (2 Co 1,22; E 1,13; 4,30), an illumination, which takes a man out of the darkness of sin into the light* of Christ (E 5,8-14; Hb 6,4), a new circumcision joining him to the new people of God (Col 2,11; cf E 2,11-22). All this is summed up in his status as a son* of God (1 Jn 3,1), which confers on him an incomparable dignity. It is not a question of a new static condition, but of an entry into a dynamic state, a higher life from which the Christian must never fall away. This is why constant efforts must be made to make the death to sin and the life for God always more effective (R 6,12ff). The emphasis is at times laid on the union with the Passion and at others on the resurrection: these two aspects refer to the unique paschal reality and remain indissolubly linked. United to the Passover of Christ by his efforts and a generous faithfulness, the baptized person prepares to enter into His glorious kingdom (Col 1,12f) and to take possession of the heavenly inheritance of which he possesses the first fruits in the gift of the Spirit (2 Co 1,22; E 1,14).

→Anointing III 5.6—Body of Christ III 1—Church III 2 b, IV, V 1—Circumcision NT—Clothing II 4—Confession NT 1—Death NT II 1, III 1—Dove 3—Election NT I—Faith NT II 2.3—Fire NT II—Flood 3—Holy NT II, III —John the Baptist—Joy NT II o—Life IV 4—Light & Dark NT II 2—Name NT 3 a—New III 3 b—Pardon II 3—New Birth—Pardon II 3—Passover III 2—Pentecost II 2 a e—Pure NT II 2—Repentance/Conversion NT I, III, IV 1—Resurrection NT II 2—Salvation NT II 2—Seal 2 b—Sin IV 2 e. 3 c—Spirit of God NT I 1—Taste 2—Trial/Temptation NT II—Water IV 2—White 2—Worship NT II 2, III 2.

FA pjb

BEASTS & BEAST

1. *Origin of the symbolism.* There is no question in the Bible of a symbolism analogous to that of the bestiaries of the middle ages; at most the Bible provides a sketchy symbolism with regard to some animals*. Nevertheless these animals, enemies of man, have a place in religious thought; and they furnish some of the graphic representation which one finds from Genesis to the Apocalypse. There is no reflection on the mystery of the animal kingdom; on the other hand all the repulsive and dangerous animals are there, including the legendary ones: savage beasts, lions, wolves, and panthers (Ho 5,14; Ha 1,8), hyenas and jackals (Is 13,22); beasts of prey and birds that haunt ruins (Is 13, 21; 34,11ff; Zp 2,14), reptiles from the basilisk to the crocodile (Ps 91,13; Ez 29); destructive insects like grasshoppers and crickets (Na 3,15ff) ...A thoroughly evil faun, connected with the presence of demons* (cf the satyrs of Is 13, 21; 34,12-14; Lv 17,7), stands face to face with man. This is not to mention the huge sea monsters (Gn 1,21), prototypes of the beast *par excellence*; the dragon, the fugitive serpent, Rahab or Leviathan (Is 27,1; Jb 7,12; Is 51,9). The latter, which personifies the sea* in the symbolism of oriental mythology, stands face to face with Yahweh Himself as the adversary of His plan of salvation.

2. *Origins.* Some texts, taking up a now demythologized imagery, represent the creative* act of God as a victorious combat against the primordial monster, the incarnation of disorder: Rahab or Leviathan (Ps 74,13f; 89,10f; Jb 9,13; 25,12; Ns 51,9). This war*, set outside the sphere of history, serves to give a meaning to all the historical confrontations; the drama of Paradise* (Gn 3). In Genesis, the cunning adversary of God and men is no longer called by his true name; but behind the earthly serpent there lies hidden the prototype serpent, the dragon which is the devil and Satan* (Ws 2,24; Ap 12,9; 20,2). The beast accursed among all beasts thus is the

great representative of the curse, and history will be the lists of the tilting field where he will test his strength against the posterity of the woman*, over which he has acquired a certain power (Gn 3,14ff).

3. The struggles of the beast against man.

a) Beasts as scourges of God. This war takes place initially at the temporal level: the malicious beasts lay the blame at sinful humanity's door. But they do not act with full independence; God knows how to turn their deeds to His own ends; they are craftsmen of His judgment* against Egypt (Ex 7,26—8,28; 10,1-20; Ws 16,1-12); they execute His curses against His unfaithful people (Dt 28,26.42; Lv 26,22; cf Jr 15,3). The stereotyped situation of towns abandoned and handed over to the wild beasts is also used to suggest the punishment of human communities (Is 34,11f; Jr 9,10; 10,23; 49,33; 50,39; 51,37; Ze 2,14f...). In the desert, blazing serpents sting those who murmur (Nm 21,5-7); in the promised land grasshoppers devour the crops, a terrible army whose invasion announces the day* of Yahweh (Jl 1—2). One also finds symbolic grasshoppers among the eschatological scourges, strange horsemen who devastate sinful humanity (Ap 9,3-10; cf Na 3,15ff; Jr 51,27). At their head strides the angel of the abyss (Ap 9,11), and no one will escape them if he is not marked out for salvation (Ap 9,4; cf 7,3).

b) The triumph of the beast. But the beast has other triumphs. Satan* has men adore him in his disguise. In their blindness, they prostrate themselves before "every kind of image of reptile and repulsive animals" (Ez 8,10). Proscribed in Israel by the Law (Dt 4,16ff), this form of idolatry ravages the pagan peoples (Ws 11,15; 12,24; 13,10.14; R 1,23), drawing down on themselves the rigors of the divine wrath* (Ws 16,1-9; R 1,24ff). Still again, the beast incarnates itself in some way in the great pagan empires which undertake to dominate the world, making war* on the people of God and manifesting a sacrilegious arrogance (Dn 7,2-8). Thus the primordial struggle is repeated here below since it is from the dragon, the prince of this world*, that the beast in question holds his power (Ap 13,4). Before the king, he draws himself up as Antichrist* blaspheming, persecuting the saints and making them adore him (Ap 13,1-9); and no one has any right to live here below unless he is stamped with his number (Ap 13,16ff; number*). This claim to totalitarian empire is not the work of Antiochus Epiphanes alone, nor of pagan Rome: men will see it renewed throughout the history of the Church.

c) The defeat of the beast. But the triumph of the beast is only apparent and momentary. As early as the OT, victory* of the faithful is affirmed. Moses raises the sign of the brazen serpent (Nm 21,9) for Israel in the desert, and whoever looks at it remains among the living (Ws 16,6). In the face of the pagans' animal worship, Israel is able to defend her faith in the one living God (Dn 14,23-42). She faces without weakening the peril of lions, and God delivers her from it (Dn 6); for whosoever puts his trust in God is guarded by His angels*, and he can crush evil beasts underfoot (Ps 91,11-13). These anticipated victories proclaim the victory of Jesus: when He repulsed Satan (Mt 4,1-11 p), He remained in the desert "with the wild beasts," served by angels (Mk 1,13). To His disciples too He can communicate "the power to crush underfoot serpents, scorpions, and all the power of the enemy," for Satan is now fallen from heaven and the evil spirits* themselves are made subject to the envoys of Jesus (Lk 10,17ff; cf Mk 16,17f). If the defeat of the beast is not yet public, it is nonetheless an accomplished fact.

4. *The death of the beast.* The judgment* which will put an end to history will entail the consummation of this defeat: the beast will be slain and his body given over to the fire (Dn 7,11-27).This is how the defeat of the primordial Serpent, which is the devil and Satan, will take place (Ap 12,9). This will be the last combat of Christ (Ap 19,11-16) in which He defends His holy city* against the exasperated nations* (Ap 20,8f). Then Satan and death* and hell, and the beast and his false prophet, and all the adorers of the beast—followers of the Antichrist—will be flung together into the lake of fire and brimstone, which is the second death (Ap 19,19ff; 20,10.14). Finally, the drama, which was started in the beginning, will end.

→Animals—Antichrist OT 1; NT 3—Babel/Babylon 6—Blasphemy—Evil Spirits OT—King NT II—Kingdom OT III—Numbers II 2—Satan III—Sea 1.2—Victory OT 1; NT 2—War OT IV.

PG pjb

BEATITUDE

Man wants happiness, which he calls life*, peace*, joy*, rest*, blessing*, and salvation*. All these benefits are included differently in the formula with which one declares someone happy or unhappy. When the "wise man" proclaims: "Happy are the poor! Unhappy the rich!" he does not wish to pronounce either a blessing* which gives happiness or a curse* which produces unhappiness; he rather wishes to exhort the people in the name of his experience of happiness to follow the paths which lead to it.

To comprehend the scope and the meaning of numerous maxims of wisdom which seem commonplace to us, they must be situated in the religious climate in which they were enunciated. Indeed if beatitude always supposes God as its source, it has experienced a slow evolution from the earthly to the heavenly.

1. GOD AND BEATITUDE

1. *Happiness and glory in God.* In contrast to the Greek gods, ordinarily hailed by the title of "happy" because they incarnate the dream of man, the Bible does not linger on the happiness of God (cf 1 Tm 1,11; 6,15) which has nothing in common with that to which biblical man aspires. Above all it sees Yahweh as a God of glory*, who desires to share His glory with men. And so there is another difference: while the Greek gods rejoiced in their happiness without particularly troubling themselves with the lot of men, Yahweh leans with solicitude to all men, especially to His people; the beatitude of man derives from God's grace*, it is a participation in His glory.

2. *Beatitude is God Himself.* In going through the proclamations which abound in wisdom literature, the reader of the Bible discovers in what true happiness consists and why he must seek it. Happy the man who fears Yahweh; he will be powerful and blessed (Ps 112,1f), he will have numerous children (Ps 128,1ff). If he wishes to be assured of life, well-being, blessing, wealth (Pr 3,10), he must follow the divine paths (Ps 1,1), walk in the Law (Ps 119,1), listen to wisdom (Pr 8,34f), find it (Pr 3,13f), practice himself in it (Si 14,20), look after the poor (Ps 41,2); in a word, be just.

In his development of these incentives to lead his disciples along the way* of true happiness, the wise man does not usually look be-yond the prospect of immediate reward*. It is for the pious and the poor* of Yahweh to proclaim this step forward: they will understand that with God they possess everything and that total abandonment and limitless confidence* is the way to happiness: no expressed motif, but a simple affirmation. "Happy are those who hope in him" (Is 30,18). "Happy the man who has confidence in you" (Ps 84,13; cf Ps 2,12; 65,5; 146,5). For the true Israelite, then, to fear God, to observe the Law and to listen to Wisdom means to expect happiness as a reward. For the more spiritual it even means possessing it already; it means being with God for ever, tasting "unbounded joy in your presence" (Ps 16,11; cf 73,23ff).

II. FROM EARTHLY TO HEAVENLY HAPPINESS

Thus the divine summit of beatitude has been defined. But to discover that God alone is happiness, every man treads a path leading from disappointment to disappointment* (Ps 118,8f; 136,38; 146,3f) and slowly purifying his desires.

1. *Earthly beatitude.* Happiness is life*, a life which has long been identified with terrestrial life. The beatitude of a people who have Yahweh as God is to have big sons, beautiful daughters, full granaries, numerous herds, and finally peace* (Ps 144,12-15). The sacred texts spell out these goods of man in the national, familial or personal sphere. To have a king worthy of the name (Qo 10,16f), a spouse of good sense (Si 25,8) who is outstanding (Si 26,1), a large fortune acquired honestly and possessed without being enslaved to it (31,8); to be prudent (25,9), not to offend by speech (14,1), to have pity on the unfortunate (Pr 14,21), to have nothing with which to reproach oneself (Si 14,2). In brief, happiness is to have a life worthy of the name and to be educated to that by God Himself (Ps 94,12). It is certainly right to grieve over one who has just died, but the tears must not last too long because a funereal gloom would hinder the full enjoyment of happiness here below (Si 38,16-23).

2. *Toward heavenly beatitude.* Given and blessed by Yahweh, the earthly goods of the covenant were the signs of a life shared with God. When belief in eternal life became established, the limitations and dangers of these goods became more apparent; and at the price

of this purification they then came to signify eternal life itself. At the same time the new hope led to new values, such as the spiritual fruitfulness* of the childless man and woman: and this hope led to the reversal of the old order of values. Past experience shows that the happiness of a man should not be judged befor his final hour (Si 11,28). With an unheard of boldness foreshadowing the Gospel, the Book of Wisdom declares that the childless are blessed if they are just and virtuous (Ws 3,13ff). The wise men simply restated, then, what the psalms of the poor* were already proclaiming when they saw in confidence in Yahweh the absolute good (vg Ps 73,23-28).

NT

With the coming of Christ, all goods are virtually given and happiness finds in Him both its ideal and its fulfillment. For He is the kingdom already present and He gives His faithful the supreme good: the Holy Spirit, as a pledge of the heavenly inheritance.

1. BEATITUDE AND CHRIST

Jesus is not merely a wise man of great experience; He is the one who lives fully the beatitude which He proposes.

1. The *"beatitudes,"* placed at the beginning of Jesus' inaugural discourse, offer the program for Christian happiness according to Mk 5,3-12. In Luke's version they are coupled with declarations of unhappiness, thus extolling the superior value of certain conditions of life (Lk 6,20-26). However these two interpretations cannot be reduced to the beatification of virtues* or states of life. They complement one another; above all they only reveal their truth if they are reported in the sense that Jesus Himself gave them. In effect Jesus came on God's behalf to give solemn "yes" to the promises of the OT; the kingdom of heaven is given, needs and afflictions are suppressed, mercy and life are reconciled in God. In fact, if certain beatitudes are pronounced for the future, the first one ("Happy the poor..."), which virtually contains the others, looks to its actualization from the present moment forward.

But that is not all. The beatitudes are a "yes" given by God in Jesus. Whereas the OT came to identify beatitude and God Himself, Jesus presents Himself in turn as the one who fulfills* the aspiration for happiness: the kingdom* of heaven is present in Him. What is more, Jesus wished to "incarnate" the beautitudes by living them perfectly, by showing Himself "meek and humble of heart" (Mt 11,29).

2. *The other gospel pronouncements* all tend equally to show that Jesus is at the center of beatitude. Mary is "beatified" to have given birth to the Savior (Lk 1,48; 11,27), because she believed (1,45); in so doing, she declared the beatitude of all those who, hearing the Word of God (11,28), will believe without having seen* (Jn 20,29). Woe to the Pharisees (Mt 23, 13-22), to Judas (26,24), and to the unbelieving towns (11,21)! Happy is Simon to whom the Father has revealed in Jesus the Son of the living God (Mt 16,17)! Happy the eyes that have looked upon Jesus (13,16)! Happy above all the disciples who, awaiting the return of the Lord, will be faithful, vigilant (Mt 24,46), and devoted to the service of one another (Jn 13,17).

II. THE VALUES OF CHRIST

While the OT timidly forced itself to add to the earthly values of wealth and success the value of justice in poverty and failure, Jesus, for His part, denounces the ambiguity of an earthly representation of beatitude. Henceforth, the happy ones of this world would no longer be the rich, the highly esteemed, the flattered, but those who are hungry and who weep, the poor and the persecuted (cf 1 P 3,14; 4,14). This reversal of values was possible for Him who is all value.

Two chief beatitudes include all the others: poverty with its retinue of works* of justice*, humility*, meekness*, purity*, mercy*, and solicitude for peace*; then persecution* for the love of Christ. But these values of themselves are nothing without Jesus who gives them all their meaning. And only he who has put Christ at the heart of his faith can hear the beatitudes of the Apocalypse. Happy is he if he does hear them (Ap 1,3; 22,7), if he remains vigilant (16, 15), because he has been called to the nuptials of the Lamb (19,9), to the resurrection (20,6). Even if he must give his life in testimony*, let him not lose heart: "Happy are the dead who die in the Lord!" (14,13).

→Blessing II 3—Console—Death NT III 4—Glory IV 1—Heaven VI—Inheritance OT II 2; NT II—Joy—Laugh 2—Meal IV—Paradise—

Peace—Poor NT I, II—Promises III 1—Rest—
Sadness NT 2—Suffering NT I 2.

JLA & XLD pjb

BLASPHEMY

Any insult to a human being deserves to be
punished (Mt 5,22). How much more should
blasphemy, an insult to God be punished! It is
the opposite of the adoration* and praise* that
man owes to God, the most notable sign of
human impiety.

OT

The presence of one blasphemer among the
people of God was enough to defile the whole
community. This is why the Law says: "Whoever blasphemes the name of Yahweh will die,
the entire community will stone him" (Lv 24,16;
cf Ex 20,7; 22,27; 1 K 21,13). More frequently,
blasphemy is found on the lips of the pagans
who insult the living God when they attack His
people: a Sennacherib (2 K 19,4ff.16.22; Tb 1,
18), an Antiochus Epiphanes (2 M 8,4; 9,28; 10,
34; Dn 7,8.25; 11,36), from whom, without a
doubt, the picture of Nebuchadnezzar in the
Book of Judith is suggested (Jdt 9,7ff). So also
the Edomites who applaud the destruction of
Jerusalem (Ez 35,12f) and the pagans who insult the anointed of Yahweh (Ps 89,51f). In regard to these, God reserves to Himself the
handing out of deserved punishments: Sennacherib will fall by the sword (2 K 19,7.28.37)
like Antiochus, the Satanic beast* (Dn 7,26;
11,45; cf 2 M 9); and the land of Edom will be
turned into a desert (Ez 35,14f). On the other
hand, the people of God must beware not to
provoke these blasphemies of the pagans (Ez
36,20; Is 52,5), for God would take vengeance*
for this profanation of His name.

NT

1. The same drama surrounds *the person of
Jesus* in the NT. He honors His Father*, but
the Jews accuse Him of blasphemy because He
calls Himself the Son* of God (Jn 8,49.59; 10,
31-36), and it is for this reason that He will be
condemned to death (Mk 14,64 p; Jn 19,7). In
reality, this very blindness perfects the sin of
the Jews because they dishonor the Son (Jn 8,
49), and they overwhelm Him with blasphemies
on the cross (Mk 15,29 p). If this were nothing

more than a mistake about the identity of the
Son* of Man, the sin would be forgivable (Mt
12,32) on the grounds of ignorance (Lk 23,34;
Ac 3,17; 13,27). But it is a more serious disregard because the enemies of Jesus attribute to
Satan* the signs which He performs through the
Spirit of God (Mt 12,24.28 p): there is, therefore, blasphemy against the Spirit*, and this
can be forgiven neither in this world nor in the
next (Mt 12,31f p) since it is a deliberate refusal
of the divine revelation*.

2. The drama goes on. Now, however, it is
centered around the *Church* of Jesus Christ*.
Paul was a blasphemer when he persecuted her
(1 Tm 1,13); when, afterwards, he preaches the
name* of Jesus, the Jews oppose him with
blasphemies (Ac 13,45; 18,6). Their opposition,
thus, has the same character that it had on
Calvary. To these is soon added the hostility
of the persecuting Roman Empire, a new manifestation of the beast* with its mouth full of
blasphemies (Ap 13,1-6), a new Babylon, adorned with blasphemous titles (Ap 17,3). Finally,
false doctors, teachers of error*, introduce blasphemy even among the faithful (2 Tm 3,2; 2 P
2,2.10.12), to the extent of making it necessary
at times to deliver these masters over to Satan
(1 Tm 1,20). Thus the blasphemies of men
against God are moving toward a clash which
will coincide with the final crisis in spite of the
signs which announce the divine judgment* (Ap
16,9.11.21). Faced with this situation, Christians
turn away from the example of the faithless
Jews* "because of whom the name of God is
blasphemed" (R 2,24). They will avoid anything which provokes the insults of the pagans
against God or His Word (1 Tm 6,1; Tt 2,5).
Their good conduct should lead men to "glorify
the Father who is in heaven" (Mt 5,16).

→Godless Man — Curse — Name — Human
Speech.

RD pjb

BLESSING

I. RICHES OF BLESSING

The word *blessing* often calls to mind only
the most superficial forms of religion; muttered
formulae, practices almost devoid of meaning,
clung to all the more as they have less of faith.

47

On the other hand, even living Christian tradition has scarcely retained any but the less rich in meaning of the biblical usages, classifying the more important ones in the categories of grace and thanksgiving. Hence arises a real indifference to the words of blessing and even to the reality which they can designate.

Yet the last visible action of Christ on earth, which He bestowed on His Church and which Christian Byzantine and cathedral art has stylized, is His blessing (Lk 24,50f). To detail the riches of the biblical blessing is really to illumine the marvels of the divine generosity and the religious quality of the wonder which this generosity awakens on the part of the creature.

Blessing is a gift* which touches life and its mystery, and it is a gift which is expressed by the word and its mystery. Blessing is word* as much as gift, *speaking* as much as *good* (cf gr. *eu-logia*, lat. *bene-dictio*), because the good which it carries with it is not a precise object, a definite gift; because it belongs not to the sphere of *having* but of *being*; and because it stresses not the action of man but the creation of God. To bless is to speak a creative and vivifying gift whether prior to its being produced under the form of a prayer, or whether after the event under the form of thanksgiving. But while the prayer of blessing anticipates the divine generosity, thanksgiving has seen it revealed.

II. THE VOCABULARY OF BLESSING

In Hebrew, as in English, in spite of the weakening which the word has undergone among us, one single root (*brk*, perhaps connected to knee* and to adoration*, perhaps also to the vital force of the sexual organs) serves to designate all forms of blessing at every level. Blessing, being at one and the same time a thing given, a gift of some thing, and the formulation of this gift, is expressed by three words: the substantive *berākā*, the verb *bārak*, and the adjective *barûk*.

1. *Blessing* (*berākā*). Even in its most profane, its most material sense, that of *gift*, the word carries a very perceptible nuance of human encounter. The gifts offered by Abigail to David (1 S 25,14-27), by David to the tribe of Judah (1 S 30,26-31), by the cured Naaman to Elisha (2 K 5,15), by Jacob to Esau (Gn 33,11), are all aimed at ratifying a union or a reconciliation*. But the far more frequent usage of the word is in a religious context: if the word of

blessing is chosen even to designate the most material riches it is in order to trace the gifts back to God and to His generosity (Pr 10,6.22; Si 33,17), or even to the esteem people have of blessing as a good (Pr 11,11; 28,20; Si 2,8). Blessing evokes the image of a holy prosperity, but also of generosity to the unfortunate (Si 7, 32; Pr 11,26) and always of the benevolence of God.

This abundance and this comfort are what the Hebrews call peace*, and the two words are often associated. But if they both express the same fullness of richness, the essential richness of blessing is that of life* and fecundity; blessing blooms (Si 11,22 hb.) like an Eden (Si 40, 17). Its privileged symbol is water* (Gn 49,25; Si 39,22); water is itself an essential, indispensable blessing (Ez 34,26; Ml 3,10); simultaneously with that life which it nourishes on earth, it evokes by its heavenly origin the generosity and largess of God, His vivifying power. The oracle of Jacob about Joseph gathers together all these images—fecund life, water, and the sky: "The blessings of the heavens above, the blessings of the abyss below, the blessings of the breasts and the womb" (Gn 49,25). This sensitivity to the generosity of God in the gifts of nature prepared Israel to accept the generosities of His grace*.

2. *To bless.* The verb admits of a very wide range of use, from the commonplace greeting addressed to a stranger on the street (2 K 4,29) or the customary formulae of courtesy (Gn 47, 7.10; 1 S 13,10) to the highest gifts of the divine favor. The one who blesses is more often God, and His blessing always makes life gush forth (Ps 65,11; Gn 24,35; Jb 1,10). Moreover only living beings are eligible to receive it; inanimate objects are consecrated to the service of God and sanctified by His presence, but not blessed.

After God, the source of life is the father*, and it falls to him to bless. More than any other, his blessing is efficacious, as his curse* is fearful (Si 3,8); and Jeremiah must have been at the end of his rope to dare to curse the man who came to announce to his father that a boy had been born to him (Jr 20,15; cf Jb 3,3).

By a strange paradox, it often happens that the weak bless the powerful (Jb 29,13; Ps 72, 13-16; Si 4,5), that man dares to bless God. This is because, if the poor* man has nothing to give to the rich man and man has nothing to give to God, a blessing establishes between beings a vital and reciprocal relation which enables the lesser one to see the generosity of the powerful one pour out upon him. It is not absurd to bless God who is "above all bless-ings" (Ne 9,5); it is simply to confess His generosity and to render thanks to Him; this is the creature's first duty (R 1,21).

3. *Blessed.* The participle *barûk* is the strong-est of all the words of blessing. It makes up the center of the typical formula of Israelite blessing: "Blessed be N...!" Neither a simple statement nor a pure wish, and even more en-thusiastic than beatitude*, this formula pours out like a cry before a person in whom God has just now revealed His power and His generosity and whom He has chosen "among all": Jael, "among the bedouin women" (Jg 5,24); Israel, "among the nations" (Dt 33,24); and Mary, "among women" (Lk 1,24; cf Jdt 13,18). It is amazing what God can do in His elect*. The blessed being is in the world as a revelation* of God, he belongs to God by a special title, he is "blessed of Yahweh" as cer-tain beings are "holy to Yahweh." But while the holiness* which consecrates to God separ-ates from the profane world, a blessing makes the being, which God designates, a rallying-point and a source of radiation. The "holy one" and the "blessed one" both pertain to God; but the "holy one" reveals more His inacces-sible grandeur, the "blessed one" His inex-haustible generosity.

As frequent and as spontaneous as the cry: "Blessed be N...!" is the parallel formula: "Blessed be God!" It stems equally from a shock experienced at an act in which God comes to reveal His power. It stresses less the magnitude of the act than its marvelous appro-priateness, its character of sign. Once again the blessing is a human reaction to the revelation of God (cf Gn 14,20, Melchizedek; Gn 15,2, Eliezer; Ex 18,10, Jethro; Rt 4,14, Boaz to Ruth).

Finally, more than once, the two cries: "Blessed be N...!" and "Blessed be God!" are united and echo each other: "Blessed be Abraham by the most high God, creator of heaven and earth!—and blessed be the most ·high God who has delivered your enemies into your hands!" (Gn 14,19f; cf 1 S 25,32f; Jdt 13,17f). In this complete rhythm the true nature of blessing appears. It is a raptured outburst before an elect of God, but it does not stop at the elect; it mounts right to God who has re-vealed Himself in this sign. He is the *barûk* beyond all others, the blessed one; He possesses all blessing in its fullness. To bless Him is in no way to believe that anything whatsoever is added to His richness, but it is rather to allow oneself to be swept away by the trans-port of this revelation and to invite the world to praise* Him. A blessing is always a public confession* of divine power and a thanksgiv-ing* for its generosity.

III. HISTORY OF BLESSING

The whole history of Israel is the history of the blessing promised to Abraham (Gn 12,3) and given to the world in Jesus, the "blessed fruit*" of the "blessed womb" of Mary (Lk 1, 42). At the same time, in the books of the OT the dimensions of blessing involve many nuan-ces; and blessing assumes diverse postures.

1. *Up to Abraham.* Blessed in the beginning by the Creator (Gn 1,28), the man and the woman unloosed the curse of God by their sin. Still, if the serpent (3,14) and the earth (3,17) are cursed, neither the man nor the woman are. By their labor, by their suffering, often at the price of anguish, life will continue to spring up (3,16-19). After the flood, a new blessing gave power and fertility to humanity (9,1). Still, sin did not cease to divide and destroy humanity; the blessing of God on Shem has for its counterpart the curse of Canaan (9,26).

2. *The blessing of the patriarchs.* The blessing of Abraham is, on the contrary, a new kind. Without doubt, Abraham will have enemies* in a divided world, and God will show His fidelity in cursing whoever (as an individual) shall curse him, but this case must remain an exception; the intention of God is to bless "all the nations* of the earth" (Gn 12,3). All the narratives of Genesis are the history of this blessing.

a) Blessings pronounced by fathers, a more archaic procedure, shows them, generally at the moment of death, calling down on their sons the powers of fecundity and of life*, "the heavens' dew and the earth's fatness" (Gn 27, 28), streams of milk and the "blood of grapes" (49,11f), the strength to crush their enemies (27,29; 49,8f), a land in which to settle (27,28; cf 27,39; 49,9) and to perpetuate their name* (48,16; 49,8...) and vigor. One perceives in these rhythmic fragments and in these narra-tives the dream of nomad tribes in search of a homeland, avid to defend their independence, but already conscious that they form a com-munity about some chiefs and privileged clans (cf Gn 49). All in all it is the dream of blessing which all men spontaneously desire and which they are ready to obtain by any sort of means, including violence and trickery (27,18f).

b) On these refrains and popular narratives, Genesis superimposes the promises and *the blessings pronounced by God Himself*, not to disavow the narratives, but rather to situate them in their place in the activity of God. Present also is the question of a powerful name* (Gn 12,2), of an uncountable posterity (15,5), of a land where they are installed (13, 14-17); but here God takes in hand the future of His own: He changes their name (17,5.15), He makes them pass through temptation (22,1) and faith (15,6), and already He imposes upon them a commandment (12,1; 17,10). He knows well how to fulfill the desire* of man, provided, of course, it is in accordance with faith.

3. *Blessing and covenant.* This bond between blessing and commandment is the principle of the covenant also: the Law* is the means of making a people lead a life that is "holy to God" and as a consequence "blessed of God." That is what the covenant rituals express. Worship* is, in the religious mentality of the times, the privileged means of assuring oneself of the divine blessing, of renewing by contact with sacred places, times, and rites the vital power of man and of his world, so short and so fragile. In the religion of Yahweh the worship is only authentic in the covenant and fidelity to the Law. The blessings of the Covenant Code (Ex 23,25), the threats of the assembly of Shechem under Joshua (Js 24,19), the great blessings of Deuteronomy (Dt 28,1-14)—all suppose a treaty of union, proclaiming the divine will, then the *loyalty* of the people, and finally the cultic act which seals the agreement and gives it its sacred worth.

4. *The prophets and blessing.* The prophets* hardly knew the language of blessing. Even though they are men of the Word* and its efficacy (Is 55,10f), and even though they know themselves as called and chosen by God, as signs of His work (Is 8,18), still His action in them is too interior, too weighty, too little visible and communicable to provoke in and around them the cry of blessing. And their message, which consists in recalling the terms of the covenant and denouncing their violations, scarcely inclines them to bless. Among the literary forms which they utilize, that of

cursing is familiar to them, that of blessing practically unknown.

It is all the more remarkable to see arise on occasion even at the heart of a curse in the classical manner, an image or an affirmation proclaiming that the promise of blessing remains intact, that from desolation life will spring up like a "holy seed" (Is 6,13). It is thus that the promise of the cornerstone in Zion blazes out in the middle of the curse against the senseless rulers who believe the city to be invulnerable (Is 28,14-19); and that in Ezekiel the great prophecy of the outpouring of the Spirit, all full of images of blessing—water, earth, harvests—concludes with a divine logic the condemnation of Israel (Ez 36,16-38).

5. *Hymns of blessing.* Blessing is one of the major themes of the prayer* of Israel; it is the response to all the work of God, which is revelation. It is very close to thanksgiving*, praise or confession* and builds on the same schema, but it is closer than these to the event in which God comes to reveal Himself, and it generally possesses a simpler tone: "Blessed be Yahweh, who has done marvelous things for me!" (Ps 31,21), "who did not yield us a prey to their teeth" (Ps 124,6), "who forgives all your sins" (103,2). Even the hymn of the three children in the furnace, which invokes the universe to sing the glory of the Lord, does not lose sight of the work which God just accomplished: "For He has saved us from the fire" (Dn 3,88).

IV. BLESSED IN CHRIST

How could the Father, having delivered His own Son for us, refuse us anything (R 8,32)? In Him He has given us everything; we lack no gift* of grace* (1 Co 1,7) and are, "with the believing Abraham*" (G 3,9; cf 3,14), "blessed with every sort of spiritual blessing" (E 1,3). In Him we give thanks to the Father for His gifts (R 1,8; E 5,20; Col 3,17). The two movements of blessing, the grace which descends to us and the thanksgiving which ascends, are recapitulated in Jesus Christ. There is nothing beyond this blessing, and the throng of elect assembled before the throne and before the Lamb to chant their final triumph proclaims to God: "Blessing, glory, wisdom, thanksgiving ...forever and ever!" (Ap 7,12).

If the whole NT is nothing but the perfect blessing received from God and returned to

Him, the book is not filled with words of blessing. These are relatively rare and used in precise contexts, which serve to determine exactly the sense of the biblical blessing.

1. *Blessed is He who comes!* The gospels offer only one example of a blessing, addressed to Jesus: the cry of the crowd at His entry into Jerusalem on the eve of His passion: "Blessed is He who comes!" (Mt 21,9 p). Surely no one ever answers to the description of a blessed being like Jesus, in whom God reveals with brilliant signs His power and bounty (cf Ac 10, 38). His arrival in the world stirs up a wave of blessings—in Elizabeth (Lk 1,42), in Zechariah (1,68), in Simeon (2,28), and in Mary herself (without using the actual word, 1,46f). He is obviously the center of blessing: Elizabeth proclaims "Blessed is the fruit of thy womb!" (1,42). He Himself is never blessed directly, with the one unique exception of Palm Sunday. This lack cannot be mere accident. Perhaps it reffects the distance spontaneously established between Jesus and other men, for to bless someone is in a certain sense to be united with him. Perhaps too it marks the incomplete nature of the revelation of Christ as long as His work was not consummated, the opaque quality which surrounded His person up to His death and resurrection. On the other hand, in the Apocalypse when the Lamb, who has been slain, comes to take possession of His power over the world by receiving the book in which is sealed the fate of the universe, the whole of heaven acclaims Him: "the Lamb that was sacrificed is worthy to be given power...glory and blessing" (Ap 5,12f). In this context blessing has the same extent and the same importance as the glory* of God.

2. *The chalice of blessing.* Before multiplying the loaves (Mt 14,19 p), before distributbing the bread which became His body (Mt 26,26 p), and before the breaking of the bread at Emmaus (Lk 24,30), Jesus pronounces a blessing; and we also "bless the chalice of blessing" (1 Co 10,16). Whether the blessing designates in these texts a special action or a particular formula distinct from the eucharistic words* properly so-called, or whether it is only the title given to the words which follow, is of little importance here. The fact is that the eucharistic narratives closely associate blessing and thanksgiving, and that in this association blessing represents the ritual and visible aspect, the action and the formula, while thanksgiving expresses the content of the actions

and the words. The rite is the only one preserved to us of all those that the Lord could have performed during His life because it is the rite of the new covenant (Lk 22,20). In it blessing finds its final fulfillment. It is a gift expressed in an immediately efficacious word. It is the perfect gift of the Father to His children—all His grace—and the perfect gift of the Son offering His life to the Father—all our thanksgiving united to His. It is a gift of fecundity, a mystery of life and communion.

3. *The blessing of the Holy Spirit.* If the gift of the eucharist contains the whole blessing of God in Christ, if His last act is the blessing which He leaves the Church (Lk 24,51) and the blessing which He stirs up in her (24,53), nevertheless the NT nowhere says that Jesus Christ is the blessing of the Father. Actually, blessing is always a gift*, a life received and assimilated. Now the gift beyond all others is the Holy Spirit*. Not that Jesus Christ is less given to us than the Holy Spirit, but the Spirit is given in order to be in us the gift received from God. The vocabulary of the NT is meaningful. It is true that Christ is ours, but it is above all true that we are Christ's (cf 1 Co 3,23p; 2 Co 10,7). Many a time it is said of the Holy Spirit, on the other hand, that He is given to us (Mk 13,11; Jn 3,34; Ac 5,32; R 5,5), that we receive Him (Jn 7,39; Ac 1,8; R 8,15) and possess Him (R 8,9; Ap 3,1) to the point where one speaks spontaneously of "the gift of the Spirit" (Ac 2,38; 10,45; 11,17). The blessing of God, in the full sense of the word, is His Holy Spirit. Now this divine gift, which is God Himself, exhibits all the traits of blessing. The great themes of blessing—water which regenerates, birth and renewal, life and fecundity, plenitude and peace, joy and communion of hearts—all are equally the fruits* of the Spirit.

→Abraham I 3, II 4—Beatitude—Confession OT 1—Curse—Election OT I 3 b—Eucharist I—Fruit—Fruitfulness I 1—Good & Evil II 2—Grace II 3—Harvest I—Imposition of Hands OT; NT I—Joy OT II 1—Life II 1—Oil—Peace —Praise—Right Hand 2—Taste 2—Thanksgiving—Vintage I—Water II 1—Wealth I 1—Will of God OT o.

JG pjb

BLOOD

In late Judaism and the NT, the phrase "flesh* and blood" is used to mean man in his perishable nature (Si 14,18; 17,31; Mt 16,17; Jn 1,13), the condition taken up by the Son of God in coming down to earth (He 2,14). But except for this usage, the Bible speaks only of spilled blood (in the sense of the Latin *cruor*), always connected with the loss or sacrifice of life. Greek thought, by contrast, connected blood (in the sense of the Latin *sanguis*) with man's generation and his emotional life.

OT

Like all ancient religions, the religion of Israel found blood something sacred, for blood is life* (Lv 17,11.14; Dt 12,23), and everything touching life is in close contact with God, the sole Master of life. From this recognition, three consequences proceed: the prohibition of murder, the dietary prohibition of blood, the use of blood in official worship.

1. *Prohibition of murder.* Man is made in the image of God, and only God has power over his life; if anyone spills a man's blood, God will demand an accounting of it (Gn 9,5f). This is the religious foundation of the decalogue precept "Thou shalt not kill" (Ex 20,13). In the case of murder, the blood of the victim, like that of Abel*, "calls for vengeance*" against the murderer (Gn 4,10f; cf 2 S 21,1; Ez 24,7f; 35,6). Customary law considers "blood-vengeance" (Gn 9,6) legitimate. It seeks only to avoid the unlimited blood-feud (cf Gn 4,15.23f) and assigns rules for such feuds (Dt 19,6-13; Nm 35,9-34). God Himself sometimes makes such vengeance His proper responsibility, bringing the blood of the innocent on the heads of those who spill it (Jg 9,23f; 1 K 2,32). This is why the persecuted faithful appeal to God to avenge the blood of His servants (Ps 79,10; 2 M 8,3; cf Jb 16,18-21), and He Himself promises that this vengeance will be had when His day* comes (Is 63,1-6).

2. *Dietary prohibition of blood.* The prohibition against eating blood and meat not ritually drained (Dt 12,16; 15,23; cf 1 S 14,32-35) was in force well before biblical revelation (cf Gn 9,4). Whatever the original meaning of the proscription, it received precise motives in the

OT: blood, like life, belongs only to God; blood has its proper place in sacrifice (Lv 3,17); man must not use it except for purposes of expiation (Lv 17,11f). This prohibition remained in force for some time in early Christianity to facilitate the use of a common table by converted Jews and pagans (Ac 15,20-29).

3. *Use of blood in official worship.* The sacred character of blood calls, finally, for its diverse uses in official worship.

*a) The covenant** between Yahweh and His people was sealed by a blood-rite: half the blood of the victims was poured on the altar* which represented God, half on the people. Moses explained the rite: "this is the blood of the covenant Yahweh has made with you..." (Ex 24,3-8). Thus an indissoluble bond was established between God and His people (cf Ze 9,11; He 9,16-21).

*b) In sacrifices** blood was likewise an essential element. Whether it was a matter of a holocaust, a communion sacrifice, or consecratory rites, the priest poured blood on the altar and all around (Lv 1,5.11; 9,12; etc.). In the paschal rite, the blood of the lamb* took on another value: it was put on the lintel and the uprights of the door (Ex 12,7.22) to preserve the house from the destructive scourges (12, 13.23).

c) Blood-rites had a place of special importance in the *liturgy of atonement*, for "blood atones" (Lv 17,11). The blood is poured by sprinkling (4,6f, etc.). On the Day of Atonement in particular, the high priest enters the holy of holies with the blood of a victim offered for his sins and those of the people (16).

d) Finally, sacrificial blood has a *consecratory value*. In the rites of consecration for priests (Ex 29,20f; Lv 8,23f.30) and the altar (Ez 43,20), it marks them out as belonging to God.

NT

If the NT puts an end to the bloody sacrifice of Jewish worship, and abrogates the legal dispositions relating to blood-vengeance, it is because it recognizes the value and meaning of "innocent blood," of the "precious blood" (1 P 1,19), poured out for the redemption of men.

1. *The synoptic gospels.* Full in the face of His coming death, Jesus thinks of Jerusalem's responsibility: the prophets had been murdered of old, He Himself will be handed over, His envoys will be killed in their turn. God's judgment on the guilty city must be severe: all the just blood poured out here below since the blood of Abel will come on the head of this generation (Mt 23,29-36). The passion is drawn in this dramatic perspective: Judas knows he has betrayed innocent blood (27,4); Pilate washes his hands of this blood while the mob takes responsibility for it (27,24f). But there is another side to the action as well. At the last supper, Jesus presents the cup of the eucharist* as "the blood of the covenant, poured out for many in remission of sins" (26,28 p). His body offered and His blood shed shall make of His death a doubly significant sacrifice: a sacrifice of the covenant* substituting a new covenant for that of Sinai; a sacrifice of atonement according to the prophecy of the Servant of Yahweh. Thus innocent blood unjustly spilled becomes the blood of redemption*.

2. *St. Paul.* Paul finds ready expression of the meaning of the cross* of Christ in speaking of His redemptive blood, Jesus, covered with His own blood, henceforth plays on behalf of mankind the role sketched of old by the propitiatory in the ceremony of expiation (R 3,25). He is the localization of the divine presence; He assures the forgiveness of sins. For His blood has the power of salvation*: through Him justification* comes to us (R 5,9), through Him we are ransomed (E 1,7), and acquired by God (Ac 20,28); the unity* of Jew and pagan is realized in Him (E 2,13), as is that between man and the celestial powers (Col 1,20). Men can share in this blood of the new covenant when they drink of the eucharistic cup* (1 Co 10,16f; 11,25-28). In this way a deep bond with eschatological emphasis is formed between them and the Lord: His death is recalled and His coming announced (11,26).

3. *The epistle to the Hebrews.* The epistle to the Hebrews takes the entrance of the high priest into the holy of holies with the blood of expiation as a prophetic figure* of Christ entering heaven with His own blood to obtain our redemption (He 9,1-14). This image blends with that of the covenant sacrifice Moses offered on Sinai. The blood of Jesus, the blood of the new covenant, is offered for the forgiveness of men's sins* (He 9,18-28). Through it,

sinners obtain access to God (10,19); this blood, more eloquent than the blood of Abel (12,24), assures their sanctification (10,29; 13,12) and their entry into the flock of the good shepherd (13,20).

4. *St. John.* The Apocalypse echoes the traditional doctrine when it speaks of the blood of the Lamb*: this blood has washed us of our sins (Ap 1,5; cf 7,14) and, ransoming us for God, has made us a royal priesthood (5,9). In a vision all the more important because of the particular time it was presented, Babylon*, the city of evil, gluts herself on the blood of the martyrs* (18,24). The martyrs have vanquished Satan because of the blood of the Lamb (12, 11), but their spilled blood nonetheless cries for justice. God will take vengeance* in giving spillers of blood blood to drink (16,3-7), awaiting the time when their blood will be spilled in turn to become the triumphal attire of the Word in His zeal for justice (19,13; cf Is 63,3).

John the evangelist presents a completely different meditation on the blood of Jesus. He has seen water and blood run from the side of Christ pierced by the lance (Jn 19,31-37), a double witness of the love of God which corroborates the testimony of the Spirit (1 Jn 5,6ff). But this water* and blood continue to exercise their life-giving power in the church. Water is the sign of the spirit who causes regeneration and quenches thirst (Jn 3,5; 4,13f). The blood is distributed to men in the celebration of the eucharist*. "Whoever eats my flesh and drinks my blood has everlasting life...he remains in me and I in him" (Jn 6,53-56).

→Abel—Circumcision OT 2—Covenant OT I 3; NT I—Cup 3—Eucharist—Expiation—Flesh I 1.3 b—Lamb of God 2—Life II 3—Magic 2 a c —Martyr—Passover I 6 b—Persecution—Pure NT II 2—Redemption NT 1.2—Sacrifice— Soul I 1—Vengeance 1.4—Violence—Wine II 2 b—Witness NT III 2.

CS & PG ecu

BODY

Strikingly different from a common impression, the body is not just the compound of flesh and bone a man possesses during his earthly existence, puts off at death, and takes up again on the day of resurrection. In his theology of the body, Paul has outlined a far higher dignity than this. Not only does the body give unity to a totality of parts (this is the sense of the Greek, which it seems that Paul keeps, following on the fable of the members of the body, in 1 Co 12,14-27) but it symbolizes the person in his most significant phases: his native state as a sinner, his consecration to Christ, his life of glory.

I. "BODY" AND "FLESH"

In the OT, *flesh* and *body* are designated by the same word (*basar*). Their subsequent distinction in NT Greek (*sarx* and *soma*) can be fully appreciated only in the perspective of faith.

1. *Dignity of the body.* As in most languages, *body* often indicates the same reality as *flesh.* Thus, the life of Jesus should be manifest in our body, as well as in our flesh (2 Co 4,10f). A Semite has the same regard for the body as for the flesh* since both signify the whole man.

Paul stresses the dignity of the body. He avoids using the term *body* to indicate a corpse —quite different from other NT authors (vg Mt 27,52.58f; Lk 17,37; Ac 9,40). Paul reserves for the body one of man's human dignities, the power to beget life (R 1,24; 4,19; 1 Co 7,4; 6,13-20). Further, when Paul speaks of the transient and ephemeral element in man, all that is purely human—and especially the sinful human component—he attributes these aspects not to the body but to the flesh. Thus, he does not draw up a catalogue of sins of the body. (The reference to "a sin against the body" in 1 Co 6,18 probably refers to a sin against the total human person.) In itself the body is to be respected by man because it is an expression of the person.

2. *The body controlled by the flesh.* But the flesh, where sin dwells (R 7,20), takes control of the body. Henceforth there is a "sinful body" (6,6), just as there is a "sinful flesh" (8,3). Sin is capable of dominating the body (6,16) so that the body itself leads to death (7,24). Thus the body is reduced to a lowly state (Ph 3,21), a mean condition (1 Co 15,43); full of unholy cravings (R 6,12), the body performs sensual acts (8,13). In this Pauline theology, the body is subject to three powers which have reduced the flesh to slavery: the Law*, sin*, and death* (cf 7,5). In this light, the "body" does not ex-

press the human person as he comes from the Creator's hands, but the person as enslaved by the flesh and sin.

II. THE BODY AND THE LORD

1. *The body is for the Lord.* The Corinthians to whom Paul wrote had been tempted to think of fornication as an indifferent act, without serious implications. Paul's response does not appeal to the fact that the soul is spiritual nor to a distinction between a vegetative life and an elevated form of life imperiled by this type of conduct. He writes, "Food is for the stomach and the stomach for food, but God will put an end to both. However the body is not made for fornication. The body is for the Lord, and the Lord is for the body" (1 Co 6,13). In contrast to the stomach, which is in the domain of flesh that is transitory (cf Ph 3,19) and incapable of inheriting the kingdom* of God (1 Co 15,50), the body will rise again as did the Lord (1 Co 6,14); for the body is a member of Christ (6,15), the temple* of the Holy Spirit (6,19). For these reasons, man should give glory to God by means of his body (6,20). While the flesh is destined for dust, the body is consecrated to the Lord. This is the source of its incomparable dignity.

2. *The body of Christ.* To be more precise, the dignity of the body comes from the fact that the body has been redeemed by Christ. Jesus took on the "body of flesh" (Col 1,22) which made Him subject to the Law (G 4,4). Because Jesus entered into the "form of sinful flesh" (R 8,3), He became "a curse* for us" (G 3,13); He has "been made sin* for us" (2 Co 5,21). Finally, He was subject to the power of death*, but His death was a definitive and final death to sin (R 6,10). Thus, He conquered death, the flesh, and sin so that the powers which crucified Jesus were stripped of their might (1 Co 2,6.8; Col 2,15). He condemned sin (R 8.3) and changed the curse of the Law into a blessing (G 3,13f; E 2,15). Not only did He thus free us from bondage, but in the strict sense He incorporated us into Himself. The sweeping import of His life and redemptive suffering is that there is now but "one" body, the body* of Christ.

2. *The body of the Christian.* For these reasons, every believer united to Christ is capable of conquering through the body of Christ the

powers to which he was at one time subject—the Law, sin, and death. He is "dead to the Law" (R 7,4), his "body of sin is destroyed" (R 6,6) so that he has "stripped off the fleshly body" destined for death (Col 2,11). In receiving baptism the Christian has in brief form been subjected to the total life of Christ, hence the Christian should pattern his daily life after that of Christ: he should "offer his body" as a living sacrifice (R 12,1).

The dignity of the body is not realized on earth, for the body of earthly misery and sinfulness will be transformed into the glorious* body (Ph 3,21), into a "spiritual body" (1 Co 15,44), one not subject to decay. Thus will man "reassume the likeness of the heavenly Adam*" (1 Co 15,49). We may anticipate the transition from the mortal body to the body of the heavenly Lord taking place by a direct transformation "at the blink of an eye," as on the day of Christ's final coming. At the same time we must prepare for another aspect of our destiny, the painful transition that is death*. Therefore, we should "prefer to leave this body to go to dwell with the Lord" (2 Co 5,8) and await the resurrection whereby we will finally and perpetually constitute the one body of Christ.

→Adoration O, I, II 3—Apparitions of Christ 6 —Body of Christ—Clothing—Death OT I 2; NT I 2, III 4—Flesh—Man—Resurrection—Sexuality II 2, III 2—Soul.

XLD wjw

BODY OF CHRIST

In the NT, the body of Christ is of paramount importance in the mystery of the redemption. The term itself, however, has a variety of meanings. Sometimes the phrase indicates the individual body of Jesus, sometimes His eucharistic body, and other times that body of which we are members and which is the Church.

I. THE INDIVIDUAL BODY OF JESUS

1. *Jesus and His bodily life.* The fact that Jesus shared our bodily life is apparent on every page of the NT. According to the flesh,

Paul asserts, Jesus is a descendant of the patriarchs, of the line of David (R 1,3; 9,5), born of a woman (G 4,4). In the gospels the reality of Jesus' human nature is everywhere so evident that it is not necessary to make explicit mention of His body. He experiences hunger* (Mt 4,2 p), fatigue (Jn 4,6), thirst (Jn 4,7), sleep* (Mk 4,38), and suffering*. To emphasize the same facts John speaks rather of the flesh* of Jesus (cf Jn 1,14) and hurls an anathema at those who deny "that Jesus came in the flesh" (1 Jn 4,2; 2 Jn 7).

2. *The bodily death of Jesus.* References to the body of Jesus are intensified in the passion narratives. During the meal at Bethany, His body is anointed for His burial (Mt 26,12 p). Finally He dies on the cross (Mt 27,50 p) and is placed in a tomb (Mt 27,58ff p; Jn 19,38ff). But this prosaic human end, identical with that of every human being, has nonetheless a special meaning in the mystery of salvation*; for on the cross* Jesus bore our sins* in His body (1 P 2,24), and God reconciled us to Himself in this corporeal body by handing it over to death* (Col 1,22). This body of Christ, the real paschal Lamb* (1 Co 5,7), has been the instrument of our redemption*; from His pierced side have poured forth the blood* and the water* (Jn 19,33ff). The epistle to the Hebrews likewise gives particular attention to the body of Jesus in order to portray the sacrifice* of Christ. At His entry into the world, Jesus was disposed to offer Himself, since God had "fashioned a body" for Him (He 10,5); and ultimately it was by "the offering of His body" that He sanctified us once and for all (He 10,10).

3. *The glorified body of Jesus.* This mystery, to be sure, was not complete with the bodily death of Jesus, but only with His resurrection*. While the evangelists stress the reality of the body of the risen Christ in their accounts of the apparitions* (Lk 24,39.42; Jn 20,27), they also indicate that it is no longer under the same limitations as before His passion (Jn 20,19.26). No longer "a physical body" (1 Co 15,44), it is a "body of glory" (Ph 3,21), a "spiritual body" (1 Co 15,44). Thus in striking fashion is revealed the sacred meaning of the body of Jesus in the new dispensation that began with the incarnation. This body, which was destroyed and then in three days rebuilt, now takes the place of the temple* of old as the sign of God's presence* among men (1 Jn 2,18-22).

II. THE SACRAMENT OF THE BODY OF CHRIST

1. *"This is my body."* After the resurrection, the body of Christ does not enjoy only an invisible heavenly existence "at the right* hand of God" (He 10,12). Before His death, Jesus instituted a rite for perpetuating through the use of signs the earthly presence* of His sacrificed body. The narratives of the institution of the eucharist* show that this rite had been instituted in the perspective of the cross that was at hand and it thus reveals the meaning of the bodily death of Jesus: "This is my body which is given for you" (1 Co 11,24 p); "This is my blood of the covenant which is shed for many" (Mk 14,24 p). Thus the sign of bread* and wine* now make present on earth the body of Jesus which was delivered up and His blood which was shed.

2. *The eucharistic experience of the Church.* When this same rite is renewed in the Church it is a commemoration of the death of Christ (1 Co 11,24ff). At the same time, the memorial is located in the light of the resurrection by which Christ's body became "a life-giving spirit" (15,45). Furthermore, the eucharist has an eschatological dimension since it proclaims the return of the Lord and invites men to look forward to this (11,26). By this rite, therefore, the Church participates in a singular experience, the "sharing in the body of Christ," which causes the Church to live once again all the elements essential to the mystery of salvation.

III. THE CHURCH, THE BODY OF CHRIST

1. *Members of a single body.* By reception of the eucharist we become aware that we are members of the body of Christ. "Is not the bread we eat a sharing in the body of Christ? Then since there is only one bread, so we make up only one body" (1 Co 10,16f). Hence we should understand our union with Christ in a very real sense. We are truly His members, and the Christian who commits fornication "takes a member of Christ to unite it to a prostitute" (1 Co 6,15). When Paul says that all of us make up one single body (1 Co 12,12), that we are parts of one another (R 12,5), he is not speaking metaphorically, as in the Greek fable of the stomach and other bodily parts which Paul exploits on this occasion (1 Co 12,14-26).

Christ's own body unites the diverse members of the one body who are joined together by baptism* (1 Co 12,13.27) and by eucharistic communion* (1 Co 10,17). In this body each Christian has his own function for the total good (1 Co 12,27-30; R 12,4). In short, it is about the individual body of Jesus that the unity of mankind becomes a reality as all men are called to join themselves to that body.

2. *The Body of Christ which is the Church.* In the captivity epistles, Paul once again presents this doctrine and gives a more complete picture, stressing even more that Christ is the head of the body and so of the Church (Col 1,18). At the same time he insists on His cosmic role insofar as He is the Creator (1,16f; E 1,22) and on His superiority with regard to the angels (Col 1,16; 2,10; E 1,21). Just as a husband, the head (E 5,28) and superior of the body, loves his wife "as his own body" (5,23), so Christ has loved the Church and given Himself for her (5,25) as her savior (5,23). Thus the Church is His body and His fullness* (E 1,23; Col 1,24), while He is the head (Col 1,18; E 1,22) that guarantees the unity of the body (Col 2,19). In this body of which we are members (E 5,30) we are all one (Col 3,15). Whatever our origin, we have all been restored to God's friendship so as to become one people*, a single new man* (E 2,14-16). Such is the magnitude and extension of the body of Christ. The Christian experience is established both in the historical fact of the incarnate Christ and in the eucharistic rite—an experience that then allows on this point an opening up of the mystery of the Church in all its richness.

3. *The body of Christ and our body.* Our very bodies* even are called to enter into a new world because they have been grafted onto Christ as His members, have become temples of the Holy Spirit (1 Co 6,19), and will rise with "Christ who will transform our body of misery to make it resemble His glorious body" (Ph 3,20f). Here the function of the body of Christ in our redemption will be fully accomplished.

→Apparitions of Christ 4 b—Body II 2.3—Bread—Build III—Church—Communion NT—Eucharist—Fulness 3—Head 3—Jesus Christ II 1 d—Man I 2 c—Schism NT—Temple NT I 2, II 2—Unity III—Vine 3.

FA wjw

BOOK

I. WRITING AND BOOKS

Writing and books are connected with one another, but they are not coterminous. A book is a coherent set of writings which adds to Scripture a unified subject. This is the reason why a book is normally given a title, even if in biblical usage it does not appear at the beginning of the book. A book involves a title and a subject because it is a synthesis, not merely a series of lines and columns of writing; it is an organic work in which a succession of events are collected into a continuous account by gathering related writings, poems, songs, sentences, parables, and prophecies into one collection.

The book makes its appearance early in Israel's history. Some of the ancient narratives know of and use two old collections of epic and lyric songs, "The Book of the Wars of Yahweh" (Nm 21,14) and "The Book of the Just Man" (Js 10,13; 2 S 1,18). The existence of these two collections shows that Israel was conscious very early of the originality of its destiny and of the continuity which God would give to its history. The number of closely unified books of various types which this small people produced in a few centuries testifies to the vigor of their faith which led them to express and master the problems presented to them. They wrote historical syntheses, juridical works, poetical and liturgical collections, and reflections upon the problems of human existence.

II. THE BOOK,
A MEMORIAL AND SACRED WITNESS

Among the books produced by Israel, there are many whose origin we can discover, and we find that this origin is sacred; such are the legislative and prophetic books. The Law* and the prophets* form an essential structure of the Bible.

"The two tablets of the testimony" (Ex 31, 18), containing "the law and the commandments" (24,12) which Moses received from God and carried in his hand (32,15) can hardly be called a book in the proper sense of the word. These tablets of stone, though of a better material, appear analogous to the clay tablets on which the scribes wrote. Still, this work is destined to be preserved and to bear testimony to the will* of God, its author. The tablets are like an outline and central core of those collections which develop progressively and come to be called "Book of the Covenant" (Ex 24,7; 2 K 23,2.21), "Book of the Law" (Dt 28,58.61; 29,20; Js 1,8; 8,34), "Book of Moses" (2 Ch 25,4; 35,12; Ezr 6,18; Mk 12,26). The purpose of the book is to preserve God's commands and to serve as a permanent witness against those who would betray their commitments (Dt 31,26f; cf Js 24,27).

The collections of the prophets are made in response to a similar need. It is not enough for Isaiah to assemble his disciples and bury his testimony in their hearts (Is 8,16) and so to remain among his people as a "revelation and witness" (8,20); he receives a command "to write in a book, that it may serve in the days to come as a witness forever" (30,8). Jeremiah twice dictated to Baruch a resumé of all his words for the past twenty years in the hope that this terrifying synthesis of "the wrath* and fury with which Yahweh has threatened His people" will lead them to repentance (Jr 36, 2.7).

Thus the books of Israel are seen both in their literary aspect and in their singular originality not so much as a witness to the past history and proper genius of a people as a witness which God gives to His own justice* and man's sin*. This is precisely the role which St. Paul assigns to Scripture: "to conclude all things under sin" (G 3,22).

III. BOOKS FROM EARTH,
FROM HEAVEN

Once the prophetic books are said to contain the Word* of God, it is natural that a visionary like Ezekiel, when he begins to dream of his prophetic mission*, sees himself eating a scroll from heaven and repeating on earth the text written from on high (Ez 2,8—3,3). In a vivid way which avoids the strict literalism of so many later commentators, Ezekiel's vision points up the nature of an inspired book—a work entirely from God and entirely composed by a human author.

There are other books, too, more mysterious, whose content God has reserved to Himself more or less exclusively. Such, for example, is the "Book of Citizenship" in which pagans are enrolled among the citizens of Zion (Ps 87,5f; Is 4,3) and from which the names of false prophets are deleted (Ez 13,9). Since one who is enrolled as a citizen of Jerusalem* is "destined to live on" (Is 4,3), this book coincides with the "Book of Life*" (Ps 69,29) in which God has written down the names of those whom He predestines* to live on earth (Ex 32, 32f) and in heaven (Dn 12,1; Lk 10,20). And if a book exists in which our days and all our actions are inscribed even before they take place (Ps 139,16), it is different from one of those books that will be brought forward and opened in the hour of judgment* (Dn 7,10; Ap 20,12). Throughout all these images, the question is not so much one of counting and calculating as one of proclaiming the supreme justice of God's interest in men and the infallible execution of His plan*. If anything is counted up in His book, it is our tears (Ps 56,9).

IV. THE SEALED BOOK

The book sealed with seven seals, which He who sits upon the throne holds in His hands and which the Lamb alone is able to open and read (Ap 5,1-10), is certainly, according to the OT tradition, a prophetic book (cf Is 8,16; 29, 11f; Ez 2,9) and probably the sum total of Israel's Scriptures. All these books take on a new and unsuspected meaning in Jesus Christ. Until then they were seen mainly as a Law*, a compendium of divine commandments forever violated, a crushing testimony to our infidelity. But when He comes who is spoken of "in the scroll" and says, "Behold, I come to do your will, O God" (He 10,7=Ps 40,9), then God's will* shall be fulfilled to the last iota (Mt 5,18) and His words* will be seen to be an immense promise* kept at last, a unique plan* brought to completion. In Jesus Christ, all the different books (gr. *biblia* in the plural) become one book, the Bible (lat. *biblia* in the singular).

→Law *B*—Predestine 3.4—Tradition OT II 2 —Word of God—Writing.

JG mjm

BREAD

Bread, a gift of God, is for man a source of strength (Ps 104,14f), a means of subsisting so essential that to lack bread is to lack everything (Am 4,6; cf Gn 28,20). Thus in the prayer which Christ teaches His disciples, bread seems to sum up all the gifts* which are necessary for us (Lk 11,3); indeed, it was chosen as a sign of the greatest of gifts (Mk 14,22).

I. DAILY BREAD

1. *In everyday life*, a situation is characterized by saying what taste it gives to bread. A suffering person and one whom God seems to abandon eats a bread "of tears," of anguish, or "of ashes" (Ps 42,4; 80,6; 102,10; Is 30,20); it is eaten by the joyful man in joy (Qo 9,7). Of the sinner it is said that he eats a bread of impiety or of falsehood (Pr 4,17); and of the sluggard, a bread of idleness (Pr 31,27). On the other hand, bread is not only a means of subsistence: it is intended to be shared. Every meal* supposes a gathering and likewise a communion*. To eat bread regularly with someone is to be his friend*, an intimate friend (Ps 41,10=Jn 13,18). The duty of hospitality* is sacred, making of each one's bread the bread of the passerby, sent by God (Gn 18,5; Lk 11,5.11). After the exile* particularly, accent is placed on the necessity of sharing one's bread with the hungry: here Jewish piety* finds the best expression of fraternal charity (Pr 22,9; Ez 18,7.16; Jb 31,17; Is 58,7; Tb 4,16). When Paul commends to the Corinthians the collection on behalf of "the saints," he reminds them that every gift comes from God, beginning with bread (2 Co 9,10). In the Christian church, the "breaking of bread" designates the eucharistic rite, as it is broken on behalf of all: the body of the Lord becomes the very source of the unity of the Church (Ac 2,42; 1 Co 10,17).

2. *Bread, gift of God*. God, having created man (Gn 1,29), and again after the flood (9,3), makes known to him what he may eat; and it is at the price of hard labor that sinful man will be assured of what is necessary: "you will eat your bread in the sweat of your brow" (3,19). From then on, abundance or scarcity of bread will have the value of a sign: abundance will be a blessing* from God (Ps 37,25; 132,15; Pr 12,11), and scarcity a punishment* of sin (Jr 5,17; Ez 4,16f; Lm 1,11; 2,12). Man must therefore humbly ask his bread from God and await it with confidence. In this respect, the accounts of multiplication of loaves are significant. The miracle worked by Elisha (2 K 4, 42ff) well expresses the superabundance of the divine gift: "They shall eat and have some

left." Humble confidence is also the first lesson of the gospel accounts; borrowing from a psalm (78,25) the formula: "They shall all eat and be filled" (Mt 14,20 p; 15,37 p; cf Jn 6,12), they recall the "bread of the strong" with which God filled His people in the desert. In the same context of thought, Jesus invited His disciples to ask for "daily bread" (Mt 6,11), as sons who confidently await everything from their heavenly Father (cf Mt 6,25 p).

Finally, bread is the supreme gift of the eschatological period, whether for each one in particular (Is 30,23), or in the Messianic banquet promised to the elect (Jr 31,12). The meals* of Jesus with His own were thus a prelude to the eschatological banquet (Mt 11,19 p), and especially the eucharistic* meal where the bread Christ gives to His disciples is His body*, true gift of God (Lk 22,19).

II. BREAD IN WORSHIP

1. The priestly legislation accords a great importance to the loaves "of proposition," placed in the temple on a table with jars intended for the libations (1 K 7,48; 2 Ch 13,11; cf Ex 25, 23-30). Their origin seems ancient (1 S 21,5ff). Perhaps it is a reflection of the old religious feeling which offered nourishment* to the divinity. For Israel, whose God refuses all nourishment (Jg 13,16), these loaves become the symbol of communion* between God and His faithful; and the priests will consume them (Lv 24,5-9).

2. *The bread of new grain* made up part of the offering brought to the festival of Weeks (Lv 23,17). The phrase, "as a gesture of presentation" shows that it signifies acknowledgment of the divine gift, as every liturgy of first-fruits (cf Ex 23,16.19). It is given in entirety, naturally, to the priest, the representative of God (Lv 23,20; cf Ez 44,30; Nm 18, 13). It is likewise an intention of thanksgiving which inspires the offering of bread and wine made by the king-priest Melchizedek to God the Creator (Gn 14,18ff).

3. Beginning with the oldest codes, unleavened loaves accompany the sacrifices (Ex 23,18; 34,25) and constitute Israel's nourishment during the feat of springtime (23,15; 34, 18). The leaven was excluded from the cultic offerings (Lv 2,11); perhaps a symbol of corruption was seen in it. In any case, when the agrarian festival of the unleavened bread was united to the immolation of the Pash, the custom of unleavened bread was related to the departure from Egypt: it was supposed to recall the hasty departure which had prevented them from making the dough rise (Ex 12,8.11. 39). Perhaps the origin of the rite is simply a custom of nomad life, carried over to the sedentary life in Canaan. It is eventually joined to the idea of a renewal, since the old leaven must disappear (12,15). St. Paul employs this image to convince the baptized to live as new* men (1 Co 5,7f). The use of bread in worship finds its fulfillment* in the eucharist*. After having multiplied the loaves with some liturgical gestures (Mt 14,19 p), Jesus enjoins during the supper the renewal of the action through which He makes from bread His sacrificed body and the sacrament of unity of the faithful (1 Co 10,16-22; 11,23-26).

III. BREAD OF THE WORD

In announcing hunger for the Word* of God, the prophet Amos (8,11) compares bread to the Word (cf Dt 8,3 with regard to the manna). Later, in recalling the Messianic banquet, prophets and wise men speak of the bread which stands for the living Word of God (Is 55,1ff), divine wisdom in person (Pr 9,5f; Si 24,19-22, cf 15,1ff). For Jesus, too, bread evokes the divine Word by which man must live daily (Mt 4,4). To the desire of the bread to be eaten in the eschatological kingdom (Lk 14,15), Jesus responds by the parable of those invited to the banquet. From the outset this parable presupposes acceptance of the person and His message. In giving a very strong teaching context to the first account of the multiplication of the loaves, it seems that St. Mark wishes to suggest that the loaves are the symbol of the Word of Jesus, and at the same time a symbol of His body handed over for us (Mk 6,30.34). According to St. John, Jesus reveals the meaning of this miracle in affirming that He is the true bread (Jn 6,32f). He presents Himself at first as the Word in which one must believe (6,35-47). Since this Word incarnate is offered in sacrifice, the adherence in faith necessarily brings with it communion with the sacrifice in the eucharistic rite (6.49-58). As necessary food and gift of God even in its materiality, the bread the faithful man daily asks God for can signify, with the development of faith, the divine Word and the very person of the immolated Savior, who is the true bread from heaven, the bread of life, living and life-giving (6,32.35.51).

→Communion NT — Eucharist — Hunger & Thirst—Life IV 2—Manna—Meal—Nourishment.

DS pmcm

BROTHER

The word *brothers*, in its strictest sense, means men who are the issue of the same maternal womb (Gn 4,2). But in Hebrew, as in many other languages, it is applied by extension to the members of one same family (Gn 13,8; Lv 10,4; cf Mk 6,3), or of the same tribe (2 S 19,13), of the same people (Dt 25,3; Jg 1,3), by opposition to strangers* (Dt 1,16; 15,2f). Finally it means people descended from the same ancestor, as Edom and Israel (Dt 2,4; Am 1,11). Alongside of this fraternity founded on flesh, the Bible is acquainted with another where the bond is of the spiritual order: fraternity by faith (Ac 2,29), sympathy (2 S 1,26), similar function (2 Ch 31,15; 2 K 9,2), contracted covenant (Am 1,9; 1 K 20,32; 1 M 12,10)...

This metaphorical use of the word shows that the human brotherhood, as a lived reality, is not limited to a simple relationship of blood, although this constitutes its natural foundation. Revelation does not begin from the philosophical reflection on the "community of nature" which makes brothers of all men. Not that it rejects the ideal of universal brotherhood; but it knows that it is unrealizable and holds its pursuit as deceptive, as long as it is not sought in Christ. For besides, this is the ideal which the OT envisages through the elementary fraternal communities—family, people, religion; and it is this the NT begins to realize in the community of the Church.

OT

TOWARD UNIVERSAL BROTHERHOOD

1. *The beginnings.* In creating the human race "from one sole principle" (Ac 17,26; cf Gn 1—2), God placed in the heart of men the dream of brotherhood in Adam*; but this dream was not to come true until after a long wayfaring. For, to begin with, the history of the sons of Adam is that of a broken fraternity; jealous of Abel*, Cain kills him. He does not even wish to know where his brother is (Gn 4,9). Since Adam's day humankind was sinful. With Cain is unmasked in men a visage of hatred which they sought vainly to veil behind the myth of an original human goodness. Man must recognize that sin has tapped at the door of his heart (Gn 4,7); and he must triumph over it if he does not wish to be dominated by it.

2. *Brotherhood in the covenant.* Before Christ makes sure of this triumph the chosen people are going to have a long apprenticeship in brotherhood. Not all at once is there a fraternity among all men; but there was a fraternity among the sons of Abraham* through faith in the same God and through the same covenant*. This is the ideal which the Law of Holiness laid down: "Thou shalt not hate thy brother...thou shalt love thy neighbor*" (Lv 19,17f). No disputes, no spites, no vengeance! A positive assistance like that which the law of the levirate requires with regard to the essential duty of fecundity: when a man dies childless, his nearest relative must "raise up a posterity to his brother" (Dt 25,5-10; Gn 38,8.26). Patriarchal traditions hand on the beautiful examples of this fraternity: Abraham and Lot avoid disagreement (Gn 13,8), Jacob is reconciled with Esau (33,4), Joseph forgives his brothers (45, 1-8).

But the putting into practice of such an ideal meets ceaselessly with the hardness of human hearts. The Israelite society, such as the prophets see it, remains far removed from brotherhood. There was no fraternal love (Ho 4,2); "no one spares his brother" (Is 9,18ff); injustice is universal, there is no confidence possible (Mi 7,2-6); no one can "trust a brother, for every brother wishes to supplant the other" (Jr 9,3), and Jeremiah is himself persecuted by his own brothers (Jr 11-18; 12,6; cf Ps 69,9; Jb 6,15). To this hardened world, the prophets recall the demands of justice*, of kindness, of compassion (Ze 7,9f). Having their Creator as a common Father* (Ml 2,10), does not this bestow on all members of the covenant a brotherhood more real even than their descent from Abraham (cf Is 63,16)? Similarly the sages extol true brotherhood. Nothing is more painful than to be abandoned by one's brothers (Pr 19,7; Jb 19,13); but a true brother loves always even in adversity (Pr 17,17); one cannot exchange him for gold (Si 7,18), because "a brother helped by a brother is a strong fortress" (Pr 18,19 LXX). God hates quarrels and loves harmony (Si 25,1). "Ah, how sweet it is for brothers to dwell together!" (Ps 133,1).

3. *Toward the reconciliation of estranged brothers.* The gift of the divine Law does not suffice, however, to remake a brotherly world. It is at all levels that the human fraternity has failed. Beyond individual quarrels, Israel sees the bond of the tribes dissolve (cf 1 K 12,24); and the consequence of the schism is fratricidal wars (vg Is 7,1-9). Exteriorly, it clashed with its brother-nations who were nearest, such as Edom which it was in duty bound to love (Dt 23,8), but which on its part did not spare Israel (Am 1,11; cf Nm 20,14-21). What is to be said of nations further removed which opposed each other with a rigorous hate*? In the presence of this collective sin, the prophets turn to God. He alone could restore human brotherhood when He would bring about eschatological salvation*. Then He would reunite Israel and Judah in one single people (Ho 2,2f.25), for Judah and Ephraim will be jealous of each other no more (Is 11,13f); He will gather all of Jacob (Mi 2,12); He will be the God of all the clans (Jr 31,1); the "two peoples" will walk in agreement (Jr 3,18), thanks to the king* of justice (23,5f); and there will be only one kingdom (Ez 37,22). This fraternity will finally extend to all the nations*; reconciled among themselves, they will find peace* and unity* (Is 2,1-4; 66,18ff).

NT

ALL BROTHERS IN JESUS CHRIST

The prophetic dream of a universal brotherhood becomes a reality in Christ, the new Adam*. Its earthly realization in the Church, imperfect as it still is, is the tangible sign of its final accomplishment.

1. *The first-born of a multitude of brothers.* By His death on the cross* Jesus became "the eldest of many brothers" (R 8,29). He reconciled* with God and between themselves the two factions of mankind: the Jewish* people and the nations* (E 2,11-18). Together they now have access to the Kingdom*, and the elder brother—the Jewish people—should no longer be jealous of the prodigal at last returning to the Father's house (Lk 15,25-32). After His resurrection, Christ can call His disciples brothers (Jn 20,17; Mt 28,10). This is now the reality: all who receive Him become children of God (Jn 1,12), brothers not by descent from Abraham according to the flesh, but by faith*

in Christ and the fulfillment of the will* of the Father (Mt 12,46-50 p; cf 21,28-32). In this way men become brothers of Christ, not in any figurative sense but by a new birth* (Jn 3,3). They are re-born of God (1,13), with the same origin as Christ who has made them holy and "openly calls them brothers" (He 2,11). In fact Christ has become in all things like us, in order to make us sons with Him (2,10-17). Sons of God in the full sense of the word and capable of calling Him "Abba," we are also co-heirs with Christ, for we have become His brothers (R 8,14-17) and are far more closely related to Him than we could be to brothers according to the flesh.

2. *The community of brothers in Christ.* While He was still living, Jesus Himself laid the foundation and announced the law of the new community of brothers. He has taken up and perfected the commandments which concerned the relations between brothers (Mt 5,21-26), making a notable place for the duty of fraternal correction (Mt 18,15ff). If this last text gives us a glance of a limited community from which the faithful brother can be excluded, we see however that it is open to all (Mt 5,47). Each one should show his love for the smallest of his unfortunate brethren, for in them it is always Christ he meets (Mt 25,40). After the resurrection, when Peter has "confirmed his brethren" (Lk 22,31f), the disciples constitute between them a "brotherhood" (1 P 5,9). Certainly, at the beginning they continue to give the name of "brothers" to the Jews, their racial companions (Ac 2,29; 3,17...). But Paul does not yet see more in them than his brethren "in the flesh" (R 9,3). For a new race had come to birth, beginning with the Jews and the nations (Ac 14,1f), reconciled in their faith in Christ. Nothing more will divide them as members, not even the difference of social condition between masters and slaves (Phm 16). They are all one in Christ, all brothers, well-beloved faithful of God (vg Col 1,2). Such are true sons of Abraham (G 3,7-29) constituting the body of Christ (1 Co 12,12-27); they have found in the new Adam* the foundation and the source of their brotherhood.

3. *Fraternal love.* It is in the bosom of the believing community that fraternal love* is first exercised. This "sincere philosophy" is not simply a natural philanthropy. It can only come from the "new* birth" (1 P 1,22f). It has nothing Platonic; for if it seeks to reach all

men, it is at the interior of the small community that it is exercised: avoidance of dissensions (G 5,15), mutual support (R 15,1), almsgiving* (2 Co 8—9; 1 Jn 3,17) and delicacy (1 Co 8,12). It is what comforts Paul on his arrival at Rome (Ac 28,15). In his epistle, John seems to keep the restricted meaning of the word 'brother', that is, a member of the believing community. Fraternal love is the opposite of Cain's attitude (1 Jn 3,12-16); it is the indispensable sign of love of God (1 Jn 2,9-12).

4. *Toward perfect brotherhood.* The community of believers, however, is never realized in its perfection here below; unworthy members can be found in it (1 Co 5,11), false brethren may be introduced (G 2,4f; 2 Co 11,26). But it knows that one day the devil, the accuser of all the brethren before God, will be cast down (Ap 12,10). While awaiting this final victory, which will be the fullness of self-realization, it already is giving witness that the human fraternity is marching toward the new man* dreamed of from the beginning.

→Abel 1—Almsgiving—Community OT 5; NT I—Education III 2— Enemy—Fathers & Father —Hate—Hospitality—Love II—Mary II 5— Mercy O; OT II; NT II—Neighbor—Shame II 2—Slave I—Stranger I—Tenderness 3— Unity I—Vengeance 2 a.

AN & XLD wjy

BUILD

The themes of construction and of an edifice that one builds occupy an important place in the Bible, the book of a people* who themselves constructed and built their houses*, their cities*, their temple*. To make things is a natural desire of man; God will make this desire one of the axes of His plan for salvation.

I. THE BUILDING OF ANCIENT ISRAEL

1. *To build a family and to construct an edifice.* The first meaning of the Hebrew verb *banah* is construction of material edifices—an altar (Gn 8,20), a house (33,17), a city (4,17). God does not condemn such undertakings, as long as they are not destined to set man up

against God, as it was at Babel (Gn 11,1-9). The divine presence is indispensable for preventing the work from inevitable failure (Ps 127,1). The "pagan" constructions are not important in God's eyes. He will destroy them when He wills, no matter how beautiful and solid they may seem (Am 3,13ff; Zp 2,4ff; Ze 9,3ff).

Building is applied to a family as it is to masonry. God builds woman out of Adam's side (Gn 2,22); a mother is "built" by the children she brings into the world (16,2; 30,3). But it is God who does this building (1 K 11,38). The transition from the person to the family, to the tribe, and to the people, especially if they are conceived as a house*, is easy and natural. Here also it is God who acts in order to build the dynasty of David* (2 S 7,11), the house or the people of Israel* (Jr 12,16; 24,6; 31,4).

2. *To construct and destroy.* In blessing "the work of man's hands" (Dt 14,29; 15,10), God puts the finishing touches to it and gives it solidity; He "builds" it. But if man forgets God, He will destroy the work that was built without Him (Jr 24,6; 42,10). The annihilation of persons, of dwelling places, of towns, and of peoples will be the witness of His chastisements; Jeremiah, the prophet of this destruction, is sent "to uproot and to pull down, to build and to plant" (Jr 1,10).

But God who is faithful and who builds (cf the proper name *Yibneya*, "Yahweh builds," 1 Ch 9,8) does not destroy completely and irrevocably. At the very moment He directs the destructive flow of His wrath* (Is 28,18; 30,28) toward human grandeur (Is 2,11), He still continues to do constructive work (Is 44,26; 58,12). The fallen hut of David will be rebuilt (Am 9,11); the people will return from exile and rebuild their cities (Jr 30,4.18); Jerusalem* and the temple* will be restored (Hg 1,8; Ze 6,13; Jr 31,38). The imagery itself depicts material reconstructions and the restoration of the people, the houses rising and the population abounding (Is 49,19-21; Jr 30,18f).

II. THE NEW FOUNDATION

The new edifice, the new* people*, is indeed the continuation of the old—of Israel and of her institutions—but it does not rest on them. It is founded on an essential element, the rock* which God destined to be the pinnacle and crown of all the works built by God in Israel (Is 28,16; Ze 4,7). But the workers entrusted with the work have rejected this stone which is a stumbling block to them (cf Ps 118,22; Mt 21,41f p). The marvel is that this rejected stone was of such quality in the original process of construction that in putting it at the base of the new edifice (Ps 118,22), God resumes and completes all the previous work. Because of the workers' bad will, God in person builds "a work admirable to behold," an incredible masterpiece. The rejected stone become "the cornerstone" (1 P 2,7) is Jesus Christ, "the only foundation" possible (1 Co 3,11).

Jesus Christ is also the new temple*. As Jeremiah (cf Jr 7,12-15), so Jesus prophesies the destruction of the magnificent edifice, pride of Israel, that has become "a den of thieves" (Jr 7,11; Mt 21,12). He prophesies the restoration in three days, that is, in less than no time, of another temple, His own body. He will be the constructor of this building (Jn 2,19-22).

III. THE BUILDING OF THE BODY OF CHRIST

1. *I will build my Church.* As the cornerstone and holy temple, Jesus is not only the new edifice; He is also its builder. The edifice is His work, it is "His Church" (Mt 16,18). He chooses its materials and puts them in place; thus does He put Peter* as its foundation. In His glory, "it is He also who gives" to each one his place and ministry. He gives to all the parts of the edifice "concord and cohesion" and thus constructs His own body* in charity (E 4,11-16).

2. *The builders.* First, there are those whom Christ has placed as "foundations": the apostles* (E 2,20). They are both the "foundations" and "founders" of the Churches* to which they give birth. Just as for Jeremiah to build is part of the prophetic ministry (Jr 1,10; 24,6), for Paul it is a characteristic of the apostolic charism* (2 Co 10,8; 12,19; 13,10). As "cooperators with God" (1 Co 3,9), the apostles have to plant (3,6), to "place the foundation" who is Jesus Christ (3,10f).

3. *The body which is built.* Under the direction of the head, Christ, the entire body "builds itself" (E 4,15f) in all its parts. The ministry of building the Church is given not only to the "prophets, evangelists, pastors and doctors" (E 4,11), who are entrusted with definite responsibilities; but all the "holy* ones" who are "God's field and building" (1 Co 3,9) have to take active part in this building. It is a common and mutual work*, each building the other, giving him his full value in the edifice, and receiving from him help and strength (R 14,19; 15,2; 1 Th 5,11; Jude 20). It is an important duty and an essential criterion in the discernment of charisms*, the most precious of which are those that build up the assembly (1 Co 14,12). To edify their brothers is to build the Church, on condition, of course, that they remain "rooted and built" in Christ and in His authentic tradition (Col 2,6f). On the last day* fire* will prove the quality of the materials used (1 Co 3,10-15).

4. *The new edifice* is the holy city, the new Jerusalem* (Ap 21,2). It comes down from heaven*, from God, for in this city none of those things which sin produces will be found any longer: neither death, nor weeping, nor wailing, nor pain. And it is all the work of God (Ap 21,4). Nevertheless "it rests on the twelve pillars, each bearing the name of one of the Lamb's twelve apostles" (21,14). "Over its doors are inscribed the names of the twelve tribes of Israel" (21,12). This clearly is the edifice founded by Jesus Christ and entrusted by Him to His apostles. It is the Church built by the labor of all the saints. It is indeed the spouse. Its ornaments are "the flax of shining whiteness" and all its jewels, which everywhere reflect and send back the light of the divine glory (21,19-23). These are "the good works of the faithful" (19,8). Everything in this edifice is God's work, and it is entirely constructed by the saints. Such is the mystery of grace*.

→Exhort—Growth 2 d—House I 2—Stone 4— Temple OT I 2.3; NT I—Works NT II 3.

JMF & JG gsa

BURIAL

From prehistoric times there is evidence of the care taken by the most primitive men over the burial of the dead. In its various forms this care is a sign of the belief in some sort of survival of man after death*.

1. *In Israel*, as amongst its neighbors, to be deprived of burial is regarded as a terrible misfortune (Ps 79,3). It is one of the most fearful

punishments with which the prophets threaten the wicked (1 K 14,11ff; Jr 22,18-19).

And so the Israelite takes great care over the preparations for his burial, like Abraham (Gn 23, the account of the founding of the patriarchal tomb). Burial is the principal duty of the son of the dead man (Gn 25, 8ff; 35,29; 50,12f; Tb 4,3f; 6,15; 14,10ff). It is a work of piety incumbent on the army in time of war (I K 11,15) and on every faithful Israelite (the Book of Tobit insists on this duty: 1,17-20; 2,4-8; 12, 12f).

The rites of mourning are extremely complex and are to be found among the neighboring peoples too: fasting (1 S 31,13; 2 S 1,12; 3,35), torn clothes (Gn 37,34; 2 S 1,11; 3,31; 13,31), the wearing of sackcloth (Gn 37,34; 2 S 3,31; 14,2; Ez 7,18), the cutting of hair and self-inflicted wounds (Am 8,10; Mi 1,16; Is 22,12; Jr 7,29; 16,6; 48,37; 49,3; this practice will be forbidden by Dt 14,1 and Lv 19,27f, probably because it was part of the Baal cult), and lamentation (2 S 1,12.17-27; 3,33f; 13,36; 1 K 13,30; Am 5,16; Jr 22,18; 34,5). These different customs are not only signs of sorrow; they have also a ritual aspect, though we do not know the original meaning (the cult of the dead, protection against their evil spells...). In Israel, where the cult of the dead is altogether excluded by the yahwist faith, these rites are mainly designed to procure a peaceful condition for the dead person by "gathering him to his people" (Gn 25,8; 35,29), when he "sleeps with his ancestors" (1 K 2,10; 11,43).

2. *In the Gospels* we see that the contemporaries of Jesus preserve the OT customs for burial (Mk 5,38; Jn 11,38-44).

Jesus does not condemn these customs, even when He says that the call to follow Him is more important than the sacred duty of burying one's father (Mt 8,21f). Before it happens, He is deeply affected by the shame of His death as a criminal, deprived of funeral honors (Mk 14,8).

In fact these honors will be paid to Him by Joseph of Arimathea in all haste because of the approaching feast (Mk 15,46f). But when the women come on Easter morning to complete this hasty burial by an anointing* with perfumes (Mk 16,1f; in Jn 19,39f the body of Jesus has already received this anointing on the eve of His death), they hear the angel tell them: "He is risen, he is not here." The traditional Christian custom of burying the dead in the catacombs and the cemeteries ("sleeping places:" cf I Th 4,13) is based on these accounts. It draws its inspiration from the honors paid to the body consecrated by the action of the Spirit, and still more from the prospect of hope opened up on Easter day.

→Anointing I 2—Death OT I 3—Fasting 1.

AG ems

C

CALAMITY

The human family is constantly running into collective misfortunes; it is always surprised by their suddenness, their extent, and their blind determinism. The whole Bible echoes this suffering: war*, famines, flood*, storms*, fire*, sickness*, and death*. The apocalypses reveal to man, who cannot be satisfied with a natural explanation of these phenomena, their mysterious dimension, and thus reveal man to himself.

1. *Calamity in God's plan.* Deep down as well as on the surface, calamity is an imbalance. Related as it is to chastisement, in the sense that in the final analysis it flows from man's sin*, nevertheless it is distinct from it because it affects all creation, and because it manifests more clearly the face of Satan* to whom the world is subjected during its time of trial* (Jb 1,12; Mt 24,22). Calamity is a collective "blow" (*naga'*, to strike) that manifests to what extent sin is at work in human history (Ap 6; 8,6—11,19).

War, famine, pestilence, death; these scourges are not presented by the Apocalypse as simply a component of time. For if, following its literary relationships, we analyze former apocalypses we find a current which, from the later books of Judaism (Ws 10—19; Dn 9,24-27; 12,1), passing through the psalms (Ps 78; 105) and the prophets (Ez 14; 21; 38; Is 24; Zp 1,2f), reaches back to the scourges of Egypt* (Ex 7—10). Then the meaning of calamity becomes clear: it is a part of the great judgment* that is the Passover*. The eschatological liberation which we are living is prefigured by the liberation of the first Passover and the first exodus.

Seen under this paschal light, calamity loses its mask: the moment in which sin's power of death triumphs in calamity sounds the beginning of its defeat and of the victory* of Christ. In the name of God's love that works through the cross*, calamity changes its meaning (R 8, 31-39; Ap 7,3; 10,7).

2. *Man faced by calamity.* If this is what calamity is, man should regard it with an honest attitude. He should not blaspheme (Ap 16,9) nor turn to some idol to deliver him from it (2 K 1,2-17; Is 44,17; 47,13). He should recognize in it a sign of the times* (Lk 12,54ff), the expression of his slavery* to sin and the announcement of the Savior's visit* which is quite near (Mt 24,33). Calamity, as an anticipation of the day* of Yahweh, is an ultimatum with a view to conversion (Ap 9,20f), a summons to watch (Mt 24,44). But above all, it is the beginning of our complete liberation: "When this begins to happen, straighten up and raise your head because your deliverance is near" (Lk 21,28).

In this same eschatological line it is normal that calamity accompanies the development of the Word* in the world (Ap 11,1-13) since in this way it expresses the parallel development of the mystery of Antichrist*. But above all, the Christian should endure it with the certainty that he is loved (Lk 21,8-19) and in the power of Christ (2 Co 12,9). The properly eschatological state of soul which calamity should preserve in us is, then, expectation; in fact, it testifies to the birth of a new world* and to the work of the Spirit* who advances the whole of creation toward total redemption* (Mt 24, 6ff; R 8,19-23).

→Flood—Judgment OT I 2, II 1—Punishments —Suffering—Visit—Wrath *B.*

JCo pjb

CALLING

Among the most impressive pages of the Bible are scenes in which there is a call. The call of Moses by the burning bush (Ex 3), of Isaiah in the temple (Is 6), the dialogue between Yahweh and young Jeremiah (Jr 1)—all these present God in His majesty and mystery and man in what he really is, his fear and generosity, his power to resist or respond. Since accounts of vocation are so important in Scripture, in God's revelation of Himself, and in man's salvation, God's call must be a moment of singular importance.

I. CALLING AND MISSION IN THE OT

Every OT call has a mission* as its object. Whenever God summons someone, He sends him. To Abraham (Gn 12,1), to Moses (Ex 3, 10.16), to Amos (Am 7,15), to Isaiah (Is 6,9), to Jeremiah (Jr 1,7), and to Ezekiel (Ez 3,1.4), He repeats the same command: a call is a direct summons in which God makes clear to man that He has chosen and destined the man for a particular work in His plan of salvation and in the destiny of His people. A divine choice, then, is the basis of a call; its purpose is to accomplish the divine will*. The idea of calling, however, adds something to that of choice and mission, that is the note of personal challenge directed to the deepest level of the individual's sense of moral responsibility. The call upsets the man's existence, not merely in external fashion, but in the inmost area of his being, for it makes him a different man.

This personal aspect of God's calling is textually verified. God speaks the name of the one He calls (Gn 15,1; 22,1; Ex 3,4; Jr 1,11; Am 7,8; 8,2). As a better indication of the fact that He is taking possession of and altering a man's existence, God gives His chosen one a new name* (Gn 17,1; 32,29; cf Is 62,2). And God awaits a response to His appeal, a voluntary consent given in faith and obedience. Sometimes acceptance is instantaneous (Gn 12,4; Is 6,8). But often the man is gripped with fear and tries to shun the call (Ex 4,10ff; Jr 1,6; 20,7) which normally puts the one called apart from other men and makes him appear strange to his friends (Gn 12,1; Is 8,11; Jr 12,6; 15,10; 16,1-9; cf 1 K 19,4).

God's call is not directed to everyone chosen to be His instrument. The kings*, for example, are the Lord's anointed but they hear no such call from God. It is Samuel who informs both Saul (1 S 10,1) and David (16,12). Nor do priests receive their priesthood* through a divine calling but rather because of their birth. Even though Aaron himself is "called by God," according to He 5,4, Moses is the intermediary of the call (Ex 28,1); nothing is said of Aaron's interior acceptance. While there is no explicit statement in the epistle to the Hebrews, it is not out of keeping with the tenor of that epistle to see in the indirect indisposition of Aaron's call a sign that the Levitical priesthood, even in the case of Aaron, is inferior to the priesthood referred to by God's words: "You are my Son... You are a priest... according to the order of Melchizedech" (He 5,5f).

II. ISRAEL'S CALL
AND THE CALL OF JESUS CHRIST

Did Israel receive a call? In the current sense of the word, the answer is evident. In exact biblical terms, although a people* may not be so clearly treated or undergo the reactions of a single person, nevertheless, God does act toward Israel just as He acts toward those whom He calls. Certainly God speaks to Israel by personal agents; especially is Moses a mediator. Apart from this difference imposed by the nature of things, Israel has all the elements required for a calling. The covenant* is primarily a call from God, a word of direct address to the heart. The Law* and the prophets are full of the sense of calling: "Hear, O Israel" (Dt 4,1; 5,1; 6,4; 9,1; Ps 50,7; Is 1,10; 7,13; Jr 2,4; cf Ho 2,16; 4,1). These words pledge the people to a distinct type of life in which God is their warranty (Ex 19,4ff; Dt 7,6); hence His prohibition against reliance on anything but God (Is 7,4-9; cf Jr 2,11ff). God's call to Israel waits for a response, a commitment of the heart (Ex 19,8; Js 24,24) and of its entire life. All these characteristics are typical of a calling.

In a sense it is true that these marks of a calling are found in their fullness in the person of Jesus Christ. He is the perfect Servant* of God who always listens* to the Father's voice and obeys it. But as a matter of fact the NT does not use the terminology proper to a calling when speaking of Christ. Though Jesus does consistently mention His mission from the Father, nowhere is it said that God called Him —a significant omission. A calling supposes a change in being since God's call catches a man at his ordinary work, intercepts him in the midst

of his friends, and involves him in a project known to God alone—go to "the land I will point out to you" (Gn 22,1). In the case of Jesus Christ His baptism is both a scene of royal investiture—"You are my son" (Mk 1,11)—and God's introduction of the Servant in whom He is perfectly satisfied. But there is no hint here or elsewhere in the gospels of typical scenes of calling. Throughout the gospels Jesus is perfectly aware of His origin and His destination (Jn 8,14). He goes where others cannot follow and His destiny is absolutely unique. This is not because of a calling but rather proceeds from His being itself.

III. THE CALLING OF THE DISCIPLES
AND THE CALLING OF CHRISTIANS

There is no voice of God which extends a call to Jesus. But Jesus Himself offers a large number of calls to follow Him. It is by means of a call that Jesus surrounds Himself with the twelve (Mk 3,13). A similar call is made to others (Mk 10,21; Lk 9,59-62). All His preaching involves what might be termed a calling: a call to follow Him along a new path known only to Him: "If anyone wishes to come after me..." (Mt 16,24; cf Jn 7,17). While "many are called, but few chosen," this is because the invitation to the kingdom is a personal call to which some remain deaf (Mt 22,1-14).

The Church in its infancy at once recognized that the Christian is one who is called. Peter's first sermon at Jerusalem is a call to Israel, similar to that made by the prophets. Peter seeks to stimulate a personal option: "Save yourselves from this perverse generation*!" (Ac 2,40). For Paul there is a real parallelism between himself, "the apostle* who is called," and the Christians of Rome or Corinth, "the saints* who are called" (R 1,1.7; 1 Co 1,1f). To restore the Corinthians to what they should be, Paul reminds them of their calling. For this calling gives the Corinthian community whatever worth it has: "Consider your call. Not many are wise in the eyes of men" (1 Co 1,16). As a norm of conduct in this world whose shape is passing away, Paul induces each of them to remain "in the state of life in which he was called" (7,24). The life of the Christian is a calling because it is a life in the Spirit*. And the Spirit is the source of a totally new world. This Spirit is "united to our spirit" (R 8,16) to make us responsive to the Word* of the Father and to awaken in us the response of sons.

Because the vocation of the Christian is born by the Spirit and because the Spirit is the one source of life for the entire body of Christ, there is at the heart of the one Christian vocation "a diversity of gifts...of ministries*...of works..." Yet in this variety of charisms*, there is ultimately but one body* and one Spirit (1 Co 12,4-13). The Church*, the community of those who are called, is herself *Ekklēsia*, "the called," as well as *Eklektē*, "the one chosen" (2 Jn 1). Therefore, all Christians who hear the call of God in the Church and respond each according to his call actually give answer to the call of the total Church which hears the voice of the spouse and answers: "Come, Lord Jesus!" (Ap 22,20).

→Abraham I—Apostles II 1—Charisms II 2—David 1—Disciple NT 2 a—Election—Follow—Grace IV—Marriage NT II—Mission—Moses 1—Name OT 1; NT 4—People *A* I 1—Peter I—Predestine 2—Prophet OT II 1—Seek III—Will of God O.

JG dfb

CAPTIVITY

I. THE TRIAL OF THE CAPTIVITY

Since the beginning of its history, Israel experienced in Egypt an "original captivity" when the land that had welcomed the patriarchs became for their descendants a "house of servitude" (Ex 13,14; Dt 7,8). In strict terms, however, the Hebrews were the slaves* of Pharaoh rather than captives or prisoners. More than once afterwards, the people of God knew *deportation*, a practice which Amos denounced as a crime (Am 1,6.9) even though it was common in the ancient East. This was the lot of the Northern tribes after the destruction of Samaria (2 K 17,6.23), and then that of Judah at the beginning of the sixth century (2 K 24—25). In both cases there was a question of chastisements which punished the people of God for their infidelities. In traditional language, the Babylonian* captivity will in a special sense always be *the* captivity, even though it was more a deportation or an exile*.

Alongside of these collective trials, the Bible mentions in various contexts the lot of individual captives or prisoners. For some of them, imprisonment is a real punishment (cf Mt 5,25; 18,30), but for others it is a *providential trial*

(cf Ap 2,10). Such is the case of Joseph (Gn 39, 20ff) whom God's wisdom "did not abandon in his chains" (Ws 10,14); it is also the lot of more than one of the prophets (cf 1 K 22,26ff), of Jeremiah (Jr 20,2; 32,2f; 37,11-21; 38,6), of John the Baptist (Mt 14,3), and finally of Jesus who was bound (Jn 18,12; Mt 27,2) and certainly thrown into prison. In the Church the same destiny is in store for the apostles (Ac 5, 18; 12,3ff; 16,23f); and Paul, able to go into captivity of his own accord (Ac 20,22), can call himself at a later date literally "the prisoner of Christ" (E 3,1; 4,1; cf 2 Co 11,23). Yet "the Word of God will not be fettered" (2 Tm 2,9; cf Ph 1,12ff), and miraculous deliverances (Ac 5,19; 12,7-11; 16,26) will make it clear that prison cannot hold the gospel captive.

For God is concerned about prisoners. If He demands His faithful to "break the unjust chains" (Is 58,6) and if visiting prisoners is one of the works* of mercy (Mt 25,36.40; cf He 10, 34; 13,3), He shows Himself solicitous for "His prisoners" (Ps 69,34), even for those who had scornfully defied His commands (Ps 107,10-16). To His captive people especially He promises liberty* (Is 52,2) which is, as it were, a foretaste of the gospel (Is 61,1).

II. THE SPIRITUAL CAPTIVITY OF THE SINNER

It happens that, through their experience of temporal captivity, the people of God perceive another captivity of which the former becomes an expressive symbol: the captivity of sinners. On this level also, there is a mingling between captivity and slavery*, Jesus' peremptory affirmation: "whoever commits sin is a slave" (Jn 8,34), was hinted at in the OT: God abandoned His faithless people to their enemies (Jg 2,14). He "delivered them to the power of their crimes" (Is 64,6 LXX); according to the teaching of the sages, sin* is a sort of estrangement: "The wicked is caught by his own misdeeds, he is held in the bonds of his own sin" (Pr 5,22; cf 11,6).

But it is the apostolic writings that reveal above all the depth of the human distress from which Jesus was to announce deliverance (cf Lk 4,18; cf Is 61,1). "I am a being of flesh, sold into the power of sin," I am like a "captive subject to the law of sin that is in my members" (R 7,14.23): that is, according to St. Paul, every man's condition before he is justified*. After all, sin is not an abstraction: sinners are definitely caught "in the devil's snare which holds them captive and subject to his will" (2 Tm 2,26).

Another concrete manifestation of this spiritual captivity is found in "the cords of Sheol" and "the snares of death" (cf Ps 18,6) that are so dreadful to man (cf He 2,14f). Jesus' liberating action also extended that far: having tasted* death*, He "descended into hell" to proclaim the good news of salvation also "to the spirits that were detained in prison" (1 P 3, 19).

Finally, Paul does not hesitate sometimes to consider the Law* itself as a kind of "prison," in which "we were shut up before faith came" (G 3,23; cf R 7,6): perhaps these expressions are somewhat excessive, nevertheless they do help us understand better the true liberation* that Jesus Christ acquires for us.

What becomes of these sinners set free by Christ? A new paradox: they are made *the "captives" of the Lord.* Paul proclaims that the slaves of sin become the slaves of justice* (R 6,12-23; 1 Co 7,22); he considers himself as chained by the Spirit (Ac 20,22); he also wants to make "every thought captive so as to lead it to obey Christ" (2 Co 10,5; cf R 1,5). In reality, Jesus has, like the generals of old, "led away captives" (E 4,8=Ps 68,19) in His victorious train. However it is to distribute His gifts to them and make them share in His own victory* (cf 2 Co 2,14).

→Babel/Babylon 4 — Exile — Exodus OT — Liberation / Liberty — Redemption — Sin — Slave—Trial/Temptation OT I 3.

LR pjbg

CARES

1. *Exhortations to care.* Care is first the concern that a man brings to the completion of a work or of a mission. The Bible admires and recommends this intelligent and active attention of man to all his duties. First the humbler tasks; for example, those of the house (Pr 31, 10-31), of one's profession (Si 38,24-34), or of public responsibilities (50,1-4). The Bible places care for spiritual duties higher still: the search for wisdom (Ws 6,17; Si 39,1-11) or for moral progress (1 Tm 4,15; cf Tt 3,8; 1 Co 12,25), the solicitude of the apostle (2 Co 11,28; cf 4,8f). Here the supreme example is Jesus Himself, who gives Himself without reserve to the accomplish-

ment of His mission (Lk 12,50; 22,32). Further, care for "the affairs of the Lord" is of so lofty an order that it can lead, at Christ's call, to the renunciation of the cares of this world* in order to care directly and completely for the "one thing necessary" (1 Co 7,32ff; cf Lk 10,41f).

2. *Cares and faith.* In all areas the Bible condemns negligence and laziness. But it also knows that man runs the risk of allowing himself to be absorbed by the cares of this world to the detriment of spiritual concerns (Lk 8,14 p; 16,13 p; 21,34 p). Jesus has denounced this danger: He calls His disciples to care only for the kingdom* of God. The liberty of spirit necessary to them will not come from carelessness—the tasks of this world remain a duty—but from confidence* in the paternal love of God (Mt 6,25-34 p; cf 16,5-12).

Besides, whatever may be the area they deal with, cares are of themselves a call to confidence and to faith*. If a task well accomplished allows one in certain instances to "laugh* at the day to come" (Pr 31,25), the cares which it involves are more often an occasion for a man to take cognizance of his limitations in uncertainty, fear*, or anguish. The suffering* thus engendered is the common lot of all men (Ws 7, 4). It invites them to trust to the Lord the "burden" of their cares (Ps 55,23; cf 1 P 5,7), even if this burden results from their sins (Ps 38,19; cf Lk 15,16-20), in a faith which knows that "the most high takes care of them" (Ws 5, 15). They will then be able to "use this world" with all necessary care "as if they did not really use it" (1 Co 7,31). Beyond all cares in fact, "The peace* of God, which surpasses all understanding, will take their hearts and their thoughts in Christ Jesus under its protection" (Ph 4,6f).

→Anguish—Confidence—Fear of God II— Providence 1—Sadness OT 1—Wealth I 2— Work.

JDu jpl

CHARISMS

The word *charism* is the English counterpart of the Greek *charisma* which means "free gift" and is connected with the same root as *charis*, "grace." In the NT, the word does not always have a technical sense. It can denote all the gifts of God, which He bestows without changing His mind (R 11,29), especially this "gift of grace" which comes to us through Christ (R 5, 15f) and opens out into eternal life (R 6,23). In fact, God has in Christ "filled us with grace" (E 1,6: *charitoō*) and "will bestow on us every kind of gift" (R 8,32: *charizō*). But the first of His gifts is the Holy Spirit Himself who has been poured into our hearts and there produces charity (R 5,5; cf 8,15). The technical use of the word *charisma* is essentially understood in the perspective of this presence of the Spirit, which makes itself known by all sorts of "gratuitous gifts" (1 Co 12,1-4). The use of these gifts poses some problems which are examined especially in the epistles of St. Paul.

I. THE EXPERIENCE
OF THE GIFTS OF THE SPIRIT

In the OT, the presence of the Spirit* of God manifested itself in the men He inspired by extraordinary gifts* ranging from prophetic discernment (1 K 22,28) to raptures (Ez 3,12) and mysterious transports (1 K 18,12). In a more general way, Isaiah also attributed to the Spirit the gifts promised to the Messiah (Is 11,2), and Ezekiel the change of men's hearts (Ez 36,26f), while Joel announced the universality of His outpouring on men (Jl 3,1f). These eschatological promises* should be kept in mind so as to understand the experience of the gifts of the Spirit in the early Church: for she is the fulfillment of these promises.

1. *In the Acts of the Apostles*, the Spirit makes itself known right from the day of Pentecost* when, in accord with the Scriptures (Ac 2,15-21), the apostles proclaim in all languages the wonderful works of God (2,4.8-11). It is the sign that Christ has been exalted at the right hand of God and has received from the Father the promised Spirit and has poured it on mankind (Ac 2,33). After this, the presence of the Spirit shows itself in different ways: by the repetition of the signs of Pentecost (Ac 4,31; 10,44ff), especially after baptism and the imposition of hands (Ac 8,17f; 19,6); by the action of prophets* (11,27f; 15,32; 21, 10f), teachers (13,1f), preachers of the gospel (6,8ff); by miracles* (6,8; 8,5ff) and visions (7,55). These particular charisms are bestowed in the first place on the apostles, but they are also encountered among the people around them, sometimes in connection with the exercise of certain official functions (Stephen, Philip, Barnabas), always directed toward the good of the community which believes under the influence of the Holy Spirit.

2. *In the Pauline churches*, the same gifts of the Spirit form part of the common experience. The apostle's preaching is accompanied by the Spirit and the works of power*, that is by miracles (1 Th 1,5; 1 Co 2,4); he himself speaks in languages (1 Co 14,18) and has visions (2 Co 12,1-4). The communities know that the Spirit has been given to them by the wonders which He accomplishes in their midst (G 3,2-5), and by the very different gifts that He bestows upon them (1 Co 1,7). Since the beginning of his apostolate, Paul has high regard for these gifts of the Spirit; his only concern is to discern those that are genuine. "Do not stifle the Spirit, do not despise prophecies, but test everything: keep what is good and avoid the bad of whatever kind" (1 Th 5,19-22). This advice will receive further development when Paul runs into the pastoral problem which the charisms present.

II. CHARISMS IN THE CHURCH

The problem is posed within the community at Corinth by the undue importance attached to "speaking in languages" (1 Co 12—14). The religious enthusiasm that expresses itself in speeches "in different languages" (cf Ac 2,4) is not without ambiguity. The drunkenness* caused by the Spirit runs the risk of being confused by spectators with the drunkenness caused by wine (Ac 2,13), or even with the folly of madness (1 Co 14,23). Due to its apparent similarity to the transports of enthusiasm practiced by pagans in certain orgiastic cults, it also runs the risk of leading to irresponsibility those among the faithful who do not distinguish between the influence of the divine spirit and its counterfeits (1 Co 12,1ff). But in settling this practical issue, Paul raises the discussion higher and presents a doctrine that is very general.

1. *Unity and diversity of charisms.* The gifts of the Spirit are as diverse as the ministries* in the Church and the operations of men. The profound unity* between them lies in the fact that they come from one Spirit, as the ministries come from one Lord*, and the forms of work from one God* (1 Co 12,4ff). Men, each following his own charism, are the administra-

tors of a divine grace* which is one and multiplex (1 P 4,10). Comparison with the human body helps us understand more easily how all divine gifts are directed to the same goal: they are given in view of the common good (1 Co 12,7); they contribute together to the utility of the Church*, body of Christ*, in the same way as all the members cooperate for the good of the human body, each by fulfilling its role (12,12-27). The distribution of the gifts is the Spirit's doing (12,11) and, at the same time, Christ's, who give divine grace as He sees fit (E 4,7-10). But in the use of these gifts, each one should think first of all of the common good.

2. *Classification of charisms.* Paul was not concerned with giving us a reasoned classification of charisms although he enumerates them several times (1 Co 12,8ff.28ff; R 12,6ff; E 4,11; cf 1 P 4,11). But we can recognize the different spheres of application where the gifts of the Spirit find place. In the first instance, some charisms are related to the functions of the ministry (cf E 4,12): those of apostles*, prophets*, teachers, evangelists, and pastors (1 Co 12,28; E 4,11). Others concern the different activities that are useful to the community: service, teaching, exhortation, works of mercy (R 12,7f), words of wisdom or knowledge, outstanding faith, the gift of healing or working miracles, speaking in languages, and discernment of spirits (1 Co 12,8ff)...

Evidently, these charismatic activities which manifest the active presence of the Spirit do not constitute particular ecclesiastical functions; one can meet them in people who have other functions. Thus Paul, an apostle, speaks in languages and works miracles. Prophecy* is sometimes mentioned as an activity open to all (1 Co 14,29ff.39ff), at other times it is presented as a function (1 Co 12,28; E 4,11). The particular vocations of Christians are likewise founded on charisms: one is called to celibacy, another receives some other gift (1 Co 7,7). Finally, the practice of charity, which is the first Christian virtue, is itself a gift of the Holy Spirit (1 Co 12,31—14,1). As is clear, charisms are not exceptional things even though some of them, like the power to work miracles, are outside the common run. The whole life of Christians and the whole functioning of Church institutions depend entirely on them. It is through them that the Spirit of God governs the new people on whom He has been poured in abundance. To some He gives power and

grace to fulfill their functions, to others He gives power and grace to respond to their vocation and to be useful to the community so that the body of Christ might be built up (E 4,12).

3. *Rules for their use.* If one must not "stifle the Spirit," nevertheless one has to test the genuineness of the charisms (1 Th 5,19f) and "test the spirits*" (1 Jn 4,1). This discernment, itself a fruit of grace (1 Co 14,10), is essential. Paul and John set down an principal rule on this point, which provides an absolute criterion: the true gifts of the Spirit are known by this— that one confesses that Jesus* is the Lord (1 Co 12,3), that Jesus Christ, having come in the flesh, is from God (1 Jn 4,1ff). This rule permits the elimination of every false prophet whom the spirit of the Antichrist* animated (1 Jn 4,3; cf Co 12,3). Furthermore, the use of charisms ought to be subordinated to the common good; it ought also to respect the hierarchy. Ecclesiastical functions are classified according to the order of importance, at the head of which come the apostles (1 Co 12, 28; E 4,11). The activities to which all the faithful can aspire ought themselves be appreciated, not according to their spectacular character but according to their effective utility. All ought first to seek charity, then the other spiritual gifts*. Among these, prophecy* comes in the first place (1 Co 14,1). Paul delays considerably in showing its superiority to speaking in different tongues; for, as long as the religious enthusiasm manifests itself in such an unintelligible way, the community is not edified by it, and this edification of all remains essential (1 Co 14,2-25; cf 1 P 4,10ff). Even the authentic charisms must be subjected to some practical rules so that good order reigns in religious assemblies (1 Co 14, 33). Paul also gives the community of Corinth some instructions which are to be observed strictly (1 Co 14,26-38).

4. *Charisms and ecclesiastical authority.* This intrusion of the apostle into a domain in which the activity of the Spirit manifests itself shows that in all cases the charisms remain subjected to ecclesiastical authority (cf 1 Jn 4,6). As long as the apostles* are living, their power in this matter comes from the fact that the apostolate is the primary charism. After them their delegates participate also in the same authority as the instructions gathered from the pastoral epistles show (especially 1 Tm 1,18—4,16). This

is because these delegates themselves have received a particular gift of the Spirit by the imposition* of hands (1 Tm 4,14; 2 Tm 1,6). If they are not able to possess the charism of the apostles, nevertheless they have no less a charism of government which gives them the right to prescribe and to teach (1 Tm 4,11) and which no one ought to look down on (1 Tm 4,12). In the Church everything remains subjected to a hierarchy of government which is itself of charismatic order.

→Apostles—Church IV 1.2, VI—Exhort O—Grace IV—Ministry—Miracle III 3 b—Pentecost II 1—Prophet OT I; NT II 3—Schism NT —Sickness/Healing NT II 1—Sign NT II 2—Spirit of God V 2—Teach NT II 3—Tongue 2 —Virginity NT 3.

AG & PG pjb

CHILD

Like all healthy people, Israel sees in fruitfulness* a sign of God's blessing*. Children are "the crown of old men*" (Pr 17,6), sons are "the olive plants around the table" (Ps 128,3). But unlike certain moderns, the biblical authors do not forget that the child is an unfinished being, and they remember the importance of a firm education. Folly is anchored in his heart (Pr 22,15), caprice is his law (cf Mt 11,16-19); and lest he be tossed about by all winds (E 4, 14), he must be kept under tutelage (G 4,1ff). In view of these statements, the biblical affirmations about the religious dignity of the child are all the more remarkable.

I. GOD AND CHILDREN

In the OT, by reason of his native weakness and imperfection, the child seems to be a *privileged one of God*. The Lord Himself is the protector of the orphan and the avenger of his rights (Ex 22,21ff; Ps 68,6). He showed His paternal tenderness* and His care for the education of Israel, "When he was a child" from the time of the exodus from Egypt and the sojourn in the desert (Ho 11,1-4).

Children are not excluded from the *worship* of Yahweh. They participate even in penitential supplications (Jl 2,16; Jdt 4,10f), and God prepares for Himself praise from the mouths of children and very young ones (Ps 8,2f=Mt

21,16). He will likewise go into the heavenly Jerusalem, where the elect will have the experience of the "maternal" love of God (Is 66,10-13). Even a psalmist, to express his confident abandonment to the Lord, did not find a better image than that of a young child who sleeps on his mother's bosom (Ps 131,2).

Moreover, God does not hesitate to choose certain children as the first beneficiaries and messengers of His revelation* and of His *salvation**. Little Samuel receives the Word of Yahweh and faithfully passes it on (1 S 1—3); David is singled out in preference to his older brothers (1 S 16,1-13); young Daniel shows himself wiser than the ancients of Israel in saving Susanna (Dn 13,44-50).

Finally, a high point of Messianic prophecy is the birth of Emmanuel, the sign of deliverance (Is 7,14ff); and Isaiah proclaims the royal child who will re-establish right and justice together with the kingdom of David (9,1-6).

II. JESUS AND THE CHILDREN

Was it not fitting therefore that to inaugurate the new covenant the Son of God should make Himself a little child? Luke has carefully marked the stages of His childhood, a survey of which is as follows: newly born in a manger (Lk 2,12), a little child presented in the temple (2,27), a child obedient to His parents, and yet mysteriously independent of them in His dependence on His Father (2,43-51).

As an adult, Jesus adopts the same attitude toward children as God has. Just as He pronounced the beatitude* of the poor* He blesses* the children (Mk 10,16), thus revealing that they are on the same level when it comes to entering the kingdom. Children are the symbols of *the genuine disciples**; "It is to such as they that the kingdom of heaven belongs" (Mt 19,14 p). Indeed one should "accept the Kingdom as a little child" (Mk 10,15) and receive it in all simplicity as a gift of the Father instead of demanding it as due. He must "return to the state of children" (Mt 18,3) and consent to be "reborn" (Jn 3,5) in order to get into this kingdom. The secret of true grandeur is "making oneself little" like a child (Mt 18,4). Such is the true humility* without which one cannot become a son* of the heavenly Father.

The true disciples are precisely "the very little ones" to whom the Father has graciously wished to reveal, as He did before to Daniel, His secrets which are hidden from the wise (Mt

71

11,25f). In the language of the gospel, moreover, *little* and *disciple* seem at times to be equivalent (cf Mt 10,42 and Mk 9,41). Blessed are those who receive one of these little ones (Mt 18,5; cf 25,40), but woe to one who scandalizes* or despises them (18,6.10).

III. THE APOSTOLIC TRADITION

Paul is particularly aware of the state of imperfection that childhood represents (1 Co 13, 11; G 4,1; E 4,14). He urges Christians to concentrate on their growth* in order to arrive at the "fullness of Christ" (E 4,12-16). He reproaches the Corinthians for their childish behavior (1 Co 3,1ff) and warns them against a false idea of spiritual childhood. This seems to be a reaction to a false interpretation of the words of Jesus (1 Co 14,20; cf Mt 18,3f). However Paul is not unaware of the privilege of the little ones: "whatever is weak in the world, that is what God has chosen" (1 Co 1,27f). In his apostolic charity his own spontaneous attitude toward his neophytes, his "little children," is the tenderness of a mother (1 Th 2,7f; G 4, 19f; cf 1 Co 4,15).

He 5,11-14 contains a similar doctrine on the law of growth that is a part of Christian life; for there is no question of remaining at the stage of the little child feeding only on milk*. If 1 P 2,2 does urge the newly baptized* to long for the milk of God's word, like new born babes, it is in order that they should grow up to salvation. As for John, he speaks less of spiritual childhood than of the new birth* of the adopted sons* of God (1 Jn 3,1); but he speaks just as much like a father as Paul, when he addresses his "children" (2,1.18; cf Jn 13,33).

→Authority OT I 1.2; NT II 2—Confidence—Education—Humility III—Life II 1—Milk 3—Mother—New Birth—Old Age—Poor NT II—Simple.

LR gsa

CHURCH

If many contemporaries hardly go beyond the human aspect of the Church—a society in the world quite well defined by men united in faith and in cult—Scripture addresses faith and describes the Church as a mystery*, formerly hidden in God but now revealed and partly realized (E 1,9f; R 16,25f). It is the mystery of a people, though still sinners, who possess the pledge of salvation, since they are the extension of the body of Christ, the entrance to love. It is the mystery of a human-divine institution in which man can find light, pardon, and grace "for the praise of God's glory" (E 1,14). To this absolutely novel institution the first Greek-speaking Christians gave the biblical name of *ekklēsia*. The term indicated a continuity between Israel and the Christian people, and at the same time was suitable to take on a new meaning,

I. IMPLICATIONS OF THE WORD

In the Greek world, the word *ekklēsia*, of which *church* is only an equivalent translation, refers to the assembly of the *dēmos*, the people as a political force. This profane sense (cf Ac 19,32.39f) colors the religious sense when Paul treats of the current behavior of a Christian assembly* united "in church" (vg 1 Co 11,18).

In the LXX, on the contrary, the word describes an assembly convened for a religious act, often of worship (vg Dt 23, 1 K 8, Ps 22,26). It corresponds to the hb. *qāhāl*, which is used especially by the Deuteronomic school to describe the assembly at Horeb (vg Dt 4,10), on the steppes of Moab (Dt 31,30), or in the promised land (vg Js 8,35; Jg 20,2). It is also used by the Chronicler (vg 1 Ch 28,8; Ne 8,2) to describe the liturgical assembly of Israel during the time of the kings or after the exile. But if *ekklēsia* always translates *qāhāl*, this latter word is at times rendered by other words, particularly by *synagôgē* (vg Nm 16,3; 20,4; Dt 5,22), which more often translates the sacerdotal word *'ēdāh*. *Church* and *synagogue* are two almost synonymous terms (cf Jm 2,2); they will not be opposed in meaning until the Christians will appropriate the first for themselves and reserve the second for the obstinate Jews. The choice of *ekklēsia* by the LXX was doubtless influenced by the assonance *qāhāl ekklēsia*, but also by the etymological influences. *Ekklēsia* comes from *ekkaleô (I call from, I convoke)*; of itself it indicates that Israel, the people of God, was the assembly of men convoked by divine initiative. And it recalled a sacerdotal expression in which the idea of call was expressed: *klētē hagia*, the literal translation of *miqrā'qodeš*, "religious assembly" (Ex 12,16; Lv 23,3; Nm 29,1).

It is only natural that Jesus, in founding a new people of God which was a continuation of the old, should have called it by a biblical name for religious assembly (He must have said in Aramaic either 'edta or kenista, most frequently translated by synagōgē, or more probably qehala), a name translated by ekklēsia in Mt 16,18. Likewise the first Christian generation, which knew itself as the new people* of God (1 P 2,10), prefigured by "the church in the desert" (Ac 7,38), adopted a scriptural term which was very suitable to point them out as the "Israel* of God" (G 6,16; cf Ap 7,4; Jm 1,1; Ph 3,3). This term had, moreover, the advantage of including the theme of the call God gratuitously gives in Jesus Christ to the Jews, then to the gentiles, to form "the holy assembly" of the last time (cf 1 Co 1,2; R 1,7: "these called holy").

II. PREPARATION FOR AND COMPLETION OF THE CHURCH

For a long time God has prepared for the reunion of His scattered children (Jn 11,52). The Church is the community of men who are heirs of salvation* in Jesus Christ (Ac 2,47): "we, the saved," writes Paul (1 Co 1,18). Now the divine plan* of salvation, if it culminates in this community, was nonetheless conceived "before the creation of the world" (E 1,4) and outlined among men since Abraham, even since Adam's appearance.

1. *First creation and new creation.* From the beginning man was called to society (Gn 1,27; 2,18) and to propagation (1,28) while living at ease with God (3,8). But sin* cuts across the divine plan. Instead of remaining head of a people called to live with God, Adam is the father of a humanity divided by hate* (4,8; 6,11), dispersed by pride* (11,8f), fleeing its creator (3,8; 4,14). There will be need, then, of a new Adam* (1 Co 15,45; Col 3,10f) to start a new creation* (2 Co 5,17f; G 6,15), where the life of friendship with God will be restored (R 5,12...), where humanity will be again unified (Jn 11,52), and its members reconciled (E 2,15-18). Such will be the Church prepared by Israel. The Bible situates the history of Abraham and his descendants in the universal history of the world where sin displays its consequences. In this way the Bible shows that the Church, the true people of Abraham (R 4,11f), should insert itself in the world and there be

the answer to sin, to its discords, and the death* proceeding from sin. Deluge traditions have already provided Israel with the example of a just man placed by God at the beginning of a new creation after the widespread diffusion of sin. This universal salvation given by means of the water* to Noah's descendants was a figure* of that salvation, rich in another way, which Christ would bring by baptism* (1 P 3,20f).

2. *Old and new Israel.* The election* of Abraham, sealed by covenant* (Gn 15,18), starts the decisive process of forming a people* of God. From this blessed race of which He is the origin will come Christ. He will fulfill all the promises* (G 3,16). He will found the people who are the real spiritual descendants of Abraham* the believer (Mt 3,9 p; Jn 8,40; G 4,21-31; R 2,28f; 4,16; 9,6ff). By entrance into the Church of Jesus Christ through faith all nations* will be blessed in Abraham (G 3,8f= Gn 12,3 LXX; cf Ps 47,10).

Between Israel, the carnal descendant of the patriarchs, and the Church there is both break and continuity. Accordingly the NT applies to the new people of God names of the old, but by way of transpositions and contrasts. The two are the ekklēsia, but the word now signifies the mystery, unknown in the OT, of the body* of Christ (E 1,22f); its worship* of God is completely spiritual (R 12,1). The Church is Israel*, but the Israel of God (G 6,16), in a spiritual, not a physical sense (1 Co 10,18). She is a purchased people—purchased by the blood* of Christ (Ac 20,28; 1 P 2,9f; E 1,14) and also taken from among the heathen (Ac 15,14). She is the bride, the one without flaw (E 5,27), no longer the adulterous spouse (Ho; Jr 2—3; Ez 16). She is the vine*, no longer wild (Jr 2,21) but fruitful (Jn 15,1-8). She is the holy remnant* (Is 4,2f). She is the flock, not to be called together once (Jr 23,3) and later dispersed (Ze 13,7ff), but the last flock of her immolated and resurrected shepherd* (Jn 10). She is the Jerusalem* from on high, free now from slavery (G 4,24f). She is the people of the new covenant* predicted by the prophets (Jr 31,31ff; Ez 37,26ff). The new covenant, however, is sealed by the blood of Christ (Mt 26.28 p; He 9,12ff; 10,16), who is its mediator* for all nations (Is 42,6). The charter of the Church's covenant is no longer the law* of Moses, incapable of giving life (G 3,21), but the law of the Spirit* (R 8,2) inscribed in the heart (Jr 31,33f; Ez 36,27; cf 1 Jn 2,27). She is the kingdom* of the saints announced by Daniel and prefigured by the Davidic assembly of the Chronicler. She is no longer an organization for the material welfare of one nation (Jn 18, 36), but a life principle visible everywhere, a spiritual suggestion of an invisible, eternal kingdom where death will be destroyed (1 Co 15,25f; Ap 20,14). Finally, the temple* of the new economy is the resurrected body* of Christ (Jn 2,21f). It is not made by human hands (Mk 14,58) nor is it destructible (Mt 16,18). Since the Church is the body of Christ, it is equally the new temple (2 Co 6,16; E 2,21; 1 P 2,5); it is the place of a presence* and a worship*, surpassing the old and universally accessible (Mk 11,17).

III. FOUNDATION OF THE CHURCH BY JESUS

The OT prepares for the Church and prefigures it. Jesus reveals and founds the Church.

1. *The stages of the Church*. The mind of Jesus is registered in His proclamation of the kingdom* of heaven. In this framework He reveals, in a prophetic language where diverse elements are not always distinguishable, that the heavenly phase of the kingdom (Mt 13,43; 25,31-46) will be preceded by a phase of slow earthly growth (13,31f). And during the period of waiting for the harvest* the cockle of sin sown by the Evil One must grow together with the good grain (13,24-30.36-43). Two stages will mark the earthly period. First is the mortal life of Jesus. By His preaching, His action over Satan, and the formation of the Messianic community, He establishes the kingdom as present (Mt 12,28; Lk 17,21). The second stage is the time of the Church in the strict sense (Mt 16,18). Three major events will begin the time of the Church: first, the sacrifice* of Jesus setting up (Mt 26,28) this "community of the new covenant" eager for the perfect cult (cf Ml 3,1-5). Jeremiah had hoped for this pure form of worship in the time of Josiah (2 K 23) but transposed it to the eschatological future (Jr 31). Groups at Qumrân and at Damascus believed they represented the purified cult. Secondly there is His resurrection, after which He will gather together His scattered flock once more in Galilee (Mk 14,27f). And finally there is the destruction of Jerusalem (Mt 23, 37ff; cf Lk 21,24), the sign of the Church taking the place of the Jewish people as well as a prelude to the last judgment.

2. *Calling and training the disciples*. During His mortal life, Jesus collects and trains disciples*, to whom He reveals mysteries* of the kingdom (Mt 13,10-17 p). They are the "small flock" (Lk 12,32) of the good shepherd (Jn 10) announced by the prophets, the kingdom of the saints (Dn 7,18-22). Jesus envisaged the group's survival and increase after His death, and He gives the broad outlines of its future status. He intends His prophecies about the persecution of His followers (Mt 10,17-25 p; Jn 15,18...), and probably His parables on the mixing of the just and sinners too (Mt 22,11f; 13,24-30.36-43.47-50), to look beyond the time of His earthly life. And above all His instructions to the twelve suppose a certain period of time.

a) *The twelve*. Jesus chooses from His disciples twelve intimates who will be the nucleus and the leaders of the new Israel (Mk 3,13-19 p; Mt 19,28 p). He subjects them to an apprenticeship: the baptismal rite (Jn 4,2), preaching, fighting the evil spirits* and sicknesses* (Mk 6,7-13 p). He teaches them to prefer service to holding first place (Mk 9,35), to give priority to the "lost sheep" (Mt 10,6), not to fear inevitable persecutions (10,17...), to gather together in His name* for common prayer (18,19f), to forgive one another (18,21-35), and not to expel known sinners from the congregation without first trying persuasion (18,21-18). In tracing back to Jesus some of its most ancient practices (eg compare Mt 18,15-20 with 1 Co 5,1-13; 2 Co 13,1; 1 Tm 5,19) the Church has shown that it is by reference to the pre-paschal experience of the twelve that she has to discover her rules of life.

b) *Universal mission of the twelve*. The early missionary period of the apostles* does not exceed the confines of Israel (Mt 10,5f). Only after Jesus' resurrection will they be commanded to teach and baptize all nations* (Mt 28,19). But even before His death Jesus announces that the heathen can enter the kingdom. The "sons of the kingdom" (Mt 8,12), that is, the Jews*, who had a priority, will see this priority taken away (Mt 21,43) since they refused to be "gathered" (Mt 23,37) by Christ. In place of the Jewish people, excluded provisionally (cf Mt 23,39; R 11,11-32), pagans will enter (Mt 8,11f; Lk 14,21-24; Jn 10,16) on equal footing (Mt 20,1-16) with the Jewish nucleus of repentant sinners who have believed in Jesus (Mt 21,31ff).

Thus the Church, the first real kingdom not of this world (Jn 18,36), will fulfill and surpass the most daring universalistic prophecies of the OT (vg Jon; Is 19,16-25; 49,1-6). Jesus does not link the Church in any way with the earthly triumph of Israel, in which He Himself is not interested. A hard lesson for the multitude (Jn 6,15-66) and even for the twelve (Ac 1,6); they will understand it well only after Pentecost. Still the twelve will not attempt to structure their universal mission on a retaliation against their own nation. They will preach loyalty to imperial authorities (R 13,1...; 1 P 2,13f). The norm for Church-State relations they will find in Christ's saying: "Give to Ceasar the things that are Caesar's and to God the things that are God's" (Mt 22,21 p). To the emperor, the tax and everything required by the just demands of the State for the national temporal good (R 13,6f); to God the rest, that is, our whole being. For it is God's sovereign right preached by the Church which creates, surpasses, and judges Caesar's right (R 13,1).

c) *Authority of the twelve.* Leaders need power. Jesus promises it to the twelve: Peter* is the rock* that insures Church stability; he has the responsibility of the major-domo who opens or closes the gates* of the heavenly city, and has the exercise of disciplinary and teaching powers (Mt 16,18f; cf Lk 22,32; Jn 21). The apostles are to repeat the Lord's Supper (Lk 22,19); beyond this they have the same power "to bind and loose," which will pass judgment especially on men's conscience (Mt 18,18; Jn 20,22f). These texts already reveal the nature of the Church of which Jesus Christ is creator and Lord. She will be an organized and visible society, inaugurating here below the kingdom of God. She is constructed on the rock. She perpetuates Christ's presence by exercising apostolic powers and by the eucharist. She will conquer hell* and seize its victims. Thus is the Church the source of life and of mercy.

In Jesus' mind the Church's mission* will last as long as the world. The same will be true of the visible structure and the powers given for this mission. Certainly a large segment of the apostolic office cannot be passed on. The location of the apostles* as witnesses* of Jesus during His life and after His resurrection is unique in history. But when the risen Jesus, according to Matthean theology, commands the twelve to teach, baptize, direct, and when He promises to be with them always until the end of the world (Mt 28,20), He lets them see the permanence of these powers throughout all future generations,

even after the apostles' death. Thus will the early Church understand the powers. Apostolic powers will there continue to be exercised by leaders whom the apostles will choose and consecrate for this task by the imposition* of hands (2 Tm 1,6). Today, too, the episcopal powers have no source other than these words of Jesus.

IV. BIRTH AND LIFE OF THE CHURCH

1. *Passover and Pentecost.* The Church is born at Christ's Passover*, when He "passes" from this world to His Father (Jn 13,1). With Christ delivered from death and becoming a "life-giving spirit" (1 Co 15,45), a new* humanity (E 2,15; G 6,15), a new creation* arises. The fathers often said that the Church, the new Eve, was born from Christ's side during the death sleep, just as the old Eve came from the side of Adam asleep. John's testimony about the effects of the spear thrust (Jn 19,34f) suggests this view, if it is true for John that the blood and water symbolize first the sacrifice of Christ and the Spirit which animates the Church, then the sacraments of baptism and the eucharist which give her life.

But the Church body lives only when it is the body* of Christ resurrected* ("awakened," cf E 5,14), diffusing the Spirit* (Ac 2,33). This outpouring of the Spirit begins on the day of Easter (Jn 20,22) when Jesus "breathes" the revivifying Spirit (Jn 20,22; cf Gn 1,2) on the disciples whom He has finally reassembled (cf Mk 14,27) as leaders of the new people of God (cf. Ez 37,9). Luke for his part makes Pentecost* day, which in Judaism was a commemoration of the Passover and the gift of the covenant*, the occasion of the great charismatic outpouring (Ac 2,4), with an eye both to the witness* of the twelve, and to the manifestation of the Church to the world at large. This day is for her like an official birthday. Pentecost is for her a little of what it had been for Jesus—conceived of the Holy Spirit (Lk 1,35), anointed* by this Spirit at the dawn of His Messianic mission (Ac 10,38; Mt 3,16 p); and what it is for each Christian—the gift of the Spirit by the imposition* of hands, the seal* of His work in baptism (Ac 8,17; cf 2,38).

2. *Spread of the Church.* The Church grows rapidly after Pentecost. Entrance is first by accepting the word* of the apostles (Ac 2,41), which engenders faith* (2,44; 4,32) in Jesus resurrected, Lord and Christ (2,36), leader and

savior (5,31); then by receiving the baptism* of water (2,41), followed by an imposition of hands which confers the Spirit and His charisms* (8,16f; 19,6). According to Luke (Ac 2,42), a fourfold fidelity is needed for living membership: faithfulness to the teaching* of the apostles which deepens the first faith engendered by the proclamation of the message of salvation, faithfulness to the fraternal communion* (koinônia), to the breaking of bread*, and to common prayer. Especially by the breaking of bread, that is, by the eucharistic* meal (cf 1 Co 11,20.24), is one mind (Ac 2,46) created. Here is felt the presence of the resurrected Christ who so recently ate and drank with the twelve (Ac 10,41). Here His sacrifice is "proclaimed" and hope for His return kept alive (1 Co 11,26).

At Jerusalem, the communion* of spirit goes so far as to inspire a voluntary community of material goods (Ac 4,32-35; He 13,16), recalling what was of obligation at Qumrân. But Luke himself allows a glance at some shadows in the picture (Ac 5,2; 6,1). The faithful are grouped under the authority of the apostles*. Peter is in command (Ac 1,13f), exercising in concert with them the primacy he received from Christ. An assembly of elders has a subordinate share in the authority of the apostles (Ac 15,2); then, after their departure, in the authority of James (21,18), who becomes head of the local Church. Seven men filled with the Spirit, among whom are Stephen and Philip, are put in charge of attending to the "Greek-speaking" Christians (6,1-6).

The fearlessness of these men filled with the Spirit, especially of Stephen, causes their dispersion (Ac 8,1.4). The dispersion permits the spread of the Church, from Judea (8,1; 9,31-43) to Antioch (11,19-25); from Antioch "to the ends of the world" (Ac 1,8; cf R 10,18; Col 1,23), or at least to Rome (Ac 28,16-31). The reverses Paul meets from the Jews facilitate grafting the wild pagan stock to the trunk pruned of the chosen people (R 11,11-18). But neither Paul nor Peter, who in baptizing Cornelius made a decisive gesture not contradicted by certain excessive concessions made to the Judaizers (G 2,11-14), allows pagans entering the Church to be subjected to Jewish practices still observed by the "Jewish" Christians (Ac 10,14; 15,29).

3. Thus the originality of the Church in the face of Judaism is affirmed, her catholicity achieved, the missionary command received

from Christ carried out. Her unity* dominates places and peoples, for all the communities know they are cells of one single ekklēsia. The extension of this biblical world, from its original application to the Christians in Jerusalem, to the pagan-Christian gatherings; contributions to the collection by Paul's converts for the Jerusalem Christians (2 Co 8,7-24); the appeal to Church practice to determine a point of discipline (1 Co 11,16; 14,33); mutual interest and concern (Ac 15,12; 21,20; 1 Th 1,7ff; 2,14; 2 Th 1,4); and greetings (1 Co 16,19f; R 16,6; Ph 3,2f)—all of these are signs characterizing a true awareness of a Church.

V. CHRISTIAN REFLECTION ON THE CHURCH

1. All the communal aspects of salvation in Jesus Christ interest the Church. Paul is, however, the only inspired writer who investigated the mystery for himself and in his own name. In his Damascus vision he had there and then the revelation of a mysterious identity between Christ and the Church (Ac 9,4f); reflection stimulated by experience is added to this first intuition. Indeed, as he builds* up the Church, Paul discovers all her dimensions. First of all, he reflects on the vital union which converts contract with Christ and with one another by the baptismal rite, and which the Spirit makes almost tangible by His charisms*. To the Corinthians, who turn the gifts* away from their "building" and unifying role, he recalls this fundamental point: "We are all baptized in one Spirit to form one Body" (1 Co 12,13). The baptized constituting the Church are, therefore, members of this one body* of Christ, and the eucharistic bread is the bond of living cohesion (1 Co 10,17). This unity of faith and of baptism makes it impossible for anyone to say he follows Cephas or Apollos or Paul, as if Christ could be divided (1 Co 1,12f; 3,4). To demonstrate and consolidate this unity Paul organizes a collection for the "saints" in Jerusalem (1 Co 16,1-4; 2 Co 8—9; R 15,26f).

Somewhat later, captivity and the cosmic speculations he has to fight at Colossae take Paul away from more immediate problems. Both contribute to a broadening of his horizons. The entire divine plan he sees with the eyes of the apostle* of the gentiles (G 2,8f; R 15,20) appears in all its splendor (E 1). Then the Ekklēsia in general is no longer one or other local community (as it was shortly before, with the possible exceptions of 1 Co 12.28; 15,9; G 1,13). It is in its amplitude and universality the body of Christ, the place of reconciliation for Jews and Gentiles forming a single perfect man* (Col 1,18-24; E 1,23; 5,23ff; cf 4,13). On this basic idea Paul superimposes the image of Christ, head of the Church. Christ is distinct from His Church, but she is united to Him as to her head (E 1,22f; Col 1,18); in this she shares the condition of the angelic powers (Col 2,10). Above all the Church is united to Christ as her principle of life, cohesion, and growth* (Col 2,19; E 4,15f): the incomplete Body grows "toward the One who is the Head," the glorious Christ (4,15). Frequently the image of the temple*, built on Christ as the cornerstone and on the apostles and prophets as foundations (E 2,20f), interjects itself into the body motif to form a verbal *chassé* (a dance set to partners): the building grows (E 2,21) and the body is built (4,12.16). In E 5,22-32, ideas of body and head combine with the biblical image of the bride: Jesus*, leader (=head) of the Church, is also the Savior who loved the Church as a *fiancée* (comp 2 Co 11,2); He sacrifices Himself to communicate to her by baptism, sanctification, and purification, to bring her resplendent before Himself, and to take her as His bride. Finally, a last notion merges with the preceding ideas to define the Church according to Paul: the Church is the choice part of this fullness* (*plērōma*) which resides in Christ because He is God (Col 2,9), savior of men brought into His body (E), and head of the whole universe ruled by cosmic powers (Col 1,19f). She herself can be called *plērōma* (E 1,23); this she is because Christ "fills" her and she in turn "fills" Him in completing His body by her progressive growth (E 4,13). The beginning and end of all this is the fullness of God Himself (3,19).

2. Without using the word, John insinuates a profound theology of the Church. His allusions to a new exodus* (Jn 3,14; 6,32f; 7,37ff; 8,12) call to mind a new people of God, which the biblical images of bride (3,29), of flock (10, 1-16), and of vine* (15,1-17) directly describe. The small group of disciples set apart from the world (15,19; cf 1,39.42f) constitutes the new people in embryo. The passage from this group of disciples to a Church is effected by the death and resurrection of Jesus. Christ dies "to bring together the dispersed" (11,52) into one flock with no distinction among Jews, Samaritans, and Greeks (10,16; 12,20.32; 4,21ff.30-42). He

goes up to His Father to give the Spirit to His followers (16,7; 7,39), especially to His representatives responsible for forgiving sins (20,21f). The Church will reap the harvest* which Christ sowed (4,38) and thus extend Christ's mission* (20,21). John is in a position to testify to this, he who touched the Word made flesh (1 Jn 1,1) and gave the Spirit to Philip's converts (Ac 8, 14-17—contrast this with Lk 9,54). But by native disposition and preference John is attracted to the Church's interior life. Members of the Church are united under the staff of Peter (21). They draw the wellsprings of life from union with Christ, the vine (15); this union is made real in baptism (3,5) and the eucharist (6). They meditate together on the words of Christ under the direction of the Spirit (14,26); by mutual love (13,33-35) they bear the fruit* God expects of them (15,12.16f). By all of this the Church shows her unity* which has for its source and model that very unity of the divine persons who are present in one and all (17). Familiar with persecution* (15,18—16,4), she faces it with triumphant confidence; since victory* over the world* and its prince is already won (16,33).

The last idea is central in the Apocalypse. There the Church is represented alternately as the holy city (Ap 11,1-3), then as the woman* struggling with the dragon (Satan*) (Ap 12), who uses the beast* (the pagan empire) to persecute the saints but whose days are numbered; then as the temple and its environs, in which a square of true believers is preserved while in the public place the beast kills two prophet-witnesses (11,1-13). Does not the millenium of ch. 20, which is not a time of earthly triumph for the Church, describe an interior spiritual renovation (comp 20,6 and 5,10; and cf Ez 37,10=Ap 11,11), or the happiness of martyrs even before the general judgment? At all events, it is above all for the new Jerusalem*, heaven*, that the Church aspires (3,13; 21,1-8; 21,9—22,5). "The Spirit and the Bride say: Come!" (22,17).

In the heavenly life, when all that the prophets foretold will be fulfilled, sin will be totally eliminated (Is 35,8; Ap 21,27), as well as suffering and death (Ap 21,4; cf Is 25,8; 65,19); and then the dispersion* of Babel*, of which Pentecost* is already the antithesis, will be given its final answer (Is 66,18; Ap 7,9f). Then too all caricatures will disappear: arrogant empires, "synagogues of Satan" (Ap 2,9; 3,9). Only "the abode of God with men" (21,3) will remain, "the new universe" (v 5).

VI. OUTLINE
OF A THEOLOGICAL SYNTHESIS

The Church is created by God, built up by Christ, and inhabited by the Spirit (1 Co 3,16; E 2,22). As such the Church is entrusted to men, to the apostles "chosen by Jesus through the Holy Spirit" (Ac 1,2), then to those who will receive by the imposition of hands the charism to govern (1 Tm 4,14; 2 Tm 1,6).

The Spirit (Jn 16,13) guides the Church, the "pillar and support of truth" (1 Tm 3,15), the Church perpetually capable of "guarding the deposit of sound instruction" received from the apostles (2 Tm 1,13f). This power of protecting the deposit of faith is the power to enunciate it and make it explicit without error. Formed into the body of Christ by means of the gospel (E 3,6), born of one baptism (E 4,5), nourished with one bread (1 Co 10,17), she gathers into one people (G 3,28) the children of one God and Father (E 4,6). The Church eliminates human divisions and unites into one people Jews and pagans (E 2,14ff), civilized and barbarian, masters and slaves, men and women (1 Co 12,13; Col 3,11; G 3,28). This unity is catholic, as has been said since the 2nd century. The Church is made to reconcile all human diversities (cf Ac 10,13: "Kill and eat"), to adapt herself to all cultures (1 Co 9,20ff), to embrace the whole universe (Mt 28,19).

The Church is holy* (E 5,26f), not only in her head and structure, but also in her members sanctified by baptism. There are sinners* in the Church (1 Co 5,12); but they are personalities torn between their sin and the demands of their entry into the assembly of the "saints" (Ac 9, 13). The Church, like Christ, does not turn them away but offers them pardon* and purification (Jn 20,23; Jm 5,15f; I Jn 1,9); the noxious weed can always become wheat before the visit of the reaper (Mt 13,30). The Church is not an end in itself, rather she leads to the definitive kingdom* which the parousia of Christ will substitute for her. Nothing defiled will enter this kingdom (Ap 21,27; 22,15). Persecutions* intensify the Church's aspiration to be transformed in the heavenly Jerusalem*.

The perfect model of the Church's faith, hope, and charity is Mary*; she witnessed the Church's birth on Calvary (Jn 19,25) and in the Cenacle (Ac 1,14). Paul is filled with an intense (1 Co 4, 15; G 4,19) and practical love of the Church. He is consumed with "care* for all the Churches" (2 Co 11,28) and with a desire to mediate the infinite fruits of the cross* by his great suffering*

(1 Co 4,9-13; 2 Co 1,5-9). Thus he "completes in himself what is lacking to Christ's trials* for His body the Church*" (Col 1,24). His life as "a worker for the Church" (1,25) is an example*, particularly for those who will continue the apostolic work.

All the members of the Christian people (*laos*), not merely leaders, are called to serve* the Church by using their charisms. They are called to live on the vine like branches loaded with the fruit* of charity. They are asked to be a credit to their priesthood* (1 P 2,5) by the sacrifice* of faith (Ph 2,17) and a pure life according to the Spirit (R 12,1; 1 Co 6,19; Ph 3,3). The Christian must take active part in the worship* of the assembly. If he has received the particular charism of virginity*, he must adhere solely to the Lord; if married, he is to model conjugal life on the nuptial union of Christ and His Church (E 5,21-33). The holy city which Jesus loved as a fertile bride (5,25) and whom "every man calls: 'Mother'" (Ps 87,5=G 4,26), deserves our filial love. We love her, however, insofar as we continue to build* her up.

→Apostles—Apparitions of Christ 5.7—Authority NT II—Body of Christ III—Brother NT—Build III—Calling III—Charisms II—Communion NT 1—Dispersion 2—Election NT II —Flood 3—Fruitfulness III 3—Fullness 3—Growth 2 d. 3—Head 3.4—Heresy—House III —Israel NT 2—Jerusalem NT II 3—Jesus Christ I 3; II 1 d. 2 b c—Kingdom NT III 2—Mary V—Mediator II 2—Ministry—Mission NT II—Mother II 3—Mystery NT II 2—Nations NT II—Peace III 4—Pentecost II 3—People *C*—Peter 3 a—Plan of God NT—Prophet NT II 3—Remnant NT—Revelation NT I 2 a—Schism NT 2— Shepherd & Flock NT 2—Sign NT II 3—Spirit of God NT IV, V 4 —Spouse NT—Temple NT II 2, III 2—Time NT II—Tradition NT II 2—Trial/Temptation NT II—Unity III—Vine 3—Virginity NT 1.3—War NT II—Woman NT 3—Worship NT II 2 —Works NT II 3.

PT gsa

CIRCUMCISION

OT

1. *Circumcision as a sign* of membership in a community.* Circumcision was a practice of

many peoples, usually in connection with formal entry into the adult community or with marriage. Israel must have received circumcision as an ancient custom; it appears in texts that seem to be very ancient, suggesting the use of flint knives (Ex 4,24ff; Js 5,2-9); and yet it is nowhere prescribed in the really ancient texts. Circumcision, then, is a fact that is not discussed or justified. Later, it was a cause of shame* not to be circumcised (Js 5,9; Gn 34, 14). Israel always felt repelled by the uncircumcised (1 S 17,26.36; Jg 14,3; 1 Ch 10,4; Ha 2, 16; Ez 44,7ff): the uncircumcised is not really a man. Thus circumcision is a rite signifying membership in a community.

2. *Circumcision as the sign of the covenant.* This rite cannot, however, help having a religious meaning, for it is ordered by Yahweh (Js 5,2) under threat of His wrath (Ex 4,24). A significant step was taken especially in the priestly literature where circumcision becomes the physical sign of the covenant*, a sign that every male Israelite must carry in his flesh from the eighth day after his birth. And the blood* then shed (cf Ex 4,26) will often (at least in later Judaism) be called "covenant-blood."

Circumcision is connected with Abraham, the father of the people (Gn 17,9-14; 21,4), and is prescribed by the Law (Lv 12,3). It is a necessary condition for admission to celebration of the Passover* where Israel affirms itself a people redeemed and saved by Yahweh (Ex 12,44.48). When persecuting pagan authorities forbid it (1 M 1,48), circumcision will become a symbol of the choice open to the Jews. Some will seek to hide their circumcision (1 M 1,15), while others will risk their lives by circumcising their children (1 M 1,60; 2 M 6,10) and forcing circumcision on those who hesitate (1 M 2,46).

3. *Circumcision of the heart.* Israel could be tempted to consider circumcision sufficient to gain a share in the blessings promised* in the covenant. Jeremiah was clearly the first to make the point that physical circumcision was practiced by many peoples and so had no value in itself (Jr 9,24). What mattered was to strip off the foreskin of the heart* (Jr 4,4), according to the metaphor in wide use (6,10; Lv 19,23). The Deuteronomist makes the same call to circumcision of the heart, by which he means an exclusive love of Yahweh and the practice of fraternal charity (Dt 10,12-22), a call that finds its echo in the priestly tradition itself (Lv 26,41; Ez 44,7ff). This circumcision of the heart which

Israel of itself cannot achieve will be given on the day* of salvation by God. "The Lord will circumcise your heart. . .so that you may love the Lord. . .and thus you will live" (Dt 30,6). In this same sermon (30,12), Paul will rightly find the proclamation of salvation by grace* and by faith* (R 10,6ff).

NT

1. *The practice of circumcision.* Jesus, like John the Baptist, was circumcised (Lk 1,59; 2, 21). As His disciples, He was first (Mk 7,27) "at the service of the circumcised" (R 15,8). But His gospel also had to be proclaimed to the nations* (R 15,9-12), a fact which would call into question the practice of circumcision. Must all submit to his rite of belonging to the posterity of Abraham? As frequently happens, a practical answer preceded theory. In some places, converted pagans were baptized without an obligation to be circumcised (Ac 10—11). In spite of pressure from the Jewish-Christians, the Jerusalem council approved by decree the freedom which had been authorized by Peter's vision (Ac 10,45ff) and had already been practiced in this matter of circumcision (Ac 15).

This decision could have been based on the practical need to facilitate the entry of pagans who might be repelled by an act thought to be a mutilation. But the decision had doctrinal significance, as Paul made clear at the time of a similar crisis in Galatia. The uncircumcised pagan was admittedly far from God (cf Col 2, 13): but if he were circumcised he must bear the whole burden of the Law, which no man could do (G 3,2; 5,10; 6,13). For both reasons he is heading toward destruction. Furthermore, to make circumcision necessary for salvation is to void the gratuitous promise God made to Abraham before his circumcision. Circumcision came later, not as the source but as the seal of the justice* given by God's promise and Abraham's faith (G 3,6-29; R 4,9-12). To require circumcision would render valueless the cross* of Christ, which saves by fulfilling God's gratuitous promise (G 5,11f).

2. *Spiritual circumcision.* Henceforth, the prophets' call for "circumcision of the heart," for an inner ratification of the external rite, is fulfilled by wiping out the racial distinctions presupposed by the rite. "Neither circumcision nor lack of circumcision has any value, but only faith working in charity" (G 5,6). What matters is "being a new creation" (G 6,15), and

"observing the commandments of God" 1 Co 7,19). A man's state before his call makes no difference, since faith justifies the circumcised as well as the uncircumcised. God is the God of all (R 3,29); Christ is all in all (Col 3,11).

Though the rite was suppressed, the word continued to have a meaning. Believers could say, "We are the circumcised for we worship in the Spirit of God" (Ph 3,3). Thus the prophetic oracles are fulfilled* by a true circumcision that was hidden, spiritual, interior (R 2,28f), not done by the hand of man (Col 2,11). It is identical with baptism* which assimilates the believer to "Christ's circumcision, stripping off the body* of flesh" (Col 2,11f) and bringing him to live with Christ forever.

→Abraham II 4—Baptism I 2, IV 4—First Fruits II—Heart I 3, II 1—Jew I 1—Law C II, III 1—Sexuality II 1—Sign OT II 2; NT II 1.
CW wjw

CITY

As one way in which social life is experienced in a certain type of civilization, city life is a human reality with which biblical revelation cannot fail to come into contact. It may do so in order to pass a value-judgment upon it, or it may use it as a point on which to base revelations.

OT

1. *From nomadic life to city life.* Israel is aware that city life goes back far beyond the Hebrew patriarchs. After contrasting the pastoral life of Abel and the agricultural life of Cain (Gn 4,2), Genesis credits the latter with the foundation of the first city, which he names after his son Enoch (a play on the word meaning "dedication" 4,17). But it is only after the break caused by the flood that we see the foundation of the great cities around which the Mesopotamian empires are organized (10, 10f). Abraham's ancestors lived in their territory (11,31). But in the time of the patriarchs pastoral life is essentially nomadic or semi-nomadic, on the fringes of the cities of Canaan. During the time spent in Egypt the cities built by the enslaved Hebrews are Egyptian fortresses (Ex 1,11). Thus the Exodus generation takes up again the traditional nomadic life in the steppes. It is only with the conquest of Canaan that Israel becomes accustomed once

and for all to agricultural and urban life: they receive towns, houses and plantations as a gift from God (Dt 6, 10f; Js 24,13). Only in a few fringe groups will there remain any attachment to the old nomadic customs, and in these cases it will be seen as a form of protest against the corruption of civilization (as with the Rechabites: Jr 35,6-10; cf 2 K 10,15ff).

2. *The ambiguity of urban civilization.* In spite of everything this new form of life is of ambiguous value from the religious point of view. For the peasants the town is a refuge against raiding parties or foreign armies; and many towns include a place of worship that is consecrated to Yahweh from now on. This is especially the case with Jerusalem, the city of David* (Ps 122,5) and centre of political power (Is 7,8), but also the city of the Great King* (Ps 48,4; cf 46,5), the place where the tribes assemble for worship and the sign of unity for all the people* (Ps 122,3f). However, this urban civilization falls an easy prey to the sins of Canaan (Am 3,9f; 5,7-12; Is 1,21-23), in the same way as important cities like Ninive and Babylon had been corrupted by paganism. And so the prophets promise the main cities and towns of Israel the same fate that they had promised to so many cities of the pagan world (Am 6,2; Mi 3,12): a ruin like that of Sodom and Gomorrah (cf Gn 19). Nor does this announcement of God's Judgment* spare the pagan cities: Tyre, Sidon and Babylon are the objects of similar threats.

3. *The two cities.* Nevertheless prophetic eschatology continues to allow a special place to the new Jerusalem* (Is 54; 60; 62), the religious centre of the holy land (cf Ez 45), while it foresees the final fall of the wicked cities, of which Babylon* is the type (Is 47). And finally apocalyptic literature will sketch the contrasting picture of the two cities: the city of nothingness (Is 24,7-13), the stronghold of the proud (25,2; 26,5), and the strong city, the refuge of the people of God, who are made up of the poor (26,1-6). These contrasting images of Judgment* and of Salvation* are the answer to the fundamental ambiguity of urban civilization, which is accepted as a gift from God but which is at the same time capable of bringing out the worst.

NT

1. *Salvation and the judgment of God.* The

background of urban civilization is present throughout the NT, both in Palestine and in the Roman Empire. And the proclamation of the Gospel* is adapted to this social situation, both in the time of Jesus and in the time of the apostles. But the welcome accorded to the Word* of God is very different in the different situations: Jesus is rejected by the cities of Galilee; Athens refuses the Gospel (Ac 17,16ff), while Corinth welcomes it (18,1-11); in Ephesus there are opportunities and opposition (1 Co 16, 8f). This is why Jesus repeats the anathemas of the prophets against the lakeside towns (Mt 11, 20-24 p) and against Jerusalem (Lk 19,41ff; 21,20-24 p; 23,28-31), which stand for their unbelieving inhabitants.

2. *The two cities.* Finally, even though the Jewish capital experiences God's judgment* already in apostolic times (Ap 11,2.8), Christian eschatology continues to be built around the theme of the two cities, when the Church of Jesus has to face the persecuting Roman Empire. The Apocalypse foretells the fall of the new Babylon (17,1-7; 18; 19,2), while at the end of time the new Jerusalem comes down from heaven to earth so that all the elect may be gathered together there (21). Moreover, the baptized have already come near it here below (He 12,22), since they have the rights of citizens (Ph 3,20). The city from above is even now their mother (G 4,25f); that is why they have no abiding city here below, for they are looking for the city of the future (He 13,14). Thus, the human experience of urban life makes it possible to bring out one essential aspect of the world of the future, toward which we are making our way (cf 11,16).

→Abide—Babel/Babylon—Build III 4—Church V 2—David 1—Earth—Gate OT I—Heaven VI — Holy NT V — House — Jerusalem — Stranger.

PG ems

CLOTHING

Along with food and shelter, clothing is a basic element of human existence (Si 29,21). Food and clothing are a blessing of God (Dt 10,18; cf Gn 28,20); whereas hunger and nakedness come as a punishment (Dt 28,48). Since clothing is a protection against the inclemencies of the weather, the poor man's cloak must not be kept in pawn when the night's cold begins to descend on him (Ex 22,25). In addition to these rudimentary observations, the symbolism of clothing develops in two other dimensions: it is a sign of a definite order coming from the Creator and likewise a symbol recalling the promise of a glory lost in Paradise.

I. CLOTHING: A REFLECTION OF THE DIVINE ORDER OF THE WORLD

The Creator brought the universe out of a primal chaos and gave every single thing its place in an ordered world. Thus it is that clothing appears as a sign of the human person both in his identity and individuality.

1. *Clothing and the human person.* At its first level, clothing protects the body from the weather and from glances which could reduce the person to an object of sexual* lust; such looks return the human person to the chaos of lack of personal individuality from which the Creator brought him. On this is based the prohibition of "lifting the robe," a protection for the family circle in itself (Gn 9,20-27), and in its maternal (Gn 34; 2 S 3) and conjugal (Dt 22, 13-24) aspects. Clothing here protects the private life of each individual.

Clothing also ensured the distinction of sexes and can symbolize their relations. Man and woman must wear different clothes (Dt 22,5; cf Lv 19,19). The woman veils her face for definite reasons, such as in premarital meeting of man and woman, where it is a kind of ritual consecration to the one who has chosen her (Gn 24,65). Wearing the veil corresponds to the gesture of the prospective bridegroom sharing what he has with the woman by "spreading the loose part of his cloak over her" (Rt 3,9; cf Dt 23,1). He is not thus thereby taking "possession" of her (cf Rt 4,7; Dt 25,9; Ps 60,10), but rather conferring on his chosen one the honor of his own person.

Clothing reflects the type of life lived in the social unit. For each part of the community clothing acts as a sign of harmonious life born of working together (sheep shearing: 1 S 25,4-8; weaving: Pr 31,10-31; Ac 18,3; tailoring: Ac 9, 39), of wise administration (Pr 31,30), and of mutual help. Giving one's cloak is a sign of brotherhood. Jonathan seals his covenant with David in this way (1 S 18,3f) because clothing is intimately united with the person, a union evident to those who love the person (Gn 37,33);

CLOTHING

in some cases this union is evident even by the scent of the clothes (Gn 27,15.27; Ct 4,11). The ostentatious luxury which is a shameless indictment of social disproportion and does nothing to remedy the different (Si 40,4; Jm 2,2), draws the curse of prophets and apostles. To clothe the naked is a command of justice (Ez 18,7) pertaining to the life of the community; its violation invites community disintegration. More than "making its members warm again" (Jb 31,20), this act makes a man enter anew the community life (Is 58,7); it is reproducing in the case of the naked man God's activity toward all men (Dt 10,18f)—it takes him out of the chaos. Without this act of justice, charity is dead (Jm 2,15). When Christ says "give even your cloak!" (Mt 5,40), He means that one must give his own person to the one who requests it.

2. *Clothing and human activities.* The same clothing is not worn at all times. Occasions are varied; for example, the profane and the sacred, work and the periods of celebration. If some work demands the removal of clothes (Jn 21,7), there is on the other hand a wide variety of festive garments.

A change of clothing can denote a transition from the profane to the sacred, as is the case of the people awaiting God's appearance (Ex 19,10; Gn 35,2), the priests on entering and leaving the inner sanctuary (Ex 28,2f; Lv 16,4; Ez 44.17ff; Ze 3); this is true also of the various divisions of the clean and unclean (Lv 13—15). Clothing too distinguishes the higher functions in Israel. Among the royal attire (1 K 22,30; Ac 12,21) there is a purple robe with gold clasps (1 M 10,20.62.64; 11,58; 14,44). To show approbation of the anointed king the people spread their garments under his feet (2 K 9,13; Mt 21, 8), for it is his task to cover them with glory (cf 2 S 1,24). The prophet wears a mantle over a cloth of skin (Ze 13,4; Mt 3,4 p), like the cloak Elijah threw over Elisha in giving him the prophetic vocation (1 K 19,19). This investiture can communicate the prophetic charism (2 K 2,13ff). The high priest is invested by "putting on the sacred vestments" (Lv 21,10). With these symbolic garments (Ex 28—29; Lv 16; Ez 44; Si 45,7-12) a "man beyond reproach" can "face the divine wrath, and the destroyer yields" (Ws 18,23ff; cf 1 M 3,49).

II. CLOTHING AND NAKEDNESS: SPIRITUAL SYMBOLS

Clothing is also a sign of the spiritual side of man, as is indicated in the Paradise narrative and in the accounts of sacred history.

1. *In Paradise.* Forbidden knowledge opened the eyes of Adam and Eve, and they knew they were naked (Gn 3,7). Until that moment, they had felt themselves in harmony with the divine atmosphere by a kind of grace which clothed them like a garment. Henceforth not their sex, but their entire body is signed with want before God's presence. A grass skirt no longer suffices to cover it. The sinners hide among the trees of the garden because their shame arises in the presence of the divine majesty: "I was afraid because I am naked." Now they no longer have a sign justifying a familiarity of approach to God, for they have lost the sense of belonging to the Lord. They are perpetually surprised by their nakedness, like a mirror which does not reflect God's image.

God, however, does not dismiss the sinners without clothing them in skin tunics (Gn 3,21), a covering that does not suppress their nakedness but is more a sign of their permanent call to the dignity they lost. Clothing will now indicate duality: the affirmation of fallen man's dignity and the possibility of once more clothing himself with a lost glory.

2. *The history of the covenant* is often symbolized with the help of clothing, which then means either the glory lost or promised. God begins an intimate communication of His glory through the covenant. As a shepherd He wraps the infant found in the vast desert waste (Dt 32,10). As a king, the skirts of His robe fill the temple (Is 6,1). As a spouse He spreads the skirt of His mantle over His people (Ez 16,8ff) and clothes them, not in the skins of animals, but "in fine linen and silk" as if He were to make them priests (cf Ex 28,5.39.42). Though Yahweh communicates His own splendor to His people (Ez 16,13f), the royal bride does not remain faithful. Ezekiel refers to the idolatrous customs of the high places; he frankly pursues the allegory and points to the bride exhibiting her nakedness and giving herself to everyone. "With her clothes she makes herself gaily colored shrines," and plays the harlot to all who pass by (16,15ff; cf Ho 2,9ff). When her clothing should not have been worn out, as once in the long sojourn in the desert (Dt 8,4), then

82

God watches as it decays, is tattered (Is 50,9), and is consumed by worms and moths (51,8).

Yet God's plan will be achieved by a counter measure drawing out of evil its remedy. First, Yahweh makes a naked land of Israel by turning the lust of her lovers to destructive fury (Ez 16,37; Jr 13,26) until only a remnant* finally reaches in utter destitution the benefit of restoration. Then, a Servant* "without beauty or eminence" is sent by Him to cure His people of their passions by humbling Himself even to death (Is 53,12). Thus Zion "as a bride" will be girded both by her destroyers and her rebuilders (49,17f). Then Yahweh, clothed with justice* as a shield, with vengeance* as a tunic, and draped in jealousy (59,17), comes to adorn His bride with the mantle of justice (61,10).

3. *Christ clothed in glory.* In order that Israel be thus adorned, Christ, the real Servant, must be stripped of His clothing (Mt 27,35; Jn 19,23), be given up to a parody of kingly investiture (Jn 19,2f...), and become an indistinguishable "man," deprived of legal status. But this man is the Son of God whose glory is incorruptible. Already at the transfiguration* His body is shown as glorious in the resplendence of His clothing (Mt 17,2). And He was able to restore the clothes of the possessed man at Gerasa (Mk 5,15; cf Ac 19,16). After the resurrection, like the announcing angels (Mt 28,3 p), the Lord keeps only His essential garment—radiance, a sign of His glory* (Ac 22,6-11; 10,30; cf 12,7). And the as yet unopened eyes of Mary Magdalene and of the travelers to Emmaus first see nothing more than a gardener or a fellow traveler (Jn 20,15; Lk 24,15f), for this glory is evident only to a rich faith. For the believer, Christ makes a burning, passionate advance, clothed in a mantle bearing the inscription, "King of kings and Lord of lords" (Ap 19,16).

4. *The clothing of the elect.* The orderly arrangement of the created universe is now apparent to the eyes of faith. As Paul says, the angels* perceive the total order (1 Co 11,10) and Adam reflects the glory of God in his unveiled face (2 Co 3,18), as does Christ who is his head (1 Co 11,3f). Eve was created as a complement rather than a copy of Adam (11,8f) and therefore should wear some sign of self-mastery in her subordinate role. Thus the veil by which she refuses to subject her "glory" (11,6.10.15) to indiscriminate looks (11,5.13; cf 1 Tm 2,9.14). This veil indicates an entire self-possession in her consecration—the opposite of alienation from self. Only on resurrection day will this glory of hers be made evident.

Actually, every man is called to enter in the movement toward glory started by Christ. If God can make a splendid crop from a bare and tiny seed tossed in the earth, He can make the body of each man incorruptible (1 Co 15,37.42); over the perishable clothing that is the human body He can clothe the man with the imperishable (2 Co 5,3ff). When this occurs, humanity leaves its naked condition for freedom, sonship, and the right of divine inheritance by "putting on Christ." Then God makes a perfect and single community of those who by faith and baptism (G 3,25ff) have put off the old man and put on the new man (Col 3,10; E 4,24); they are one in Christ (G 3,28), living by a new principle, the Spirit. The members of this community still have to struggle, but using the "armor of light" (R 13,12) so that even nakedness itself will not be able to separate them from Christ (R 8,35).

The victorious "have washed their robes and whitened them in the blood of the Lamb" (Ap 7,14; 22,14). Then the bride can in no way be deficient, for the long course of history is a process of adornment for the marriage. "She has been permitted to wear glistening white linen" (19,7f). God shall one day roll up heaven and earth as a fabric that has served its time and replace them with the new heaven and earth (He 1,11f). The protagonists, for the most part in white* garments, will be in their places. Then shall the new Jerusalem be dressed as a bride (Ap 21,2) and finally advance to meet her spouse. Then "the city can do without the light of the sun and moon, for the glory of God has illumined it, and the Lamb is its lamp" (2,23).

→Glory I, V—Transfiguration 2—White.

EH dfb

CLOUD

Like the night* or the darkness, the cloud can signify a twofold religious experience: the beneficent proximity of God or the chastisement of Him who hides His face. Furthermore, it is a privileged symbol for signifying the mystery of the divine presence: it manifests God while veiling Him completely. The natural symbolism of clouds, which helps to promote the contemplation of the all-powerful Wisdom (Jb 36,22—37,24), should help to convey the experience of the divine presence. The clouds have, in fact, two principal aspects. Light and rapid (Is 60,8), they are messengers—sometimes illusory (Jb 7,9; Ho 6,4; 13,3; Jude 12)—more often harbingers of beneficial rain (1 K 18, 44f; Is 5,6; Ps 78,23). From this, it is understandable that they can become "the chariot of Yahweh" (Ps 104,3). On the other hand, dark, dense, heavy as a mist, they form an opaque veil around heaven (Jb 22,13f) and the divine dwelling place (Ps 18,12), and they cover the earth with a terrifying shadow (Ez 34,12; 38, 9.16), threatening a hurricane (Na 1,3...; Jr 4,13).

1. *The column of cloud and of fire.* According to the Yahwist account of the exodus, the Hebrews were led by a "column" which assumes a double aspect: "Yahweh preceded them, by day under the form of a column of cloud to indicate to them the route, and by night in the form of fire* to give them light" (Ex 13,21f). The Lord is present to His people at all times so that they can pursue their journey. He assures them as well of His protection against their enemies; the column modifies its appearance no longer according to time, but according to men: "the cloud was dark on one side and bright on the other" (Ex 13,21, Sym); even a "column of fire *and* of cloud" is spoken of (14,24), thus showing the twofold portrait of the divine mystery: inaccessible holiness to the sinner, proximity of grace for the elect. In God, contradictions are resolved; with man, they express the presence or absence of sin. This coexistence of the cloud and of fire, so dear to mystical piety, has been repeated in later tradition (Dt 1, 33; Ne 9,12; Ps 78,14; 105,39; 2 M 2,8; Ws 17, 20—18,4): God has spoken not from an image manufactured by man, but "from the midst of fire, of the cloud and of darkness" (Dt 5,22).

2. *The cloud and the glory of Yahweh.* It is from Sinai that God has spoken; a cloud had covered the mountain during six days when Yahweh descended in the form of fire (Ex 19, 16ff). According to the Elohist and priestly traditions, the column of cloud was "the Angel of God" (14,19), while one awaited the "Holy Spirit...of Yahweh" to be present (Is 63,14); thus the cloud serves to heighten the divine transcendence. There is no more fire and cloud, but fire in the cloud: the cloud becomes a veil which protects the glory* of God against impure glances; there is a wish to emphasize not so much a difference between men as the dis-

tance between God and man. Accessible and impenetrable at the same time, the cloud permits contacts with God without seeing Him face to face, the fatal vision (Ex 33,20). From the cloud which covers the mountain, Yahweh calls Moses who alone can penetrate there (24,14-18). On the other hand, if it protects His glory, the cloud also manifests it; "the glory of Yahweh appeared in the form of a cloud" (16,10); it remains immobile at the entrance of the tent of meeting (33,9f) or it determines the movements of the people (40,34-38). Taking up again, to a slight extent, the preceding symbolism, it is linked to the glory which is fire (Nm 9,15): in it blazes a fire during the night (Ex 40,38).

Later, after its consecration by Solomon, the temple* was "filled" by the cloud, by the glory (1 K 8,10ff; cf Is 6,4f). Ezekiel will see this cloud protecting the glory which is going to leave the temple (Ez 10,3f; cf 43,4), and Judaism will dream of its return with that of the glory.

3. *Eschatological clouds.* As in the theophanies of the exodus, the day* of Yahweh is accompanied by mists and clouds; the latter signify the coming of God as judge (cf Nm 17,7), whether through their natural symbolism or by the aid of the metaphor of the heavenly vehicle. For example, it is a "thick fog" (Js 24,7) which serves to describe the coming of the Lord: it is "a day of clouds and darkness" (Zp 1,15; Ez 30,3.18; 34,12; Na 1,3; Jl 2,2). The cloud here announces a storm (Jr 4,13), which having passed, leaves behind the memory of a veil behind which Yahweh is hidden: "You have enveloped yourself in a cloud so that prayer may not pass by" (Lm 3,44). Clouds can also indicate the time of a beneficent new exodus (Is 4,5) and assure the hope of salvation: "Let the clouds rain down justice!" (Is 45,8).

Starting with the metaphor which presented Yahweh coming on His chariot (Ps 104,3), "mounted on a light cloud" (Is 19,1), among those who form His escort (2 S 22,12; Ps 97,2), an image is apocalyptically portrayed: "Behold Him coming upon the clouds of heaven, as a Son of Man*" (Dn 7,13) whose empire will never pass away.

4. *Christ and the cloud.* Before He comes on the clouds of heaven, the Son of Man is conceived of the Virgin Mary, covered by the shadow* of the Holy Spirit and by the power of the most high (Lk 1,35). When Jesus is trans-

figured*, the cloud, as in the OT, reveals the presence* of God, but also the glory* of the Son (Mt 17,1-8 p). It then removes Him from the gaze of the disciples, proving that He dwells in heaven, beyond visible things (Ac 1,9), but present to His witnesses (7,5f). As in the OT again, the cloud will be His celestial chariot, when the Son of Man* will come on the last day*, "with" or "on" the clouds (Mt 24,30 p; 26,64 p). Meanwhile, the seer of the Apocalypse contemplates a Son of Man "seated on a white cloud" (Ap 14,14) and coming, escorted by clouds (1,7): such is the equipment of the Lord of history.

5. *Christians in the cloud.* At the Transfiguration the cloud covers not only Jesus and the visitors from heaven, but also the disciples (Lk 9,34); it unites heaven and earth, consecrating the assembly of disciples inaugurated by Jesus round His word. Once they have entered into the heavenly cloud, the disciples know that from now on they form one community with Jesus and even with heaven, insofar as they listen to His word. According to another tradition, figures* give way to reality, as the prophecy had foretold (Is 63,14). Whereas the Hebrews had been "baptized in (the name of) Moses in the cloud and in the sea*" (1 Co 10,1f), the Christian is baptized in (the name of) Christ in the Holy Spirit and in water. The true cloud is the Spirit* who reveals (Jn 14,26), who directs (16,13). The "veil" which, like the cloud, covered the face of Moses, radiating a temporary glory, fell down for those who turned themselves toward the Lord who is the Spirit (2 Co 3,12.18). It remains true, however, that the image of the eschatological clouds retains its value to signify that at the last day, believers will also be those snatched up from the earth to go before the Lord who comes (1 Th 4,17; cf Ap 11,12).

→Ascension I, II 4, III—Fire OT I 2—Glory III 2—Heaven IV—House II 1—Night OT 1 —Presence of God OT II—Shadow—Storm—Temple OT I 1.

XLD pmcm

COMMUNION

In eucharistic communion the Christian manifests the originality of his belief; that is, the certitude of an intimate and real contact with God that is beyond description. There is a word for this experience: although the OT has no special word for it, in the NT the Greek word *koinōnia* expresses the relationship of the Christian with the true God revealed by Jesus and that of Christians among themselves.

The quest for communion with the godhead is nothing new to man; religion, which appears in him as a desire for union with God, often takes the form of sacrifices or sacred meals, in which the god is thought to share the food of his faithful. On the other hand the covenant meals aim to seal the bonds of brotherhood or friendship between men.

Only Jesus Christ, the sole mediator*, can fulfill this desire for communion. But the OT, even while jealously protecting the vast distance between God and man, insuperable before the incarnation, still prepared for the fulfillment of man's desire.

OT

1. *The worship** of Israel manifests the need to enter into union with God. This necessity is expressed especially in the "peace offerings," in which part of the victim is returned to the one making the offering. In eating this part man is admitted to the table of God. Many translations have called these simply "communion sacrifices" (cf Lv 3), although the OT never speaks explicitly of communion with God, only of a repast taken "before God" (Ex 18,12; cf 24,11).

2. *The covenant.* The need for communion would remain an empty dream if God had not given His people a structure for real exchange and a community of life. In the covenant* Yahweh takes charge of the existence of Israel and makes Israel's interests His own (Ex 23,22). He seeks to encounter Israel (Am 3,2) and to win her heart (Ho 2,16). This plan for communion is evident from the covenant and is clear from the structure God uses to implement His initiative: His long conversations with Moses (Ex 19,20; 24,12-18) and the very name of "the Tent of Meeting" where He encounters Moses (Ex 33,7-11).

3. *The Law.* The Law* is the charter of the covenant and is meant to teach Israel God's way of response (Dt 24,18; Lv 19,2). Obedience to the Law and a manner of life guided by its precepts is the discovery of God and union

with Him (Ps 119). Conversely, the love* and search for God is the observance of His commandments (Dt 10,12f).

4. *Prayer.* The Israelite living faithful to the covenant encounters God still more intimately in two fundamental forms of prayer*: (1) in the spontaneous outbursts of admiration and joy at God's great works, leading to blessing*, praise*, and thanksgiving*; and (2) in ardent petition to experience God's presence (Ps 42,2-5; 63,2-6) in a union that would endure beyond death* (Ps 16,9; 49,16; 73,24).

5. *Communion of hearts among the people* is the result of the covenant. The natural solidarity of family, clan, and tribe becomes a community of thought and life in the service of the God who brought Israel together. Loyalty to this saving God involves considering a fellow Israelite as a "brother*" (Dt 22,1-4; 23,20) and being liberal to the classes with no inheritance of their own (24,19ff). The liturgical assembly of the priestly tradition is also seen as the national community advancing toward its divine destiny (cf Nm 1,16ff; 20,6-11; 1 Ch 13,2), the "community of Yahweh" and of "all Israel" (1 Ch 15,3).

NT

In Christ, communion with God becomes a reality, as Jesus gives men a share in His divine nature (2 P 1,4); for He Himself shares the nature common to all men, even in its weakness (He 2,14).

1. *Communion with God as experienced in the Church.* At the beginning of His public life Jesus joins to Himself twelve companions who are to share in close solidarity with Him His mission of teaching and mercy (Mk 3,14; 6,7-13). He says His followers must share His suffering to be worthy of Him (Mk 8,34-37 p; Mt 20,22; Jn 12,24ff; 15,18). He is the true Messiah*, the king* joined to His people. At the same time, He emphasizes the basic unity of the two great commandments of love (Mt 22,37ff).

The fraternal union of the first Christians is the result of their common faith in the Lord Jesus, of their desire to imitate Him together and of their love* for Him, a love to which their mutual love necessarily leads. They only have "one heart and one soul" (Ac 4,32). This communion between them is realized in the first place in the breaking of bread (2,42). In the

Jerusalem church it results in the sharing of their goods (4,32—5,11), and then, between the communities that came from paganism and Jerusalem, in the collection urged by Paul (2 C 8—9; cf R 12,13). The material aid provided for the preachers of the Gospel shows this communion in a special light by giving it the character of spiritual gratitude (G 6,6; Ph 2,25). Suffering persecution together brought about a unity* of heart (2 Co 1,7; He 10,33; 1 P 4,13), as did cooperation in spreading the gospel (Ph 1,5).

2. *The meaning of this communion.*

a) For *St. Paul*, the believer attached to Christ by faith* and baptism* shares in His mysteries* (cf verbs with the prefix *sun-*, "with, in"). The Christian dies to sin with Christ and arises with Him to a new life (R 6,3f; E 2,5f). By his own sufferings and death a Christian is made like Christ in His passion, death, and resurrection (2 Co 4,14; R 8,17; Ph 3,10f; 1 Th 4,14). The sharing in the eucharistic* body of Christ (1 Co 10,16) brings about at one and the same time the "communion with the Son" (1,9) and the union of the members of the Body (10,17). The gift of the Holy Spirit* to all Christians sets the seal on the intimate communion between them (2 Co 13,13; Ph 2,1).

b) For *St. John*, the disciples who welcome the announcement of the "Word of Life" enter into communion with its witnesses (the apostles) and through them with Jesus and the Father* (1 Jn 1,3; 2,24). Finally Christians, united among themselves, abide* in the love of the Father and the Son, as the Father and the Son abide in one another and are only one (Jn 14, 20; 15,4.7; 17,20-23; 1 Jn 4,12). The observance of Jesus' commandments is the authentic sign of the desire for this permanent communion (Jn 14,21; 15,10): the power of the Holy Spirit brings it about (Jn 14,17; 1 Jn 2,27; 3,24; 4,13) and the eucharistic bread* is its essential nourishment (Jn 5,56).

Thus the Christian has a foretaste of an unending joy which is the dream of every human heart and was the hope of Israel: "to be with the Lord, forever" (1 Th 4,17; cf Jn 17,24), sharing His glory (1 P 5,1).

→Abide II 3—Altar 3—Body of Christ II 2, III 1—Bread—Church—Covenant—Cup 1—Desire IV—Eucharist—Imposition of Hands OT—Know NT 2—Love II NT 3—Meal—

Presence of God NT II—Sacrifice—Solitude II —Unity—Worship OT I; NT III 2.

DS & JG wjw

CONFESSION

In the language of today, *confession* suggests almost exclusively the sacrament of penance and the confessional. But this current and ordinary meaning is a secondary and very specific use of the word. In both the OT and NT, and in Christian tradition, the holy persons who "confess their faith" are those who proclaim God's majesty and His deeds of salvation by a public and official acknowledgment of faith* in God and in His actions. The confession of sins is authentic only by including an acknowledgment of the holiness* of God.

The confession of his faith is an essential disposition for the religious man. It does not necessarily involve a distinct knowledge and a complete account of God's deeds, but it does imply a practical attitude of openness and readiness to welcome the divine initiative. The priest Eli showed this attitude in simultaneously acknowledging the sins of his own sons and the greatness of God: "It was the Lord" (1 S 3,18). This attitude ordinarily leads from knowledge of God to the subsequent reaction of giving thanks. Thus, openness to God is both the reason for and the public expression of thanksgiving* and praise* (Ps 22,23). Like gratitude and praise, confession is addressed directly to God, in contrast with witness* which also deals with God's deeds, but is rather addressed to men.

OT

1. *To confess God's name.* Confession, praise, thanksgiving and blessing* are always connected. For their starting-point they have the works* of God. There are quite a number of short confessions that follow the simple formula: "Blessed be Yahweh who..." (Ex 18, 10; 1 K 1,48; Ps 28,6; 31.22...). The recital of His wonders (Ps 26,7) is the central element of confession and most often begins with a hymn, an invocation of Yahweh (Ex 15,1; Ps 118,1). Above all the phrase "I give you thanks" is used, but also "I praise you: I sing your praises." In the main part of the recital God is addressed with epithets like "my rock*; my strength*; my salvation*..." He is called in-

comparable (Ex 15,11; Ps 18,32); and the duty performed in this way toward His great name (Jr 10,6; Ps 76,2) ensures that the remembrance will last for ever and that Israel's faith will be handed on (Dt 6,6-9).

Pre-Christian Judaism was loyal to this tradition in a daily confession of faith by a prayer composed of three passages from the Pentateuch. The first of these proclaimed the fundamental belief in the one God* who had made a covenant with Israel (Dt 6.4f).

2. *The confession of sins* expresses a basic conviction that every sin is committed against Yahweh (Lv 26,40), even faults immediately against one's neighbor (Lv 5,21; 2 S 12,13f). Sin* is an obstacle to the relationship God wants to establish with man. The personal (Pr 28,13) or collective (Ne 9,2f; Ps 106) disavowal of this act against God by the guilty party's recognition of responsibility reaffirms the unshakable rights of God which sin had called in question. When God's rights, coming primarily from God's initiative in the covenant* relationship, are reaffirmed, pardon* is granted (2 S 12,13; Ps 32,5); and the separation from God, as well as its concomitant misery, is ended (Js 7,19ff).

NT

I. TO CONFESS JESUS CHRIST

While the act of the believer remains essentially the same, the object of his confession of faith undergoes a real transformation. The grandeur of God shines forth in all its splendor. The oldest confessions of Israel's faith (Dt 26. 50; Js 24,2-13) recall the events of the exodus from Egypt. But the liberation achieved by Christ affects the whole of humanity. His victory destroyed man's worst enemy, sin, which threatens man from within. In contrast to temporary national liberations of the past, Christ's is a definitive salvation*.

The confessions of faith of Peter (Mt 16.16 p; Jn 6.68f) and of the man born blind (9,15ff. 30-33) show how this faith is the result of living contact with Jesus of Nazareth. In the Church Jesus, by His death and resurrection. is the object of the profession of faith as the essential actor in the drama of salvation. This can be seen from the early formulas "maranatha" (1 Co 16.22) and "Jesus is Lord*" (1 Co 12.3; Ph 2,11). which are a summary of the faith and serve as liturgical acclamations. The object of faith proclaimed in the preaching according to a stereotyped schema (*kerygma*) also expresses itself in the beginnings of a credo (1 Co 15,3-7) and in liturgical hymns (1 Tm 3,16). Jesus is recognized as the only Savior (Ac 4,12), God (Jn 20,28), Judge of the world to come (Ac 10, 42), the apostle of God and our High Priest (He 3,1). In the adherence of faith to the one sent by God as Messiah* and Savior, the Christian's confession is directed to God Himself.

It is not enough that the Word be received and dwell* in us (1 Jn 2,14); it must be confessed. At times professing the Word is simply acceptance of the word, in contrast to the denials of those who deny the mission of Jesus (1 Jn 2,22f). But more frequently, even normally, confessing the Word is public acknowledgment. Such confession is necessary for salvation (R 10,9f), always praiseworthy (He 13,15), and modeled on Jesus' testimony to the truth (Jn 18,37; 1 Tm 6,12f). This confession accompanies baptism* (Ac 8,37) and is of obligation in those circumstances when failure to confess would be equivalent to denial of the faith (Jn 9,22). In spite of persecution* a Christian must confess his faith in the presence of authority, as Peter did (Ac 4,20), even to the point of martyrdom*, as Stephen (Ac 7,56). The punishment is being disowned by Jesus before His Father (Mt 10,32f; Mk 8,38) if one has put human esteem before divine approbation (Jn 12,42f).

Because confession is the reflection of the divine activity in man and goes back to God, every genuine confession is the product of the Holy Spirit* (1 Co 12,3; 1 Jn 4,2f): this is especially true in professions of faith made in the presence of persecuting authority (Mt 10,20).

II. CONFESSION OF SINS

The practice of disclosing one's sins to a man who has received the power to forgive them does not seem to be attested in the NT: both fraternal correction and community admonitions are intended to make the guilty one acknowledge his external faults (Mt 18, 15ff). The mutual confession recommended in Jm 5,15 is perhaps inspired by a Jewish practice, and 1 Jn 1,9 does not give the precise form that the necessary admission has to take.

Still, the confession of one's sins is always the sign of repentance and a normal condition for pardon. The Jews who went to John the Baptist confessed their sins (Mt 3,6 p). Peter declared himself a sinner, unworthy to approach Jesus (Lk 5,8). Jesus Himself describes the repentance of the prodigal son and includes the avowal of his sin (Lk 15,21). When Jesus forgives sin, admission of sin is a condition for pardon*, as appears in the words of Zaccheus (19,8), or the actions of the sinful woman (7,36-50), or in the silence under accusation of the woman taken in adultery (Jn 8,9-11). These cases are the starting point for the practice of sacramental confession. Every man is a sinner and must acknowledge himself as such in order to be cleansed (1 Jn 1,9f). But this acknowledgment of unworthiness and confession with the lips* have their value from repentance in the heart*; and the confession of Judas is useless (Mt 27,4).

Thus, in the two covenants, the person who confesses his faith in the saving God, like the man who confesses his sin—each is freed by faith* (G 3,22) in fulfillment of the word of Jesus: "Your faith has saved you" (Lk 7,50).

→Adoration—Ashes—Baptism IV 3—Blessing II 2.3, III 5, IV—Election OT I 2—Faith—Feasts—Jesus (Name of) III—Jesus Christ II 1 a—Lips—Lord—Martyr—Pardon I, II 3—Plan of God OT I, III—Praise—Repentance/ Conversion — Responsibility 4 — Silence — Thanksgiving—Tongue—Witness OT III, NT II, III—Worship.

PS wjw

CONFIDENCE

As a person faces the tasks and dangers of life, he has need of support on which he can rely (hb. *bātāḥ*) and of a haven where he can take refuge (hb. *hāsāh*); in order not to be paralyzed by anguish* but to persevere through trials and keep up hope of reaching the goal, confidence is required. But where should confidence be placed?

1. *Confidence and faith in God.* Man has faced this problem from the beginning and God has given the answer. When God forbade man the fruit of the tree of knowledge, He equivalently asked man to put his trust in God Himself as the judge of good and evil (Gn 2, 17). To believe in God's Word is to choose between two wisdoms; that is, to confide in God's wisdom and to forsake reliance on self

in the strict meaning of the term (Pr 3,5). Belief in the divine Word is confidence in the all-powerful Creator who made all things in heaven and on earth (Gn 1,1; Ps 115,3.15). Man then has nothing to fear from creatures; rather, his is the mission to subject them to himself (Gn 1,28).

But man and woman preferred to put their trust in a creature, and they learned by experience that such an action is trusting a lie (Gn 3, 4ff; Jn 8,44; Ap 12,9). Both of them tasted the fruit of this empty confidence as they felt fear of God and shame in each other's presence. The fruitfulness of the woman and of the soil became laborious and painful. Finally, they would experience death (Gn 3,7.10.16-19).

The people of Israel did not learn from the example of Abraham, who was confident up to the moment of sacrifice that "God will provide" (Gn 22,8-14; He 11,17). They relied not on the all-powerful God who had freed them, nor on the love of Him who freely called them to sonship (Dt 32,6.10ff). But when they found themselves without earthly support in the desert (Ex 16,3), they yearned for slavery again and murmured against the Lord. All through its history, Israel chose not to rely on its God (Is 30,15; 50,10), but preferred the idols denounced by the prophets as "impostures" (Jn 13,25) and "nothingness" (Is 59,4; cf Ps 115,8). The sages stress the folly of confidence in riches (Pr 11,28; Ps 49,7f), in physical force (Ps 62,11), and in earthly princes (Ps 118,8f; 146,3). Only the fool trusts his own judgment (Pr 28,26). "Cursed is he who trusts in man... Blessed is he who trusts in the Lord" (Jr 17,5.7).

Jesus stresses the need to follow the above maxim when He recalls the need for an initial · option rejecting every lord and master but the one whose power, wisdom, and fatherly love make Him deserving of absolute confidence (Mt 6,24-34). Instead of trusting in his own justice (Lk 18,9.14), man must seek the justice of the kingdom (Mt 5,20; 6,33), a justice that God gives only to the man of faith (Ph 3,4-9).

2. *Confidence and humble prayer.* This confidence in God rooted in faith is as firm as a person's humility. To have confidence, it is not necessary to underrate the power of evil forces seeking to control this earth (Mt 4,8f; 1 Jn 5, 19). Still less need man forget that he is a sinner. The point at issue here is to acknowledge the omnipotence and the mercy of the Creator who wishes to save all men (1 Tm 2,4) and make them His adopted sons in Jesus Christ (E 1,3ff).

Judith both taught and gave an unforgettable example of absolute confidence (Jdt 8,11-17; 13,19). She called on God both as the savior of those whose position is desperate and as the God of the lowly (9,11). This inseparable connection of confidence and humility is expressed in the prayer of poor people like Susanna, defenseless and in mortal danger, whose heart hoped in God (Dn 13,35). It is from "the depths of the abyss" (Ps 130,1) that the confident petitions of the psalms arise: "Though I am needy and miserable, the Lord thinks of me" (Ps 40,18); "in your love I am confident" (13,6); "He who trusts Yahweh is surrounded by kindness" (32,10); "blessed be the man trusting in Him" (2,12). Psalm 131 is the purest expression of this humble confidence to which Jesus is going to give its perfection.

He calls on His disciples to open themselves like children to the gift of God (Mk 10,15). Prayer to our heavenly Father is certain to obtain everything (Lk 11,9-13 p), including the gift of justification and salvation (Lk 7,50; 8, 13f). This prayer restores to man his power over creation (Mk 11,22ff; cf Ws 16,24). Still the children of God must expect that the godless will deride and persecute them precisely because of their childlike confidence. This was Jesus' own experience (Mt 27,43; cf Ws 2,18) as He consummated His sacrifice and died with a cry of confidence on His lips (Lk 23,46).

3. *Confident and joyous trust.* By this act of trustful love, Jesus won the victory over all the forces of evil and drew all men to Himself (Jn 12,31f; 16,33). He not only evoked their confidence, but gave foundation to their trust. Thus the confident disciple becomes a faithful witness whose trust rests on God's own reliability, for he is sure that God's grace will complete its work (Ac 20,32; 2 Th 3,3f; Ph 1,6; 1 Co 1,7ff). St. Paul manifests this confidence even in times of crisis (G 5,10), and it gives him unfailing strength to proclaim the Word of God in absolute freedom (*parrēsia*) (1 Th 2,2; Ac 28,31). The first disciples were witnesses endowed with great confidence; it was confidence and prayer that made them such witnesses (Ac 4,24-31).

This unshakable trust is a condition for fidelity (He 3,14) and gives the earliest witnesses for Christ a joyful and noble courage (3,6). They are aware of access to the throne of grace (4,16) along the path opened by the blood of Jesus (10,19). They possess a certain daring that shows no fear (13,6), and they know in whom they have placed their trust (2 Tm 1,12);

for nothing will separate them from the love of God (R 8,38f) who has first justified them, then poured His love out into their hearts to make them justifiably proud and constant in trials (R 5,1-5). In all of this they were convinced that all things were working together for their benefit (R 8,28).

This confidence which is a condition for fidelity to the Christian obligations is in turn strengthened by fidelity itself. Preserving fulfillment of Christ's commandments is the proof of a love (Jn 15,10) which then gives confidence a new and more complete dimension. Only those who persevere in love will have full assurance on the day when Christ comes as judge, for perfect love eliminates fear (1 Jn 2,28; 4, 16ff). Perseverance in love assures the Christian now that God listens and answers his prayer, and that his present sadness will be turned to joy, a joy that no one can take because it is the joy of the Son of God (Jn 16,20ff; 17,13).

→Anguish 3—Beatitude OT I 2, II 2—Cares—2—Child I, II—Creation IV 2—Disappointment—Faith—Fear of God II—Flesh II 1—Hope—Humility II, III—Liberation/Liberty III 3 a—Persecution II—Prayer II 3—Pride O; NT 2—Providence—Rock 1—Salvation OT II; NT II 3—Shame I 1, II 1—Silence 2—Sleep I 1—Unbelief I 2.

MFL wjw

CONSCIENCE

The word conscience means the intuitive faculty by which we judge an act, whether it is something that has already been done or yet to be done. It is more than a theoretical knowledge of good and evil*; it is the practical judgment by which we state that this is (was) good or bad for me.

The Bible contains no special word for conscience until it comes into contact with the Greek world. In fact *syneidēsis* only appears in Qo 10,20 (where it means a man's thoughts) and Ws 17,10 (where it means the internal admission of wickedness). It is not found in the Gospels, but it is used especially by Paul. But the reality behind the word is present throughout the Bible; this is what permits us to note the difference between Pauline thought and the Hellenistic mentality.

1. *"My heart does not reproach me at all."*

When it is stated explicitly, the function of conscience is attributed to the heart* or the loins*. "David's heart misgave him for having taken a census of the people. 'I have committed a grave sin,' he said" (2 S 24,10). It was the same when he had cut the border off the cloak of the Lord's Anointed (1 S 24,6), or when he was told that he might regret having shed blood (25,31). At first the pangs of conscience are associated with the covenant* that had been made with the Lord. For it is in the sight of Yahweh that the actions of kings are judged (1 K 16,7), in the sight of that Yahweh who probes the loins and the hearts (Jr 11,20; 17, 10; Ps 7,10) and to whom all the actions of men are present (Ps 139,2).

But is the judgment of "conscience" based solely on this idea of the nearness of God? The drama of Job seems to suggest otherwise. Job can cry out to his detractors and even to God Himself that his heart is pure: "I take my stand on my integrity, I will not stir: my conscience gives me no cause to blush for my life" (Jb 27,6), and this can be loosely translated: "My heart does not reproach me at all." And yet he must do penance in dust and ashes (42,6). However deep within a man conscience may be, it does tend to measure the mystery of God according to the knowledge that it has of His will* as expressed in the Law*.

The Pharisees* whom Jesus condemns have a different view of justice from Job; they have projected the consciousness of their justice into an outward practice of the Law. Jesus does not abolish the Law, but He shows that its practice must be governed by purity of intention. He makes it clear where conscience comes in, when He teaches men to judge from the heart (Mt 15,1-20 p), with the help of a sound eye (Lk 11,34ff), and in the presence of the Father who sees in secret (Mt 6,4.6.18). In doing this, Jesus prepares the way for a free conscience, for the day when, with Paul, the Law will no longer be something that is only outside man but will find its true meaning and power with the help of the Spirit that is poured out in men's hearts.

2. *Conscience according to Paul.*

a) Paul borrowed the word *syneidēsis* not from any literary source, nor from Stoic philosophy (the word does not appear in Epictetus, Plutarch or Marcus Aurelius), but from the religious language of the time. It was meant to express the reflex and autonomous judgment that belonged to the biblical notion of heart.

The passage from one idea to the other can be seen clearly in the advice given to Timothy: "The only purpose of this instruction is that there should be love, coming out of a pure heart, a clear conscience and a sincere faith" (1 Tm 1, 5). Heart, conscience and faith* are in their different ways at the root of every charitable action. If the intention is right, if faith gives a firm conviction, then conscience will be satisfied. Thus, the Christian obeys* civil authority* "not only for fear of being punished, but also for conscience's sake," for his faith shows him how this authority is "in God's service" (R 13, 4f). And so Paul often states that he considers his conscience "clear" (2 Co 1,12; cf Ac 23,1; 24,16).

It does not follow that this conscience is autonomous, as the Stoics would have it. For them, conscience is free because of our knowledge of the laws of nature. For Paul, the judgment of conscience is always subject to that of God; "True, my conscience does not reproach me at all, but that does not prove that I am acquitted; the Lord alone is my judge" (1 Co 4,4). His claims to a clear conscience are normally followed by the mention of God (2 Co 4,2) or the witness of the Holy Spirit (R 9,1). Conscience is "theonomous." When it is described as "clear" and "pure," it is radically enlightened by genuine faith (1 Tm 1,5.19; 3,9; 4,1f; 2 Tm 1,3; cf He 13,18; 1 P 3,16).

b) And so the believer achieves perfect *liberty**. While the Law imposed on the Jews the choice between this meat and that, between this feast and that, for the Christian "everything is clean" (R 14,20; Tt 1,15), "there are no forbidden things" (1 Co 6,12; 10,23). Faith has given the "knowledge" (8,1) that allows a man to recognize the goodness of every creature (3,21-23; 8,6; 10,25f). The Christian with an enlightened conscience finds himself, then, liberated from the ritual prescriptions of the Law of Moses: "where the Spirit of the Lord is, there is freedom" (2 Co 3,17), a "freedom that does not depend on somebody else's conscience" (1 Co 10,29). His conscience makes him as free as the Stoic, but in a different way and within limits that must now be defined.

After saying: "There are no forbidden things," Paul adds at once: "but not everything does good" (1 Co 10,23). In fact a conflict can arise between consciences that have not developed in the same way or to the same degree. In the eyes of certain believers, meat consecrated to idols remains unclean; and because of this conviction they ought not to partake of it: such is the verdict of their conscience. The believer who is "strong" (R 15,1) will have to go to any lengths rather than shock his brother who is still weak: "you are certainly not free to eat what you like if that means the downfall of someone for whom Christ died" (R 14,15). "Of course all food is clean, but it becomes evil if by eating it you make somebody else fall away" (14,20; 1 Co 8,9-13). Knowledge, then, must give way to brotherly love.

Conscience must also restrict liberty because of the divine presence that gives it its meaning. "I agree there are no forbidden things for me," said Paul to the Corinthians, but he added: "but I am not going to let them dominate me" (1 Co 6,12). Nor is it permitted for me to associate with a prostitute: my body does not belong to me. Here again knowledge and liberty are limited by someone who at first appears to be as someone other than myself, but who gradually reveals Himself in faith as the true fulfillment of myself.

Thus Paul is not governed by written and unchangeable norms; what binds his conscience is his relationship with the Lord and with his brethren. What he recognizes is not a rigid framework imposed by a written law, but the flexible and far more compelling relationship with the Word of God and with other people. Moreover, this does not affect the usefulness of written laws, but removes from them that absolute quality that they sometimes assume in the eyes of the timid.

c) Clearly Paul had reflected a long time on the new liberty that had been won in Christ, when, with the experience gained from his contact with the pagan world, he made the following statement: "Pagans who have never heard of the Law* but are led by reason to do what the Law commands, may not actually 'possess' the Law, but they can be said to 'be' the Law. They can point to the substance of the Law engraved on their hearts—they can call a witness, that is, their own conscience—they have accusation and defense, that is, their own inner mental dialogue...' (R 2,14f).

Seen in its context, this statement means first of all that God's judgment does not fall on the knowledge of good and evil but on its practice. And this is determined in the last resort not by the revealed Law but by the consciousness of good and evil; in this the will of God becomes manifest. So it is that Adam, having disobeyed God, realizes his nakedness and flees from His face (Gn 3,8ff). This again supposes, according to Paul, that God's plan is written in the heart of every man even before revelation makes it clear beyond any doubt. Even if God has not been recognized as the Creator (R 1, 19ff), even if there is no revealed Law, man is born in a dialogue with God and, confronted by His initiative, reacts according to God's plan.

3. *Conscience purified by worship.* The Letter to the Hebrews normally uses the term in a sacrificial context. The sacrifices* of the OT did not have "the power to make the worshipper perfect in his conscience" (He 9,9); otherwise, if those taking part in this act of worship had no longer any consciousness of sin, worship would have come to an end (10,2). In contrast, "the blood* of Christ purifies our conscience from dead works so that we may offer worship to the living God" (9,14). This purification* now takes place at baptism (10, 22), for, according to Peter, it is baptism which ensures the "pledge made to God from a good conscience, through the resurrection of Jesus Christ" (1 P 3,21). Finally, only the blood of Christ and the resurrection make a clear conscience possible.

→Good & Evil—Heart OT 3.4—Law *A* 2; *B* IV; *C* III 2.3—Liberation/Liberty I, III 3 c— Loins 2—Man II 1 d—Pure OT II; NT II 3— Responsibility—Sin I 2—Spirit OT 3.4.

XLD ems

CONSOLE

In sadness*, sickness*, grief, and persecution* man needs comfort; he looks for someone to console him. There are, of course, always people who avoid a person in distress as they would one with a communicable disease. But, at least relatives and friends of the afflicted are touched with pity and come to share his sorrow and to lighten it (Gn 37,35; 2 S 10,2f; Jn 11,19.31). By words and customary gestures they strive to console (Jb 2,11ff; Jr 16,5ff); but often these well-intentioned words are more of a burden than a comfort (Jb 16.2; 21,34; Is 22, 4), for they cannot bring back the departed one who is mourned (Gn 37.35; Mt 2,18). In sorrow man stands alone (Jb 6,15.21; 19,13-19; Is 53,3);

even God seems far removed (Jb; Ps 22,2f; Mt 27,46).

1. *Waiting for God the consoler.* In the course of her history Jerusalem had experienced complete dereliction. When the city was ravaged and the people exiled*, not only did Jerusalem receive no consolation from her old allies (Lm 1,19), but she felt forgotten by God Himself (Is 49,14; 54,6ff), and lost heart.

But as a matter of fact, God's abandonment was "for just a moment" (Is 54,7) as a reminder that He is the only real source of consolation. Then He returns to Jerusalem. "Console, give consolation to my people, says your God" (Is 40,1; 49,13...). Thus Yahweh answers the cry of the abandoned city. After the chastisement involved in the exile, He will intervene for her to work out the promises* made by His prophets (Jr 31,13-16; cf Si 48,24). This saving intervention is motivated by a love* expressed in diversified figures of speech. God consoles His people with the kindness of a shepherd* (Is 40,11; Ps 23,4), with the affection of a father*, the fervor of a lover or spouse* (Is 54), with the tenderness* of a mother* (Is 49,14f; 66,11ff).

Hence Israel will express its hope of eschatological salvation* as expectation of a decisive consolation (Ze 1,13). A mysterious delegate, the Servant*, will accomplish the work (Is 61, 2); and Jewish tradition, as verified in the gospel itself, will call the Messiah* *Menahēm*, "the Consolation of Israel" (Lk 2,25f). While waiting for the time of the Messiah, the faithful* of Israel know that God has not left them alone. To console them in their earthly sojourn, He gives them His promise* (Ps 119,50), His love (119,76), the Law and the prophets (2 M 15,9), and the Scriptures (1 M 12,9; R 15,4). With these sources of comfort, they nourish a hope in their trials*.

2. *Christ, consoler of the afflicted.* In Jesus, the God of consolation draws near to men. Jesus puts Himself forth as the awaited Servant: "The Spirit of the Lord is upon me..." (Lk 4,18-21). To the oppressed and the poor*, He brings a message of consolation, the good news* of felicity in the kingdom* of their Father (Mt 5,5). He comes to instill courage in those submerged in sin* or in sickness*, the sign of sin (Mt 9,2.22). He offers rest* to those bent and bowed with burdens (Mt 11,28ff).

Consolation is to continue after Jesus' departure to be with the Father; Jesus does not abandon His own. The Spirit of Pentecost, whom He has given them, never ceases to fill the Christian community with interior encouragement and this enables them to face obstacles and persecution* (Ac 9,31). The pastors to whom He has entrusted His Church also add their words of comfort (15,31). And finally the miracles of the Lord on behalf of His followers are signs* from God the consoler and they generate joy* in the hearts of the faithful (Ac 20,12).

The apostle Paul installed the groundwork for a theology of consolation through his discovery that even in suffering as fearful as death consolation can come from the desolation itself when this desolation is united to the suffering of Christ (2 Co 1,8ff). This consolation is found among the faithful (1,3-7), since it is nourished by the one and only source of consolation, the joy* of the risen Christ. He is the origin of all solace (Ph 2,1), especially for those separated from their dear ones by death (1 Th 4,18). The work of the consoler is essential to the Church in her role as witness to the fact that God always consoles the poor and afflicted (1 Co 14,3; R 15,5; 2 Co 7,6; cf Si 48,24).

→Beatitude—Exhort—Hope OT II 2—Joy—Laugh 2—Paraclete O—Sadness OT 4; NT 2.3 —Suffering.

CA wjw

COVENANT

God wishes to lead all men to a life of communion with Himself. It is this idea, fundamental to the doctrine of salvation*, which the theme of the covenant expresses. In the OT, it dominates all religious thought, but we see it deepen with the passing of time. In the NT it acquires an unparalleled fullness, for henceforth it has as its content the total mystery of Jesus Christ.

OT

Before being concerned with the relations of men with God, the covenant (*berith*) pertains to the social and juridical experience of men. Men were bound among themselves by agreements and contracts implying rights and duties that were usually reciprocal. There were pacts among groups or equal individuals who wanted

to help one another: these are the covenants of peace (Gn 14,13; 21,22ff; 26,28; 31,43ff; 1 K 5,26; 15,19), the covenants of brothers (Am 1, 9), the agreements of friendship (1 S 23,18), and marriage itself (Ml 2,14). There are unequal treaties, in which the powerful promises his protection to the weak, while the latter engages himself to serve the former: the ancient East used to practice from time to time these acts of vassalage, and biblical history offers many examples (Js 9,11-15; 1 S 11,1; 2 S 3,12ff). In these cases, the inferior can seek a covenant; but the powerful agrees to it according to his own good pleasure and dictates the conditions (cf Ez 17,13f). The conclusion of the agreement often was made by a ritual consecrated by usage. The parties pledged themselves by oath*. Someone would then cut in two some animals and one would pass among the pieces while pronouncing imprecations against all future transgressors (cf Jr 34,18). Finally they would set up a memorial: a tree would be planted or a stone set up which would henceforth be the witness of the pact (Gn 21,33; 31,48ff). Such is the fundamental experience by which Israel has represented her relations with God.

I. THE COVENANT OF SINAI

The theme of covenant is not introduced late in the OT: it is the beginning of all the religious thought and makes it different from all the surrounding religions, which were directed toward nature divinities. At Sinai, the delivered people entered into a covenant with Yahweh, and it is thus that the worship of Yahweh became its national religion. The covenant in question clearly is not a pact between equals; it is analogous to the treaties of vassalage; Yahweh decides with a sovereign liberty to grant His allegiance to Israel and He dictates His own conditions. Nevertheless, the comparison should not be pushed too far; for the Sinaitic covenant, because it shows God as the initiating cause, is of a type apart: it reveals straight off an essential aspect of the plan* of salvation.

1. *The covenant in the plan of God.* Right from the vision of the burning bush, Yahweh simultaneously revealed to Moses His name and His plan* for Israel: He wants to deliver Israel from Egypt to set her up in the land of Canaan (Ex 3,7-10.16f); for Israel is "His people" (3,10), and He wants to give her the land promised to her Fathers (cf Gn 12,7; 13,

15). This already supposes that, on the part of God, Israel is the object of election* and the depository of a promise*. The exodus* comes thereupon to confirm the revelation of Horeb: in effectively freeing His people, God shows that He is the master and that He is capable of imposing His will; thus the delivered people answers to the event by its faith (Ex 14,31). With this point secured, God can now reveal His own plan of a covenant: "If you hear my voice and observe my covenant, you will be my people privileged among all peoples. For all the earth is mine, but you, you will be for me a priestly kingdom and a consecrated nation" (Ex 19,5f). These words emphasize the gratuity of the divine election*: God has chosen Israel without merit on its part (Dt 9,4ff), because He loved her and wanted to keep the oath He made to her fathers (Dt 7,6ff). Having separated her from the pagan nations*, He reserved her for Himself exclusively. Israel would be His own people*, she would serve Him with her worship*, she would become His kingdom*. In return, Yahweh assures her aid and protection. Had He not already, at the time of the exodus, "borne her on the wings of eagles and brought her to Himself" (Ex 19,4)? And now, looking to the future, He renews His promises to her: the angel* of Yahweh will walk before her to facilitate the conquest of the promised land; there God will fill her with His blessings* and assure her of life* and peace* (Ex 23,20-31). As the pivotal moment in the plan of God, the covenant thus sets in motion the total future development, the individual details of which are nevertheless not totally revealed from the beginning.

2. *The clauses of the covenant.* While giving His covenant to Israel and making promises to her, God also imposes some conditions which Israel will have to observe. The mingled accounts in the Pentateuch furnish many formulations of these clauses which match the agreement and constitute the Law*. The first concerns the worship of Yahweh alone and the proscription of idolatry* (Ex 20,3ff; Dt 5,7ff). The rejection of all compromises or of all treaty with the pagan nations* derives immediately from this stipulation (cf Ex 23,24; 34,12-16). But it also follows that Israel should accept all the divine desires*, which envelop her entire existence, both political and religious, by a close network of prescriptions: "Moses made clear all that God had commanded to him. Then all the people answered: 'Everything that Yah-

weh has spoken we will observe'" (Ex 19,7f). This is a solemn commitment. Respect for this commitment will forever condition the historical destiny of Israel. All the people of Yahweh are at the crossroads. If they obey, they are assured of the divine blessing*; if they go back on their word, they vow themselves to curses* (cf Ex 23,20-33; Dt 28; Lv 26).

3. *The conclusion of the covenant.* The complex story of the exodus preserves two different rituals for the conclusion of the covenant. In the first, Moses, Aaron, and the ancients of Israel eat a sacred meal in the presence of Yahweh whom they contemplate (Ex 24,1f.9ff). The second seems to reproduce a liturgical tradition preserved in the sanctuaries of the north. Moses raises twelve sacred pillars for the twelve tribes and an altar* for sacrifice. He offers some sacrifices, pours a part of the blood on the altar, and sprinkles some on the people, to mark the union which is made firm between Yahweh and Israel. Then the people bind themselves solemnly to observe the conditions of the covenant (Ex 24,3-8). The blood* of the covenant plays an important role in this ritual.

Once the pact was concluded, diverse objects would perpetuate its memory, witnessing to the centuries the initial agreement of Israel. The ark* of the covenant is a small coffer in which are placed the "tablets of witness" (that is, of the Law); it is the memorial of the covenant and the sign of the presence of God in Israel (Ex 25,10-22; Nm 10,33-36). The tent in which it was placed, figure of the future temple*, is the place of encounter between Yahweh and His people (Ex 33,7-11). The ark of the covenant and Tent of Meeting mark the place of central worship where the confederation of the tribes offer to Yahweh the official homage of the people whom He has chosen for Himself, without prejudice to other places of worship. By this is marked the perpetual bond of Israelite worship with the initial act which founded the nation: the covenant of Sinai. It is this bond which gives to the Israelite worship its particular significance, despite all the borrowings one notices there, in the same manner as the entire law has sense only because of the covenant which declares the stipulations of the law.

4. *Meaning and limits of the Sinaitic covenant.* The Sinaitic covenant has revealed in definitive fashion an essential aspect of the plan of salvation: God wishes to bring men to Himself by making of them a community of worship dedi-

cated to His service, ruled by His Law, the depository of His promises. The NT will realize this divine project in its fullness. At Sinai the realization begins, but it remains in many respects ambiguous and imperfect. Although the covenant is a free gift* of God to Israel (in other words: a grace*), its contractual form seems to bind the plan of salvation to the historical destiny of Israel, and it risks making salvation appear as the payment for a human fidelity. Besides, its limitation to a single nation does not fit well with the universality of God's plan which is so clearly affirmed elsewhere. Finally, the temporal scope of the divine promises (the earthly happiness of Israel) also risks masking the religious objective of the covenant: the establishment of the kingdom of God in Israel, and, through Israel, on the entire earth. Despite these limits, the Sinaitic covenant would govern the rest of the life of Israel and the further development of revelation.

II. THE COVENANT IN THE LIFE AND THOUGHT OF ISRAEL

1. *The renewals of the covenant.* It would be imprudent to affirm that the covenant was renewed annually in Israelite worship. However, Deuteronomy preserves the fragments of a liturgy which supposes a renewal of this type, with a statement of ritual curses (Dt 27,2-26) and a solemn reading from the Law (Dt 31,9-13.24-27; 32,45ff); but this last point is provided for only every seven years (31,10) and its practice in that ancient period is unverifiable. It is easier to determine an effective renewal of the covenant at certain crucial turning points in history. Joshua renewed it at Shechem and the people resumed their commitment to Yahweh (Js 8,30-35; 24,1-28). The pact of David* with the elders of Israel (2 S 5,3) is followed by a divine promise: Yahweh grants His covenant to David and to his dynasty (Ps 89,4f.20-38; cf 2 S 7,8-16; 23,5) only on the condition that the covenant of Sinai be faithfully observed (Ps 89,31ff; 132,12; cf 2 S 7,14). The prayer and the blessing of Solomon at the dedication of the temple* are bound at the same time to this Davidic covenant and to that of Sinai of which the temple is a memorial (1 K 8,14-29.52-61). One finds the same renewals under Joash (2 K 11,17), and especially under Josiah, who followed the Deuteronomic ritual (2 K 23,1ff; cf Ex 24,3-8). The solemn reading of the Law by Ezra presents quite a similar context (Ne 8). Thus the thought of the covenant is the directing idea which serves as a basis for all religious reforms.

2. *Prophetic reflection.* The message of the prophets* refers constantly to the covenant. If they unanimously denounce the infidelity of Israel toward her God, if they preach the catastrophies which threaten a sinful people, it is because of the pact of Sinai, of its demands and its curses, to which she had agreed. But to keep alive the doctrine of the covenant in the spirit of their contemporaries, the prophets brought out some new aspects which the ancient tradition contained only in a virtual state. Originally, the covenant appeared primarily under a juridical aspect: a pact between Yahweh and His people. The prophets enlivened it with emotional overtones by searching human experience for other analogies to explain the mutual relationships of God and His people. Israel is the flock, and Yahweh the shepherd*. Israel is the vine*, and Yahweh the vinedresser. Israel is the son*, and Yahweh the father*. Israel is the spouse, and Yahweh the bridegroom. These images, especially the last, make the Sinaitic covenant appear as an encounter of love* (cf Ez 16,6-14): the attentive and gratuitous love of God, calling in return for a love which will translate itself into obedience*. The Deuteronomic spirituality gathers the fruit of this deepening experience: if it unceasingly recalls the demands, the promises, and the threats of the covenant, it it better to emphasize the love of God (Dt 4,37; 7,8; 10,15) which waits for the love of Israel (Dt 6,5; 10,12f; 11,1). Such is the background in which henceforth would be heightened the fundamental expression of the covenant: "You are My people and I am your God." Here again Israel's love for God should naturally show itself in obedience. In this respect the people are forced to make a decision, which is for them a choice between life and death (Dt 30,15...). This too is a result of the covenant into which they have entered.

3. *The syntheses of sacred history.* Parallel to the preaching of the prophets, the reflection of the sacred historians on the past of Israel has for its beginning the doctrine of the covenant. Already the Yahwist linked the covenant of Sinai with the more ancient covenant concluded by Abraham*, the framework of the first promises (Gn 15). The Deuteronomic writers, in

retracing the history which had transpired from the time of Moses to the destruction of Jerusalem (from Js to 2 K), have no other end in view but to make the reader grasp, in the events, the application of the Sinaitic covenant: Yahweh has fulfilled His promise; but the infidelity of His people has also forced Him to inflict on them the threatened chastisements. This is the meaning of the twofold destruction of Samaria (2 K 17,7-23) and of Jerusalem (2 K 23,26f). While, during the captivity, the priestly historian retraces the plan of God from the creation to the Mosaic era, the divine covenant serves him as a guide-wire: after the first check of the creative plan and the catastrophe of the flood, the covenant of Noah* takes on a universal amplitude (Gn 9,1-17); after the second failure and the dispersion of Babel, the covenant of Abraham restricted the plan of God exclusively to the offspring of the patriarch (Gn 17,1-14); after the trial of Egypt, the Sinaitic covenant prepared the future by founding the people of God. Israel thus grasps the meaning of its history by referring itself back to the covenant of Sinai.

II.   TOWARD THE NEW COVENANT

1. *The break-up of the old covenant.* The prophets did more than deepen the doctrine of the covenant in emphasizing the implications of the Sinaitic agreement. Turning their eyes to the future, they presented in its totality the drama of the people of a God who bound Himself to them. In consequence of the infidelity of Israel (Jr 22,9), the ancient pact was found broken (Jr 31,32), just like a marriage* which fails because of the adulteries of the wife (Ho 2,4; Ez 16,15-43). God did not take the initiative in this breach, but He drew from it the consequence: Israel will undergo in its history the just penalty for her infidelity; this will be the meaning of her national trials*: destruction of Jerusalem*, exile*, dispersion*.

2. *Promise of the new covenant.* Despite all this, the plan of the covenant revealed by God remains unchanged (Jr 31,35ff; 33,20f). There will be, therefore, at the end of these times, a new covenant. Hosea called this to mind under the aspects of a new betrothal, which would bring to the bride love*, justice*, fidelity, knowledge* of God, and which would re-establish peace* between man and the rest of creation (Ho 2,20-24). Jeremiah states precisely that the

human heart* will be changed, for the Law of God will be inscribed in it (Jr 31,33f; 32,37-41). Ezekiel announces the conclusion of an eternal covenant, of a covenant of peace (Ez 36,26), which will renew that of Sinai (Ez 16, 60) and that of David (34,23f), and will bring about a change of hearts and the gift of the divine spirit* (36,26ff). Thus would the program outlined earlier be achieved: "You will be My people and I will be your God" (Jr 31,33; 32, 38; Ez 36,28; 37,27).

In the Message of Consolation, this eschatological covenant again assumes the traits of the wedding of Yahweh and the new Jerusalem* (Is 54): a covenant firm as that which was sworn to Noah (54,9f), a covenant made of the graces promised to David (55,3). The one who made the covenant was the mysterious Servant* whom Yahweh set up as the "covenant of the people" and the light of the nations*" (42,6; 49,6ff). Thus is the vision magnificently expanded. The plan of the covenant which dominates all human history will find its culmination at the end of time. Revealed in an imperfect way in the patriarchal, Mosaic, and Davidic covenants, it will finally materialize in perfect form, at once interior and universal, by the mediation* of the Servant of Yahweh. Assuredly the history of Israel will follow its course. Because of the covenant of Sinai, the Jewish institutions will bear the name of the holy covenant (Dn 11,28ff). But this history will in fact be turned toward the future, toward the new covenant, toward the NT.

NT

In using the word *diathēkē* to translate the Hebrew *berīth*, the Septuagint made a significant choice which must have had considerable influence on the Christian vocabulary. In the language of Hellenistic law this term designated the act by which one disposes of one's goods (will) or declares the provisions which he intends to effect. Emphasis rests less on the nature of the juridical agreement than on the authority of the person therein who determines the course of events. In using this word, the Greek translators emphasized both the divine transcendence and the condescension at the origin of the people of Israel and their Law.

I.   ESTABLISHMENT
OF THE NEW COVENANT BY JESUS

The word *diathēkē* figures in the four stories

of the last supper in a context of unique importance. After having taken bread and distributed it saying, "Take and eat, this is my body," Jesus took the cup of wine, blessed it, and passed it around. The shortest formula is preserved by Mark: "This is my blood, the blood of the covenant, which will be shed for many" (Mk 14,24); Matthew adds: "for the remission of sins" (Mt 26,28). Luke and Paul say: "This cup is the new covenant in my blood" (Lk 22, 20; 1 Co 11,25); and Luke alone: "which is going to be shed for you." The passing of the cup is a ritual gesture. The words pronounced bind it to the act which Jesus is on the verge of accomplishing: His death* accepted freely for the redemption* of many.

From this last feature it is evident that Jesus regards Himself as the suffering Servant* (Is 53,11f) and understands His death as an atoning sacrifice* (cf 53,10). It is thus that He becomes the mediator* of the covenant which the Message of Consolation hints at (Is 42,6). But the "blood of the covenant" recalls also that the covenant of Sinai had been concluded in blood* (Ex 24,8): for the sacrifices of animals was substituted a new sacrifice, the blood of which would efficaciously achieve a definitive union between God and men. Thus was fulfilled the promise of the "new covenant" announced by Jeremiah and Ezekiel: through the blood of Jesus, human hearts will then be changed and the Spirit of God will be given. The death of Christ, at once sacrifice of Passover*, sacrifice of the covenant, and atoning sacrifice, will lead to their fulfillment the figures* of the OT which outlined the death in various ways. And because this act will henceforth be rendered present in a ritual gesture which Jesus commanded to "do again in memory* of Him," it is by the eucharistic* participation, accomplished by faith, that the faithful will be united most intimately to the mystery of the new covenant and that they will benefit from its graces.

II. CHRISTIAN REFLECTION ON THE NEW COVENANT

1. *St. Paul.* Placed by Jesus Himself at the heart of Christian worship, the covenant theme is the background for the whole NT, even where it is not explicitly noted. In his argumentations against Judaizers who hold as necessary the observance of the Law given in the Sinaitic covenant, Paul says that even before the Law came into being, another divine disposition (*diathēkē*) had been announced in proper and due form: the promise* made to Abraham. The Law could not annul this disposition. But Christ is the fulfillment of the promise (G 3,15-18); it is therefore by faith* in Him that salvation is obtained, not by the observation of the Law. This view of salvation emphasizes one fact: the old covenant was itself inserted into a gratuitous economy, an economy of promise which God had freely instituted. The NT is the point at which that economy is brought to a head. Paul did not contest that the "disposition" set up at Sinai came from God: the renewed "covenants" were one of the privileges of Israel* (R 9,4), to which the nations* were, up to then, strangers (E 2,12). But when one parallels this disposition to that which God had just revealed in Christ, the superiority of the new covenant over the old is clear (G 4,24ff; 2 Co 3,6ff). In the new covenant, sins are taken away (R 11,27); God dwells among men (2 Co 6,16); He changes the heart of men and He places in them His Spirit (R 5,5; cf 8,4-16). It is thus no longer the covenant of the letter, but that of the Spirit (2 Co 3,6), which brings with it the liberty* of the sons of God (G 4,24). It reaches the nations as it reaches the people of Israel, for the blood* of Christ has remade the unity* of the human race (E 2,12ff). Taking up again the perspectives of the prophetic promises, which he sees accomplished in Christ, Paul thus elaborates a general picture of human history, the key to which is the covenant theme.

2. *The letter to the Hebrews*, from a slightly different point of view, fashions a parallel synthesis from the same elements. By the cross*, Christ, the priest, has entered the sanctuary of heaven. There He is forever before God, interceding for us and inaugurating our communion with Him. This new covenant announced by Jeremiah is thus realized (He 8,8-12; Jr 31,31-34); a "better" covenant endowed with the distinguished quality of its mediator (He 8,6; 12,24); a covenant sealed in blood just like the first (He 9,20; Ex 24,8), no more the blood of animals but that of Christ Himself, poured out for our redemption* (9,11f). This new dispensation had been prepared by the preceding, but it has made the old null and void; and it would be vain to attach oneself to that which was going to disappear (8,13). Just as a testamentary disposition takes effect at the death of the testator, so the death of Jesus has put us in possession of the promised inheritance* (He 9,

15ff). The old covenant therefore was imperfect because it remained on the level of shadows and figures*, assuring only imperfectly the encounter of man with God. On the contrary the new covenant is perfect because Jesus, our high priest, assures us of everlasting access to the presence of God (He 10,1-22). The wiping away of sins, the uniting of man to God—such is the result obtained by Jesus Christ, who "by the blood of an eternal covenant has become the great shepherd* of the sheep" (He 13,20).

3. *Other texts.* Without any need to cite explicitly the OT, the other books of the NT allude to the fruits of the cross of Christ in terms which recall the covenant theme. Better than Israel at Sinai, we have become "a royal priesthood* and a holy nation" (1 P 2,9; cf Ex 19,5f). This privilege is now extended to a community of which men "of every race, tongue, people and nation" have become a part (Ap 5, 9f). Yet here on earth the carrying into effect of the new covenant brings with it some limitations. It is necessary therefore to contemplate the covenant in the eschatological perspective of the heavenly Jerusalem*: in this the "living of God with men," "they will be His people and, He, God-with-them, will be their God" (Ap 21,3). The new covenant is consummated in the wedding of the Lamb* and the Church*, His spouse* (Ap 21,2.9).

At the end of the doctrinal development, the theme of the covenant thus blends again all the motifs, from the OT to the NT, which have served to define the relations of God and men. To show its content, we must speak of sonship, of love*, of communion*. More especially must we go back to the act by which Jesus founded the new covenant: by the sacrifice* of His own body and by His own blood poured out, He has made of men His own body*. The OT did not yet know this gift of God; however OT history and institutions obscurely outlined its characteristics, because everything there already concerned the covenant between God and men.

→Abraham II 1—Adultery 2—Ark of the Covenant—Blessing III 3, IV 2—Blood—Calling II—Circumcision OT 2—Communion OT 2—David o.3—Election—Eucharist IV, V—Faith OT I—Faithfulness—Flood 1.3—Friend 1 Inheritance OT—Israel OT 1; NT 2—Joy OT II—Know OT 3—Law *A* 1; *B*—Liberation/liberty II 2—Love I—Marriage OT II 3—Mediator—Meal II, III—Memory—Moses o. 2.3—New II 3, III 3—Noah 1—Peace I 1.2, II

3 a—Pentecost I 2—People *A* II, II 1; *B* I; *C* I —Piety OT 2—Presence of God OT I, III 2— Plan of God OT I—Redemption OT—Sacrifice OT III 1; NT 1—Salt 2.3—Servant of God I, II 2—Sin II 1—Spouse—Truth OT 1.2—Unity II—Worship.

JGi & PG jjk

CREATION

OT

I. THE CREATOR OF HEAVEN AND EARTH

The earliest biblical literature gives the impression that the ancient Israelites were more accustomed to consider God as savior of Israel and author of the covenant* than as creator of the world* and of man*. Still, it is certain that the concept of creation does go back to the earliest days of Israel. As a matter of fact, the idea of creation already existed in the Near-Eastern milieu of biblical revelation well before the time of Abraham. In Egypt we find the narrative of creation by Atum inscribed on the walls of the pyramids. In Mesopotamia there are Akkadian texts which depend on Sumerian traditions and which gave several accounts of creation. At Ugarit the supreme god El was called "creator of creatures." Doubtless, in all three of these instances, the origin of the world was bound up with polytheistic ideas. In Mesopotamia creation was an organic part of a war of the gods which mythology located at the beginning of time. Nonetheless, these myths attest to preoccupations and ideas that could not have been foreign to Israel.

One hypothesis is that the divine name* Yahweh originally had a causative sense, as "He who brings to be," therefore, "the Creator." But Genesis provides a more important hint. Melchizedek blesses Abraham "by God most high, who created heaven and earth" (Gn 14,19), exactly the expression which occurs in Phoenician texts. Then Abraham himself took as his witness "God most high, who created heaven and earth" (Gn 14,22). Thus the patriarchs found their own God in the creator-god of the King of Salem, in spite of the polytheism that had modified the traits of this deity.

II. THE BIBLICAL REPRESENTATION OF CREATION

The Book of Genesis opens with two complementary accounts of creation. They are placed there as a preface to the covenant with Noah, Abraham, and Moses—or rather as the first act in the history of salvation*, starting the dramatic interplay of God's various manifestations of goodness and man's infidelity.

1. *The older narrative* (Gn 2,4-25) is concerned principally with the creation of the first human couple and their immediate surroundings. God draws forth water from the ground to make the earth fruitful, and He plants there the Garden of Eden as a paradise*. He then fashions the body of the man from the dust of the earth and subsequently the bodies of the animals*. After this He forms the woman* from the body of the man. Thus, all that exists is a result of God's personal activity; and the narrative in its own way stresses the concrete character of this activity, showing God at work in the manner of a human artisan. But the work* of God is completely perfect, for man is created to live in happiness with the animals to serve him, and to live with the woman, his other self, as his companion. Only sin will introduce disorder and a curse* into a world which in its beginning is good*.

2. *The priestly account* (Gn 1) has a more majestic setting. In the beginning, God draws the universe (heaven and earth) out of primeval chaos (Gn 1,1). Then He brings forth all that gives richness and beauty to the universe. The author of this account had been struck by the order of creation, especially in the distinction between its different parts, in the regular movement of the stars, and in the laws of reproduction. All of this is the work of the Creator, who had put everything in its place simply by the power of His Word* (Ps 148,5). The climax of this work is the creation of him who will be the image* and likeness of God and who should rule the universe. When His work was finally completed God rested, and thereby blessed the seventh day and destined it to be a day of rest*. This final element gave to the life of man the sacred rhythm of the week*, a rhythm based on the temporal order of creation. Thus, the creative activity of God is the model of all human work*.

This second account has certain elements in common with the Babylonian traditions: the victory over the abyss, the separation of the upper and lower waters, the creation of the stars. But there is no trace of mythology in this chapter of Genesis. God acts alone, deliberating only with Himself. His victory over chaos is not the outcome of a real struggle. The abyss (*tehôm*) is not an evil deity like the Babylonian Tiamat. There are no monsters or demons that God defeats or imprisons. Creation is an action spontaneously initiated by the God of all power* who works according to a plan and for the benefit of the man He created in His image.

3. *The biblical tradition.* The generic idea of the creation evidenced in this account controlled Israelite thought even before the biblical narratives had taken their present form. The prophets appeal to this concept of creation in their polemic against idols*, which they attack as lifeless products of human hands, without power to save (Jr 10,1-5; Is 40,19f; 44,9-20), while Yahweh is the creator of the world (Am 4,13; 5,8f; 9,5f; Jr 10,6-16; Is 40,21-26).

After the exile the sages advance theological reflection on creation. The editor of Proverbs is not content to affirm that God had created the world with wisdom, intelligence, and knowledge (Pr 3,19f; cf Ps 104,24), but goes on to speak of personified Wisdom* as the first work that God produced at the very earliest beginning (Pr 8,22ff). Wisdom was present when all things were created, working as the master artisan (Pr 8,24-30). She delighted in the universe before taking pleasure in the company of men (Pr 8,31). Ben Sira was nourished by this doctrine, and he too stresses the fact that Wisdom is created before all else (Si 1,9; 24,9). Similarly, the Book of Wisdom saw Wisdom as the craftsman of the universe (Ws 8,6; cf 9,9). A closely related stream of thought appears in the authors of the psalms who attribute creation to the personified Word* and Spirit* of God (Ps 33,6; 104,30; cf Jdt 16,14). These new horizons are important preludes to the revelation of the Word and of the Holy Spirit.

Finally, in the Greek period, we reach the explicit idea of a world created from nothing: "Look at the heaven and the earth and see all that is in them, and know that God has made them from nothing, and that the human race came to be in the same way" (2 M 7,28). At this time the theology of creation is involved in Jewish apologetics. Faced with a pagan world for which all things were gods except God Himself, Israel stresses the greatness of the one

God who gives glimpses of Himself through His works* (Ws 13,1-5).

III. CREATION IN THE PLAN OF GOD

1. *Creation and history.* The OT interest in creation is not that of human curiosity pursuing the problem of the origin of things. In creation the OT sees above all the starting point for the plan* of God and the history of salvation; creation is the first of those great divine deeds which continue throughout the history of Israel. Creative power* and mastery of history are correlative. Since He is creator and master of the world, Yahweh can choose Nebuchadnezzar (Jr 27,4-7) or Cyrus (Is 45,12f) to carry out His plans on earth. Events happen only in dependence on Him. Quite literally, He makes them (Is 48,6f). This is especially true of the great events that shaped the destiny of Israel: the election* of the people of God who were made and formed by Him (Is 43,1-7), their deliverance in the exodus* (cf Is 43,16-19). For this reason the psalmists, in their reflections on sacred history, add these great events to the marvels of creation in order to depict an adequate picture of God's miracles* (Ps 135,5-12; 136,4-26).

Placed into the foregoing context, God's creative act completely escapes being disfigured by the mythical ideas of the ancient Near East. From this time on the sacred writers could safely represent creation in a poetic manner by borrowing images from the old myths from which the venom had been removed. The Creator becomes the hero of a gigantic struggle against the beasts* Rahab and Leviathan, the personification of chaos. These monsters God crushed (Ps 89,11), pierced (Is 51,9; Jb 26,13), and shattered into pieces (Ps 74,13). Still, they are not finally destroyed, but only quieted (Jb 3, 8), imprisoned (Jb 7,12; 9,13), and relegated to the sea (Ps 104,26). In these terms creation was God's first victory*. And in history there followed a series of struggles which could be described by use of the same images. Will not the exodus be a new victory over the great abyss (Is 51,10)? By the mediation of symbols there is the recurring comparison of God's great deeds in history to His first great action.

2. *Salvation and a new creation.* Sacred history does not stop with the present but moves on to the term depicted by prophetic eschatology. To understand exactly the meaning of ultimate salvation* one must refer to God's creative act. The conversion of Israel will be true re-creation. "The Lord creates something new* on the earth: the woman seeks out her husband" (Jr 31,22). Likewise for the future deliverance (Is 45,8) which will be accompanied by the marvels of a new exodus (Is 41,20). And in the new Jerusalem* the people will experience the joys of paradise (Is 65,18). The constancy of the laws established by God in the universe is a sure sign that this new order to come will last forever (Jr 31,35ff). Finally, the whole universe will share in this total renewal of all things, for Yahweh will create new heavens and a new earth (Is 65,17; 66,22f). This is a majestic view in which the term of God's plan is joined to the perfection of His original creation after the long parenthesis opened by man's sin. Ezekiel does not use the explicit term *create*, but he is in close agreement to the above when he shows Yahweh changing the heart* of man in the last times so as to re-introduce him into the joy of Eden (Ez 36,26-35; cf 11,19). Therefore the psalmist relies on this promise to beg God to "create in him a pure heart" (Ps 51,12). In such a renovation of his being, he rightly urges a concrete anticipation of the new creation to be made in Jesus Christ.

IV. MAN BEFORE THE CREATOR

1. *Man's predicament.* The biblical doctrine of creation is neither speculative nor abstract theology, but a religious sentiment that calls forth a spiritual reaction. Through creation, man discovers the Creator (cf Ws 13,5) and is led to profound feelings of wonder and gratitude. In some psalms, contemplation of the beauty in creation leads to enthusiastic praise (Ps 19,1-7; 89,6-15; 104). In other places man is overwhelmed by the divine majesty appearing in His marvelous works. This is the meaning of God's discourse in the book of Job (38—41). With such realistic reminders should not Job be submerged in profound humility (42,1-6)? Thus man* comes to acknowledge his real situation as a creature. God has kneaded, molded, and formed him like clay (Jb 10,8ff; Is 64,7; Jr 18, 6). What is he before the God whose mercy is so necessary (Si 18,8-14)? It is a futile effort to flee the divine presence*, for at every instant man is in his Creator's hands, and nothing created escapes God (Ps 139). This is the basic attitude of genuine piety*, a mentality that pervades all OT devotions.

2. In this awareness of his true condition before God, man can find *access to confidence**. Isaiah returns again and again to the fact that this same God who created heaven and earth now intends to destroy the enemies* of His people, to grant His people salvation, and to restore the new Jerusalem (Is 44,24-28; cf Is 51, 9ff). The believer should eliminate all fear, for his help comes from the Lord who made heaven and earth (Ps 121,2).

NT

I. GOD THE CREATOR

The concept of God the Creator elaborated in the OT retains its essential place in the NT and is there even further developed.

1. *The OT heritage.* When He created the world by His Word* (cf 2 Co 4,6), God called into being what did not exist (R 4,17). This first activity continues as He animates creatures; for in Him we have life, movement, and being (Ac 17,28; 1 Tm 6,13). He created the world "and all that is in it" (Ap 10,6; Ac 14,15; 17,24; He 2,10); all exists by Him and for Him (1 Co 8,6; R 11,36; Col 1,16). Therefore everything created is good, and all that is from God is pure* (1 Co 10,25f; cf Col 2,20ff). Therefore the laws of the natural order must be observed by man. For example, divorce contradicts the plan of Him who made man and woman in the beginning (Mt 19,4-8).

Naturally these principles are emphasized in Christian preaching to the pagans, in which the primitive Church is only passing on the doctrine of Judaism (Ac 14,15; 17,24-28). For "by faith we know that the world has been formed by one word of God" (He 11,3), just as God's invisible perfections are quite obvious to anyone who is able to understand the significance of creatures (R 1,19f). In the believer, this principle leads to praise* (Ap 4,8-11) and is the ground of confidence (Ac 4,24).

2. *Jesus Christ and creation.* In one important respect the NT perfects what was implicit in the OT: God the Creator with whom Israel was acquainted is now revealed as the Father* of Jesus Christ. Jesus is closely associated with the Father in His creative activity, and therefore is "the one Lord* through whom all things exist and by whom we are" (1 Co 8,6). He is the first of the works of God (Ap 3,14). Since He

is the Wisdom of God (1 Co 1,24), He is "the reflection of God's glory and the image of His being" (He 1,3), "the image of the invisible God and the first-born of all creatures" (Col 1, 15). Since in Him all things were created and now subsist (Col 1,16f), He it is who "sustains the universe by His powerful word" (He 1,3). He is the Word* of God existing with God from the beginning before becoming flesh in the fullness of time (Jn 1,1f.14); He has made all things and is from the beginning life* and light* in the created universe (Jn 1,3f). Thus the concept of creation is completed by a reflection on the Son* of God who is the artisan, the model, and the end of all things.

II. THE NEW CREATION

1. *In Christ.* The NT is still more aware than the OT of the dramatic effects introduced into the perfection of creation as a consequence of human sin, as it is cognizant of the fact that the present world is destined to dissolve and disappear (1 Co 7,31; He 1,11f; Ap 6,12ff; 20,11). But in Christ a new* creation has already begun, as the oracles of the prophets had indicated. This new creation is primarily in man*, who is renewed interiorly in baptism* according to the image of his Creator (Col 3,10), who becomes in Christ "a new creature" (G 6, 15), a new being after the passing away of the old (2 Co 5,17). But the new creation extends also to the universe, because the plan* of God is to bring all things under Christ as the one head (E 1,10), to reconcile all things in and with Him (2 Co 5,18f; Col 1,20). Thus, in describing Christ's relation to the world, there is a subtle movement from His action in the original creation to His action in the eschatological re-creation of creatures. Creation and redemption* thus merge, for we are "the work of God, created in Christ Jesus for a life of good works" (E 2,10).

2. *From the first to the final creation.* Because of the striking parallel between the first and the final creation, it is possible to describe in greater detail the course by which this creation of a new humanity in Jesus Christ comes about (cf E 2,15; 4,24). In the beginning, God made Adam the head of the human race and entrusted the world to his dominion. In the end time, the incarnate Son of God entered history as the new Adam* (1 Co 15,21.45; R 5,13). God made Christ the head of redeemed humanity which is His body*

(Col 1,18; E 1,22f), giving Him all power on earth (Mt 28,18; Jn 17,2). All has been entrusted to His hands, and He is made heir of all things (He 1,2; 2,6-9), so that all things—heavenly as well as earthly beings (E 1,10)—are to be unified in Him. Because Christ has in Himself the fullness* of the Spirit (Mk 1,10 p; Lk 4, 1), He communicates this Spirit to other men for their spiritual renovation and to make of them a new creature (R 8,14-17; G 3,26ff; cf Jn 1,12).

3. *In the expectation of victory.* This new creation begun on Pentecost has not yet reached completion. The man who is interiorly renewed still longs for the redemption of his body* on the day of resurrection (R 8,23). The surrounding world is now subjected to frustration and seeks freedom from its servitude to inevitable corruption in order to enjoy the glorious liberty of the children of God (R 8,18-22). History is tending to this destiny, to the new heaven and the new earth proclaimed by Scripture (2 P 3, 13). This the Apocalypse anticipates in a striking description: "The first heaven and the first earth have disappeared...Then He who sits on the throne declared, 'See I am making all things new'" (Ap 21,1-5). This will be the final creation of a transformed universe when the definitive victory of the Lamb is achieved.

→Adam I—Adoration O—Animals I—Arm & Hand 1—Church II 1—Dove 3—Earth OT I 1—Figure OT II 3—Flesh I—God OT I—Growth 1—Glory III 1—Know OT 4; NT 3—Light & Dark OT I 1; NT I 3—Life II 1—Man I 1, III 4—New—Paradise—Passover I 6 a—Power II—Reconciliation II 1—Revelation OT I 3, II 2—Sea 1.2—Stars 2—Time intro; OT I 1—Week 2—Wisdom OT III 3—Woman OT 1 —Word of God OT II 2 b—Work i 1, IV 2.4—Works OT I 2—World OT I; NT I 1.

PA wjw

CROSS

Jesus died by crucifixion. Thus the cross was the instrument of redemption and it has become, with death*, suffering*, and blood*, one of the essential terms calling to mind our salvation*. The cross is no longer a sign of disgrace, but a challenge and the way to glory, first for Christ, then for all Christians.

I. THE CROSS OF JESUS CHRIST

1. *The scandal of the cross.* "We preach Christ crucified, a scandal for the Jews and folly* for the pagans" (1 Co 1,23). In these words Paul expresses the spontaneous reaction of every man introduced to the redeeming cross. Could salvation come to the Graeco-Roman world by crucifixion, a punishment reserved for slaves (cf Ph 2,8), and not only a cruel death, but a disgrace (cf He 12,2; 13,13)? Could salvation come to the Jews through a dead body, contact with which brought an impurity which must be removed as soon as possible (Js 10,26f; 2 S 21, 9ff; Jn 19,31)? Could salvation come from a condemned man, bearing the mark of a divine curse*, hanging on a gibbet (Dt 21,22f; G 3,13)? The witnesses at Calvary might well have made sport of the crucified, calling on Him to come down from His cross (Mt 27,39-44 p). As for Christ's disciples, it is a simple matter to predict their horrified reaction. Peter, who had just acknowledged Jesus as Messiah, could not tolerate mention of His suffering and death (Mt 16, 21ff p; 17,22f p). How much greater would be his abhorrence of crucifixion. Also, on the eve of His passion, Jesus announced that all would be scandalized by this subject (Mt 26,31 p).

2. *The mystery of the cross.* If Jesus, and His disciples after Him, did not try to soften the scandal of the cross, it was because a hidden mystery present in the cross gave it new meaning. Before Easter, Jesus alone affirmed the cross as necessary, as part of His obedience* to the will* of the Father (Mt 16,21 p). After Pentecost, enlightened by the glory of the risen Lord, the disciples themselves preached the necessity of the cross and rightly located the scandal of the cross as part of the plan* of God. If the Messiah* had been crucified (Ac 2, 23; 4,10) and "hung from a tree" (5,30; 10,39) in a shocking way (cf Dt 21,23), it was because of the hatred of His brethren. In the clarifying light of prophecy, this fact acquired a new dimension as the fulfillment* of "what was written about the Christ" (Ac 13,29). For this reason the gospel accounts of Jesus' death are filled with references to the psalms (Mt 27,33-60 p; Jn 19,24.28.36f). "The Messiah had to suffer," according to the Scriptures, as the risen Lord will explain to the disciples going to Emmaus (Lk 24,25f).

3. *The theology of the cross.* Paul was heir to the primitive tradition that "Christ died for our

sins according to the Scriptures" (1 Co 15,3). This fact of tradition furnished a basis for his theological reflection in which he found the cross to be true wisdom*; consequently he wished to know only Christ crucified (2,2). In the cross shines forth the wisdom of God's plan*, already spoken of in the OT (1,19f), in which the power* of God appears through the weakness of man (1,25). Developing this basic insight, Paul discovers meaning even in the details of the crucifixion. Jesus was "hung from a tree" as one cursed, so that we might escape the curse of the Law (G 3,13). His body, exposed on the cross, "in the likeness of sinful flesh*," allowed God to "condemn sin in the flesh" (R 8,3). As the verdict of the Law* was carried out, at the same time God "cancelled it by nailing it to the cross, disarming the principalities and powers" (Col 2,14f). "By the blood of the cross" God reconciled* all things to Himself (Col 1,20). Thus He has overcome the old divisions caused by sin; He has established peace* and unity* between Jews and pagans so that they form but one body* (E 2,14-18). Thus the cross stands as the boundary between the two economies, the dispensation of the OT and the NT.

4. *The cross, elevation to glory.* In the thought of St. John, the cross is more than suffering* and humiliation which has meaning in the plan of God because of its salutory effects. The cross is already an anticipation of the glory* of God. Tradition earlier than John had always spoken of the cross in connection with the consequent glorification of Jesus. But in the eyes of John, it is in the cross itself that Jesus is triumphant. To indicate this victory John had recourse to the words that hitherto denoted the exaltation of Jesus to heaven (Ac 2,35; 5,31). Therefore, the Son* of Man is "raised up" (Jn 8,28; 12,32f); it is as the new brazen serpent, as the sign of salvation (3,14; cf Nm 21,4-9). In the Johannine passion narrative, Jesus moves toward the cross with majesty. He ascends it triumphantly because it is on the cross that He founds His Church by "giving the Spirit*" (19,30), and by permitting blood* and water* to flow from His side (19,34). Henceforth, one must "look upon Him who was pierced" (19,37), since faith* is directed to the crucified one, and the cross is the living sign of salvation. In this same tenor, the Apocalypse appears to have seen in this saving "wood" "the wood of life," and in the tree of the cross, "the tree of life" (Ap 22, 2.14.19).

II. THE CROSS AS THE SIGN OF THE CHRISTIAN

1. *The cross of Christ.* With the revelation that the two witnesses were martyred "there where the Lord was crucified" (Ap 11,8), the Apocalypse identifies the lot of the disciples* with that of the master. This is what Jesus had called for: "If a person wishes to come after me, let him deny himself and take up his cross and follow* me" (Mt 16,24 p). The disciple must not only die to himself, for the cross he carries is moreover a sign of death to the world*. It is a sign that he has broken all natural ties (Mt 10,33-39 p) and accepted the fate of persecution* in which he may well lose his life (Mt 23,34). At the same time, however, the cross is also a sign of anticipated glory (cf Jn 12,26).

2. *The crucified life.* According to Paul, the cross of Christ marks off the two dispensations of the Law* and of faith*. And in the heart of the Christian, the cross marks the boundaries of the two worlds, the flesh* and the spirit*. In the cross alone is justification* and wisdom*. If the Christian is converted it is because Jesus Christ on the cross appears before his eyes (G 3,1). If he is justified, it is not by works* of the Law, but by faith in the crucified one; for he himself has been crucified with Christ in baptism* and is therefore dead to the Law to live in God (G 2,19) and to have no more to do with the world* (G 6,14). Thus, he puts his confidence* only in the strength* of Christ; otherwise he would be "an enemy of the cross" (Ph 3,18).

3. *The cross, the glory of the Christians.* In the daily Christian life "the old man* is crucified" (R 6,6), so that he is entirely free from sin. His judgment is transformed by the wisdom of the cross (1 Co 2). In accord with this wisdom, he follows the example* of Jesus, humble and "obedient* unto death, even the death of the cross" (Ph 2,1-8). For a general pattern of life, he should look to Jesus as the model "on the wood of the cross who bore the burden of our sins in His body, so that we might die to our faults and live for justice" (1 P 2,21-24). Finally, the Christian must dread apostasy in which a person "crucifies again on his own account the Son of God" (He 6,6). And his confident cry must be that of St. Paul, "As for me, I want never to boast of anything but the cross of our Lord Jesus Christ, on which

the world was crucified for me, and I to the world" (G 6,14).

→Blood NT 2—Death NT II, III—Follow 2 b —Folly—Jesus Christ II 1 b—Joy NT I 2, II 2— Love I NT 2 b—Persecution—Plan of God NT I 1, II, III 1—Preach II 3—Punishments 3— Redemption NT—Sacrifice NT I, II 1—Scandal I—Servant of God III—Sign NT I 2—Suffering —Tree 3—Trial/Temptation NT I—Unbelief II 2—Victory NT 1—Way III—Wisdom NT II 1.

JA & XLD wjw

CUP

1. *The cup of fellowship.* The oriental custom of passing a cup during a meal* for all to drink is itself a sign of communion*. But at sacrificial banquets, man is invited to the table of God; and thus the overflowing cup (Ps 23,5) that is offered is a sign of fellowship by the faithful partners of the covenant* (Ps 16,5) with the God of the covenant. But the godless* refuse to worship God and will not drink from the cup He offers. They prefer the cup of demons (cf Dt 32,17; 1 Co 10,20f) with whom they are united in idolatrous worship.

2. *The cup of wrath.* This godlessness draws down the wrath* of God. To express the consequences of divine wrath the prophets use the symbol of a cup. This cup contains a wine* that brightens the heart of man; but abuse of the cup leads to shameful drunkenness*, a drunkenness which is God's chastisement reserved for the godless (Jr 25,15; Ps 75,9; cf Ze 12,2). Their part of the cup, which is the death potion they must drink, is the wine of God's wrath (Is 51,17; Ps 11,6; Ap 14,10; 15,7 —16,19).

3. *The chalice of salvation.* God's wrath is reserved for those whose hearts are hardened, and only by conversion is there the possibility of reprieve. In the OT, the sacrifices of atonement express repentance and conversion. The blood* of the victims, collected in the cup of sprinkling (Nm 4,14) was poured on the altar and over the people as a renewal of the covenant between God and a now purified people (cf Ex 24,6ff). These rites prefigured the sacrifice* in which the offering of Christ's blood brought about full expiation and an eternal

covenant with God. This sacrifice is the cup that the Father gives His Son Jesus to drink (Jn 18,11). In filial obedience* Jesus accepts the cup for the salvation of men; He drinks it and gives thanks to His Father on behalf of all those He is saving (Mk 10,39; Mt 26,27f.39-42 p; Lk 22,17-20; 1 Co 11,25).

For all time this cup is the chalice of salvation* (Ps 116,13) offered to all men both to give them a share in the blood of Christ until He comes again and to allow them to bless forever the Father who will ultimately have them drink at the table of His Son in the kingdom (1 Co 10,16; Lk 22,30).

→Blessing IV 2—Blood NT 2—Covenant NT I — Drunkenness 1 — Eucharist — Hunger & Thirst NT 1—Vintage 2—Wine II 2 a.

PEB wjw

CUPIDITY

The word "cupidity" is the closest to the Greek *pleonexia* (from *pleon echein*, to have more), which in the LXX and the NT means the desire to possess more and more without concern for others and even at their expense. Cupidity is to a great extent the same as covetousness, the perversion of desire* (*epithymia*) but seems to lay stress on certain characteristics; it is a violent and almost frenzied covetousness (E 4,19), and is especially opposed to love of neighbor and above all of the poor. In the first place it is concerned with material goods, wealth and money.

Like the Greek philosophers, the Bible describes the evils caused by cupidity, but it goes to the religious heart of the matter when it judges it from a standpoint too high for paganism to reach: apart from the fact that cupidity causes harm to one's neighbor, it offends the God of the covenant and so is nothing less than idolatry.

OT

1. *Manifestations and consequences.* Narrators, prophets and wise men condemn the attacks on the rights of one's neighbor to which cupidity leads. This is what leads the merchant, who is often dishonest (Si 26,29—27,2), to give short measure, to speculate and to make money at all costs (Am 8,5f); leads the rich man to blackmail (5,12), to accumulate property (Is 5,

8; Mi 2,2.9; cf 1 K 21), to exploit the poor (Ne 5,1-5; cf 2 K 4,1; Am 2,6), even by refusing to pay the wages they have earned (Jr 22,13); and leads the prince and the judge to demand bribes (Is 33,15; Mi 3,11; Pr 28,16) in order to pervert the course of justice* (Is 1,23; 5,23; Mi 7,3; 1 S 8,3).

Thus, it is seen to be the direct opposite of love of neighbor, and especially of the poor*, whom the Law is supposed to protect against this sort of thing (Ex 20,17; 22,24ff; Dt 24,10-21). While Yahweh says: "Do not harden your heart...against that poor brother" (Dt 15,7), the covetous man has a shrivelled up soul (Si 14,8f) and shows himself to be pitiless (27,1). Concerned only with their own interests, the covetous princes, "like wolves tearing their prey," even resort to violence* to increase their gains (hb. *besa'*, gr. *pleonexia*: Ha 2,9; Jr 22,17) and to assert their lust for power (Ez 22,27).

2. *Religious meaning.* But the sheep torn by the wolves belong to Yahweh the God of the covenant (Ez 34,6-16). In the end it is He who is offended by cupidity: it is a blasphemy that spurns God (Ps 10,3). Moreover, the OT recognizes that it is idolatrous and the Yahwist tradition describes as cupidity (Gn 3,6) the act by which Adam and Eve tried to be "like gods" (3,5) and refused to put their trust in God and admit their dependence as creatures. In this way Genesis suggests that cupidity is at the root of every sin* (cf Jm 1,14f). In wanting to enjoy and keep only for himself something that comes from God's love for His service, the sinner puts a created good, and ultimately himself, in the place of God. This is why the Targum in its commentary on the commandment against covetousness (Ex 20,17; Dt 5,21), identifies the pagans, the sinners *par excellence* (G 2,15), with "those who covet." And Paul probably has the Genesis story in mind when he sums up the whole Law in the same commandment (R 7,7) and sees all the sins of the desert generation (1 Co 10,6) as a matter of covetousness (cf Nb 11,4.34), an expression of their rejection of the spiritual experience through which God had made them pass (Dt 8,3; cf Mt 4,4). The covetous man runs after precarious goods (Qo 6,2; Pr 23,4f; 28,22), is always unsatisfied (Pr 27,20; Qo 4,8) and will be punished because he has spurned God and done wrong to his neighbor. "Covetousness ruins those in whom it takes root" (Pr 1,19), while "he who hates avarice will lengthen his days" (28,16).

NT

The NT develops the message of the OT in three main ways. By revealing the full scope of the *agapē*, the very opposite of covetousness, and by disclosing the hidden idolatry of covetousness, it goes straight to the heart of its malice. By revealing the secrets of the future life and thus showing the real value of earthly goods, it points out how stupid is the whole approach of the covetous man.

1. *Manifestations and consequences.* The only occasions where the word *pleonexia* appears in the *Gospels* are in Mk 7,22, in a list of sins where Jesus is pointing out the interior source, and in Lk 12,15: "Be on your guard against all covetousness." This half verse, summarizing a doctrine that is dear to Luke, forms a bridge between the refusal of the Master to arbitrate in a dispute about an inheritance (vv 13f) and the parable about the thoughtlessness of the rich man who is complacent about his store of supplies as if tomorrow belonged to him (vv 15b-21). And so, according to Luke, covetousness consists in wanting always to increase one's possessions, even at the expense of other people, and at the same time in being attached by "avarice" (cf 2 Co 9,5) to the goods already possessed.

Paul mentions the word more often and associates it with sexual disorders (1 Co 5,10f; 6,9f; R 1,29; Col 3,5; E 5,3.5; cf 1 Th 4,6: *pleonektein*, "to exploit," with regard to impurity). This is a significant parallel: whether it is a question of material profit or of sensual pleasure, the point is that one's neighbor is being used instead of being served. In both cases it is a matter of culpable "covetousness," which stifles the Word of God (Mk 4,19) and puts the sinner on the side of paganism (R 1,24.29), of the world* (Tt 2,12; 1 Jn 2,16f; 2 P 1,4), of evil (Col 3,5), of the flesh* (G 5,16; R 13,14; E 2,3; 1 P 2,11), of the old man (E 4,22) and of the perishable body (R 6,12). The covetous man sacrifices others to his own interests, by means of violence if necessary: "you want something and you haven't got it; so you are prepared to kill" (Jm 4,2). Unlike Christ, who in His love for us "did not regard his equality with God as something to be grasped" (Ph 2,6), He "grasps" and guards jealously anything that arouses his desire. Unlike Jesus, who "was rich, but...became poor for your sake, to make you rich out of His poverty" (2

105

Co 8,9), he deprives the poor for his own profit (Jm 5,1-6; Lk 20,47 p).

Cupidity is unworthy of any Christian but it would be particularly scandalous in the case of an apostle, who is bound by his vocation to make himself the "slave of all" (Mk 10,44; 1 Co 9,19). For his part, Paul declares that there has never been any thought of covetousness in his mind (1 Th 2,5); far from coveting the goods of the faithful (Ac 20,33), he has worked* with his own hands to avoid living at their expense, although he has the right to do this (20,34; 1 Th 2,9; 1 Co 9,6-14; 2 Co 11,9f; 12, 16ff), and in this way to put his lack of self-interest beyond suspicion (1 Co 9,12; cf Ph 4, 17). This conduct should serve lesser ministers* as an example (Ac 20,34f). Bishops (1 Tm 3,3; Tt 1,7) and deacons (1 Tm 3,8) should not be fond of money and shameful gain!

On the other hand false teachers can be recognized by their greed (Tt 1,11; 2 Tm 3,2), for under the pretext of piety they are trying to make profit and are not content with what they have (1 Tm 6,5f). In 2 P 2,3.14 "covetousness" is the word used to describe the use of lying speeches, sometimes with immoral intentions (2,2.10.18; 3,3; cf Jude 16).

It will always be the ideal of the true servants of the Gospel to be considered as people who have nothing, while possessing everything (2 Co 6,10).

2. *Religious content.* If Paul considers cupidity to be especially serious, it is because he has clearly understood what the OT only hinted at: "covetousness is idolatry*" (1 Co 3,5). In this he is following Jesus, for whom to be a "lover of money" (Lk 16,14) is to set one's heart on created goods when it belongs to God alone (Mt 6,21 p), and to make these goods one's masters, while spurning the only true Master, who is God (6,24 p).

The proverb: "the love of money is the root of all evils" (1 Tm 6,10), then, gets a deeper and a tragic meaning. By choosing a false god a man cuts himself off from the only true God and condemns himself to perdition (6,9), like Judas the covetous traitor (Jn 12,6; Mt 26,15 p), "the son of perdition" (Jn 17,12). On the other hand perishable goods are now seen for what they are really worth in view of the future life (Lk 6,20.24), which was unknown to the wise men. And so the NT can show better than these how senseless the behavior of the covetous man really is (12,20; E 5,17; cf Mk 8,36 p): Mammon is "tainted" (Lk 16,9.11),

that is to say—according to the Aramaic word that probably lies behind this—false and deceiving. It is folly to depend on perishable goods (Mt 6,19f), for death, the gateway to the eternal life that wealth makes a man forget, leads to a reversal of situations (Lk 16,19-26; 6,20-26).

→Desire II—Flesh II 1. 2b—Folly—Idols II 3 —Justice *A* I OT 1—Poor OT II, III—Sexuality III—Sin—Violence II—Virtues & Vices— Wealth II, III.

PT ems

CURSE

The vocabulary of cursing is rich in Hebrew. It expresses the violent reactions of a fiery temperament. Men curse in anger (*z'm*), and in humiliating (*'rr*), in contempt (*qll*), in execration (*qbb*), in oaths (*'lh*). The Greek Bible is especially inspired by the root *ara*, which describes a prayer, vow, or imprecation, and which really suggests recourse to a stronger power against the thing cursed.

A curse brings into play profound forces which are beyond man. Through the power of the spoken word which seems to develop its deadly effects automatically, the curse calls forth the dreaded power of evil and sin*, the inexorable logic which leads from evil to misfortune. Also, in its full form a curse implies two closely linked terms, the cause or condition involving the effect: "Because you have done this (if you do this)...such a misfortune will come upon you."

One cannot curse thoughtlessly without the danger of letting loose upon oneself the evil one calls on another (cf Ps 109,17). To curse someone, you must have a claim upon his whole being, a claim of legal or paternal authority, a claim of suffering or unjust oppression (Ps 137, 8f; cf Jb 31,20.38f; Jm 5,4), a claim of God.

I. PREHISTORY: CURSE ON THE WORLD

Right from the beginning a curse is present (Gn 3,14.17), but against this was the primary motif of blessing (1,22.28). The curse is like a reverse echo of the supreme blessing, which is the creative Word* of God. When the Word, which is light, truth, and life, touches the prince of darkness, the father of lies and of death, the blessing that He brings shows up the murderous refusal of Satan* and will by this contact be turned into a curse. Sin is an evil which the Word did not create but which the Word does lay bare and bring to naught. The curse is already a judgment*.

God blesses because He is the living God*, the source of life* (Jr 2,13). The tempter who defies Him (Gn 3,4f) and draws man into sin, draws him also into his curse. Instead of the divine presence* there is an exile far from God (Gn 3,23f) and from His glory (R 3,23); instead of life there is death* (Gn 3,19). But always only the chief culprit, the devil (Ws 2,24), is "cursed forever" (Gn 3,14f). Women will continue to give birth and the earth to bear fruit. The original blessing on all fruitfulness (3,16-20) has not been withdrawn, but the curse casts over it the shadow of suffering*, burdensome work* and agony. And yet life remains stronger, an omen of the ultimate failure of the curse (3,15).

The curse reaches from Adam to Abraham, involving death, of which man himself became the author (Gn 4,11; on the binding force of the blood curse, cf 4,23f; 9,4ff; Mt 27,25); and corruption, which ended in the destruction (Gn 6, 5-12) of the flood* where water*, the primordial life, became the abyss of death. Yet in the very midst of the curse, God sent His consolation*, Noah, the first-fruits* of a new human race, to whom blessing is promised forever (8,17-23; 9,1-17; 1 P 3,20).

II. THE PATRIARCHS
CURSE UPON THE ENEMIES OF ISRAEL

Although a curse destroyed Babel and dispersed* the men leagued against God (Gn 11,7), God raised up Abraham to reunite all the peoples around him and his lineage, for their blessing or for their woe (12,1ff). Though the blessing drew the chosen race away from the twofold curse of a sterile* womb (15,5f; 30,1f) and from a hostile land (27,27f; 49,11f.22-26), the curse called down on them by the enemies of the chosen race drove them "far from the fat of the earth...and from the dew which falls from the sky" (27,39). Their curse came to be reprobation, exclusion from the one blessing. "Cursed be the one who curses you!" Pharoah (Ex 12,29-32), then Balak (Nm 24,9) experienced this. The height of irony—Pharoah is reduced to pleading with the children of Israel "to ask for a blessing upon (him)" from their God (Ex 12,32).

III. THE LAW:
CURSE UPON GUILTY ISRAEL

The more the blessing advanced, the more was the curse revealed.

1. *The Law* gradually unveils sin (R 7,7-13), proclaiming along with the commands and prohibitions the deadly consequences of their violation. From the Covenant code to the august liturgies of Deuteronomy, the threats of the curses gain each time in precision and in their tragic extent (Ex 23,21; Js 24,20; Dt 28; cf Lv 26,14-39). The blessing is a mystery of election*; the curse is a mystery of rejection: the elect who prove unworthy seem to be cut off from a choice (1 S 15,23; 2 K 17,17-23; 21,10-15), which nevertheless concerns them forever (Am 3,2).

2. *The prophets*, witnesses of the hardness* of heart of Israel (Am 6,1...; Ha 2,6-20), of their blindness in the face of imminent disaster (Am 9,10; Is 28,15; Mi 3,11; cf Mt 3,8ff), are forced to announce "violence and spoil" (Jr 20,8), and to return continually to the language of cursing (Am 2,1-16; Ho 4,6; Is 9,7—10,4; Jr 23,13ff; Ez 11,1-12.13-21). They are forced to see the curse compass all of Israel and spare nothing or no one; not the priests (Is 28,7-13), the false prophets (Ez 13), the wicked shepherds (Ez 34,1-10), the nation (Mi 1,8-16), the city (Is 29,1-10), the temple (Jr 7,1-15), the palace (22,5), the kings (25,18).

Yet never is the curse total. At times, without apparent reason and with no transition, in a burst of tenderness, the promise* of salvation follows a threat (Ho 2,8.11.16; Is 6,13). But more often, right in the very heart of the curse, shines forth the blessing (Is 1,25f; 28,16f; Ez 34,1-16; 36,2-12.13-38).

IV. THE CALLING DOWN
OF CURSES BY THE JUST

From this remnant* through which God passed on the blessing of Abraham, cries of malediction were raised up, by Jeremiah (Jr 11,20; 12,3; 20,12) and by the psalmists (Ps 5,11; 35,4ff; 83,10-19; 109,6-20; 137,7ff). Undoubtedly these calls for vengeance, which shock us, as if we knew how to pardon*, include a certain amount of personal or nationalistic resentment. But once they have been purified, these cries can be taken up in the NT; for they express not only the distress of mankind subjected to the curse of sin, but they call for the justice* of God, which necessarily implies the destruction of sin. Can God refuse to listen to the imprecation uttered by a person who at the same time confesses his own sin (Ba 3,8; Dn 9,11-15)? The Servant goes as far as to renounce the right of vengeance belonging to the innocent man who is persecuted. "Without opening his mouth" (Is 53,7), he offers himself up to the curse for our sins (53, 3f); his intercession will be a guarantee of salvation for sinners, while waiting for the end of sin to come; then "there shall be no more curse" (Ze 14,11).

V. JESUS CHRIST, CONQUEROR OF THE CURSE

"There is no more condemnation for those who are in union with Christ Jesus" (R 8,1) nor is there any curse. Having become "sin" (2 Co 5,21) and "curse" for us, by allowing Himself to be identified with sin and with the curse incurred by sin, Christ "has bought us back from the Law's curse" (G 3,13) and put us in possession of the blessing and of the Spirit* of God. The Word can then inaugurate the new times, when there will be no more curses properly so called (gr. *katara*) uttered by Jesus but the declaration of a state of unhappiness (gr. *ouai*), which is now coupled with the beatitude* (Lk 6,20-26). It does not reject but attracts (Jn 12,32), it does not scatter but brings together (E 2,16). The Word frees man from the accursed chains—Satan, sin, anger, death—and enables him to love. The Father, who has forgiven everyone in His Son, can teach His children how to conquer the curse by pardon (R 12,14; 1 Co 13,5) and by love (Mt 5,44; Col 3,13). The Christian can no longer curse (1 P 3,9). As opposed to the "cursed be the man who curses you!" of the OT, following the Lord's example he should "bless those who curse you" (Lk 6,28).

Though conquered by Christ the curse remains a reality, no longer a deadly fate as it was without Him, but still a possibility. The supreme manifestation of blessing, even in its

most intense emotion, brings the rancor of the curse, which follows in its footsteps from the beginning. The curse, taking advantage of the final days which are numbered for it (Ap 12, 12), lets loose all its poison at the time when salvation* is consummated (8,13). Therefore, the NT contains a good number of formulas of cursing. The Apocalypse can at the same time proclaim, "There will no longer be any curse" (22,3), and still hurl the definitive curse, "Out...with all who love evil!" (22,15), out with the dragon (12), the beast and the false prophet (13), the nations, Gog and Magog (20,7), the prostitute (17), Babel (18), death and Sheol (20,14), the darkness (22,5), the world* (Jn 16,33), and the powers* of this world (1 Co 2,6). This total curse, "Out!" without recourse, is uttered by Jesus Christ. What makes it dreadful is that it is not for Him a passionate vengeance*, nor a reasonable demand for retaliation. It is more pure and more terrifying; it leaves to their choice those who have cut themselves off from love*.

Not that Jesus came to curse and condemn (Jn 3,17; 12,47); rather He brings blessings. Never during His life did He curse anyone. Of course, He did not refrain from making the most foreboding threats against the satiated people of this world (Lk 6,24ff), against the unbelieving cities of Galilee (Mt 11,21), against the scribes and pharisees (Mt 23,13-31), against "this generation*" in which all the sins of Israel are concentrated (23,33-36), against "that man by whom the Son of Man is handed over" (26,24). But these were always warnings and sad prophecies and never outbursts of wrath*. A curse in the proper sense of the word does not come to the lips of the Son of Man except at His final coming, "Depart from me, you cursed!" (Mt 25,41). Yet even at that hour, He warns us that there will be no change in His attitude. "If anyone hears my words and disregards them, it is not I who shall condemn him...The message I have given will judge him on the last day" (Jn 12,47f).

→Anathema NT—Beatitude—Blessing—Beasts & Beast 2—Blasphemy—Earth OT I 3—Good & Evil II 2—Hell OT II; NT I—Sickness/Healing OT I 3—Suffering O; OT II; NT I 2—Vintage I—Wealth III 1—Wrath *B* NT I 2, III 1.

JCo & JG hjb

D

DAVID

The figure of David, as man and king, stands out in such a way that he ever remains for Israel the type of Messiah who is to be born of his race. From David's time onward the covenant* with the people became the covenant with the king*, as Ben Sira recalls at the end of the section in which he describes it (Si 47,2-11). The throne of Israel is therefore the throne of David (Is 9,6; Lk 1,32). His victories* foretell the triumph the Messiah*, filled with the Spirit who rested on the son of Jesse (1 S 16,13; Is 11, 1-9), will win over injustice. By the victory of His resurrection, Jesus will fulfill the promises made to David (Ac 13,32-37) and will give history its meaning (Ap 5,5). How did the person of David achieve this chosen place in salvation history?

1. *The chosen of God.* David is called by God and consecrated by anointing* (1 S 16,1-13). David is consistently the "blessed*" of God, the one whom God assists with His presence*. Because God is with him he succeeds in all his undertakings (16,18); in his struggle with Goliath (17,45ff), in his wars in the service of Saul (18,14ff), and in those he will conduct as king and liberator of Israel: "Everywhere he went, Yahweh gave him the victory" (2 S 8,14).

Like Moses*, David was commanded to be the shepherd* of Israel (2 S 5,2). He inherits the promises* made to the patriarchs; first of all, that of possessing the land of Canaan. He engineers the taking possession by his battle against the Philistines, begun in the time of Saul and continued during his own reign (5,17-25; cf 10—12). The definitive conquest is perfected by the taking of Jerusalem* (5,6-10), which will be called the "City* of David." This city becomes the capital of all Israel. Around it is effected the union of the tribes. Jerusalem is where the ark* brought in by David created a new holy city (6,1—19). And David there fulfills the priestly functions (6,17f). Thus "David and the whole house of Israel" form one sole people* around their God.

2. *The hero of Israel.* David answers his call-ing with a deep attachment to God. His religion is characterized by expectancy of the hour of God. He therefore restrains himself from making an attempt on Saul's life, even though he has the opportunity to rid himself of his persecutor (1 S 24; 26). He allows himself to be entirely ruled by God's will and is ready to accept whatever comes from Him (2 S 15,25f), hoping that the Lord will change all the evils he has to undergo into blessings (16,10ff). He remains the lowly servant, overwhelmed by the privileges God gives him (2 S 7,18-29); hence he is the model of the "poor" who, in imitation of his surrender to God and his most certain hope, continue his prayer in the praises and petitions of the Psalter. But the deep insights gained by his piety do not prevent us from seeing the archaic nature of his religion, whether it is a question of the use of an ephod as a divining instrument (1 S 23,9; 30, 7) or of the presence of a teraphim in his house (19,13).

To the "singer of Israel's songs" (2 S 23,1), the Levites attribute, besides numerous psalms, the plan of the temple (1 Ch 22; 28) as well as the organization of the cult (23—25) and of its songs (Ne 12,24.36), and even, already in the time of Amos, the invention of musical instruments (Am 6,5).

David's religious fame should not make one overlook the man. He had his weaknesses and his greatnesses. He was a rough soldier, deceitful too (1 S 27,10ff). He did grave wrongs and showed himself weak with his sons even before his old age. His morals still lacked refinement: during his stay with the Philistines he acted as a robber chief (1 S 27,8-12) and was even cunning enough not to let Achish notice anything unusual, even after more than a year (29,6f). Nor can we pass over in silence his merciless reaction after the burning of Ziklag (30,17) or in his struggle with Moab (2 S 8,2). And finally, although he was bound by his word not to deal severely with all who had done him harm, he left his posthumous revenge in the hands of Solomon (1 K 2,5-9). But what magnanimity in his faithful friendship* for Jonathan, in the respect that he ever manifested toward Saul. Some details reveal his greatness of soul: reverence for the ark (2 S 15,24-29), respect for the lives of his soldiers (23,13-17), generosity (1 S 30, 21-25), and forgiveness (2 S 19,16-24). He was moreover, a shrewd statesman who won for himself the friendship of Saul's court and of the elders of Judah (1 S 30,26-31) when he disapproved the assassination of Abner (2 S 3,28-37) and avenged the murder of Ishbaal (4,9-12).

3. *The Messiah, son of David.* The success of David could have made one think that God's promises were achieved. Then a new and solemn prophecy gives fresh impetus to Israel's hope (2 S 7,12-16). As David projects the building of a temple*, God informs him that He wishes to build for him an everlasting lineage (*bānāh*: "build*"; *bēn*: "son"); "I will build you a house" (7,27). Thus God turns Israel's attention toward the future. It is an unconditional promise which does not destroy the covenant* of Sinai but strengthens it by concentrating it in the person of the king (7,24). Henceforth, it is through the Davidic dynasty that God, present in Israel, would lead and maintain her in unity. Psalm 132 sings of the bond set up between the ark, symbol of the divine presence, and the lineage of David.

Thus is understood the importance of the problem of succession to the Davidic throne and the intrigues it arouses (cf 2 S 9—20; 1 K 1). So, too, is better understood the place of David in the prophetic oracles (Ho 3,5; Jr 30,9; Ez 34,23f). Mention of David in them is affirmation of the jealous love of God for His people (Is 9,6) and His faithfulness to His covenant (Jr 33,20ff), "an everlasting covenant, made of favors promised to David" (Is 55,3). None could question this faithfulness*, even in the midst of trial* (Ps 89,4f.20-46).

At the fullness of time, Christ therefore is called "Son of David" (Mt 1,1). Jesus never rejected this Messianic designation, but it failed to express fully the mystery of His person. Therefore, since He came to fulfill the promises made to David, Jesus proclaims that He is greater than David: He is David's Lord* (Mt 22,42-45). Jesus is not merely "David the servant," shepherd of the people of God (Ez 34, 23f) and His faithfulness to His covenant (Jr 33,20ff), He is God Himself who comes to feed and save His people (34,15f), "shoot of the race of David," for whom the Spirit and the spouse wait and for whose return they pray (Ap 22,16f).

→Anointing III 2—Covenant OT II 1—Election OT I 3 c—House II 1—Israel OT 2 a—Jerusalem—Jesus Christ II 1 c—King—Kingdom OT II—Melchisedech 2—Messiah—Number II 2—Prayer II 1—Promises II 3—Servant of God I—Shepherd & Flock OT 2—Strength O—Temple OT I 2—Unity II.

RM jrc

DAY OF THE LORD

The believer does not see history as continually making a new beginning; rather it is a progression which the visitations* of God divide into seasons, days, hours*, and privileged moments. The Lord has come; He does not cease to come; and He will come to judge* the world and to save the faithful. In this total view of history, "the day of the Lord" is a special expression used to designate God's solemn intervention in the course of that history. Sometimes the expression is shortened to "the day" or "that day." It has a twofold meaning. First of all, it is an historical event, the day which will witness the triumph of God over His enemies. It also has a cultic meaning, i.e., the day especially set aside for the worship of God. These two meanings are not unrelated. Worship* commemorates and proclaims God's intervention in history. The historical event, because it comes from God, transcends time; it belongs to God's eternal present, which worship must actualize in historical time*.

OT

I. THE PROCLAMATION OF THE DAY OF YAHWEH

The expectation of an unmistakable intervention of Yahweh on Israel's behalf seems to have found very early expression in popular belief: the expectation of a "day of light*" (Am 5,18). Indeed, in the different uses of this idea by the prophets, from the eighth to the fourth century, the same pattern can be seen describing the day of the Lord. Yahweh shouts His battle cry (Zp 1,14; Is 13,2): "The day of Yahweh is at hand!" (Ez 30,3; Is 13,6; Jl 1,15); and He assembles His enemies for battle (Is 13,3ff). It is a day of clouds (Ez 30,3) and fire (Zp 1,18; Ml 3,19); the heavens are overturned (Is 34,4), the earth trembles (Jl 2,1-11), the world is laid waste (Is 7,23) and plunged into a solitude like that of Gomorrah (Zp 2,9) and the desert (Is 13,9). Panic lays hold of men (Is 2,10.19); they hide themselves (Is 2,21), filled with confusion (Ez 7,7), frightened (Is 13,8), struck blind (Zp 1,17); their arms hang useless at their sides (Ez 7,17);

they lose heart (Is 13,7); they are unable to stand on their feet (Ml 3,2). This is the destruction of everything (Zp 1,18), the judgment, the selection (Ml 3,20), the purification (3,3); it is the end (Ez 7,6f).

Although after the exile this description is applied to the last day, its first application is to the course of historical events. Thus the destruction of Jerusalem was a "day of Yahweh" (Ez 13,5; 34,12; Lm 1,12; 2,22). The origin of this description is not to be found in some myth about a war* among the gods (even though the imagery of the day preserves some mythical traits). Nor will the origin be found in Israel's cult (though religious festivals were called "days of Yahweh"). Behind all this there is an historical experience: the intervention of Yahweh fighting on behalf of His people. Such interventions are the "day of Midian," when Yahweh distinguishes Himself by giving Israel a marvellous victory* (Is 9,3; cf Jg 7,15-25); the day of Joshua* (Js 10,12f); the day of Jezreel (Ho 2,2) and many other "days" of victory (Is 28, 21; cf 2 S 5,17-25). According to the tradition of the holy war* Yahweh would enter the battle with a battlecry (Nm 10,35f; Ps 68,2); He would stop the sun if need be (Js 10,12ff; cf Ex 14,20; Js 24,7), and press into His service the clouds (Jg 5,4f), the thunder (1 S 7,10) or stones from heaven (Js 10,11); He would strike terror into the enemy ranks and wipe them out (Ex 15,14f; 23,27f; Js 2,9; 5,1...). Israel built up the idea of the Day of the Lord from the memories of their national epic, and through these images they affirmed their faith: Yahweh is the Lord of history.

II. EXPECTATION OF THE LAST DAY

Yahweh directs history to its final outcome. Hence, the proclamation for Israel of a day of Yahweh will become a proclamation of such a day for the whole world. This day will not occur in the course of time, but at the end of time and of our present world.

Originally, the day of Yahweh extended only to Israel. The prophets, in their struggle against the false sense of security of a people who thought they had a right to be delivered unconditionally from all their troubles, went contrary to the popular hope, whether or not they used the term "day of Yahweh" (Am 5,18ff; Ho; Is 28,14ff; Mi 1,2f; Jr 4). Only for a remnant* will the day mark the victory of Israel.

With the prophet Zephaniah (6th century)

the scope of the day of Yahweh is enlarged. It will affect the enemy nations* (Zp 2,4-15); it will prepare for their conversion and the restoration of Israel (3,9-18). At the time of the exile, when the Day of Yahweh's wrath* has arrived for Jerusalem (Lm 1,12), the double idea of the Day which means judgment* for the nations* and victory for the Remnant* of Israel becomes established. This day overtakes Babel (Is 13) and Edom (Is 34). For Israel, which must always be cleansed (Ml 3,2; Ze 13,1f), it is an assurance of protection (Ze 12, 1-4), the gift of the Spirit (Jl 3; Ze 12,10), a new paradise* (Jl 4,18; Ze 14,8). Israel will take vengeance on her enemies (Jr 46,10) when the hour of the nations has sounded (Ez 30,3f). Such is the "day of vengeance* of Yahweh" (Is 34,8).

The same tendency that extends the Day of Yahweh to the nations also refers it to the end of time. Even as early as the time of Ezekiel the day is thought of as marking an "end" (Ez 7,6f). In Daniel it is the "end of the world" (Dn 9,26; 11,27; 12,13), and it will be preceded by "the time of the end" (8,17; 11,35.40; 12,4.9). The images of Yahweh's war* against the enemies of Israel (cf Ze 14,12-20) are enriched with cosmic images representing Yahweh's original battle, when He triumphed over the beasts* and the chaos. Nevertheless, the account remains in contact with history. The coalition assembled from the four corners of the earth to oppose Jerusalem (Ze 12,3) will be crushed by Yahweh, who will be acknowledged as judge of the whole world (Ps 94,2; 96,13). The entire earth will be stripped of its peoples (Is 24,1), and the people of God shall be destroyed (Ez 38) like the gods who inspire them. Thus the day of Yahweh will mark the definitive victory of God over His enemies. The kingdom psalms put this hope in the form of a prayer, appealing to the God of vengeance (Ps 94) or announcing His reign (Ps 93; 96—99).

NT

With the coming of Christ, time* acquires a new dimension which is reflected in a complexity of terms. The NT authors speak of a day of visitation* (1 P 2,12), a day of wrath* (R 2,5), a day of judgment* (2 P 2,9), "that day" (Mt 7,22), the day of the Lord (1 Th 5,2; 2 Th 2,2). These authors also speak of the day of the Lord Jesus (1 Co 1,8), the day of Christ (Ph 1,6.10), the day of the Son of Man (Lk 17, 24ff). They also use the words *apokalypsis* (2 Th

1,7; 1 P 1,7.13), *epiphaneia* (1 Tm 6,14; Tt 2,13), *parousia* (Mt 24,3.27; 1 Th 2,19; 2 Th 2,1; 1 Co 15,23; Jm 5,7f; 1 Jn 2,28). *Parousia* ordinarily means "presence" (2 Co 10,10) or "coming" (2 Co 7,6f); in the Graeco-Roman world the word was used to designate the official visitations of emperors. In the NT the use of *parousia* can also derive from the apocalyptic tradition of the OT concerning the "coming of the Lord" (vg Ze 9,9). As the NT vocabulary shows, the Day of the Lord is from now on the Day of Christ. Certain texts (2 Tm 1,10) anticipate the "epiphany" of the Lord and even apply it to the Incarnation; others reveal a tendency to a more spiritual approach, while preserving the apocalyptic apparatus of the OT.

I. THE COMING OF THE LORD

The question is whether the coming of the Lord is fully realized with the appearance on earth of Jesus of Nazareth, now that He has become Lord. A certain tension remains between the traditional eschatology and its actualization. It is the Judge of the end of time who "comes" according to the Baptist's announcement (Mt 3,11); and the Spirit "comes" on Jesus at His baptism (3,16). And yet John wonders whether Jesus is "the one who is to come" (11,3). "The kingdom of heaven is here," says Jesus, using a formula like the one used in the OT to proclaim the Day of the Lord; "the kingdom of God has overtaken you" (12, 28). Pentecost fulfills the prophecy of Joel: the Day of the Lord inaugurates "the last days" (Ac 2,17). And the entry of the Gentiles into the Church fulfills the prophecy of Amos (Ac 15,16ff). However neither the Passover nor Pentecost are called "Day of the Lord," except in liturgical usage. Although this expression is realized in a certain way in the "days" of the Lord Jesus, it continues to sustain the hope of Christians, who are awaiting His return.

1. *The day of the Son of Man.* For the one whom they expect at the end of time is Jesus, glorified like the Son of Man* in Daniel, as He Himself foretold (Lk 17,24ff). In these sayings Jesus uses the classical descriptions of the OT with its imposing theophanies, especially in "the synoptic apocalypse" (Mt 24 p). We recognize the elements of war (24,6ff), cosmic events (24,29), the rising up of idolatry (24,15), the selectivity of the judgment (24,37-43), the suddenness and unpredictability of the day (24,44).

The element added to the OT tradition is the coming of the Son of Man in glory (24,30f). Similar images are found in other apocalyptic texts of the NT. Thus Paul speaks of a trumpet and the archangel of the end (1 Th 4,16f; 1 Co 15,52); he recalls that the day will come like a thief, bringing with it terrible sufferings (1 Th 5,3), and that it will mark the final victory over the enemy (1 Co 15,24-28). But Paul also adds that then will occur the resurrection of the dead and the meeting with Christ descending from heaven (1 Th 4,16f). The Apocalypse also preserves the context of war (wrath, armies, cries of victory) and judgment (Ap 20,11ff) and of cosmic events (21,1). In short, on the Day of the Lord, the triumph of God (OT) through His Son Jesus (NT) will be celebrated. With salvation in sight (1 P 1,4f), all things will be restored (Ac 1,6; 3,19f), and our bodies will be transformed into His body of glory (Ph 3,20f).

2. *Light shed on our daily life.* This future event has a determining effect on the behavior of the believer here below. The parousia allows us to evaluate men at their true worth (1 Co 1,18), to judge the importance of human works (4,3ff), and to calculate the stability of this world whose "shape passes away" (7,31). The prospect of the parousia sheds light on many of Paul's decisions (cf 6,12ff; 7,26...); it sustains the Christian in hope (Tt 2,13); it helps him to accept persecution joyfully as an anticipation of the last day (1 P 5,13f); and it should be positively desired: "May the reign of God come!" For God will bring the work of salvation to its conclusion (Ph 1,6) by making His faithful strong and blameless (1 Co 1,8; Ph 1,9f; 2 Tm 1,12.18), as they await with love this final "epiphany" (2 Tm 4,8). This confidence, which the Apocalypse, following Paul, wants to inspire, is the basis of the Christian's pride* at the prospect of the imminent return of the Lord (1 Jn 2,28; 4,17), even though he is already faced by the manifestations of the Antichrist* (4,1-4).

II. IMMINENCE AND DELAY OF THE PAROUSIA

The expectation of the parousia, understood as the coming of the Lord, is ambiguous. Although the faithful are assured that "Jesus will come in the same way in which He was seen going to heaven" (Ac 1,11), still they do not at all know when He will come (Mt 24,42).

Its perpetual imminence impresses itself on their conscious faith with such force that they are spontaneously led to assume an early date for His coming. The NT tradition preserves the note of imminence amidst a "delay" that becomes more and more evident. Imminence is not exactly the same as chronological proximity.

1. *Proximity of the parousia.* It seems that in the early days of the Church the faithful, surrounded by the light of Easter and Pentecost, thought that Christ was going to return shortly. The community at Thessalonica reflected this conviction in some enlightening excesses: the dead would have no part in the blessing* of the parousia (1 Th 4,13...); work was no longer necessary, since the Lord was coming (2 Th 3,6); then the parousia would already have taken place. In correcting their illusions Paul never says that the parousia will come in the distant future; on the contrary, he fosters the hope of being alive at the time (1 Th 4,17). He teaches especially the duty to watch* because "the day comes like a thief in the night" (1 Th 5,2). Then, too, the note of imminence is hard to express without becoming involved in considerations of time; what is imminent seems to be "soon" to come. Thus the NT authors present the parousia as "closer" at hand now than it was formerly (R 13,11): the day has drawn near, the judgment is at hand (1 P 4,5ff); a little while longer and the day will come (He 10,25. 37). Jesus says: "I am coming soon" (Ap 22,20).

2. *Delay of the parousia.* The result is that the parousia appears to the believer to be slow in coming. Jesus had proclaimed this delay (Mt 25,5.19) and for that reason preached a constant vigilance (24,42-51), which permits the keeping of the commandment without spot (1 Tm 6,15). The time before the parousia ought to be spent in making one's talents profitable (Mt 25,14-30) and in helping other men (25,31-46) according to the new commandment which Jesus taught at the time of His departure and promise to return (Jn 13,33-36). "And so," St. Paul concludes, "while we still have time, let us do good" (G 6,10; cf Col 4,5; E 5,16). If the parousia is slow in coming, one must guard against listening to false teachers, for it will surely come (2 P 3,10). If today nothing appears to have changed (3,4), it is because we await the chastisement of the world by fire* (3,7). If the parousia keeps us waiting, it is because the Lord does not measure time as men do (3,8) and because He patiently hopes for the conver-

sion of all men (3,8f). The believer ought to pray, therefore, for the coming of the parousia, since that will be the coming of the kingdom* in all its fullness. "Come, Lord!" was the prayer of the first Christians (1 Co 16,22; Ap 22,17.20).

III. EASTER AND THE PAROUSIA

Although it is of great significance that history is brought to completion by the coming of the Lord, still that coming must not blind the faithful to the meaning of Easter and Pentecost. Christ is already in His glory; in some way or other, His day is with us right now.

1. *"Sons of the day"* (1 Th 5,5). In using this expression Paul reflects the common faith. Since Christ has arisen, the believer no longer belongs solely to the night*, but to the day. No more is the day to be awaited only in the imminent future—a fact which was already affecting the conduct of the Christian; but it is interiorized spiritually in the believer to the extent that he becomes "a son of the light" (E 5,8).

A similar conviction is expressed elsewhere in theological terms: we are already arisen with Christ through baptism (R 6,3f), salvation is already ours (E 2,5f), our life is hidden in God (Col 3,3f).

2. *In the fourth gospel,* the tension between future and present is preserved, although the present reality of salvation outweighs the expectation of it in the future. The classical themes of eschatology are found: Messianic tribulation (Jn 13,19; 14,1...; 16,1-4), the last day (6,39f. 44.54; 11,24; 12,48), the coming of Jesus (21, 22f), resurrection to judgment (5,28; 11,24), fire (15,6), the casting out of the enemy (12,31). But it is "now" (5,25; 12,31) that everything is accomplished. The voice of the Son of Man replaces the trumpet of judgment (5,25); judgment is passed and wrath abides with the unbeliever (3,36); eternal life is given (5,24); His glory is made manifest (1,14; 2,11; 11,40), for the hour* of the glorious passion of the Son of Man has arrived (12,27.31; 13,1; 17,1). Thus an act of faith in Jesus who presents Himself to men makes the day of judgment actually present (5,24; 6,47). Finally, the Church is the place of Christ's presence when she keeps the commandment of love (13,35). Without rejecting the imminence of the parousia, John has thus spiritualized the tradition in making the day of the Lord actually present through faith.

3. *Sunday, the day of the Lord.* The parousia is also rendered present in worship. In the apocalypse, John speaks of a "day pertaining to the Lord," *dies dominica* (Ap 1,10), during which he had his vision. It is the "first day of the week" (1 Co 16,2; Ac 20,7), in the course of which Christians honored the Lord. This day fell on the day after the Sabbath*: if it was chosen, it was not with the intention of taking the place of the Sabbath but in order to commemorate an historical event—the day of Easter, according to the precise form given at the beginning of the second century. Sunday recalls the victory of the Lord on the great day of the resurrection. On the other hand, as the day of the eucharistic celebration, it proclaims the return of the Lord, His parousia (1 Co 11, 26). Tradition will fill out this interpretation by calling Sunday "the eighth day," which recalls the fact that on the day of Easter, which anticipates the parousia, God's creation of the first day has achieved its fullness.

→Calamity 2—Cloud 3.4.5—Elijah OT 5—Fear of God I—Feasts NT II—Fire OT III; NT I—Fulfill OT 3; NT 3—Harvest III 1.2 c—Hope NT II—Jesus Christ I 3—Judgment—Light & Dark OT II 3—Night OT 2; NT 3—Passover III 1—Perfection NT 6—Pilgrimage OT 2—Plan of God NT IV—Repentance/Conversion NT I, IV 2—Resurrection NT II 1—Sabbath NT 2—Salvation OT I 2; NT II 3—Sign NT II 4—Son of Man—Suffering NT II—Time OT III 2; NT II 3, III—Visit—Watch I—Wrath.

PA & XLD mjm

DEATH

OT

I. PRESENCE OF DEATH

1. *The experience of death.* Every man experiences death. Far from having the effect of turning men aside to take refuge in illusory dreams, biblical revelation, at whatever level it is examined, begins by clearly facing the fact of death: the death of loved ones, which, after farewell* has been said (Gn 49), distresses those left behind (50,1; 2 S 19,1...); death is something which each man must envisage for himself since he also "will see* death" (Ps 39,49; Lk 2,26; Jn 8,51), "will taste* death" (Mt 16, 28 p; Jn 8,52; He 2,9). This is a bitter thought

for one who enjoys the goods of this world, but a desirable prospect for him who is overwhelmed by the trials of life (cf Si 41,1f). Thus, while Hezekiah wept over his fast approaching death (2 K 20,2f), Job cried aloud for its consummation (Jb 6,9; 7,15).

2. *After death.* The dead "are no more" (Ps 39,14; Jb 7,8,21; 7,10): the first impression is one of non-existence, for what happens after death escapes the grasp of the living. According to the belief of primitive peoples, long conserved in the OT, death is, nevertheless, not total annihilation. While the body* is placed in an earthen grave, something of the dead person, a shadow*, persists in Sheol (*šeōl*). But these hells* are conceived in a very rudimentary manner: a gaping hole, a deep pit, a place of silence (Ps 115,17), of perdition, darkness, and oblivion (Ps 88,12f; Jb 17,13). There all the dead share the same miserable lot (Jb 3,13-19; Is 14,9f), even though there are degrees of ignominy (Ez 32,17-32); they are given over to dust (Jb 17,16; Ps 22,16; 30,10) and vermin (Is 14,11; Jb 17,14). Their existence is but a sleep* (Ps 13,4; Dn 12, 2): gone is hope, knowledge of God, experience of His miracles, and praise offered to Him (Ps 6,6; 30,10; 88,12f; 115,7; Is 38,18). God Himself forgets the dead (Ps 88,6). And once the gates* of Sheol are entered (Jb 38,17; cf Ws 16,13) there is no return whatsoever (Jb 10,21f).

Such is the desolate perspective which death presents to man on the day when he has to be "reunited with his forebears" (Gn 42,29). These images do no more than give concrete form to the spontaneous impressions which are universal and are held even today by so many of our contemporaries. That the OT remained at this level of belief to a rather late date is a sign that when it encountered Egyptian religion and Greek spiritualism, it refused to devaluate this mortal life in order to place all hope in an imaginary immortality. It rather waited for a clear revelation, through proper channels, of the mystery of the after-life.

3. *The cult of the dead.* Funeral rites are a universal phenomenon: since the dawn of history man has honored his dead and maintained some contact with them. The OT conserves the essentials of this secular tradition: deeds of mourning translate the grief of the living (2 S 3,31; Jr 16,6); ritual burial (1 S 31, 12f; Tb 2,4-8), prompted by a dread of death without burial (Dt 21,23); care of tombs, which touches closely on familial piety (Gn 23; 49,29-

32; 50,12f); funeral banquets (Jr 16,7); even offerings on the tombs of the dead (Tb 4,17), although they are placed "before mouths forever closed" (Si 30,18).

However, revelation already imposes some limits on these customs which are bound up with the superstitious beliefs of neighboring peoples. Hence the prohibition against ritual incisions (Lv 19,28; Dt 14,1), and especially the proscription of necromancy (Lv 19,3; 20,27; Dt 18,11). It was a serious temptation at a time when magic* flourished and conjuring up the dead was widely practiced (cf Odyssey), not unlike today's devotees of spiritualism (1 S 28; 2 K 21,6). We do not find in the OT a cult of the dead properly so-called, such as existed among the Egyptians. The absence of knowledge about life beyond the grave was doubtless an aid in guarding the Israelites from this practice.

4. *Death, man's destiny.* Death is the common lot of mankind, "the way of all the earth" (1 K 2,2; cf 2 S 14,14; Si 8,7). In putting an end to each man's life, death leaves its impression on man's personality: the death of the patriarchs "filled with days" (Gn 25,8; 35,29), the mysterious death of Moses (Dt 34), the tragic death of Saul (1 S 31)...But before this inevitable necessity, how can one help but feel that life, so ardently desired, is but a fragile and fugitive good*? It is a shadow*, a sigh, a nothing (Ps 39,5ff; 89,48f; 90; Jb 14,1-12; Ws 2,2f); it is vanity, since the final lot of all is the same (Qo 3; Ps 49,8...), even of kings (Si 10,10)! A melancholy truth, resulting sometimes in a disillusioning resignation when faced with an inevitable destiny (2 S 12,23; 14,14). Yet, true wisdom goes further; it accepts death as a divine decree (Si 41,4), which underlines the lowliness of the human condition when faced with an immortal God: what is dust returns to dust (Gn 3,19).

5. *The influence of death.* Despite all this, a living man senses in death an inimical force. Spontaneously he gives it a countenance and personifies it. Death is the melancholy shepherd who in hell pens men up (Ps 49,15); he penetrates into homes to cut down young children (Jr 9,20). True, in the OT death also wears the garb of an exterminating angel, executing divine vengeance* (Ex 12,23; 2 S 24,16; 2 K 19,35), and even plays the role of the divine Word* which exterminates God's adversaries (Ws 18,15f). But this purveyor of the insatiable fires of hell (cf Pr 27,20) more often has the traits of another power whose sly approach is suspected in every sickness and danger. Alas, the sick man already sees himself as "reckoned among the dead" (Ps 88,4ff); the man in peril of death is encompassed by the waters* of death, the torrents of Belial, the cords of Sheol (Ps 18,5f; 69,15f; 116,3; Jon 2,4-7). Death and Sheol are not only realities of the lower world; they are powers* at work in this world—and heaven help the man who falls into their clutches! What, after all, is life if not man's anguished struggle against death?

II. THE MEANING OF DEATH

1. *The origin of death.* Although the experience of death does awaken such resonant chords in man, it is impossible to reduce it to a simple natural phenomenon whose objective observation entirely exhausts its content. We cannot deny meaning to death. Violently contradicting our natural desire to live, death oppresses us like a chastisement; this is why we instinctively see in death the penalty of sin*. From this intuition, common to ancient religions, the OT constructs a firm doctrine which highlights the religious significance of an extremely bitter experience. Justice wills that the impious perish (Jb 18,5-21; Ps 37,20.28.36; 73,27); the sinful soul must die (Ez 18,20).

This fundamental principle already clarifies the enigmatic fact of death in this world: as to its origin, the sentence of death was not pronounced against man until after the sin of Adam*, our first parent (Gn 2,17; 3,19). For God did not make death (Ws 1,13); He created man to be incorruptible, and death only entered the world through the envy of the devil (Ws 2, 23f). The influence which death exercises over us possesses the value of a sign: it manifests the presence of sin in this world.

2. *The way to death.* Once this connection between sin and death has been discovered, a new aspect of our existence is revealed in its true colors. Not only is sin an evil in that it is contrary to our nature and to the divine will; but it is also concretely for us the "way* to death." Such is the teaching of the sages. He who pursues evil, marches to his death (Pr 11, 19). The one who allows himself to be seduced by Dame Folly* travels toward the valleys of Sheol (7,27; 9,18). Already the gates of hell open wide to swallow up the sinner (Is 5,14), as they did for Korah and his followers who

descended alive into hell (Nm 16,30...; Ps 55, 16). The godless* man is indeed walking a slippery path (Ps 73,18f). He is already virtually dead since he has made a pact with death and has chosen his portion (Ws 1,16); and his final lot will be to become an object of opprobrium forever amidst the dead (Ws 4,19). This law of providence had practical repercussions in the life of Israel. Men guilty of the gravest sins must be punished with death (Lv 20,8-21; 24,14-23). In the case of sinners, death is certainly not a natural destiny. Privation of the most cherished gift of God, life*, takes on the character of damnation.

3. *The enigma of the just man's death.* What then shall we say of the death of the just*? That a father's sins should be punished by the death of his sons is still somewhat comprehensible when one considers the solidarity of mankind (2 S 12,14...; cf Ex 20,5). But if it is true that every man pays for his own crimes (cf Ez 18), how can we justify the death of the innocent? Apparently God allows the just to perish in the same way as the guilty (Jb 9,22; Qo 7,15; Ps 49,11). Is there any meaning left in their death? Here the faith of the OT ends in an enigma. For its solution the mystery of death requires light from above.

III. DELIVERANCE FROM DEATH

1. *God saves man from death.* It is not within man's power to save himself from death: this requires God's* grace since He alone is, by nature, life itself. Thus, when the influence of death over man manifests itself, in whatever way it happens, man can only appeal to God (Ps 6,5; 13,4; 116,3). If he is a just man, he can then cherish the hope that God "will not abandon his soul to Sheol" (Ps 16,10), that He "will redeem his soul from the clutches of Sheol" (Ps 49,16). Once healed or saved from peril, he gives thanks to God for deliverance from death (Ps 18,17; 30; Jon 2,7; Is 38,17), for he has had concrete experience of this liberation. Even before the perspective of his faith has gone beyond the limitations of this life, he will know that the divine power* surpasses that of death and Sheol. This is the first landmark of a hope* which will ultimately expand into a perspective of immortality.

2. *Conversion and deliverance from death.* Moreover, in the context of this present life God does not accord this deliverance from death in a capricious way. Certain stringent conditions are necessary. The sinner is dying precisely because of his sins; and God is not pleased by his death. He prefers that the sinner be converted and live (Ez 18,33; 33,11). If by sickness God puts a man in danger of death, this is to correct him. Once converted from his sin, He will snatch him from the infernal pit (Jb 33,19-30). This shows the importance of prophetic* preaching, which, by inviting man to be converted, strives to save his soul from death (Ez 3,18-21; cf Jm 5,20). The same is true of the teacher* who corrects a child in order to withdraw him from evil (Pr 23,13f). God alone delivers man from death; but not without man's cooperation.

3. *The definitive deliverance from death.* In the last analysis any hope of deliverance from death will be vain unless this deliverance surpasses the bounds of terrestrial life. The anguish of Job and the pessimism of Ecclesiastes bear witness to this fact. But at a later date the OT revelation did go further. It announced an ultimate triumph of God over death, a definitive deliverance of man snatched from the dominance of death. Then, when He sets up His eschatological kingdom, God will destroy forever that death which He did not make in the beginning (Is 25,8). At that time, the just who sleep in dust will rise from their graves in order to participate in His kingdom eternally, while the wicked will remain in the eternal horror of Sheol (Dn 12,2; cf Is 26,19). In this new perspective, the lower regions will have become a place of eternal damnation, our hell*. Conversely, the idea of life after death has also been clarified. Already the psalmists are formulating the hope that God will deliver them forever from the power of Sheol (Ps 16,10; 49,16; 73,20). This desire now becomes a reality. Just as Enoch was taken up without seeing death (Gn 5,24; cf He 11,4), the just will be raised up by the Lord, who will take them into His glory (Ws 4,7...; 5,1-3.15). This is why, here below, their hope* is for full immortality (Ws 3,4). And so, we have an explanation of how the martyrs in the time of the Maccabees, animated with such a faith, could heroically bear their torments (2 M 7,9.14.23.33; cf 14,46), while Judas Maccabeus, animated by this same thought, inaugurated prayers for the dead (2 M 12,43ff). From then on the present life counted for less than eternal life.

4. *Fruitfulness of the just man's death**. Even before it opened to all men the new perspective, revelation had given new clarity to the problem of the just man's death by attesting to its fecundity. The fact that the just one, the Servant* of Yahweh, should suffer death and "be cut off from the land of the living," is not totally devoid of meaning. His death is an expiatory sacrifice* offered voluntarily for the sins of men; through it the plan* of God is accomplished (Is 53,8-12). Thereby was revealed in advance the most mysterious trait in the economy of salvation* which the life of Jesus set in motion.

NT

In the NT the dominant lines of prior revelation converge toward the mystery of Christ's death. There all of human history appears like some gigantic drama of life and death; until the coming of Christ, and without Him, there is only the kingdom of death. Christ comes, and by His death triumphs over death itself; from that instant, death takes on a new meaning for the new humanity which dies with Christ in order to live with Him eternally.

I. THE REIGN OF DEATH

1. *Recalling its origins.* The drama began at the beginning of human history: through man's fault sin* entered the world, and through sin, death (R 5,12.17; 1 Co 15,21). Since that time all men "die in Adam*" (15,22), so that death rules the world (R 5,14). This sense of the presence of death, which the OT expresses in such a striking manner, truly corresponds to an objective reality, and behind the universal reign of death lurks Satan*, "the prince of this world," "a murderer from the beginning" (Jn 8,44).

2. *Humanity under the empire of death.* What gives force to the empire of death is sin. It is the "sting of death" (1 Co 15,56=Ho 13,14); for death is its fruit, its end, its wages (R 6,16. 21.23). But sin itself finds in man an accomplice: lust (7,7); it is lust which gives birth to sin; and sin, in turn, brings forth death (Jm 1, 15); in other words, it is the flesh*, whose desire* is death and which fructifies in death (R 7,5; 8.6). By this our body, God's creature, becomes a "body of death" (7,24). In vain does the Law enter on the scene in this drama of the world in order to set up a barrier against the instruments of death which are at work in us.

For sin takes occasion from the Law to seduce us and more surely procure our death (7,7-13). By acknowledging sin (3,20), though powerless to overcome it, and by explicitly condemning the sinner to death (cf 5,13f), the Law has become the "force of sin" (1 Co 15,56). This is why the ministration of that Law, which is holy and spiritual in itself (R 7,12.14) but whose simple letter does not confer the power of the Spirit*, had in fact become a ministration of death (2 Co 3,7). Without Christ, humanity was therefore plunged into the shadow* of death (Mt 4,16; Lk 1,79; cf Is 9,1). Death, therefore, has always been one of the major factors in human history, and it still remains one of the calamities* which God inflicts on a sinful world (Ap 6,8; 8,9; 18,8). This causes the tragic character of our condition. Through our own fault we are delivered up mercilessly to the influence of death. How then shall the perspective of hope which the Scriptures open up to our gaze be realized in our lives?

II. CHRIST'S DUEL WITH DEATH

1. *Christ takes on Himself our death.* Thanks to Christ, the promises of Scripture find their realization. In order to free us from the sway of death He willed first to take on Himself our mortal nature. His death was not an accident. He foretold it to His disciples in order to prevent their being scandalized* (Mk 8,31 p; 9,31 p; 10.34 p; Jn 12,33; 18,32); He desired it like a baptism which would plunge Him into the waters of hell (Lk 12,50; Mk 10,38; cf Ps 18,5). Though He trembled before death (Jn 12,27; 13,21; Mk 14,33 p), as He shuddered before the tomb of Lazarus (Jn 11,33.38), though He besought His Father who could preserve Him from death (He 5,7; Lk 22,42; Jn 12,27), in the end He accepted this cup* of bitterness (Mk 10,38 p; 14,30 p; Jn 18,11). In order to do the Father's will* (Mk 14,36 p), He was "obedient* unto death" (Ph 2,8). This He did in order "to fulfill the Scriptures" (Mt 26,54). Was He not the very Servant* foretold by Isaiah, the just one placed in the ranks of evildoers (Lk 22,37; cf Is 53,12)? In fact, though Pilate could find nothing about Him deserving of death (Lk 23,15.22; Ac 3,13; 13,28), He accepted a death which appeared to be the chastisement required under the Law (Mt 26,66 p). For, "being born under the Law" (G 4,4) and having taken on "flesh like the flesh of sin" (R 8,3), He was united with His people and the entire human race.

"God made Him sin for our sake" (2 Co 5,21; cf G 3,13), so that the punishment merited by the sin of mankind should fall on Him. This is why His death meant "death to sin" (R 6,10), though He Himself was innocent; for He took on to the very end the lot of sinners, "tasting death" as they all must do (He 2,8f; cf 1 Th 4,14; R 8,34) and descending with them "into hell." But by thus placing Himself "among the dead," He brought them the good news that life would be restored to them (1 P 3,19; 4,6).

2. *Christ died for us.* In fact, the death of Christ was fruitful like the death of the grain of wheat cast on the ground (Jn 12,24-32). Though apparently imposed as a chastisement for sin, His death was really an expiatory sacrifice* (He 9; cf Is 53,10). Fulfilling literally, but in another sense than intended, the unwitting prophecy of Caiaphas, Christ died "for the people" (Jn 11, 50f; 18,14), and not only for His people, but "for all men" (2 Co 5,14f). He died "for us" (1 Th 5,10), when we were sinners (R 5,6ff); thereby He gave us a manifestation of supreme love (5,7; Jn 15,13; 1 Jn 4,10). For us, and not only in our place, but also for our benefit, He died. For by dying "for our sins" (1 Co 15,3; 1 P 3,18), He reconciled* us with God (R 5,10) so completely that we are enabled to receive the promised heritage (He 9,15f).

3. *Christ's triumph over death.* Where does the salutary efficacy of Christ's death come from? From this fact, that having confronted the ancient enemy of mankind, He triumphed over him. In His living body we perceive manifestations of that future victory*, when He will recall the dead to life (Mt 9,18-25 p; Lk 7,14f; Jn 11). In the kingdom* of God which He will inaugurate, death will retreat before Him who is "the resurrection and the life" (Jn 11,25). Once and for all, Christ faced death on its own ground and conquered it at the very moment when death thought it vanquished Him. In hell, He entered as master and left at will, "having received the keys of death and Hades" (Ap 1, 18). Because He suffered death, God crowned Him with glory (He 2,9). In Him was realized that resurrection* from the death foretold in the Scriptures (1 Co 15,14). He has become the "first-born among the dead" (Col 1,18; Ap 1, 5). Now that he has been "delivered by God from the terror of Hades" (Ac 2,24) and from infernal corruption (Ac 2,31), it is clear that death has lost all sway over Him (R 6,9). At the same time, the devil, who had power over death,

was reduced to impotence (He 2,14). That was the first victorious act of Christ. "Death and life confronted one another in an awesome struggle. The Lord of life died: and, living, He reigns" (Easter Hymn).

From that moment man's relation to death was changed; for the vanquishing Christ illumined for all time to come "those who sit in the shadow of death" (Lk 1,79). He freed them from that "law of sin and death" to which they had previously been slaves (R 8,2; cf He 2,15). Finally, at the end of time, His triumph will have a dazzling consummation in the general resurrection*. Then will death be destroyed forever, "swallowed up in victory" (1 Co 15, 26.54ff). For death and Hades must then yield up their prey, after which they will be hurled with Satan into the pool of fire and brimstone which is the second death (Ap 20,10.13f). Such will be the final triumph of Christ: "O death, I shall be your death: Hell, I shall be your sting" (Antiphon from the old breviary).

III. THE CHRISTIAN CONFRONTED WITH DEATH

1. *Dying with Christ.* In taking on our nature Christ did not merely assume our death for the sake of being united with our sinful condition. As head of a new humanity, the new Adam* (1 Co 15,45; R 5,14), He contained all men in His death on the cross. Hence, in a certain manner "all men die" in His death (2 Co 5,14). And yet, it is necessary that this death become an effective reality for each man. This is the meaning of baptism* whose sacramental efficacy unites us to Christ on the cross: "baptized into Christ's death," we are "buried with Him in death," "conformed to His death" (R 6,3ff; Ph 3, 10). Henceforth we are dead and our life is hidden with Christ in God (Col 3,3). This is a mysterious death which is the negative aspect of the grace* of salvation. For what we thereby die to is that entire order of things by which the rule of death manifests itself on this earth: we die to sin (R 6,11), to the old man* (6,6), to the flesh* (1 P 3,18), to the body* (R 6,6; 8,10), to the Law (G 2,19), to all the elements of the world (Col 2,20)...

2. *From death to life.* This dying with Christ is, in reality, a dying to death itself. When we were captives of sin, it is then that we were dead (Col 2,13; cf Ap 3,1). Now we are alive, "returned from the dead" (R 6,13) and "delivered

from dead works" (He 6,1; 9,14). As Christ said: whoever hears His word passes from death to life (Jn 5,24). Whoever believes in Him need fear death no more: though he be dead, he shall live (Jn 11,25). Such is the stake of faith*. On the other hand, he who will not believe will die in his sins (Jn 8,21.24); the sweet odor of Christ becomes for him the scent of death (2 Co 2,16). The drama of humanity struggling with death is acted out in every man's life; its conclusion depends on our choice when faced with Christ and His gospel: for some it will be eternal life, for Jesus said "whoever keeps my word will not see death forever" (Jn 8,51); for others it will be the horror of a "second death" (Ap 2,11; 20,14; 21,8).

3. *Dying each day.* Nevertheless our union with the death of Christ, realized sacramentally in baptism, must be continually actualized every day of our lives. This is the meaning of asceticism, by which we "mortify"—that is: we "cause to die" in ourselves—the works of the body (R 8,13), our earthly members with their passions (Col 3,5). This is also the meaning of all that manifests in us the power of natural death, for death has changed its meaning since Christ made it an instrument of salvation. The fact that the apostle of Christ appears to men, in his weakness, as one dying (2 Co 6,9), that he is in constant peril of death (Ph 1,20; 2 Co 1,9f; 11,23), that he "dies each day" (1 Co 15,31), all this is no longer a sign of defeat: he bears in himself the mortality of Jesus might also be manifest in his body; he is freed from death because of Jesus, in order that the life of Jesus might be manifested in his mortal flesh. When death does its work in him, life is operative in the faithful (2 Co 4,10ff). This daily dying really makes the death of Jesus present and prolongs its fruitfulness in His Body, which is the Church.

4. *In the face of bodily death.* In this same perspective, bodily death takes on a new meaning for the Christian. It is no longer only an inevitable destiny to which one resigns oneself, a divine decree one accepts, a condemnation incurred because of one's sins. The Christian "dies for the Lord" just as he lived for Him (R 14,7f; cf Ph 1,20). And if he dies a martyr* of Christ, shedding his blood in testimony of Him, his death is a libation having the value of a sacrifice* in God's eyes (Ph 2,17; 1 Tim 4,6). This death, by which he "glorifies God" (Jn 21, 19), earns him the crown of life (Ap 2,10; 12,

11). From an anguishing necessity, death has become an object of beatitude*: "Blessed are they who die in the Lord! Let them henceforth rest from their labors." (Ap 14,13). Death for the just is an entry into peace* (Ws 3,3), into eternal rest, into perpetual light*. *Requiem aeternam dona eis, Domine, et lux perpetua luceat eis!*

The hope of immortality and resurrection which come to light in the OT has now found a solid foundation in the mystery of Christ. For not only has union with His death made us live with a new life, but it has also given us assurance that "He who raised Christ Jesus from the dead will also give your mortal bodies life" (R 8,11). Then, by the resurrection, we shall enter into a new world where "death shall be no more" (Ap 21,4); or rather, for the elect who rise again with Christ there will be no "second death" (Ap 20,6; cf 2,11): this will be reserved for the reprobate, the devil, death and Hades (Ap 21,8; cf 20,10.14).

This is why dying for the Christian is, in the last analysis, a gain, since Christ is his life (Ph 1,21). His present condition which binds him to his mortal body* is oppressive to him. He would prefer to quit this life in order to go and be with the Lord (2 Co 5,8); he is anxious to put on the clothing* of glory* of the risen, in order that whatever in him is mortal might be absorbed by life (2 Co 5,1-4; cf 1 Co 15,51-53). He desires to leave in order to be with Christ (Ph 1,23).

→Anguish—Ashes—Baptism IV 1.4—Body—Body of Christ I 2, II 1—Burial—Calamity—Cross — Curse — Eucharist IV 1 — Farewell Speeches—Good & Evil I 1.4—Hell—Jesus Christ I 3, II 1 b—Liberation/Liberty III 2 b—Life—Man II 1 c—Martyr—Night OT 3—Old Age 1—Persecution—Prophet OT II 4—Punishment 1—Redemption NT 2.3.4—Rest II 2—Resurrection—Sacrifice NT I, II 1—Sadness OT 1; NT 1—Shadow I—Sickness/Healing O—Sin I 2—Sleep—Soul II 2.3—Sowing I 2 b—Suffering—Water II 2, IV 2—Wrath *B* OT I 1.

PG tms

DECEPTION / DISAPPOINTMENT

The Bible is not only aware of the existence of deception and disappointment, but it turns readily to the subject. The Greeks too are very conscious of the failures and frustrations that are part of existence; but, although they frequently return to the subject of this aspect of man's lot, they do so almost furtively and principally with the idea of bearing it in a dignified manner. However, the Bible shows little of this discretion; in fact, it seems to take pleasure in letting the complaints of Job and the sarcasms of Ecclesiastes be heard. This is an example of the difference in temperament and culture between the restraint of the Greek and the passion of the Hebrew. There is above all a difference of religious attitude: because of its faith Israel has a keen sense of the value of creation but also of its precarious nature; a feeling of failure, which is a matter for sorrow but always with a sense of resignation, and an absolute certainty of final victory.

I. SHAME, LIE AND VANITY

In the Hebrew vocabulary for the idea of deception and disappointment, stress is laid on two shades of meaning in particular: the *vanity or futility* of the object that deceives and the *confusion* of the subject that is deceived.

1. *The falsehood of vain things.* The Hebrew experiences a profound need for stability and a horror of inconsistency and illusory appearances. When lying* is condemned, it is perhaps less the idea of disloyalty than its fundamental nothingness that is condemned. Lie, vanity, nothingness are the usual words to describe things that deceive, things that produce nothing, the "sons of Belial" (the LXX has transcribed the word without translating, cf Dt 13,14). And the most frequent images are those of wind (*hebel*, the "vanity" of Ecclesiastes), of dust (*'aphar*) and of emptiness (*riq*).

2. *The shame of being confounded.* In a world where all life is lived under the eyes of others, deception inevitably covers its victim with shame*: the one who has put his confidence* in something that did not merit it finds himself publicly confounded. This is a terrible trial for man's pride*, for his need to be recognized by his peers. And the most popular equivalents used to describe deception are the words for shame and confusion, especially those derived from the root *buš*. We allow this essential nuance to escape our attention too easily; and so we usually translate Paul's saying by: "hope does not deceive" (R 5,5), when it would be better to say: "hope does not lead to confusion"

(in Greek: *ou kataiskynei*), which explains the Apostle's pride in proclaiming the Gospel and the cross.

II. ALL IS DECEPTION

There are two types of being that are particularly deceiving, because they claim that they deserve men's confidence and can assure their destiny: the great powers and the false gods, in other words Egypt and the idols. Beneath a brilliant exterior, Egypt*, "Rahab-do-nothing," is in fact "futile and empty" (Is 30,7); its powerful cavalry is only flesh*, and the Egyptian is only a man (Is 31,1ff; cf Jr 2,37). These horses and these soldiers are, however, real beings, but the false gods are nothing, and their idols* are a lie and powerless. That is why their servants and their makers are bound to be covered with shame (Jr 2,28; Is 44,9ff).

But Qoheleth goes further and makes this sense of deception a general one: "Vanity of vanities...all is vanity...under the sun," he repeats (1,2.14, etc). So much does he feel that life is a deception that he attributes this conviction to Solomon, the king who possessed all the gifts*. However, he does not despise the things of this world; on the contrary, he expects a great deal of them and this is the cause of his basically bitter attitude, which, however, does see a solution: to learn to accept everything from God, the bad as well as the good (7,13f).

III. GOD DOES NOT DECEIVE

Man is a source of deception for his fellowman (Jr 17,5; Ps 118,8), but he is also a source of disappointment to God. The vine* that He had nurtured with love produced nothing but sour grapes (Is 5,4). Jesus, who "could tell what a man had in him" (Jn 2,25) experienced this deception: ignored by His neighbors (Mk 6, 3f), He saw men shut their hearts the more He tried to reach them (Mt 23,37f; Jn 12,37-40), and He saw Himself deserted by His disciples just as He was giving Himself up for them (Mk 14,50).

At certain times God Himself seems to deceive. His most faithful servants are familiar with the temptation of thinking that their efforts have failed and that God has left them to their own devices. Elijah wanted to die, having discovered that he was no better than his fathers (1 K 19,4). Jeremiah was even driven to question

God's dependability: "Do you mean to be for me a deceptive stream with inconstant waters?" (Jr 15,18, to be contrasted with Jr 2,13; Is 58, 11). And Jesus Himself experienced the lengths to which abandonment by God could go (Mk 15,34).

To say that God alone does not deceive is to take a step that goes beyond all appearances; it is an experience of faith*, an experience that often enough is lived out in a state of darkness and gained at the price of deceptions that are bitterly felt. This fundamental certainty cannot be experienced by man unless he clings to the salvation* brought by Jesus Christ, who committed His spirit into the hands of the Father (Lk 23,46) and so revealed the faithfulness* of a God, who seemed absent and indifferent. Supported by this faith, we can no longer be deceived by anything (cf R 8,31-39), because God is faithful. And the pledge of this faithfulness, the assurance against all deception, is the gift of His Son, in whom we are called and preserved until His Coming (1 Co 1,9; 1 Th 5,23f).

→Confidence—Hope—Lie II 1—Sadness—Shame I 1.

JG ems

DESERT

The religious significance of the desert is conceived differently according to its orientation as a geographical place or as a privileged epoch in salvation history. In the first viewpoint, the desert is a land which God has not blessed. Water is rare there, as in the Garden of Paradise before the rain (Gn 2,5), vegetation scanty, living impossible (Is 6,11). To make a land into a desert is to make it like the original chaos (Jr 2,6; 4,20-26); the sins of Israel deserve this (Ez 6,14; Lm 5,18; Mt 23,38). In this barren land live evil spirits* (Lv 16,10; Lk 8,29; 11,24), satyrs (Lv 17,7), and other malevolent beasts* (Is 13,21; 14,23; 30,6; 34,11-16; Zp 2,13f). In short, viewed in this light, the desert is opposed to inhabited land as curse* is opposed to blessing*.

Now the dominant biblical view is that God wished to make His people pass through this "dreadful land" (Dt 1,19) to make them enter the land flowing with milk and honey. This event is going to transform earlier symbolism. If the desert always maintains its character as a desolate place, above all else it calls to mind one stage in sacred history: the birth of the people of God. The biblical symbolism of the desert cannot, then, be confused with some mystique of solitude* or of flight from civilization. It does not aim at a return to the desert ideal but at a passing through the desert period, of which Israel's exodus is the definitive type.

OT

I. SETTING OUT
FOR THE PROMISED LAND

Unlike memories of the exodus from Egypt properly so called, those of the journey through the desert were idealized only at a later date. In their present form the traditions show that this was both a time of trial for the people, and even of apostasy, but also a time of glory for the Lord. Three elements govern these memories: the plan of God, the unfaithfulness of the people, the triumph of God.

1. *The plan of God.* A twofold intention directed the desert crossing. It was the way* expressly chosen by God, though not the shortest (Ex 13,17), because God wished to be the guide of His people (13,21). Finally it is in the Sinai desert that the Hebrews are to adore God (Ex 3,17f=5,1ff). There they receive the Law* and receive the covenant* that made these wanderers a true people* of God: one can even take a census (Nm 1,1ff). God wished His people to be born in the desert. However, He promised them a land, and so made the desert sojourn a privileged but provisional period.

2. *The unfaithfulness of the people.* The way chosen by God had nothing comparable to the fruitful earth of Egypt*, where nourishment and security were never lacking. It was rather the way of pure faith in Him who was guiding Israel. Right from the start of the journey the Hebrews murmur against the Lord's arrangement: no security, no water, no meat! These complaints run all through the narratives (Ex 14,11; 16,2f; 17,2f; Nm 14,2ff; 16,13f; 20,4f; 21, 5), raised alike by the first and second generation in the desert. The theme of complaint is clear: they miss the ordinary life. As laborious as it was in Egypt, they would prefer it to this extraordinary life surrendered to the care of God alone. Better life as a slave than impending death; rather bread and meat than tasteless

manna*. Thus the desert reveals the heart of man unable to withstand the trial* to which he is subjected.

3. *The triumph of the divine mercy.* But if God permits to perish in the desert all who are hardened* in unfaithfulness and lack of trust, He does not therefore abandon His plan, but draws good from evil. To the people that murmur He gives wonderful food and water. If He must chastise sinners, He offers unexpected means of salvation, such as the brazen serpent (Nm 21,9). Always God makes His holiness and glory shine forth (20,13). The latter would especially be evident when a true people would enter the promised land with Joshua. The final triumph lets us see in the desert not so much the period of the people's unfaithfulness as the season of God's merciful faithfulness—God who always forestalls the rebellious and accomplishes His plan.

II. THE DESERT PERIOD IN RETROSPECT

Established in the promised land, the people soon succeeded in transforming it into a place of idolatrous and wicked prosperity. They tended to prefer the covenant gifts to the covenant giver. Later on the desert period will be idealized, enhanced by the divine glory.

1. *Call to conversion.* Thematizing by means of memory*, Deuteronomy makes the desert events live in the present (Dt 8,2ff.15-18): it is a wonderful time of the paternal solicitude of God. The people had not perished there, but God had tested them there that they might realize that man does not live by bread alone but by every word that proceeds from the mouth of God. Likewise, the sobriety of worship in the desert period urges Israel not to be content with a formalistic piety (Am 5,25=Ac 7,42). Inversely the memories of disobedience are a call to conversion and trust in God alone —at least they should now stop being stiff-necked and tempting God (Ps 78,17f.40; 95,7ff; Ac 7,51), and learn to adapt themselves in patience to God's way of doing things (Ps 106, 13f) and marvel at the triumph of His mercy (Ne 9; Ps 78; 106; Ez 20).

2. *The wonderful works of God.* Though one might call to mind these infidelities, there was no thought of presenting the desert sojourn as a chastisement. Still less was it regarded as a recollection of marvels that accompanied the time of God's betrothal with His people. It was the idyllic time of the past in contrast to the present period in Canaan. And so when Elijah goes to Horeb, he goes not solely to seek a refuge in the desert but a place of refreshment (1 K 19). Since chastisements do not succeed in bringing back the unfaithful spouse*, God is going to take her into the desert and there speak to her heart (Ho 2,16). Once again it would be a time of betrothal (2,21f). Past marvels are embellished in memory: the manna* becomes a heavenly nourishment* (Ps 78,24), a bread* for every taste (Ws 16,21). Now these gifts are also the pledge of a current presence since God is faithful. He is a loving Father (Ho 11), a shepherd* (Is 40,11; 63,11-14; Ps 78,52). Because of this period when the people lived so close to God, how could one not have complete trust in Him who guides and nourishes (Ps 81,11)?

3. *The desert ideal.* If the desert period is an ideal time, why not prolong it endlessly? It is for this reason that the Rechabites used to live in tents in order to show their rejection of the Canaanite civilization (Jr 35), and that the monks of Qumrân broke with the official priesthood in Jerusalem. This mystique of the flight to the desert has its grandeur—it can even give a meaning to a persecution situation (1 M 2, 28ff; He 11,38)—but in the measure in which it would isolate itself from the concrete event in which it originates, it may tend to degenerate into a sterile evasion—God has not called Israel to live in the desert, but to traverse the desert to live in the promised land. Furthermore, the desert keeps its figurative* value. The salvation hoped for by the exiles in Babylon is conceived as a new exodus*: the desert will blossom beneath their feet (Is 32,15f; 35,1f; 41,18; 43,19f). In some apocalyptic accounts salvation at the end of time is presented as the transformation of the desert into paradise*; the Messiah will then appear in the desert (cf Mt 24,26; Ac 21, 38; Ap 12,6.14).

NT

I. CHRIST AND THE DESERT

While the Essene communities, like that at Qumrân, extolled separation from the city* and fled to the desert, John* the Baptist did not wish to consecrate any desert mystique. If he preaches his message there, it is to revive the privileged time. And when water had renewed their hearts, he sent the baptized back to their work (Lk 3,10-14). The desert was only a means of conversion with an eye to the coming Messiah.

1. *Christ in the desert.* Jesus wished to live again the various episodes of God's people. As the Hebrews of old He is driven by the Spirit of God into the desert to be tested there (Mt 4,1-11 p). But in contrast to His forefathers, He overcomes the trial and remains faithful to His Father. He prefers the Word of God to bread, trust to a striking miracle, the service of God to all hope of earthly domination. The trial which had miscarried at the time of the exodus now finds its meaning: Jesus is the first-born Son in whom is fulfilled the destiny of Israel. It is not impossible that the theme of paradise regained may be read in the Markan narrative (Mk 1,12f).

2. *Christ, our desert.* In the course of His public life, Jesus without doubt used the desert as an escape from the crowds (Mt 14,13; Mk 1, 45; 6,31; Lk 4,42), an apt place for solitary prayer (Mk 1,35 p). But these actions are not described as pertaining directly to desert symbolism. On the other hand, Jesus is presented as one who fulfills in His person the marvelous gifts of yesterday. He is the living water, the bread from heaven, the way and the guide; the light in the night, the serpent who gives life to all who look on it to be saved. He is, finally, the one in whom is fulfilled the intimate knowledge of God, by sharing in His flesh and blood. In a certain sense, it can be said that Christ is our desert—in Him we have overcome the trial, in Him we have perfect communion with God. Henceforth the desert as place and time is fulfilled in Jesus. Here figure gives way to reality.

II. THE CHURCH IN THE DESERT

The symbolism of the desert continues to play a role in understanding the state of the Church. She lives hidden in the desert until the return of Christ who will end the power of Satan (Ap 12,6.14). The symbol, however, enjoys a more intimate relation with its biblical background when Jesus multiplies loaves in the desert to show His disciples not that it is necessary to live in the desert, but that a new time is inaugu-

rated in which man lives in a superior way by the very word of Christ (Mt 14,13-21 p).

Paul takes the same perspective. He teaches that the events of old were for the instruction of us who have come to the climax of time* (1 Co 10,11). Baptized in the cloud and in the sea, we are nourished by living bread and steeped in the water of the Spirit which pours out of the rock*. And this rock is Christ. It is no illusion. We still live in the desert, but sacramentally. The figure of the desert remains, therefore, indispensable if we are to understand the nature of Christian life.

This life is lived beneath the sign of trial as long as we have not entered into the rest* of God (He 4,1). Therefore, recalling events of the past, let us not harden* our hearts. Our "today" is sure of victory, because we are "sharers in Christ" (3,14), who will remain faithful in time of trial.

→City OT 1—Elijah OT 1—Evil Spirits OT 1—Exodus OT 1—Hunger & Thirst OT i a b—Manna 1—Mountain III 1—Rock 2—Salt 1—Solitude II 2—Trial/Temptation OT I 1; NT I —Unbelief I 1—Water III 1—Way I.

CT & XLD jrc

DESIRE

For Buddhism the supreme perfection is "to kill desire." How distant the men of the Bible, even those closest to God, seem from this ideal! The Bible is, on the contrary, filled with the tumult and conflict of every form of desire. Certainly it is far from approving them all; and the purest desires must know a radical purification. This is how desire has power and gives to man's existence all its value.

I. THE DESIRE TO LIVE

At the root of all human desires is man's basic indigence and his fundamental need to possess life* in the fullness* and expansiveness of his being. This datum of nature is proper, and God has consecrated it. The saying of Ben Sira, "Do not bypass present good fortune, do not let any object of legitimate desire escape" (Si 14,14), does not express the highest biblical wisdom*. If not canonized as an ideal, it is, however, at least presupposed by Jesus Christ as a normal reaction. For if He lay down His life, it is that

His sheep "might have life and have it more abundantly" (Jn 10,10).

Scriptural language confirms both the presence of this natural tendency and its positive value. Numerous comparisons manifest most intense desires: "As a deer yearns for running water" (Ps 42,2); "as the eyes of a maidservant are on the hand of her mistress" (123,2); "more than a watchman awaits the dawn" (130,6), "send me the sound of rejoicing and feasting" (51,10). More than once the prophets and the Deuteronomist base threats or promises on the permanent aspirations of man: planting, building, marrying (Dt 28,30; 20,5ff; Am 5,11; 9,14; Is 65,21). Even the old man whom God has "made see so many evils and troubles" is not to neglect waiting until He comes again "to refresh his old age and console him" (Ps 71,20f).

II. PERVERSIONS OF DESIRE

Since desire is essential and ineradicable, it can be for man a lasting and perilous temptation. If Eve sinned*, it was because she let herself be seduced by the forbidden tree*, which was "sweet to the taste, pleasant to the eyes, pleasing to look upon" (Gn 3,6). Because she has thus yielded to desire, woman* will henceforth be the victim of the desire that bears her toward her husband and will be subject to the sway of her husband (3,16). In the human race sin is like a savage desire ready to spring loose; we must perforce stand in awe of it (4,7). This unchained desire is covetousness or cupidity*, "concupiscence of the flesh*, concupiscence of the eyes, the empty pomp of wealth*" (1 Jn 2, 16; cf Jm 1,14f). Its kingdom over mankind is the world*, the realm of Satan*.

The Bible is a history of man and is filled with desires that sweep away the sinners. As the Word of God, the Bible describes the deadly consequences of desire. Hungry* in the desert, Israel does not feed on faith* in the Word of God (Dt 8,1-5). It thinks only of weeping for the foods of Egypt and of pouncing upon the quail—and the guilty perish, victims of their concupiscence (Nm 11,4.34). David yields to desire and seizes Bathsheba (2 S 11,2ff), unleashing a series of sins and disasters. On the advice of Jezebel, Ahab yields to desire, seizes the vineyard of Naboth, and thus pronounces the death sentence on his dynasty (1 K 21). Two old men desire Susanna "to the point of uncontrolled desire" (Dn 13,8.20) and pay for the sin with their lives.

More categorically does the Law, seeing the heart* as the source of sin, forbid sinful desire: "Do not covet your neighbor's goods...his wife" (Ex 20,17). Jesus will reveal the scope of this prohibition; He will not create it (Mt 5,28).

III. THE CONVERSION OF DESIRE

The novelty of the gospel is primarily its absolutely clear delineation of obscure elements in the OT: "What makes a man unclean is that which comes forth from the heart" (Mt 15,18). The newness of the gospel is its unwavering proclamation of liberation* from the concupiscences that used to fetter man. These concupiscences, this "desire of the flesh is death*" (R 8,6). But the Christian who possesses the Spirit* of God is able to follow the "desire of the spirit," "to crucify the flesh with its passions and concupiscences" (G 5,24; cf R 6,12; 13,14; E 4,22), and to let himself "be led by the Spirit" (G 5,16).

This "desire of the spirit," freed by Christ, was already present in the Law*, which is "spiritual" (R 7,14). The entire OT is permeated with a profound desire for God. Beneath the desire to acquire wisdom* (Pr 5,19; Si 1,20), beneath the longing for Jerusalem* (Ps 137,5), beneath the desire to go up to the holy city (128,5) and to the temple* (122,1), beneath the desire to know the Word of God in all its forms (119,20.131.174), runs a thoroughgoing desire which polarizes all energies, which enables one to unmask the illusion and the counterfeit (cf Am 5,18; Is 58,2), to surmount all deceptions—it is the unparalleled desire for God. "What have I in heaven save you? Apart from you, I desire nothing on earth. My flesh and my heart waste away, stronghold of my heart, God, my share forever" (Ps 73,25f; cf 42,2; 63,2).

IV. DESIRE FOR COMMUNION

If it is possible for us to desire God more than anything else in the world, it is in union with the desire of Jesus Christ. Jesus was possessed by a burning, anguished desire that only His baptism*, His passion (Lk 12,49f), would appease. It was the desire to give glory* to His Father (Jn 17,4) and to show the world the magnitude of His love (14,30). But this desire of the Son* reaching out to His Father* cannot be separated from the desire that directs Him toward His own. While He was moving to His passion, it made Him "desire with great desire to eat the Passover* supper with them" (Lk 22,15).

This divine desire for communion* with men —"I will be near to him and he near to me" (Ap 3,20)—arouses a profound echo in the NT. The Pauline epistles especially are filled with the apostle's desire for his "brothers so greatly loved and longed for" (Ph 4,1), all of whom he "longs for with the tenderness of Christ" (1,8). They are filled with his joy to experience, by the testimony of Titus, the Corinthians' "ardent longing" (2 Co 7,7) for him, a positive effect of God's activity (7,11). This preceding desire alone is able to counterbalance the basic longing of Paul for Christ; more precisely, for communion with Him, "the desire to depart and be with Christ" (Ph 1,23), "to live with the Lord" (2 Co 5,8). For the desire of the new man, baptized in the death and resurrection of Christ, finds its fulfillment in the hope of communion with God, as can be seen throughout the Bible. The cry of the "Spirit and the Bride" is "Come!" (Ap 22,17).

→Beatitude OT II—Cupidity—Gift—Hope— Hunger & Thirst—Prayer—See OT 1—Seek— Sexuality I 1, III 2.

PMG & JG jrc

DISCIPLE

A person who freely puts himself in the school of a teacher and shares his views is a disciple. This word, almost absent from the OT, is used frequently in later Judaism (hb. *talmîd*), as the development of a biblical tradition. It is found likewise in the NT (gr. *mathētēs*) but with the original meaning that Jesus gave it.

OT

1. *Disciples of prophets and of wise men.* From time to time writers point out that an Eliseus attached himself to Elijah (1 K 19,19ff) or that a group of fervent disciples surrounded Isaiah, receiving as a trust his witness and his revelation (Is 8,16). More often the wise men had disciples whom they call their "sons" (Pr 1,8.10; 2,1; 3,1) and in whom they inculcate the traditional teaching. But neither prophets nor wise men dared by their teaching* take the place of the Word* of God. On this alone and not on

the traditions of master and disciple is the covenant founded.

2. *Disciples of God.* Since the divine Word* is the source of all wisdom, the ideal is not, therefore, to attach oneself to a human master but to be a disciple of God Himself. Personified divine Wisdom* thus calls men to hear it and to follow its lessons (Pr 1,20ff; 8,4ff.32f). The eschatological oracles announce that in the last days God would make Himself master of hearts: they will no longer have need of earthly masters (Jr 31,31-34), but will be "disciples of Yahweh" (Is 54,13). The Servant of Yahweh Himself, though charged to teach the divine injunctions (Is 42,1.4), waits with open ear each morning and receives the tongue of a disciple (Is 50,4). Faithful to this prophecy, the psalmist would therefore pray without growing weary: "Lord, teach me!" (Ps 119,12.26f.33f; 25,4-9...).

3. *Teachers and disciples in Judaism.* At the return from exile, when the Law* becomes the primary object of teaching, the masters responsible for this basic institution are called "doctors of the law." Now, to the authority of the Word of God upon which they commented is added little by little their own personal authority (Mt 23,2.16-22), especially when they pass on the tradition* that they themselves have received from their masters. Post-biblical Judaism would group itself on the basis of this *talmud* ("teaching"). At the time of the NT, Paul recalls that he himself had been a disciple of Gamaliel (Ac 22,3).

NT

1. *Disciples of Jesus.* Apart from a few mentions of the disciples of Moses (Jn 9,28), of the Baptist (vg Mk 2,18; Jn 1,35; Ac 19,1ff), or of the Pharisees (vg Mt 22,16), the NT restricts the name of disciple to those who have acknowledged Jesus as their master. In the gospels the twelve are from the first so designated (Mt 10,1; 12,1...). Beyond this intimate circle, one who follows Jesus (Mt 8,21), principally the seventy-two whom Jesus sent on the mission* (Lk 10,1), receives the name. These disciples were undoubtedly numerous (Lk 6,17; 19,37; Jn 6,60), but many gave up (Jn 6,66). No one might pretend to become the master: if he was "to make disciples" (Mt 28,19; Ac 14,21f), this was not on his own account but only for Christ. Thus, little by little, from chapter six of the Book of Acts the simple appellation of "disciple" in-

cludes every believer, whether or not he had known Jesus during His early life (Ac 6,1f; 9,10-26...); the faithful were, then, from this point of view, likened to the twelve themselves (Jn 2,11; 8,31; 20,29).

2. *Characteristics.* Whatever the apparent similarity to the Jewish doctors of His time, Jesus specified unique requirements for His disciples.

a) Calling. To become His disciple, intellectual or even moral aptitudes were not important. What matters is a call, the initiative of which comes from Jesus (Mk 1,17-20; Jn 1,38-50) and behind Him the Father, who "gives" Jesus His disciples (Jn 6,39; 10,29; 17,6.12).

b) Personal attachment to Christ. To become a disciple of Jesus it is not required to be a man of superior caliber. Indeed the relation which unites disciple and master is not exclusively, or even primarily, one of an intellectual order. He says to the disciple: "Follow me!" In the gospels the verb *follow** always expresses attachment to the person of Jesus (vg Mt 8, 19...). To follow Jesus is to sever with the past, with a complete break if it is a question of privileged disciples. To follow Jesus is to fashion one's conduct on His, to listen to His lessons, and to conform one's life to that of the Savior (Mk 8,34f; 10,21 p.42-45; Jn 12,26). They were different from the disciples of the Jewish doctors who, having been instructed in the Law, were able to break away from their master and teach on their own. The disciple of Jesus is not bound to a doctrine but to a person: he cannot leave Him who henceforth is for him more than father and mother (Mt 10,37; Lk 14,25f).

c) Destiny and dignity. The disciple of Jesus is, therefore, called to share the very destiny of the master: to carry His cross (Mk 8,34 p), to drink His cup (Mk 10,38f), finally, to receive from Him the kingdom (Mt 19,28f; Lk 22,28ff; Jn 14,3). Therefore, from this time on, whoever would give him simply a glass of water as a disciple would not lose his reward (Mt 10,42 p); on the other hand, what a sin "to scandalize one of these little ones!" (Mk 9,42 p).

3. *Disciples of Jesus and disciples of God.* If the disciples of Jesus are thus distinguished from those of the Jewish doctors, it is because God Himself speaks to men through His Son. The doctors passed on merely human traditions, which at times "voided the Word of God" (Mk

7,1ff); Jesus is divine Wisdom incarnate who promises to His disciples rest* for their souls (Mt 11,29). When Jesus speaks, the prophecy of the OT is fulfilled: it is God Himself whom they hear, and thus all can become "disciples of God" (Jn 6,45).

→Apostles—Calling III—Child II—Church III 2—Education—Example—Faithfulness NT 2—Follow—Friend 2—John the Baptist—Listen 1 —Persecution—Shepherd & Flock NT—Teach —Tradition OT II 2—Word of God OT III; NT I 2, II 2, III 2.

AF jrc

DISPERSION

From the first chapters of Genesis the dispersion of men on the earth appears as an ambiguous fact. The result of the divine blessing* by which man was to multiply and fill the earth (Gn 9,1; cf 1,28), it is fulfilled in unity*; the punishment for sin, it becomes the sign of the division between men (Gn 11,7f). This double perspective is found again in the history of salvation.

1. *Dispersion of the people-nation.* God chose for Himself a people* to whom He gave a land. But, unfaithful to God, Israel was dispersed (2 K 17,7-23); it returns to exile* as formerly in Egypt* (Dt 28,64-68). The misfortunes that accompany the Exile are described in the Septuagint by the word *diaspora* (Dt 28,25; 30,4; Is 49,6...), and this term, which really means "dispersion," then becomes applied to all the Jews spread over the pagan world after the Babylonian captivity. The purpose of this dispersion is purification (Ez 22,15); as soon as this purification has taken place, the return would come to pass (Ez 36,24). In the meantime dispersion remains a sorrowful fact that tortures holy souls (Ps 44): if only the time would come when God would gather together all the members of His People (Si 36,10)!

From this evil, however, God draws a much greater good: dispersed Israel makes the true faith known to outsiders (Tb 13,3-6); from the exile proselytism begins (Is 56,3); during the Greek epoch the author of Wisdom wishes to be heard by pagans; for such is, according to him, the calling of Israel (Ws 18,4). In this new perspective Israel tends to disengage herself from her stature as a nation to take the form of a church; it is no longer the race but the faith that assures her of the living unity of which the pilgrimages to Jerusalem are the sign (Ac 2,5-11).

2. *Dispersion of the people-church.* With Christ the people of God pass beyond the Jewish national framework and become properly the Church*. At Pentecost* by the gift of tongues* and by charity the Spirit insures the communion of nations*. Henceforth it is no longer here nor there but "in Spirit and in truth" (Jn 4,24) that men adore the God who unites mankind. The faithful no longer fear the persecution that scatters them far from Jerusalem (Ac 8,1; 11,19), and they are going to radiate their faith according to the command of the risen one to gather together all nations in one faith by one baptism (Mt 28,19f).

For the Jewish diaspora is substituted, therefore, a different diaspora, willed by God for the conversion of the world. It is to this subject that James addresses his epistle (Jm 1,1). It is this that Peter finds among the pagan converts who with the faithful Jews (1 P 1,1) formed the new people of God in order to lead dispersed mankind (Ac 2,1-11) back into unity. For Christians, the unity of faith* triumphs unceasingly by the dispersion. The children of God are gathered together by the sacrifice of Christ (Jn 11,52): in whatever place they find themselves, hereafter, Christ, "lifted up from the earth," will draw them all to Himself (Jn 12,32), bestowing on them the Spirit* of love which unites them in His own body* (1 Co 12).

→Exile—Pentecost II 2 c—Punishments— Schism OT 1—Solitude—Stranger I—Unity.

RM jrc

DOVE

1. Turtle-dove, wood-pigeon, pigeon or dove are the main varieties of flying creatures, wild or otherwise, that the Bible groups under the generic name of dove (hb. *yonah*). It is the only bird offered in sacrifice in the temple. It is the offering of the poor and it is used above all in the purification* rites (Lv 1,14; 5,7.11; Nb 6,10; Lk 2,24, quoting Lv 12,8). Hence, the presence in the temple of the dove-sellers (Mt 21,12 p; Jn 2,14.16).

2. As they are familiar with the habits of the

dove, the Jews make great use of them in *comparisons.* When Israel is waiting for the salvation that does not come, their lament is like the moaning of the dove (Is 38,14; 59,11; Na 2,8). When they are discouraged, they would like to fly off into the desert (Ps 55,7f). The seasonal migrations show that the dove has an instinctive knowledge, the sort of knowledge that Israel does not display with regard to God (Jr 8,7). These migrations suggest flight into exile at one moment (Ez 7,16) and gathering together in a resting place the next (Ho 11,11; Is 60,8). On the other hand "Ephraim is like a silly, witless dove" (Ho 7,11), frightened by danger. Not one of these comparisons is used directly by Jesus; he uses contrasts and tells His disciples to show themselves "cunning as serpents and yet as harmless as doves" (Mt 10,16).

3. Finally, in the Bible as with many poets, the dove can be a *symbol* of love. In the eyes of the lover the beloved is "my dove" (Ct 2,14; 5,2...). Israel calls itself by this name: "Do not betray your turtle-dove to the beast" (Ps 74,19). At the baptism of Jesus, the Spirit of God descends like a dove and comes on Jesus (Mt 3,16 p). It has not proved possible to find any certain interpretation of this symbol. It is most probably not a reference to the dove returning to Noah's Ark (Gn 8,8-12). Some critics, with the support of Jewish traditions, identify the dove with Israel. But is it not rather a suggestion that the love of God is descending symbolically on earth? And lastly, in accordance with some other Jewish traditions that saw the Spirit of God hovering over the waters (Gn 1,2) as a dove, some critics consider that we have here a suggestion of the new creation that is taking place at the baptism of Jesus.

→Animals—Baptism III 2—Simple 2—Spirit of God NT I 1—Temple NT I 1.

XLD ems

DREAMS

Both antiquity and modern science attach great importance to dreams, but for different reasons. Antiquity saw in them a way for man to get in touch with the supernatural world; while modern science sees in them a manifestation of the depths of man's personality. These two views are not incompatible: if God acts on man it is in the very depths of his being.

OT

The peoples who preceded and surrounded Israel saw dreams as a divine revelation*; and they happened often enough for the kings of Egypt and Mesopotamia to have in their service official interpreters of dreams (Gn 41,8; Jr 27,9).

The OT mentions that in Israel too revelation took place in dreams, to which must be added the words* and visions* of God in the night. These revelations were sometimes addressed to private individuals (Jb 4,12-21; Si 34,6), even to pagans (Gn 40—41; Dn 4). But most of them concerned God's plan* for His people: they gave guidance to the patriarchs (Gn 15,12-21; 20,3-6; 28,11-22; 37,5-11; 46,2-4: and this is the way it always is in the elohist tradition), to Gideon (Jg 6,25f), Samuel (1 S 3), Nathan (2 S 7,4-17) and Solomon (1 K 3). After the Exile Zechariah (1—6) and Daniel (2; 7) were told in dreams of the coming of salvation. And Joel promised dreams for the time of the outpouring of the Spirit (3,1).

Unlike their pagan neighbors Israel did not seem to have had official interpreters of dreams. Abraham, Isaac, Jacob, Samuel, Nathan and Solomon. . .understood them without help; nor were interpreters to be found in the temple or in the court of the kings. But, when Yahweh sent dreams to pagan kings, it was the servants of the true God who explained their mysteries, which remained inaccessible to non-Jewish interpreters (Gn 41; Dn 2; 4). In this way the pagans were forced to recognize that Yahweh alone was the master of mysteries; and He only revealed them to His own.

Just as the prophets reflected on the distinction between true and false prophets, they also condemned lying dreams (Dt 13,2-6; Jr 23,25-32; Ze 10,2), without, however, denying the divine origin of the dreams of their ancestors. But the fact that the Bible does not mention dreams during the centuries that elapsed between Solomon and Zechariah, throughout the great epoch of the prophets, has its meaning: it suggests that at this time the dream was seen as a secondary form of revelation, designed either for the individual (in earlier days the patriarchs had had dreams, but at that time neither the people nor the prophetic movement existed) or for pagans. On the other hand the prophetic Word was the supreme form of revelation addressed to the people.

NT

The NT does not report any dream of Jesus: probably because it does not dwell on the psychology of the Master, but more still because it sees in Him the one who "knows" the Father without the need for any intermediary.

However, dreams are not altogether absent from the NT. At Pentecost Peter announced the fulfillment of the prophecy of Joel (3,1), in which dreams were seen as a manifestation of the Spirit in the last days (Ac 2,17). The Book of Acts records several nocturnal visions of Paul (16,9f; 18,9; 23,11; 27,23); these apparitions strengthened and guided the apostle in his mission but did not bring him any doctrinal message. Matthew reports several dreams similar to those of the OT; either to convey revelation to pagans (Mt 27,19), or to guide Joseph during Jesus' childhood (1,20; 2,13.19.22: these are three appearances of the Angel of the Lord in the manner of the OT). Thus, the NT recognizes this means of revelation used by God in the earlier ages of the OT. It sees in them, like the prophets, a revelation designed to enlighten an individual (and sometimes a pagan). But it considers them subordinate to the Word, which was addressed to the whole Church and revealed in a supreme way in Jesus Christ.

→Apparitions of Christ 1—Mystery OT 2 a—Revelation OT I 1—Sign OT II 3—Sleep I 2—Visitation OT 2—Word of God OT I 1.

AG ems

DRUNKENNESS

We find the dangers of drunkenness described in a number of accounts. Such a state hands a man over to the power of his passions or into the hands of his enemies. Among the prophets, drunkenness is frequently associated with unlawful rites (Am 2,8; Ho 4,11; cf Ap 17,2) or with a degraded condition of society. From certain existential aspects, drunkenness can take on a symbolic value.

1. *Drunkenness and misfortune.* Drunkenness exposes a person to derision; but the Bible has always seen in misfortune an aspect of shame*. The drunken man and the man struck by misfortune "lose face*," poise, and everything which preserves good appearances. Both men become an object, a spectacle. A person can

"make another drink" so as to bring him to shame. Ha 2,15f takes up such a situation to describe the misfortune that Yahweh prepares. One then can drink "the cup of wrath" (Jr 25,27f; 51,7). Jeremiah becomes as one drunk, "because of Yahweh and His holy words" (Jr 23,9), because they announce the coming misfortune in such an extreme way. It seems as if the earth itself weaves beneath one's feet (Is 24, 19f), that all resistance is in vain, and that all familiar landmarks disappear: it seems as if the last day is already upon us.

2 *Drunkenness and watchfulness.* A moral warning—drunkenness brings about forgetfulness, and may be followed by even more penetrating realities. The mother of the Arab king, Lemuel, sees in strong drinks a means of forgetting: one can give them to those who have suffered disaster, but kings and princes shun them from fear of forgetting their own pronouncements and misinterpreting justice (Pr 31,4-7). Isaiah goes further. That which the drunken man forgets is the plan* of Yahweh (Is 5,12). Drunkenness is a symptom and image of lassitude and incoherence (Is 19,14; 29,10; Jr 13,13; Jl 1,5). In the same vein the NT sees in drunkenness an abandonment of watchfulness by which the Christian is firmly grounded in the salvation which takes place and will take place on earth. The person who has enough of waiting and gets drunk finds that it is then that Christ comes (Mt 24,45-51 p). So as not to be

unaware of the coming of Christ, we should be sober and watchful*, following the advice of St. Peter (1 P 5,8) taken up in the office of Compline, and be on guard with eyes wide open: "sleepers sleep at night and drunkards are drunk at night" (1 Th 5,6ff; R 13,13).

3. *Drunkenness and the Spirit.* Drunkenness shuts one off from the kingdom (1 Co 5,11; 6,10; R 13,13; G 5,21; 1 P 4,3). Nevertheless, it tries to penetrate into the realm of the sacred; the Corinthians came drunk to their agapes (1 Co 11,21). Among those in the crowd of Jerusalem at the day of Pentecost*, some through mockery would have attributed to drunkenness the effects of the Spirit* (Ac 2,13-15). However, that which brought on the mockery here is no longer a misfortune but the liberating presence of the Spirit. St. Paul suggests the same connection when he commands shunning drunkenness to seek the fullness of the Spirit (E 5,18). Man seeks in drunkenness knowledge of his innermost self and to become free from what hampers his freedom of expression and his entire being. He finds in that state a joy* that the Canticle of Canticles associates with that of love (Ct 5,1). But the Spirit alone can bring him this fullness in truth.

→Charisms II 0—Noah I—Nourishment I— Vintage—Wine.

PBp jrs

E

EARTH

The life of man depends completely on the riches which the earth conceals and on the fertility of its soil. It is the providential framework of his life: "The heavens belong to Yahweh, but the earth he has given to the sons of Adam" (Ps 115,16). However, the earth is not only the framework of man's life: there is an intimate bond between him and it. He came forth from this *adamah* (Gn 2,7; 3,19; cf Is 64,7; Jr 18,6) and gets his name from it:

Adam*. Every ancient civilization saw this intimate connection between the earth and man, to the extent of expressing it through the very realistic image of mother-earth or earth-woman: Israel did so too. God even makes use of the experience that, through the covenant, man is going to have of his connections with the earth, in order to lead him to discover the bonds that, through it, He wants to establish with him.

And so it is not surprising to see the earth and its material goods occupying an important place in revelation*. It is associated with man in the whole history of salvation, from the beginning of time to the expectation of the Kingdom to come.

OT

I. THE MYSTERY OF THE BEGINNINGS

1. *The earth, creation and property of God.* "In the beginning," God created heaven and earth (Gn 1,1). The Bible gives two successive representations of this beginning, which was previous to man but ordered to him. In the first, God separates from the waters the mainland, which he calls "earth" and which he then peoples (1,9-25); in the second, the earth is an empty and sterile desert (2,4-6) in which God is going to plant a garden in which to place man. In either case, the earth is completely dependent on Him; it is His possession: "To Him belongs the earth" (Ps 24,1; 89,12; cf Lv 25,23). Because He is the creator of the earth, God has an absolute right over it and He alone disposes of its goods (Gn 2,16f), establishes its laws (Ez 23,10), and causes it to bear fruit (Ps 65; 104). He is its Lord (Jb 38,4-7; Is 40,12.21-26); it is His footstool (Is 66,1; Ac 7, 49). Like all creation, it owes Him praise (Ps 66,1-4; 96; 98,4; Dn 3,74); this praise takes form and voice on the lips of man (Ps 104).

2. *The earth, domain of man.* If God has drawn man from the earth and made him emerge from it by breathing the breath of life into him, it is in order to entrust this earth to him and make him master of it. Man is to rule over it (Gn 1,28f); it is like a garden of which he is made the steward (2,8.15; Si 17,1-4). Hence, between them, we have that reciprocal shaping that leaves so many echoes in Scripture. On the one hand, man leaves his mark on the earth by his work*; on the other, the earth is a vital reality which in some ways shapes the psychology of man. His thought and his language ceaselessly return to images of the earth: "Do you sow* justice? Reap a harvest of goodness. . .Why have you ploughed evil?" (Ho 10,12f). Isaiah, in his parable of the cultivator (Is 28,23. . .), explains the trials necessary for supernatural fruitfulness*, beginning from the laws of cultivation, while the psalmist compares his anguished soul to a land made thirsty for God (Ps 63,2; 143,6).

3. *Earth cursed because of sin.* If the bond between man and the earth is so close, what is the source of this hostility between man and ungrateful nature which all generations can successively experience? Earth is no longer a paradise* for man. A mysterious trial has intervened, and sin* has corrupted their relations. Assuredly the earth is still governed by the same providential laws which God established in the beginning (Gn 8,22), and this order of the world bears witness to the Creator (R 1,19f; Ac 14,17). But sin has brought a true curse* upon the earth which makes it bring forth "brambles and thorns" (Gn 3,17f). It is a place of trial, where man suffers* until he finally returns to the ground from which he has been drawn (3,19; Ws 15,8). Thus the solidarity of man with the earth continues to be affirmed both for better and for worse.

II. THE PEOPLE OF GOD AND ITS LAND

Bound to man from its beginnings, the earth will preserve its role in biblical revelation. In its way it will remain in the center of the history of salvation.

1. *Experience of the patriarchs.* Between Babylon*, a strange and threatening land from which God draws Abraham (Gn 11,31—12,1), and Egypt*, a tempting land and a place of slavery from which God will draw his posterity (Ex 13, 9. . .), the patriarchs are going to find in Canaan a place of sojourn which will remain the promised land "flowing with milk and honey" (Ex 3,8) for their posterity. God, in fact, promises this land to Abraham (Gn 12,7). Following him, the ancestors of Israel will wander over it before it becomes their inheritance* (Gn 17,8). They will be there only as strangers in a temporary dwelling place, for they are guided by the needs of their flocks alone. But they find more than pastures or wells in the land. They find in it the place in which the living God* manifests Himself to them. The oak trees (Gn 18), the wells (26,15ff; cf 21,3f), and the altars* erected (12,7) are witnesses* which preserve the memory of these manifestations. Certain of these places bear His name: Bethel, "house* of God" (28,17ff); Penuel, "face of God" (32,31). With the grotto of Machpelah (23), Abraham first takes juridical possession of a portion of this promised land. Isaac, Jacob, and Joseph will desire to rest there, thus making Canaan their fatherland*.

2. *The gift of the land.* The renewed promise*
of God (Gn 26,3; 35,12; Ex 6,4) has maintained
among the Hebrews hope* for the land in which
they will settle. Yahweh causes them to go forth
from Egypt, a foreign land (cf Gn 46,3). Nevertheless, in order to enter the promised land,
they must first experience destitution, "the blazing solitude of the desert*'" (Dt 32,10). Israel,
the "people chosen from among the nations
which are upon the earth" (Dt 7,6), must not
have any possession other than God. Once
purified, it can then, under Joshua's* lead,
conquer Canaan, "a place where nothing of
what can be had on earth is lacking" (Jg 18,
10). Yahweh intervenes in this conquest and
it is He who gives the land to His people (Ps
135,12). Obtained without fatigue (Js 24,13),
the land is a free gift, a grace*, like the covenant from which it flows (Gn 17,8; 35,12; Ex
6,4.8). Israel becomes enthusiastic over the land,
for God has not deceived His people. "It is
a good, a very good country" (Nm 14,7; Jg
18,9), which contrasts with the aridity and the
monotony of the desert: it is the earthly paradise* found again. Thus the people at once
become attached to this "happy land of brooks
and springs, the land of wheat and barley, of the
vine, of fig trees and pomegranate trees, of olive
trees, of oil, of honey, the land where bread is
not measured" (Dt 8,7ff). Does it not hold
the land as an inheritance* from God (Dt 15,4),
whom it wishes to serve alone (Js 24,16ff)?
The earth and its goods will thus be a permanent
reminder to it of the love* of God and of His
fidelity to His covenant. He who possesses the
land also possesses God. For Yahweh is no
longer only the God of the desert, but Canaan
has become His dwelling place. As the centuries
run along, men come to believe that this dwelling place is so closely bound to the land of
Israel that David does not believe it possible
to adore Yahweh abroad in the land of other
gods (1 S 26,19); and Naaman brings a bit
of the land of Israel to Damascus in order to be
able to render worship to Yahweh (2 K 5,17).

3. *The drama of Israel in its land.*

a) The law of the land. The promised land
has been given to Israel as its "domain"
(Dt 12,1; 19,14), a domain which is to bring
it prosperity, though not without effort on its
part. Work* is a law for him who wishes to
receive the divine blessings, and Scripture is not
gentle toward the slothful "who sleep during
the harvest" (Pr 10,5; 12,11; 24,30-34). Tenant

of God on a land in which it remains "stranger*
and guest" (Lv 25,23; Ps 119,19), Israel must
in addition fulfill various obligations. In the
first place, it must manifest to God its praise*,
its thanksgiving*, its dependence. This is the
meaning of the agrarian feasts* (Ex 23,14. . .),
which associate its life of worship with the very
rhythms of nature: the feasts of Azymes, of the
reaping, of the first-fruits* (Ex 23,16), of the
harvest. Furthermore, the use of the products
of the soil is subject to precise rules; and the
poor and the stranger must be allowed to glean
(Dt 14,29; 24,19-21). In order not to exhaust
the soil, its produce must be given up every
seventh year (Ex 23,11). This law of the land,
simultaneously religious and social, is a sign of
the authority of God, to whom the soil belongs
by right. Its observance must differentiate
Israel from the pagan peasants who surround
it.

b) Temptation and sin. Now, it is precisely
here that Israel is going to be exposed to trial*
and temptation. It has bound its activity and its
life to its land: field, house, wife, are its points
of contact (Dt 20,5ff). Once it has become
sedentary and bound to the earth, Israel will
easily bring back its way of understanding God
in the dimensions of its field and vineyard.
It experiences the earth-mother and the earth-
woman, in the pagan sense of these images. At
the same time that it learns from the Canaanites
the laws of its agricultural life, it tends to adopt
the materialistic and idolatrous religious customs of this life. Yahweh often tends to become
for it a protecting Baal (Lord of the country)
and guarantor of fertility (Jg 2,11). This produces the violent reaction of Gideon (6,25-32)
and later that of the prophets scourging "those
who add house to house and join field to field"
(Is 5,8). They will put the people on guard
against the dangers of becoming settled and
landed, in which they will see a source of thefts
(cf 1 K 21,3-19), of plunderings (Mi 2,2), of
injustices, of class differences, and of enrichment which causes pride and envy (cf Jb 24,2-
12). How can the holy God stand these things?
Is it not evident that in place of finding in its
land a sign of the goodness of God in order to
elevate its heart to Him, or an occasion of
entering into dialogue with Him, Israel has selfishly become attached to it, like all the other
members of sinful humanity? This summons to
a dialog comes from the significant picture
used by the prophets, not of the earth-woman,
but of the earth-spouse (Ho 2,5; Is 45,8; 62,4;

cf Ct 4,12; 5,1; 6,2.11). Here the earth stands for men, for, if God is its Spouse, it is not for its sake but for their sake (cf 2 M 5,19).

c) *Warnings and chastisements.* But Israel still does not understand this, and so, in the face of this situation, the warnings of the prophets join the cries of anguish of the Deuteronomist: "Be careful not to forget Yahweh your God!" (Dt 6,12; 8,11; 11,16). Indeed, the people that enjoys a marvelous country (6,10f) has forgotten the source of this blessing: "It is because Yahweh has loved your fathers. . .that He has given you entry into this country" (4,37f; 31, 20). What other reason is there for these journeyings across foreign lands, if not to receive in the end the gift of the land and to experience divine love? "Remember your wanderings which Yahweh caused you to make during forty years in the desert in order to humble you and to know the depth of your heart" (8,2). The land belongs to God. His authority is demanding and jealous, like His love. Man should remain humble, faithful, and obedient (5,32— 6,25). If he does so, he will receive blessings* in return: "The products of your land shall be blessed. . .the increase of your flocks" (28,4. . .), for "Yahweh takes care of this land. . .His eyes are fixed on it from the beginning of the year even to its end" (11,12). On the other hand there will be a curse* if Israel turns away (Dt 28,33; Ho 4,3; Jr 4,23-28)! There is even a glimpse of that worst of all threats, the loss of the land: "You will be snatched from the land you are about to enter" (Dt 28,63). This threat, which the prophets specify with vehemence (Am 5,27; Ho 11,5; Jr 16,18), is finally accomplished as a severe divine chastisement in the midst of the agonies of war* and of exile*.

4. *Promises for the future.* Nonetheless this chastisement, however radical it may be, is never regarded by the prophets as absolute and definitive. It will be a purifying trial, like that of the desert long before. Beyond it there remains a hope* whose object shows all the marks of past experience: the land still plays a major role. This land will first be the land of Israel to which the new people* will be restored by Yahweh. Purified and completely consecrated (Ez 47,13—48,35; Ze 14), this "holy land" (Ze 2,16; 2 M 1,7; Ws 12,3) can be called, like Jerusalem its capital, the bride of Yahweh (Is 62,4). But beyond the holy land the entire earth will share with it in salvation. Religiously centered on Jerusalem* (Is 2,2ff; 66,18-21; Ps 47,8ff), it will become the "land of pleasures" (Ml 2,12), of a new humanity in which the nations* will be joined to Israel in order to rediscover their primitive unity*. To put it more clearly, the beginnings alone will offer an adequate representation of this transfigured earth. The "new heavens and the new earth" which God will then create (Is 65,17) will give to the abode of men the characteristics of the primitive paradise* with its fertility and its marvelous conditions of life (Am 9,13; Ho 2,23f; Is 11,6-9; Jr 23,3; Ez 47,1f; Jl 4,18; Ze 14,6-11).

In this perspective, the possession of the land then takes on an eschatological meaning. This is accentuated still more by the passage from the collective level to the individual level, which is initiated in Isaiah 57,13; 60,21, and is developed by the wise men: "the earth" then designates both the land which was promised to Abraham and to his descendants and the other and higher, but still vague, reality which is the portion of the just man who puts all his faith in God (Ps 25,13; 37,3. . .). Progressively raised from earthly preoccupations to purer spiritual aspirations, Israel is ripe for receiving the message of Jesus: "Blessed are the meek, for they shall inherit the earth" (Mt 5,4).

NT

I. JESUS AND THE EARTH

Jesus shares in God's lordship over the earth (Col 1,15; E 4,10) because nothing has been made without Him (Jn 1,3): "all power has been given to Him in heaven and on earth" (Mt 28,18). However, as a man among men, He is bound to the land of Israel by all the fibers of His being.

1. It is a message of universal salvation which He comes to reveal to men, but He does so with the language of a particular country and civilization. The landscapes and the customs of Palestine have in some way shaped the imagination of Him who created them: the image of the sower* and of the harvest*, of the vine* and the fig tree, of the cockel and the grain of mustard, of the shepherd* and the sheep, of fishing on the lake. . .without counting the instructions which He gives on observing the sights of life: "Behold the birds of the sky. . . and the lilies" (Mt 6,26ff), the plucked ears of corn (Mt 12,1-8 p), the barren fig tree (Mt 21, 19).

2. But beyond these images, Jesus provides a teaching on this world here below. The desire to possess the land becomes with Him a desire to enter into possession of spiritual goods (Mt 5,4). The earthly kingdom gives place to the reality which it prefigured, the kingdom of heaven (Mt 5,3). Henceforth man must be able to deprive himself of his fields for the sake of Christ and of the gospel (Mk 10,29f). The narrowly terrestrial aspects of the prophetic promises are now definitively surpassed. Not that the things of this earth on which we live are condemned in themselves, but they are put in their true place, which is secondary in regard to the expectation of the kingdom (Mt 6,33). If this is done, everything is established in order and the will of God is accomplished "on earth as it is in heaven" (Mt 6,10). In this paradoxical manner, Jesus gives its sacred value to the land of men, which is the work of the hands of God and the sign of His presence* and of His love. Though men have used it and will still use it in order to turn themselves away from God, to "bury their talent in it" (Mt 25,18), Christ takes charge of it with love (cf Col 1,20) and makes it capable of bearing His mystery. He goes so far as to take bread*, the fruit of the earth (Ps 104,14), in order to leave here below the presence of His body* under a sign.

3. He has come to bring fire* on the earth (Lk 12,49). It is among the mass of the peasants of Galilee and Transjordan that He found His first disciples in order to spread this fire: they are "the salt of the earth" (Mt 5,13). The gospel then is strongly implanted in a particular corner of our world, namely, this same holy land which God has given to Israel. There also at Jerusalem*, its capital, He will plant His cross in order to inflame the entire world: then "lifted up from the earth, I will draw all men to me" (Jn 12,32). The holy land will thus remain forever the geographic center from which salvation will have gone forth to gain all of humanity.

II. THE NEW PEOPLE AND THE EARTH

1. Thenceforward the plan of universal salvation sketched out in the beginning is restored. The gospel is going to be extended from the land of Israel to the entire world according to the plan indicated by Jesus: "You will be my witnesses in Jerusalem, in all Judea and Samaria and all the way to the limits of the earth (Ac 1,8; cf Mt 28,16ff).

2. Jesus thus achieves not only the passage from the land of Israel, shut up in its limits, to the universe, but also that from the material earth to that earth of which it is the figure: the Church and the kingdom of heaven. The people of the OT had believed in the promises in order to enter into possession of the land of rest, but that was but a figure* of the salvation to come. It is now we who enter by faith into the true land of rest* (He 4,9), the heavenly abode where Jesus dwells since His resurrection and of which we have a foretaste in His Church.

3. In this new perspective there is revealed the meaning which is henceforth attached to human work* and to the liturgy. Following Christ, the new people has already penetrated in hope into the land of rest which was destined for it. This involves a transformation of its earthly activity. It must still "rule the earth," it still risks being trapped in the prosperity which the land brings it (Lk 12,16-34). But, with eyes fixed on Christ ascended into heaven*, it must henceforth "think of the things that are above, not of those of the earth" (Col 3,2); not in contempt, but in order to "use them as though not using them" (1 Co 7,31). The heavenly gaze of the believer does not deny, but rather fulfills the earth by giving it its true meaning. Liturgical prayer in fact gives a voice to the earth, to all that it contains and to what it allows to be produced by work. By this prayer man in some way raises the earth up and makes it ascend toward God. For the new people has not lost its earthly roots. On the contrary, it "rules over the earth" (Ap 5,10), and as long as it accomplishes its pilgrimage here below it cannot remain deaf to the "groaning" of material creation which also awaits salvation (R 8,22).

III. THE EARTH IN CHRISTIAN HOPE

The earth is indeed associated with the history of the new people, just as long as it is drawn into the drama of sinful humanity. It also "awaits" "the revelation of the sons of God. . . with the hope* of being itself delivered from the slavery of corruption in order to enter into the liberty and the glory of the children of God" (R 8,19ff). United with man from the beginning, it remains so unto the end. It is, like him, an object of redemption*, although in a mysterious way. For the earth in its present state "will pass away" (Mt 24,35 p): "it will be consumed with the works which it includes" (2 P 3,10). But that will be in order that it may be replaced by the "new earth" (Ap 21,1) "which we await according to the promise of God and in which justice will dwell" (2 P 3,13).

→Abide—Adam I 1—City—Desert—Election OT I 3 c—Exile—Exodus—Fatherland—Feasts OT I; NT II—First Fruits I—Flesh I 3—Heaven —House II 1—Inheritance—Jerusalem OT I 2 —Joshua—Kingdom—Life III 1—Milk 2— Paradise 2—People A II 4; B II 3.4—Rest II 1 —Sowing I 1—Unbelief I 2—Vine—World OT O.

GB jpl

EDUCATION

God's plan is accomplished in time*. It is by a slow maturation that the chosen people will reach its full stature, its perfection*. St. Paul has compared this "economy" of salvation to an education: the child becomes an adult. Israel lived under the tutelage of the Law*, like a child attended by a pedagogue, until the fullness* of time came. Then God sent His own Son to confer on us filial adoption. To this the gift of the Spirit testifies (G 4,1-7; 3,24f). But the education of Israel does not end with the coming of Christ. We ought "to be the essence of the perfectly mature man* who reaches the fullness of Christ" (E 4,13). From the beginning to the end of time the divine work is to educate the chosen people.

Comprehending by faith the total pattern of the divine pedagogy, the Christian can mark its stages and characteristics. In fact this could be done by uniting the scattered articles of this book. Love*, a dialogue between two persons, is the foundation of all education. The educator teaches*, reveals*, exhorts*, promises*, chastises, rewards*, gives the example*. For this reason he should show himself faithful* to his plan and patient* before the looked-for result. However it seems preferable to restrict ourselves and stay within the very restricted vocabulary apropos of education. The word *mūsār* means instruction (gift of wisdom) as well as correction (reprimand, chastisement). It is found in the books of Wisdom for family education, and among the prophets (and Deuteronomist) to characterize divine behavior. In translating this word as *paideia* (cf lat. *disciplina*), the LXX did not intend to make education, as it appears in the Bible, Hellenic. Greek education seeks to awaken the human personality within a rather limited earthly horizon.

In the Bible, God is the supreme educator. He seeks by precepts and by trials* to obtain from His people (and secondarily from individuals) a ready obedience to the Law or obedience in faith*. If the education given by wise men or by the family seems profane, the context of the books of Wisdom definitely shows that the training is only an expression of divine education (Pr 1,7; Si 1,1). God is the model of teachers. His work of education occurs in three stages which show how the educator exercises a growing influence on the character of the person being educated.

I. GOD EDUCATES HIS PEOPLE

1. *As a father educates his son:* thus has the Deuteronomic reflection characterized God's way of acting in freeing and forming His people. "Understand then that Yahweh your God corrects you as a father corrects his son" (Dt 8,5). The preacher shows himself heir of the prophets. Hosea announced before: "When Israel was a child, I loved him... I taught Ephraim to walk; taking them up in my arms ... I led them with light bonds, with cords of love... I bent over them and fed them" (Ho 11,1-4). Such love is seen in the education of the child found by the roadside in Ezekiel's allegory (Ez 16). This is but a logical picturesque deduction from the basic point in revelation: "Thus Yahweh speaks: Israel is my first-born son" (Ez 4,22).

To understand what is implied by these words, it is important to know the cultural context of the education of children in Israel. It is characterized by two aspects: its end is wisdom*, its preferred means is correction. The teacher should teach his pupil wisdom, understanding, and "discipline" (Pr 23,23). This last term properly designates the fruit of education: tact (1,2), a way of handling oneself well in life, which one must learn and retain (4,13; cf 5,23; 10,17). To succeed in life one must apply his heart to "discipline" (23,12f; cf Si 21,21). Parents and teachers are for children an authority sanctioned by the Law (Ex 20,12). One must listen* to the father and mother (Pr 23,22) under pain of heavy sanctions (30,17; Dt 21,18-21). Education is a difficult art, for "folly is anchored in the child's heart (Pr 22,15). Depraved society entices to evil (1,10ff; 5,7-14; 6,20-35), so that parents are afflicted with cares* (Si 22,3-6; 42,9ff). Remonstrances are then necessary, even the whip, which does not first demand the favorable circumstances necessary for remonstrance: "the crack of the whip and correction is always wisdom" (Si 22,6; 30,1-13; Pr 23,13f). Such is the basic experience which permits us to understand Yahweh's teaching method.

2. *The education of Israel by Yahweh* reflects the two aspects of family pedagogy, instruction in wisdom and correction. Because of sin the two aspects are transposed.

a) "Yahweh's lessons" to His people are the signs accomplished in the heart of Egypt, the miracles in the desert, the whole great work of liberation* (Dt 11,2-7). Israel must, therefore, reflect on the trial* undergone during the journey across the desert*. It suffered hunger* to understand that "man does not live by bread alone but by everything coming from the mouth of Yahweh." This experience of daily dependence should teach Israel to recognize the solicitude of Yahweh, its Father. Their clothes* were not worn out, their feet were not swollen in the course of the forty years (Dt 8,2-6). This test was destined to reveal the depths of Israel's heart and to start a dialogue with Yahweh. Besides this, the Law* is also presented as God's means of education: "He made you listen to His voice from heaven to instruct you" (Dt 4,36), not only to express His divine will* under the form of objective commandments but to make you recognize that God loves you (4,37f) and that He wishes to give you "happiness and long life in a land He is giving you forever" (4,40). Good educator that He is, Yahweh promises to reward* the observance of the Law. Finally, as in the case of a test, the Law ought to signify the presence of the very word of the educator. The Word* is not in the distant heavens nor beyond the seas but "very near you, in your mouth and in your heart" (30, 11-14).

b) Correction, which can range from threat to reprimand to punishment, ought to assure the effectiveness of "Yahweh's lessons"; for sin made Israel a stiff-necked people, very much as folly is anchored in the child's heart. Yahweh, therefore, seizes the hand of a prophet who will turn from the path followed by the people (Is 8,11). This prophet will be of indestructible patience*. As the mouth of God Himself, he will continually—morning and evening—recall God's will and God's love. Hosea shows

the learning value of punishments sent by Yahweh (Ho 7,12; 10,10) by alluding to the fruitless endeavors of the husband who seeks to win back his unfaithful wife (2,4-15; cf Am 4,6-11). Jeremiah unceasingly repeats this idea: "Take warning, Jerusalem" (Jr 6,8). But to no avail. The rebellious children do not welcome the lesson; they refuse to be taught (2,30; 7,28; Zp 3,2.7). "They put up a front harder than rock" (Jr 5,3). Then correction becomes punishment which falls down thick and fast (Lv 26,18.23f.28), but fairly. It is not the wrath* which kills (Jr 10,24; 30,11; 46,28; cf Ps 6,2; 38,2); conversion can follow. Israel ought to acknowledge: "You have corrected me, and I have submitted to the correction like a young untrained bull"; and its sorrow should end in a prayer: "Make me return, oh, that I may return, for you are my God" (Jr 31,18). The psalmist recognizes the value of divine correction: "My loins* taught me in the night" (Ps 16,7). And the wise man says: "Happy the man whom God corrects! Be docile to the lesson of Shaddai!" (Jb 5,17), for it is God's way of governing peoples (Ps 94,10; cf Is 28,23-26).

c) The education, however, will be finished only on the day when the Law will be imbedded in the heart*: "They will no longer have to teach one another. . .they will all know me, from the least to the greatest" (Jr 31,33f). To obtain this result, it will be necessary that correction fall on the Servant*: "The chastisement which gives us peace is on Him, and it is thanks to His wounds that we are healed" (Is 53,5). Then will it be understood to what point the "heart of Yahweh was moved" when He had to utter threats over "His beloved Son" (Jr 31,20; cf Ho 11,8f).

II. JESUS CHRIST, TEACHER OF ISRAEL

The Servant presents Himself to His people with the characteristics of a rabbi who educates his disciples* as sons. Through Him it is God in person who reveals the fulfillment of His plan. In addition, the Servant takes upon Himself the corrections which we deserve. He is the redeemer of Israel. Doubtless there is no specific vocabulary to affirm this double aspect, but one can be guided by the OT figurative* expressions.

1. *The revealer.* To set up an account of Jesus' "pedagogy," it is sufficient to look at the retro-

spective accounts given by the evangelists, especially by Matthew. Jesus, who teaches faith to the disciples, progressively brings them to know Him as the Messiah. According to Matthew, this teaching is divided into two sections. "From the day" Peter confesses* Him as the Christ, He will change His manner of acting (Mt 16,21). First He wishes His contemporaries to identify the announced kingdom with His person (cf 4,17). He thus raises a pertinent question by His authoritative teaching (Mt 7,28f; Mk 1,27) and by His miracles (Mt 8,27; Lk 4,36), even if this procedure raises a doubt in John the Baptist (Mt 11,3). He teaches according to the disposition of the audience. For example, in parables*, which were intended not only to instruct but also to arouse a demand for an explanation (Mt 13,10-13.36), He teaches until the points are finally "understood" (13, 51). He makes the disciples "realize" their inability and His own ability to give bread in the desert (14,15-21); from the bread He draws the lesson they should have "understood" (16, 8-12). After He has given them definite instructions (10,5-16), He lets them take part in His mission* and He asks a report of the work they did (Mk 6,30; Lk 10,17). And then, when He has been recognized as the Christ, He can reveal a mystery that is very difficult to accept: the cross*. His education then becomes more and more exacting. He corrects Peter who dares to reprimand Him (Mt 16,22f); He laments the lack of faith in His disciples (17,17), but gives them the reason for their failure (17,19f). He draws a lesson from the jealousy which is manifested in the small group (20,24-28). His whole procedure is a way of teaching that tends to impress the lesson forever. Thus by the question three times asked of Peter, "Do you love me?" He intends to heal the heartfelt wound of the triple denial (Jn 21,15ff).

2. *The redeemer.* Jesus is not content with telling what must be done; perfect teacher that He is, He has given the example*: of poverty for He does not have a place to rest His head (Mt 8,20); of faithfulness* to His mission, which makes Him stand up against the Jews and their leaders, for example, by driving the vendors from the temple, a zeal* which will bring Him to death (Jn 2,17); of fraternal charity, Himself washing the feet of His disciples, He the master (Jn 13,14f).

Now this example is extended still further. Jesus identifies Himself with those He has to teach, taking upon Himself their "correction,"

the chastisement which weighs on them (Is 53,5). He bears their infirmities (Mt 8,17), He takes away the world's sin (Jn 1,29). Thus He wished to know our weaknesses, "He who has been tested in every way just as we have, with the exception of sin" (He 4,15), He who, "though He was Son, learned obedience from His sufferings. . .and was made perfect" (5,8f). By His sacrifice Jesus brought to conclusion the education of Israel. Apparently He failed: He had clearly foretold what must come about (Jn 16, 1-4), but He could not by Himself make His disciples clearly understand (Jn 16,12f). It is proper that He goes away and gives way to the Spirit (17,7f).

III. THE CHURCH, STUDENT AND TEACHER

1. *The Holy Spirit as educator.* It is really the Paraclete* who brings God's work of education to completion. The Law is no longer our teacher (G 3,19; 4,2); but it is the Spirit, perfectly within us, who makes us say: "Abba! Father!" (G 4,6). We are no longer servants, but friends* (Jn 15,15) and sons* (G 4,7). This is the work the Paraclete achieves in recalling Jesus' teachings to the memory* of believers (Jn 14,26; 16,13ff), in defending Jesus' cause against persecutions of the world* (16,8-11). All are then "docile" to the Father's call (6,45). Such is the effectiveness of the anointing* in the Christian heart (1 Jn 2,20.27). The real educator, after all, is God, who is perfectly invisible and interior to man.

2. *Instruction and Correction.* Nevertheless, up till the end of time, education retains its OT corrective aspect. The epistle to the Hebrews recalls to Christians: "It is as sons that God treats you. And who is the son whom his father does not correct? If you are exempt from this correction, it is because you are illegitimate sons" (He 12,7f). We should then expect, if we are tepid, to be visited* by correction (Ap 3,19). These are divine judgments*, which do not kill (2 Co 6,9) and which save one from condemnation (1 Co 11,32); after the suffering they give joy* (He 12,11). Scripture also is a source of instruction and correction (1 Co 10,11; Tt 2,12; 2 Tm 3,16). Paul himself educates the people he writes to by urging them to imitate his example (1 Th 1,16; 2 Th 3,7ff; 1 Co 4,16; 11,1). Finally, the believer should practice fraternal correction according to Jesus' precept (Mt 18,

15; cf 1 Th 5,14; 2 Th 3,15; Col 3,16; 2 Tm 2,25). Paul does this with vigor, not hesitating to use the rod (1 Co 4,21), nor to hurt feelings if there is cause (2 Co 7,8-11). He incessantly instructs and warns his children (1 Co 4,14; Ac 20,31). In the education of their children, parents are only the representatives of the sole educator, God. They should not exasperate the children, but rebuke and correct as God Himself would (E 6,4).

→Authority OT I 2; NT II 2—Child—Example —Exhort—Fathers & Father—Mary III 2— Mother—Patience I—Punishments 3—Teach— Trial/Temptation—Wisdom OT II 1—Woman OT 2—Worship OT II.

XLD gsa

EGYPT

1. *The role of Egypt in sacred history.* Among the foreign nations* with which Israel has had any dealings, perhaps none shows the ambiguity of temporal powers more than Egypt. This land of abundance is the providential refuge of the starving patriarchs (Gn 12,10; 42ff), of exiles (1 K 11,40; Jr 26,21), of defeated Israelites (Jr 42f), of Jesus in His flight (Mt 2,13); but for the same reason she provides easy temptation for peoples without ideal (Ex 14,12; Nm 11,5 . . .). An empire proud of her strength*, she earlier oppressed the Hebrews (Ex 1—13); yet in spite of this she keeps her prestige in the eyes of Israel during the centuries when Israel aspires to temporal grandeur. David (2 S 20,23-26) and above all Solomon (1 K 4,1-6) copy the Egyptians in their organization of the royal court and in the administration of the kingdom. Egypt's help is sought in times of crisis by Samaria (Ho 7,11) as well as by Jerusalem (2 K 17,4; 18,24; Is 30,1-5; Jr 2,18. . .; Ez 29,7. . .). As the home of culture she contributed to the education of Moses (Ac 7,22); use of her literature (notably Pr 22,17—23,11). But, on the other hand, she is a land of idolatry and magic (Ws 15,14-19) whose fatal seduction alienates the Israelites from their God (Jr 44,8. . .).

2. *Egypt before God.* It is not therefore surprising that there should be a judgment* of God against Egypt: at the time of the exodus, to make her free Israel (Ex 5—15; cf Ws 16—19); during the period of the kings, to punish this proud power who gave Israel an empty promise of aid (Is 30,1-7; 31,1-3; Jr 46; Ez 29-32); to humiliate this pagan nation which was led astray by her wise men (Is 19,1-5). Under all these titles, she will continue to represent symbolically the human collectivities doomed to God's wrath (Ap 11,8).

Yet, because she was a land of welcome, Egypt is not always excluded from the assembly of Yahweh (Dt 23,8f). Even after He punishes her thus, God exercises moderation in her regard: the Egyptians remain His creatures, and He would like above all to turn them from evil (Ws 11,15—12,2). That is why He plans to convert Egypt in the end and to unite her with His people, that she in turn might learn to serve Him (Is 19,16-25; Ps 87,4-7). Although judged by her sins, she will nevertheless share in salvation as all the other nations*.

→Captivity I—City OT 1—Deception/Disappointment II—Desert OT I 2—Exodus—Liberation/Liberty II 1—Nations OT II 1 a—Slave I—Wisdom O; OT I 1—Work II.

RM & PG gsa

ELECTION

Without election it is impossible to understand anything about God's plan* and will* regarding man. But the sinner, incurably distrustful of God and envious of his brothers, is always reluctant to accept God's grace* and generosity: he blames them when another profits from them (Mt 20,15); and when it is he, he avails himself of them as if they had a value which only he gives them. Between Cain's fury against his brother (Gn 4,4f) and the cry of Paul, tortured for his brothers according to the flesh (R 9,2f) and emptying his anguish in thanksgiving for "the unfathomable decrees and the incomprehensible ways of God" (11,33), there is a total way which leads from sin to faith; it is the entirety of redemption; it is the fullness of Scripture.

OT

I.   THE EXPERIENCE OF ELECTION

1. *The initial fact.* The experience of the election is that of a destiny different from that of other peoples, of a unique condition due not to a blind concatenation of circumstances or to

a series of human successes, but to a deliberate and sovereign initiative of Yahweh. If the classic vocabulary of the election (hb. *bāḥar* and its derivatives) appears relatively late, at least in this precise and particular sense, the awareness of this divine activity dates back to the beginning of Israel's existence as the people* of Yahweh. This awareness is inseparable from the covenant*, and it speaks at the same time of her unique character (the only one from among so many others) and of her interior secret (chosen by God). Thus does it give the covenant its religious depth, the dimension of mystery*.

2. *The first confessions** of divine choice go back to the oldest expressions of the faith of Israel. The ritual of the first-fruits narrated in Dt 26,1-11 includes a very old *credo*, the substance of which is the divine initiative which brought the Hebrews out of Egypt to lead them to a land of blessing*. The account of the covenant concluded at Shechem under Joshua makes the history of Israel go back to an election—"I took your father Abraham. . ." (Js 24,3)—and underlines the fact that the answer to this initiative can be only a choice: "Choose whom you will serve" (24,15). Doubtless the formulas of the covenant on Sinai—"You will make of us your inheritance" (Ex 34,9), "I will regard you as my own among all the peoples" (19,5)—are more recent; but the faith that they express is already found in one of Balaam's oracles: "How can I curse one whom God has not cursed. . .Behold a people who live apart and who are not counted among the nations" (Nm 23,8f), and soon again in the song of Deborah who alternated the wonders of "Yahweh, the God of Israel" (Jg 5,3.5.11) with the generosity of the combatants who offered themselves "for Yahweh" (Jg 5,2.9.13.23).

3. *The election as a continued event.* All these confessions recall a history and sing the continuity of a unique plan*. The election of the people seems to be prepared for by a series of previous election, and it is constantly developed by the choice of individuals newly chosen.

a) *Before Abraham*, the outline of the history of man, if it includes God's preferences (Abel, Gn 4,4), privileged treatments (Enoch, 5,24), the unique case of Noah* who was "the only just one before me in this generation" (7,1), the blessing given Shem (9,26), does not yet contain an election properly so called. But the historical outline constantly supposes election. All this history is constructed in order that from the midst of this human multitude which is a prey to sin and which dreams of "reaching heaven" (11,4), God, who sees all generations, may one day choose Abraham to bless in him "all the nations of the earth" (12,3).

b) To the *patriarchs*, God shows the continuation of His plan of election. He chose a race and keeps this choice. But in this race it is not the natural heir, Eliezer, Ishmael, Esau, or Ruben, who gets His blessing. Each time a particular impulse of God designates His choice: Isaac (Gn 18,19), Jacob, and Judah. The whole of Genesis has for its theme the paradoxical encounter between the normal consequences of the initial election of Abraham and the actions by which God overturns man's projects and thus remains at the same time faithful to His promises* and the sovereign priority of His choice.

In these accounts a permanent characteristic of election is affirmed. Although in men's eyes the privilege of the elect automatically entails the forfeiture of those who have been bypassed —witness the refrain which punctuates the oracles pronounced by the fathers: "May your brothers be your slaves!" (9,25; 27,29; 27,40)— in the divine promises God's Word over His elect makes them a blessing for the whole earth (12,3; 22,18; 26,4; 28,14).

c) Within the chosen people, God constantly chooses men to whom He entrusts a mission*, temporary or permanent. This choice, which sets them apart and consecrates them, reproduces the characteristics of the election of Israel. To the *prophets** election is shown often through the calling*, the direct appeal of God proposing a new manner of existence and demanding an answer. The typical case is Moses (Ex 3; cf Ps 106,23: "His elect"); but Amos (Am 7,15), Isaiah (Is 8,11), Jeremiah (Jr 15,16f; 20,7), all have the same experience. They were seized, taken away from their ordinary life, from the society of men, and forced to proclaim God's point of view and to set themselves against their people.

The *kings** were chosen, as Saul (1 S 10,24), and especially David, who was chosen by Yahweh at the very moment that Saul was rejected (1 S 16,1), and chosen forever with his descendants, who will perhaps be severely chastised but never rejected (2 S 7,14ff). There is now no more call heard; the divine choice is made known to the king by the prophet (1 S 10,1) who has it from the Word* of God (1 S 16,6-12; Hg 2,23); and it is often by a play of events that God brings to the throne the king He has chosen; for example, Solomon in preference to Adonijah (1 K 2,15). But there is surely a question of an election (Dt 17,15), not only because of the royal dignity and the sacred character of the anointing*, but also because the choice of the anointed one of Yahweh is always linked with God's covenant with His people (Ps 89,4) and because the essential function of the king is to keep Israel faithful to her election.

Priests and Levites are likewise the object of an election. The ministry entrusted to them of "keeping themselves in Yahweh's presence" supposes a "separation" (Dt 10,8; 18,5), a form of existence different from that of the rest of the people. Now it is a divine initiative that is at the origin of this consecration. God took the Levites for Himself in place of the first-born who belonged to Him by right (Nm 8,16ff), thus showing that His sovereignty is not at all a blind and indifferent domination, but that it is interested in the quality of the partners and it expects from them a joyous ratification. Chosen by Yahweh to be His portion and inheritance*, the Levites should busy themselves with taking Him for their portion and their inheritance (Nm 18,20; Ps 16,5f). And if there is a continuity between the election of the priests and the Levites and that of Israel, it is that Yahweh has chosen His people to be entirely "a kingdom of priests and a consecrated nation" (Ex 19,6).

As He has chosen His people, Yahweh has chosen the *earth** and the holy places He destines for Himself; for He is not, like the Canaanite Baals, a prisoner of the springs or the mountains where He acts. Just as "He has chosen the tribe of Judah," He has, because He loves it, "chosen the mountain* of Zion" (Ps 78, 68) and has "chosen it for His abode" (Ps 68,17; 132,13). Above all, He has chosen "for a dwelling place of His name" the temple* of Jerusalem (Dt 12,5...; 16,7-16).

II. THE MEANING OF ELECTION

Deuteronomy, which has perpetuated the vocabulary of election around the root *bḥr*, has equally evolved the meaning of the root.

1. The *origin* of election is a gratuitous initiative of God: it is Yahweh who "set His heart on you and chose you" (Dt 7,7), and not you who chose Him. The explanation of this grace*

is love*; no merit, no excellence justifies it. Israel is the last of the peoples, "but...Yahweh has loved you" (7,7f). Election creates a close relation between God and His people: "You are sons" (Dt 14,1). Yet this parentage has nothing natural about it, as is often the case between the divinity and its believers in paganism. It is the result of Yahweh's choice (14,2) and expresses the transcendence of Him who is always "the first to love" (1 Jn 4,19).

2. The *purpose* of election is to constitute a holy* people, consecrated to Yahweh, "raised above all nations in honor, renown, and glory" (Dt 26,19), making the grandeur and the generosity of the Lord radiate among the peoples. The Law*, particularly by the barriers it sets up between Israel and the nations*, is the means to assure this holiness (7,1-6).

3. The *result* of an election which sets Israel apart from other peoples is to bind her to a destiny that has nothing in common with theirs: either extraordinary prosperity or unparalleled misfortune (Dt 28). The word of Amos remains the charter of election: "From among all the families of the earth I have known only you; therefore I will punish you for all your iniquities" (Am 3,2).

III. THE NEW, ESCHATOLOGICAL ELECTION

1. *Election and rejection.* This threat, though serious, retains a note of reassurance: for God to chastise His people thus, He must not renounce it. Its effect would be more dreadful if God should annul the election and let Israel be lost among the peoples. Just as He slighted the seven older sons in favor of David (1 S 16,7), just as He rejected Ephraim in favor of Judah (Ps 78,67f), does He not venture to "reject the city He has chosen, Jerusalem" (2 K 23,27)? The prophets, particularly Jeremiah, are forced to envisage this outcome. Israel is like silver that cannot be purified, and is condemned to the rubbish heap (Jr 6,30; cf 7,29); "Have you therefore rejected Judah?" (14,19).

The final answer is negative: "If the heavens above could be measured and the foundations of the earth below fathomed, then could I reject the whole race of Israel" (Jr 31,37; cf Ho 11,8; Ez 20,32). It is true that the unfaithful bride has been "repudiated for her sins," but God can still ask: "Where then is the letter of repudia-

ELECTION

tion of your mother?" (Is 50,1). The election continues but in a new form: "Yahweh will again elect Jerusalem" (Ze 1,17; 2,16), He "will once more choose Israel" (Is 14,1) in spite of her sin and destruction, in the form of a remnant* which will not be the effect of chance but of God's power: "holy seed" (Is 6,13), "the branch" (Ze 3,8), "the seven thousand men who have not bent their knee before Baal" (1 K 19,18) and whom, according to St. Paul's interpretation, God has reserved for Himself (R 11,4, adding "for me").

2. *Behold my elect.* To this new Israel the title of elect is very often given in Second Isaiah, always by God Himself (either "my elect," Is 41, 8; 43,20; 45,4; or "my elects," 43,10; cf 65, 9.15.22). It perfectly describes the creative initiative of God who is capable of making a completely idolatrous people become devoted to the service* of the true God. At the center of the world and of its history, God chose this people; and it is of them He thinks and for them that He governs the whole earth, choosing a Cyrus (45,1) and making him a conqueror "for the sake of Israel, my elect" (45,4).

At the heart of this work, God makes a mysterious personage appear to whom He does not give a name other than "my Servant" (42,1; 49,3; 52,13) and "my elect" (42,1). He is neither a king* nor a priest* nor a prophet*, for all these are chosen from among men, before they are conscious of their mission. They hear the call of a vocation, they receive an anointing*. But He heard God's call "from His mother's womb" (cf Jr 1,5) and His name* is not given by men but designated by God alone (49,1). His whole existence is from God; it is but an election, and that is why it is also service and consecration: the elect is necessarily the Servant*.

NT

I. JESUS CHRIST, GOD'S ELECT

Although the title is rarely given to Jesus in the NT (Lk 9,35; 23,35; probably Jn 1,34), it is always at a solemn moment; baptism*, the transfiguration*, or the crucifixion; and always it calls forth the image of the servant. God Himself in pronouncing it attests that in Jesus of Nazareth He finally comes to the end of the work He had undertaken in choosing Abraham and Israel. He has found the only elect who

fully merits this name, the only one to whom He could confide His work and who is capable of fulfilling His wish. Isaiah's "Behold my elect!" proclaimed God's triumph in then possessing one who would never deceive Him. The "Behold my elect!" of the Father over Jesus reveals the secret of this certitude. It is this man of flesh who, from His mother's womb, has been sanctified and called His Son* (Lk 1,35), and who, "from the creation of the world," has been destined to "gather all things unto Himself" (E 1,4.10; 1 P 1,20). Only Christ is the elect of God, and there are no chosen ones except in Him. He is the chosen rock*, the only one capable of supporting the building* that God constructs (1 P 2,4ff).

Although he never utters this name, Jesus has the clearest conviction of His election: the certainty of coming from elsewhere (Mk 1,38; Jn 8,14), of belonging to another world (Jn 8,23), of having to live a unique destiny, that of the Son* of Man, and of accomplishing God's very work (Jn 5,19; 9,4; 17,4). All Scripture relates the election of Israel, and Jesus knows that everything points to Him (Lk 24,27; Jn 5,46). But this perception arouses in Him only the will to serve* and to fulfill* to the end what must be achieved (Jn 4,34).

II. THE CHURCH, A CHOSEN PEOPLE

1. *The choice of the twelve* early shows that Jesus wishes to accomplish His work by having "with Him those whom He wished" (Mk 3,13f). Around Him they represent the twelve tribes of the new people*. This people has for its origin the choice of Christ (Lk 6,13; Jn 6,70), which reverts to the Father's choice of Christ (Jn 6,37; 17,2) and takes place under the action of the Spirit (Ac 1,2). From the beginning of the Church as with the origin of Israel there is the election by God: "It is not you who have chosen me" (Jn 15,16; cf Dt 7,6). The elections of Matthias (Ac 1,24) and of Paul (Ac 9,15) show that God does not intend to build His Church* except on the witnesses* He has set up (Ac 10,41; 26,16).

2. *The divine election continues in the Church* as a lived reality. The Christian communities and their leaders make choices and confer missions (Ac 6,5), but these choices only confirm God's choices and acknowledge His Spirit (6,3). If the twelve impose their hands on the seven (6,6), if the Church of Antioch sets apart Paul

and Barnabas, it is because the Spirit has designated them as those whom He calls for His work (13,1ff). The presence of charisms* in the Church reveals that the election is not abrogated.

Gathering together and establishing in one body these individual callings*, the Church is chosen. The gift of faith*, the acceptance of the Word* are not explained by human wisdom* nor by power nor by birth, but only by God's choice (1 Co 1,26ff; cf Ac 15,7; 1 Th 1,4f). It is natural that the Christians, conscious of having been "called from darkness" to form "a chosen race. . .a holy people" (1 P 2,9), are called simply "the elected" (R 16,13; 2 Tm 2,10; 1 P 1,1), and that *Ekklēsia* and *Eklektē*, *Church* and *Elect*, are placed together not simply because of their pleasing assonance (cf 2 Jn 13; Ap 17,14).

III. CHOSEN OR REJECTED

As for the chosen, the NT speaks of the "chosen of God," thus affirming the personal character and the sovereignty of this choice (Mk 13,20.27 p; R 8,33). Yet it also speaks simply of the elect in eschatological contexts, and thus sees beyond the trials those to whom election has become like a visible and revealed reality (Mt 22,14; 24,22.24): and it is the same with damnation.

The OT knew a rejection anterior to election, the rejection of one who is not chosen; but this rejection is somewhat provisional, since the choice of Abraham is to be a blessing for all nations*. At the heart of election, the successive rejection of the guilty and the unworthy does not impair the promise. The divine choice is irrevocable. In Jesus Christ the election of Abraham is fulfilled and the rejection of the nations ends. In Him Jews* and Greeks, after being reconciled (E 2,14ff), have been chosen, "designated" to form only one people, "the people whom God has acquired" (E 1,11.14); election has absorbed all.

It is possible, however, "after one has received the knowledge of the truth," for him to "trample under foot the Son of God. . .to profane the blood of the covenant. . .to fall, a dreadful thing, into the hands of the living God" (He 10,26-31). There is possible rejection which is not a repudiation of election, but which express in the election itself the judgment* of the elect who does not know His own. His "I do not know you" (Mt 25,12) does not annul the "I have known you" (Am 3,2) of the election. It ex-

presses God's earnestness: "Therefore will I visit you for all your iniquities."

This rejection no longer belongs to time but to eschatology. That is why it did not fall on the Jewish people. True there is a sin in their history. The children of Israel stumbled on the rock* that had been chosen and placed by God (R 9,32f); they rejected His elect. Yet they remain, "according to the election, beloved because of their fathers" (11,28); and their error, as was that of the nations in the old covenant, is provisional and providential (11,30f). As long as the Lord has not come, they are always called to conversion until, after all the pagans have entered in the election, all Israel* receives again her election (11,23-27).

→Abraham I 1—Calling I, III—Church II 2—Covenant OT I 1—Grace II 2.3, IV—Holy NT IV—Israel OT 1 c—Know OT 1—Love I—People *A* I 1—Plan of God OT I—Predestine—Pride OT 1—Remnant—Will of God O.

JG gsa

ELIJAH

"Yahweh is living before I am!" Eliyyahu readily writes, realizing in his existence what his name* signifies: "Yahweh is my God." A prophet like fire*, he will restore the covenant of the living God; "for having been inflamed with zeal for the Law, he was carried off to heaven" (1 M 2,58) "in a whirlwind of fire, on a chariot drawn by fiery horses" (Si 48,9).

OT

1. *Return to the desert.* The desert* where Elijah has to flee reveals to him the solicitude of his God (1 K 17,2ff; 19,4-8), who lets him go as far as Horeb. There God manifests Himself to him in the very same place where Moses saw Yahweh "from the back" (19,9-14; cf Ex 33, 21.23). And like Moses, the Tishbite becomes by his encounter with Yahweh the source of holiness for the people (1 K 19,15-18).

2. *The champion of God and of the oppressed.* "I am filled with a jealous zeal for Yahweh, the God of hosts" (19,10). Nothing less than this devouring zeal was necessary for confronting the potentates of the day. Intoxicated by military victories, the splendor of the new capital, and the prosperity of the cities, they are

141

immersed in a climate of proud self-sufficency and of national exaltation (16,23-34). At the royal palace, "the house of ivory" (22,39), Jezebel, Ahab's pagan wife, contemplates only blasphemous projects. Does she not keep in Baal's temple some hundred false prophets charged with propagating the worship of idols! Elijah takes up the challenge and confounds his adversaries with Yahweh's marvelous intervention on Mount Carmel (18). Thus, every time that the rights of his God are at stake, Elijah enters the lists with thundering invectives (2 K 1). His cause is not only true worship but also justice* and the lot of the weak. Elijah thunders against Ahab, murderer of the peace-loving Naboth, in such a way that the king, frightened, ends up in repentance (1 K 21). Such a figure well deserves to be always characterized by this thundering trait in Scripture: "Elijah rises like a fire, his word burns like a torch" (Si 48,1).

3. *Witness of God among the pagans.* For many Israelites of the 9th century, God's benefactions ought to be reserved to the chosen people. But for God who sends Elijah, the work of salvation* goes beyond the limits of the covenant. A pagan is saved from famine (1 K 17,10-16), her son is snatched from death (17, 17-24).

4. *Translation of Elijah to heaven.* The man of God mysteriously disappears from the eyes of his friends, lifted up by "the whirlwind," "the Chariot of Israel and its team of horses," leaving his prophetic spirit to Elisha to continue God's work (2 K 2,1-18).

5. *The precursor.* To the mysterious translation will correspond an eschatological return: "Behold I send you the prophet Elijah before the great and formidable day* of Yahweh comes." His work of "bringing back the heart of the fathers to their sons and the hearts of sons back to their fathers" (Ml 3,23f) will be the last delay determined by God "to appease the anger before it bursts" (Si 48,10).

NT

1. *John the Baptist and Elijah.* This eschatological expectation (cf Mk 15,35f p) is fulfilled in John* the Baptist (Mt 17,10-13), but in a mysterious way; for John is not Elijah (Jn 1, 21.25), and if his preaching brings back the hearts of sons to their fathers, it is not he who appeases God's wrath*.

2. *Jesus and Elijah.* John the Baptist realizes the figure* of Elijah in what concerns the penance practiced in the desert (Mt 3,4; cf 2 K 1,8), but it is Jesus who fulfills the major characteristics. From the episode at Nazareth, He defines His universal mission* by reference to that of Elijah (Lk 4,25f). The miracle at Sarepta is linked in imagery with that of Naim (Lk 7, 11-16; cf 1 K 17,17-24). Elijah causes an avenging fire to descend from heaven (2 K 1,9-14; cf Lk 9,54); Jesus brings a new fire, that of the Holy Spirit* (Lk 12.49). On the Mount of Olives, Jesus is consoled* and comforted by an angel, as was Elijah in the desert (Lk 22,43; cf I K 19,5.7); but unlike Elijah He did not ask for death. Elijah, raised up to heaven while "his spirit rests on Elisha" (2 K 2,1-15), prefigures the ascension* of Christ who will send to His disciples "what His Father has promised" (Lk 24,51; cf 9,51).

3. *The believer and Elijah.* James makes the intercession of Elijah, "a man like us," the model of the prayer of the just* (Jm 5,16ff). The conversation of the prophet with Jesus during the transfiguration (Mt 17,1-8 p), as it was before with Yahweh "in the sound of a light breeze" (1 K 19,12), remains for the Christian tradition an example* of the intimacy to which the Lord calls all believers.

→Ascension I, II 4—Fire OT I 1, II 2.3—John the Baptist 1—Prophet OT—See OT I 1—Transfiguration 2—Zeal II 1.

FG gsa

ENEMY

I. THE FACT OF ENMITY

1. *Constancy and limits.* Biblical man is always confronted by his enemy. This is a fact about which there is no question. In the family circle, a stirring enmity opposes Cain and Abel (Gn 4,1-16), Sarai and Hagar (Gn 16,1-7), Jacob and Esau (Gn 27—29), Joseph and his brothers (Gn 37,4), Hannah and Peninnah (1 S 1,6f). In the city, the prophets as well as the psalmists complain of their enemies (Ps 31; 35; 42,10; Jr 18,18-23). These could be relatives (Mi 7,6; Jr 12,6) or old friends* (Ps 55,13ff). This has become the framework of thought: behind every adversity, one finds an adversary; and the sick* man of the psalms is almost always one

who is persecuted* (Ps 13; 38,1-16). But the Law sees in the enemy, if he belongs to the community of Israel, a subject of rights (Ex 23,4; Nm 35,15). The nation itself is built in this world of enmity. But hostility has degrees: it is without mercy in the case of the Canaanites or the Amalekites (Ex 17,16; 1 S 15), but it ends up merely as a cold war against Moab and Ammon (Dt 23,4-7), and Deuteronomy lets us understand that, in the case of Edom and of Egypt (Dt 23,8), *stranger** does not necessarily mean *enemy*.

2. *Origin*. How explain the permanence of such a fact in sacred history? Actually it is simply a fact of history after sin introduced hatred. Israel is conscious of herself being in a merciless world. To dream of seeing herself exempted from this relation would be to wish her to be of a nature different from that of contemporaneous humanity. God takes man where he is. The Canaanites are attacked because they are idolators (Gn 15,16; Dt 20,16ff), and because they occupy the place—the promised land (Dt 2,12). At this period a certain identification is seen between the enemies of God and the enemies of the nation: "I will be the enemy of your enemies" (Ex 23,22).

II. LIGHT ON THE WORLD OF ENMITY

1. *A typical case*. Saul's struggle with David is the most detailed account we have of personal enmity. Saul alone is the enemy there. He wants David's life (1 S 18,10f; 19,9-17) and opposes a plan that is at once divine and earthly; the royalty of his rival. The deep motive of his hate is that which the Bible most frequently presents: envy. But David avoids being contaminated by Saul's hate. His attitude is such that, were a Christian to attempt it, he has first a large task even to equal it. Indeed some of God's friends have to live, according to their capacity, a drama similar to that of David, where the signs of a moral refinement abound. Fully inserting itself into their desire to live, the call of God has led them to shake themselves from their egoism without losing their hold on existence.

2. *The experience of defeat*. Israel as a nation has a similar enough experience. For one war* she inflicts on others (as that of conquest), what wars she suffers! With time the image of enemy is gradually confused with that of op-

pressor. There is no reason then to entertain dreams of power! Israel has learned by then that Yahweh, rather than give more strength* to the just man, prefers to liberate him Himself (Ex 14,13f.30). The enemy is not conquered by the just or oppressed; he perishes as his own victim (Ps 7,13-17; cf Saul, Aman...). While waiting for his own defeat, he does not triumph without reason; he chastises in God's name and, without meaning to, teaches. His total annihilation is linked with the fullness of blessing* (Gn 22,17; 49,8; Dt 28,7). Now, in the course of history, Yahweh lets him continue to be strong (Jg 2,3; 2,20-23; Dt 7,22). This continuance is the sign of two things: the level of fulfillment of the promise*, and that of the faithfulness* of the people. On both accounts the time of the fullness* has not yet come.

3. *The work of time*. Those who would repeat the curses* of the psalmist long after him would not be able to do it in the name of the same particular interests nor concerning the same persons; there has already been a purification. One senses such an evolution in the Book of Wisdom (Ws 10—19) which sees in history conflicts more of ideologies than of interests. When the Maccabees, resuming the tradition of the holy war*, fight "for their life and for their laws" (1 M 2,40; 3,21), they do it with a clear consciousness of the double purpose which is expressed by the formula which this phrase unites without confusion. To sum up, on the one hand the juridical principle of retaliation (the talion), which puts a check on vengeance* (cf Gn 4,15.24), is never denied, and the victory of Israel is seen as the destruction of her enemies (Es). On the other hand, experience and divine light orient the heart toward love*. Among the counsels of prudence, Ben Sira demands that man pardon* in order to be pardoned by God (Si 28,1-7; cf Pr 24,29). This is the demand of Jesus Himself.

III. JESUS TRIUMPHS OVER ENMITY

1. *Commandment and example*. "Love your enemies, do good to those who hate you" (Mt 5,44 p). This commandment stands out among the newest demands (cf 5,43) of Jesus. He Himself had enemies who did not "want Him to be king," as one parable says (Lk 19,27). They put Him to death; and on the cross He pardoned them (Lk 23,34). So should the disciple* do in imitation of his master (cf 1 P 2,23), in imitation

of the heavenly Father* (Mt 5,45ff), from whom he would then be able to obtain pardon (cf Mt 6,12). The Christian who pardons has no illusions about the world in which he lives, no more than Jesus had illusions about the Pharisees* or about Herod. But he practices to the letter the counsel of Scripture: to heap coals of fire on the head of his enemy (R 12,20=Pr 25,21f). This is not vengeance*: this fire* will change into love if the enemy consents to it. The man who loves his enemy intends to change him into a friend* and he chooses means wisely. In this antecedent activity, God Himself has preceded him: when we were His enemies, He reconciled* us to Him by the death of His Son (R 5,10).

2. *The victory over enmity.* Jesus does not come to deny enmity but to show it in its full dimension at the moment of conquering it. It is not an ordinary fact, but a mystery, the sign of the reign of Satan*, the enemy above all others. After the Garden of Eden, enmity sets him up against the sons of Eve (Gn 3,15). As the enemy of men and of God, he sows tares here below (Mt 13,39). That is why we are exposed to his attacks. But Jesus has given to His own disciples authority over all power* which comes from the enemy (Lk 10,19). They hold this authority from the combat in which Jesus triumphed by His very defeat, having offered Himself to the blows of Satan given by His enemies, and having conquered death* by death itself. He thus knocks down the "wall of enmity" which ran across humanity (E 2,14-16). While waiting for the day* when Christ, to put "all His enemies under His feet," will destroy death forever, the "last enemy" (1 Co 15,25f), the Christian fights with Jesus against the old enemy of the human race (E 6,11-17). With Him no one would act like an enemy of the cross of Christ (Ph 3,18), but rather He knows that the cross brings Him to triumph. This cross* is the place outside of which there is no reconciliation* either with God or among men.

→Animals O—Antichrist—Brother OT 3—Curse II—Friend—Hate—Love II OT; NT 2—Pardon III—Persecution—Satan—Stranger O—Vengeance—Victory—Violence IV 2—War.

PBp gsa

ERROR

Error is not equivalent to ignorance. It is not in the gropings or in the miscalculations of the intellect where the Greeks put it. It is not reduced to misunderstanding created by deceptive circumstances (Gn 20,2-7; Ws 13,6-9), nor to the inadvertence which causes evil and injustice (Lv 4,2.13.22.27). It is above all unfaithfulness*, the rejection of truth*. Wandering will be its effect and chastisement: Cain a vagabond (Gn 4,12), Israel wandering (Ho 9,17), the sheep without a shepherd (Is 13,14; 53,6; Ez 34,16) to bring them back to the fold (Lk 15,4-7; 1 P 2,25).

OT

Error is located in the area of the religious: a disobedience that blinds. Error is "straying far from the way* designated by Yahweh" (Dt 13,6.11). Linked with the apostasy of Israel, error leads to idolatry* (Am 2,4; Is 44,20; Ws 12,24), and generally proceeds from the abandonment of Yahweh (Ws 5,6). In effect, the just* alone walk with assurance (Ps 26,1.3; 37, 23.31); the godless* are delivered to wander (Is 63,17; Pr 12,26), which God sanctions in abandoning them to it (Ez 14,6-11; Jb 12,24), lest they be converted (Ba 4,28; Ez 33,12). Otherwise, with the hardness* of heart which augments it, error proliferates (Ws 14,22-31); a growth* for which the leaders of the people (Is 9,15)—the Levites (Ez 44,10-13), the false prophets* (Ho 4,5; Is 30,10f; Jr 23,9-40; Lm 4, 13ff; Mi 3,5; Ez 13,8.10.18)—are the most responsible. This announces the diabolic error of the last times (cf Dn 11,33ff).

NT

The eschatological error announced by the prophet comes to its climax upon contact with Jesus Christ, who is truth in person (Jn 14,6). Jesus denounces the errors of His contemporaries (Mt 22,29). And the apostles put the faithful on guard against them (1 Co 6,9; 15,33). But the master (Mt 27,63f; Jn 7,12.47) and His disciples (2 Co 6,8) will in their turn be denounced as imposters. So are deceived the Pharisees who let themselves be blinded (Jn 9, 41) and "the princes of this world who, if they had known God's wisdom*, would not have crucified the Lord of glory" (1 Co 2,8).

However, in spite of being checked before truth, error remains active among sinners. It makes them "at the same time deceivers and deceived" (2 Tm 3,13). Thus there is need to watch* (Jm 1,16; 1 Jn 2,26f), to distrust the fables spread by false teachers (1 Tm 1,4; 2 P 2, 1f), by the trickery of men (E 4,14.25; Tt 1,14) which late Judaism put under the command of the powers* of error, the fallen angels*. Moreover, it is everyone's duty to bring back the sinner who is straying far from the truth (Jm 5, 20).

In foreseeing the end of time, Jesus forewarned His faithful against the seduction of false prophets (Mt 24,5.11.24 p). In fact, this spirit of error (1 Jn 4,6), this "mystery of impiety" (2 Th 2,7) grows* until the end of time (2 P 2,15-18; Ap 20,8), when it will show its true face, that of the Antichrist* (2 Jn 7), that of Satan* who inspires him (2 Th 2,9ff), that of the devil, "seducer of the whole world" (Ap 12,9). But finally, the beast*, the false prophet and the devil will all be cast into the pool of fire (19,20; 20,3.10).

→Antichrist NT—Heresy 3—Lie II, III—Teach NT II 3—Truth NT 2 c. 3.

JR gsa

EUCHARIST

I. MEANING OF THE TERM

1. *Thanksgiving and blessing.* Of itself *eucharist* means the gratitude which is the source of thanksgiving. This meaning, the most ordinary use in profane Greek, is also found regularly in the Greek Bible, especially in human relations (Ws 18,2; 2 M 2,27; 12,31; Ac 24,3; R 16,4). In regard to God, thanksgiving* (2 M 1,11; 1 Th 3,9; 1 Co 1,14; Col 1,12) usually takes the form of a prayer (Ws 16,28; 1 Th 5, 17f; 2 Co 1,11; Col 3,17; etc.), as in the beginnings of the Pauline epistles (vg 1 Th 1,2). It then unites naturally with the blessing* which praises the "wonders" of God, because these wonders are expressed for man in the favors which color the praise* of thankfulness; in these conditions, thanksgiving is accompanied by a "remembrance" in which the memory* recalls the past (Jdt 8,25f; Ap 11,17f), and *eucharistein* is equivalent to *eulogein* (1 Co 14, 16ff). This blessing-thanks is found particularly in Jewish meals where the blessings both praise and thank God for the good which He has given men. Paul speaks in this sense of eating with

"thanksgiving" (R 14,6; 1 Co 10,30; 1 Tm 4,3f).

2. *The usage of Jesus and Christian usage.* In the first multiplication of loaves, Jesus pronounces a "blessing" according to the synoptics (Mt 14,19 p), a "thanksgiving" according to Jn 6,11.23. In the second multiplication, Mt 15, 36 mentions a "thanksgiving" while Mk 8,6f speaks of a "thanksgiving" over the bread and a "blessing" over the fish. This practical equating of the two dissuades us from distinguishing at the last supper between the "blessing" over the bread (Mt 26,26 p; cf Lk 24,30) and the "thanksgiving" over the cup* (Mt 26,27 p). Paul, in any case, speaks of them inversely, with the "thanksgiving" over the bread (1 Co 11,24) and the "blessing" over the cup (1 Co 10,16).

In fact, it is the word *eucharist* which has prevailed in Christian usage to designate the act instituted by Jesus on the eve of His death. But one should remember that this term expresses praise* for the wonders of God as much or more than thanks for the good which men have drawn from them. By this decisive act in which He entrusts to food the eternal value of His redemptive death, Jesus consummated and established for all ages this homage of Himself and of everything to God; this is proper to "religion" and is essential to His work of salvation. In His person offered on the cross and in the eucharist, humanity in its entirety and all the universe make a return to the Father. This wealth of the eucharist is at the center of Christian worship*. We find it in the compressed texts which must now be closely analyzed.

II. INSTITUTION
AND EARLY CELEBRATION

1. *The accounts.* Four NT texts report the institution of the eucharist: Mt 26,26-29; Mk 14,22-25; Lk 22,15-20; 1 Co 11,23ff. The one which Paul "hands on" after having "received" it seems to be a liturgical tradition. The same should be said of the synoptic texts, whose pithy conciseness determines the context. They are valuable reflections of the way in which the early Churches celebrated the supper of the Lord. Their resemblances and differences are explained by this origin. The very Aramaic wording of Mark can be a reproduction of the Palestinian tradition, while Paul's redaction, a

bit more Greek, would reflect the tradition of the churches of Antioch or Asia Minor. Matthew undoubtedly represents the same tradition as Mark with some variants or additions which also may have a liturgical origin. As for Luke, he poses some delicate problems solved in different ways: vv 15-18 can represent an ancient tradition quite different from the others, or even more probably, an amplification drawn by Luke himself from Mark 14,25. Verses 19-20 should be considered authentic, against the evidence which would omit 19b-20; for one can see in these verses a combination of Mk and 1 Co made by Luke himself. Thus we have another form of the tradition of the Hellenistic churches which would then make a third liturgical witness alongside Mk/Mt and 1 Co. The variants between these different texts are, however, of minor importance, apart from the command to repeat the eucharist, which is omitted by Mk/Mt; but the attestation of this fact by 1 Co/Lk and internal probability incline us to accept it as primitive.

2. *The historical framework*. Another problem on which the interpretation of these texts depends is their historical background. For the synoptics, it was certainly a paschal meal (Mk 14,12-16 p). But according to Jn 18,28; 19,14.31, the Pasch was not celebrated until the following day, Friday evening. Everything has been done to explain this lack of agreement. Some place the blame on John who put it a day back in order to obtain the symbolism of Jesus dying at the hour of the immolation of the paschal lamb (Jn 19,14.36). Some claim that the Pasch that year was celebrated on Thursday and on Friday by different groups of Jews. And finally some suggest that Jesus might have celebrated the Pasch on Tuesday evening, following the Essene calendar. The best explanation is certainly to admit that Jesus, knowing that He would die at the very moment of the Pasch, anticipated a day. His own last supper, then, called to mind the paschal rite sufficiently for him to graft upon it His own new rite which would be the paschal rite of the NT. This solution respects the chronology of John and gives a satisfactory account of the synoptic presentation.

3. *Religious meal and the Lord's meal*. A paschal perspective seems, then, to underlie the passages of institution, much more than the perspective of some solemn Jewish feast, namely an Essene meal, by which some have wished to explain the passages. The immediate sequence of bread/wine in the last supper as in the Qumrân meals is a superficial connection and without bearing, because it could result in the gospel texts from a liturgical abridgement where only the two important elements of the last supper of Jesus would have been preserved, the bread at the beginning and the third cup at the end, with all that intervenes being supressed. We have, moreover, a trace of this interval revealed in the words "after the meal," which in 1 Co 11,25 precedes the cup. Furthermore the Essene meals of Qumrân lack the paschal theology to which the words of Jesus allude, and it is certainly gratuitous to consider these words as a later element deriving from the influence of Paul or the Hellenistic churches. The clearly fixed ceremonial of the Essene meal, similar to that of many meals of Jewish confraternities of the time, can, at the most, suggest the ordinary meals of Jesus and His disciples and the meals after the resurrection when they were reunited again around their master, but now confident of having Him always with them as their forever living and risen Lord.

It would not be necessary, in fact, always to find the eucharist in these daily meals which the first Jerusalem brethren took together in joy, while breaking bread in their homes (Ac 2,42. 46). This "breaking of bread" may only be an ordinary meal, though certainly religious as were all Semitic meals. It would focus on the remembrance and expectation of the risen master. The eucharist properly so-called would be added when they renewed the words and actions of the Lord in order to share His mysterious presence through the bread and wine. So there would be a transforming of an ordinary meal into the "Lord's meal" (1 Co 11,20-34). Breaking away from the Jewish rite, this eucharist certainly becomes more than annual, perhaps weekly (Ac 20,7.11). But unfortunately we also recognize that we are unable to determine in many passages whether it is a matter of an ordinary "breaking of the bread" or of the eucharist properly so-called (Ac 27,35; and previously in Lk 24,30.35).

III. THE EUCHARIST, SACRAMENT OF NOURISHMENT

1. *The meal, religious sign*. The eucharist is a rite of food, instituted in the course of a meal. From earliest times, especially in the Semitic world, man has attributed to food a sacred

value, sustaining life thanks to the munificence of the divinity. Bread, water, wine, fruits, etc. are all goods for which one blesses God. The meal itself has religious value, because eating in common establishes sacred ties between the dinner companions, as well as between them and God.

2. *From symbols to reality*. In biblical revelation, food* and meal* serve, therefore, to express the communication of life which God gives to His people. The manna* and the quails of the exodus*, as well as the water* gushing from the rock of Horeb (Ps 78,20-29), are symbolic realities (1 Co 10,3f), and as such they prefigure the true gift* which comes from the mouth of God (Dt 8,3; Mt 4,4), the Word*, the true bread* come down from heaven (Ex 16,4).

These figures are now fulfilled in Jesus. He is the "bread of life," first by His Word which opens up eternal life to those who believe (Jn 6,26-51a), and then by His flesh* and His blood* given for us to eat and drink (Jn 6,51b-58). Jesus spoke these words which promise the eucharist after He had miraculously fed the crowd in the desert (Jn 6,1-15). The gift which He promises, and which He opposes to the manna (Jn 6,31f.49f), is in this way linked up with the wonders of the exodus, and at the same time is set in the horizon of the Messianic banquet, the image of heavenly happiness familiar to Judaism (Is 25,6; rabbinic writings) and to the NT (Mt 8,11; 22,2-14; Lk 14,15; Ap 3,20; 19,9).

3. *The meal of the Lord, memorial and promise*. The last supper is in the nature of an ultimate preparation for the Messianic banquet where Jesus will again find His own after the coming trial. The "Pasch fulfilled" (Lk 22,15f) and the "new wine" (Mk 14,25 p) which he will taste with them in the kingdom of God, He prepares for them at the last supper when He makes the bread and wine signify the new reality of His body and His blood.

The rite of the paschal meal presents Him with the appropriate and desired occasion for this. The words which the father of the family pronounced on this occasion over the different foods, most especially over the bread and the third cup, bestowed on them a power of recalling the past and stirring up hope for the future such that by receiving them the guests really relived the trials of the exodus and lived by anticipation the Messianic promises. In His turn Jesus makes use of this creative power which the Semitic mind recognized in the word, and He added still more to it by His sovereign authority. In giving to the bread and wine their new meaning, He does not explain them; He transforms them. He does not interpret; He determines, He decrees: this is my body (i.e. it will be that from now on). The copula "to be," which no doubt is missing in the original Aramaic, would not by itself justify this realism, because it can be used simply to express a figurative meaning: e.g. "the harvest is the end of the world; the reapers are the angels" (Mt 13,39). But here we have a situation which demands a strong meaning. Jesus is not proposing a parable* where concrete objects would help to make clear an abstract reality. He is presiding over a meal where the ritual blessings confer on the food a value of another order. And, in the case of Jesus, this value has an unprecedented fullness and realism, which come to it from the pledged reality of a redemptive death leading through a resurrection to the eschatological life.

IV. THE EUCHARIST, SACRAMENT OF A SACRIFICE

1. *Announcement of the redemptive death*. The death is known to be redemptive because the body will be "given for you" (Lk; 1 Co has only "for you," with variants of slight weight); the blood will be "poured out for you" (Lk) or "for a multitude" (Mk/Mt). The very reality of the bread and wine separated on the table points to the violent separation of the body and blood. Jesus announces clearly His coming death and He presents it as a sacrifice*, comparable to the sacrifice of the victims whose blood sealed the first covenant* at Sinai (Ex 24,5-8), and to the paschal lamb* in the measure in which Judaism of those days considered it also as a sacrifice (cf 1 Co 5,7).

But in speaking of the blood "poured out for man" in view of a "new covenant," Jesus must be thinking also of the Servant* of Yahweh whose life was "poured out," who bore the sins of "many" (Is 53,12), and whom God designated as a "pledge to the people and a light of the nations" (Is 42,6; cf 49,8). Already before this time, He had attributed to Himself the role of Servant (Lk 4,17-21) and had claimed a similar mission of giving His life "as a ransom for many" (Mk 10,45 p: cf Is 53). Here He lets it be known that His approaching death is going to replace the sacrifices of the old covenant and free men not only from temporal captivity* but also from the bond of sin*. For such a work God had need of the Servant. He is going to found this "new covenant" which Jeremiah had proclaimed (Jr 31,31-34).

2. *Communion in the sacrifice.* But newest of all is the fact that Jesus enclosed within the food the richness of this sacrifice. The people of Israel like all ancient peoples were accustomed to reap the fruits of a sacrifice by consuming the victim. They did it to unite themselves to the offering and to God who accepted it (1 Co 10,18-21). By eating the immolated body of Jesus and by drinking His blood, the faithful shared in His sacrifice, making their own His offering of love and profiting by the return to grace which it effected. So that they might be able to do this everywhere and at all times, Jesus chose very ordinary foods and made of them His flesh and blood in the condition of a victim. He commanded His disciples to repeat after Him the words which, by His authority, will effect this change. He thereby gives to them a delegated participation in His priesthood*.

Henceforth each time they re-enact this event or take part in it, Christians "announce the death of the Lord, until the time when He comes" (1 Co 11,26), because the sacramental presence which they bring about is that of Christ in His condition of sacrifice. They do this "in His memory*" (1 Co 11,25; Lk 22,19), that is to say, they recall by faith His redemptive act, or better, perhaps, they recall it to God's memory (cf Lv 24,7; Nm 10,9f; Si 50,16; Ac 10,4.31) as an offering renewed without end which begs for His grace. This is an *Anamnēsis* which brings with it a wonderful reminder and acknowledges the marvels of God of which the greatest is the sacrifice of His Son offered to restore salvation to men. Wonder of love in which they share by uniting themselves in communion* to the body of the Lord, and in Him to all His members (1 Co 10,14-22). The sacrament of the sacrifice of Christ, the eucharist is the sacrament of charity, of union in the body* of Christ.

V. THE EUCHARIST,
THE ESCHATOLOGICAL SACRAMENT

1. *Permanence of the sacrifice of Christ in the new world.* The thing which gives realism to the symbolism of these actions and words is the reality of the new world to which they are an introduction. The death of Christ opens up on a new life* which never finishes (R 6,9f). This is the eschatological era, of the period of "future goods," compared to which the present era is only a "shadow*" (He 10,1; cf 8,5; Col 2,17). His sacrifice is made "once and for all" (He 7,27; 9,12.26ff; 10,10; 1 P 3,18). His blood has definitively replaced the inefficacious blood of the old covenant victims (He 9,12ff.18-26; 10, 1-10). The new covenant, for which He is the mediator* (He 12,24; cf 13,20), has suppressed the old (He 8,13) and obtains the eternal inheritance* (He 9,15). Henceforth, our high priest sits at the right hand of God (He 8,1; 10,12), "having won for us eternal redemption*" (He 9,12; cf 5,9), "always living to intercede in our favor" (He 7,25; cf 9,24) by His "unchangeable priesthood" (He 7,24). Past, as far as its contingent realization in the time of our transitory world, His sacrifice is always present in the new world where it has entered by the offering of Himself which He continues to make to His Father.

2. *Through the eucharist, the Christian communicates with this new world.* The eucharist now puts the believer in contact with this high priest who lives always in His condition of victim. The transition which is effected here from the bread to the body and from the wine to the blood, reproduces in its sacramental way the transition of the old world to the new world* which Christ passed through in going by His death to life. The paschal rite, like the exodus which it commemorated, was already itself a rite of transition—from the captivity of Egypt to the freedom of the promised land; and then, more and more, from the captivity of suffering, sin, and death, to the freedom of happiness, justice, and life. But the Messianic blessings remained in the paschal rite an object of hope*, and the foods which they blessed allowed them to taste* of these blessings only in a symbolic way. In the Pasch of Christ this is changed, because the Messianic era has actually arrived through His resurrection, and in it the promised blessings are obtained. The words and actions which formerly could only symbolize future blessings can now bring about present blessings as well.

The eucharistic body and blood are not, then, only the symbolic memorial of a completed event. They are the whole reality of an eschatological world in which Christ lives. The eucharist procures for the believer, still immersed in the old world, physical contact with Christ in all the reality of His new, risen, "spiritual" being (cf Jn 6,63). The whole sacramental order, in which the eucharist is the center, achieves this contact also. The foods which the eucharist assumes change their existence and become the true "bread of angels" (Ps 78,25; cf Ws 16,20), the sustenance of the new era. By their presence on the altar, Christ dead and risen again is really present in His eternal disposition of sacrifice. This is why the Mass is a sacrifice, identical with the historical sacrifice of the cross, through the loving offering of Christ who instituted the Mass which is different only by the accidental circumstances of the time and the place where it is reproduced. Through the Mass, the Church* unites in every place and until the end of the world the praises and offerings of men to the perfect sacrifice of praise and offering—in a word, to the "eucharist" which alone has value before God and itself alone gives value to them (cf He 13,10.15).

→Blessing IV 2—Blood NT—Body of Christ II, III 2—Bread—Communion O; NT—Covenant NT I—Day of the Lord NT III 3—Feasts NT II—Figure NT I—Flesh I 3 b—Manna 3 —Meal III—Nourishment III—Passover II, III —Priesthood NT III 1—Sacrifice—Thanksgiving NT—Wine II 2 b—Worship NT II, III 1.2.
PBe afmcg

EVIL SPIRITS

The portrait of the evil spirits, malevolent spiritual beings, comes to light only slowly in revelation. At the outset, biblical texts employed certain elements borrowed from popular beliefs, without as yet setting them in relation to the mystery of Satan*. At the end, the developed whole has taken on meaning in the light of Christ who has come here below to liberate men from Satan and his subordinates.

OT

1. *Origins of the belief.* The ancient Orient gave personalities to the thousand obscure forces whose presence was suspected to be behind the evils that assail man. Babylonian religion had an involved demonology; in it were practiced many exorcisms to deliver bewitched persons, things, and places. These basically magic rites constituted an important part of medicine since every sickness* was attributed to the action of an evil spirit.

From its beginning the OT acknowledged the existence and action of beings of this type. It uses the folklore that peopled ruins and deserted* places with disturbed presences mingled with savage beasts: shaggy satyrs (Is 13,21; 34,12), Lilith, the demon of night (Is 34, 14). . .It dedicates to them cursed places like Babylon (Is 13) or the land of Edom (Is 34). The atonement ritual prescribes handing over to the demon Azazel the he-goat loaded with the sins of Israel (Lv 16,10). Likewise evil powers crowd around the sick man and torment him. Originally such evils as the pestilence (Ps 91,6; Ha 3,5) or fever (Dt 32,24; Ha 3,5) were looked upon as plagues of God. He sends them upon the guilty as He sends His evil spirit upon Saul (1 S 16,14f.23; 18,10; 19,9) and His destroying angel* upon Egypt, Jerusalem upon the Assyrian army (Ex 12,23; 2 S 24,16; 2 K 19,35).

But after the exile, there was a clearer distinction between the angelic and diabolic world. The Book of Tobit knows it is evil spirits that torment man (Tb 6,8) and that angels have the task of combating them (Tb 8,3). But to represent the worst demon, the one who kills, the author did not hesitate to call on Persian folklore, giving it the name of Asmodeus (Tb 3,8; 6,14). It is clear that the OT, as convinced of the existence and operation of the evil spirits as of the angels*, had for a long time only a rather vague concept of their nature and relation to God.

2. *Divinized evil spirits.* Now for the pagans it was a constant temptation to seek to conciliate the lower spirits by offering them sacrificial worship—in a word, to make them gods. Israel was not sheltered from this temptation. Abandoning its Creator, it turned to "other gods" (Dt 13,3.7.14), or in different terms, to the evil spirits (Dt 32,17), going so far as to offer them human sacrfices (Ps 106,37). Israel prostituted herself to the satyrs (Lv 17,7) which haunted the unlawful high places (2 Ch 11,15). The Greek translators of the Bible have systematized this demoniacal interpretation of idolatry*, identifying the pagan gods with the evil spirits (Ps 96,5; Ba 4,7), introducing them even into contexts where the original Hebrew did not speak of them (Ps 91,6; Is 13,21; 65,3). Thus the world of the evil spirits became a world competing against God.

3. *The satanic army.* Later Judaic thought organizes this world more systematically. Evil spirits are regarded as fallen angels, accomplices

of Satan* who have become his helpers. To call to mind their fall, sometimes mythical imagery of the war* of the stars* (cf Is 14,12) is used, or the primordial battle between Yahweh and the beasts* which personify the sea*. Sometimes the old tradition of the sons of God falling in love with mortal women (Gn 6,1ff; cf 2 P 2,4) appears. Elsewhere we find evil spirits in sacrilegious rebellion against God (cf Is 14,13f; Ez 28,2). In any case evil spirits are looked upon as impure spirits characterized by pride and lust. They torment men and strive to lead them to evil. To fight them, one resorts to exorcism (Tb 6,8; 8,2f; cf Mt 12,27). These exorcisms are no longer magical, as formerly in Babylon, but deprecatory: it is hoped, indeed, that God will repress Satan and his allies, if appeal is made to the power of His name* (cf Ze 3,2; Jude 9). It is known, moreover, that Michael and his celestial army are in perpetual conflict with evil spirits and that the former come to the assistance of men (cf Dn 10,13).

NT

1. *Jesus, victor over Satan and his spirits.* The life and activity of Jesus takes place in the perspective of this duel between two worlds where the final stake is man's salvation. Jesus personally confronts Satan and scores a victory over him (Mt 4,11 p; Jn 12,31). He also faces evil spirits who have power over sinful mankind and routs them in their own domain.

This is the meaning of many episodes which feature possessed persons: the demoniac in the synagogue at Capharnaum (Mk 1,23-27 p) and the one at Gerasa (Mk 5,1-20 p); the daughter of the Syrophoenician woman (Mk 7,25-30 p) and the epileptic son (Mk 9,14-29 p); the mute demoniac (Mt 12,22ff p) and Mary Magdalen (Lk 8,2). Most of the time diabolic possession and sickness are intermingled (cf Mt 17,15.18). Consequently sometimes Jesus is said to heal the possessed (Lk 6,18; 7,21), sometimes to drive out evil spirits (Mk 1,34-39). Without casting doubt on those cases of possession which are clear-cut (Mk 1,23f; 5,6), account must be taken of the opinion, current in those times, which attributed directly to the evil spirits certain phenomena which would be in the field of present-day psychiatry (Mk 9,20ff). Above all one must keep in mind that every sickness* was a sign of Satan's power over man (cf Lk 13,11).

When He confronts sickness, Jesus confronts Satan*. When He heals, He triumphs over Satan. The evil spirits thought they were placed here below as masters of the earth; Jesus came to destroy them (Mk 1,24). Because of the authority He shows with regard to evil spirits, the crowds are astonished (Mt 12,23; Lk 4,35ff). His enemies accuse Him: "It is by Beelzebub, the prince of the evil spirits, that He casts out evil spirits" (Mk 3,22 p). "Is He not Himself possessed by the evil spirits?" (Mk 3,30; Jn 7,20; 8,48f.52; 10,20f). But Jesus gives the true explanation: it is by the Spirit of God that He casts out evil spirits, and that proves the kingdom* of God has come to men (Mt 12,25-28 p). Satan thought himself strong, but he was dislodged by one yet stronger (Mt 12,29 p).

Henceforth exorcisms will be performed in the name* of Jesus (Mt 7,22; Mk 9,38f). When He sends the disciples on their mission*, He communicates to them His own power over the evil spirits (Mk 6,7.13 p). They, indeed, observe evil spirits are subject to them, clear proof of Satan's fall (Lk 10,17-20). Throughout the centuries, expulsion of demons, together with miracles, will be one of the signs accompanying preaching the gospel (Mk 16,17).

2. *The battle of the Church.* Actually, deliverance of the possessed reappears in the Acts of the Apostles (Ac 8,7; 19,11-17). However, the duel between the emissaries of Jesus and the evil spirits takes other forms in Acts: a struggle against magic and superstitions of all kinds (Ac 13,8ff; 19,18f) and the belief in divining spirits (Ac 16,16); the struggle against idolatry, in which the evil spirits are adored (Ap 9,20) and invite men to their table (1 Co 10,20f); the struggle against false wisdom (Jm 3,15), against deceptive diabolic doctrines of all ages (1 Tm 4,1), against those engaged in the service of the beast* (Ap 16,13f) and who work deceiving prodigies. Satan and his helpers are behind every human deed opposing the progress of the gospel. Even the trials of the apostle are attributable to an angel of Satan (2 Co 12,7). But because of the Holy Spirit, men now know how to distinguish the spirits (1 Co 12,10) and no longer permit themselves to be deluded by the deceptive fascination of the diabolic world (cf 1 Co 12,1ff). As was Jesus, the Church is involved in a war to the death and holds fast to an invincible hope: Satan, already conquered, now has only limited power; the end of time will see him and his helpers definitely vanquished (Ap 20,1ff.7-10).

→Angels OT 2—Beasts & Beast 1—Desert O—

Idols II 2—Power III 2—Satan O—Sea 2.3—
Sickness/Healing OT I 2; NT I 1—Spirit OT
4; NT 1—Stars 4.

JBB & PG jrc

EXAMPLE

If the word* enlightens, then example
attracts. Therefore God, being a good educator*, gives man examples to follow*, models to
imitate.

OT

God's ways and human examples. God adapts
Himself to the weakness of men, who are
children that have to be formed and at the
same time sinners that have to be reformed.
It is not yet possible to put forward for their
imitation the one who yet created them in His
own image (Gn 1,26f), for the model would seem
inaccessible because of its transcendence. To
claim to be like God is the act of a sinner (3,5);
the just man's only concern is to answer the call
of his Creator by walking with Him, that is by
living the life of perfect uprightness demanded
by His presence* (17,1; cf 5,22; 6,9). In the
same way we have in the divine command: "Be
holy, for I am holy*" two distinct kinds of
holiness: that of God, which is the transcendence of His mystery, and that of man, which
is the purity demanded by divine worship and
by the presence of the thrice-holy in the midst
of His people (Lv 19,2; cf Ex 29,45). So this
is not a call to imitate God. Nevertheless the
teaching of the prophets allows us to see that
God requires man to follow ways* along which
He Himself is pleased to walk (Jr 9,23; cf Mi
6,8).

The people will find the examples they need
by looking at their fathers*: judging the tree
by its fruits, they will see in their behavior
what they must imitate and what they must
avoid. On the one hand there is the faith and
the faithfulness of Abraham* (Gn 15,6; 22,12-
16), and on the other the doubt and disobedience of Adam* and Eve (Gn 3,4ff). There are
many of these characters in history, whose
example is enlightening and whom the wise
men parade before the eyes of their disciples*
(Si 44,16-49; cf 1 M 2,50-60). The elders, then,
must, like Eleazar, feel their responsibility
toward the people and especially the young;
they have to set a noble example, even if that

means dying a martyr's death (2 M 6,24-31).

NT

*From the human examples to the divine
model.* The NT still calls the past to mind:
one must not imitate the murderer Cain (1 Jn
3,12) nor the disobedient generation in the
desert (He 4,11), but take as one's model the
patience of the prophets (Jm 5,10), the faith
and perseverance of a cloud of God's witnesses
(He 12,1). Besides, the believers have witnesses*
of this sort before their eyes (6,12): let them
imitate the faith of their leaders (13,7) and the
conduct of those who are models, like Paul (Ph
3,17). The apostle often urges the faithful* to
become his imitators (1 Co 4,16; G 4,12), especially by working as he did to give them an
example (2 Th 3,7ff). Let the elders be models as
he was (1 Tm 4,12; Tt 2,7; 1 P 5,3), so that
their communities may in their turn be examples
(1 Th 1,7; 2,14).

But for the believer there is only one perfect
model, of which the others are simply a reflection: Jesus Christ*. Paul himself must only be
imitated because he imitates Christ (1 Co 4,16;
11,1). This is the fundamental novelty:
thanks to Jesus, Son* of God made man, man
is able to imitate his Lord (1 Th 1,6) and thus
imitate God Himself (E 5,1). In fact Jesus is
the source and the model of this perfect faith,
which is trust and faithfulness (He 12,2); to
anyone believing in Him He gives the grace of
becoming a child* of God and of living from
His life (Jn 1,12; G 2,20). Henceforth, man
can imitate the example of the Lord and follow
Him along the path of the humble love* that
made Him offer up His own life (Jn 13,15; E
5,2; 1 P 2,21; 1 Jn 2,16; 3,16); he can love
his brethren as Jesus loved them (Jn 13,34;
15,12).

But Jesus loved them as His Father loved
Him (Jn 15,9). To imitate Jesus is to imitate
the Father; to answer our calling to become
true images of Christ (R 8,29), the perfect image
of His Father (Col 1,15), is to renew ourselves
in the likeness of our Creator (3,10; cf Gn
1,26f; this comparison reveals the deep and
hitherto hidden meaning of this passage). We
can and should become holy as our heavenly
Father is holy (1 P 1,15f, quoting Lv 19,2
and giving it a new meaning). In doing this we
are carrying out the command of Christ Himself, for He wants us to imitate the Father, His
perfect goodness (Mt 5,48) and His merciful
love (Lk 6,36; cf E 4,32). If we do this, one day

151

He will come and we shall be like Him whom we have imitated, because we shall see Him as He really is (1 Jn 3,2).

→Disciple—Education II 2—Figure—Follow 2 c—Image—Way.

JR & MFL ems

EXHORT

Exhortation (gr. *paraklēsis*) occurs only once (R 12,8) in the lists of charisms*. Yet it was one of the essential works of the apostles, the prophets, and the presbyters. It is rooted in the religious life of the OT and Judaism, and it continues on in the Church of the present time.

OT

God's witnesses are never content to expound the divine plan* of salvation* dispassionately: the priestly discourses (such as those in Dt 4—11), the prophetic discourses (as in Is 1,16...), and the sapiential discourses (as those of Pr 1—9), speak to the heart* as well as to the mind of the hearers. They invite the hearers, encourage them, and, on the part of God, stimulate them to listen*, to be converted, and to seek God. From the earliest times to the days of the Maccabees, we find the same movement, the same appeal: there is no preaching* without exhortation to a courageous faithfulness* toward Yahweh and toward His Law* (Dt 5,32; 6,4ff; 32,45ff), especially in persecutions* (2 M 7,5), or in time of a holy war* (2 M 8,16; 13,12.14).

NT

At the threshold of the NT, John the Baptist continues this tradition: "with many exhortations, he kept on preaching the gospel to the people" (Lk 3,18). Likewise Jesus is not content simply to proclaim the message of the kingdom* present in His own person, and to reveal its mysteries*. He calls on men to enter in, He invites them earnestly to repent, to believe in the gospel*, to follow* it, to keep its word*. So too, the apostles "beseech and exhort" the crowds to receive their message and to be baptized (Ac 2,40). In the Christian communities, the propet* "builds up, exhorts, encourages" (1 Co 14,3), as Timothy and Titus also must do (2 Tm 4,2; Tt 1,9). This only serves to prolong one of the essential works of the apostolic ministry (Ac 11,23; 14,22; 15,32; 16,40; 1 Th 3,2), a work about which Paul explains himself clearly: "it is as if God was exhorting through us" (2 Co 5,20; cf 1 Th 2,13). The writings of the NT, therefore, include numerous exhortations. To exhort, in fact, is the essential purpose of the epistle to the Hebrews (He 13,22) and of the first epistle of Peter (1 P 5,12). The ordinary Christians, moreover, should exhort one another (2 Co 13,11; He 3,13; 10,25) in view of the building* up of the Church.

→Charisms — Console — Education — Preach —Teach.

RD afmcg

EXILE

In the ancient Orient, deportation was a practice frequently used against conquered peoples (cf Am 1). From 734, certain cities of the kingdom of Israel underwent this painful experience (2 K 15,29); then, in 721, the whole of the kingdom (2 K 17,6). But the deportations which left the greatest mark on the history of the people of the covenant are those which Nebuchadnezzar carried out as a result of his campaigns against Judah and Jerusalem in 597, 587, 582 (2 K 24,14; 25,11; Jr 52,28ff). It is these deportations into Babylon for which the name *exile* has been reserved. The material state of the exiles was not always terribly hard; it grew milder with time (2 K 25,27-30). But the way of return remained as closed as ever. They had to wait for the fall of Babylon and the edict of Cyrus in 538 for a way to be opened for them (2 Ch 36,22f). This long period of trial left a powerful impression on the religious life of Israel. By it God revealed to them His uncompromising holiness and His overwhelming faithfulness.

I. THE EXILE, CHASTISEMENT FOR SIN

1. *Exile, extreme chastisement.* By the logic of sacred history, the possibility of an exile seemed unimaginable. It was the reversal of the whole plan* of God, achieved during the exodus at the cost of so many miracles. It was a denial of all the promises* made: a surrender of the promised land, deprival of the Davidic king, aliena-

tion from the demolished temple. Even after the exile had taken place, the natural reaction was not to believe it and to think that the proper state of affairs would be re-established without delay. But Jeremiah denounced this illusion: the exile would be prolonged (Jr 29).

2. *The exile, a revelation of sin.* The continuance of the catastrophe was necessary so that the people and their leaders would become well aware of their incurable perversion (Jr 13,23; 16,12f). The threats of the prophets, taken lightly up till then, were now fulfilled to the very letter. The exile now appeared as a chastisement for failings so often denounced: faults of the rulers, who instead of relying on the divine covenant*, had recourse to human political deals (Is 8,6; 30,1f; Ez 17,19ff); faults of the powerful who, in their cupidity, had destroyed the fraternal unity of the people through violence and fraud (Is 1,23; 5,8. . .; 10,1); faults of all, immorality and scandalous idolatry* (Jr 5,19; Ez 22), which had made of Jerusalem an evil place. The wrath* of the most holy God, continually provoked, had ended by crying out: "there was no longer a remedy" (2 Ch 36,16).

The vineyard of Yahweh had become corrupt and was then ravaged and uprooted (Is 5). The adulterous spouse* had been stripped of her finery and was severely chastised (Ho 2; Ez 16,38). The recalcitrant and rebellious people had been driven from their land and dispersed* among the nations* (Dt 28,63-68). The severity of the sanction manifested the gravity of the fault. It was no longer possible to maintain the illusion, nor to keep face before the pagans: "Today we have shame on our face" (Ba 1,15).

3. *Exile and confession.* From this time on, a humble confession* of sins will become habitual in Israel (Jr 31,19; Ezr 9,6. . .; Ne 1,6; 9,16.26; Dn 9,5); the exile had become something like a "negative theophany," an unprecedented revelation of the holiness of God and of His detestation of evil.

II.   THE EXILE, A FRUITFUL TRIAL

Rejected from the holy land, deprived of their temple and worship, the exiles could believe themselves completely abandoned by God and plunged into a fatal discouragement (Ez 11,15; 37,11; Is 49,14). In reality, at the very heart of the trial*, God remained present, and His wonderful faithfulness* was already at work to raise up His people (Jr 24,5f; 29,11-14).

1. *The comfort of the prophets.* The actualization of the threatening oracles had led the exiles to take the ministry of the prophets seriously. But now, precisely by repeating to themselves these words, they found in them reasons for hope*. The announcement of the punishment, in fact, always included both a call to conversion and a promise of renewal (Ho 2,1f; Is 11,11; Jr 31). It is like an expression of a jealous love which is therein manifested by the divine severity. Even while punishing, God desires nothing so much as to see the first tenderness flourish anew (Ho 2,16f). The cries of the chastened infant overwhelm the heart of the Father (Ho 11,8ff; Jr 31,20). Hardly listened to in Palestine, now these messages found eager acceptance in the groups of exiles in Babylon. Jeremiah, formerly persecuted, now became the most esteemed of the prophets.

Among the exiles themselves, God raised up successors for them, who would guide and support the people in the midst of difficulties. The victory of the heathen armies seemed to be a victory for their gods. So the temptation was great to let themselves be fascinated by the Babylonian worship. But the prophetic tradition told the exiles to despise the idols* (Jr 10; Is 44,9. . .; cf Ba 6). Still better, a deported priest, Ezekiel, received in majestic vision a revelation of the "mobility" of Yahweh, whose glory* is not locked up in the temple (Ez 1) and whose presence* is an invisible sanctuary for the exiles (Ez 11,16).

2. *Preparation of the new Israel.* The Word of God, the presence of God: on this basis a worship* could be organized and developed— not a sacrificial worship but a liturgy of the synagogue. It would consist of uniting themselves to listen* to God (by means of a reading and a commentary on the sacred texts), and to speak to God in prayer*. Thus was formed a spiritual community of poor* men completely oriented to God and hoping for salvation from Him alone. Within this community, the priestly class took care to recount the sacred history and to teach the Law. This work resulted in a priestly document, a compilation and renewal of the remembrances and ancient precepts which had made Israel a sacred nation and the priestly kingdom of Yahweh.

Far from letting itself be contaminated by idolatry, this renovated Israel became the herald of the true God in a pagan land. Israel opened itself to its new vocation as "light to the nations*" (Is 42,6; 49,6), and orientated itself toward the eschatological hope of the universal reign of Yahweh (Is 45,14).

3. *A new exodus.* But as this hope remained centered on Jerusalem*, its realization demanded that the exile must come to an end. This is really what God then promised to His people in the Book of Consolation (Is 40—55), which describes beforehand the wonders of a second exodus*. Once again Yahweh will make Himself shepherd* of Israel. He Himself will go to search for the exiles, and precisely as a shepherd (Ez 34,11ff) will lead them to their fold (Is 40,11; 52,12). He will purify them of all their defilements and give to them a new heart* (Ez 36,24-28). He will conclude an eternal covenant with them (Ez 37,26; Is 55,3), and fill them with all good things (Is 54,11f). It will be a great triumph for Yahweh (Is 42,10-17). All the prodigies of the exodus from Egypt will be eclipsed (Is 35; 41,17-20; 43,16-21; 49,7-10).

Actually in 538 the edict of Cyrus was promulgated. A burst of enthusiasm lifted up the fervent Jews. A volunteer group of important men, the ones "saved from the captivity" (Ezr 1,4), returned to Jerusalem. These men had a decisive influence on the organization of the Jewish community and its spiritual orientation. In the midst of so many difficulties, this was the resurrection* of the people (cf Ez 37,1-14), an astonishing witness proclaiming the faithfulness of God and sung joyfully in the presence of the wondering nations (Ps 126).

4. *Exile and the NT.* The experience of death and resurrection, the departure into exile and the triumphant return, have more than a simple relation to the central mystery of the plan of God (cf Is 53). These events continue to be rich in lessons for Christians. Certainly a living way* assures them free access henceforth to the true sanctuary (He 10,19; Jn 14,6). But to have free access is not the same as to be at the final goal. In one sense, "to dwell in this body is to live in exile far from the Lord" (2 Co 5,6). Being in this world* without being of this world (Jn 17,16), Christians should at all times recall to mind the holiness* of God, who cannot compromise with evil (1 P 1,15; 2,11f); and they should rely on the faithfulness* of God who, in Christ, will lead them to the heavenly fatherland* (cf He 11,16).

→Babel/Babylon 2.4—Captivity I—Earth OT II

3 c—Exodus OT 2—Fatherland OT 2—Liberation/Liberty II 2—Punishments—Repentance/Conversion OT III—Temple OT II 2.3—Trial/Temptation OT I 2.3—Way I 2.

CL & AV afmcg

EXODUS

The word *exodus* means "a way out," hence "the action of leaving, departure." In the Bible it designates especially the departure of the Hebrews from Egypt, or, according to a broader meaning, the long journey of forty years which led them from Egypt across the desert* (Ex 3,7-10) into the promised land. The various stages of the journey are related in the Pentateuch (Ex, Nm, Dt). In Jewish and Christian thought this event becomes the type and pledge of every deliverance brought about by God in favor of His people.

OT

1. *The first exodus.* The exodus marked the real birth of the people of God, a birth accomplished in blood * (Ez 16,4-7). It is at this time that God will beget Israel (Dt 32,5-10), and even more than Abraham, will become for Israel a father* full of love and solicitude (Ho 11,1; Jr 31,9; Is 63,16; 64,7). The exodus, as a sign of divine love, is in itself a pledge of salvation*. As He once delivered His people from captivity* in Egypt, so God will save them again at the moment of the Assyrian danger (Is 10,25ff; Mi 7,14f) or the Babylonian peril (Jr 16,14f; Is 63—64; cf Ps 107,31-35; Ws 19). But Israel returned only ingratitude (Am 2,10; Mi 6,3ff; Jr 2,1-8; Dt 32; Ps 106; cf *Popule Meus* during the adoration of the cross on Good Friday) in response to this divine solicitude, instead of remaining faithful to the ideal of life to which they were led in the desert (Ho 2,16; Jr 2,2f).

2. *The new exodus.* To the people, once again captive and exiled to Babylon because of their infidelities, the deliverance was announced as a renewal of the exodus. Once again God would redeem His people (Is 63,16). The crippled and the weak all recover their strength and prepare for the departure (Is 35,3-6; 40,1f; 41,10; 42,7-16; Zp 3,18ff). A way* will be mapped out in the desert (Is 35,8ff; 40,3; 43,19; 49,11; 11,16). God will make the water spring forth there as it once did at Meribah (Is 35,6f; 41,18; 43,20;

44,3; 48,21; cf Ex 17,1-7) and the desert will be transformed into an orchard (Is 35,7; 41,19). The Euphrates will be divided, just as the Red Sea of old, to let the caravan of the new exodus pass through (Is 11,15f; 43,16f; 51,10). God will carry the group on His wings (Is 46,3f; 63,9; cf Ex 19,4; Dt 32,11) and then will be their guide (Is 52,12; cf Ex 14,19).

NT

In making John* the Baptist "the voice of Him who cries: In the desert prepare the way of the Lord" (Mt 3,3 p; Is 40,3), the apostolic tradition wished to affirm that the work of the redemption* brought about by Christ was the fulfillment of the mystery of salvation* prefigured by the exodus. With this same intention, the tradition considered Jesus also as the new Moses* foretold in Dt 18,18 (Ac 3,15.22; 5,31; 7,35ff).

1. *St. Paul* only touches upon this theme: Jesus is the true paschal Lamb* immolated for us (1 Co 5,7), and the marvels of the exodus (the passage through the Red Sea, the manna*, the rock*) were figures of the spiritual realities produced by Christ (1 Co 10,1-6).

2. *St. Peter* develops this theme in a more ecclesial perspective. Christians have been redeemed by the blood of the spotless Lamb (1 P 1,18f; cf Ex 12,5; Is 52,3), and "called" (1,14f; cf Ho 11,1) from the darkness into the light (2,9; cf Ws 17—18). They have been freed from the dissolute life which they once led in paganism (1,14.18; 4,3) in such a way as to be made the new people* of God (2,9f; cf Ex 19,6; Is 43,20f), governed by the law of holiness* (1,15f; cf Lv 19,2). Having been purified by the sprinkling of the blood* of Christ, they vowed obedience* to God from that time on (1,2.14.22; cf Ex 24,6ff), offering Him a spiritual worship* (2,5; cf Ex 4,23). Girding up their loins* (1,13; cf Ex 12,11), they are ready to walk along the way* which should lead them to their fatherland* in heaven (1,17).

3. *St. John* offers a more elaborate theology. Christians have been rescued from servitude of the devil by the blood of the paschal Lamb (Jn 1,29; 19,36; 8,34ff; 8,44; 1 Jn 3,8), and are now on route to the kingdom of heaven. They are nourished by Christ, the living bread* descended from heaven (Jn 6,30-58); cf Ex 16), and they are refreshed by the water* which

gushes from His side (7,37f; 19,34; cf Ex 17,1-7). When wounded, they are healed by "looking upon" Christ raised up on the cross (3,14; 19,37; cf Nm 21,4-9). By following* Him who is the light* of the world (8,12; cf Ex 13,21f), they will one day come before the Father (12, 26; 13,8; 14,3; 17,24). After His resurrection, in fact, Jesus became the first to achieve the Passover*, His "leaving this world to go to the Father" (13,1) where, "raised up from the earth," He draws all men to Himself (12,32). They, in their turn, will come to a final exodus when they "shall pass" from the world below to the world above (8,23).

4. *The Apocalypse* takes a viewpoint quite like that in the first epistle of Peter. By the blood* of the Lamb*, Christians have been freed from the "earth," from an evil world* subject to Satan (Ap 14,3), so that they might form the kingdom of priests foretold by God in Ex 19,6 (Ap 5,9f). This is the renewal of the ancient covenant* (11,19; cf Ex 19,16). Though written in a time of persecution, the Apocalypse sounds like a song of victory. Memories of the Red Sea (15,3ff; cf Ex 14—15) stir up thoughts of the approaching disaster of the enemies of God's people, enemies who will be destroyed by the Word* of God just as the first-born of Egypt once were (19,11-21; cf Ws 18,14-18). God is coming to dwell among His people (15,8) and to bring victory* to them because He is called "He is," and all creatures merely as nothing (11,17; 16,5; cf Ex 3,14). During the paschal night, Christians call to mind even now this epic of the exodus in the song of *Exsultet*.

→Cloud 1—Desert—Exile II 3—Flood 2— Lamb of God 2—Liberation/Liberty II 1— Moses—New II 1—Passover I 2.4—Pilgrimage —Redemption OT 1—Salvation OT I 1—Sea 2 —Way I, III.

MEB afmcg

EXPIATION

English translations of the Bible frequently use the term *expiation* or sometimes *propitiation* (hb. *kipper*; gr. *hilaskesthai*) in the OT, either with respect to sacrifices* "for sin" or when the priest is said "to fulfill the rite of expiation" (vg Lv 4). Even more especially the term is used in respect to the annual feast of the 10 *tishri*, usually called "the day of expiations" or "the great day of expiation," a day whose ritual Lv 16 describes in detail.

In the NT, though the term is rare (R 3,25; He 2,17; 1 Jn 2,2; 4,10), the idea is found frequently, not only in the whole epistle to the Hebrews, which likens the redemptive* role of Christ to the function of a high priest on the "day of expiations," but more or less certainly each time that Christ is said "to die for our sins" (vg 1 Co 15,3) or "to pour forth His blood for the remission of sins" (vg Mt 26,28).

1. *Expiation and sin.* In English, as in a number of modern languages, the notion of expiation tends to be confused with that of chastisement which was not medicinal. But this is not accurate, for all the ancients (and the meaning of the word *expiare* in the Vulgate and its use in the liturgy follows them) *to expiate* means essentially "to purify," or even more exactly, to render an object, place or person "pleasing to the gods, from being displeasing before" (Lachelier). Every expiation, therefore, presupposes the existence of a sin which it was to destroy.

This sin* is not thought of as a material stain which man would have the power to obliterate, but it is identified with the very rebellion of man against God, so that the expiation erases the sin by newly reuniting the man to God and "consecrating" him to God according to the sense of the sprinkling of blood*. Just as on one hand sin provokes the wrath* of God, so each expiation terminates this wrath. It "renders God propitious." But the Bible usually attributes this role to prayer with the sacrifice of expiation having rather the purpose of "rendering man pleasing to God."

2. *Expiation and intercession.* In the few passages where the two terms *expiation* and *wrath* are found associated, it is prayer*, in fact, which is involved: such is the expiation of Moses (Ex 32,30; cf 32,11ff), or that of Aaron (Nm 17,11ff) according to the interpretation of Ws 18,21-25; so also is that of Phinehas (Ps 106, 30) according to the Targum, and still more clearly the expiation of the "Servant of Yahweh" whose role as intercessor is mentioned four times (Targum Is 53,4.7.11.12). And it is in virtue of this very notion of expiation that St. Jerome, following in this the usage of the Old Latin versions, in the stereotyped formula which concludes each of the sacrifices for sin, was able to translate the Hebrew word which means "to carry out the rite of expiation" by a word meaning "to pray" or "to intercede"

(Lv 4,20.26.31; etc).

It is not surprising, then, that the epistle to the Hebrews, in describing Christ entering into heaven to perform the essential duty of His priesthood*, defined as an "intercession" (He 7,25; 9,24), is able to compare this to the high priest going through to the other side of the veil to perform the most pre-eminent sacrifice, the sprinkling of blood onto the propitiatory. Christ's death itself is also seen as a supreme "intercession" (He 5,7).

Such an interpretation stresses the fact that in every instance authentic expiation can have no value independent of the interior dispositions of the one who offers it. It is first of all a spiritual act which the exterior action expresses but cannot supply. It also excludes pretention on man's part to force God to become favorable to him. In describing the intercession of Aaron, the book of Wisdom carefully explains that his prayer consisted of "reminding God of His promises and oaths" (Ws 18,22), so that such a prayer amounted to an act of faith in God's faithfulness*. Conceived in this way, expiation in no way tends (except perhaps in the eyes of the man himself) to change God's dispositions, but to dispose man to receive the gift of God.

3. *Expiation and pardon.* In the religious consciousness of the Jews, the "day of expiations" was considered even more as the "day of forgiveness." When St. John in two different places alludes first to the heavenly intercession of Christ before the Father (1 Jn 2,2), and then to the work accomplished here below by His death and resurrection (1 Jn 4,10), he declares that He is or that the Father has made Him a "*hilasmos* for our sins." This term certainly carries the same meaning which it always has in OT Greek (vg Ps 130,4) and which the Latin word *propitiatio* also always conveys in the liturgy: through Christ and in Christ, the Father achieves the plan of His eternal love (1 Jn 4,8) in "showing Himself propitious," that is, in "pardoning" men, by an efficacious pardon* which really destroys sins, which "purifies" man and communicates to him God's own life (1 Jn 4,9).

→Blood—Cup 3—Fasting 2—Feasts OT II 3; NT I—Imposition of Hands OT—Lamb of God 1—Martyr 1—Pardon II 2—Priesthood OT II 1 —-Punishments 3—Pure OT I 2—Redemption— Repentance/Conversion OT I 2, III 1—Servant of God—Sin III 3—Suffering OT III.

SL afmcg

F

FACE

1. *The face and the heart.* "As the reflection of the face in water, so the heart of man reflects man" (Pr 27,19). The mirror of water discloses the paradox of the human countenance. It is for the person at the same time that by which he sees and that which is seen. Face to face human encounters symbolize and awaken interior recognition in the hearts.

The face is the mirror of the heart*. One reads there not only grief (Jr 30,6; Is 13,8), weariness (Dn 1,10) or affliction (Ne 2,2), but also the joy (Pr 15,13) one has on a holiday (Si 13,26; Ps 104,15). One reads there the strictness which a father must display toward his daughters (Si 7,24), but also the ruthless hardness (Dt 28,50) of a father stubborn with pride (Ez 2,4; Dn 8,23). In short, "the heart of a man shapes his countenance whether for good or bad" (Si 13,25). But the mirror of the face can be misleading. God alone looks to the heart (1 S 16,7; Jm 2,9) and judges human actions accordingly (Si 35,22; Mt 22,16).

2. *The face of the prince.* The relations of subject to prince express themselves in a kind of game of countenances. One asks to see the face of the king (2 S 14,32). But in his presence one prostrates oneself on the ground, "falling on his face" (2 S 1,2; 14,33). To be able to look upon the face of the king (Es 1,14) is a conspicuous privilege, and a favor anxiously awaited is to see him light up in a smile (Jb 29,24f) because "in the light of his royal countenance is life" (Pr 16,15).

3. *To seek the face of God.* Though God is not a man (Nm 23,19) and no creature can give an idea of His glory (Is 40,18; 46,5), He has, nevertheless, plans and intentions, just as men do. He wants to enter into communication with man. And so even He has a face. He is able in turn to show His countenance in His kindness (Ps 4,7; 80,4.8.20) and to hide it in His wrath* (Is 54,8; Ps 30,8; 104,29).

This divine countenance dwells in the midst of Israel. Though invisible it is nonetheless full of the extraordinary vitality of the living God*, and this presence* of the divine face is the strength of His people (Ex 33,14; 2 S 17,11; Dt 4,37; Is 63,7). This is what gives meaning to the cultic desire to see* the face of God (Ps 42,3) and to "seek the face of God" (Am 5,4; Ps 27,8; Ps 105,4). But because the face of Yahweh is that of a holy and just God, only "the upright will behold His face" (Ps 11,7).

4. *Face to face with God.* The face of God is mortally fearful to man (Jg 13,22; Ex 33,20) because of his sin (Is 6,5; Ps 51,11). And yet it is the life and salvation of man (Ps 51,13f). By way of exception, "Yahweh would speak with Moses* face to face, as a man speaks with his friend*" (Ex 33,11). But when Moses asked to see God's glory, he only saw God's back (33,18-23). "To follow someone is to see him from the back. Moses, who burned to see the face of God, understood how it is that one sees God: to follow God wherever He leads—this is how one sees God" (Gregory of Nyssa).

5. *Upon the face of Christ,* God has made His own face to shine upon us and to be gracious to us (cf Nm 6,24). On this face the glory* of God radiates forth (2 Co 4,6). The glory of the transfiguration (Mt 17,2 p) is the sign that in Jesus, God Himself assumes a face (cf Ap 1,16) and in Him the face which "no one has ever seen" (Jn 1,18) now appears: "Whoever has seen me has seen the Father" (Jn 14,9). It is a human face, scoffed at, blindfolded (Mk 14, 65 p), and disfigured (cf Is 52,14); but it is "the image of the divine substance" (He 1,3).

Once he has seen the glory of this face, the Christian, through the Holy Spirit* dwelling within him, remains continually illumined and transformed, not just by a passing manifestation (2 Co 3,7f), as was true of the face of Moses, but by a ray of life and salvation. "All of us, reflecting the splendor of the Lord in our unveiled faces; are being transformed into His very image, from glory to glory, as though the Spirit of the Lord" (2 Co 3,18). It is this "glory of God that is on the face of Christ" which the service of the gospel* makes shine "upon every human conscience" (2 Co 4,2-6).

Christians, who have been transfigured in this way in the Spirit by the glory of the Lord, have the certitude that they will one day see "face to face" Him whom they have until now known only "in a mirror," and they will know as they are known (1 Co 13,12), and they will "see God" (Mt 5,8). Thus will be fulfilled the desire* which drew Israel to the temple: "The throne of God and of the Lamb will be mounted, and servants will adore them. They will see His face" (Ap 22,3f).

→Glory IV—God NT III—Grace II 3—Heart I 1—Light & Dark OT II 2—Presence of God —Pride—See—Seek I.

FG & JG afmcg

FAITH

For the Bible faith is the source and center of all religious life. By faith man should respond to the plan which God works out in time. In the footsteps of Abraham, "father of those who believe" (R 4,11), the exemplary personages of the OT have lived and died in the faith (He 11) which Jesus "brings to its perfection" (He 12,2). The disciples of Christ are "those who have believed" (Ac 2,44) and "who believe" (1 Th 1,7).

The variety of the Hebrew vocabulary of the faith reflects the complexity of the spiritual attitude of the believer. Two roots are, however, dominant: *āman* (cf amen*) suggests solidity and sureness; *bāṭaḥ*, security and confidence*. The Greek vocabulary is still more diverse. Greek religion, in fact, hardly allows any place to faith. The LXX not having at their disposal, therefore, appropriate words for the rendering of the Hebrew, have groped. To the root *bāṭaḥ* correspond especially: *elpis, elpizō, pepoitha* (Vulg. *spes, sperare, confido*); to the root *āman*: *pistis, pisteuō alētheia* (Vulg. *fides, credere, veritas*). In the NT later Greek words relative to the domain of knowledge become clearly predominant. Study of the vocabulary already reveals that faith, according to the Bible, has two poles: the confidence which is directed to a "faithful" person and involves the whole man; and, on the other hand, a movement of the intelligence to which a word or signs* permit access to realities that are not seen (He 11,1).

Abraham, father of believers. Yahweh calls Abraham*, whose father "served other gods" in Chaldea (Js 24,2; cf Jdt 5,6ff), and promises him a land and a numerous posterity (Gn 12,1f). Contrary to all likelihood (R 4,19), Abraham "believes in God" (Gn 15,6) and in His Word; he obeys this call* and wagers his existence on this promise*. On the day of trial*, his faith was capable of sacrificing the son in whom the promise was already realized (Gn 22); for his faith, in fact, the Word of God is truer even than its fruits: God is faithful* (cf He 11,11), and all-powerful* (R 4,21).

Abraham is henceforth the type itself of the believer (Si 44,20). He foretells those who will discover the true God (Ps 47,10; cf G 3,8) or His Son (Jn 8,31-41.56), those who will place their salvation in God alone and in His Word (1 M 2,52-64; He 11,8-19). One day the promise will be fulfilled in the resurrection of Jesus, posterity of Abraham (G 3,16; R 4,18-25). Abraham will then be the "father of a multitude of peoples" (R 4,17f; Gn 17,5): all those whom the faith will unite to Jesus.

OT

I. FAITH, A DEMAND OF THE COVENANT

The God of Abraham visits* His unhappy people in Egypt (Ex 3,16). He summons Moses, reveals Himself to him, and promises him "to be with him" in bringing Israel into its land* (Ex 3,1-15). "As if he saw* the invisible," Moses answers this divine proposal by a faith which "will hold firm" (He 11,23-29) in spite of eventual weaknesses (Nm 20,1-12; Ps 106, 32f). As mediator* he communicates God's plan to the people, while his miracles* indicate the origin of his mission*. Israel is also called "to believe in God and in Moses, His servant" (Ex 14,31; He 11,29) with an absolute confidence (Nm 14,11; Ex 19,9).

The covenant consecrates this engagement of God in the history of Israel. In return Israel was asked to obey the Word* of God (Ex 19, 3-9). Now, "to hear Yahweh" is first of all "to believe in Him" (Dt 9,23; Ps 106,24f); the covenant, then, asks for faith (cf Ps 78,37). The life and death of Israel will depend henceforth on its free fidelity (Dt 30,15-20; 28; He 11,33) in maintaining the Amen of faith (cf Dt 27,9-26) which has made of it the people* of God. In spite of innumerable infidelities which permeate the history of the crossing of the desert, the conquest of the promised land, and the setting up in Canaan, this epoch may be summarized thus: "By faith the walls of Jericho fell. . .and time would fail me if I were to speak of Gideon, Barak, Samson, Jephthah, David" (He 11,30ff).

According to the promises of the covenant (Dt 7,17-24; 31,3-8), the all-powerful fidelity of Yahweh was always manifested in the service of Israel when Israel had been faithful to it. From then on the proclaiming of these wonders of the past, and above all of the Exodus, as the activity of the invisible God was for Israel a confession* of faith (Dt 26,5-9; cf Ps 78; 105) handed on from generation to generation, especially on the occasion of the great annual feasts* (Ex 12,26; 13,8; Dt 5,20). In this way the people kept alive the memory* of the love of their God (Ps 136).

II. THE PROPHETS AND THE FAITH OF ISRAEL IN PERIL

The difficulties of the existence of Israel until the exile* were a severe temptation for its faith. The prophets denounced idolatry* (Ho 2,7-15; Jr 2,5-13) which suppressed faith in Yahweh alone, the formalism of worship (Am 5,21; Jr 7,22f) which fatally limited its demands, the seeking of salvation by force* of arms (Ho 1,7; Is 31,1ff).

Isaiah was the most striking of the heralds of the faith (Is 30,15). He called Ahaz from fear* to peaceful confidence* in Yahweh (7,4-9; 8,5-8) who will keep His promises to the House of David (2 S 7; Ps 89,21-38). He inspired Hezekiah with the faith which permitted Yahweh to save Jerusalem (2 K 18—20). It was in faith that he uncovered the paradoxical wisdom* of God (Is 19,11-15; 29,13—30,6; cf 1 Co 1,19f).

The faith of Israel was especially threatened at the taking of Jerusalem and the exile*. "Wretched and poor" (Is 41,17) Israel ran the risk of attributing its lot to the impotence of Yahweh and of turning toward the gods of victorious Babylon. The prophets then proclaim the omnipotence of the God of Israel (Jr 32,27; Ez 37,14), Creator of the world (Is 40,28f; cf Gn 1), Lord of history (Is 41,1-7; 44,24f), rock* of His people (44,8; 50,10). The idols* are nothing (44,9-20). Yahweh "excepted, there is no god" (44,6ff; 43,8-12; cf Ps 115,7-11); in spite of all appearances, He always deserves complete confidence (Is 40,31; 49,23).

III. THE PROPHETS AND THE FAITH OF THE FUTURE ISRAEL

1. *Faith, reality to come.* Taken as a whole, Israel did not listen to the appeal for faith made by the prophets (Jr 29,19). In order to hear it, they would first have had to believe in the prophets (Tb 14,4) as once they had believed in Moses (Ex 14,31). But at this point Israel was faced by a double obstacle. In the first place the existence of false prophets (Jr 28,15; 29,31) caused difficulties. How were they to be distinguished from genuine ones (23,9-32; Dt 13,2-6; 18,9-22)? Then there was faith itself with its paradoxical outlook and the difficulty of its practical demands.

The faithful* God could not fail to carry out His promises*, but in the context of the covenant this fulfillment depended on faith, and this faith was lacking in historical Israel. For the prophets, then, faith became a reality of the future, which would be granted by God to the Israel of the New covenant. One day God will renew their hearts* (Jr 32,39f; Ez 36, 26), which will thus be enabled to pass from hardness* (Is 6,9ff) to faith (R 10,9f; cf Jn 12,37-43). He will fill them with knowledge* (Jr 31,33f) and obedience (Ez 36,27), of which faith is the source.

2. *Faith, the bond of the future Israel.* Like Abraham* and Moses*, the prophets, for their part, based their lives on faith in Yahweh, in their calling and in their mission (cf He 11,33-40). This faith was often unshakable from the beginning (Is 6; 8,17; 12,2; 30,18). Sometimes it was slow to assert itself in the face of the trial* of a call that was too demanding (Jr 1; cf Ex 3,10ff; 4,1-17) or when God seemed absent (1 K 19; Jr 15,10-21; 20,7-18), before arriving at last at a definitive firmness (Jr 26; 37—38).

This faith of the prophets spread in each case through a greater or smaller group of disciples (cf Is 8,16; Jr 45) and hearers. In this way it seemed more and more like a personal engagement and frame of mind, which was already gathering together the Remnant* foretold by the prophets.

These see the Israel to come foreshadowed in these little communities. Reunited by their faith in the mysterious stone* of Sion (Is 28,16; cf 1 P 2,6f), they will be a people* made up of the poor* brought together by their faith in God (Mi 5,6f; Zp 3,12-18). Only "the upright man will live by his faithfulness (LXX: by his faith)" (Ha 2,4). The prophets, then, foresaw

159

no longer a nation saved as such, but already a church*, a community of the poor, bound together by personal faith. The Servant* of Yahweh will be an exemplary figure for this people of faith. In the midst of a trial* that will mean even death* (Is 50,6; 53), he sets his face "like flint" in absolute faith in God (50,7ff; cf Lk 9,51), which the future will justify (53,10ff; cf Ps 22).

3. *The faith of the nations.* The mission of the Servant* extends to the nations* (Is 42,4; 49,6). Thus, if the Israel of the future is united above all by faith, it will be able to open its ranks to the nations. In faith they too will come to know the one God (43,10), will confess Him as such (45,14; 52,15f; cf R 10,16; Is 56,1-8) and will await their salvation from His power (51,5f).

IV. TOWARD THE GATHERING OF BELIEVERS

In the centuries after the exile the historical Israel tended to shape itself according to the future Israel foretold by the prophets, yet without ever reaching the stage of ceasing to be a nation and becoming a real "assembly of believers" (1 M 3,13).

1. *The faith of the wise, of the poor, and of the martyrs.* Like the prophets, the wise men of Israel knew for a long time that they should count on Yahweh alone to be "saved" (Pr 20, 22). When all salvation disappears from the visible plane, wisdom* requires a total confidence in God (Jb 19,25f), in a faith which "knows" that God remains all-powerful (Jb 42,2). The wise are here very close to the poor* who have chanted their confidence in the psalms.

The whole Psalter proclaims the faith of Israel in Yahweh, sole God (Ps 18,32; 115), Creator (8; 104), all-powerful (29), faithful Lord (89), and merciful (136) for His people (105), universal king of the future (47; 96—99). Many psalms express Israel's confidence in Yahweh (44; 74; 125). But the highest testimonies of faith are the prayers* in which the faith of Israel expands in an individual confidence of rare quality. The persecuted just man's faith in God who will save him sooner or later (7; 11; 31; 62); confidence of the sinner in the mercy of God (40,13-18; 51; 130); peaceful assurance in God (4; 23; 121; 131) stronger than death (16; 49; 73): such is the prayer of the poor gathered

together by the certainty that beyond all trial (22) God reserves for them the good news (Is 61,1; cf Lk 4,18) and the possession of the land (Ps 37,11; cf Mt 5,4).

For the first time doubtless in its history (cf Dn 3), Israel is exposed after the exile to a bloody religious persecution* (1 M 1,62ff; 2, 29-38; cf He 11,37f). Martyrs* do not die only in spite of their faith, but because of it. Faced with this supreme absence of God, the faith of the martyrs, however, did not weaken (1 M 1,62); it deepened, even to hoping, through God's fidelity, in the resurrection* (2 M 7; Dn 12,2f) and immortality (Ws 2,19f; 3,1-9). Thus, strengthening itself ever more, personal faith gathered little by little the remnant* that was the beneficiary of the promises (R 11,5).

2. *Faith of the pagan converts.* At the same period a missionary current flowed through Israel. As Naaman of old (2 K 5), a number of pagans believe in the God of Abraham (cf Ps 47,10). It is then that the history of the Ninivites is written whom the preaching of a single prophet—to the shame of Israel—leads to "believe in God" (Jon 3,4f; cf Mt 12,41); that of the conversion of Nebuchadnezzar (Dn 3—4) or of Achior who "believes and enters the house of Israel" (Jdt 14,10; cf 5,5-21): God gives the nations* time "to believe in Him" (Ws 12,2; cf Si 36,4).

3. *Imperfections of the faith of Israel.* Persecution certainly raised up martyrs, but also fighters who refused to die without a struggle (1 M 2,39ff) to free Israel (2,11). In the unequal struggle they counted on God to give them victory* (2,49-70; cf Jdt 9,11-14). Though it was admirable in itself (cf He 11,34.39), their faith existed side by side with a certain amount of confidence in human strength*.

Another imperfection threatened the faith of Israel. Martyrs and fighters died because of their fidelity to God and the Law* (1 M 1,52-64). Israel in fact had ended by understanding that faith involved obedience* to the demands of the covenant. Along this line it was threatened by the danger to which so many of the Pharisees* succumbed, formalism which was more attached to ritual demands than to the religious and moral appeals of Scripture (Mt 23,13-30), pride* relying more on men and their works* than on God alone to be justified* (Lk 18,9-14).

The confidence of Israel in God then was not pure, partly because of the veil that hung between its faith and God's plan announced by Scripture (2 Co 3,14). Moreover, the true faith had been promised only to a future Israel. The pagans on their part found it difficult to share a faith which first opened on a national hope*, or on very heavy ritual demands. What, moreover, would they have to gain by adopting it (Mt 23,23)? Approaching the faith of the poor, in fact, could not make the pagans participate in a salvation which was still only a hope. Israel and the nations could only await Him who would bring the faith to its perfection (He 12,2; cf 11,39f) and receive the Spirit, "object of the promise" (Ac 2,33).

NT

I. FAITH IN THE THOUGHT AND THE LIFE OF JESUS

1. *The preparations.* It is the faith of the poor* (cf Lk 1,46-55) which receives the first announcement of salvation. Imperfect in Zechariah (1,18ff; cf Gn 15,8), exemplary in Mary (Lk 1,35ff.45; cf Gn 18,4), shared little by little by others (Lk 1—2 p), humbleness of appearance does not veil from faith the divine initiative. Those who believe in John the Baptist are also the poor conscious of their sin, and not the proud Pharisees* (Mt 21,23-32). This faith causes them to gather unknowingly around Jesus, who is among them (3,11-17 p), and orients them toward faith in Him (Ac 19,4; cf Jn 1,7).

2. *Faith in Jesus and in His Word.* All were able "to hear and see" (Mt 13,13 p) the Word* and the miracles* of Jesus who preached the coming of the kingdom (11,3-6 p; 13,16-17 p). But to hear the Word* (11,15 p; 13,19-23 p) and to "do" it (7,24-27 p; cf Dt 5,27), to see* truly, in a word, to believe (Mk 1,15; Lk 8,12; cf Dt 9,23) was peculiar to the disciples* (Lk 8,20 p). Words and miracles, on the other hand, posed the question: "Who is He?" (Mk 5,41; 6,1-6.14ff p). This question was a trial* for John the Baptist* (Mt 11,2f) and a scandal* for the Pharisees (12,22-28 p; 21,23 p). The faith demanded for miracles (Lk 7,50; 8,48) was only a partial response in recognizing the omnipotence of Jesus (Mt 8,2; Mk 9,22f). Peter gave the true answer: "Thou art the Christ" (Mt 16,13-16 p). This faith in Jesus henceforth unites the disciples with Him and among themselves in making them share the secret of His person (16,18-20 p).

Round about Jesus who was a poor* man (11,20) and who addresses Himself to the poor (5,2-10 p; 11,5 p), a community of poor men, of "little ones" (10,42), is thus set up, whose bond, more precious than all, is faith in Him and in His Word (18,6-10 p). This faith comes from God (11,25 p; 16,17) and one day will be shared by the nations* (8,5-13 p; 12,38-42 p). The prophecies are fulfilled.

3. *The perfection of faith.* When Jesus, the Servant*, took the road to Jerusalem to be obedient* unto death* (Ph 2,7f), He "set His face" (Lk 9,51; cf Is 50,7). In the presence of death, "He brought to its perfection*" (He 12,2) the faith of the poor (Lk 23,46=Ps 31,6; Mt 27,46 p=Ps 22), showing an absolute confidence in "Him who could," by the resurrection, "save Him from death" (He 5,7).

Despite their knowledge of the mysteries* of the kingdom (Mt 13,11 p), the disciples only with difficulty followed the way in which, in faith, they should follow* the Son* of Man (16,21-23 p). The confidence which excludes all worry and all fear (Lk 12,22-32 p) was not theirs habitually (Mk 4,35-41; Mt 16,5-12 p). From then on the trial* of the passion (Mt 26,41) will be a scandal* for them (26,33). What they then see makes great demands on their faith (cf Mk 15,31f). The faith of Peter himself, while not disappearing—for Jesus had prayed for it (Lk 22,32)—did not have the courage to assert itself (22,54-62 p). The faith of the disciples had still to take a decisive step to become the faith of the Church.

II. FAITH OF THE CHURCH

1. *The paschal faith.* The step was taken when the disciples, after many hesitations in the face of the apparitions* of Jesus (Mt 28,17; Mk 16,11-14; Lk 24,11), believed in His resurrection*. Witnesses* of all that Jesus has said and done (Ac 10,39), they proclaim Him "Lord and Christ" in whom the promises were invisibly fulfilled (2,33-36). Their faith is now capable of going "as far as blood" (cf He 12,4). They call their hearers to share in it to benefit from the promise by obtaining the remission of their sins (Ac 2,38f; 10,43). The faith of the Church is born.

2. *Faith in the Word.* Belief is first of all to

receive the preaching* of witnesses, the gospel* (Ac 15,7; 1 Co 15,2), the Word* (Ac 2,41; R 10,17; 1 P 2,8), by confessing* Jesus as Lord* (1 Co 12,3; R 10,9; cf 1 Jn 2,22). This initial message, transmitted as a tradition* (1 Co 15, 1-3), will be able to enrich itself and become more precise in a teaching* (1 Tm 4,6; 2 Tm 4,1-5): this human word will be always for faith, the very word of God (1 Th 2,13). To receive it is for the pagan to abandon his idols* and to turn to the living and true God (1 Th 1,8ff), it is for all to recognize that the Lord* Jesus fulfills God's plan (Ac 3,21-26; 13,27-37; cf 1 Jn 2,24). It is in receiving baptism* to confess the Father, the Son, and the Holy Spirit (Mt 28,19).

This faith, as Paul will see it, opens the understanding "to the treasures of wisdom* and of knowledge*" which are in Christ (Col 2,3); the wisdom itself of God revealed by the Holy Spirit (1 Co 2), so different from human wisdom (1 Co 1,17-31; cf Jm 2,1-5; 3,13-18; cf Is 29,14) and the knowledge of Christ and of His love (Ph 3,8; E 3,19; cf 1 Jn 3,16).

3. *The faith and life of the baptized.* Led by faith to baptism* and the imposition* of hands, which make him a full member of the Church, he who has believed in the Word participates in the teaching, the spirit, the "liturgy" of this Church (Ac 2,41-46). For it is in her that God realizes His plan* by working the salvation of those who believe (2,47; 1 Co 1,18): faith expands by obedience* to this plan (Ac 6,7; 2 Th 1,8). It unfolds in the activity of a moral life (1 Th 1,3; Jm 1,21f) faithful to the law* of Christ (G 6,2; R 8,2; Jm 1,25; 2,12); it acts through fraternal love* (G 5,6; Jm 2,14-26). It maintains itself in a fidelity capable of meeting death after the example of Jesus (He 12; Ac 7,55-60) as a confidence* in Him that is absolute, in Him "in whom it has believed" (2 Tm 1,12; 4,17f). Faith in the Word, obedience in confidence—such is the faith of the Church, which separates those who are lost from those who are saved (2 Th 1,3-10; 1 P 2,7f; Mk 16,16).

III. ST. PAUL, AND SALVATION BY FAITH

For the newly born Church as for Jesus, faith was a gift of God (Ac 11,21ff; 16,14; cf 1 Co 12,3). When the pagans were converted it was then God Himself who "purified their hearts by faith" (Ac 11,18; 14,27; 15,7ff). "For having believed," they received the same Spirit as the believing Jews (11,17). They were then received into the Church.

1. *Faith and the Jewish Law.* But a problem was soon raised: must they submit to circumcision* and the Jewish Law* (Ac 15,5; G 2,4)? Agreeing with those in charge (Ac 15; G 2,3-6), Paul thought it absurd to oblige the pagans to "Judaize", for it was faith in Jesus Christ that had saved the Jews themselves (G 2,15f). When they wished to impose circumcision on the Christians of Galatia (5,2; 6,12), Paul readily saw that it was preaching another gospel* (1,6-9). This new crisis was for him the occasion of deep reflection on the role of the Law* and of the faith in salvation history.

From Adam's time (R 5,12-21) all men, pagans or Jews, are guilty before God (1,8—3,20). Made for life, the Law itself only begot sin* and death* (7,7-10); G 3,10-14.19-22). The coming (G 4,4f) and the death of Christ put an end to this situation by manifesting the justice* of God (R 3,21-26; G 2,19ff) which is obtained by faith (G 2,16; R 3,22; 5,2). The role of the Law was then brought to an end (G 3,23—4,11). It was the regime of the promise*—now fulfilled in Jesus—which took over (G 3,15-18): like Abraham the Christians are justified by faith, without the Law (R 4; G 3,6-9; cf Gn 15,6; 17,11). According to the prophets, moreover, the just man should live by faith (Ha 2, 4=G 3,11; R 1,17), and the remnant* of Israel (R 11,1-6) be saved by faith alone in the rock* placed by God (Is 28,16=R 9,33; 10,11), that which permitted it to be opened to all nations* (R 10,14-21; 1 P 2,4-10).

2. *Faith and grace.* "Man is justified by faith without the works* of the Law*" (R 3,28; G 2, 16). This statement of Paul's asserts the uselessness of the practices of the Law under the regime of faith. But more profoundly still it means that salvation is never something owed but a grace* of God received through faith (R 4,4-8). Paul certainly is not unaware that faith must "work" (G 5,6; cf Jm 2,14-26) in docility to the Spirit received at the time of baptism (G 5,13-26; R 6; 8,1-13). But he strongly emphasizes the fact that the believer cannot either "boast" (pride*) of "his justice" or find support in his works, as Saul the Pharisee did (Ph 3,4.9; 2 Co 11,16—12,4). Even if "his conscience does not reproach him" before God (1 Co 4,4), he counts on God alone "who works

in him both to will and to accomplish" (Ph 2, 13). He, therefore, works out his salvation "in fear and trembling" (Ph 2,12) but also with a joyful hope (R 5,1-11; 8,14-39). His faith assures him "of the love of God manifested in Christ Jesus" (R 8,38f; E 3,19). Thanks to Paul the paschal faith lived by the primitive community was lived with a clear conscience. It was freed from the impurities and the limitations which affected the faith of Israel. It is completely the faith of the Church.

IV. FAITH IN THE WORD MADE FLESH

At the end of the NT, the faith of the Church, together with St. John, meditates on its beginnings. The better to face the future, it returns to Him who has given it its perfection. The faith of which John speaks is the same as that of the synoptics. It groups the community of disciples about Jesus (Jn 10,26f; cf 17,8). Oriented by John the Baptist (1,34f; 5,33f), it discovers the glory of Jesus at Cana (2,11). It "receives His words" (12,46f) and "hears His voice" (10,26f; cf Dt 4,30). It asserts itself by the lips of Peter at Capernaum (6,70f). The passion is a trial for it (14,1.28f; cf 3,14f) and the resurrection its decisive object (20,8.25-29).

But the fourth gospel is much more even than the synoptics the gospel of faith. First of all the faith is there explicitly centered on Jesus and His divine glory*. Belief in Jesus (4,39; 6,35) and in His name* (1,12; 2,23) is necessary. Belief in God and in Jesus is all one (12,44; 14,1; cf 8,24=Ex 3,14). For Jesus and the Father are one (10,30; 17,21). This unity* itself is the object of faith (14,10f). Faith should approach the invisible reality of the glory of Jesus without having need of seeing* the signs (miracles*) which make it known (2,11f; 4,48; 20,29). But if in fact it has need of seeing (2,23; 11,45) and of touching (20,27), it is no less called to open itself in the knowledge* (6,69; 8,28) and the contemplation (1,14; 11,40) of the invisible.

John insists besides on the present character of the invisible consequences of faith. For him who believes there will be no judgment* (5,24). He is already risen (11,25f; cf 6,40), walks in the light (12,46), and possesses eternal life (3,16; 6,47). On the other hand, "he who does not believe is already condemned" (3,18). Faith also insists on the tragic grandeur of an urgent choice between death and life, light* and darkness; and of a choice all the more difficult

because it depends on the moral conduct of him to whom it is proposed (3,19-21).

This insistence of John on faith, on its proper object, on its importance, is explained by the purpose itself of his gospel: to bring his readers to share his faith by believing "that Jesus is the Christ, the Son of God" (20,30), to become children of God through faith in the Word made flesh (1,9-14). The choice of the faith remains possible through the actual testimony of John (1 Jn 1,2f). This faith is the traditional faith of the Church: it confesses Jesus as Son* in fidelity to the teaching received (1 Jn 2,23-27; 5,1) and ought to expand in a life without sin (3,9f), animated by fraternal love (4,10ff; 5,1-5). Like Paul (R 8,31-39; E 3,19), John judges that it leads to the recognition of God's love for men (1 Jn 4,16).

Faced with the combats to come, the Apocalypse exhorts believers to "the patience* and the fidelity of the saints" (Ap 13,10) unto death. At the source of this fidelity there is always the paschal faith in Him who could say, "I have been dead, and behold I am living forever and ever" (1,18), the Word of God who establishes His kingdom* irresistibly (19,11-16; cf Ac 4, 24-30).

The day* when faith comes to an end and "we shall see God as He is" (1 Jn 3,2) is, therefore, the faith of the Pasch which will be again proclaimed: "Such is the victory which has triumphed over the world: our faith" (5,4).

→Abraham I 1.2, II 3.4—Amen—Anointing III 6—Apparitions of Christ—Baptism IV 3—Cares 2—Confession OT 1; NT 1—Confidence—Conscience 2 a—Faithfulness OT 2; NT 2—Fear of God II—Follow 1.2 c—Fruitfulness III 2—Gospel IV 3—Heart II 2 b—Heresy—Hope—Hospitality 2—Jesus (Name of) III—Jesus Christ I 2.3—Joy NT II 1—Justice *B* 1—Justification I, III—Know NT 3—Law *C* III 1.3—Liberation/Liberty III 1—Listen O 1—Mary IV —Messiah NT II—Miracle I 3, II 3, III 1. 2 b. 3 b—Name NT 3 a—New Birth 3 a—Noah 3—Obedience II, IV—Peter 3 b—Poor OT III—Pride NT 2.3—Promises—Repentence/Conversion NT III 1—Reward II 3 c—Salvation OT II 1; NT I 1 a, 2 a, II 2—Schism OT 2—See OT I; NT I 2—Seek II—Sign—Trial/Temptation OT I 1—Truth NT 2 a.3—Unbelief—Witness NT III—Word of God OT III 2; NT I 2, II 2, III 2—Works NT II 1.2.

JDU wjy

FAITHFULNESS

Fidelity or faithfulness (hb. *'emet*), a major attribute of God (Ex 34,6), is frequently associated with His paternal goodness (hb. *ḥesed*) toward the people of the covenant. These two complementary attributes indicate that the covenant* is at one and the same time a free gift and a lien, the solidity of which has stood the proof of centuries (Ps 119,90). To these two attitudes, in which the ways of God are summarized (Ps 25,10), man should respond by conforming to them. The filial piety* which he owes to God would have as proof of its truth* his fidelity in observing the precepts of the covenant.

All through salvation history God's fidelity is shown to be immutable in contrast to the constant infidelity of man until Christ, faithful witness* of the truth (Jn 18,37; Ap 3,14), communicates to man the grace with which He is filled (Jn 1,14.16) and makes him capable of meriting the crown of life by imitating His fidelity unto death (Ap 2,10).

OT

1. *God's fidelity.* God is the "rock" of Israel (Dt 32,4). The name symbolizes His unchangeable fidelity, the truth of His words*, the solidity of His promises*. His words will not pass away (Is 40,8), His promises will be kept (Tb 14,14); God does not lie, nor does He retract (Nm 23, 19). His plan is carried out (Is 25,1) by the power of His word which leaves His mouth, and does not return until after having accomplished its mission (Is 55,11). God does not change (Ml 3,6). He also wishes to unite to Himself the spouse He has chosen by a bond of perfect fidelity (Ho 2,22) without which one cannot know God (4,2).

It is not enough therefore to praise the divine fidelity which surpasses the heavens (Ps 36,6), nor to proclaim it in order to invoke it (Ps 89, 1), or to remind God of His promises (Ps 89, 1-9.25-40). We must pray to the faithful God to obtain fidelity from Him (1 K 8,56ff), and to stop answering His fidelity by our impiety (Ne 9, 33). Only God, in fact, can convert His faithless people, and give it happiness by making the fidelity which ought to be its fruit sprout from the earth (Ps 85,5.11ff).

2. *Man's fidelity.* Of His people God requires faithfulness to the covenant which He freely renews (Js 24,14); priests should be especially faithful (1 S 2,35). If Abraham and Moses (Ne 9,8; Si 45,4) are models of fidelity, Israel as a whole imitates the faithlessness of the generation of the desert (Ps 78,8ff.36f; 106,6). Where one is not faithful to God, fidelity to men disappears; no one can be relied on (Jr 9,2-8). This corruption is not found in Israel alone, for the proverb is valid for all places: "Who shall find a faithful man?" (Pr 20,6).

Israel, therefore, chosen by God to be His witness, has not been a faithful servant; they have remained blind and deaf (Is 42,18ff). But God has chosen another Servant* on whom He has sent His Spirit (Is 42,1ff), to whom He has given hearing and speech. This chosen one faithfully proclaims the justice* without which trials* could make Him faithless to His mission* (Is 50,4-7), for God is His strength (Is 49,5).

NT

1. *Fidelity of Jesus.* The faithful Servant thus announced is Christ Jesus, Son and Word of God, true and faithful, who comes to fulfill the Scripture and the work of His Father (Mk 10, 45; Lk 24,44; Jn 19,28.30; Ap 19,11ff). By Him are kept all the promises of God (2 Co 1,20); in Him are the salvation and glory of the elect (2 Tm 2,10); with Him men are called by the Father to enter into communion*, and it is by Him that believers will be strengthened and made faithful to their vocation until the end (1 Co 1,8f). The fidelity of God (1 Th 5,23f), whose gifts* are without repentance (R 11,29), is therefore manifested in Him in its plenitude and this fidelity directs men to follow* the constancy of Christ in order to make them more faithful (2 Th 3,3ff).

We should imitate the fidelity of Christ by holding firm until death, and count on His fidelity to live and reign with Him (2 Tm 2,11f). Still more, even if we are unfaithful, He remains faithful; for although He can deny us, He cannot deny Himself (2 Tm 2,13). Today, as yesterday and always, He remains what He is (He 13,8), the merciful and faithful high priest (He 2, 17) who grants access with assurance to the throne of grace (He 4,14ff) to those who, relying on the fidelity of the divine promise, keep unfailing faith* and hope* (He 10,23).

2. *The faithful of Christ.* The title "faithful" is sufficient to designate the disciples* of Christ, those who have faith* in Him (Ac 10,45; 2 Co 6, 15; E 1,1). Of course it includes the natural virtues of loyalty and good faith which Chris-

tians should be careful to practice (Ph 4,8). It designates, moreover, this religious fidelity which is one of the major prescriptions whose observance Christ asks (Mt 23,23) and which characterizes those whom the Holy Spirit moves (G 5,22). It appears in the details of life (Lk 16,10ff) and thus dominates the whole of social life.

In the new covenant this fidelity has a soul, and it is love*. Inversely, it is the proof of genuine love. Jesus insists on this point: "Remain in my love. If you keep my commandments, you will remain in my love, as I have kept the commandments of my Father and I remain in His love" (Jn 15,9f; cf 14,15.21.23f). John, faithful to the teaching of Christ, inculcates it in his "children," when he invites them "to walk in the truth*," that is, in fidelity to the commandment of mutual love (2 Jn 4f); but he adds at once: "For love consists in living according to the commandments of God" (2 Jn 6).

It is to this fidelity that the reward of sharing in the joy of the Lord is reserved (Mt 25,21.23; Jn 15,11). But this fidelity demands a struggle against the tempter, the evil one, a struggle which requires watchfulness and prayer (Mt 6, 13; 26,41; 1 P 5,8f). In the last times the trial of this fidelity will be fearful; the saints will have to exercise constancy (Ap 13,10; 14,12), grace for which will come from the blood* of the Lamb (Ap 7,14; 12,11).

→Abraham II 2—Adultery—Amen—Confidence 3—Covenant—Desert OT I 2.3; NT I 1 — Deception / Disappointment III — Error — Example — Faith — Follow 1 — Grace II 1.2 — Hope—Joy OT II 2—Justice—Love I—Marriage OT II 3; NT I—Mary IV 2—Obedience II 3—Patience—Piety OT—Promises—Providence 2—Remnant OT 3.4; NT—Rock 1—Servant of God II—Truth—Virtues & Vices 1—Witness.

CS & MFL wjy

FAREWELL SPEECHES

In the OT as in the NT there are cases of people on the point of death taking leave of their heirs with farewell speeches that amount to last wills and testaments.

OT

The people whose farewell speeches are re-

ported are mostly those who are responsible for the people of God: Jacob, Moses, Joshua, Samuel, David...(and, in later Judaism, the twelve patriarchs). Apart from the special characteristics that are occasioned by the different circumstances, their farewell speeches have much in common. The dying man recalls God's gifts to His people; he foresees the promised salvation (Gn 49,8-12; Dt 32,36-43; Test. of the 12 Patr.); he urges his successors to be faithful (Dt 31—32; Js 24; 1 S 12); in the most recent texts (1 M 2,51-61; Test. of the 12 Patr.) he lays stress on the example of the fathers*.

And so the fathers and leaders of Israel are seen as witnesses* of the covenant. They hand on the tradition that they have received and the task and the powers entrusted to them; and they invite their successors to carry on their work.

NT

1. *Farewell speeches of Jesus.* The eschatological discourse (Mk 13) is the last teaching given by Jesus to the people. He urges the faithful to prepare themselves for the fulfillment of the promises that He has been announcing. But, by the radical novelty of His person, He introduces an original theme: the prophecy of His parousia, which turns the farewell into an aurevoir.

The Last Supper is the classical example of Jesus' farewell speeches. In Mt and Mk the institution of the Eucharist* finishes on a note of meeting again in the Kingdom (Mk 14,25 p). In Luke it continues with a discourse urging the Twelve to follow the example of Jesus' service (22,24-27) and promising them, in the form of a testament, a share in His royal power (Lk 22, 28-30). In John the long account (Jn 13—17) opens with the washing of the feet, when Jesus gives an example of His service. Two parallel discourses (14 and 16,16-33) form the farewell speeches properly so called: in them Jesus foretells the sorrowful separation that lies ahead and the joy of His return (in the "paschal apparitions" in 16; in His presence in the Church in 14). He urges His disciples to faith, love and peace. His absence is only for a time; it is only an apparent absence.

Like the farewell speeches of Moses, Samuel and David, the apparitions* of the risen Christ to the Twelve include a handing on of powers. On these occasions Jesus entrusts to His followers the task of carrying on His mission*: He instructs them to preach, to baptize and to pardon (Mt 28,19 p). He promises them His presence throughout time (28,20).

2. *The farewell speeches of the apostles*, servants carrying out God's plan, are closer to those of the OT characters.

The second epistle to Timothy is a real last will and testament. Paul, seeing that his death is not far off (2 Tm 4,6-8), reminds his faithful disciple of the salvation that has been brought about in Jesus (1,9-10), warns him of the danger of heresy (2,16-18) and looks forward full of hope to the coming of the Day of the Lord (1,12.18; 2,11-12). The same themes appear in the second epistle of Peter: the approaching death of the apostle (2 P 1,12-15), the salvation that has been granted (1,3-4), the fact of heresy* (2,1-3.10-22) and the expectation of the Day of the Lord (1,16.19; 3,8-10.12-13.18).

But the most distinctive testament is the one of Paul to the presbyters of Ephesus (Ac 20,17-38). Here we find mention of Paul's example (vv 18-21,31-35), the prospect of his coming arrest (vv 22-24), the solemn statement that he has carried out his task (vv 25-27), the invitation to carry on his work in the service of the Church (v 28) and to defend the flock against the heretics (vv 29-30).

Unlike those of Jesus, the speeches of the apostles do not contain any suggestion of meeting again. It is not that they do not hope to meet their faithful followers again on the Day of the Lord*; but, when they think of this day, it is of the meeting with their Master that they are thinking more than anything else. He alone is the conqueror of death* and of every absence.

→Apparitions of Christ 4—Death OT I 1 Meal III—Presence of God NT I.

AG ems

FASTING

Fasting consists in depriving oneself of all food and drink, and even of sexual* relations, for one or more days, from one sunset to the next.

Today, in the West, even Christians find it difficult to appreciate its value. If they value moderation in drinking and eating, fasting seems to them dangerous to health, and they do not at all perceive its spiritual usefulness. This attitude is opposed to the one that historians of religion uncover to some degree everywhere.

Whether from motives of asceticism, or purification or mourning or supplication, fasting occupies an important place in religious rites. In Islam, for example, it is the best means to find out the divine transcendence. The Bible, which is the foundation for the attitude of the Church, on this point agrees with all the other religious currents. But it specifies the meaning of fasting and regulates its practice. Along with prayer* and almsgiving*, it is one of the essential acts which express to God man's humility*, hope*, and love*.

1. *The meaning of fasting.* Since man is both body and soul, it would be useless to imagine a purely spiritual religion. To become involved, the soul* needs bodily acts and attitudes. Fasting, always joined to suppliant prayer, helps express humility before God. Fasting (Lv 16,31) is equivalent to "humbling one's soul" (16,29). Fasting, then, is not an ascetical adventure; it does not aim at acquiring a state of psychological or religious exaltation. These purposes have been attested to in the history of religion; but in the biblical context, when a man abstains from eating for a whole day (Jg 20,23; 2 S 12,16f; Jon 3,7), when he considers food as a gift from God (Dt 8,3), this privation is a religious act and we must correctly understand its motives. And the same can be said of conjugal relations (Jl 2,16).

We turn to the Lord (Dn 9,3; Ezr 8,21) with an attitude of dependence and total abandonment. This is the case before undertaking a difficult task (Jg 20,26; Es 4,16), when pardon is being asked for a fault (1 K 21,27), or a cure is being sought (2 S 12,16.22), in the case of mourning after being widowed* (Jdt 8,5; Lk 2, 37) or after a national disaster (1 S 7,6; 2 S 1,12; Ba 1,5; Ze 8,19), to obtain the end of some calamity (Jl 2,12-17; Jdt 4,9-13), to open one's mind to divine light (Dn 10,12), to await the grace necessary to accomplish some mission (Ac 13,2f), and to prepare oneself to meet God (Ex 34,28; Dn 9,3).

Occasions and motives are varied. But it is always a question of establishing oneself with faith in an attitude of humility* in order to receive the action of God and to place oneself in His presence. This deep intention unveils the meaning of the forty-day fast of Moses (Ex 34, 28) and Elijah (1 K 19,8). The forty-day fast of Jesus in the desert*, which was modeled on Moses' and Elijah's fast, was not motivated by an opening up to the Spirit of God since Christ was already filled with the Spirit (Lk 4,1). If the Spirit drives Him to fasting, it is in order to inaugurate His Messianic mission* by an act of confident surrender to His Father (Mt 4,1-4).

2. *The practice of fasting.* The Jewish liturgy had a "great fast" on the Day of Atonement (cf Ac 27,9). Its practice was a proper condition of belonging to the people of God (Lv 23, 29). There were also other group fastings on the anniversaries of national calamities. Furthermore, pious Jews fasted out of personal devotion (Lk 2,37), as for example the disciples of John the Baptist and the Pharisees (Mk 2,18), some of whom fasted twice a week (Lk 18,12). They sought to accomplish in that way one of the elements of justification* as defined by the Law and the prophets. If Jesus did not prescribe anything like this for His disciples (Mk 2,18), it is not because He looked down on this justification or that He wanted to do away with it; but He came to fulfill* it. That is why He forbade any display of fasting and why He invites His disciples to surpass this justice in certain instances (Mt 5,17.20; 6,1). Jesus insists even more on detachment as far as wealth is concerned (Mt 19,21), on voluntary continence (19,12) and above all on self-renunciation in order to carry one's cross (10,38-39).

Actually, the practice of fasting involves certain dangers. It involves the danger of formalism which the prophets had already denounced (Am 5,21; Jr 14,12), and the danger of pride and ostentation if one fasts "in order to be seen by men" (Mt 6,16). To be pleasing to God, true fasting must be united with love of neighbor and should include a search after true justice (Is 58,2-11). Like prayer, it cannot be separated from almsgiving. Finally, it should be done for the love of God (Ze 7,5). Jesus invites His followers to fast with perfect discretion. Known only to God, this fasting will be the pure expression of hope in Him. A humble fasting opens the heart to interior justice which is a work of the Father who sees and acts in secret (Mt 6,17f).

The apostolic Church preserved, in this matter of fasting, the customs of Judaism, but performed it in the spirit defined by Jesus. The Acts of the Apostles mentions some religious celebrations involving fasting and prayer (Ac 13,2ff; 14,22). During his overwhelming apostolic labors, Paul was not content with suffering hunger and thirst when circumstances forced them on him. He added repeated fastings (2 Co 6,5; 11,27). The Church has remained faithful to this tradition and seeks by the practice of fasting

to place the faithful in an attitude of total openness to the grace of the Lord, while waiting for His return. For if the first coming of Jesus filled up the explication of Israel, the time that follows His resurrection is not that of total joy without any penitential acts. Defending his non-fasting disciples against the Pharisees, Jesus Himself said: "Can the friends of the bridegroom fast, as long as the bridegroom is with them? But the days will come when the bridegroom will be taken from them, and then they shall fast in those days" (Mk 2,19f p). True fasting, then, is the fasting of faith, the absence of the sight of the Beloved and the continuing search for Him. While waiting for the bridegroom to come back to us, penitential fasting has its place in Church practice.

→Almsgiving NT 1—Burial 1—Hunger & Thirst OT 2—Nourishment III—Perfume 1—Repentance/Conversion OT I 2.

RG jrs

FATHERLAND

A fatherland, "land of the fathers," is one of the essential aspects of the experience of a people. For the people* of the OT, the fatherland held an important place in their faith and hope. Nevertheless, the fatherland of the OT is only a preparatory stage in God's revelation, for God ultimately revealed another fatherland to which all men are destined.

OT

1. *The experience of a fatherland.* The history of God's people began with an uprooting: Abraham had to leave his fatherland and go to another country about which he knew nothing (Gn 12,1f). But the realization of the new establishment of his race was delayed. During their stay in Canaan, the patriarchs were foreigners and guests (Gn 23,4; He 11,13); the inheritance of the country was promised to them (Gn 12,7), but not yet given. Moreover, Egypt*, where they were sojourning, was also a strange country for them (cf 15,13). It was only after the exodus* and the covenant* of Sinai that God's promise was fulfilled and Canaan became their own land, a land full of religious meaning. It was not only received as a gift from God; it not only contained the tombs of their fathers (Gn 47,30; 50,5; Ne 2,3-5); but the fact that God also

possessed it as His place of residence—the sanctuary for the ark* and then the temple* of Jerusalem—conferred a sacred value upon it. It appeared linked to the faith under all these titles.

2. *The experience of being uprooted.* But Israel also suffered the very opposite experience. A double national disaster ultimately ravaged this beloved fatherland. At the same time, the people were transported far away from it, and had to suffer the experience of being uprooted. The exile* only strengthened the Jews' attachment to the fatherland (Ps 137,1-6) whose misfortunes they mourned (cf Lm). Then they understood that the cause of this great catastrophe was the great national sin that God had punished in an exemplary manner (Lm 1,8.18f; Is 64,4. . .; Ne 9,29ff). As long as the trial lasted the humiliated and distant fatherland occupied a central place in their prayer (Ne 9,36f), in their cares (2,3), and in their hopes for the future (Tb 13,9-17; Ba 4,30—5,9). Attached to the institutions of the past, they unceasingly labored to resurrect them, and they succeeded in this to some extent. But at the same time, they discovered a transfigured image of the future fatherland in the oracle of the prophets. It is the new holy land and the new Jerusalem*, the center of a reunited land, which takes on the aspect of a restored paradise*. Thus, the fatherland was for the Jews both a concrete reality analogous to all other human fatherlands, and an ideal conception that affects all the nationalistic ideologies with its purity and grandeur. In it all human dreams are crystalized. Without being multinational, like the concept of the Roman Empire at the same epoch, it tends toward universality by means of the vocation of Israel*: in Abraham all the families of the earth must be blessed (Gn 12,3), and Zion must become the mother* of all fatherlands (Ps 87).

NT

1. *Jesus and His fatherland.* In order to be completely human, Jesus also had the experience of a fatherland. His was not any country at all, but the land that His Father had given as an inheritance to His people. He loved the fatherland with every fibre of His being; all the more as His mission to it was for Him the occasion of a new drama. In fact, as Israel had ignored the voice of the prophets in the past, ultimately the Jewish fatherland scorns the one who reveals its true vocation to it. At Nazareth, His father's village, Jesus is rejected; no prophet is received in his own country (Mt 13,54-57 p; Jn 4,44). At Jerusalem, the national capital, Jesus knew that He was going to die (Lk 13,33). He also wept over the city that had failed to recognize the time of God's visitation (Lk 19,41; cf 13,34f p). The terrestial fatherland of the Jews goes irreparably toward its ruin, for it has not done what God expected from it. A new catastrophe will be a sign for all eyes to see that God has taken away the mission with which, until that time, it was charged according to the plan of salvation (Mk 13,14-19; Lk 19,43f; 21,20-23).

2. *The new fatherland.* The new people, the Church, will not suppress incorporation into an earthly fatherland, as certain current ideologies try to do. Love of fatherland will always remain a duty for the Christian, together with the prolonging of family love. Thus, the Christians of Jewish origin remained attached, as Jesus was, to the fatherland of Israel. On another level, St. Paul revindicated the right of Roman citizenship that he possessed by reason of his birth (Ac 22,27f). But the fatherland of Israel no longer has its sacred character which was now transferred to a higher reality. The Church* is the Jerusalem which is above, whose sons we are (G 4,26), as the Israelites were the sons of the earthly Jerusalem. It is in heaven that we have the rights of citizenship (Ph 3,20). In that way all men can share the experience of the new fatherland. Formerly, the pagans were strangers* to the city of Israel (E 2,12); but now they share with the Jews the honor of being fellow citizens with the saints (2,19). Thus, heaven* is the true fatherland for which Israel, chosen from among the earthly fatherlands, was only the figure*, meaningful, but temporary. We have no permanent dwelling place here, and we seek that which is to come (He 13,14). This is the fatherland that God prepared for the patriarchs in former times; and they, beyond the land of Canaan, were already hoping with all their faith for this better fatherland (He 11, 14ff). All men must do as they did and see beyond the corner of earth where they have taken root with their families, see the new fatherland where they will live with them forever.

→City NT 2—Earth—Exile—Fathers & Father I, II 1—Jerusalem OT—People *A* II 4—Stranger.

PG rco'c

FATHERS & FATHER

To a world that aims to establish "a brotherhood without a father," the Bible reveals that God is essentially a father. Beginning with the experiences of earthly fathers and spouses for whom family life furnishes the means of exercising authority in a spirit of love, and in contrast with the aberrant manner in which paganism transferred these human realities to its gods, the OT reveals the love* and authority of the living God by means of the images of father and spouse*. The NT takes up both of these images, but perfects the concept of father by revealing the unique sonship of Jesus and by adding the unheard of notion that this filiation procures the paternity of God over all men.

I. THE FATHERS OF THE CARNAL RACE

1. *Master and lord.* On the plane that could be called horizontal, the father is the uncontested head of the family, the one whom the spouse recognizes as master (*ba'al*, Gn 20,3) and lord* (*'ādōn*, 18,12), upon whom depends the education* of the boys (Si 30,1-13), the marriage* settlements (Gn 24,2ff; 28,1f), the freedom of the girls (Ex 21,7), and indeed (in time past) the life of the children (Gn 38,24; 42,37); in the father the whole family is incarnate, and he is the assurance of its unity (vg 32,11). Consequently, the family was called *bēth ab*, "father's house" (34,19).

Through an analogy, once the term *house** began to designate a clan (vg Ze 12,12ff), an important fraction of the people (vg "the house of Joseph"), or even the entire people (vg "the house of Israel"), the authority of the leader of these groups was conceived in the image of the father of the family (cf Jr 35,18). In the monarchy, the king* was the "father" of the nation (Is 9,5), just as Nabonidus at Babylon was characterized the "father of the fatherland." The name of father was equally applied to priests (Jg 17,10; 18,19), to the royal counselors (Gn 45,8; Es 3,13f; 8,12), to the prophets (2 K 2, 12), and to the wise men (Pr 1,8, etc; cf Is 19, 11), because of their authority as educators. By their influence on the horizontal plane, the earthly "fathers" prepared Israel as a unique people* to receive God's salvation and to recognize God as its father.

2. *Ancestor of a line.* On the vertical plane, the father was head of a line of descendants and the link with the line. By procreating, he perpetuated himself (Gn 21,12; 48,16); he contributed to the continuance of his race, assuring that the family possessions would go to his heirs, his issue (15,2f). If he died without a son, he was considered as having been punished by God (Nm 3,4; 27,3f).

At the head of the line the ancestors were the fathers *par excellence*, those in whom the future of the race was previously formed. As the curse* on the son of Ham included the subordination of the Canaanites to the sons of Shem, in the same way the greatness of Israel was included beforehand in the election and blessing* of Abraham (Gn 9,20-27; 12,2). The stages in the lives of Abraham, Isaac, and Jacob were marked by the promise of innumerable descendants and a fertile country; for the history of Israel was written in the intricate details of their lives, just as the history of the neighboring people was written into the history of Lot, Ishmael, or Esau, who were excluded from the promises (Gn 19,30-38; 21,12f; 36,1). In like manner, each tribe attributed to its ancestor of the same name the responsibility for its place at the tribal meetings (Gn 49,4). The genealogies, while expressing relationships other than or more complex than ties of blood (Gn 10), systematized the paternal lineages and stressed the importance of ancestors whose actions had involved the future and the rights of their descendants. The genealogies of sacerdotal traditions (Gn 5; 11) notably order the sequence of the generations in relationship with the divine election and salvation by showing a continuity between Adam himself and the patriarchs.

II. THE FATHERS OF THE SPIRITUAL RACE

Although the patriarchs were the fathers *par excellence* of the chosen people, properly it was not by reason of their physical paternity but because of the promises* which, going beyond considerations of race, shall be attained ultimately by all who will imitate their faith. Their paternity "according to the flesh" (R 4,1) was only the temporary condition of a spiritual and universal paternity based on the permanence and coherence of the salvific plan of a God unceasingly at work from the election of Abraham* until the glorification of Jesus (Ex 3,15; Ac 3,13). St. Paul is the theologian of this spiritual paternity, but the idea was prepared in the OT.

1. *Transcending primacy of race.* The spiritual aspect of the paternity of ancestors takes on increasing importance in the OT to the extent that the idea of solidarity in good and evil is deepened. The ancestry of the "fathers," which is increased with each generation, does not include only the patriarchs, nor even only the ancestors who were praised in the second century (Si 44—50; 1 M 2,51-61); also included are some rebels; and some prophets put Jacob himself in the first rank of these rebels, the eponymous ancestor of the nation (Ho 12,3ff; Is 43,27). But these rebels involved their descendants, who are considered one with them, in their disobedience and their chastisement (Ex 20,5; Jr 32,18; Ba 3,4f; Lm 5,7; Is 65,6f; Dn 9,16). Because they were fathers according to physical parentage, they thought that it necessarily followed that their descendants, through a veritable moral paternity, were made heirs to their faults or at least to the chastisements that those faults incurred. Jeremiah announces (Jr 31,29f) and Ezekiel proclaims as imminent (Ez 18) the emptiness of this automatic idea of reward*: punishment will be measured according to a man's own sin.

Beginning with the exile, a similar development was made toward a solidarity in the line of goodness. God never appeared so clearly as the one Father of His people as He did at that very moment when Abraham and Jacob, whose heritage (cf Ez 33,24) had been taken over by some intruders, seemed to forget their posterity (Is 63,16). The reason was that in the midst of the trial a "qualitative Israel" was being formed, an Israel to which not all the sons of Abraham according to the flesh belonged, but only those who imitate Abraham's search for justice* and his hope* (Is 51,1ff). Moreover, is not the race of Israel impure from the beginning according to the lineage of the fathers as well as the mothers (Ez 16,3)? Does not the writer of Chronicles himself admit the relationship of some of his people with pagan clans (1 Ch 2,18-55)? Do not the prophets proclaim the possibility of the proselytes being joined to the people of the promises (Is 56,3-8; cf 2 Ch 6, 32f)? The time is not far away, notwithstanding the nationalist uprisings, when the salutary paternity of Abraham and the great ancestors will be actualized by faith and no longer by race.

2. *From the nation to the universe.* To the extent that the fatherhood of ancestors was conceived as something spiritual, it also became more universal. This was clearly indicated with regard to Abraham. According to the sacerdotal tradition, his name means "father of a multitude," that is, a multitude of peoples (Gn 17,5). Moreover, the promise of Gn 12,3: "Through you will all the nations of the earth bless themselves" becomes in the Greek translation: "In you will be blessed..." (cf Si 44,21; Ac 3,25; G 3,8). Instead of magnifying the chosen race, the LXX suggests the idea that all the nations will one day share in the blessing of Abraham.

These universalist currents, which were often enough counterbalanced by the opposite tendency to make the race an absolute (Ezr 9,2), were ended by John the Baptist and Jesus. John said: "From these stones, God can raise up children to Abraham" (Mt 3,9 p). For Jesus, if there is a filiation with Abraham that is necessary for salvation, it is not membership in the race which constitutes it, but repentance* (Lk 19,9), imitation of the patriarch's works*, that is, his faith* (Jn 8,33.39f). And Christ let it be understood that God would raise up to the fathers, through the call to the pagans, a spiritual posterity of believers (Mt 8,11).

3. *From the prediction to the actual fulfillment.* By giving an early fulfillment to Jesus' proclamation, the life of the Church permitted the teacher of the pagans, who was spurred on by the crisis of the Judaizers (1 Tm 2,7), to develop the same themes. Certainly for Paul, the members of Israel "according to the flesh" (1 Co 10, 18), "cherished for the sake of the fathers" (R 11,28), keep by virtue of the promises* made to them (Ac 13,17.32f) a priority in the call to salvation (R 1,16; cf Ac 3,26); although many refused to believe in the supreme heritage of the promises (G 3,16) and in that way made themselves slaves like Ishmael (G 4,25). But at the very heart of "God's Israel" (G 6,16) there was no difference between Jews and gentiles (E 3,6); circumcised or not, all become by "claiming to be" of "the faith* of Abraham, the father of us all," sons of the patriarch and beneficiaries of the blessings promised to Abraham and his descendants (G 3,7ff; R 4,11-18). At baptism*, a new spiritual race of Abraham's children is born according to the promise (G 3, 27ff), a race whose first representatives did not hesitate to call themselves "fathers" (2 P 3,4).

III. THE FATHERHOOD OF THE GOD OF THE FATHERS

1. *From fathers to the Father.* The progressive

spiritualization of the idea of the fatherhood of man had made possible the revelation of the idea of the fatherhood of God. If the fatherhood of the patriarchs seemed inoperative during the exile, it was the occasion to exalt the permanence of Yahweh's fatherhood (Is 63,16). In spite of the contrast, fatherhood could then be attributed simultaneously to ancestors and to God. This also sprang from "sacerdotal" history: by placing Adam, created in the image of God (Gn 1,27) and himself generating others in his own image (5,1ff), at the top of the ladder of generations*, it suggested that the line of ancestry went back to God. Later Luke does this same thing (Lk 3,23-38). For Paul, God is the supreme Father to whom all *paternity* (descent from one ancestor) owes its existence and value (E 3,14f). Thus, between human fathers and God a likeness exists which permits the name of father to be applied to the latter. Further, this divine paternity alone gives to human paternities their full meaning in the plan of salvation.

2. *Transcendence of the divine paternity.* It was not, however, a process of reasoning by analogy that led Israel to call God its Father; it was a lived experience, and perhaps a reaction against neighboring peoples.

All the ancient nations invoked God as their Father. With the Semites, such a custom went far back into their history, and the paternal quality of the god included the role of protector and lord and often creator. In the Ugaritic texts (from the XVI century), El, the supreme god of the Canaanite pantheon, was called "King Father Shunem." By this his control over gods and men was expressed. The very name "El," which is also the name of the God of the patriarchs (Gn 46,3), originally was the designation for the sheik. In this case it denoted the authority over what was sometimes called his "clan."

According to this original meaning, the idea of divine paternity passed into the Bible. But another meaning existed that was rejected by the OT. In fact, the Phoenician El, who was likened to a bull similar to the Egyptian Min, fecundated his spouse and begot other gods. Baal, son of El, had specialized in the fecundation of human couples, animals, and the soil, on the condition of ritual imitation of his union with a goddess. Yahweh, however, is unique; He has neither sexual activity nor female associate, nor son in the carnal sense. If the poets sometimes say "Son of God" of the angels

(Dt 32,8; Ps 29,1; 89,7; Jb 1,6. . .), the princes, and the judges (Ps 82,1.6), it is a sign of their Syro-Phoenician sources and their way of submitting these simple creatures to God to whom no physical paternity is attributed. If Yahweh is a procreator (Dt 32,6), it is clearly in the moral sense since He is not the father of the gods and the spouse of a goddess, but at one and the same time (and therefore in the figurative sense) the father and the spouse (Ho, Jr) of His people. Although He is also Father insofar as He is Creator (Is 64,7; Ml 2,10; cf Gn 2, 7; 5,1ff), it is not through monstrous theogonies, as in the Babylonian myths. Finally, the God who sovereignly "calls the wheat" (Ez 36,29) has nothing in common with the fecundating Baal and the magic of his erotic cults that horrified the prophets. He does not want to be invoked in the way in which Baal is invoked by his followers (Jr 2,27). Everything indicates that the leaders of Israel wished to purify the notion of divine paternity, so strong among their neighbors, from all its sexual overtones and to retain the valuable aspect transferable to God of a social terminology concerning family heads and ancestors.

3. *Yahweh, Father of Israel.* At the beginning, it was especially in a collective and historical perspective that the divine fatherhood was conceived. God was revealed as Father of Israel at the moment of the exodus* when He showed that He was its protector and the one who provided food, as well as its master. The basic idea was that of a beneficent sovereignty that demanded submission and confidence (Ex 4,22; Nm 11,12; Dt 14,1; Is 1,2ff; 30,1.9; Jr 3,14). Hosea and Jeremiah kept the idea, but enriched it by stressing the immense tenderness of Yahweh (Ho 11,3f.8f; Jr 3,19; 31,20). At the beginning of the exile, while the same theme of the fatherhood of God founded on divine election continued to be exploited (Is 45,10f; 63,16; 64, 7f; Tb 13,4; Ml 1,6; 3,17), and while the canticle of Moses added the idea of adoption (Dt 32,10), certain psalmists (Ps 27,10; 103,13) and certain wise men (Pr 3,12; Si 23,1-4; Ws 2,13-18; 5,5) considered every just man as a son* of God, that is, an object of His tender* protection. The individual application of this idea would not be altogether novel, if it was certain that, in the old theophoric names* like Abi-ezer (Js 17,2), the syllable after the *ab* (Father) stood for the first person suffix, so that it could be translated: "My Father is assistance."

4. *Yahweh, Father of the king.* Since David's time, the fatherhood of Yahweh was claimed especially with regard to the king* (2 S 7,14f; Ps 2,7; 89,27f; 110,3 LXX), through whom the divine favor reached the whole nation that he represented. All the kings of the ancient Near East were considered as adopted sons of their god; and the words of Ps 2,7: "You are my son," are found literally in a Babylonian formula of adoption. But, in places other than Israel, the demands of the gods were usually caprices, as can be seen in the demands made on Kemosh according to the stele of Mesha (cf 2 K 3). In Egypt the god is a father according to the flesh. Yahweh, on the contrary, transcended the order of the flesh and sanctioned the moral conduct of the kings (2 S 7,14).

These texts concerning the royal sonship prepared for the revelation of Jesus' unique sonship, to the extent that through the line of kings of Judah there was already outlined the definitive Messiah*. Another approach to the revelation was given after the exile through the portrayal of Wisdom* (Pr 8) personified as God's daughter preceding every creature, and summing up in herself the hope attached, since Nathan's prophecy, to the dynastic succession of David.

IV. JESUS REVEALS THE FATHER

With the approach of the Christian era, Israel was well aware that God was Father of His people and of each of His faithful. Very rare in apocalyptic literature and the Qumrân texts, which perhaps fear the Hellenistic use of the term, the name "father" is frequently found in the rabbinic writings where the very formula "our Father, who art in heaven" (Mt 6,9) was discovered.

Jesus perfected* the best of the Jewish reflection on the fatherhood of God. Like the poor* man in the psalm for whom the community of "men of pure heart" alone represents the true Israel (Ps 73,1), "the race of the sons of God" (73,15), Jesus dreamed of a community (we must say "our Father," not "my Father") who have become "little ones" (Mt 11,25 p), to whom the Father reveals His secrets, each one of them personally being a son of God (Mt 6,4.6.18). But He added something new by going beyond even the universalism which a late current of Judaism had attained. Although the latter attached the quality of creator to the paternity of God, it had not yet concluded that God was the Father of all men and that all men are brothers* (cf Is 64,7; Ml 2,10). Moreover, although it was thought that divine mercy extended to "all flesh" (Si 18,13), the qualification was generally added that only the sons of God, the just of Israel, received the full effect of that mercy (Ws 12,19-22; cf 2 M 6,13-16). Concretely, they were the only ones to whom the theme of Deuteronomy (Dt 8,5) concerning a "correction from Yahweh" inspired by paternal love was applied (Pr 3,11f; cf He 12,5-13). For Jesus, on the contrary, the community of the "little ones," still limited in fact to only the repentant Jews who do the Father's will (Mt 21,31ff), also included the pagans (Mt 25,32ff), who will supplant the "sons of the kingdom" (Mt 8,12).

For this new Israel*, which by right was already opened to all, the Father provided generously the necessary goods (Mt 6,26.32; 7, 11), above all, the Holy Spirit (cf Lk 11,13), and showed the immensity of His tender mercy (Lk 15,11-32). The only thing necessary was that one humbly acknowledge this unique paternity (Mt 23,9) and live like a child* who prays to his Father (7,7-11), trusting in Him (6,25-34), submitting to Him, while imitating His universal love (5,44f), His tendency to pardon* (18,33; cf 6,14f), His mercy (Lk 6,36; cf Lv 19,2), and His perfection itself (Mt 5,48). Although this theme of imitation of the Father is not new (Lk 6,36 is found again in a targum), the insistence on its application to mutual pardon and love of enemies* is new. God is never so much our Father as when loving and forgiving, and we are never so much sons as when we act in the same way toward our brothers*.

V. THE FATHER OF JESUS

1. *God is revealed by Jesus as Father of an only Son.* That God is His Father in a unique sense, Jesus made known by His way of distinguishing "my Father" (vg Mt 7,21; 11,27 p; Lk 2,49; 22,29) from "your Father" (vg Mt 5,45; 6,1; 7,11; Lk 12,32); by presenting Himself as the "Son*" (Mk 13,32), beloved Son, that is, unique (Mk 12,6 p; cf 1,11 p; 9,7 p); and especially by expressing consciousness of a union so close between them both that He penetrated all the secrets of the Father, secrets that He alone could reveal (Mt 11,25ff). The transcendent meaning of those words *Father* and *Son*, which (at least in the formula "Son of God" that was usually avoided by Jesus) was not in itself evident and was not perceived by His

questioners (in Lk 4,41 Son of God stands for Christ), was confirmed by the meaning of the title "Son* of Man" and through the claim of an authority that went beyond human authority. It was also confirmed by the prayer which Jesus addresses to His Father, saying "Abba" (Mk 14, 36), which is equivalent to our "papa": a familiarity of which there is no example before Jesus, and which manifested an intimacy that is without equal.

2. *In the mystery of His paternity*, God gives Himself an equal. The early theologians make explicit what the synoptics said about "the Father of Our Lord Jesus Christ" (R 15,6; 2 Co 1,3; 11,31; E 1,3; 1 P 1,3). They speak of Him often by His name of Father, and they are also thinking about Him when they simply say *ho Theos* (vg 2 Co 13,13). Paul treats of the relations of Father and Son as actors in salvation. However, when he speaks of the "proper Son of God" in comparing Him with adopted sons (R 8,15.29.32), and when he attributes to the "beloved Son" the creative work itself (Col 1, 13.15ff), this presupposes that there is in God* a mystery of transcendent paternity.

John went still further. He called Jesus the only-begotten, that is, the only and beloved Son* (Jn 1,14.18; 3,16.18; 1 Jn 4,9). He stressed the unique character of the fatherhood corresponding to that sonship (Jn 20,17); the perfect unity of wills (5,30) and activities (5,17-20) of the Father and the Son, manifested by the miraculous works* that one gave the other to accomplish (5,36); their mutual immanence (10, 38; 14,10f; 17,21); their mutual intimacy of knowledge* and love (5,20.23; 10,15; 14,31; 17, 24ff); their mutual glorification (12,28; 13,31f; 17,1.4f). The Jews, passing from the plane of action to the plane of being, understood Jesus' declaration concerning equality with God (5, 17f; 10,33; 19,7). They were right: God is truly Jesus' "own Father"; Jesus existed before Abraham (8,57), as the divine Logos, destined to manifest the Father (Jn 1,1.8).

3. *In His incarnate state, the Son remains submissive to the Father*. Although His dignity as Son made Jesus equal to God the Father, according to Christ Himself (vg Mt 26,39 p; 11, 26f; 24,36 p) and the authors of the NT the Father is not any less the possessor of His paternal prerogatives. It is to the Father that the early kerygma (vg Ac 2,24) and Paul (vg 1 Th 1, 10; 2 Co 4,14) attributed Jesus' resurrection. The Father has the initiative regarding salvation. He is the one who chooses and calls the Christian (vg 2 Th 2,13f) or the apostle (vg G 1,15f). He is the one who justifies (vg R 3,26.30; 8,30). Jesus is only the necessary mediator*; and the Father sends Him (G 4,4; R 8,3; Jn *passim*), delivers Him (R 8,32), gives Him a work to do (vg Jn 17,4), words to speak (12,49), men to save (6,39f). The Father is the beginning and end of all things (1 Co 8,6). The Son who acts only in dependence on Him (Jn 5,19; 14,10; 15,10) will submit to Him (1 Co 15,28) as to His leader (11,3) at the end of time.

VI. FATHER OF CHRISTIANS

If men have the power to become children of God (Jn 1,12), it is because Jesus is by nature a child of God. The Christ of the synoptics brought the first glimmer of light on this point by identifying Himself with His own (vg Mt 18, 5; 25,40), by calling Himself their brother (28, 10), and once by even designating Himself with them under the common name of "sons" (17, 26). But the full light came to us through Paul. For it is Paul who tells us that God freed us from slavery* and adopted us as sons (G 4,5ff; R 8,14-17; E 1,5) through baptismal faith which makes us a single being in Christ (G 3,26ff); and Christ is the eldest son, who shares with His brothers* the paternal heritage (R 8,17.29; Col 1,18). The Spirit*, because He is the interior agent of this adoption, is also its witness; and He attests to it by inspiring in us the same prayer of Christ to whom He conforms us, "Abba" (G 4,6; R 8,14ff.29). Since the resurrection, the Church by reciting the "Our Father" expresses the awareness of being loved by the very love with which God embraces His only Son (cf 1 Jn 3,1); and that is what Luke undoubtedly suggests by making us say only: "Father!" (Lk 11,2) as Christ did.

Our filial life, manifested in prayer, is also expressed by fraternal charity; for if we love our Father, we cannot fail to love His children, our brothers: "Whoever loves the one who begot him, loves also the one who is born of him" (1 Jn 5,1).

→Abraham I 3, II 2—Authority OT I 1.2; NT II 2—Blessing II 2, III 2, IV 2.3—Brother OT 2 —Burial 1—Earth OT II 1—Education I 1— Election OT I 3 b—Example—Farewell OT— Fatherland OT 1—Fruitfulness—Generation— God NT IV—House I 1—Jesus Christ I 2— Love I NT 4—Man I 1 d. 2 a—Mercy O; NT I

FEAR OF GOD

The OT is usually characterized as a law of fear, while the NT is called the law of love. This rough approximation omits important distinctions. If fear is especially important in the OT, the basic principles of the law of love are nonetheless present. On the other hand, the new law does not abrogate a fear which is the heart of any genuinely religious disposition. In both Old and New Testaments there is a real though diverse blending of fear and love*. It is more important to distinguish religious fear from the natural human fright experienced by every man in the face of calamities of nature or attacks from an enemy (Jr 6,25; 20,10). Only religious fear pertains to biblical revelation.

I. FROM HUMAN FRIGHT TO THE FEAR OF GOD

When a man experiences imposing, extraordinary, or terrifying phenomena, he spontaneously senses a presence that is superior to him and before which he is reduced to insignificance. This is an ambiguous sentiment, where the sacred is revealed under the aspect of the *tremendum* without further and more exact precision. The OT balances this sentiment with a genuine knowledge of the living God* who shows His greatness through many events in the created universe. The religious fear of Israel when God appears at Sinai (Ex 20,18f) has for its source the majesty of the one God, the same cause of Moses' fear at the burning bush (Ex 3,6) and Jacob's fear after his vision in the night (Gn 28,17). Nonetheless, when fear arises, on the occasion of cosmic signs indicating God's wrath* (storms* and earthquake), there is a certain admixture of a dread which is less than purely religious and which is characteristic of the traditional description of the day* of the Lord (Is 2,10.19; cf Ws 5,2). Such, for example, was the emotion of the guards at the sepulcher on Easter morning (Mt 28,4). But reverential fear, which shows itself in adoration*, is quite different in that it is the normal reaction of the believer before divine manifestations, as in the case of Gideon (Jg 6,22f), of Isaiah (Is 6,5), or of those who witnessed the miracles of Jesus (Mk 6,51 p; Lk 5,9-11; 7,16) and of the apostles (Ac 2,43). The fear of God involves different converging properties which together serve to draw a man toward deeper faith*.

II. FEAR OF GOD AND CONFIDENCE IN GOD

In the true life of faith, fear is held in balance by an opposite feeling which is confidence* in God. Even God's appearances to men are not meant to terrify but to reassure: "Fear not!" (Jg 6,23; Dn 10,12; cf Lk 1,13.30), a phrase Christ uses again when He walks on the waters (Mk 6,50). God is not a tyrant wary of His power, but a father whose providence surrounds men and provides for their needs. His "Fear not" accompanies His promises* to the patriarchs (Gn 15,1; 26,24) and is again heard in the eschatological promises to His afflicted people (Is 41,10.13f; 43,1.5; 44,2), as well as in Jesus' promises to His "little flock" which was to receive the kingdom from the Father (Lk 12,32; Mt 6,25-34). God spoke in similar terms to the prophets to strengthen them for their mission. They will meet opposition, but they should not fear (Jr 1,8; Ez 2,6; 3,9; cf 2 K 1,15).

So it is that faith in God is the source of an assurance that completely expels purely human fear. When Israel has to meet its enemies in war, the divine message is the same, "Fear not!" (Nm 21,34; Dt 3,2; 7,18; 20,1; Js 8,1). In times far more dangerous, Isaiah repeats this to Ahaz (Is 7,4) and to Hezekiah (Is 37,6). To the apostles facing persecution Jesus says not to fear those who kill the body (Mt 10,26-31 p). A lesson so often repeated finally translates itself into life so that with confidence in God the true believers banish all fear from their hearts (Ps 23,4; 27,1; 91,5-13).

III. FEAR OF GOD'S CHASTISEMENTS

There is another aspect of God's dealing with men that easily instills in them a salutary fear. In the OT God reveals Himself as judge*, and the proclamation of the law* of Sinai is accompanied by a threat of sanctions (Ex 20,5ff; 23, 21). Throughout her history, Israel's disappointments are proposed by the prophets as so many palpable and providential indications of God's anger—a weighty motive for standing in fear before God! In this light, the law of God is rightly a law of fear. Similarly, Ps 2 recalls the threat of divine chastisement in order to bring foreign nations to submit to the Lord's anointed one (Ps 2,11f).

This portion of biblical teaching should not be minimized since the NT itself stresses the wrath* and judgment* of God. This frightening prospect only those hardened in evil need fear (Jm 5,1; Ap 6,15f; Lk 23,30). For others who know the depths of their sinfulness (cf Lk 5,8) but who trust in the justifying grace* of God (R 3,23f), the NT opens up a new state of mind, not that of servile fear but the attitude of adopted sons of God (R 8,15), where an inner disposition of love* expels fear. Fear supposes a punishment (1 Jn 4,18); but he who loves no longer fears punishment, even if in his own heart he knows he deserves to be condemned (1 Jn 3,20f). This is the sense in which the NT is a law of love. At the same time, even in OT times there were men who lived under the law of love, just as now there are those who have not advanced beyond the law of fear.

IV. FEAR OF GOD AND RELIGION

On the whole, the fear of God can be understood in so wide and profound a sense that it is simply identified with religion itself. It is characteristic of Deuteronomy to associate the fear of God with love of God, with the observance of His commandments, with the service of God (Dt 6,2.5.13), while Is 11,2 sees in the fear of God one of the gifts of the Spirit* of God. The sages speak of it as the beginning of wisdom* (Pr 1,7; Ps 111,10), and Ben Sira composes a litany which shows that fear of God is practically equivalent to piety* (Si 1,11-20). In this sense it merits the happiness extolled in several pslams (Ps 112,1; 128,1), for "the mercy* of God extends from age to age to those who fear Him" (Lk 1,50; cf Ps 103,17). While the day of judgment* causes sinners to tremble with fear, it is also the day in which God "will reward those who fear His name" (Ap 11,18).

Though the NT does preserve the shade of meaning of reverential fear stirred by the constant prospect of God as judge (2 Co 7,1; E 5,21; Col 3,22), especially when there is question of people "who do not fear God" (Lk 18,2.4; 23, 40), ordinarily the NT rather understands fear of God in the deeper sense of a basic virtue. "God shows no partiality, but in every nation

favors men who fear Him and live justly" (Ac 10,34f). Such fear of God is the way to salvation through faith.

→Abraham I 2—Adoration—Anguish—Beatitude OT I 2—Cares 2—Confidence—Holy OT II—Piety OT 2; NT 2—Presence of God OT II —Wisdom OT I 3.

PA & PG wjw

FEASTS

In all religions, a feast is an essential element of worship*. The congregation pays homage, usually in a spirit of joy*, for one or other aspect of human life, through certain rites designated for certain times*. They return thanks and implore the favor of the divinity. Characteristic of the feast in the Bible is its relation to sacred history, because it achieves contact with God who is constantly acting on behalf of His chosen people; yet these feasts are also rooted in the common ground of humanity.

OT

I. ORIGIN OF JEWISH FEASTS

The recurrence of the lunar cycle, which determined the Israelite month, quite naturally provided an occasion for feasts: sometimes it was the full moon (Ps 81,4), usually the new moon (*Neomenia:* 1 S 20,5; 2 K 4,23; Am 8,5), and finally the Sabbath* which established a weekly* rhythm (Ex 20.8-11). The solar cycle brought in the feast of the New Year, a feast known to all civilizations. This feast was joined first to the feast of the Harvest in autumn (Ex 23,16), then the Passover* in the spring (Ex 12, 2). And from this liturgy are derived certain rites of the Day of Expiation* (cf Lv 16).

In addition to this structure established by the rhythm of the stars*, the daily life of the Israelite, pastoral and later agricultural, determined feasts which tend to become confused with the above feasts. On the occasion of the Passover*, the pastoral feast of spring, the offering of the first-fruits* of the flock took place. The working of the land gave rise to three great feasts: the Azymes in spring, the Harvests* or Weeks in summer, the Harvest or vintage* in autumn (Ex 23,14-17; 34,18.22). Deuteronomy unites the Passover to the Azymes and gives to the feast of the Harvest the name of the feast of Tents (Dt 16,1-17). Certain rites of the current feasts can only be understood by reason of their pastoral or agrarian connections.

After the exile some secondary feasts appeared: Purim (Es 9,26; cf 2 M 15,36f), Dedication and the Day of Nicanor (1 M 4,52-59; 7,49; 2 M 10,5f; 15,36f).

II. THE MEANING OF THE JEWISH FEASTS

The different feasts take on a new meaning in terms of the past which they recall, the future which they proclaim, and the present whose demands they reveal.

1. *Celebration acknowledging the great works of Yahweh.* Israel praises its God with different titles. The Creator is commemorated each Sabbath (Ex 20,11); the deliverer from Egypt is present not only on the day of the Sabbath but also when the feast of the Passover is celebrated (Dt 5,12-15; 16,1); the feast of Tents recalls the journey in the desert* and the time of Israel's betrothal to Yahweh (Lv 23,42f; cf Jr 2,2); and finally, late Judaism attached the gift of the Law at Sinai to the feast of Weeks (in Greek, Pentecost*). Thus the agrarian feasts become commemorative feasts: in the prayer of the Israelite offering his first-fruits, thanksgiving stands for both the gifts of the earth and the great deeds of the past (Dt 26,5-10).

2. *A joyous anticipation of the future.* The feast makes real by an authentic hope* the final goal of salvation. God's past acts assure the future of the people. The commemoration of the exodus foretells and guarantees a new* exodus*: Israel will be finally and completely freed one day (Is 43,15-21; 52,1-12; 55,12f), and the reign of Yahweh will extend to all the nations* who will go up in pilgrimage* to Jerusalem for the feast of Tents (Ze 14,16-19). How "completely taken up in joy*" the people will then be (Ps 118; 122; 126): are they not then in the presence of God (Dt 16,11-15; Lv 23,40)?

3. *Present needs.* But this joy is genuine only if it comes from a contrite and purified heart. Even the psalms of joy remind men of these needs: "O my people, if you would but listen!" is spoken at the time of the feast of Tents (Ps 81,9ff). More exactly, the feast of Expiation speaks of the desire* for a profound conversion through collective confessions* (Ps 106; Ne 9, 5-37; Dn 9,4-19). For their part, the prophets protest incessantly against the illusory security which a joyous liturgy offered by unfaithful hearts can give: "I hate, I despise your feasts. . ." (Am 5,21; cf Ho 2,13; Is 1,13f). By these seemingly destructive oracles, an appeal is made not for an actual suppression of the feasts, but for the fullness of their meaning, an encounter with the living God (Ex 19,17).

NT

I. FROM THE JEWISH FEASTS TO THE ETERNAL FEAST

Jesus certainly observed the Jewish feasts of His time, but first He indicated that His person and His work alone give them their full meaning: so with the feast of Tents (Jn 7,37ff; 8,12; cf Mt 21,1-10 p) or the dedication (Jn 10,22-38). Most importantly, He deliberately put the new covenant of His sacrifice within a paschal setting (Mt 26,2.17ff.28 p; Jn 13,1; 19,36; 1 Co 5,7f). By this new and final Passover, Jesus also completed the offering of the feast of Expiation because His blood gives access to the true sanctuary (He 10,19) and to the great festive assembly of the heavenly Jerusalem (12,22f). From this time on the true feast is celebrated in heaven. With palms in hand, as at the feast of Tents (Ap 7,9), the multitude of the chosen people, redeemed by the blood of the true paschal Lamb* (5,8-14; 7,10-14), sing continually a new* hymn (14,3) to the glory of the Lamb and His Father. The feast of the Passover has become the eternal feast of heaven.

II. CHRISTIAN FEASTS

If the heavenly Passover has restored the numerous Jewish feasts to an eschatological unity, it now also gives a new meaning to the many feasts of the Church on earth. In contrast with the Jewish feasts, the Church's feasts commemorate an event completed once and for all and which has eternal value. But like the Jewish feasts, the Christian feasts continue to be subject to the rhythm of the seasons and the earth while attached to the major events in the life of Christ. While one must take care not to give an excessive value to these feasts (cf G 4,10) which remain as a shadow of the true feast (cf Col 2,16), nevertheless the Church need not worry about this multiplicity of feasts.

The Church focuses first of all on the observance of the paschal mystery commemorated in the eucharist* which brings together the community each Sunday, the day* of the resurrection of the Lord (Ac 20,7; 1 Co 16,2; Ap 1,10). It is the beginning of the week* which ended on the Sabbath, and it indicates the radical novelty of the Christian feast, a unique feast whose radiance illumines the entire year, and whose riches are developed in a festive cycle centered on Easter.

In addition, the Church will be able to rediscover the natural cycles (vg the Ember days) by calling on the riches of its Jewish patrimony. All this will come through re-enacting it through the life of Christ and by orientating the mystery to the eternal heavenly feasts.

→Day of the Lord NT III 3—Harvest I—Joy OT II 1—Meal II, III—Passover—Pentecost—Pilgrimage—Rest I 3—Sabbath—Time OT I 2; NT II 3—Vintage 1—Week—White—Worship.
DS & MFL afmcg

FIGURE

The Greek word *typos* and Latin *figura* are used by theologians to designate the most original symbolisms to be found in the language of the Bible—prototypes. The sacred books employ many other terms for the same purpose, terms that express the same connected ideas: *antitypos* (an answer to the *typos*), *hypodeigma* (example, hence that which announces, reproduces, anticipates), *paradeigma* (example), *parabolē* (symbol), *skia* (shadow), *mimēma* (imitation). In a general sense, all these terms are related to image (*eikōn*), model *typos*: 1 Th 1,7; but they most frequently admit a particular shade of meaning which brings them close to type/figure.

OT

Like every religious language the language of the OT has frequent recourse to symbolism, without waiting to define its nature and sources. But one easily identifies the fundamental concepts from which it draws its use of symbols. That is all that need concern us here.

I. EXEMPLARIST SYMBOLISM: THE HEAVENLY MODEL AND ITS EARTHLY IMITATIONS

In the wake of all the ancient religions, the OT represents the divine world, the celestial world, as the sacred prototype for the image from which the world here below is organized. Like a king, God dwells in a heavenly palace (Mi 1,3); He is surrounded by a court of servants (Is 6,1ff), etc. And since the end of worship is to put man in relation with God, one tries to reproduce this ideal model, so that the celestial world becomes in some sort placed within the reach of man. It is thus that Jerusalem and its temple are an imitation of the divine palace with which it is in a certain manner identified (cf Ps 48,1-4). That is why the priestly code shows God on Sinai communicating to Moses a model to which he must conform the tabernacle (hb. *tabnīt*; gr. *typos*, Ex 25,40, or *paradeigma,* Ex 25,9). This model is a kind of architect's plan (cf 1 Ch 28,11: *tabnīt, paradeigma*) set up by God after His own dwelling. Likewise, according to Ws 9,8, the temple built by Solomon is an "imitation *(mimēma)* of the sacred tent which God had prepared for Himself from the beginning." The exemplarist symbolism is not altogether removed from the Platonic theory of *Ideas*. Indeed, on this point, all Plato did was to work out philosophically an idea that was current in the religious traditions of the ancient East.

II. ESCHATOLOGICAL SYMBOLISM: THE HISTORY OF SALVATION AND ITS FINAL CONSUMMATION

1. *The biblical concept of sacred history.* The ancient mythologies applied the same exemplarist principles to the cosmic cycles (return of days and seasons, etc.) and to the fundamental experiences of human history (royal accession, war, etc.). Here and there they saw the earthly reflections of a divine history which took place before all time, a primordial archetype of all the cosmic future and all human activity. This archetype, indefinitely imitated in time, endowed the things of earth with their sacred meaning. That is why the myth was enacted in worship by a ritual drama, in order to put men in connection with the activity of the gods. Now biblical revelation, by eliminating polytheism, emptied of its content the only sacred history known by the neighboring

pagans. For them God's activity was limited to His creation. But in a new perspective, they discovered another kind of sacred history, of which paganism was entirely ignorant: the history of God's plan*, which from the beginning develops in time* in a straight line and not in a circle until its full realization, which will come at the end of time, when all things come to an end.

2. *The meaning of the events of sacred history.* The end of God's plan will be clearly revealed only when He takes a body in the eschatological event. However, God has already begun to give an obscure knowledge of it to His people beginning with the events of their history. Experiences such as the exodus*, the covenant* of Sinai, the entry into the promised land*, etc., were not mere accidents devoid of meaning. Acts of God in human history, they bore in themselves the mark of the end which God was pursuing in directing the course in history, in sketching progressively its characteristics. That is why they could already nourish the faith of the people of God. That is why the prophets also, evoking in their eschatological prophecies the purpose of God's plan, show a most perfect resumption of past experiences: new* exodus* (Is 43,16-21), new covenant* (Jr 31,31-34), new entry into the promised land toward a new Jerusalem* (Is 49,9-23), etc. Thus, therefore, sacred history with all its component elements (events, persons, institutions) possesses that which might be called an eschatological symbolism: a partial manifestation of God's plan on a level hitherto imperfect, it shows in a veiled manner the term toward which this plan is moving.

3. *Eschatology and beginnings.* The same principle is eminently applied to the beginning of sacred history, the creation*. For if there is nothing more in the biblical revelation of a divine primordial history, it keeps alive that primordial act by which God began His plan, unveiling from the beginning the ends He wished to pursue here below. Eschatology, God's final act, ought to find its characteristics in God's initial act. According to the prophetic oracles, it will not be merely a new exodus, etc. It will be a new creation (Is 65,17), similar to the first, since it will take up again the same design; it will be more perfect, since it will remove the obstacles, sin* and death*, which caused the first plans of God to fail. They are, therefore, the same images of perfection and of

happiness which serve to evoke, at both ends of time, the primitive paradise* and paradise regained (vg Ho 2,20-24; Is 11,5-9; 51,3; 65,19-25; Ez 36,35). Between the two, sacred history unfolds, consciously lived by the people of the old covenant, who await its consummation in the new covenant.

4. *Worship and sacred history.* Worship* in the OT is not mythical history of the gods to be made present in a ritual drama to make men participate in the history. But since sacred history remains a divine action accomplished in human time, the liturgical feasts* acquired little by little the function of commemoration of (and in this sense of "making present" for the faith of Israel) the lofty deeds of which it was made up. The Sabbath* becomes a memorial of creation (Gn 2,2f; Ex 31,12ff); the Pasch, a memorial of the exodus (Ex 12,26f); Pentecost*, a memorial of the covenant on Sinai (in post-biblical Judaism); Tabernacles, a memorial of the wandering in the desert (Lv 23,42f). And since, on the other hand, these past events were omens of final salvation, their cult commemoration is a bearer of hope: Israel recalls the historic blessings of God only to await with greater faith the eschatological blessing of which they are the veiled announcements woven into the web of history.

III. MORAL EXEMPLARISM

Finally, the OT knew a moral exemplarism in which typical men of the past are models provided by God for the instruction of His people. It is thus that Enoch was an example *(hypodeigma)* of penitence (Si 44,16). An example of this kind is frequently exploited in the sapiential books. It acquires a peculiar strength when it rests on the eschatological symbolism of sacred history, such as we have just now defined it (cf Ws 10—19).

It is clear that the doctrine of prefigurations is already quite alive in the OT. Flowing from a concept of sacred history which properly belongs to biblical revelation, it differs profoundly from the simple exemplarist symbolism which the OT knew and exploited as occasion offered. It gives a language to the prophetic oracles, thanks to which they can evoke in advance the mystery of salvation. It is also bound even to the dialectic of revelation. The NT will finish the demonstration.

I. THE ATTITUDES OF JESUS

Jesus is aware of bringing the time of preparation to its end (Mk 1,15) and of beginning here below the state of things announced by the prophetic oracles (cf Mt 11,4ff; Lk 4,17ff). Henceforth all sacred history that transpired under the rule of the first covenant acquires its definitive meaning in the deeds He accomplishes, the institutions He establishes, the drama He lives. Thus, to define His work and make it intelligible, He compares it intentionally with the figurative elements contained in that history. The community He created will be called a Church* (Mt 16,18), that is to say, an assembly for worship, similar to that of Israel in the desert (cf Ac 7,38); it will rest on twelve apostles*, whose number* recalls that of the tribes, the fundamental structure of the people of Israel* (cf Mt 19,28). The same is to be said for the supper, which explains the meaning of His cross and makes the reality present under the sacramental signs—it is understood in relation to the Pasch (Lk 22,16 p) and to the covenant on Sinai (Lk 22,20); the promised bread of life, His body, surpasses in its effects the manna* which was an imperfect image of it (Jn 6,58). These examples show how Jesus, accepting the eschatological symbolisms of sacred history, exploits them to evoke concretely the mystery of salvation come at the end of time, inaugurated in His person and in His life, called to be rendered present in the history of His Church and to be consummated in eternity when human time shall have come to an end. By that He makes it understood how in Him the events and the institutions of the OT acquire their full meaning, veiled in part until then, but now completely unveiled by the event toward which they were tending.

II. DEVELOPING BIBLICAL FIGURES

Following Jesus, the sacred authors of the NT as a whole made an unceasing appeal to the figurative principle, sometimes to show that the mystery of salvation was developing "in conformity with the Scriptures," sometimes to define it in a language enriched with religious significance. It is thus that Matthew transfers to Jesus what Hosea said about Israel, "Son of God" (Mt 2,15; cf Ho 11,1), while John applies to Christ on the cross the description of the Paschal Lamb* (Jn 19,36). In both cases the

fulfilling* of the Scriptures I the fulfilling of the biblical a number of places the do the NT also takes its point historical experience of the peop whether it be because the prophetical oracles have transposed their data in referring them to eschatology (thus Ap 21 takes up Is 62), or that this transfer of texts belongs properly to the authors of the NT (thus 1 P 2,9, referring to Ex 19,5f). However, we must wait for St. Paul and the epistle to the Hebrews to see the theological principle of the prefigurations clearly defined.

III. ST. PAUL

For Paul, the personages and the facts of sacred history contain the figures (it is the meaning which he gives to the word *typos*) announcing the mystery of Christ and of Christian realities. From the beginning Adam* was a figure of the Adam to come (R 5,14). Later, the events of the exodus* happened figuratively (1 Co 10,6); they are "figures which concern us upon whom the ends of the world have come" (1 Co 10,11). The reality prefigured by these types is our effective participation in the mystery of Christ made sure by the Christian sacraments. In 1 P 3,21, also, baptism is called an antitype of the *flood*. Moral exemplarism flows easily from this figurative interpretation of sacred history. The chastisements of our fathers in the desert are a lesson for us (cf 1 Co 10,7ff), and they announce the definitive condemnation of unfaithful Christians. The destruction of Sodom and the preservation of Lot are an example *(hypodeigma)* for the godless of the future (2 P 2,6). Inversely, the faith of Abraham* "is aimed at us also" (R 4,24) so that "they who profess the faith are sons of Abraham" (G 3,7).

In prolonging the lines of such a typology, Paul allows himself to allegorize certain pages of Scripture, where he finds symbols of Christian realities. He says so explicitly in G 4,24, when he transfers to Christians that which Genesis said of Isaac, child of the promise. This allegorization is not confused purely and simply with the typology which is its foundation. It remains a practical method used to adapt biblical texts to another object than that which they had in view at first, and free to place secondary meaning on all the details they contain. Paul, moreover, was aware that the biblical figures were no more than deficient images with to the realities now unveiled. Thus, ‚sh worship contained only "the shadow of ‚ngs to come" *(skia),* the reality *(sōma)* being ‚he body of Christ (Col 2,17).

IV.   THE EPISTLE TO THE HEBREWS

In St. Paul, it was the eschatological symbolism, already employed by the prophetic oracles, which flowed in pairs of words like *typos/antitypos* and *skia/sōma.* In the epistle to the Hebrews this eschatological symbolism crosses with an exemplarist symbolism common to oriental religions, to Platonism, and to the OT itself. This is because the mystery* of Christ, the sacrifice which He accomplishes, the salvation which He brings, are at once heavenly things (He 8,5; 9,23; 12,22), eternal by nature (5,9; 9,12; 13,20), and the "things to come" (6,5; 10,1), come at the end of ages (9,26). These are the true realities (8,2; 9,24), to which our fathers in the faith, the men of the OT, could only aspire (11,16.20), while we Christians have already tasted of them by the initiation of baptism (6,4). In fact, the first covenant* contained only anticipated reproductions of them *(hypodeigma,* 8,5; 9,23), shadows *(skia,* 8,5), replicas *(antitypos,* 9,24) of a model which then existed in heaven, although it was to be revealed here below only by Christ. This model *(typos)* which was shown to Moses on the mountain when he built the tabernacle (8,5=Ex 25,40; cf Ac 7,44) is the sacrifice* of Christ, who has entered the heavenly sanctuary as high priest of the blessings to come in order to accomplish the new covenant (9,11f). The ecclesial realities no longer only enclose a shadow *(skia)* of blessings to come, but an image* *(eikōn)* which contains all their substance and permits a mysterious participation in them. Thus we have defined the sacramental economy of the new covenant, in opposition to the old economy and its figurative worship.

In this technical language the word *typos* is clothed with a meaning different from that which it had in St. Paul, since it no longer designates the prefigurations of the NT in the OT, but the act of Christ, who, at the end of time, effects the event of salvation. There is here a clear trace of exemplarist symbolism, the relation of the OT to the mystery of Christ being the same as that of the cultic things of the earth to their heavenly archetype. However, since this archetype is at the same time the end of sacred history, it is so in virtue of an eschato-

logical symbolism of which the things of the OT are replicas *(antitypos):* in Christ who belongs at once to time and to eternity, the relation of earth to heaven and the relation of figurative history to its term are blended, or rather identified.

As a matter of fact, we discover in other passages that the author of the epistle is as attentive as Paul to the horizontal dimension of typology, even if his language suggests above all the vertical dimension. He discovers in fact in the events of the OT the prefiguration of the event of salvation: Isaac on the block is a symbol *(parabolē)* of Christ dead and risen (11, 19); the rest* of the promised land in which our Fathers entered symbolizes the divine repose to which the Christian economy introduces us (4, 9f; cf 12,23). From this eschatological symbolism flows naturally a moral exemplarism: the Hebrews in the desert* are for us an example *(hypodeigma,* 4,11) of disobedience, and their punishment foretells that which awaits us if we like them are unfaithful. On the contrary, the saints of the OT are for us an example of faith (11).

The principle of prefigurations, sketched in the OT, constantly employed in the NT, explicitly defined (with appreciable nuances) by St. Paul and the epistle to the Hebrews, is then essential to biblical revelation, the development of which it permits us to understand. From the one to the other Testament, it sheds light on the continuity of a life of faith led by the people of God at different levels, of which the first foretold "by means of figures" that which was to follow it.

→Adam II 2—Fulfill—Image—Revelation OT II 1 a—Sign.

PG wjy

FIRE

From the time of Abraham's election, the symbol of fire shines out in the history of God's relations with His people (Gn 15,17). This biblical revelation has a different dimension from the philosophies of nature of the religions which divinize fire. Israel undoubtedly shares with all the ancient peoples the theory of four elements; but in its religion, fire has value only as a sign, which men must transcend in order to find God. In fact it is always in the course of a personal dialogue that Yahweh manifests

Himself "in the form of fire;" yet this fire is not the only symbol which is used to translate the essence of divinity. Sometimes fire is seen associated with contrary symbols such as breath, water, or wind; or else it changes itself into light*.

OT

I. THEOPHANIES

1. In the *fundamental experience* of the people in the desert*, fire expresses not the glory* of God in the first place, but the holiness*, which is both attractive and yet to be feared. On Mount Horeb Moses is drawn by the sight of a bush enveloped in fire yet not "consumed" by it. But the divine voice tells him that he would not be able to approach it if God had not called him and if he had not been purified (Ex 3,2f). On Sinai the mountain smokes from the fire which surrounds it (19,18) without being destroyed. Although the people tremble with fear and are not allowed to go near, Moses is again called to go up before God who reveals Himself. When God, therefore, manifests Himself as a devouring fire, He does so not to consume everything along the way, since He calls those whom it purifies.

Further experience occurring at the same place helps to show more clearly the symbolic value of fire. Elijah*, the prophet full of a zeal* that is similar to fire (Si 48,1), seeks the presence of Yahweh on Sinai. Following the hurricane and the trembling of the earth, he sees fire. But "Yahweh was not within the fire." Here is a different symbol which makes known the passing of God: a light breeze (1 K 19,12). Then later when Elijah was carried to heaven in a fiery chariot (2 K 2,11), the fire will only be one symbol among others to express the visitation of the living God.

2. The *prophetic tradition* tends also to place the sign of fire within a context of religious symbolism. Isaiah sees only smoke after his call*, and he feels he may die for having come near the divine holiness*; but as he comes out of the vision, his lips* have been purified by a glowing coal of fire (Is 6). In the inaugural vision of Ezekiel, storm* and fire are associated with the rainbow which gleams in the clouds, but then the appearance of a man emerges from it. This emergence recalls the luminous cloud* of the exodus rather than the theophany of Sinai (Ez 1). In the Apocalypse of Daniel, fire makes up part of the background in which the divine presence* shows itself (Dn 7,10), but it plays a special role in the description of the judgment* (7,11).

3. In interpreting the theophany of the desert, *the Deuteronomic and priestly traditions* make explicit the double significance of the symbol of fire: the revelation* of the living God and the demand for purity by the holy God. God spoke (Dt 4,12; 5,4.22.24) and gave the tablets of the Law (9,10) from the midst of fire in order to make Israel understand that He is not to be represented by images*. But there is also question here of a destructive fire (5,25; 18,16) which terrifies men (5,5). Only the chosen of God knows for certain that he can encounter this presence without dying (4,33). Once they reached this stage Israel could, without running the risk of confusing God with a natural element, regard their God as "consuming fire" (4,24; 6,15). This expression is simply another way of describing the theme of divine jealousy (Ex 20,5; 34,14; Dt 5,9; 6,15). Fire symbolizes the intransigence of God before sin*. It consumes what it encounters, just as God does the hardened sinner. He acts otherwise with His chosen people, but always in such a way that He must transform anyone whom He approaches.

II. IN THE COURSE OF HISTORY

1. *Sacrifice by fire.* An analogous representation of God as a devouring fire is also found in the liturgical use of holocausts. Perhaps it is Israel's desire for complete purification, and even more its desire to make in this way an irrevocable gift, which it expressed in the consumption of a victim the smoke of whose burning rose up to heaven. Here again the fire has only a symbolic value and its use does not sanctify any rite: it is forbidden to consume by fire a first-born son (Lv 18,21; cf Gn 22,7). But this symbolic value is of great importance in the official worship. A perpetual fire must be provided on the altar (Lv 6,2-6), without being made by the hand of man. There was a curse on anyone who dared to substitute a "profane" fire for the fire of God (Lv 9,24—10,2). Did not God miraculously intervene after the famous sacrifices of Abraham (Gn 15,17), Gideon (Jg 6,21), David (1 Ch 21,26), Solomon (2 Ch 7,1ff), and Elijah (1 K 18,38) awaiting the amazing combustion of stagnant water into a new perpetual

fire (2 M 1,18ff)? It is, then, by fire that God accepts the sacrifice of man and ratifies a covenant of worship with him.

2. *Prophets and fire.* Though the people willingly offered sacrifices, they did not want to look upon the fire of Sinai. But in the meantime the divine fire comes down among men in the person of the prophets*, most often in order to avenge the divine holiness by purifying or chastising. Moses softens the glare of divine fire, which shone forth on his face, by using a veil (Ex 34,29). But he burns with fire the "sin" which is the golden calf (Dt 9,21), and it is through fire that he takes revenge on the rebels (Nm 16,35), as he had done earlier on the Egyptians (Ex 9,23). After Moses, Elijah appears to prevail upon the lightning at will in order to annihilate the proud (2 K 1,10-14): here is a "living torch" (Si 48,1).

The literary prophets proclaim and frequently describe the wrath* of God as a fire: punishing the ungodly (Am 1,4—2,5), setting the sinful nations on fire in a gigantic holocaust which calls to mind the Canaanite liturgies of Topheth (Is 30,27-33). The conflagration in the forest of Israel reaches a point where the wickedness itself becomes fire (Is 9,17f; cf Jr 15,14; 17,4.27). But the fire is intended not merely to destroy. It purifies, and the very existence of prophets who have approached God without being consumed by it acts as a witness. The remnant* of Israel will be like a brand snatched out of the fire (Am 4,11). If Isaiah, whose lips were purified by fire (Is 6,6), begins preaching the Word without any apparent torment of soul, Jeremiah holds the Word within his heart as if it were a devouring fire which he cannot constrain (Jr 20,9). He becomes a crucible commissioned to test the people (6,27-30). He is the spokesman of God who said: "Is not my word a fire?" (23,29). In the same way on the last day, the leaders of the people must become brands of fire in the stubble (Ze 12,6), carrying out themselves the divine judgment.

3. *Wisdom and devotion.* The individuals themselves benefit from this religious experience. Second Isaiah had already spoken about the crucible of suffering which was the essence of the exile (Is 48,10). So the sages liken the chastisements which fall upon man to the effects of fire. Job is like the tragic revolt in the desert or like the victims of Elijah's fire (Jb 1,16; 15,34; 22,20); he undergoes fire as well as the great destructive waters (20,26.28). But along with this terrifying aspect of fire, there is a purifying and transforming aspect. The furnace of humiliation or of persecution tests the elect (Si 2,5; cf Dn 3). The fire itself becomes the symbol of the ardor which triumphs over all: "love* is a flame of Yahweh, and the great waters cannot extinguish it" (Ct 8,6f). Here two major symbols, fire and water, are opposed to one another. The fire prevails.

III. AT THE END OF TIME

The fire of judgment becomes a chastisement without remedy, a real fire of wrath* when it falls upon the hardened sinner. But then—for such is the force of a symbol—this fire which can no longer destroy the impurity still burns the cinders. In this way revelation shows what the life of a creature can be who refuses to be purified by the divine fire but remains burned by it. We have here something more than there is in the tradition which tells of the destruction of Sodom and Gomorrah (Gn 19,24). Taking, perhaps, as a starting point the sacrilegious rites of Gehenna (Lv 18,21; 2 K 16,3; 21,6; Jr 7,31; 19,5f), and then thoroughly deepening the prophetic images of fire (Is 29,6; 30,27-33; 31,9) and metal melting, there is progress from this to a representation of the eschatological judgment* as fire (Is 66,15f). It is a fire which tests the ore (Ze 13,9). The day* of Yahweh is like the fire from a foundry (Ml 3,2), burning like a furnace (Ml 3,19) and devouring the whole earth (Zp 1,18; 3,8), beginning with Jerusalem (Ez 10,2; Is 29,6). For this fire appears to burn from within, like that which "comes forth from the midst of Tyre" (Ez 28, 18). Within the dead bodies of the men who rebelled "the worm shall not die nor shall their fire be quenched" (Is 66,24; cf Mk 9,48). "Fire and the worms shall be within their flesh" (Jdt 16,17). But we also find here a certain ambivalence regarding the symbol: while the ungodly are delivered up to their inner fire and worms (Si 7,17), the survivors from the fire find themselves surrounded by a wall of fire which for them is Yahweh (Is 4,4f; Ze 2,9). Once they are purified Jacob and Israel themselves become a fire (Ob 18), as they participate in the life of God.

NT

With the coming of Christ, the last time* has begun, although the end of time has not yet arrived. In the NT also, fire keeps its traditional, eschatological value. But the religious reality which it signifies has already been realized in the time of the Church.

I. ESCHATOLOGICAL PERSPECTIVES

1. *Jesus*. Though He was announced as the winnower who throws the chaff into the fire (Mt 3,10) and who baptizes with fire (3,11f), Jesus rejects completely the role of judge, and He kept His hearers in expectancy of the fire of judgment by using again the classical language of the OT. He speaks of the "gehenna of fire" (5,22) and of the fire into which fruitless weeds will be thrown (13,40; cf 7,19) as well as vine branches (Jn 15,6). It will be an unquenchable fire (Mk 9,43f), where "their worm" does not die (9,48), a real blazing furnace (Mt 13,42.50). This is nothing else than a solemn echo of the OT (cf Lk 17,29).

2. *The first Christians* held on to this language while adapting it to different situations. Paul uses it to depict the end of time (2 Th 1,8). James describes rotted and rusted wealth being given over to the destructive fire (Jm 5,3). The epistle to the Hebrews shows the dreadful prospect of a fire which must devour the rebellious (He 10,27). We can also call before our imaginations the final fire for which "the heavens and earth are stored up" (2 P 3,7,12). It is in terms of this eschatological fire that faith must be purified (1 P 1,7), as well as apostolic work (1 Co 3,15), and the Christian's life tested by persecution (1 P 4,12-17).

3. *The Apocalypse* recognizes two aspects of fire: the fire of theophanies and the fire of judgment. The Son of Man appears with flaming eyes and dominates the scene (Ap 1,14; 19,12). On the one hand we find the theophany: a sea of crystal mixed with fire (15,2); on the other there is the punishment: a fiery sulphurous lake for the devil (20,10), the second death (20,14f).

II. IN THE AGE OF THE CHURCH

1. *Jesus* inaugurated a new era. He did not act immediately as John the Baptist had anticipated, to the extent that John found himself questioning his own faith (Mt 11,2-6). Jesus is opposed by the sons of thunder who wanted

Him to make fire fall from heaven upon the inhospitable Samaritans (Lk 9,54f). But if He had not been an instrument of avenging fire during His earthly life, He did fulfill the prediction of John in His own way. He did it when He declared in a sermon which is difficult to interpret, "I have come to bring fire upon the earth and how I wish it were kindled already! I have a baptism to undergo. . ." (Lk 12,49f). Was not the death of Jesus His baptism* in spirit and fire?

2. Since then *the Church* has lived by this fire which inflames the world, thanks to the sacrifice of Christ. It burned in the hearts of the travelers to Emmaus when they heard the resurrected one spoken of (Lk 24,32). It descended upon the disciples gathered together on the day of Pentecost* (Ac 2,3). This fire from heaven is not the fire of judgment. It is the fire of the theophanies which bring about the baptism of fire and spirit (Ac 1,5). Fire now symbolizes the Spirit, and if this Spirit is not explicitly said to be charity itself, the account of Pentecost* shows that His mission was to transform those who must propagate to every nation* the same message, that of the Spirit.

The Christian life is also under the sign of cultic fire, no longer that of Sinai (He 12,18), but of the fire which consumes the holocaust of our lives in worship* acceptable to God (12,29). This fire continues to be a consuming fire as it transposes the divine jealousy into a cultic consecration at every moment. But for those who have received the fire of the Spirit, the distance between man and God is overcome by God Himself who is present in the very depths of man. Perhaps this is the meaning of the enigmatic words: one becomes faithful when one has been "salted* with fire," the fire of judgment and that of Spirit (Mk 9,48f). According to a saying attributed to Jesus by Origen: "He who is close to me is close to fire; whoever is far from me is far from the kingdom."

→Baptism II, IV 1—Calamity—Cloud 1.2—Elijah OT 2; NT 2—Glory III 2—Hell—Judgment OT II 2; NT II 1—Light & Dark OT I 2—Pentecost I 1—Salt 2—Spirit of God O; NT I 1—Storm—Wrath *B* OT I 1; NT I 1—Zeal.

BR & XLD afmcg

FIRST-FRUITS

I. THE FIRST-FRUITS

1. *The Law.* We derive the term *first-fruits* (hb. *bikkūrīm*, root. *bkr*, "to be born before") from levies laid on the "first" products of the soil (hb. *rēšīt*, gr. *aparchē*), which we consider as the "best" of the crop. In Israel, as among other peoples (Egyptians, Babylonians, Greeks, Romans), the people would offer these first-fruits to a divinity. Hebrew law slowly determined this obligation and the aspects of this offering, which in the beginning was accomplished freely without precise ritual (Gn 4,3f). We could follow the steps of this evolution in the texts of different periods: Ex 22,28, the offering of "the abundance of the threshing mill and the new wine," of "the best of the first of earth's products" (Ex 23,19; cf 34,26); detailed description of the ceremony in Dt 26, 2. . .; the extension of the law to what is made from or taken from the first-fruits (Nm 15,20; Ez 44,30; Lv 23,17.20; cf 2 K 4,42; Dt 18,4; cf Tb 1,6). The sacerdotal legislation mentions two offerings of a more solemn kind, that of the first sheaf of barley in the course of the paschal week (Lv 23,10f), that of the first-fruits of the wheat harvest during Pentecost* (Ex 34,22; Lv 23,17), called for this reason the "day of the first-fruits" (Nm 28,26).

2. *The aspects of the rite.* The liturgical rite, joined to a sacrifice* in Lv 2,12, has a complex meaning. This offering is equivalent to a gesture of thanksgiving to God, the master of nature and source of all fruitfulness. The profession of faith which, according to Dt 26,3, expresses the meaning of the ceremony, adds an important precision. It contains an explicit reference to the journey from Egypt and the entrance into possession of the land of Canaan: "Behold, I bring now the first-fruits of the earth's products which Yahweh has given me" (Dt 26,10). The offering of the Hebrew is a response to the divine generosity throughout the course of history. The gift* of God calls for the gift* of man. Here is a principle of universal import.

The rite contained another aspect: the consecration to God of the first of the fruits sanctifies the whole harvest, since the part stands for the whole (R 11,16). So, by this symbolic gesture, the goods of the earth in their totality pass from the profane order into the domain of the sacred. Sanctified fruits* for a holy people! The idea

that a part, once consecrated, exercises a sanctifying influence on the mass is found elsewhere in the Bible, but dealt with on a higher level. Thus Israel (Jr 2,3), the Christians (Jm 1,18), and especially the first converts (R 16,5; 1 Co 16,15) or the virgins (Ap 14,4), are compared to the first-fruits levied on the masses and offered to God or to Christ. In the plan of salvation, a consecrated elite plays an active role in the sanctification of the world. According to 1 Co 15,20.23, Christ rises as the "first-fruits" so that all who now sleep may follow Him in glory. It is possible that Paul, in Col 1,15ff, was inspired by Pr 8,22, where the divine Wisdom is called the "first-fruits" of the divine work or power. In the order of creation, as in that of redemption, Christ fulfills the two aspects contained in the notion of first-fruits: priority and influence. The image evolves in R 8, 23, where the first-fruits of the Spirit define the anticipation and the guarantee of the ultimate salvation of Christians.

3. *Tithes.* The OT often associates the tithe with first-fruits (hb. *ma'asēr*, root "ten," or, perhaps, in the beginning, "libation." The oldest legislation makes no mention of this custom (Ex 20—23), though it had been in use for a very long time (Am 4,4; cf Gn 28,22). The tithe seems at first to be confused with the first-fruits (Dt 12,6.11.17; 14,22); on the other hand, in certain later texts (Ez 44,30; Nm 18,12. . .), the sacrificial aspect of the offering of the first-fruits weakened and people tended to reduce the first-fruits to a tax set apart for the benefit of the clergy (Ml 3,10; cf Si 45,20; Ne 10,36...). Finally, the tithe was clearly distinguished from the first-fruits and consisted of a fee of one-tenth of the fruits of the earth and one-tenth of the flocks.

II. THE FIRST-BORN

The offering of the first-born of animals *(bekorîm)* and of men, that is, "all that opens the womb," is a particular application of the law concerning first-fruits. The Code of the Covenant prescribes the "gift" to Yahweh of the first-born of man and of cattle and sheep (Ex 22,28f). The Code of Worship assigns this reason for it: "Every being that comes first from the maternal womb belongs to me: every male, every first-born of your cattle and your sheep" (Ex 34,19). But, as in the case of the first-fruits, an historical motif is superimposed on the fundamental principle of the absolute sovereignty of God: the gift is addressed to the Lord, liberator of His people, and it perpetuates the memory of the night in which Yahweh "caused to perish the first-born of the land of Egypt: those of men and those of beasts" (Ex 13,15).

If the law applies at the same time to the first-born of both animals and man, it realizes its purpose differently in each case. One sacrificed (Ex 13,15; cf Dt 15,20; Nm 18,17) or redeemed (Ex 13,13; 34,20; Lv 27,27) every first-born of the animals. As regards the first child, man "gives" it, that is to say, according to the exegesis of Ex 13,2, "consecrates" it to the Lord. How? They thought of circumcision. The barbarous custom of the immolation of children, attested to by the excavations of Gezer and of Taanach, have led certain authors to admit the existence of such sacrifices in Israel also. In primitive times they would have considered them legitimate. It is certain that, under the Phoenicians' influence, these practices were introduced among people (1 K 16,34) at an age of religious syncretism. Ahaz "makes his son pass through fire" (2 K 16,3), Manassah imitates him (2 K 21,6), and Mi 6,7 alludes to this cruel custom. But the Israelite ritual expressly condemns this aberration (Dt 12,31; 18,10ff; Jr 7,31; 19,5; 32,35; Lv 18,21; 20,2ff). Certainly, the Lord has a right to the first-fruits of life (Gn 22,2), but He refuses the sacrifice of man's children, and so the first-born will not be immolated but redeemed. The story of the sacrifice of Isaac illustrates the law of redemption-substitution prescribed by Ex 13,13; 34,20. Later, this redemption was assured by the Levites who took the place of the first-born (Nm 3,11ff; 8,16). The day came when Jesus, the first-fruits of humanity, offered Himself to the Father through the hands of Mary (Lk 2,22ff). He then gave their full value to the prescriptions of the ancient Law.

→Bread II 2—Fruit II—Gift OT 2—Hope NT III—Meal II—New I—Pentecost I 1.

CH jjk

FLESH

In the eyes of some people man's carnal aspect seems to indicate a state of inferiority and even an evil. This thinking depends only very indirectly on the Bible. In fact, Scripture never considers flesh as intrinsically evil; its judgment is clarified not by a philosophical speculation about the nature of man, but by the light of revelation: flesh has been created by God, flesh has been assumed by the Son of God, flesh is transfigured by the Spirit of God, and that is why the Christian can say: "I believe in the resurrection of the flesh." In the inspired pages from the beginning to the end, flesh *(basar)* designates the status of creature; but with St. Paul this sense is no longer the only one: although it certainly does not designate an evil nature, flesh can also denote man's condition as sinner; it follows that at the end of this development the term *sarx* hides the ambiguity which it is important to expose.

I. THE CREATURE BEFORE GOD

For the NT as well as for the OT, man* is not understood as a being composed of two distinct elements: "matter" (the flesh or the body) and "form" (the body or the soul), which animates it. He is aware of the unity of his personal being. To say that he is flesh is to speak of him according to his external aspect, corporeal, earthly, according to the thing that allows him to express himself through this flesh, which is his body, and which characterizes the human person in his earthly condition.

1. *Dignity of the flesh.* Fashioned by God as by a weaver (Jb 10,11; Ps 139,13ff) or a potter (Gn 2,7; Jr 1,5; Jb 10,8f), the flesh is, under this title, worthy of our admiration (Qo 11,5; 2 M 7, 22f); whether it be an element of our corporeal being—flesh and blood (Si 14,18; Mt 16,17), bone and flesh (Gn 2,23; Lk 24,39), heart and flesh (Ps 84,3; 73,26)—or whether it denotes the body* as a whole, for example in its sickness (Ps 38,4; G 4,14), in suffering (2 Co 12,7), or in tribulations (1 Co 7,28), a hint of contempt is never found in its regard; on the contrary, flesh cannot be hated (E 5,28f). The eulogy of the flesh reaches its climax when Ezekiel announces that God will replace Israel's hardened and stony heart* with "a heart of flesh" (Ez 36,26), docile and affable.

2. *The corporeal person.* There is yet a more basic dignity: the flesh can also denote man in his concrete totality. In the same way as they use the term *soul**, Semites speak objectively of "all flesh" to mean the whole animated creation (Gn 6,17; Ps 136,25; Si 40,8), mankind

(Is 40,5f=Lk 3,6; Jl 3,1=Ac 2,17; Mk 13,20; Jn 17,2). By the term they can also denote the essence of the person; thus Adam sees in the woman that God brought to him another self; but he does not say that she has a soul like his; he exclaims: "She is bone of my bones and flesh of my flesh" (Gn 2,23; cf Si 36,24). These last words express the awareness of deep communion, which can extend to every relationship (Gn 29,14; 37,27; R 9,3), and more especially to the new being, the "one flesh" which the spouses become (Gn 2,24=Mt 19, 5 p; 1 Co 6,16; E 5,31). Thus it happens that the same term can signify the person himself, the *ego* (Qo 4,5; 5,5; 2 Co 7,5), and even his activities of a psychological order, no doubt hinting at the corporeal but not in the bad sense: the flesh suffers (Jb 14,22), is afraid (Ps 119,120), languishes with desire (Ps 63,2), or shouts with joy (Ps 84,3); it lives by the teaching of the wise (Pr 4,22); it is even endowed with a will (Jn 1,13).

3. *The earthly condition.* Finally, to designate concrete man by his flesh is to manifest his earthly origin. This shade of meaning is demanded when the term is used in contrast to the heavenly world of God and the spirit.

a) *The creature.* Outside God* everything is flesh, even an angel (Ez 10,12); Jude (7) finds no more difficulty in this statement than several fathers of the Church: he is satisfied with specifying that the flesh of angels is different from ours. It is then in no way offensive to add "according to the flesh" when speaking of the patriarchs (R 9,5), our father Abraham (R 4,1), or earthly masters (Col 3,22=E 6,5). In the same way, to live "in the flesh" (2 Co 10,3; G 2,20; Ph 1,22ff; Jm 4,1f) simply means to live on earth, to be visible (Col 2,1), concretely present (Col 2,5). To denote the time of Jesus' life on earth (1 Jn 4,2; He 5,7), it is said that He took flesh and blood (He 2,14).

b) *Limitation and powerlessness.* Ordinarily, to speak of flesh is to speak of the frailty of a creature. "All flesh is grass...but the word of God remains forever" (Is 40,6f). Flesh is to spirit* as the earthly is to the heavenly; thus Jesus Christ, "descended from the line of David according to the flesh, has been proven Son of God with power according to the Spirit of holiness" (R 1,3f; cf 1 Tm 3,16). As creature, man is unable of himself to enter the kingdom of God: "what is born of the flesh is flesh, what is born

of the spirit is spirit" (Jn 3,6; cf 1 Co 15,50). Man as "flesh and blood" can no longer of himself know divine realities (Mt 16,17; cf G 1, 16; E 6,12); and, if he presumes to judge them by his reason, he shows himself "wise according to the flesh" (1 Co 1,26). Truly, therefore, "it is the spirit that gives life, the flesh is good for nothing" (Jn 6,63); for example, in the case of seeing behind the eucharistic rite the person of the Savior.

Such is the earthly condition that the Son* of God has willed to take on; in the words of John: "the Word became flesh" (Jn 1,14), a real man of this world with human limitations; but He was also a man in whom the believer recognizes the Savior and the Son of God (1 Jn 4,2; 2 Jn 7) and whose flesh and blood he is willing to eat to gain eternal life (Jn 6,53-58).

4. *The world of the flesh.* Thus, through his flesh which is no more than "dust" (Gn 3,19; Qo 12,7) man belongs to the terrestrial world; through the breath which God lends him, he is related to the celestial world. This idea of belonging to two worlds led the Jewish writers to make a distinction between the world of spirits and the world of flesh; thus under the pen of the Greek translator of the Bible "the God of the spirits which animate all flesh" becomes "the God of the spirits *and* of all flesh" (Nm 16,22; 27,16), as He 12,9 will oppose "the Father of the spirits" to the "fathers according to the flesh." But this cosmic dualism should not be confused with an anthropological dualism according to which man united within himself the two worlds of the spirit and the flesh as two component substances. →It is important to find the correct interpretation of the two texts that seem to be an exception. In R 7,25 the reason of which Paul speaks is not a faculty in control of itself as in Greek thought, but a spectator powerless in the face of the disorder of sin ingrained in the flesh. In Mt 26,41b the "generous" spirit is not a part of man but a gift made by God (cf Ps 51,14). Nowhere is flesh one of the elements of the "composite" whole that is man. Only toward the II/III century with the beginning of rabbinic thought was anthropological dualism adopted in the Jewish world.

II.   THE SINNER BEFORE GOD

There is, however, a dualism of another order, a moral dualism. This must still be carefully distinguished according to the milieu from which it is derived. For some Greeks, the body is a prison for the soul and one should try to escape from it as from a bad situation. Later, as a consequence of the Epicurean controversy, the flesh becomes the seat of sensuality, identified with sexuality considered as evil and degrading for the spirit. The licentious gnosis against which Jude fought probably presents some resemblance to these Epicurean theories (Jude 4. 7...): the flesh, evil by nature, has to be conquered. If for their part the writers of late Judaism and of the NT preach such a struggle, they do it with a wholly different perspective: the flesh—this creaturely condition in which man has placed his trust—ends up by characterizing a world where the spirit of evil reigns.

1. *Sinful trust in the flesh.* Isaiah proclaims that God should be our only support: "The horses of the Egyptian are flesh and not spirit" (Is 31,3): Jeremiah contrasts the two types of trust: "Woe to the man who trusts in man, who makes his flesh his support and whose heart strays from Yahweh" (Jr 17,5ff). Paul follows suit: "let no flesh glory before God" (1 Co 1, 29); contrary to the Jews whose pride* is in the privilege of circumcision (R 2,25-29; G 6,12ff), Paul does not want to glory* except in Christ (Ph 3,3f). Consequently, although he lives in the flesh, he behaves no more according to the flesh (2 Co 10,2f) so that he does not glory in it (2 Co 11,18); by so acting one does not deserve to be called carnal (1 Co 3,1.3; 2 Co 1,12) either in his will (2 Co 1,17) or in his knowledge of Christ (2 Co 5,16). For it is possible to judge Christ according to the flesh, as Jesus reproached the Jews for doing (Jn 8,15): since their eyes were flesh (Jb 10,4), they judge by appearances (Jn 7, 24) and thus transform their frail condition of creature into a condition of sin. John also will end up describing the world* as sinful and denouncing the lust of the flesh (1 Jn 2,16). That is not an accusation against flesh as such, but against the will of man which has made it sinful. One can distinguish two "spirits," of good and evil, each with a world under its dominion and each claiming the heart of man (as at Qumrân); but this is not an affirmation of a natural dualism, as if this struggle had to last forever with the spirit of good being unable to triumph over evil.

2. *Sinful flesh and the Spirit of holiness.* Paul has systematized this struggle and this victory by using the pair of words, *flesh/spirit.* It is only in appearance that such a contrast between the flesh and the spirit corresponds to that which the Greeks place between the soul and the body, between purity and impurity. In fact it draws directly on the Semitic opposition between earthly and heavenly, but it is transformed by two experiences: that of the Holy Spirit* who is given to Christians and that of sin* to which our flesh has brought us.

a) *The struggle between flesh and spirit.* We find the literary antithesis describing this conflict develops in two stages, which stand out in the letters to the Galatians and to the Romans.

Paul declares that the believers are children of Abraham by Sarah according to the spirit and not by Hagar according to the flesh (G 4, 21-31). The OT and the NT are marked out as two contrasting periods in the history of salvation which the Law* and faith* characterize. From this comes the distinction between two worlds in which the believer takes part: the flesh appeared as the residue of sin which the Law has caused to multiply, the spirit as the personification of all that was good in the purpose of the Law and which was accomplished by the gift of the Spirit. The antagonism between these two powers is unyielding within the heart of a Christian (G 5,17): he can live according to the flesh, he should live according to the spirit; from which follows the continual risk of perverting a situation which, however, has been established by the Holy Spirit.

In the seventh and eighth chapters of his epistle to the Romans, Paul shows how the two sources of death and life are at work. These two powers which dwell in man in succession (R 7,17-20; 8,9ff) bring about in the believer a twofold way of living (8,4-17), even though through Christ he has done away with sin. The possibility of living according to the flesh is the trace which sin leaves within us, and this it does through the flesh, in which sin formerly dwelt.

b) *The dominion of the flesh.* When adopted as the norm of existence, the flesh dictates man's conduct. It acquires a real autonomy, inheriting from the power of sin* both its prerogatives and its desires; it makes slaves of those who obey "the law of sin" (R 7,25). With insolence (Col 2,23), it then manifests its desires* (R 8,5ff), its lusts (R 13,14; G 3,3; 5,13.16f); it brings forth evil works* (G 5.19). Such is life according to the flesh (R 7,4) to the point that even the understanding becomes carnal (Col 2,18;

cf 1 Co 3,3). It is the same with the body, in itself neutral, when, under the command of the flesh, it acquires the name of "the body of the flesh" (Col 2,11); it becomes identified with this "body of sin" (R 6,6); it is truly fashioned by the "flesh of sin" (R 8,3).

c) *The triumph of Christ.* But sin has been conquered by Christ, who took this "body of flesh" (Col 1,22) and was made sin (2 Co 5,21); He took upon Himself a state which labored under sin and passed judgment against sin within that very flesh (R 8,3). Henceforth the Christian has, in Christ, crucified his flesh (G 5,24); the fight that he carries on (6,8) does not end fatally, rather is he assured of victory* according to the measure in which he recognizes his real condition of creature and puts his trust not in the flesh, in his weakness, but in the strength* of the Savior's death, which is the source of the Spirit of life.

→Blood O—Body I—Body of Christ I 1—Cupidity NT 1—Death—Desire II, III—Man—Resurrection—Sexuality III 2—Sin—Soul—Spirit OT 3—Stone 2—Word of God NT III.
XLD pjb

FLOOD

1. *The ancient flood.* The recollection of a catastrophic flood which went back to a far removed past was preserved and augmented in Sumerian and Babylonian myths of various times. The biblical tradition sorted out the material of this popular heritage in the light of its monotheistic belief and gave it a moral and religious significance. What was attributed to the caprice of jealous gods appeared henceforth as the proper work of the one God. The idea of disaster gave way to that of a purification directed to salvation*, represented by the saving ark. Beyond irresponsible forces appeared a divine judgment* that strikes the sinner and makes the just man the seed of a new humanity. The adventure of Noah* thus ceases to be an incidental episode; it summarizes and symbolizes the whole history of Israel and likewise the history of mankind.

Only Noah is called just (Gn 7,1); but, like Adam*, he represents all of his household and saves them and himself (Gn 7,1.7.13). By this free election* God reserves for Himself a small remnant*, the survivors who would be the origin of a new people. If the hearts of the men He had saved are still drawn to sin, God avows that He is patient: His mercy is opposed to purely vindictive punishment* and opens the way to conversion (Gn 8,15-22). Condemnation by the waters* thus terminates in a new covenant* which guarantees faithfulness of God to all mankind as well as to the family of Noah (Gn 9,1-17).

2. *Type of the future.* Prophetic theology had seen in the deluge, as in the liberation by the waters of the Red Sea after the exodus*, the prototype of God's salvific judgments. The return of the remnant from exile—the seed of a new people—appears not only to be a new exodus, but the resumption of the work of Noah leaving the ark: "With an eternal love, I have taken pity upon you, said God; it is for me as in the days of Noah, when I swore that the waters of Noah would never again cover the earth" (Is 54,7ff). The thought of a saving judgment was evoked by the sages: "Noah was found blameless and upright; in the time of tribulation he healed all. Thanks to him a remnant remained upon the earth after the flood. Everlasting agreements were set up with him" (Si 44,17f; cf Ws 10,4f; 14,6). The Messianic images of the healer and of the remnant already make Noah the type of Jesus Christ who will one day be the beginning of a new creation*.

3. *The flood of the new era.* To herald the eschatological judgment, Jesus recalls the flood (Mt 24,37ff). This judgment is, moreover, anticipated here below. Christ indeed, like a new Noah, descends into the deep waters* of death* and arises victorious from them—He and a multitude of the redeemed. Those who immerse themselves in the water of baptism will come forth saved and conformed to the risen Christ (1 P 3,18-21). If, then, the flood prefigures baptism, the liberating ark could appear to the fathers as the type of the Church* which floats over the waters of a sinful world and receives all those "who desire to be saved from this wicked generation" (Ac 2,40).

However, the last judgment which threatens the wicked has not yet come. As in the days of the flood, this delay reveals the enduring mercy of God; the eschatological judgment is put off until the Messianic community achieves its fullness (cf P 2,5.9; 3,8f). Throughout the apocalyptic images of his time, the author of the second epistle of Peter distinguishes three stages of salvation history: the ancient world which was judged by water, the present world which will perish in fire, and the future world with the new heaven* and the new earth* (2 P 3,5ff.11ff). The old covenant with Noah will thus find perfect fulfillment in a new order where the creative work of God will succeed in bringing purified man and the purified universe to live in harmony.

→Baptism I 1—Calamity O—Noah—Punishments—Water II 3.

LS jrc

FOLLOW

To follow God is to walk in the ways of God, following the ways* by which He has led His people in the time of the exodus*, the ways which His Son will trace in leading all men to the term of the new, the true exodus.

1. *The calling of Israel.* In going forth from Egypt, the people was responding to Yahweh who called it to follow Him (cf Ho 11,1). In the desert, Israel walks behind Yahweh, who guides it in the pillar of cloud and the pillar of fire (Ex 13,21), who sends His messenger to trace out a path for His people (Ex 23,20.23). Ceaselessly Israel hears this call to follow Yahweh, as the betrothed follows her bridegroom (Jr 2,2), as the flock follows its shepherd* (Ps 80,2), as the people follows its king* (2 S 15,13; 17,9), as the faithful man follows his God* (1 K 18,21).

Following expresses in fact a total attachment and an absolute submission, that is to say faith* and obedience*. Thus Caleb, the man who never doubted, is rewarded for having followed Yahweh perfectly (Dt 1,36). David, who observed the commandments, remains the model of those who follow God with all their heart (1 K 14,8). When King Josiah and all the people undertake a commitment to live according to the covenant, they determine to "follow Yahweh." Thenceforth the ideal of the believer will always be to follow "the ways of the Lord" (Ps 18,22; 25,4...).

To follow Yahweh is then a demand of fidelity. Yahweh is truly a jealous God: He forbids the following of other gods, that is, rendering worship to them and imitating the practices of their believers (Dt 6,14). But Israel lends an ear to local gods; it has hardly arrived in Canaan when the Baals contend for its heart with the God of Sinai (Dt 4,3). Israel "hobbles on two legs," to such an extent that the voice

of the prophets resounds with violence: "If it is Yahweh who is God, follow Him; if it is Baal, follow him" (1 K 18,21). Following Elijah, the prophets ceaselessly rebuke Israel for "prostituting herself by turning away from following Yahweh" (Ho 1,2) and for "following strange gods" (Jr 7,6.9; 9,13; 11,10). Preaching conversion, they invite Israel to take up again the path she followed in the time of the exodus (Ho 2,17), to come back again to follow Yahweh.

2. *In the footsteps of Christ.*

a) *The first steps.* "Follow me," says Jesus to Simon and Andrew, to James and John, to Matthew; and His word, full of authority, draws their adherence (Mk 1,17-20; 2,14). Once they become disciples* of Jesus, they are going to be initiated progressively into the secrets of His mission and the mystery of His person. To follow Jesus, in fact, is not only to attach oneself to a moral and spiritual teaching, but to share His destiny. The disciples are certainly ready to share His glory: "We have left all to follow you; what then shall we receive?" (Mt 19,27)—but they must learn that they must first share His trials and His passion. Jesus demands total detachment: the renunciation of riches and security, the surrender of one's own family (Mt 8,19-22; 10,37; 19,16-22) without thought of dividing one's heart or of turning back (Lk 19,61f). This is a demand to which all can be called; but not all respond to it—for example, the rich young man (Mt 19,22ff).

b) *Even to sacrifice.* Having thus renounced his possessions and his worldly attachments, the disciple learns that he must follow Jesus even to the cross*. "If anyone wishes to follow me, let him renounce himself, take up his cross, and follow me" (Mt 16,24 p). In demanding such a sacrifice from his disciples, a sacrifice not only of their possessions but also of their persons, Jesus reveals Himself as God and succeeds in revealing how far the demands of God reach. But the disciples will only be able to meet those demands when Jesus has first accomplished the deed of sacrifice*. This is what Peter, who is ready in spirit to desire to follow Jesus wherever He will go and who is no less ready to abandon Him like the other disciples (Mt 26,35.56), can understand only "later" (Jn 13,36ff), when Jesus has opened the way by His death and His resurrection: Peter then will go where he did not expect to go (Jn 21,18f).

c) To believe and to imitate. The theologians of the NT have transposed the metaphor. For Paul to follow Christ is to conform himself to Him in the mystery of His death and resurrection. This conformity, to which we are predestined by God from all eternity (R 8,29), is begun in baptism (R 6,2ff) and must be deepened by imitation (1 Co 11,1), the voluntary sharing in His suffering, in the midst of which the power of the resurrection displays itself (2 Co 4,10f; 13,4; Ph 3,10f; cf 1 P 2,21).

In John's view, to follow Christ is to grant Him one's faith, a complete faith founded on His Word alone and not on external signs (Jn 4,42), a faith which can overcome the hesitations of human wisdom (Jn 6,2.66-69); it is to follow the light of the world by taking Him as a guide (Jn 8,12); it is to place oneself among the sheep which the one shepherd gathers into one flock (Jn 10,1-16).

Finally, the believer who follows the apostles* (Ac 13,43) begins to follow Christ "wherever He goes" (Ap 14,4; cf Jn 8,21f), while he waits to follow in His footsteps "beyond the veil, where He has entered as a precursor" (He 6,20). Then the promise of Jesus will be fulfilled, "If anyone serves me, let him follow me, and where I will be, there also will my servants be" (Jn 12,26).

→Calling III—Cross II 1—Disciple NT 2 b—Example—Faith NT I, II—Faithfulness NT—Jesus Christ I 2.3—Love I NT 2 a—Perfection NT 3.

CA jpl

FOLLY

Folly in the Bible is opposed to wisdom* (vg Pr 10,1.14) and like it is defined with relation to the conduct of life* and the knowledge* of God. The fool is therefore the dolt and the imprudent, and also the godless* man (Pr 1,22-32; Si 22,9-18) who recognizes neither the Law (OT) nor Christ (NT).

1. *The wise men* put the inexperienced young man on guard against the seductions which will lead him to foolish behavior: that of depraved women (Pr 7,5-27), that of Dame Folly, the personification of godlessness* (Pr 9,13-18). They draw the portrait of the fool to show their disciples what they will become if they neglect discipline (Si 21,14-20). Did not fools come to

the point of thinking that the Lord did not act justly, or that He saw nothing (Si 16,17-23), or even that He is not (Ps 14,1)? Consequently they would hold the just to be fools (Ws 5,4) and their death an irreparable misfortune (Ws 3,2).

2. *Faced with the kingdom of God*, present in the person of Christ, folly consists not only in the godlessness which rejects the law of God, but in a wisdom which closes itself to His grace. A radical conversion is necessary for all to receive the words of Christ and to put them into practice—failure to do this makes one a fool (Mt 7,26). It is folly to find support in one's riches (Lk 12,20); folly not to respond to the demands of God, like the foolish virgins (Mt 25,1-13), or to try to twist them, like the Pharisees* (Mt 23,17). Anyone admitting a connection between sickness, sin and evil spirits could see the story of the madman of Gerasa as a symbol of the folly that turns into love. This is the story of a violent maniac who now wants to follow Jesus his savior, after having terrorized the neighborhood (Mt 8,28-33 p). For Paul the real folly is not to believe in the wisdom of God who reveals Himself in Christ crucified and the folly of His preaching* (1 Co 1,18-29). But the believer should submit to be taken, as Christ Himself was (Mk 3,21), for a fool in the eyes of the world (1 Co 3,18ff); Paul has also been taken for a fool (1 Co 4,10; Ac 26,24); and every apostle of Christ crucified will have the same lot; for he preaches a salvation* which is the work of the folly of God, folly of love, which is the supreme wisdom (1 Co 1,25).

→Covetousness NT 2—Cross I 1—Education I—Godless Man OT 2—Laugh 1—Scandal I 4—Simple 1—Wisdom.

JA wjy

FRIEND

1. "The faithful friend is priceless" (Si 6,15f; 7,18), for "he loves at every moment" (Pr 17,17), making life sweet (Ps 133; Pr 15,17). How can one forget the marvelous friendship which united David and Jonathan in a spontaneous effusion (1 S 18,1-4), which endured in trial (1 S 19—20) up to death (2 S 1,25f) and survived in the memory* of the heart (2 S 9,1; 21,7)?

But if there are some such friendships, there also exist others which are illusory. Why do the rich have so many friends, and the poor, the sick, and the persecuted have so few (Pr 14, 20; cf Ps 38,12; 55,13f; 88,19; 109,4f; Jb 19,19)? Why "does he who partakes of my bread take up vengeance against me" (Ps 41,10)? These sad experiences teach men to be clear-minded in the choice of their friends, even to the point where it is best to be on one's guard at times (Si 6,5-13; 12,8—13,23; 37,1-5). Though sincere (Jb 2,12f), cannot friendship be deceiving (Jb 6,15-30), even able to draw one to evil (Dt 13,7; Si 12,14; cf 2 S 13,3-15)?

Thus friendship gains by growing old: "New wine, new friend; if it has grown old, you will drink it with joy" (Si 9,10); friendship appreciates open reprimand (Pr 27,5f); friendship is especially nourished on the fear* of God: "he who fears the Lord makes for himself true friends; for such as one is, such is the friend that he has" (Si 6,16f). Actually (cf love*), the model and source of true friendship is the friendship which God seals with man, with an Abraham (Is 41,8; Gn 18,17ff), a Moses (Ex 33,11), the prophets (Am 3,7).

2. In sending His Son among us, God has shown Himself a "friend of men" (Tt 3,4); and Jesus has depicted Him as one who allows Himself to be disturbed by an importunate friend (Lk 11,5-8). Especially, Jesus has given to this friendship a face of flesh: He loved the young rich man (Mk 10,21), He loved Lazarus tenderly, and in him all those who were to rise from the tomb by faith (Jn 11,3.11.35f). He has some "companions" who shared His life (Mk 3, 14) but not all of them became His "friends" (gr. *philos*); thus Judas is still called "companion" (gr. *hetairos*) (Mt 26,50; cf 20,13; 22,12), while to the others Jesus has just declared: "I do not any longer call you servants*, but friends" (Jn 15,15); they have shared His trials, they are ready to face the night of the passion (Lk 22, 28f); thus Jesus shares with them the secrets of His Father (Jn 15,15) as among friends. The type of the friend of Jesus, faithful up to the cross, is "the disciple whom Jesus loved" (Jn 13,23) and whom He entrusted to His very own mother (19,26).

Those whom the Lord has chosen to be His friends cannot help feeling bound by friendship toward one another. Of course there are some stormy moments: Paul, for example, who is bound by so many strong ties to his brethren (cf R 16,1-16) and constantly anxious about anything to do with them (cf 1 Th 2,7f; 2 Co 11,28f), experiences serious difficulties in his relationship with Barnabas (Ac 15,36-39) and even with Peter himself (G 2,11-14). And at the end of his life he is going to feel almost alone and deprived of all friendship (2 Tm 4,9-14). But apart from all these crises there remains the certainty that brotherly love* between His followers is the Lord's will (Jn 15,2f). The picture of the friendship that existed in the early community (Ac 2,44f; 4,32) is still an ideal and a source of strength for all Christians.

3. *The friend of the bridegroom.* Marriage* customs in Israel call for the presence of a "friend of the groom" whose task it is to prepare the nuptial meeting and to act as go-between for the young couple until the time of the marriage, when he presents the young girl to her bridegroom. Allusions to this custom can be found in the text in which the Lord is described as the Spouse* of Israel. It is the prophet's role to be His friend and to lament the unfaithfulness of the bride (Is 5,1-7). It is also the role of John the Baptist, who prepares men to meet the Lord and then retires into the background, overjoyed at their mutual happiness (Jn 3,28f). And lastly it is the role of Paul who "espouses" the community at Corinth to Christ (2 Co 11,2). But later, when he takes up the image again, the Apostle will realize that it is in fact the spouse who always takes the initiative: "He presents to Himself" the bride, who cannot be pleasing to Him unless He first showers her with all His gifts (E 5,27). And so the spouse Himself takes the part that before had belonged to the "friend."

→Brother—Enemy—John the Baptist 2—Love —Neighbor—Meal I, III—Servant of God III 3—Serve III 2.

CW jjk

FRUIT

Whether in its proper sense it means fruitfulness* (vg the fruit of the womb: Lk 1,42), or in a figurative sense the result obtained (vg the fruit of one's actions: Jr 17,10), the word *fruit* means that which is produced by a living being—more precisely by a creature; for if God plants and sows as a man, we do not say that He bears fruit: He harvests* the fruit which ought to manifest His glory.

I. THE DUTY OF BEARING FRUIT

The creative act which has placed in every being a seed of life is a triumphant blessing*. The earth should produce fruit trees giving fruit according to their species (Gn 1,11f); animals and man receive the commandment: "Fructify and multiply!" (Gn 1,22.28). Sown in earth, life* is superabundantly fruitful. Now, one of the signs of life is that he who plants harvests the fruit (Is 37,30; 1 Co 9,7; 2 Tm 2,6). God, then, claims the fruits of His vineyard: all inactivity is reprehensible (Jude 12), unproductive branches are cast into the fire, and they burn (Jn 15,6; cf Mt 3,10); the vineyard will be entrusted to other vine-dressers (Mt 21,41ff). The barren figtree has no longer any right to occupy the soil (Lk 13,6-9). Finally, according to an old oriental institution concerning commercial affairs, the owner has the right to punish him who has not lived up to his contract: "Trade till I come" (Lk 19,13).

II. MAN'S COOPERATION WITH GOD

1. *God, lord of life.* But God does not ask His creatures for fruit without giving them the means of producing it. As he cooperates by his labor in the production of fruit, man should recognize that it is primarily God's work*. Adam is told to cultivate and gather the fruits of the trees in the Garden of Eden, in which God has set him. But he is forbidden to touch the fruit of the tree* of life (Gn 3,22), and this suggests among other things that he was being told that God alone is the source of life. All through its history, Ephraim (whose name means "who makes (Joseph) fruitful": Gn 41,52) will have to understand that, if it bears fruit, it is thanks to Yahweh, verdant cypress, veritable tree of life (Ho 14,9). Israel should then offer its first-fruits* as a sign of thanksgiving (Dt 26,2); it should above all have recourse to the divine wisdom* whose flowers give such marvelous fruit (Si 24,17).

2. *The life-giving water.* In this same Garden of Eden, to make the vegetation grow, it was necessary also for God to cause rain to fall, and to fashion a man to cultivate the soil (Gn 2,5). According to the symbolism of the Bible, the earth could not, under the cultivation of man, produce its fruits, unless water made the seed germinate. Without water* the earth remains sterile*. It is the desert, as at Sodom, where "the trees bear fruit, but ripen not" (Ws 10,7). Without Yahweh, the only faithful rock, man is not able to bear fruit; "his grapes are poison" (Dt 32,32); he ought then to pray, as did Elijah, so that thanks to the rain, "the earth may give its fruit" (Jm 5,17f). Then the earth will receive God's blessing and produce useful herbs (He 6,7f), and the just man, like "a tree planted on the edge of a stream" (Jr 17,8; Ps 1,3) "continues to bear fruit in its old age" (Ps 92,14f).

3. *The role of man.* If the water depends above all upon God, the choice and cultivation of the land are entrusted to man. Sown among thorns the grain does not come to maturity (Lk 8,14); and it will bear more or less fruit according to the quality of the soil where it fell (Mt 13,8). But in every instance the growth* does not depend upon man's efforts: the earth produces its fruits "of itself" (gr. *automatē*) (Mk 4,26-29). Doubtless it was necessary to labor to cultivate wisdom, but one could count on its excellent fruits (Si 6,19). There is at the same time the lesson of labor in the toil, and the lesson of patience* in awaiting the fruit.

III. GOOD AND BAD FRUIT

Not having wished to receive from God alone the fruit of life which had been destined for him, Adam finds himself obliged to cultivate a cursed soil instead of garden trees "pleasant to the eye and good to eat" (Gn 2,9); it will bring forth thorns and thistles (Gn 3,18). Having tasted of the fruit of the tree of the knowledge of good and evil, Adam pretends to determine for himself what is good and what is evil. His action became ambiguous, even in his own eyes. But God who sounds the loins and the hearts, judges His vineyard Israel by the fruit it bears. He expected grapes from it, but found them sour (Is 5,1-7). The fruit proclaims the quality of the orchard, as the world reveals the thoughts of the heart (Si 27,6). John the Baptist denounces the illusion of those who bragged about being sons of Abraham, but bear no good fruit (Mt 3,8ff). Jesus proclaims "that by its fruit a tree is known" and reveals a malignant sap underneath the pharisaical bark (Mt 12,33ff). He teaches His disciples to discern false prophets: "By their fruits you shall know them. One does not gather grapes from thorns, or figs from thistles" (Mt 7,16). More generally, then, an ambiguity is at the heart of a man who wishes "to bear fruit for death" when he ought to "bear fruit for life" (R 7,4f).

IV. THE VIGOR OF CHRIST AND THE FRUIT OF THE SPIRIT

But Christ has submitted to this ambiguity. He has lived the law of fructification which He declared before the world: "Unless the grain of wheat falling into the ground die, it remains alone. But if it die, it will bring forth much fruit" (Jn 12,24); it has accepted the hour* of sacrifice and has been glorified by the Father. The law of nature has become, through the mediation of Christ, the law of Christian existence. "I am the true vine, and my Father is the vine-dresser. Every branch that is in me and bears not fruit, He will cut away" (Jn 15, 1f), for to bear fruit it must remain on the vine (15,4), that is to say, faithful* to Christ. The union with Jesus should be fruitful, generous: "Every branch which bears fruit the Father will purge that it may bring forth more fruit" (15,2). Such is the divine way, the superabundance which supposes the continual purification of the disciple, and his patience* (Lk 8,15). Then will come "to full maturity the fruit of justice which we bear through Christ for the glory and praise of God" (Ph 1,11; cf Jn 15,8).

The eschatological prophecy is then fulfilled. The vineyard of Israel, formerly magnificent (Ex 17,8), then dried up (19,10-14; cf Ho 10,1; Jr 2,21), again gives its fruit, and the earth its produce (Ze 8,12); one could become intoxicated with wisdom (Si 1,16) and even become a source of life: "of the fruit of justice is born a tree of life" (Pr 11,30). The NT permits us to specify the contents of the fruit of the Spirit, borne by the sap of Christ. It is not multiple, but it multiplies; it is charity, flowering into all kinds of virtues (G 5,22f). Love is not only a "fruit sweet to the palate" of the spouse (Ct 2,3). The well-beloved Himself may "enter into His garden and taste* its delicious fruits" (Ct 4,16). At the end of time, the prophet had seen that the regularity of the seasons (Gn 8,22; Ac 14,17) would be renewed: each month the trees standing at the edge of the torrent that springs from the side of the Temple would give their fruits (Ez 47,12). Connecting this vision with that of paradise*, the Apocalypse contemplates only one tree* of life, that which has become the tree of the cross*, capable of curing the pagans themselves (Ap 22,2).

→First Fruits I—Fruitfulness—Growth—Harvest — Sowing — Sterility — Tree — Vine — Vintage—Virtues & Vices 2—Work III, IV 2 —Works.

CS & XLD wjy

FRUITFULNESS

God, whose superabundant fullness is fruitfulness beyond all measure, created Adam in His own image*, in the image of His only Son who, however, in Himself alone exhausts the divine and eternal fruitfulness. To achieve this mystery, man, when transmitting life*, communicates his own image in the course of time, thus surviving through the generations.

I. THE CALL TO FRUITFULNESS

Continuously from the beginning of time, the call of the Creator has resounded: "Increase and multiply!" and let the creatures fill the earth.

1. *Command and blessing.* In so commanding God gives the power of response. Such is the sense of the blessing* which makes man and woman capable of "creating" beings in their own image, after the command has taken effect among plants and animals. The joy of fecundity makes Eve, the mother* of the living, exult after her first infant: "I have given birth to a son, thanks to Yahweh" (Gn 4,1). The Book of Genesis is the history of the generations* of man: genealogies, anecdotes, births desired, difficult ones, impossible ones, marriage plans, the true way to childbearing—like a symphony developing a bass chord played by the Lord at the daybreak of time. The Lord punctuates this history with blessings which, in addition to the promised land, announces a "posterity as numerous as the stars of the heaven and the sands of the shores of the sea*" (Gn 22,17). It will be the same with Jerusalem after the exile, seeing her children come toward her from afar (Is 49,21; 54,1ff; 60,4.15; 62,4).

2. *Protection of the sources of life.* Among their other lessons, two narratives show the respect with which the origins of life must be surrounded. It is not permissible to look upon the nakedness of one's father when he is drunk, under pain of incurring the curse* (Gn 9,20-27). God Himself intervenes when the wombs of the wives of the patriarchs are threatened. Since Sarah and Rebecca must be the mothers of the godly people of Israel, how does the Pharaoh (Gn 12,12-20) or Abimelech (Gn 20; 26,7-12) dare to mix his human acts with the action of God? And if in his selfishness Onan diverts

his seed* and prevents it from creating life, it is he who loses his life (Gn 38,8ff).

3. *Laws and hymns.* Later the law comes to protect human fecundity by formulating certain prohibitions: rules concerning the periods of the woman (Lv 20,18), protection of young girls and their fiancés (Dt 22,23-29), and sanctions on certain acts (vg Dt 25,11f)...Even if these rules, which are undoubtedly of pre-Mosaic origin, derive from instinctive taboos, they are taken up and directed by a consideration of the fecundity of the chosen people. And the Law concludes: "If you are faithful to Yahweh, blessed will be the fruit of your wombs" (Dt 28,4).

Subsequently the psalms repeat in chorus: "Lo, children are an inheritance from the Lord; the fruit of the womb is a reward" (Ps 127,3; cf Ps 128,3; Pr 17,6). And then there is the classic wish addressed to the young spouse: "Our sister, may you increase to thousands of thousands!" (Gn 24,60; cf Rt 4,11f).

II. IN SEARCH OF POSTERITY

Animated by the divine blessing and the desire of men, each man's dream is to perpetuate his name* after death.

1. *The profound desire of nature* is expressed in a story which appears scandalous but was admired in later rabbinic tradition (Gn 19,30-38). It concerns the daughters of Lot who were living alone. Rather than allow themselves to wither away without bearing any offspring, they arranged that their father, without knowing what he was doing, raise up for them a progeny. This tale of incest which was certainly condemned by the Law (cf Lv 18,6-18) was intended as a satire against the Moabites, but it gave an opening for a certain admiration of the cunning of these daughters of Eve who in this way fulfilled the wish of the Creator.

2. *The Levitate law* (Dt 25,5-10) defends the man who dies without offspring (Rt 4,5.10). The brother-in-law of a childless widow must, under certain conditions, produce in her a child. The poem of Ruth is written to honor fecundity which he assured in spite of death or exile. It extends the history of Tamar who does not hesitate to disguise herself as a prostitute in order to achieve fertility, in spite of the egoism of her brother-in-law, Onan, and the

injustice of her father-in-law, Judah (Gn 38, 6-26; cf Rt 4,12; Mt 1,3).

3. In contending against sterility*, the Jews had recourse to *adoption* by means of a device, then legal, which consisted in making the servant give birth to a child, that is, one who was then considered as her own son by the wife (Gn 16,2; 30,3...) or daughter (Rt 4,16f). The *genealogies* take little care to trace the line of generations* from father to son. If the physical giving of life is the basis for paternity, this is not its only meaning because the divine blessing is not handed down exclusively according to bonds of blood. When Genesis relates how the earth was peopled, the genealogies are able to make one man the father of a whole city or nation. By this the author wants to say that in the origin of nations there was question not only of the extension of one family stock but of immigrations, of marriages, of covenants, and of conquests. The strictly racial line could be broadened and take on a spiritual meaning; in the posterity of Abraham proselytes would be joined to the privileged clan.

Considered in this way, biblical history is first of all a genealogy. According to this notion of existence man is entirely directed toward the future, toward Him who is to come. Such is the meaning of the impulse placed in him by His Creator: not merely to survive, but that he may one day contemplate the perfect image of God in a son of man.

III. FRUITFULNESS IN CHRIST

This image of God is made manifest in Jesus Christ who does not suppress this desire for fruitfulness but fulfills it and gives it its full significance.

1. *Jesus Christ and human generations.* According to the OT, the history of man is achieved in his descendants (cf Gn 5,1; 11,10; 25,19...), and the whole of history looks anxiously to the future where this promise will be fulfilled. Jesus Himself, has no descendants according to the flesh, but He does have ancestors and a spiritual posterity.

a) Christ comes at the end of sacred history, in the fulness of time* (Gn 4,4). According to the apocalyptic calculations of the Book of Enoch, he inaugurates the seventh week, that of the Messiah, since the call of Abraham.

Perhaps this is Matthew's intention in recounting the 3 × 14 generations* that make up Christ's genealogy (Mt 1,1-17). Jesus presents Himself as the final heir for whom all generations have waited through the ages.

b) *Christ fulfills the universalism* outlined in the OT. Four names of women break into the genealogy. They are not names of the wives of patriarchs, but those of foreigners or of mothers who bore children under unusual conditions: Tamar (Gn 38) and Rahab (Js 2,11), Ruth (Rt 1,16; 2,12) and Bathsheba (2 S 11,3). The flower of Israel has in its ancestry some who are attached to a non-Jewish, non-righteous soil; and they are made to inherit it at the time of glory and the sinfulness of men. In contrast with this fruitfulness according to the flesh is the completely pure and divine maternity of the Virgin who bears a child through the work of the Holy Spirit.

c) *Christ is the end of history*, because He is the new Adam* whose "descent" Matthew records (Mt 1,1; cf Gn 5,1). The future has already come in Him who was to come. In Him, the past finds meaning. Jesus fulfills in a spiritual generation the earthly transmission of the blessings of God. Israel increases with the birth of new sons of man: the Body* of Christ grows through the spiritual birth of sons of God.

2. *The life of faith and virginal fruitfulness.* Jesus did not judge it opportune to repeat the commandment of Genesis regarding the duty of fecundity. Rather He broke with Jewish tradition which had once proclaimed: "Not to procreate is to shed human blood," and instead He even encouraged voluntary sterility* (Mt 19,12). What is more, He revealed the meaning of fecundity itself.

First of all He did this with respect to Mary*. He does not deny the beauty of her vocation to motherhood. But, to the woman who was so exultant over such good fortune, He revealed its deep significance: "Rather happy are those who hear the Word of God and keep it!" (Lk 11,27). Mary is blessed because she believed; by her virginal maternity she is the model for all who by their faith adhere to God alone.

Jesus even specifies in what sense faith* is spiritual fruitfulness. He wants to overlook His parents according to the flesh, and He asks: "Who is my mother? who are my brothers? Whoever does the will* of God, he is my brother, my sister and my mother" (Mt 12,48ff p). In begetting His Son, God has said and done everything. The believer who unites himself to God shares, then, in the generation of the Son. Spiritual fruitfulness presupposes virginity of faith.

3. *The fruitfulness of the Church*. In providing for their own spiritual fruitfulness the believers are only sharing in the fruitfulness of the whole Church. Their work is that of the woman* who gives birth to a child, the mother* of the male child (Ap 12). This is primarily the function of an apostle, as Paul showed in a privileged manner by his words and life. Like a mother, he gave birth anew in pain (Gn 4,19), he nourished his little ones and took care of them (1 Th 2,7; 1 Co 3,2). As their sole father, he begot them in Christ (1 Co 4,15), and he exhorts them firmly (1 Th 2,11). These images are not just metaphors. They express an authentic experience of the apostolate in the Church.

Each believer must also bring forth fruit* in the Church as a true branch of the true vine (Jn 15,2.8). It is through these works* that the believer glorifies the Father* who is in heaven (Mt 5,16), the Father who is the source of all fruitfulness.

→Blessing—Child—Death OT III 4; NT II 2, III 3—Fathers & Father I, II—Fruit—Generation—Grace V—Growth—House I 2—Life—Marriage—Mother—New Birth—Sexuality I 1 —Solitude I 2, II 2—Sow II 1—Sterility—Storm 1.3—Vine 2—Virginity—Visit OT 1—Woman OT 2; NT 1—Works OT II 2.

XLD afmcg

FULFILL

Abortive projects and weak decisions mark human life, which is stamped with human weakness and inconstancy. The all-powerful and faithful God is not satisfied with unfinished works: the Bible totally and entirely witnesses to the accomplishments of His designs. *Accomplish* says more than *do*; the terms which the word translates evoke the idea of fullness* (hb. *mālē'*, gr. *plēroun*), or that of achievement (hb. *kālāh*; gr. *telein*) and of perfection* (hb. *tāman*; gr. *teleioun*). One accomplishes a work begun (1 K 7,22; Ac 14,26), that is to say that one brings it to a desirable completion. One accomplishes a word, command, or promise* or oath*: the word is like a hollowed mold in which the reality should be cast; it is the first step of an action which ought to follow through and achieve its end.

OT

PERSPECTIVES OF FULFILLMENT

1. *Word of God and Law.* More than any other word, the Word* of God tends to fulfillment: "The word which comes from my mouth never returns without result" (Is 55,11). God "does not speak in vain" (Ez 6,10). His Law*, His orders demand obedience (Ex 20 etc) and in the end will obtain it (Dt 4,30f; 30, 6ff; Ez 36,27).

2. *Prophecies.* The divine prophecies sooner or later are realized: "Long ago I had revealed ...suddenly I have acted, and it has happened" (Is 48,3; cf Ze 1,6; Ez 12,21-28). Fulfillment is the mark of God who guarantees the calling of a prophet and the authenticity of His message (Dt 18,22). The OT testifies more than once that such and such an event has happened "to accomplish the word of Yahweh" transmitted by a prophet. Thus are presented the maintaining of the line of David and the building of the temple (1 K 8,24), the departure into exile and the return to rebuild the temple (2 Ch 36,21ff; Ezr 1,1f). These past achievements are the guarantee of the accomplishments to come.

3. *The times are fulfilled.* Sudden as it was at times, fulfillment is not achieved haphazardly, but "in its time" (Lk 1,20), at the end of a kind of gestation. That the Word be accomplished, it is necessary that "the time for it be achieved" (vg Jr 25,12); and for the plan* of God to be wholly and entirely accomplished, it will be necessary for the fullness of time to have arrived (E 1,10; G 4,4; cf Mk 1,15).

NT

"IT IS ACCOMPLISHED"

The incomparable time of fulfillment is that of the NT. Of this the evangelists, especially Matthew, seek to convince the readers.

1. *Prophecies.* The formula "that it may be accomplished which had been said by..." recurs ten times in Mt—for the virginal con-

ception and the flight into Egypt, for the healing of the sick, the teaching in parables, the triumphant entry into Jerusalem, the betrayal of Judas...Analogous formulas appear in the other gospels. These detailed observations aim at making us understand that all the OT was orientated to the revelation of Jesus; fulfillments there emphasized were only a slow preparation for the full realization of the plan of God during the earthly existence of Jesus.

In Jesus' existence itself all these fulfillments are not on the same level. One among them, and one alone, is designed as a "complete work"; that is the death of Jesus on the cross. In the formula of Jn 19,28 "that the Scripture may be fulfilled," the verb *teleioun* replaces the usual *plēroun,* and the context stresses completeness by the repetition of "it is consummated" (19,30). Lk uses the latter verb only in reference to the passion (Lk 12,50; 18,31; 22, 37); and according to the epistle to the Hebrews it is by His passion that Jesus has been fulfilled, brought to completion (He 2,10; 5,8f).

All the events of sacred history have, therefore, been orientated toward the coming of Christ, and in the life of Christ all the deeds of Scripture culminate in His sacrifice*; thus it is that in "Him all the promises* of God have had their *yes*" (2 Co 1,20).

This fulfillment does more than bring about what had been foreseen. In fact the law of divine fulfillments itself is that they should always exceed anything that could have been imagined beforehand. The result of this is that the fulfillment of the OT in the NT cannot be explained simply in terms of correspondence and continuity, but includes at the same time differences and breaks, demanded by the move to a higher plane. This *threefold relationship* (resemblance, difference, superiority) is made particularly clear by the author of Hebrews, when he compares Moses and Christ (3,1-6), the old priesthood and the priesthood of Christ (5, 1-10; 7,11-28), the old worship and the sacrifice of Christ (9,1-14) etc. However, the same idea necessarily underlies the whole of the NT. The latest fulfillment is itself a revelation; by integrating words spoken in the past into a synthesis that could not have been foreseen until then, it gives them a new depth of meaning. Jesus Christ is indeed, then, the promised successor of David (2 S 7,12f; Lk 1,32f) but His kingdom is not of this world (Jn 18,36f), for in Him we see the realization of the prophecy of the Servant* who dies a humiliating death (Is 53; 1 P 2,24f) and also of the heavenly Son of

Man* (Dn 7,13f; Mt 26,64), the triumphant Lord (Ps 110; Mt 26,64). He builds a new temple, to which the riches of the pagans flow (Hg 2,6-9; Is 60,7.13). But this is a temple "not made by human hands" (Mk 14,58), His risen Body (Jn 2,21), of which we become members (1 Co 12,27). The sometimes disconcerting way in which the NT uses the writings of the OT can often be explained in this way: the authors are less concerned with the original context of each of the words than with the new context fixed by God Himself through the events.

2. *The Law.* The Word of God is not only promise; it is also demand. In the Sermon on the Mount, speaking of the Law*, Jesus proclaims that He has not come "to abolish, but to fulfill" (Mt 5,17).

The context gives us to understand that, far from suppressing the Mosaic Law, Jesus deepens its precepts: He extends its demands into the world of intention and hidden desire. But above all He renews the Law, makes it "perfect" (Jm 1,25), by revealing fully the primary demand which provides the key to all the others, the commandment of love*. Therein do the Law and the prophets find themselves summed up and raised to their perfection (Mt 7,12; 22,40 p).

In order to "fulfill the Law," Jesus is not content, moreover, to promulgate His command; He to whom "it belongs to accomplish all justice" (Mt 3,15), He Himself achieves in His own person, and in that of His believers, all that He demands; His sacrifice is the pinnacle of love (Jn 15,13) and it also is the source of love as well. "Having arrived at the fulfillment" (He 5,9), Christ has in the same action "brought to fulfillment those whom He sanctifies" (He 10,14; cf Jn 17,4.23).

A similar fulfillment of the old Law can, without paradox, be presented as its annulment. When that which is perfect occurs, that which is merely partial comes to an end (cf 1 Co 13, 10). Such is Paul's point of view. On the one hand, the charity which sums up the Law rules it and informs it and thus suppresses by this act the slavery to legal prescripts. "He who loves others has fulfilled the Law" (R 13,8; cf R 13, 10; G 5,14). On the other hand, the legalist spirit is cut away at the root; man is no longer able by fulfilling the Law to forge his own perfection. "In order that the justice of the Law be fulfilled in us," it was necessary that God send us His Son (R 8,3f) and that, through His Son, we should receive the Spirit. By this

act "we are no longer under the Law, but under grace*" (R 6,15).

The performance of works is something demanded by the very dynamism of grace (Col 1,10f). In works* faith* is fulfilled (Jm 2,22; cf G 5,6), and likewise the love of God (1 Jn 2,5; 4,12). But the execution of works is poles apart from the legalism attacked by Paul. There is no longer a question of human display; at issue is the divine fruitfulness* (G 5,22f; Jn 15,5).

3. *End of time.* The work accomplished on the cross of Christ is thus displayed in time, until "the end of the world" comes (Mt 24,3 p) which was announced by the OT and the NT (day* of the Lord) and will be the complete manifestation of the consummation of the plan* of God in Christ (cf 1 Co 15,23f).

→Figure NT—Fullness—Growth NT 1—Jesus Christ I—Kingdom NT III 3—Law *C*—Memory 4 a—New—Oath—Perfection NT 2—Plan of God—Preach I 3 a—Promises—Prophet NT I—Revelation NT I 3, II 3, III 3—Seal 2—Time NT—Will of God NT—Works NT I 2—Writing IV.

A V jjk

FULLNESS

The word *fullness*, which signifies perfection* in abundance, is particularly apt to describe the saving power of Christ who has received all power in heaven and on earth. Nevertheless, the underlying Greek noun (*plērōma*) offers a much greater variety of meaning, signifying basically either the content which fills up a space—the sea (1 Ch 16,32) or the earth (Ps 24,1; cf 1 Co 10,26)—or that which completes something (Mt 9,16; Mk 2,21; Col 1,24); it can designate equally well either the container or the totality (R 11,12), abundance (R 15,29), fulfillment (R 13,10).

1. *The fullness of time.* Just as for Elizabeth (Lk 1,57) and Mary (Lk 2,6) the "days were fulfilled" in which they should bring forth children, so for the earth the time is "fulfilled*" (Mk 1,15), and we can speak of the fullness of the Messianic and eschatological times* (G 4,4; E 1,10). This measure, at last full, which makes us think of the content of a box packed with sand, does not correspond to a maturity or a

perfection reached by men, but to a time fixed by God. Thus Jesus "fills out," "fulfills*" the prophecies.

2. *The fullness which exists in Christ.* God was pleased to make all fullness dwell in the risen Christ (Col 1,19). To explain this expression two interpretations among others are worthy of note. According to the first, a more static interpretation, the "pleroma" would be the universe filled with the presence* of God. In this case, Paul would have been influenced by both the Stoicism which was widespread and by the sapiential milieu. Wisdom, in effect, "fills the universe and holds all things united" (Ws 1,7). According to the second interpretation, which is more dynamic, Paul would reflect other images of the sapiential literature: Wisdom, like the waters of the greatest rivers, swells to the heights of its banks, overflows and breaks loose. More vast than the sea, deeper than the abyss, Wisdom fills the sage; and he, at first a simple channel and tributary, is himself transformed into a river and a sea (Si 24, 25-31; cf Pr 8,12ff). Elsewhere, God has made Wisdom live in Israel (Si 24,8-12). Precisely in Christ, in whom lives the complete fullness (Col 1,19; 2,9), are found hidden all the treasures of Wisdom (Col 2,3). These treasures have nothing in common with hoarded and avariciously preserved riches, but like living waters which spread abroad, they are the fullness of life* which opposes the emptiness of death* (Ph 2,7), the power*, saving and superabundant, which pours from the name* over every other name (Ph 2,9). This superabundance is transparent everywhere in the Pauline epistles, especially in the more lyrical passages like R 5,15-21; 8,31-39; 11,33-36; Ph 2,9ff. It is most particularly striking in the hymn to the Ephesians in which the inexhaustible style struggles to translate the overflowing richness of the grace* with which God has crowned us in His well-beloved Son.

3. *The Church, fullness of Christ.* Christ is in complete possession of the divine omnipotence (Col 1,19; 2,9), and the faithful share in His fullness (2,10; 3,19). In fact, the external life and the superabundant sanctification existing in the glorified Body of Christ (2,9) are shared by the Church, which becomes His Body. And this is why from this time on the Church can be called the fullness of Christ (E 1,23). These two titles, Body and Fullness, do not apply to the universe but only to the Church. She must, however, still develop in order to arrive at the maturity of the fullness of Christ (4,13). This growth will be both in depth (cf 4,14ff) and in extension. The Church is in fact destined to reach out to the whole of creation, which is groaning in expectation (cf R 8,19-23), in order to gather together and save all things. In this way Christ progressively fills the universe with His fullness through the Church (E 1,20ff; 4, 10).

In his prologue, St. John restates this doctrine in simpler terms: in His glory, the only Son "full of grace and truth" (Jn 1,14) pours out upon men the inexhaustible abundance of the divine goodness. "Yes, from the fullness of Christ we have all received" (Jn 1,16).

→Blessing—Body of Christ III 2—Church V 1 —Figure NT—Fulfill—Growth—Numbers II 1 —Perfection NT 6—Plan of God NT I— Revelation NT I 3, II 3, III 3—Time NT— Wealth.

PL jjk

G

GATE

When open, the gates allow people to come and go, allowing free circulation: they express welcome (Jb 31,32) and the offering of an opportunity (1 Co 16,9). When shut, they prevent people from passing; they protect (Jn 20, 19) or they are a sign of refusal (Mt 25,10). Thus, they also suggest the idea of sorting out.

OT

I. GATE OF THE CITY

The city guards its entrance by a huge fortified gate, protecting inhabitants from the attacks of the enemy and allowing friends to come in: "the stranger who is within the gates" (Ex 20,10) shares in the privileges of Israel. Thus, the gates ensure the security of the inhabitants and allow the town to set itself up as a community. The life of the city is centered on the gates: this is where meetings take place (Jb 29,7; Ps 69,13), business matters are settled (Gn 23,11-18; Rt 4,1-11), political maneuvers are worked out (2 S 15,1-6); the place from which departures are made in time of war (1 K 22,10) and above all where judgments are made (Dt 21,19; 22,15; 25,7; Am 5,10.15; Jb 5,4; 31,21; Pr 22,22; 24,7). The gates stand for justice and security (Is 28,6). The gates, then, are in some way identified with the city, and the word can stand for the town itself (Dt 28,52-57); it can even stand for the power* of the city. To take possession of the gates means to make oneself master of the city (Gn 22,17) and to free the captives (Ps 107,16; Is 45,2); to receive the keys of the city is a sign of being invested with power (Is 22,22). By analogy, one speaks of the gates of sheol or of death* to denote that mysterious abode to which every man is led (Ps 107,18; Is 38,10) and to which God alone knows the entrance (Jb 38,17), but also to denote the power that He alone is capable of conquering (Ps 9,14; Ws 16,13; cf Mt 16,18).

Jerusalem is *the* town, with the ancient gates (Ps 24,7ff) that God loves especially (Ps 87), because He has Himself strengthened them (147,13). The pilgrim* passing through them experiences a sense of unity and peace (122). Reputed to be impregnable, Jerusalem can offer its inhabitants security by shutting its gates; however, justice is not always done at these gates (Is 2,21f; 29,21). The prophets, then, glimpse a new Jerusalem, both open to the nations and established in peace and justice (Is 26,1-5; 60,11; Ez 48,30ff; Ze 2,8f).

II. GATE OF HEAVEN

Yahweh does of course open the gates of heaven in order to send down rain, manna (Ps 78,23) and every kind of blessing* on to the earth (Ml 3,10); but since the closing of paradise man no longer communicates familiarly with God. It is worship that establishes relations between the two worlds, divine and earthly: thus, Jacob recognized in Bethel "the gate of heaven" (Gn 28,17). The Israelite presenting himself at the gates of the temple wants to approach Yahweh (Ps 100,4); but he will hear the priest remind him of the conditions for entry: faithfulness to the covenant and justice (15; 24; Is 33,15f; cf Mi 6,6-8; Ze 8,16f): "This is Yahweh's gateway, through which the virtuous may enter" (Ps 118,19f). For his part, Jeremiah takes up his stand at these very gates and states that these conditions are far from being fulfilled: the meeting with God is illusory and the temple will be rejected (Jr 7; cf Ez 8—11). Jerusalem loses the very reason for its existence. It is by "removing the evil from its midst" rather than by shutting its gates to the nations that the city will be holy. When the temple is destroyed, Israel understands that man cannot climb the heavens; and so, in prayer, they ask God to tear open the heavens and to come down Himself (Is 63,19): they ask Him to go ahead of the flock and lead it through the gates (Mi 2,12f; cf Jn 10,4).

NT

Jesus answers this appeal; at His baptism the heavens are opened and He Himself becomes the true gate of heaven, come down on earth (Jn 1,51; cf Gn 28,17), the gate leading to pastures where divine blessings will be offered freely (Jn 10,9), the only Mediator. Through Him God communicates Himself to men; through Him men have access to the Father (E 2,18; He 10,19). But at the same time Jesus holds the keys of David (Ap 3,7) and He makes demands: entry into the kingdom, of which He entrusts the keys to Peter (Mt 16,19), entry into life, into the salvation, represented as a town or a banqueting-hall, means entrance through a narrow gateway, conversion (Mt 7,13f; Lk 13,24), faith (Ac 14,27; E 3,12). Those who do not take care will find the door shut (Mt 25, 10; Lk 13,25). But Jesus holds the keys of death and of hell (Ap 1,18), has overcome evil and has made His Church stronger than the powers of evil (Mt 16,18).

At the end of time, city and heaven become one and the same. The Apocalypse shows us the fulfillment of the prophecies of Isaiah, Ezekiel and Zechariah: the heavenly Jerusalem has twelve gates; they are always open and yet evil no longer enters in. Peace and justice abound there; and there is the perfect

GIFT

exchange between God and humanity (Ap 21, 12-27 and 22,14-15).

→Death OT I 2—Hell—Salvation NT I 1—
Shepherd & Flock NT 1.

JB ems

GENERATION

Beginning with the meaning of begetting, of procreation, the word *generation* tends to express the solidarity which unites men among themselves. As in English, this solidarity could group those who live at one and the same period (contemporaries). But the Hebrew adds an historical nuance to this sociological meaning; it is the solidarity of those who are descendants of one and the same family or of one and the same race (descent, lineage). By this word and by the use of genealogies, the Bible wishes to emphasize the solidarity of men, in blessing or in sin, from Adam to Christ and even to the end of time.

1. *Community of race.* Every man is born in a generation; it is that that marks the *tōledōth* (from the root *yālad*, to beget), or genealogical lists (Gn 5,1; 11,10; 1 Ch 1—9). He inherits blessings* and divine promises* granted his ancestors. When there is question of Jesus Christ, Son of Abraham and Son of Adam, promises and blessings find their fulfillment in Him (Mt 1,1-17 p). These generations constitute the history, and consequently are not simply an empty framework to be filled by the actions of men. They ought to sing of God and His works (Ps 145,4) and proclaim blessed the mother of Jesus (Lk 1,48).

2. *Free solidarity.* Man inherits the blessings, but also the sin of preceding generations (Mt 23,35f). There exists a "wicked and perverse generation" (Dt 32,5) which Jesus recognizes in that of His contemporaries (Mt 12,39; 17,17), and especially in the Pharisees* whom He terms a brood of vipers (Mt 12,34; 23,33); it has the devil for father (Jn 8,44-47), its hardness* of heart provokes the disgust and the wrath* of God (He 3,7-19; Ps 95,8-11). But belonging to this generation is no longer fatal since Christ has sent the Spirit for the forgiveness of sins. "One can be saved from it" (Ac 2,40) and belong to the generation of Abraham* the believer (R 4,11f), to be the "chosen generation" (1 P 2,9; cf Is 43,20) of those who believe

in the Son of God and are born of God (Jn 1, 12f; 1 Jn 5,1). There are, therefore, two generations or two "worlds*" which are not unrelated; and it is the duty of Christians "to make themselves blameless and pure, children of God in the midst of a wicked and perverse generation, in a world in which they shine as sources of light, offering to it the Word of life" (Ph 2,15; cf Lk 16,8).

→Fathers & Father I 2, II, V 2—Fruitfulness—
Sowing II 1.

AB wjy

GIFT

At the origin of every gift the Bible teaches us to recognize the divine initiative. "Every good gift...comes from the Father of lights" (Jm 1, 17; cf Tb 4,19). God it is who takes the initiative for creation and who gives all men nourishment and life (Ps 104). Again, it is God who takes the initiative for salvation (Dt 9,6; 1 Jn 4, 10). As a result, generosity goes astray when it pretends to precede grace* (cf Jn 13,37f). The primary attitude required of man is to open himself to the gift of God (Mk 10,15 p). When he receives it he becomes capable of a genuine generosity and is called to practice giving in his turn (1 Jn 3,16).

OT

1. *The gifts of God.* The OT is not a time of gifts but rather of promise*. The gifts themselves function only to prefigure and prepare for the definitive gift.
"I will give this land to your posterity," said Yahweh to Abraham (Gn 15,18). The echo of this word resounds throughout the Pentateuch. The book of Deuteronomy sets out to give an appreciation of such a gift (Dt 8,7; 11, 10), but it declares also that unfaithfulness will bring on evil; another gift is necessary: circumcision* of heart, the condition for return and for life (Dt 29,21—30,6).
Through Moses God gives to His people the Law* (Dt 5,22), the gift beyond all others (Ps 147,19f), for it is a participation in His own wisdom (Si 24,23; cf Dt 4,5-8). But the Law is powerless if the heart which receives it is evil (cf Ne 9,13.26). Israel needs a new heart*; such is the coming gift to which the prophets direct their hopes (Jr 24,7; Ez 36,26ff).
So it was with all the gifts of the OT: some

200

seem to fall short (the Davidic dynasty, the presence of the glory* in the temple), and successive disappointments force their hopes to look further. Others are nothing more than memories which stir up their desires—bread* from heaven (Ws 16,20f), water* from the rock (Ps 105,41). Israel had received much, but it awaits yet more.

2. *Gifts to God.* To recognize His sovereign rule and His benefits, Israel offers to Yahweh the first-fruits*, tithes (Dt 26), and sacrifices* (Lv 1...). Likewise she offers gifts to make up for her unfaithfulness to the covenant (Lv 4; 5) and to find favor once again with Yahweh (2 S 24,21-25). The offerings to God are located, therefore, in the framework of reciprocity (Si 35,9f).

3. *Reciprocal gifts.* It is in the same perspective that the gift among individuals, families, or nations, is most often understood. When one gave, one showed *hesed*, that mutual good will and beneficence that is the rule between allies or friends. One who accepts the gift accepts the covenant* and is prohibited from any attitude of hostility (Gn 32,14; Js 9,12ff; 2 S 17,27...; 19, 33...). But the gifts that were intended as bribes are sharply censured (Ex 23,8; Is 5,23). The attitude is, therefore, not without nobility, since the reciprocity of the offerings normally witnesses to the reciprocity of good feeling.

The gift to the poor, recommended in glowing terms (alms*), itself tends to become similar to reciprocal giving. The hope is that some day the poor man would be able to return the gift (Si 22,23) or that Yahweh would make up for it (Pr 19,17). Giving to the wicked is clearly discouraged (Tb 4,17): such a gift would be sheer waste (Si 12,1-7). The OT was careful to join a reasonable prudence to a very real generosity.

NT

"If you knew the gift of God..." (Jn 4,10). Setting in full light the foolish generosity of God (R 5,7f), the NT overturns human values. This was indeed the time of the gift.

1. *The gift of God in Jesus Christ.* The Father reveals His love* for us by giving us His own Son (Jn 3,16); and in His Son the Father gave Himself, for Jesus is filled with all the riches of the Father (Jn 1,14): words and deeds, power to judge and to give life, name, glory, love—all

that is the Father's is given to Jesus (Jn 17).

In His faithfulness* to the love that unites Him to the Father (Jn 15,10), Jesus achieves the complete gift of Himself: "He gives His life" (Mt 20,28 p). "The true bread of heaven given by the Father," He gives "His flesh for the life of the world" (Jn 6,32.51; cf Lk 22,19; "This is my body given for you"). By His sacrifice, He brings it about that the promised Spirit* is given to us (Ac 2,33), "the gift of god" *par excellence* (Ac 8,20; 11,17). Right on this earth we thus have the pledge of our inheritance*: we are made rich with every spiritual gift (1 Co 1,5ff), with a variety of charisms (12), with the gifts of the risen Christ (E 4,7-12); never will the superabundance of the gift of grace* be sufficiently praised (R 5,15-21). In a hidden but true manner (Col 3,3f), we already live by the eternal life*, "the free gift of God" (R 6,23).

2. *The gift to God in Jesus Christ.* Since the sacrifice of Christ, at one and the same time the gift of God to mankind (Jn 3,16) and the gift of mankind to God (He 2,16f), men need no longer offer other gifts. The perfect victim is eternally sufficient (He 7,27). But they must join themselves to this victim and, offering themselves to God (R 12,1), place themselves at His disposal for the service of others (G 5, 13-16; He 13,16). For grace is not received like a present in which a man can shut himself up; it is received to bring forth fruit* (Jn 16; cf Mt 13,12).

3. *The gift without return.* The motion of giving to others takes on, then, a fullness and intensity never before known. The "lust" that opposes it must be fought unceasingly. Henceforth, instead of seeking reciprocity of pledges, one must rather fly from it (Lk 14,12ff). When a person has received so much from God, any calculating, any narrowness of heart becomes scandalous (Mt 18,32f). "Give to whoever asks of you" (Mt 5,42). "Freely you have received, freely give" (Mt 10,8). Whether material goods or spiritual gifts, the Christian is called to look upon all as riches for which he is merely the steward and which have been entrusted to him for the service of others (1 P 4,10f). In an extraordinary invitation Jesus asks the man who wishes perfection to give away his entire fortune (Lk 18,22). The gift of God in Jesus Christ sweeps us along even further: Jesus "gave up His own life for us," His grace induces "us to offer our life also for our brothers" (1 Jn 3,16); "there is no greater love..." (Jn 15,13).

This gift brings about union in love and arouses thanksgiving* in all (2 Co 9,12-15). The one giving thanks God as much as and more than the beneficiary, for he knows that his generosity itself is a grace (2 Co 8,1), a fruit of the love that comes from God (cf 1 Jn 3,14-18). And this is why, finally, "it is more blessed to give than to receive" (Ac 20,35).

→Almsgiving — Blessing — Bread — Charisms —Earth OT II 2—First-Fruits—God NT V— Grace—Inheritance—Justification II 3—King-dom NT II 3—Love I NT 1; II NT 2—Pre-destine 4—Presence of God OT III 2; NT I— Promises—Sacrifice—Spirit of God OT I 3; NT III—Thanksgiving—Wealth—Wisdom OT III 4.

AV jrc

GLORY

I. GLORY IN GENERAL

In the Hebrew Bible the word that signifies glory, *kabod*, implies the idea of weight. The weight of a being in existence defines its importance, the respect which it inspires, its glory. For the Hebrew, therefore, glory does not designate so much the renown as the real value, estimated according to its weight.

The basis of glory could be riches. Abraham was said to be "very glorious" because he possessed "cattle, silver, and gold" (Gn 13,2). Glory also designates the high social position occupied by a man, and the authority which it confers on him. Joseph says to his brothers: "Tell my father all the glory I have in Egypt" (Gn 45,13). Job, ruined and humiliated, cries: "He has despoiled me of my glory!" (Jb 19,9; 29,1-25). With power* (Is 8,7; 16,14; 17,3f; 21,16; Jr 48,18), glory implies radiance. It designates the flash of beauty*. One speaks of the glory of the vestments of Aaron (Ex 28, 2.40), of the glory of the temple (Hg 2,3.7.9) or of Jerusalem (Is 62,2), or of the "glory of Lebanon" (Is 35,1f; 60,13).

Glory is, *par excellence*, the property of the king. It speaks, with its riches and its power, of the luster of his reign (1 Ch 29,28; 2 Ch 17,5). Solomon receives from God "riches and glory such as no other among the kings" (1 K 3, 9-14; cf Mt 6,29). Man, king of creation, is "crowned with glory" by God (Ps 8,6).

II. CRITIQUE OF HUMAN GLORY

The OT has seen the fragility of human glory: "Be thou not afraid when a man shall be made rich, and when the glory of his house shall be increased. For when he shall die, he shall take nothing away: nor shall his glory descend with him" (Ps 49,17f). The Bible has known how to tie glory to moral and religious values (Pr 3,35; 20,3; 29,23). Obedience to God excels all human glory (Nm 22,17f). In God is the only solid foundation of glory (Ps 62,6.8). The wise man who has meditated on the ephemeral glory of the godless does not want "to have" anything more for his glory than God: "In your glory you will receive me" (Ps 73,24f). This attitude will be, in its perfection, that of Christ. When Satan offers Him "all the kingdoms of the world with their glory," Jesus answers: "The Lord your God shall you adore and Him only shall you worship" (Mt 4,8ff).

III. THE GLORY OF YAHWEH

The expression "the glory of Yahweh*" means God* Himself, insofar as He is revealed in His majesty, His power, the glow of His holiness, the dynamism of His being. The glory of Yahweh is therefore epiphanic. The OT knows two types of manifestations or epiphanies of the divine glory: the lofty deeds of God and His manifestations.

1. *The lofty deeds of God.* God manifests His glory by His striking interventions, His judgments*, His "signs" (Nm 14,22). Such is *par excellence* the miracle* of the Red Sea (Ex 14, 18); such also, that of the manna* and the quail: "In the morning you will see the glory of Yahweh" (Ex 16,7). God comes to the aid of His own. The glory is then almost synonymous with salvation* (Is 35,1-4; 44,23; comp Is 40,5 and Lk 3,6). The God of the covenant* uses His glory to save and relieve His people. His glory is His power at the service of His love* and His fidelity: "When Yahweh will rebuild Zion, He will be seen in His glory" (Ps 102,17; cf Ez 39,21-29). His creative work also manifests the glory of God. "The glory of Yahweh fills all the earth" (Nm 14,21); among natural phenomena, the storm* is one of the most expressive of His glory (Ps 29,3-9; cf 97, 1-6).

2. *The apparitions of "the glory of Yahweh."*

In the second type of divine manifestations, the glory, the visible reality (Ex 16,10), is the flashing radiance of the divine being. Hence, the prayer of Moses: "Give me the grace to see* your glory!" (Ex 33,18). On Sinai the glory of Yahweh took on the aspect of a flame crowning the mountain* (Ex 24,15ff; Dt 5,22ff). From having drawn near in the cloud*, Moses returns, "the skin of his face radiant" (Ex 34,29), "with such a glory," says Paul, "that the children of Israel were not able to gaze upon him" (2 Co 3,7). After Sinai the glory clothes the sanctuary: "It will be consecrated by my glory" (Ex 29,43; 40,34). The glory of Yahweh is enthroned there on the ark of the covenant*. From then Israel is at the service of this glory (Lv 9,6.23f); it lives, moves and triumphs under its radiance (Nm 16,1—17,15; 20,1-13; 40,36ff). The ark and the glory are closely connected. For Israel, to lose one is to lose the other (1 S 4,21f). Later the glory will fill the temple* (1 K 8,10ff) and it is from here that it will withdraw at the time of the exile* as a sign of rebuke (Ez 9—11). Between this local and ritual concept of the glory and the active and dynamic concept, the relation remains close. In both instances God is revealed as present* to His people* to save them, to sanctify them, and to rule them. The bond between the two notions appears clear at the time of the consecration of the sanctuary. God then said: "They will know that it is I, Yahweh, their God, who made them leave the land of Egypt to remain among them" (Ex 29,46).

It is under the aspect of a royal glory that Isaiah contemplates the glory of Yahweh. The prophet sees the Lord*, His throne elevated, His retinue filling the sanctuary, His court of Seraphim crying His glory (Is 6,1ff). This is a devouring fire*, holiness which lays bare the stains of the creature, its nothingness, its radical weakness. It does not triumph, however, to destroy, but to purify and to regenerate; and it wishes to invade all the earth. The visions of Ezekiel speak of the transcendent liberty of the glory, which deserts the temple (Ez 11,22f), then radiates over a community renewed by the Spirit* (36,23ff; 39,21-29).

The last part of the Book of Isaiah unites the two aspects of glory: God reigns in the holy city, then regenerated by His power* and illumined by His presence*: "Arise; be enlightened, O Jerusalem, for your light* is come and the glory of the Lord is upon you" (Is 60,1). Jerusalem is seen "raised up in glory in the midst of the earth" (62,7; cf Ba 5,3). From her the glory of God radiates over all the nations*, who come to her dazzled (Is 60,3). Among the prophets of the exile, in the psalms of the kingdom, in the apocalypses, glory reaches to a certain universal dimension of an eschatological character: "I come to gather the nations of all tongues. They will come to behold my glory" (66,18f; cf Ps 97,6; Ha 2,14).

Against this luminous background is detached the figure "without beauty, without glory" (Is 52,14) of the one who is nevertheless charged to make the divine glory radiate to the extremities of the earth: "You are my Servant* for in you will I glory" (49,3).

IV. THE GLORY OF CHRIST

The essential revelation of the NT is the connection of glory with the person of Jesus. The glory of God is entirely present in Him. Son* of God, He is the "splendor of His glory, the figure of His substance" (He 1,3). The glory of God is "on His face" (2 Co 4,6); from Him it radiates on men (3,18). He is "the Lord of glory" (1 Co 2,8). It was already His glory that Isaiah contemplated, and "it was of Him he spoke" (Jn 12,41).

1. *Eschatological glory*. The full manifestation of the divine glory in Jesus will take place at the parousia. "The Son* of Man will come in the glory of His Father with His angels*" (Mk 8, 38; cf Mt 24,30; 25,31) and will manifest His glory by the consummation of His work*, at the same time as judgment* and salvation*. The NT has tended toward this "apparition of the glory of our great God and Savior, Christ Jesus" (Tt 2,13f), toward "eternal glory in Christ" (1 P 5,10), to which God has called us (1 Th 2, 12) and which is "going to be revealed" (1 P 5, 1), "for that which is at present momentary works for us beyond measure exceedingly an eternal weight of glory" (2 Co 4,17). The whole of creation* yearns for the revelation of this glory (R 8,19). John sees the new Jerusalem* descending from heaven*, streaming with light: "The glory of God has illumined it, and the Lamb holds the place of a torch" (Ap 21,23).

2. *Paschal glory*. By the resurrection and the ascension* Christ has already "entered" (Lk 24, 26) into the divine glory, which the Father, in His love, has "given Him before the creation of the world" (Jn 17,24) and which belongs to Him as Son, equal to the Father. The Man-God

has been taken into the divine cloud*, "taken up" (Ac 1,9.11), "taken up in glory" (1 Tm 3, 16), "God has raised...and has given Him glory" (1 P 1,21). He has "glorified His Servant Jesus" (Ac 3,13). This glory, as the "glory of Yahweh" in the OT, is a sphere of transcendent purity, of holiness, of light, of power, of life. The risen Jesus radiates this glory in all His being. Stephen dying saw "the glory of God, and Jesus standing at the right* hand of God" (7,55). Saul was blinded by His "luminous glory" (22,11). By comparison, the glory of Sinai is nothing (2 Co 3,10). The glory of the risen Christ blinds Paul as the light* of a new creation*: "For God who commanded the light to shine out of darkness, has shined in our hearts to give the light of the knowledge of the glory of God which is in the face* of Christ Jesus" (4,6).

3. *Glory in the earthly ministry and the passion of Christ.* The glory of God is manifested not only in the resurrection, but in the life, the ministry, and the death of Jesus. The gospels are doxophanies, especially that of Luke among the synoptics. In the scene of the annunciation the coming of the Holy Spirit* upon Mary evokes the descent of the glory, in the sanctuary of the OT (Lk 1,35). At the nativity, "the glory of the Lord" surrounds the shepherds with its light (2,9f). This glory is visible at the baptism of Jesus and at His transfiguration* (9,32.35; 2 P 1,17f), in His miracles*, His Word*, the eminent holiness of His life, His death. This was not merely the means introducing the Messiah to His "glory" (Lk 24,26): the signs which accompany it reveal in the crucified Himself "the Lord* of glory*" (1 Co 2,8).

In John the revelation of glory in the life and death of Jesus appears still more explicit. Jesus is the Word incarnate. In His flesh* dwells and is revealed the glory of the only Son of God (Jn 1,14.18). It manifests itself from the very first "sign" (2,11). It appears in the transcendent union of Jesus with the Father who sends Him, better still in their unity* (10,30). The works* of Jesus are the works of the Father, who "accomplishes" them in the Son (14,10) and there reveals His glory (11,40), light*, and life* for the world*. Above all this glory shines forth throughout the passion. It is the hour* of Jesus, the loftiest of theophanies. Jesus "consecrates" Himself to His death (17,19) in all clearness (13,1.3; 18,4; 19,28) by obedience to the Father (14,31) and for the glory of His name* (12,28). He makes a free gift of His life (10,18) out of love for His own (13,1). The cross* transfigured becomes the sign of "the elevation" of the Son of Man (12,23.31). Calvary offers to the gaze of all (19,37) the mystery of the divine "I am" of Jesus (8,27). The water* and the blood* springing from the side of Christ, symbolize the fruitfulness* of His death, source of life*. Such is His glory (7,37ff; 19,34.36).

4. *The ecclesial glory.* The glorification of Christ is completed in Christians (Jn 17,10). In them the sacrifice of Jesus bears its fruit* to the glory of the Father and the Son (12,24); 15,8). The Holy Spirit*, sent by the Father and the Son, is, with the sacramental water and blood (1 Jn 5,7), the artisan of this glorification. Christians enter by Him into the knowledge* and the possession of the riches of Christ (Jn 16,14f; 2 Co 1,22; 5,5). Already the glory of the risen Christ is reflected in them, transforming them to His image* "of glory unto glory" (3,18; Col 1,10f; 2 Th 1,12). By the Spirit even suffering* is transfigured (1 P 4,14).

5. *Christian honor.* The consciousness of this glory begets the feeling of Christian dignity and of Christian honor. Already in the OT it is the greatness of Israel to be the people to whom God has revealed His glory. To Israel* "belongs the glory" (R 9,4). God is "his glory" (Ps 106,20). Already fidelity to God is in Israel colored by a religious sense of honor. The divine commandment is the glory of Israel (Ps 119,5f); idolatry* its supreme sin: Israel then "barters" His glory for the idol" (106,20). In the midst of a world which is lost for not having wished to give to God the glory that is His due (R 1,21f), Christians are saved, "citizens of heaven" (Ph 3,20); "risen with Christ" (Col 3,1), "they shine as lights* in the world" (Ph 2,15f). It is their honor that "men, in seeing their good works*, give glory to (their) Father who is in heaven" (Mt 5,16). Before the glory of the Christian name*, all feeling of social inferiority disappears: "Let the brother* of low condition glory in his exaltation, and the rich in his being low" (Jm 1,9), for there is no longer room for "considerations of persons" (Jm 2,1ff). The feeling of Christian pride* extends even to the body*, in which Christians should "glorify God" (1 Co 6,15,19f). Finally, to suffer for the Christian name* is a glory (1 P 4,15f). It is the seeking of worldly honor which, according to John, has denied access to faith* to more than one (Jn 5,44; 12,43). Jesus Himself opened up the way to the Christian

understanding of honor. Indifferent to glory among men (5,41), He "despised the infamy of the cross*" (He 12,2). His unique honor was to fulfill His mission*, "not seeking His own glory," but "the glory of Him who sent Him" (Jn 7,18), putting His honor in the hands of His Father alone (8,50.54).

V. PRAISE OF GLORY

The duty of man is to recognize and praise the divine glory. The OT sings the glory of the creator,* king*, savior, and saint of Israel (Ps 147,1). It deplores the sin* which puts a veil before the divine glory (Is 52,5; Ez 36,20ff; R 2,24). It burns with the desire of seeing the divine glory recognized by all the world (Ps 145,10f; 57,6.12).

In the NT the doxology has Christ for its center. "It is through Him that we say our Amen* to the glory of God" (2 Co 1,20). Through Him arises "to God the only wise... glory forever and ever" (R 16,27; He 13,15). Glory is given to God for His birth (Lk 2,20), for His miracles (Mk 2,12...), and for His death (Lk 23,47). The doxologies measure the progress of His message (Ac 11,18; 13,48; 21,20), as they punctuate the dogmatic explanations of Paul (G 1,3f; etc.). The doxologies of the Apocalypse summarize in a solemn liturgy the whole drama of redemption (Ap 15,3f). Finally, as the Church* is "the people* whom God has acquired for the praise* of His glory" (E 1,14), to the Father is given "glory in the Church and in Christ Jesus unto all generations world without end!" (3,21).

To the liturgical doxology, the martyr* adds the doxology of blood. "Despising his life even unto death" (Ap 12,11), the believer thus professes that fidelity to God excels all human glory and worth. At the price of his blood*, like Peter, he "glorifies God" (Jn 21,18).

The final doxology, at the end of history, is the chanting of the "marriage of the Lamb*!" (Ap 19,7). The spouse* appears clothed "in a robe of linen of blinding whiteness" (19,8). In the fire of the "great tribulation," the Church is apparelled for the eternal bridals, with the only glory worthy of her spouse: the virtues, the offerings, the sacrifices of the saints.

And yet the glory of the bride comes to her entirely from her spouse. It is in His blood* that the robes of the elect have been made "white*" (7,14; 15,2); and if the bride wears this striking apparel, it is because "it has been given her" to do so (19,8). She is left to clothe herself day after day with the "good works* which God has prepared in advance, that we should walk in them" (E 2,10). The love of Christ is at the beginning of this glory, for "Christ has loved the Church and delivered Himself for her...: He wished to present her to Himself all resplendent with glory, without spot or wrinkle or anything of the kind, but holy and immaculate" (5,25.27). In this mystery of love* and of holiness* is consummated the revelation of the glory of God.

→Angels—Apparitions of Christ 1—Ark of the Covenant III—Ascension—Beatitude OT I 1—Blessing IV 1—Clothing II—Cloud 2.4—Cross I 4, II 1.3—Day of the Lord NT I 1, III 2—Face 5—Fire OT I—God NT III—Heaven III—Hope NT III, IV—Humility IV—Image V—Jesus Christ II 1 a b; II 2 d—Light & Dark OT I 2; NT I 3—Moses 4—Name OT 4; NT I—Power—Presence of God OT II; NT III—Pride NT 3—Resurrection NT I 2.4—Reward II 4—Right Hand 2—See—Son of Man—Spirit of God NT V 1—Storm 2—Strength II—Suffering NT III 2—Thanksgiving O; OT 2; NT 1—Transfiguration—Victory NT 2—White—Works OT II 3.

DM wjy

GOD

The Bible is not a treatise on God; it does not withdraw and stand apart as if to describe an object; it does not invite us to speak of God. Rather the Bible calls us to hear Him and to answer Him by acknowledging His glory and serving Him. If we live in the spirit of obedience and with gratitude, it is possible to formulate what God has said about Himself in the Bible. He does not speak of Himself in the same way in the OT and the NT, when He speaks to us through the prophets and through His Son (He 1,1f). More than with any other subject the distinction between the OT and the NT must here be rigorously observed; for "no one has ever seen God; only His only begotten Son, who is in the bosom of the Father, has made Him known" (Jn 1,18). One must first reject the heretical opposition between the vindictive God of the OT and the God of love of the NT. One must then likewise hold fast that only Jesus* unlocks the secret of the one God of the two Testaments.

OT

I. GOD IS FIRST

Since "the beginning" (Gn 1,1; Jn 1,1), God exists and His existence forces itself on us as an initial fact which needs no other explanation. God had no origin, no becoming. The OT does not know those theogonies which, in the religions of the ancient East, explain the beginning of the world by the birth of the gods. Because He alone is "the first and the last" (Is 41,4; 44,6; 48,12), the world is entirely His work, His creation*.

Because He is first, God does not have to introduce Himself. He demands recognition by man's spirit through the sole fact that He is God. In no way should there be thought of a discovery of God, a graduated approach of man resulting in the acknowledgment of His existence. To know Him is to be known (cf Am 3, 2) and to discover Him at the source of one's own existence; to fly from Him is to find oneself yet followed by His gaze (Gn 3,10; Ps 139,7).

Because God is first, as soon as he makes Himself known His personality, His reactions, His plans are sharply defined. Let a person come to know Him just a little and he knows, from the moment when he discovers Him, that God wishes something very specific and that He knows precisely where he goes and what he does.

This absolute priority of God is expressed in the traditions of the Pentateuch in two complementary ways. The so-called Yahwist tradition places Yahweh on stage from the beginning of the world and, well before the episode of the burning bush, depicts Him pursuing His own plan*. The Elohist traditions, on the contrary, underscore the novelty produced by the revelation to Moses of the divine name*; but at the same time these traditions indicate that beneath these different names, which are almost always terms descriptive of the divine name El, God was already making Himself known. Indeed Moses was able to recognize Yahweh as the true God only because already, obscurely but clearly, he knew God. This identity of the God of reason with the God of revelations*, this priority of God, present to the spirit of man as soon as he awakened to it, is indicated throughout the Bible by the immediate and constant identification between Yahweh and Elohim, between the God who reveals Himself to Israel and the God whom the nations* are able to name.

This is why whenever Yahweh reveals Himself in apparitions He names and defines Himself by pronouncing the name El/Elohim, with all that expression calls to mind: "the God of your father" (Ex 3,6), "the God of your fathers" (Ex 3,15), "your God" (Ex 6,7), "God of tenderness and mercy" (Ex 34,6), "your (intimate form) God" (Is 41,10; 43,3), or simply, "God" (1 K 18,21.36f). Between the name of God and that of Yahweh a living relation is established, a dialectic: in order to be able to reveal Himself as Yahweh, the God of Israel poses as God; but in revealing Himself as Yahweh, He said in an entirely new manner who God is and what He is.

II. EL, ELOHIM, YAHWEH

In practice, *El* is the archaic and poetical equivalent of *Elohim*. Like *Elohim* and our word *God*, *El* is simultaneously a common name designating the divinity in general and a proper name designating the individual and definite person who is God. *Elohim* is a plural; not a plural of majesty—Hebrew was unaware of that—nor further a polytheistic survival, unlikely in the Israelite mentality on this particular point. But the idea is probably a trace of a common Semitic conception that perceived the divinity as a plurality of forces.

1. *El*. El was known and adored outside of Israel. As a common name, it designates the divinity in almost the whole Semitic world. As a proper name it was that of a great god who seems to have been the supreme god in the western sector of the world, in particular in Phoenicia and in Canaan. Was El, from its Semitic origins, a common god, supreme and unique, whose pure but fragile religion would have been later eclipsed by a more seductive and corrupt polytheism? Was he rather the chief god and guide of the different Semitic clans, an individual god for each clan, but without being able to make his unicity prevail when he clashed with other groups, finally degraded into one of those figures of the pagan pantheon? This history is obscure but the fact is certain that the patriarchs, under different titles— El 'Elyôn (Gn 14,22), El Rōï (16,13), El Shaddai (17,1; 35,11; 48,3), El Bethel (35,7), El 'Ōlām (21,33)—call their god El; and that, in the case of El 'Elyôn especially, the God of Melchizedech, king of Salem, this El was treated as identical with the God of Abraham (14,20ff). These facts show not only that the God of Israel is the "judge of all the earth" (18,25), but also

that He is capable of being recognized and adored in reality as the true God even outside the chosen people.

This recognition, however, is exceptional. In most cases, the gods of the nations were not gods (Jr 2,11; 2 K 19,18). El/Elohim is for practical purposes known as the true God only by revealing Himself to His people under the name of Yahweh. The unrivaled personality of Yahweh endowed the divine face, always more or less pale and constantly disfigured by the different paganisms, with a consistency and life that compelled recognition.

2. *Yahweh*. In Yahweh God reveals what He is and what He does, His name and His operation. His operation is wonderful, unheard of, and His name mysterious. Since the manifestations of El to the patriarchs occur unexpectedly in a familiar country, in simple and familiar forms, Yahweh reveals Himself to Moses in the savage surroundings of the desert* and in the distress of the exile in the formidable figure of fire* (Ex 3,1-15). The complementary revelation of Ex 33,18-23; 34,1-7 is not less terrifying. However, this God of consuming holiness is a God of fidelity and salvation. He remembers Abraham and his progeny (3,6), it attentive to the misery of the Hebrews in Egypt (3,7), is determined to deliver them (3,8) and to grant them prosperity. The name of Yahweh under which He manifests Himself corresponds to the work in which He is engaged. This name, certainly, involves a mystery*; it speaks of something inaccessible: "I am who am" (3,14). No one can force Him, nor even penetrate to Him. But it also asserts something positive, an extraordinarily active and attentive presence*, an invulnerable and liberating power*, an inviolable promise: "I am."

III.   GOD SPEAKS OF HIMSELF

Yahweh is the echo, repeated by men in the third person, of the revelation* made by God in the first person: *'ehyeh*, "I am." This name which says everything is constantly commented upon by God Himself in the diverse formulas He gave of Himself.

1. *The living God*. In the mouth of God the formula "I am living" is perhaps a late creation of Ezekiel. It is in any case the reverberation of a very ancient and popular formula of the faith of Israel: "Yahweh is living" (Jg 8,19;

1 K 17,1...), "the living God" (1 S 17,26.36; 2 K 19,16...). It well expresses the impression had by a man in the presence of Yahweh, that of an extraordinarily active presence of an immediate and total spontaneity "which is never tired or weary" (Is 40,28), "who slumbers not nor sleeps" (Ps 121,4), who reacts the moment anyone touches His followers (1 S 17,26.36; Ho 2,1; Dn 6,21). His language at Horeb, at the moment when He reveals His name, translates quite well this intensity of life*, this attention to His works: "I saw...I have lent my ear... I know...I am determined...I send you" (Ex 3,7-10). The "I am" prepared by these revelations cannot be less dynamic than they.

2. *The Holy God*. "I swear it by my holiness" (Am 4,2), "I am the holy one" (Ho 11,9). This irresistible but totally interior vitality, this ardor that simultaneously consumes and gives life is holiness*. God is holy (Is 6,3), His name is holy (Am 2,7; Lv 20,3; Is 57,15...), and the radiance of His holiness sanctifies His people (Ex 19,6). His holiness opens before God an abyss that cannot be crossed by any creature. No one can abide His coming; the firmament reels, the mountains* melt (Jg 5,4f; Ex 19,16...), and all flesh* trembles, not only the sinful man who sees himself condemned, but even the flaming seraphim, unworthy to appear before God (Is 6,2).

3. *"I am a jealous God"* (Ex 20,5). The jealous zeal* of God is another aspect of His interior intensity. It is the passion that He brings to all He does and to all that He touches. He cannot tolerate a foreign hand coming to profane anything of importance to Him, anything that His care "sanctifies" and makes holy. He cannot bear that any of His undertakings should fail (cf Ex 32,12; Ez 36,22...); He cannot "yield His glory to anyone" (Is 48,11). When the prophets discover that this passion of God for the work of His hands is the passion of a spouse*, the theme takes on a new intensity and intimacy. The divine jealousy is at one and the same time a fearful wrath* and a vulnerable tenderness*.

4. *"You shall have no other gods but me"* (Ex 20,3). The jealousy of God has for its essential object "other gods." Israelite monotheism is not the fruit either of a metaphysical reflection or of a political integration or of a religious evolution. In Israel it is an affirmation of faith as ancient as its belief, that is, the certitude

of its election*, the certainty of having been from among all the nations chosen by a God to whom all nations belong. This monotheism of the faith was for a long time able to reconcile itself with representations implying the existence of "other gods," of Chemosh, for example, in Moab (Jg 11,23f), or the impossibility of adoring Yahweh outside the boundaries of "His heritage" (1 S 26,19; 2 K 5,17). But from the beginning Yahweh could not tolerate their concurrent presence; and the whole history of Israel narrates His victories* over His rivals, the gods of Egypt, the Baals of Canaan, the imperial divinities of Ashur and of Babylon, until the definitive triumph which makes clear the nothingness of false gods. It was a victory sometimes obtained by miracles, but which is permanently that of the faith. Jeremiah, who foretells the total downfall of Judah and Jerusalem, notes simply in passing that the gods of the nations "are not even gods" (Jr 2,11), but "those that exist not" (5,7). In the midst of exile, faced with the fascination of idolatry*, from the bosom of a defeated and dishonored people burst forth the definitive cries: "Before me, no god was formed and there will be none after me; I, I, I am Yahweh, there is no other savior than I" (Is 43,10f...) The memory of Horeb appears evident and the spiritual continuity between texts so profoundly different is significant: Yahweh is the only God because He is the only one able to save, "the first and the last," always at hand, always attentive. If idolatry attacks Him "mortally," that is because it questions His ability and His will to save, because it denies that He is ever present and active, that He is Yahweh.

5. *"I am God and not man"* (Ho 11,9). God is absolutely different from man. He is spirit* and man is flesh* (cf Is 31,3), fragile and perishable like the grass (Is 40,7f). This difference is so radical that man is always misinterpreting it. In the power* of God he sees efficacious strength* but not faithfulness* of heart (cf Nm 23,19); in His holiness*, he sees only distance that cannot be crossed, without suspecting that it is at the same time proximity and tenderness: "I am the holy one in the midst of you and I do not love destruction" (Ho 11,9). The incomprehensible transcendence of God brings it about that He is at the same time "the most high" in His "elevated and holy abode" and He "who lives with the contrite and humbled man" (Is 57,15). He is the all-powerful and the God of the poor; He makes

His voice heard in the din of the tempest (Ex 19,18ff) and in the whisper of the breeze (1 K 19,12); He is invisible and even Moses did not view His face* (Ex 33,23); but when appealing to the desires of the human heart in order to reveal Himself, He hands over His own heart. He forbade any likeness of Himself, any image* of which man would make an idol* by adoring the work of his hands, but He is presented to our imagination beneath the most concrete aspect. He is "the wholly other" who defies comparison (Is 40,25), but He is everywhere at home and He is in no way a stranger to us. His reactions and His behavior are translated by our most familiar activities: He "modeled" with His own hands the clay which would be man (Gn 2,7), He bolted the door of the ark after Noah (Gn 7,16) to be certain that none of its inhabitants might be lost. He has the victorious outburst of the leader in war* (Ex 15, 3...) and the solicitude of the shepherd* for his sheep (Ez 34,16). He holds the universe in His hand, and He shows toward tiny Israel the affection of the vinekeeper for his vineyard (Is 5,1-7), the tenderness of a father (Ho 11,1) and of a mother (Is 49,15), the passion of a man in love (Ho 2,16f). The anthropomorphisms can be naive, but they always express in a profound manner an essential trait of the true God: if He created man to His own image*, He is able to reveal Himself through the reactions of man. Without genealogy, spouse, or sex—if He is other than us—it is not because He is less a man than we; He is on the contrary the perfect ideal that we dream about for man: "God is not a man, to lie, nor a son of man, to withdraw" (Nm 23,19). God always surpasses us and always in the way that we least expect it.

IV. THE NAMES GIVEN TO GOD BY MAN

The God of the OT reveals Himself finally in the demeanor of those who know Him and in the names that they give Him. At first sight it might be thought that it is possible to distinguish official titles used in the communal worship and the names created by personal piety. As a matter of fact, the same titles are found, together with the same overtones in collective as well as individual prayer. God is as much "the rock* of Israel" (Gn 49,24; 2 S 23,3...) as "my rock" (Ps 18,3f; 144,1) or simply "rock" (Ps 18,32), "my shield" (Ps 18,3; 144,2) and "our shield" (Ps 84,10; 89,19), "the shepherd* of His people" (Mi 7,14...) and "my shepherd" (Ps 23,1). These are signs that the encounter with God is personal and living.

These epithets are astonishingly simple, borrowed from the domestic realities of daily life. The Bible did not know the endless litanies of Egypt or of Babylon, the titles that are multiplied for the pagan divinities. The God of Israel is infinitely great, but He is always within reach of hand and voice. He is the most high (*'Elyôn*), the everlasting (*'Ōlām*), the holy one, but at the same time "the God who sees me" (*El Rôï*, Gn 16,13). Almost all His names define Him by His relation to His own: "the terror of Isaac" (Gn 31,42.53); the mighty One of Jacob" (49,24); the God of Abraham, of Isaac, and of Jacob (Ex 3,6); the God of Israel; our God; my God; my Lord. Even the epithet "the holy one," which rigorously sets Him apart from all flesh, becomes on His lips "the holy one of Israel" (Is 1,4...) and makes of this holiness something which belongs to the people of God. In this reciprocal possession appears the mystery of the covenant and the proclamation of the relation which unites to His only-begotten Son the God of our Lord Jesus Christ.

NT

I. IN JESUS CHRIST, ACCESS TO THE FATHER

In Jesus* God is revealed in a definitive and complete manner: having made us the gift of His own Son. He has nothing more to save for Himself and nothing more to give (cf R 8,32). The basic certitude of the Church, the discovery which illumines the entire NT, is that with the life, death, and resurrection of Jesus, God fulfilled His supreme act and that every man is henceforth able to have access to Him. This unique and definitive act can take diverse names, depending upon one's perspectives. The most archaic formulas simply proclaim: "This Jesus who was crucified...God has made Lord and Christ...the promise is for you, for your children, and for those who are at a distance" (Ac 2,36-39); "through Him, repentance and remission of sin" (Ac 5,31). These expressions appear unassuming, but, though less explicit, they already bear as far as the fullest Pauline formulas on the "mystery* of God, which is Christ" (Col 1,27; 2,2), "in whom we have...access to the Father" (E 2,18; 3,12); or as far as those of John: "No one has ever seen God; the only-begotten Son* who is in the bosom of the Father, He has made Him known" (Jn 1,18). Since the first day the Christian faith has known that on the Son* of Man, the heavens, abode of God, are opened (Ac 7,56; Jn 1,51; cf Mk 1,10). Under varied forms and diverse names, "revelation of the justice* of God" (R 3,21), "reconciliation*" (R 5,11; E 2,16), "radiance on our faces of the glory* of God" (2 Co 3,18), "knowledge of God" (Jn 17,3), the basis of our Christian experience is the same: God is within reach; by an unheard of demonstration of power and love, in the person of Christ, He offers Himself to those who will receive Him.

It is, therefore, all one—to adhere to Jesus Christ in faith* and to know* the true God: "eternal life is...to know the one true God and (His) envoy, Jesus Christ" (Jn 17,3). Confronted with the event of Jesus Christ, the man who approaches the faith, whether he comes from Judaism or paganism, whether he has been formed by reason or by the tradition of Israel, discovers the true countenance and the living presence of God.

II. IN JESUS CHRIST REVELATION OF THE TRUE GOD

1. *The idolater.* Placed by Paul in opposition to the gospel (R 1,16f), the idolater discovers in Christ the true countenance of God and that of his own sin. The gospel of Christ unmasks at one and the same time both the perversion of the pagan wisdom which "changes the glory of the incorruptible God for an image of a corruptible being" (R 1,23) and the source of this perversion, "the preference being given to the creature rather than to the Creator" (1,25), "the refusal to give Him glory" (1,21); and its fatal climax, the degradation of man and death (1,32). In "renouncing idols...to await" Jesus Christ, the pagan discovers "the living and true God" (1 Th 1,9); he finds in the face* of Christ the glory* of God (2 Co 4,6) from which he was exiled (R 3,23).

2. *For the pagan who seeks* God gropingly (Ac 17,27) and remains able by wisdom to lay hold of God (1 Co 1,21; R 1,20), the discovery that he makes in Christ is not less new, the change is not less profound. In the God of Jesus Christ he finds, certainly, the divine "nature," eternal, unchangeable, all-powerful, omniscient, infinitely good and desirable. But these attributes no longer possess the impartial

and distant light of metaphysical proof; they have the flashing and mysterious revelation of the initiatives by which God has manifested His grace* and has turned His face* toward us (cf Nm 6,25). His omniscience becomes a personal glance that follows us in secret (Mt 6,4ff) and examines the depths of our hearts (Lk 16,15); His omnipotence is His ability to "raise up from these stones children to Abraham" (Mt 3,9), "to call nothingness into existence" (R 4,17), whether it is a matter of giving rise to creation, of causing the birth of a son to Abraham, or of raising from the dead the Lord Jesus (R 4,24). His eternity is the faithfulness of His Word* and the firmness of His promise*; it is "the kingdom which God has prepared for His own from the beginning of the world" (Mt 25,34). His goodness is the unheard of marvel that "God has loved* us first" (1 Jn 4,10.19) when we were as yet His enemies (R 5,10). For the natural knowledge* of God which, real as it is, is only in the last analysis a deeper knowledge of the world, the revelation of Jesus Christ substitutes the immediate presence, the personal embrace of the living God. For to know God is to be known by Him (G 4,9).

3. *The Jew* who awaited God knew Him already. By personal choice, God had made him understand his calling*. In the covenant* He had taken charge of his existence. Through His prophets* He had truly spoken to him His Word (He 1,1). God was before him as a living being who called him to dialogue. But to what extent this dialogue is to go, to what involvement on the part of God, what answer from man, the OT is unable to say. There is still the distance between the Lord and His most faithful servants. God is a "God of tenderness and mercy" (Ex 34,6); He has the passion of a spouse and the tenderness of a father; but behind these images that can in some vague way feed our dreams while still hiding from us the reality, what secret has God in store for us?

The secret is revealed in Jesus Christ. Through Him the judgment takes place, the sharing of hearts. Those that refuse to believe in Jesus say in vain of His Father: "He is our God"; they do not know Him and they are nothing but liars (Jn 8,54f; cf 8,19). Those that believe are no longer held back by any secret, whatever it may be; or rather they have entered into the secret, into the impenetrable mystery of God; they are at home in this mystery, they understand the Son when He takes them into His confidence: "All that I have heard from my Father, I have made known to you" (Jn 15,15). No more figures or parables, for Jesus speaks of His Father with complete openness (16,25). No more questions to be put to Him (16,23), no more disquiet (14,1); the disciples "have seen the Father" (14,7).

4. *God is love.* Such is the secret (1 Jn 4,8.16), to which no one comes except through Jesus Christ, "recognizing" in Him "the love which God has for us" (4,16). The OT had been able vaguely to sense that love*, since it is the great commandment (Dt 6,5; Mt 22,37) and the supreme good (Ct 8,6f), should be the most accurate definition of God (cf Ex 34,6). But it was yet a matter of language created by man, of images that must be transposed. In Jesus Christ, God Himself gives us the decisive proof, free from any equivocation, that the event on which the destiny of the world depends is a work of His love. By handing over "His well-beloved Son" (Mk 1,11; 12,6) to death for us, God gave us proof (R 5,8) that His definitive attitude toward us is "to love the world" (Jn 3,16) and that, by this supreme and irrevocable act He loves us with the same love with which He loves His only-begotten Son, and makes us capable of loving Him with the love that His Son bears Him; He makes us a gift of the love that unites Father and Son and which is their Holy Spirit.

III. THE GLORY OF GOD ON THE FACE OF JESUS CHRIST

The Christian certitude of having been admitted to the very secret of God does not rest on a deduction. Reason can make it explicit: "He who has handed over His only-begotten Son, will He not give us everything?" (R 8,32); but its force does not come from our logic; it comes from the unconditioned revelation that the presence of the Word living in our flesh enacts for us, men living in the flesh. In Christ has really "appeared the love of God for man" (Tt 3,4). Him whom "no one has ever seen" (Jn 1,18), Jesus has not only described and depicted for us; He has not merely given us a clear idea of Him. "Radiance of the Father's splendor, image of His substance" (He 1,3), He has made us see* Him as it were made visible: "Who sees me sees the Father" (Jn 14,9). It is not a question merely of a reproduction, though perfect, of a copy identical with the original. Since He is the only-begotten Son, is in the

Father*, and possesses in Himself the Father (14,40), Jesus could not say one word, make one move without turning to His Father, without receiving from Him His impulse and orientating His every action toward Him (5,19f.30). As He could do nothing without looking upon the Father, He could not say what He is without referring Himself to the Father (Mt 11,27). There is, at the source of all He does and all He is, the presence and love of His Father. This is the secret of His personality, of the glory* that streams from His face (2 Co 4,6) and stamps His every deed.

IV. THE GOD OF OUR LORD JESUS CHRIST

The God of Jesus Christ is His Father. When Jesus addresses Him, He does so with the familiarity and impulse of a child: *"Abba."* But He is also His God because the Father, possessing the divinity without receiving it from any other, gives it entirely to the Son* whom He begets from all eternity and to the Holy Spirit in whom both are united. Jesus thus reveals to us the identity of the Father* and of God, a mystery of divinity and a mystery of trinity. Three times Paul repeats the formula that expresses this revelation: "the God and Father of our Lord Jesus Christ" (R 15,6; 2 Co 11,31; E 1,3). Christ reveals to us the divine Trinity in the one way that is accessible to us (if one dare say it), in that to which God has predestined us by creating us to His image*, that of filial dependence.

Because the Son in the presence of His Father is the perfect exemplar of the creature in the presence of God, He reveals to us in the Father the perfect image of a God who makes Himself known with righteous wisdom and who revealed Himself to Israel. The God of Jesus Christ possesses, in a fullness and with an originality of which man would never dream, the traits that He revealed of Himself in the OT. He is for Jesus as He is for none of us "the first and the last." He from whom Christ comes and to whom Christ returns, He who is the explanation of all things and from whom all things come, He whose will is to be achieved at all costs and who is ever sufficient. He is the holy one, the only good, the only Lord. He is the sole one, in comparison with which nothing else counts. And Jesus, to show what the Father is worth, "that the world might know that (He loves His) Father" (Jn 14,31), sacrifices all the splendors of creation and faces the power of Satan, the horror of the cross. He is the living God, ever active, attentive to all His creatures, passionately fond of His children. It is this fire that consumes Jesus as long as He has not restored the kingdom to His Father (Lk 12,50).

V. GOD IS SPIRIT

This encounter of Father and Son takes place in the Holy Spirit*. In the Spirit, Jesus Christ hears the Father say, "You are my Son"; and He receives His joy (Mk 1,10). In the Spirit, He makes His joy at being the Son return to the Father (Lk 10,21f). Since He can only be united with the Father in the Spirit, Jesus Christ can no longer reveal the Father without simultaneously revealing the Holy Spirit.

Revealing that the Spirit is a divine person, Jesus Christ also reveals that "God is spirit" (Jn 4,24) and what this means. If the Father and the Son are united in the Spirit, they are not united in order to rejoice in the possession of one another but in the giving; their union is a giving and produces a giving. But if the Spirit who is the gift thus seals* the union of Father and Son, then they are essentially gifts themselves, their common essence is to give itself, to exist in the other. Now this power of life, communication, and liberty is the Spirit. God is spirit and this means that He is at one and the same time omnipotence and total disposability, sovereign affirmation of Himself and complete detachment; this means that in taking possession of His creatures He makes them exist in all their originality. It is an entirely different thing from not being made of matter; it is above all barriers and all retreats. It is to be eternally and at every moment a new, intact force of life and communion.

dom OT III; NT I 2—Word of God—Worship —Yahweh.

JG jrc

GODLESS MAN

With a variety of vocabulary both in the Hebrew and in the Greek, the Bible describes a spiritual attitude which is the contrary of piety*. To hatred for God and for His Law, it adds the nuance of hostility and bluster. Paul tells of the coming of the "impious man" *par excellence* who in the last days "will lift himself up over everyone and will show himself as God" (2 Th 2,3f.8). He adds that the "mystery* of godlessness is already at work" in the world (2,7). In fact, it has been at work since the beginning of history, since Adam* despised God's command (Gn 3,5.22).

OT

1. *Impious men in the sight of God.* Impiety is a universal fact for sinful humanity: the godlessness of the generation of the deluge (Gn 6,11; cf Jb 22,15ff), of those who built the tower of Babel (Gn 11,4), of the inhabitants of Sodom (Ws 10,6), and so on. But it asserts itself with peculiar clearness among the pagan peoples who were the enemies of Israel. For example—the persecuting Pharaoh (cf Ws 10,20; 11,9), the Canaanite idolaters (Ws 12,9), the blaspheming Sennacherib (Is 37,17), proud Babylon* (Is 13, 11; 14,4), and the persecuting Antiochus Epiphanes (2 M 7,34). Even so, the people of God are not exempt from this same impiety, as is seen by their revolts in the desert (Ps 106,13-33), their infidelities in the promised land (Ps 106, 34-40). God actually sends the pagans to punish this sinful and impious nation (Is 10,6; cf 1,4). Despite a national conversion, the psalmists and wise men will still denounce even after the exile the presence of impiety among the faithful people. The Maccabean crisis will draw attention to certain Jews who have strayed from the right path (cf 1 M 2,23; 3,15; 6,21, etc.).

2. *The impious and the just.* In the sapiential literature, the human race appears divided into two groups: the just and wise as opposed to the impious and foolish. Between these two is an opposition and fratricidal battle which already gives a sketch of the separate activities of the two realms. Having begun with Cain and Abel

(Gn 4,8...), this battle extends to all periods. The godless man gives free rein to his instincts: trickery, violence, sensuality, pride (Ps 36,2-5; Ws 2,6-10). He condemns God (Ps 10,3f; 14,1). He sets upon both the just and the poor* (Ps 10,6-11; 17,9-12; Ws 2,10-20). He has apparent success which sometimes can be lasting and is a source of genuine anguish for religious people (Ps 94,1-6; Jb 21,7-13). Out of a concern for justice*, first of all, the persecuted ask God for the destruction of these misguided wicked people (Ps 10,12-18; 31,18f; 109,6...), and in advance they take delight in a vengeance* which astonishes us (Ps 58,11).

3. *Retribution of the impious.* Those faithful to the covenant know very well that the impious are headed for ruin (cf Ps 1,4ff; 34,22; 37,9f.12-17.20). But this calm statement of retribution*, which still is pictured in a temporal setting, clashes with some scandalous facts. There are some impious men who prosper (Jr 12,1f; Jb 21,7-16; Ps 73,2-12) as if there were no divine sanction (Qo 7,15; 8,10-14). Prophetic eschatology gives assurance that the last days will see the Messiah*-King destroy the godless (Is 11,4; Ps 72,3); and God will exterminate them at the time of his judgment* (cf Is 24,1-13; 25,1f). But, while it looks forward to this last day, it does not explain precisely how the wicked must expiate their crimes.

However, the question will be settled on the individual level for all, and we have to wait until a late date for the solution. In the time of the Maccabees, we know that finally all the godless will appear personally before the tribunal of God (2 M 7,34f) and there will be no resurrection* to life for them (2 M 7,14; cf Dn 12,2). And so the Book of Wisdom can paint the picture of their final chastisement after death* (Ws 3,10ff; 4,3-6; 5,7-14). This solemn attestation is the source of a salutary reflection. Actually, God does not want the godless to die, but to be converted and to live (Ez 33,11; cf 18, 20-27 and 33,8-19). A similar merciful outlook will be found in the NT.

NT

1. *True impiety.* In the Greek vocabulary of the NT the spiritual attitude already stigmatized by the OT is indicated in a more exact way. It is godlessness (*asebeia*), injustice (*adikia*), and the rejection of law (*anomia*). Throughout the discussions between Jesus and the Pharisees, however, two ideas of this scorn for God are

met. For the Pharisees* the touchstone of piety* is the practice of legal prescriptions and the traditions* which surround them. Ignorance of this matter is already impiety (cf Jn 7,49). Jesus, therefore, was wrong to eat with sinners (Mt 9,11 p), to be their friend (Mt 11,19 p), to lodge with them (Lk 19,7). Yet Jesus knows very well that every man is a sinner, and that none can say of himself that he is pious and just. The gospel* which He brings gives sinners the possibility of repentance* and salvation (Lk 5,32). The touchstone of true piety will be the attitude one adopts toward this gospel.

2. *The call of the impious to salvation.* The problem is exactly the same since Christ has consummated His sacrifice* by dying "at the hands of the wicked" (Ac 2,23). He died, "a just man for the unjust" (1 P 3,18), although He willed "to be reckoned among the wicked" (Mk 15,28 p). He died for the godless (R 5,6) in order that they might be justified by faith in Him (R 4,5). The just* of the NT are the impious who have been justified by grace*. Recognizing the call to salvation in the gospel, they renounced their impiety (Tt 2,12) to turn to Christ. Henceforth the truly impious are those who refuse this message or who corrupt it: the false teachers who trouble the faithful (2 Tm 2,16; Jude 4.18; 2 P 2,1ff; 3,3f) and who merit the name of Antichrist* (1 Jn 2,22): the indifferent who live in voluntary ignorance (2 P 3,5; cf Mt 24,37; Lk 17,26-30); and especially the pagan powers who excite supreme impiety against the Lord (2 Th 2,3.8). Such is the context for the revelation of the mystery of impiety.

3. *God's anger on the impious.* More so than in the OT, the chastisement of impiety is now a certainty. The anger of God reveals itself in a permanent way against all impiety and human injustice (R 1,18; cf 2,8). This is all the more true in the perspective of the last days and the last judgment*. Then will the Lord reduce the impious to nothingness by the splendor of His coming (2 Th 2,8). All who take part in the mystery* of impiety will be confounded and punished (Jude 15; 2 P 2,7). If punishment comes late it is because God makes use of patience to allow the wicked to be converted (2 P 2,9).

→Antichrist—Arrogance 3—Blasphemy—Error OT—Folly—Hate—Hypocrite 2—Lie II 2 a —Persecution I 1—Piety—Sin—Unbelief— Wealth II.

ADa & PG jrs

GOOD & EVIL

"God saw that all He had made was very good" (Gn 1,31). And yet to hasten the coming of the eschatological kingdom, Christ tells us to ask in the Our Father: "Deliver us from evil" (Mt 6,13). The opposition between these two formulas poses a problem for the modern-day believer, a problem to which the Bible itself offers the elements of solution: in this world which was created good, whence does evil come? When and how will it be overcome?

I. GOOD AND EVIL IN THE WORLD

1. For one who sees or experiences them, *some things are subjectively good or bad.* The Hebrew word *ṭôb* (translated both by the Greek words *kalos* and *agathos*—beautiful and good [cf Lk 6,27.35] indicates basically persons or objects which call forth pleasant sensations or a feeling of general well-being: a good meal (Jg 19,6-9; 1 K 21,7; Rt 3,7), a beautiful young girl (Es 1, 11), generous people (Gn 40,14)—in brief anything that brings happiness or makes life* easier in the physical or psychological order (cf Dt 30, 15). On the other hand, anything that leads to sickness*, to suffering* under any form, and, above all to death* is bad (hb. *ra'*, gr. *ponēros* and *kakos*).

2. *Can the objective goodness of creatures*, as the Greeks understood it, *be also spoken of?* For everything they imagined an archetype which was to be imitated or realized; they presented to man an ideal, the *kalos-kagathos*, who possesses within himself all moral, esthetic, and social qualities; and is therefore open, agreeable, and useful to the city*. In this particular perspective, how are we to conceive evil? As an imperfection, a purely negative thing, an absence of good? Or, or the contrary, as a reality within its own right and flowing from that evil principle which played an important part in Iranian thought. When the Bible attributes a real goodness to things, it does not understand it in this way. When it says: "God saw that it was good" (Gn 1,4...), it shows that this goodness is not measured in view of any abstract good, but in relation to God the Creator, who alone gives things their goodness.

3. *Man's goodness* is a particular case. In fact, it depends partly on himself. At the beginning of creation*, God placed him before "the tree*

of the knowledge* of good and evil," leaving him the possibility of obeying and of enjoying the tree of life or of disobeying and being drawn to death (Gn 2,9.17), a conclusive test of the liberty* which is given to every man. If he rejects evil and does good (Is 7,15; Am 5,14; cf Is 1,16f), by observing the law* of God and by conforming himself to His will* (cf Dt 6,18; 12,28; Mi 6,8), he will be good and will be pleasing to Him (Gn 6,8); otherwise he will be bad and will be displeasing to Him (38,7). Because he is responsible*, his choice, made in conscience*, will determine his moral quality and, consequently, his destiny.

4. Now, seduced by the evil one (cf Satan*), *man* has from the beginning chosen evil.* He has looked for his good in creatures "good to eat and alluring to see" (Gn 3,6), but beyond the will* of God—and this is the very essence of sin*. In these creatures he has found only the bitter fruits of suffering and death (Gn 3,16-19). As a result of his sin, evil was brought into the world and it proliferated there. The children of Adam have become so bad that God is sorry that He made them (Gn 6,5ff): there is no one who does good on earth (Ps 14,1ff; R 3,10ff). This too is the experience of man: he feels frustrated in his insatiable desires (Qo 5,9ff; 6,7), prevented from fully enjoying the goods of the earth (Qo 5,14; 11,2-6), even incapable of "doing good without ever sinning" (Qo 7,20) because evil flows from his own heart* (Gn 6,5; Ps 28,3; Jr 7,24; Mt 15,19f). He is affected in his freedom (R 7,19f), a slave of sin (6,17); even his reason is affected: inverting the order of things, he calls good evil and evil good (Is 5,20; R 1,21-25). Finally, discouraged and deceived, he observes that "everything is vanity" (Qo 1,2); he experiences in the hard way that "the whole world lies in the power of the evil one" (1 Jn 5,19; cf Jn 7,7). In fact, evil is not simply the absence of good, but a positive force which subdues man and corrupts the universe (Gn 3,17f). God did not create it, but now that it is here it stands in opposition to Him. A never-ending war* begins and will last throughout history: to save man, the all-powerful God will have to triumph over evil and the evil one (Ez 38—39; Ap 12,7-17).

II. GOD ALONE IS GOOD

1. *God's goodness* is one of the main revelations of the OT. Having known evil in its greatest degree during the slavery in Egypt, Israel discovers good in Yahweh, her liberator*. God snatches her away from death (Ex 3,7f; 18,9), then leads her to the promised land, "the good country" (Dt 8,7-10) "which flows with milk* and honey" and "on which Yahweh keeps His eyes continually." Israel will find happiness there (cf Dt 4,40) if she remains faithful to the covenant* (Dt 8,11-19; 11,8-12; 18,28).

2. *God imposes a condition on His gifts.* Like Adam in the Garden of Eden, Israel finds herself facing a choice which will decide her destiny. God places before her blessing* and curse* (Dt 11,26ff) because both physical and moral good are equally connected with God: if Israel "was to forget Yahweh," to cease loving Him, no longer observed the commandments and broke the covenant, she would be deprived immediately of these earthly goods (Dt 11,17) and sent back into slavery until her land became a desert* (Dt 30,15-20; 2 K 17,7-23; Ho 2,4-14). Israel tests the truth of this basic doctrine of the covenant in the course of her history: as in the drama of Paradise the experience of sin is followed by the experience of misery.

3. *The success of the impious and the misery of the just.* But the doctrine seems to fail in an important point: does not God seem to favor the impious and leave good men in misery? The just* suffer, the Servant* of Yahweh is persecuted, the prophets* are put to death (cf Jr 12,1f; 15,15-18; Is 53; Ps 22; Jb 23—24). The experience of suffering* is painful and mysterious and we do not see its meaning right away. Yet through it, the poor* of Yahweh learn slowly to detach themselves from "the goods of this world*" which are unstable and of short duration (Zp 3,11ff; cf Mt 6,19ff; Lk 12,33f). They learn to find their strength*, their life*, and their good in God who alone remains to them when everything has gone and to whom they adhere with heroic faith* and hope* (Ps 22,20; 42,6; 73,25; Jr 20,11). Without a doubt they are still subject to evil, but they have on their side the Savior who in the day of salvation* will triumph; then, they will receive the goods that God has promised to those who are faithful to Him (Ps 22,27; Jr 31,10-14). In all truth, God "alone is good" (Mk 10,18 p).

III. GOD TRIUMPHS OVER EVIL

In revealing Himself as Savior, God already announced His future victory* over evil. This victory had yet to be affirmed in a definitive way by making man good and removing him from the power of the evil one (1 Jn 5,18f), the "prince of this world*" (Lk 4,6; Jn 12,31; 14,30).

1. *Of course God had already given the Law**, which was good and destined to bring life (R 7,12ff): if he observed the commandments, man would be doing good and would gain eternal life (Mt 19,16f). But of itself this Law remained ineffective so long as the heart* of man, a prisoner of sin, was not changed. To will the good is within man's* reach, but to accomplish it is not: he does not the good he desires but the evil which he does not desire (R 7,18ff). Concupiscence drags him, as it were, in spite of himself; and the Law, which was made for his good, turns out in the end to be his downfall (R 7,7.12f; G 3,19). This interior struggle leaves him infinitely unhappy; who then will deliver him (R 7,14-24)?

2. Only *"Jesus Christ our Lord"* (R 7,25) can reach evil at its roots by triumphing over it in the very heart of man (cf Ez 36,26f). He is the new Adam* (R 5,12-21) without sin (Jn 8,46) over whom Satan has no power. He has made Himself obedient even up to dying on the cross* (Ph 2,8), He has given His life so that His sheep may find a place to graze (Jn 10,9-18). He has made Himself "a curse* for us so that through faith we may receive the promised Spirit" (G 3, 13f).

3. *The fruits of the Spirit.* It is thus that, by renouncing life and earthly goods (He 12,2) and sending us the Holy Spirit, Christ has obtained for us the "good things" which we should ask for from the Father (Mt 7,11; cf Lk 11,13). It is no longer a question of material goods like those once promised to the Hebrews, but of "the fruits* of the Spirit" within us (G 5,22-25). From now on, man, transformed by grace*, can "do good" (G 6,9f), "perform good works*" (Mt 5,16; 1 Tm 6,18f; Tt 3,8.14), "conquer evil by good" (R 12,21). To become capable of these new goods, he has to pass through privation, "to sell his goods" and follow* Christ (Mt 19,21), "to deny himself and carry his cross with him" (Mt 10,38f; 16,24ff).

4. *The victory of good over evil.* In choosing to live in such a way with Christ so as to obey the inspirations of the Holy Spirit, the Christian breaks away from solidarity with Adam's choice. In this way moral evil is truly conquered in him. Its physical and psychological consequences certainly remain as long as the present world lasts, but man now glories in his tribulations. Through them he acquires patience* (R 5,4) and considers that "the sufferings of the present time are not to be compared with the glory* that has to be revealed" (8,18-25). Thus, through faith and hope he is already in possession of the incorruptible riches (Lk 12,33f) which are conferred through Christ's mediation*, who is the "high priest of the goods to come" (He 9,11; 10,1). It is only a beginning, for believing is not seeing*; but faith guarantees the goods that are hoped for (He 11,1), those of the better fatherland* (He 11,16), those of the new world which God will create for His elect (Ap 21,1ff).

→Babel/Babylon 3—City OT 3; NT 2—Conscience—Curse—Fruit III—Growth 2 a—Hate III 3—Lie III— Light & Dark NT II—Persecution — Responsibility — Reward — Satan — Sin — Suffering — Taste — Tongue 1 — Trial/Temptation—Vengeance—Virtues & Vices—War—Way II—Wisdom OT I 2, II 1; NT III 2—Works NT I 3—World.

JdV pjb

GOSPEL

For us, the gospel designates either the account which relates the life of Jesus, or the section of it which is read at each Mass. In profane Greek, *gospel* signifies "good news," especially an announcement of victory. The Roman peace, the principal events of the life of the emperor, who was a god and savior, were extolled as so many gospels. On the other hand, there is no doubt that the word *gospel* was borrowed from the OT by Christian language with the particular meaning which it already possessed, to announce salvation.

I. OLD TESTAMENT

Hebrew uses a word to signify the announcement of good news regarding a private person or the life of the nation: the death of an enemy (2 S 18,19f.26), victory (Ps 68,12), the salvation of Judah (Na 2,1). This word assumes its specifically religious value in Is 40—66. The "herald of good news" announces at the end of the exile the coming of the kingdom of God (Is 52,7). His message is one of consolation*, pardon for sin, and the return of God to Zion (40,1f.9). This "gospel" is a divine force in action (52,1f). Proclaimed from a mountain top (40,9), it concerns all the nations* (52,10; cf Ps 96,2). It reaches beyond even the horizon of the century. Over and above return from exile, it proclaims the victory* and ultimate reign of God.

II. JESUS

1. *The herald of good news.* In His answer to the men sent by the Baptist (Mt 11,4f p), as in the scene at the synagogue in Nazareth (Lk 4,16-21), Jesus applies to Himself the text of Isaiah 61,1f: "Anointed by God with the Holy Spirit and with power" (Ac 10,38; Mt 3, 16f), He comes "to preach the gospel to the poor*."

2. *The good news.* "The time is fufilled. The reign of God is at hand" (Mk 1,15): such is the essence of the message. But this time the very person of the messenger becomes the center of the good news. The gospel is Jesus Himself (cf Mk 1,1). The angels proclaimed His birth as a gospel (Lk 2,10f). With Him the reign of God becomes present (Mt 12,28). The man who abandons all for the sake of Jesus and "for the sake of the gospel" receives "a hundred-fold now in this life" (Mk 10,30). We see also the crowds pressing upon this bearer of good news and trying to detain Him. But the gospel must be spread abroad: "I must preach the good news of the kingdom of God to other towns also, for that is what I was sent to do" (Lk 4, 43).

3. *Response to the gospel will be repentance* and faith** (Mk 1,15). God offers a grace of forgiveness (Mk 2,10 p; 2,17 p), and of renewal (Mk 2,21f). He expects from the man who will confess and renounce his sin that he risk his life for the gospel: "He who would save his life will lose it, and he who loses his life for my sake and for the gospel's sake will save it" (Mk 8,35). These followers born of the gospel are the "poor in spirit" (Mt 5,3 p; Mk 10, 17-23 p), the "little ones" (Mt 11,28; Lk 9,48; 10,21), even sinners (Lk 15,1f; 18,9-14; Mt 21,

31), even pagans (Mt 8,10f; 15,21-28 p). Consciousness of their need predisposes them to listen and to sense the divine compassion out of which the gospel proceeds (Mt 9,36; 14,14 p; Lk 1,41-50; 19,1-10).

III. THE APOSTLES

1. *The messengers.* The risen Jesus commands His apostles "to go throughout the whole world proclaiming the gospel to all of creation" (Mk 16,15), "to every nation" (Mk 13,10). The Book of Acts describes the stages of this preaching (or kerygma). In spite of obstacles the good news diffuses itself "even to the ends of the earth" (Ac 1,8). Through the grace of the Spirit the Church announces the good news "confidently" (2,29; 4,13.31; 28,31). This work is so important that to perform it suffices to gain for one the name of evangelist: thus the deacon Philip is called "evangelist" (Ac 21,8; cf E 4,11; 2 Tm 4,5).

2. *The message.* The good news is always that of the kingdom of God (Ac 8,12; 14,21f; 19,8; 20,25; 28,23). It proclaims that "the promise made to our fathers has been fulfilled" (13,32). It is the grace of forgiveness, the gift of the Spirit (2,38; 3,26; 10,43; 13,38; 17,30). But henceforth it can equally be called "the good news of Jesus" (8,35; 17,18), "of the name* of Jesus Christ" (8,12), "of the Lord* Jesus" (11,20), and "of peace* through Jesus Christ" (10,36). The resurrection of Christ becomes the center of the gospel.

3. *Reception of the gospel.* The good news is accompanied by "signs" promised by Jesus (Mk 16,17; Ac 4,30; 5,12.16; 8,6ff; 19,11f). It is propagated in an atmosphere of poverty, simplicity, community charity, and joy (Ac 2,46; 5,41; 8,8.39). The gospel everywhere encounters hearts* of one accord in "desiring to hear the Word* of God" (13,7.12), and eager to know what must be done in order to be saved (16, 29f). They have the common quality of "listening*" (2,22.37; 3,22f; etc.), "receiving" (8,14; 11,1; 17,11), and of "obeying" (6,7). On the other hand, contemptuous conceit (13,41), jealousy (13,45f), and fickleness (17,32) close the hearts of men to the gospel.

IV. ST. PAUL

1. *The messenger.* Paul is incomparably the

man of the gospel. God had "set him apart to declare the gospel" (R 1,1). He revealed to Paul His Son that he might "declare Him among the pagans" (G 1,15f). He "entrusted the gospel" to him (1 Th 2,4). As a "minister" of the gospel (Col 1,23), Paul must preach it (1 Co 9,16). In doing so he renders to God "a spiritual worship*" (R 1,9) and exercises a "sacred office" (R 15,16).

2. *The message.* Paul refers to this gospel simply as "the gospel" or as the gospel "of God," "of His Son...Jesus Christ our Lord" (R 1,3ff.9), "of Christ" (R 15,19f; 2 Co 2,12; etc.), "of the glory of Christ" (2 Co 4,4), or of His "unfathomable riches" (E 3,8).

a) *The power of salvation.* Paul's gospel, like that of the whole Church, centers upon the death and resurrection of Christ (1 Co 15,1-5). But it does so with a singular energy and is directed toward Christ's glorious coming (1 Co 15,22-28). It is the new economy of salvation insofar as it is propagated and developed by the apostolic preaching* and by the divine energy intrinsic to it: "it is a power* of God unto salvation" (R 1,16). "The gospel thrives and bears fruit all over the world" (Col 1,6). A spectacular growth of churches, a superabundance of charisms*, and an unprecedented spiritual renewal are all joined to the supernatural "assurance" of the apostle himself—the witness of His power which is about to conquer the world (G 3,5; 4,26f; 2 Co 2,12; 3,4; 1 Th 1,5). Paul works with his hands and "bears all things ...rather than offer any hindrance to the gospel of Christ" (1 Co 9,12).

b) *Fulfillment of the Scriptures.* Paul emphasizes the continuity of the gospel with the OT: it is "the disclosure of a mystery* enveloped in silence* for long ages, but now revealed and through the Scriptures brought to the knowledge of all the nations" (R 16,25f). The promise* made to Abraham (Gn 12,3) was a "fore gospel" which now is being accomplished in the conversion of the pagans (G 3,8; E 3,6).

3. *Human response to the gospel.* The gospel can only exercise its saving power when men respond to it with faith*; "It is a power of God for salvation for all who believe...In it is revealed God's justice from faith to faith" (R 1,16f; 1 Co 1,18.20). It is the occasion for an option. Since it displays its saving power in seeming weakness and prolongs the mystery of

the cross* (1 Co 1,17—2,5), for some it is a scandal*, "foolishness" (1 Co 1,18.21.23; R 9, 32f; G 5,11); and it "remains concealed." Blinded by "the god of this world" these men "do not see the gospel resplendent with the glory of Christ" (2 Co 4,4). They do not obey* it (2 Th 1,8). But others receive the gospel in "the obedience of faith" (R 1,5; 2 Co 10,5). In the grace of the gospel, they open themselves to "the gospel of grace" (Ac 20,24).

V. ST. JOHN

Neither the gospel nor the epistles of John make use of the word *gospel. Word** and *witness** take its place. Their object is truth*, life*, and light*. But in the Apocalypse, John has a vision of "an angel flying in air, with eternal good news to announce to those who live on the earth" (14,6f), a gospel of the final coming of the kingdom of God.

CONCLUSION

When, in the course of the second century, the word *gospel* comes to designate the written account of the life and teachings of Jesus, it does not, therefore, lose its primitive meaning. It continues to signify the good news of salvation and of the kingdom of God in Christ. "This gospel," writes St. Irenaeus, "the apostles first of all preached. Then, by the will of God, they handed it on to us in the Scriptures so that it might become the basis and pillar of our faith." When the priest or deacon intones the formula: "Continuation of the holy gospel...," he is declaring to the world, just as the prophet or the apostle, the good news of his liberation by Jesus Christ. In the liturgical responses: "Glory to you, O Lord! Praise be to you, Christ!" we find, if we are attentive to the meaning of the words, all the enthusiasm and joy of the first encounter of the world with the newness of the gospel.

→Apostles II 1—Exhort—Israel NT 1—Jesus (Name of) III—Jesus Christ II 2—Kingdom NT I—Mystery II—Preach—Revelation NT—Salvation NT—Tradition NT I 2—Witness NT III 1—Word of God NT I, II.

DM afmcg

GRACE

I. THE MEANING OF THE WORD

The word which designates grace (gr. *charis*) is not a pure creation of Christianity; it appears in the OT. But it is the NT which has fixed its meaning and determined its extension. It has made use of this precise term to characterize the new order begun by Jesus Christ, and to oppose it to the old economy; the latter was governed by the Law* (R 6,14f; Jn 1,17).

Grace is the gift* of God which contains all other gifts, the giving of His Son* (R 8,32). But grace is more than just the gift. It is the gift which radiates the generosity of the giver and envelops with this generosity the creature who receives His gift. It is through grace that God gives and he who accepts God's gift finds grace and complacence in the sight of God.

By a significant conjuncture, the Hebrew word and the Greek word, translated into Latin by *gratia*, and into English by *grace*, lend themselves to designate at the same time the source of the gift in Him who gives and the effect of the gift in him who receives it. Indeed the supreme gift of God is not totally alien to the exchanges by which men are united among themselves and by which there exists between Him and us the bonds which reveal His image* in us. While the Hebrew *ḥēn* designates first the favor, the gratuitous benevolence of a highly placed person, then the concrete witness of this favor, shown by Him who gives and bestows favors, received by him who receives and finds grace, and finally the charm which draws the attention and retains the favor—the Greek *charis*, by an almost inverse movement, designates first the radiant seduction of beauty, then the radiance together with the interior of the beauty, and finally the gifts which are the witness of this generosity.

II. GRACE IN THE OT

Revealed and given by God in Jesus Christ, grace is present in the OT as a promise* and as a hope*. Under various forms, under different names, always uniting God who gives and man who receives, grace appears everywhere in the NT. The Christian reading of the OT such as St. Paul proposes to the Galatians, consists in recognizing in the ancient economy the acts and the features of the God of grace.

1. *Grace in God.* God gives His own definition of Himself: "Yahweh, God of tenderness and of grace, slow to wrath and rich in mercy and fidelity" (Ex 34,6). Grace in God is at the same time mercy* bent over misery (*ḥēn*) generous fidelity to His own (*ḥesed*), unshakable solidity in His engagements (*'emet*), tenderness* of heart and attachment of his whole being to those whom He loves* (*raḥamin*), inexhaustible justice* (*ṣedeq*), capable of assuring all His creatures the plenitude of their rights, and of fulfilling all their aspirations. That God could be the peace*, and the joy* of His own, is the effect of His grace: "How precious is your grase (*ḥesed*), O God! Men take refuge in the shadow of your wings, they are filled with the superabundance of your house, and you make them drink of the torrents of your delights" (Ps 36,8ff), "for your grace (*ḥesed*) is better than life" (63,4). Life*, the most precious of all blessings, pales before the experience of the divine generosity, this inexhaustible source. The grace of God could, therefore, be a life richer and fuller than all our experiences.

2. *Manifestations of God's grace.* The generosity of God is spread over all flesh (Si 1,10); His grace does not remain a treasure jealously guarded. But the striking sign of this generosity is the election* of Israel. It is an initiative altogether gratuitous, which is justified by no merit in the people elect, by no preliminary worth, either of number (Dt 7,7), or of good conduct (9,4), or "of the strength of its hand" (8,17), but only the "love for you and fidelity to the oath sworn to your fathers" (7,8; cf 4,37). At the beginning of Israel, there is but one explanation, the grace of the faithful God who keeps His covenant* and His love* (7,9). The symbol of this grace is the land which God gives to His people, "a land of torrents and of springs" (8,7), "of mountains and valleys watered by rain from heaven" (11,11), "cities which you did not build...houses which you have not filled, wells which you have not dug" (6,10f).

This gratuitousness is not without a purpose, blindly pouring out riches, as it were from an unusable abundance. The election has for its purpose the covenant. The grace which chooses and which gives is a gesture of knowing*; it attaches itself to him whom it chooses, and it awaits a response from him, thanks and love. This is the preaching of Deuteronomy (Dt 6,5. 12f; 10,12f; 11,1). The grace of God looks for partners, an exchange, a communion*.

3. *God's grace on His elect.* The word which undoubtedly best translates the effect produced on man by God's generosity is *blessing**. Blessing is much more than an external protection. It maintains in him who receives it life*, joy*, fullness* of strength*; it establishes between God and His creature a personal encounter; it makes the smile and regard of God rest upon man, the radiance of His face* and of His grace (*ḥēn*, Nm 6,25); this bond has something that is vital, for it touches on the creative power. It belongs to the father* to bless; and if the history of Israel is that of a blessing destined for all nations (Gn 12,3), it is because God is a father and fashions the destiny of His children (Is 45, 10ff). God's grace is the love of a father; it creates sons*. Because this blessing is that of a holy* God, the bond which it sets up with His elect is that of a consecration. The election is a call to the holiness and promise of consecrated life (Ex 19,6; Is 6,7; Lv 19,2).

From this filial response, from this consecration of life and heart, Israel holds off (cf Ho 4,1f; Is 1,4; Jr 9,4f). "As a cistern makes its water cold, so (Jerusalem) made her wickedness cold" (Jr 6,7; cf Ex 16; 20). Then God is discovered doing what man is radically incapable of doing, and bringing it about that man himself should be its author. Of a corrupted Jerusalem, He will make a just city (Is 1,21-26); of incurably rebellious hearts (Jr 5,1ff) He will make new* hearts capable of knowing* Him (Ho 2,21; Jr 31,31). This will be the work of His Spirit* (Ez 36,27); it will be the coming into the world of His own justice* (Is 45,8.24; 51,6).

III. THE GRACE OF GOD IS REVEALED IN JESUS CHRIST

The coming of Jesus Christ shows how far the divine generosity can go; even to giving us His own Son* (R 8,32). The source of this unheard of action is the mingling of tenderness, fidelity, and mercy by which Yahweh defined Himself, and to which the NT will give the specific name of grace, *charis*. The desire of God's grace (which is nearly always accompanied with His peace*, the great Semitic desire being thus associated with the typically Greek ideal of *charis*) introduces nearly all the apostolic letters and shows that, for Christians, it is the supreme gift*, that which summarizes all God's action and all that we could desire for our brethren.

In the person of Christ, "grace and truth have come to us" (Jn 1,17), we have seen* them (1,14), and suddenly we have known that "God is love*" (1 Jn 4,8); thus, on seeing Jesus Christ we know that His action is grace (Tt 2,11; cf 3,4).

Although the evangelical tradition common to the synoptics does not know the word, it is fully conscious of the reality. For it also Jesus is the supreme gift of the Father (Mt 21,37 p), delivered for us (26,28). The sensitivity of Jesus to human misery, His emotion in the presence of suffering, translate, moreover, the tenderness and the mercy by which the God of the OT is defined. And St. Paul, to encourage the Corinthians to generosity, reminds them of "the liberality (*charis*) of Jesus Christ...being rich he made Himself poor for us" (2 Co 8,9).

IV. THE GRATUITY OF GRACE

If God's grace is the secret of the redemption*, it is also the secret of the concrete way in which each Christian (R 12,6; E 6,7) and each Church receive and live it. The Churches of Macedonia have received the grace of generosity (2 Co 8,1f), the Philippians have received their part of the grace of the apostolate (Ph 1,7; cf 2 Tm 2,9), which explains the entire activity of Paul (R 1,5; cf 1 Co 3,10; cf G 1,15; E 3,2).

Through the variety of charisms* is revealed the election*, the choice coming from God, prior to all human options (R 1,5; G 1,15), which is the introduction to salvation* (G 1,6; 2 Tm 1, 9), which consecrates to a particular mission* (1 Co 3,10; G 2,8f).

For Paul the initial gratuity of election (R 11,5) will mark the whole of Christian existence. Salvation is a gift of God and not the reward due to work done (4,4); otherwise "grace would not be grace at all" (11,6). If salvation is due to any observance at all, then God's grace no longer has any object, "faith is pointless and the promise worth nothing" (4,14). Only faith* in the promise* respects the real nature of God's work, which is to be primarily a grace.

The concrete conditions in which grace is given make it even more gratuitous. It is an enemy* that God chooses, a condemned man whom He reprieves: "we were still helpless... still sinners...still enemies," unable to free ourselves from the power of sin, "when we were reconciled to God by the death of His Son" (5,6-10). And God's grace is not content to save us from death by a gesture of acquittal (3,24; E 2,5;); it extends generosity beyond all limits.

Where sin proliferated, grace abounds more than ever (R 5,15-21). Without reserve it opens up the inexhaustible wealth* of divine generosity (E 1,7; 2,7) and spreads it without counting the cost (2 Co 4,15; 9,14; cf 1 Co 1,7). From the moment that God delivered up His own Son on our behalf, how could "He refuse anything that He can give?" (R 8,32).

V. FRUITFULNESS OF GRACE

God's grace is not "fruitless" (1 Co 15,10). It enables faith to produce works*, to complete its work (1 Th 1,3; 2 Th 1,11), to "operate by charity" (G 5,6) and to produce fruits* (Col 1,10), "the good works God has prepared in advance for us to produce" (E 2,10). For the apostles grace is an inexhaustible source of activity (Ac 14,26; 15,40): it makes Paul all that he is and it works in him all that he does (1 Co 15,10), so much so that whatever is most personal in him, "what I am," is precisely the work of this grace.

Because grace is the principle of transformation and action it calls for constant collaboration. "Since we have been...entrusted with this work of administration, there is no weakening on our part" (2 Co 4,1), always on the alert "to obey grace" (1,12) and to "respond" to it (R 15,15; cf Ph 2,12f). Grace is never lacking; it is always "sufficient," even in the direst distress, for it is then that its power* is most obvious (2 Co 12,9).

Thus, grace is a birth* into a new life (Jn 3,3ff), the life of the Spirit* who loves the sons* of God (R 8,14-17). Paul often uses juridical terms to describe this existence, which are meant to prove the reality of the Christian regime instituted by grace. The Christian is "called in grace" (G 1,6), "established in grace" (R 5,2) and lives under its reign (5,21; 6,14). But this existence is not only a fact, having a juridical status fixed by authority: it is a life* in the fullest sense of the word, the life of those who have "returned from the dead" and live a new life with the risen Christ (6,4.8.11.13). Although Paul approaches the matter from a different angle, his experience at this point matches John's exactly: the grace of Christ is the gift of life (Jn 5,26; 6,33; 17,2).

This experience of life is that of the Holy Spirit*. The regime of grace is the regime of the Spirit (R 6,14; 7,6): man is freed from sin and bears the fruits of sanctification (6,22; 7,4). The Spirit, who is the gift* of God *par excellence* (Ac 8,20; 11,17), "bears witness to our spirit" (R 8,16), through an unquestioned experience, that grace really makes us sons of God, able to address God as Father*: Abba. This is the justification that is worked out by grace (3,23f): to be able to be in God's eyes exactly what He expects of us, sons before their Father (8,14-17); 1 Jn 3,1f). Realizing in this way that God's grace is the source of all his actions, the Christian adopts the right attitude with regard to men, genuine pride*. This does not consist in boasting that one has anything at all of one's own, but of having received everything by grace, and above all of having been granted justice. Paul is fond of linking together pride and grace (R 4,2ff; 5,2f; 2 Co 12,9; cf E 1,6). In the grace of God man succeeds in becoming himself.

→Beatitude OT I 1—Blessing—Charisms—Faith NT III 2—Gift—Good & Evil III 3—Justice—Justification II 3—Law *B* III 5; *C* III 1—Liberation/Liberty I, III 2 a c—Mercy—Salvation NT — Tenderness — Thanksgiving—Works NT II 1.

JG wjy

GROWTH

1. *Growth in creation**. Growth is the law of life*. God gives both men and animals the command to multiply. But men are not only to increase in number, they are to increase their control of the world (Gn 1,22.28; 9,7). Moreover, they must not forget that their growth depends on God, just as the growth of the rushes depends on the water (Jb 8,11ff). The blessing* of the Creator remains the principle of life and of its progress. Man's sin draws down a divine curse and would bring life on earth to an end (Gn 3,17; 6,5ff), if God did not show His mercy by renewing His blessing (9, 1-7), which, through Abraham, is to reach all nations (12,3; G 3,8).

2. *Growth in the history of salvation.*

a) *Growth of evil in the world.* Not only is evil present in creation but it increases there. War sets brother against brother and the innocent perishes (Gn 4,8); the spirit of revenge increases beyond measure and multiplies murders (4,24); wickedness grows in the heart of man and violence invades the earth; and if punishments of various sorts do point out the

220

malice of godless men (6,13; 11,9; 19,24f) very often these men see their prosperity (Ps 73,3-12; Jr 12,1) and their posterity (Jb 21,7f) increase. Not only does God tolerate this scandal, but He prevents His servants from stopping the growth of evil by claiming that He will wipe out the wicked (Mt 13,30). His method is to triumph over evil by good (R 12,31); where sin abounds He makes His grace abound even more (5,20).

b) Growth of the chosen people. From the midst of the sinful world God chooses for Himsel a people born of Jacob. Just as He granted that his descendants should increase (Gn 35, 11), He will be pleased to make His people grow if they are faithful to the covenant; otherwise He will bring them to ruin (Lv 26,9; Dt 28,63; 30,16). It is true that in His goodness God does not treat Israel like other peoples: He corrects them before their sins reach their full measure (2 M 6,12-16). The object of this punishment is a conversion opening their hearts to salvation; then God will let His people increase in numbers and in glory (Jr 30,19; Ez 36,10f.37f; Is 54,1ff).

c) Growth of the Savior and of His word.* To carry out this plan of salvation, God sends His Son Jesus into the world, full of grace and truth. But He is subject to the laws of the human condition; He is at first a child increasing in wisdom and strength (Lk 2,40.52); and if His preaching does reveal the mystery of His mission and person to men, it does so progressively and meets with opposition. This opposition goes on increasing until the hour when darkness* seems to triumph (Lk 6,11; 11,53f; 19,47f; 22,2.53); but it is at this hour that Jesus completes His work by reaching the peak of His love and revealing fully to men how much the Father loves them (Jn 3,16; 13,1; 15,13; 17,4; 19,30). As the grain that falls on the earth dies there and so multiplies (12,24), so the good Shepherd dies in order to give His sheep the superabundance of life (10,10f). His Word, sown in their hearts, will bear fruit (Lk 8,11.15); and that is why Luke expresses the progress of the infant Church sometimes by saying that the number of believers is increasing (Ac 2,41; 5,14; 6,7; 11,24) and sometimes by speaking of the growth of the Word (6,7; 12,24; 19,20).

d) Growth of the Church and of the Christian in it.* Growth is the law of Christian life

as of all life. The Christian must grow, not in isolation but in the Church in which he is inserted as a living stone*. While he is growing toward salvation, the spiritual house, which is the Church, is being built up (1 P 2,2-5). Paul urges the Christian to grow in faith (2 Co 10,15) and the knowledge of God by bearing fruit in all good works and growing in charity (Col 1, 10; Ph 1,9; Th 3,12). This progress in the knowledge of God is in the first place growth in His grace (2 P 3,18), for it is the Savior who is its author: the apostles, God's faithful collaborators, do but plant and water; it is God who give the increase (1 Co 3,6-9).

It is God too who gives each of the saints the grace to make progress toward Christ, their Head*, by the practice of true charity and by cooperating in this way in the building up of the Body of Christ, which effects its own growth by building itself up in charity (E 4,11-16). For the growth of each depends on the progress of his union with Christ; each individual must decrease, as John the Baptist said, so that Christ may increase and grow in him to his full stature (Jn 3,30; E 4,13), and so that, in the Lord and in the Spirit, the Church may be built up and ascend as a holy temple inhabited by God (2,21f).

3. *Toward the Kingdom* of God.* If the believer is constantly aiming at the goal (Ph, 3, 12ff) and anxious to advance from spiritual infancy to perfection (1 Co 3,1f; He 5,12ff), and if the Gospel must constantly bear fruit and grow in the world (Col 1,6), does this mean that the kingdom of God has to grow? Of course the parables* present this kingdom as the end of a movement: the movement of the leaven's action in the dough (Mt 13,33), the growth of the seed until the harvest, even the growth of a tree (13,23.32), and all this through the power that is in it (Mk 4,28). But does not this mean less the growth of the kingdom itself than the growth of the Church toward the kingdom, which it proclaims, of which it is the seed and which it awaits as a gift from God? Everyone should receive this gift* like a little child by believing in the Gospel which is its proclamation (10,15; cf 1,15), in order to be able to enter into that communion with God in which the kingdom consists, when the Son of Man comes in His glory to judge the world (Mt 25,31-34). It is then that God will reign, for communion with Him will be perfect: He will be all in all (1 Co 15,24-28). His kingdom does not grow: it is the goal at which all

spiritual growth aims and it is the desire for this goal that gives rise to this growth. Its arrival, like the resurrection* of Jesus, is the gift of the Father.

→Build—Church III 2—Fruitfulness—Fruit II —Fulfill—Fullness—Kingdom NT II 2—Harvest—New Birth 3—Perfection—Sow.

JR & MFL ems

H

HARDNESS OF HEART

The progressive sclerosis of the man who is separated from God is called hardness of heart, blindness. To harden the heart is to fatten the heart*; to stop the ears; to coat the eyes; to sleep; to throw a fit of giddiness, or torpor, or of falsehood so that one has a stiff neck and a heart of stone. This state can affect all men—pagans, Israelites, and even the disciples of Jesus.

I. AT THE SOURCE OF HARDNESS OF HEART

1. *The fact.* Two major texts—from Exodus and Isaiah—have exercised the religious reflection of Israel. If Pharaoh does not let Israel go, it is because God hardens his heart (Ex 4,21; 7,3; 9,12; 10,1.20.27; 11,10; 14,4) or he hardens it himself (Ex 7,13f.22; 8,15; 9,7.34f). Now these two interpretations are juxtaposed in the texts so that one cannot attribute to the second the intention of correcting the first. Hence a theological problem: if it is not surprising that man is the cause of his hardness of heart, how admit that God favors this attitude and even causes it? Now Paul clearly affirms: "God is merciful to whomever He wishes and hardens the heart of whomever He wishes" (R 9,18).

In the OT God gave Isaiah a mission: "Go, and say to this people: 'Listen but without understanding; look but without seeing!' Dull the heart of this people, make them hard of hearing, blindfold their eyes, lest their eyes see, their ears hear, their heart understand, they be converted and be cured" (Is 6,9f). Far from being set aside as offensive, this text was substantially used again by Jesus (Mt 13,13) and by His disciples (Mt 13,14f p; Ac 28,25ff), to explain the refusal with which Israel opposed Christ.

2. *Meaning.*

a) Does it suffice then to say that the hardness of heart of the people was not directly willed, but only foreseen by God? True the language of the Semite attributes to God a positive will to do what He is content with permitting; but this answer, valid to a certain point, seems to be an evasion. Instead of trying to excuse God, it is proper to consider the context in which these threats and verifications of hardness of heart are formulated. To harden the heart is not to disapprove; it is to bring judgment on a state of sin*; it is to wish that this sin bear visible fruits. Hardness of heart therefore is not due to an initiative of the divine wrath*, predestining* a man to damnation; He punishes the sin of which man does not repent. When man hardens his heart, he commits a sin; when God hardens the heart, He is not the source but the judge of sin. Hardness of heart characterizes the state of the sinner who refuses to be converted and who remains separated from God. It is the immanent sanction of sin, which shows the evil nature of the sinner: "Can an Ethiopian change his skin? A leopard its spots? And you, can you act right, you who have been accustomed to evil?" (Jr 13,23).

b) Paul tried to find a meaning in such a state of affairs. First of all, he goes into the providential plan* of God. Nothing escapes God. Pharaoh, whose personal fate Paul does not consider, is instrumental in the end in making the divine glory shine forth (Ex 9,16; 14,17f). By her hardness of heart Israel permits the entry of the pagan nations* into the Church (R 9). Moreover, God's plan is entirely ordered to the remnant* which must survive. Next, Israel's hardness of heart shows the severity of God, the edge of His anger. It is not for fun that God makes a covenant with a people. How would He tolerate heedlessness (Lk 17,26-29 p),

222

self-sufficiency (Dt 32,15), pride (Dt 8,12ff; Ne 9,16)? Finally, this hardness of heart shows God's patience*. He does not destroy the sinner, He continuously extends His hands toward a rebellious people (R 10,21 citing Is 65,2; cf Ho 11,1f; Jr 7,25; Ne 9,30). Thus, whether He seeks to attract the sinner or abandons him to himself, God shows His mercy* again and again.

II.   TOWARD THE VICTORY OF GOD

1. *Ambivalent situation.* John suggests perhaps an even more profound understanding of this fact from the metaphor of light*. Light blinds those who are not disposed to receive it (Jn 3,19ff). In the same way God, by the continual presence of His love, stimulates in the sinner a reaction of refusal. That is why miracles*, God's predisposing works, harden Pharaoh's heart and remain valueless in the eyes of the Israelites who murmur against Moses in the desert (Nm 14,11; Ps 106,7) and against Jesus after the multiplication of loaves (Jn 6, 42f). They cannot be understood even by Jesus' disciples, since these have their spirits choked (Mk 6,52; 8,17-21). In the same way the divine chastisements, which are medicinal in purpose (Am 4,6-11), or the prophetic appeals to conversion remain ineffective and at times even produce the contrary effect (2 K 17,13f; Jr 7, 25ff), so that men come to grieve the Holy Spirit (Is 63,10; Ac 7,51).

2. *God has the last word.* This hardness of heart, this determinism of sin which is nourished from its own substance, cannot cease except by conversion: "If you hear the voice of God, do not harden your hearts" (Ps 95,7f = He 3,7f.12). But how could the hardened sinner be converted? "Why, Lord, do you let us wander far from your ways and our hearts be hardened against fear of you? Come back, for the sake of your servants and of the tribes of your heirs" (Is 63,17). The believer knows that God can break the fatality of evil and find the way to His bride's heart (Ho 2). The last word belongs to God alone. Therefore did the prophet announce that men's heart* of stone would be replaced one day by a heart of flesh (Ez 36, 26) and that the Spirit* of God would make possible what is impossible to men (Ez 36,26f). In effect Christ is come; He has given the Spirit which makes one docile to the teachings of God. And so the Church, the heiress of Israel, prays God in His mercy to compel even our rebellious wills (liturgical prayer).

→Curse III 2—Error OT—Fire OT III—Hypocrite 2—Punishments 2.3—Repentance/Conversion—Sin—Unbelief—Wrath *B* OT I 1.

XLD gsa

HARVEST

Like the vintage*, the harvest* in general signifies for the peasant the fruit* of his labor and the measure of his yearly subsistence. This judgment which nature passes on human labor can also signify the judgment* of God.

I.   THE JOY OF THE HARVESTERS

The barley harvest (April) and the wheat harvest (May) are occasions of popular rejoicing: from hill to hill the song of the reapers spreads, making them oblivious of their hard lot of toiling with the scythe in the withering heat of the sun (Rt 2; Is 9,2; Jr 31,12; Ps 126,6). In this joy*, Yahweh is not forgotten: the harvest time is the sign and fruit of divine blessing*. To God who gave the increase (1 Co 3,6f) thanks* are returned (Ps 67,7; 85,13); they are expressed by the liturgical feast of the harvest of Pentecost* during which the first-fruits of the harvest are offered (Ex 23,16; 34,22), especially the first sheaf (Lv 23,10).

The reaper must also allow others to share in his joy by showing himself to be liberal. The Law prescribed that "You must not muzzle an ox when he is treading the grain" (Dt 25,4; 1 Co 9,9) and especially that "you must not reap to the very corners, nor gather the gleanings" (Lv 19,9; Dt 24,19), in order to leave a portion for the poor and the stranger*. It was this liberality which brought Boaz to meet and espouse Ruth, the stranger, considered to be the grandmother of David and of the Messiah (Rt 2,15ff; Mt 1,5).

Nevertheless this legitimate and fraternal joy should not fix the peasant's attention on the land. Undoubtedly the Law wishes to inculcate this by the sabbatical* year which stipulates that the land be left fallow every seventh year (Lv 25,4f), thus inviting the peasant to return to a pastoral life and thereby place himself once more solely in God's hands. Jesus made this explicit: one should abandon oneself to the heavenly Father like "the birds of the air who neither sow nor reap" (Lk 12,24 p). The peasant must not place his security or his hopes in his grain-filled barns, nor should he lay up treasure for himself, but "in God's eyes" who one day will harvest his soul (Lk 12,16-21; cf Jr 17,11).

II. THE HARVEST AND THE SOWING

1. The harvest is the fruit of the sowing*. Between the two there is a correspondence on many points. A man harvests what he has sown (G 6,7); without labor there is no harvest (Pr 20,4); "He who sows crime will reap calamity" (Pr 22,8); to sow justice is to reap a harvest of goodness (Ho 10,12f). All this signifies that "God renders to every man according to the fruit of his works" (Jr 17,10). It is useless to protest with the lazy servant: "God reaps where He has not sown" (Lk 19,21), for in creating and redeeming man, God has sown His Word in the hearts of all (Jm 1,21; Mk 4,20).

2. If the harvest is related to the sowing, yet it is often realized in a different spiritual climate. "May those who sow in tears reap with shouts of joy!" (Ps 126,5). It also differs in measure. Certainly, "the man who sows sparingly will reap sparingly, and the man who sows generously will reap generously" (2 Co 9,6); but, since God is always superabundant in His works, the harvest may be greater than the sowing and by as much as a hundredfold, as in the case of Isaac (Gn 26,12) because of the good ground which receives the Word of God (Mt 13,8.23 p).

3. Finally, though the ideal would be to reap what one sows (Is 37,30), God has so arranged the time for sowing and reaping (Gn 8,22; Jr 5,24) that man must await patiently* the ripening of the grain (Mk 4,26-29), but with full confidence despite the proverb: "One man sows, another reaps" (Jn 4,37).

III. THE HARVEST, GOD'S JUDGMENT

In harvesting the deeds of men, God judges* according to His justice*. This judgment which will occur at the end of time is anticipated in the coming of Christ.

1. *The day of Yahweh.* The harvest has a twofold aspect. There is the harvest, and this is the joyous aspect; the grain is cut, bundled, threshed, and finally the straw is burned (Is 28,27f), and this is the chastisement.

Such a harvester is God who cuts down, tram-ples, and winnows when He punishes Israel (Is 17,5; Jr 13,24) or Babylon (Jr 51,2.33). And when the malice of men reaches its peak, He must "put in the sickle, for the harvest is ripe" (Jl 3,13), that of the people's judgment. And yet at the same time, through a radical contrast which is reflected in prophetic oracles, there comes the prophecy of a joyous harvest, following closely upon the labor (Jl 3,18; Am 9,13; Ho 6,11; Ps 126,5f).

2. *In Messianic times.* This announcement becomes a reality with the coming of Christ.

a) The sower and the reaper. Since for the precursor Christ is the winnower who clears his threshing floor and separates the grain from the chaff (Mt 3,12 p), for Christians Jesus is both the sower who sows the Word in the hearts of men (Mk 4,3-9 p) and the reaper who plies His scythe to the field where the crop is ripe (4,29). There is no reason for waiting: "the fields are white for the harvest...; the sower also shares in the joy of the reaper" (Jn 4,35f).

b) The laborers of the harvest. Since the harvest is already ripe, the master invites to the task (Mt 9,38 p). The disciples, sent into the world, will gather the fruits of their predecessors' labors, and especially those of Jesus who has paid with His blood for the multiplication of the grain of wheat. In this the proverb which distinguishes between sower and reaper (Jn 4,37) remains true. Nevertheless, the reapers themselves will "pass through the sieve" of trials* and persecution* (Lk 22,31).

c) In the expectation of the final harvest. While it is true that the new Pentecost* inaugurates the harvest of the Church, this will only be completed on the day* of the Lord, when the Son of Man will put His scythe to the crop which has fully ripened (Ap 14,14ff; Mk 4,29). Until then the cockle will remain mixed with the good grain. The Church must judge and condemn evil, but she has no mission to cast the evildoer into the flames. It is the Son of Man who will, at the end of time, send His angels to carry out the judgment which He will pass on the works of men (Mt 13,24-30.36-43).

→Feasts OT I—Fruit—Joy OT I—Judgment OT II 2—Pentecost I 1—Sowing—Vintage.

RG tms

HATE

Hate is the contrary of love, but it is also closely allied to it. If the love of Amnon for Tamar suddenly turns to violent aversion, it is because he burned with passion (2 S 13,15). Many biblical formulas which absolutely oppose the pair love/hate (Gn 29,18.31; Mt 5,43; 6,24), suppose that it is a natural reaction of love to hate the very thing it prizes most. This is the state of soul which Deuteronomy supposes in the case of the husband who repudiates his wife (Dt 22,13.16). This violence of reaction is at the base of Semitic language which has free recourse to pairs of opposite words while making no note of intermediate differences in meaning. But the reality does not always correspond to the strength of the language, and it can be said of a polygamous household about the woman who is not preferred, or who simply is less loved, that she is hated (Dt 21,15; cf Gn 29,31ff). These remarks serve to explain certain surprising formulas (Lk 14,26; cf Mt 10,37); they leave untouched the religious problem which hate proposes: Why and how does hate introduce itself into humanity? What does the Bible mean when it applies the notion to God? What attitude did Christ take toward hate?

I. HATE AMONG MEN

1. *A world given over to hate.* Hate among men has been a fact. Genesis notes its presence from the first human generation (Gn 4,2-8) and men of wisdom know how to look at it with a clear eye (Pr 10,12; 14,20; 19,7; 26,24ff; Si 20,8). But the Bible passes a value judgment upon this fact. Hate is evil, the fruit of sin, because God has made men brothers* who are to live together in mutual love*. The case of Cain shows well the process of hate; born of jealousy, it tends to supress the other and lead to homicide. That is enough to denounce its satanic origin as the Book of Wisdom explains: envious of the happiness of men, the devil has hated them and brought about their death (Ws 2,24). Since then the world has been delivered over to hate (Tt 3,3).

2. *The just man is the object of hate.* Since its distant origins, the pattern of "envy-hate-murder" applies always in the same sense: it is the godless* one who hates the just* man and who carries on as his enemy*. Thus it was with Cain toward Abel, Esau toward Jacob, the sons of Jacob toward Joseph, the Egyptians toward Israel (Ps 105,25), the godless kings toward the prophets (1 K 22,8), the evil ones toward the just in the psalms, foreigners toward the anointed one of Yahweh (Ps 18; 21), toward Zion (Ps 129), toward Jerusalem (Is 60,15). So it is a permanent law that the one who loves God is hated, whether his being placed apart arouses envy, or whether it constitutes a living reproach to sinners (Ws 2,10-20). At any rate, God Himself is seen in his chosen one and becomes the object of hate (1 S 8,7; Jr 17,14f).

3. *Will the just man be able to hate?* In return for the hate which victimizes him, will the just man be able to hate? For the people of God, there is a law that one must love his neighbor (Lv 19,17f); there is also a law demanding the death of the murderer who has killed out of hate (Dt. 19,11ff), at the very moment when the law is endeavoring to soften the practice of blood-vengeance* by establishing cities of refuge (Dt 19,1-10).

There are nevertheless other instances: that of the evil men who hate the just; that of the enemies of God's people. They both behave as God's enemies (Nm 10,35; Ps 83,3). The conduct which the love of God prescribes here can seem surprising. Israel will hate the enemies of God so as not to imitate their conduct; that is the meaning of the holy war* (cf Dt 7,1-6). The unhappy just one who would be tempted to envy the evil ones and to imitate them (Pr 3,31; Ps 37; 73) will hate the group of sinners in order to keep himself from sin (Ps 26,4f; 101,3ff). "To love those who hate Yahweh" (2 Ch 19,2) would be the same as falling in with the impious and becoming unfaithful (Ps 50,18-21). An undivided love should be the response to God's jealous love (Ps 119,113; 97,10). His cause must be espoused in all things. What He loves, must be loved; what He hates, must be hated (Am 5, 15; Pr 8,13; Ps 45,8). How can one fail, then, to hate those who hate Him (Ps 139,21f)?

This attitude is not without ambiguity and danger, for will we not easily come to look upon every personal or national enemy as an enemy of God in order to take away selfishly the privileges of divine election*? The danger was not imaginary, for in vowing an "eternal hate" for the cause of Belial, the Qumrân sect actually identified the "cause of God" with their own closed group. "You must love your neighbor and hate your enemy" (Mt 5,43): that was not the letter of the ancient Law, but many admitted this abusive interpretation dictated by a narrow exclusivism.

II. IS THERE HATE IN GOD?

How can one talk about hate in connection with the God of love? Actually, God cannot hate any of the beings He has made (Ws 11,24). To say that He could would be as much an injury as to accuse Him of hating His people (Dt 1,27; 9,28). But the God of love is also the holy* and the jealous God. Even His love implies a violent rejection of sin*. He hates idolatry*, be it that of the Canaanites (Dt 12,31; 16, 22) or that of Israel (Jr 44,4). He hates hypocrisy* in worship (Am 5,21; Is 1,14), plundering, and crime (Is 61,8), false oaths (Ze 8,17), repudiation (Ml 2,16), and in general the collection of sins enumerated in Pr 6,16-19. Now in a certain way the sinner becomes one with sin. He places himself in the position of an enemy* (i.e., of one who hates God: Ex 20,5; Dt 7,10; Ps 139,21; R 1,30). The total incompatibility which, by his faults, he sets up between God and himself is translated in the Bible in terms of hate: God hates the violent (Ps 11,5), idolater (Ps 31,7), hypocrite (Si 27,24), and all doers of evil in general (Ps 5,6ff). He hates unfaithful Israel (Ho 9,15; Jr 12,8) as He hates the Canaanites because of their crimes (Ws 12,3). The case is a little more complex when He declares: "I have loved Jacob and hated Esau" (Ml 1,2; R 9,13); in this case Jacob stands for Israel and Esau for Edom (Ml 1,2; cf Gn 25,30; 32,28). Thus, God condemns the violence of Edom toward Israel (cf Ps 137,7; Ez 25,12ff; Ob 10-14). He also indicates by the use of this expression that election* implies preference, like that of the man who "loves" one of his spouses and "hates" the other (cf Gn 29,31ff; R 9,11ff).

But if this preference and this repulsion are positive realities wherein God declares Himself with all His force, still we cannot call them hate except on the condition that we purify the word of all that it means in our sinful world: its evil rancor, its intention to harm and destroy. So if God hates sin, can we say that God, "who desires not the death of the sinner, but that he be converted and live" (Ez 18,23), hates the sinner? By election* and chastisement God follows out a unique plan of love for all men. His love* will have the final word. It is fully revealed in Jesus. The NT never speaks of hate in God.

III. JESUS FACED WITH HATE

1. *The world's hate for Jesus.* Appearing in a world which stirs up the passion of hate, Jesus sees the different forms of that hate converging toward Him. There is the hate of the chosen one of God who is envied (Lk 19,14; Mt 27,18; Jn 5,18); the hate of the just man whose presence is a condemnation (Jn 7,7; 15,24); the heads of Israel hate him also because in their jealousy they want to reserve the divine election for themselves (cf Jn 11,50). Behind them there is also the whole evil world* which hates Him (Jn 15,18); they hate the light* in Him because their works* are evil (Jn 3,20). And so is accomplished the mystery announced in the Scripture of the blind, unreasonable hate (Jn 15,25). Beyond Jesus this hate looks to the Father Himself (Jn 15,23f). Jesus dies the victim of hate, but by His death He kills hate (E 2,14.16) because this death is an act of love* which reintroduces love into the world and establishes it there once and for all.

2. *The world's hate for Christians.* Whoever follows* Jesus will experience the same lot. The disciples* will be hated "because of His name*" (Mt 10,22; 24,9). They should not be frightened by that (1 Jn 3,13); they should even rejoice at it (Lk 6,22), because by it they are associated with the destiny of their master. The world hates them because they are not of the world (Jn 15, 19; 17,14). Thus there is revealed the enemy* who was active since the beginning (Jn 8,44); but Jesus has prayed for them not that they be taken out of the world, but that they be protected from the evil one.

3. *To hate evil but not men.* Just as in the case of Jesus over whom the prince of this world has no power (Jn 14,30; 8,46), and just as in the case of the holy God, the holy Father (Jn 17,11), the disciples will hate evil. They will know the radical incompatibility between God and the world (1 Jn 2,15; Jm 4,4), between God and the flesh* (R 8,7), between God and money (Mt 6,24). To suppress in them all complicity with evil, they will renounce all things and will go so far as to hate themselves (Lk 14,26; Jn 12,25). But with regard to other men, they shall hold no hate in their hearts: "whoever hates his brother is in darkness" (1 Jn 2,9.11; 3,15). Love is the only rule, even in relation to one's enemies (Lk 6,27).

Thus, at the end of this history of hate the situation is clear for the Christian and a straightforward course of action lies before him: to love all men and to hate himself. Without Christ (E 2,11; Tt 3,3f) man could imagine that he was using hate as a means of affirming himself. But the time of Cain has passed and the Christian knows that only love gives life and makes a man like God (1 Jn 3,11-24).

→Brother OT 1—Enemy—Love—Persecution I 1—Revenge—Sin IV 2 c—Violence—War NT II 1—Wrath.

JB jrs

HEAD

The interest of this word comes to a great extent from its christological use in the Pauline epistles. To describe the sovereignty of Jesus Christ* Paul is not afraid of playing on the complexity of this theme and of making different uses of this image.

1. *Christ, the head of the corner.* Apart from the proper sense of the Hebrew *ro's* and of the Greek *kephalē*, which mean the head of a man or an animal, apart from their use in describing attitudes and feelings of joy, of mourning or of mockery, a metaphorical use can be seen in the application of this word to everything that comes first in the inanimate world (the beginning of a road, of a year, the façade of a building), the best or the highest (the top of a tree, of a mountain, or of a monument: Gn 11,4; Ze 4,7). It is probably in this last sense that we must understand the image used in Ps 118,22: "it was the stone rejected by the builders that proved to be the keystone." But this image is often taken up by the NT authors and applied to Christ: is He not the main stone crowning the new Temple*, assuring it of cohesion and giving it its meaning (Mt 21,42 p; Ac 4,11; 1 P 2,7; E 2,20)? However, some authors prefer to see this cornerstone as the foundation on which the whole building rests.

2. *Christ, the head of the universe.* According to another metaphorical use the word head is applied to men who walk ahead (cf the head as opposed to the tail in Dt 28,14.43f; Is 9,13) and above all to the leaders (Ex 6,14; 1 S 15,17; Jb 29,25; Dn 7,6; Ap 12,3). This meaning is found again in 1 Co 11,3: "Christ is the head of every man, man is the head of woman, and God is the head of Christ." And it is no doubt to this idea of leadership that the allusions to the primacy of Christ over all beings refer (1 Co 11,3; Col 2,10; cf E 1,10.22).

3. *Christ, the head of the Church.* When Paul calls Christ the head of the Body, that is of the Church (Col 1,18; 2,19; E 1,22f; 4,15), it seems that this picture, in which it must be noted that the head is not one member among others but a principle of life, of cohesion and of growth (Col 2,19; E 4,15f), is a development of Pauline ecclesiology. In fact, according to 1 Co, the Church, through baptism and the Eucharist, is united to Christ in such a way that it becomes His Body*. However, within this unity there exists a real difference between Christ, who has already reached the goal and is now exercising His life-giving activity, and the mass of Christians who receive everything from Him. It is probably to allow for this difference in the unity that Paul came to see in Christ the head of the Body, just as in E 5,23 he sees in Christ the Spouse, that is the head, of the Church.

4. *The connection between these ideas.* However, Paul often connected these various representatives of Christ, the head of the corner of the new Temple, the head of the universe and the head of the Body of the Church. The first title, certainly the oldest and the most traditional (Ac 4,11; Mt 21,32 p), appears, especially in E, in association with the third (see the parallelism in the vocabulary between the description of the Temple in E 2,20f and that of the Body in E 4,16. Note in this last verse as well as in v 12 the use of the word construction). Finally, it is not by accident that Christ is seen in the Pauline epistles as both the head of the Church and the head of the universe. As we have seen, these two ideas are not the same, and only the Church is that part of the universe that can be honored with the title of the Body of Christ and of the Spouse of Christ: so it is in a privileged sense that Christ is its head. However, before even accepting union with the Church and thus allowing itself to be transformed into the Body of Christ, as a spotless bride and a holy temple, the universe, whether it likes it or not, finds itself subject to the primacy of the one who has brought back all things under one Master (E 1,10) and wants to purify them, give them life under one head and ensure the cohesion of this holy temple through Himself.

→Authority—Body of Christ III 2—Church V 1 —Spouse NT 1—Stone 4—World II 2.

PL ems

HEART

The connotations of the word "heart" are not the same in Hebrew and English. Naturally the physiological sense is the same (2 S 18,14; Ho 13, 8), but the other uses of the word are very different. In our present use of the word hardly anything is suggested except the affective life; while in the Hebrew the heart is understood as the "inside" of man in a far wider sense. Apart from feelings (2 S 15,13; Ps 21,3; Is 65,14), the heart contains memories and ideas, plans and decisions. God has given men "a heart to think with" (Si 17,6), and the psalmist speaks of the "thoughts of the heart" of God Himself, meaning His plan of salvation, which lasts from age to age (Ps 33,11). A "big heart" (1 K 5,9) suggests extensive knowledge; "give me your heart" can mean "give me your attention" (Pr 23,26); and a "hardened heart" includes the idea of a closed mind. According to the context the meaning can be restricted to the intellectual aspect (Mk 8,17) or on the contrary extend beyond it (Ac 7,51). Often it is necessary to go back beyond the psychological distinctions to the core of man's being, to the place where he enters into dialogue with himself (Gn 17,17; Dt 7,17), accepts his responsibilities and opens himself or closes himself to God. In the concrete and global anthropology that we find in the Bible, man's heart is the very source of his conscious*, intelligent and free personality, the place of his decisive choices, the place of the unwritten Law (R 2,15) and of the mysterious action of God. In the OT as in the NT the heart is the place where man meets God, an encounter which becomes fully effective in the human heart of the Son of God.

I. THE HEART OF MAN

1. *Heart and external appearance.* In personal relationships it is clear that what counts most is the inner attitude, the heart, though it is hidden from view. Normally, a person's outward expression should reveal what is in his heart. Thus one knows the heart indirectly, from the facial expression (Si 13,25), from words on the lips* (Pr 16,23), and from a person's actions (Lk 6, 44). But it can be that words and conduct hide rather than reveal the heart (Pr 26,23-26; Si 12, 16), since man has the dangerous capacity of deception. In this case the heart itself is deceitful, since it shows forth one expression on the face while harboring wholly different sentiments within. Such duplicity is a great evil and is vigorously denounced by the Bible (Si 27,24; Ps 28,3f).

2. *God and the heart.* Finding himself called by God, a man tries to escape through duplicity. "God is a consuming fire" (Dt 4,24); how can one meet His radical demands? The chosen people themselves never stop dodging their obligations. To avoid sincere conversion, they seek to placate God by external worship* (Am 5, 21...) and beguiling words (Ps 78,36f).

But this attempt is an illusion. God cannot be deceived as man can: "Man looks to appearances, but the Lord sees the heart" (1 S 16,7). God "searches the heart and tests the loins*" (Jr 17,10; Si 42,18). He uncovers their lie* and observes: "This people honors me with their lips, but their heart is far from me" (Is 29,13). Before God, man realizes he is called in question down to the depths of his being (He 4,12f). To approach God is "to risk one's heart" (Jr 30,21).

3. *The need for a new heart.* Gradually, Israel learned that external religion is not enough. To find God, one must "seek* Him with all one's heart" (Dt 4,29). Israel learned that she must once and for all "fix her heart on the Lord" (1 S 7,3) and "love* God with her whole heart" (Dt 6,5). This involves profound submission to the Law*. But her entire history witnesses to her radical inability to live according to this ideal. Her evil extends to her heart. "This people has a stubborn and rebellious heart" (Jr 5,23), an "uncircumcised heart" (Lv 26,41), a "deceitful heart" (Ho 10,2). Rather than trust in God, "they followed the bent of their wicked heart" (Jr 7,24; 18,12). Consequently, unending calamity befell them. All they can do is "rend their heart" (Jl 2,13) and present themselves before God with a "broken and contrite heart" (Ps 51, 19) to beg their Lord to "create in them a clean heart" (Ps 51,12).

II. THE NEW HEART

1. *Promised.* This is exactly God's plan and its proclamation gives solace to Israel. The fire* of God is a fire of love that prevents Him from allowing the destruction of His people. The mere thought of this overwhelms His heart (Ho 11,8). When He led His unfaithful spouse into the desert, it was to speak again to her heart (Ho 2,16). There will be an end to these

trials and a new age will dawn, an age of inner renewal brought about by God Himself. "He will circumcise* your heart and that of your posterity, to bring you to love the Lord your God with your whole heart and your whole soul, so that you may live" (Dt 30,6). The Israelites will rebel no more, for God will establish with them a new covenant and He will "place the Law in the depths of their being and write it on their hearts" (Jr 31,33). Better still, God will give them a new heart (Jr 32,39), a heart with which to know* Him (Jr 24,7; comp Dt 29,3). After the command, "Form in yourselves a new heart" (Ez 18,31), God Himself promises to achieve what He requires of them. "I will cleanse you. I will give you a new heart, and put within you a new spirit*. I will take out of your body the heart of stone* and I will give you a heart of flesh*'" (Ez 36,25f). Thus is insured a lasting union of God and His people.

2. *Given.* It is by Jesus Christ that this promise was fulfilled.

a) In the *synoptic* Gospels Jesus carries on the teaching of the prophets, opposes the formalism of the Pharisees* and points out that the real evil is that coming from the heart: "Out of the heart come wicked plans, murders, adultery. . .; these are the things that defile a person" (Mt 15,19f). Jesus recalls God's requirement of interior generosity: man must receive the word in a heart that is well disposed (Lk 8,15); he must love God with his whole heart (Mt 22, 37 p) and pardon his brother from the heart (Mt 18,35). To the pure of heart, Jesus promises the vision of God (Mt 5,8). But He who is "meek and humble of heart" (Mt 11,29) goes far beyond the prophets, since He who is purity gives this purity* to His disciples (Mt 9,2; 26, 28). After His resurrection He illumines their hearts. While He spoke to them, their hearts were on fire within themselves (Lk 24,32).

b) Henceforth, it is faith* in Christ, an acceptance in the heart, that brings about this interior renewal which is otherwise not achieved. This Paul announces: "If in your heart you believe that God has raised Him from the dead, you will be saved. It is faith coming from the heart that leads to justification" (R 10,9f). By faith, the eyes of the heart are illumined (E 1,18), and Christ dwells in the heart (E 3,17). Into the hearts of believers a new* spirit is sent, "the Spirit of the Son who

cries, 'Abba, Father'" (G 4,6), and with the Spirit, "the love of God" is poured out (R 5,5). Thus "God's peace surpassing all understanding will guard our hearts" (Ph 4,7). This is the new covenant, one founded on the sacrifice of Him whose heart was bruised with insults (Ps 69, 21).

c) *John* speaks of the heart only to drive from it all trouble and fear (Jn 14,27). But he announces in other terms the fulfillment of the same promises. He speaks of knowledge* (1 Jn 5,20; cf Jr 24,7) and of communion* (1 Jn 1,3), of love and of eternal life. All these come to us through the crucified and glorified Jesus. Within Jesus (Jn 7,38; cf 19,34), there springs up a source of interior renewal for the believer (4,14). Jesus personally enters within His followers to give them life (6,56f). According to John, it could even be said that Jesus *is the heart* of the new Israel, the heart that brings a close relation with the Father and establishes unity among all: "I in them, and you in me, that they may be perfectly one" (17,23; cf 11,52; Ac 4,32); "that the love with which you have loved me may be in them and I in them" (Jn 17,26).

→Circumcision OT 3; NT 2—Conscience 1.2 a —Desire II, III—Face 1—Hardness of Heart —Judgment NT I 2—Know OT 3—Law *A*; *B* IV; *C* III 3, IV 1—Lips 1—Loins 2—Love I OT 2, NT 3; II NT 1—Pure OT II 3; NT I 3— Repentance/Conversion—Simple 2—Soul I 3— Spirit—Spirit of God OT IV; NT V 4—Tongue —Virtues & Vices.

JdF & AV wjw

HEAVEN

If today *heaven* can indicate the domain of astronomers and astronauts, as well as the place where God assembles the saved, this is in no way due to a gross misunderstanding in the simple language of the Bible. Rather, it is the simple language of a universal human experience: God reveals Himself to man through the whole of creation*, including its visible structures. The Bible transmits this revelation* in a sometimes complex form, but one rather free from confusion. The Bible distinguishes clearly this physical sky, which is of the same order as the earth*, and God's heaven. There is the heaven of "heaven and earth" and the heaven distinct from the earth. But it is more especially the first which enables us to conceive the second.

I. HEAVEN AND EARTH

For the Hebrews, as for us, the sky is a part of the universe, different from the earth, though in contact with earth. It is for them a global hemisphere covering the earth, with the two together making up the universe. For lack of a specific term, this is called "heaven and earth" (Gn 1,1; Mt 24,35).

If the Israelite is struck by the splendor of this heaven, and delighted in its light* and transparency (Ex 24,10), he is even more impressed by the unshakable solidity of the firmament (Gn 1,18). For him the sky is built as solidly and ordered as well as the earth. It rests on columns (Jb 26,11) or foundations (2 S 22,8), and is provided with reservoirs for rain, snow, hail, and wind (Jb 38,22ff; 37,9ff; Ps 33,7). Through its "windows" and "gates" the elements pass at the proper times from their storehouses (Gn 7,11; 2 K 7,2; Ml 3,10). The celestial bodies fixed in the firmament, that vast army of the stars* (Gn 15,5), give testimony by their magnificent regularity to the grandeur of the whole plan (cf Is 40,26; Jb 38,31f).

II. HEAVEN DISTINCT FROM THE EARTH

Man's experience of the sky with its vastness, light, marvelous and inexplicable harmony, forces on him an enduring, natural, and direct sense of the impenetrable mystery* of the universe. Though the depths of the earth and the abyss below are equally inaccessible to man (Jb 38,4ff.16ff), still the inaccessibility of the sky is continually exposed to him and, as it were, visibly revealed. Man belongs to the earth* and heaven is closed to him: "No one has gone up to heaven" (Jn 3,13; cf Pr 30,4; R 10,6). The folly of the king of Babel was to dream of ascending to heaven (cf Gn 11,4); this is making oneself equal to the almighty (Is 14,13f). Thus, a natural relation exists between the sky and God*. The sky is His home: "The heavens are the heavens of the Lord, but the earth He has given to mankind" (Ps 115,16).

This spontaneous religious sentiment evoked by the sky explains the frequent use in the LXX of the plural "heavens." Judaism and the NT emphasized the religious significance of this plural form to the extent that "kingdom* of heaven" (plural form) becomes identical with "kingdom of God." Still, neither in the OT nor in the NT can a strict rule be laid down that the singular is the physical sky and the plural the dwelling of God. Eventually this plural may have come to indicate the widespread oriental notion of different "heavens" lying one above the other (cf 2 Co 12,2; E 4,10). But more frequently the plural simply expresses a lyrical and poetic enthusiasm (cf Dt 10,14; 1 K 8,27). The Bible does not acknowledge two heavens, one physical and the other spiritual. Rather it is in the visible heavens that the Bible discovers the mystery of God and His work.

III. HEAVEN, THE DWELLING OF GOD

Heaven is the dwelling which God first stretched out like a tent, and above the waters He raised the beams of His palace (Ps 104,2f). Then He came forth riding on the clouds (Ps 68,5.34; Dt 33,26) and raising His voice over the great waters* in the tumult of the storm* (Ps 29,3). In heaven He has His throne and there He convokes His court, "the army of heaven," that carries out His orders even to the ends of the earth (1 K 22,19; cf Is 6,1f.8; Jb 1,6-12). He is in truth the God of heaven (Ne 1,4; Dn 2,37).

These expressions are not childish images or poetic exaggerations; but they stem from a vision, poetic yet profoundly true, of the reality of our world. They tell of a universe entirely ruled by God's sovereign power and wholly penetrated by His knowledge. Since the Lord* "reigns in heaven," He can laugh at the kings of earth with their plotting (Ps 2,2ff; cf Gn 11, 7); and "His searching glance tests the sons of Adam" (Ps 11,4). He has His lofty vantage point in "glory above the heavens" from which to deal justly with all, "lifting the poor man from the dust" (Ps 113,4ff). Seated on high, He can receive "the supplication of every man, and of all His people Israel" (1 K 8,30. . .). Though He is a God near at hand, still He is also distant (Jr 23,23f); not only because "His glory fills all the earth" (Is 6,3), but also because nothing in the world can contain Him, not even "the heavens or the heaven of heavens" (1 K 8,27).

While this heavenly dwelling of God does primarily suggest His total transcendence, it also equally indicates His presence* to man, like the omnipresence of the sky above. More than one text explicitly relates His infinite distance and His nearness. From the ladder Jacob saw at Bethel "set up on the earth with its top reaching to heaven" (Gn 28,12), to the prophetic oracles, like this one of Isaiah, God's distance and proximity are joined: "The heavens are my throne. . .What kind of house could you build for me?. . .Yet the man on whom I gaze is one who is poor and contrite of heart" (Is 66,1f; cf 57,15).

IV. "RAIN DOWN, YOU HEAVENS. . ."

Since the God of Israel is a saving God whose home is in heaven, He is there with His truth* (Ps 119,89f), His grace*, and faithfulness* (Ps 89,3). He is there to pour salvation* on the earth. As the sky represents God's sovereign and all-embracing presence, so also it is the symbol of salvation made ready for the earth. From the sky, moreover, comes the blessing* of life-giving rain and the dew, both signifying God's generosity and largesse. Thus, natural signs and historical memories converge to make the hope* of Israel an expectation of an event coming downward from heaven: "O that you would rend the heavens and come down" (Is 63,19; cf 45,8: an antiphon from the Advent liturgy).

Furthermore, the ascensions of Enoch (Gn 5, 24) and Elijah (2 K 2,11) drew men's minds upward in search here for the everlasting communion with God to which these two had been admitted. In their turn, the apocalyptic seers Ezekiel, Zechariah, and especially Daniel receive from the God of heaven revelations of mysteries* about the destiny of the nations (Dn 2,28). From that time, the salvation of Israel is inscribed in heaven and will descend from there. From heaven, Gabriel came to Daniel (9,21) to promise the end of desolation (9,25). On the clouds of heaven the Son of Man must appear so that dominion may be given over to the holy ones (7,13.27). Finally, it is from heaven, where "he stands before God" (Lk 1,19), that Gabriel is sent to Zechariah and to Mary. To heaven return the angels* who sang "glory to God in the heights of heaven and peace on earth" (2,11-15). This presence of His angels in our midst is the sign that God has rent the heavens and that He is Emmanuel, God with us.

V. JESUS CHRIST: HEAVEN PRESENT ON EARTH

1. *Jesus speaks of heaven. Heaven* is a word frequently on the lips of Jesus. But it never indicates a reality that would exist by itself, independently of God. Jesus speaks of the kingdom* of heaven, of the reward stored in heaven (Mt 5,12), of one's treasure laid up in heaven (6,20; 19,21). This usage always stems from Jesus' thoughts of the Father* in heaven (5,16.45; 6,1.9), who knows, who "is there in the secret place to see" (6,8.18). Thus heaven is the invisible yet attentive paternal presence* that surrounds the world with inexhaustible bounty (7,11), even for the birds of the air (6,26), both for just men and unjust (5,45). Since men are normally blind to this presence, Jesus has come to tell what He knows and to testify to what He has seen (Jn 3,11). Thus heaven becomes a living and triumphant reality; the kingdom of heaven arrives on this earth.

2. *Jesus comes from heaven.* When He speaks of heaven, Jesus does not talk about a distant striking reality, but of a familiar world that is His own, a reality as deep and serious to Him as our world is to us. He possesses the secrets of the kingdom of heaven (Mt 13,11) and He knows as His own Father the one who is our Father in heaven (12,50; 16,17; 18,19). To speak in this way of heaven, He must have come down from heaven. "No one ever went up to heaven but the one who has come down from heaven, the Son of Man who dwells in heaven" (Jn 3,13).

Since He is the Son* of Man with His destiny in heaven and a man come from heaven to return there (Jn 6,62), the works* of Jesus are of heaven. His essential work, the sacrifice of His flesh and blood, is the bread* which God gives, bread from heaven (Jn 6,33-58) which gives eternal life*, the life of the Father, the life of heaven.

3. *On earth as it is in heaven.* If Jesus comes from heaven and is going back there, if it is also true to say that Christians are already in heaven with Him and that the Father has "raised them and made them sit in heaven" (E 2,6; cf Col 2,12; 3,1-4), then Jesus' work is still continuing. It consists in joining together earth* and heaven forever; to see to it that the "kingdom of heaven comes" and that God's will* is done, "on earth as it is in heaven" (Mt 6,10), "so that by Him all things, whether

on earth or in heaven, are reconciled" (Col 1,20). Given "all power on heaven and earth" (Mt 28,18) at His resurrection*, and having entered the heavenly sanctuary by the blood of His sacrifice* (He 4,14; 9,24), He is exalted "higher than the heavens" (7,26) and is seated at the right hand of God. There He has sealed a new covenant between heaven and earth (9, 25). As He entrusts His power to His Church, He promises to ratify in heaven what it does on earth (Mt 16,19; 18,19).

4. *Heaven opened*. The reconciliation achieved by Jesus is attested to us by signs: the heavens open over Him (Mt 3,16), the Spirit descends (Jn 1,32), and eventually His followers have the same experience. With a great roar (Ac 2,2) and in a flash of vision (Ac 9,3; 10,11), heaven is opened over them and the Spirit descends. Christ fulfills His promise: "You will see heaven open. . .upon the Son of Man" (Jn 1,51).

VI.   HOPE FOR HEAVEN

"Our citizenship is in heaven, whence we long for the Lord Jesus Christ, our Savior, who will come to transform our lowly body into a likeness of His glorious body, by the power that enables Him to subject the entire universe to Himself" (Ph 3,20f). This text includes all the aspects of the heaven for which Christians hope*. Heaven is a city* or community made for us, the new* Jerusalem* (Ap 3,12; 21,3.10ff). We belong to heaven now, for there is built the dwelling for which we aspire (2 Co 5,1). Heaven is a new universe (Ap 21,5), made up like ours of "new heavens and a new earth" (2 P 3,13; Ap 21,1). But it contrasts with ours since nothing remains of "death, tears, crying, or pain" (Ap 21,4), nothing "unclean" (21,27), no "night" (22,5), for these give way to everlasting happiness and joy. When it appears, the old universe, "the first heaven and earth," will have vanished (21,1) in flight (20,11) as a scroll is rolled up (6,14).

Heaven will be our new universe, since ours is forever that of the Word made flesh* and of His body. There would be no heaven for us without communion* with the Lord* (1 Th 4, 17; 2 Co 5,8; Ph 1,23) who subjects all things to Himself in order to hand over all to God the Father (1 Co 15,24-28).

→Abide I—Angels—Ascension—Beatitude OT

II 2—City NT 2—Cloud—Earth NT I 2, II 2— Fatherland NT 2—Feasts NT—Gate OT II; NT —Hope NT IV—House II 2.3—Inheritance NT II—Jerusalem OT III 3; NT II—Joy NT III— Kingdom NT I 1—Light & Dark NT II 4— Manna 2.3—Passover III 3—Paradise 3.4—Rest III 3—Reward III 1—See NT II—Stars— Temple—White 1—World O.

JMF & JG wjw

HEBREW

The primitive meaning of the name of the Hebrews is not clear. In Genesis, it always means men sojourning as strangers* in a land which is not their native country. Examples are Abraham (Gn 14,13), Joseph (39,14; 41,12), Jacob and his sons (40,15; 43,32). Since their eponymous ancestor Eber lived well before Abraham (Gn 10,25; 11,14), the term could be applied to a large portion of Semitic peoples.

In Exodus the Hebrew descendants of Jacob (Ex 1,15; 2,6. . .) were separated from the Egyptians by their race, origin, and religion (Yahweh is the "God of the Hebrews," 7,16; 9,1). In the same way the Hebrews, Semites living in Canaan, are different from their Philistine oppressors (1 S 4,6. . .; 13,3.19; 14,11; 29,3; cf Nm 24,24); but it is not sure that they are all Israelites (cf 1 S 14,21). Deuteronomic law about Hebrew slaves (Dt 15,12f; Jr 34,14) depicts them as brothers of the Israelites, but this could still be taken in a larger sense (cf Gn 24,27). Thus, up to the captivity, the term does not seem ever to be used as a common name of the people nor as a title with a religious meaning.

It is different, however, in later texts. In Jon 1,9, Jonah presents himself to the pagan sailors as "a Hebrew and servant of the God of heaven"; in 2 M 7,31; 11,13; 15,37, the term *Hebrew* means the Jews* settled in the holy land. In these two cases the religious overtone is not absent, but it is colored by a national meaning.

When Paul calls himself "a Hebrew, son of Hebrews" (Ph 3,5; 2 Co 11,22), he does so to insist on the Palestinian origin and Hebraic language of his family. For the Judaeo-Christians these same criteria distinguish the Hebrews from the Hellenists (Ac 6,1). But it is clear from Jn 19,13.17 that the word "Hebrew" can also be used to refer to the Aramaic language. But in these cases the word does not carry a directly religious connotation. That is why it has not passed into the Christian vocabulary to designate the spiritual posterity of Abraham (cf R 4,16).

→Israel—Jew—People *A* II 1.

PG jrs

HELL

Jesus Christ descended into the nether world, and the damned descend into hell: these two expressions of faith refer to two different actions and suppose two different conditions. The gates* of the nether world where Christ descended were opened to let its captives escape, while the hell where the damned descend is forever closed after them. Nevertheless, the word used is the same, not by accident or by an arbitrary comparison, but for a very logical reason and as the expression of a major truth. The nether world, like hell itself, is the kingdom of death*. Without Christ there would be in the world only one hell and one death, the eternal death, the death that is all powerful. If there is a "second death" (Ap 21,8), separable from the first, it is because Jesus Christ by His death has broken the reign of death. Because He descended into the nether world, the nether world is no longer hell; but it continues to bear its features. That is why at the last judgment* the nether world, Hades, rejoins hell and assumes its normal place in the pool of fire (Ap 20,14). That is the reason why, although the images of hell in the OT remain ambiguous and do not yet have their absolute character, nevertheless Jesus Christ uses them to describe eternal damnation, because they are more than mere images; they are the reality of what the world would be without Him.

OT

I. THE BASIC REPRESENTATIONS

1. *The nether world, abode of the dead.* In ancient Israel, the nether world, *sheol*, is "the meeting place of all the living" (Jb 30,23). Like many other peoples, Israel imagines the afterlife of the dead as a shadow* of existence, without value and without joy. Sheol is the frame which assembles these shadows. It is pictured as a tomb, "a hole," "a pit," "a ditch" (Ps 30,10; Ez 28,8), in the deepest regions of

the earth (Dt 32,22), beyond the subterranean abyss (Jb 26,5; 38,16f), where a deep obscurity reigns (Ps 88,7.13), where "brightness itself resembles dark nights*" (Jb 10,21f). It is there that all the living "descend" (Is 38,18; Ez 31, 14). From there they will never rise (Ps 88,10; Jb 7,9). They can no longer praise God (Ps 6,6), hope in His justice (88,11ff) or in His fidelity (30,10; Is 38,18). It is total destitution (Ps 88,6).

2. *The infernal powers let loose on earth.* To descend into this nether world filled with days at the end of a happy old age, there "to meet again their fathers*" (Gn 25,8), is the common lot of humanity (Is 14,9-15; Jb 3,11-21) and none can complain. But often enough Sheol does not wait for this hour. Like an insatiable monster (Pr 27,20; 30,16), it lies in wait for its prey and carries it away in full vigor (Ps 54,16). "In the midst of his days," Hezekiah sees "the gates* of Sheol" open (Is 38,10). This invasion of the infernal forces "into the land of the living" (38,11) is the tragedy and the scandal (Ps 18,6; 88,4f).

II. THE HELL OF SINNERS

This scandal is one of the provinces of revelation. The tragic aspect of death* shows the disorder of the world, and one of the axes of the Israelitic religious thought is the discovery that this disorder is the fruit of sin*. According as this consciousness is affirmed, the features of hell take on a more and more sinister aspect. It opens its jaws to swallow up Korah, Dathan, and Abiram (Nm 16,32f); it puts in motion all its power to devour "the glory of Zion and its noisy crowd, its cries, its joy" (Is 5,14); it makes godless* men disappear in terror (Ps 73,19).

Of this terrifying end, Israel knew two especially expressive images: the burning of Sodom and Gomorrah (Gn 19,23; Am 4,11; Ps 11,6) and the devastation of the site of Topheth, in the valley of Gehenna, the place of pleasure which is destined to become a place of horror, where "they will see the corpses of those who rebelled against me, where the worms will not die nor the fire be quenched" (Is 66,24).

Death in fire* and indefinite continuance in corruption are the gospel images of hell. It is a hell which is no longer the so-called "normal" hell that Sheol was, but a hell which can be said to have fallen from heaven*, "come from Yahweh" (Gn 19,24). If it brings together the bottomless abyss" and "the rain of fire" (Ps 140,11), the image of Sheol and the memory of Sodom, it is because this hell is kindled by "the breath of Yahweh" (Is 30,33) and "the intensity of His wrath*" (30,27).

This hell promised to sinners could not be the lot of the just, especially when these latter, for remaining faithful to God, had to suffer persecution* from sinners and at times death. It is logical that the godless awake to "the eternal horror" of the "country of dust," the traditional Sheol, where the intermingled gathering of the holy and the godless sleep, while their victims awake "to eternal life*" (Dn 2,12). And while the Lord gives to the just their reward, "He arms creation for punishing His enemies" (Ws 5,15ff). Hell is no longer localized in the lowest depths of the earth; it is "the universe let loose against the foolish" (5,20). The gospels take up these images: "In the abode of the dead" where he is "tortured with flames," the rich man perceives Lazarus "in Abraham's* bosom"; but between them is dug "a great abyss" that is unbridgeable (Lk 16,23-26). Fire and abyss, the wrath* of heaven and the opening of the earth*, the curse* of God and the hostility of creation*: this is hell.

NT

I. CHRIST SPEAKS OF HELL

Jesus attaches more importance to the loss of life, the separation from Himself, than to the description of hell current among His contemporaries. If it is perhaps dangerous to see in the parable of the wicked rich man any decisive statement on the subject of hell by the Lord, in any case Jesus must be taken seriously when He uses scriptural images of the most violent and merciless kind in this context: "weeping and gnashing of teeth in the burning furnace" (Mt 13,42), "gehenna, where the worm does not die and the fire* is not quenched" (Mk 9,43-48; cf Mt 5,22), where God can "destroy the soul* and the body*" (Mt 10,28).

What gives weight to these affirmations is the fact that they are uttered by the very man who has power to cast into hell. Jesus does not speak of hell only as a threatening reality; He announces that He Himself "will send His angels to cast the workers of iniquity into the burning furnace" (Mt 13,41f), and He will pronounce the curse*: "Begone from me, ye cursed, into eternal fire!" (Mt 25,41). It is the Lord who declares: "I do not know* you"

(25,12); "Cast him into the exterior darkness" (25,30).

II. JESUS CHRIST DESCENDED INTO THE NETHER WORLD

Christ's descent into the nether world is an article of faith, and it is in fact an assured datum of the NT. If it is very difficult to determine the value of certain texts, to discover what was "His preaching to the spirits in prison, to those who had refused to believe before. . .in the days when Noah was constructing the ark" (1 P 3,19f), the certain fact is that this descent of Jesus into the nether world signifies the reality of His death* as man as well as His triumph over it. If "God has delivered Him from the terrors of Hades" (that is to say, from Sheol, Ac 2,24), it is after plunging Him there, but without abandoning Him there forever (2, 31). If Christ, in the mystery of the ascension, is "raised up above all the heavens," it is because He has also "descended into the lower regions of the heart"; and He had to make this sinister descent in order to "fulfill all things" and reign as Lord of the universe (E 4,9f). The Christian faith confesses that Jesus Christ is the Lord in heaven after being raised from among the dead (R 10,6-10).

III. THE GATES OF HELL BROKEN

By His death Christ triumphed over the last enemy, death* (1 Co 15,26); He broke open the gates of hell. Death and Hades had always been naked in God's eyes (Am 9,2; Jb 26,6); now they are forced to give back the dead they keep (Ap 20,13; cf Mt 27,52f). Hell was until the death of the Lord "the rendez-vous of all flesh, the fatal meeting place of a humanity exiled from God, and one could not get out of it before Christ, "the first-fruits of those who have fallen asleep" (1 Co 15,20-23), "the first-born from among the dead" (Ap 1,5). Redemption* is for humanity, condemned in Adam* to death and to separation from God, the opening of the gates* of hell, the gift of eternal life. The Church* is the fruit and the instrument of this victory (Mt 16,18).

But Christ, even before His coming, was already promised and hoped for. In the measure that he accepts this promise, the man of the OT sees the nether world brightened by a light that becomes certitude. On the contrary, in the measure that he rejects it, the nether world becomes hell, and he sinks into an abyss where the power of Satan* prevails in horror. Finally, when Jesus Christ appears, "those who do not obey His gospel. . .are punished with eternal loss, banished from the face of the Lord" (2 Th 1,8f); they rejoin death and Hades "in the pool of fire" (Ap 20,14f).

→Captivity II—Curse—Death—Fire OT III; NT I 1—Gate OT I; NT—Judgment—Punishments—Reward—Satan—Sin—Wrath *B* OT I 2.

JMF & JG gsa

HERESY

1. *Schism and heresy.* The words schism* and heresy both refer to a grave and persisting division within the Christian people, but at two different levels: a schism is a rupture in the sphere of hierarchical communion, while heresy is a rupture in the sphere of faith itself.

In the OT the intellectual content of the faith was too limited and too little worked out for there to be room for heresy. The temptation of Israel was not to "choose" *(hairein)* arbitrarily from a body of precise doctrine but to "follow other gods" (Dt 13,3): apostasy or idolatry* rather than heresy. Those who led people astray and those who followed them cut themselves off from Yahweh, the only God and Savior of Israel, but did not cause a split in the unity of the holy people; they were asking to be cut off from them (Dt 13,6).

The strict sense of the word "heresy" only appears in certain late writings of the NT (2 P 2,1; Tt 3,10). For Paul, the *haireseis* of 1 Co 11,19 are scarcely different from the *schismata* of v 18. Nevertheless, a certain difference of degree is probable. Ruptures *(schismata)* within the community tend to crystalize into real rival parties or sects *(haireseis)* with their own special theories, as they existed in Judaism: the Sadducees (Ac 5,17), the Pharisees (15,5; 26,5) and the Nazarenes (24,5.14; 28,22), or in the Greek world with its schools of rhetoric (also called *haireseis*).

So the Church was familiar with two different situations in this matter of doctrinal error. In the first place its unity was threatened by the Judaizing crisis. And later on certain people cut themselves off from faith in Christ (1 Jn 4,3), "but they had never really belonged" (2,19); they were like the disciples who refused to believe in Jesus at Capharnaum (Jn 6,36.64) and left Him (v 66).

2. *The Judaizing crisis.* The admission of pagans into the Church very soon gave rise to questions about the value of Jewish observances, which the Jewish Christians continued to follow. To impose them on Gentile converts to Christianity would have been to see them as necessary for salvation. And indeed this was what the judaizers claimed (Ac 15,1). But, according to Paul, this claim made Christ pointless and stripped the cross of all its value. To seek justice in the Law meant breaking with Christ, falling from grace (G 5,1-6). The Church was threatened by a split, and Paul wanted at all costs to obtain the agreement of the Jewish-Christian Church, above all of "James, Cephas and John" (2,9), about the liberty of pagan Christians (2,4; 5,1). And he obtained it at the Council of Jerusalem in 49 (Ac 15; G 2,1-10); if he had not, he would have "run in vain" (G 2,2), that is to say the apostolic revelation (cf E 3,3-5) would have contradicted itself: "if anyone preaches a version of the Good News different from the one we have already preached to you. . .he is to be condemned" (G 1,9).

3. *Incipient heresies.* But Paul's message was also to offend Greek wisdom. The infatuation of the Corinthians with this wisdom was not without doctrinal implications: they thought that they could choose between Paul, Apollos and Cephas, as others chose between the various schools *(haireseis)* of itinerant philosophers, and they remained deaf to the "language of the cross" used by all the apostles (1 Co 1,17f). Or else they disputed the resurrection of the dead, emptying in this way both preaching and faith of their essential content: the resurrection of Christ (15,2.11-16).

Later, Judaic speculations combined with borrowings from Hellenism to threaten the faith of the Colossians in the primacy of Christ (Col 2,8-15; cf E 4,14-15) and to take them back to the rule of darkness (Col 2,17).

Toward the end of the apostolic age the danger of pre-gnostic ideas, borrowed from heterodox Judaism or paganism (1 Tm 1,3-7.19f; 4,1-11; 6,3-5; 2 Tm 2,14-26; 3,6-9; 4,3f; Tt 1,9-16; Jude; 2 P 2; 3,3-7; Ap 2,2.6.14f.20-25), became more pressing. Certain "false prophets" (1 Jn 4,1) even denied that Jesus was the Son of God "come in the flesh" (2,22f; 4,2f; 2 Jn 7).

Whether at Corinth (1 Co 4,18f), at Colossus (Col 2,18) or elsewhere (1 Tm 6,4; 2 Tm 3,4), these deviations, which give rise to arguments and divisions (1 Tm 6,3ff; Tt 3,9; Jude 19), result from the stubborn pride of those who refuse to submit to the doctrine preached unanimously throughout the Church (R 6,17; 1 Co 15,11; 1 Tm 6,3; 2 P 2,21) and change it by wanting to improve on it with speculations of their own (2 Jn 9). And so the most dangerous of them are excommunicated (Tt 3,10; 1 Tm 1,20; Jude 23; 2 Jn 10).

This severity of the NT toward false teachers shows how valuable is faith that is not wrecked (1 Tm 1,19; 2 Tm 3,8) and attaches us firmly to the Church, which is always victorious over the errors that threaten the treasure of "sound teaching" received from the apostles (2 Tm 1,13f).

→Church IV 3—Error NT—Faith NT III 1—Jew I—Nations NT II—Schism—Teach NT II 3—Truth NT 2 c—Unity III.

PT ems

HOLY

The liturgy acclaims God thrice holy; it proclaims Christ as alone holy; it celebrates the feast of saints. We also speak of the holy gospels, of holy week; and we are called to become holy. Holiness, then, appears to be a complex reality which touches on the mystery of God, but also on worship and morality. It includes the notions of *sacred* and *pure*, but transcends them. It seems to be inaccessibly reserved to God, but it is constantly attributed to creatures.

The Semitic word *qōdeš* (holy thing, holiness), derived from a root which undoubtedly means "to cut off, separate," points toward the idea of separation from the profane; holy things are those which one does not touch or approach except on certain conditions of ritual purity*. Imbued with a dynamism, with a mystery and a majesty in which the supernatural can be seen, they evoke a feeling of mixed terror and fascination which makes man aware of his pettiness before these manifestations of the "numinous."

The biblical notion of holiness is even much richer. Not content with describing the reactions of man confronted with the divine, and with defining holiness by negating the profane,

the Bible contains the revelation of God* Himself; it defines holiness at its very source, God, from whom all holiness is derived. But with this fact Scripture poses a problem on the nature of holiness, which in the end is that of the mystery of God and of His communication with man. At first exterior to persons, places, and objects which it makes "sacred," this derived holiness becomes real and interior only by the gift of the Holy Spirit Himself; then love*, which is God Himself (1 Jn 4,18), will be communicated, triumphing over sin* which was obstructing the radiation of His holiness.

OT

I. GOD IS HOLY, HE MANIFESTS HIS HOLINESS

The holiness of God is inaccessible to man. In order for man to discover it, God must "be made holy," that is, "show Himself to be holy" by manifesting His glory*. Creation, theophanies, trials*, chastisements, and calamities* (Nm 20,1-13; Ez 38,12ff), but also miraculous protection and unhoped for deliverances reveal the sense in which God is holy (Ez 28, 25f).

Made manifest first through the series of majestic theophanies at Sinai (Ex 19,3-20), the holiness of Yahweh appears as a power at once terrifying and mysterious, ready to destroy all who approach (1 S 6,19f), but also capable of blessing those who give shelter to the ark where it resides (2 S 6,7-11). It is not to be confused, then, with the divine transcendence or wrath*, since it manifests itself in love* and pardon* as well: "I will not give vent to the fury of my wrath. . .For God—not man—am I: present before you is the holy one" (Ho 11,9).

In the temple, Yahweh appears to Isaiah as a king* of infinite majesty, as the creator* whose glory fills the whole earth, as the object of worship such as only the seraphim are capable of rendering Him. Moreover, even they are not holy enough to contemplate His face*; and man cannot see* it without dying (Is 6,1-5; Ex 33,18-23). Nevertheless, this inaccessible God fills the chasm that separates Him from creatures: He is the "holy one of Israel," the joy*, strength*, support, salvation*, and redemption* of this people with whom He is united by the covenant* (Is 10,20; 17,7; 41,14-20).

Thus, far from being reduced to separation or transcendence, the divine holiness includes all the riches and life, power, and goodness that

God possesses. It is more than just one divine attribute among others: it characterizes God Himself. From that time on, His name* is holy (Ps 33,21; Am 2,7; cf Ex 3,14); Yahweh swears by His holiness (Am 4,2). Language itself reflects this conviction when, ignoring the adjective "divine," it considers the names "Yahweh" and "the holy one" as synonyms (Ps 71,22; Is 5,24; Ha 3,3).

II. GOD WISHES
TO BE RECOGNIZED AS HOLY

Jealous of His exclusive right to worship* and obedience*, God wants to be recognized as holy, to be treated as the one true God, and thus to manifest His own holiness through men. If He minutely regulates the details of sacrifices (Lv 1—7) and the conditions of purity* necessary for worship (Lv 12—15), if He demands that His holy name be not profaned (Lv 22,32), it is because a liturgy, well celebrated, both brilliantly displays His glory (Lv 9,6-23; 1 K 8,10ff; cf Lv 10,1ff; 1 S 2,17; 3,11ff) and throws in relief His majesty. But this worship has value only if it expresses obedience to the Law* (Lv 22,31ff), profound faith (Dt 20,12), personal praise (Ps 99,3-9): this is what it means to fear* God, to acknowledge His holiness (Is 8,13).

III. GOD SANCTIFIES,
HE COMMUNICATES HOLINESS

1. *Holiness and consecration.* By prescribing rules of worship* by which His holiness is manifested, Yahweh has reserved certain places (holy land, sanctuaries, temple*), persons (priests, Levites, first-born, officials, prophets*), objects (offerings, vestments, and objects of worship*), times* (Sabbaths*, jubilee years), which are consecrated to Him by formal rites (offerings, sacrifices*, dedications, anointings*, blood sprinklings) and which are, by this very fact, prohibited from profane usages. Thus, the Levites must not even look at the ark* of the covenant (Nm 4,1.20); the Sabbaths must not be "profaned" (Ez 20,12-24); the deportment of priests is governed by specific regulations more exacting than the ordinary laws (Lv 21).

All these things are holy, but their degree of holiness varies according to the bond which unites them to God. The holiness of these consecrated persons and objects is not of the same nature as that of God. In fact, in contradistinc-tion to contagious defilement (Lv 11,31; 15,4-27), it is not received automatically by contact with the divine holiness. It is the result of a free decision of God, according to His law, according to rites fixed by Him. The infinite distance which separates it from the divine holiness (Jb 15,15) is expressed in the rites: thus the high priest may penetrate into the holy of holies only once a year after minute purifications (Lv 16,1-16). It is necessary, then, to distinguish between true sanctity which is proper to God and the sacred character which frees certain persons and objects from the profane and elevates them to an intermediate state, which at the same time veils and manifests the holiness of God.

2. *The holy people.* Chosen and set apart from the other nations*, Israel becomes the particular domain of God, the priest*-people, the "holy people." Thanks to an inexplicable love, God lives and walks in His people's midst (Ex 33, 12-17); He manifests Himself to them in the cloud*, the ark* of the covenant, the temple*, or simply in His glory* which accompanies them even in exile (Ez 1,1-28): "in your midst, I am the holy one" (Ho 11,9). This active presence* of God confers a holiness on the people which is not simply a ritual holiness, but a genuine dignity, calling for moral holiness. It is in order to sanctify His people that Yahweh promulgates the Law* (Lv 22,31ff). Israel, for example, must not allow herself to indulge in the vices of the Canaanite tribe; Israel must refuse all marriage with the young women of other nations and destroy by anathema* all that can defile her (Dt 7,1-6). Her strength* resides, not in armies or shrewd diplomacy, but in her faith in Yahweh, the holy one of Israel (Is 7,9). He it is who gives her not only the character that distinguishes her from other peoples, but also all the security (Is 41,14-20; 54,1-5), pride (Is 43,3-14; 49,7), and perseveringly invincible hope (Is 60,9-14) that she possesses.

IV. ISRAEL MUST SANCTIFY HERSELF

Israel should respond to the free choice of God who wishes her sanctification by sanctifying herself.

1. She should first *purify herself*, that is, wash from herself any defilement that is incompatible with God's sanctity, before assisting at the theophanies or participating in worship (Ex 19,10-

15). But considering all things, it is God alone who gives her purity*, through the blood of the sacrifice (Lv 17,11), or by purifying her heart (Ps 51).

2. The prophets and Deuteronomy constantly repeated that sacrifices for sin were not sufficient to appease God; but that justice*, obedience*, and love* were needed (Is 1,4-20; Dt 6,4-9). And so, the commandment: "Be ye holy, for I, Yahweh, am holy" (Lv 19,2; 20,26), looks not only for a purity in worship, but also for a *lived holiness*, that is, a holiness which is lived according to the many familial, social, and economic, as well as ritual, prescriptions contained in the various codes (vg Lv 17—26).

3. Finally, men's sanctification is *susceptible of progress*; also, only those who pass the trial* and benefit from the eschatological kingdom (Dn 7,18-22) can be called "saints." They are the men of wisdom who feared Yahweh (Ps 34, 10), the "small remnant" of people of Zion who escaped, those whom God has "written down for survival" (Is 4,3).

NT

The apostolic community assimilated the doctrines and vocabulary of the OT. Thus, God is the holy Father (Jn 17,11), the transcendent *Pantocrator*, and the eschatological judge (Ap 4, 8; 6,10). Holy is His name (Lk 1,49), and likewise His law (R 7,12) and covenant (Lk 1,72). Holy also are the angels (Mk 8,38), the prophets, and the sacred writers (Lk 1,70; Mk 6,20; R 1,2). Holy is His temple, and likewise the heavenly Jerusalem (1 Co 3,17; Ap 21,2). Since He is holy, the elect* should also be holy (1 P 1,15f=Lv 19,2), and the holiness of His name* should be manifested in the coming of His kingdom (Mt 6,9). However, Pentecost*, the manifestation of the Spirit of God, seems to be at the origin of the properly NT conception of holiness.

I. JESUS, THE HOLY ONE

The holiness of Christ is intimately bound up with His divine sonship* and with the presence of the Spirit of God in Him: "conceived of the Holy Spirit, He will be holy" and will be called the Son of God (Lk 1,35; Mt 1,18). When John baptized Him, the "well-beloved Son" received the anointing* of the Holy Spirit (Ac 10,38;

Lk 3,22). He drives out unclean spirits, and they proclaim Him "the holy one of God" or "the Son of God" (Mk 1,24; 3,11), these two expressions being henceforth equivalent (Jn 6, 69; cf Mt 16,16). "Filled with the Holy Spirit" (Lk 4,1), Christ manifests Himself through His works*; His miracles and proofs are intended more as signs of His holiness than as signs of an awe-inspiring power; before Him, as before God, one becomes aware of one's own sinfulness (Lk 5,8; cf Is 6,5).

Christ, the "holy Servant*" of God (Ac 4,27. 30), who suffered death although He was author of life, is the incomparably "holy one" (Ac 3,14f). Therefore "God has exalted Him" (Ph 2,9); being raised from the dead in the spirit of holiness (R 1,4), He is not of this world (Jn 17,11). From then on, He who is seated at the right hand of God (Mk 16,19) can be called "the holy one," as God can be (Ap 3,7; 6,10). The holiness of Christ is therefore of a different order from that—entirely relative—of the holy personages of the OT; it is identical with that of God, His holy Father (Jn 17,11): the same spiritual power, the same prodigious manifestations, the same mysterious profundity; it makes Him love His own even to communicating to them the glory He has received from the Father and even to sacrificing Himself for them; this is how He shows His holiness: "I sanctify myself—so that they may be sanctified" (Jn 17,19-24).

II. CHRIST SANCTIFIES CHRISTIANS

Differing from the victims and worship of the OT, which purified the Hebrews only exteriorly (He 9,11-14; 10,10), the sacrifice* of Christ sanctifies the faithful "in truth" (Jn 17,19), truly communicating holiness to them. The Christians really participate in the life of the risen Christ by faith* and baptism* which give them "the anointing which has come from the holy one" (1 Co 1,30; E 5,26; 1 Jn 2,20). They are likewise "holy in Christ" (1 Co 1,2; Ph 1,1), through the presence of the Holy Spirit in them (1 Co 3,16f; E 2,22); they are indeed "baptized in the Holy Spirit," as John the Baptist had announced (Lk 3,16 p; Ac 1,5; 11,16).

III. THE HOLY SPIRIT

The principal agent in the sanctification of the Christian, then, is the Holy Spirit*. He fills the first communities with gifts* and charisms*. His action in the Church, however, differs from that of the Spirit of God in the OT. The fullness and universality of His outpourings signify that the Messianic times have been accomplished since Christ's resurrection (Ac 2,16-38). On the other hand, His coming is bound up with baptism and with faith in the mystery of the dead and risen Christ (Ac 2,38; 10,47; 19,1-7). His presence is permanent, and Paul can affirm that the redeemed are "temples of the Holy Spirit" and "temples of God" (1 Co 6,11.20; cf 3,16f) and that they have a true communion with Him (2 Co 13,13). And as "all those whom the Spirit of God animates are sons of God" (R 8,14-17), the Christians are not only prophets subject to the temporary action of the Spirit (Lk 1,15; 7,28), but children of God who have the source of the divine holiness always within them.

IV. THE SAINTS

Used absolutely, the word "holy" or "saint" was exceptional in the OT; it was reserved to the elect of eschatological times. In the NT, it designates the Christians. Attributed first to the members of the original community of Jerusalem and especially to the small group of Pentecost* (Ac 9,13; 1 Co 16,1; E 3,5), it was extended to the brethren of Judea (Ac 9,31-41), and then to all the faithful (R 16,2; 2 Co 1,1; 13,12). Indeed through the Holy Spirit, the Christian actually participates in the divine holiness itself. The Christians, who form the true "holy people" and the "royal priesthood*" and who constitute the "holy temple" (1 P 2,9; E 2,21), must give God true worship* by offering themselves with Christ in "holy sacrifice" (R 12,1; 15,16; Ph 2,17).

Finally, the holiness of the Christians, which accrues from an election* (R 1,7; 1 Co 1,2), demands that they cut themselves off from sin* and pagan customs (1 Th 4,3); they must act "according to the holiness which comes from God and not according to the wisdom of the flesh" (2 Co 1,12; cf 1 Co 6,9ff; E 4,30—5,1; Tt 3,4-7; R 6,19). This demand for holy living is the basis of the whole Christian ascetical tradition; it rests not on the ideal of a law which remains exterior, but on the fact that the Christian "captivated by Christ" should "share His sufferings and death in order to arrive at His resurrection" (Ph 3,10-14).

V. THE HOLY CITY

Although already achieved by right, in reality the holiness of God struggles with sin. The time has not yet come when "the saints will judge the world" (1 Co 6,2f). The saints can and should continue to sanctify themselves to be prepared for the parousia of the Lord (1 Th 3,13; Ap 22,11). On that day* will appear the new Jerusalem, the "holy city" (Ap 21,2) in which the tree* of life will blossom, and from which all that is impure and profane will be excluded (Ap 21—22; cf Ze 14,20f): and the Lord Jesus will be glorified in His saints (2 Th 1,10; 2,14), "for God is love*" (1 Jn 4,8). This is certainly the secret of the mystery of the inaccessible holiness of God that is communicated to men.

→Altar 3—Anathema OT—Blessing II 3—Church VI—Example—First-Fruits I 2 b—Glory III—God OT III 2.5, IV—Justice O; *A* NT 2—New I, III 3 b—Paraclete 1—Perfection OT—Pure—Sacrifice—Sexuality II—Spirit of God—Truth NT 3 c—Worship OT III—Wrath *A* 2; *B* OT II; NT III 1—Writing III—Zeal I.

JdV ecu

HOPE

To speak of hope is to call to mind the place the future holds in the religious life of the people of God. The future was to be one of happiness to which all men are called (1 Tm 2,4). God's promises* gradually revealed to His people the splendor of this future, a reality in this world but in "a better country—I mean, the heavenly one" (He 11,16). It will be "eternal life" and men will be "like God" (1 Jn 2,25; 3,2).

It is confidence* in God and His faithfulness* and faith in His promises that guarantees the reality of this future (cf He 11,1) and permits one at least to guess at its wonders. So it is possible for the believer to desire this future or, more precisely, to hope for it. In fact, participation in this certain future remains problematic, for it depends on a faithful and patient love* and this is a difficult thing to ask from a sinful freedom*. The believer cannot, then, have any absolute confidence in his own ability to achieve this future. He can only confidently hope that the God in whom he believes and who alone can make his freedom capable of loving will give it to him. Rooted in this way in faith and trust, hope can open out toward the future and sustain the whole life of the believer with its dynamism.

Faith, trust, hope and love, therefore, are different aspects of one spiritual complex. The same Hebrew roots often express one or other of these ideas. The vocabulary for hope is primarily connected to the roots *qāwāh, yāhal* and *bāṭah,* which translators have done their best to express in Greek (*elpizō, elpis, pepoitha, hypomenō...*) and in Latin (*spero, spes, confido, sustineo, expecto...*). The NT (probably St. Paul) sets up the triad of faith, hope, and charity in all its sharpness (1 Th 1,3; 1 Co 13,13; G 5,5f).

OT

I. HOPE FOR YAHWEH'S BLESSINGS

Though the mysterious promise God originally makes to sinful humanity (Gn 3,15; 9,1-17) proves that God never leaves man without hope, the history of biblical hope really begins with Abraham*. The future assured by the promise* is quite simple: a land and a posterity impossible to count (Gn 12,1f; fruitfulness*). For centuries Israel's hope will center on earthly objects: "the land flowing with milk and honey" (Ex 3,8.17), with every form of prosperity (Gn 49; Ex 23,27-33; Lv 26,3-13; Dt 28).

But this vigorous impetus toward material goods does not make Israel's religion a simple ethics of worldly prosperity. These earthly goods are considered by Israel as blessings* (Gn 39,5; 49,25) and as gifts* (Gn 13,15; 24,7; 28,13) of a God demonstrating in this way faithfulness to His promise and covenant (Ez 23,25; Dt 28,2). And earthly goods must be sacrificed unhesitatingly (Js 6,17-21; 1 S 15) when faithfulness to Yahweh demands it. Abraham's sacrifice was always the example of perfect hope in the promise of the almighty (Gn 22), an indication that Israel would one day know a "better hope" (He 7,19) to which God would slowly lead His people.

II. YAHWEH, HOPE OF ISRAEL AND OF THE NATIONS

Progress here was chiefly the prophets' work. They purified and maintained Israel's hope, but at the same time opened new horizons.

1. *False hope.* Israel often forgot that a future happiness was a gift of the God of the covenant* (Ho 2,10; Ez 16,15ff). Then was Israel tempted to guarantee its future as did the nations*; by a formalistic worship*, by idolatry*, by power*, and by covenants*. The prophets denounce this illusory hope (Jr 8,15; 13,16). Without faithfulness there is no hope of salvation* (Ho 12,7; Is 26,8ff; 59,9ff). The day* of Yahweh would be "the day of wrath*" (Zp 1, 15ff), "darkness without a glimmer of light" (Am 5,20). Jeremiah (1—29) typifies this aspect of the prophetic ministry.

2. *True hope.* At times the future seems to be closed to the Israelites, who are tempted to say: "Our hope is ruined" (Ez 37,11; cf Lm 3,18). At such times the prophets saw hope as hidden from sight (cf Is 8,16f), but it would not vanish. A remnant* will be saved (Am 9,8f; Is 10,19ff). Thus does God's plan continue its forward movement. At the moment of its chastisement, announcement of this "future filled with hope" (Jr 29,11; 31,17) breaks in upon Israel (Jr 30—33; Ez 34—48; Is 40—55) for her permanent consolation* and hope (Ps 9,19). Even Israel's unfaithfulness should not hinder hope. God will pardon* her (Ho 11; Lm 3,22-33; Is 54,4-10; Ez 35,29). Salvation is no less certain for being slow (Ha 2,3; Zp 3,8). For the faithful* and merciful* Yahweh is the "hope of Israel" (Jr 14, 8; 17,13f).

3. *A new hope.* The prophetic idea of the future is highly complex. The prophets preach peace*, salvation*, light*, healing, and redemption. They had an imperfect notion of a wonderful and definitive renewal of paradise*, of the exodus*, of the covenant*, and of the reign of David. Israel "will have its fill of blessings*" (Jr 31,14) from Yahweh (Ho 2,23f; Is 32,15; Jr 31), and she will see the "wealth* of the nations" (Is 61) flowing to her. Since the prophets were close to Israel's past, they place Israel and her earthly happiness (beatitude*) at the mid-point of the future.

The prophets also long for the day when Israel will be filled with a knowledge* of God (Is 11,9; Ha 2,14), because first God will renew their hearts* (Jr 31,33ff; Ez 36,25ff) and the nations* will be converted (Is 2,3; Jr 3,17; Is 45,14f). This future age will be the period of a finally perfect worship* (Ez 40—48; Ze 14) in which all nations will participate (Is 56,8; Ze 14,16f; cf Ps 86,8f; 102,22f). The peak of worship is to contemplate Yahweh and live with

Him (Ps 63; 84). For the prophets, God Himself (Is 60,19f; 63,19; 51,5) and His reign (Ps 96—99) are the hope of Israel and of the nations. Still, the anticipated future happiness of Israel is earthly; without exception (Ez 18) it is happiness for the total community, though its coming depends on individual observance.

III. HOPE IN PERSONAL SALVATION AND IN THE HEREAFTER

At this point progress in the hope of the OT comes from the pious and the wise as they work in the context of faith in personal reward*. This faith, however, runs directly into the problem raised by the just* man's suffering*. Probably toward the end of the Babylonian exile, or a little later, a prophet had indeed taught that this suffering should beget rather than impede hope, because it was a redemptive suffering (Is 53). But this early OT prophecy was short-lived. In spite of certain vague feelings (Jb 13,15; 19,25ff), Job's hope, for example, opens out on the dark night (Jb 42,1-6).

The hope of the mystics was filled with the presence* of God; hence they feel that they have arrived at their goal. For such hope suffering and death are relatively unimportant (Ps 73; 49,16; cf 139,8; 16). The martyrs' faith begets hope for the resurrection* (Dn 12,1ff; 2 M 7); a collective hope centered about the "Son* of Man" (Dn 7). Hope for the wise looked more to peace* (Ws 3,3), to rest* (4,7), to salvation* (5,2); these gifts are not to be found on earth but in immortality (3,4), in the presence of the Lord (5,15f). Thus hope becomes personal (5,5) and is oriented to the world to come.

Jewish hope in the time of Jesus differed according to the religious currents of the period. Reflecting the various forms and the successive stages of Israel's hope, it expected a future both material and spiritual—one centered on God and on Israel and, therefore, temporal and eternal, collective and individual. The actualization of this future in the person of Jesus would demand that hope be still more purified.

NT

I. THE HOPE OF ISRAEL FULFILLED BY JESUS

Jesus announces the arrival of the kingdom* of God (Mt 4,17) in the world. But this kingdom is a spiritual reality accessible only to faith. If Israel's hope is to be fulfilled, she must re-

nounce all the material aspects of her expectations. Jesus requires His disciples to accept suffering* and death* as He did (Mt 16,24ff). On the other hand, the kingdom already present is, in another sense, still to come. Hope, therefore, continues; but its orientation now is exclusively toward eternal life* (18,8f), toward the glorious coming of the Son* of Man "who will reward everyone according to his works" (16, 27; 25,31-46). While awaiting this day*, the Church is strengthened by the promises (16,18) and by the presence of Jesus (28,20). It should fulfill the hope of the prophets by opening the kingdom and its hope to the nations* (8,11f; 28,19).

II. JESUS CHRIST, HOPE OF THE CHURCH

The hope of the Church is an assured hope in faith, for the gift of the Spirit* has achieved fulfillments of the promises* made (Ac 2,33.39). The whole force of the Church's hope focuses upon the expectation of Jesus' return (1,11; 3, 20). This return is called the parousia (Jm 5,8; 1 Th 2,19), the day* of the Lord, the visitation*, the revelation*. It is a future near at hand (Jm 5,8; 1 Th 4,13ff; He 12,18ff; 1 P 4,7); there is frequently surprise at its delay (2 P 3,8ff). But it will really come "as a thief in the night*" (1 Th 5,1ff; 2 P 3,10; Ap 3,3; cf Mt 24,36). The uncertainty calls for vigilance (1 Th 5,6; 1 P 5,8) and resolute patience* in trial and suffering* (Jm 5,7ff; 1 Th 1,4f; 1 P 1,5ff; cf Lk 21,19). The Church's hope is joyful (R 12,12), even in suffering (1 P 4,13; cf Mt 5,11f). Because the anticipated glory is so great (2 Co 4,17), it is reflected in the present moment (1 P 1,8f). Hope engenders a certain seriousness (1 Th 5,8; 1 P 4,7) and detachment (1 Co 7,29ff; 1 P 1,13; Tt 2,13). These are, in fact, the earthly benefits leading to the hope of "participating in the divine nature" (2 P 1,4). Finally, hope excites prayer* and fraternal love* (1 P 4,7f; Jm 5,8f). Anchored firmly in the world to come (He 6,18), hope permeates the whole of Christian life.

III. THE PAULINE DOCTRINE OF HOPE

St. Paul shares the hope of the Church, but the wealth of his thought and of his own spiritual life contribute elements of special value to the common treasury.

An instance is the place which he gives to the "redemption* of our body" (R 8,23), whether in the transformation of the living (1 Co 15,51;

cf 1 Th 4,13-18), or even more especially in the place he gives to the resurrection* of the dead. Not to believe in this resurrection is for Paul to be "without hope" (1 Th 4,13; 1 Co 15,19; cf E 2,12).

Glory will only be awarded to those who "persist in doing good" (R 2,7f; cf He 6,12). But human freedom is weak (R 7,12-25). Can the Christian then really hope to take part in the promised inheritance* (Col 4,24)? He can and should hope as Abraham* did, "hoping against all hope." He can hope because of his faith* in the promises* (R 4,18-25) and in virtue of his trust in the faithfulness* of God who strengthens the faithfulness of man (1 Th 5,24; 1 Co 1,9; cf He 10,23) from the time of his initial calling* to the attainment of glory* (R 8,28-30).

The fulfillment of these promises in Jesus Christ (1 Co 1,20) plays a fundamental role in Paul's thought. The glory awaited is present reality (2 Co 3,18—4,6) though invisible (2 Co 4,18; R 8,24f). One who is baptized* is already arisen (R 6,1-7; Col 3,1) in the Spirit, whom he has received as the pledge (2 Co 1,22; 5,5; E 1,4) and the first-fruits* (R 8,11.23) of the world to come, and already possesses in this world. Thus "all bounds to hope" are removed (15,13). God has given the grace* of justification* to men whom Adam had dragged toward death*. But now "much more" will their solidarity with His Son lead them to life* (R 5). This fulfillment in Christ of Israel's hope is a fuller revelation of the basis for Christian hope: a love* such that in no way can it be taken from the Christian (R 8,31-39).

Paul's own personal hope gives us an excellent example. It appears in his soul with an extreme intensity. It laments that it is not yet achieved (2 Co 5,5; R 8,23) and rejoices in the thought of the awaited future (1 Co 15,54ff). In this light even the most legitimate of human hopes lose all their value (Ph 3,8). Drawing its support only from the grace of God and not from works* (1 Co 4,4; 15,10; R 3,27), hope provides by its dynamism the strength needed for the race (Ph 3,13f) and the combat (2 Tm 4,7) which Paul carries on in order to achieve his mission, while at the same time he guards against being "disqualified himself" (1 Co 9,26f). Hope awakens new hopes (Ph 2,19; 2 Co 1,9f; 4,7-18), but always "in the Lord." When Paul's death seems near, he looks forward to the reward (Ph 3,14) which will crown his race (2 Tm 4,6ff; cf 1 Co 3,8). But he knows that his recompense is Christ Himself (Ph 3,8). His hope is above all to be with Him (Ph 1,23; 2 Co 5,8).

The Apostle is no longer looking forward to his personal happiness but quite simply to being with someone he loves. This fundamental disinterestedness of his hope appears again in his work for the salvation of "others" (2 Tm 4,8; 2,7), whether Christians (1 Th 2,19) or pagans, to whom he wants to reveal Christ, "the hope of his glory" (Col 1,24-29). Paul's hope, therefore, embraces in all its fullness (cf R 8,19ff) the plan of God, and it answers "with love" (2 Tm 4,8) to the love of the Lord.

IV. THE MARRIAGE FEAST OF THE LAMB

The Johannine hope does not cease to be an expectance of the return of the Lord (Jn 14,3; 1 Jn 2,18), and of the resurrection and judgment (Jn 5,28f; 6,39f). But it prefers to rest in the possession of an eternal life* already given to the believer (3,15; 6,54; 1 Jn 5,11ff) who is already arisen (Jn 11,25f; 1 Jn 3,14) and judged (Jn 3,19; 5,24). The Christian's passage into eternity will only be the peaceful manifestation (1 Jn 4,18) of a reality already existing (1 Jn 3, 2).

In the Apocalypse the perspectives are completely different. The risen Lamb, surrounded by Christians (Ap 5,11-14; 14,1-5; 15,2ff), is already triumphant in heaven whence will come the Church, His spouse* (21,2). But this spouse is at the same time on the earth (22,17) where is enacted the drama of Christian hope at grips with history. The apparent triumphs of satanic powers threaten to wear down this hope. In reality, however, the invincible Word fights and reigns at the side of His people (19,11-16; 20, 1-6) and the decisive victory* is near (Ap 1,1; 2,5; 3,11; 22,6.12). The hope of Christians should, then, be triumphant till the coming of the "new world" which will finally give full and definitive realization to the prophecies of the OT (Ap 21—22).

At the end of the book the bridegroom promises: "My return is near." And the bride answers Him: "Come, Lord Jesus!" (Ap 22, 20). This cry takes up again an Aramaic prayer of the Church in its early days: "Marana tha!" (cf 1 Co 16,22). Christian hope will never find better expression, because it is in essence only the ardent desire of a love which hungers for the presence of the Lord.

→Anguish 3—Ascension IV—Confidence—Consolation 1—Day of the Lord OT II; NT II —Death OT III 1.3; NT III 4—Deception/Disappointment—Desire—Earth OT II 4; NT III—Faith—Fasting—Heaven VI—Inheritance—Joy OT II 3; NT II 1—Liberation/Liberty II 3—Life III 3, IV 5—Night OT O.2—Patience II 1—Persecution II—Promises—Providence—Remnant—Resurrection NT II—Salvation OT II 2; NT II 3—See NT II—Sow I 2 b—Time OT III; NT III—Watch I—Word of God OT III 2.

JDu afmcg

HOSPITALITY

1. *Hospitality as a work of mercy*. The visitor who passes through and asks for the housing he needs (Pr 27,8; Si 29,21f) reminds Israel of her former condition as an enslaved stranger* (Lv 19,33f; cf Ac 7,6). It also reminds her of her present condition of a traveler upon earth (Ps 39,13; cf He 11,13; 13,14). This visitor needs to be welcomed and treated with love* in the name of God who loves him (Dt 10,18f). No sacrifices, however great, will be refused when it is a question of his defence (Gn 19,8; Jg 19,23). Nor will a man hesitate to inconvenience his friends, if he himself does not have the means of satisfying the needs of an unexpected guest (Lk 11, 5f). This eager and religious welcome of which Abraham is the type (Gn 18,2-8), in which Job prides himself (Jb 31,31f) and which is approved by Christ (Lk 7,44ff) is an aspect of fraternal charity which makes the Christian very aware of his debt to others (R 12,13; 13,8).

2. *Hospitality as a witness to faith*. At the last judgment Jesus will reveal to everyone the mystery of this hospitality, a form of charity. Through and in the visitor, Christ Himself is welcomed or sent away (Mt 25,35.43), recognized or unrecognized, just as when He came unto His own. It is not only at His birth that there was not room for Him in the inn (Lk 2,7). It is right up to the end of His life that the world did not recognize Him and His own did not receive Him (Jn 1,9ff). Those who believe in Him receive His ambassadors "in His name*" (Jn 13,20), as well as all men, even the most humble (Lk 9,48). They see in every visitor not only an ambassador of the Lord, an "angel*" (Gn 19,1ff), but also the Lord Himself (Mt 10, 40; Mk 9,37).

Hence far from treating the visitor as a debtor (Si 29,24-28) or as unwelcome and to be mistrusted (Si 11,34) and the object of murmuring

(1 P 4,9), pleasure is taken in welcoming those who cannot make any return for the services rendered (Lk 14,13). Every Christian (1 Tm 5, 10), and especially the bishop (1 Tm 3,2; Tt 1,8), must see in the one knocking at his door (cf Ap 3,20) the Son of God who has come with His Father to bestow on and establish with Him His dwelling place (Jn 14,23). These divine visitors will in turn introduce him into their home not as a guest, but as a child of the house (Jn 14,2f; E 2,19). Happy will be the watchful servants who will open the gate* to the master when He knocks at the time of the parousia! He will reverse the roles and manifest the mystery of hospitality by serving at table (Lk 12,37) and by sharing His meal* (Ap 3,20).

→Brother—House I 1, III 2—Meal—Neighbor—Perfume 1—Poor NT III 1—Stranger I.

PMG & MFL jrs

HOUR

The Bible story is divided into ages, months, days, and hours. But frequently time, day, and hour go beyond the chronological meaning and give evidence of a religious meaning. Just as in the case of the time* of Yahweh's visitation* or the day* of salvation, *hour* means the decisive stages in the plan* of God.

1. *The eschatological hour*. Jewish apocalyptic was convinced of the nearness of the end time, the fullness* of time. It analyzed this foreseen time of the divine intervention into days and hours. All the moments count when the end arrives. Daniel learns that his vision concerns the "hour of the time" and that wrath* will be active "for the hours of the final time" (Dn 8, 17.19), "because time hastens toward those hours" (11,35). In fact, there will be a definitive hour of consummation which will see the ruin of the enemy* (11,40.45; cf Ap 18,10.17.19). In the same way, the apocryphal Book of Henoch counts the hours in which the sheperds of Judah follow one another.

It is in this atmosphere that Jesus announces the hour of final triumph for the Son of Man. Perfectly unknown to men, it is the hour of judgment* (Mt 24,36.44.50 p; Jn 5,25.28) and the hour of the harvest* (Ap 14,15ff). Equally unforeseen will be the hour of the different visitations* which will announce the final hour. These will be either general trials (Ap 3,10) or particular ones (9,15). The believer has to be ready for that precise hour no matter how undetermined it may be (Mt 25,13). He knows, besides, that the hour is near and that, in one sense, it has already arrived (Jn 4,23) and is under way (5,25.28). It is the "final hour" (1 Jn 2,18), that of active vigilance (R 13,11), but also of perfect worship* in the intimate relation with the Father through the Spirit (Jn 4,23).

2. *The Messianic hour.* In a less spectacular way, the hour comes with Jesus—the hour when the kingdom is announced (perhaps Jn 2,4), especially the hour of His passion and glory, which brings to accomplishment the salvific plan of God.

The synoptics designate it with a simple and solemn statement: "Behold, my hour has come, etc..." (Mt 26,45 p). Not any precise moment of time, it is the entire supreme phase of His activity which it crowns, much as happens in the pregnant woman's hour of delivery when pain marks the arrival of new life (Jn 16,21). It is an hour of suffering, and when it comes it begins a violent interior struggle (Mk 14,35). It is also the hour of the enemy* and the apparent triumph of darkness (Lk 22,53). But it is even more the hour of God decided by Him alone and lived out by Jesus according to the will of the Father. Since He came to do this will*, He accepts this hour in spite of the anguish it gives Him (Jn 12,27). Is it not also the hour of His glory* (12,23) and of His full saving activity (12,24)?

So much does Jesus make this will of God His own that He Himself calls it on one occasion, according to John, "my hour" (2,4). No one, not even His own mother, can turn Him from the plan of God and ask Him for a miracle without His making reference to His hour (either to affirm it or to deny it, according to the different opinions of the critics). It is in terms of this hour that He organizes all His wonderworking and prophetic activity. In speaking of "His hour" the evangelist generalizes. Every attempt to arrest Him or to stone Him is in vain, so long as His hour has not yet come (7,30; 8,20). Human plans break down against this divine determination. But when "the hour to pass from this world to the Father" (13,1) has come, the hour of a love carried to its term, the Lord goes freely to His death, with power over the events, just as a priest fulfills the rites of the liturgy (cf 14,29f; 17,1).

Thus, though the events appear to follow one another without coordination, everything is directed toward a purpose which will be attained in its own time, day, and hour. The hours of this movement are carefully recorded just as they would be today for an economic or political plan. They have their sorrowful moments as when Jesus was abandoned by His disciples (Jn 16,32), but they all tend toward His glory, and His glorious return. They are all an accurate witness of God's plan* which directs history (Ac 1,7).

→Day of the Lord—Plan of God NT I 1— Time NT I 1—Visitation.

RM jrs

HOUSE

In order to live man needs a favorable surrounding and a protecting shelter, a family and a home. Both of these are expressed by the same Hebrew word *bayith* (*bēth* in compound words, vg *Beth-el*, house of God). But God was not satisfied with giving man a natural family and a material dwelling. He wanted to bring man into His own home, not only as a servant, but as a son. Therefore, after dwelling in the heart of Israel in the temple, God sent His only Son to build men a spiritual abode, a home made of living stones and open to all men.

I. THE HOME OF THE CHILDREN OF MEN

1. *The family home.* Man looks forward to having a place where he can be "at home," a nest, as the old proverb says (Pr 27,8), a roof which protects his private life (Si 29,21). He wants this in his own country (Gn 30,25) where his father's home is, a heritage which no one should take from him (Mi 2,2), or even covet (Ex 20,17 p). In his well-kept home the charm of his wife makes things bright (Si 26,16), but a wicked wife makes it uninhabitable (25,16). A man lives in his home with his sons who are part of it, whereas his servants can leave it (Jn 8,35). He likes to welcome guests there, even constraining them if need be (Gn 19,2f; Ac 16, 15). A home is worth so much that a man who has just built one should not be kept from enjoying it. A very humane law in Israel dispensed him from the risks of war, even a holy war (Dt 20,5; 1 M 3,56).

2. *The one who builds and the one who de-*

stroys. Furthermore, to construct a home is not just to build* its walls, but it is to establish a hearth and to beget a lineage and to pass on to them religious teaching and examples of virtue. It is a work of wisdom (Pr 14,1) and a task for which a virtuous woman is irreplaceable (31,10-31). It is even a divine task which a man by himself cannot bring to completion (Ps 127, 1). But by his wickedness a man can bring ruin upon his home (Pr 17,13), and a foolish wife tears it down (14,1). Before destroying the home, sin has already brought on another collapse, that of the man himself, a fragile dwelling of clay (Jb 4,19) brought to life by the breath of God (Gn 2,7). Sinful man must die and return his breath to God before going to rejoin his fathers in the grave, the house of eternity (Gn 25,8; Ps 49,12.20; Qo 12,5ff); yet he lives on in his progeny, the house which God built for His friends (Ps 127). This shows why building a house without being able to dwell in it is a sign of the punishment of God which infidelity merits (Dt 28,30). The elect, on the other hand, will dwell in eschatological joy in their homes forever (Is 65,21ff).

II. THE SYMBOLIC HOUSE OF GOD

1. *House of Israel and house of David.* God wishes to dwell once again among men who have been cut off from Him by sin. He began His plan by calling Abraham* to serve Him and by drawing him from the midst of men who served other gods (Js 24,2). Therefore Abraham had to leave his country and the home of his father (Gn 12,1). He and his sons with him would live in a tent as wanderers (He 11,9.13) until the day when Jacob and his sons settled down in Egypt. Soon, however, Israel longed to leave this "house of bondage" and God delivered them from it, to make a covenant with them and to dwell in the midst of His people in the tent which He had them make. There rested the cloud* which veiled His glory* and manifested His presence* to all the house of Israel (Ex 40,34-38). This name likewise belonged to the descendants of Jacob, who became more numerous than the stars (Dt 10,22).

The people gathered about the tent of their God, which for that reason was called Tent of Meeting (Ex 33,7). It was there that God spoke to Moses*, His servant, who had constant access to His house (33,9ff; Nm 12,7), and guided the people to the promised land. Yahweh wished to make of this land, which was entirely "His house" (Ho 8,1; 9,15; Jr 12,7; Ze 9,8), the stable domicile of His people (2 S 7,10). David, in turn, wished to install God in a house similar to the palace in which he himself dwelt (7,2), but God would have none of this, because the tent sufficed Him (7,5ff). But He blessed the intention of His anointed. If He did not desire to dwell in a house of stone, He wished to build a house for David, and settle his descendants on his throne (7,11-16). To build a house for God was reserved for the Son of David, who would have God for His Father (7,13f).

2. *From the house of stone to the heavenly temple.* Solomon applied this mysterious prophecy to himself. While proclaiming that the heavens* of the heavens could not contain God who dwelt in them (1 K 8,27), he would build a house for the name* of Yahweh in which He would be invoked, and for the ark*, the symbol of His presence (8,19ff.29). But God is not tied down to any place or any house. And He had it proclaimed by Jeremiah in the very house which bears His name (Jr 7,2-14). He proved this to Ezekiel by two visions: in one God's glory* leaves His profaned house (Ez 10,18; 11, 23); in the other, the glory appears to the prophet over the pagan land where the house of Israel is exiled (Ez 1). But to this house which has stained His name, God announced that He would purify it, bring it together again, unite it, and set up His dwelling within it once more (36,22-28; 37,15f.26ff). All of this would be the effect of the pouring out of His Spirit* upon the house of Israel (39,29). This major prophecy gives one a glimpse of the true house of God, not the material and symbolic temple described minutely by the prophet (40—43), but the house of Israel itself, the spiritual dwelling of its God.

3. *The dwelling of the God of the lowly.* Moreover, upon return from the exile, a twofold lesson was to be taught to the people, to free them from their provincialism and formalism. On the one hand, God opened His house to all the nations* (Is 56,5ff; cf Mk 11,17). On the other hand, He announced that His house is transcendent and eternal and that to enter it one must have a humble and contrite heart (Is 57, 15; 66,1f; cf Ps 15). But who can lead man into this heavenly dwelling? Divine Wisdom* itself is going to come among men to build its house and invite men to enter (Pr 8,31; 9,1-6).

III. THE SPIRITUAL HOUSE
OF THE FATHER AND HIS SONS

1. Jesus Christ is in fact the Wisdom of God (1 Co 1,24). He is the Word* of God who came to dwell among us, being made flesh* (Jn 1,14). He is of the house of David and comes to rule over the house of Jacob (Lk 1,27.33). But at Bethlehem, the city of David, where He was born, He found no house to receive Him (2,4.7). Though he lived at Nazareth in the home of His parents (2,51), at the age of twelve He stated that He was concerned with the affairs of His Father (2,49), whose house is the temple (Jn 2,16). In this house He will intervene with the authority of the Son who is at home there (Mk 11,17 p). He knows, however, that it is destined for destruction (13,1f p); and He has come to build another, His Church* (Mt 16,18; cf 1 Tm 3,15).

2. While working out His mission, He will not have a home of His own (Lk 9,58), nor a family (8,21). He will be invited and will invite Himself to the homes of sinners and publicans (5,29-32; 19,5-10). He will find in the homes of those who receive Him a welcome sometimes cold, sometimes friendly (7,36-50; 10,38ff). But He will always bring to these homes the call to conversion, the grace of forgiveness, the revelation of salvation, the one thing necessary. To the disciples, who at His call left their homes and renounced all to follow Him (Mk 10,29f), He will give the mission to bring peace* to the homes that welcome them (Lk 10,5f) and likewise to call others to follow Christ, the way leading to the home of His Father, where He promises to bring us (Jn 14,2-6).

To gain access for us to this house which God built and of which He Himself as Son is the head (He 3,3-6), Christ our high priest goes before us, entering by means of His sacrifice (6,19f; 10,19ff). This house of the Father, this heavenly sanctuary, is furthermore a spiritual reality not far from us. "We ourselves are that house," as long as we do not fail in hope (3,6).

3. Certainly we will not reach this house of God till we have left our earthly dwelling and put on our eternal and heavenly dwelling, our glorious and immortal body (2 Co 5,1f; cf 1 Co 15,53). But right now God invites us to work with Him to build this house, which has Jesus Christ as foundation (1 Co 3,9ff), the living cornerstone, and which is made of living stones, those who believe (1 P 2,4ff). By giving us access to the Father, Christ did not have us enter His home only as guests; He has made us belong "to the household" (E 2,18f), to be united into the construction of the building and to grow with it. For everyone becomes a house of God when he is united with his brethren in the Lord by the Spirit (2,21f). This is the reason why in the Apocalypse the heavenly Jerusalem no longer has a temple (Ap 21,22). In its entirety it is the house of God with men who have become His sons (21,3.7) dwelling with Christ in the love of His Father (Jn 15,10).

→Abide—Build—City—Fathers & Father I 1—Hospitality—Presence of God OT III 1—Temple OT I 2; NT I 1.

JMF & MFL hjb

HUMAN SPEECH

Following a notion that is common in antiquity, the biblical world does not consider human speech only as empty sound, a simple means of communication among men; speech expresses the person, participates in his dynamism, and somehow is efficacious. Hence, its importance in human behavior. According to its quality, it reflects honor or confusion upon the speaker (Si 5,13); life and death are in its power (Pr 18,21). In judging a man's worth, speech is a touchstone by which he can be tested (Si 27, 4-7). It is known that the masters of wisdom inculcated good use of speech and denounced faulty usage. On this point the NT will only repeat the teaching of the OT.

1. *Concerning bad use of speech.* There is the chatterbox (Pr 10,19; 29,20), who gabbles away in his stupidity (10,8; 13,3) and indiscretion (20,19), and who makes himself detested (Si 20, 5-8), the fool who is recognized by his tricky speech (20,18ff), the false friend who offers only "windy words" for consolation (Jb 6,26). Still worse is the speech of the wicked that is like a bloody ambush (Pr 12,6). The wise man must guard himself from slander (Si 5,14), for the tongue* causes more victims than the sword (Pr 12,18; Si 28,17f). The words of the talebearers are often received like "sweets" (Pr 26, 22), but they wound cruelly; the psalmists, with the insistence of people who have suffered much, continually denounce the slander and calumny that strikes them (Ps 5,10; 10,7). In the NT, the epistle of St. James considers these same coun-

sels on faults of speech (Jm 3,2-12): to guard one's tongue is one of the first demands of Christian wisdom (cf 1,26 and 3,2).

Other perils are to be feared; notably, impure speech (Si 23,12-21) and false oaths*. The Mosaic Law forbade the latter (Ex 20,7; Nm 30, 3; Dt 23,22...). Fearing that oaths would be used thoughtlessly, the author of Ecclesiastes advises that restraint be used regarding the number of oaths (Si 23,7-11). Jesus taught an ideal of truthfulness that made oaths useless (Mt 5, 33...), and this ideal was retained by the apostolic Church (Jm 5,12; 2 Co 1,17f). Among the sins of speech there is also to be included the sin of superstitiously trusting in its magical effect. Common in the ancient East, known in the biblical milieu (word of evil fortune: Nm 22,6; phantom words: Is 29,4), it is forbidden by the Law under pain of death and under the same title as the other magical rites (Lv 20, 6.27).

2. *Good use of speech.* Contrary to the sinners and fools, the wise man must know exactly how to control his speech. A fitting speech or an opportune response is a treasure and a joy (Pr 15,23; 25,11), for "there is a time to speak and a time to keep silent" (Qo 3,7). He must restrain his speech (Si 1,24), weigh his words, put a latch on his mouth (Si 28,25; Ps 39,2; 141,3), and be slow to speak (Jm 1,19). To all this he must unite wisdom and goodness, as does the perfect woman (Pr 31,26). Human speech then is like deep water, an overflowing torrent, a source of life (Pr 18,4; cf Dt 32,1f); for the mouth speaks from the abundance of the heart, and in such a way that a good man brings out a treasure from within him (Lk 6,45). Speaking under the action of the Holy Spirit, he can edify, exhort, and console his brothers (1 Co 14,3); for his human speech then expresses the Word* of God.

→Amen 1—Heart I 1—Lie—Lips—Oath—Preach II—Silence 2—Tongue—Truth OT 2; NT 1—Witness OT I.

AF & PG rco'c

HUMILITY

I. HUMILITY AND ITS DEGREES

Biblical humility is, in the first place, modesty as opposed to vanity. Without any foolish pretention the modest person is not wise in his own conceits (Pr 3,7; R 12,3.16; cf Ps 131,1). The humility which is opposed to pride* is at a deeper level. It is the attitude of the sinful creature before the almighty and thrice holy one. The humble man recognizes the fact that he has received all from God (1 Co 4,7). A worthless servant (Lk 17,10) of himself is nothing (G 6,3) except a sinner (Is 6,3ff; Lk 5,8). God will glorify this humble person (1 S 2,7f; Pr 15,33) who is open to His grace (Jm 4,6= Pr 3,34).

Incomparably deeper yet is the humility of Christ who saves us by His self-abasement and who invites His disciples to serve their brothers in love (Lk 22,26f) so that God will be glorified in all of them (1 P 4,10f).

II. THE HUMILITY OF THE PEOPLE OF GOD

Israel first learns humility by experiencing the almighty power* of God who saves them and who alone is their most high. Israel keeps this experience alive by commemorating God's deeds in their worship*. This worship is a school of humility. By praise and thanksgiving the Israelite imitates the humility of David who advanced before the ark (2 S 6,16.22) to glorify God to whom he owed everything (Ps 103).

Israel has also had the experience of poverty either in the collective trial of defeat and of exile* or in the individual trial of sickness* and oppression of the weak. These humiliations have made it take notice of man's deep-seated impotence and of the sinner's misery as he separates himself from God. Thus man is inclined to turn to God with a contrite heart (Ps 51,19), with the humility that is based on a total dependence and confident docility and which inspires the supplications of the psalms (Ps 25; 106; 130; 131). Those who praise God and beg Him to save them are frequently called the "poor*" (Ps 22,25.27; 34,7; 69,33f). This word means first of all the social class of unfortunates, but it takes on a religious meaning in Zephaniah: to seek* God is to seek poverty which is humility (Zp 2,3). After the day of Yahweh, the "remnant" of the people of God will be "humble and poor" (Zp 3,12; gr. *praüs* and *tapeinos*; cf Mt 11,29; E 4,2).

In the OT, the models of this humility are Moses*, the most humble of men (Nm 12,3), and the mysterious Servant* who by his humble submission even to death accomplishes God's plan (Is 53,4-10). After the return from exile, the prophets and wise men will preach humility. The most high dwells with the one who has a humble spirit and a contrite heart (Is 57,15; 66,2). "The fruit of humility is the fear of God, riches, glory, and life" (Pr 22,4). "The greater you are, the more you have to humble yourself in order to find favor with the Lord" (Si 3,18; cf Dn 3,39: the offertory prayer "in the spirit of humility"). Finally, in the words of the last prophet, the Messiah will be a humble king; He will enter Zion mounted on an ass (Ze 9,9). Truly the God of Israel, the king of creation is the "God of the humble" (Jdt 9,11f).

III. THE HUMILITY OF THE SON OF GOD

Jesus is the humble Messiah whom Zechariah announced (Mt 21,5). He is the Messiah of those humble ones whom He proclaimed blessed (Mt 5,4=Ps 37,11; gr. *praüs*=the humble one who has been made patient* and kind by his submission to God). Jesus blesses the children* and offers them as models (Mk 10,15f). In order to become one of these little ones to whom God has revealed Himself and who alone will enter into the kingdom* (Mt 11,25; 18,3f), it is necessary to join the school of Christ, "The teacher who is meek and humble of heart" (Mt 11,29). But this master is not only a man; He is the Lord who has come to save sinners by taking on flesh just like theirs (R 8,3). Far from seeking His own glory (Jn 8,50), He humbles Himself even to the point of washing the feet of His disciples (Jn 13,14ff). Though He is the equal of God, He empties Himself to the extent of dying on the cross for our redemption (Ph 2,6ff; Mk 10,45; cf Is 53). In Jesus we have a revelation not only of divine power without which we would be nothing, but also of divine charity without which we would be lost (Lk 19,10).

This humility ("the sign of Christ" as Augustine said) is the humility of the Son of God, the humility of charity. We have to follow the way of this "new" humility in order to practice the new commandment of charity (E 4,2; 1 P 3,8f; "wherever humility is, there is also charity" says Augustine). "Those who in their mutual relationships clothe themselves with humility" (1 P 5,5; Col 3,12) seek the interest of others, and take the last place for themselves (Ph 2,3f; 1 Co 13,4f). In the list of the fruits* of the Spirit, Paul places humility alongside of faith (G 5,

22f). These two attitudes (which were the essential characteristics of Moses according to Si 45,4) are actually connected since they are both attitudes of being open to God, of confident submission to His grace and His Word.

IV. GOD'S WORK IN THE HUMBLE

God regards the humble and bends down toward them (Ps 138,6; 113,6f). Taking glory only in their weakness (2 Co 12,9) they open themselves up to the power of God's grace which is not sterile in them (1 Co 15,10). The humble person not only obtains pardon for his sins (Lk 18,14), but also the wisdom* of the almighty loves to manifest itself by means of the humble person whom the world despises (1 Co 1,25.28f). We have only to think of the humility shown by the one whom the Lord sends to prepare the way for Him and whose only thought is to retire into the background (Jn 1,27; 3,28ff). God makes the humble virgin, who wants only to be a servant, the mother of His Son, our Lord (Lk 1,38.43).

Whoever humbles himself by undergoing trials under the all-powerful hand of the God of all grace, and whoever joins in the fellowship of Christ crucified, will, like Jesus, be exalted by God in his hour, and will have a share in the glory of the Son of God (Mt 23,12; R 8,17; Ph 2,9ff; 1 P 5,6-10). With all the humble he will sing eternally the holiness and love of the Lord who has done great things in them (Lk 1,46-53; Ap 4,8-11; 5,11-14).

In the OT, the Word of God leads man to glory by the path of humble submission to God, his Creator and Savior. In the NT, the Word of God is made flesh in order to lead man to the heights of humility which consists in serving God in men, in humiliating oneself by love in order to glorify God while also saving men.

→Arrogance 5—Ashes—Child II, III—Confidence 2—Creation OT IV 1—Fasting—Joy OT II 2; NT I 1—Mary IV 3—Meal III—Patience II 2—Perfection NT 3—Poor OT III; NT I, II —Pride O—Strength II—Sweetness 2—Virtues & Vices 3.

MFL jrs

HUNGER & THIRST

Because they express a vital need, hunger and

thirst reveal the meaning of human existence before God; and this gives them a certain ambivalence (Pr 30,9). To suffer hunger and thirst is a positive experience that ought to make a man open to God; but the condition of the hungry is an evil not wanted by God and one that should be eliminated. When it assumes the proportions of a collective event (as in the case of a famine for example), the Bible sees it as a calamity*, a sign of divine judgment*.

OT

1. *Hunger and thirst, a test of faith.*

a) *In the desert,* God made His people undergo hunger in order to test them, and to get to know their inmost hearts (Dt 8,1ff). Israel had to learn that it depended entirely for its existence on Yahweh who alone gives them His food and drink. But beyond and beneath these physical needs, Israel must discover in itself a need more vital still, its need for God. The manna* which comes from heaven appropriately calls to mind that which goes forth from the mouth of God—His Word, His Law in which the people must find life (Dt 30,15ff; 32,46f). But the people fail to understand this and they think only of the meats of Egypt: "Oh, what memories!" (Nm 11,4f). And so instead of the salutary test by hunger God is compelled to gorge Israel with meat "until it comes out of their nostrils" (11,20; cf Ps 78,26-31).

b) *Once established in their land* and surrounded with good things, Israel forgets the lesson of the desert* and attributes these things to their own merit, and they gloried in them in the presence of Yahweh (Dt 32,10-15; Ho 13, 4-8). So God must again lead His people back into the desert (Ho 2,5) so that the heart* of Israel, fainting of thirst and weeping for its lost grain and ruined vineyards (2,11.14), will be awakened (2,16) and will again feel keenly the essential hunger and thirst, that of "hearing the word of Yahweh" (Am 8,11).

c) *The prophets and the sages accept these lessons.* The need and the desire for good things which God reserves for those who love Him is continually expressed in images of a meal, of bread, of water, or of wine. One hungers for the banquet which Yahweh prepares for all the nations upon His mountain (Is 25,6). One thirsts for the wisdom* which refreshes (Pr 5,15; 9,5)

and for the inebriating wine* which is love (Ct 1,4; 4,10). One hurries to receive from God, "without cost," drink for the thirsty and food which satisfies (Is 55,1ff). But it is for the most pure water* that one has a thirst, and for the wine alone whose intoxication brings life—God Himself (Ps 42,2). God holds Himself ready to fill this desire: "Open wide your mouth, and I will fill it" (Ps 81,11).

2. *Hunger and thirst, a call to charity.* The trial of hunger and thirst should remain the exception. The poor*, who will not disappear from the country (Dt 15,11), are living appeals to all who come near them. One of the primordial obligations of an Israelite is to give bread and water to his brother*, to his fellow citizen (Ex 23,11), to anyone in need (Tb 4,16f), even to his enemy* (Pr 25,21). This is what it means to practice justice* (Ez 18,5.16) and to make one's fasting* pleasing to God (Is 58,7.10). In the end, Yahweh Himself will intervene in favor of the hungry to invite them to a banquet which will completely satisfy their hunger and thirst (Is 25,6; cf 65,13).

NT

1. *Jesus Christ,* Messiah of the poor (Lk 1,53), announces to those who hunger and thirst that they will have their fill (6,21). He begins His mission by taking upon Himself the condition of one who hungers and thirsts. Put to the test, as Israel in the desert, He affirms and proves that man's essential need is the Word of God, the will of the Father (Mt 4,4) which He makes His food and by which He lives (Jn 4,32ff). On the cross, once He has drunk "the cup which the Father had given Him" (Jn 18,11), His thirst in crucifixion is inseparable from His desire to "fulfill the entire Scripture" (Jn 19,28) and to complete the work of His Father, but also to "stand before His face" (Ps 42,3).

2. *Jesus alleviates and arouses hunger and thirst.* As God of old in the desert, Jesus eases the hunger of the people who follow Him (Mk 8,1ff), while at the same time He is preoccupied with awakening a desire for the Word of God, for the true bread* which is Jesus Himself (Jn 6), the desire for the living water* which is His Spirit* (Jn 7,37ff). He stirs up this thirst in the Samaritan woman (Jn 4,1-14), just as He invites Martha to desire His Word as the one thing necessary (Lk 10,39-42).

3. *The Christian and the hungry.* For the followers of Jesus, the duty of feeding the hungry is more demanding than ever. A torturing thirst in Gehenna awaits him who did not see the hungry at his door (Lk 16,19-24). The reward is for the man who gave a glass of water to one of Jesus' disciples (Mt 10,42). On this point will man be judged, because to feed the hungry and to give drink to the thirsty is to alleviate, through His brothers*, the hunger and thirst of Jesus (Mt 25,35-42). We ought always to thirst for this charity with which we ease the sufferings of others. The source of this charity is open and free to souls of desire, souls athirst for God and for the vision of His face, and athirst for the true life (Is 55,1ff; Ap 21,6; 22,17).

→Beatitude NT II—Bread—Desert—Desire II —Meal—Nourishment—Water.

JB afmcg

HYPOCRITE

Following in the steps of the prophets (vg Is 29,13) and the sages (vg Si 1,28f; 32,15; 36,20), but with unequaled vigor, Jesus laid bare the roots and consequences of hypocrisy, especially that of those who at that time formed the intelligensia, the scribes, the Pharisees and the doctors of the Law. Clearly a hypocrite is one whose actions do not correspond to the thoughts of his heart*. He is also called blind by Jesus (comp Mt 23,25 and 23,26). There is a connection that seems to justify both meanings. By trying to deceive others, the hypocrite deceives himself and himself becomes blind, unable to see the light.

1. *The formalism of the hypocrite.* Religious hypocrisy is not simply a lie*; it deceives another in order to win his esteem by means of religious deeds which are not performed from a simple* intention. The hypocrite seems to be acting for God, but actually is acting for himself. Highly recommended practices like almsgiving, prayer, fasting, are thereby perverted by the anxious care of "making a show" (Mt 6, 2.5.16; 23,5). This habit of putting a distance between the heart and the lips* teaches how to cover up bad intentions with a crafty air, as when under cover of a question of law one wished to lay a trap for Jesus (Mt 22,18; cf Jr 18,18). Wanting to save face* the hypocrite knows how to select certain laws or to arrange

them by a clever casuistry. In this way he can strain out a gnat and swallow a camel (Mt 23, 24), or turn the divine prescriptions to his own rapacious profit and intemperance (23,25): "Hypocrites! Isaiah prophesied well of you when he said: 'This people honors me with their lips, but their heart is far from me'" (15,7).

2. *The blind man who deceives himself.* Formalism can be cured, but hypocrisy is close to hardness* of heart. The whited sepulchers end up taking as true what they would like others to believe. They think they are just* (cf Lk 18,9) and they become deaf to every call to conversion. Like an actor in the theatre (gr. *hypocritēs*) the hypocrite continues to play his role, and all the more so if he holds a higher position and people obey his word (Mt 23,2f). Fraternal correction is helpful, but how could the hypocrite remove the beam which blocks his sight when all he thinks of is getting rid of the speck in his neighbor's eye (7,4f; 23,3f)? Spiritual guides are necessary here on earth, but are they not taking God's place when they go substituting human traditions for the divine Law? There are the blind men who pretend to guide others (15,3-14) and their doctrine is nothing more than a bad leaven (Lk 12,1). These blind men are incapable of recognizing the signs of the times*; that is, they cannot see in Jesus God's ambassador. They call for a "sign from heaven" (Lk 12,56; Mt 16,1ff). Blinded by their own malice, they do not want any part of the goodness of Jesus; rather they attempt to keep Him from doing good by appealing to the law of the Sabbath (Lk 13,15). With evil hearts incapable of speaking the truth (Mt 12,24.34), they dare to imagine that Beelzebub is at the origin of Jesus' miracles. In order to break down the gates of their hearts, Jesus makes them lose face before others (Mt 23,1ff) by denouncing their basic sin and secret rottenness (23,27f). This is better than letting them share in the lot of the wicked (24,51; Lk 12,46). No doubt that Jesus uses here the Aramaic term *ḥānēfa*, which ordinarily in the OT means "perverse, wicked." The hypocrite is on the way to becoming wicked. The fourth gospel changes the term *hypocrite* to *blind*. The sin of the Jews* is to say "We see," when actually they are blind (Jn 9,40).

3. *The permanent risk of hypocrisy.* It would be an illusion to think that hypocrisy is proper only to the Pharisees*. The synoptic tradition had already extended to the crowd the accusation of hypocrisy (Lk 12,56; 13,15). John aims

at the unbelievers of every age by attacking the Jews*. The Christian, especially the one in a position of leadership, also runs the risk of becoming a hypocrite. Even Peter does not escape this danger in the episode at Antioch which puts him at odds with Paul. His conduct was an "hypocrisy" (G 2,13). And Peter recommends

to the believer to live simply as a newly born infant, knowing that hypocrisy lies in wait (1 P 2,1f) to lead him to fall into apostasy (1 Tm 4,2).

→Lie—Pharisee 1—Pride 1—Simple 2—Unbelief II 1.

XLD jrs

I

IDOLS

I. TURNING AWAY FROM IDOLS

In one sense, the Bible is the story of God's people who are constantly turning themselves away from idols. One day, Yahweh "took" Abraham who "was serving other gods" (Js 24,2f; Jdt 5,6ff). But this breaking off, no matter how radical it was, was not accomplished once and for all. Abraham's descendants would always have to repeat it (Gn 35,2ff; Js 24,14-23). They would have to renew their choice again and again and follow* the one God in place of "pursuing vanity" (Jr 2,2-5).

Idolatry can actually creep into the inner workings even of Yahwism. Israel learned from the decalogue that it must not make images* (Ex 20,3ff; Dt 5,7ff), because only man* is the authentic image of God (Gn 1,26f). For example, the bull which man makes to symbolize the divine power* (Ex 32; 1 K 12,28; cf Jg 17—18) will draw upon itself God's wrath* and the scathing irony of the prophets (Ho 8,5; 13,2). Whether it is a question of false gods or of His own image, God punishes infidelity (Dt 13); He abandons those who abandon Him or make caricatures of Him, by sending national calamities on them (Jg 2,11-15; 2 K 17,7-12; Jr 32, 28-35; Ez 16; 20; 23).

When the exile comes as the tragic confirmation of this prophetic historical vision, the people reform; but the idolaters do not disappear (Ps 31,7), nor do those who deny God (Ps 10,4.11ff). Finally, in the time of the Maccabees, to serve idols (1 M 1,43) is to adhere to a pagan humanism which is incompatible with the faith* that Yahweh expects from His people. They have to choose between the idols and martyrdom* (2 M 6,18—7,42; cf Dn 3).

The NT describes the same situation. Torn away from idols and having turned to the true God (1 Th 1,9), the believers are constantly tempted to fall back into the paganism which infiltrates daily life (cf 1 Co 10,25-30). They have to flee idolatry to enter into the kingdom (1 Co 10,14; 2 Co 6,16; G 5,20; 1 Jn 5,21; Ap 21,8; 22,15). The Church, in which the ruthless struggle between Jesus and the world* continues, has a history marked by the temptation to adore "the image of the beast" (Ap 13,14; 16,2), to accept the setting up in the temple of the "devastating idol" (Mt 24,15; cf Dn 9,27).

II. THE MEANING OF IDOLATRY

Israel was not content with trying to respond faithfully to God's call, but it reflected on the nature of the "dumb idols" (1 Co 12,2) which tempted it. Gradually Israel will express in precise terms the nothingness of idols.

1. *The "other gods."* By this expression which was current up to the time of Jeremiah, Israel seems to admit the existence of gods other than Yahweh. This is not a question of the equivocal remains of other religions which mixed into popular Yahwism, such as the "domestic idols" (*terāphām*) undoubtedly reserved to women (Gn 31,19-35; 1 S 19,13-16), or the serpent Nehushtan (2 K 18,4). Rather it is a question of the Canaanite Baals which the Israelites meet when they are installed in the promised land. It is a death struggle against these Baals. Gideon had the everlasting honor of substituting Yahweh's altar* for the altar which his father dedicated to Baal (Jg 6,25-32). So if Israel speaks about "other gods" it still does not doubt that Yahweh is the only God (cf Ex 20,3-6; Dt 4,35).

This is how it qualifies other beliefs (cf 2 K 5,17).

2. *The nothingness of idols.* The death struggle against the idols continues but now in the spirit of one who is faithful to Yahweh, so that he will recognize that "the idols are nothing" (Ps 81,10; 1 Ch 16,26).

At the risk of his life Elijah makes fun of the gods that cannot consume the holocaust (1 K 18,18-40). The exiles understand clearly that the idols know nothing since they are incapable of telling the future (Is 48,5). Nor can they save (45,20f). "Before me was no God formed, and after me there shall be none" (43,10). If this is the case it is because they do not truly exist but are only the inventions of men. When the prophets hurl their attacks against the idols of wood, stone, or gold (A 5,26; Ho 8,4-8; Jr 10,3ff; Is 41,6f; 44,9-20), they are not denouncing just a figurative expression but a real perversion. Instead of adoring the Creator, the creature adores his own creation.

The Book of Wisdom brings to light the consequences of this idolatry (Ws 13—14). It is the fruit of death because it signifies the abandonment of Him who is life. At the same time it offers the believer an explanation of the origin of this perversion. It is the divinization of the dead or of famous people (14,12-21), or it is the adoration of natural forces which were destined to lead man to their author (13,1-10).

Paul follows up this criticism of idolatry by associating it with the cult of demons. To sacrifice to idols is to sacrifice to demons (1 Co 10,20f). Finally, in a terrible indictment, he denounces the universal sin* of men who instead of recognizing the Creator in His creation, have exchanged the glory of the incorruptible God for a representation of His creatures. From this follows their fall in all areas (R 1,18-32).

3. *Idolatry, a permanent temptation.* Idolatry is not an attitude which is overcome once and for all. It comes back in different forms. Whenever one ceases to serve the Lord, one becomes a slave* of created realities: money (Mt 6,24 p), wine (Tt 2,3), the desire to dominate one's neighbor (Col 3,5; E 5,5), political power (Ap 13,8), pleasure, envy, hate (R 6,19; Tt 3,3), sin (R 6,6), even the merely material observance of the Law (G 4,8f). All this leads to death (Ph 3,19), whereas the fruit of the Spirit is life (R 6,21f). Behind these vices which constitute idolatry is hidden an ignorance of the one God who alone deserves our confidence*.

→Adoration I 3, II 1—Adultery 2—Anathema OT—Animals I 1—Babel/Babylon 1—Beasts & Beast 3 b—Cupidity OT 2; NT 2—Deception/ Disappointment II—Egypt 1—Error OT—Evil Spirits OT 2; NT 2—God OT III 4; NT II 1— Heresy 1—Image I—Lie II 1—Magic 1—Meal II—Nations OT II 1 b—Shame I 4—Sin II 1, IV 3 a—Stars—Stone 1—Unbelief—Virtues & Vices 3—Wealth III—Zeal I 1.

CW jrs

IMAGE

No one on earth has seen nor is able to see* God the Father; He makes Himself known in His images (cf Jn 1,18). Before He made the full revelation of Himself in the perfect image of His Son, Jesus Christ, He began to make His revealing glory* shine forth before men under the old covenant. The Wisdom* of God which is "the pure emanation of His glory" and "the image of His excellence" (Ws 7,25f) already reveals certain aspects of God. Also, man who was created with the power of ruling over nature and who was gifted with immortality, already constitutes a living image of God. Nevertheless, the prohibition of images in Israelitic worship* was a hollow expression of the seriousness of this title given to man and was a negative preparation for the coming of the God-Man, the only image in which the Father revealed Himself fully.

I. THE PROHIBITION OF IMAGES

The precept of the Decalogue (Dt 27,15; Ex 20,4; Dt 4,9-28), applied with more or less rigor down through the ages, constitutes a fact which is easy to justify when it is a question of false gods (idols*); but it is more difficult to explain in the case of images of Yahweh. The sacred authors were used to anthropomorphisms and so were not reacting principally against a sensible representation, but rather they wanted to combat idolatrous magic and preserve the transcendence of God*. God does not manifest His glory by means of golden calves (Ex 32; 1 K 12,26-33) and images made by the hand of man, but through the works of His creation* (Ho 8,5f; Ws 13; R 1,19-23). God is not appeased by the intercession of images which men use as they please, but rather God exercises His saving action freely in the hearts of men through wisdom and through His Son.

II. MAN, THE IMAGE OF GOD

OT

The strength of this expression does not come so much from the word itself, which was already used in connection with the creation of man in some Babylonian and Egyptian poems, but rather from the general context of the OT. Man* is in the image not only of a god who is himself conceived of after the likeness of man, but also of a God so transcendent that it is forbidden to make an image of Him. Only man can lay claim to this title which expresses his highest dignity (Gn 9,6).

According to Gn 1,26-29 to be in the image of God, in His likeness, implies the power to rule over all earthly creatures, and also, seemingly, if not to create, at least to procreate living images (Gn 1,27f; 5,1ff; cf Lk 3,38). Ordinarily, the texts of the OT (Ps 8; Si 17) develop the first theme, that of domination. At the same time the notion of the image of God, whether used explicitly in these texts or not, is enriched by clarification and addition. In Ps 8, it seems to be identified with a state of "glory and splendor," "slightly inferior to that of a divine being." In 2,23 man is no longer only *in* the image of God, an imprecise expression which leaves the meaning open to certain rabbinic interpretations, but he properly *is* the image of God. Finally, in this same passage, an important element of resemblance between God and man has become explicit—that of immortality. Alexandrian Judaism (cf Philo) distinguished two creations according to the image of God; the earthly man is drawn from dust. This speculation about the two Adams was taken up and changed by St. Paul (1 Co 15).

NT

The NT not only frequently applies the expression *the image of God* to man (1 Co 11,7; Jm 3,9), but also makes frequent use of this theme and develops it. Thus, for example, the command of Christ: "Be ye perfect as your heavenly Father is perfect" (Mt 5,48) appears to be a necessary consequence of the doctrine about man, the image of God. The same holds true for a saying attributed to Christ and reported by Clement of Alexandria: "to see your brother is to see God." This conviction imposes respect for others (Jm 3,9; cf Gn 9,6) and is the foundation of our love for them: "Whoever does not love his brother* whom he sees will not be able to love God whom he does not see" (1 Jn 4,20). But man, an imperfect and sinful image, needs something more which has been sketched by the OT Wisdom and realized by Christ.

III. WISDOM,
THE IMAGE OF GOD'S EXCELLENCE

Man is only an imperfect image, but on the contrary Wisdom is "a stainless mirror of the activity of God, an image of God's excellence" (Ws 7,26). Since Wisdom exists "from the beginning, before the origin of the earth" (Pr 8, 23), we can conclude that Wisdom presided at the creation of man. We can, then, understand certain speculations of Alexandrian Judaism which have their echo in Philo. For Philo, the Logos is the image of God; he is the instrument which God used in creating, the archetype, the exemplar, the principle, the eldest son according to whom God created man.

IV. CHRIST, THE IMAGE OF GOD

This expression is found only in the epistles of Paul, though the idea is present in the gospel according to St. John. Between Christ and the one who sends Him, between the only Son* who reveals His Father and the invisible God* (Jn 1,18), the union is such (Jn 5,19; 7,16; 8,28f; 12,49) that it supposes something more than a simple delegation. The mission* of Christ surpasses that of the prophets* to become joined with that of the Word* and of divine Wisdom*. It supposes that Christ is a reflection of God's glory (Jn 17,5.24). It supposes between Christ and His Father* a resemblance which is clearly expressed in this affirmation which contains, if not the word, at least the theme of image: "Whoever has seen me, has seen the Father" (Jn 14,9).

St. Paul uses the Genesis doctrine about man (1 Co 11,7), but he also knows how to make use on occasion of some interpretations of the Rabbis and of Philo about the two Adams*. He applies these here to Christ Himself (1 Co 15,49) and later to the new man (Col 3,10). In the end, however, it is in the light of Wisdom, the perfect image, that he sees in Christ the title of the image of God (2 Co 3,18—4,4). Without abandoning these different sources of inspiration, Paul is at pains to discern still more accurately the mystery* of Christ. In R 8,29, Christ is the image because of His sonship. According to Col 3,10 He presides, insofar as an image, at the creation* of the new man*. As a result of the convergence of old elements and new, the notion of the image of God as applied by Paul to Christ, especially in Col 1,15, becomes very rich and complex. There is a resemblance, but a spiritual and perfect resemblance, because of His sonship* which is prior to creation. In the strongest sense of the word He is the representation of the invisible Father. He is the cosmic sovereignty of the Lord* who sets His imprint on the visible and invisible world. He is the image of God according to immortality, the first-born from among the dead, the one and only image who assures the unity of all beings and the unity of the divine plan. He is the principle of creation and the principle of its restoration by a new creation.

V.   THE CHRISTIAN TRANSFORMED ACCORDING TO THE IMAGE OF CHRIST

All these elements constitute so many forces of attraction on man who, as an imperfect and sinful image, needs this perfect image of Christ to find again and accomplish his original destiny. After putting on the likeness of the earthly Adam, what he must now do is to put on the image of the heavenly Adam (cf 1 C 15,49). Between these two "images," united in one and the same divine plan (cf R 8,29; E 1,3-14), there is, then, a hidden link, a break caused by sin and a dynamic relation. This dynamism can be seen also and above all in the Christian: from now on he has become one being with Christ (R 6,3-6; Col 3,10) and so is a child of God (1 Jn 3,2) and, under the action of the Lord, he is transformed from glory to glory in this image of the Son, the first-born of a multitude of brothers (2 Co 3,18; R 8,29). The goal of this process of glorification is the resurrection, which allows the Christian to put on once and for all the image of the heavenly Adam (1 C 15,49) and to "transfigure these wretched bodies of ours into copies of His glorious Body" (Ph 3,21).

→Adam I 1.3—Example—Face 5—Figure—

God OT III 5—Idols—Jesus Christ II 1 d—Man—See—Worship OT I.

PL jrs

IMPOSITION OF HANDS

The hand, along with the word*, is one of the most expressive means of language that man has. By itself it ordinarily symbolizes the power* (Ex 14,31; Ps 19,2) and even the Spirit* of God (1 K 18,46; Is 8,11; Ez 1,3; 3,22). To impose hands on someone is more than just lifting the hands into the air, even if it were to bless someone (Lv 9,22; Lk 24,50). It is actually to touch the other and to communicate something of yourself to him.

OT

As a sign of blessing, the imposition of hands expresses realistically the character of the blessing* which is not just a word but an act. Thus Jacob transmitted to his entire posterity the richness of blessing which he himself had received from his ancestors, Abraham and Isaac: "Let them increase and multiply upon the earth!" (Gn 48,13-16).

As a sign of consecration, the imposition of hands indicates that the Spirit of God has set aside a being whom He has chosen, that He has taken possession of him, that He has given him authority and aptitude for exercising some function. Thus were the Levites set apart as a holy offering (Nm 8,10); thus did the Spirit of Wisdom fill Joshua (Dt 34,9), preparing him to take over as head of the people with full power (Nm 27,15-23).

As a symbol of identification, the imposition of hands establishes a union between the one who offers a victim in sacrifice and the victim itself. The victim is consecrated to God and is ordered to take on the sentiments of the one who makes the offering—thanksgiving, sorrow for sin, or adoration. This was the case in the sacrifices of expiation (Lv 1,4), of communion (3,2), of remission of sin (4,4), or again, in the consecration of the Levites (Nm 8,16). In the scapegoat rite on the Day of Atonement there is no consecration. By the imposition of hands, Israel communicates its sins to the animal which then as impure cannot be offered to Yahweh in sacrifice and so is exiled into the desert (Lv 16,21f).

NT

INHERITANCE

1. *In the life of Jesus.* As a sign of benediction Jesus placed His hands upon the little children* (Mk 10,16), and conferred on them the beatitude* which He had announced to the poor* (Mt 5,3), thereby obtaining from His Father the reward of His own "prayer" (Mt 19,13). The imposition of hands was also a *sign of deliverance.* By it Jesus cured the sick*: "Woman, you are delivered from your infirmity," He said to the stooping woman, and He laid His hands upon her and immediately she stood upright (Lk 13,13). It was the same for the healing of the blind man at Bethsaida (Mk 8,23ff) and for each of the many sick who came to Him at sundown (Lk 4,40).

2. *In the life of the Church.* According to the promise of the risen one the disciples "will impose hands on the sick, and they will be healed" (Mk 16,18). It was by such a gesture that Ananias returned the sight to the converted Saul (Ac 9,12) and that Paul, in turn, restored health to the governor of Malta (28,8). As well as being a sign of liberation, the imposition of hands was used in the infant Church as a sign of consecration. By it are transmitted the divine gifts, especially that of the Holy Spirit*. Peter and John conferred this gift on the Samaritans, who had not yet received it (Ac 8,17). Paul did likewise for the people at Ephesus (19,6). Simon the magician was so struck with admiration for the power of this gesture that he wanted to buy it with money (8,18f). From that time on, this gesture appeared as a visible sign which carried a powerful, divine reality.

By this same gesture, the Church transmits a spiritual power adapted to a precise mission*, set up for some determined functions. This was the case for the institution of the seven (6,6) consecrated by the apostles, and for the mission of Paul and Barnabas (13,3). Paul, in turn, imposed hands on Timothy (2 Tm 1,6f; cf I Tm 4,14), and Timothy repeated this gesture on those whom he had chosen for the ministry* (1 Tm 5,22). Thus the Church continues to impose hands with the meaning specified each time by a formula. This gesture continues to carry with it the gifts of the Spirit.

→Arm & Hand 2—Charisms II 4—Faith NT II 3—Joshua 1—Ministry II.

JBB jrs

INHERITANCE

The biblical notion of inheritance goes beyond the juridical meaning of the English word. It means the possession of some goods by a stable and permanent title. It is not just any goods but those which allow a man and his family to expand their personalities without being at the mercy of another. Concretely, in an agricultural and pastoral civilization, this means a minimum of some land and flocks. As for the manner of entering on the possession of this inheritance, that will vary in different cases: by conquest, by gift, by division regulated according to law, and by inheritance in the strict sense of the term (cf 1 K 21,3f). Such are the data of human experience which give the basis for the religious usage of the OT and the NT to express a fundamental aspect of God's gift to man.

OT

I. ORIGIN OF THE THEME

From the beginning the notion of inheritance was closely linked to that of covenant*. In the divine plan it characterizes a triple relationship: Israel is the inheritance of Yahweh, the promised land is the inheritance of Israel, and it thereby becomes the inheritance of Yahweh Himself.

1. *Israel, the inheritance of Yahweh.* Of these three relationships, the first is the most fundamental: Israel is the inheritance of Yahweh (cf Ex 34,9; 1 S 10,1; 26,19; 2 S 20,19; 21,3). This expression suggests an intimate relation between God and His people which is "His very own" (Ex 19,5). The formula of the covenant, "You will be my people and I will be your God" (Jr 24,7; Ez 37,27), means practically the same thing. But the notion of inheritance adds the idea of a special belonging which takes Israel out of the sphere of the profane (the sphere of other peoples) and into the world of God.

2. *The promised land, the inheritance of Israel.* This second relation is equally linked to the theme of covenant as is clear from the recital of the patriarchal covenant given in Gn 15. There the promise* of God to Abraham has a double object: an heir who is Isaac and his line of descendants, and an inheritance, the land of

Canaan. Naturally the heirs of Abraham will also inherit that promise (Gn 26,3; 35,12; Ex 6,8). Note the fact that Canaan has not yet been given to Abraham as an inheritance, but is only promised to his heirs. It is this promise and Israel's expectancy which results from it which will allow a gradual deepening of the inheritance theme. The disappointments which follow upon the excessively material hopes which were never realized will allow an elevation of the level of Israel's expectancy until the point at which it desires its true inheritance, the only one which can satisfy man's heart.

3. *The promised land, the inheritance of Yahweh.* From the first two relationships flows a third: the promised land* is the inheritance of Yahweh. The formula does not express a natural connection between Yahweh and Canaan. In this respect Israel is different from the surrounding peoples who see their different countries as the domains proper to different gods. Actually, the whole earth belongs to Yahweh (Ex 19,5; Dt 10,14). If Canaan has become His inheritance by a special title, it is because He has given this land to Israel, and has, consequently, chosen to establish his residence there (cf Ex 15,17). This gives us the profound meaning of the division of the holy land in which each tribe of Israel receives its lot, its share of the inheritance (Js 13—21). The share is received from God, and the limits of each share are intangible (cf Nm 36). In case of forced sale, the jubilee year will allow the return of each land to its original owner (Lv 25,10): "The land must not be sold in perpetuity; for the land is mine, since you are only resident aliens and sojourners with me" (Lv 25,23). Israel is on its own land the farmer of God; Israel ought to live on it not for itself but for God.

II. DEVELOPMENT OF THE THEME

The development of the theme in the OT involves two aspects: its relation to the eschatological context and its spiritualization.

1. *Eschatological inheritance.* The conquest of Canaan might seem like a realization of the promise of Gn 15. Now, starting with the eighth century, the inheritance of Yahweh passes bit by bit to the power of the pagans. God did not go back on His promises, but the sins of Israel have temporarily compromised the results of those promises. It will only be in the final times

that the people of God, reduced to a remnant*, will possess the land as its inheritance forever, and will enjoy in it perfect happiness (Dt 28, 62f; 30,5). This teaching in Deuteronomy appears again in the prophets at the time of the exile (Ez 45—48; note the allusion to Gn 15 in Ez 47,14), and after the exile (Ze 8,12; Is 60,21): only the just will be the final beneficiaries of the inheritance (cf Ps 37,9.11.18.22.34; 25,13; 61,6; 69,37).

In this transformation of the hope* of Israel, there is room to mention the special place granted to the king*, the anointed of Yahweh. It is possible that at an early date the psalmist promised the living monarch "the nations* as his inheritance, and the extremities of the earth for his domain" (Ps 2,8). But once reread after the exile, the promise has been understood of the future king, of the Messiah* (cf Ps 2,2).

The inheritance of the land, the inheritance of the nations: this type of eschatology does not always result from earthly perspectives. This final stage will come about slowly when the doctrine of reward* after death has taken shape. And so the entrance into the possession of the inheritance promised by God to the just (Dn 12,13; Ws 3,14; 5,5) will be after death in the "world to come." This is, however, a question of a transfigured inheritance.

2. *Spiritualized inheritance.* The beginning of the spiritualization of the inheritance is the condition of the Levites who, following a formula of Dt 10,9, "do not have an inheritance with their brothers, because Yahweh is their inheritance." Originally this formula was understood in a rather material way: the inheritance of the Levites was made up of the offerings of the faithful (Dt 18,1f). But it gradually acquires a deeper meaning and comes to be applied to the people as a whole: Yahweh is its inheritance (Jr 10,16; cf the name *Hilqiyah*, "Yahweh is my share"). This conviction takes its entire meaning from the time when the material inheritance, the land of Canaan, was taken from the people of God (cf Lm 3,24).

That was the beginning of the complete spiritualization of the notion of inheritance. When the psalmists say "Yahweh is my share" (Ps 16,5; 73,26), they thereby point out the perfect good the possession of whom satisfies their heart. It is clear that this entirely interior inheritance is reserved for the faithful remnant*. It is no longer an extrinsic reward granted for faithfulness*, but it is the very joy* which results from this fidelity (cf Ps 119). In this new perspective the old formula "to possess the land" becomes more and more a conventional expression of perfect happiness (cf Ps 25,13) which forms the prelude of the second gospel beatitude* (Mt 5,4; cf Ps 37,11 LXX). It is also clear that the possession of God by the believer anticipates in some way the inheritance that he will receive in "the world to come."

NT

I. HEIR OF THE PROMISES

1. *Christ, the only heir.* In the OT the heir of the promise was reserved first of all only to the people of God, then to the remnant of the faithful. In the NT it is clear first of all that this remnant is Christ. In Christ the descendants of Abraham are concentrated (G 3,16). As Son* He possesses by birth the right of inheritance (Mt 21,38 p), He was constituted by God the "heir of all things" (He 1,2), because He inherited a name* higher than that of the angels (1,4), the name of Yahweh Himself (Ph 2,9).

Nevertheless, in order to enter into the actual possession of this inheritance, Jesus had to go through His passion and death (He 2,1-10; cf Ph 2,7-11). He thereby showed what obstacle prevented the accomplishment of the ancient promises: the state of slavery* in which men found themselves (G 4,3.8; 5,1; Jn 8,34), the regime of tutelage to which God subjected them (G 3,23; 4,1ff). By His cross* Jesus ended this temporary situation so we could pass from the condition of slaves to that of sons, and therefore heirs (G 4,5ff). Thanks to His death we can now receive the eternal inheritance promised to us (He 9,15).

2. *The believers, heirs in Christ.* This is, in fact, the present condition of Christians. They are the adopted sons of God because the Spirit of God animates them, and therefore they are heirs of Gods and co-heirs of Christ (R 8,14-17). They inherit the promise made to the patriarchs (He 6,12.17), just as Isaac and Jacob had (11,9), because they are the true descendants of Abraham (G 3,29). Submission to the Mosaic Law is now worthless for inheritance, as is membership in Israel* according to the flesh*. The only thing that counts is adherence to Christ by faith (R 4,13f). The result is that in the mystery* of Christ, "the pagans are admitted to the same inheritance, beneficiaries of the same

promise" (E 3,6; cf G 3,28f). A new people* is formed around Christ, the sole heir. By grace* (R 4,16) the right of inheritance is given to this people.

II. THE PROMISED INHERITANCE

The inheritance which "God gives to men with those who are sanctified" (Ac 20,32), "the inheritance among the saints" in light (E 1,18), shows at the same time its true nature. The land of Canann was not the adequate object of the promises. It was only a figure* of the heavenly city (He 11,8ff). The inheritance "prepared" by the Father for His chosen ones "from the beginning of the world" (Mt 25,34) is grace* (1 P 3,7); it is salvation* (He 1,14); it is the kingdom of God (Mt 25,34; 1 Co 6,9; 15,50; Jm 2,5); it is eternal life* (Mt 19,29; Tt 3,7).

These expressions stress the transcendental character of the inheritance. It is not within the grasp of "flesh* and blood," but demands a being who is transformed according to the image* of Christ (1 Co 15,49f). As the kingdom*, it is a participation in His universal royalty (cf Mt 5,4; 25,34; R 4,13 which is close to Gn 15 and Ps 2,8). As eternal life*, it is a participation in the life of the risen Christ (cf 1 Co 15,45-50) and by that in the life of God Himself. We will gain it perfectly after death when we join Christ in glory. Right now we have only the hope* of that glory (Tt 3,7). Nevertheless, the Holy Spirit* who has been given to us is our pledge of that glory (E 1,14) as we wait for the parousia when Christ will give us the full possession of it.

→Abraham II 4—Body II 1—Earth OT II 1.2.4; NT I 2—Faithfulness III 1 a—Fatherland OT 1; NT 2—Gift NT 1—Hope—Kingdom NT II 2.3, III 3—People *A* II 4—Promises II 1, IV—Reward III 2—Salvation NT II 3—Son of God NT II 2—Vine 2.

FD & PG jrs

ISRAEL

OT

Israel (probably meaning "God struggles," "God is strong") designates in the OT either a people or its eponymous ancestor, identified with the patriarch Jacob (Gn 35,10.20f; 43,8;

50,2 etc.). The story that explains the double name of the patriarch is based on the popular etymology for Israel: "he wrestled with God" (Gn 32,29; Ho 12,4).

1. *Israel, a covenant people.*

a) Israel, a sacred name. Israel is not only the name of a tribe like Edom, Aram, and Moab. It is a sacred name*, the name of the covenant people*. The covenant people forms the "community of Israel" (Ex 12,3.6), and under this title it hears the speeches recorded in Deuteronomy ("Hear, O Israel!..." Dt 5,1; 6,4; 9,1; cf Ps 50,7; 81,9) as the prophetic promises (Is 41,8; 43,1; 44,1; 48,1).

b) Israel, a people of twelve tribes. For its fundamental national structure, Israel has the twelve tribes which bear the name of the twelve sons of Jacob right from the formation of the covenant (Ex 24,4). If the list of tribes has known minor variations (cf Gn 49, Dt 33, Jg 5, Ap 7,5...), still their number* is sacred and is related to the cultic service of the twelve months of the year. This is the first historical form that the people of God took in this world.

c) Yahweh is the God of Israel and Israel is the people of Yahweh. Through the covenant, God is in some way joined to Israel. He is their God (Is 17,6; Jr 7,3; Ez 8,4), their holy* one (Is 1,4; 44,14; Ps 89,19), their strong one (Is 1,25), their rock* (Is 30,29), their king (Is 43,15), and their redeemer (Is 44,6). The God* of revelation thereby enters into the history of religions as the God proper to Israel. In return it is Israel alone that He chooses to make the trustee of His plan* of salvation. Once again, the titles given to Israel are significant. Israel is the people* of Yahweh (Is 1,3; Am 7,8; Jr 12,14; Ez 14,9; Ps 50,7), His Servant* (Is 44,21), His chosen one (Is 45,4), His first-born Son* (Ex 4,22; Ho 11,1), His holy one (Jr 2,3), His inheritance* (Is 19,25), His flock (Ps 95,7), His vineyard (Is 5,7), His domain (Ps 114,2), His spouse* (Ho 2,4). Therefore Israel does not belong only to the political history of humanity. By divine choice it is at the very center of religious history.

2. *Israel and Judah.*

a) Political duality of Israel. The sacred league of the twelve tribes concealed a political duality which is clearly seen during the royal epoch. David became successively the king of Judah, in the South, and then of Israel in the North (2 S 2,4; 5,3). When Solomon died, Israel broke off from the house of David (1 K 12,19) with the cry: "To your tents, Israel!" (2 K 12,16; cf 2 S 20,1). In this way the people of God are broken up. The language of the prophets adapted itself to a condition that was contrary to the doctrine of the covenant, and which in the future distinguished Judah from Israel, which was frequently identified with Ephraim, the dominant northern tribe (Am 2,4; Ho 4,15f; Is 9,7ff...; Mi 1,5; Jr 3,6ff).

b) Israel and Judaism. After the fall of Samaria, Judah became the center for the regrouping of all Israel (2 K 23,19...; 2 Ch 30, 1ff). After the fall of Jerusalem, the ideal image of the national restoration is sought for in the former league of the twelve tribes. The preponderant role of Judah in this restoration explains why the name of Jew* is given from then on to the members of the dispersed people, and why the name of Judaism will be given to the institution which groups them together again (G 1,13f). But the name of Israel recovers at the same time its sacred value (Ne 9,1f; Si 36,11; cf Mt 2,20f; Ac 13,17; Jn 3,10).

3. *The promise of a new Israel.* The eschatological oracles of the prophets have truly announced for the future of Israel a return to its original unity: a reunion of Israel and Judah (Ez 37,15...), a reassembly of the dispersed Israelites who belong to the twelve tribes (Jr 3,18; 31,1; Ez 36,24...; 37,21...; Is 27,12). This is a fundamental theme of Jewish hope (Si 36,10). But the profit to be derived from these promises* will be reserved for a remnant* of Israel (Is 10,20; 46,3; Mi 2,12; Jr 31,7). Yahweh will make a new* Israel of this remnant. He will deliver it (Jr 30,10) and re-establish it in its country (31,2); He will make a new covenant* with it (31,31) and a new king* (33,17). Then, Israel will become the center of the union of nations* (Is 19,24f). These nations, seeing in Israel the presence of the true God (45,15) will turn toward Him; their conversion will coincide with the salvation (45,17) and glory of Israel (45,25).

NT

1. *The gospel and ancient Israel.* The order

of providence has willed that the outcome of salvation be realized in Israel, and that Israel, as the covenant people, receive the first announcement of it. That is already the purpose of John's baptism (Jn 1,31). During His lifetime, the Savior's mission, as well as that of His disciples, confined itself to Israel only (Mt 10,6.23; 15,24). After His resurrection, the good news was first brought to Israel (Ac 2,36; 4,10). Israel and the nations, which participated together in the drama of the passion (4,27), have both received the call to faith (9,15), on an equal footing but in a different order: first the Jews who are "Israelites" by birth (R 9,4), then the others (cf R 1,16; 2,9f; Ac 13,46). The salvation brought by the gospel fulfills the hope of those who are waiting for the consolation* of Israel (Lk 2,25), the salvation* of Israel (Lk 24,21), the restoration of the kingdom for Israel (Ac 1,6). Through Jesus, God has come to bring help to Israel (Lk 1,54), to show it mercy* (Lk 1,68), to grant it a conversion and the remission of sins (Ac 5,31). Jesus is the glory* of Israel (Lk 2,32), its king* (Mt 27,42 p; Jn 1,50; 12,13), its Savior (Ac 13,23f). The new hope based on His resurrection* is none other than the hope of Israel itself (Ac 28,20). In short, Israel constitutes the organic link which joins the realization of salvation to all human history.

2. *The new Israel.* In the meantime since the time of Jesus, the new Israel announced by the prophetic promise has appeared here below. To make it a positive institution, Jesus chose twelve apostles, thereby modeling His Church* after the old Israel which was formed of twelve tribes. Further His apostles will judge the twelve tribes of Israel (Mt 19,28 p). This Church is the eschatological Israel for which God reserved the new covenant* (He 8,8ff). In it is accomplished the reassembling of the chosen ones in the twelve tribes (Ap 7,4). It is a holy city which rests on the foundation of the twelve apostles, and it has the names of the twelve tribes inscribed on its gates (Ap 21,12; cf Ez 40,30ff).

3. *The ancient Israel and the new Israel.* The Church, the new Israel, is therefore the fulfillment of the old Israel. In the old Israel, membership was by birth (Ph 3,5), and pagans were excluded from its citizenship (E 2,12). But it is no longer enough to belong to the "Israel according to the flesh" (1 Co 10,18) in order to become part of the "Israel of God," for "all the descendants of Israel are not Israel" (R 9,6). Confronted with Jesus and the gospel, a sorting takes place (cf Lk 2,34f): the fall of those who look for the justice* of the Law and who harden their hearts when they hear the announcement of justification by faith (R 9,31; 11,7), and the rescue of those others, the "true Israelites" (Jn 1,48), who constitute the remnant* of Israel announced by the Scriptures (R 9,27ff) and who are joined to the new Israel by the converted pagans. The old Israel has not been definitively rejected, but at the time her incomprehension of the gospel was manifested God wishes to awaken her jealousy (R 10,19). When the pagans are converted in their totality, the partial hardening of Israel's heart will cease, "and thus all Israel will be saved" (R 11,26). It will belong once again to that spiritual Israel which has entered into the way of salvation.

→Calling II—Church II 2, III 2 b—Circumcision—Covenant OT—Egypt—Election—Faith OT—Hebrew—House II 1.2—Inheritance OT I 1—Jew—Kingdom OT I, II—Law *B*—Mission OT I 2, II—Nations—People—Plan of God NT III 2—Power I 1—Promise II—Schism OT 2—Servant of God II 1.2—Shadow II 3—Sin II—Son of God OT I—Stranger—Unbelief III —Vine 2.

PG jrs

J

JERUSALEM

Jerusalem is a "holy city," venerated by Jews, Christians, and Moslems for motives which in part coincide. But in the eyes of Christians, its role in the divine plan belongs to the past. Now there remains for it only the profound meaning uncovered in the NT.

OT

I. VOCATION

1. The Canaanite city of Urushalim ("Foundation of the god Shalem") is known from Akkadian documents of the 14th century (Tell-el-Amarna letters). Biblical tradition recognizes in it the city of Melchizedek, a contemporary of Abraham (Gn 14,18ff), and identifies its site with Mount Moriah where Abraham offered his sacrifice (2 Ch 3,1). In the time of the judges Jerusalem was still a pagan city (Jg 19,11f), since the Israelites had failed in their first attempt at conquest (Jg 1,21). David* finally took it from the Jebusites (2 S 5,6ff). He called his citadel "City of David" (5,9), fortified it, and made it the political capital of his kingdom. In bringing the ark of the covenant there (6), he established the sanctuary of the confederacy of the twelve tribes, which had previously been at Shiloh. Nathan's promise confirmed that God would approve this place of residence (7), and Solomon brought his father's work to completion in this location by building the temple and solemnly dedicating it (1 K 6—8). In this way the town's religious destiny became settled.

2. In the holy land* Jerusalem occupies a special place. A personal possession of David's dynasty, it remains outside the sphere of the tribes. As a political capital, it represents concretely the national unity of the people* of God. As a religious capital, it is the spiritual center of Israel, because Yahweh resides there on Mount Zion, which He has chosen as His abode (Ps 78,68f; 132,13-18). And it is to this place that the faithful go up in frequent pilgrimages*. Hence the double significance which grounds its character as a holy city and gives it a principal role in the faith and hope of Israel.

II. DRAMA

Because of this significance, Jerusalem is drawn into the drama which jolted all the institutions of God's people during the royal epoch: it experiences alternately God's favor and wrath.

1. Immediately after the peak of Solomon's reign, Jerusalem underwent the repercussion of the schism which followed on his death. The Book of Kings sees in this the providential chastisement of the monarch's infidelities (1 K 11). Attached to Judah, the city remained the capital of a reduced kingdom and kept its temple. But Jeroboam installed official sanctuaries in Israel which competed with it (12,26-33), and soon the founding of Samaria (16,24) set up a rival capital. The unity of the political role and the religious role realized by David is thus disrupted.

For all that, the significance of Jerusalem endures, especially in the eyes of faithful Judahites. After the fall of Samaria, hopes turn to Jerusalem, and Hezekiah tries to rally the northern tribes to it. A first religious reform is effected (2 K 18,1-4; cf 2 Ch 29—31), and under his rule the town experienced an extraordinary deliverance at the time of Sennacherib's invasion (2 K 18,13—19,36). The memory of it will stay imprinted in their minds, to the glory of the holy city (Ps 48,5-9). A century later, Josiah tried anew to regroup all the Israelites around a sanctuary where worship would from then on be strictly centralized (2 K 22,1—23,25). This was the final attempt to save the national work of David.

2. As it turns out: "God did not relent from the heat of wrath..." He says: "I will reject this city which I have chosen, Jerusalem, and the temple of which I said: 'There will my

name be'" (2 K 23,26f). In spite of temporary reforms, Jerusalem is still a city unfaithful to its God, and that decides its destiny. It is unfaithful in its kings*, who give themselves up to idolatry (2 K 16,2ff; 21,3-9); it persecutes the prophets (2 Ch 24,21; cf Jr 36—38). It is unfaithful in its priesthood* which despises the prophetic teaching (Jr 20) and lets idolatry establish itself in the temple (2 K 21,4f.7; Ez 8). It is unfaithful in its people*, attracted by pagan alliances, indifferent to the Law of God (Is 1, 16f; Jr 7,8ff). "How has she become a prostitute, the faithful city?" (Is 1,21). Without a sincere conversion, the wrath of God will turn on her: Isaiah sees salvation only for a holy remnant* (Is 4,2f); Jeremiah promises for its temple the lot that befell Shiloh (Jr 7,14); Ezekiel, summarizing the city's infidelities, announces its imminent chastisement (Ez 11,1-12; 23; 24,1-14), because Yahweh has resolved to abandon it (10,18ff).

3. These threatening oracles clarify the meaning of its final destruction under the blows of Nebuchadnezzar. It is God's "judgment which is being accomplished" (cf Ez 9,1—10,7). Once given this outcome, the "daughter of Zion" has only to admit her long-standing guilt (Lm 1—2); her children beg God to make the pagans suffer the same evil which they have perpetrated on Jerusalem, His heritage (Ps 79). At the end of this drama the problem which arises from then on concerns the future.

III. TOWARD THE NEW JERUSALEM

1. In parallel fashion in the unfolding of the drama and to the extent that they were announcing its end, the prophets were turning their eyes toward another Jerusalem. Isaiah saw it, after its trial, as becoming once more a "city of justice and a faithful city" (Is 1,26f). Jeremiah perceived the day when the restored people of Israel would come back to adore God in Zion (Jr 31,6.12). Ezekiel minutely described the future city reconstructed around its temple (Ez 40—46), the center of a paradisal country (47,1—48,29), wide open to the twelve tribes (48,30-35), and having for its name "Yahweh is there" (48,35). During the time of the exile, these views of the future developed into grandiose promises: Jerusalem, once the cup of the divine wrath* is emptied, is going to find again its festal garments (Is 51,17—52,2). Magnificently rebuilt (54,11f) and again the spouse*

of Yahweh (54,4-10), she will see her children multiply marvelously (54,1ff; 49,14-26).

2. The subsequent restoration by the edict of Cyrus (Ezr 1—3), then the rebuilding of the temple (5—6) seem to put the fulfillment of these oracles within reach. The contemporary prophets announce the glory of the city and its temple, called to become the religious center of the universe (Hg 2,6-9; Is 60,62). In fact the picture soon manifests some prosaic realities and becomes mixed with the image of paradise* regained (Is 65,18): Zion is going to give birth to the new people* with joy unsurpassed (66, 6-14). For all that, the concrete situation remains less bright, and the city continues to experience its share of trials: the walls remain in ruins for a long time (cf Ps 51,20; 102,14-18), and the energy of Nehemiah is needed to rebuild them (Ne 1—12). Under the drive of its restorers it becomes the "fortress of the Torah," as isolated as possible from foreign influences (cf Ne 13). But from then on this capital of a tiny province is stripped of every politically important role.

3. It is on the religious level that Jerusalem now fulfills its essential mission. From every side Jews turn to it (Dn 6,11). People go up to it on pilgrimages (Ps 122) and rejoice at being able to remain there (Ps 84). This is the period of the formation of beautiful liturgies in the temple (Si 50,1-21). The psalms celebrate Yahweh's residing there (Ps 46; 48); Jerusalem is called to become the mother* of all the nations* (Ps 87). Playing on its name (Yerušalaïm), they wish it Peace (šalôm: Ps 122,6-9) and invite one another to praise God (Ps 147,12ff). The last prophetic texts make it the theater of the eschatological judgment* (Jl 4,9-17) and of the feast of joy offered to all humanity (Is 25,6ff); they see it as the final deliverance and transfiguration (Ze 12; 14). Describing beforehand in lyric terms the happiness which God is reserving for it (cf Tb 13), they invite one another to confidence (Ba 4,30—5,9). It will still encounter trial under King Antiochus, who will profane it (1 M 1,36-40). But, in contrast with this historic reality, frequently not too bright, Jewish apocalypses will present a more and more fantastic image of the future city. For them, there will exist henceforth a heavenly Jerusalem of which the Davidic town is only the imperfect copy. In the last times this Jerusalem will be revealed by God and will descend to earth. How better express the transcendence of

the future order than by comparison with an historical experience which already enclosed its meaningful figure*?

NT

I. THE EARTHLY JERUSALEM AND THE ACCOMPLISHMENT OF SALVATION

From Mark to John, Jerusalem occupies a growing place in the gospels. But it is in Luke that its role is more heavily underlined, as the hinge between the gospel and the Acts.

1. According to *Mark*'s gospel, the echo of John the Baptist's preaching reaches all the way to Jerusalem (Mk 1,5). But it is in Galilee that the gospel of the kingdom announced by Jesus begins and is at first confined there (1, 28.39). Jesus turns toward Jerusalem only after meeting with the disbelief of the Galilean towns (6,1-6; 8,11ff; 9,30) and having announced His passion three times. He goes up there only to compete His sacrifice (10,32ff). From that point on the drama unfolds: Jesus triumphantly enters the city in conformity with the Scripture (11,1-11), and in cleansing the temple He acts as a prophet (11,15-19). Success without a morrow, since He encounters the opposition of Jewish authorities (11,27—12,40). This is why, in the context of His approaching death (12,6-9), He foretells the punishment of the city and the profanation of its temple (13,14-20), the end of an outdated religious economy and a prelude to the final consummation (13,24-27). Actually rejected by the people (15,6-15), condemned by their leaders (14,53-64), Jesus is crucified outside the city (15,20ff). While He is dying the veil of the temple is torn, to signify that the ancient sanctuary has lost its sacred character (15,33-38). Jerusalem is here the place of the great denial.

2. To this schema *Matthew* adds a number of traits. The future drama is applied to Jesus' infancy. Although pagans guided by a star (cf Nm 24,17) come to Bethlehem to adore the Messiah (Mt 2,1f.9ff), the scribes do not know how to recognize in Jesus the one whom their Scriptures announced (2,4ff)—and King Herod is already plotting His death (2,16ff). The totally human excitement of Jerusalem, then (2,3), does not lead up to an act of faith. The capital is uncrowned to the benefit of Bethlehem and Nazareth. The Son of David, Jesus, will not

bear the name of Jerusalem, the city of His ancestor, but of Nazareth (2,23). In the course of His public ministry, the worst adversaries of Jesus come from Jerusalem (15,1). This is why He laments over the lot which awaits the city, this city which puts the divine envoys to death (23,37ff). Consequently, it is in Galilee that the final apparitions take place, in the course of which the risen Jesus sends His apostles to all nations (28,7.16-20).

3. Into this rather conventional outline *John* introduces more complex historical observations which center on the more frequent journeys made by Jesus to Jerusalem. It is there that the largest part of the drama unfolds. John dwells at length on the incredulity of his people (Jn 2,13-25), the difficulty in believing felt by their best teachers (3,1-12), the miracles Jesus accomplishes there, and the contradictions He has to meet (5; 7—10). His final miracle takes place at the gates of Jerusalem, like a final testimony to His saving work; but Jesus retires from there when He knows they are conspiring against Him (11,1-54). He returns only to accomplish His hour* (12,27; 17,1). The great refusal is underlined here still more than in Mark.

4. In joining a sketch of Christian origins to the gospel account, *Luke* evinces another facet of this sacred drama centering in Jerusalem. In Jesus' life it is the place where everything leads. The child Jesus is presented there and faithful souls there know how to recognize Him (Lk 2,22-38); He goes up there at the age of twelve and manifests His wisdom in the midst of doctors of the Law (2,41-50). These are veiled announcements of His manifestation and coming sacrifice. Because Jerusalem is the end of His life: "it is not fitting that a prophet die outside of Jerusalem" (13,33). Luke also sets in high relief Jesus' journey up to the city where He must accomplish His departure (9,31; 9,51; 13,22; 17,11; 18,31; 19,11). Before the definitive refusal opposed to His mission, He announces its downfall in terms more precise than in Mark and Matthew (19,41-44; 21,20-24). But the context of an intermediate period, the "pagans' time," clearly separated this event from the final consummation (21,24-28).

In fact, if the story of Jesus is completed at Jerusalem with His sacrifice, apparitions, and ascension (24,36-53; Ac 1,4-13), it is from there that the story of apostolic testimony begins. At Jerusalem they receive the Spirit (Ac 2). From that time they have the mission* of carrying the gospel* from Jerusalem to Judea, to Samaria, and to the limits of the earth (1,8; cf Lk 24,47f). They actually announce the good news first in the city and establish the Christian community there (Ac 2—7). There the Sanhedrin renews against them the hostility which caused Jesus' death (4,1-31; 5,17-41). Moreover, through the mouth of Stephen, God announces the destruction of the temple made by the hand of man, in punishment for Israel's resistance to the Holy Spirit and for her rejection of Jesus (7,44-53). The persecution stirred up by these words results in the dispersion of a part of the community (8,1); and at the same time by a paradoxical consequence, there is a new expansion of the gospel in Samaria (8,2-40), at Caesarea (10), then all the way to Antioch (11,19-26), where the first pagans are received into the Church. In the same way, the death of the first witness of the gospel results in the conversion of Saul the persecutor, who will become a choice instrument in the hands of God (7,58—8,1ff; 9,1-30). From that point Saul leaves Jerusalem to begin his role as a missionary (9,30; 11,25f); Peter also leaves it after his imprisonment (12,17); Jerusalem thus ceases to be the center of evangelization and proceeds toward the destiny predicted for it by Jesus, while the gospel will reach to the "limits of the earth."

II. FROM THE EARTHLY TO THE HEAVENLY JERUSALEM

1. *St. Paul*, the "choice instrument" converted on the road to Damascus (Ac 9), is the first to emphasize that the old Jerusalem has been supplanted by a new Jerusalem which is rooted in heaven. To the Galatians he presents this spiritual Jerusalem, our mother, heiress of the divine promises*, persecuted by the earthly Jerusalem which is called on to give way to her presence (G 4,24-31).

2. *The epistle to the Hebrews* takes up the same image. This heavenly Jerusalem, city of the living God (He 12,21ff), which Christians have already drawn near to by baptism, is the divine home where the temple "not made by hands of man," the end of Christ's mission, is found (9,24; cf 9,11f). This temple was the model (*typos*: 8,5), of which the temple here below was only the copy, the shadow, the reproduction, the figure (8,5; 10,1): a transcendental

reality of which the Jewish apocalypse spoke in magnificent terms.

3. The Johannine *Apocalypse* takes up the description of it to contemplate the Church in its final perfection: the spouse* of the Lamb* (Ap 21,1—22,5), a shining marvel, and city of dreams. The prophetic texts which described the new Jerusalem, notably those of Ezekiel and the Book of Isaiah, are taken up here and reinterpreted in such manner that the earthly city is lost to view. Its heavenly model alone is seen; but the Church on earth already bears its image because it partakes in its mystery: it is this holy city which the pagans trample under foot by persecution (11,2). At the end of the NT, the capital of Israel, Yahweh's ancient place of residence here below, no longer has the value of a figure. At the very moment when the new tragedy announced by Jesus is being realized for it, the promises of which it was the provisional depository are passing to another Jerusalem, now existing but at the same time tending to its final perfection, the definitive fatherland of all the redeemed: "Jerusalem, heavenly city, blest vision of peace!" (Hymn for the Dedication of Churches).

→Babel/Babylon 6—Build III 4—Church V 2 —City—David 1—Earth OT II 4—Fatherland OT 2; NT 1.2—Gate—Mother II 3—Mountain III 1.2—New IV—People II 4—Pilgrimage— Spouse NT—Stone 6—Temple OT I.

MJL & PG jrs

JESUS (NAME OF)

The intention of this article is simply to show what the name of Jesus, one name amongst many others, suggests and signifies.

I. "THIS JESUS"

The name signifies first of all what is ordinarily indicated in human language and particularly in biblical thought by a name: the being Himself in His singularity, His concrete and personal individuality: He and no other, He and all that He is—this Jesus, as He is named in several places (Ac 1,11; 2,36; 5,30; 9,17). This demonstrative, expressed or not, conveys almost all the basic Christian affirmations—the continuity between the individual who appeared in the flesh and the divine being confessed by faith. "This Jesus whom you have crucified, God has made both Lord and Christ" (Ac 2,36). "He who has been taken from you—this same Jesus—shall come in the same way" (1,11). "He who has been made a little lower than the angels, Jesus, we see crowned with eternal glory" (He 2,9). The revelation which converted Paul on the road to Damascus is of the same type: "I am Jesus whom you are persecuting" (Ac 9,5; 22,8; 26,15). It not only reveals to His persecutor, inseparable as he is from his own people, the presence of their Lord, but it makes him understand that the heavenly being whose power he has just experienced and the Galilean blasphemer whom he was persecuting with such hatred are indeed one. He has been once for all "laid hold of by Christ" (Ph 3,12). All former personal distinction seems as nothing to him when he thinks of the "knowledge of Christ Jesus his Lord" (Ph 3,8). The imposing Christ who fills the universe with the divine fullness (Col 1,15-20) remains "the Christ whom you have received, Jesus the Lord" (2,6).

II. JESUS OF NAZARETH

A being of the flesh, "born of a woman, born subject to the Law" (G 4,4), Jesus appeared in the world at a given date, "while Quirinius was governor of Syria" (Lk 2,2), in a human family —that of "Joseph, of the house of David" (1,27); He lived "in a village of Galilee, called Nazareth" (1,26). The name which He received at circumcision, as every Jewish child did (Lk 1,31; 2,21; Mt 1,21.25), was not exceptional in Israel (cf Si 51,30). But since in this infant God becomes Emmanuel, "God with us" (Mt 1,23), God accomplished in Him the promise made to the first Jesus, Joshua*, to be with Him and to reveal Himself as "Yahweh* the Savior" (Dt 31,7f). His origin seems so common; in order to designate Him, they do not normally join to His name, as in the case of a well-known family, the name of His father* and His ancestors (cf Si 51,30), but simply that of Nazareth, His home town. The genealogies of Matthew and Luke stress later the royal line of Jesus. The first proclamations of faith insist rather on the current manner of designating Him and the remembrance they had of Him after He left: "Jesus of Nazareth" (Jn 19,19; Ac 2,22; 4,10; 6,14; 22,8).

III. JESUS IN THE GOSPELS

Jesus is the name ordinarily used by the gospels to designate Christ and to relate His activity. It also seems that He was generally called "Rabbi," master (Mk 4,38; 5,35; 10,17); and after His death and entrance into glory He is called "Lord*." But with some few definite exceptions (cf Mt 21,3 and especially the purely Lucan sections: Lk 7,13; 10,1; etc.), the gospels always speak simply of Jesus. This is not an artificial attempt to restore a language anterior to faith from the time when Jesus had not yet completed His self-revelation and when most people saw Him only as a man. Without the slightest artifice, the gospels follow the same movement of faith* which always consists in applying to "this Jesus," to the concrete person, salvific and divine titles like those of Lord* (Ac 1,21; 2,36; 9,17; etc.), Christ (2,36; 9,22; 18,28; etc.), Savior (5,31; 13,23), Son* of God (9,20; 13,33), and Servant* of God (4,27.30). Whenever they speak of Jesus, the gospels are right in the line where they want to be: the gospel* is the announcement of the good news of Jesus (8,35), of Christ Jesus (5,42; 8,12), of the Lord Jesus (11,20; cf 15,35). John's gospel, which is the most careful to point out constantly the divine quality of Christ and to show in each of His acts the glory* of the only Son (Jn 1,14) and the sovereignty entrusted to the Son of Man (1,51; 3,14), does not miss a chance to pronounce the name of Jesus, even repeating it in the simplest of conversations when it seems superfluous (Jn 4,6.21; 11,32-41). Through the desire to "confess* Jesus Christ who has come in the flesh*" (1 Jn 4,2) each time the name comes up, this attention reveals the certitude that the name touches and reveals the richness of the "Word of Life" (1,1).

IV. THE NAME
ABOVE EVERY OTHER NAME

If the Christian faith cannot break away from Jesus and from all that this name implies about abasement and concrete humanity, the reason is that this name has become "the name above every other name," the one before which "every knee* bends, in heaven, on the earth and under the earth" (Ph 2,9ff). The name of Jesus has become the proper name of the Lord. When Israel called on the name of the Lord to find salvation* (Jl 3,5), it pronounced the name that God had given Himself, Yahweh, the name which is always with His people to deliver them (Ex 3,14f). This name evoked a personality extraordinarily emphatic and vigorous which it would have been vain to wish to constrain or flatter. The name of Jesus evokes the same divine omnipotence, the same invulnerable vitality, but with the traits that are familiar to us; and we discover ourselves in the presence of someone who has given Himself to us forever and who belongs to us.

The unique salvation of humanity (Ac 4,12), the unique richness of the Church (3,6), the unique power* at her disposal, is Jesus: "Jesus Christ* heals you" (9,34). The whole mission of the Church is to "speak in the name of Jesus" (5,40). Thus, in the synagogue at Damascus on the day after his conversion, Paul "preaches Jesus" (9,20). In the Agora of Athens "he announces Jesus and the resurrection" (17,18). At Corinth, he announces "Jesus Christ, the one who has been crucified" (1 Co 2,2). All Christian existence consists in "dedicating one's life to the name of our Lord Jesus Christ" (Ac 15,26), and the supreme joy* is being "judged worthy to undergo outrages" (5,41) and to "die for the name of the Lord Jesus" (21,13).

→Adoration II 2—Confession NT 1—Faith NT I 2—Jesus Christ—Joshua 2—Knee I—Lord—Messiah NT—Name NT 2.3—Power V—Salvation NT I 2 b.

JG jrs

JESUS CHRIST

These two words, a personal name—Jesus*—and the name of a function—Christ—are put together by the early Church (not only Paul, but also Mt 1,1.18; 16,21; Mk 1,1; Jn 1,17; 17,3; Ac *passim*), which is not satisfied with giving Jesus the title of Messiah*, which is what it does with other titles: Lamb of God, David, Son of God, Son of Man, Mediator, Word of God, Prophet, Holy, Savior, Lord, Servant of God...When it says Jesus Christ, the Church brings together in a close relationship the title proclaimed by believers and the historical person who lived on the earth, the interpretation and the original fact. Any presentation which absorbs one of the two terms in the other does not do justice to the Gospel. Criticism, then, must separate the movement leading to the knowledge of Jesus into two periods of time: and by prayerful meditation it must reconstruct it in order to come into contact with a living Person. This article does not go into details about "all that Jesus did," for the whole world would not be big enough to contain the books that could be written on this subject (Jn 21,25). It concentrates on the person of the Master Himself. To try to reach Jesus of Nazareth with all the rigor of literary criticism is to listen to the question that Jesus Himself asked: "and, you, who do you say that I am?" (I), a question which the authors of the NT are trying to answer (II). And this answer always brings one back to the historical person who raised the question.

I. JESUS OF NAZARETH

The Gospels* are not lives of Jesus edited according to the principles that govern the writing of history today. Written by believers to arouse and strengthen faith, they bring together and arrange memories that have indeed had light shed upon them and been transformed by the paschal faith but, which, when subjected to careful criticism, allow us to reach the person of Jesus of Nazareth with certainty.

1. *The eschatological situation of Jesus.* The Good News announced by Jesus is that the kingdom of God is being inaugurated by His very Word: "Happy are your eyes because they see, your ears because they hear! I tell you solemnly, many prophets and holy men longed to see what you see, and never saw it; to hear what you hear, and never heard it" (Mt 13,16f p). What is it, then, that they have seen and heard? In the first place exorcisms, which are interpreted by Jesus Himself: 'but if it is through the finger of God that I cast out devils, then know that the kingdom of God has overtaken you" (Lk 11,20 p); in fact, the enemy has been conquered: "I watched Satan fall like lightning from heaven" (10,18). Then there are the miracles*, which prove, according to Jesus, that a new era has begun: "the blind see again, and the lame walk, lepers are cleansed, and the deaf hear, and the dead are raised to life." Finally, they have heard the decisive choice that Jesus makes and this is more important still: "the Good News is proclaimed to the poor" (Mt 11,5 p). For, when Jesus speaks in this way, He is saying that the prophecy of Isaiah has

been fulfilled (Is 29,18f; 35,5f; 61,1).

The fact is that in His eyes the proclamation is eschatological: it fulfills* God's plan by epitomizing it. In this way Jesus takes up His position with regard to the OT. He admires John as the last and greatest of the prophets: "I tell you solemnly, of all the children born of women, a greater than John the Baptist has never been seen;" but since the rule of God has ushered in a new era Jesus continues: "yet the least in the kingdom of heaven is greater than he is" (Mt 11,11f).

The radical novelty of the Kingdom of God does not only consist in the fact that it is there, but in its nature. "Since John the Baptist came, up to this present time, the kingdom of heaven has been subjected to violence and the violent have taken it by storm [from those who want to enter it]" (Mt 11,12). And so Jesus must take a stand against the upholders of the sabbatical and ritual order which has been established by the doctors of the law with their casuistry and subtlety (Mt 15,1-20; 23,1-33). But at the same time He must purify the hopes of His contemporaries, who confuse the kingdom of God with national and earthly liberation (Mt 16,22; 20,21; 21,9 p; Lk 19,11; 22,38; 24,21; Jn 6,15; Ac 1,6). Jesus even differs in His approach from John the Baptist (Mt 11,3): like John, He demands full conversion*, but instead of announcing imminent condemnation by a vengeful God (Mt 3,7-12), He proclaims a year of grace (Lk 4,19). This is the unique situation in which Jesus considers Himself to be. Joy* is promised to those who discover the treasure (Mt 13,44f). Happy are those who experience this hour!

2. *Decision with regard to Jesus.* There is no point in wondering when this hour will come: "the coming of the kingdom of God does not admit of observation and there will be no one to say, 'Look here! Look here!' for, you must know, the kingdom of God is among you" (Lk 17,20f). The reign of God is no longer simply a thing of the future, it is within the grasp of all: it is enough to recognize the messianic times and to look at Jesus. Who, then, is He?

This Jesus is no ordinary rabbi explaining the scriptures, for He teaches with authority (Mk 1,22). Unlike the prophets*, He does not simply announce God's oracle, He says: "But I say this to you..." (Mt 5,22.28.34.39.44), prefacing what He says with a solemn declaration: "I tell you solemnly," as if in reply to some secretly heard question. He even dares to compare Himself with illustrious figures from the

OT: "There is someone greater than Jonas here...there is someone greater than Solomon here" (Mt 12,41f; Lk 11,31f).

This is why conversion to God means following* Jesus, deciding for or against Him. "He who is not with me is against me, and he who does not gather with me scatters" (Mt 12,30). To hear Jesus is to hear God Himself, for it means "building one's house on rock" (7,24). But when confronted by Jesus with His baffling behavior, how can such a decision be made? Jesus knows this well enough: "Happy is the man who does not lose faith in me" (11,6 p).

Therefore, Jesus has to justify His claim. Not by refusing to admit His identity, but by revealing that He has a unique relationship with His Father. Everything is possible to Him because He believes (Mk 9,23), with a faith that will be called the prototype of all faith* (cf He 12,2). What is more, He speaks to God as to His own "Daddy" (Mk 14,36), and associating Himself with the apocalyptic tradition of Daniel (Dn 2,23-30), He dares to say that the mysteries are revealed to Him because He is "the Son" in a unique relationship with "the Father" (Mt 11, 25ff p). For all that He does not claim knowledge of all things (Mk 13,32) and He submits His will to His Father's (14,36; cf Mt 20,23). Nevertheless, claiming a special position in the long list of God's messengers (Mk 12,6), He identifies the Kingdom of God with His own person; this, for example, is what the parable of the sower suggests (Mt 13,3-9 p) and what His behavior toward the poor and the sinners shows, a symbol of God's own attitude (Lk 15).

3. *Jesus and the future.* Jesus' life is that of a good Jew. But He rises above the Jewish traditions, and He assesses their importance according to the will* of God, with whom He enjoys the unique relationship that has already been mentioned. He comes to fulfill the Law and the prophets (Mt 5,17). The ideal of absolute love that He puts forward dismisses the subtleties of casuistry and remains impracticable to anyone who does not follow* Jesus. It can only be aimed at and achieved by a close dependence of Him: "Come to me...my yoke is easy and my burden light" (Mt 11,28f). Jesus is also faithful to the prophetic tradition when He announces, in spite of His contemporaries, that the pagans too will receive salvation (Lk 13,28f p).

Did Jesus think that the Church would carry on where He had left off, in order that this object might be achieved? It would be naive to believe that Jesus founded the Church in the form that we know it today; but it is wrong to claim that Jesus thought that at His death there would be no room for any intermediate stage before the parousia (cf Day of the Lord*).

By gathering round Him the circle of the disciples (Lk 10,1f p) and more particularly the group of the Twelve (Mk 3,12), who were to follow after Him (Lk 9,57-61 p) in order to extend His action and His presence—this is a recognized historical fact, even though it is difficult to date it with any precision—Jesus certainly did not intend to inaugurate a Church* after the manner of the separatist community at Qumrân but to foreshadow the definitive people of God (Mt 19,28 p). On the other hand, He certainly realized, unlike John the Baptist, that the establishment of God's rule would be progressive (Mk 4,29; Mt 13,24-30), that Simon would have to strengthen his companions in their faith (Lk 22,32) and that His disciples would have to suffer after His death (Mt 9,15 p; Mk 8,34 p; Lk 6,22 p). This is why the word *ekklesia*, the equivalent of the Aramaic word sod or *'edah*, used at Qumrân to describe the eschatological community of God's elect, may very well have been used by Jesus, even though it only appears on two occasions in the Gospels (Mt 16,18; 18,17). It would be an over-simplification of the facts of the NT to deny that Jesus had any idea of a period of time after His death. But this does not in any way exclude the personal conviction that, with His death, the end would take place (cf Mk 9,1).

In order to appreciate the meaning of this last statement, other sayings of Jesus must be taken into account. Jesus foresaw that He was going to die soon, as is clear from the prophecies that do not mention the resurrection (Lk 13, 31ff; cf 17,25; Mk 9,12). He saw this death as part of God's plan, as a service, as a sacrificial ransom (Mk 10,45); and on the eve of His death He bequeaths to His followers His legacy of mutual service (Lk 22,25ff).

These are indications that prevent us from making Jesus a man who against His will suffered death at the hands of enemies stronger than Himself. Many exegetes go further and think that Jesus identified His life with that of the Servant of God*, and it is true that Jesus speaks of His destiny, the destiny of the Son of Man*, in the very terms of the Servant songs of Isaiah (52,13—53,12): His obedience is expressed by "he must" (Lk 17,25), the sacrifice of His life is offered for many (Mt 20,28 p; 26, 28 p; Lk 22,16.18.30b), and it is the covenant that He is establishing (Lk 22,20).

If Jesus did understand His death in this way, why should He not have had an inkling of His resurrection? The precise details of the three great prophecies of the passion and resurrection of Jesus (Mt 16,21 p; 17,22f p; 20,18f p; cf Lk 24,25f.45) no doubt reflect the influence of the primitive community; but Jesus' faith in His resurrection within a short time can also be seen from His sayings. Like every faithful Jew, He knew that He was to rise at the end of time (Mt 22,23-32 p); moreover, He claimed a special place, even at the end of time, as we have already noted. On the other hand Jesus was convinced of His unique relationship with God and with all men and so how could He have doubted the final success of His mission and a special intervention by His Father in His favor? Of course such confidence in the resurrection does not mean that He did not share the human condition: He was overcome by anguish* and trembled in Gethsemani (Mk 14,36), and felt Himself abandoned even by God (15,34); but he knew that He was "the Son."

One last question remains. In order to reveal who He was, did Jesus take a short cut and use the formulas that were current in Judaism, such as Messiah, Son of God, Son of Man? In the Gospels the equivalents of these titles are used by Jesus. However, except in the case of the titles "the Son" and "the Son of Man," where it is impossible to state categorically that they were not used by Jesus, the critics believe that the infant Church did not distort but rather clarified Jesus' thought when it made Him say that He was "the Son of God" or "the Messiah." Jesus did not take the initiative in proclaiming Himself Messiah, for this was a title whose ambiguity would only be removed by the death on the cross; but He put His contemporaries on the right road to recognizing Him when He forbade His disciples to disclose His true identity (Mk 8,27-30 p), when He allowed Himself to be acclaimed the Son of David on the occasion of His entry into Jerusalem (Mt 21,1-9 p), or when to the question of the High Priest: "Are you the Son of God?" He replied with those mysterious words of the most ancient matthean formula: "You say it" (Mt 26,64). In His role as revealer, Jesus attached no importance to these "titles," which would most probably have given a false picture of the authentic relationship that He wished to establish with men. When He introduced Himself as the man with a unique relationship with God and a unique relationship with all men, Jesus put the ultimate question: "Who do you say I am?" (Mt 16,15 p).

II. JESUS, LORD, CHRIST AND SON OF GOD

To this question the disciples were unable to find the correct answer until Jesus had died on the cross and then showed Himself to them alive in the apparitions*. As they responded through their faith* to Jesus' initiative, the disciples discovered the meaning of the life and the mystery of the person of Jesus of Nazareth. In order to explain this meaning they spoke of Jesus with the help of titles taken from the traditional language, but they gave them a new sense. The efforts at expressing this are varied and groping, according to the gifts of each writer and the circles in which they lived. This christology certainly has a history, but we cannot retrace it with any certainty, since the sources are a combination of the palestinian foundation and hellenistic interpretations. It is possible, however, to pick out the first attempts at expressing the mystery of Jesus, and also the individual points of view of the different evangelists.

1. *First expressions of the mystery.* In the different ways in which the paschal experience is expressed it is possible to pick out four points of view, which may be a reflection of a certain historical evolution. The idea of the parousia confirms the heavenly exaltation of Jesus the Christ. The idea of the reedeeming cross* concentrates attention on the Servant. And finally questions are asked about the man Jesus, firstly in the mystery of His person and then in His relationship with the universe. This exposé will make use primarily of the confessions of faith and the hymns, which both represent material of an earlier date than either Pauline theology or the Gospel presentations. Nevertheless the developments made by NT theology will be mentioned in references (cf).

a) *Jesus raised to the heavens, Lord and Christ.* After their contact with the living Jesus, the disciples proclaim: "God has raised him from the dead" (1 Th 1,10; R 10,9; cf 8,11; G 1,1; 1 P 1,21; Ac 4,10). This statement is not the result of reflection on any text of scripture (cf 1 Co 15,4); it is an immediate expression, using the Jewish theological language of the resurrection*, of the belief that the paschal ex-

perience demands the exaltation and the enthronement of Jesus, as is clear from the experience of Stephen (Ac 7,56) and of Paul (7,3; 22,6; 26,13).

Corresponding to this early evidence of Chistian faith, there is the very ancient Aramaic acclamation "Marana tha" (1 Co 16,22; Ap 22,20; cf the echo of this in 1 Co 11,26), that is, according to the most probable interpretation: "Our Lord, come!" It makes it clear that this Jesus, exalted and enthroned in heaven, is the eschatological "Judge"; apart from this, it gives the true meaning of the coming of the glorified Jesus (Ac 1,11), a coming which is not a simple "return" at the end of time, but a continual manifestation throughout the course of human history: Jesus is the Lord of history (cf Mt 28,20).

Another ancient expression, probably the product of the hellenistic churches, is the confession of faith*: "Jesus [is] Lord" (1 Co 12,3; R 10,9; Ph 2,11), also "proclaimed" in a liturgical context. Here is no dry formula of faith, but an act of recognition and of submission to the Lord, which is what Jesus has become.

The nature of the event announced in this way will be made clear through the scriptures. Thus, with the help of the messianic prophecies (2 S 7,14; Ps 2,7; 110,1), they come to realize that Jesus has been "made Lord and Christ" (Ac 2,36), that He "has been appointed Son of God" (R 1,4; Ac 13,33); He is seated at the right hand of God (Ac 7,56; perhaps 2,33ff; 5,31; Mk 14,62 p; R 8,34...), and finally, He shares the divine omnipotence (Mt 28,18).

From the point of view of exaltation, the titles Messiah*, Son of God* and Lord* have originally an analogous meaning: they are not directly connected with the death or earthly life of Jesus: they simply state that Jesus of Nazareth fulfills Israel's hopes and becomes the Lord of all times.

The theological developments of the NT authors start from here. And so Paul does not only accept the transfer to Jesus of the title *Kyrios*, which in the LXX refers to God (R 10,2f; [Ph 2,11]; 1 Co 2,8; cf 15,25; E 1,20), but he also contrasts Jesus with the "Lords" of the pagans (1 Co 8,5f; 10,21); this is the origin of the expression "*Our* Lord Jesus Christ." And so the evangelists have people address Jesus not simply as "Rabbi" but as "Lord" (cf Mt 8,25 p; Lk 7,19 p).

b) *The salutary death of Jesus.* In view of the scandal occasioned by the shameful death of Jesus, the paschal faith searches the scriptures for a possible meaning. During His life on earth Jesus had, in a veiled way, interpreted His destiny by reference to the prophecy of the suffering and exalted servant. The early Church gives its Lord the title of servant* (Ac 3,26; 4,25-30) and conveys the meaning of the events that have taken place through the words of Isaiah (52,13—53,12). Jesus has been exalted (Ac 2,33; 5,31), "glorified" (3,13); the passion is described in this way in a text earlier than the epistle of Peter (1 P 2,21-25) and in the catechesis of Philip (Ac 8,30-35). Finally one of the most ancient formulas of faith states that Jesus "died *for* our sins, in accordance with the scriptures" (1 Co 15,3). The preposition *hyper*, here as elsewhere (G 1,4; 2 Co 5,14f.21; R 4,25; 8,32; 1 P 3,18; 1 Jn 2,2) and especially in the eucharistic terminology (Lk 22,20; 1 Co 11,24), refers to the salvific value of Jesus' death.

Other titles, with a meaning analogous to that which the title Servant came to have, are made to express the same reality. Jesus is "the Just One" (Ac 3,14), the one who leads men to life (3,15; cf 5,31), the spotless Lamb of God (1 P 1,19f; cf Jn 1,29.36). He is the sinless High Priest, the mediator of the New Testament (He 2,14-18; 4,14).

From this point on, the combined influence of the hellenistic religions leads to the title of "savior" appearing in the latest pauline letters (Tt 1,4; 2,13; 3,6; 2 Tm 1,10). From this time also we see the development of the pauline mystique of the baptized person united with the death and resurrection of Christ (G 2,19; R 6,3-11), leading to a deeper understanding of the doctrine of propitiation, etc. (R 3,23f...).

c) The man Jesus. As it becomes more concerned with the origins of the one whom it knows to be alive today after His death, the apostolic Church soon turns its attention to the earthly existence of Jesus.

Thus, the Gospel tradition takes shape in response to a double need, to make known the life of the one whom it believes to have risen (Ac 10,37f) and to put it forward as an example of how believers should live. This is how memories are gradually gathered together and clarified, with faith in the Lord Jesus always the unifying factor. In this light, which surrounds it with a halo and transfigures it, the figure of the man Jesus emerges.

Paul is less interested in His earthly existence than in His teaching and His redeeming death.

The Epistle to the Hebrews also explains the meaning of Christ's sufferings*. Jesus voluntarily accepted His death (He 10,7), "he was made perfect by sufferings" (2,10); He endured the cross instead of joy (12,2) and He learned obedience from what He suffered (5,7f): He is the one "who leads us in our faith and brings it to perfection" (12,20).

This movement of return to the beginnings includes questions about the origins of Jesus, probably with the help of recourse to prophecies like that of Nathan (2 S 7,12ff) or of Ps 16,10f. The existence of Jesus involves two modes of being: one earthly in the flesh and the other heavenly through the Spirit (R 1,3f; 1 P 3,18; 1 Tm 3,16a). Transformed inwardly by the Spirit, Jesus receives an anointing*, understood in the first place as a royal anointing on the occasion of His enthronement (He 1,9), then as a prophetic* anointing on the occasion of His baptism with a view to His ministry (Ac 10,38; cf 4,27; Lk 4,18). The resurrection, understood as a fulfillment of the promise made to David (Ac 2,34f; 2 Tm 2,8), leads to Jesus being seen as the Son of David (R 1,3f; 2 Tm 2,8; Ac 13,22f; 15,16 and perhaps Mk 12,35ff). By an analogous procedure the genealogies of Jesus are worked out (Mt 1,1-17; Lk 3,23-37). The same is true of the prologues to the Gospels formed by the traditions about the infancy of Jesus (Mt 1—2; Lk 1—2), although here it is a case of a more explicit christology, the fulfillment of the scriptures. The anecdotal history that they give reveals a profound theology, of which the main concern is to ask the following question: what was the origin of the one whom we now adore as the Lord?

d) The first-born of all creation. Going back still further leads to the discovery of the pre-existence of Jesus, in a step that must have been inspired not by the gnostic myth of the Savior-God but by Jewish apocalyptic traditions, anxious to show the unity of creation and of the end-time. Thus, in the Book of Enoch the pre-existence of the Son of Man* is stated (Enoch 39,6f; 40,5; 48,2f; 49,2; 62,6); and elsewhere certain Jewish circles used to mediate on Wisdom at the beginning of creation (Jb 28,20-28; Ba 3,32-38; Pr 8,22-31; Si 24,3-22; Ws 7, 25f). The very ancient hymn, which lies behind Ph 2,6-11, describes the three successive states of Jesus, who was in "the form of God" before emptying Himself in the course of His life on earth, then being exalted to heaven. This passage does not state that a certain human nature was

269

"assumed" by a divine person; it is trying to show that the presence of Jesus extends to the whole duration of time. Jesus is the one "through whom everything exists and through whom [we come to God]" (1 Co 8,6); He is the rock that accompanies the people in the desert (10,4). And finally, perhaps before the development of Paul's theology, Jesus is called "the image* of the unseen God and the first-born of all creation" (Col 1,15), the one in whom "lives the fullness* of divinity" (2,9).

After the assertion of the perfect justice and sanctity of Jesus (Ac 3,14), the NT proceeds to the proclamation of His divinity, He is the "Son of God," in a sense that makes explicit the allusions made by Jesus of Nazareth and which goes beyond the messianic sense, since it is based on the pre-existence of the Son whom God revealed to Paul (G 1,12) and whose Gospel Paul proclaims (R 1,9). Jesus is "the Son of God": this is the belief of the Christian (1 Jn 4,15; 5,5), proclaimed constantly in the Gospels (Mk 1,11; 9,7; 14,61; Lk 1,35; 22,70; Mt 2,15; 14,33; 16,16; 27,40.43), echoing the words of Jesus on "the Son" (Mt 11,27 p; 21, 37ff p; 24,36 p). The climax of this progressive revelation is the proclamation (perhaps already in R 9,5, in all probability in He 1,8; Tt 2,13 and certainly in Jn 1,1.18; 20,28) that Jesus is God* with God.

As a corollary of the pre-existence, the ecclesial and cosmic dimension of Jesus is revealed in its turn. He is the Head* of the Church, which is His Body* (Col 1,18); His Lordship extends over the whole world, for He has traveled through its three spheres: earth, hell and heaven (Ph 2,10). Is He not the "Lord of glory" (1 Co 2,8), because He is "the first to be born from the dead" (Col 1,18)?

Various titles are associated with this point of view. Jesus is the New Adam* (1 Co 15, 15.45; R 5,12-21), the one in whom God brings together (anakephalaio) all things (E 1,10), the one who has established peace* by making one single man* (2,13-16); He is the mediator of the new covenant (1 Tm 2,5; He 9,15; 12,24)...

2. *Gospel presentation of the mystery.* We have grouped together in quite an artificial way the first attempts at grasping the mystery of Jesus; in fact only the Gospels are authentic christologies. Before the four Gospels were written, the Gospel tradition was at work interpreting the mystery of Jesus; it can be recognized at the christological point of each Gospel pericope as well as in the different presynoptic arrangements. Interest in the earthly life of Jesus is, then, significant in itself, independently of any biography of Jesus. More precisely, it reveals a double concern. In the first place against any gnostic attempt to reduce it to some sort of myth, it is determined to maintain the revelation of Jesus as rooted in history; then against any archeological attempt, concentrating only on digging up the past, it expresses itself by means of a conviction: the one who lived is still living and speaks to the Christians of the present time. The Gospels are all "actualizations" of the event that was Jesus of Nazareth.

If there is any christology in the NT, then it is the Gospel* before the gospels. This christology was not worked out in any systematic form nor in any collection of letters, but with the sole intention of presenting and making present the mystery of Jesus, now become Lord. As for the four Gospels, they offer different aspects of this presentation, always referring back to the one Gospel proclaimed in the Holy Spirit. This survey will end with a few brief notes on this subject.

a) *St. Mark* invites his readers to recognize in Jesus of Nazareth the Son of God, the one who has saved us by triumphing over Satan. He insists on the actual happening of the personal meeting with God in Jesus at the end of time. We should note Mark's reserve, compared with Mt or Lk, in the use of the expression "Son of God." Apart from the confession made by the demons in one story (Mk 5,7) and in a summary of exorcisms (3,11), the title only occurs at the three climaxes of revelation: in the words spoken by God at the baptism (1,11), and at the Transfiguration (9,7), and finally on the lips of the centurion. The veil of the Temple has been torn, the time of Judaism has come to an end; it is then that the efficacity of Jesus' death is proclaimed in the name of the pagans: "Truly this man was the Son of God" (15,39).

b) *St. Matthew* brings the Gospel to a climax with the "manifesto" of the risen Christ: "all authority...has been given to me...and know that I am with you always; yes, to the end of time" (Mt 28,18ff). Jesus introduces Himself as the Son of Man, foretold by the prophet Daniel (Dn 7,13f), who has been given universal sovereignty. The Gospel tries to show how Jesus, having refused to accept this sovereignty from Satan (Mt 4,8ff) because the Father has put all things in His power (11,27), has triumphed over His enemies: the reign of God is the reign of Christ. In order to show this, Matthew stresses the scriptural argument of the early Church, for Jesus comes to crown Israel's past. He has written the ecclesiastical Gospel *par excellence*, making the events of the past present for his time (vg 14,33).

c) *St. Luke* in his book about the Acts of the Apostles shows the interest he has in the Church and gives a firm indication that there is a time of Jesus, which comes between the time of the prophetic announcement and the time of the Church (cf Lk 16,16; 22,35-38; Ac 2,1). The life of Jesus takes on an importance for the time of the Church. It was the first act of God's plan in the Church, an act that has a typical value. The time to come that follows is constantly based on it: an event of the past remaining for ever present. On the other hand the picture of Christ is more that of the merciful Savior (Lk 3,6; 9,38.42; Ac 10,38) addressing Himself to the poor (Lk 4,18), to sinners (15), to the disinherited of the earth. Finally he gives a strict meaning to the title "Son of God" and clearly distinguishes it from the title of Christ (1,35; 22,70).

d) *St. John* begins his presentation with the traditional statement of the pre-existence and shows the glory* of the Father, in Jesus, the glory of the resurrection that can be seen already in the signs that He works in the course of His passage through this world. The Son of man, who is in heaven, is present here and returns to heaven (Jn 3,13.31; 6,62; cf 13,1; 14,28; 16,28; 17,5). He is the Word* of God manifested in the mortal flesh of Jesus (1,14). He is the absolute and definitive Revealer, and to give one's faith to Him is to live (3,16f.36; 11,25f...): from His lips come the statements of eternity (8,58; 10,38) or of immanence in the Father (10,38; 14,9f.20; 17,21).

The book of John is still more different from the others and can be called the Gospel *par excellence*, insofar as it leads the believer back again and again to the person and the earthly activity of Jesus of Nazareth, without which no ecclesial existence can have any meaning: and the same is true of the sacramental life, baptism (3,22-30) and the Eucharist (6).

CONCLUSION

Before we finish we must make some reference to the *Apocalypse*. It is the meeting place of many currents and especially of the liturgical life, and it shows the living Christ, the Lord who leads and rules the Church (Ap 1—3). Above all stands the figure of the Lamb, bearing the marks of the passion that He has suffered (5). He ensures that the Church triumphs over her enemies (6,15ff; 17,14) and fixes His marriage with her for the end of time (19,7f; 21,9). Lord of human history, He is the first and the last (1,17), the beginning and the end (22,13), the Alpha and the Omega (1,8; 21,6), the Amen (3,14), the Anointed of God, and finally the King of kings and the Lord of Lords, to whom all honor and glory are due (19,19; 17,14).

These presentations of the mystery of Jesus of Nazareth, now become Lord and Christ, cannot be reduced to a single system; but they do reveal one single movement: the intention of making the presence of this Jesus, who lived and died for us, real for a certain group of people. Orthodoxy is assessed by the firmness of the link between the Christian interpretation and the fact of Jesus: "Every spirit which acknowledges that Jesus Christ has come in the flesh is from God" (1 Jn 4,2). In order to express itself and communicate itself, the faith in its infancy showed itself dependent on the various cultures of its time: and so on palestinian Judaism, on the diaspora or on the surrounding hellenism. In adapting itself in this way to the different civilizations, the Church opens the way to and foreshadows every future interpretation. And after the NT, hermeneutics carries on the movement; for example there are in due course discussions about the "self-consciousness" of Jesus, of His "nature" and person, without any suggestion that the interpretation is being fixed for all time. And even today it must be practised in the various cultures where faith in Jesus Christ is to be found.

→Abraham II 4—Adam II—Apparitions of Christ—Ascension—Blessing IV 1—Body of Christ—Church III—Covenant NT—Creation NT I 2, II—Cross I—Day of the Lord NT—Desert NT I—Education II—Election NT I—Elijah NT 2—Example NT—Fathers and Father IV, V—Fulfill NT 1—Fullness—God NT—Gospel II—Head—Holy NT I—Image IV —Jesus (Name of)—King NT—Lamb of God —Law *C* I—Light & Dark NT I—Life IV—

Lord NT—Love I NT 2—Man I 2, II 2, III—
Mediator II—Messiah NT—Mission NT I
—Mystery NT II 2—Obedience III—Plan of
God NT I 1—Peace III—Prayer IV—Predes-
tine—Presence of God NT I—Priesthood NT
I—Redemption NT—Resurrection NT I—
Revelation NT I 1, II 1, III 1—Sacrifice NT—
Salvation NT I 1—See NT I—Servant of God
III—Shepherd & Flock NT 1—Son of God NT
I—Son of Man NT—Spirit of God NT I—
Spouse NT 1—Suffering NT I, II—Teach NT
I—Temple NT I—Truth NT 3 a—War NT I
—Way III—Will of God NT I 2—Wisdom NT
I—Witness NT II—Word of God NT I 1, III 1
—Works NT I.

XLD ems

JEW

In the earliest days of the NT, the term *Jew*
was often synonymous with *Israelite* or
Hebrew*, though these latter terms were more
especially reserved for religious usage. With
Paul and John, the word *Jew* sometimes had
real theological meaning, and this is a source of
possible confusion for the inattentive reader.

I. JEW AND PAGAN IN ST. PAUL

Paul, as did the prophets, sees mankind
divided into two camps, the chosen people and
the nations*, "Jew and Greek" (G 3,28). This
basic distinction was at the same time both
preserved and abolished by the coming of
Christ.

1. *The advantages of being a Jew.* The name
Jew is itself a glorious title (R 2,17). The
etymology of the word derives from Judah:
"I will give glory to Yahweh" (Gn 29,35) and,
by reason of the blessing of Jacob, "your
brothers shall praise you" (49,8). The privileges
of the Law* and circumcision have their meaning in reference to the Jew (R 2,17-29). Paul
claims to be a Jew as a point of honor: "We
are Jews by birth, and not sinful heathens" (G
2,15). This cry of Paul helps us in understanding
the devout Jew's daily prayer of thanks for not
being born *gōy*, pagan. Paul, Christian though
he was, called himself an Israelite (R 11,1;
Ph 3,5). And according to Luke he solemnly
announced in Jerusalem: "I am a Jew" (Ac

22,3); and Apollos, a convert to Christianity,
is spoken of as "a Jew" (18,24).

God's gifts, wonderful as they are in every
way, do impose obligations on the recipient.
Paul accuses the Jews of not keeping the Law
which they teach to others and of causing God's
name to be blasphemed* among the nations
rather than praised (R 2,17-24). Circumcision
is of value only if one is circumcised in heart,
as the prophets taught (Jr 4,4; Dt 30,6; Lv
26,41). The unbelieving Jew is a Jew in appearance only (R 2,28), a usurper of a glorious
name (Ap 2,9; 3,9). The Christian is the truly
circumcised (Ph 3,2), "the Jew in Spirit" (R
2,29). At the end of the list of charges brought
by Paul against everybody, it seems that the
privileges of the Jew are abolished: all men
alike are sinners, Jews and Greeks (3,9).

2. *The converted pagan and the unbelieving
Jew.* The relationships between "Jew and
Greek" are complex. From one point of view
all differences between the two disappear, not
only on the level of sin, but even on the level
of grace: "There is neither Jew nor Greek"
(G 3,28), for in Christ we form but one being;
faith*, not the observance of the Law, is the
source of our justice (cf Col 3,11). It is in
these circumstances that the reconciliation* of
the nations, which the prophets foretold, can be
accomplished: "God is also God of the pagans"
(R 3,29; 10,12).

On the other hand, Paul jealously maintains
the priority of Jew over pagan in receiving
both punishment and reward; tribulation or
glory goes "to the Jew first, then to the Greek"
(R 2,9f; 1,16; Mt 15,24 p; Ac 13,46; 18,6). The
converted pagan, who might be tempted to think
that he has replaced the Jew in God's plan, is
reminded of this priority. The "superiority" of
the Jew (R 3,1) remains because God does not
repent of His gifts (11,29). Jews converted to
Christianity form the "natural branch" of the
olive tree, while the Christians of pagan origin
have been "grafted on contrary to nature" (11,
24). Even in its obdurate condition, Israel has
a role in the Church of Christ; for Israel is
something lacking to the Church, which ought
to cause a "great sadness and continual sorrow
in the heart" of every believer (9,2).

II. ST. JOHN
AND THE UNBELIEVING JEW

The fourth evangelist, like the others, speaks

about the Jews of Jesus' time (vg Jn 3,1; 12,9). Nevertheless, at the time when John was writing, the Church and the synagogue formed two completely separate communities. The newborn Church's struggle with the Jews no longer existed, except within the broader framework of the world's incredulity toward Christ. For the most part, John does not use the word *Jew* as an ethnic designation, but as a theological term with an historical foundation. He uses the term first of all to designate those who crucified Jesus, but then, in a more profound sense, to signify all unbelievers. There are various indications that John tends to make the Jew a "type" of the unbeliever; i.e., he tends to make *Jew* a category of religious thought.

John speaks in his gospel of the Jewish customs and festivals as though they belonged to a foreign people (Jn 2,6.13; 5,1; 6,4; 7,2...). As opposed to His manner of speaking to Nicodemus (7,51), Jesus speaks to the Jews as though they were foreigners (8,17; 10,34; cf 7,19.22). Ordinarily, the term *Jew* designates the adversaries of Jesus (2,18.20; 5,16.18; 6,41...). conversely, anyone who follows Jesus or truly concerns himself with Him is treated as an enemy of the Jews, even though he be of Jewish origin (5,15; 7,13 in comp with 7,11; 1,19). For John the "Jews" come to be a type-form of unbelief*, a feature of the fourth gospel which involves the danger of its being put to an anti-Semitic usage.

Such an interpretation can certainly not find any support in John. To the extent that *Jew* refers to those who took part in Jesus' crucifixion, the world* has already taken their place by persecuting in turn the disciples of Christ. Just as Jesus has been appointed judge of the Jews (19,13) who would not have Him as their king (19,14.19-22), so must the Christian judge the world that wants to judge him; for that purpose, he listened unceasingly to the testimony of the Paraclete*, the defender of Jesus.

→Circumcision—Election—Hebrew—Israel OT 2 b—Nations—People—Pharisees 2—Stranger I —Unbelief III.

XLD mjm

JOHN THE BAPTIST

As a witness to Jesus, John is more than a prophet (Lk 7,26 p). A messenger who precedes the Lord (Lk 1,76; Mt 11,10 p; cf Ml 3,1), he inaugurates the gospel (Ac 1,22; Mk 1,1-4);

"until him, it was the Law and the prophets; since then the kingdom of God is proclaimed" (Lk 16,16 p). Prophet without equal, he prepares the ways of the Lord (Mt 11,11; Mk 1,3 p) whose "precursor" he is (Ac 13,24f) and to whom he is the witness (Jn 1,6f).

1. *The precursor and his baptism.* John, before being born of a mother who had been childless up to that time, is consecrated to God and filled with the Holy Spirit (Lk 1,7.15; cf Jg 13,2-5; 1 S 1,5.11). John, who is destined to be a new Elijah* (Lk 1,16f), recalls the great prophet by his clothing* and by the austere life (Mt 3,4 p) he leads in the desert from his youth (Lk 1,80). Was he trained by a community such as Qumrân? However that may be, there finally comes the time of his manifestation to Israel, carefully dated by Luke (3,1f). John appears as a master surrounded by his disciples (Jn 1,35), teaching them to fast and pray (Mk 2,18; Lk 5,33; 11,1). His powerful voice unsettles Judea; he preaches a conversion signified by a ritual washing accompanied by the confession of sins, which moreover calls for a renewal of life (Mk 1,4f); for it is useless to be Abraham's sons if you do not practice justice* (Mt 3,8f p), the laws of which he gives to the multitude of the humble (Lk 3,10-14).

But the Pharisees and lawyers do not believe in him; some treat him as if he were possessed (Mt 21,32; Mk 11,30ff p; Lk 7,30-33); thus, when they come to him, he tells them that the wrath* of God will consume every sterile tree (Mt 3,10 p). He denounces the adultery of King Herod and gets himself imprisoned and, finally, put to death (Mt 14,3-12 p; Lk 3,19f; 9,9). Because of his zeal* John is very much the new Elijah that was expected and who must prepare the people for the coming of the Messiah (Mt 11,14); but he is not recognized and his witness* will not prevent the passion of the Son of Man (Mk 9,11ff p).

2. *The witness of the light and the friend of the bridegroom.* The witness of John consists first of all in proclaiming himself the simple precursor. The crowd asks him in effect if he is not the Messiah* (Lk 3,15). To one official enquiry, the Baptist replies that he is not worthy to untie the sandals of the one that he precedes and "who is before him" (Jn 1,19-30; Lk 3,16f p). The one "who comes" and who will baptize in the Spirit (Mk 1,8) and in fire (Mt 3,11f) is Jesus on whom the Spirit descended after His baptism (Jn 1,31-34).

By proclaiming Him the Lamb* of God who takes away the sin* of the world (Jn 1,29), John is not foreseeing how Christ will take away the sin, any more than he understands why Christ had wished to be baptized by him (Mt 3,13ff). To take away sin, Jesus will have to receive a baptism of which John's was only a figure*, the baptism of His passion (Mk 10,38; Lk 12,50). Jesus will thus fulfill all justice (Mt 3,15), not by doing away with sinners, but by justifying the multitude whose sins He would bear (cf Is 53,7f.11f). Before the passion, the attitude of Jesus astonishes John and his disciples who were expecting a minister of justice. Christ recalls to their minds the prophecies of salvation which He fulfills and urges them not to be scandalized* (Mt 11,2-6 p; cf Is 61,1).

But some of John's disciples will not become disciples of Jesus. In the gospels there are traces of the polemic between the sect of the Baptist and the early Church (vg Mk 2,18). The Church, to show the pre-eminence of Christ, has only to appeal to the witness of John himself (Jn 1,15). True friend of the bridegroom and filled with joy at His appearance, John effaces himself before Jesus (3,27-30) and, by his words, invites his own disciples to follow Christ (1, 35ff). Jesus in return glorified His witness, a lamp* burning brightly (5,35), the greatest prophet born of woman (Mt 11,11); but He went on to say, the least in the kingdom* of heaven is greater than he. He preferred the grace of the sons of the kingdom to the prophetic charism, without at the same time depreciating the holiness of John.

The glory of this humble friend of the bridegroom is proclaimed in the prologue of the fourth gospel which relates John to the Word made flesh: "John was not the light* but the witness of the light"; the prologue also relates John to the Church: "He comes to give witness to the light in order that all might believe through him" (Jn 1,7f).

→Baptism II—Elijah NT 1—Friend 3—Humility IV—Jesus Christ I 1—Joy NT I 1—Prophet NT II 1—Repentance/Conversion NT I—Visitation NT 1—Witness NT II.

MFL jrs

JOSHUA

1. *Leader of Israel.* From the OT point of view the work of Joshua represents an essen-

tial stage in the history of salvation. As the servant of Moses (Ex 17,9; Nb 11,28), he went up Mt. Sinai with him (Ex 24,13) and lived close to the sanctuary (33,11). This was the source of the deep-seated loyalty, which he displayed in the affair of the spies sent to Canaan (Nb 13); and Caleb and he were to be the only ones of the desert generation to enter the Promised Land (14,30.38). He was chosen by God as Moses' successor as the leader of Israel, and he received the Spirit of God when Moses laid hands on him (27,15-23; Dt 31,7f.14-23). And so at the death of Moses he was able to assume the leadership of the people. Then we see him, full of valor (Js 1,6), showing his courage in the conduct of the holy war. However, in this war there is a heavenly leader and Joshua is only His representative (5,13ff); the assistance He gives can be seen when the powers of nature are put at the service of Israel to help them in their battles (6,20; 10,10-14). The objective of the conquest is not, however, to destroy the Canaanites but to give God's people the land of the pagans as their heritage (Ps 78,54f; 105,44f): was not this the country of their ancestors, the Promised Land*? But Israel was only led into it in order to maintain the Covenant with God and to observe His Law. With an absolute religious intransigence (23) Joshua himself gave an example in this matter and led Israel along the way of fidelity (8,30-35; 24).

2. *The figure of the Savior.* In their meditations the wise men will frequently return to this part of exemplary history: as the successor of Moses in his prophetic office Joshua was well named (hb.="Yahweh saves") and saved God's elect (Si 46,1). And yet this first "Jesus" was only the dim foreshadowing of another Savior to come, who would also have the same name* (Mt 1,21). His activity was only a preparatory episode in the long history of salvation (Ac 7,45); today, with Jesus Christ dead, risen and raised to the heavens, the real salvation* is revealed to God's people. The Promised Land reached by Joshua is only a stage, not the end, a foreshadowing, not the real place of rest (He 4,8). A better place of rest* is promised to us: that of the seventh day, a sharing in God's own rest. Joshua, the man of courage, encourages us to fight to reach this place of rest, where we shall find the reward of our labors (Ap 14,13).

→Earth OT II 2—Imposition of Hands OT 2—
Jesus (Name of) II—Salvation OT I o.

PG ems

JOY

God's revelation of Himself as Creator and
Savior arouses in man a tremendous joy. How
can one contemplate creation* without proclaiming "My joy is in the Lord" (Ps 104,34)
and desiring that "God rejoice in His works*"
(104,31)? In the presence of God and His works
in human history, joy seizes every man who is
not without feeling (92,5ff) and makes itself
known: "Come, let us shout with joy to the
Lord...the rock of our salvation" (95,1); "Let
the heavens rejoice! And let the earth be
glad...before the face of the Lord, for He is
coming" (96,11ff). And if He comes, it is to
invite His faithful servants to enter into His
own joy and to prepare the way for them (Mt
25,21).

OT

I. THE JOYS OF LIFE

The joys of human life are a part of God's
promises* to men (Dt 28,3-8; Jr 33,11); their
privation is a punishment for infidelity (Dt
28,30-33.47f; Jr 7,34; 25,10f). Man's humble joy
in the woman he loves (Qo 9,9), in the fruit of
his labors (3,22), and in eating and partaking of
good times (2,24; 3,12f) is spared the merciless
criticism of Qoheleth. He praises that joy which
allows a man to forget the troubles of this life
(8,15); this is the joy that God Himself gives
(5,17ff). The purpose of wine* is to bring joy
(Jg 9,13; Ps 104,15) to those who use it with
moderation (Si 31,27). Moreover, the time of
vintage* is one of joy (Is 16,10), as is the time
of harvest* (Ps 126,5f). The great joy that a
woman brings to her husband by her beauty
and virtue (Pr 5,18; Si 26,2.13) is seen as the
image of the highest possible joy (Is 62,5).
Fecundity is a cause of gladness for husband
and wife (1 S 2,1.5; Ps 113,9; cf Jn 16,21),
especially if their son is wise (Pr 10,1).

Along with the tumultuous joys of festive
occasions—the coronation of a king (1 K 1,40),
victory (1 S 18,6), or the return of prisoners
(Ps 126,2f)—there are other joys so intimate
that they cannot be communicated to strangers

(Pr 14,10). The wise man knows the value of
that joy of heart which brings good health
(17,22) and for which a kind word (12,25) or a
friendly look (15,30) does so much. God condemns only perverse joys of the evildoer (2,14),
particularly that evil joy which the just man's
enemies derive from his misfortune (Ps 13,5;
35,26).

II. JOYS OF THE COVENANT

God, the source of the wholesome joys of
this life, offers the highest possible joys to His
people: the joys which are found in fidelity to
the covenant.

1. *Joys of community worship.* Israel finds
in her worship* the joy of praising* God (Ps
33,1), who deigned to be her king (Ps 149,2)
and who invites her to rejoice in His presence*
(Dt 12,18). In this way she also experiences
the sweetness of fraternal unity (Ps 133). Thus
Israel finds an effective means for resisting the
temptation of the Canaanite cults, whose sensual rites are an abomination to God (Dt 12,30f;
23,18f). The feasts*, celebrated in an atmosphere of enthusiasm and jubilation (Ps 42,5;
68,4f; 100,2), recall to the people "the day*
which the Lord has made for its joy and gladness" (Ps 118,24). Some of these celebrations
are recorded in history; e.g., the Passover of
Hezekiah (2 Ch 30,21-26), the celebration of the
return from exile (Ezr 6,22), and especially the
festival of Tents at which Ezra, after the book
of the Law was read, proclaimed: "This day
is holy...Do not be sad; the joy of the Lord
is our strength" (Ne 8,10). It is precisely to
preserve this plenitude of joy that the Law
commands the people to take their joy from its
sources in the three annual festivals at Jerusalem, where they are to go to receive the divine
blessings* (Lv 23,40; Dt 16,11.14f). From this
source God wants all the nations* to draw their
joy (Is 56,6f).

2. *Joys of personal fidelity.* This joy, which
is offered to all men, is the special portion of
the humble who constitute the true people of
God (Ps 149,4f). Like Jeremiah, they feed upon
the Word* of God, which is the delight of their
hearts (Jr 15,16). They find their joy in God
(Ps 33,21; 37,4; Jl 2,23) and in His law (Ps
19,9), which is their treasure (119,14.111.162)
and which remains as their delight even in the
midst of bitter anguish (119,143). The humble

seekers* after God can rejoice (34,3; 69,33; 70,5; 105,3), because they are justified by the grace* (Ps 32,10f) and the mercy* of God (51,10.14). Their confident union with the Lord, their sole good* (16,2; 73,25.28), gives them a glimpse of eternal joy (16,9ff). Their intimate union with the divine wisdom is a foretaste of eternal joy (Ws 8,16).

3. *Eschatological joys.* Israel truly lived in an atmosphere of hope. If their worship reminds them of the great deeds of God and the exodus above all, it is to arouse in them a desire for a new exodus* in which God will reveal Himself without equal, the savior of all men (Is 45,5-8.21f). That will be a time of Messianic joy. Isaiah had proclaimed its superabundance (9,2): the desert shall rejoice (35,1), and when God acts the heavens will shout with joy and the earth shall rejoice (44,23; 49,13). Captives shall be set free and shall come to Zion, shouting for joy (35,9f; 51,11), to be clothed with the garments of salvation and justice (61,10) and to taste the eternal joy (61,7) which will fulfill all their hopes (25,9). Then will the servants of God raise their voices in songs of heartfelt joy amidst a creation* that has been renewed, for God will make Jerusalem "joy" and His people "gladness," that He may rejoice in them and provide them with an everlasting jubilation (65, 14.17ff; 66,10). Such is the joy that Jerusalem expects from God, the holy and eternal one; His mercy is going to save her (Ba 4,22f.36f; 5,9). The master craftsman of this work of salvation is to be Jerusalem's king, who will come to her in humility and whom she will welcome in exultation (Ze 9,9).

NT

I. THE JOY OF THE GOSPEL

This humble king is Jesus Christ, who preaches the joy of salvation to the lowly and gives it to them through His sacrifice.

1. *The joy of salvation is preached to the lowly.* The coming of the Savior creates an atmosphere of joy which Luke has underlined more than the other evangelists. Even before the rejoicing at His birth (Lk 1,14), the precursor leaped for joy in his mother's womb when Mary came (1,41.44). The Virgin, for whom the greeting of the angel was an invitation to joy (1,28: gr. *chaire*=rejoice!) praises, as much with joy as humility, the Lord who has become her son to save the humble (1,42.46-55). The birth of Jesus is a cause of great joy to the angels who announce it and to the people He came to save (2,10.13f; cf Mt 1,21). It fulfills the expectation of just men (Mt 13,17 p) who, like Abraham, had already rejoiced in the contemplation of it (Jn 8,56).

The kingdom of God is already present in Jesus (Mk 1,15 p; Lk 17,21). He is the bridegroom whose voice brought a rapture of joy to the Baptist (Jn 3,29) and whose presence prevents His disciples from fasting* (Lk 5,34 p). They have the joy of knowing that their names are inscribed in heaven (10,20), for they are among the poor* to whom the kingdom of God belongs (6,20 p), a treasure for which one gladly gives up everything (Mt 13,44). And Jesus taught them that persecution*; by confirming their certitude of possessing the kingdom, ought to intensify their joy (5,10ff p).

The disciples rightly rejoice at the miracles* of Jesus which bear witness to His mission (Lk 19,37ff), but they are wrong to rejoice in the miraculous power which Jesus had given them (10,17-20). That power is only a means, and its purpose is not to provide curiosity seekers like Herod with some empty pleasure (23,8) but to bring just men to the praise of God (13,17) and to attract sinners to the Savior, disposing them to receive Him with joy and to be converted (19,6.9). This conversion is a cause of joy for the disciples, as true brothers (15,32), just as it is for the Father in heaven and the angels (15,7.10.24) and for the good shepherd* whose love has saved His wandering sheep (15, 6; Mt 18,13). But to share in His joy, one must love as He has loved.

2. *The joy of the Spirit, the fruit of the cross.* Jesus, who rejoices that the Father revealed Himself to the humble through Him (Lk 10,21f), gives His life for these little ones, His friends*, to bring them that joy whose source is in His love (Jn 15,9-15). At the same time His enemies display their perverse joy at the foot of His cross (Lk 23,35ff). Jesus goes to the Father through the cross*, and the disciples ought to rejoice if they love Him (Jn 14,28) and understand the purpose of His going, which is to send the Spirit (16,7). Thanks to the gift of the Spirit, they will live with the life of Jesus (14, 16-20); and because they will ask in His name*, they will obtain everything from the Father. Then their sadness* will be changed to joy; and their joy will be perfect and nothing will be able to take it away from them (14,13f; 16,20-24).

But the disciples did not understand that the

passion leads to the resurrection. The passion so demolished their hopes (Lk 24,21) that the joy of the resurrection* seemed unbelievable (24,41). And yet, once the risen one had ascended into heaven, after pointing out to them the fulfillment of the Scriptures and promising them the strength of Spirit (24,44.49; Ac 1,8), they were filled with joy (Lk 24,52f). The coming of the Spirit gave them strength both to speak out (Ac 2,4.11) and to remain steadfast; "they were glad to be judged worthy of suffering for the name" of the Savior to whom they bore witness (5,41; cf 4,12; Lk 24,46ff).

II.   THE JOY OF THE NEW LIFE

The Word of Jesus has produced its fruit. Those who believe in Him have the fullness of His joy (Jn 17,13). The life of the community is one of simplicity and gladness (Ac 2,46), and the preaching of the good news is everywhere a special source of joy (8,8). Baptism fills the faithful with the joy of the Spirit (13,52; cf 8,39; 13,48; 16,34), which makes the apostles sing out even in their worst trials (16,23ff).

1.   *The sources of spiritual joy.* Joy is indeed a fruit* of the Spirit (G 5,22) and a characteristic mark of the kingdom of God (R 14,17). This is not that passing enthusiasm which is aroused by the Word* but quickly destroyed by persecution (cf Mk 4,16). It is that spiritual joy of the faithful who in the time of trial* are an example* to others (1 Th 1,6f) and who, by their joyful spirit of generosity (2 Co 8,2; 9,7), by their perfection* (2 Co 13,9), by their union (Ph 2,2), by their docility (He 13,17), and by their fidelity to the truth* (2 Jn 4; 3 Jn 3f) are now and will be until the day* of the Lord the joy of their apostles (1 Th 2,19f).

That charity by which the faithful are united in the truth (1 Co 13,6) brings them an enduring joy which nourishes their prayer* and their unceasing thanksgiving* (1 Th 5,16; Ph 3,1; 4,4ff). How is it possible to thank the Father for being brought into the kingdom of His beloved Son and not be full of joy (Col 1,11ff)? Diligent prayer is a source of joy because it is enlivened with hope* and because the God of hope answers it by filling the believer with joy (R 12,12; 15,13). Thus Peter bids the believer to bless God with exultation; for his faith*, proven by trial but certain of obtaining salvation, brings him an ineffable joy which is the foretaste of glory (1 P 1,3-9).

2.   *The witness of joy in time of trial.* This joy belongs only to a faith that has been proven. If the disciple is to be glad when the glory of Christ is revealed, his joy must be proportioned to the measure in which he participates in Christ's sufferings* (1 P 4,13). Like his master, he will prefer the cross* to joy in this life (He 12,2); he will joyfully accept having his possessions taken away (He 10,34); and he will consider it the supreme joy to be subjected to all sorts of trials (Jm 1,2). For the apostles, just as for Christ, poverty and persecution* lead to perfect joy.

Paul experienced the joy of the cross during his apostolic ministries. Indeed, it is an element of his witness: though "sorrowful," the servants of God are "ever joyful" (2 Co 6,10). The apostle is filled with a superabundant joy during his trials (2 Co 7,4). With complete lack of concern for himself, he rejoices as long as Christ is preached (Ps 1,17f); and his joy is to suffer for the faithful and for the Church (Col 1,24). He even invites the Philippians to share the joy which is to be his in shedding his blood in the final testimony to the faith (Ph 2,17f).

III.   COMMUNION IN ETERNAL JOY

Trial will come to an end, however, and God will avenge the blood* of His servants by passing judgment upon a Babylonian grown drunk with it. Then there will be joy in heaven (Ap 18, 20; 19,1-4) where the nuptials of the Lamb* will be celebrated, and those who take part in them will rejoice in giving glory to God (19,7ff). This will be the full manifestation of that perfect joy which from now on belongs to the children of God. For the Spirit which has been given to them will bring them into communion with the Father and His Son Jesus Christ (1 Jn 1,2ff; 3,1f.24).

→Anointing I 1—Beatitude—Blessing—Confidence — Console — Drunkenness 3 — Feasts Harvest I, III 1—Laugh 2—Meal—Oil 2—Perfume 1—Persecution II 3—Praise—Rest—Run —Sadness NT 3—Suffering NT III 2—Thanksgiving O; OT 2—Vine—Vintage I—White—Wine.

AR & MFL mjm

JUDGMENT

The expectation of Christ's return as judge of the living and the dead has become part of the

Christian *Credo*. Every man will appear before Him to render an account of his actions. Such a theme is not unusual in the history of religion; Egypt and Greece also were aware of a "judgment of the dead." But the manner in which the NT conceives Christ's judgment on the last day can be understood only in relation to its previous development. The judgment of God was already an article of faith in the OT. History presented many concrete examples of it, and eschatology implied its glorious realization.

OT

The root *šāphaṭ*, though it regularly means to "judge," can have the broader meaning of *šōphēṭ*, i.e., a governor who guides his people (cf Dn 9,12). The *suffetes* of Carthage were such; so also were the judges of Israel from the time of the conquest to that of the kings (cf Jg 2,16). One of the important duties of all the governors is to render just decisions in lawsuits, so that justice* will prevail in society. They must pass the decrees (*mišpāṭ*) which defined the rights of each party and, when needed, re-established right order by condemning offenders. This judicial function—which is expressed by the two roots *šāphaṭ* and *dīn*—was exercised by Moses and the elders who assisted him (Ex 18,13-16), by Samuel (1 S 7,16f; 8,3), by the kings (2 S 15,1-6; 1 K 3,16-28), by some local magistrates, and especially some priests (Dt 16, 18ff; 17,8-13). In practice, despite the regulations laid down, injuries were far from being always redressed, nor were the rights* of each man always respected and justice always exactly observed. But that was the ideal, which is never missing either from the portraits of the King-Messiah (Ps 72,1f; Is 11,3f; Jr 23,5) or from the descriptions of the eschatological people (Is 1, 17.26). The sacred writers are inspired by this human experience when they speak of the judgment of God.

I. THE JUDGMENTS OF GOD IN HISTORY

1. *Faith in the judgment of God* is never put in doubt. Yahweh rules the world, and men in particular. His Word* determines the law and establishes the rules of justice. He "searches the mind and the heart" (Jr 11,20; 17,10), knowing perfectly the just and the sinners. Since He dominates events, He cannot fail to shape them in such a way that in the end the just will escape from their trials and the wicked will be

punished (cf Gn 18,23ff). And so one spontaneously has recourse to Him as to the supreme dispenser of justice and repairer of injuries (Gn 16,5; 31,49; 1 S 24,16; Jr 11,20). In fact this is the main idea of His function as sovereign judge. When one submits one's case to Him by appealing to Him for vengeance*, it is not so much out of vindictiveness as to repair a violated right. Some of the psalms contain appeals to God from just men suffering persecution (Ps 9,20; 26,1; 35,1.24; 43,1, etc.). Sometimes they praise Him because He judges the whole earth (1 S 2,10; Ps 67,5); at other times they urge Him to defend against the injustices of human judges (Ps 82).

2. *History* provides the believer with concrete examples of the divine judgment to which all men and peoples are subject. At the time of the exodus*, God "judged Egypt," which means that He punished the oppressor of Israel whom He wished to set free (Gn 15,14; Ws 11,10). The chastisements of Israel in the desert, as tangible evidence of God's wrath*, are all judicial sentences against an unfaithful people. The annihilation of the Canaanites during the conquest is another example which demonstrated both the severity and the moderation of the divine judgment (Ws 12,10-22). An investigation of past history shows a decision of the divine judge at the root of all the catastrophes which descend upon a sinful race; this is true of the destruction of Sodom (Gn 18,20; 19,13), of the deluge (Gn 6,13), of original sin (Gn 3, 14-19)...Hence, the judgment of God constitutes a permanent threat hung over the head of mankind, not in the world to come but in present history. No sinner can escape.

II. THE ESCHATOLOGICAL JUDGMENT

1. The summons to an ominous judgment and the announcement of its imminent coming form part of the essential *prophetic themes*. God has entered into trial proceedings with His people; He turns them over to His tribunal and pronounces a sentence which He prepares to execute (Is 3,13ff). This idea underlies all the prophecies of punishment (cf Is 1,24f; 5,5f). From the time of Amos on, it transforms the expectation of the day* of Yahweh by adding an element of terror (Am 5,18ff). Israel, the unfaithful spouse, will be judged according to the law applying to adulterers (Ez 16,38; 23,24); her sons will be judged according to their behavior and their works (36,19). If this prospect seems

somber, it must not be forgotten that in executing His judgment God will distinguish between the just and the sinful; His intent in punishing the sinful is to deliver the just (Ez 34,17-22). And so in His people a remnant* of the just men will escape the judgment. Moreover, God's judgments will not be directed solely toward Israel; all peoples are subject to them, as is seen in Amos' strictly judicial style (Am 1,3—2,3) which can be found even in Ezekiel (Ez 25,1-17). Jeremiah depicts the broad outlines of this judgment of the nations* (Jr 25,30-38). In the background of the prophecies of future calamities lies the expectation of historical events which will signify, on the level of experience, God's revulsion toward sin*. The most important of these will be the destruction of Jerusalem and the dispersion of Israel.

2. Among the post-exilic prophets, whose modes of expression tend toward apocalyptic, the necessary prelude to oracles of salvation* is a prophecy of the *last judgment*, encompassing the sinners of the whole world and all the collective hostilities toward God and His people. God is going to judge the world by fire* (Is 66, 16). He will assemble the nations in the valley of Jehoshaphat ("God-Judge"); this will be the time of the eschatological harvest* and vintage* (Jl 4,12ff). The Book of Daniel describes, in imaginary terms, this judgment which will put a close to time and open the eternal reign of the Son* of Man (Dn 7,9-12.26). The final times extend beyond the earth and history. It is the same in the Book of Wisdom, where the just and unjust appear together to render an account (Ws 4,20—5,23). But only sinners need to fear then, for the just will be protected by God Himself (4,15f; cf 3,1-9); the holy ones of the most high will have a share in the kingdom of the Son of Man (Dn 7,27). Thus God's sentence upon a sinful humanity is not realized solely in those particular judgments which affect individuals and nations during the course of history. History will terminate in a final confrontation which will constitute the judgment *par excellence*, when the day* of Yahweh will come.

3. It is necessary to keep this prophetic perspective in mind when reading the *post-exilic psalms*. Their appeal to the God-Judge frequently seems to be an effort to hasten the hour of the last judgment: "Rise up, O Judge of the earth! Render to the proud their deserts!" (Ps 94,2). The psalmists sing in advance of the glory of this solemn trial (Ps 75,2-11; 96,12f;

98,7ff), certain that God will bring justice to the poor and suffering (Ps 140,13f). And so Israel, victim of impious men and slave of the pagans, awaits the judgment with hope*. Nevertheless, it remains a formidable prospect: "Enter not into judgment with your servant; for in your sight no living man can be innocent!" (Ps 143, 2). Every man is a sinner. How can he contemplate without fear his confrontation with God? Who will be able to escape the judgment, except by the mercy* of God?

NT

At the time of Jesus the expectation of the judgment of God, understood in its eschatological sense, was well established, although the concrete representation of it was by no means uniform and coherent. The opening of the gospel shows John the Baptist appealing to it when he threatens his hearers with the wrath* to come and exhorts them to receive his baptism as a sign of their penitence (Mt 3,7-12 p). The preaching of Jesus and that of the apostles, while closely adhering to this understanding of the judgment, makes some important modifications, since, from the moment of Jesus'* appearance in the world, the final times* are begun. The eschatological judgment is already present, although it is necessary to await the glorious return of Christ to see it accomplished completely.

I. GOSPEL DESCRIPTIONS OF THE JUDGMENT

1. *In the synoptic gospels*, Jesus frequently refers in the course of His preaching to the judgment on the last day. At that time all men must give an account of their lives (cf Mt 25, 14-30). A severe condemnation awaits the hypocritical scribes (Mk 12,40 p), the cities around the sea of Galilee which have not listened to Jesus' preaching (Mt 11,20-24), the unbelieving generation* which was not converted at the sound of His voice (12,39-42), and the cities that will not receive His representatives (10,14f). The judgment of Sodom and Gomorrah will be nothing in comparison with theirs; they will suffer the judgment of Gehenna (23,33). These threats set in relief the principal motive of God's judgment, viz., the attitude of men toward the gospel. Man's attitude toward his neighbor will count just as much. In the Mosaic Law, every murderer was subject to human judgment; according to the law of the gospel, one can be

guilty of far less than murder and still be in danger of hell (Mt 5,21f)! Every slanderous word must be accounted for (12,34-38). Everyone will be judged according to the way he has judged his neighbor (7,1-5). The description of the solemn sessions in which the Son of Man is the dispenser of justice (25,31-46) shows men welcomed into the kingdom* or delivered over to eternal punishment according to the love or indifference which they have shown for one another.

Still there is one crime which, more than all the rest, calls down the divine judgment. This crime, in which human unbelief* reached the summit of its malice in a sham display of legal judgment, is Jesus' trial and condemnation to death (Mk 14,63 p; cf Lk 24,20; Ac 13,28). During this unjust trial Jesus commended Himself to Him who judges justly (1 P 2,23), and in raising Him to life again God restored what was rightfully His. But the execution of that unjust sentence has brought with it God's sentence against a sinful mankind. It is indicative that in Matthew's account the setting of Jesus' death agrees with the traditional description of the judgment in OT eschatology (Mt 27,45.51ff). The death of Jesus, therefore, is the moment of judgment upon the world. Subsequent history, even to the last day, will do no more than make that judgment manifest. According to the testimony of Jesus Himself, the judgment will affect first of all "those who are in Judea," the leaders in guilt (24,15ff p). But that will only be a prelude and a sign of the final coming of the Son of Man as judge (24,29ff). He who was condemned, the victim of the world's sin, will Himself pronounce a striking condemnation of the sinful world.

2. *The gospel of John* develops this theology by an insistence on the presence of judgment at the very heart of history, i.e., during the time of Jesus. John is not unaware of the fact that the Father has established Jesus, the Son of Man, as judge on the last day (Jn 5,26-30). But really the judgment is present from the moment the Father sends the Son into the world*. He is not sent to judge the world; on the contrary, He comes to save it (3,17; cf 8,15f). But according to each one's attitude toward Jesus, the judgment is immediately present. He who believes will not be judged; he who does not believe is already judged because he has refused the light* (3,18ff). The judgment, then, is not so much a divine sentence as a revelation of the secret of human hearts. Those whose works* are evil prefer darkness to the light (3,19f);

God needs only allow these self-sufficient men, who boast of their clear vision, to blind themselves. But Jesus comes to heal the eyes of the others (9,39) so that acting in the truth* they might come to the light (3,21). The last judgment will openly reveal this division already present in human hearts.

John is no less attentive to the meaning of the trial and death of Jesus. In his account, the trial is accorded as much space as the ministry itself. Jesus strives in vain to bring the Jews*, who are the instruments of Satan and the evil world, to "judge with justice" (7,24). Indeed, He will be delivered to Pilate to be condemned to death (19,12-16). But the death of Jesus will signal the judgment of the world and Satan's defeat (12,31), as though the elevation on the cross anticipated in some way the glorious return of the Son* of Man. Beginning with His death, He will be able to send the Spirit to His faithful ones, and the Paraclete will permanently confound the world by bearing witness to the fact that the world's prince has already been judged, that is, condemned (16,8.11). This is the way in which the eschatological judgment foretold by the prophets is realized. Since the time of Christ the judgment is an accomplished fact, continually present, of which there is awaited only the final consummation.

II. THE JUDGMENT IN APOSTOLIC PREACHING

1. All the evidence of the apostolic preaching as found in the discourses from Acts to the Apocalypse concurs in giving an essential place to the proclamation of the judgment with its summons to conversion. God has set a day* for the judgment of the world through Christ, whom He has raised from the dead (Ac 17,31; cf 24,25; 1 P 4,5; He 6,2). Even after conversion, the constant imminence of this judgment (Jm 5,9: "The judge is at the door") dictates a proper attitude, for the judgment will begin with the house of God before being extended to evildoers (1 P 4,17), and God will judge each one according to his works and without respect for persons (1 P 1,17; cf R 2,6). This is a fearful prospect which ought to make sinners tremble (He 10,27-31; cf R 12,19)! Fornicators and adulterers will be subjected to a severe judgment (He 13,4), as will those who have refused to believe and have sided with evil (2 Th 2,12), the impious, false teachers, and even the fallen angels (2 P 2,4-10), the wicked "superintendents" (1 Tm 3,6) and unfaithful widows who

have not remained in their widowed state (5,12). On that day of wrath* the just judgment of God will be revealed (R 2,5). It will be impossible to flee (2,3) because God will judge even the hidden actions of men (2,16; 1 Co 4,4). Christ is the one who will then be the judge of the living and the dead (2 Tm 4,1; cf R 2,16; Ap 19,11). The Apocalypse paints a terrifying picture of the final judgment (Ap 20,12f; cf 11,18; 16,5...), of which an historical prelude is found in the judgment of Babylon*, the enemy city of God (14,8; 17,1; 18,2—24). In responding to the pleas of the martyrs* to judge their cause (6,9f; 18,20), God will take vengeance on Babylon for the blood of His servants (19,2). Finally, at the end of time, all men will be subjected to fire* to prove the value of their works (1 Co 4,5; 2 P 3,7). And what will be the norm for that examination? For those who claim to know it, the norm will be the Mosaic Law (R 2,12); those who have not known the Law of Moses will be judged by the natural law (2,14f); but those who have accepted the gospel will be judged by the law of liberty (Jm 2,12). But ill fortune awaits him who shall have judged his neighbor (R 2,1ff), for he will be judged with the same severity with which he judged others (14,10ff; Jm 2,13; 4,11ff; 5,12)!

2. Allowance must be made for imagery in these descriptions of the last judgment. But the most important question is *who can escape the judgment* if it is as depicted. Who will be saved? In effect, history reveals the wrath* of God as directed against all mankind; no one is innocent before Him (R 3,10-20; cf 1,18). Since the day that sin entered the world through the fall of the first man, all men have been judged worthy of condemnation (5,16.18). No one can escape by his own merits. But when Jesus, the Son of God become flesh, died as a result of our sins, God condemned the sin of the flesh to free us from its yoke (8,3). Now is the justice* of God revealed, not the justice which punishes, but that which brings justification* and salvation* (3,21). All men deserve judgment, but all are gratuitously justified if only they believe in Jesus Christ (3,24ff). The faithful are no longer condemned (8,1). If they are justified by God, who will condemn them (8,34)? In the old Law the ministry of Moses was one of condemnation, but the ministry of the servants of the gospel is one of grace* (2 Co 3,9) and reconciliation* (5,19ff). Our confidence in the day of judgment (1 Jn 4,17) comes from God's love for us already manifested in Christ, so that we have nothing more to fear. The threat of judgment now weighs only upon evil men. Jesus has come to deliver us from judgment.

→Babel/Babylon 2.5.6—Baptism II, IV 1—Calamity 1—Conscience—Curse I, V—Day of the Lord—Egypt 2—Fear of God III, IV—Fire —Flood—Hardness of Heart I 2 a—Harvest III —Hour 1—Justice—Justification I—Kingdom OT III—Nations OT III 1; NT III 2 a—Paraclete 3—Prophet OT IV 1—Punishments— Repentance/Conversion NT I, IV 2—Reward—Rights/Laws OT 1—Shame—Son of Man—Time OT III 1 — Trial — Vintage 2 — Visit —War OT III 2, IV 2; NT III 1—Word of God NT I 2, II 2, III 2—Works NT I 3—World OT III 1; NT III 3—Wrath *B* NT I 1,2, II 1.

JCo & PG mjm

JUSTICE

The word *justice* calls to mind a juridical order in which a judge dispenses justice by enforcing observance of custom or law*. The moral notion of justice is broader, extending itself to the fact that justice gives everyone his due, even though this due is not fixed by custom or law. The natural-law obligation of justice is based on an equality of exchange or distribution. In the religious context of man's relations with God, the vocabulary associated with justice finds only limited applications in modern languages. It is in current usage, of course, to call upon God as the just judge and to speak of judgment* as the final confrontation between man and God. But, in comparison with biblical language, modern religious usage of words pertaining to justice seems extremely restricted. Although close in meaning to several other terms (rectitude, holiness, uprightness, perfection, etc.), the word *justice* is central to a quite limited set of words, such as just, justify, justification* (hb. *ṣdq*; gr *dikaios*).

In one of the main biblical themes, justice is the familiar moral virtue with its scope so enlarged as to extend to the total observance of all God's commandments, but which is always conceived as entitling man to a just return before God. Correlatively, God demonstrates His justice in that He is a model of integrity; first of all, in His judicial function of guiding the people and each individual person; and then as the God of retribution, either punishing or rewarding according to one's works. This concept of justice, from the viewpoint of the judgment*, is treated in section *A* below.

Another biblical theme, or perhaps a more profound view of the order which God intends to produce in His creation, gives justice an extended meaning and a more immediately religious value. Human integrity is never merely the reflection or product of God's supreme sense of proportion or the wonderful delicacy with which He manages the universe and fills His creatures. The justice of God, which man attains through faith*, ultimately coincides with His mercy*; and, like the divine mercy, designates at times a divine attribute, at other times the concrete gifts of salvation* which this mercy dispenses. This extension of the ordinary meaning of justice is certainly perceptible in English translations of the Bible, but this hieratic English does not extend beyond the technical language of theology. Upon reading R 3,25, does even the educated Christian suspect that the justice which God revealed in Jesus Christ is precisely His salvific justice, i.e., His merciful fidelity? Section B will present the specifically biblical concept of justice from the perspective of mercy*.

A. JUSTICE AND JUDGMENT

I. HUMAN JUSTICE

OT

1. *Civil justice.* The ancient legislation of Israel already required judges to show integrity in the performance of their duties (Dt 1,16; 16,18.20; Lv 19,15.36). Similarly, the earliest proverbs praise the justice of the king (Pr 16, 13; 25,5). Some analogous texts speak of the "just man" as the claimant (Ex 23,6-8), or even at times as the righteous judge (Dt 16,19), who must justify the innocent person by acquitting him or restoring his rights (Dt 25,1; Pr 17,15).

The pre-exilic prophets frequently and forcefully denounce the injustice perpetrated by judges and kings in their oppression of the poor*, and they foretell evil in payment for such disorders (Am 5,7; 6,12; Is 5,7.23; Jr 22,13.15). They force a consideration of the moral and religious dimensions of injustice; what had been viewed merely as a violation of rules or customs now becomes an insult to the holiness of a personal God. This is why injustice carries with it far more than the customary sanctions; it entails a punishment prepared by God Himself. The just man of the prophetic reproaches is again the claimant, but he is almost always presented in the concrete as one poor* and oppressed (Am 2,6; 5,12; Is 5,23; 29,21).

The prophets frequently add positive exhortation to their reproaches to "do what is right and just" (Ho 10,12; Jr 23,3f). Knowing the weakness of human justice, they look above all to the future Messiah* as the righteous prince, who will administer a faultless justice (Is 9,6; 11,4f; Jr 23,5; cf Ps 45,4f; 7f; 72,1ff.7).

2. *Justice as fidelity to the Law.* Prior to the exile, justice signified complete observance of the divine precepts, i.e., conduct in conformity with the Law*. This is seen in a large number of proverbs (Pr 11,4ff.19; 12,28), in several narrative accounts (Gn 18,17ff), and in Ezekiel (Ez 3,16-21; 18,5-24). In the same context, the just man is the pious man, the irreproachable servant*, the friend of God (Pr 12,10; *passim*; Gn 7,1; 18,23-32; Ez 18,5-26). After the exile this pietistic concept of justice is most evident in the lamentations (Ps 18,21.25; 119,121) and hymns (Ps 15,1f; 24,3f; 140,14).

3. *Justice as reward.* Conduct in conformity to the Law is a source of merit and prosperity. The word *justice*, which describes this conduct, underwent a semantic evolution prior to the exile and came to signify also the various rewards for justice. Thus an act of kindness becomes justice in the eyes of Yahweh, which could almost be translated "merit" (Dt 24,13; cf 6,24f). In Pr 21,21, "he who follows justice and mercy shall find life, justice and glory," the last three words here being synonymous. In Ps 24,3ff, the justice which one receives from God is the divine blessing in reward for devoted service of the pilgrim (cf Ps 112,1.3.9; 37,6).

4. *Justice, wisdom, and goodness.* In the final books of the OT are found, with some new nuances, all the traditional themes of the earlier books. To the notion of strict justice, which ought to govern man's dealings with his fellows (Jb 8,3; 35,8; Qo 5,7; Si 38,33), a new aspect is added in Ws 1,1.15 where justice is wisdom* put into practice. Greek influence is evident in Ws 8,7, where *dikaiosynē* has the meaning of strict justice and where wisdom teaches temperance, prudence, justice, and fortitude, the four classical cardinal virtues.

In certain late texts, justice takes on the meaning of almsgiving*: "Water quenches a flaming fire, and almsgiving atones for sins" (Si 3,30; Tb 12,8f; 14,9ff). The reason for this semantic evolution can be found in the Semitic view of justice, where it is not so much a passive attitude of impartiality as it is a passionate commitment of a judge to the cause of the party in the right. It is this positive commitment which determines in each case whether there shall be condemnation or deliverance, and not a neutral and ambivalent act of "rendering justice." In accord with this view of justice, the just man* is kind and charitable (Tb 7,6; 9,6; 14,9), and "it is proper for the just man to be humane" (Ws 12,19).

NT

1. *Jesus.* The exhortation to a juridical type of justice is not central to Jesus' message. The gospel does not lay down regulations regarding the *duties of justice*, it makes no insistent appeal to an oppressed group, nor does it present the Messiah as the righteous judge. There are good reasons for this silence: the codes of the OT, expressions of God's will, were also the charter of a society. In Jesus' time, justice is exercised by the Romans. Jesus did not set Himself up as a social reformer or national Messiah. The most serious fault of His contemporaries is no longer social injustice, but the more specifically religious vice of formalism and hypocrisy. Jesus' denunciation of pharisaism corresponds to the prophets' denunciations of injustice. Jesus must have exhorted the men of His time to the practice of "ordinary" justice, but little trace of this remains (Mt 23, 23: the judgment*, *krisis*, signifies strict justice).

In Jesus' manner of speaking, justice preserves its biblical meaning of *fidelity to the Law*. Although this is not the central point of His message, Jesus does not hesitate to define the moral life as true justice, as spiritual obedience to God's commandments. It is possible to discern here two principal lines of thought. On the one hand, there is the condemnation of the false justice of the Pharisees; Jesus denounces, even more than the great prophets did, the hypocritical observance of a human and haughty religion (Mt 23). On the other hand, His inaugural discourse defines the true justice of His disciples (Mt 5,17-48; 6,1-18). And so, the life of the disciple, freed from a narrow and literal interpretation of the precepts, still remains a life of justice, i.e., of fidelity to the laws which, promulgated anew by Jesus, recapture the Mosaic spirit, the true and perfect will of God.

2. *The apostolic Church. Justice in the strict sense* is not one of the preoccupations of early Christianity. The new Church is less like the community of Israel than even the world of the gospels was. The Church's problems are Jewish incredulity and pagan idolatry rather than questions of social justice. Nevertheless, when occasion offers, concern for justice remains a vital force (1 Tm 6,11; 2 Tm 2,22).

The conception of *justice as holiness* is also found in the early Church. Fidelity to the Law on the part of Joseph (Mt 1,19) and Simeon (Lk 2,25) disposes them for the Messianic revelation (cf Mt 13,17). When Matthew writes that Jesus, at His baptism, "fulfilled all justice," he appears to proclaim a major theme of his gospel; viz., that Jesus brings to culmination the ancient justice, which is the religion of the Law* (Mt 3,15). Matthew's version of the beatitudes* reveals in Christianity a renewed form of Jewish piety (5,6.10); the justice which one must desire and for which one must suffer seems to be fidelity to a rule of life which remains a law. Finally there is one peculiarity of vocabulary, already seen in the OT, that appears again in the apostolic letters, where justice sometimes means the *reward* for observances. Justice is seen as a fruit (Ph 1,11; He 12,11; Jm 3,18) and a crown (2 Tm 4,8); it is like the substance of eternal life (2 P 3,13).

II.   DIVINE JUSTICE

OT

The ancient warrior and religious poems praise divine justice in its concrete setting, either as God's punitive judgment against Israel's enemies (Dt 33,21) or (especially in the plural form: justices) His deliverance of the chosen people (Jg 5,11; 1 S 12,6f; Mi 6,3f). The prophets take up this form of expression and give it new depth. God sends His chastisements—His justice—not so much against the enemies of the people as against sinners, even Israelites (Am 5,24; Is 5,16; 10,22...). On the other hand, God's justice can also be a favorable judgment*, the deliverance of the claimant (Jr 9,23; 11,20; 23,6), from which comes the corresponding usage of *justify* (1 K 8,32). The same twofold meaning is found in the lamentations. There the author sometimes begs God, in His fidelity, to deliver him (Ps 71,1f); at other times he confesses* that God, in punishing him, has revealed His incorruptible justice (Dn 9,6f; Ba 1,15; 2,6) and is shown to be just Himself (Ezr 9,15; Ne 9,32f; Dn 9,14). The hymns, as is natural, especially praise the favorable aspect of justice (Ps

7,18; 9,5; 96,13); the just God is the merciful God (Ps 116,5f; 129,3f).

NT

In contradistinction to the prophets and psalmists, the NT says little about the interventions of God's judicial justice in the life of the believer or of the community. Rather, it directs our attention to the last judgment. It is understood that in this supreme judgment God shows Himself just, but the vocabulary of justice occurs only rarely. This is because Jesus, without excluding the traditional vocabulary of the last judgment (Mt 12,36f.41f), reveals salvation* as a divine gift bestowed according to one's faith* and humility*.

Though the apostolic Church preserves this latter thought (Jn 16,8.10f; 2 Tm 4,8), still it is found to insist on the severity of God's judgment. It is possible to detect a return to the language of a morality of works* (Mt 7,13f; 13,49; 22,14; Lk 13,24) and a juxtaposition of the theme of the judgment* with the gospel message of salvation through faith. Further, some traces of this irreducible duality are found in St. Paul himself. Beyond doubt, he presents the doctrine of grace* and faith* in all its fullness, but even Paul continues to speak in Jewish terms of the just judgment of God, who will reward each one according to his works (2 Th 1,5f; R 2,5).

B. JUSTICE AND MERCY

I. THE JUSTICE OF MAN

OT

The very foundation of legalism is to identify justice and observance of the Law, and this identification is found long before the exile. The Law is the norm of the moral life; the justice of the faithful Jew is his title to prosperity and glory. Hence, it is all the more important to point out certain passages which declare this legalistic justice vain and ineffective. Some ancient texts speak of the conquest of the promised land in terms which foreshadow the Pauline conception of salvation* through faith*: "Say not in thy heart...justice has caused Yahweh to give me possession of this land..." (Dt 9,4ff).

It is in this same light that the famous passage of Genesis is to be explained: "(Abraham) believed Yahweh and it was credited to

him as justice" (Gn 15,6). Whether justice is understood in this passage as conduct pleasing to God or, according to the evolution of the word indicated above, as reward and something almost like merit, in both cases faith* is extolled as the way to please God. The essential link between justice and surrender to God prevents us, as St. Paul well emphasized, from conceiving justice in a legalistic fashion. The words of Genesis are cited in 1 M 2,52, and their echo is heard in 1 M 14,35 where justice is Simon's fidelity to his people.

Finally, it is possible to see in Job's dramatic questions and in the "inspired pessimism" of Qoheleth, which cast doubt on the doctrine of retribution, a preparation for a higher revelation. "It is the just man who perishes in his justice..." (Qo 7,15; cf 8,14; 9,1f). "How will man appear just before God?" (Jb 9,2; cf 4,17; 9.20...).

NT

1. *The message of Jesus* attributes the greatest importance to trust in God rather than to observance of the commandments; but, without giving a new turn to the vocabulary of justice, Jesus seems to have taken over a new meaning for such terms as *poor**, *humble, sinner*. Nevertheless, it is possible that Jesus called faith the true justice, designated the sinner as the truly just man (cf Mt 9,13), and defined justification* as the pardon* promised to the humble (Lk 18,14).

2. *Paul*, prior to his conversion, pursued the justice of the Law (Ph 3,6). Man acquires this justice in proportion to his good works* (R 9, 30f; 10,3); as such, it can be called a justice coming from the Law* (R 10,5; G 2,21; Ph 3,9) or from works* (R 3,20; 4,2; G 2,16). Paul did not make a complete break from these ideas at the outset of his conversion. Nevertheless, the dispute at Antioch marks a decisive turning point; In G 2,11-21, Paul opposes the two systems of justification* and gives the term *to be justified* its Christian meaning. "We believe in Christ Jesus, that we may be justified by the faith of Christ and not by the works of the Law" (G 2,16). From this point on, Paul's notion of justice completely changes. Man henceforth believes in God, and God "justifies" him, i.e., assures him of salvation through faith and union with Christ. Hereafter the word *justice* and its derivatives will designate the Christian realities of salvation*. Indeed, the assurance of God's favor is had in a tangible

way; the Spirit* (G 3,2) and life* (2,19ff) both guarantee justification and constitute it at the same time. The center of interest changes from the last judgment to justice viewed as a present state of man, but which still remains eschatological in its expectation of the rewards of heaven.

II. DIVINE JUSTICE

OT

In the exercise of His judicial justice, God is most fresuently seen as delivering the oppressed. In itself this liberation* remains within the framework of judicial justice, but viewed as a divine favor it opens up a richer conception of God's justice. On the other hand, the OT has foreseen that man cannot win divine favor by his own justice and that faith is of greater value for finding acceptance with Yahweh. This point of view provides another reason for conceiving God's justice as a witness to His mercy* and as a means of approaching the mystery of justification.

This concept of justice develops very quickly. According to the Deuteronomist, God is not content to do justice to the orphan; He loves the stranger* and gives him food and clothing (Dt 10,18). In Ho 2,21, God promises to betroth Himself to His people "in justice and judgment, in mercy and tenderness." The author of the lamentations, in his appeal to God's justice, expects much more than a just sentence: "In your justice grant me life*" (Ps 119,40.106. 123; 36,11); moreover, he hopes for that justice which is the forgiveness of sin (Ps 51,16; Dn 9, 16). But justification of the sinner is a paradoxical act and even contrary to judicial teaching, where justification of the guilty party is the greatest error. An analogous paradox is seen in many of the psalms, wherein God manifests His justice by His gratuitous and occasionally universal favors, which completely surpass all that man has a right to expect (Ps 65,6; 111,3; 145,7.17; cf Ne 9,8).

In Is 40—66, the expression *justice of God* takes on a prominence and importance which foreshadows the great theme of St. Paul. In these chapters of Isaiah God's justice is sometimes the salvation* of the captive people, at other times the divine attribute of mercy* and of fidelity. This salvation is a gift* far surpassing the idea of deliverance or reward; it includes the bestowal of heavenly blessings such as peace* and glory* upon a people whose only

"merit" is to be the chosen people of Yahweh (Is 45,22ff; 46,12f; 51,1ff.5.8; 54,17; 56,1; 59,9); the whole tribe of Israel will be justified, i.e., glorified (45,25). Thus does God show Himself just in the sense that He manifests His mercy and graciously fulfills His promises* (41,2.10; 42,6.21; 45,13.19ff).

NT

1. *Jesus.* When Jesus wants to give expression to the revelation of divine salvation which His coming into the world brought about, He does not speak, as did Deutero-Isaiah or St. Paul, of a manifestation of God's justice, but He does use the equivalent term "kingdom* of heaven." Non-Pauline Christianity, which adhered closely to the language of Jesus, did not use the phrase "justice of God" to express the actual revelation of divine grace* in Jesus Christ.

2. *St. Paul.* On the other hand St. Paul develops the idea of God's justice with great clarity. This development does not coincide, however, with the beginning of his ministry; his epistles to the Thessalonians and Galatians make no mention of it. In conformity with primitive preaching, Paul's earliest message of salvation is strictly eschatological (1 Th 1,10). The emphasis in these places is placed more on deliverance than on wrath*, but this deliverance is merely the favorable aspect of judgment and it remains within the framework of God's judicial justice. Nevertheless, the controversies with the Jewish Christians led Paul to define true justice as a grace bestowed in the present time. In his epistle to the Romans, Paul is led to define Christian life as the justice of God, an expression which has the advantage of preserving some of the eschatological meaning originally associated with *salvation* and *kingdom*, and at the same time of emphasizing, by opposition to the justice of works, the fact that it is a present grace*. The justice of God, therefore, is divine grace, in itself eschatological and even apocalyptic, but really and presently anticipated in the Christian life. Paul will say that the justice of God comes down from heaven (R 1,17; 3,21f; 10,3) and that it comes to transform mankind. It is a blessing belonging essentially to God, one which becomes ours without ceasing to be from heaven.

At the same time Paul implies that this communication of justice is rooted in God's fidelity to His Covenant*, or, in a word, in His mercy*. And sometimes this idea is even stated explicitly, giving rise to the second Pauline meaning of "justice of God" as the divine attribute of mercy. This meaning appears in R 3,25f: "God reveals His justice at the present time, so that He is just Himself and justifies him who believes in Jesus." In R 10,3, the two meanings of justice are brought together: "Ignorant of the justice of God (the grace bestowed on Christians) and seeking to establish their own, they have not submitted to the justice of God (mercy)."

Thus the biblical message about the nature of justice presents a twofold aspect. In view of the divine judgment which works itself out in the course of history, man ought to "do justice." This duty is understood in an ever more interior manner, terminating in an "adoration in spirit and in truth." On the other hand, considering the plan of salvation, man sees that he cannot acquire this justice by his own works, but that he receives it as a gift of grace. God's justice cannot be reduced to an act of judgment; above all else it is a merciful fidelity to His salvific will. It creates in man that justice which it demands from him.

→Conscience 1—Fasting 2—Grace II 1.3—Holy OT IV 2—Judgment—Justification—Law *B* III 5; *C* III 2—Paraclete 3—Peace—Perfection OT —Persecution—Piety—Poor OT II; NT III 3—Pride OT 3—Punishments 3—Reward—Rights/ Laws OT 2.3—Salvation OT I 2—Seek I, II—Trial—Truth OT 2; NT 1—Vengeance—Victory O 3 b; NT 2—Violence I, III 1, IV 2.3—Virtues & Vices 1—Works OT II 3—Wrath *B* NT II 1.

ADes mjm

JUSTIFICATION

Normally a person is justified when he makes his own cause triumph over that of an opponent and makes the justice of his cause known. It is not necessary that the encounter take place before a court of law or that the opponent be an enemy*. The scope of justice extends far beyond that of law or even custom. Every human relation entails its own justice* and its own norm. When one respects that special justice and norm, he treats everyone he deals with in the precise manner proper to each. This is determined not only by externals, position in society and deeds accomplished, but also according to the more profound merit of each one's very being, his talents and his needs. A person is just when he treats everyone in the way suited to each. A jerson is justified in a trial* or dispute when he demonstrates not so much his inno-

cence as the propriety of his conduct; in this way he makes his justice known.

I. BEING JUSTIFIED BEFORE GOD

The desire to appear justified before God and to think one can win out against him seems unthinkable. Far from even daring to risk such a thing, one dreads that God Himself will initiate proceedings whose outcome is doomed from the start: "Enter not into judgment with your servant, for in your sight no man living shall be justified" (Ps 143,2); for "if you remember iniquities...who shall withstand it?" (Ps 130,3). The wise course is to confess one's sins and in silence allow God to manifest His justice: "You are just in your pronouncements" (Ps 51,6).

It is not strange that man can never be justified in God's sight. The wonder is rather that he can think himself justified, and that the Bible does not seem to find it preposterous. Job was well aware that "man cannot be right against God" (Jb 9,2), that "God is not a man...," and that it is "impossible to debate with Him and to appear together in a court of justice" (9,32). Still he cannot forego "proceeding with his case, conscious of his right" (13,18f). Since God is just, Job has nothing to fear in a confrontation in which "God will face a just man for an adversary" and in which Job "shall bring his cause to victory" (23,7). In fact, God Himself, in reducing Job to silence and in convincing him of folly and inconstancy (38,2; 40,4), ultimately does not say he is wrong. Job discovers in the faith* of Abraham* an act by which, without taking advantage of God, Abraham corresponds exactly to everything expected of him (Gn 15,6).

The OT, therefore, makes man's justification before God both an unattainable supposition and a state for which man has been made. God is just, which means that He is never in the wrong and that no one can argue with Him (Is 29,16; Jr 12,1). But perhaps it also means that, knowing the clay from which He has fashioned us and the union for which He has created us, even in His justice and out of regard for His creatures, God does not refuse to make it possible for them to be just in His sight, as they ought to be.

II. JUSTIFIED IN JESUS CHRIST

1. *The powerlessness of the Law.* Jewish legalism, in which the Pharisee* Paul was raised, believed that if it did not actually profess that

view which may have been hinted at in the OT, at least it ought to incline toward it; viz., that the Law* is the expression of God's will* and is within man's capabilities (cf Dt 30,11 —indeed, within man's intellectual capabilities: understandable and easy to know) and that, as a result, it is enough for man to observe the Law perfectly to be able to present himself before God and be justified. The Pharisee's error does not lie in thinking that he can treat God according to justice, as He deserves to be treated; his error lies in his belief that he can achieve this by his own powers and in his desire to find in himself the disposition which attains to God and which God expects of us. This essential perversion of heart in which one wants "the right to be glorified in God's sight" (R 3,27) comes from a fundamental error in interpreting the covenant*. This misinterpretation separates the Law* from the promises*; it sees in the Law a means of being justified before God, and it forgets that fidelity to the Law can itself only be the work* of God, the accomplishment of His Word*.

2. *Jesus Christ.* Now Jesus Christ was truly "the just one" (Ac 3,14). In God's sight He appeared exactly as God wanted, the Servant* in whom the Father could finally be pleased (Is 42,1; Mt 3,17). He knew right to the end how to "accomplish all justice" (Mt 3,15) and He died so that God would be glorified (Jn 17,1.4); i.e., so that God would appear before the world in all His grandeur and dignity, worthy of all sacrifice and lovable above all else (Jn 14,31). In His death, in which He appeared as an outcast (Is 53,4; Mt 27,43-46), Jesus was truly justified; and God acknowledged His completed work (Jn 16,10) by raising Him up and putting Him in full possession of the Holy Spirit (1 Tm 3,16).

3. *Grace.* But the purpose of Jesus' resurrection* is "our justification" (R 4,25). That which the Law was unable to accomplish and which it categorically excluded, the grace of God has given us in Christ's redemption* (R 3,23f). This gift of justification is no mere pretense, no condescension on God's part whereby, in view of Christ's perfect justification, He is willing to consider us as though we were justified because of our association with His Son. When Paul wanted to indicate a simple verdict of pardon and acquittal, he did not use a word connected with justification, for that would signify the recognition of a positive legal right and the confirmation of the correctness of one's position. Paul

did not attribute God's action in justifying us to His justice, but to His pure mercy*. The truth is that God, in Christ, "has willed to show His justice...to be just Himself and to justify him who puts faith in Jesus" (R 3,26).

4. *Children of God.* Clearly God manifests His justice first of all toward His Son* who was "delivered for our sins" (R 4,25) and who, by His obedience* and justice, has merited for many justification and justice (R 5,16-19). But the fact that God gave Jesus Christ the power to merit our justification does not mean that God, out of regard for His Son, only consents to treat us as though we were just. It means that in Jesus Christ He makes it possible for us to have the precise disposition that He expects from us, to treat Him as He deserves and to render effectively that justice to which He is entitled—in a word to be truly justified before Him. Thus God is just toward Himself, yielding none of the honor and glory* to which He has a right; and He is just toward His creatures whom He allows, purely through His grace which penetrates to their very depths, to be justly disposed toward Him and to treat Him for what He is, their Father*, that is to say, to be truly His children (R 8,14-17; 1 Jn 3,1f).

III. JUSTIFIED BY FAITH

The regeneration by which God justifies us is no magical transformation. It truly occurs within us in our movements and reactions by ridding us of our attachments to ourselves and our own glory (cf Jn 7,18) and by binding us to Jesus Christ in faith* (R 3,28ff). To believe in Jesus Christ is in fact to know Him whom the Father has sent. By this faith one cherishes His words, risks everything for His kingdom, "accepts the loss of everything...for the sake of gaining Christ," sacrifices "(one's) own justice which is from the Law" to receive "the justice ...which comes from God and is based on faith" (Ph 3,8f). One who believes in Jesus Christ "knows the love which God has for us" and confesses that "God is love*" (1 Jn 4,16). The believer has arrived at the heart of the mystery* of Christ; He is just.

→Faith NT III 2—Godless Man NT 2—Grace VI—Judgment OT II 3; NT II 2—Justice— Law *B* III 5; *C* III 1—Pardon II 2—Predestine 2—Reconciliation I 2—Sin III 3, IV 3 a c— Trial—Works NT II 1.

JG mjm

K

KING

In the ancient Orient, the institution of kingship was always intimately connected with the mythical understanding of royalty as divine, an idea common to the diverse civilizations of the period. Thus, as a sacred institution kingship belongs, to a greater or lesser extent, in the sphere of things divine. In Egypt the reigning Pharaoh was taken for an incarnation of Horus. All his acts were, therefore, divine by nature, and the exercises of cult by right accrued to him. In Babylon, the king was the elect of Marduk and was delegated by him to the rule of the "four regions," that is to say of the entire earth; civil and military head, he is also high priest of the city. In both these cases the kingship made of its possessor a born mediator* between the gods and men. Not only was it his duty to assure these latter of justice, victory, and peace; it was through his mediation that all divine blessings came, including the fertility of the earth and the fecundity of man and beast. And so, the institution of kingship was of a piece with polytheistic mythologies and cults. In a later era, the Greek and Roman empires took up these ideas in divinizing their sovereigns.

Biblical revelation, in all its originality, steps out of this background. The theme of the kingdom* of God occupies a leading place in both Testaments. The notion of human kingship develops on the basis of Israel's experience, and serves, finally, to define the kingship of Jesus Christ. But this ideology undergoes a radical twofold purification which places it in harmony with the revelation of the one God*. On the second point it is even totally transformed. On the one hand, the kingship as a temporal institution was, from the beginning, detached from the area of things divine; on the other hand, by the time doctrinal development has been completed, the kingship of Christ is of an order other than that of the political world.

OT

Kingship does not belong to the most funda-mental institutions of the people* of God, a confederation of tribes joined by the covenant*. Nevertheless, it existed in Canaan from the time of the patriarchs (Gn 20) and among the neighboring people from the time of the exodus and the judges (Gn 35,31-39; Nm 20,14; 21,21. 33; 22,4; Js 10-11; Jg 4,2; 8,5). But though Israel adopted royal display to apply to its God, it did not draw any implications for its political institutions: Yahweh* reigned over Israel in virtue of the covenant (cf Jg 8,23; 1 S 8,7; Ex 19,6), but no human king incarnated his presence in the midst of his people.

I. THE EXPERIENCE OF KINGSHIP

1. *Institution of the kingship.* In the time of the judges, Abimelech tried to institute a kingship of the Canaanite type at Shechem (Jg 9,1-7); the institution encountered strong ideological opposition (9,8-20) and ran aground miserably (9,22-57). It was in the face of the Philistine peril that the elders of Israel began to desire a king "to judge them and conduct their wars" (1 S 8,19). The institution was an ambiguous one which risked making Israel like the "other nations" (8,5.20); also, one of the accounts of the fact made Samuel's attitude one of opposition (8,6; 10,17ff; 12,12). In conferring anointing* on Saul (9,16f; 10,1) and presiding at his enthronement (10,20-24; 11,12-15), Samuel gave the new institution a thorough religious consecration. But the monarchy was inserted in a larger context whose fundamental traits were always fixed by the covenant pact. Saul was, like the judges, a charismatic leader whom the Spirit* of Yahweh guided (10,6ff) and who conducted a holy war* (11). It was likewise as a charismatic leader of proven value that David succeeded him, first in Judah (2 S 2,1-4), then in Israel (5,1ff). However, with him the monarchy went one step further: the kingdom was politically organized on the model of neighboring states; and above all, the prophecy of Nathan made of the Davidic dynasty a permanent institution of the people of God, a receptacle

of the divine promises (7,5-16) Thenceforth the hope of the people of God attached itself to Davidic royalty, at least in the South of the country (cf Nm 24,17; Gn 48,8-12) where the institution always kept its dynastic form. In the North, on the contrary, religious conditions tended to keep the kingship in its charismatic form; and prophets were to be found raising up kingly vocations (1 K 11,26-40; 2 K 9).

2. *Royal functions.* In Israel, the king does not belong in the area of things divine, as was the case in surrounding civilizations. Like other men, he remained subject to the exigencies of the covenant and the Law, a fact which the prophets do not fail to remind him of on occasion (cf 1 S 13,8-15; 15,10-30; 2 S 12,1-12; 1 K 11,31-39; 21,17-24). However, the king plays a sacred role, and his anointing* must be respected (1 S 24,11; 26,9). From the time of David, the king's position with respect to God gains in precision: God makes the king His adopted son* (2 S 7,14; Ps 2,7; 89,27f), depository of His powers, and virtually established as the head of all the kings of the earth (Ps 89,28; cf 2,8-12; 18,44ff). God promises that He will protect the king if he is faithful. By his victories* over external enemies he will assure the prosperity of his people (cf Ps 20; 21), and victory over domestic enemies shall make justice* reign (Ps 45,4-8; 72,1-7.12ff; Pr 16,12; 25,4f; 29, 4.14). Thus his temporal tasks rejoin the fundamental goal of the covenant and the Law*. Further, as leader of the people of God, he occasionally exercises some of the functions of worship (2 S 6,17f; 1 K 8,14.62f), and this allows mention of a royal priesthood (Ps 110,4). Thus, in a manner, the ideal of the faithful king (Ps 101), just and peaceful, crowns the whole national ideal; the exercise of the kingly power should make this ideal issue in deeds.

3. *Ambiguity in the experience of kingship.* But the historical and prophetical books bring out the ambiguity of the experience of kingship. Insofar as the kings respond to the ideal assigned them, they receive the support of prophets and the praise of the historians: such was the case with David (Ps 78,70; 89,20-24), Asa (1 K 15,11-15), Jehoshaphat (1 K 22,43), Hezekiah (2 K 18,3-7), Josiah (2 K 23,25). But the glory of Solomon is already equivocal (1 K 11,1-13). Finally, bad kings are numerous in Israel (1 K 16,25ff.30-33) as well as in Judah (2 K 16,2ff; 21,1-9). The constant temptation of the Israelite royalty was indeed, especially in the North, that of aligning itself with the example of surrounding pagan monarchies. This took the form not only of imitating their despotism (which 1 S 8, 10-18 denounces) but also of adoption of the idolatry* favored elsewhere by the mythical concept of divine royalty. For this reason, the prophetic movement ceaselessly denounced the abuses of kingship and showed in national calamities the chastisement merited by the kings (cf Is 7,10ff; Jr 21—22; 36—38; 2 K 23,26f). Hosea condemned the very institution of kingship (Ho 8,4). Deuteronomy, in trying to regulate it, sets the monarchs on guard against the imitation of pagan kings (Dt 17,14-20).

4. *Pagan kings.* Holy writ adopts a modified attitude in respect to the pagan kings. As is true of all earthly* authority, they hold their power from God. Elisha even intervenes in the name of God to stir up the revolt of Hazael at Damascus (2 K 8,7-15; cf 1 K 19,15). They can hold providential missions* toward the people of God: God gave Nebuchadnezzar hegemony over all the Orient, including Israel (Jr 27); then He raised up Cyrus to humble Babylon and free the Jews (Is 41,1-4; 45,1-6). But all remain subject to God's claims, and He pronounces His judgments to chastise their sacrilegious arrogance* (Is 14,3-21; Ez 28,1-19) and their blasphemies* (Is 37,21-29). When the hour comes, they also shall bend the knee before his supreme royalty and before the power of His anointed one (Ps 2; 72,9ff).

II. TOWARD THE FUTURE ROYALTY

1. *The prophetic promises.* Judging the experience of kingship from a purely religious point of view, several prophets finally evaluated it as a disaster. Hosea announced its end (Ho 3,4f). Jeremiah decidedly envisaged the humbling of the Davidic dynasty (cf Jr 21—22), to which Isaiah still showed so much attachment. It is in the perspective of the "last times" that the prophets as a whole would have us glimpse the perfect realization of a divine plan manifested by the calling of David and sketched in figure* in some rare successes. In the eighth century, Isaiah turned his eyes toward the future king whose birth he hailed (Is 9,1-6): he would give the people of God joy*, victory*, peace*, and justice*. This scion of Jesse animated by the Spirit of Yahweh would make justice* reign to such an extent (cf 32,1-5) that the land would become an earthly paradise* (11,1-9). Micah professed the same confidence in His coming (Mi 5,1-5). Jeremiah at

the very hour of the dynasty's fall, announced the future reign of the just seed of David (Jr 23, 5f). Ezekiel, for all his profession of the same fundamental faith, marks a turning point. He accords the new David, shepherd* of Israel, only the less brilliant title of prince (Ez 34,23f; 45,7f); going back once more beyond the kingly era, the prophet seeks Israel's ideal in the theocracy of Mosaic times. Similarly placing its hopes in this theocracy (cf Is 52,7), the Book of Consolation likewise does not discount the accomplishment of the promises made to David (Is 55,3; cf Ps 89,35-38).

2. *Awaiting the promises*. The experiment with the kingship ended in 587. It was not, all in all, anything more than a parenthesis in the history of Israel. But it left profound marks on her consciousness. During the exile she suffered the humiliation of the dynasty (Lm 4,20; Ps 89, 39-52) and prayed for its restoration (Ps 80,18). Zorobabel's mission (Ezr 3) gave a moment's hope that this "seed of David" would re-establish the national monarchy (Ze 3,8ff; 6,9-14); but the hope was short lived. Reorganized under a theocratic form, post-exilic Judaism was subject to the authority of pagan kings who liberally protected Israel's autonomy (cf Ezr 7, 1-26) and for whom she offered official prayer (6,10; 1 M 7,33). As the period of national trial stretched longer, eyes turned the more toward the "last times" announced by the prophets. Expectation of the kingdom* of God constituted the central point of eschatological hope. And in this context expectation of the future king always held an important place. The ancient royal psalms were applied to him (Ps 2; 45; 72, 110), and his reign was presented in their light. The image appearing on the horizon was that of a just, victorious, and peaceful king (Ze 9,9f). As for the pagan kings, sometimes they were depicted submissive to his rule and participants in the worship of the true God (cf Is 60,16); sometimes their judgment and condemnation were announced (Is 24,21f) if they should raise themselves against the reign of Yahweh (Dn 7,17-27).

3. *On the threshold of the NT*. The restoration of the monarchy by the Hasmonaean dynasty, just when the apocalyptic current was taking refuge in the expectation of a miraculous intervention by God (cf Dn 2,44f; 12,1), is not in the line of the traditional hope. Though the revolt of Judas was attached to the ideology of the ancient "holy wars*" (cf 1 M 3), the concentration of power in Simon's hands (1 M 14) finally appeared as an innovation. Besides, the Hasmonaean dynasty quickly adopted the customs and methods of government holding sway among the pagan kings. Likewise, the Pharisees* broke with this dynasty out of fidelity to the Davidic royal line from which the Messiah* was destined to come (cf Psalms of Solomon). Again, the Essene movement was opposed to a priesthood* which it considered illegitimate, and awaited the coming of the "two Messiahs of Aaron and Israel" (the high priest and the Davidic king who would be subordinated to him). After the Hasmonaeans, kingly power later passed to the Herodian dynasty acting under Roman control. With the exception of the Sadducees who accommodated themselves to this state of things, the expectation of an eschatological king remained strong in the whole Jewish people. But while this expectation retained its religious objective—the final reign of God—it generally assumed a rather strong political coloring: the kingly Messiah was expected to free Israel from foreign oppression.

NT

The message of the NT centers around the essentially religious theme of the kingdom* of God. The theme of a royal Messiah, rooted in the experience of Israel and founded on the prophetic promises, serves further to define the role of Jesus as human artisan of the kingdom. But in fully taking its place in the history of salvation* the theme is stripped of all its political overtones.

I. JESUS' KINGSHIP DURING HIS EARTHLY LIFE

1. *Was Jesus a king?* During His public ministry, Jesus did not once give way to the Messianic enthusiasm of the multitude so mixed with human hopes and temporal aspirations. He gave no opposition to the authority of the tetrarch Herod, who nevertheless suspected a competitor in Him (Lk 13,31ff; cf 9,7f); nor did He oppose Himself to the authority of the Roman emperor, to whom tribute was due (Mk 12,13-17 p): His mission* is of another order. He does not contradict Nathanael's act of Messianic faith ("You are the king of Israel" Jn 1,49); but He turns His attention toward the parousia of the Son* of Man. When the multitude wanted to take Him and make Him king after the multiplication of the loaves, He stole away (Jn 6,15). Once, at the time of His trium-

phal entry into Jerusalem, He countenanced a public demonstration: appearing in the midst of a humble train conforming to the prediction of Zechariah (Mt 21,5; cf Ze 9,9), He permitted Himself to be acclaimed king of Israel (Lk 19,38; Jn 12,13). But this very success sped the hour of His passion. Finally, as the passion is about to commence, it is in a purely eschatological perspective that He speaks to His own of His kingdom (Lk 22,29f).

2. *The passion and Jesus' kingship.* Jesus' interrogation during His religious trial* bears on His character as Messiah* and Son* of God. On the other hand, in His civil trial before Pilate, His royalty is under question; the evangelists take the opportunity of making the passion its paradoxical revelation. Questioned by Pilate ("Are you the king of the Jews?" Mk 15,2 p; Jn 18,33.37), Jesus does not reject the title (Jn 18,37), but He specifies that His "kingdom* is not of this world" (Jn 18,36), so that He is no competitor of Caesar (cf Lk 23,2). In the blindness of their misbelief, the Jewish authorities came to recognize the exclusive political hegemony of Caesar so as the better to reject the royalty of Jesus (Jn 19,12-15). But His kingship was revealed by the very acts which mocked Him: after the scourging, the soldiers saluted Him as king of the Jews (Mk 15,18 p); the inscription on the cross read: "Jesus of Nazareth, king of the Jews" (Jn 19, 19ff p); the bystanders were intent on deriding this mock royalty (Mt 27,42 p; Lk 23,37); but, seeing His true nature, the good thief prayed that Jesus "remember him when He came into His kingdom" (Lk 23,42). Indeed, Jesus will know a kingly glory, but it will be after His resurrection* and His coming on the last day. Come like the claimant in the parable to receive the kingship, and rejected by His fellow countrymen, He will nevertheless be invested and will return to ask for an account and take vengeance* on His enemies* (Lk 19,12-15.27). Jesus' royalty shines out on the cross if one knows how to see things from the viewpoint of faith: *Vexilla Regis prodeunt, fulget crucis mysterium*, "The standards of the King appear, the mystery of the cross shines out in glory" (Passiontide hymn).

II. THE KINGSHIP OF THE RISEN CHRIST

1. *The present kingship of the Lord.* The risen Christ entered into His kingdom. But it was necessary for Him first to make His witnesses* understand this Messianic reign so different from that of the Jews' expectation. There is no question of His restoring the kingship for the benefit of Israel (Ac 1,6); His kingdom will be established by the preaching of His gospel* (Ac 1,8). Nevertheless, He is king, and the Christian preaching* proclaims this in applying the prophetic writings to Him. He is the king of justice of Ps 45,7 (He 1,8), the priestly king of Ps 110,4 (He 7,1). King He was in a mysterious manner from the beginning of His earthly life, as the evangelists emphasize in recounting His infancy (Lk 1,33; Mt 2,2). But this kingship, "which is not of this world*" (Jn 18,36), and which is not represented by any human monarchy to which Jesus might have delegated His powers, does not in any way rival the kingship of earthly kings. Christians become subjects of the kingdom when God "snatches them from the power of darkness to transfer them to the kingdom of His Son, in whom they have redemption" (Col 1,13). This does not keep them from submitting to the kings of this world and paying them honor (1 P 2,13.17), even if these kings are pagan: such kings are depositaries of authority and it suffices that they do not oppose the spiritual authority of Jesus. Conflict arises when they sometimes raise themselves against Him, fulfilling the prophecy of Ps 2,2. This had been the case in the passion (Ac 4,25ff). It is the case throughout history when these earthly kings, committing fornication with Babylon* (Ap 17,2) and letting her reign over them (17,18), participate in the satanic kingship of the beast* (17, 12); then, drunk with their power, they become persecutors of the Church and her children, as Babylon herself drank her fill of the blood of the martyrs* of Jesus (17,6).

2. *The reign of Christ at the parousia.* The Apocalypse paints a symbolic presentation of the last times in which the final crisis will be initiated by a campaign of all the kings against the Lamb*. Having given their might over to the beast* (Ap 17,13), they will muster at the coming of the great day* (16,14); but the Lamb will conquer them (cf 19,18f), "for He is the king of kings and the Lord of lords" (17,14; 19, 1ff; cf 1,5). His parousia will be a striking manifestation of His kingliness as well as of the kingdom of God (11,15; 2 Tm 4,1): following the prophecy of Is 11,4, the royal son of David will annihilate the Antichrist* by the manifestation of His coming (2 Th 2,9). He will then return the kingdom to His Father*, for, following the text of Ps 110,1, He is to reign "until

God has placed all His enemies under His feet" (1 Co 15,24f). The outcome of the eschatological war* which He will wage as Word of God will be that He shall rule His enemies, according to Ps 2,9, with a rod of iron (Ap 19,15f). Then, sharing His reign (cf 1 Co 15,24), all the martyrs, decapitated because they have refused to adore the beast*, will revive to reign with Him and with God (Ap 20,4ff; cf 5,10). Thus they will share in the eternal reign of the Son* of Man, in keeping with the promise of Dn 7, 22.27. Is this not what Jesus Himself promised the twelve at the last supper: "I will prepare you the kingdom, and you will sit on thrones to judge the twelve tribes of Israel" (Lk 22,29f; cf Ap 7,4-8.15)?

→Anointing III 2—Ascension II o—Authority OT II 1—Calling I—Clothing I 2—David—Election OT I 3 c—Fathers & Father I, III 4—Glory I, III 2—Jesus Christ II 1 c—Kingdom—Lord OT; NT 2—Mediator I 1—Melchizedek 2—Messiah—Mother I 3—Oil 2—Prayer I 2—Priesthood OT I 3, III 2—Prophet OT I 3—Shadow II 1—Shepherd & Flock O—Son of God OT II.

PG ecu

KINGDOM

"The kingdom of God is at hand": such is the principal aim of John the Baptist's and Jesus' preaching (Mt 3,1; 4,17). To know in what this mysterious reality that Jesus came to establish here below consists, what is its nature and what its demands are, we must have recourse to the NT. Nevertheless, the theme has its source in the OT, which had sketched its major lines while announcing and preparing its coming.

OT

The divine kingship is an idea common to all the religions of the ancient East. The mythologies used it to confer a sacred worth on a human king*, the earthly representative of the god-king. But treating this idea of the divine royalty, the OT gives it special meaning in keeping with its monotheism, its conception of political power, and its eschatology.

I. ISRAEL, KINGDOM OF GOD

The idea of Yahweh*-King did not appear right from the beginning of the OT. The God of Abraham, Isaac, and Jacob does not have kingly traits, even when He comes to reveal His name* to Moses (Ex 3,14). But after the installation of Israel in Canaan, recourse is had very quickly to this symbolic representation in order to show the respective situation of Yahweh and His people. Yahweh reigns over Israel (Jg 8,23; 1 S 8,7). His worship* is a service that His subjects carry out here below as do His angels* on high. And here is found the fundamental idea that one recognizes in the lyricism of worship (Ps 24, 7-10) as well as in the prophets (Is 6,1-5), and whose various aspects the sacred authors detail. Yahweh reigns forever (Ex 15,9) in heaven (Ps 11,4; 103,19), on earth (Ps 47,3), and in the universe He has created (Ps 93,1f; 95,3ff). He reigns over all the nations* (Jr 10,7.10). Among them, however, there is one people* that He has chosen as His particular domain. This is Israel, which He has made by His covenant* a priestly kingdom and a consecrated nation (Ex 19,6). Therefore, Yahweh's reign is manifested especially in Israel, His kingdom. There the great king resides, in the midst of His own (Ps 48,3; Jr 8,19) at Jerusalem*. From there He blesses them (Ps 134,3), guides them, protects them, gathers them, as a shepherd* his flock (Ps 80; cf Ez 34). Thus, the doctrine of the covenant finds for itself an excellent expression in the theme of the divine kingship, to which it gives a completely new meaning. If, in fact, Yahweh Lord of Hosts (Is 6,5) rules the world because He governs its course, and rules its events because He guides them and exercises judgment* on them, He wishes that, in His people, His Reign may be recognized in an effective manner by the observance of His Law*. This first demand gives to His reign not a political but a moral character, which cuts off all the old representations of the divine kingship.

II. THE KINGDOM OF GOD AND ISRAELITE KINGSHIP OF ISRAEL

Israel, kingdom of God, has, however, a political structure, which evolves with the times. But when the people give themselves a king* the institution of this human royalty ought to subordinate itself to the royalty of Yahweh, ought to become an organ of the theocracy based on the covenant. This fact explains, on the one hand, the current of opposition which manifests itself against the monarchy (1 S 8,1-7.19ff), and, on the other hand, the intervention of divine envoys who manifest the choice of Yahweh for Saul (10,24), for David (16,12), and finally, for the Davidic dynasty (2 S 7,12-16). From now on the kingdom of God has for temporal support a human kingdom, enmeshed like all its neighbors in international politics. Without doubt the Israelite kings do not maintain an ordinary kingship. They hold their kingship from Yahweh, whom they ought to serve (2 Ch 13,8; cf 1 Ch 28,5). And Yahweh regards the descendants of David as His sons* (2 S, 7, 14; Ps 2,7). Still, the experiment of monarchy remains indecisive: the cause of God's rule does not coincide with the earthly ambitions of the kings, especially since they fail to recognize the divine law. And so the prophets recall unceasingly the subordination of the political order to the religious order; they reproach the kings for their sins and announce the punishments which will follow (the instance of David in 2 S 12; 24,10-17). The history of the kingdom of Israel is thus written in tears and blood, until the day when the destruction of Jerusalem comes to close the experiment, definitively bringing with it the great confusion of the faithful Jews (Ps 89,39-46). This fall of the Davidic dynasty has for its root cause the break of the human kings with the king from whom they are holding their power (cf Jr 10,21).

III. AWAITING THE FINAL REIGN OF YAHWEH

At the time when the Israelite kingship collapses, the religious guides of the nation are looking, beyond the monarchical epoch, toward the original theocracy they wish to restore (cf Ex 19,6). And the prophets announce that Israel, at the end of time, will again recover its characteristics. Certainly, in their promises, they make a place for the future king*, for the Messiah*, son of David. But the theme of the kingship of Yahweh takes on anew a much greater importance, especially from the end of the exile on. Yahweh, as a shepherd*, proceeds to busy Himself with His flock in order to save it, reassemble it, and lead it into His land (Mi 2,13; Ez 34,11...; Is 40,9ff). The good news *par excellence* which is announced to Jerusalem is: "Your God reigns" (Is 52,7; cf Zp 3,14f). And one glimpses there a progressive extension of this rule to the entire earth: from everywhere, men will come to Jerusalem to adore the king Yahweh (Ze 14,9; Is 24,23).

Transferring these radiant promises to a place of worship and orchestrating the themes of certain older psalms, the post-exilic lyricism sings in advance the eschatological rule of God, a universal rule, proclaimed and recognized in all the nations, manifested by the divine judgment* (Ps 47; 96—99; cf 145,11ff). Finally, at the time of the persecution of Antiochus Epiphanes, the apocalypse of Daniel comes to renew solemnly the prophetic promises. The transcendent reign of God will be established on the ruins of human empires (Dn 2,44...). The symbol of the Son* of Man coming on the clouds of heaven serves to evoke it, by contrast with the beasts* who represent the political powers here below (Dn 7). His coming will be accompanied by a judgment*, after which the kingship will be given forever to the Son of Man and the people of the saints of the most high (7,14.27). Thus, the rule of Yahweh will take the concrete form of a kingdom of which the people* will be the depository (cf Ex 19,6); but the kingdom will no longer be of "this world." It is such a promise that the Book of Wisdom echoes: after the judgment, the just "will command the nations and rule the peoples, and the Lord will rule over them forever" (Ws 4,8).

After centuries of preparation, the Jewish people will live henceforth in the expectation of the reign, as the non-canonical literature shows. Often, this expectation is concretized in a political form: they await the restoration of the Davidic kingdom by the Messiah*. But the most religious souls know how to see here a reality essentially interior: it is by obeying the Law, according to the rabbis, that the "just man takes on himself the yoke of the kingdom of heaven." Such is the hope, strong but yet ambiguous, to which the gospel of the kingdom will respond.

NT

I. THE GOSPEL OF THE KINGDOM OF GOD

1. *Jesus* gives the kingdom of God the first place in His preaching. What He announces in the small towns of Galilee is the good news of the kingdom (Mt 4,23; 9,35). "Kingdom of God" writes Mark; "kingdom of heaven" writes Matthew in conforming himself to the phrases of the rabbinical language. The two expressions are equivalent. Accompanying the preaching, the miracles* are the signs of the kingdom's presence and they make us glimpse its meaning. With its coming the domination of Satan*, of sin*, and of death* over man is at an end. "If it is by the Spirit of God that I

chase the evil spirits*, then the kingdom of God has come to you" (Mt 12,28). It follows that there must be a decision; it is necessary to be converted, to embrace the demands of the kingdom in order to be a disciple* of Jesus.

2. *The apostles*, from living with their master, receive the mission to proclaim in their turn this gospel* of the kingdom (Mt 10,7). After Pentecost also, the kingdom remains the final object of the evangelical preaching, even with St. Paul (Ac 19,8; 20,25; 28,23.31). If the faithful who are converted suffer a thousand tribulations, it is "in order to enter the kingdom of God" (Ac 14,22), because God "has called them to His kingdom and His glory" (1 Th 2, 12). Henceforth, only the name* of Jesus is added to the kingdom of God to constitute the complete object of the gospel (Ac 8,12): to reach the kingdom one must believe in Jesus.

II. THE MYSTERIES
OF THE KINGDOM OF GOD

The kingdom of God is a mysterious reality whose nature Jesus alone can make known. Yet He reveals it only to the humble and the small, not to the wise and prudent of this world (Mt 11,25)—to His disciples*, not to the people outside, for whom all remains a mystery (Mk 4, 11 p). The pedagogy of the gospels is constituted in great part by the progressive revelation of the mysteries* of the kingdom, notably in the parables*. After the resurrection this pedagogy will be completed (Ac 1,3), and the action of the Holy Spirit will terminate it (cf Jn 14,26; 16,13ff).

1. *The paradoxes of the kingdom*. Judaism, taking the eschatological oracles of the OT literally, represented the coming of the kingdom as striking and immediate. Jesus understands it in a completely different manner. The kingdom comes when the Word* of God is addressed to men; such a seed, thrown on the ground, ought to grow (Mt 13,3-9.18-23 p). It will grow* by its own power, like a grain of wheat (Mk 4,26-29). It will lift up the world, like the leaven put in the dough (Mt 13,33 p). Its humble beginning thus contrasts with the future promised to it. Jesus, in fact, does not address the Word to the Jews of Palestine only; and among them, it is even only to a "small flock" of disciples that "the kingdom is given" (Lk 12,32). But the same kingdom ought to become a great tree where all the birds of heaven will nest (Mt 13,31f p); it will receive all nations* into its bosom, because it is not bound to any of them, not even to the Jewish people. Existing here below in the measure that the Word* of God is received by men (cf Mt 13,23), it could pass for an invisible reality. In fact, its coming is not allowed to be observed as any worldly phenomenon (Lk 17,20f). However, it is manifested in the exterior as the wheat mixed with the tare in a field (Mt 13,24 ...). The "little flock" to which it is given (Lk 12,32) takes on an earthly appearance, that of a new Israel, of a Church* founded on Peter*; and he even receives "the keys to the kingdom of heaven" (Mt 16,18f). It is only necessary to note that this earthly structure is not that of a human kingdom: Jesus hides Himself when they wish to make Him king* (Jn 6,15), and it is in a completely special sense that He permits Himself to be called by the title of Messiah.

2. *The successive phases of the kingdom*. That the kingdom may be said to grow supposes that it should be aware of the times. Certainly, in one sense, the time* is accomplished and the kingdom is here; since John the Baptist, the era of the kingdom is open (Mt 11,12f p); it is the time of the wedding (Mk 2,19 p; cf Jn 2,1-11) and of the harvest* (Mt 9,37ff p; cf Jn 4,35). But the parables of growth* (the seed, the mustard-seed, the leaven, the tares and good wheat, the fish: cf Mt 13) allow a delay to be seen between this historical inauguration of the kingdom and its full realization. After the resurrection of Jesus, the dissociation of His entry in glory and His return as judge (Ac 1,9ff) will finish by revealing the nature of this intermediary period; this will be the time of witness* (Ac 1,8; Jn 15,27), the time of the Church. At the end of that time, the kingdom will arrive in its plenitude (cf Lk 21,31): the Passover* will be consummated (Lk 21,14ff); this will be the eschatological meal* (Lk 21,17f) where those invited from everywhere will celebrate with the patriarchs (Lk 13,28f p; cf 14,15; Mt 22,2-10; 25,10). From the beginning of this kingdom to its consummation, the faithful are called to "inherit" it (Mt 25,34), after the resurrection and transformation of their bodies (1 Co 15,50; cf 6,10; G 5,21; E 5,5). In the meantime, they invoke its coming with their prayers: "May your kingdom come" (Mt 6,10 p).

3. *The entrance of men into the kingdom*. The kingdom is God's outstanding gift, the essential prize that must be acquired at the cost of all

one possesses (Mt 13,44ff). But to receive it, certain conditions must be fulfilled. Not that it may ever be considered a reward due in justice: God freely engages men in His vineyard, and He gives to His workers what He pleases (Mt 20,1-16). Nevertheless, if all is grace*, men ought to respond to grace: sinners hardened in evil "will not inherit the kingdom of Christ and of God" (1 Co 6,9f; G 5,21; E 5,5; cf Ap 22,14f). Poverty of soul (Mt 5,3 p), a child-like attitude (Mt 18,1-4 p; 19,14), an active search for the kingdom and its justice* (Mt 6, 33), bearing persecution (Mt 5,10 p; Ac 14,22; 2 Th 1,5), the sacrifice of all one possesses (Mt 13,44ff; cf 19,23 p), perfection greater than that of the Pharisees* (Mt 5,20); in a word, the accomplishment of the Father's will* (Mt 7,21), especially in the matter of fraternal charity (Mt 25,34): all this is asked of him who wishes to enter the kingdom and finally inherit it. For if all are called to it, not all will be chosen; the guest without a wedding garment will be cast out (Mt 22,11-14). At the beginning a conversion* is required (cf Mt 18,3), a new* birth, without which one cannot "see the kingdom of God" (Jn 3,3ff). Belonging to the Jewish people is no longer a necessary condition, as in the OT: "many will come from the East and the West to sit at the table in the kingdom of heaven, while the subjects of the kingdom will be cast outside..." (Mt 8,11f p). The prospect of judgment*, which certain parables present in concrete form: the sorting of the tare and the good grain (Mt 13,24-30), the sorting of the fish (Mt 13,47-50), the rendering of accounts (Mt 20,8-15; 25,15-30): all this constitutes a demand for vigilance (Mt 25,1-13).

III. THE KINGDOM OF GOD AND THE KINGSHIP OF JESUS

In the NT, the two themes of the kingdom of God and the Messianic kingship are joined more closely because the Messiah-King is the Son of God Himself. This place of Jesus at the center of the mystery of the kingdom is found in three successive stages through which the latter must pass: the earthly life of Jesus, the time of the Church, and the final consummation of things.

1. *During His lifetime,* Jesus shows Himself very reserved in the use of a king's* title. If He accepts it as the Messianic title responding to the prophetic promises (Mt 21,1-11 p), he must strip it of its political overtones (cf Lk 23,2) to reveal the kingdom "which is not of this world" and which is manifested by the witness given to the truth (Jn 18,36f). On the other hand, He does not hesitate to identify the cause of God's kingdom with His own: to leave all for God's kingdom (Lk 18,29) is to leave all "for His name*" (Mt 19,29; cf Mk 10,29). Describing in advance the eschatological reward which awaits men, He identifies the "kingdom of the Son* of Man" and the "kingdom of the Father" (Mt 13,41ff), and He assures His apostles that He will give them the kingdom as His Father has given it to Him (Lk 22,29f).

2. His royal enthronement will not take place, however, until the hour of His resurrection*: it is then that He sits on the same throne with His Father (Ap 3,21), that He is exalted at the right hand of God (Ac 2,30-35). In the fullness of the *Church's time,* God's kingship is exerted over men by means of Christ's kingship, He who is universal Lord* (Ph 2,11); the Father has constituted His Son "king of kings and Lord of lords" (Ap 19,16; 17,14; cf 1,5).

3. *At the end if time,* Christ, conqueror of all His enemies, will hand over the kingdom to God the Father (1 Co 15,24). Then this kingship "will be fully secured to our Lord and His Christ" (Ap 11,15; 12,10), and the faithfull will receive "the inheritance in the kingdom of Christ and of God" (E 5,5). It is thus that God, master of all, will take complete possession of His kingdom (Ap 19,6). The disciples of Jesus will be called to share the glory of this kingdom (Ap 3,21), because here below Jesus has made of them "a kingdom of priests for their God and Father" (Ap 1,6; 5,10; 1 P 2,9; cf Ex 19,6).

→Church—Earth NT I 2—Gospel—Growth 3 —Heaven II, V—Hope NT I—Inheritance NT II—Jesus Christ I 1.2—Justice B II NT—King —Meal IV—Messiah OT II 3; NT II 1—Miracle II 2—Mystery NT I—Parable I 2, II 2, III— People *A* I 2; *C* I—Plan of God OT IV; NT— Repentance/Conversion NT I, II—Son of Man OT II 1—Tree 2—Violence IV 1.3.

RD & PG ecu

KNEE

1. *To bend the knee* before someone is to express symbolically that one is not on a footing of equality with him, to confess one's inferiority, to mark submission. Thus on the passing of Haman all had to bend the knee and prostrate themselves (Es 3.2) This gesture could be given a religious touch, vg before Elijah, man of God (2 K 1,13). The first Christians had to recognize a true gesture of adoration (Mt 8,2) in the attitude of the leper who "bent his knee" (Mk 1,40), or "falls upon his face" (Lk 5,12), and a sacrilegious parody in the mockery of the soldiery (Mt 27,29 p). This gesture explicitly signifies adoration* to the eyes of "those who have not bent the knee to Baal" (1 K 19,18=R 11,4), or when Yahweh wishes that it be reserved for Him alone (Is 45, 23; cf Mt 4,9). Finally, the Christian knows that at the name* of Jesus every knee must bend (Ph 2,10) to recognize that Jesus is Lord*.

2. *Kneeling during prayer*—a form more simple that a complete prostration—characterizes an attitude of soul different from that which one has when either sitting or standing. The prayer* which one makes then has nothing of discourse, of exhortation, or of blessing; it is an imploring, sometimes silent, a profound supplication. Four instances of such prayer, official or private, are reported in the OT. At the end of the dedication of the temple, Solomon turns toward the congregation which is standing, blesses it, and makes a short speech (1 K 8,14-21); then he turns toward the altar, and throughout his long prayer (8,22-53) remains "kneeling, his hands extended toward heaven" (8,54). Finally, he gets up, stands, and blesses the people while exhorting them (8,55-61). After his victory over the priests of Baal, Elijah senses the end of the drought with which Israel's apostasy had been punished. "He climbed to the top of Carmel and bowed down to the earth, putting his face between his knees" (1 K 18,42); and rain fell. Many centuries later at the news of marriage contracted by Jews with strangers, Ezra remains "seated, crushed, until the evening offering"; then "I came out of my prostration, fell to my knees, extending my hands to heaven, and said. . ." (Ezr 9,4f) a prayer in which the people joined weeping (10,1). Finally Daniel, alone in his lofty chamber, "three times a day fell to his knees praying and blessing God; he had always done so" (Dn 6,11).

We do not see Jesus Himself kneeling except for the prayer of the agony (Lk 22,41), "thrown to the ground" (Mk 14,35), "His face to the earth" (Mt 26,39). But kneeling is frequently pointed out by Luke in solemn circumstances: Stephen, at the moment of forgiving his tormentors (Ac 7,60), Peter before the raising of Tabitha (9,40), Paul after his long farewell discourse to the elders of Ephesus (20,36), and all the Christians in choir on the shore at the moment of separation (21,5). Kneeling is a normal posture to express supplication in adoration (E 3, 14).

→Adoration—Blessing II o—Jesus (Name of) IV.

XLD wjy

KNOW

The initial biblical invitation addressed to the heart of man is to know God in the total context of life rather than as the result of speculation. Knowledge (hb. *yd'*) for the Semite is more than a recondite process of understanding because it involves an existential relationship. To know an object is to have a completely real experience of it as is well exemplified by a "knowledge" of suffering (Is 53,3), of sin (Ws 3,13), of war (Jg 3,1), of peace (Is 59,8), of good and evil (Gn 2,9.17), where there is a true personal involvement with far-reaching repercussions. To know an individual is to participate in a personal relationship admitting a variety of form, embracing many stages. "Knowledge," therefore, can have a wide range of meaning—denoting the close fellowship of the family (Dt 33,9) as well as marital relations (Gn 4,1; Lk 1,34). Knowledge of God is attained when man feels the touch of divine judgment (Ez 12,15) or, in a wholly different fashion, when man shares in God's covenant (Jr 31,34) and is gradually led to close acquaintance with God.

OT

1. *The divine initiative.* Religious knowledge begins with God's initiative. Before knowing God, man is known to God. This is the mystery of divine election* and concern as appears when God is said to know Abraham (Gn 18,19), as well as His people: "I have known only you out of all the families of the earth" (Am 3,2).

Even before their birth God knows the prophets (Jr 1,5) and all those whom He predestines* to be His adopted sons (R 8,29; 1 Co 13,12). Here He distinguishes individuals, knows them by name (Ex 33,17; cf Jn 10,3), and consequently makes Himself known to them. He reveals His name* (Ex 3,14), instills in them fear* of Him (Ex 20,18ff); but above all He displays tender care by delivering them from enemies, by giving them a land (Dt 4,32...; 11, 2...), and by imparting to them a knowledge of His commandments, the one path to prosperity (Dt 30,16; Ps 147,19f).

2. *Man's misunderstanding.* In answer to the divine initiative, the people should have known God, should have been united to Him in true love (Ho 4,1; 6,6). But from the very beginning they were incapable of this reaction (Ex 32,8). "A people with an errant heart, this nation has not known my ways" (Ps 95,10). Misunderstanding God consistently implicated the people in trials* (Nm 14,22; Ps 78). Less wise than pack animals, "Israel knows nothing" (Is 1,3; Jr 8,7). She revolts, violates the covenant (Ho 8,1), prostitutes herself "to gods unknown to her" (Dt 32,17).

Even when Israel fancies that she "knows Yahweh" (Ho 8,2), she is deluded, for her relation to Him is superficial and perfunctory (Is 29,13f; Jr 7). A genuine understanding of God should pervade the heart and appear in the realities of daily life (Ho 6,6; Is 1,17; Jr 22,16; cf Mt 7,22f). The prophets often repeat this message but "the nation does not listen* to the voice of its God and would not tolerate instruction" (Jr 7,28). Consequently, Israel will be punished "for its lack of knowledge" (Is 5,13; Ho 4,6).

God will, then, make Himself known in a frightful manner through the horrors of destruction and exile*. Ezekiel punctuates his preaching of these punishments* with the ominous refrain, "And you will know that I am the Lord." In a confrontation with herself and with God in the stark reality of the event, Israel could continue in her delusion no longer. She must acknowledge the holiness of God as well as her own sin* (Ba 2).

3. *Knowledge and a new heart.* Israelite hope anticipated a stupendous restoration in which "the land would be filled with the knowledge of Yahweh, just as the waters cover the sea" (Is 11,9). But how can this come about? Israel does not pretend any longer that she could

achieve this herself for she is aware of her "evil and uncircumcised heart*" (Jr 7,24; Lv 26,41) and conscious that true knowledge of God demands a pure heart*. Deuteronomy stresses the need for a spiritual transformation which can come from God alone. "Up to now, Yahweh has not given you a mind to understand" (Dt 29,3); but after the exile, "He will circumcise* your heart and the hearts of your descendants" (Dt 30,6).

Jeremiah applies this same promise to those in exile (24,7). The essence of the new covenant* announced by Jeremiah (Jr 31,31-34) is a thorough purification—"I will pardon their crime"—which will make a thorough docility possible in which "I will place my law in the depths of their being and I will write it upon their hearts." In this assurance, the mutual dedication "I will be their God and they will be my people," will be the fountainhead of unambiguous knowledge. "They will no longer need to teach each other or say to one another 'Know the Lord.' But all will know me from the least to the greatest."

Ezekiel completes this prospect by indicating the role of the Spirit* of God in the inner renewal: "I will give you a new heart; I will place in you a new spirit...I will give you my spirit" (Ez 36,26f). This will be the resurrection of the people* of God (Ez 37,14). By these means God will make Himself known, not just to Israel (Ez 37,13), but to the pagan nations* as well (Ez 36,23).

Second Isaiah foreshadows this salvation to come and also stresses its unlimited reverberations. Idolatry will suffer an unprecedented blow (Is 45—46). At the time of a new exodus* God will give evidence of His mastery over history and "all flesh will know that I, Yahweh, am your savior" (Is 49,26). To the Israelites God says, "You are my witnesses...so that people may come to know me" (Is 43,10); to His Servant, "I will make you the light of the nations" (Is 49,6).

4. *Wisdom from above.* Meanwhile, another line of thought was emerging and developing in a similar direction when Israel's sages were seeking and assembling maxims for the good life (Pr). Their fixed conviction was that God alone knows the secret (Jb 28). "He has scrutinized the whole road to understanding" (Ba 3,37), so "all wisdom* comes from the Lord" (Si 1,1). Assuredly, God in His kindness gave the source of wisdom to Israel, "that is, the Law* given through Moses" (Si 24,23f). Because

this is a gift external to man (cf Ws 9,5), it is necessary to implore God's assistance to perfect His work by providing the inner gift of His "spirit of wisdom" (Ws 7,7; 9). "What man, really, can know the plan of God?" (Ws 9,13).

The men of Qumrân show that they thirst for the "knowledge of divine mysteries." They give thanks to God for the light that has already been granted to them (1 QH 7,26f) and they long for the time of the final manifestation, which will enable the just to "understand the knowledge of the Most High" (1 QS 4,18-22).

As they come into contact with the Greek world, the Jews of the Dispersion begin to develop an argument of a more philosophical nature to combat idolatry and spread the knowledge of the one true God. The author of Wisdom states that the sight of nature should lead men to recognize the existence and the power of the Creator (Ws 13,1-9).

NT

The fully informed knowledge of God promised for the age of the new covenant comes to men in Jesus Christ.

1. *The synoptics.* Jesus alone was capable of revealing the Father* (Lk 10,22) and of interpreting the mystery of the kingdom* of God (Mt 13,11). He taught with authority (Mt 7,29), and He would not appease sterile curiosity (Ac 1,7). His teaching was not doctrinaire but rather the "good news" and a call for conversion (Mk 1,14f). Because God is at hand men should note the signs of the times (Lk 12,56; 19,42), and be disposed to receive Him (Mt 25,10ff). To His preaching Jesus added miracles as marks of His mission (vg Mt 9,6).

All this, however, was still only prologue. Christ's enemies (Mk 3,5) as well as His disciples had closed minds (Mk 6,52; Mt 16,23; Lk 18,34). Only when He had poured out the blood of the new covenant (Lk 22,20 p) did the fullness of light finally dawn: "Then He opened their minds" (Lk 24,45) and gave the Holy Spirit (Ac 2,33). Thus the final age began, the age of genuine knowledge of God.

2. *St. John.* John traces the stages of this revelation* even more clearly than the synoptics. Openness to the teaching of the Father is first required; those who are tractable are drawn toward Jesus (Jn 6,44f) and there is a mutual recognition (10,14). Jesus then leads them toward the Father (14,6). Still, all Jesus' words

and deeds remain somewhat enigmatic (16,25) until the time He is lifted up on the cross. Only this elevation leading to glory brings out His meaning (8,28; 12,23.32) and secures for the disciples the gift of the Spirit (7,39; 16,7). The Spirit divulges to them the full scope of the words and deeds of Jesus (14,26; cf 2,22; 12,16) and guides them to truth in its entirety (16,13). Thus the disciples know Jesus, and through Jesus they know the Father (14,7.20).

In accord with Jeremiah's prediction, a new relationship is established with God: "The Son of God has come and given us understanding to know the true one" (1 Jn 5,20; 2,14). There is no other definition of life* eternal than "to know you the one true God and Jesus Christ whom you have sent" (Jn 17,3) in an unequivocal knowledge that justifies the statement that Christians "no longer need to be taught" (1 Jn 2,27; cf Jr 31,34; Mt 23,8). This knowledge includes a capacity for discernment and John gives its main characteristics (1 Jn 2,3ff; 3,19.24; 4,2.6.13), and warns against false doctrines (2, 26; 4,1; 2 Jn 7). However, when it is understood in its full breadth, this knowledge of God can rightly be called "communion" (1 Jn 1,3), since it is a share in the same life (Jn 14,19f), a union perfect in the truth of love (Jn 17,26; cf 1 Jn 2,3f; 3,16. . .).

3. *St. Paul.* To a Greek world in avid pursuit of philosophical and religious theories (*gnosis*), Paul boldly preaches the cross* of Christ (1 Co 1,23). Salvation is not found in any type of human wisdom, but in faith* in Christ crucified, "the power and wisdom of God" (1 Co 1,24). Men can come to a knowledge of God through creation, but "their empty minds were darkened" and they gave themselves over to idolatry, thus deserving God's anger (R 1,18-22). From now on they must give up their pretensions (1 Co 1,29) and recognize that by themselves they are unable to penetrate the secrets of God (1 Co 2,14), and submit to the good news (R 10,16) transmitted "by the folly* of the gospel" (1 Co 1,21; R 10,14).

Baptism and faith in Christ open the door to a completely different type of understanding, to the "greatest benefit possible, the knowledge of Christ Jesus." This knowledge is not abstract but living; it is "to know Him in the power* of His resurrection and by sharing His sufferings" (Ph 3,8ff). Thereby man's understanding is "recreated" and made capable of "seeing what is the will* of God, what is good and pleasing to Him, what is perfect" (R 12,2). Resisting gnostic tendencies, which appear here and there among Christians (1 Co 1,17; 8,1f; Col 2,4.18), Paul leads them toward a more authentically religious knowledge, the knowledge that comes from the Spirit* of God and enables us really to "know the gifts that God has given us" and express them in a language "taught by the Spirit" (1 Co 2,6-16).

Before "the incomparable riches of Christ" (E 3,8), Paul's astonishment can only increase with the years; and it is his desire that Christians have "the full expansion of understanding to enable them to comprehend that mystery* of God in which are hidden all the treasures of wisdom and knowledge" (Col 2,2f). Still, he is not oblivious to the fact that "knowledge inflates" while "it is charity that builds" (1 Co 8,1; 13,2). Consequently what Paul has in mind is not an arrogant gnosis but an understanding of "the love* of Christ surpassing all knowledge" (E 3,19). He longs for the time when the imperfect will yield to the perfect, and he shall know even as he is known (1 Co 13,12).

Thus, for Paul, in company with all biblical thought, knowledge is entrance in the vast tides of life and light that emanate from the heart of God and lead back to Him.

→Apparitions of Christ 4.6.7—Dreams NT—Faith—Folly—Heart O, II 1.2 a—Love O; NT 3; II OT—Mary II 4—Mystery—Predestine—Prophet OT IV 4—Revelation—See—Spirit of God OT I 3; NT V 5—Spouse OT 1—Taste—Teach—Truth OT 3; NT 2.3—Will of God NT II 1—Wisdom.

JCo & AV wjw

L

LAMB OF GOD

In many books of the NT (Jn, Ac, 1 P, and especially Ap), Christ is identified as a lamb; this theme proceeds from the OT according to two distinct perspectives.

1. *The Servant of Yahweh.* Persecuted by his enemies, the prophet Jeremiah compared himself to a "lamb which one leads to the slaughter" (Jr 11,19). Subsequently this image was applied to the Servant* of Yahweh who, dying that He might pay for the sins of His people, appeared "as a lamb led to the slaughter, like a sheep before the shearers, silent and not opening its mouth" (Is 53,7). This text, emphasizing the humility and resignation of the Servant, announces perfectly the destiny of Christ, as Philip explains to the eunuch of the queen of Ethiopia (Ac 8,31.35). The evangelists look back to this when they point out that Christ "kept silent" before the Sanhedrin (Mt 26,63) and answered nothing to Pilate (Jn 19,9). It is possible that John the Baptist also refers to this when, according to the fourth gospel, he points out Jesus as the "Lamb of God who takes away the sins of the world" (Jn 1,29; cf Is 53,7.12; He 9,28).

2. *The paschal Lamb.* When God had decided to deliver His captive* people from the Egyptians, He ordered each family of Hebrews to immolate a lamb "without blemish, male, and one year old" (Ex 12,5), to eat it at night and to mark with its blood the lintels over their doors. Thanks to this "sign," they would be spared by the exterminating angel coming to strike all the first-born of the Egyptians. Enriching the primitive theme, Jewish tradition later on gave a redemptive value to the blood of the lamb: "Because of the blood of the covenant of circumcision, and because of the blood of the Pasch, I have delivered you from Egypt" (Pirqe R. Eliezer 29; cf Mekhilta on Ex 12). It is because of the blood* of the paschal* lamb that the Hebrews were freed from the slavery* of Egypt and that thereafter they were able to become a "consecrated nation," "a kingdom of priests" (Ex 19,6), bound to God by a covenant* and governed by the law of Moses.

Christian tradition has seen in Christ "the true Lamb" of the Passover (Preface of the Mass of Easter), and His redemptive mission is fully described in the baptismal catechesis which underlies the first epistle of Peter, and which is echoed in the Johannine writings and the epistle to the Hebrews. Jesus is the Lamb (1 P 1,19;

Jn 1,29; Ap 5,6) without blemish (Ex 12,5), that is to say, without sin (1 P 1,19; Jn 8,46; 1 Jn 3,5; He 9,14), which delivers men at the price of its blood (1 P 1,18f; Ap 5,9f; He 9,12-15). He has thus delivered them from the "earth" (Ap 14,3), from the evil world* given over to the moral perversion which springs from the worship of idols* (1 P 1,14.18; 4,2f), in the sense that they are able from now on to avoid sin* (1 P 1,15f; Jn 1,29; 1 Jn 3,5-9) and to form the new "royal priesthood," the true "consecrated nation" (1 P 2,9; Ap 5,9f; cf Ex 19,6), offering to God the spiritual worship* of an irreproachable life (1 P 2,5; He 9,14). They have left the darkness of paganism for the light of the kingdom* of God (1 P 2,9): this is their spiritual exodus*. Having, thanks to the blood of the Lamb (Ap 12,11), overcome Satan, of whom Pharaoh was the type, they can intone the "canticle of Moses and of the Lamb" (Ap 15,3; 7,9f.14-17; cf Ex 15) which celebrates their deliverance.

This tradition, which sees in Christ the true paschal Lamb, goes back to the very origins of Christianity. Paul exhorts the faithful of Corinth to live as if on unleavened bread "in purity and truth," because "our Pasch, Christ, has been immolated" (1 Co 5,7). He does not propose here a new teaching about Christ the Lamb; he is referring to the liturgical traditions of the Christian Pasch, therefore well before 55-57 A.D., the date when the apostle was writing this letter. If we trust the Johannine chronology, the very event of the death of Christ would have furnished the foundation of this tradition. Jesus was put to death the night before the feast of Unleavened Bread (Jn 18,28; 19,14.31), thus the day of the Pasch, in the afternoon (19,14), at the very hour when, according to the prescriptions of the Law, the lambs were being immolated in the temple. After His death, they did not break His legs, as they did to the other condemned men (19,33); and the evangelist sees in this fact the realization of a ritual prescription concerning the paschal lamb (19,36; cf Ex 12, 46).

3. *The heavenly Lamb.* While thoroughly protecting the theme of Christ the paschal Lamb (Ap 5,9f), the Apocalypse establishes a striking contrast between the weakness of the immolated Lamb and the power* which His exaltation to heaven confers on Him. A lamb in His redemptive death, Christ is at the same time a lion whose victory* has liberated the people of God who were captives of the powers of evil (5,5f; 12,11). Enjoying now the throne of God

(22,1.3), receiving with Him the adoration of the celestial beings (5,8.13; 7,10), He is now invested with divine power. It is He who executes the decrees of God against the impious (6,1...) and His wrath* plunges them into terror (6,16). It is He who leads the eschatological war* against the united powers of evil, and His victory will consecrate Him the "king of kings and Lord of lords" (17,14; 19,16...). He will recover again His original gentleness only when the nuptials will be celebrated with the heavenly Jerusalem, which symbolizes the Church (19, 7.9; 21,9). The Lamb will then appear as shepherd* to conduct the faithful to the sources of living water* of the heavenly blessedness (7,17; cf 14,4).

→Animals O; II 3—Blood OT 3 b; NT 4—Exodus NT—Jesus Christ II 1 b; concl.—Passover I 6 b, II, III 2.3—Redemption NT 1.4—Sacrifice NT I, II 1—Servant of God III 2—Shepherd & Flock NT 1—Spouse NT—Victory NT.

MEB jjk

LAMP

Lamp, by reason of its light, symbolizes the living presence both of God and of man.

1. *Symbol of the divine presence.* "Thou, O Lord, art my lamp" (2 S 22,29). Thus does the psalmist proclaim that God alone can give light and life. Is not the creator of the Spirit that is in man just such a "lamp of Yahweh" (Pr 20, 27)? Like a lamp, it lights up the believer's path with its Word* (Ps 119,105) and its command (Pr 6,23). The prophetic writings are "a lamp which shines in a dark place, until the day begins to break and the morning star arises in our hearts" (2 P 1,19). When the final day* comes, "there will be no more night*; the elect will have no need of the light of lamp or sun," for "the Lamb will be their lamp" (Ap 22,5; 21,23).

2. *Symbol of human presence.* The lamp is also used to symbolize human presence. Yahweh promises David a lamp, meaning a perpetual line of offspring (2 K 8,19; 1 K 11,36; 15,4). On the other hand, if the nation is unfaithful, God threatens to extinguish the "light of the lamp" (Jr 25,10); then the best that the evil man can hope for is that his lamp will be

extinguished quickly (Pr 13,9; Jb 18,5f).

As a sign of its fidelity to God and the continuity of its prayer*, Israel kept a lamp perpetually lit in the sanctuary (Ex 27,20ff; 1 S 3,3). If the lamp were allowed to go out, it would be a sign to God that He had been abandoned (2 Ch 29,7). But blessed are they who watch* in expectation of the Lord, such as the prudent young women (Mt 25,1-8) or the faithful servant (Lk 12,35), whose lamps remained lit.

But God expects still more. Instead of hiding his lamp under a bushel (Mt 5,15f p), the loyal servant must let his light shine forth in the midst of an evil world (Ph 2,15), as did Elijah whose "word shone like a torch" (Si 48,1) and John* the Baptist, "that lamp which burned brightly" (Jn 5,35) as a witness to the true light (1,7f). So also the Church, founded upon Peter and Paul, "the two olive trees and the two lamps that stand in the presence of the Lord of the earth" (Ap 11,4), must manifest the glory of the Son of Man until the end of time (1,12f).

→Light & Dark OT II 2; NT II 3—Watch.
JBB mjm

LAUGHTER

"Laughter," the name of Isaac, is the occasion for a variation on a theme which might thus be presented: what is more complex than laughter? All through Gn 17,17; 18,12-15; 21, 6..., Scripture plays on two aspects of laughter: a laugh of unbelief* which can be transformed into a laugh of joyous amazement at a wonderful divine work. Certainly, biblical man knows how to laugh: a strong sense of comedy is concealed in more inspired narratives than commonly imagined. But this humor is marked by the roughness of the Israelite of those days and seldom swerves from a note of challenge, derision, or satisfied boasting. Biblical texts more often subject the reader to the laugh of the fool, the man who is not behaving according to the demands of truth, than to the laugh of the just man.

1. *The laugh of the fool.* This is the wanton (Si 27,13) or simply exaggerated (21,20) laugh, while that of the wise man is discreet. Especially is the fool's laugh the laugh of the scoffer. This term has a very precise meaning. It signifies a man rebellious against correction (Ps 1,1; Pr 13,1; 15,12...), instruction, or acceptance of faith*. The scoffer is the opposite of the wise man (Pr 9,12; 29,8): he responds to the Word of God with raillery (Jr 20,7f), for example, to the reform of Hezekiah (2 Ch 30,10). Later he sneers when the resurrection of the dead is preached (Ac 17,32). In the last days, "mockers full of mockery" (2 P 3,3) will doubt the promises. Mockery, then, is almost equivalent to the refusal to believe. The just man is subject to it especially if he suffers (Ps 22,8; 35,26; Lm 3,14...). The nations mock Israel. Mockers are also heard on Calvary (Mk 15,29f; Lk 23,35f).

2. *The laugh of the believer.* Qoheleth declares that laughter is absurd (Qo 2,2). He expects more from tears (7,3). Yet he recognizes that there is a "time to laugh" (3,4). Actually, laughter changes meaning according to persons and times. The just man will laugh at the godless* man (Ps 52,8) at some appropriate time just as God makes game of the scoffer (Ps 2,4; Pr 3,34). Ridicule is a weapon against false gods and is employed both by Elijah at Carmel (1 K 18,27) and by the book of Baruch (Ba 6); the Maccabean martyrs use sarcasm against their persecutor (2 M 7,39). At the same time, the just man's laugh can be free from polemic and can express the consolation of the soul blessed by God (Ps 35,27; 126,2; Jb 8,21). Laughter can be confident, as the strong woman who "laughs at tomorrow" (Pr 31,25).

Jesus said that one kind of laughter, that of those satisfied with the present time (Lk 6,25; cf Jm 4,9), would not last; but to those who are now weeping He promised the laughter accompanying permanent joy (Lk 6,21). The final state of laughter will echo the perfectly pure laugh of Wisdom, which from the beginning is "at play" (here "to play" is the same word as to laugh: Pr 8,30f) in the presence of God and man.

→Incredulity O—Joy.
PBp ecu

LAW

The Hebrew word *Tōrāh* has a broader and less strictly juridical meaning than the Greek *Nomos*, which is its LXX translation. It designates an "instruction" given to men by God for the regulation of their conduct and is primarily applied to that body of legislation which the OT tradition associates with Moses. The NT adopts this meaning of the term and calls Law the whole economy based on the Jewish legislation (R 5,20), as opposed to the regime of grace* instituted by Jesus Christ (R 6,15; Jn 1, 17). Nevertheless, the NT also speaks of the "Law of Christ" (G 6,2). Moreover, Christian theology distinguishes the two Testaments by the terms "old Law" and "new Law". To take in the whole history of salvation*, the NT further recognizes the "natural law" (cf R 2, 14f) for all men not subject to either of the preceding laws. Thus the three essential stages of God's plan* are characterized by the word *law*, a word which emphasizes their ethical and institutional aspect. The following discussion of law will proceed according to three stages: natural law, old Law, new Law.

A. PRIOR TO MOSES: THE NATURAL LAW

The expression *natural law* is not used in Scripture in so many words, but the reality is clearly present under various forms.

1. *Old Testament.* Gn 1—11 (and the rare parallel texts) present a picture of man's religious regime up to the decisive time of the promises* (Abraham and the patriarchs) and of the Law (Moses). From the beginning man is confronted with a positive precept of God's will* (Gn 2,16f). It is precisely this precept that constitutes the trial in Paradise, and its transgression entails the entrance of death into the world (3,17ff; cf Ws 2,24; R 5,12). From these consequences it is clear that God did not leave man without law. Man is governed by a moral law, of which God reminds Cain (Gn 4, 7), and which was violated by the generation of the deluge (6,5). There are also certain religious precepts contained in Noah's covenant with God (9,3-6), as well as certain forms of worship* instituted by the men of that time (4,3f; 8,20). Men are just (4,3; 5,24; 6,9) or wicked (4,4; 6,5.11f; 11,1-9; cf Ws 10,3ff) according to their attitudes toward this embryonic law.

2. *New Testament.* Paul's concept of the plan of salvation* includes the stage of sacred history from Adam to Moses (R 5,13f). In fact, the pagan nations which have had no part in Israel's vocation are still subject to the pre-Mosaic religion. Though God allowed them to go their own ways (Ac 14,16; cf R 1,24-31)

and to grope for Him (Ac 17,27) during the time of their ignorance (17,30), still they were not for all that without knowledge of His will. His will was revealed to them by their conscience (R 2,14f). In his use of the word *law* in this context, Paul's basic meaning is the prescriptions of the moral order. God judges the pagans according to these prescriptions (1, 18; 2,12) and condemns them for violating the moral order, since they know God's verdict against human crimes (1,32; cf Am 1,2—2,3). Paul strikes at the root of moral disorder and inveighs against that religious sin which reveals the true nature of disobedience to the Law, i.e., knowing God but not giving Him glory (R 1,21).

B. MOSES AND THE OLD LAW

God separated the people of the OT from the other nations* and placed them under a regime of positive law which He Himself revealed, the Torah of Moses.

I. DIVERSITY OF THE LAW

1. The Law of Moses is found exclusively in *the five books of the Pentateuch*. The sacred history of God's plan* from the beginning to the death of Moses is interwoven with legislative texts. These texts are found within the framework of creation (Gn 2,2f), the covenant of Noah (9,1-7), the covenant of Abraham (17, 9-14), the exodus* (Ex 12,1-28.43-51), the covenant of Sinai, and the sojourn in the desert (Ex 20,1-17; 20,22—23,32; 25—31; 34,10-28; 35—40; the whole of Lv; Nm 1,1—10,28; 15; 17—19; 26—30; 35; almost all of Dt).

2. This comprehensive body of legislation, the Torah, regulates the life of God's people at all levels. The moral prescriptions, especially the Decalogue (Ex 20,2-17; Dt 5,6-21), sum up the fundamental demands of the human conscience with an accuracy and sureness rarely attained by the pagan philosophers. The juridical regulations, found in several different codes, control the various civil institutions (familial, social, economic, judicial). Finally, there are regulations for Israel's worship with its rites, its ministers, and its prerequisites (rules regarding cleanness). Nothing is left to chance; since the people of God are supported by the social structures of a particular nation, even their temporal

institutions are affected by positive, religious law.

3. There is a corresponding variety in the literary *formulation of the law*. Those of the casuistic type (vg Ex 21,18...) belong to a genre current in the ancient oriental codes and deriving from particular judicial decisions. Others (vg Ex 21,17) recall the popular maledictions which accompany the ceremonial renewal of the covenant (Dt 27,15...). The apodictic commandments (vg the Decalogue) are the direct orders by which God makes His will* known to the people. Finally, there are certain motivated precepts similar to the teachings of Wisdom (vg Ex 22,25f). But it is the commandments which set the tone for the whole collection of laws. In this way the Torah of Israel is clearly different from other codes which are merely collections of judicial decisions. The Torah appears above all else as the obligatory teaching given in the name of God Himself.

4. Because of this variety of the law, the OT has various names for it: instruction (*Tōrāh*), witness, precept, commandment, decision (or judgment), word*, will*, way of God (cf Ps 19, 8-11; 119 passim). It is clear that the Law exceeds all the limits of human legislation.

II. ROLE OF THE LAW IN THE OT

1. *The Law is closely connected with the covenant**. When God by entering into the covenant makes Israel His special people, He joins certain promises* to this election*, the fulfillment of which will dominate subsequent history (Ex 23,22-33; Lv 26,3-13; Dt 28,1-14). But God also sets down certain conditions for His promises. Israel must obey His voice and keep His commands; otherwise God's curses* will descend upon the people (Ex 23,21; Lv 26,14-45; Dt 28,15-68). In effect, the ceremony of the covenant involves an agreement to keep the divine law (Ex 19,7f; 24,7; cf Js 24,21-24; 2 K 23,3). The Law, therefore, is the basic element of religious economy to prepare Israel for the coming of salvation*. Its demands, difficult as they seem, are really a divine favor; for their intent is to make Israel a wise people (Dt 4,5-8) and to put them in contact with the will* of God. Thanks to the harsh schooling of the Law, the "stiff-necked people" begin to learn of that holiness which God expects of them. This is especially true of the moral commands of the Decalogue,

the heart of the Torah, but it also applies to the prescriptions dealing with civil matters and worship which translate the ideal into the concrete framework of Israel's institutions.

2. The bond between the Law and the covenant explains the fact that Israel has *no law other than that of Moses*. Moses* is the mediator* of the covenant upon which the old order was based; hence, he is also the mediator through whom God reveals to His people the demands which follow from His covenant (Ps 103,7). This essential fact is brought out in two ways. First, no human legislator, even at the time of David and Solomon, ever substitutes or adds his own authority to that of the Creator of the nation (even Ez 40—48, though Mosaic in inspiration, is not incorporated into the Torah). Then there is the inverse of this, that all legislative texts are ascribed to Moses and placed within the context of the sojourn at Sinai.

3. This does not mean that the Torah undergoes no *development* with the passage of time. Internal criticism correctly distinguishes sections of varying tone and character. This indicates that the Mosaic heritage was transmitted in various streams of tradition corresponding to the sources of the Pentateuch. Several times it was revised and brought up to date. The Decalogue (Ex 20,1-17) and the Code of the Covenant (Ex 20,22—23,33) are thus taken up and amplified by the Deuteronomist (Dt 5,2-21; 12—28), who shows that the love of Yahweh is the first commandment toward which all the others are directed (6,49). The Code of Holiness (Lv 17—26) is an attempt at another synthesis whose theme is the imitation of the holy God (19,1). The various reforms under the kings (1 K 15, 12ff; 2 K 18,3-6; 22,1—23,25) always base their development and deepening of the Law upon the Mosaic Torah. The final work of Ezra, which was probably done in connection with the definitive fixing of the Pentateuch, does no more than consecrate the validity and authority of the traditional Law (cf Ezr 7,1-26; Ne 8) whose foundation and essential orientation was established by Moses.

III. ISRAEL BEFORE THE LAW

The presence of the Law is felt throughout the OT. Its demands constantly confront the people; it is always implicit in the sacred writers' thoughts.

LAW

1. The *priests* are, *ex officio*, the custodians and specialists of the Torah (Ho 5,1; Jr 18,18; Ez 7,26). Their duty is to teach* the people the decisions and instructions of Yahweh (Dt 33,10). This instruction, which is given at the sanctuary (Dt 31,10f), clearly concerns matters of cult (Lv 10,10f; Ez 22,26; Hg 2,11ff; Ze 7,3); but everything else concerned with the conduct of life lies within its scope. The priests, as interpreters of the sacred deposit, are commissioned to pass on a knowledge of the ways of Yahweh (Ho 4,6; Jr 5,4f). They are the ones, therefore, who compile the legislative codes; and the Torah develops under their authority.

2. The *prophets**, men of the Word*, impelled by the Spirit* of God, recognize the authority of the Torah, and they reproach even the priests for neglecting it (cf Ho 4,6; Ez 22,26). Hosea knows many of the Torah's numerous precepts (Ho 9,12), and the sins which he denounces are mainly violations of the Decalogue (4,1f). Jeremiah, in support of the Deuteronomic reform (2 K 22), preaches obedience to the "Words of the Covenant" (Jr 11,1-12). Ezekiel gives a list of sins which seems to be taken from the Code of Holiness (Ez 22,1-16.26). The morality which they esteem so highly is simply a more profound insight into the demands of the Mosaic Torah.

3. It is not surprising to find the same state of mind also among Israel's *historians*. These compilers of the ancient traditions view the covenant of Sinai as the beginning of the nation. The Deuteronomic historians (Dt, Jg, S, K) look for the meaning of past events in light of the criteria furnished by the Deuteronomist. The priestly historian of the Pentateuch is governed by the legislative tradition of his milieu. The author of Chronicles, in his revision of the history of Israel's theocracy, allows himself to be guided by the ideal of the Pentateuch, which had at last been fixed. The men of former times are blamed or praised according to their regard for the Torah. History of this sort becomes a living exhortation for the people of God to remain faithful.

4. *Among the men of wisdom,* the teaching of the same Torah appears under new forms. There are the maxims of Proverbs and Ben Sira and the biography of Tobit. Moreover, Ben Sira makes the explicit statement that true Wisdom is nothing else than the Law (Si 24, 23...) and that its tent was pitched in Israel when Moses gave the Law (24,8...). Once

Judaism became faithful after the trial of the exile, the psalmists could sing of the grandeur of the divine law (Ps 19,8...), the supreme gift which God gave to no other nation (Ps 147,19f). Their declarations of love for the Law (Ps 119) reveal their love for God Himself. In this way they passed on the basis of Jewish piety* at that period.

5. After the time of Ezra, *the community of Israel* definitively established the Torah at the center of its life. The ardor of their attachment to the Law can be measured by the martyrdoms endured for love of the Torah (1 M 1,57-63; 2,29-38; 2 M 6,18-28; 7,2...) when Antiochus Epiphanes attempted to change the sacred seasons and the Law (Dn 7,25; 1 M 1,41-51). No doubt there were some Hellenized traitors among them; but the revolt of the Maccabees, incited by "zeal for the Law" (1 M 2,27), finally restored the traditional order which would never again be brought into question. The only problem which will cause division between the teachers and the sects will be the interpretation of the Torah, in which everyone recognizes the one and only divine rule for life. While the Sadducees, who consider their priests to be the only true interpreters, will cling to the written Torah, the Pharisees will acknowledge an equal authority in the oral Torah, i.e., in the tradition* of their ancestors. The sect of Qumrân (probably Essenes) will go still further in their cult of the Legislator (i.e., of Moses), whom they will interpret according to their own norms.

Judaism derives its greatness from its devotion to the Law. Still, such an attachment to the Law has its dangerous aspects. One danger is to put all the precepts on a par, religious and moral, civil and ritual, without properly subordinating them (Dt 6,4). The cult of the Law, once transformed into a meddling formalism and abandoned to the subtleties of the casuists, places an impossible burden on men (Mt 23,4; Ac 15,10). Another danger, more basic than the first, is to base man's justice* before God not on divine grace*, but on obedience* to the commandments and the practice of good works*, as though man were able to justify himself. The NT will make a frontal attack upon these two abuses.

IV. TOWARD A NEW LAW

While the OT itself was testifying to the final times, the Law, under the new covenant, was undergoing a profound change. Did not the Torah, which the God of Israel taught the people on the holy mountain* (Is 2,3), and the order which the Servant* of Yahweh would bring upon the earth (Is 42,1.4), surpass in religious value those of Moses? The prophetic oracles do not define precisely the contents of the new covenant; only Ezekiel attempts to outline it in the traditionalist spirit (Ez 40—48). But what is affirmed is that man's relationship to the Law will be modified. It will no longer be a matter only of an exterior Law written on tablets of stone; the Law, written in men's hearts*, will bring to everyone that knowledge of Yahweh (Jr 31,33) which was missing under the old covenant (Ho 4,2). Men's hearts will also be changed; under the interior impulse of the divine Spirit*, men will finally obey the laws and ordinances of God (Ez 36,26f). Such will be the new Law which Christ will bring to the world.

C. JESUS AND THE NEW LAW

I. THE PERSONAL ATTITUDE OF JESUS

1. Jesus' attitude toward the old Law is clear, though it allows of differences. He violently opposes the tradition* of the ancients which the scribes and Pharisees* taught, but He does not act in the same way toward the Law. Quite the contrary, He repudiates that tradition because it leads men to violate the Law and annul the Word* of God (Mk 12,28-34 p). In the kingdom* of God, the Law is not to be abolished, but fulfilled* to the last iota (Mt 5,17ff), and Jesus Himself obeys it (cf 8,4). To the extent that the scribes are faithful to Moses, their authority must be acknowledged, even though their conduct is not to be imitated (23,2f).

Nevertheless, in preaching the gospel* of the kingdom, Jesus inaugurates a religious regime which is fundamentally new*. The Law and the prophets have come to an end with John* the Baptist (Lk 16,16 p); the wine of the gospel cannot be poured into the old skins of the Sinaitic regime (Mk 2,21f p). Jesus' fulfillment of the Law consists, first of all, in the establishment of order among the various precepts. This order is far different from that hierarchy of values established by the scribes who neglect the principal duties (justice, mercy, honesty) while insisting on the accessory details of the Law (Mt 23,16-26). Moreover, the imperfections permitted under the old Law "because of hard-

ness of hearts" (19,8) are to be no more in the kingdom; the rule of conduct will be the law of perfection* in imitation of God's perfection (5,21-48). This is an unattainable ideal in man's present condition (cf 19,10). But even as He imposes this Law, Jesus provides an effective example* and the interior strength* of the Spirit (Ac 1,8; Jn 16,13) necessary for its observance.

Finally, the Law of the kingdom incorporates the twofold commandment of the old Law to love God and love one's neighbor as oneself (Mk 12,28-34 p); everything is subordinated to this commandment and derived from it. This golden rule of positive charity embodies the Law and the prophets (Mt 7,12) for men's dealings with one another.

2. In His various pronouncements upon the Law, Jesus already appears as a legislator. Without contradicting Moses*, Jesus explains and perfects the Mosaic teachings, as when He proclaims that man is greater than the Sabbath* (Mk 2,23-27 p; cf Jn 5,18; 7,21ff). Still, He went beyond the letter of the Law and even opposed it with new norms. For example, He reverses the prescriptions of the code of cleanliness (Mk 7,15-23 p). Teachings such as this surprise His hearers, for they undercut those of the scribes and reveal an awareness of a unique authority (1,22 p). Moses is superseded, for in the kingdom there is only one teacher (Mt 23, 10). Men must hear His Word and act upon it (7,24ff), for only in this way will they fulfill the will* of the Father (7,21ff). Just as the faithful Jews, following the rabbinic teachings, took upon themselves the yoke of the Law, so now one must take up the yoke of Christ and learn from Him (11,29). Prior to this, man's eternal fate was determined by his attitude toward the Law; from now on it will be settled on the basis of his attitude toward Jesus (10,32f). Without any doubt, here is one greater than Moses; the new Law foretold by the prophets is now promulgated.

II. THE PROBLEM IN PRIMITIVE CHRISTIANITY

1. Jesus had not condemned the practice of the Jewish Law; He essentially obeyed it Himself, as in the matter of the temple tax (Mt 17, 24-27) or the Law of the Pasch (Mk 14,12ff). At first this was also the attitude of the apostolic community, who were faithful at the temple services (Ac 2,46) "and who were highly re-

garded" by the Jewish people (5,13). Although they made use of certain liberties authorized by the example of Jesus (9,43), they observed the legal prescriptions and even imposed on themselves extra practices of piety (18,18; 21,23f). And among them there were found devotees of the Law (21,20).

2. A new problem arose when uncircumcised pagans were directly converted to the faith without any Jewish background. Peter himself baptized the centurion Cornelius after a vision in which he was commanded to regard as clean whatever God purified by faith* and the gift of the Spirit (Ac 10). The opposition of those who were zealous for the Law (11,2f) crumbled before the evidence of a divine intervention (11, 4-18). But a mass conversion of Greeks at Antioch (11,20), supported by Barnabas and Paul (11,22-26), rekindled the controversy. Some observers from Jerusalem, and more precisely from the company of James (G 2,12), wanted to oblige the converts to observe the Torah (Ac 15,1f.5). During his visit to the Church at Antioch, Peter hedged on this difficulty (G 2, 11f). Paul alone held his ground and affirmed the liberty* of the pagan converts with regard to the practices of the Law (G 2,14-21). In a plenary council held at Jerusalem, Peter and James finally agreed with him (Ac 15,7-19). Paul's companion Titus was not even bound to undergo circumcision*. The only condition placed on Christian communion was an alms for the mother Church (G 2,1-10). A practical rule was also added to facilitate community of table in the churches of Syria (Ac 15,20f; 21,25). But this decision to grant freedom to the pagans left a hard core among the devotees of the Law who were ill-disposed toward Paul (cf 21,21).

III. THE THOUGHT OF ST. PAUL

In the course of his apostolic journeys to pagan lands, Paul soon met with opposition among the Jewish Christians, especially in Galatia, where the opposition organized a countermission (G 1,6f; 4,17f). This gives Paul the opportunity to reveal his thoughts on the Law.

1. Paul preaches only one gospel. According to this gospel, man is justified only by faith* in Jesus Christ, not by the works* of the Law (G 2,16; R 3,28). The import of this principle is twofold. First, Paul proclaims the futility of the ritual practices of Judaism—circumcision

(G 6,12) and observances (4,10); the Law understood in this way is limited to the institutions of the old covenant. Then Paul attacks a false understanding of the economy of salvation* according to which man merits his own justification* by his observance of the divine Law, whereas in reality he is gratuitously justified by the sacrifice* of Christ (R 3,21-26; 4,4f); here also commandments in the moral order are under dispute.

2. In light of this teaching, a question arises concerning the place of the Law in the plan* of salvation. There is no doubt that the Law is from God. Although it was given to men through the intermediary of angels, which is a sign of its inferiority (G 3,19), still it is something holy and spiritual (R 7,12.14), one of the privileges of Israel (9,4). But of itself it is powerless to save the carnal man, who is the slave of sin (7,14). Even considering the Law in its moral aspect, it only gives a knowledge of what is good, not the strength to do it (7,16ff); it only tells us what sin is (3,20; 7,7; 1 Tm 1,8), not how to escape from its power. The Jews who possess it and seek its justice* (R 9,31) are sinners no less than the pagans (2,17-24; 3,1-20). Instead of freeing men from evil, the Law can be said to involve them in it; it brings a curse* upon men from which only Christ can rescue them by taking it upon Himself (G 3,10-14). The Law served as a pedagogue and tutor to God's people in their infancy (3,23f; 4,1ff). It taught them to desire a justice which was impossible to attain so that they would better understand their absolute need of their only Savior.

3. Once this Savior has come, the people of God are no longer subject to the pedagogue (G 3,25). By freeing man from sin (R 6,1-19), Christ also frees him from the tutelage of the Law (7,1-6). He removes that interior contradiction which makes the human conscience* a prisoner of evil (7,14-25). He thus brings to an end the provisional regime of the Law; He is Himself the termination of the Law (10,4), since He causes believers to assent to the justice of faith* (10,5-13).

Does this mean that hereafter there will be no concrete rule of conduct for those who believe in Christ? By no means. Even though it is true that the juridical and ritual regulations pertaining to the institutions of Israel are no longer valid, the moral ideal of the commandments remains; but now that ideal is incorporated into the commandment of love, which is the complete fulfillment of the Law (13,8ff). But this ideal itself is detached from the old economy and is transfigured by the presence of Christ who made the ideal a reality in His own life. As the "Law of Christ" (G 6,2; cf 1 Co 9,21), it is an ideal no longer exterior to man; the Spirit* of God imprints it on our hearts when He fills them with His love (R 5,5; cf 8,14ff). The practical fulfillment of the ideal of the commandments is the normal effect of the Spirit (G 5,16-23). St. Paul adopts this point of view when He depicts the moral ideal imposed on the Christian. He is able, therefore, to list rules of conduct all the more demanding because their goal is Christian sanctity (1 Th 4,3); he can even discuss individual cases, seeking a solution to them in the words of Jesus (1 Co 7,10). Unlike the old Law, the new Law fulfills the promises of a covenant written in the heart (2 Co 3,3).

IV. OTHER APOSTOLIC WRITINGS

1. *The epistle to the Hebrews* regards the Law (i.e., the old economy) from the viewpoint of worship*. The author is familiar with the ceremonies prescribed by the Law (He 7,5f; 8,4; 9,19.22; 10,8), but he also knows that this Law has been unable to attain the end toward which it was directed, the sanctification of men; the Law has brought nothing to perfection (7,19). As an imperfect type of the sacrifice of Jesus, it contains but a shadow of the good things to come (10,1). On the other hand, the new economy contains the reality of these good things, and it brings them to us under an image (10,1) which communicates them by rendering them perceptible. This is the reason why the substitution of Jesus' priesthood for the provisional priesthood brought about a change in the Law (7,12). Thereby was fulfilled the prophetic promise of a Law inscribed on our hearts (8,10; 10,16).

2. *The epistle of James* speaks of the Law only under the aspect of its moral prescriptions endorsed by the teaching of Jesus. Thus understood, the Law is no longer an element of the old economy henceforth abrogated. It is the perfect Law of liberty* to which we are subject at all times (Jm 1,25). Its peak of perfection is the sovereign law of love* (2,8). But not one of its other prescriptions is to be ignored; otherwise one becomes a transgressor and shall be judged accordingly (2,10-13; cf 4,11). The new Law is no less demanding than the old.

3. *In the vocabulary of John, Law* always refers to the Law of Moses (Jn 1,17.45; 7,19.23), the Law of the Jews (7,49.51; 12,34; 18,31; 19,7), "your Law," as Jesus calls it (8,17; 10,34). *Commandment* is the word opposed to the pejorative *Law*. Jesus Himself has received commands from His Father and He keeps them, for they are eternal life (12,49f). He has received the command to lay down His life, which is the greatest act of love (15,13); now, this command itself is a sign of the Father's love for Him (Jn 10,17f). Christians in their turn must keep the commandments of God (1 Jn 3,22), which consist in believing in Christ (1 Jn 3,23) and living in truth (2 Jn 4). These commands are the same as those of Christ, whose teaching comes from the Father (Jn 7,16f). It is one and the same thing to obey God's commands and to give witness* to Jesus (Ap 12,17; 14,12).

John is also concerned to recall to mind the personal commands of Jesus. These must be kept in order to know Him truly (1 Jn 2,3f), to have His love within us (1 Jn 2,5), to dwell in His love* (Jn 14,15; 2 Jn 5), just as Jesus keeps the commands of His Father and dwells in His love (Jn 15,10). Keeping the commandments—this is the sign of true love (Jn 14,21; 1 Jn 5,2f; 2 Jn 6). And there is one among all the rest of the commandments which is supreme in both Old and New Testaments, the command of fraternal love (Jn 13,34; 15,12; 1 Jn 2,7f) flowing from the love of God (1 Jn 4,21). Thus the testimony of John is united with that of Paul and the other evangelists. When the old Law was abolished after Jesus' condemnation according to its prescriptions (Jn 18,31; 19,7), a new Law was born, a different type of Law, one which depends upon the Word of Jesus. This Law forever remains the rule of Christian life.

→Authority OT I 2—Book II—Captivity II—Conscience—Covenant OT I 2; NT II 1—Death NT I 2—Education O, 2 a, III 1—Faith NT III 1—Flesh II 2 a—Fulfill OT 1; NT 2—Good & Evil III 1—Grace O—Jew I 1—Justice—Justification II 1—Liberation/Liberty II 2 c—Light & Dark OT II 2.3—Moses o.3—Obedience II 3, IV—Perfection OT 3; NT 1—Pharisees—Priesthood OT II 2; NT I 1—Promises II 2—Prophet OT III 1—Pure OT I; NT I 1—Responsibility 2—Revelation OT II 1 a—Rights/Laws OT 1; NT—Slave—Teach—Way I 2—Will of God O;

OT I 1—Wisdom OT I 3—Witness OT II 2, III—Word of God OT II 1 a—Works NT II 1 —Writing V.

PG mjm

LEPROSY

In the same category as leprosy properly so called (*nega'* has the primary meaning of "wound, blow"), the Bible groups together under various names several particularly contagious diseases of the skin, and even the moldiness of clothes and walls (Lv 13,47..., 14,33...).

1. *Leprosy, uncleanness, and divine punishment.* According to the Law*, leprosy is a contagious impurity whose victim is excluded from the community until he has been healed and ritually purified, for which a sin offering is required (Lv 13—14). Leprosy is the "plague" *par excellence* with which God strikes (*nâga'*) sinners. Israel is threatened with it (Dt 28,27. 35); the Egyptians are afflicted with it (Ex 9, 9ff), as are Miriam (Nm 12,10-15) and Uzziah (2 Ch 26,19-23). In principle, therefore, it is a sign of sin. Yet if the suffering Servant is struck (*nâgûa'*; Vulg.: *leprosum*) by God and men turn away from Him as from a leper, the reason is that despite His innocence, He bears the sins of men who will be healed by His wounds (Is 53,3-12).

2. *Healing the lepers.* The healing of leprosy can take place through natural processes, but it can also happen through a miracle, as in the case of Naaman in the waters of the Jordan (2 K 5), which was a sign of the divine favor and of prophetic power. When Jesus heals the lepers (Mt 8,1-4 p; Lk 17,11-19), He triumphs over the plague; He heals men whose illnesses He takes upon Himself (Mt 8,17). By purifying the lepers and restoring them to the community, He miraculously abolishes the division between the clean and the unclean. If He prescribes the legal offering it is to give witness: the priests will thus see His respect for the Law as well as His miraculous power. Along with His other cures, therefore, curing leprosy is a sign that He is indeed "the one who is to come" (Mt 11,5 p). Thus, when the twelve are sent out on their mission, they receive the command and the power to show by this sign that the kingdom of God is at hand (Mt 10,8).

→Pure OT I—Sickness/Healing OT I 1.

PG mjm

LIBERATION/LIBERTY

"Brothers, you have been called to liberty" (G 5,13). This message is an essential part of the gospel of salvation*; Jesus has come "to proclaim release for prisoners and restore liberty to the oppressed" (Lk 4,18). Jesus' coming brings deliverance not only to the ancient pagans who felt themselves ruled by fate and to the Jews who refused to admit being slaves (Jn 8,33), but also to the men of today who in a confused way aspire to a definitive liberation. But there is liberty and liberty, and the Bible gives no definition. It does, however, at least affirm implicitly that man is endowed with the power of responding by a free choice to God's plans for him (I); and above all it shows the path of genuine freedom: Yahweh intervenes, in the OT, to assure the liberation of His people (II); and in the NT the grace of Christ brings the freedom of the children of God to all men (III).

I.   THE LIBERTY OF MAN

It might seem that certain biblical texts ignore the existence in man of any real freedom of choice, since the sacred authors lay so much stress on the sovereignty of God's will* (Is 6,9f; R 8,28ff; 9,10-21; 11,33-36). But in these cases it is important to make allowances for the tendency of semitic thought to go straight to divine causality without mentioning the secondary causes, which are, however, not denied (cf Ex 4, 21; 7,13f: the hardening* of Pharaoh's heart). On the other hand we must also distinguish the different degrees and modalities in the will of God. He does not will the salvation of all men (1 Tm 2,4) and the eternal death of the impenitent sinner in the same way (cf Ez 18,23). Paul's assertion of the "freedom of divine choice" (R 9,11) and of predestination* (8,29f) does not give us the right to conclude that human freedom is illusory.

In fact the whole of biblical tradition supposes that man is capable of taking free decisions: it constantly appeals to his power of choice and at the same time stresses his responsibility*, from the story of the first sin onward (Gn 2—3; cf 4,7). It is incumbent on man to choose between blessing and curse, life and death (cf Dt 11,23ff; 30,15-20), to be converted*; and this is so to the end of his life (Ez 18,21-28; R 11,22f; 1 C 9,27). It is up to each individual to set out on the way that leads to life and to persevere on it (Mt 7,13f). Siracides expressly rejects the excuses of the fatalist: "Do not say: 'The Lord was responsible for my sinning,' for He is never the cause of what He hates. . .If you wish you can keep the commandments: to behave faithfully is within your power" (Si 15,11-15; cf Jm 1,13ff). And Paul protests indignantly against the blaspheming words of the sinner who thinks he can accuse God of injustice, when in fact He condemns justly (R 3,5-8; 9,19f).

The sacred authors have not entirely removed the apparent contradiction between divine sovereignty and human freedom, but they have said enough to show us that God's grace and man's free obedience are the two things needed for salvation. Paul sees this to be true of his own life (Ac 22,6-10; 1 C 15,10), as in the life of every Christian (Ph 2,12f). In our eyes it is a mystery, but God knows the secret of moving our heart without subjecting it to violence and of drawing us to Himself without forcing us (cf Ps 119,36; Ez 36,26ff; Ho 2,16f; Jn 6,44).

II. THE LIBERATION OF ISRAEL

1. *The exodus from Egypt.* Their liberation by God from the servitude in Egypt (Ex 1—15) was the fundamental event marking the beginning of the chosen people. In speaking of this event, the OT gives special emphasis to two verbs; the first gaal: Ex 6,6; Ps 74,2; 77,16) refers to familiar rights*, while the second (*pādāh*: Dt 7, 8; 9,26; Ps 78,42) ordinarily concerns commercial rights ("to deliver something for an equivalent payment"). But the two verbs are practically synonymous when God is their subject, and in the vast majority of cases the LXX used the same word to translate them (*lytrousthai*, frequently rendered in Latin by *redimere*). The etymology of the Greek verb (*lytron*: ransom) should not mislead us regarding its meaning. All the biblical texts show that the first redemption* was a victorious liberation for which Yahweh payed no ransom to Israel's oppressors.

2. *God, the "Gō'ēl" of Israel.* After the infidelities of God's people had brought about the destruction of Jerusalem and the exile*, the liberation of the Jews in Babylon was a second redemption, the good news of which is the main message of Is 40—55. Yahweh, the holy one of Israel, is its "liberator," its "*gō'ēl*" (Is 43, 14; 44,6.24; 47,4; cf Jr 50,34).

In ancient Hebrew law, the *gō'ēl* is the near relative upon whom falls the duty of defending the family interests when there is a question of maintaining the patrimony (Lv 25,23ff), freeing a "brother" fallen into slavery (Lv 25,26-49), protecting a widow (Rt 4,5), or avenging an assassinated kinsman (Nm 35,19ff). The use of the title *gō'ēl* in Is 40—55 suggests that a bond of relationship still persists between Yahweh and Israel; in virtue of the covenant* made at the time of the first exodus* (cf Ex 4,22), the chosen nation, despite its sins, remains the spouse of Yahweh (Is 50,1). The parallelism between the two liberations is clear (cf Is 10, 25ff; 40,3); as was true of the exodus, the return from exile is a complete favor (Is 45,13; 52,3), and God's mercy* is still more evident in the latter case, since the exile was meant as a punishment of the people for their sins.

3. *Expectation of the definitive liberation.* Still other trials would beset the chosen people, who, in their troubles, will never cease calling upon God for aid (cf Ps 25,21; 44,27) and recalling their first deliverance, the pledge and type of all the others: "Do not forsake that role which is yours, for you have been redeemed from the land of Egypt" (prayer of Mordecai in Es 4,17g LXX; cf 1 M 4,8-11). The centuries immediately preceding the coming of the Messiah are marked by an expectation of the "definitive liberation" (translation from the Targum in Is 45,17; cf He 9,12), and the official prayers of Judaism beg the *gō'ēl* of Israel to hasten the day of its coming.

Moreover, the Jews were looking especially for freedom from the yoke which the nations had imposed upon the holy land. This was probably the concept which the disciples traveling to Emmaus had of the task of "him who was to deliver Israel" (Lk 24,21). As a result, only a spiritual elite (cf Lk 2,38) was able to put a more authentically religious content into their hope* of deliverance, as did the psalmist: "The Lord will deliver Israel from all its sins" (Ps 130,8). True liberation implied the purification of the remnant, which was summoned to participate in the holiness of its God (cf Is 1,27; 44,22; 59,20).

4. *Personal and social prolongations.*

a) On the personal level, God's liberation of His people is perpetuated and renewed somehow or other in the life of each of the faithful (cf 2 S 4,9: "As the Lord lives, who has delivered me from every distress"), a theme frequently heard in the psalms. Sometimes the psalmist expresses this in general terms without specifying the particular danger to which he is or has been exposed (Ps 19,15; 26,11); at other times he says that he is struggling with adversaries who seek his life (Ps 55,19; 69,19), or again his prayer is that of a seriously sick man who would soon be dead without the intervention of God (Ps 103,3f). But there are already some prayers of expectation which express a more profoundly religious hope (cf Ps 31,6; 49,16).

b) On the social level, biblical legislation itself reflects the remembrance of Israel's first deliverance, especially in the Deuteronomist tradition, when it sets down that the Hebrew slave* should be set free after seven years in memory of Yahweh's deliverance of His people (Dt 15, 12-15; cf Jr 34,8-22). The Law was not always observed, however; and even after the return from exile Nehemiah would have to rise up against certain of his compatriots who did not hesitate to lead their "ransomed" brethren back into slavery (Ne 5,1-8). Nevertheless, "setting the oppressed free, breaking every yoke" is one of the forms of "fast which is pleasing to Yahweh" (Is 58,6).

III. THE LIBERTY OF THE CHILDREN OF GOD

1. *Christ our liberator.* The liberation of Israel only foreshadowed Christian redemption. In reality, Christ is the one who will establish a rule of perfect and definitive liberty for all, Jew and pagan, who unite with Him in faith and charity.

Paul and John are the chief heralds of Christian liberty. Paul preaches it especially in his letter to the Galatians; "Christ set us free that we might remain free men...Brothers, you have been called to be free men" (G 5,1.13; cf 4,26. 31; 1 Co 7,22; 2 Co 3,17). John emphasized the principle of true liberty, the faith that receives the Word* of Jesus: "The truth has set you free;...if the Son set you free, you will indeed be free" (Jn 8,32.36).

2. *The nature of Christian liberty.* Although it has repercussions on the social plane, to which the letter to Philemon bears excellent witness, Christian liberty is located beyond social structures. Available to slaves* as well as free men, it presupposes no change in one's state (1 Co 7,21). In the Graeco-Roman world, where civil liberty formed the very basis of personal integrity, this fact of Christian liberty was a paradox; but in this way the profound value of the deliverance which Christ offered was made clear. No longer is this deliverance to be confused with the ideal of the sages, Stoics, and others, who sought through their philosophizing and moral endeavors to acquire a perfect mastery over themselves and an imperturbable interior peace. Far from being the product of an abstract and timeless doctrine, Christian liberty is the result of an historical event, the victorious death of Jesus, and of contact with a person, union with Christ in baptism.

The believer is free in the sense that, in Christ, he has received the power of living from now on in the intimacy of the Father, without being impeded by the bonds of Sin, Death and the Law.

a) Sin is the true despot from whose yoke Jesus Christ wrests us. In R 1—3, Paul describes sin's universal tyranny over the world, but he does so to set in greater relief the superabundance of grace* (R 5,15.20; 8,2). By uniting us to the mystery of Christ's death and resurrection, baptism* has put an end to our slavery (R 6,6). This liberation accomplishes the essential element of the OT expectation, as the elite of Israel understood it (cf Lk 1,68-75). In citing the LXX version of Is 59,20, Paul draws out of it its spiritual meaning: "From Zion shall come the deliverer; He shall remove wickedness from Jacob" (R 11,26). The apostle reveals to the pagans the "mystery" of their full admission to the privileges of the chosen people; the wonderful deeds of the first deliverance are renewed for all of us: "God rescued us from the domain of darkness and brought us into the kingdom of His beloved Son, in whom we have redemption and the forgiveness of sins" (Col 1,13f).

b) Death, the inevitable accompaniment of sin (Gn 2,17; Ws 2,23f; R 5,12), has also been overcome; it has lost its sting (1 Co 15,56). Christians are no longer enslaved by fear of it (He 2,14f). Deliverance from the fear of death, of course, will be perfect only at the glorious resurrection* (1 Co 15,26.54f); we are still "awaiting the redemption of our body" (R 8, 23). But, to some extent, the final times have already begun and "we have passed from death to life" (1 Jn 3,14; Jn 5,24) to the degree that we live in faith* and charity.

c) *The Law.* By the same token "we are no longer under the Law*, but under grace*" (R 6,15). As surprising—or as commonplace—as that statement of Paul may seem, it cannot be minimized without distorting the apostle's gospel of salvation. Since we have died mystically with Christ, we are henceforward redeemed from the Law (R 7,1-6); and we cannot find the principle of our salvation in the fulfillment of an exterior law (G 3,2.13; 4,3ff). We are in a new regime, and docility toward the Spirit poured into our hearts now constitutes the norm for our conduct (cf Jr 31,33; Ez 36,27; R 5,5; 8,9.14; 2 Co 3,3.6). It is true that Paul still speaks of a "law of Christ" (G 6,2; cf 1 Co 9,21), but this law is summed up in love (R 13,8ff) and, under the influence of the Spirit, we carry it out spontaneously, for "where the Spirit of the Lord is, there is freedom (2 Co 3,17).

3. *The exercise of Christian liberty.*

a) Set free, the Christian is filled with a *bold confidence,* a pride*, which the NT calls *parrēsia.* This typically Greek word (literally: freedom to say everything) designates a characteristic attitude of the Christian and still more of the apostle. This confidence leads a man to act like a son in God's presence (cf E 3,12; He 3,6; 4,16; 1 Jn 2,28; 3,21), for what was received at baptism is the "spirit of an adopted son" and not the "spirit of a slave" (R 8,14-17); and in the presence of men, the Christian attitude instills complete confidence in preaching the gospel message (Ac 2,29; 4,13; etc.).

b) *Liberty is not license or libertinism.* "Brothers, you have been summoned to liberty; only do not turn that freedom into license for the flesh*" (G 5,13). From the very beginning, the apostles had to denounce certain distortions of Christian liberty (cf 1 P 2,16; 2 P 2,19), and the danger seems to have been particularly serious in the community at Corinth. The gnostics there may have adopted a Pauline formula as a motto: "Everything is permitted to me." But they falsified its meaning, and Paul was obliged to clarify his statement and point

out that the Christian cannot forget that he belongs to the Lord and that he is destined for the resurrection (1 Co 6,12ff).

c) *The primacy of charity.* "All things are lawful, but not everything edifies" (1 Co 10,23). Our conscience may tell us to renounce our rights if the good of our neighbor demands it (1 Co 8—10; R 14). Properly speaking, this is not a limitation on our liberty, but a more perfect way of exercising it. Freed from their former slavery in order to serve God (R 6), Christians will put themselves "through charity at the service of one another" (G 5,13), as the Holy Spirit moves them (G 5,16-26). By making himself a servant* and in a sense the slave of his brethren (cf 1 Co 9,19), Paul does not cease to be free; but he imitates Christ (cf 1 Co 11,1), the Son who became a Servant.

→Calamity—Captivity—Cares 2—Conscience 2 b—Death OT III; NT II 3—Exodus—Good & Evil I 3—Imposition of Hands NT I—Judgment OT II 1—Law C II 2, III 3, IV 2—Moses 2—Passover—Predestine 2—Pride O; NT 2—Providence 2—Redemption OT 1; NT 1—Repentance/Conversion — Responsibility — Rest —Salvation—Serve III 2—Sin—Slave—Trial/Temptation—Way I—Will of God—Work III —Wrath B OT III 2; NT III 1.

LR mjm

LIE

The biblical use of the word *lie* covers two different meanings depending on whether the relations of man with his neighbor or his relations with God are concerned.

I.   THE LIE IN RELATIONS WITH THE NEIGHBOR

1. *In the OT.* The prohibition of lying in the Law aims originally at a precise social context, that of false witness in trials (Decalogue: Ex 20,16; Dt 5,20; repeated in Ex 23,1ff.6ff; Dt 19,16-21; Lv 19,11); given under oath*, the lie is besides a profanation of the name* of God (Lv 19,12). The restricted meaning subsists in the moral teaching of the prophets and the sages (Pr 12,17; Ze 8,17). But the sin of lying has also a much broader extension: it is deceit, cheating, the disagreement between thought and

tongue* (Ho 4,2; 7,1; Jr 9,7; Na 3,1). Yahweh holds all that in horror (Pr 12,22), He who cannot deceive (Jb 13,9); the liar also is going to destruction (Ps 5,7; Pr 12,19; Si 20,25). Even the wily Jacob who got away with the paternal blessing was in his turn tricked by his father-in-law Laban (Gn 29,15-30).

2. *In the NT*, the obligation of a total loyalty is clearly formulated by Jesus: "Let your language be yes, yes and no, no" (Mt 5,37; Jm 5,12); and Paul makes it his rule of conduct (2 Co 1,17f). The teachings of the OT are also repeated; not, however, without receiving a deeper motivation: "Lie not to one another, stripping yourselves of the old man with his deeds and clothing yourselves with the new man" (Col 3,9f); "Tell the truth, for we are members of one another" (E 4,25). Lying would be a return to a perverted nature; it would go against our solidarity in Christ. One understands that according to Acts, Ananias and Sapphira in lying to Peter lied in reality to the Holy Spirit (Ac 5,1-11): the perspective of social relations was overstepped when the Christian community was concerned.

II. THE LIE IN RELATIONS WITH GOD

1. *Disregard of the true God.* Yahweh is the God* of truth. To disregard Him by turning to deceitful idols is the lie *par excellence*—no longer that of the lips* but that of life. The sacred authors denounce without end this imposture, aiming ironic couplets at it (Jr 10,1-16; Is 44,9-20; Ps 115,5ff), mocking stories (Dn 14), ignominious epithets: nothingness (Jr 10,8), horror (4,1), vanity (2,5), impotence (2,11)...In their eyes, every conversion supposes first of all that one confesses the lying and deceitful character of the idols that one has served (16, 19). This is Paul's understanding when he urges the pagans to turn from their lying idols (R 1,25) in order to serve* the living and true God (1 Th 1,9).

2. *Sin of lying and religious life.*

a) The OT also knew a more subtle manner of disregarding the true God. It was to adopt a fixed habit of lying in one's life. Such was the way of acting of the godless*, enemies of man and of good; they were knaves (Si 5,14) with nothing but lies in their mouths (Ps 59,13; Si 51,2; Jr 9,2), they trusted in the lie (Ho 10,

13), they were attached to it to the point of refusing conversion (Jr 8,5), and even their apparent conversions are lies (3,10). Useless to entertain illusions about the man left to himself: he is spontaneously a liar (Ps 116,11). On the other hand, the true faithful man keeps lying out of his life so as to be in communion with the God of truth (Ps 15,2ff; 26,4f). So will act at the last times the Servant* of Yahweh (Is 53,9), just as the whole humble remnant* whom God will then leave to His people (Zp 3,13).

b) The NT finds this ideal realized in Christ (1 P 2,22). That is why the putting aside of all lying is the first requirement of the Christian life (1 P 2,1). We understand by that not only the lie of the lips, but that which is included in all vices (Ap 21,8): that type of lie the elect, companions of Christ, have never known (14,5). He especially merits the name of liar who disregards the divine truth* which is revealed in Jesus: Antichrist who denies that Jesus is the Christ (1 Jn 2,22). With him the lie is no longer in the moral order, it is essentially religious, just like that of idolatry.

3. *The supporters of lying.*

a) Now, to overthrow men in this lying universe which rises before God in an attitude of defiance, there exist deceitful guides at all periods. The OT knew lying prophets*, whom God mocked on occasion (1 K 22,19-23), but whom the true prophets more often denounced in severe terms: thus Jeremiah (5,31; 23,9-40; 28,15f; 29,31f), Ezekiel (13), and Zechariah (13, 3). Instead of the Word* of God they bore to the people messages that were falsified.

b) In the NT Jesus likewise denounced the blind guides of the Jewish people (Mt 23,16...). These hypocrites who refuse to believe in Him are liars (Jn 8,55). They are a prelude to other liars who will rise throughout the centuries to turn men away from the gospel: Antichrists (1 Jn 2,18-28), false apostles (Ap 2,2), false prophets (Mt 7,15), false Messiahs (Mt 24,24; cf 2 Th 2,9), false doctors (2 Tm 4,3f; 2 P 2,1ff, cf 1 Tm 4,1f), without counting the Jews who prevent the preaching of the gospel (1 Th 2,14ff), and false brethren, enemies of the true gospel (G 2,4)...They are so many supporters of the lie whom Christians ought to face, as Paul did in the case of the magician Elymas (Ac 13,8ff).

III. SATAN, FATHER OF LIES

Thus the world is divided into two camps: that of good and that of evil, that of the truth and that of the lie—in the twofold sense, moral and religious. The first is concretely that of God. The second has also a head, Satan*, the old serpent who seduces the entire world (Ap 12,9) since the day when he seduced Eve (Gn 3,13) and in separating her from the tree of life was a "murderer from the beginning" (Jn 8,44). It is he who urged Ananias and Sapphira to lie to the Holy Spirit (Ac 5,3); and Elymas the magician is his "son*" (Ac 13,10). The incredulous Jews who refused to believe in Christ depend on Satan: they are sons of the devil, liar and the father of lies (Jn 8,41-44). And so they also wished to kill Jesus, because "He had spoken the truth* to them" (Jn 8,40). It is he who aroused the false doctors, enemies of the truth of the gospel (1 Tm 4,2); he who in order to wage war against the Christians (Ap 12,17) gave his powers to the beast* of the sea, the "totalitarian" empire, to the mouth full of blasphemies (13,1-8); and the beast of the earth, which played the role of false prophets to deceive men and have them adore the lying idol, still depends on him (13,11-17). The axis of the world passes between these two camps, and it is important that Christians do not allow themselves to be misled by the tricks of the devil to the point that their faith is corrupted (2 Co 11,3). To remain in the truth, they must, therefore, pray God to deliver them from the evil one (Mt 6,13).

→Antichrist NT 2—Deception / Disappointment I 1—Error—Evil Spirits NT 2—Heart I 2—Human Speech 1—Hypocrite—Idols—Lips 1—Satan I 2, III—Sin IV 2 b—Tongue 1—Truth—Witness OT I; NT I.

JCa & PG wjy

LIFE

The living God calls us to eternal life. From the beginning to the end of the Bible, there is a profound appreciation of life in all its forms and an unadulterated concept of God. These attitudes indicate that man hopefully and untiringly pursues life as a sacred gift of God, one in which the mystery and liberality of God breaks forth.

I. THE LIVING GOD

To invoke "the living God" (Js 3,10; Ps 42, 3...), to be taken for the "servant of the living God" (Dn 6,21; 1 K 18,10.15), to swear "by the living God" (Jg 8,19; 1 S 19,6...), is not simply to proclaim that the God* of Israel is a powerful and active God. Such procedure gives God one of the names* He favors most (Nm 14,21; Jr 22,24; cf Ez 5,11...), calls to mind His extraordinary vitality, His consuming emotional warmth "which neither tires nor wearies" (Is 40,28). The title recalls that "He is the everlasting king...His wrath* none can bear" (Jr 10,10); that it is He "who endures forever... who saves and delivers, who performs signs and wonders in the heavens and on the earth" (Dn 6,27). The high estimate the Bible has for the title of the "living God" is an indication of Scripture's regard for life.

II. THE VALUE OF LIFE

1. *Life is something precious.* Life appears at the last stages of creation* as its crowning point. On the fifth day are born "the sea-monsters, the living things that glide and move in the waters" (Gn 1,21), and the birds. The earth then brings forth other living creatures (1,24). Finally, God creates the most perfect living thing in His image—man*. To assure continuity and growth* to his life now in birth, God bestows His blessing* (1,22.28). Therefore, even though life is a time of hard work (Jb 7,1), man is ready to sacrifice everything to preserve life (2,4). The lot of a soul* in the lower region seems so tragic that to desire death* can only be explained as the after effect of an incredible and shattering misfortune (Jb 7,15; Jon 4,3). To enjoy the present state of life for a long time (cf Qo 7,17; 11,8f), to be on this "land of the living" (Ps 27,13), and only to die, as Abraham," at a happy old age, advanced in years and replete with days (Gn 25,8; 35,29; Jb 42,17) is the ideal. Parents intensely desire to have offspring (cf Gn 15,1-6; 2 K 4,12-17) because children are a source of joy to their parents (cf Ps 127; 128) and a sort of extension of their life. Therefore it is pleasant to see large groups of elderly people and of children in public (cf Ze 8,4f).

2. *Life is fragile.* Man, and other living creatures on the same scale, have a tenuous grip on life; death is part of their nature. Their life

is dependent on the involuntary and easily vulnerable process of respiration. All are subject to death by nature. This breath of air is a gift of God (Is 42,5) in continual dependence on Him (Ps 104,28ff) "who slays and brings to life" (Dt 32,39). So life is short (Jb 14,1; Ps 37,36), a wisp of smoke (Ws 2,2), a shadow* (Ps 144,4), as nothing (Ps 39,6). In comparison with earlier days life seems to be getting even shorter (cf Gn 47,8f). One hundred and twenty years or one hundred years, even eighty or seventy have become the maximum (cf Gn 6,3; Si 18,9; Ps 90,10).

3. *Life is sacred.* While it is true that all life comes from God, man's power to breathe comes from God in a very special manner; for to make man a living individual, God breathed in his nostrils the breath of life (Gn 2,7; Wi 15,11), the same breath that He withdraws at death (Jb 34,14f; Qo 12,7 after the uncertainty manifest in 3,19ff). Therefore God gives man's life His special protection by forbidding murder (Gn 9,5f; Ex 20,13), even the murder of a Cain (Gn 4,11-15). Even the life of an animal* is somewhat sacred though man can eat flesh* of animals. All the blood should be drained out because "the life of the flesh is in the blood" (Lv 17,11), the source of the living and breathing soul (Gn 9,4). Moreover, it is through the blood of sacrifice* that man enters into contact with God.

III. THE PROMISES OF LIFE

1. *The law of life.* God "takes no pleasure in the death of anyone" (Ez 18,32) because He has not created man for death but for life (Ws 1,13f; 2,23). Moreover, God put at man's disposal an earthly paradise* in which the fruit of the tree* of life would make him "live forever" (Gn 3,22). When sinful man sought life by his own devices God forbade access to the tree of life; but He did not deny life itself to man. Before God gives life to men through the death of His Son, He offers His people "the ways* of life" (Pr 2,19...; Ps 16,11; Dt 30,15; Jr 21,8).

These ways proferred are "the laws* and ordinances" of Yahweh; those "who fulfill them shall find life therein" (Lv 18,5; Dt 4,1; cf Ex 15,26), as well as the "completion of the entire number of his days" (Ex 23,26); the obedient will have "length of days and of life, light for his eyes, and peace" (Ba 3,14). Because these are the ways of justice* and "justice leads to life"

(Pr 11,19; cf 2,19f...), "the just man shall live by his faithfulness*" (Ha 2,4); but the heathen shall be crossed out of the book* of life (cf Ps 69,29). For a long time Israel's hope for the promised life centered upon a life on this earth* as the land Yahweh gave to His people. "The life and length of days" which God reserves for a faithful Israel (Dt 4,40...; cf Ex 20,12) represent a happiness unique in the world, "superior to that of all the nations of the earth" (Dt 28,1).

2. *God, source of life.* Though this life promised by God is lived entirely on earth, it is not fostered primarily by earthly goods, but by attachment to God, "the fountain of living water" (Jr 2,13; 17,13), "the source of life" (Ps 36,10; cf Pr 14,27); "His love is better than life" (Ps 63,4). For this reason the higher type of Israelite comes to prefer above anything else the happiness of living his entire life in His temple where one day before His face*, consecrated to His praise, "is worth more than a thousand" (Ps 84,11; cf 23,6; 27,4) other days elsewhere. For the prophets life is "seeking Yahweh" (Am 5,4f; Ho 6,1f).

3. *Life beyond death.* The sinful Israelite nation experiences more of death* than the happiness of life on earth. But through death Israel finds out the persistence of God's call to life. From the utter darkness of exile, Ezekiel announces that God "does not take pleasure in the death of a sinner," but rather calls him "to conversion and life" (Ez 33,11). Ezekiel knows that Israel is like a collection of corpses, but he still preaches that God will make His Spirit* breathe in these dried-out bones which then come to life once again (37,11-14). Also from the period of the exile, Second Isaiah sees the Servant* of Yahweh "cut off from the land of the living...for the crime of His people" (Is 53,8); "He offers His life as a sacrifice* of expiation" and beyond His death "sees a posterity and prolongs His days" (53,10). A flaw, therefore, courses through the fatal sin-death combination. One can die for his sins* and still expect something of life. One can die for something other than his sins and, in dying, find life.

The persecutions of Antiochus Epiphanes came as a confirmation of the prophets' statements that death could come from one's fidelity to God. Such a death accepted for God was not separation from Him, but a path leading to life through the resurrection*: "God will give them back again breath and life...They drink of an inexhaustible life" (2 M 7,23.36). From the dust in which they sleep "shall they arise. . .to shine with the magnificence of the stars," while their persecutors "shall sink down into everlasting horror" (Dn 12,2f). The Book of Wisdom expands this hope to a transformation of the entire life of the just. While the wicked, like living dead, "are hardly born before they cease to be" (Ws 5,13), the just are "in God's hand" (3,1) and will receive from Him "everlasting life. . .the kingly crown of glory*" (5,15f).

IV. JESUS CHRIST: I AM THE LIFE

The promises become reality with the Savior's coming.

1. *Jesus preaches life.* For Jesus life is something valuable, "more so than food" (Mt 6,25). "Saving a life" is more important even than the Sabbath* (Mk 3,4 p) because "God is not a God of the dead, but of the living" (Mk 12, 27 p). Christ cures and restores life almost as if He could not tolerate the presence of death. Had He been present Lazarus would not be dead (Jn 11,15.21). This power to give life shows His power over sin (Mt 9,6) and indicates that He brings a life that does not die—"life everlasting" (19,16 p; 19,29 p). This is the true life, one that can be called without qualification "life" (7,14; 18,8f p. . .). Entrance to and possession of this life demands that one follow the narrow path, sacrifice all his wealth*, even his body and his present life (cf Mt 16,25f).

2. *In Jesus is life.* Christ, the eternal Word, possessed life from all eternity (Jn 1,4). As man, He is "the Word of life" (1 Jn 1,1). He is rightfully the complete master of all life (Jn 5,26) and gives it in abundance (10,10) to all those His Father has given Him (17,2). He is "the way, the truth, and the life" (14,6), "the resurrection and the life" (11,25). He is "the light* of life" (8,12); He gives a living water* which in the recipient becomes "a spring of water bursting forth to eternal life" (4,14). Christ is "the bread* of life"; to those who eat His body* He gives the power to live by Him as He lives by the Father (6,27-58). Living in Christ presumes faith*, for "whoever lives and believes in Him shall not die" (11,25f); but the non-believer "will never see life" (3,36). Living in Christ demands a faith which receives and follows Christ's word, just as Christ Himself obeys His Father because "His command is eternal life" (12,47-50).

3. *Jesus Christ, sovereign of life.* What Jesus asks of others He Himself does first. The content of His message is something He Himself bestows on man. Freely and because of love for the Father and for His own, "He gives His life" ("His soul*," Jn 10,11.15.17f; 1 Jn 3,16) as the good shepherd* does for his sheep. But Jesus gives His life "to take it up again" (Jn 10,17f), so that afterwards He becomes "a life-giving spirit (1 Co 15,45), capable of bestowing the gift of life on all who believe in Him. Jesus Christ, dead and risen, is "the prince of life" (Ac 3,15); the Church's mission is "to announce this life boldly to the people" (Ac 5,20). This was the series of events lived out by the first Christians.

4. *To live in Christ.* The passing from death to life is repeated in the person who believes in Christ (Jn 5,24): "baptized in His death" (R 6,3) and "returned from death" (6,13), the believer lives henceforth for God in Jesus Christ (6,10f). With a living principle of knowledge he now knows* the Father and the Son whom He sent. Precisely this is eternal life (Jn 17,3; cf 10,14). The believer's "life is hid with Christ in God" (Col 3,3), in the living God whose temple he is (2 Co 6,16). Thus does he participate in the nature of God (2 P 1,4) and in a life hitherto alien to him (cf E 4,18). In possession of the Spirit* of God from Christ, his own spirit is life (R 8,10). No longer is the believer subject to the limits of the flesh*. For he can pass through death unharmed to live forever (cf 8,11.38), no longer for himself, "but for Him who died and arose" for his sake (2 Co 5,15). For this man, "to live is Christ" (Ph 1,21).

5. *Death absorbed by life.* In proportion as a Christian here and now shares the death* of Christ by enduring His sufferings, will he manifest Christ's life even in his body* (2 Co 4,10). What is mortal must be absorbed into life (2 Co 5,4), the corruptible must put on immortality. For almost every individual, this process of change supposes bodily death (cf 1 Co 15, 35-55). Instead of preventing life, this death establishes life permanently and expands it in God, swallowing up death in its victory* (15 54f).

The Apocalypse sees the souls of martyrs already in heaven (Ap 6,9) and Paul wishes for death "to be with Christ" (Ph 1,23; cf 2 Co 5,8). Life with Christ, therefore, is a fruit of the resurrection* (cf 1 Th 5,10) and is possible immediately after death. At that time one can be like God and see* Him as He is (1 Jn 3,2), face* to face (1 Co 13,12). This vision is the essence of eternal life.

The full perfection of the life to come will be reached only when the body itself arises glorified and shares eternal life. Then "Christ, our life" (Col 3,4) will appear in the heavenly Jerusalem, "God's abode with men" (Ap 21,3). There the river of life flows and the tree* of life flourishes (22,1f; 22,14.19). "At that time, no longer will there be death" (21,4), for it will be "hurled into the fiery pond" (20,14). Everything will be subject to God who "will be all in all" (1 Co 15,28). That will be a new paradise* where the saints will taste* forever the very life of God in Jesus Christ.

→Baptism IV 2.4—Beatitude—Blessing—Blood —Creation—Death—Desire I—Fruit—Fruitfulness—Gift NT 3—God OT III 1—Grace II 1, V—Growth—Joy OT I—Lamp 2—Light & Dark OT II 1; NT I 2—Man I 1 a—Mother I 1, II 1—New Birth—Old Age 1—Paradise—Resurrection—Run 2—Salvation—Sexuality I 1 —Soul I 1.2—Spirit of God NT V 3—Strength —Tree—Victory NT 1—Violence O—Water—White o—Wisdom OT II 1—Woman OT 1.2.

AAV & JG dfb

LIGHT & DARK

The theme of light runs through the whole of biblical revelation. The separation of light and darkness was the first act of the Creator (Gn 1,3f). At the end of salvation history the new creation (Ap 21,5) will have God Himself as light (21,23). From the earthly physical light which alternates with night's darkness, men will pass into the unfailing light which is God Himself (1 Jn 1,5). History, occurring between these extremes, takes the form of a conflict with light and darkness confronting one another, a confrontation identical with that between life* and death* (cf Jn 1,4f). No metaphysical dualism hardens this dramatic world view, as is the case in Iranian thought. But man's stake in the conflict is not any less; his final destiny is defined in terms of light and darkness as well as in terms of life and death. The theme, there-

fore, occupies a central place in the religious symbolism employed by Scripture.

OT

I. THE GOD OF LIGHT

1. *The Creator of light.* Light, like everything else, exists only as a creature of God; the light of day, for instance, which emerges from the original chaos (Gn 1,1-5), or the light of the stars* illuminating the earth day and night (1,14-19). God sends it forth and calls it back, and the light obeys trembling (Ba 3,33). The alternating darkness is also in the same situation, since the same God "fashioned light and darkness" (Is 45,7; Am 4,13 LXX). Therefore, light and darkness sing the same hymn of praise to the Creator (Ps 19,2f; 148,3; Dn 3,71f). Thus all mythical notions are radically removed. This does not, however, stop light and darkness from having a symbolic meaning.

2. *The God clothed in light.* Like other creatures, light is a sign which visibly manifests some aspect of God. It is like a reflection of His glory*. As such, it is part of the literary device used to suggest theophanies. Light is God's clothing* (Ps 104,2). When He appears, "His brilliance is like the day, and rays of light shine from His hands" (Ha 3,3f). The vault of heaven on which His throne rests is flashing like crystal (Ex 24,10; Ez 1,22). And He is portrayed as surrounded by fire* (Gn 15,17; Ex 19,18; 24,17; Ps 18,9; 50,3) and hurling lightning in the storm* (Ez 1,13; Ps 18,15). This picturesque and symbolic portrait establishes a connection between the divine presence and the impression a dazzling light makes on men. As for darkness, it does not exclude God's presence*, since He probes and sees what happens there (Ps 139,11f; Dn 2,22). Nevertheless the most perfect darkness, that of Sheol, is where men are "cut off from His hand" (Ps 88,6f.13). In the darkness, then, God sees but is not seen; He is present, but not openly.

3. *God is light.* In spite of the above recourse to light symbolism, one must wait till the Book of Wisdom for its application to the divine essence. Wisdom*, a pouring out of God's glory, is a reflection of the eternal light, "and is superior to all created light" (Ws 7,27.29f). Here the symbolism attains a level of development which the NT will employ more fully.

II. LIGHT, A GIFT OF GOD

1. *Light of the living.* "Light is sweet, and it is good for the eyes to see the sun" (Qo 11,7). Everyone has had this experience. From this common experience comes the close association between light and life*; to be born is to "see the day" (Jb 3,16; Ps 58,9). The blind man who does not see the "light of God" (Tb 3,17; 11,8) has a foretaste of death (5,11f). But the sick man snatched by God from death rejoices to see again "the light of the living" shining on him (Jb 33,30; Ps 56,14), since Sheol is the kingdom of darkness (Ps 88,13). Light and darkness thus have opposite meanings for men; this is the basis of their symbolism.

2. *Symbolism of light.* First of all, the light of theophanies involves an existential meaning for the participants; light may emphasize the majesty of God on intimate terms with men (Ex 24,10f), or make man feel His forbidding character (Ha 3,3f). To this mysterious suggestion of the divine presence, the metaphor of the luminous appearance adds a reassuring note of benevolence (Ps 4,7; 31,17; 89,16; Nm 6,24ff; cf Pr 16,15). But the presence of God with men is above all a protecting presence. By His Law* He illumines the paths of men (Pr 6,23; Ps 119, 105); He is, therefore, a guiding lamp* (Jb 29,3; Ps 18,29). He saves from peril by lighting up the eyes (Ps 13,4). He is thus man's light and salvation (Ps 27,1). Finally, He leads the just man to the joy of a luminous day (Is 58,10; Ps 36,10; 97,11; 112,4), while the evil man stumbles in the darkness (Is 59,9f) and sees his lamp extinguished (Pr 13,9; 24,20; Jb 18,5f). In the end, light and darkness represent the two destinies awaiting man, happiness and misery.

3. *Promise of light.* It is not surprising to find the symbolism of light and darkness recurring in the prophets, now in an eschatological perspective. Darkness, the threatening scourge for the Egyptians (Ex 10,21...), is one of the signs announcing the day* of Yahweh (Is 13,10; Jr 4,23; 13,16; Ez 32,7; Am 8,9; Jl 2,10; 3,4; 4,15). For a sinful world this day will be darkness and not light (Am 5,18; cf Is 8,21ff).

Nevertheless the day of Yahweh will also have another aspect, the day of deliverance for the remnant* of the lowly and distressed just ones. Then "the people who walk in darkness will see a great light" (Is 9,1; 42,7; 49,9; Mi 7,8f). The image has an obvious meaning and allows many applications. It suggests first the clearness of a wonderful day (Is 30,26), without the alternation of day and night (Ze 14,7), a day brightened by the "sun of justice" (Ml 3,20). Yet the dawn which will rise over the new Jerusalem* (Is 60,1ff) will be of another order from that of our present world. The living God Himself will shine upon His own (60,19f). His Law* will enlighten His people (Is 2,5; 51,4; Ba 4,2). This Servant* will be the light of the nations* (Is 42,6; 49,6).

On this supreme day, therefore, will re-occur for the just and for sinners the two destinies strikingly exemplified in the history of the exodus*: darkness for the heathen, but a day of bright light for the saints (Ws 17,1—18,4). The just will shine like the sky and the stars, while the heathen will dwell forever in the dark horror of Sheol (Dn 12,3; cf Ws 3,7). The perspective opens upon a world transfigured by the image of the God of light.

NT

I. CHRIST, LIGHT OF THE WORLD

1. *Fulfillment of the promise.* The eschatological light promised by the prophets became a reality in the NT. When Jesus began preaching in Galilee, the prophecy of Is 9,1 was fulfilled (Mt 4,16). When He rose according to the prophecies, it was "to proclaim the light to the people and to the pagan nations" (Ac 26, 23). Thus do the canticles preserved in Luke proclaim in Him right from infancy the rising sun which will illumine those who are in darkness (Lk 1,78f; cf Ml 3,20; Is 9,1; 42,7), the light which will enlighten the nations (Lk 2,32; cf Is 42,6; 49,6). Paul's vocation to proclaim the gospel to the gentiles will be along the lines of the same prophetic texts (Ac 13,47; 26,18).

2. *Christ revealed as light.* It is primarily by His words and deeds that Jesus reveals Himself as the light of the world. Cures of the blind (cf Mk 8,22-26) have a special meaning here, as John stresses in recording the episode of the man born blind (Jn 9). Jesus states there, "As long as I am in the world, I am the light of the world" (9,5). In another place, "Whoever follows me does not walk in darkness, but he will have the light of life" (8,12); "I, the light, have come into the world in order that whoever believes in me will not walk in darkness" (12,46). His illuminating action proceeds

from what He is in Himself, the very Word* of God, the life* and light of men, the true light which enlightens every man by coming into this world (1,4.9). Likewise the drama which goes on around Him is a confrontation of light and darkness. The light shines in the darkness (1,4), and the evil world* tries to put it out; for men prefer darkness to the light since their works* are evil (3,19). Finally, at the hour of the passion, when Judas leaves the Cenacle to hand over Jesus, John intentionally observes, "It was night" (13,30); and Jesus, at the time of His arrest, declares, "This is your hour, and the power of darkness" (Lk 22,53).

3. *Christ transfigured.* While Jesus dwelt on earth, the divine light He carried within Him was hidden under the lowliness of flesh*. There was, nevertheless, one occasion where it became visible to the privileged witnesses in an extraordinary vision, the transfiguration*. His face shone, His clothes were brilliant as light (Mt 17,2 p)—they are no longer simply part of mortal humanity. Here is an anticipation of Christ's risen state when He will appear to Paul in a shining light (Ac 9,3; 22,6; 26,13). The transfiguration is dependent on the symbolism proper to OT theophanies. The light which shone on the face* of Christ is that of the glory of God Himself (cf 2 Co 4,6). It is precisely as Son* of God that He is "the reflection of His glory" (He 1,3). Through Christ, the light, is revealed something of the divine essence. Not only does God "dwell in inaccessible light" (1 Tm 6,16), not only can He be called "the Father of light" (Jm 1,5), but, as St. John explains, "He is light itself, and in Him is no darkness at all" (1 Jn 1,5). Therefore, everything which is light comes forth from Him, from the creation of physical light on the first day (cf Jn 1,4) to the illumination of our hearts by the light of Christ (2 Co 4,6). Anything alien to this light pertains to the kingdom of darkness; the darkness of night, the darkness of Sheol and of death, the darkness of Satan.

II. SONS OF LIGHT

1. *Men between darkness and light.* The revelation of Jesus as the light of the world brings into relief the darkness-light antithesis, not in a metaphysical perspective, but on a moral plane. Light defines the kingdom of God and of Christ as that of goodness and justice. Darkness specifies the domain of Satan* as one of evil and ungodliness (cf 2 Co 6,14f), although Satan sometimes disguises himself as an angel of light to deceive man (11,14). Man exists between these two; he must choose, so that he might become "a son of darkness" or "a son of light." The Qumrân sect already used this description for the eschatological war*. Jesus employs it to distinguish the present world* from the kingdom* He is founding. For Him men are divided into "sons of this world" and "sons of light" (Lk 16,8). The division is clarified when Christ, the light, appears. Those who do evil flee the light lest their works* be revealed. Those who act in truth come to the light (Jn 3,19ff) and they believe in the light in order to become sons of the light (Jn 12,36).

2. *From darkness to the light.* By birth all men pertain to the kingdom of darkness, especially the pagans "darkened in their thoughts" (E 4,18). It is God who "has called us from darkness to His marvelous light" (1 P 2,9). He took us from the kingdom of darkness, He has transferred us to the kingdom of His son to share the destiny of the saints in the light (Col 1,12f). This was the decisive grace experienced at baptism when "Christ shone upon us" (E 5,14) and we were "brought into the light" (He 6,4). Once we were darkness, but now we are light in the Lord (E 5,8). This determines our standard of conduct: "to live as sons of light" (E 5,8; cf 1 Th 5,5).

3. *The life of the sons of light.* The Pauline exhortation above had already been enjoined by Jesus (cf Jn 12,35f). A man should not allow his interior light to grow dark, just as he should not neglect his eyes, the lamp* of his body (Mt 6,22f p). This advice is habitually on Paul's lips: put on the arms of light and put away deeds of darkness (R 13,12f) lest the day* of the Lord surprise you (1 Th 5,4-8). All his moral teaching easily fits this perspective: the product of light is all that is good, just, and true; "sterile deeds of darkness" include sins of all kinds (E 5,9-14). Johannine doctrine is the same. "Walk in the light" to be in union with God who is light (1 Jn 1,5ff). Fraternal love* is the criterion for judging whether a man is in the darkness or in the light (2,8-11). The man who lives as a true son of the light makes the divine light present in him shine before men. Light of the world in his turn (Mt 5,14ff), man thus assumes the work given him by Christ.

4. *Toward the eternal light.* Committed to the

light, man can hope for the marvelous transformation God promised the just in His kingdom (Mt 13,43). The heavenly Jerusalem* where they finally arrive will reflect on them the divine light, according to the prophetic texts (Ap 21, 23ff; cf Is 60). Then the elect, contemplating the face of God, will be illumined by this light (Ap 22,4f). Such is the hope of the sons of light; such also is the prayer which the Church addresses to God for her deceased members.

→Baptism IV 4—Cloud—Day of the Lord NT III 1—Death OT I 2—Fire—Glory—Hardness of Heart II 1—Lamp—Life IV 2—Night—Oil—Revelation—See—Shadow—Sin IV 2 a—Stars 4—Truth OT 3; NT 3—Watch I 2—White—Word of God NT I 1.

LIPS

The lips are a thread of scarlet upon the face of the beloved (Ct 4,3); they distill the unctuous honey of the word (4,11); they are even said to be the word itself (Jb 16,5) as it is formed. Unlike the tongue*, which plays an active role in the speech process, the lips and mouth passively await their opening to express the depths of the heart*.

1. *Lips and heart*. The lips are at the service of the heart, whether it be good or evil (Pr 10, 32; 15,7; 24,2). They reveal its qualities; the grace of the ideal king (Ps 45,3) or the deceitful allure of the adulterous woman (Pr 5,3; 7,21). The lips of the sinner serve his evil designs by their lies*, deceits, and calumnies (Pr 4,24; 12, 22; Ps 120,2; Si 51,2); they can conceal profound wickedness behind a pleasant face*; "Polish upon an earthen pot is the flattering lip joined to an evil heart" (Pr 26,23). This deceit even affects man's dealings with God: "This people honor me with their lips but their heart is far from me" (Mt 15,8=Is 29,13).

The opposite of the deceitful man is the one whose lips are always sincere and just (Ps 17,1; Pr 10,18-21; 23,15f). But to keep them from lies (Ps 34,14=1 P 3,10), God Himself must instruct them (Pr 22,17f); they must be lifted up to the lips of God through obedience* and fidelity (Ps 17,4; Jb 23,12). "Set a guard, O Lord, over my mouth; keep watch at the gate of my lips!" (Ps 141,3; cf Si 22,27f).

2. *"Lord, open my lips!"* The psalmist knows that he must have recourse to God for the grace of simplicity in his speech with others. But in the presence of God man can do nothing but acknowledge his profound corruption: "Woe to me, I am lost; for I am a man of unclean lips, and I dwell among a people of unclean lips, and my eyes have seen the king, the Lord of hosts" (Is 6,5). He knows that he ought to glorify and acclaim God (cf Ps 63,4.6) and offer Him true praise (Ho 14,3), but he is also aware of his basic uncleanness. He does not simply wait for God to deign to open his lips so that he might respond (Jb 11,5); to remove his sin, his lips must be purified by fire (Is 6,6). When His day* comes, God "will give the people pure lips" (Zp 3,9), as He will create in them a new heart* (Ez 36,26). Today this hope is realized in Jesus Christ, "through whom we can offer a sacrifice of praise for all time, that is, the tribute of lips which acknowledge His name*" (He 13,15). Therefore, with the certainty of being heard, every man can pray: "Lord, open my lips, and my mouth will proclaim your praise!" (Ps 51,17).

→Confession NT 2—Heart I 1.2—Human Speech—Lie—Tongue.

CL & XLD mjm

LISTEN

The biblical revelation* is essentially the Word* of God to man. And that is why, although in the Greek mystery religions and oriental gnosticism the relation of man to God is based above all on vision, in the Bible "faith comes by hearing" (R 10,17).

1. *Man is to hear God.*

a) Listen, cries the prophet with the authority of God (Am 3,1; Jr 7,2). Listen, repeats the wise man in light of his own experience and of his knowledge of the Law* (Pr 1,8). Listen, Israel, says the pious Israelite daily in order to be penetrated by the will* of his God (Dt 6,4; Mk 12,29). Listen, says Jesus Himself, the Word of God, in His own turn (Mk 4,3.9 p).

Now according to the Hebraic meaning of the word *truth**, to listen, to receive the Word of God, is not only to lend it an attentive ear but also to open one's heart* to it (Ac 16,14); it is to put it into practice (Mt 7,24ff), that is, to obey.

319

Such is the obedience of faith* which preaching that is heard demands (R 1,5; 10,14ff).

b) But man does not wish to listen (Dt 18,16. 19), and that is his tragedy. He is deaf to the calls of God; his ears and his heart are uncircumcised (Jr 6,10; 9,25; Ac 7,51). This is the sin of the Jews that Jesus encounters: "You are unable to hear my Word...Whoever is of God hears the Word of God; if you do not understand, it is because you are not of God" (Jn 8,43.47).

Only God, in fact, can open the ear of His disciple* (Is 50,5; cf 1 S 9,15; Jb 36,10), "to hollow" it that he might obey (Ps 40,7f). And so in the Messianic age the deaf will hear and the miracles of Jesus signify that finally the deaf people will understand and obey the Word of God (Is 29,18; 35,5; 42,18ff; 43,8; Mt 11,5). It is what the voice of heaven declares to the disciples: "This is my beloved Son; hear Him" (Mt 17,5 p).

Mary*, accustomed to keep the words of God faithfully in her heart (Lk 2,19.51), was beatified by her son Jesus, when He revealed the profound meaning of her motherhood: "Blessed are those who hear the Word of God and keep it" (Lk 11,28).

2. *God listens to man.* In his prayer* man asks of God to listen to him, that is, to hear him favorably. God does not listen to the unjust or sinners (Is 1,15; Mi 3,4; Jn 9,31). But He hears the poor, the widow and the orphan, the humble and imprisoned (Ex 22,22-26; Ps 10,17; 102,21; Jm 5,4). He listens to the just, those who are devout and do His will (Ps 34,16.18; Jn 9,31; 1 P 3,12), those who ask in accordance with His will* (1 Jn 5,14f). And if He does listen, it is because He listens "always" to His son Jesus (Jn 11,41f), through whom the prayer of the Christian is always transmitted.

→Calling—Disciple—Faith OT I; NT I 2— Follow — Know OT 2 — Obedience — Transfiguration 2—Word of God.

CA jrc

LOINS

The word often stands for a man's physical strength (1 K 12,10), his procreative power, and refers to the middle region of the body, the hips or the seat of the generative functions (2 S 7,12; Ps 132,11; He 7,5.10). It means also the seat or source of the passions, secret thoughts and feelings (Ps 72,21; Ap 2,23). So there are two different types of meaning, one being a call to action and the other a reminder of God's power over the most hidden part of our personality.

1. The vital strength of a man is concentrated *in the lumbar region.* Just as for a journey or physical combat one attaches a money bag (Gn 37,34), or a loin cloth is put on by means of a belt to the outer clothes or dress (1 K 20,31; Mt 3,4), or weapons (2 S 20,8), so in the service of God the loins must be girt. The Hebrews were thus equipped for the exodus (Ex 12,11); so also was Jeremiah girded for opposition (Jr 1,17). The valiant woman is always hard at work (Pr 31,17); the Messiah's strength will consist in justice and constancy (Is 11,5). The disciple of Jesus ought to keep his loins girt and a lamp* burning in his hand (Lk 12,35). The Christian is urged to fight "with the girdle of truth and justice for his coat of mail" (E 6, 14). St. Peter concludes: "Be like men stripped for action, perfectly self-controlled" (1 P 1,13).

2. *In the loins, the internal organs,* the deepest feelings are expressed. In that area are formed hidden designs, and violent passions are enkindled. The heart of the master rejoices when he hears his disciple speaking well (Pr 23,16). A man's loins can be stirred by apostasy (1 M 2, 24), transfixed by a trial (Jb 16,13). Man's Creator (Ps 139,13) can use these organs to instruct the conscience of a man in prayer (Ps 16,7). Ordinarily associated with the heart*, the loins designate a region which escapes the attention of men and hence is little spoken of. Only "God sounds the depths of the heart and the loins" (Ps 7,10; Jr 11,20; Ap 2,23); and in the same fashion, it is Jesus who knows what is in man (Jn 2,25). God alone penetrates to the depths of one's being. Jeremiah, the prophet of the interior life, as well as the psalmist, did not fear to be tested by the divine scrutiny: "Try me, O Lord, test me, examine my mind and my heart" (Ps 26,2; Jr 17,10; 20,12). For they knew that, unlike their enemies, their loins testified to what their lips* had spoken (Jr 12,2f). God hears human speech, but He is also "witness of the loins and a true searcher of the heart" (Ws 1,6). So the liturgy words its prayer in the same spirit: "Enkindle, O Lord, our loins and our hearts with the fire of the Holy Spirit."

→Conscience 1—Heart I 2.

RF jab

LORD

In its liturgy the Church addresses every prayer to God the Father through Jesus Christ our Lord. The title of Lord was bestowed on Jesus from the beginning, as is clear from the evidence of Paul, who recalls the primitive creed of the Christian faith: "Jesus is Lord" (R 10,9). This name expresses the mystery of Christ, Son of Man and Son of God, and the OT shows in fact that *Lord (Adonay=Kyrios)* is not only a royal title but also a divine name.

OT

The lordship of Yahweh is not limited to the people whom He has chosen and over whom He is king (1 S 8,7f; 12,12); Yahweh is the "Lord of lords" because He is the God* of gods (Dt 10,17; Ps 136,3). His lordship is not that of a Canaanite divinity, bound to the earth of which it is the *Baal* (a term which designates the possessor and by extension the husband, master, and lord of his wife). The name of Baal cannot apply to the God of Israel (Ho 2,18; if it is used in Is 54,5, this is to designate God as spouse not of a territory but of His people).

As universal Lord, God exercises His dominion in every place for the benefit of His people (Dt 10,14-18). Two names express His authority: *melek* and *'ādōn*. The first means "king" (Is 6,5; Ps 97,5); and the kingship of the God of Israel extends to all of His creation (Ps 95,3), even to the pagans themselves (Ps 96,10). The second name means "Lord": God is the Lord of all the earth (Js 3,11; Mi 4,13; Ps 97,5). God is invoked by addressing Him as "my Lord"; this is a royal title (*Adōnī*), which habitually takes the form *Adōnāy* (plural of intensity) when it is applied to God. This invocation, already present in ancient texts (Gn 15,2.8), expresses the confidence which the servants of God place in His absolute sovereignty (Am 7,2; Dt 9,26; Js 7,7; Ps 140,8). This title, frequently employed, finally became a proper name for God.

When, out of respect, the name of Yahweh* was no longer pronounced in the liturgical readings, it was replaced by *Adōnāy*. For this reason it doubtless came about that the LXX uses *Kyrios*, the Greek equivalent of *Adonai*, to translate Yahweh. The title of *Kyrios* then can, for this reason, have two meanings: sometimes it designates the sovereignty of Yahweh, sometimes the incommunicable name of the one true God.

NT

The NT transfers the title *Kyrios* to Christ. To explain this transference is to define the Christian faith.

1. *The faith of the infant Church.* Beginning from the expression found in Ps 110,1, Jesus had wished to make people understand that, while being a son of David, He was superior to him and existed before him (Mt 22,43ff; cf Lk 1, 43; 2,11). Relying on this same psalm, the infant Church proclaims the lordship of Christ which is made effective by His resurrection (Ac 2,34ff). In its prayer, it preserved for a long time the primitive Aramaic invocation: *Marana tha*: "Our Lord, come!" (1 Co 16,22; Ap 22,20). The light of Easter and reflection on Scripture are the sources of the first Christian profession of faith: "Jesus is Lord" (R 10,9; 1 Co 12,3; Col 2,6). Jesus deserves the supreme title of *Marana* and *Kyrios* in as much as He is the Messiah* enthroned in heaven, inaugurating His kingdom by the gift of the Spirit (Ac 2,33), and always present to His Church in the eucharistic assembly, while it awaits the judgment* (10,42). But this lordship of Christ, in the forefront in the title *Kyrios*, is that of God Himself, so much so that what belonged to Yahweh alone, for instance, the invocation of the name* (2,20f) or the gestures and formulas of adoration* (Ph 2,10=Is 45,23; Jn 9,38; Ap 15,4), was transferred to the "Lord of all" (10,36).

2. At Corinth *Paul* passes on the *Marana tha* of Palestinian Christianity, showing by this that he receives his conception of Jesus-Lord from it and not from Hellenism which gave this title to the gods and to the emperor (cf Ac 25,26). Like Peter in his preaching, he relies on Psalm 110 (1 Co 15,25; Col 3,1; E 1,20) and gives to *Kyrios* a double value, both human and divine. As king*, Jesus is Lord of all men (R 14,9), of all His enemies, the powers* (Col 2,10.15), and death* (1 Co 15,24ff.57; cf 1 P 3,22), and of the human masters who represent to their slaves the only true master (Col 3,22—4,1; E 6,5-9). Finally He is Lord of the Church, His own body which He rules and nourishes (Col 3,18; E 1, 20ff; 4,15; 5,22-32). Also all the universe; heavens, earth, and hell proclaim that Jesus is Lord (Ph 2,10f). This last text assures the divine value of the title: after Jesus, who was of "divine state," has made Himself a slave, He is exalted by God and receives from Him "that name* which is above every name," a radiation

of the divinity over His glorified humanity which lays the foundation for His universal sovereignty.

Considered in terms of this double significance, both royal and divine, the formula of faith "Jesus is Lord" takes on a note of protest against the imperial claims to divinity. There are *kyrioi* among the "false gods," but Jesus is the only absolute *Kyrios* (1 Co 8,5f), to whom the others are subject. The Apocalypse makes it clear also that the title "Lord of lords," which is attested for a very long time in the East (from about 1100 B.C.), does not belong to the deified emperor, but to Christ alone, as to the Father (Ap 17,14; 19,16; cf Dt 10,17; 1 Tm 6,16).

Casting the light of Easter back over the events of the life of Christ, Luke likes to designate Jesus by His title of Lord (Lk 7,13; 10,39. 41...). John uses it less often (Jn 11,2), but he recalls how the disciple Jesus loved recognized the Lord in the person standing on the shore (21,7); and especially how Thomas, speaking for the whole Church, fully recognized the divinity of the risen Jesus in His lordship over believers: "my Lord and my God" (20,28).

→Adoration II 2—Authority NT I—Body II— David 3—God—Glory—Jesus (Name of) III— Jesus Christ II—King NT II 1—Kingdom NT III 2—Man I 1 d. 2 b—Messiah NT II 2—Name OT 4; NT 3—Yahweh 3.

PT jpl

LOVE

"God is love." "Love one another." Before arriving at this summit of NT revelation, man should purify the completely human concepts he has made for himself about love, in order to grasp the mystery of divine love—and this takes place through the cross. The word *love* actually signifies a mixture of different things, carnal or spiritual, passionate or thoughtful, serious or light, expansive or destructive. One loves something pleasant; an animal, a companion in one's work, a friend, relatives, his children, finally a woman. The biblical man knew all that. Genesis (cf Gn 2,23f; 3,16; 12,10-19; 22; 24; 34), the history of David (cf 1 S 18,1ff; 2 S 3,16; 12,15-25; 19,1-5), the Canticle, are, among many others, the witnesses of all kinds of sentiment. Sin is often mixed in; but one also finds modest uprightness, depth, and sincerity expressed in words habitually sober and modest.

Little given to intellectual abstraction, Israel

often gives to the words an affective coloring: for her, to know* is already to love; her fidelity* to social and familial (*hesed*) ties is completely impregnated with spirit and a liberal spontaneity (cf Gn 24,49; Js 2,12ff; Rt 3,10; Ze 7,9). *To love* (hb. *āhab*; gr. *agapan*; among the Greek words for love the Septuagint has chosen this less usual verb, which is to become an exclusively religious word in the NT) has as many overtones as the English word.

In short, the biblical man knows the value of affection (cf Pr 15,17), although he is not ignorant of its risks (Pr 5; Si 6,5-17). When the notion of love penetrates his religious psychology, it is totally charged with a human experience both rich and concrete. At the same time love raises numerous questions. Can God, so great, so pure, lower Himself to love man, small and sinful? And if God condescends to love man, how could man respond to this love by love in return? What relationship exists between love of God and the love of men? All religions make an effort in their own ways to answer these questions, usually by falling into one or the other of two opposed extremes: to maintain the distance between God and man, they relegate the divine love to an inaccessible sphere— or to make God present to man, they profane the love of God into a totally human love. The Bible gives a clear answer to this religious anxiety on man's part. God has taken the initiative by a dialogue of love with men; in the name of this love He binds them and teaches them to love each other.

I. THE DIALOGUE OF LOVE BETWEEN GOD AND MAN

OT

Although the word *love* does not appear here, the creation narratives (Gn 1; 2—3) hint at the love of God through the goodness of which Adam and Eve are the object. God wishes to give them life* in its fullness, but this gift supposes free adherence to His will*; it is by the expedient of a commandment that God engages in the dialogue of love. Adam wanted to make himself master of that which was destined for him as a gift: he sinned. Then the mystery of goodness is deepened by mercy* to the sinner in the promises* of salvation*; progressively the ties of love which united God and man will be re-established. The story of Paradise is already an indication of the whole of sacred history.

1. *Friends and confidants of God.* In calling Abraham, chosen from among the pagans (Js 24,2f), to become His friend (Is 41,8), God expresses His love in the form of friendship: Abraham becomes the confidant of His secrets (Gn 18,17). If such is the case, it is so because Abraham responded to the demands of divine love: he left his country at the request of God (12,1); he must soon enter into the mystery of fear* of God who is love, for he is called upon to sacrifice his only son, and with him, his human love: "Take your son, him whom you love" (Gn 22,2).

Moses* did not have to sacrifice his son; but his whole people is called into question by conflict between divine sanctity and sin; he is torn between God, whose representative he is, and the people whom he represents (Ex 32,9-13). If he remains faithful, it is because from his calling (3,4) to his death, he did not cease to advance in intimacy with God, dealing with Him as with a neighbor* (33,11); he had had the revelation of the tremendous tenderness of God, of a love which without sacrificing anything of its holiness is mercy* (34,6f).

2. *Prophetic revelation.* Confidants of God themselves (Am 3,7); personally loved by God, whose choice laid hold of them (7,15), sometimes tore then asunder (Jr 20,7ff), but also filled them with joy (20,11ff); the prophets* are witnesses of a drama of the love and the anger of Yahweh (Am 3,2). Hosea, then Jeremiah and Ezekiel, reveal that God is the bridegroom of an always unfaithful Israel; this passionate and jealous love (cf zeal*) is rewarded only with ingratitude and betrayal. But love is stronger than sin; it must suffer (Ho 11,8); it pardons* and recreates in Israel a new* heart* capable of love (Ho 2,21f; Jr 31,3.20.22; Ez 16, 60-63; 36,26f). Other images, as that of the shepherd* (Ez 34) or the vine* (Is 5; Ez 17,6-10), express the same divine ardor and the same drama.

Promulgated no doubt (2 K 22) at the moment when the people seem to prefer definitely the worship of idols* to the love of God, Deuteronomy unwearyingly recalls that the love of God for Israel is gratuitous (Dt 7,7f) and that Israel should "love God with all its heart" (6,5). This love is expressed in acts of adoration* and of obedience* (11,13; 19,9) which suppose a radical choice, a costly uprooting

(4,9-28; 30,15-20). But it is possible only if God in person comes to circumcise* the heart of Israel and to render it capable of love (30,6).

3. *Toward a personal dialogue.* After the exile*, Israel, purified by the trial*, discovers more and more that life with God is a dialogue of love. It is no doubt in this frame of mind that they re-read the Song of Songs: with the alternating ideas of possession and seeking, the Spouse* and the bride are shown to love one another with a love "strong as death" (Ct 8,6).

After the exile there is even greater awareness that God is addressing Himself to the heart of each man. He does not only love the group (Dt 4,7) or its leaders (2 S 12,24) but each individual Jew, and above all the just* man (Ps 37,25-29; 146,8), the poor* and the lowly (Ps 113,5-9). And gradually we see the emergence of the idea that apart from the Jew Yahweh's love even embraces the pagans as well (Jon 4, 10f), and in fact every creature (Ws 11,23-26).

Thus, as the time for the arrival of Christ draws near, the pious* Jew (hb. *hasid*: Ps 4,4; 132,9.16) meditates on the Bible and realizes that he is loved by a God whose merciful fidelity to the covenant* (Ps 136; Jl 2,13), whose goodness (Ps 34,9; 100,5) and grace* (Gn 6,8; Is 30,18) and tenderness* (Ps 86,15; Ws 15,1) he sings. In return, he repeats unceasingly his love for God (Ps 31,24; 73,25; 116,1) and for all that belongs to Him: His name*, His Law*, His wisdom* (Ps 34,13; 119,127; Is 56,6; Si 1,10; 4,14). This love should often prove itself in the face of the example and pressure of the ungodly (Ps 10; 40,14-17; 73; Si 2,11-17); and this can go all the way to martyrdom, as was the case in the time of the Maccabees (2 M 6—7); and also later in the case of Rabbi Akiba, dying for his faith in 135 A.D.: "I have loved Him with my whole heart, He will say, and with all my fortune; I had not yet had the occasion to love Him with my whole self (cf soul*). The moment has arrived." When this sublime word was pronounced, the full revelation had already been given to men by Jesus Christ.

NT

The love between God and men had been revealed in the OT through a series of events: divine initiatives and refusals by man, the suffering of rejected love, sad excesses for one who was at the level of love and was accepting the grace of love. In the NT, divine love is expressed in a unique fact, the very nature of which transfigured the facts of the situation: Jesus came to live as God and as man, the dramatic dialogue of love between God and man.

1. *The gift of the Father.* The coming of Jesus is first of all an act of the Father. According to the prophets and the promises of the OT, "being mindful of His mercy" (Lk 1,54f; He 1,1), God made Himself known (Jn 1,18); He manifests His love (R 8,39; 1 Jn 3,1; 4,9) in Him who is not only the expected Messiah* savior (Lk 2,11), but His own Son* (Mk 1,11; 9,7; 12,6), He whom He loves (Jn 3,35; 10,17; 15,9; Col 1,13).

The love of the Father expresses itself then in a manner which nothing can surpass. Here we have the realization of the new covenant* and the eternal wedding of the bridegroom* with humanity is concluded. The divine generosity, which has been in evidence since Israel's beginnings (Dt 7,7f), reaches its peak. In welcoming the Son, man cannot help renouncing all pride*, all arrogance*, based on his own merits; the gift of love made by God is absolutely free (R 5,6f; Tt 3,5; 1 Jn 4,10-19). This gift is definitive, going beyond the earthly existence of Jesus (Mt 28,20; Jn 14,18f); this gift is pushed to the extreme, because it consents to the death of the Son that the world* may have life (R 5,8; 8,32) and that we may be sons* of God (1 Jn 3, 1; G 4,4-7). If "God so loved the world that He gave His only Son" (Jn 3,16), it is that men may have eternal life*; but they themselves condemn themselves, those who refuse to believe in Him who has been sent and who "love more" the darkness than the light (3,19). The choice is inevitable: either love through faith in the Son, or anger through the refusal of faith (3,36).

2. *The perfect love revealed in Jesus.* It is not only on the occasion of contact with Jesus, but through His person, that henceforth the drama of love is enacted. By His very existence, Jesus is the concrete revelation of love; Jesus is the man* who fulfills the filial dialogue with God and bears witness of it to men. Jesus is God who comes to live out His love in the fullness of humanity and who came to make us understand the ardent appeal of love. In His very person man loves God and is loved by Him.

a) The entire life of Jesus witnesses to the twofold dialogue. Given over to the Father from the beginning (Lk 2,49; cf He 10,5ff), living in prayer and thanksgiving (cf Mk 1,35; Mt 11,25),

and above all in perfect conformity to the divine will* (Jn 4,34; 6,38), He is untiring in listening* to God (5,30; 8,26.40), which assures Him of being heard by God (11,41f; cf 9,31). In regard to men, His life is completely given, not only to certain friends* (cf Mk 10,21; Lk 8,1ff; Jn 11,3.5.36), but to all (Mk 10,45). He went about doing good (Ac 10,38; Mt 11,28ff), in total disinterestedness (Lk 9,58) and in attention to all, including especially the most despised and the most unworthy (Lk 7,36-50; 19, 1-10; Mt 21,31f); He chose freely those He wished (Mk 3,13), to make them His friends (Jn 15,15f).

This love calls for reciprocity; the commandment of Deuteronomy is still in force (Mt 22,37; cf R 8,28; 1 Co 8,3; 1 Jn 5,2), but it is through Jesus that one obeys it; in loving Him, man loves the Father (Mt 10,40; Jn 8,42; 14,21-24). Finally, to love Jesus is to keep His Word* in its entirety (Jn 14,15.21.23) and to follow* Him in renouncing all (Mk 10,17-21; Lk 14,25ff). Henceforth a division is operative throughout the gospel (Lk 2,34) between those who accept and those who refuse this love before which one cannot remain neutral (Jn 6,60-71; cf 3,18f; 8,13-59; 12,48).

b) On the cross, love reveals in a decisive way its intensity and its drama. Jesus had to suffer* (Lk 9,22; 17,25; 24,7.26; cf He 2,8) to reveal fully His obedience* to His Father (Ph 2, 8) and His love of His own (Jn 13,1). Completely free (cf Mt 26,53; Jn 10,18), throughout the temptation and the apparent silence* of God (Mk 14,32-41; 15,34; cf He 4,15) in the starkly human solitude* (Mk 14,50; 15,29-32), nevertheless He pardons and is still open to all men (Lk 23,28.34.43; Jn 19,26). Jesus arrives at the unparalleled instant of the "greatest love" (Jn 15,13). Without reserve He here gives all to God (Lk 23,46) and to all men without exception (Mk 10,45; 14,24; 2 Co 5,14f; 1 Tm 2,5f). By the cross, God is completely glorified (Jn 17,4); "the man Jesus" (1 Tm 2,5), and with Him all mankind, merits to be loved by God without reserve (Jn 10,17; Ph 2,9ff). God and man are incorporated in a unity*, according to the final prayer of Jesus (Jn 17). It is still necessary that man freely accept so total and demanding a love which should lead him to self-sacrifice after the example of Christ (17,19). He finds on his path the scandal* of the cross* which is nothing else than the scandal of love. It is there that is manifested in its fullness the gift of the bridegroom to His spouse (E 5,25ff;

G 2,20); but there also for all men is the supreme temptation to infidelity.

3. *Universal love in the Spirit.* If Calvary is the place of perfect love, the manner of its manifestation is a decisive test; the friends of the crucified abandon Him (Mk 14,50; Lk 23, 13-24); this is because fidelity to divine love is not a matter of a physical encounter nor of human reasoning; in short, of "knowledge according to the flesh*" (2 Co 5,16); here is required the gift of the Spirit*, who creates a "new* heart*" (cf Jr 31,33f; Ez 36,25ff). Sent forth at Pentecost* (Ac 2,1-36) as Christ had promised (Jn 14,16ff; cf Lk 24,49), the Spirit since that time has been present in the world (Jn 14,16) through the Church (E 2,21f); and He teaches* men what Jesus has told them (Jn 14,26), making them understand from within, by a true religious knowledge. Witnesses* or not of the earthly life of Jesus, men are here equal, without distinction of time or race. Every man has need of the Spirit to be able to say "Father" (R 8,15) and to glorify Christ (Jn 16, 14). There is diffused among us a love (R 5,5) which controls us (2 Co 5,14), a love from which nothing can separate us (R 8,35-39) and which prepares us for the definitive encounter with love in which "we will know as we are known" (1 Co 13,12).

4. *God is love.* Led by the Spirit to live with his Lord in a dialogue of love, the Christian, then, comes close to the very mystery of God*. For God does not reveal Himself for what He is at the first encounter: He speaks, calls and acts, and in this way man arrives at a deeper understanding. When He gives His Son, God reveals that He is the one who gives Himself in love (cf R 8,32). Living with His Father in a dialogue of absolute love and so revealing that the Father and He are "one" from all eternity (Jn 10,30; cf 17,11.21f) and that He is Himself God (Jn 1,1; cf 10,33.38; Mt 11,27), "the only Son who is nearest to the Father's heart" helps us to get to know the God whom "no one has ever seen" (Jn 1,18). This God is His Father and Himself in the unity of the Spirit. And the "beloved disciple," the one who has experienced what charity and faith really mean, can say what must be the last word on the subject: "God is love" (1 Jn 4,8.16). Of all human words, with their richness and their limitations, it is this word "love" that gives the best idea of the mystery of God the Trinity, the eternal and reciprocal gift of the Father, Son and Spirit.

II. FRATERNAL CHARITY

OT

In the OT, the commandment of the love of God is completed by the "second commandment": "You shall love your neighbor as yourself" (Lv 19,18). Actually this commandment is presented in a less solemn fashion than the other (comp Lv 19,1-37 and Dt 6,4-13); and the term *neighbor** there has, assuredly, a rather narrow meaning. But the Israelite is already asked to turn attention to "others." In the most ancient texts, it is an offense against God to be indifferent or hostile to one's neighbors (Gn 3, 12; 4,9f); and the Law adds to the demands which concern the relations with God those which pertain to the relations among men: thus the Decalogue (Ex 20,12-17), or the "Covenant Code," which abounds in prescriptions about attention to the poor* and the lowly (Ex 22,20-26; 23,4-12). The whole prophetic tradition (Am 1—2; Is 1,14-17; Jr 9,2-5; Ez 18, 5-9; Ml 3,5) and the entire sapiential tradition (Pr 14,21; 1,8-19; Si 25,1; Ws 2,10ff) terminate at the same point: it is impossible to please God without respecting other men, especially the most forsaken, the least "interesting." Never did anyone believe he could love God without being interested in men: "He practiced justice and the law...He judged the cause of the poor and of the downcast. Is this not to know* me?" (Jr 22,15f). The oracle concerns Josiah, but touches all Israel (cf Jr 9,4).

That this duty should explicitly be called *love* is not often said (Lv 19,18; 19,34; Dt 10,19). Already however, in speaking of love for the stranger* [resident alien] the command is founded on the duty to act as Yahweh did at the time of the exodus*: "Yahweh loves the stranger to whom He gives bread and clothing. Love the stranger, for in the land of Egypt you were strangers" (Dt 10,18f). The motive is not a simple natural solidarity, but the history of salvation.

Before the coming of Christ, Judaism deepened the nature of fraternal love. In the love of the neighbor was included the Jewish adversary, even the pagan enemy*; love became more universal, although Israel kept to its central role. "Love peace," said Hillel. "Long for peace. Love creatures, lead them to the Law." There is the discovery that to love is to prolong the divine action: "Just as the holy one—may He be blessed!—clothes the naked, consoles the afflicted, buries the dead, likewise, you also clothe the naked, visit the sick, etc." It was from that time easy to make the connection between the two commandments of love for God and for the neighbor; that is what a scribe one day would do upon approaching Jesus (Lk 10,26f).

NT

If the Jewish conception could let one believe that fraternal love is put on a level of equality with the other commandments, the Christian vision gives it the central, or rather, the unique position.

1. *The two loves.* From the beginning to the end of the NT, the love of neighbor* seems to be inseparable from the love of God: the two commandments are the zenith and the key of the Law (Mk 12,28-33 p). Brotherly love is the fulfillment of all moral demands (G 5,22; 6,2; R 13,8f; Col 3,14): it is in fact the only commandment (Jn 15,12; 2 Jn 5), the unique and many-sided work* of all living faith* (G 5,6. 22). "A man who does not love the brother whom he can see cannot love God, whom he has never seen...we love God's children if we love God Himself (1 Jn 4,20f; 5,2). It is impossible to improve on the statement that fundamentally there is only one love.

So the love of one's neighbor is essentially religious: it is not simply philanthropy. Moreover it is religious because of its model: the love of God itself (Mt 5,44f; E 5,1f.25; 1 Jn 4, 11f). And lastly and above all it is so because of its source, for it is the work of God in us: how would we be merciful like the heavenly Father (Lk 6,36) if the Lord did not teach us (1 Th 4,9), if the Spirit did not spread it in our hearts (R 5,5; 15,30)? This love comes from God and exists in us from the very fact that God took us for His sons* (1 Jn 4,7). Having come from God, this love returns to Him. In loving our brothers, we love the Lord Himself (Mt 25,40), since we all together form the body* of Christ (R 12,5-10; 1 Co 12,12-27). Such is the manner in which we can respond to the love with which God has first loved us (1 Jn 3,16; 4,19f).

While awaiting the coming of the Lord, charity is the essential activity of the disciples of Jesus, according to which they will be judged (Mt 25,31-46). Such is the patrimony left by Jesus: "Love one another, as I have loved you" (Jn 13,34f). Christ's act of love continues to find expression through the acts of His disciples.

This commandment, though ancient because linked to the very sources of revelation (1 Jn 2, 7f), is new*. In fact, Jesus has inaugurated a new era by His sacrifice, founding the new community which the prophets had announced; and He has given to man the Spirit who creates new hearts. If therefore the two commandments are united, it is because the love of Christ continues to be expressed through the charity which His followers manifest among themselves.

2. *Love is a gift.* Christian charity is seen, especially by the synoptics and by Paul, in the image of God gratuitously giving His Son for the salvation of all sinful men, without any merit on their part (Mk 10,45; R 5,6ff). It is therefore universal, not allowing any social or racial barrier to exist (G 3,28), not despising anyone (Lk 14,13; 7,39); rather, it demands the love of enemies* (Mt 5,43-47; Lk 10,29-37). Love cannot be discouraged: it expresses itself in pardon* without limit (Mt 18,21f; 6,12.14f), the spontaneous act toward an opponent (Mt 5,23-26), patience*, the return of good for evil (R 12,14-21; E 4,25—5,2). In marriage* it is expressed under the form of a total gift after the image of the sacrifice of Christ (E 5,25-32). For all it is a mutual enslavement (G 5,13), in which man renounces himself with Christ crucified (Ph 2,1-11). In his "hymn to charity" (1 Co 13), Paul manifests the nature and grandeur of love. Without in the least neglecting its daily demands (13,4ff), he affirms that without charity nothing has value (13,1ff), that it alone will survive everything. In loving as Christ loved, we live already a divine and eternal reality (13, 8-13). By love the Church is built up (1 Co 8,1; E 4,16); by it man becomes perfect for the day* of the Lord (Ph 1,9ff).

3. *Love is communion.* John does of course also mention the universality and gratuity of love (Jn 3,16; 15,16; 1 Jn 4,10), but being more conscious of the communion* of the Father and the Son in the Spirit he stresses the consequences of this for the love of Christians for one another. Their brotherhood ought to be a total communion, in which each takes part to the limit of his capacity for love and faith. In the face of the world*, in which he cannot love the kingdom of the "evil one" (1 Jn 2,14f; cf Jn 17,9), the Christian will love his brothers* with an exacting and practical love (1 Jn 3,11-18), in which the law of renouncement and of death moves freely, without which there is no true fruitfulness* (Jn 12,24f). By this charity, the

believer lives in communion with God (1 Jn 4, 7—5,4). Such was the last prayer of Jesus: "That the love with which you have loved me may be in them and I in them" (Jn 17,26). Lived by the disciples in the midst of the world to which they do not belong (17,11.15f), this fraternal love is the witness* by which the world can recognize Jesus as sent by the Father (17,21): "By this all will know you as my disciples: by this love which you will have for one another" (13,35).

→Adultery 1 — Almsgiving — Brother — Communion — Confidence 3 — Covenant—Desire—Dove 3—Election OT II 1—Enemy II 3, III—

Example NT—Faithfulness 3—Fathers & Father—Fear of God O, III—Fire OT II 3—Friend—Gift—God NT II 4, III—Grace—Hate—Heart—Hope—Hospitality—Humility III—Know—Law B II 3; C—Marriage—Meekness 3—Mercy—Miracle I 2 c—Neighbor—Pardon—Patience—Perfection NT 2.4—Perfume 1—Piety OT 2; NT 2—Predestine—Providence—Redemption NT 5—Reward III 2—Rights/Law NT—Sacrifice NT II 1—Schism NT—Seek III—Sexuality—Shepherd & Flock—Spouse—Tenderness — Unity — Violence IV 2.3 — Virginity—Virtues & Vices—Will of God—Works NT II 2—Wrath—Zeal.

CW jjk

M

MAGIC

1. *Magic and magicians.* When he is confronted by a world that overwhelms him and by beings that terrify him or that he wishes to control, man tries to acquire a power that goes beyond his own strength and makes him master of the divinity and so of his own destiny. If today the methods have changed, the tendency and the desire to master the unknown remain rooted in man's heart and lead to similar practises.

Divination (hb. *qsm*: Ez 31,26) and sorcery (hb. *ksj*: Mi 5,11; Na 3,4; gr. *pharmakia*: Dt 18, 10; cf Ws 12,4; Ap 18,23), these form the "magic arts" (*magike techne*: Ws 17,7), not to be confused with the astrological science of the "magi" (Mt 2,1-12). Included in magical practises are charms (Ps 58,6; Jr 8,17; Qo 10,11), the use of knots and bonds (Ez 13,17-23), the "evil eye," which bewitches (Ws 4,12; cf 2,24; G 3,1), etc. Hebrews and Jews had contact with Egyptian and Chaldean magicians (Ex 7—9; Is 47,12f), diviners (Gn 41,8.24; Is 44,25) and wise men and sorcerers (Ex 7,11). There is evidence of magic in all countries, even in Israel.

One typical case is described at length: the case of the witch of Endor, who conjures up the shades of Samuel to prophecy to Saul his tragic death (1 S 28,3-25). Mention is also made of the sorcery of Jezebel (2 K 9,22) and of the

superstitious practises of Kings Ahaz (16,3) and Manasseh (21,6), which are opposed by Josiah (23,24). Normally the facts are related in order to show the superiority of Yahweh or, later, of the Lord Jesus over the dark forces, which magic and divination are trying to enlist.

2. *Struggle against magic.* This is in fact the reason why the laws were made and the memories handed down, showing the judgment of divine revelation on this important point.

a) Prohibitions. The three great mosaic codes of law forbid magic under pain of death (Lv 19; Dt 18; Ex 23). Similarly practices connected with magic are also forbidden (Dt 22,5.11; Lv 19,19), for example the Canaanite rite of cooking a kid in its mother's milk (Ex 23,19; 34,26; Dt 14,21). Also forbidden and viewed with horror are the sacrifices of children (Dt 18), particularly in the rites surrounding the foundation of cities (1 K 16,34), in the rites of preservation (2 K 3,27) or of initiation (Ws 12, 3ff). And finally there are many prohibitions about the use of blood, for to drink blood would be to take to oneself the vital power that is reserved to God alone (Gn 9,4; Lv 3,17; Ac 15, 29). These practises are simply classed with idolatry* (G 5,20; Ap 21,8).

b) In a number of stories *the magicians are*

outwitted by the divine power. Thus Joseph gets the better of the diviners (Gn 41) and Moses of the Egyptian magicians (Ex 7,10-13.19-23; 8, 1-3.12-15; 9,8-12). Together with his she-ass, Balaam is forced to serve Yahweh and the Hebrew people (Nb 22—24). Daniel confounds the Chaldean wise men (Dn 2; 4; 5; 14). Similar stories, which aim to edify by recounting a story and, if need be, making use of legendary material, like the story of Jannes and Jambres (2 Tm 3,8), are also to be found in the NT. Simon the magician turns humbly to Peter (Ac 8,9-24); Barjesus-Elymas is reduced to silence by Paul (13,6-11), and it is the same with the girl with the python spirit at Philippi (16,16ff) or the Jewish exorcists of Ephesus (19,13-20).

The fact is that miracles* and prophecies* allow men to do without the practices of magic, for they make God's presence felt in a sure way (Dt 18,9-22; cf Nb 23,23); on the other hand sorcerers turn men away from the service of the true God (Dt 13,2-6) and miracle-workers falsify doctrine (Mt 24,34; Ap 16,12-16...). And so the prophets vigorously oppose the magicians of the nations (Is 19,1ff; 44,25; 47,12f; Jr 27,9; Ez 21,34).

The temptation to use magic is strong and, in a certain way, Jesus wanted to undergo it. Satan invites Him to make use of His divine power in order to assuage His hunger and so astonish the Jews; but Jesus does not want to accept power over the world from him: "You must worship the Lord your God, and serve Him alone" (Mt 4,1-11).

c) *Magic practises and ritual.* It is certain that the ritual of the OT contained certain practises borrowed originally from magic, but only after purifying them: it was one way of subordinating them to the worship of the true God. And so, while the profane use of blood is forbidden, the priest, in the name of God, performs the rites of expiation* (Lv 17,11) and of the covenant* (Ex 24,8) with blood; and blood must drown the voice of the sins crying out to God (Jr 17,1; Lv 4). Taken into this new context, the rite changes its meaning. Nevertheless, whenever a rite becomes a matter of superstition, it is abolished eventually: the bronze serpent was destroyed as soon as it became the object of idolatrous worship (2 K 18,4). And even the use of the divine name*, at first given to the whole people (for, unlike the Egyptian gods, Yahweh is not afraid of falling under the control of sorcerers), is in the end reserved to the priest (Nb 6,27). And it is known from the

Greek papyri found in Egypt that the ancient magicians did not hesitate to make use of this divine name, thus speaking the name of God in vain (cf Ex 20,7 LXX).

Man was created free and capable of choosing God, and received from God Himself mastery over the world; and so he does not have to have recourse to magic, that hybrid art, which tries to combine artificially religion and esoteric knowledge, but which can in fact only parody nature and corrupt the effects of faith.

→Death OT I 3—Egypt 1—Human Speech 1—Idols—Miracle I 2 a, II 1—Mystery O—Name OT 4—Power III 2—Revelation OT I 1—Sickness/Healing O; OT II 1—Sign OT II 3; NT II 4.

XLD ems

MAN

The elements of a biblical anthropology are given in a number of different articles: soul*, heart*, flesh*, body*, spirit*. This synthetic conception expresses the whole man in his different aspects. This is quite different from the common mentality of our day which views the body and the soul as the two component parts of man. The soul means man insofar as he is animated by the spirit of life. The flesh indicates that he is a perishable creature. The spirit signifies his openness to God. Finally, the body is man's external expression. To this first difference between the two mentalities there must be added another and deeper one. In the view of Greek philosophy, the concern is to analyze man, this microcosm who unites two worlds, the spiritual and the material.

Biblical theology, on the other hand, looks at man only in his relation to God whose image* he is. Instead of enclosing itself in a natural and closed world, the Bible opens up the scene to the dimensions of history in which the principal actor is God, the God who created man and Himself became man in order to redeem him. Already linked to theology, this anthropology becomes inseparable from a Christology. Thus the various ways in which men behave in the course of history is summed up in the two categories of the sinner and the new man. And these become real in the two figures revealed at certain privileged moments of sacred history: Adam and the Servant of Yahweh, and are fulfilled by Jesus Christ. The authentic type, therefore, of living man is not Adam, but Jesus Christ; it is not one who has come from earth, but who has come down from heaven. It is Jesus Christ who was prefigured in Adam, the heavenly Adam who was portrayed in the earthly Adam.

I. THE IMAGE OF GOD

1. *The earthly Adam.* The second chapter of Genesis is concerned not only with the history of a single man, but with the history of all humanity, as is clear from the meaning of the word *Adam**, which means "man." For the Semitic mind, the ancestor of a race carries in himself the collectivity "which has come from him." All the descendants are really expressed in him; they are incorporated in him. This is what has been called "the corporate personality." According to Gn 2, man appears in Adam with his three essential relationships: to God, to the earth, and to his brothers.

a) Man and his Creator. Adam is neither a fallen God, nor a particle of spirit which has fallen from heaven into a body. He is a free creature with a constant and essential relation to God. This is what is shown by his origin. Though sprung from the earth, he is not limited to it; his existence depends on the breath* of life which God has breathed into him. So he becomes a living soul*, that is, a personal being and at the same time a being dependent on God. Religion does not come as a complement to his already existing human nature, but from the beginning is part of his very make-up. It would be nonsense to speak about man without his relation to God.

To the breath, which constitutes the living man, God joins His Word, and this first word takes the form of a prohibition: "From the tree of the knowledge of good and evil you must not eat; for the day that you eat of it, you shall certainly die" (Gn 2,16f). In the course of his existence man continues to be bound to God his Creator by obedience* to His will*. To man this commandment seems to be a prohibition, a limitation. Actually, it is necessary for his fulfillment; it allows man to understand that he is not God, that he depends on God who gives him life—this breath which animates him without his being aware of it.

Man is, then, united to the creator by a relationship of vital and fundamental dependence, which his liberty* must express in the form of obedience. This law* written in man's heart is conscience, through which the living God speaks with His creature.

b) Man at the head of the universe. God places man in a good and beautiful creation (Gn 2,9), to develop and guard it, as His steward. He wishes Adam to establish control over the animals* by giving them names* (2,19f; cf 1,28f). By this He indicates that nature is not to be divinized, but dominated and brought under control. The duty to work* on the earth does not follow upon the duty of obedience to God, but constantly refers back to it. The first account of creation tells of it in its own way: the seventh day, the day of rest*, marks the limit of man's work, because the work* that man does with his hands should mirror the work of the Creator.

c) Man in society. Finally, man is a social being by his very nature (cf flesh*) and not by virtue of some extrinsic command. The fundamental difference of the sexes* is at one and the same time the type and the source of life in society, which is founded not on force but on love. God sees this relation of the sexes as a mutual helping of one another. And man, recognizing the expression of himself in the woman whom God has given him, is ready for the dangerous outgoing of self which constitutes love*. Every encounter with one's neighbor has its ideal in this first relation. This is so true that God Himself will express the covenant He has made with His people by the image of a marriage*.

Without their clothing*, man and woman are "naked without shame, one before the other." The significance of this is that the social relationship is still without a shadow because communion* with God is fullness radiant with glory. Thus, man has no fear of God, but is at peace* with Him who walks as a friend in his garden. He is in a state of unclouded dialogue with his companion, with the animals and with the whole of creation.

d) In the image of God. The priestly account of creation (Gn 1) resumes the affirmations of the Yahwist account by showing that the creation of man is the crown of the universe and by pointing to the purpose God had: "Let us make man to our image, to our likeness...Be fruitful...Subdue the earth and have dominion over all the animals" (Gn 1,26ff). Created in the image* of God, man can enter into dialogue with Him. He is not God, but lives dependent upon God in a relation analogous to that of a son to his father (cf Gn 5,3). But there is this difference, that the image cannot subsist independently of the one whom it should express. This is the meaning of the term *breath* in the creation account. Man exercises his role as image in two major activities: as image of the divine paternity, he ought to multiply and fill the earth; as image of the divine lordship*, he ought to subject the earth to his domination. Man is the lord of the earth; he is the presence of God on the earth.

2. *The heavenly Adam.* Such is God's plan. But this plan is perfectly realized only in Jesus Christ, the Son of God. Christ inherits the attributes of wisdom*, "the reflection of the everlasting light, a spotless mirror of the activity of God, and a likeness of His goodness*" (Ws 7,26). Adam was created in the image of God, but only Christ is "the image of God" (2 Co 4,4; cf He 1,3). Paul comments: "He is the image of the invisible God, the firstborn of all creation, for in Him all things have been created, in the heavens and on the earth ...all has been created through Him and for Him. He is before all things and everything subsists in Him; and He is also the head of the body, that is, of the Church" (Col 1,15-18). The triple relationship of Adam occurs once again, clear but elevated.

a) *The Son before the Father.* It is the Son who is the image of God that Paul has just spoken of (Col 1,13). He is not simply the visible image of the invisible God, but He is the Son* always united to His Father. As He said of Himself: "The Son cannot do anything of His own accord, but only what He sees the Father doing...I am not seeking to do what I please, but what pleases Him who has sent me" (Jn 5,19f.30; cf 4,34). Jesus realizes perfectly what Adam should have been, a creature in a constant relation of filial dependence upon God. Whoever sees Jesus, sees the Father (14,9).

b) *Christ and the universe.* Man accomplishes the work of his own hands, but Jesus accomplishes the work of His Father. "My Father is still at work and I work too" (Jn 5,17). Now this work* is in reality creation* itself. "All has been created through Him"; under His sight, creation gets life and becomes the parable of the kingdom of heaven. Just as in the account of creation which was totally ordered to man,

so here "everything has been created for Him"; in fact, His lordship extends not only over the animals, but over every creature.

c) *Christ and humanity.* He is finally the "leader, the head of the body." This means first of all that He is the one who gives it life, the "second Adam" (1 Co 15,45), this heavenly Adam whose image we have to put on (15,49). He is the head of the family which is the Church*, a perfect human society. Better yet, He is the principle of unity in the society that men make up (E 1,10).

Adam finds the meaning of his being and his existence only in Jesus Christ, the Son of God who became man so we may become sons of God (G 4,4f).

II. THROUGH A DISFIGURED IMAGE

The ideal fixed by creation and to which we must always refer back cannot be attained any more, cannot even be directly aspired after. Henceforth man must pass from the mutilated image of the sinner to the ideal likeness of the Servant of God. Such are the new conditions in which the life of man in the concrete unfolds.

1. *Adam the sinner.* The author of Gn 3 did not want to paint a picture of a defeat, but to announce victory* after the battle. Before pronouncing the change which is going to affect man in his three dimensions, God sows hope in his heart: the posterity of the woman will undoubtedly be touched by the heel of her adversary, but it will crush the head of the serpent's breed (Gn 3,15). This proto-evangelium colors the somber news that follows and assures man of God's final triumph.

a) *Divisions in the human family.* The first thing that Adam, the sinner, discovers is that his nudity (Gn 3,7.11), which until then is only symbolized, becomes a separation. When he is questioned by God, Adam blames his wife and thus dissociates himself from her (3,12). God then tells them that their unity has been destroyed: their relations will be governed by the force of instinct, by covetousness and by domination; and the fruit of their love* will only be given to them at the cost of the pains of childbirth (3,16). The following chapters of Genesis show how the separation of the first couple has repercussions that cut across all social bonds: between Cain and Abel, brothers* who are enemies (Gn 4), and in the men at Babel who no longer understand one another (Gn 11,1-9). Religious history is a tissue of divisions, a succession of wars* between the people and the nations*, between the members of this people* itself, between the rich and the poor...But the promise of victory remains—the dawn after the night—and the prophets will not cease to announce the prince of peace who will reconcile men to one another (Is 9,5f).

b) *The universe hostile to man.* Because of Adam's sin, the land will henceforth be cursed; man will have to eat his bread no more as the spontaneous fruit of the earth, but by dint of labor and in the sweat of his brow (3,17f). Creation, then, in spite of itself, is subject to corruption (R 8,20): in place of voluntary submission, it revolts against man. No doubt that in any situation the earth would have trembled and would have produced thorns, but these brambles and these calamities* no longer mean only that the world is decrepit, but also that man is a sinner. Nevertheless, the prophets announce a state of paradise* (Is 11,6-9), thereby showing how much alive in man is this nature as it came forth from the hand of the Creator. Hope is not dead (R 8,20).

c) *Man delivered over to death.* "You are dust, and to dust you shall return" (Gn 3,19). Instead of receiving the divine life as a gift, Adam wanted to dispose of his life and become a god by eating the fruit of the tree*. Through this disobedience man broke off the source of his life. When death* would have been only a simple passing to God, it is no longer only a natural phenomenon. Now fatal, it signifies punishment*, eternal death. This is also signified by the exile* from Paradise. By rejecting the interior law (theo-nomy), which is the presence of God in him, man is delivered over to himself, to his fallacious autonomy. History tells of the repeated failures of the one who thought he could be equal to God and became only a mortal. All the same, this did not mean the end of the dream of a full life. Once again God opens up the way to the tree* of life to man (Pr 3,18; 11,30): His Law*, His wisdom* are all sources of fruitfullness for anyone who puts them into practise. But this Law has left his heart and from now on seems to him forever exterior (hetero-nomy).

d) *Division of conscience*.* In fact the Law points the way to salvation without being able to give it, and so it creates within man a division which is at one and the same time deadly and salutary. The Adam who was united in communion with the creator flees from himself when he flees from God. He hides from the One who calls him (Gn 3,10). This fear, which is a caricature of the authentic fear of God*, is contagious. It points to a division of conscience.

Only an interiorly unified man could lay hold of and dominate this intimate division. Paul, enlightened by the Spirit, has stated this. In the epistle to the Romans, he describes the "I" delivered over to the empire of sin, and existing without the Spirit which is nevertheless indispensable to it. Like someone beheaded but still alive, he is aware of his disruption: "I am a being of flesh sold into the power of sin. What I do I do not understand, because I do not do what I want, but I do what I hate." Without stopping in conscience to sympathize with God's Law, man who has allowed sin to set itself up in him sees the flesh* pass its "carnal" judgment (Col 2,18), harden its heart* (E 4,18), and tyrannize its body* to the point of making it produce evil works* (R 8,13). It seems to him that he is going irretrievably toward death. This is not the case, however, because an act of faith can save the sinner from the domination of the flesh. But until this act of faith, the sinner lives in a state of alienation. He lacks his principle of unity and personalization, the Spirit*. By the mouth of Paul, the sinner calls on the Savior with the cry which had rung out all through the OT: "What a wretched man I am! Who can save me from this doomed body?" (R 7,24).

With this call, the sinner completes his journey. Having refused to receive life as a gift, having realized his inability to get hold of himself by his own powers, he turns finally to the one who gives grace*. Here he is once again in the fundamental attitude of the creature. But the dialogue which begins again is hereafter that of a sinner with his Savior.

2. *The Servant of God.* Following the lead of the primitive community, Paul has recognized this Savior as the one announced by Isaiah under the traits of the Servant* of God. Actually, after the paschal triumph the Christians did not turn themselves toward some grandiose description of the Messiah-King*, or the glorious Son* of Man. They did not need a superman, but a man who bears and bears away the sin of the world.

a) *Faithful to God until death*. God is pleased with His Servant and "has sent His Spirit upon Him so that He will carry justice to the nations with fidelity" (Is 42,1ff). When He feels that He has used up His strength and has grown tired without profit, He knows that God glorifies Him unceasingly (49,4f). He is obedient like any disciple each morning when God opens His ear. He does not resist, not even when insulted, because His confidence* in God is not shaken (50,4-7). And as the hour of sacrifice comes, "frightfully handled, He humbles Himself; He does not open His mouth but is like the lamb led to slaughter" (53,7). Fully accepting the will of the Lord which allows the crimes of men to fall on Him, He delivers Himself to death (53,12). Such is the faithful Servant, the last remnant* of humanity, who by His obedience* re-established the bond broken by Adam and manifests the absolute character of this bond by accepting death.

b) *The man of sorrows*. Adam the sinner is clearly afflicted with pain and suffering; the Servant carries our sufferings* and our sorrows (Is 53,3). What is more, the one who was to rule over the animals has become like them; "he no longer has human appearance" (Is 52, 14), he is "a worm and no man" (Ps 22,7).

c) *Before society*. "An object of hate and avoided by man" (Is 53,3), the Servant is finally rejected by everyone. His contemporaries are horrified because of him and consider him to be a failure (52,14); but, through His prophet, God makes them recognize and confess* the expiatory and salutary value of this sacrifice. "He has been pierced for our sins, and broken for our crimes...The punishment which brings peace to us is upon Him. Thanks to His wounds we are healed" (53,5). In the man of sorrows the prophet foresees the intercessor who prays for sinners and the victim who justifies* the multitude (53,11). Through the death of the Servant, Adam can admit himself defeated by sin; and it is at the moment when he renounces his righteousness that salvation starts. God's action only becomes effective through the final passion of the man abandoned by men. Life is certainly not the result of any covetousness, but the fruit ever new of a gratuitous gift.

d) *Jesus Christ the Servant*. The prophecy of the Servant underlies a number of early Christian hymns. These review the existence of Jesus in a diptych which pictures both the misery and grandeur of the man: His abasement and His exaltation (Ph 2,6-11; He 1,3; R 1,3f; etc). He, who during His entire life was nourished on the will of the Father, far from clinging jealously to the level which made Him equal to God, took the condition of a slave. Becoming like unto men, He humbled Himself still more, obeying unto death, to death on a cross. Perfectly obedient, Jesus behaved as a true Adam, entering into perfect solitude* to become the father of the new race, the source of eternal life. This is the one whom Pilate displayed in the dress of a mock king on the balcony: "Behold the man" (Jn 19,5): such is the way of glory*. In this image disfigured by his sin, man should recognize the Son of God who "has been made sin so that we may become in Him the justice of God" (2 Co 5,21).

III. IN THE IMAGE OF CHRIST

A sinner, Adam cannot fully become once again what he was by right—"in the image of God." He is modeled anew "in the image of Christ:" not simply of the Word, but of the crucified, conqueror of death. The values seen in the second chapter of Genesis will be found again, now transferred to the person of Christ.

1. *Obedience of faith to Jesus Christ*. It is no longer directly to God that man must address his obedience and his homage, not to the Law which was mercifully given to sinful man, but to Him who has come to take on human form (R 10,5-13). The only work to be done is to believe in Him whom God has sent (Jn 6,29). For the "only mediator* between God and man is Jesus Christ, Himself a man" (1 Tm 2,5). There is only one Father to whom the believers are led so that they might have life in abundance and forever through the Son.

2. *The primacy of Christ*. If Jesus gives the life of the Father, it is because He is "the beginning, the first-born among the dead...God was pleased to have dwell in Him all the fullness*, and to reconcile* by Him to Himself all beings by making peace through the blood of the cross" (Col 1,18ff). The divisions which affect sinful humanity are not overlooked, but they are hereafter overcome and placed in relation to a new* creature, according to a new dimension, being in Christ: "There is no longer Jew nor Greek, nor slave nor free man, nor man, nor woman, for you are all made one in

Christ Jesus" (G 3,28). The difference between the sexes had become a conflict; the separation of the man and wife spread to social and racial divisions. As he rediscovers his unity in Christ, man can dominate human situations: freedom or slavery, marriage* or virginity* (1 Co 7), each has its meaning and its value in Christ Jesus.

The confusion of languages which symbolized the division and dispersion* of men is overcome by the language of the Spirit whom Christ gives unfailingly. This charity expresses itself through a variety of charisms* for the glory of the Father.

3. *The new man.* The new man is first of all Christ in person (E 2,15), but also everyone who believes in the Lord Jesus. His existence is no longer subjected to the flesh*; it is a continual victory by the spirit* over the flesh (G 5,16-25; R 8,5-13). United to Him who took a "body of flesh" (Col 1,22), and sharing in the baptism* into the death of Christ (R 6,5f), the body* of the Christian is dead to sin (R 8,10). His body of misery will become a body of glory (Ph 3,21), a "spiritual body" (1 Co 15,44). His understanding is renewed and changed (R 12,2; E 4,23); he knows how to judge (R 14,5) in the light of the Spirit, the experience of whom he can express intelligently. Does he not even have the understanding of Christ (1 Co 2,16)? If man is no longer a simple mortal because faith has planted in his heart the germ of immortality, he must still die unceasingly to the "old man" in union with Jesus Christ who died once for all men. His life is a new* one. Thus because for us there is no veil over the face, we all reflect as in a mirror the splendor of the Lord; thus we are transfigured into His likeness from splendor to splendor; such is the influence of the Lord who is Spirit (2 Co 3,18). The new man must always make progress by letting himself be taken over by the unique image which is Christ. Through the disfigured image of the old man there appears the ever better and glorious image of the new man, Jesus Christ our Lord. In this way man "is made again in the image of his Creator" (Col 3,9f).

4. *Creation*, at last, which in spite of itself was subject to vanity and which to this day groans within us in the pains of childbirth, still keeps the hope* of being freed from the slavery to corruption in order to enter into the glorious freedom of the children of God. If, because of sin, work remains burdensome, it has been

given new value by the hope of being transfigured in final glory (R 8,18-30). And when the final enemy, death, is destroyed, the Son will hand back His kingship to God the Father, and thus God will be all in all (1 Co 15,24-28).

→Adam — Animals — Body — Clothing — Creation OT II 1.2, IV—Earth OT I; NT II 3 —Flesh—God OT III 5—Good & Evil I 3— Image—Jesus Christ II 1 c—Marriage—New III 3—Responsibility—Sexuality I—Solitude I —Son of God NT II—Son of Man OT I— Soul—Spirit—Trial/Temptation OT II—Wisdom OT II 2—Woman—Work—Works OT II —World.

XLD jrs

MANNA

Manna is a nourishment which God gave to Israel during the wandering in the desert (Js 5,12). What matters is not the definition of what it was but the understanding of its symbolic value; the interpretation of the name, "What is it?" (hb. *man hu*; Ex 16,15), brings out its mysterious character. God wanted in fact to put His people to the test, while at the same time providing subsistence for them (16,4.28). This marvelous gift gave rise to many commentaries in tradition. The narratives in the Pentateuch (Ex 16, Nm 11,4-9), the psalms, the Book of Wisdom (Ws 16,20-29) witness to it. Thus it prepared the revelation of the true bread of heaven of which it was the promise and the type (Jn 6,31f).

1. *Manna and the trial in the desert.* Faced with the precarious situation in which they found themselves in the desert, the unbelieving people compelled God to act: "Is Yahweh in our midst, or not?" (Ex 17,7). God answered by showing forth His glory, among other ways, by the gift of the manna (16,7.10ff). And in His turn God made the manna raise a question for His people, to educate them and to try them. "Are you going to recognize that I am your God, by conforming yourselves to my commands?" (cf 16,4.28).

In giving Israel this means of subsistence, God, in effect, indicated to them His efficacious presence* (16,21); and this sign is so meaningful that they must preserve its memory by placing in the ark* a vessel of manna along with the tables of the Law (16,32ff; cf 25,21; He 9,4).

But every sign calls for a response. The gift of manna is accompanied by prescriptions intended to test the faith of Israel in the giver. They must collect it from day to day without saving any for the next day, except on the eve of the Sabbath* when the collection will be enough for two days, in order to respect the Sabbath rest*. Thus the manna was for the people the way of showing their obedience* to God and their confidence* in His Word (Ex 16,16-30). Moreover the cakes of boiled manna, without being tasteless (Nm 11,8), always had the same taste. Israel grew weary of it and complained, failing to recognize the test and its lesson. Instead of relying only on earthly food (11,4ff), man should first of all trust what comes from heaven, the mysterious food of which manna is the symbol, the Word* of God (Dt 8,2f).

2. *Manna and the eschatological expectation.* Israel, when thinking over its past in prayer before God, sang of the favor of the manna, "wheat and bread from heaven," "the bread of the strong," of the angels who dwell in heaven (Ps 78,23ff; 105,40; Ne 9,15). In praising this miraculous gift, the sages imagined the qualities which heavenly nourishment* must have, which the Creator would give to His children at the time of the eschatological banquet. This is the nourishment, the object of Israel's expectation, of which the author of Wisdom is thinking in his inspired commentary (midrash) on Exodus. The future manna will accommodate itself to the taste* of each individual and will be adapted to the desires* of the children of God. In tasting it, they will taste even more the meekness* of the Creator who puts creation at the service of those who believe in Him (Ws 16,20f.25f). The Apocalypse speaks of this same manna. It is promised to those whose faith and witness will have made them conquerors of Satan and the world (Ap 2,17; cf 1 Jn 5,4f).

3. *Manna and the true bread of God.* Christ in the desert confirmed the lesson of the OT, by living it out: "Man does not live on bread alone, but on every word which comes from the mouth of God" (Mt 4,1-4 p; cf Dt 8,3). He renewed this teaching when He fed the people of God with a miraculous bread*. This bread which satisfied the people (Mt 14,20; 15, 37 p; cf Ps 78,29) stirred up an enthusiasm that had nothing to do with the faith* which Jesus demanded (Jn 6,14f). The disciples did not understand the meaning of the gift and the

miracle any better than the crowd. As for the unbelieving Pharisees and Sadducees, they demanded at that very moment "a sign coming from heaven" (Mt 16,1-4 p; cf Jn 6,30f; Ps 78,24f).

But the true bread "come down from heaven," is not the manna which allows death, but Jesus Himself (Jn 6,32f) who is received by faith (6,35-50): it is His flesh given "for the life of the world" (6,51-58). Paul also saw this same "spiritual food" prefigured by the manna of the desert (1 Co 10,3f). Therefore with good reason does the eucharistic liturgy take up the biblical images which refer to the manna. In receiving the mysterious bread of the eucharistic meal*, apparently, like manna, always the same, the Christian responds to a sign of God and gives witness to his faith in His Word which descended from heaven. And therefore from this time on he is "fed by the bread of angels, become the bread of wayfarers" (*Lauda Sion*). It satisfies all their needs and responds to all their tastes, during the new exodus of the people of God. The believer, furthermore, is already the victor in the battle which he must carry on during his wandering, for he is already fed by the bread of God Himself, and he lives by His eternal life (Jn 6,33.54.57f; Ap 2,17).

→Bread III—Desert OT I 2—Eucharist III 2—Hunger & Thirst OT 1 a—Jesus Christ II 1 a—Lord NT—Nourishment II.

MFL hjb

MARRIAGE

OT

I. MARRIAGE IN THE PLAN OF CREATION

Both accounts of creation end with a scene which gives a basis for the institution of marriage. In the Yahwist account (Gn 2), the divine purpose is made explicit in these words: "It is not good for man to be alone; I will make a helper for him who is like him" (2,18). Man, being superior to all the animals (2,19f), cannot find a helper except in one who is "flesh of his flesh and bone of his bone" (2,21ff). Such a one God created for him. This is why, leaving father and mother, he attaches himself to her by love and they become "but one flesh"

(2,24). Sexuality* thus gets it meaning from considering the unity in the flesh of two beings whom God calls to assist each other in mutual love. In the original integrity it was free from all feeling of shame (2,25), but it became an occasion of disturbance as a result of sin (3,7). Thereafter the life of a human couple will be hounded by suffering and by passionate or dominant temptations (3,16). But in spite of this, for the "mother of all living beings" (3,20), fertility will remain a lasting divine blessing (4,1.25f). The priestly version (Gn 1) is less charged with dramatic elements. Man, made to the image of God in order to rule over and people the earth, is in fact the couple (1,26f). Bearing offspring there appears as the very purpose of sexuality, which is an excellent thing, like all of creation (1,31). The divine ideal for the institution of matrimony is thus affirmed before sin has corrupted the human race.

II. MARRIAGE AMONG THE PEOPLE OF GOD

When God undertook to educate His people by giving them His Law*, the institution of marriage was no longer at the level of this primitive ideal. And so, in practice the Law was adapted partially to the demands of their hardness of heart (Mt 19,8). Having children was considered as the first and foremost value, to which all else was subordinated. But with this aspect assured, the institution preserved the trace of ancestral customs far removed from the prototype of marriage in Gn 1—2.

1. *Conjugal love and social constraint*. The ancient texts are strongly marked by a mentality in which the community takes precedence over the individuals upon whom it imposes its laws and its demands. Parents arrange marriages for their children without consulting them (Gn 24,2ff; 29,23; Tb 6,13). The group excludes certain marriages within the relationship (Lv 18,6-19) or outside the nation (Dt 7,1-3; Ezr 9). Certain unions are required by the necessity of perpetuating the race, as that of the childless widow with her closest relation (levirate: Dt 25,5-10; Gn 38,13-15; Rt 2,20). In spite of all, under these appearances of constraint, the spontaneity of love remained quite lively. Sometimes the heart agreed with the imposed union (Gn 24,62-67; Rt 3,10); sometimes a man and woman were united because they

made their own choice (Gn 29,15-20; 1 S 18,20-26; 25,40ff), in some cases against the will of their parents (Gn 26,34f; Jg 14,1-10). Homes united by deep love are found (1 S 1,8), loyalties remaining freely beyond the grave (Jdt 16, 22). In spite of the dowry provided by the family of the woman (Gn 34,12; Ex 22,15f) and the title of master or owner which the husband bore (*baal*), the woman is not simply a commodity which is bought and sold. She appears capable of assuming responsibilities, and she can actively contribute to the success of the marriage and to the reputation of her husband (Pr 31,10-31). The love of two free partners in a passionate dialogue, unhampered by constraint, is presented in the Song of Songs. Even if it is allegorical and is concerned with the love of God and of His people, this book speaks of love with words and attitudes which were at that time those of human love (cf Ct 1,12-17; 6,4—8,4).

2. *Polygamy and monogamy*. The ideal of fecundity and the concern to have a powerful family caused the desire for very many children (cf Jg 8,30; 12,8; 2 K 10,1). This naturally led to the practice of polygamy. The Yahwist, for whom the ideal was monogamy (Gn 2,18-24), stigmatizes polygamy when he attributes its origin to the initiative of the barbarian Lamech (4,19). Nevertheless, all throughout the Bible the practice of having two wives appears (1 S 1,2; cf Dt 21,15), or the practice of taking concubines and female slaves (Gn 16,2; 30,3; Ex 21,7-11; Jg 19,1; Dt 21,10-14). The kings contracted a large number of unions, for love (2 S 11,2ff) or for political reasons (1 K 3,1). Thus appeared the large harems (1 K 11,3; 2 Ch 13, 21) where true love was impossible (cf Es 2,12-17).

But exclusive attachment was not at all rare, from Isaac (Gn 25,19-28) and Joseph (Gn 41, 50), to Judith (Jdt 8,2-8) and Tobit and his son (Tb 11,5-15), including Ezekiel (Ez 24,15-18) and Job (Jb 2,9f). The wisdom literature recalls the joys and difficulties of the monogamous home (Pr 5,15-20; 18,22; 19,13; Qo 9,9; Si 25, 13—26,18). In the Song of Songs the love of the two spouses is obviously undivided. All this denotes a real evolution in morality. By the time of the NT monogamy is the current rule for Jewish marriages.

3. *The stability of marriage and the fidelity of the spouses*. It is again the concern for having offspring which could introduce the practice of

repudiation because of sterility*. But polygamy allowed this difficulty to be resolved (Gn 16). In regulating the practice of divorce, the Law did not define what "defect" can permit a man to repudiate his wife (Dt 24,1f). After the exile, however, the wise men sang of fidelity toward "the wife of one's youth" (Pr 5,15-19) and they eulogized conjugal stability (Si 36,25 ff). Comparing the marriage contract (*berith*) with the covenant* (*berith*) of Yahweh with Israel, Malachi even stated that God "hates repudiation" (Ml 2,14ff). Though on the way to the stricter ideal, Judaism at the time of the NT still admitted the possibility of divorce; and the teachers discussed the causes which could make it legitimate (cf Mt 19,3). The custom concerning conjugal fidelity (Gn 38,24), which was later sanctioned by the written Law (Dt 22,22; Lv 20,10), punished by death every woman guilty of adultery, as well as her accomplice. But this prohibition of adultery (Ex 20, 14) aimed first at making the rights of the husband respected, since nothing formally prohibited the man from having relations with unmarried women or prostitutes. The practice of polygamy made such tolerance more readily admissible. But just as there was a trend toward monogamy, so too there was progress on this point: adultery was also forbidden to the man (Jb 31,9; Si 9,5.8.9; 41,22ff). Within these limits the practice of adultery was severely denounced by the prophets (Ez 18,6), even when the guilty party was King David himself (2 S 12). The wise men furthermore put young men on their guard against the seductions of stray women (Pr 5,1-6; 7,6-27; Si 26,9-12) in order to form them for conjugal fidelity.

4. *The religious ideal of marriage.* Although marriage was above all a matter of civil law and although the ancient texts make no allusion to a religious rite, the Israelite knew well that God led him in the choice of a spouse (Gn 24,42-52) and that God assumed under the name of the covenant the precepts which regulated marriage (vg Lv 18). The Decalogue, the fundamental law of Israel, guarantees the sanctity of the institution (Ex 20,14; cf Pr 2,17). After the exile the Book of Tobit presented a highly spiritual picture of the home prepared by God (Tb 3,16), built upon faith and prayer under His view (7,11; 8,4-9), following the model traced by Genesis (8,6; cf Gn 2,18), protected by daily fidelity to the Law (14,1.8-13). Once arrived at this level, the biblical ideal of marriage surpassed the imperfections which

were provisionally sanctioned by the Mosaic Law.

NT

The view of marriage in the NT is dominated by the paradox of the life of Jesus. "Born of a woman" (G 4,4; cf Lk 11,27), He consecrated by His life at Nazareth (Lk 2,51f) the family such as it had been prepared by the whole OT. But born of a virgin mother, and living Himself a life of virginity, He gave witness to a value superior to marriage.

I. CHRIST AND MARRIAGE

1. *The new Law.* With explicit reference going beyond the Law of Moses to the creative plan of Genesis, Jesus affirmed the absolute character of marriage and its indissolubility (Mt 19,1-9). God Himself has joined together man and woman, bestowing upon their free choice a consecration which goes beyond them. They are "one flesh*" in His eyes. Even repudiation, which had been tolerated "because of the hardness of hearts," must be excluded from the kingdom of God in which the world returns to its original perfection. The exception of the "case of fornication" (Mt 19,9) probably does not envisage a justification of divorce (cf Mk 10,11; Lk 16,18; 1 Co 7,10f). It is probably concerned with the dismissal of an illegitimate spouse, or with a separation which cannot be followed by another marriage. This explains the consternation of the disciples before the rigor of the new Law. "If such is the relation of man to his wife, it would be better not to marry" (Mt 19,10).

This insistence upon principles does not rule out mercy for sinful men. On several occasions Jesus encountered adulterers or those who were unfaithful to the ideal of love (Lk 7,37; Jn 4,18; 8,3ff; cf Mt 21,31f). He welcomed them, not to approve their conduct, but to lead them to a conversion and a pardon which emphasized the value of the ideal that had been betrayed (Jn 8,11).

2. *The sacrament of marriage.* Jesus was not satisfied to bring back the institution of marriage to that primitive perfection which human sin had obscured. He gave it a new foundation which conferred upon it a religious meaning in the kingdom of God. By the new covenant which He formed in His own blood (Mt 26,28),

He Himself because the spouse* of the Church. Likewise for Christians who are temples of the Holy Spirit from their baptism (1 Co 6,19), marriage is "a great mystery in relation to Christ and the Church" (E 5,32). The submission of the Church to Christ and the redemptive love of Christ for the Church, which He saved by delivering Himself up for it, are thus the living rule which the spouses should imitate. They will be able to do so because the grace of the redemption touches their very love by assigning it its ideal (5,21-33). Human sexuality, whose normal demands must be appreciated with prudence (1 Co 7,1-6), is now assumed in a sacred reality which transfigures it.

II. MARRIAGE AND VIRGINITY

"It is not good for man to be alone," says Gn 2,18. In the kingdom of God inaugurated by Jesus, a new ideal comes to light. Men will make themselves "voluntary eunuchs" for the kingdom (Mt 19,11f). This is the paradox of Christian virginity*. Between the time of the OT, when bearing offspring was a primary duty to perpetuate the people of God, and the parousia, when marriage will be abolished (Mt 22, 30 p), two forms of life coexist in the Church: marriage, transfigured by the mystery of Christ and the Church; and consecrated celibacy, which Paul considered better (1 Co 7,8.25-28). It is not a question of undervaluing marriage (cf 7, 1), but of living to the full this nuptial mystery in which every Christian already participates by his baptism (2 Co 11,2). By becoming attached undividedly to the Lord to please Him alone (1 Co 7,32-35), one bears witness that the structure of the present world, to which the institution of marriage is correlated, is moving toward its end (7,31). Within this perspective, of course Paul wishes that "those who have a wife live as if they did not have one" (7,29) and that widows* should not remarry. But it all depends in the end on the Lord. It is a question of different and complementary vocations in the Body* of Christ. In this sphere as in others "everybody has his own particular gift from the Lord, one with a gift for one thing and another with a gift for the opposite" (7,7; cf Mt 19,11).

→Adam II 2—Adultery I—Circumcision OT I —Clothing I 1—Flesh I 2—Friend 3—Fruitfulness—Mary II 4—Sexuality—Spouse—Sterility —Unity I, III—Virginity—Widows 2—Woman OT 2; NT 2.

CW hjb

MARTYR

Martyr (gr. *martys*), etymologically means *witness**, whether it is a matter of testifying historically, juridically, or religiously. But in the use established by Christian tradition, the name of martyr is applied exclusively to one who gives witness in blood. This use is already attested in the NT (Ac 22,20; Ap 2,13; 6,9; 17, 6); the martyr is one who gives his life through his fidelity in giving testimony to Jesus (cf Ac 6,56).

1. *Christ martyr.* Jesus is Himself by an eminent title the martyr of God, and consequently the prototype of martyrs. In his willingly accepted sacrifice* He gives in fact the supreme witness of His fidelity to the mission* entrusted to Him by the Father. According to St. John, Jesus not only knew His death in advance, but freely accepted it as the perfect homage given to the Father (Jn 10,18); and at the moment of His condemnation, He declared: "I am born and I have come into the world to bear witness to the truth" (18,37; cf Ap 1,5; 3,14).

In the passion of Jesus, St. Luke sets in relief the features which shall henceforth define the martyr: the comfort of God's grace in the hour of agony (Lk 22,43); silence* and patience* before accusations and insults (23,9); innocence admitted by Pilate and Herod (23,4. 14f.22); overlooking His own sufferings (23, 28); welcome given to the repentant sinner (23,43); pardon granted to Peter (22,61) and to His persecutors themselves (22,51; 23,34).

More profoundly still, the whole of the NT recognizes in Jesus the suffering Servant* foretold by Isaiah. In this perspective the passion of Jesus seems essential to His mission. Likewise, in fact, so that the Servant should suffer and die "to justify many" (Is 53,11), Jesus must pass through death "to bring to the multitudes redemption from sin" (Mt 20,28 p). Such is the meaning of "I must" which Jesus repeats on different occasions: God's plan of salvation passes through the suffering* and death* of His witness (Mt 16,21 p; 26,54.56; Lk 17,25; 22,37; 24,7.26.44). Have not all the prophets*, moreover, been persecuted and put to death (Mt 5,

12 p; 23,30ff p; Ac 7,52; 1 Th 2,15; He 11, 36ff)? This cannot be a mere accident; Jesus recognizes it as a divine plan which finds its fulfillment in Him (Mt 23,31f). Thus, He moves "resolutely" toward Jerusalem (Lk 9,51) "for it cannot be that a prophet perish out of Jerusalem" (13,33).

His passion made of Jesus the expiatory victim which replaces all ancient victims (He 9, 12ff). The believer discovers in Him the law of martyrdom: "Without the shedding of blood there is no remission" (He 9,22). We understand why Mary*, so closely associated with the passion of her Son (Jn 19,25; cf Lk 2,35), was later hailed as queen of Christian martyrs.

2. *The Christian martyr.* The glorious martyrdom of Christ founded the Church: "When I shall be lifted up from the earth," Jesus had said, "I shall draw all men to me" (Jn 12,32). The Church, the body* of Christ, has been called upon in her turn to give God the witness* of blood for the salvation of men. Already, the Jewish community had had its martyrs, notably at the time of the Maccabees (2 M 6—7). But in the Christian Church martyrdom took on a new meaning, which Jesus Christ Himself revealed: it is the full imitation of Christ, the participation perfected in His witness and in His work of salvation: "The servant is not above his master; if they have persecuted me, they will also persecute you!" (Jn 15,20). To His three intimate companions Jesus foretold that they would follow in His passion (Mk 10,39 p; Jn 21,18ff), and to all He revealed that only the grain that dies in the earth bears much fruit* (Jn 12,24). Thus the martyr Stephen who recalled so vividly the passion brought about the first spread of the Church (Ac 8,4f; 11,19) and the conversion of Paul (22,20). Finally, the Apocalypse is really the Book of Martyrs, of those who have given the Church and the world the witness of their blood, following the example of the true and faithful Witness (Ap 3,14). The whole book is a celebration of their trials and their glory, and the passion and glorification of the two witnesses of the Lord are a symbol of this (Ap 6, 9f; 7,14-17; 11,11f; 20,4ff).

→Blood NT 4—Confession NT I—Death NT III 4—Persecution—Trial III 3—Trial/Temptation NT II—Witness NT III 2.

CA wjy

MARY

The important role which the mother of Jesus holds in Christian tradition has been outlined from scriptural revelation. If the twelve centered their interest upon the ministry of Jesus from His baptism to Easter (Ac 1,22; 10, 37ff; 13,24ff), this was because they could only speak of events in which they had taken part and they had to answer the more urgent needs of the mission. It was to be expected that the narratives about the infancy of Jesus only appeared after this. Mark ignored them, being content to mention the mother of Jesus twice (Mk 3,31-35; 6,3). Matthew was aware of them but centered them in Joseph, the descendant of David, who received the heavenly messages (Mt 1,20f; 2,13.20.22) and gave the name Jesus to the child of the Virgin (1,18-25). With Luke, Mary comes into full view. At the beginning of the gospel, she is who plays the leading role, with a genuine personality. At the birth of the Church, she takes part with the disciples in the prayer in the Cenacle (Ac 1,14). Finally John frames the public life of Jesus between two Marian scenes (Jn 2,1-12; 19,25ff). At Cana as on Calvary Jesus authoritatively defined the role of Mary, first as obedient, then as mother of His disciples. This gradual growing awareness of the role of Mary should not be explained simply by psychological motives. It reflects an ever deepening understanding of the very mystery of Jesus*, inseparable from the "woman*" of whom He willed to be born (G 4,4). Several titles will make it possible to assemble the scattered material of the NT.

I. DAUGHTER OF ZION

1. Mary appears first of all as *similar to her contemporaries.* As the inscriptions of the times and the numerous Marys of the NT show, her name*, already borne by the sister of Moses (Ex 15,20), was common during the period of Jesus. In the Aramaic it probably means "Princess," "Lady." Relying on Palestinian traditions, Luke shows Mary as a pious Jewish woman, faithfully subject to the Law (Lk 2,22. 27.39), expressing in the very terms of the OT her replies to the divine message (1,38). Her Magnificat, in particular, is a selection from the psalms and is inspired principally by the song of Hannah (1,46-55; cf 1 S 2,1-10).

2. But, again for Luke, Mary is not a simple

Jewish woman. In the scenes of the annunciation and the visitation (Lk 1,26-56), he presents Mary as *the daughter of Zion,* in the sense this expression had in the OT, the personification of the people* of God. The "rejoice" of the angel (1,28) was not the ordinary greeting. It recalls the promises* of the coming of the Savior to His holy city (Zp 3,14-17; Ze 9,9). The title "crowned with favor," object *par excellence* of the divine love, can call to mind the spouse of the Song of Songs, a very traditional figure of the chosen people. These literary indications correspond to the role which Mary played in these scenes. She alone, in the name of the house* of Jacob, received the announcement of salvation. She accepted it and thus made possible its fulfillment. In her Magnificat, finally, she quickly goes beyond her personal gratitude (1,46-49) to lend her voice to the race of Abraham in gratitude and joy (1,50-55).

II. VIRGIN

1. *The fact of Mary's virginity* in the conception of Jesus is stated by Mt 1,18-23 and Lk 1, 26-38 (there is a hint of it in some ancient versions of Jn 1,13: "He whom neither blood nor flesh but God begot"). The obvious independence of the accounts of Mt and Lk leads us to the conclusion that this information goes back to a more ancient tradition, on which both depend.

2. *In the palestinian milieu* the place accorded to virginity in the coming of the Messiah seems to be a new factor. Up to this point the Bible attributed no religious value to virginity* (Jg 11,37f). The Essenes of Qumrân seem to be the first Jews to bind themselves to continence in an evident concern for legal purity*.

3. *Matthew* confines himself to seeing the fulfillment of the oracle of Is 7,14 (following the gk. text) in the virginal conception of Jesus.

4. *Luke,* on the other hand, attaches great importance to Mary's virginity, and throughout his work he shows his interest in continence (Lk 2,36; 14,26; 18,29) and in virginity (Ac 21, 9). He does, it is true, report Mary's marriage with Joseph (Lk 1,27; 2,5), for he sees this as the basis of the messianic legitimacy of Jesus (3,23ff). But the first thing he says about the young spouse is that she is a virgin (1,27); according to palestinian custom her marriage

had to take place quite some time before her introduction into her husband's house (cf Mt 25,1-13).

The virginity of Mary at the moment of the Annunciation is stressed by the objection that she makes to the angel when he tells her that she is going to be the mother of the Messiah: "But how can this come about, since I do not know man?" (Lk 1,34). The expression "to know a man" is in fact a normal way in the Bible of speaking of conjugal relations (Gn 4,1.17.25; 19,8; 24,16...). In this way Luke emphasizes that Mary is a virgin at the moment that she conceives Jesus.

Is Luke also trying to say that before the Annunciation Mary wanted to preserve her virginity? Since St. Augustine, many have thought so. They have translated her question to the angel by paraphrasing it: "since I do not want to know man," considering this nuance necessary to justify Mary's question. Since she is the wife of a son of David, all that she needs to do to become the mother of the Messiah is to consummate her marriage; if she sees any difficulty here, it is because she wants to preserve her virginity.

However, this interpretation rests on a debatable assumption: it supposes that Mary married Joseph against her will. And above all it overlooks the strict meaning of Mary's question, which means: "I have not actually had conjugal relations." Luke is suggesting by this that Mary understands that she is to become a mother immediately, just as the mother of Samuel conceived as soon as the angel announced her maternity (Jg 13,5-8). Her objection is that her marriage has not yet been consummated. Her question leads the angel to tell her that the conception of Jesus is virginal. This is revealed to her at the same time as the divine sonship, of which it is the sign. The Spirit of God, which presided at the creation of the world (Gn 1,2), is about to inaugurate the creation of the new world in the conception of Jesus.

Thus the virginal conception is seen in Luke as the necessary consequence of the divine sonship of Jesus. And it is in the announcement of her mysterious maternity that Mary learns of her vocation as a virgin.

5. *The reference to Jesus' brothers* (Mk 3,31 p; 6,3 p; Jn 7,3; Ac 1,14; 1 Co 9,5; G 1,19) has led several critics to think that Mary did not preserve her virginity after the birth of Jesus. This opinion is not met anywhere in the ancient

tradition when mention is made of Jesus' brothers, and it clashes with several Gospel texts. James and Joseph, brothers of Jesus in Mt 13,55 p, seem to be the sons of another Mary (Mt 27,56 p). And when Jesus is dying He entrusts His mother to the care of a disciple (Jn 19,26f), which seems to suggest that she has no other son. Apart from this it is known that in the semitic world the name brother* is applied to close relations and relations by marriage.

III.   MOTHER

At all levels of the gospel tradition Mary is first and foremost "the mother of Jesus." Several texts call her by this simple title (Mk 3, 31f p; Lk 2,48; Jn 2,1-12; 19,25f). It defines her whole function in the work of salvation.

1.   *This maternity is voluntary.* The narrative of the annunciation brings this out clearly (Lk 1,26-38). Considering the unheard of vocation which the angel announces to her, Luke shows that the Virgin is anxious to reconcile this new call of God with the call to virginity which she has already heard. The angel reveals to her that a virginal conception will permit her to respond to both calls at the same time. Fully enlightened, Mary accepts. She is the servant of the Lord, like Abraham, Moses, and the prophets. As with them, so with Mary, and even more so, service is freedom.

2.   When Mary gave birth to Jesus, her work, like that of all mothers*, was just beginning. She had *to rear Jesus.* With Joseph who shared her responsibilities, she brought Jesus to the temple to present Him to the Lord, to express the offering of which His human consciousness was still incapable. She received for Him from Simeon the announcement of His mission* (Lk 2,29-32,34f). Lastly, she was His educator*, conscious of her authority (Lk 2,48), and Jesus was subject to her as also to Joseph (2,51).

3.   Mary remained mother *when Jesus arrived at adulthood.* She was found near her Son at the time of painful separations (Mk 3,21.31; Jn 19,25ff). But her task assumed then a new form. Luke and John make us conscious of two major stages in the maturing of Jesus. At twelve years, an Israelite by right, Jesus tells His earthly parents that He belongs first of all to the worship of His heavenly Father (Lk 2,49).

When He opened His mission at Cana, His words to Mary, "Woman, leave me alone" (Jn 2,4), are less those of a son than those of one responsible for the kingdom. Thus He claims His independence as a messenger of God. From that time, during the period of her life on earth, the mother effaces herself behind the faithful companion (cf Mk 3,32-35 p; Lk 11,27f).

4.   This self-privation is completed *at the cross.* Simeon, when he revealed the destiny of Jesus to Mary, had told her that a sword would pierce her soul in the division of Israel and the test of its faith (Lk 2,34f). On Calvary we see the fulfillment of her maternity, as John shows in a scene in which each detail is significant (Jn 19,25ff). Mary is standing at the foot of the cross. Jesus addresses to her again the solemn "woman" which marks His authority as Lord of the kingdom. By designating to His mother the disciple who was present, "Behold your son," Jesus calls her to a new maternity, which will from then on be her role for the people of God. Perhaps Luke wished to suggest this mission of Mary in the Church when he showed her in prayer with the twelve, awaiting the Spirit (Ac 1,14). This universal maternity at least responds to his intention which saw in Mary the personification of the people of God, the daughter of Zion (Lk 1,26-55).

IV.   THE FIRST BELIEVER

Far from making Mary's greatness consist in her exceptional lights, the evangelists show it in her faith*, subject to the same obscurities, to the same progress, as that of the lowliest believer.

1.   *The revelation made to Mary.* From the annunciation, Jesus is offered to Mary as the object of her faith, and this faith is enlightened by the messages which have their roots in the prophecies of the OT. The child will be called Jesus*; He will be the Son of the most high; the son of David, the king* of Israel; the promised Messiah. At the presentation in the temple, Mary hears the prophecies of the Servant of God applied to her Son, a light to the nations and a sign of contradiction. To these few explicit words must be added, even though the texts say nothing of it, that Mary had to learn to see the poverty of the Messiah in the wretched and silent life of her Son. When Jesus speaks to His mother, it is the abrupt tone of prophetic oracles. Mary must have recognized

in them the independence and authority of her Son, the superiority of faith to the human motherhood.

2. *The faithfulness of Mary.* Luke has taken care to observe the reactions of Mary in the face of divine revelations; her consternation (Lk 1,29), her difficulty (1,34), her amazement at the prophecy of Simeon (2,33), her lack of understanding at the word of Jesus in the temple (2,50). Faced with a mystery* which goes beyond her understanding, she reflects on the message (1,29; 2,33); she comes back again and again to the events in which she has taken part, preserving her memories, pondering over them in her heart (2,19.51).

Attentive to the Word* of God, she welcomes it, even if it upsets her plans and throws Joseph into a quandary (Mt 1,19f). Her answering of the divine calls, the visitation, the presentation of Jesus in the temple, are so many acts by which Jesus acts through His mother. He sanctifies the precursor; He offers Himself to His Father. Faithful, Mary remains so in silence when her Son enters His public life; she remains so even to the cross.

3. *The Magnificat.* In the song of Mary, Luke transmits a Palestinian tradition which is less concerned with reporting the words of the Virgin than with expressing the thanksgiving of the community. But Luke makes it into a prayer of Mary (especially by v 48). Using the classic form of a psalm of thanksgiving, and with the help of traditional themes from the Psalter, Mary sings of a new event. The kingdom is present. She appears as totally at the service of the people of God. In her and by her, salvation is announced; the promise is fulfilled. In her own poverty the mystery of the beatitudes* is realized. The faith of Mary is the very same as that of the people of God; a humble faith which is constantly deepened through obscurities and trials, by the meditation of salvation, by the generous service which little by little enlightens the gaze of the faithful (Jn 3,21; 7,17; 8,31f). It is because of this faith, careful to preserve the Word of God, that Jesus Himself proclaimed her blessed who bore Him in her womb (Lk 11,27f).

V. MARY AND THE CHURCH

It is possible to make a brief summary of biblical theology by gathering together and drawing out the preceding information.

1. *Virgin.* Mary, the type of the believer, called to salvation in faith by the grace of God, redeemed by the sacrifice of her Son like all other members of our race, occupies nevertheless a unique place in the Church. In her we see the mystery of the Church lived to the full by a soul which welcomes the Word of God with all her faith. The Church is the spouse* of Christ (E 5,32), a virgin spouse (cf Ap 21,2) which Christ Himself sanctified when He purified it (E 5,25ff). Each Christian soul, participating in this vocation is "affianced to Christ as a pure virgin" (2 Co 11,2). Now, the fidelity of the Church to this divine call appears first in Mary, and that in the most perfect way possible. This is the whole meaning of the virginity* to which God invited her, and which her maternity did not diminish, but consecrated. In her, therefore, is revealed on an historical level the existence of this virgin-Church, which by its attitude is the counterpoise of Eve (cf 2 Co 11,3).

2. *Mother.* Furthermore, by her relation to Jesus, Mary is in a special situation which does not pertain to any other member of the Church. She is the mother*; she is that point of humanity where the Son of God became a human child. This is the function which makes it possible to compare her to the daughter of Zion (Zp 3,14; cf Luke 1,28) and to the new Jerusalem* in her maternal role. If the new human race is comparable to a woman* of which Christ, the head, is the first-born (Ap 12,5), can we forget that just such a mystery is concretely accomplished in Mary; and that this woman, this mother, is not merely a symbol, but that, thanks to Mary, she has had a personal existence? Likewise on this point, the connection between Mary and the Church is brought out with such striking force that Mary, as well as the Church, is drawn in outline behind the woman snatched by God from the attacks of the serpent (Ap 12,13-16), the counterpart of Eve, deceived by the same serpent (2 Co 11,3; Gn 3,13). Such was Mary's role in the plan of salvation. This is why tradition has rightly seen in Mary and in the Church taken together the "new Eve," just as Jesus is the "new Adam*."

3. *The mystery of Mary.* By this connection with the mystery of the Church, the mystery of Mary is best clarified by the light of the Scripture. The Church clearly reveals what in Mary

was lived in a hidden manner. On both sides there is a mystery of virginity, a mysterious wedding, where God is the spouse. On both sides there is a mystery of motherhood and of sonship, where the Holy Spirit is at work (Lk 1, 35; Mt 1,20; cf R 8,15), with respect to Christ first of all (Lk 1,31; Ap 12,5), then with respect to the members of His body (Jn 19,26f; Ap 12, 17). The mystery of virginity implies a total purity, the fruit of Christ's grace which touches a being at its very roots making it "holy and spotless" (E 5,27). This is what gives meaning to the immaculate conception of Mary. The mystery of motherhood implies a complete union with the mystery of Jesus in His earthly life, even in trial and on the cross (Lk 2,35; Jn 19,25f; cf Ap 12,13), and a union in His glory, even to a participation in His resurrection (cf Ap 21). This is the meaning of the assumption of Mary. Immaculate conception and assumption, the two terms of Mary's life, which Scripture does not explicitly mention, appear clearly, nonetheless, in its recalling of the mystery of the Church; so that the faith of the Church has been able to discover them there. Not that there is question of raising Mary to the level of Jesus, the mediatrix at the side of the mediator! She who was "full of grace" with respect to God (Lk 1,28), remains, in the perspective of the members of the Church, "full of grace in the well-beloved" (E 1,6). But by her mediation the Son of God, the unique mediator*, was made the brother of all men and has set up an organic connection with them. In the same way men can in no way reach Him without the mediation of the Church, which is His body (Col 1,18). The attitude of Christians toward Mary is dominated by this fundamental fact. This is why Mary is in such a direct relationship with their attitude toward the Church, their mother (cf Ps 87,5; Jn 19,27).

→Church VI—Humility IV—Joy NT I 1—Mediator II o.2—Mother I 4, II 2.3—Virginity NT 2—Woman NT 1.3.

AG hjb

MEAL

Several times a day, man comes to table to take a meal either in the family circle or at an official banquet. One may eat frugally or abandon oneself to an orgy. This sharing of a common meal creates a community of living among the guests. But the meal can also have a sacred character, something which is manifested in the pagan religions as well as in the Bible. One can sit at table in the presence of an idol and be united with demons, or one can take part in the Lord's meal in order to communicate in His Body and Blood. Through this symbol, man realizes a community of existence to which he aspires, either with God or with the nether world.

I. HUMAN MEALS

The simplest meal in the Bible is already an exceptional human action. As a mark of gracious hospitality (Gn 18,1-5; Lk 24,29), or a testimonial of friendship (Mt 9,11), symbol of rejoicing at the arrival of a relative (Tb 7,9), at the return of the prodigal son (Lk 15,22-32), it can also become an act of thanksgiving to the Savior God (Ac 16,34). Even though the joy* should be full and overflowing (Jn 2,1-10; cf Qo 9,7f), lavish affectation is not looked on with approval (cf Jdt 1,16), even in Solomon's court (1 K 10,5). Superfluity degenerates into senseless aberration (Mt 14,6-11; Lk 16,19), which in its turn can meet with chastisement (Jdt 13,2). Happy is the man who maintains sufficient presence of mind to heed the divine warnings on this point (Dn 5,1-20; Lk 12,19f)!

Taught by experience, the wisdom philosophers have laid out rules for conduct at meals: simple counsels of temperance (Pr 23,20f; Si 31, 12-22) or of prudence (Pr 23,1ff; Si 13,7), a care for moral rectitude (Si 6,10; 40,29). Especially have they foreseen the unhappiness of him who does not respect the laws of hospitality*, and condemned him who betrays the bond created by the table-community (Ps 41,10). One day, Satan will enter into the heart of Judas who has just accepted a morsel offered by Him whom he intends to betray (Jn 13,18.26f).

II. SACRED MEALS

The cults of the biblical East included sacred banquets of a mysterious character in which eating sacrificial food was thought to assure an appropriation of divine powers. The temptation to participate in these ritual forms, whether that of Moab (Nm 25,2), or Canaan (Ez 18,6.11. 15; 22,9), was perennial in Israel. Yahwism also had its sacred meals, in orthodox fashion (Lv 3), and in its idolatrous counterpart with the cult of the golden calf (Ex 32,6). Every meal indeed, or at least every meal in which meat was served, had a sacred character (1 S 14, 31-35). Finally, every solemn religious act included a sacrificial meal (1 S 9,12f; cf 1,4-18). The precise meaning of this sacred meal is not clear, and the meaning seems to have eluded at least partially the Israelites themselves (cf the uncertainty to which Lv 10,17f testifies). Furthermore, the prophets make no allusion to it. The animist conception of an appropriation in this manner of sacred powers is nowhere alluded to, in contradistinction to its naive counterpart, the idea of a feeding of God by sacrificial delicacies (Nm 28,2), of which the psalmist wants to hear no more (50,12).

The different traditions agree on this one point: the sacred meal was a rite intended not to create but to confirm a covenant*, which might be established among the clans (Gn 31, 53f; cf 26,26-31), or between God and His anointed (1 S 9,22), or with His priests (Lv 24, 6-9), or with His people (Ex 24,11; Dt 27,7). Hence the paschal meal is a memorial of the *mirabilia* at the beginning of the covenant (Ex 12—13); and the eating of the first-fruits* is a recalling of the continual providence* of God toward His own (Dt 26).

Deuteronomy systematizes this idea in subordinating the theme of the meal to that of the joyous feast* in the presence of Yahweh (Dt 12, 4-7.11f.18; 14,22f; 15,20; 16,10-17). The only sacred meal is that which reunites all the people in the place chosen by God for His own presence. And through this meal the people commemorate in the rite of thanksgiving the blessings of God, praising Him with His own gifts. The celebration in words, song, or dance takes priority here over the material aspects of a banquet. This evolution, which can be recognized in Christian liturgies also, was aided by the polemic of the prophets against a too materialistic conception of sacrifice*, and also by the correlative exaltation of the sacrifice of praise*, as the fruit of the lips: "Rejoice, Jerusalem. Yahweh, your God, is in the midst of you. He will rejoice over you with gladness, He will renew you in His love. He will exult over you with a shout" (Zp 3,14-17; cf Is 30,29; Ne 12,27-43). This theme will be essential for an understanding of the sacrifice of the new Law (He 13,9-16).

III. CHRIST AND MEALS

The celebration of human meals has a totally new meaning when the God-man is in attendance. He is the friend invited to the family table at the house of Lazarus (Lk 10,38-42), to the wedding feast at Cana (Jn 2,1-11). Christ accepts the invitation of the Pharisee Simon, but in the same place He accepts the avowal of the sinful woman turned penitent (Lk 7,36-50). Without hesitation, He eats with the publicans Matthew (Mt 9,10) or Zaccheus (Lk 19,2-10).

By His presence Jesus confers on meals their full value. He joins His own in the togetherness of a common meal, and He Himself says grace (Mt 14,19; 15,36). He approves the laws of hospitality (Lk 7,44ff); He recommends the humble choice of the last place (14,7-11) and the plight of the poor Lazarus (16,21). These meals already realize the Messianic tidings of the OT in making available the divine gifts: joy (Mt 9,15), pardon (Lk 7,47), salvation (Lk 19,9), superabundance, when Jesus in His own person brings forth food in the desert for the famished multitude (Mt 14,15-21). As a return to the happiness of paradise and a renewal of the miracles of the exodus (Jn 6,31ff; cf Ex 16,18), these works* of Christ likewise announce another banquet, the eucharist*, and beyond that, the eschatological feast.

In expectation of His return, Jesus inaugurates the meal of the new covenant sealed in His blood. In place of the manna*, He gives His flesh* as nourishment, the true living bread* offered for the life of the world (Jn 6,31ff.48-51). This meal was indeed a continuation of those which He habitually took in the company of His disciples, which undoubtedly consisted of bread and wine and served to gather His own about Him. But this farewell*-meal was preceded by a washing of feet which expressed symbolically the sacrificial significance of the eucharistic institution. It likewise called to mind that humility and charity are demanded for a worthy participation in the sacred banquet (Jn 13,2-20).

On Easter Sunday, it is in the course of a meal that the risen Christ appears* to His own (Lk 24,30; Jn 21,13). The primitive Jerusalem community thought to relive the meal with the risen Christ (Ac 1,4), by renewing "the breaking of the bread" in joy and fraternal communion* (Ac 2,42.46).

According to Paul, the primary condition for participation in the eucharist is in effect charity (1 Co 11,17-33). He teaches thus the double dimension of the sacred meal. In itself, it is a "sacramental" meal, for whoever eats this bread is one with the Lord and through Him one with everyone (1 Co 10,17). But this meal is still not the definitive meal since it proclaims that the Lord will return to celebrate the eschatological feast.

IV. THE ESCHATOLOGICAL BANQUET

The image of a banquet was used in the OT by the wisdom philosophers to depict the joy surrounding the feast of Wisdom (Pr 9,1f). At the end of time, Yahweh will prepare for all the people an "extraordinary" feast (Is 25,6; cf 65,13), at which will participate all those who are hungry, "even such as have no money" (55,1f). Jesus promises this beatitude* (Mt 5, 3.6) to His disciples. It will be realized at His parousia: all those who have responded by faith to the invitation of the king will take their place at the feast (Lk 22,30) to drink the new wine (Mt 26,29) with Abraham, Isaac, and Jacob in the kingdom of heaven (Mt 8,11). At least, they must have a wedding garment (22, 11-14). And if the servants are faithful in watching*, the master "will gird Himself, make them sit down at table, and passing from one to another, He will serve them" (Lk 12,37). A meal where all will be assembled together, but a meal where each will be in intimate union with the Lord: "Here I stand knocking at the door; if anyone hears my voice and opens the door, I will come in and sit down to supper with him and he with me" (Ap 3,20).

→Bread—Communion—Covenant OT I 3; NT I—Cup 1—Eucharist—Farewell Speeches NT 1—Hunger & Thirst OT 1 c—Kingdom NT II 2—Nourishment—Passover—Sacrifice OT II 1; NT II 1—Wine.

PMG jab

MEDIATOR

The intervention of Jonathan to save David whom Saul wished to kill (1 S 19,1-7) is a good example of the human mediations which we find in biblical history as in that of all humanity (1 S 25,1-35; Es 7,1-7; Ac 12,20), and which succeed sometimes in re-establishing relations which were on the way to deterioration. The mediator goes from one party to the other, he intercedes with the party who is threatening in behalf of the party threatened, and he brings peace* to the latter, when he obtains it. Thus the Law of Israel foresaw a mediation of arbitrators of this kind between two parties of equal power (Ex 21,22; Jb 9,33). Outside of these cases of conflict, normal human relations can also admit the intervention of mediators. But in this case the word has a wider meaning: it refers to the intermediaries whom a leader entrusts with occasional missions or permanent functions among his subordinates.

The OT Hebrew has no word corresponding to "mediator" (gr. *mesites*) to refer to these arbitrators or intermediaries. And in the field of relationships between God and men this peculiarity of vocabulary is significant. It was not surprising to see non-biblical ancient religions place between mankind and their supreme gods, who were not really transcendent, a whole series of secondary divinities or spirits, then men (kings, priests, etc.), who were more or less mediators or intercessors. But the God of Israel is unique, alone in His absolute transcendence. Who, then, could be a mediator between these two parties with no common ground: God and man? As St. Paul says: "Now there can only be an intermediary between two parties, yet God is one" (G 3,20). On the other hand, biblical man has frequently the very lively feeling of his own personal responsibility before God. It was already true, even at the time when the individual was still deeply immersed in the group: "If anyone has sinned against God," said the aged Eli, "who can intercede for him?" (1 S 2,25). It is, then, quite true, when Job says to God: "There is no arbiter between us (LXX: *mesites*)" (Jb 9, 33). Consequently it is paradoxical that we should find numerous mediators in the OT, even though they are only intermediaries in the broad sense, to whom God has entrusted a mission* among men. This paradox makes it clear that the one God has by no means shut Himself up in solitude but wants to enter into contact with men.

In the NT the reconciliation* between God and men is brought about by Jesus. Word* made flesh*, He can really speak and act both in the name of God and of men. Thus, for the first and only time, someone deserves in the full and strict sense the title of "mediator (*mesites*) between God and mankind" (1 Tm 2,5; cf He 8,6; 9,15; 12,24).

I. MEDIATORS IN THE OLD COVENANT

1. *Historical mediators. Abraham* is he through whom "all nations of the earth shall be blessed" (Gn 12,3); through him, the ancestor blessed of God, Israel will receive the blessings* of the earth and of posterity. According to some traditions, Abraham played the part of intercessor when he intervened in favor of the pagan king Abimelech (20,7.17f) or of Sodom (18, 22-32).

*Moses** is called by Yahweh to liberate Israel, to conclude the covenant, to give it His Law*, and to establish His worship. Responsible for his people before the Lord, he acts as head or lawmaker in the name of God, and frequently intercedes in its favor (Ex 32,11-12.31-34). No doubt he owes it to the importance of his mission that he should be the only person in the Bible, apart from Jesus, to be given the name of mediator (G 3,19)—although, it is true, in the broad sense of the word.

After the exodus, the offices assumed by Moses were divided among different personages: *the levitical priesthood** is the line chosen by God for the service of worship and of the Law. In the liturgies of Israel, it reminds the people of the lofty deeds of Yahweh in sacred history; it announces His demands; it brings down His blessing (Nm 6,24-27). It presents to God the praise and the supplication of the community and of individuals.

The *king* succeeds the judges by being clothed with the Spirit (Jg 6,34; 1 S 10,6; 16,13). The prophets revealed his election to him, for the benefit of the race (1 S 9—10; 16). He is the anointed, the Messiah* of Yahweh, who treats him as a son (2 S 7,14; Ps 2,7). His subjects look upon him as the angel* of Yahweh (2 S 14,17). Before God he represents all his people; and although he does not receive the title of priest, he exercises its cultic functions: he carries the ephod, offers sacrifices, pronounces the prayer in the name of Israel. Finally, since the God of Israel directs the history of all mankind, some prophets did not hesitate to assign to foreign kings a role in the designs of God: Nabuchadnezzar (Jr 27,6), Cyrus (Is 41, 2-5; 44,28; 45,1-6).

Differently from priest and king whose function is hereditary, the *prophet** is raised up by a personal vocation. Yahweh intervenes directly in his life to give him his mission*. Before all, he must bear His Word* to His people; His present demands, His judgment on sin, His promises for the faithful. In return, the prophet feels himself to be jointly responsible with his brethren to whom God sends him; and he intercedes constantly for them, like Samuel (1 S 7, 7-12; 12,19-23), Amos (7,1-6), Jeremiah (15,11; 18,20; 42,2…which leads to the pathetic prohibition of 7,16; 11,14; 14,11…, and the vision of Judas Maccabaeus: 2 M 15,13-16), Ezekiel finally (9,8; 11,13), who even beheld himself set up by God as a kind of sentinel to safeguard the children of His people (33,1-9; 3,17-21).

Thus, throughout the history of Israel, God caused men to arise whom He made responsible for His people, and whose office it was to insure the normal working of the covenant. By these functions, personal relations between God and individuals were not suppressed, but they were placed in the framework of the people in whose name and for whose benefit these different mediations were exercised.

2. *The eschatological mediators.* The prophetic eschatology transferred to the last days many elements of these historic mediations; it surpassed them even in painting mysterious figures who foretold in their own way the mediation of Jesus.

In the evocations of the *new people*, we find various mediators who play a role analogous to those of the past: sometimes the Messiah-king*, sometimes the prophet*, announcer of the salvation (Is 61,1ff; Dt 18,15, interpreted by Jewish tradition), more rarely the priest* of the new times (Ze 4,14, an element developed in the traditions of Qumrân).

The Servant* of God in Is 40—55 is a mysterious figure, who could, among other things, personify the remnant* of Israel in His function as mediator between God and man. He is a prophet called by God "to bring forth judgment to the gentiles" (Is 42,1), to gather dispersed Israel, to be "a light to the gentiles" (42,6; 49,5-6) and the covenant of the people (42,6; 49,8); that is to say, to set up the new people which brings together a redeemed Israel and the converted nations*. His mission is no longer only to preach the message of salvation and to intercede as did the prophets before Him. He must now "bear the sins of many" and by His own suffering* intervene in their redemption (Is 52,14; 53,12). He offers His own life as a sacrifice of expiation* (Is 53,10) and in this way seems to suggest a new type of sacerdotal mediation.

In Dn 7,13.18, *the Son* of Man* represents first "the people of the saints," oppressed by the pagan powers before being exalted by the judgment of God. Finally, He will reign over the nations (7,14.27) and will thus assure the reign of Yahweh over the world. The relation between these different eschatological mediators is not clearly established by the OT. Only the fulfillment of these prophecies in Jesus will show how these mediators are blended in the person of the only mediator of salvation.

3. *Heavenly mediators.* For a long time the pagans had felt the insufficiency of human mediators. That is why they had recourse to the heavenly intervention of lower gods. Israel rejected this polytheism, but her teaching on the angels* prepared the people of God for the revelation of the transcendent mediator. According to an old account, Jacob in a dream at Bethel saw angels of the sanctuary setting up a connection between heaven and earth (Gn 28, 12). Now, the doctrine of the angels took on (after the exile) a development that was more and more considerable. Their intercession for Israel is then described (Ze 1,12f); their interventions in its favor (Dn 10,13; 21; 12,1), the help they brought to the faithful (Dn 3,49f; 6,23; 14,34-39; Tobit) whose prayer they presented to the Lord (Tb 12,12). Malachi describes also a mysterious messenger, the angel of the covenant, whose coming to the sanctuary inaugurated the eschatological salvation (Ml 3, 1-4). It is not a question here of the mediation of a creature; through this enigmatic angel, it was God Himself who intervened to purify His people and to save them.

II. THE MEDIATOR
OF THE NEW COVENANT

At the threshold of the NT, Gabriel, a mediator from heaven, inaugurates between God and man the dialogue which is a prelude to the new covenant* (Lk 1,5-38). The decisive answer was given him by *Mary**. Speaking in the name of her people as "daughter of Zion," she is willing to become mother* of the King-Messiah, Son of God. Joseph (Mt 1,18-25), Elizabeth (Lk 1,39-56), Simeon and Anna (2, 33-38), all those who were "awaiting the consolation* of Israel" have nothing to do afterwards but accept "the Savior" (2,11), who came through Mary. It is in the first place through her that mankind gets to know Jesus and Jesus mankind. Although He is the Son (2,41-50), it is to her will and to that of Joseph

that He submits (2,51f), until the day when He will begin His ministry (Jn 2,1-12).

1. *The unique mediator.* Between God and mankind, Jesus Christ* is the mediator of the new covenant (He 9,15; 12,24), which is better than the old (8,6). It is henceforth through Him that men draw near to God (7,25). Under different forms this truth is ever present in the NT. Jesus died, rose, received the Holy Spirit in the name and to the profit of the remnant of Israel and of all men. His mediation flows back even on creation* (Col 1,16; Jn 1,3) and the history of the ancient covenant (1 P 1,11). If Jesus is mediator it is because He has been called to it by His Father (He 5,5) and has responded to this call (10,7ff). It was the same with the mediators of the OT (cf 5,4). But in the case of Jesus call and response are placed at the heart of the mystery of His being; He who was "the Son" (1,2f), He "shared in the flesh and blood" (2,14), and became "man* Himself" (1 Tm 2, 5). He thus belongs to the two parties which He reconciles in Himself.

The Son puts an end to the ancient mediations by realizing the *eschatological mediation.* In Him is the "descent from Abraham" (G 3,16), because Israel and the nations* inherit the blessings* promised to the father of God's people (G 3,15-18; R 4). He is the new Moses, the guide of the new exodus, mediator of the New Testament, head of the new people of God; but under the title of Son and no longer that of Servant (He 3,1-6). He is all at once king, son of David (Mt 21,4-9 p), the Servant of God foretold by Isaiah (Mt 12,17-21), the prophet, the announcer of salvation (Lk 4,17-21), the Son of Man, judge on the last day (Mt 26,64), the angel of the covenant who purifies the temple by His coming (cf Lk 19,45f; Jn 2,14-17). He works once and for all the freeing, the salvation, the redemption of His people. He unites in His person kingship, priesthood, and prophecy. He is Himself the Word of God. In the history of human mediations His coming brings, therefore, a radical and definitive newness. In the temple which is "not made by the hand of man" (He 9,11), He remains mediator "always living to intercede" in favor of His brethren (7,5). In fact, just as "God is unique, so also is His mediator unique" (1 Tm 2,5), mediator of the everlasting covenant.

2. *The unique mediator and His Church.* The fact that Christ is the sole mediator does not, however, put an end to the role of men in the

history of salvation. The mediation of Jesus in fact makes an appeal to men, who see themselves entrusted by Jesus with a function with regard to His Church; in a certain way He associates all the members of His Body in His mediation.

From the time of His earthly life, Jesus called men to work with Him to proclaim the gospel, to bring about the signs which manifested the presence of the kingdom (Mt 10,7f p): these envoys thus carry on the first acts of His mediation. The mission* which He entrusts to them for the period which will follow His death and resurrection will extend to the whole world and to all future centuries (Mt 28,19f) the mediation which He will then exercise in the invisible world. His apostles* will be responsible for His Word, for His Church, for baptism, for the eucharist, the forgiving of sins.

Beginning with Pentecost, He Himself communicated to His Church the Spirit whom He had received from the Father; from then on, "there has been only one body and one Spirit, as there is only one Lord and one God" (E 4, 4ff). But to incorporate new members to this body, baptism must be administered (Ac 2,38); and to communicate the Spirit there must be the imposition* of hands (8,14-17). The Spirit makes sure of the life and the growth of the body of Christ by the distribution of the charisms*. Of the recipients of these charisms some provide occasional services, others permanent services, which continue some of the functions of the apostles themselves in the organism of the Church. Those who provide these services are not mediators strictly speaking; far from exercising a mediation that would add anything to that of the one and only mediator, they are only the concrete means by which He wishes to reach all men.

Once the members of the body of Christ have rejoined their head *in glory*, this function evidently comes to an end. But then, with regard to the members of the Church who are still struggling on earth, the victorious Christians play a role of another kind. Associated with the royalty* of the Mediator (Ap 2,26f; 3,21; cf 12,5; 19,15), they present to God the prayers* of the saints on earth (5,8; 11,18), who ask God to hasten the hour of His justice (6,9ff; 8,2-5; 9,13). The final victory will be altogether that "of the blood of the Lamb and the testimony of the martyrs" (12,11). From the ascension to the parousia Jesus does not exercise His royalty without having His people participate in it, which is at one and the same time present upon

earth (12,6; 14; 22,17; cf 7,1-8) and already in glory (12,1; 21,2; cf 14,1-5).

A special place is reserved for Mary* in this exercise of the mediation of the risen Jesus. Her calling as mother at the time of the mediator's arrival on earth and her intervention on the occasion of the first sign* worked by Jesus (Jn 2,1-12) lead one to ask what invisible role she can play with regard to the Church. In the infant Church Mary is seen as one member, however outstanding, among others (Ac 1,14); she does not exercise any function that can be compared with that of the apostles or their successors. But as He dies the mediator entrusts her with a maternal mission toward His own, who are represented by the beloved disciple (Jn 19,26-27). Would this mission have ended with her death? Does she not continue to carry it out in some invisible way? Like all the elect, Mary is associated with the royalty and intercession of Jesus; but the NT at least suggests that she has a unique title to this: as mother of the Son and "mother" of His disciples.

3. *The unique mediator and the heavenly mediators.* The mediator has come from the presence of God and has returned to it. That puts Him apparently close to the heavenly mediators of the OT. This proximity led some Christians, sometimes influenced by the pagan gnosis of Asia Minor, to put Christ and the angels* more or less on the same level. These errors call for some specific explanations (Col 2,18f; He 1,4-14; cf Ap 19,10). The mediator is "the head" of the angels (Col 2,10) whom the Christians will judge with Him (1 Co 6,3). In the NT the angels continue their role of intercessors and of instruments in God's plans (He 1,14; Ap), but they do it as "angels of the Son of Man" (Mt 24,30f), the sole mediator.

Conclusion. The many mediators raised up by God between Himself and His people foreshadowed and prepared the way for the mediation that His people were to exercise between Him and all of mankind. This mediation of Israel is fulfilled in the mediation of Christ, sole mediator, alone in the unfathomable grandeur which comes to Him from being the Son. Nevertheless, head of the new Israel, it is with and through His Body that He exercises His mediation. Far from disappearing at the coming of the Son, the paradox of human mediators in the history of salvation stands out even more. The final reason for this paradox is that the one God is love (1 Jn 4,8): wishing to be with men (Mt 1,23; Ap 21,3) and to share His "divine nature" with them (2 P 1,4), it is already with them that He labors at the realization of His design; it is through the communion* of men with men that He makes a gift of communion with Himself (1 Jn 1,3).

→Covenant OT III 2; NT II 2—Gate NT—God NT I—Jesus Christ II 1 b d—King O—Law—Mary V 3—Ministry O—Moses o.2—Priesthood—Prophet OT I 3—Reconciliation—Shepherd & Flock NT 1.

AAV & JDu wjy

MEEKNESS

"Learn of me, for I am meek and humble of heart" (Mt 11,29). These are the words of Jesus, who is the supreme revelation of the meekness of God (Mt 12,18ff); He is the source of our meekness when He declares: "Blessed are the meek" (Mt 5,4).

1. *The meekness of God.* The OT sings of the boundless and merciful goodness of God (Ps 31, 20; 86,5) made evident in His rule of the universe (Ws 8,1; 15,1), and invites us to taste* of it (Ps 34,9). Sweeter than honey are the Word of God, His law (Ps 119,103; 19,11; Ez 3,3), the knowledge of His wisdom (Pr 24,13; Si 24,20), and faithfulness to His law (Si 23,27). God feeds His people with the bread* that satisfies every taste. He thus reveals His meekness (Ws 16,20f), a meekness that He makes His people, whose well-beloved spouse He is (Ct 2,3), taste, a meekness that the Lord Jesus has succeeded in revealing to us (Tt 3,4) and in making us taste (1 P 2,3).

2. *Meekness and humility*.* Moses is the model of true meekness, which is not weakness but humble submission to God, based on trust in His love (Nm 12,3; Si 45,4; 1,27; cf G 5,22f). This humble meekness characterized the 'remnant*" that God will save, and the king who will bring peace to all nations (Zp 3,12; Ze 9, 9f=Mt 21,5).

The meek who are submissive to His Word (Jm 1,20ff) God directs (Ps 25,9), upholds (Ps 147,6), saves (Ps 76,10), gives the throne of the mighty (Si 10,14), and causes to rejoice in peace on the earth (Ps 37,11=Mt 5,4).

3. *Meekness and charity.* One who is docile

to God is meek toward men, particularly toward the poor (Si 4,8). Meekness is the fruit of the Spirit (G 5,23) and the sign of the presence of wisdom from on high (Jm 3,13.17). Under its twofold aspect of calm gentleness (gr. *praütēs*) and kingly moderation (gr. *epieikeia*), meekness characterizes Christ (2 Co 10,1). His disciples (G 6,1; Col 3,12; E 4,2), and their pastors (1 Tm 6,11; 2 Tm 2,25). It is the ornament of Christian women (1 P 3,4) and brings happiness to their hearts (Si 36,23). The genuine Christian shows serene meekness to all (Tt 3,2; Ph 4,5), even in persecution (1 P 3,16); he thus attests that the "yoke of the Lord is sweet" (Mt 11, 30), since it is the yoke of love.

CS & MFL jrc

→Humility—Patience—Poor OT III; NT I—Taste—Violence II—Virtues & Vices 3.

MELCHIZEDEK

Melchizedek appears in the Bible as the protector of Abraham, the predecessor of David and the foreshadowing of Jesus.

1. *Melchizedek and Abraham* (Gn 14). Melchizedek, king* and so priest of Salem (which Ps 76,3 identifies with Jerusalem*), offers Abraham a meal of bread* and wine*, the rite of covenant* (Gn 31,44-46; Js 9,12-15); he pronounces a blessing over Abraham; and he receives tribute from Abraham in exchange for his protection.

These gestures take place in the presence of *El Elyon*, the Most High God*, the ancestral god of the Semite clans, whom Melchizedek regards at least as the supreme god and Abraham as the only God. In this episode the main part is played by Melchizedek, the non-Hebrew priest; and in his presence Abraham the Hebrew, the ancestor of the levitic priests, occupies a lower place. Rabbinic exegesis will try to forget this fact; and Christians exegesis will recall it.

2. *Melchizedek and David* (Ps 110). When David establishes himself in Jerusalem, he practises a policy of assimilation. Ps 110 portrays the Israelite king as carrying on the role of the illustrious Melchizedek. Yahweh has sworn to His anointed*: as king of Jerusalem "you are a *priest for ever*, like Melchizedek." This expression, which is hyperbolic in the case

of the ephemeral messiahs, will be true of the last Messiah*, toward whom, after the exile, Ps 110 will direct the hopes of Israel. In fact, those who read it dream of seeing a Savior rise up, uniting in His person priesthood* and royalty.

Prophets had announced that in the times to come royal power and priestly power would be brought together (Jr 33,14-22; Ze 3—6). Some people claimed a royal status for the High Priest: this was a reality for the Maccabees (1 M 10,20.65; 14,41.47); and it was a hope for the Jewish editors of the "Testaments of the Twelve Patriarchs" (especially the Test. of Levi). Others, on the contrary, faithful to the pattern suggested by Melchizedek and David, preferred to attribute the sovereign priesthood to the future King. In fact, the conjunction of a purified royalty and an authentic priesthood will only come about in Jesus Christ.

3. *Melchizedek and Jesus* (He 7; cf 5,6-10; 6,20). The man, Jesus, is descended not only from Abraham but in the first place from Adam* (Lk 3,23-38). According to the Epistle to the Hebrews, Jesus, the priest, exercises the perfect priesthood, which is not connected with the priesthood of Levi (in any case Jesus is of the tribe of Juda), but which fulfills the royal priesthood of the davidic Messiah, the successor of Melchizedek (Ps 110). From Genesis onward this priest-king is seen as superior to the levitic priests, since, in the person of their ancestor Abraham, he saw the sons of Levi bow respectfully before him, receive his blessing and pay him tribute.

Moreover, the character, the name and the titles of Melchizedek in some way foreshadow the characteristics of Jesus. He appears "without beginning or end" and in this way foreshadows Christ, the eternal priest. His name *Melchi-zedek* signifies: "my king is justice;" *king of Salem* is more or less the same as *king of Salom*, that is to say king of peace*. But does Jesus not bring justice and peace to the world? The solemn oath of Ps 110 does not apply to the levitic priests, who are sinners and mortal and therefore many, succeeding one another from one generation to another, and ministers of an outmoded covenant; it is addressed to the King-Priest, to the true Son of David, to Jesus, innocent, immortal and so unique, the minister of a new and final covenant, signified by the bread and wine, as once upon a time the pact with Melchizedek had been.

And so Melchizedek, the stranger in Israel,

a member of the "nations," but a religious person, "self-taught in the knowledge of God" (Philo), powerful friend of Abraham, adopted by David, and foreshadowing Jesus, has been the subject of an extraordinary promotion. His name appears in the Ritual (in the consecration of altars) and in the Roman Missal (in the first Eucharistic Prayer). He is still the witness of the universalism of God's plans, who makes use not only of Israel but also of the nations, in order to lead us to Christ.

→Aaron 2—Blessing II 3—Bread II 2—Creation OT I—God OT II 1—Jerusalem OT I 1—Messiah NT II 2—Nations OT II 2 b—Priesthood OT I 1.3; NT I 3.

PEB ems

MEMORY

If one were to question the Bible about the memory of man, one might find some psychological notations, such as the recalling of a blessing (Gn 40,14) or the forgetting of fatherly warnings (Tb 6,16); but what interests us here is the religious meaning of memory, its role in our relations with God.

The Bible speaks of the memory of God for man and of the memory of man for God. Every reciprocal recalling implies past *events* where one had been in *relation* with another, and the result of recalling these events is a renewal of the relation. Such is exactly the case between God and His people. Memory in the Bible refers to encounters taking place in the past and when the covenant was established. It brings to life the "today" with the intensity of presence which flows from the covenant. The recollection is here all the more in place since it is a matter of privileged happenings which decided the future and which contained it in advance. Only the faithful memory of the past can insure a good orientation for the future.

1. *Birth of memory.*

a) *The facts.* The first event is the *creation**, always a sign offered to man for the recalling of God (Si 42,15—43,33; R 1,20f). Man himself is more than a sign, he is the image* of God. He is also able to recall Him. God's successive covenants with man (Noah, Abraham, Moses,

David) have come from God's memory. He remembered then, and has promised to remember (Gn 8,1; 9,15ff; Ex 2,24; 2 S 7) to save (Gn 19,29; Ex 6,5). And the saving event which is going to orientate the people of God forever is the *Pasch* (Ho 13,4ff).

b) The memory of facts. The memory has a number of ways of prolonging in the present the effectiveness of the past. In Hebrew the meaning of the verb *zkr* in its various forms gives us some idea of it: to remember, to recall, to mention, but also to preserve and invoke—so many actions which play a most important role in the spiritual life and the liturgy.

The invocation of the name is inseparable from the memory of the Pasch (Ex 20,2), for it was in giving His name* that Yahweh inaugurated the Pasch (Ex 3); and the actual salvation which this invocation asks (Ps 20,8) is understood as the renewal of the ancient prodigies (Ps 77; Jl 3). There is also an element of memorial about *worship**, for it awakens the "memory of His covenant"; this expression which was dear to sacerdotal tradition shows clearly that God remembers His people and that the people ought to remember their God in the recurring liturgical rites (feasts*, Sabbath*) or in the places where they meet (rock*, altar*, ark*, tent, temple*). Founded on the facts of salvation, the prayer is necessarily bathed in *thanksgiving**, the normal tonality of the memory before God (Ex 15; Ps 136).

The expression of memories is insured by the *transmission of the Word**, orally or in writing (Ex 12,25ff; 17,14), especially in the books of the Law* (Ex 34,27; Dt 31,19ff). The *meditation on the Law* is for the faithful, then, the correlative form of memory (Dt; Js 1,8). This vigilant attention opens the door to Wisdom* (Pr 3,1ff). *Obedience to the commandments* is definitely the authentic expression of this memory which consists in "keeping the ways of Yahweh" (Ps 119; Ws 6,18; Is 26,8).

2. *The tragedy of forgetfulness.* But it is just there that man's memory shows its weakness, when God does not forget either His Word or His name (Jr 1,12; Ez 20,14). Despite the warnings of Deuteronomy (Dt 4,9; 8,11; 9,7): "Beware of forgetting Yahweh thy God... remember..."; the people forgot its God, and that was its sin (Jg 8,34; Jr 2,13; Ho 2,15). According to the logic of love*, God then seems to forget His faithless spouse, a misfortune

which ought to make her return (Ho 4,6; Mi 3,4; Jr 14,9). Every distress should, in fact, revive in man the memory of God (2 Ch 15,2ff; Ho 2,9; 5,15). The prophetic preaching is here added, which is a long "recalling" (Mi 6,3ff; Jr 13,22-25) destined to replace man's heart* in that state of receptiveness in which God can realize His Pasch (Ez 16,63; Dt 8,2ff).

At the same time as the recalling of faults, repentance is an appeal to the memory of God (Ez 16,61ff; Ne 1,7ff); and in pardon*, God, whose memory is that of love, recalls the covenant (1 K 21,29; Jr 31,20) and forgets the sin (Jr 31,34).

3. *From memory to expectation.* And here is the paradox: the Pasch, which has passed, is still to come. The people remember all that Yahweh has done for them: the past proves the faithfulness of God. But the present is deceptive. So too is the future, a "time to come," which will see the fulfillment of the promises already partially realized. Faithfulness and unfulfilled hopes open the minds of the people of God to the prospect of the decisive "last times." This lively concept of the future through the past characterizes the memory of the people after their return from exile. There is here a kind of mutation. The recalling becomes expectation and the memory ends in an apocalyptic imagining. The typical case is that of Ezekiel (40—48), who was followed by Zechariah, Daniel, David, the fourth evangelist, and the author of the Apocalypse.

As a community, the glorious past constitutes in the heart of the distressed present the pledge of liberation (Is 63,15—64,11; Ps 77; 79; 80; 89). Individually, the poor* man, evidently forgotten by God (Ps 10,12; 13,2), should know that he is present to His love (Is 66,2; Ps 9,19). The trial* revives his memory (1 M 2,51; Ba 4,27) and prepares it for the new event (Is 43,18f).

4. *From presence to transparency.*

a) When "Yahweh is there" (Ez 48,35; Mt 1,23), memory coincides with the present, and is its fulfillment*. The memory of the promises* and of the covenant passes to act in the coming of Christ, who summarizes time* (2 Co 1,20; Lk 1,54.72). In Him is resolved the tragedy of the two forgetfulnesses by man's return and God's forgiveness (Col 3,13). Since, in Christ, God is present and remembers man,

man has no longer to look for God in the past but in the present, in Christ (Jn 14,6f; 2 Co 5,16f). Christ, in fact, is man* definitively present to God, and God definitively present to man. Christ the Priest opens up for us the way to the Father (E 2,18; He 10,19), and His Spirit puts us in communion with Him (R 8,15-16; 8, 26-27).

b) But time is not yet consummated, and although God is from now on present in a new and everlasting covenant, man is often not present to his God and needs to remember Him. That is why the Spirit* "recalls" the mystery of Christ, not as a book* but in the personal actuality of the living Word: tradition* (Jn 14, 26; 16,13). The Spirit realizes the mystery of Christ in His body, not as a simple memorial, but in the sacramental actuality of the body, at once risen and present to the world (Lk 22, 19f; 1 Co 11,24ff): the liturgy. This "re-presentation" of the Pasch, just as in the OT, is ordained to action, to life. The Christian memory consists in "keeping the ways of Yahweh," keeping the testament of the Lord, that is to say, remaining in love* (Jn 13,34; 15,10ff; 1 Jn 3,24). Finally, as for the last accommodation of man's memory to God's, the more the Spirit enters the life of the Christian, the more He makes it vigilant, attentive to the "signs of the times," a witness who allows the active presence of the Lord to appear and reveal the approach of His coming (Ap 3,3; Ph 3,13f; 1 Th 5,1-10).

→Abraham II 1—Altar 1—Covenant OT II 1; NT I—Eucharist I 1, III 3, IV 2, V 2—Paraclete 2—Sign OT I, II—Stone 2—Time OT I 2, II 1; NT II 3—Worship OT II; NT III 1.

JCo wjy

MERCY

Modern usage, doubtless determined by Church Latin, identifies mercy with compassion or forgiveness. This identification, though valid, runs the risk of veiling the concrete richness with which Israel, in the light of her experiences, invested the word that we use in this way. In effect, mercy signified for Israel the meeting of two streams of thought, compassion and fidelity.

The Hebrew word for compassion (rahamin) expresses the instinctive attachment of one being for another. This feeling, according to Semitic thought, has its seat in the maternal bosom (raham: 1 K 3,26), in the bowels (rahamin)—we would say: the heart—of a father (Jr 31,20; Ps 103,13) or of a brother (Gn 43,30): it is tenderness*; it readily translates itself into action: it is compassion on the occasion of a tragic event (Ps 106,45) or pardon* of offenses (Dn 9,9).

The second Hebrew word (hesed), ordinarily translated by a Greek word which also signifies mercy (eleos), designates of itself piety*, a relation which unites two beings and implies fidelity. From this fact, mercy receives a solid foundation: it is not simply the echo of an instinctive goodness which may be mistaken regarding its object and its nature, but rather a conscious goodness, freely willed; it is likewise a response to an interior duty, fidelity to oneself.

English translations of these Hebrew and Greek words oscillate between mercy and love, passing through a spectrum of meanings: tenderness, pity, compassion, clemency, goodness, and even grace (hb. hēn) which, however, has a much broader sense. Despite this variety, it is not impossible to discern the biblical meaning of mercy. From beginning to end the manifestation of God's tenderness is occasioned by human misery; and man, in his turn, ought therefore to show mercy to his neighbor in imitation of his Creator.

OT

I. THE GOD OF MERCIES

Whenever man becomes conscious of his unhappy and sinful condition, then is revealed to him, more or less clearly, the face of infinite mercy.

1. Help for the miserable. The cries of the psalmist echo ceaselessly: "Have pity on me, O Lord!" (Ps 4,2; 6,3; 9,14; 25,16); or better, proclaim thanksgiving*: "Give thanks to Yahweh, for His love (hesed) is eternal" (Ps 107,1). This mercy He ceaselessly shows to those who cry to Him in their distress: for example, to navigators in peril (Ps 107,23); He shows mercy to the "sons of Adam*," whoever they be. He shows Himself the protector of the poor*, the widow, and the orphan, His privileged ones.

This firm conviction of pious men seems to originate in the experience of Israel beginning with the exodus*. Although the term *mercy* is not found in the account of this event, the liberation from Egypt is described as an act of divine mercy. The first traditions of the call of Moses clearly suggest this: "I have seen the misery of my people. I have given ear to their cries...I know their sufferings. I am resolved to deliver them" (Ex 3,7f.16f). Later, the priestly redactor will explain the decision of God by His fidelity to the covenant (6,5). In His mercy, God could not bear the misery of His chosen people; it is almost as if, in entering upon the covenant with Israel, God had made Israel a being "of His own race" (cf Ac 17,28f): an instinctive tenderness united Him to Israel forever.

2. *The salvation of the sinner.* However, what would happen if that chosen people should separate itself from Him by sin? Mercy would bring them back again so long as they had not hardened their hearts; for, moved by the chastisements which accompany sin, God wishes to save the sinner. Thus, though sin is the occasion, man enters yet more deeply into the mystery of divine tenderness.

a) The central revelation. On Sinai Moses hears the fundamental revelation of God's essence. The chosen people have just apostatized. But God, having affirmed His freedom to grant mercy to whom He would (Ex 33,19), proclaims that His divine tenderness can triumph over sin without prejudice to His holiness: "Yahweh is a God of tenderness (*raḥūm*) and grace (*ḥanūn*), slow to anger and abounding in mercy (*ḥesed*) and fidelity (*'emet*), showing kindness (*ḥesed*) to the thousandth generation, forgiving iniquity, transgression, and sin, without leaving it unpunished however, but avenging the fault... even to the third and fourth generation" (Ex 34,6f). God allows the consequences to pursue the sinner, even unto the fourth generation, thereby showing the serious nature of sin. But His mercy, remaining intact unto the thousandth generation, makes Him infinitely patient. Such is the tone that marks God's relations with His people right down to the coming of His Son.

b) Mercy and chastisement. Throughout the course of sacred history God has shown effectively that while He must chastise His people for their sins, yet He is moved to commiseration when they cry out to Him from the depths of their misery. Thus the Book of Judges is punctuated by the recurring theme of divine anger, inflamed by infidelity, and the mercy which sends a savior (Jg 2,18). The prophetic experience is going to give this history strangely human accents. Hosea reveals that if God has decided no longer to have mercy on Israel (Ho 1,6) and to punish her, His "heart turns against it, His bowels tremble and He decides not to give rein to the warmth of His anger" (11,8f): moreover one day the faithless bride will receive a new name, "has received mercy" (*Ruḥāmāh*: 2,3). Then, even though the prophets foretell dire catastrophes, they know the tenderness of the heart of God: "Is Ephraim my precious son? Is he my darling child? For as often as I threaten him, I must always think of him. Therefore my heart yearns for him, I must have pity upon him" (Jr 31,20; cf Is 49,14f; 54,7).

c) Mercy and conversion. If God thus turns away from His intention because of the misery or consequences of sin, it is only because He desires the return of the sinner to Himself, his conversion. If once again He leads His people into the desert*, it is because He wishes "to speak to their hearts" (Ho 2,16); after the exile* they will understand that Yahweh wishes their return to the land to symbolize their return to His life (Jr 12,15; 33,26; Ez 33, 11; 39,25; Is 14,1; 49,13). No, God "will not stay angry forever" (Jr 3,12f), but He wishes the sinner to recognize his evil ways: "Let the wicked return to the Lord, who will have pity on him, and to our God, for He shall abundantly pardon" (Is 55,7).

d) The appeal of the sinner. Israel certainly cherished in the depths of its heart the conviction of a mercy which had nothing that was human: "He smote, but He will bind our wounds up" (Ho 6,1). "Who is the God like thee, forgiving iniquity, and passing over transgressions? He will not hold His anger forever, for He delights in kindness. He will again show us mercy. He will tread down our iniquities. He will cast into the depths of the sea all our sins" (Mi 7,18f). Hence the cry of the psalmist rings out unceasingly, a resume of the *Miserere*: "Have pity on me, O God, in accordance with thy kindness; in thine abundant mercy wipe out my transgressions" (Ps 51,1).

3. *Merciful to all flesh.* If the divine mercy knows no other limitation except the sinner's

hardness* of heart (Is 9,16; Jr 16,5.13), it was nevertheless held to be a prerogative of the chosen people* for a long time. But by His astounding liberality, God finally shattered this remnant of human meanness (cf Ho 11,9). After the exile the lesson was understood. The story of Jonah is a satire of the narrowness of heart which could not accept the immense tenderness of God (Jon 4,2). Ecclesiasticus says clearly: "A man has mercy on his neighbor*, but the mercy of the Lord is for all mankind" (Si 18,13).

At length the unanimous tradition of Israel (cf Ex 34,6; Na 1,3; Jl 2,13; Ne 9,17; Ps 86,15; 145,8) is summed up magnificently by the psalmist with no hint of particularism: "The Lord is merciful and compassionate, slow to anger and abounding in kindness. He will not always chide, nor hold His anger forever. He has not treated us according to our sins...As a father is kind to his children, so the Lord is kind to those who revere Him. For He knows our frame; He remembers that we are but dust" (Ps 103,8ff.13f). "Happy are those who hope in Him, for He will have pity on them" (Is 30,18), because "His mercy is eternal" (Ps 136), for in Him is the source of mercy (Ps 130,7).

II. "MY WILL IS TO SHOW MERCY"

If God is tenderness, how could He not demand of His creatures the same mutual tenderness? But this sentiment is not natural for man: *homo homini lupus!* David knew this well, for he preferred "to fall into the hands of Yahweh whose mercy is great, rather than into the hands of men" (2 S 24,14). On this point, too, God had to enlighten His people gradually.

He condemns the pagans who suffocate mercy (Am 1,11). His will is that man fulfill the law of fraternal love* (cf Ex 22,26), in preference to offering holocausts (Ho 4,2; 6,6); He wills that the administration of justice* be crowned by a "tender love" (Mi 6,8). If one truly wishes to fast*, he ought to succor the poor, the widow, and the orphan in preference to hiding himself from his own flesh* (Is 58,6-11; Jb 31,16-23). True, the fraternal horizon remained limited to one's own race or belief (Lv 19,18), but the example of God Himself would little by little enlarge the human heart to the dimensions of the heart of God: "I am God and not a mere man" (Ho 11,8; cf Is 55,7). Thanks to the commandment not to indulge

one's vengeance nor to harbor hatred, the horizon would expand. But this idea would not really be set forth clearly until the last books of wisdom which sketch the rough outlines of Jesus' message on this point: pardon* must be exercised toward "every man" (Si 27,30—28,7).

NT

I. THE FACE OF DIVINE MERCY

1. *Jesus, "the merciful high priest"* (He 2,17). Before accomplishing the divine plan, Jesus wished to "become like His brethren in all things," in order that He might experience that very misery from which He came to save them. His actions too are all an interpretation of the divine mercy, even though they are not represented as such by the evangelists. Luke takes very special pains to set this point in relief. Jesus has a preference for the "poor*" (Lk 4, 18; 7,22); sinners find a "friend" in Him (7,34), for He is not ashamed to associate with them (5,27.30; 15,1f; 19,7). The mercy which Jesus bears witness to in a general way among the masses (Mt 9,36; 14,14; 15,32) takes on a personal aspect in Luke's account: it is concerned with a widow's "only son" (Lk 7,13) and with a certain bereaved father (8,42; 9,38.42). Finally, Jesus shows particular kindness to women* and strangers*. Thus is this universalism brought to its fulfillment: "all flesh shall see God's salvation" (3,6). If Jesus' compassion was such for all men, it is understandable that the afflicted would address themselves to Him as to God Himself with their cry: *"Kyrie eleison!"* (Mt 15,22; 17,15; 20,30f).

2. *The heart of God the Father.* Jesus wished to depict for all time the characteristic features of divine mercy which showed forth in His actions. To sinners, who saw themselves excluded from the kingdom of God by the pettiness of the Pharisees*, He proclaimed a gospel of infinite mercy which follows in a direct line from the authentic pronouncement of the OT. Those who please the heart of God are not the self-righteous but the repentant sinners, whom He likened to a lamb or drachma that was lost and found again (Lk 15,7.10); the father is anxiously watching for the return of his prodigal son and when he sees him in the distance he is "moved with compassion" and runs to meet him (15,20). God has waited long; He still

waits patiently for Israel who, like the barren fig tree, will not be converted (13,6-9).

3. *The superabundance of mercy.* God is indeed the "Father of mercies" (2 Co 1,3; Jm 5, 11), who showed mercy to Paul (1 Co 7,25; 2 Co 4,1; 1 Tm 1,13) and promises it to all believers (Mt 5,7; 1 Tm 1,2; 2 Tm 1,2; Tt 1,4; 2 Jn 3). Paul clearly manifests the amplitude and superabundance of the completion of the task of mercy in that salvation* and peace* which were announced in the early gospel canticles (Lk 1, 50.54.72.78). The high point of the epistle to the Romans occurs in this revelation. Seeing that the Jews, by their failure to recognize divine mercy, were misconstruing justice* to be something they could procure through their works* and observance of the Law*, Paul declares that they too are sinners and hence they also need this mercy through the justification of faith*. Before their very eyes the pagans, to whom God had made no promises, are drawn into the immense orbit of His mercy. All must acknowledge themselves sinners in order to become beneficiaries of His mercy: "God has made all men prisoners of disobedience so as to have mercy upon them all" (R 11,32).

II. BE YE MERCIFUL...

The "perfection*" which, according to Mt 5, 48, Jesus demands of His disciples, consists according to Lk 6,36 in the duty of being merciful "as your Father is merciful." This is an essential condition for entering the kingdom of heaven (Mt 5,7) which Jesus borrows from the prophet Hosea (Mt 9,13; 12,7). This tenderness should make us, like the Good Samaritan (Lk 10,30-37), neighbors* to the unfortunate person we meet on our way and full of pity toward anyone who has offended us (Mt 18,23-35), because God has had pity on us (18,32f). Thus, we shall be judged according to the mercy we have shown, perhaps unknowingly, to the very person of Jesus (Mt 25,31-46).

Seeing that the absence of mercy among pagans unleashes the divine wrath (R 1,31), the Christian ought to show love and "sympathy" (Ph 2,1), to have compassion in his heart (E 4, 32; 1 P 3,8); he cannot "close his heart" to a brother in need: the love of God is only found in those who show mercy (1 Jn 3,17).

→Almsgiving—Grace—Hardness of Heart I 2 b—Hospitality 1—Justice O; B—Love—Pardon—Patience I OT—Piety OT 2—Reward II —Shepherd & Flock—Sin IV 1 c d—Tenderness—Wrath.

JCa & XLD tms

MESSIAH

Messiah, transliterated from the Hebrew and the Aramaic, and *Christ*, transcribed from the Greek, both mean "anointed." This appellation had become in apostolic times the proper name of Jesus, and it has assumed the content of other titles claimed by Him. It highlights moreover the deep bond which joins His person to the millennial hope of the Jewish people, centered on their expectation of the Messiah, son of David. Nevertheless, the use of the word *anointed* in the OT, then in Judaism, does not yet imply the richness of meaning which the NT has given to the word *Christ*. We must go back to the origin of this vocabulary to see what transformation the NT has caused it to undergo by projecting on it the light of a revelation inscribed in the words and in the history of Jesus.

OT

In the OT the word *anointed* is first of all applied to the king. But it has been used to designate other personages, especially priests. Nevertheless, it is the first use which has left more traces in Jewish eschatology and hope.

I. FROM KING TO ROYAL MESSIAH

1. *The anointed of Yahweh in history.* In virtue of the anointing with oil which signifies his investiture by the Spirit* of God (1 S 9,16; 10,1.10; 16,13), the king* is consecrated to a function which makes of him the lieutenant of Yahweh in Israel. This anointing is an important rite in the crowning of the king (cf Jg 9,8). Thus, it is mentioned in the case of Saul (1 S 9—10), David (2 S 2,4; 5,3), Solomon (1 K 1, 39), and those of his descendants who acceded to power in a context of political crisis (2 K 11,12; 23,30). The king thus became "the anointed of Yahweh" (2 S 19,22; Lm 4,20); that is to say, a sacred personage to whom every loyal individual must manifest a religious aspect (1 S 24,7.11; 26,9.11.23; 2 S 1,14.16). Beginning with the time when the oracle of Nathan fixed

the hope of Israel on the dynasty of David (2 S 7,12-16), each king issuing from him became the actual "Messiah" by whom God wished to fulfill His plan with regard to His people.

2. *The anointed of Yahweh in prayer.* The pre-exilic psalms give a conspicuous place to the royal Messiah in the life and faith of Israel. The anointing which he received is a sign of divine preference (Ps 45,8); it has made of him the adopted son* of Yahweh (Ps 2,7; cf 2 S 7, 14). He is also certain of the protection of God (Ps 18,51; 20,7; 28,8). Revolt against him is folly (Ps 2,2), for God will not fail to intervene to save him (Ha 3,13) and "exalt his horn" (1 S 2,10). He is prayed for, nevertheless (Ps 84,10; 132,10). But in relying on the promises made to David, it is hoped that God will never fail to perpetuate his dynasty (Ps 132,17). Thus the confusion of minds was great after the fall of Jerusalem, when the anointed of Yahweh was taken prisoner by the pagans (Lm 4,20): why has God so rejected His Messiah, so that all the pagans behave outrageously to him? (Ps 89,39.52). The humiliation of the Davidic dynasty was a trial of faith, and this trial continued even after the post-exilic restoration. In fact, the hope of a dynastic re-establishment awakened for a moment by Zerubbabel was soon extinguished; Zerubbabel will never be crowned (despite Ze 6,9-14), and there will no longer be a royal Messiah at the head of the Jewish people.

3. *The anointed of Yahweh in eschatology.* Frequently severe on the reigning anointed whom they judged to be unfaithful, the prophets oriented the hope of Israel on the future king*, to whom, however, they never gave the title of Messiah. It is at the beginning of their promises that the royal Messianism is developed after the exile. The royal psalms which had already spoken of the present anointed are now sung in a new perspective which makes them refer to the future anointed, the Messiah in the strict sense of the term. They describe his glory in advance, his struggles (cf Ps 2), his victories, etc. Jewish hope rooted in the sacred texts was very much alive at the time of the NT, notably among the sect of the Pharisees. The author of the psalms of Solomon (63 B.C.) prayed for the coming of the Messiah, Son of David (Ps Sol 17; 18). The same theme is frequent in the rabbinic literature. In all these texts the Messiah is placed on the same level as the ancient kings of Israel. His reign takes place in the framework of the theocratic institutions, but it is understood in a very realistic way accenting the political aspect of his role.

II. OTHER USES OF THE WORD ANOINTED

1. *The "anointed of Yahweh" in a broad sense.* The divine anointing consecrated the king in view of a mission* related to God's plan for His people. In a broad metaphorical sense, the OT sometimes speaks of divine anointing when there is only a mission to fulfill, especially if this mission implies the gift of the divine Spirit. Cyrus, sent by God to deliver Israel from the hands of Babylon, is qualified as the anointed of Yahweh (Is 45,1) as though his royal anointing had prepared him for his providential mission. The prophets* were not consecrated for their function by an anointing with oil. Nevertheless, Elijah received the command "to anoint Elisha as prophet in his place" (1 K 19, 16). The expression may be explained by the fact that he will bequeath him "a double part of his Spirit*" (2 K 2,9). As a matter of fact, it is this anointing of the Spirit received by the prophet which is expressed in Is 61,1: it has consecrated him to announce the good news to the poor. It is also as "prophets of Yahweh" that the members of God's people are once called His anointed (Ps 105,15; cf perhaps Ps 28,8; Ha 3,13). But all these uses of the word remain occasional.

2. *The anointed priests.* No text earlier than the exile speaks of anointing for priests, but after the exile, the priesthood* saw its prestige increase. Now, since there is no longer a king, the high priest becomes head of the community. It is then that anointing is conferred upon him to consecrate him for his office. The late sacerdotal texts, to emphasize the importance of the rite, make it go back as far as Aaron* (Ex 29,7; 30,22-33; cf Ps 133,2). The anointing is later extended, moreover, to all priests (Ex 28,41; 30,30; 40,15). Beginning with this period, the high priest becomes the anointed-priest (Lv 4,3.5.16; 2 M 1,10), then a "Messiah" actually, as the king was formerly (cf Dn 9,25). Prolonging certain prophetic texts which closely associated royalty and priesthood in eschatology (Jr 33,14-18; Ez 45, 1-8; Ze 4,1-14; 6,13), some circles even awaited in later times the coming of two Messiahs: a Messiah-priest who would have pre-eminence

and a Messiah-king, charged with temporal affairs (Testaments of the Twelve Patriarchs, texts of Qumrân). But this particular form of Messianic hope seems to be restricted to Essene circles, marked by a heavy sacerdotal influence.

3. *Eschatology and Messianism*. Jewish eschatology gives, then, an important place to the expectation of the Messiah: everywhere a royal Messiah, a sacerdotal Messiah in certain places. But the scriptural promises are not reduced to this Messianism in the strict sense of the word because it is frequently tied up with dreams of temporal restoration. They equally announce the setting up of the kingdom* of God. They present also the artisan of salvation* under the features of the Servant* of Yahweh and of the Son* of Man. The coordination of all this data with the expectation of the Messiah (or Messiahs) is not easily or clearly realized. Only the coming of Jesus will dissipate the ambiguities of the prophets on this point.

NT

I. JESUS AND THE EXPECTATION OF THE MESSIAH

1. *The title given to Jesus*. Struck by the holiness, the authority, and the power of Jesus (cf Jn 7,31), His hearers asked themselves: "Is not this the Messiah?" (Jn 4,29; 7,40ff) or, which comes to the same thing: "Is not this the Son of David?" (Mt 12,23). And they urged Him to declare Himself openly (Jn 10, 24). Faced with this question, men were divided (cf 7,43). On the other hand, the Jewish authorities decided to excommunicate whoever recognized Him as the Messiah (9,22). But they who had recourse to His miraculous power, invoked Him openly as the Son of David (Mt 9,27; 15,22; 20,30f), and His Messianism was the object of explicit acts of faith: on the part of the first disciples, after the baptism (Jn 1,41.45.49); on the part of Martha, at the moment when He revealed Himself as the resurrection and the life (11,27). The synoptics give a particular solemnity to Peter's act of faith: "Who do you say that I am?"—"Thou art the Messiah" (Mk 8,29). This faith* is genuine, but it remains imperfect, for the title of Messiah runs the chance still of being understood in a perspective of temporal royalty* (cf Jn 6,15).

2. *Attitude of Jesus*. And so on this subject Jesus adopted an attitude of reserve. Except in Jn 4,25f (where the term translates, doubtless, in Christian language, an expression of Samaritan faith), He never gives Himself the title of Messiah. He allows Himself to be called Son of David, but He forbids the demoniacs to say that He is the Messiah (Lk 4,41). He accepts confessions of faith, but after that of Peter He recommends that the twelve do not say that He is the Messiah (Mt 16,20). Starting from this moment, moreover, He undertakes to purify the Messianic concept of His disciples. His career as Messiah will begin as that of the suffering Servant*; Son* of Man, He will enter into His glory by the sacrifice of His life (Mk 8,31 p; 9,31 p; 10,33f p). His disciples are disconcerted, as the Jews will be when He speaks to them of the "lifting up of the Son of Man" (Jn 12,34).

Nevertheless, on Palm Sunday Jesus intentionally allows Himself to be acclaimed as the Son of David (Mt 21,9). Then, in the controversies with the Pharisees, He emphasizes the superiority of the Son of David over His ancestor, whose Lord He is (Mt 22,41-46 p). Finally in His religious trial, the high priest demanded that He say whether He was the Messiah. Without rejecting the title, Jesus interprets it at once in a transcendental perspective: He is the Son* of Man, destined to sit at the right hand of God (Mt 26,63f). This confession was made at a moment when the passion was beginning, and it will moreover bring about His condemnation (26,65f). Thus His title as Messiah will be especially flouted (26,68; Mk 15,32; Lk 23,35. 39) at the same time as His title of king*. It is only after His resurrection that the disciples will be able to understand exactly what He was concealing: "Was it not necessary that Christ endure these sufferings and thus enter into His glory?" (Lk 24,26). Evidently, there is no longer question of temporal glory, but of something quite different. According to the Scriptures "Christ was to die and rise again, so that in His name the conversion be proclaimed to all nations for the remission of sins" (24,46).

II. FAITH OF THE CHURCH IN JESUS CHRIST

1. *The risen Jesus is the Christ*. In the light of the Pasch, the young Church, then, called Jesus the Messiah-Christ, a title which is now

freed from all ambiguity. Her reasons are apologetical and theological. The Jews must be shown that the Christ, object of their hope, has come in the person of Jesus. This demonstration rests on a very reliable theology, which emphasizes the continuity of the two covenants* and sees in the second the fulfillment of the first. Jesus appeared thus as the veritable son of David (cf Mt 1,1; Lk 1,27; 2,4; R 1,3; Ac 2,29f; 13,23), destined from His conception through the power of the Holy Spirit (Lk 1,35) to receive the throne of David His father (1,32), to lead to its completion the Israelite royalty by establishing the kingdom* of God on earth. It is the resurrection which has enthroned Him in His royal glory: now that "he has received...the Holy Spirit, who was promised" (Ac 2,33), "God hath made both Lord and Christ this same Jesus whom you have crucified" (2,36). But this glory is of the order of the new creation*; the temporal glory of the ancient anointed of Yahweh was only a distant figure* of it.

2. *The titles of Jesus Christ.* United indissolubly to the personal name of Jesus, the word *Christ* from then on had an immense broadening, for all the old titles which described Jesus were concentrated about it. He whom God has anointed is His holy Servant* Jesus (Ac 4,27), the irreproachable Lamb* pictured by Isaiah 53 (1 P 1,19; cf 1 Co 5,7). It was for that reason that it was written that He should suffer (Ac 3,18; 17,3; 26,22f), and that Ps 2 described in advance the plot of the nations "against Yahweh and against His Messiah" (Ac 4,25ff; cf Ps 2,1f). The gospel of Paul is also an announcement of Christ crucified (1 Co 1,23; 2, 2), dead for the godless (R 5,6ff); and the 1st epistle of Peter discusses at length the passion of the Messiah (1 P 1,11; 2,21; 3,18; 4,1.13; 5.1). In the Book of Isaiah the mission of the Servant was described as that of a persecuted prophet*. In fact, the only anointing which Jesus had ever claimed was the prophetic anointing of the Spirit (Lk 4,16-22; cf Is 61,1); and Peter in the Acts does not fail to recall how "God has anointed Jesus with the Spirit and power" (Ac 10,38). On the eve of His death, Jesus proclaimed His dignity as Son* of Man (Mt 26, 63f). The apostolic preaching effectively announced His return on the last day as the Son of Man who would establish the new world (Ac 1,11; cf 3,20f; Mt 25,31.24), and it is under this title that He is already seated at the right hand of God (Ac 7,55f; Ap 1,5.12-16; 14,14).

Apart from the question of attributing to Him the priestly Messianism of which late Judaism dreamed, the Apocalypse shows Him clad in priestly robes (Ap 1,13); and the epistle to the Hebrews celebrates His royal priesthood*, definitively substituted for the figurative priesthood of Aaron (He 5,5 etc.; 7). One does not hesitate to give Him the most exalted title, that of Lord* (cf Ac 2,36): He is "Christ the Lord" (Lk 2,11; 2 Co 4,5f), "our Jesus Christ" (Ac 15,26). In fact, His resurrection has brilliantly manifested that He possesses a glory greater than human: Christ is the Son* of God in the strict sense of the word (R 1,4); He is God Himself (R 9,5; 1 Jn 5,20). *Christ* is no longer for Him a title among others; it has become as His proper name (used without the article: 1 Co 15,12-23) which summarizes all the others. And those whom He has saved bear as a just title the name of "Christians" (Ac 11,26).

→Aaron 1—Anointing III 2.5—Consolation 1 —David o.3—Hour 2—Jesus Christ—John the Baptist 2—King—Kingdom OT III; NT II 1, III 1—Lord NT—Melchizedek 2—Oil 2— Passover I 6 c—Plan of God—Poor NT I— Priesthood OT III 2—Promises II 4, III 1— Redemption OT 2—Remnant OT 1—Servant of God III 1—Shepherd & Flock OT 2—Sign NT I o.1, II 3—Son of God OT II; NT I 1—Son of Man OT II—Spirit of God OT I 3; NT I 1.2— Transfiguration 1.2—Victory OT 3 a—Wine II 2 b.

PEB & PG wjy

MILK

In a pastoral civilization such as that of the Hebrews in the desert, milk, as one of nature's gifts requiring no work on man's part, is a vitally important source of nourishment*. It was always one of the normal foods of Israel (Jg 5,25; Pr 27,27; Si 39,26), and an abundance of milk was a sign of wealth (Jb 29,6). Through its association with the promises and its figurative use, the word milk assumes a symbolic significance.

1. *Divine tenderness.* A mother feeding her child is one of the most natural symbols that there is to express unlimited tenderness and devotion (1 M 7,22). It is, then, not surprising that this image should have been used in Israel to describe the infinite tenderness* and

the attentive care of Yahweh for His people, especially in the context of the exodus from Egypt and the march toward the promised land* (Nm 11,12). That is why the psalmist invites the people to abandon themselves to God, as a child rests contentedly against its mother's breast after feeding (Ps 131,2f).

2. *An image of the divine blessings and messianic promises.* Abundance of milk is part of the classic description of promises*. The land that Israel is going to enter is often described in the OT as "a land flowing with milk and honey" (Ex 3,8; 13,5; Dt 6,3; 11,9; Jr 11,5; Ez 20,6.15 etc.). "This plentiful and large region" (Ex 3,8; cf Dt 32,12ff), "this most excellent of all lands" (Ez 20,6.15), is pictured in terms of the riches of the nomadic life. In the blessing* of Judah (Gn 49,8-12), which has a Messianic perspective, the extraordinary prosperity of the land of Judah is related in terms of an abundance of wine and milk. Among the prophets this picture of prosperity serves as a description of the ideal land in the times to come (Jl 4,18; Is 55,1; 60,16); it is an image of Messianic consolation* and salvation* (Is 66,11ff). In the Song of Songs, milk symbolizes the delights of love between the bridegroom and the bride (Ct 4,11; 5,1). In the time of want, this desert nourishment will again become the basic food of Emmanuel and the survivors; its abundance will be a reminder of the promises (Is 7,15.22).

If prosperity is a gauge of divine blessings, then lack of milk and general desolation is a sign of punishment and of God's curse. Because of Israel's crimes Hosea asks God to make Israelite wombs sterile and to dry up their breasts (Ho 9,14). In view of the NT the eschatological judgment will be so awe-inspiring that, as Jesus says, women not giving milk on that day will be fortunate (Lk 23,29; cf 21, 23 p).

3. *The milk of the children of God.* Normally the NT speaks of milk in the metaphorical sense and means by it teaching considered as the food of the children* of God. For Paul, who centers his attention on the immaturity of the child, the milk given to the still carnal Corinthians is the first Christian message, as opposed to the solid nourishment of the wisdom* reserved for the perfect (1 Co 3,2; cf He 5,12ff). On the other hand, according to 1 P 2,2 the believer who has been born into the new life must continue to long for the milk of the Word* in order to grow strong and attain sal-

vation*, for he always remains a growing child and will always need the milk of God's Word. Ultimately, this Word is Christ Himself (2,3), as many of the Church fathers have taught: "We have need of the Word, the nourishment of truth*" (Clement of Alexandria).

→Child III—Land OT II 1—New Birth 3 a.
                                                    IdlP mjm

MINISTRY

The words *minister* and *ministry*, transliterated from the Latin of the Vulgate, correspond to the Greek *diakonos* and *diakonia*. These two terms do not belong to the religious language of the Septuagint, which uses them rarely in a profane sense (Es 1,10; 6,1-5). In the Vulgate *minister* renders the Hebrew *mešaret* (cf Ex 24, 13: Joshua, the servant of Moses), which could also denote priests, ministers of worship (Is 61,6; Ez 44,11; Jl 1,9). However, from the time of the OT, the reality of a religious ministry, fulfilled among the people of God by men holding title to certain religious functions, is something well attested: the kings*, the prophets*, the trustees of the priesthood are servants* of God who exercise a mediation between Him and His people. Thus St. Paul says that Moses was a minister of the first covenant (2 Co 3,7.9). In the NT Christ is the only mediator between God and men, the unique priest who offers the sacrifice of salvation, the unique bearer of the revelation* since He is the Word* of God made flesh. But in the Church which He has founded there is exercised a new kind of ministry, which is at the service of His Word and His grace.

I. MINISTRY IN THE CHURCH

1. *Ministry of the apostolate.* Jesus taught His apostles* to look upon their function as a service. The heads of nations wished to be regarded as benefactors and masters; but they, after His example, should make themselves the servants (*diakonos*) of all (Mk 10,42ff p). They are His servants, and it is under this title that He promises that they will enter with Him into the glory of the Father (Jn 12,26). From the beginning of Acts, the apostolate is therefore envisaged as a ministry (*diakonia*; Ac 1,17.25), which Matthias is called upon to fill with the

eleven others. The call of Paul to the apostolate (R 1,1) is also a call to a ministry (1 Tm 1,12; cf 2 Co 4,1), which Paul endeavors to fulfill worthily (Ac 20,24), and thanks to which God brings salvation to the pagans (21,19). Conscious of thus being a minister of God (2 Co 6, 3f) and minister of Christ (11,23), he has a lively feeling of the greatness of this function, superior to that of Moses himself, since it is a service of the new covenant, of justice, of the Spirit (3,6-9), of reconciliation (5,18), of the gospel (Col 1,23; E 3,7), of the Church (Col 1, 25).

2. *Diversity of ministries.* However, the ministry in the newborn Church goes far beyond the exercise of the apostolate properly so called. The word *diakonia* is applied first of all to the material services necessary to the community, such as serving at table (Ac 6,1.4; cf Lk 10,40) and the collection for the poor of Jerusalem (Ac 11,29; 12,25; R 15,31; 1 Co 16,15; 2 Co 8,4; 9,1.12f). Besides, a ministry is entrusted to Archippus (Col 4,17) and to Timothy (2 Tm 4,5); the title of minister (*diakonos*) is given to Apollos as to Paul (1 Co 3,5), to Timothy (1 Th 3,2; 1 Tm 4,6), to Tychicus (Col 4,7; E 6,21), to Epaphras (Col 1,7), and even to the false Judaising apostles (2 Co 11,23). This shows that there was in the Church a "diversity of ministries" (1 Co 12,5); for the Spirit "diversifies His charisms* in view of the work of the ministry" (E 4,12). Every "service" of this kind is to be used under the influence of the Spirit (R 12,7), as a mandate received from God (1 P 4,11). It remains to see in what these "services" consist. The lists of charisms* given in the letters always place at the head functions relating to the Word of God (apostle, prophet, doctor, evangelist). But this does not exclude the existence of offices that are properly pastoral, which the letter to the Ephesians mentions expressly (E 4,11).

II. HIERARCHICAL MINISTRY

1. From the time of the apostles, the NT has us assist at the birth of a *hierarchy in government* which prolongs their action. All Jewish communities had elders (*presbyteros*) at their head. Likewise, the missionaries Paul and Barnabas set up elders everywhere in the churches to direct them (Ac 14,23). At the time of the apostolic assembly at Jerusalem, we behold the elders of the local community joined to the twelve, the local community being headed by James (15,2.4.6.22f; 16,4), and we shall find them again at the time of Paul's return (21,18). Likewise, in the course of his last journey, Paul received the presbyters of Ephesus at Miletus (20,17). So, from this time, the apostles, either directly or by their delegates, set up a college of presbyters in each city (Tt 1,5), the recruitment of whom was governed by precise rules and who were established in their office by the laying on of hands (1 Tm 5,17-22). This last feature shows that the presbyterate required a special charism of the Holy Spirit. It was not, therefore, a mere administrative function. As a matter of fact, in the epistle of James, we see the presbyters praying for the sick and conferring on them the anointing with oil (Jm 5,14). It is said moreover that they exercised the presidency in the Christian assembly (1 Tm 5,17). The allusions of Paul to the presidents (*proïstamenos*) refer probably to the presbyters (1 Th 5,12f; cf R 12,8), in the same way as the mention of the heads (*higoumenos*) in the epistle to the Hebrews (He 13,7.17.24).

2. But the letter to the Philippians also mentions side by side bishops and *deacons* (Ph 1,1): there we find a hierarchy in the embryonic stage. Acts probably sees in the seven whom the twelve established to serve table (Ac 6,1-6) prototypes of the future deacons; these entered, moreover, on their office, like the presbyters, with the imposition* of hands (Ac 6,6). Their ministry, however, went beyond material service, for they preached; and Philip is explicitly qualified as an evangelist (Ac 21,8). The pastoral letters set down rules for the choice of these deacons (1 Tm 3,8-13). It was then a question of a lower ministry, the duties of which it is not easy to describe precisely. Those of Phoebe, deaconess of the Church of Cenchreae (R 16,1), are not necessarily of the same order, for the directions given by Paul on the role of women* in assemblies for worship (1 Co 11,1-16; 14,33f) are extremely strict.

3. Bishops are essentially, as their name indicates, "overseers" placed at the head of communities to exercise some vigilance over them. Such an office was not unknown in Judaism. In the community of Qumrân the *mebaqqer* (inspector) had a somewhat similar function. Primitively it was the presbyters who "exercised this vigilance" also in common in each church, for they have the mission of feeding the flock of God (Ac 20,28: 1 P 5,2f), after the image of

Christ, model of pastors (1 P 5,4), pastor and overseer of souls (1 P 2,25). But the pastoral epistles show that there is only one bishop in each community. He must be carefully chosen (1 Tm 3,1-7), apparently from among the presbyters (Tt 1,5-9). It is he doubtless who fulfills this function of pastor (cf Ac 20,28f) which Paul places among the number of charisms (E 4,11), and who recalls one of the apostolic responsibilities (Jn 21,15ff; cf Mt 18,12ff). Paul's delegates, Titus and Timothy, have authority over the presbyters, the deacons, and the bishops of the churches entrusted to them. They have responsibilities in the matter of the liturgy (1 Tm 2,1-15) and of doctrinal teaching (1 Tm 4,6.13-16; 6,3). But on this last point each bishop exercises a surveillance in his own jurisdiction (Tt 1,9). This delegation of the functions of government, first devolving on the apostles, shows that the organization of the Church was in the course of developing. Once the apostles had disappeared, it stabilized itself into a hierarchy of three ranks: a bishop, a pastor, and president of the community, surrounded by presbyters whom the deacons assisted. The necessary charism for the exercise of their functions was conferred upon them, as formerly, by the rite of the laying on of hands (cf 2 Tm 1,6).

4. Nowhere is the title of *priests* given to the ministers of the new covenant, no more than to the apostles. But their ministry puts them at the service of the priesthood* of Jesus Christ, the only high priest of men. By this title, they are, after the apostles, the stewards of God (Tt 1,7), of His mysteries (1 Co 4,2), of His grace (1 P 4,10). Such is the perspective in which the idea of the Christian priesthood is going to develop, hierarchized into three degrees (bishop, priests, deacons), identical by its functions with the ministry described in the NT, exercised by virtue of the same charismatic powers; it is derived in the last resort from the apostolic ministry in what it had that was communicable.

→Apostles II 1—Authority OT II; NT II— Charisms II 1.2—Church—Exhort—Imposition of Hands NT 2—Preach II 2 b—Priesthood OT I 4; NT III—Serve III 2—Shepherd & Flock NT —Word of God OT III 1; NT II 1.

PG wjy

MIRACLE

It is not uncommon for some Christians to consider the very notion of miracle as strictly limited, and on the contrary, for others to show themselves quite fond of false marvels. These opposed excesses have a common source which is nurtured by a certain kind of apologetic of long-standing vigor: in miracles all they see is a defiance of natural laws. What is overlooked is their role as signs* "adapted to the intelligence of all."

Everywhere in the Bible we discover the hand of God manifesting His power and love for His people. The created universe, with its fixed order (Jr 31,36f), is a "marvel" (Ps 89,6) and a "sign" (Ps 65,9), as are the unusual interventions of God in the course of history. These latter, in turn, are a renewed creation* (Nm 16,30; Is 65,18), even if today's historian considers them ordinary and explicable. Ignoring modern distinctions between "providential" actions, the exceptional convergence of natural causes; and substituting divine action for the interplay of natural agents or "secondary causes," the Bible focuses the attention of the believer on the one essential element common to all these categories: the religious significance of events. Thus, with the eyes of faith St. Augustine sees with the same clarity the mark of divine love and power in the gathering of a harvest as in the multiplication of the loaves. If he does not distinguish between them it is because one benefit is taken for granted, the other is received with astonishment. In this view a detail has no more importance than we are inclined to give it: thus, it is of no importance whether the sterile fig tree withered "instantly" (Mt 21,19) or much later (Mk 11,20); what matters is the lesson that lies hidden in this symbolic deed.

I. MIRACLES IN THE OT

1. *The facts.* Apart from the fictitious marvels of certain books or sections of books which belong to a didactic genre (Jon, Tb, the dramatic setting of Job, the Haggada of Dn 1—6, the edifying embellishments of 2 M etc.), as well as the two marvels described in the life of Isaiah (Is 37,36f; 38,7f), miracles are not numerous in sacred history except at two important periods: in the lifetime of Moses and his successor, Joshua; at the time of the founding and installation of God's chosen people; in the

lifetime of Elijah and his disciple Elisha, the restorers of the covenant of Moses.

The substantial historicity of the cycles of Elijah and Elisha makes good use of popular exaggerations (vg 2 K 1,9-16), which from one cycle to the other grow in extension and frequently lose in religious quality (vg 2 K 2,23f; 6,1-7). Despite the admittedly considerable amplifications they have undergone in the course of time, the traditional accounts of the ten plagues of Egypt or the miracles of the desert and the conquest of the promised land still retain this same quality of historicity. Those who committed them to writing, because they utilized the contemporary literary genres, were indeed compilers of tradition and freely exploited the accounts handed down to them; but they never lost sight of their religious purpose: to show the protective presence of an all-powerful God (Js 24,17) at the dawn of the history of the chosen people. Despite also the epic manner which characterizes these traditions, they remain fundamental: they recount the birth of Israel, a marvel *par excellence* and the only event besides creation (Is 65,17) which is worthy to be compared to the eschatological renewal (Is 43,16-21).

2. Miracles: divine, efficacious signs.

a) The OT shows miracles to be God's revelations and the efficacious signs of His activity. This function is indicated by the very words used: they are "signs" (hb. *'ōtōt*, gr. *sēmeia*, vg Ex 10,1), they are "signs and symbolic prodigies" (hb. *môftīm*, gr. *tērata*, vg Dt 7,19). But the very use of these terms far more commonly than that of *miracle*, clearly manifests the dimension of sign or symbol which lies hidden in every religious prodigy. Thus, the person of the prophet can be a sign, for his existence symbolizes the Word* of God made known through the actions of the prophet (Is 8,18; 20,3; Ez 12,6.11; 24,24.27).

The miraculous signs lend support to this Word, for they reveal in concrete deeds the salvation proclaimed by God's heralds and they accredit these heralds as authentic messengers of the Lord (Ex 4,1-5; I K 18,36ff; Is 38,7f; Jr 44,29f). It is this subordination of miracles to the Word which distinguishes true miracles from the tricks performed by magicians and false prophets (Ex 7,12...). The value of the message, especially manifested by the prayer* of the wonderworker (1 K 18,27f.36f), is the first sign which decides the reality of a miracle

(Dt 13,2-6); miracles only lend support to the Word once they are judged by it.

b) Among all these signs, miracles are distinguished by their efficacy and their extraordinary character. On the one hand they customarily bring to pass what they signify: such is the case of the first exodus*, an accumulation of prodigies by which God liberated His people, or the new exodus which manifests the effectiveness of His Word (Is 55,11; cf v 13). On the other hand, these works (Ps 77,13; 145,4), despite the fact that they are sometimes comprised of natural events (rain, drought...), more often go beyond what man is accustomed to witness in his world or is able to accomplish of himself. And so, the miracle is a sign particularly revelatory of God's power*; often it is referred to as an exploit (Ex 15,11), a great deed (*geburāh*, Ps 106,2), a mighty thing (Ps 106,21), an awe-inspiring event (Ex 34,10), and, above all, a marvel (*pele*, Ex 15,11; *nifla*, Ps 106,7). This last word designates feats "impossible" for man to perform—as the LXX sometimes translates—accessible to God alone (Ps 86,10), who manifests His glory* in them (Ex 15,1.7; 16,7; Nm 14, 22; Lv 10,3), a reflection of His holiness (Ex 15, 11; Ps 77,14; Lv 10,3), that is, His transcendence.

But the divine power brings only the sinful to ruin (Dt 7,17-20; Mi 7,15ff); for the people of the promise (Dt 4,37), His marvels are profitable, even when they try and humiliate (8, 16); for "Yahweh is love in all His works" (Ps 145,9). Finally, then, miracles are the efficacious signs of this love* of Yahweh (Ps 106,7; 107,8) and His gratuitous gifts (Dt 6,10ff; Js 24,11ff). In Jesus alone will the universality of that saving love be fully revealed. This He will do by simultaneously underlining the prophetic meaning of His own miracles worked on behalf of pagans (Mt 8,11ff) and by making explicit the meaning of the miracles formerly wrought through Elijah and Elisha on behalf of a Sidonian woman and a Syrian (Lk 4,25ff).

3. The miracle in reference to faith.

Beyond the astonishment which miracles arouse, they aim at provoking and confirming faith* and its accompaniments: confidence*, thanksgiving*, and memory* (vg Ps 105,5); humility*, obedience*, fear* of God, hope*. They blind those who, like Pharaoh (Ex 7.13...), look for nothing from an unknown God. But to one who already knows God and relies on Him alone there is revealed in them the powerful work of divine love and the seal of approval on the

MIRACLE

mission of God's envoy. Then, in the same movement, he believes in God's Word; he believes in God Himself (Nm 14,11).

Israel admires the grandeur of this faith in Abraham*, who obtained through it what was humanly impossible, the birth of an heir (Gn 15,6; R 4,18-22). This faith is the foundation of those constant reminders of the past contained in Dt, the prophets (vg Is 63,7-14), the psalmists (vg Ps 77; 105—107), the wisdom writers (vg Ws 10—19), which point out that the miracles of this period of God's courtship of Israel are the measure of future benefits and at the same time emphasize their educative value (vg Dt 8, 3; Ws 16,21). Yahweh nourishes this faith by instituting festivals as "memorials of these marvels" (Ps 111,4). It is this faith that animated Isaiah when only a miracle could save Judah (Is 37,34f), and Mary* when the miraculous conception was announced to her (Lk 1,45).

On the contrary, the Israelites lacked faith in the desert* (Ps 78,32) when they reacted carnally to the trials God imposed (Dt 8,2; etc.), and put Yahweh "to the test" (Ex 17,2; Ps 95, 9) in arrogantly demanding a miracle. Ahaz showed a lack of faith in his reliance on allies more than on the God of miracles (Is 7,12), and Zechariah showed a similar lack by his scepticism (Lk 1,18ff). In all these attitudes God's dominion over man is forgotten, His power and gratuitous love are ignored, and His Word is called into doubt: the miraculous has neither been accepted as a true gift nor discerned as a sign.

II. IN THE LIFE OF JESUS

1. *The facts.* Ben Sira implores: "Show signs again, and show other wonders" (Si 36,5), expressing the aspirations of post-exilic Israelites in their disappointment over a return less glorious than the new exodus which has been foretold. Jesus came to fulfill this expectation, but at the same time He discouraged an implicit taste for sensationalism and desire for revenge.

In contrast to the exodus accounts, the evangelists rely on first-hand witnesses and are very sober. By their very soberness of narration miracles seem connatural to the gospel accounts. There is an absence of effort on the part of Jesus (an absence compatible with the pedagogic use of formulas, touches, anointings, and step-by-step processes [Mk 8,23ff] which enrich the symbolism of His actions). There is a religious intent and a prayerful attitude explicit (Jn

11,41f), or suggested (Mk 6,41; 7,34; 9,29; 11, 24), which excludes all magic*. There is the very difficulty of explaining the faith of the Church without miracles. Miracles are integrated into the warp and woof of the gospel. By all these notes are the gospel miracles radically distinguished from those invented by the apocryphal writers, as well as from those which legend attributes to the rabbis, the gods (vg Asclepius), or the pagan sages (vg Apollonius of Tyana) who were contemporaneous with Christian origins. Every objective comparison brings out the historical and religious value of the gospel texts. By these deeds, not only real but truly extraordinary, Jesus "gave a sign" to His people.

2. *The miracles of Jesus as efficacious signs of Messianic salvation.*

a) By His miracles Jesus showed that the Messianic kingdom* announced by the prophets was present in His own person (Mt 11,4f); He drew attention to Himself and to the good news of the kingdom incarnate in Him; He aroused an admiration and religious fear which led men to ask who He was (Mt 8,27; 9,8; Lk 5,8ff). The question of His power to forgive sin (Mk 2,5-12 p), of His authority over the Sabbath (Mk 3,4f p; Lk 13,15f; 14,3ff), of His royal Messiahship (Mt 14,33; Jn 1,49), of His coming in the Father's name (Jn 10,36), of the power of faith in Him (Mt 8,10-13; 15,28 p)—all attest to the mission* and dignity of Jesus, but with the reservations which are imposed by the Jewish hopes of a temporal and national Messiah* (Mk 1,44; 5,43; 7,36; 8,26). The signs which St. John will later point out are already contained in these questions.

If these signs prove the Messiahship and divinity of Jesus, they do so indirectly by their witness to the fact that He really is what He claimed to be. One should not separate these signs from His *Word**: they go hand in hand with the evangelization of the poor (Mt 11, 5 p). The very titles which Jesus gives Himself, the powers He claims for Himself, the salvation He preaches and the renunciation He demands —all are seen to receive the mark of divine authenticity from His miracles by those who have not rejected the truth of His message from the outset (Lk 16,31). That this truth is thus superior to miracles we may learn from Jesus' words about Jonah (Lk 11,29-32). He imposes Himself as the first and only necessary sign (Jn 20,23) for a twofold reason: first because of the unequalled personal authority of His

herald (Mt 7,29); secondly, for the more intrinsic reason that, in fulfilling the earlier revelation (Lk 16,31; Jn 5,46f), His listeners saw
in Him the response to the appeal of the Spirit
(Jn 14,17.26). But before His work is confirmed
and illustrated by miracles He must point out
the difference between true miracles and false
signs (Mk 13,22f; Mt 7,22; cf 2 Th 2,9; Ap 13,
13). Here, as in Dt, "miracles discern doctrine
and doctrine discerns miracles" (Pascal).

b) Miracles do not bear witness to anything
exterior since they are neither arbitrary signs
nor mere ostentation: they *realize* inchoatively
what they signify, bringing out the guarantee
of Messianic salvation* which will find its
completion in the eschatological kingdom; the
synoptics also call them deeds of power*
(*dynameis*: cf Mt 11,20-23; 13,54.58; 14,2). In
fact, Jesus, moved by His human pity (Lk 7,13;
Mt 20,34; Mk 1,41), but still more by His consciousness of being the promised Servant* (Mt
8,17), effectually overcame sickness* death*,
nature's hostility to man; in short, every disorder which is caused in some degree by sin*
(Gn 3,16-19; comp Mk 2,5; Lk 13,3b and Lk 13,
2-3a; Jn 9,3) and serves the devil's work in the
world (Mt 13,25; He 2,14f). Jesus thus refuses
to perform gratuitous wonders for Satan (4,2-7),
the ill-disposed (12,38ff; 16,1-4), the jealous (Lk
4,23), or the frivolous (23,8f), since they would
have no salvific efficacy; and it is significant
that cosmic prodigies—being more relevant, it
would seem, to prophetic imagery than to
history (Ac 2,19f)—were not evoked until that
moment when Jesus, having been challenged to
save Himself by a miracle, gave His life to save
all men (Mt 27,39-54; cf 1 Co 1,22ff). The prodigies which He seems to promise in Mt 17,20 p,
are only illustrations of the power of faith.

In the light of the above, the frequent connection between *healings and exorcisms* becomes clear (Mt 8,16; etc.). The deliverance
of the possessed is a privileged case of that
victory of "the stronger man" (Lk 11,22) over
Satan which every miracle realizes in its own
way. It brings Jesus directly to grips with the
adversary in a duel which commences in the
desert (Mt 4,1-11 p), has its decisive episode
on the cross (Lk 4,13; 22,3.53), and will terminate only with the general judgment (Ap 20,10),
but in which Satan's defeat is already a fore-
gone conclusion (Mt 8,29; Lk 10,18). Exorcism
is the efficacious sign, *par excellence*, of the
coming of the kingdom (Mt 12,28).

3. *Miracles and faith.*

a) The good news of the kingdom which
Jesus preached and showed to be present in His
own person was to be received by conversion
and faith* (Mk 1,15). His miracles and exorcisms were also intended to engender conversion
and faith. By witnessing His marvelous deeds,
Chorazin and Capernaum should have been
converted and believed (Mt 11,20-24 p). John
insists on this point when he distinguishes the
varying degrees of faith (Jn 2,11; 11,15; 20,30f):
at first mild enthusiasm (2,23ff; 4,48) and selfish attractions (6,26), the "signs" lead naturally to recognition of Jesus as God's envoy
(3,2; 9,16; 10,36), prophet (4,19), the Christ (7,31),
Son* of Man (9,35-38). To have to rely too
much on His miracles in order to believe is a
sign of imperfect faith 10,38; 14,11): the word
of Jesus, since its veracity is guaranteed by a
disinterest which derives from His filial spirit
(7,16ff; 12,49f), ought to suffice, as it sufficed
for the Samaritans (4,41f) and the ruler of Capernaum (4,50), as it also sufficed for those who
believed in the Word without touching the
risen body (20,29). With all the more reason,
then, were those held inexcusable (9,41; 15,24)
who had "seen*" His miracles (6,36; 7,3; 15,
24) and still refused to believe (7,5; 12,27).

b) If many rejected the "witness*" (Jn 5,36)
of His miracles it was because spiritual dullness
(6,15.26) or legalistic pride (5,16; 7,49.52; 9,16),
jealousy (12,11) and false prudence (11,47f),
blinded them (9,39; 12,40). They did not have
those dispositions of abandonment and openness to God which in the synoptics constitute
the *faith* anterior to miracles* (Mk 5,36; 9,23;
10,52; etc.), and without which Jesus almost
seems powerless (Mt 13,58). How shall they be
able to interpret the "signs of the times" (Mt
16,3), these men who, like Israel in the desert or
Satan in the recent temptations (4,3-7), only ask
for a sign in order "to put Jesus to the test"
(16,1), and prefer to attribute His exorcisms to
the demons rather than acknowledge His supernatural power (Mk 3,22.29f p)? For hearts
hardened and closed to the Word, the signs
which they rely upon are unintelligible.

That generation* would receive no other sign
than the sign of Jonah (Mt 12,39f); Jesus makes
an appointment with His adversaries for the day
of His resurrection*, that is, the day of His most
striking sign. But this sign is also the most
easily contestable for the lovers of evidence,
since the means for verifying it are all indirect

(the empty tomb, apparitions to a few; cf Mt 28,13ff; Lk 24,11). What will prove to be the ultimate prop of faith must first be the supreme test of faith.

III. IN THE CHURCH

1. *The facts.* The sign of the resurrection*, high point of the new exodus (Jn 13,1), both gave to the Church which was born from it the key to all previous history and inaugurated a new series of signs before it led men to the faith which it founded and announced the resurrection of the dead, the plenitude of that salvation which it procured (1 Co 15,20-28; R 4,25).

2. *Pascal illumination of the gospel.*

a) The resurrection clarified for the Church, which accords it a prominent place in her kerygma and catechesis, the full meaning of prior signs. According to that kerygma, these signs "accredit" Jesus (Ac 2,22) and manifest His goodness (10,38): each synoptic develops its proper theme attesting to the progress of the Church's thought. These diverse themes can be discovered, for example, in the threefold narration of the epileptic child: Lk 9,37-43 is recounting a marvel of goodness; Mt 17,14-21 is interested in the transcendence of Jesus and the disciples sharing in His power; Mk 9,14-29 exalts the triumph of the master of life over Satan in a dramatic piece which already presages in rough outline the Johannine symbolism. And there are even clearer cases wherein such episodes receive a new depth of meaning in the light of the resurrection: it was surely the intention of the evangelists that the confession of divine filiation for which miracles had prepared the way (Mt 14,33; 27,54) should be understood in its fullest and richest sense, and that one should contemplate in certain miracles the outlines of later realities; vg the eucharist* in the multiplication of loaves, the apostolate in the miraculous draught of fishes (Lk 5,1-11).

b) *John* goes yet further. He suggests that the "signs," while accomplishing the exodus of old (Nm 14,22) and anticipating the "hour*" of the new, already manifest something of the "glory*" (Jn 2,11; 11,40) which revealed itself in Jesus' "elevation" (17,5) and which is the splendor of salvific power emanating from the incarnate Word (1,14). Each of these signs, bound up as it is with a discourse, places in relief an aspect

of that power which purifies, pardons, vivifies, illumines, and calls back to life (2,6; 5,14; 6,35; 9,5; 11,25); several even symbolize the sacraments (baptism*, the eucharist*...), which distribute the effects of that power in the Church, thus surpassing such ancient signs as manna* (6,32.49f).)What is more remarkable, these miracles are works* which the Father gives to the Son to perform (5,36) in order to manifest the intimate unity of the Father and Son (5,17; 10,37f; 14,9f). To look upon these efficacious signs of life that issued (19,34) from the side of Jesus "raised up" as the supreme sign (12, 33; cf 3,14=Nb 21,8; *semeion*), is to believe that Jesus is the Christ, the Son of God acting in the Church, and to have life in His name (20,30f). It also means to contemplate the common glory of the Father and the Son (11,4) and so to put oneself on the level of the trinitarian relations.

3. *The time of the Spirit.*

a) Since Jesus was still "with them" (Mt 28, 20), it is not astonishing that the apostles* should renew His salvific deeds (Ac 3,1-10), beginning with the divine miracles of Pentecost; for He had promised them this power, almost institutional (Mk 16,17f), and He had given them some training in its use (Mt 10,8).

The *dynameis* (Paul) which they performed manifest concretely the salvific power (*dynamis*) of the risen Jesus (Ac 3,6.12.16; cf R 1,4), and bring men to the faith by accrediting the heralds of the gospel Word (Mk 16,20; 1 Co 2, 4). Thus is confirmed the necessary connection between miracles and the Word, and their twofold purpose, apologetic and salvific. Herein we see the hierarchy of signs: the worth of an auricular witness (He 2,3f); the constancy (2 Co 12,12), the assurance, and disinterestedness (1 Th 2,2-12) of missionaries go hand in hand with these "signs and prodigies," and distinguish authentic messengers of God (Ac 8,9-24; 13, 4-12) from false prophets; all of this is accomplished through the power of the Holy Spirit (1 Th 1,5; 1 Co 2,4; R 15,19).

b) From the inception of the Church the Spirit also granted miracles to the confident prayers (cf Mt 21,21f; Jm 5,16ff) of certain of the faithful: marvelous charisms* (Jn 14,12) were subsumed under the higher gifts of teaching (1 Co 12,28f) and finally of charity, the supreme marvel of Christian life (13,2). This gift coexists with the sacraments which, in part, play the same role (cf Mk 6,13; Jm 5,13ff) but whose spiritual efficacy leaves room for signs that more directly orient the spirit toward the resurrection* and the restoration of all creation* (R 8,19-24; Ap 21,4).

The same still holds today. Certainly the world of our day has the multiform moral miracle of the Church to lead men to faith. This is seen especially in the splendor of the saints whose heroic and unifying charity is the surest sign of the divine presence (Jn 13,35; 17, 21). But physical miracles, too, continue, as in the times of the Old and the NT, to turn our attention toward the Word and the definitive kingdom, to arouse men first to conversion and then to re-conversion (Mt 18,3), and to translate divine love into living deeds. Today, as in former times, this language remains unintelligible to the proud or irreligious spirit; but it is readily understood by one who, knowing that "nothing is impossible for God" (Gn 18,14= Lk 1,37), opens his heart to the demands of faith and love when the religious context of some event indicates it is God who is "giving a sign."

→Charisms—Faith NT I 2, IV—Glory III 1—Magic—Manna—Power VI—Revelation NT III 1 b—Salvation OT I 1; NT I 2 a—Sea 3—Sickness/Healing—Sign—Word of God OT II 2; NT I 1—Works NT I 2.

PT tms

MISSION

The idea of a divine mission is not completely foreign to non-Christian religions. To say nothing of Mahomet, "the envoy of God," who claims to carry on the work of the biblical prophets, one meets this idea to a certain extent in Greek paganism. Epictetus considered himself the "envoy, inspector, and herald of the gods...sent by the gods as an example." He considered it his mission from heaven to revive the divine spark in man by his teaching and witness. In like manner, in the cult of Mercury, the initiate has a mission to make of himself "a guide for those who are worthy, in order that the human race, through his intercession, be saved by God." But in the biblical revelation, the idea of mission has very different structures. It is completely relative to salvation history. It implies a positive call of God, explicitly manifest in each particular case. It applies to collectivities as well as to individuals. Con-

nected with the idea of predestination and vocation, it is expressed by a vocabulary which centers about the verb *to send*.

OT

I. THE ENVOYS OF GOD

1. It is in the case of the prophets* (cf Jr 7, 25)—of whom Moses* is the first—that the idea of divine mission is best grasped. "I am sending you...": this phrase is at the heart of the entire prophetic calling* (cf Ex 3,10; Jr 1,7; Ez 2,3f; 3,4f). To the call of God each responds according to his personal temperament: Isaiah offers himself ("Behold, here I am, send me," Is 6,8); Jeremiah objects (Jr 1,6); Moses wishes a sign to accredit his mission (Ex 3,11ff), tries to refuse it (4,13), complains bitterly (5,22). But all obey in the end (cf Am 7,14f)—except in the case of Jonah (Jon 1,1ff), who refuses to accept his universal mission and is scandalized at the salvation of the nations*. This consciousness of a personal mission received from God is an essential trait of the true prophet. It distinguishes him from those who say: "Word of God," although God has not sent them, as those false prophets against whom Jeremiah struggled (Jr 14,14f; 23,21.32; 28,15; 29,9). In a broader sense one can also speak of a divine mission for all those who played a providential role in the history of God's people; but in order to recognize the existence of similar missions, the witness of a prophet is needed.

2. All the missions of divine envoys are relative to the plan* of salvation*. The greater part of them are directly linked with the people of Israel. But this allows room for the widest diversity. Prophets are sent to convert the hearts of the people, to announce chastisement or promises: their role is directly bound up with God's Word* which they are charged to bring to men. Other missions concern more directly the historic destiny of Israel: Joseph is sent to prepare a reception for Jacob's sons in Egypt (Gn 45,5), and Moses to lead them back (Ex 3, 10; 7,16; Ps 105,26). The same holds for all the chiefs and liberators of God's people: Joshua, the judges, David, the rebuilders of Judaism after the exile, the leaders of the Maccabean revolt...Even if the sacred historians do not speak of a mission explicitly, they evidently consider these men as divine envoys, thanks to whom the divine plan of salvation has moved toward its goal: Even the pagans can play a

MISSION

providential role: Assyria is sent to chastise unfaithful Israel (Is 10,6), and Cyrus, to conquer Babylon and liberate the Jews (Is 43,14; 48,14f). Sacred history is made up of the cross-currents of all these particular missions which ultimately lead to the same end.

II. THE MISSION OF ISRAEL

1. Should we also speak of a mission of the people of Israel? Yes, if we consider the direct connection which always exists between mission and calling*. The call of Israel defines her mission in the plan of God. Chosen from among all the nations, Israel is a consecrated people*, a priestly people charged with the service of Yahweh (Ex 19,5f). It is not said that Israel fills this role in the name of the other nations. Nevertheless, in keeping with the developing revelation, the prophetic oracles foresaw a time when all the nations* would join with Israel in order to participate in the worship of the one God (cf Is 2,1ff; 19,21-25; 45,20-25; 60): Israel is then called to become the beacon light for all of humanity. So also, if Israel is the trustee of the plan of salvation, it is with the mission of bringing all other peoples to participate in that plan: since the call of Abraham, the germinal idea was there (Gn 12, 3); it becomes more precise as revelation progressively reveals more clearly the divine purpose.

2. Starting with the exile, one can discern Israel's clear consciousness of this mission. She knows herself to be the servant* of Yahweh, sent by Him in the quality of a messenger (Is 42,19). Israel is God's witness to the pagan nations, charged with the task of making them recognize Him as the one true God (43,10.12; 44,8) and "of transmitting to the world the imperishable light of the Law" (Ws 18,4). The national calling here expands into a religious universalism. There is no longer question of dominating the pagan nations (Ps 47,4) but of converting them. The people of God thus opens itself to proselytes (Is 56,3.6f). A new spirit permeates the inspired writings. The Book of Jonah envisages a prophetic mission of which the pagans are the beneficiaries; and, in the Book of Proverbs, the envoys of divine wisdom apparently invite all mankind to His feast (Pr 9,3ff). Finally, Israel tends to become a missionary people, especially in the Alexandrian

milieu where the sacred books are translated into Greek.

III. PRELUDES TO THE NT

1. The theme of divine mission is found again in prophetic eschatology, which prepares explicitly for the NT. It is the mission of the Servant* which Yahweh designates as "a covenant of the people and a light* of the nations" (Is 42,6f; cf 49,5f). It is the mission of the mysterious prophet* whom Yahweh sends "to bring the good tidings to the poor (Is 61,1f). It is the enigmatic messenger who makes ready the way before God (Ml 3,1), and of the new Elijah (Ml 3,23). It is the mission of the converted pagans who wish to show the glory of Yahweh to their brethren (Is 66,19f). The NT will show how these Scriptures are to be fulfilled.

2. In short, the theology of the Word*, of Wisdom*, and of the Spirit* personifies in a surprising way these divine realities and does not hesitate to speak of their mission: God sends His Word in order to carry out His will here below (Is 55,11; Ps 107,20; 147,15; Ws 18, 14ff); He sends His Wisdom in order to assist man in his toils (Ws 9,10); He sends His Spirit to renew the face of the earth (Ps 104,30; cf Ez 37,9f) and make known to men His will (Ws 9,17). These expressions are also a prelude to the NT, where they will be employed to explain the mission of the Son of God who is His Word and His Wisdom, and to clarify the mission of His Holy Spirit in the Church.

NT

I. THE MISSION OF THE SON OF GOD

1. After John the Baptist, last and greatest of the prophets, the divine messenger and new Elijah foretold by Malachi (Mt 11,9-14), Jesus presents Himself to men as the envoy of God *par excellence*, the one spoken of in the Book of Isaiah (Lk 4,17-21; cf Is 61,1f). The parable of the murderous vine-dressers underscores the continuity of His mission with that of the prophets, but at the same time shows the fundamental difference between the two cases: after having sent His servants, the Father of the family finally sends His own Son* (Mk 12,2-8 p). It is for this reason that in accepting or rejecting the envoy, one accepts or rejects Him who

366

has sent Him (Lk 9,48; 10,16 p), that is, the Father Himself who has given everything into His envoy's hands (Mt 11,27). This consciousness of a divine mission which allows us to catch a glimpse of the mysterious relationships of the Father and the Son is made explicit in characteristic phrases: "I have been sent...," "I have come...," "The Son of Man has come...," to announce the gospel* (Mk 1,38 p), to fulfill* the Law and the prophets (Mt 5,17), to bring fire* upon the earth (Lk 12,49), to bring not peace but the sword (Mt 10,34 p), to call not the just but sinners (Mk 2,17 p), to seek out and save that which was lost (Lk 19,10), to serve and to give His life as a ransom (Mk 10,45 p)...All these aspects of the redemptive work accomplished by Jesus are thus allied to the mission which He received from the Father, from the preaching in Galilee to the sacrifice of the cross. In the Father's plan, however, this mission still has a limited horizon: Jesus has only been sent to the lost sheep of the house of Israel (Mt 15,24). It is in their conversion that these should themselves become aware of Israel's providential mission: to bear witness to God and His reign before all the nations of the world.

2. In the fourth Gospel, the sending of the Son by the Father recurs like a constant refrain throughout the discourses (40 times, vg 3,17; 10,36; 17,18). For the sole desire of Jesus is "to do the will* of Him who sent Him" (4,34; 6, 38ff), to accomplish His work (9,4), to speak what He has learned of Him (8,26). There is such a unity of life between them (6,57; 8,16.29) that the attitude one takes with regard to Jesus is the same one should have with regard to God Himself (5,23; 12,44f; 14,24; 15,21-24). As for the passion, the consummation of His work, Jesus looks upon it as His return to the one who sent Him (7,33; 16,5; cf 17,11). The faith He demands of men is faith in His mission (11,42; 17,8.21.23.25); this implies simultaneous faith in the Son as sent (6,29) and in the Father as sender (5,24; 17,3). Through the mission of the Son here below an essential aspect of the intimate mystery of God is revealed to men: the one true God (Dt 6,4; cf Jn 17,3), by sending His Son, revealed Himself as a Father.

3. It is not surprising to see the apostolic writings giving a central place to this mission of the Son. God sent His Son in the fullness* of time in order to redeem us and confer filial adoption on us (G 4,4; cf R 8,15). God sent His Son into the world as savior, as a propitiation for our sins, in order that we might live through Him. Such is the ultimate proof of His love for us (1 Jn 4,9f.14). Jesus is thus the envoy superior to all others (Jn 9,7), the *apostolos* of our profession of faith (He 3,1).

II. THE ENVOYS OF THE SON

1. The mission of Jesus is continued by His own envoys, the twelve who, for this reason, also bear the name of apostles*. While He was still on earth, Jesus was already sending them before Him (cf Lk 10,1) to preach the gospel and to heal (Lk 9,1 p), the very object of His own personal mission. They are the laborers sent to the harvest* by the master (Mt 9.38 p; cf Jn 4,38); they are the servants* sent by the king to call the guests to the wedding feast of his son (Mt 22,3 p). They must have no illusions about the lot that awaits them: the envoy is not greater than the one who sends him (Jn 13,16); the servant will be treated as the master was treated (Mt 10,24f). Jesus sends them "as sheep in the midst of wolves" (10,16 p). He knows that the "perverse generation*" will persecute His envoys and put them to death (23, 34 p). But what is done to them is done also to Him, and finally, also to the Father: "He who hears you hears me, he who rejects you rejects me, and he who rejects me rejects Him who sent me" (Lk 10,16); "He who receives you, receives me, and he who receives me receives Him who sent me" (Jn 13,20). In fact, the mission of the apostles is bound up intimately with that of Jesus: "As my Father has sent me, I also send you" (20,21). This word illuminates the deep meaning of the final sending of the twelve in the course of the apparitions* of the risen Christ: "Go..." They will indeed go to announce the gospel (Mk 16,15), to make disciples* of all the nations (Mt 28,19), to be His witnesses everywhere (Ac 1,8). The mission of the Son will thus reach all men effectively thanks to the mission of His apostles and His Church*.

2. It is in this light that one must understand the book of the Acts of the Apostles when it recounts the vocation of Paul. Using the classic phrases for the prophetic calling, the risen Christ says to His chosen instrument: "Go! for I am sending you far away to the gentiles" (Ac 22,21)—and this mission to the pagans traces back in a direct line to that of the Servant* of Yahweh (Ac 26,17; cf Is 42,7.16). For the Ser-

vant came in the person of Jesus, and the envoys of Jesus bring to all nations* the message of salvation which He Himself made known only to "the lost sheep of the house of Israel" (Mt 15,24). It was to this mission received on the road to Damascus that Paul always appealed in order to justify his title of apostle* (1 Co 15,8f; G 1,12). Certain of its universal extent, Paul carried the gospel message to the pagans in order to obtain from them the obedience* of faith (R 1,5), and he saw the mission of all the messengers of the gospel as vital (10,14f): was it not his labor that gave birth to faith in Christ's Word in the hearts of men (10,17)? Beyond the personal mission of the apostles stands the missionary function of the entire Church*, for thereby she is united to the mission of the Son.

III. THE MISSION OF THE HOLY SPIRIT

1. In order to accomplish their missionary function, the apostles and preachers of the gospel were not left to their own resources; they accomplish their work through the power of the Holy Spirit*. For, in order to define the exact role of the Spirit, it is again necessary to speak of a mission in the fullest sense of the word. Evoking His future coming in His discourse after the last supper, Jesus described it as follows: "The Paraclete, the Holy Spirit whom the Father will send in my name, will teach you all things" (Jn 14,26); "When the Paraclete comes whom I shall send from the Father, He will bear witness to me" (15,26; cf 16,7). The Father and the Son therefore act conjointly in sending the Spirit. Luke places emphasis on the action of Christ, whereas the Father's role consists primarily in the promise which He made, according to the witness of Scripture: "I will send you, said Jesus, Him whom my Father promised to you" (Lk 24,49; cf Ac 1,4; Ez 36,27; Jl 3,1f).

2. Such, in effect, is the meaning of Pentecost*, the initial manifestation of that mission of the Spirit which will last as long as the Church. The Spirit makes of the twelve, witnesses* of Jesus (Ac 1,8). He was given to them in order to help them fulfill their task of envoys (Jn 20, 21f). In Him will they henceforth preach the gospel (1 P 1,12), and, after them, all subsequent preachers. Thus the mission of the Spirit is inherent in the very mystery of the Church whenever she preaches the Word in fulfillment

of her missionary work. This mission of the Spirit is also found in the very source of the sanctification of men. For if, at baptism, they receive filial adoption, it is by God's sending into their hearts the spirit of His Son who cries: "*Abba!* Father..." (G 4,6). The mission of the Spirit hereby becomes the object of Christian experience. Thus is unfolded the mystery of the Godhead: after the Son, the Word and Wisdom of God, the Spirit is in turn manifested as a divine person entering into the history of men whom He transforms interiorly into the image* of the Sons of God.

→Apostles—Apparitions of Christ 2.4 c. 5.7—Authority NT II 1—Calling I, II—Cares 1—Church III 2 b c—Election OT I 3 c—Imposition of Hands NT 2—Mediator O—Nations OT IV 2; NT—Pentecost II 2 e—Peter 1.3—Preach II 2 a—Prophet—Run—Teach NT II 1.2—Trial/Temptation NT—Visit NT 2—Will of God NT I 2—Witness—Word of God OT III 1.

JP & PG tms

MOSES

For Israel, Moses is the prophet* without equal (Dt 34,10ff) through whom God liberated His people, with whom He ratified His covenant (Ex 24,8), and to whom He revealed His Law (Ex 24,3; cf 34,27). Besides Jesus, Moses is the only one to whom the NT gives the title of mediator*. But, whereas God gave the Law only to His people Israel through the mediation of His faithful servant Moses (He 3,5; G 3,19), He saves all men through the mediation of His Son (He 3,6), Jesus Christ (1 Tm 2,4ff). The Law was given to us through Moses; grace and truth have come to us through Christ (Jn 1,17). The parallelism of Moses and Jesus points up the evident differences of the two covenants.

1. *The servant and friend of God.* The calling of Moses is the crowning event of a long and providential preparation. Born of an oppressed race (Ex 1,8-22), Moses owed the daughter of the oppressing Pharaoh not only his being saved from the waters and survival (2,1-10), but also an education which prepared him for his role of leader (Ac 7,21f). Nevertheless, neither the wisdom nor the power nor the reputation thus acquired (cf Ex 11,3) would have sufficed to make him the liberator of his people. He even incurred the ill will of his own people (Ex 2,

11-15; Ac 7,26ff) and was forced to flee into the desert. There he received his call: God appeared to him, revealed to him at the same time His name*, and His plan* of salvation, made him acquainted with the plans for his mission* and gave him the means to fulfill it (Ex 3,1-15): God would be with him (3,12). In vain did he try to refuse the task: Who am I?... (3,11). The humility which led him at first to hesitate in the face of so heavy a task (4,10-13) would eventually enable him to accomplish it with unequaled meekness, despite the opposition of his own people (Nm 12,3.13). Even though his faith displayed some feebleness (20,10), God declared His servant to be most faithful (12,7f) and dealt with him as a friend* (Ex 33,11). By a singular grace God revealed to him, if not His glory*, at least His name (33,17-23). While speaking to Moses from the cloud, God accredited him as leader of His people (19,9; 33, 8ff).

2. *The liberator and mediator of the covenant.* The first act of his mission as leader was the liberation of his people. Moses had to put an end to the oppression which prevented Israel from worshipping a God whom the Pharaoh refused to acknowledge (Ex 4,22f; 5,1-18). But to achieve this end God had "to show His mighty hand" by smiting the Egyptians with formidable blows: Moses is the contriver of these calamities* which manifest the divine judgment*. At the time of the final plague it is again Moses who, filled with God's Wisdom (Ws 10,16-20), orders Israel to celebrate the Passover*. After this the people of God are delivered from the pursuing Egyptians "by the hand of Moses" (Ps 77,21): Israel crosses the sea, which engulfs the pursuers. (Ex 14). The first purpose of the exodus* is then attained: at Sinai Moses offers the sacrifice which makes Israel the people* of God (19,4ff) by sealing His covenant* with them (24,3-8; cf He 9,18ff).

To the people of the covenant are added all those who were baptized in Moses (1 Co 10,2), that is to say, those who, giving themselves to his guidance, crossed the sea with the guidance of the cloud* and experienced salvation*. Moses, "their leader and redeemer" (Ac 7,35), thus prefigures Christ, mediator of the new and more perfect covenant (He 8,6; 9,14f), the redeemer who liberates from sin those baptized in His name (Ac 2,38; 5,31).

3. *The prophet, legislator and intercessor.* As a leader of the people of the covenant, Moses speaks to them in God's name (Ex 19,6ff; 20, 19; Dt 5,1-5). Like every true prophet, he is the mouthpiece of God (Dt 18,13-20). He reveals the divine Law to Israel and teaches them how to conform their conduct to it (Ex 18,19f; 20,1-17 p). He exhorts them to fidelity to the one transcendent God who is always with them (Dt 6) and who lovingly and freely chose and saved them (Dt 7,7ff).

His role as prophet is to uphold the covenant and to educate a rebellious people (Ho 12, 14). The exercise of that mission thus makes him the first of God's persecuted servants* (cf Ac 7,52f). He sometimes complained of this to God: "Was it I who conceived this people, that you should say to me, 'Carry them in your bosom, as a nurse would carry a suckling child ...,' the task is too great for me" (Nm 11,12ff). One day, overwhelmed by the infidelity of his people (Nm 20,10ff; Ps 106,33), he allowed his faith and meekness, deep as they were, to waver (Si 45,4; He 11,24-29); and for this failing he was chastised (Dt 3,26; 1,21).

Because he is a prophet Moses intercedes for his people, with whom he feels a sense of solidarity. He is admirable in this role of intercessor: through his prayers Israel is assured of victory* over its enemies (Ex 17,9-13) and obtains pardon for its sins (32,11-14; Nm 14,13-20; 21,7ff). He thereby saves his people from death by placing himself in the path of the divine anger (Ps 106,23). "Pardon their sins or else efface me from your book" (Ex 32,31f). By this ardent charity he prefigures the qualities of the suffering Servant* who will intercede for sinners and bear their guilt (Is 53,12). He also prefigures that "prophet like himself" whose coming he foretells (Dt 18,15-18). Stephen will recall that prophecy (Ac 7,37) and Peter will proclaim its fulfillment in Jesus (Ac 3,22f). To this "prophet" *par excellence* (Jn 1,21; 6,14) Moses bears witness in the Scriptures (Jn 5,46; Lk 24,27); this is why Moses appears at Jesus' side at the transfiguration (Lk 9,30f). But Christ, the new Moses, surpasses the Law by fulfilling it (Mt 5,17); for He is the end of the old Law (R 10,4): having accomplished all that was written of Him in the Law of Moses, He rose from the dead through His Father in order to give the Holy Spirit to men (Lk 24,44-49).

4. *Moses and the glory of God.* In Christ is now revealed that glory* (Jn 1,14) whose reflection illuminated the face of Moses after his encounters with God (Ex 34,29-35). The people of the old covenant could not bear the splen-

dor of this reflection, fleeting though it was (2 Co 3,7): so Moses placed a veil over his countenance. For Paul this veil symbolizes the blindness of the Jews who read the works of Moses but neither understood them nor were converted to Christ whom they foretold (2 Co 3,13ff). For whoever truly believes in Moses also believes in Christ (Jn 5,45ff); and his countenance, like that of Moses, reflects the glory of the Lord who transforms him into His own image (2 Co 3,18). In heaven the redeemed will sing "the canticle of Moses, the servant of God, and the canticle of the Lamb" (Ap 15,3; cf Ex 15), the unique paschal canticle of the unique Savior whom Moses prefigured.

→Aaron 1—Ark of the Covenant II—Calling O, I—Covenant—Election OT I 3 c—Face 4—Faith OT I—Fire OT I 1; NT II 2—Friend 1—Joshua 1—Law—Love I OT 1—Mediator I 1—Meekness 2—Prayer I 1—Prophet—See OT I 1—Servant of God I—Transfiguration 2—Yahweh

RM & MFL tms

MOTHER

As a giver of life, the mother holds a special place in the ordinary existence of men, and also in the history of salvation.

I. MOTHER OF MEN

She who gives life ought to be loved, but the love which is borne her ought to be transfigured, after the example of Jesus, sometimes even to the point of sacrifice.

1. *Call to fruitfulness.* In calling his wife "Eve" Adam signified her vocation to be "the mother of the living" (Gn 3,20). Genesis tells us how this vocation is fulfilled in spite of the most unfavorable circumstances. Thus, Sarai has recourse to a stratagem (16,1f); the daughters of Lot to incest (19,30-38); Rachel to blackmail: "Give me children, or I die," she cried to her husband; but Jacob had to confess that he could not put himself in the place of God (30,1f). It is God alone, in fact, who has placed in the heart of woman the imperative desire to be a mother, it is He who opens and closes the maternal womb. He alone can triumph over sterility* (1 S 1,2—2,5).

2. *The mother of the home.* Having become a mother, woman exults. Eve rejoiced at her first childbirth: "I have acquired a man through Yahweh" (Gn 4,1), a rejoicing which the renown of Cain will perpetuate (from the root *acquire*). Likewise, *Isaac* recalls the laugh of Sara at the time of his birth (Gn 21,6) and *Joseph* the hope which Rachel had of having still another child (30,24). By her maternity, woman does not only enter into the history of life, she awakens a closer attachment in her spouse (Gn 29,34). Finally the Decalogue proclaims that she ought to be respected by her children quite as much as their father (Ex 20,12); failure to do this merits the same punishment (Ex 21,17; Lv 20,9; Dt 21,18-21). In their turn the sapiential books insist on the duty that everyone has to respect his mother (Pr 19,26; 20,20; 23,22; Si 3,1-16), adding that one should listen to and follow her instructions (Pr 1,8).

3. *The queen-mother.* A special role seems to be incumbent on the mother of the king*, who alone and differently from his wife enjoys a special honor before the reigning prince. She is called the great lady, as was Bathsheba (1 K 15,13; cf 2,19) or the mother of King Asa (2 Ch 15,16). This practice may clarify the appearance of maternity in the framework of royal Messianism; and it is not without interest to point out the role of the mother of Jesus who among the devout has become "our Lady" (Notre Dame).

4. *The profound meaning of maternity.* With the coming of Christ the duty of filial devotion is not suppressed but fulfilled. The apostolic catechesis maintains it clearly (Col 3,20f; E 6, 1-4). Jesus fulminates against the Pharisees who elude it under vain cultic pretexts (Mt 15,4-9 p). Henceforth, however, we must learn how to go beyond filial piety* in fulfilling it by piety toward God Himself. He has come "to separate the daughter from her mother" (Mt 10, 35), and He promises the hundredfold to him who shall have left father or mother for His sake (Mt 19,29). To be worthy of Him a man must be capable of "hating* his father and his mother" (Lk 14,26), that is to say, of loving Jesus more than his parents (Mt 10,37).

Jesus Himself gives the example of this sacrifice of maternal bonds. In the temple, at the age of twelve, He claims in the presence of His mother the right to be about the business of His Father (Lk 2,49f). At Cana, if He finally grants what His mother asks, Jesus gives her to understand that she must intervene no more with Him, either because the hour* of his public ministry has struck, or because the hour of His cross has not yet come (Jn 2,4). But if Jesus thus kept at a distance with regard to His mother, it is not that He ignored the true greatness of Mary*. On the contrary, He points it out in the faith that she shows: "Who is my mother, and who are my brethren?" And with His hand He indicates His disciples (Mt 12, 48ff). To the woman who admired the natural maternity of Mary, He insinuated that hers was a fidelity *par excellence* in hearing the Word of God and putting it into practice (Lk 11,27f). Jesus extends this maternity in the spiritual order to all of His disciples when from the height of the cross He said to him whom He loved: "Behold thy mother!" (Jn 19,26f).

II. THE MOTHER IN SALVATION HISTORY

The characteristics of a mother are used metaphorically, to express a divine attitude, or a reality of the messianic order, or again the fruitfulness of the Church.

1. *Divine tenderness and wisdom.* There is in God such a plenitude of life* that Israel gives Him the names of father* and of mother. To express the merciful tenderness* of God, *rahamim* denotes the maternal sentiments and evokes an interior emotion which a woman feels for her children (Ps 25,6; 116,5). God consoles us as a mother (Is 66,13), and if one should be found to forget the child of her womb, He will never forget Israel (49,15)—like Jesus anxious to gather together the children of Jerusalem (Lk 13,34).

Wisdom*, which is the Word* of God charged with accomplishing His plans (Ws 18,14f), in leaving His mouth (Si 24,3) relates to His children as a mother (Pr 8—9), recommending His instructions to them, nourishing them with bread* of the understanding, giving them water* to drink (Si 15,2f). His children will render Him justice (Lk 7,35) by recognizing in Jesus He who fulfills His role: "He who comes to me will never hunger, who believes in me will never thirst" (Jn 6,35; cf 8,47).

2. *Mother of the Messiah.* The protogospel already proclaims that the woman whose posterity will crush the serpent's head (Gn 3,15) is a mother. Then, in the accounts in which God is seen to triumph over sterility*, the women who gave a posterity to the patriarchs prefigured from afar the virgin mother. This virginal conception was insinuated by the prophets of the Emmanuel (Is 7,14) and of her who should give Him birth (Mi 5,2). The evangelists at any rate have recognized the fulfillment of the prophecy in Jesus Christ (Mt 1,23; Lk 1,35f).

3. *Mother of peoples.* Jerusalem* is the mother-city beyond all others (cf 2 S 20,19), she from whom the inhabitants draw nourishment and protection. From her especially are derived the justice* and the knowledge of Yahweh. Like Rebecca, for whom was wished an increase to thousands (Gn 24,60), she will become the mother of all peoples*. "To Zion each says, 'Mother,' for in her each one is born" (Ps 87, 5), whether they be of Israel or of the nations*. After the punishment which was removed by her spouse, behold her overwhelmed anew: "Give praise, O thou barren who bearest not... for many are the children of the desolate, more than of her that hath a husband" (Is 54,1; G 4,22-30). Toward her "they shall take flight like doves to their dove-cot," all the peoples of the earth (Is 2,1-5; 60,1-8).

But Jerusalem, retiring within herself on denying Christ, has been unfaithful to this spiritual maternity (Lk 19,41-44); and her children will be able to turn on her to reproach her with it (cf Ho 2,4). This is why she will be supplanted by another Jerusalem, that from on high, which is truly our mother (G 4,26), which comes down from heaven and from God (Ap 21,2). This new city is the Church, which conceives her children to the life of children of God. It is also each Christian community in particular (2 Jn 1). It is destined to give to Christ the plenitude of His body*, and to gather all peoples into the spiritual Israel*.

Participating in this motherhood, the apostles are the instruments of this fruitfulness, joyous as it is through pain (cf Jn 16,20ff). Paul tells his dear Galatians that he was in labor with them until Christ be formed in them (G 4,19), and he reminds the Thessalonians that he has surrounded them with care like a mother who nourishes her children (1 Th 2,7f). But this motherhood is valid only through that of the woman who is ceaselessly in labor and in the joy of childbirth, a figure behind whom all other mothers stand in profile—from Eve, the mother of the living, to the Church, mother of believers: through the mother of Jesus, Mary our mother (Ap 12).

MOUNTAIN

MOUNTAIN

In most religions the mountains, probably because of their height and the air of mystery which enshrouds them, are considered to be the point where heaven and earth meet. There are many countries that have their holy mountain where the world was created, or where the gods dwell, or the place from where salvation comes. The Bible retains these beliefs but purifies them. In the OT mountains are only one creature among many: thus Yahweh is undoubtedly the "God of the mountains" (probable meaning of El-Shadday), but also the God of the valleys (1 K 20,23.28); with Christ, Zion ceases to be "the umbilicus of the world" (Ez 38,12); for no longer does God wish to be adored on this or that mountain, but in spirit and in truth (Jn 4, 20-24).

I. THE CREATURE OF GOD

1. *Stability.* Men pass, the mountains remain. This experience makes it easy to see why the mountains are a symbol of God's faithful justice* (Ps 36,7); those which the patriarchs were familiar with were called "the eternal hills" (Gn 49,26; Dt 33,15). But, admirable though they are, these simple creatures must not for that reason be divinized: "Before the mountains were born, you always were, O God" (Ps 90,2; cf Pr 8,25). He who "weighed the mountains with a balance and the hills with a scale" (Is 40,12) is the Creator who "maintains them by His power" (Ps 65,7). He moves them at His good pleasure (Jb 9,5) and gives this power to the most modest believer (Mt 17,20; cf 1 Co 13,2). Let all men then proclaim: "Bless the Lord, O ye mountains and hills!" (Dn 3,75; Ps 148,9).

2. *Power.* Raised as it is above the plains which are often ravaged by calamities, the mountain offered Lot refuge in peril (Gn 19,17), and again it attracted the persecuted just who sought to flee there like the bird (Ps 11,1; cf Ez 7,16; Mt 24,16). But the just man must take care in raising his eyes to the mountains; for from Yahweh alone, Creator of heaven and earth, will he obtain help (Ps 121,1f; cf Jr 3,23). Otherwise he will be putting his trust in a creature, which, since it is purely a symbol of power* (Dn 2,35.45), would then become for him a symbol of pride*, like proud Babylon*, the overlord of the world (Jr 51,25). All pride must be humbled, God alone is to be exalted (Is 2,12-15).

3. *Before God.* "At your name, Tabor and Hermon exult " (Ps 89,13). When the Lord visits the earth, let the mountains break out into cries of joy (Is 44,23) and leap for joy before His mighty deeds (Ps 29,6), let their slopes flow with new wine* and the wheat ripen on their summits (Am 9,13; Ps 72,16)! But let them also expect to be leveled (Is 45,2; 49,11; Ba 5,7; Lk 3,5). Will they then be able to offer themselves as a safe place of refuge, on the day of wrath* (Ho 10,8; Lk 21,21; 23,30; Ap 6,14ff)? "I looked at the mountains, and lo! they were quaking" (Jr 4,24); they smoke when in contact with Him who is able to consume them by fire* (Ps 104,32; Dt 32,22); under His feet (Mi 1,4), before His face* (Is 63,19), they melt like wax (Ps 97,5), they flow away (Jg 5,5)—"and the everlasting mountains were shattered" (Ha 3,6)—dissolve away (Ez 38,20), and disappear at the end of time (Ap 6,14; 16,20).

II. THE PRIVILEGED HILLS

Though destined to a total transformation like the rest of creation*, yet certain mountains are reserved for a permanent and glorious role.

1. *The place of revelation beyond others*, "the mountain of God," Horeb, in Sinai, is the holy earth where Moses was called (Ex 3,1.5), which God sanctified by the gift of His Law (Ex 24, 12-18) and the presence of His glory* (24,16). It was there, also, that Elijah* went (1 K 19,8); he wished to listen to God speaking to him, an end doubtless envisaged by the prophets who loved to rest and pray on the mountain tops: Moses on Sinai (Ex 17,9f), Elijah, or Elisha on Mt. Carmel (1 K 18,42; 2 K 1,9; 4,25).

2. *The special place of worship*, the mountain, elevated above the ground, permitted an encounter with the Lord. Is it not on a small elevated place (the altar*) that the sacrifice must be accomplished (Ex 24,4f)? From the

mountains of Gerizim and Ebal blessings and curses were to be pronounced (Dt 11,29; Js 8, 30-35). It was likewise on a hill that the ark, returned from the Philistines, was placed (1 S 7, 1). As inheritors of a venerable tradition, Gideon (Jg 6,26), Samuel (1 S 9,12), Solomon (1 K 3,4), and Elijah (1 K 18,19f) all sacrificed with the people on the "high places" (1 K 3,2).

The Canaanite rites thus taken over were applied to Yahweh, the one true God; but the dispersion of these high places brought with it the danger of idolatry (Jr 2,20; 3,23). Thus came about the centralization of worship* in one single place (Dt 12,2-9). Here is a mountain which man has not built in order to scale the heavens (Gn 11), a hill proudly soaring skyward, which God chose from among the rugged mountains (Ps 48,2f; 68,17). Now, though all other mountains may tumble into the sea (Ps 46,3), Zion is a sure place of refuge (Jl 3,5), and imperturbable (Ps 125,1).

Man must not say: "The heavens will I scale; above the stars of God will I set up my throne; I will scale the heights of the clouds; I will be like the most high" (Is 14,13f); for he shall fall into the depths of the abyss. God has personally "established His kingdom on Zion, His holy mountain" (Ps 2,6), in the very place where Abraham sacrificed his son, on Mt. Moriah (2 Ch 3,1; cf Gn 22,2). It is that holy mountain, steeped in so many memories of divine favors, that the faithful should climb (Ps 24,3) while singing the "canticle of the mountains" (Ps 120—134); and to this mountain the faithful should constantly return (Ps 43,3) hoping to live out his days there with the Lord (Ps 15,1; 74,2).

3. *At the end of time,* what shall become of these places consecrated by God Himself? In the eschatological literature Sinai no longer finds a place; it is no longer the place it formerly was, where men were given "the words of life" (Ac 7,38), and from where God departed in order to attain His true sanctuary, Zion (Ps 68,16ff).

In contrast to Sinai which is lost in the past, Mount Zion does retain an eschatological value. "The mountain of the house of Yahweh will be established as the highest mountain, and elevated above the hills. All the nations will stream to it. 'Come, let us go up to the mount of Yahweh'" (Is 2,2f), that holy mountain (11,9; Dn 9,16). Yahweh will become king there (Is 24,23), there He shall prepare a great feast (25,6-10) for the dispersed peoples finally

reunited (27,13; 66,20), and even for strangers* (56,6f). Whereas the land shall be transformed into a plain, Jerusalem* will be exalted, thus retaining its place of prominence (Ze 14,10), and all peoples will forever be required to "go up" to Zion (14,16ff).

III. CHRIST AND THE MOUNTAINS

1. *Mountains in the life of Jesus* are diversely considered by the synoptics. They agree in showing that Jesus loved to retire to the mountains for prayer (Mt 14,23 p; Lk 6,12; 9,28); and the desert*-like solitude (comp Lk 15,4= Mt 18,12) which He sought there is doubtless a respite from the noise and bluster of notoriety (cf Jn 6,15). The synoptics are also in agreement in ignoring Mount Zion and singling out the Mount of Olives as well as the mountain of the transfiguration, but these latter are given a different perspective.

For Matthew, it is the mountains of Galilee which are the places privileged to witness the manifestations of the Savior. The life of Jesus is included between two mountain scenes; at the beginning Satan offers Jesus power over the entire world (Mt 4,8); at its close Jesus confers on His disciples the power which He has received from His Father (28,16). Between these two scenes, we again find Jesus on a "certain mountain," teaching the multitude (5,1), healing their maladies, and giving them a marvelous bread (15,29...), and finally appearing transfigured (17,1f). But one of these mountains bears a precise name; it is as if the disciple is forewarned against the temptation of ever pitching his tent on any of these mountains; only the remembrance should remain alive among the "eye witnesses of His majesty." The Scriptures are fulfilled on the "holy mountain" (2 P 1,16-19). It is not to a place in this world, but to His own person that Jesus attaches His message.

For Luke the "going up" to Jerusalem represents the way* to glory through the cross; it is no longer simply a matter of the pilgrimage which the pious Israelite makes (Lk 2,42), but of the solemn "going up" which covers a period of the life of Jesus (9,51—21,38; cf 18, 31). Ignoring the mountains of Galilee which heard the discourses and saw the miracles of Jesus, Luke concentrates his attention on the *Mount of Olives.* He does not point out the fact that Jesus pronounced the eschatological discourse there (Mt 24,3=Mk 13,3), but for him the "going up" to Jerusalem terminates there (Lk 19,29); and from there, according to apocalyptic tradition (Ze 14,3f), the Lord was to set out to conquer the world; there He is solemnly acclaimed (Lk 19,37), but also there He suffers His agony (22,39) and, finally, from there He ascends into heaven (Ac 1,12). If a precise mountain is again mentioned, it would seem that this is only done in order to teach us "to lift up our eyes" toward heaven*, or better, toward Him who has, according to Johannine theology, been "raised up" above the earth (Jn 3,13f; 19,37).

2. The other NT writings offer no unified teaching concerning *the privileged mountains* of the OT. Sinai is compared, in Pauline polemic, to the house of servitude (G 4,24ff) whence proceeds the movement toward Zion which man can now approach (He 12,18.22). In the same sense, the Apocalypse presents the Lamb as situated at the end of time on Mount Zion (Ap 14,1). Nevertheless there is a difference; the apocalyptic writer exercises a radical criticism of this holy place: the mountain is no longer envisaged, as in the vision of Ezekiel, to be the place where the city appears to be built (Ez 40,2); it is only an observation post whence one can contemplate the heavenly Jerusalem* descending from heaven (Ap 21,10).

→Ascension I—Jerusalem OT I 2—Transfiguration 2.

XLD tms

MYSTERY

The Greek word *mystērion* is not found in the Greek Bible except in a few late books (Tb, Jdt, Ws, Si, Dn, 2 M). The background of this word is the Aramaic *rāz*, which means a "secret thing" and thus corresponds to the classical Hebrew word *sōd* (found in use at Qumrân). In the NT this word is already a technical theological term. But since it was widely used in the Hellenistic milieu (philosophy, "mystery" cults, gnosis, magic), it is important to determine its precise meaning in order to avoid inexact interpretations.

OT

1. *Revelation of God's secrets.* The idea of God's secrets was familiar to Israel from the time of the prophets. These secrets were primarily concerned with the plan of salvation which God realizes in human history and which comprises the object of revelation*: "Surely He will do nothing, the Lord God, except He reveal His "secret" (*sōd*) to His servants, the prophets" (Am 3,7; cf Nm 24,4. 16). This classic doctrine abounds notably in Second Isaiah. The historic destiny of Israel corresponds to a divine plan previously revealed through the prophetic Word*, and it is this which assures the coming of salvation* at the end of time* (Is 41,21-28). Such are the antecedents of the technical and religious notion of mystery which is found in both Daniel and the Book of Wisdom.

2. *Daniel and the Book of Wisdom.*

a) The Book of Daniel is apocalyptic, that is to say, a revelation* of divine "secrets" (*rāz*: Dn 2,18f.27f.47; 4,6). Unlike other apocryphal works, these secrets do not concern creation. They rather concern things which will be realized in time, under the form of connected history, and oriented toward some end; in other words, the mysteries of the plan* of salvation. These secrets are written in heaven and will infallibly be accomplished. God may also reveal them in dreams*, visions, or by the agency of angels (cf 2; 4; 5; 7; 8; 10—12). No human wisdom can possess such knowledge of the future, but God is "the revealer of mysteries" (2,28.47). He makes known in advance "that which must come about at the end of days" (2,28); and if His enigmatic revelations remain unintelligible to men, He gives to some privileged few a wisdom* (cf 5,11), an extraordinary spirit*, thanks to which "no mystery embarrasses them" (4,6). What He thus reveals are His judgments* which are the prelude to salvation*. This object was moreover found enclosed for a long time in prophetic Scriptures. To Daniel, as he scrutinizes the Book of Jeremiah, the archangel Gabriel comes to reveal the mysterious meaning of the oracle of the seventy weeks* (Dn 9), which depends on the symbolism of numbers*. The Scriptures are here tested in the same way as dreams or visions which, elsewhere, translate the secret plans of God into enigmatic symbols.

b) The Book of Wisdom is not ignorant of the existence of mysteries in the cults of paganism (Ws 14,15.23). But, in accord with the book of Daniel, it applies the term to transcendent realities which are the object of revelation: the secrets of God in rewarding the just (2,22), the secrets relative to the origin of divine Wisdom* (6,22). These mysteries are of a soteriological order (the "world to come," the term of the divine plan) and theological (the intimate nature of God). They correspond to the matters treated by the apocalyptic authors.

3. Extra-biblical Judaism.

a) Apocryphal Apocalypses. In the apocryphal writings, Henoch, like Daniel, is reputed "to know the secrets of the saints" (Hen 106, 19): he has read the tablets of heaven whereon are written future events, and he has thereby learned the mysteries of the final lot of the just (103,2ff) and of sinners (104,10). Here, therefore, mystery is the eschatological realization of God's plan*, a notion which will again be retained in the apocalypses of Ezra and Baruch.

b) The Qumrân texts likewise attach great importance to knowledge of "the mystery of the future" which will come "on the day of visitation" and will determine the lot of the just and of sinners. They search the prophetic Scriptures for a description of this day which the teacher of righteousness has explained to them; for "God has given him knowledge of all the mysteries of the words of His servants the prophets" (cf Dn 9). Here there is question of an inspired exegesis which amounts to a new revelation: "the final times will be longer than all that foretold by the prophets, for the mysteries of God are marvelous." But this revelation is reserved to those who walk "in the perfection of the way," an esoteric revelation which must neither be communicated to the wicked nor to men outside.

NT

I. THE TEACHING OF JESUS

The synoptics used the word mystērion only once; the gospel of John, never. "To you has been entrusted the secret of the kingdom of God, but to those outside, everything is offered in parables" (Mk 4,11 p). Thus Jesus answered His disciples when they asked the meaning of the parable of the sower. Among His listeners He distinguished those capable of understanding the mystery from "those outside" whose hardness of heart prevented comprehension, according to the words of Isaiah 6,9f (Mk 4,12

p). For these latter, the coming of the kingdom remains an enigma which is not understandable by teaching through parables*. But to His disciples "the mystery is given" and the parables are made clear. The mystery in question is the coming of the kingdom* conformable to God's plan as attested to by the ancient prophets: Jesus here takes up a central theme of the Jewish apocalypses. His work consisted in establishing the kingdom here on earth and revealing in their fullness the divine secrets which concern it and which were "hidden from the foundation of the world" (Mt 13,35). With Him, the revelation* is achieved because the promises are fulfilled: the mystery of the kingdom is present on earth in His person. But by this same deed humanity is divided into two camps: the disciples receive Him; "those outside" close their hearts to Him. The proclamation of the mystery is certainly not esoteric (cf Mk 1,15 p; 4,15 p); however the veil of the parables is only raised for those who are capable of understanding (cf Mt 13,9.43). Even for these, entrance into the mystery is not a matter of human intelligence; it is a gift of God.

II. THE TEACHING OF ST. PAUL

One should place himself in this same perspective of Jewish apocalyptic literature in order to understand St. Paul's use of the word mystērion. This word suggests a profound reality, inexpressible; it reveals a glimpse of the infinite. It denotes nothing less than the object of the gospel*: the realization of salvation* by the death* and resurrection* of Christ, His implantation in history by proclaiming the Word*. But this object is characterized as a divine secret, inaccessible to human intelligence without revelation (cf 1 Co 14,2). The Word thus preserves its eschatological overtones; but it is applied to the successive stages through which foretold salvation is realized: the coming of Jesus into the world, the time of the Church, the consummation of the ages. It is in the knowledge and contemplation of this mystery that the ideal of every Christian to some extent consists (Col 2,2; E 1,15f; 3,18f).

1. The unfolding of mystery in time. In the first epistles (2 Th, 1 Co, R), these diverse aspects of mystery are seen in turn. There is found here an identity between "announcing the mystery of God" (1 Co 2,1 according to certain manuscripts) and the proclamation of

the gospel (1,17) of Jesus crucified (cf 1,23; 2,2). Such is the object of Paul's message to the Corinthians, a scandal* to the Jews and folly* to the Greeks, but wisdom to those who believe (1,23f). This divine wisdom, which takes the form of a mystery (2,7), was till then hidden. No prince of this world knew it (2,8f), but it was revealed to us by the Spirit* who searches the depths of the Godhead (2,10ff). This wisdom is inaccessible to the physical man when he is left to his natural powers alone, but it is intelligible to the spiritual man who is taught of the Spirit (2,15). However, it is only to the "perfect" (cf 2,6) and not to neophytes (3,1f) that the apostle, "the dispenser of the mysteries of God" (4,1), can "express in terms of the spirit the realities of the spirit" (2,13), in such a way that they all can understand the gifts of grace (2,12) hidden in this mystery. The gospel is given to all, but Christians are called to a progressively deeper understanding of it.

This mystery, now at work on earth for the salvation of believers, is engaged in a struggle with the "mystery of iniquity" (2 Th 2,7), that is to say, with the activity of Satan* which will culminate in the manifestation of Antichrist. Its unfolding in history comes about in paradoxical ways. Thus it was necessary that a part of Israel should be hardened in heart so that the mass of pagans might be able to be saved (R 11,25): mystery of the incomprehensible wisdom of God (11,33) which turned to good purpose the fall of the chosen people. At the end of the mystery Christ will triumph when the dead will rise and the living will be transformed in order to participate in His heavenly life (1 Co 15,51ff). The "mystery of God" encompasses all of sacred history, from Christ's coming to the parousia. The gospel is "the disclosure of the secret wrapped in silence for long ages but now revealed, and at the command of the eternal God made known through the writings of the prophets to all the heathen" (R 16,25f).

2. *The mystery of Christ and the Church.* In the captivity epistles (Col, E), Paul's attention is centered on the present aspect of the "mystery of God" (Col 2,2): the "mystery of Christ" (Col 4,3; E 3,4) effecting salvation by means of His Church. That mystery was hidden in God from the beginning (Col 1,26; E 3,9; cf 3,5); but God came to manifest it (Col 1,26), to make it known (E 1,9), to bring it to light (3,9), to reveal it to the apostles and prophets, and particularly to Paul himself (3,4f). It

becomes the object of the gospel (3,3; 6,17). It is the last word of God's plan, formed long before in order to be realized in the fullness of time*: "arranging that everything in heaven and on earth should be unified in Christ" (1,9f). The Jewish apocalyptic scrutinized the marvels of creation; Christian revelation manifests the most intimate secret of creation. In Christ, the first-born of all creatures, all things find their consistency (Col 1,15ff) and all are reconciled (1,20). The apocalyptic also scrutinized God's ways in human history; Christian revelation shows them converging toward Christ who inserted salvation into history through His Church (E 3,10). Henceforth Jews* and pagans are admitted to the same heritage, are members of the same body* and beneficiaries of the same promise (3,6). It is of this mystery that Paul has established the ministry (3,7f). In it, all things acquire a mysterious signification. Thus, the union of man and woman* is a symbol of the union of Christ and the Church (5,32). In Him the pagans as well as the Jews find a principle of hope (Col 1,27). How great is this "mystery of faith" (1 Tm 3,9), this "divine truth of our religion; He was revealed in flesh, He was vindicated by the Spirit, He was seen by the angels, He was proclaimed among the heathen, He was believed throughout the world, He was taken up in glory" (1 Tm 3,16).

A continuous progression thus leads from the mystery envisaged by the Jewish apocalypses to the "mystery of the kingdom* of God" revealed by Jesus, and finally to the "mystery of Christ" proclaimed by the apostle of the nations. This mystery has nothing in common with the mystery cults of the Greeks or oriental religions, even though Paul occasionally uses some of the technical terms employed by them in order better to oppose these particular aspects of the "mystery of iniquity" (cf 2 Th 2,7) with the true mystery of salvation; as he elsewhere opposes false human wisdom with the true divine Wisdom made manifest in the cross* of Christ (cf 1 Co 1,17-25).

III. THE APOCALYPSE OF ST. JOHN

In the Apocalypse, the word *mystērion* designates in two places the secret meaning of symbols which are explained by the seer (Ap 1,20) or the angel who speaks to him (17,7). But it is also found in two places to have a meaning very close to that which St. Paul gives it. On the brow of great Babylon*, which represents

Rome, is written a name, a mystery (17,5). This is what is at work in history, the "mystery of iniquity" which Paul already denounced (cf 2 Th 2,7). Finally, on the last day, when the seventh angel will sound the trumpet to announce the final judgment, "then God's mysterious purpose, the good news which He gave to His servants, the prophets, would be accomplished" (Ap 10,7; cf 1 Co 15,20-28).

To this consummation the Church aspires. She already lives in the mystery, but, inserted as she is in the heart of the present world, she is still torn between the divine and the diabolical powers. A day will come when the diabolical powers will be annihilated (cf Ap 20; 1 Co 15,26f) and when she will enter into the "world to come." Then the mystery of God alone will remain in a renewed universe (Ap 21; cf 1 Co 15,28). Such is the term of Christian revelation.

→Cloud—Cross I 2—Dreams OT—God NT II 3.4—Kingdom NT II—Know OT 4; NT 3—Parable—Plan of God—Presence of God OT II; NT II—Revelation—See—Sign—Silence—Spirit of God O—Truth OT 3; NT 2—Unbelief II—Wisdom.

BRi & PG tms

N

NAME

OT

For the ancients a name is not simply a conventional designation, but rather an expression of a being's place in the universe. God perfects His creation by naming creatures, day, night, heaven, earth, sea (Gn 1,3-10); He calls each star by name (Is 40,26); and He commands Adam to name each of the animals (Gn 2,20). Later on, men will frequently give meaningful names to places where important events took place. This practice accounts for some bizarre etymologies; for example, that of Babel (Gn 11,9).

1. *The names of men.* The name given at birth ordinarily expresses the man's activity or destiny: Jacob is the usurper (Gn 27,36); and Nabal is well named, for he is a fool (1 S 25,25). A name can also reflect the circumstances of birth or hint of a future glimpsed by the parents: Rachel dies calling her child "son of my sorrow"; but Jacob calls him Benjamin, "son of my right hand" (Gn 35,18). Sometimes the name is a type of prophetic wish asking help of the God of Israel for the child: Isaiah (*Yeša'-Yāhū*), "may God save!" The name always expresses man's social potential, so that *name* can also mean "renown" (Nm 16,2); to be nameless is to be worthless (Jb 30,8). On the other hand, to have several names is to be important, to have many roles to fulfill; so Solomon was also called "Beloved of God" (2 S 12,25).

Since the name is the person himself, to do something about a name is to have a hold on the being. Hence a census appears to denote servitude for the persons involved (cf 2 S 24). A change of name is a change of personality; it means the man will henceforth be a vassal (2 K 23,34; 24,17). To indicate that He is taking possession of their lives, God changes the name of Abraham (Gn 17,5), of Sarah (17,15), of Jacob (32,29). So God gives new names to a forgiven Jerusalem—City of Justice, Faithful City (Is 1,26), City of Yahweh (60,14), Desired One (62,12), My Pleasure (62,4)—this to express the new life of a city where hearts are regenerated by the new covenant.

2. *The names of God.* Among all peoples, the name of the divinity meant very much indeed; and if the Babylonians went so far as to give fifty names to Marduk, their chief god, in order to consecrate his victory at the time of creation, the Canaanites kept hidden the name of their divinities under the generic term of Baal, "master" (of such and such a place).

Among the Israelites, it is God* Himself who deigns to name Himself. Before this, the God of Moses was known only as the God of their ancestors, the God of Abraham, Isaac, and

Jacob. The angel who struggled with Jacob refused to give his name when asked (Gn 32, 30); to the father of Samson was confided only an adjective of the name: "Marvelous" (Jg 13,18). It is also through adjectives such as *Shaddai* (He of the Mountain) or expressions like *Terror of Isaac* or *Strong One of Jacob* that the God of Israel was designated in the times of the patriarchs. But one day at Horeb, God Himself revealed his name to Moses. The formula employed is taken sometimes as a refusal analogous to that which the angel made to Jacob in order not to be delivered over to him: "I am He who is" (Ex 3,13-16; 6,3). But the sacred text desired to give this formula a positive meaning. In fact, according to the context, this name should accredit the mission of Moses to the people; "*I-Am* sends me to you," Moses will say; and the people will come to adore "*He-Is*" (or "He makes to be") on the holy mountain. In any case, this name signifies that God is present among His people: He is Yahweh.

3. *To invoke the name of God.* If God revealed His name it is that He might be adored* under His true name, the only authentic one (cf Ex 3,15). Thus it will be the rallying cry of the tribes during and after the conquest (Jg 7,20). It is the name of the only true God; so will the prophets say a little later: "Before me no god was formed, and after me there shall be none. It is I, I who am Yahweh" (Is 43,10f).

It is, then, the only name which will be authorized on the lips of Israel (Ex 23,13), the only one invoked in Jerusalem when David shall have made the city his religious capital: for "Yahweh is jealous of His name" (Ex 34, 14). "To call on the name of Yahweh" is properly to render worship* to God, to pray to Him: His name is cried out (Is 12,4), He is called (Ps 28,1; cf Is 41,25), He is called upon (Ps 99,6). But if God has thus confided His proper name to Israel, she ought not "to pronounce the name of Yahweh in vain" (Ex 20,7; Dt 5,11): in fact, it is not at their disposal to be abused, and thus to end up by tempting* God: such would be to serve God no longer, but rather to make use of Him for their own purposes.

4. *The name, that is, God Himself.* God so identifies Himself with His name, that in speaking of it, He designates Himself. It is this name which is loved (Ps 5,12), praised (Ps 7,18),

sanctified (Is 29,23). It is an awesome name (Dt 28,58), eternal (Ps 135,13). It is "for His great name" (Js 7,9), on account of His name (Ez 20,9), that He acts on Israel's behalf; that is to say: for His glory*, in order to be recognized as great and holy.

In order better to emphasize the transcendence of the inaccessible and mysterious God, the name is enough to designate God. Thus, as if to avoid a localization unworthy of God, the temple* is the place where God "has made His name to dwell" (Dt 12,5); it is there that one comes into His presence (Ex 34,23), in the temple which "bears His name" (Jr 7,10.14). It is the name which, from afar, comes to make the nations pass through the crucible of destruction (Is 30,27f). Finally, in a late text (Lv 24,11-16), *the name* designates Yahweh, without further precision, just as the rabbinic language will do later on. Through a respect ever more accentuated, Judaism will tend, in fact, no longer to venture to pronounce the name revealed at Horeb. In reading, it will be replaced by *God (Elohim)* or more often *Adonai (my Lord)*. Thus the Jews will translate the Holy Scriptures from Hebrew into Greek, never writing down the name of Yahweh, but will render it by *Kyrios (Lord*)*. Just as the name of Yahweh, under the form *Yāou* or other forms, passes to a magic or profane usage, this name *Lord* will move into the NT to receive its consecration.

HC phmcn

NT

1. *The name of the Father.* Corresponding to the revelation which God has made of His name in the OT, we find in the NT the revelation through which Jesus makes known to His disciples the name of His Father* (Jn 17,6.26). In manifesting Himself as the Son*, He reveals that the name "Father" is the one that expresses the essence of God* most profoundly. This Father, whose Son Jesus is (Mt 11,25ff), also extends His fatherhood to all who believe in His Son (Jn 20,17).

Jesus asks the Father to glorify His name (Jn 12,28) and invites His disciples to ask Him to sanctify it (Mt 6,9 p): this God will do in manifesting His glory* and His power* (R 9,17; cf Lk 1,49), and in glorifying His Son (Jn 17,1. 5.23f). Christians have the duty of praising the name of God (He 13,15) and of being watchful lest their conduct cause Him to be blasphemed (R 2,24; 2 Tm 6,1).

2. *The name of Jesus.* By appealing to the name of Jesus, the disciples* heal the sick (Ac 3,6; 9,34), cast out demons (Mk 9,38; 16,17; Lk 10,17; Ac 16,18; 19,13), work all kinds of miracles* (Mt 7,22; Ac 4,30). Jesus* thus appears as His name indicates Him to be: He who saves (Mt 1,21-25), restores health to the sick (Ac 3,16), but also and above all, obtains eternal salvation for those who believe in Him (Ac 4,7-12; 5,31; 13,23).

3. *The name of the Lord.* In raising up Jesus and in making Him sit at His right hand, God has given Him the name above every name (Ph 2,9; E 1,20f), a new name (Ap 3,12) which is not distinct from that of God (14,1; 22,3f) and participates in His mystery (19,12). This ineffable name nevertheless finds translation in the appellation of *Lord**, which belongs to the risen Jesus on the same grounds as it does to God (Ph 2,10f=Is 45,23; Ap 19,13.16=Dt 10, 17), and in the designation of *Son*, which He does not share, in this sense, with any creature (He 1,3ff; 5,5; cf Ac 13,33; R 1,4 following Ps 2, 7). The first Christians did not hesitate to bestow on Jesus one of the more characteristic appellations of Judaism in speaking of God: the apostles are said to have been full of joy for having been "accounted worthy to suffer for the name" (Ac 5,41); missionaries are cited who "have gone forth on behalf of the name" (3 Jn 7).

a) *The Christian faith* consists in "believing that God has raised up Jesus from the dead," "confessing that Jesus is Lord*," "invoking the name of the Lord*": these three expressions are practically equivalent (R 10,9-13). The first Christians willingly designated themselves as "those who invoke the name of the Lord" (Ac 9,14.21; 1 Co 1,2; 2 Tm 2,22; cf Ac 2,21=Jl 3,5), signifying thereby that they recognize Jesus as Lord (Ac 2,36). In particular the profession of faith is imposed at the moment of baptism, which is conferred in the name of the Lord Jesus (Ac 8,16; 19,5; 1 Co 6,11), or even in the name of Christ (G 3,27), of Christ Jesus (R 6,3). The neophyte invokes the name of the Lord (Ac 22,16), the name of the Lord is invoked upon him (Jm 2,7); he finds himself thereby under the power of Him whose lordship he acknowledges.

In Jn, the proper object of the Christian faith is less the name of the Lord than that of Son*: in order to have life, it is necessary to believe in the name of the only Son of God (Jn 3,17f;

cf 1,12; 2,23; 20,30f; 1 Jn 3,23; 5,5.10.13), that is to say, to adhere to the person of Jesus in acknowledging that He is the Son of God, that *Son of God* is the name which expresses His true being.

b) *The apostolic preaching* has for its object the proclamation of the name of Jesus Christ (Lk 24,46f; Ac 4,17f; 5,28.40; 8,12; 10,43). The preachers will have to suffer for this name (Mk 13,13 p), and this ought to be for them a cause of joy (Mt 5,11 p; Jn 15,21; 1 P 4,13-16). The Apocalypse is addressed to those Christians who suffer for His name (Ap 2,3), but who hold fast to it (2,13) and do not deny it (3,8). The ministry of the name of Jesus is especially incumbent upon Paul: he has received it as a charge (Ac 9,15) and a cause of suffering (9, 16); he nevertheless fulfills his mission with daring and pride* (9,20.22.27f), for he had pledged his life to the name of our Lord Jesus Christ (15,26) and is ready to die for Him (21,13).

c) *The Christian life* is wholly impregnated by faith: gatherings are held in the name of Jesus (Mt 18,20), those are welcomed who present themselves in His name (Mk 9,37 p), though imposters should be guarded against (Mk 13,6 p). One gives thanks to God in the name of our Lord Jesus Christ (E 5,20; Col 3,17), conducting oneself in such a way that the name of our Lord Jesus Christ be glorified (2 Th 1,11f). In prayer, the Father is addressed in the name of His Son (Jn 14,13-16; 15,16; 16, 23f.26f).

4. *Other names.* Each creature bears the name which pertains to the role assigned it. When its mission is divine, its name comes from heaven, such as that of John* (Lk 1,13.63). Even when given by men, the name is a sign of the guidance of God: Zechariah (1,5.72: "God is mindful"), Elizabeth (1,5.73: "the oath that He swore"), Mary* (1,27.46.52: "magnified, exalted"). In giving Simon the name of Peter*, Jesus shows the role which He assigns him and the new personality which He creates in him (Mt 16,18).

The good shepherd* knows each of His flock by name (Jn 10,3). The names of the elect are inscribed in heaven (Lk 10,20), in the book of life* (Ph 4,5; Ap 3,5; 13,8; 17,8). Upon entering into glory, they will receive a new* and ineffable name (Ap 2,17); participating in the existence of God, they will bear the name of the Father and that of His Son (3,12; 14,1); God will call them His sons* (Mt 5,9), for such they are in reality (1 Jn 3,1).

→Abraham I 3—Baptism IV 2—Blasphemy—Calling I—Confession OT 1—Fathers & Father III 3—Fruitfulness II—God OT II, III, IV—Holy OT I—Jesus (Name of)—Lord—Magic 2 c—Memory 1 b—Peter 1—Prayer IV 4—Presence of God OT I—Revelation OT II 2; NT III 1 b—Sign OT II 5—Strength I 1—Woman OT 1—Yahweh.

JDt phmcn

NATIONS

In the OT perspective, the human race is divided into two parts for which biblical language reserves different appellations. On the one hand there is Israel*, the people* of God (*'ām*=gr. *laos*), to whom were given the election*, the covenant*, and the divine promises*. On the other hand there are the nations (*gōyim* =gr. *ethnē*). The distinction is not merely ethnic or political, but mainly religious. The nations are at once those who "do not know Yahweh" (the pagans) and those who do not share the life of His people (the foreigners). In the NT, the idea of the people of God evolves and broadens to become the Church, the body* of Christ. But in the face of this new people, opened to all men, humanity still seems divided: the Jews* and the nations (cf R 1,16; 15,7-12). The dialectic at play between Israel and the nations is thus a constant theme throughout the course of salvation history. On the one hand, the plan of God is introduced into human history through the election and the setting apart of Israel; on the other, the plan has always as its aim the salvation of all humanity. For this reason, the perspective oscillates constantly between particularism and universalism, until Christ comes to reunite Israel and the nations in a single new man (E 2,14ff).

OT

I. THE MYSTERY OF ORIGINS

At the beginning of the OT, the call of God rings out in a divided world where races, nations, and cultures face one another. This is a fundamental historical fact which poses many questions: did God so will it? and if not, what caused it? The Bible furnishes no scientific reply, but for this reason, it does not less closely scrutinize the original mystery of human society in order that the light of revelation might illuminate it.

1. *Unity and diversity of mankind.* The unity* of the human race underlies the schematic representations of Genesis. God made the entire race of men from a single principle (Ac 17,26). There is not only identity of abstract nature; there is also unity of blood. All genealogies begin with Adam* and Eve. After the deluge they are traced from Noah (Gn 9,18f). Nevertheless, the unity is not indistinct uniformity. Man must multiply and fill the earth (Gn 1,28); this supposes a progressive diversification of nations and races which Scripture regards as God's will (Gn 10; Dt 32,8f).

2. *The social consequences of sin.* The present condition of humanity does not, however, correspond to the divine intention. Sin* has intervened in history: Adam and Eve dreamed of "becoming like gods" (Gn 3,5). The men reunited in the countries of Shinar wished to build "a tower whose summit would reach to the heavens" (11,4). In both instances, the same boundless sacrilege is implied. And the same result also occurs, proclaimed in both cases by a divine judgment (3,14-24; 11,5-8). Man's condition, as we experience it, is the practical consequence. This is why the diversification of our race, effected in a climate of sin, results in bloody hatred (Cain and Abel: 4,1-16) and loss of spiritual unity (confusion of tongues: 11,7ff). Such are the conditions in which the nations were born into history, with the twofold vice of idolatry, which cuts them off from God, and pride*, which sets them at odds with each other. Such, too, is the background against which the call of Abraham took place. Though God chose him from among pagan nations (Js 24,2), it was to make him the father of a new people which would be His own, and in order that in the end all families of the earth might be blessed in him (Gn 12,1ff).

II. ISRAEL AND THE NATIONS IN HISTORY

Israel did not ignore its natural kinship with certain neighboring nations. The patriarchal genealogies underline this in the case of Ishmael (Gn 16) and Midian (25,1-6), Moab and the Ammonites (19,30-38), the Aramaeans (29, 1-14) and the Edomites (36). In the time of the Maccabees, the Jews even sought a relationship of race with the Spartans (1 M 12,7.21). But the attitude of Israel toward the nations was dictated by motives of another order, by the doctrine of the covenant and the plan of salvation.

1. *The nations as adversaries of God.* By reason of its national vocation, Israel is the depository of essential values: the knowledge and worship of the true God, hope of salvation included in the covenant, and the promises. But in all these matters the nations posed a double menace: that of political subjection and of religious seduction.

a) Political menace. Rare indeed were the times when Israel did not see its existence menaced. Pride and covetousness led the nations on; they were faced by questions of prestige or possession of land. Caught up in the currents of international politics, Israel had to defend tenaciously the trust confided to its keeping. Israelites knew the slavery of Egypt*. Then the wars in which Yahweh pitted them against the Canaanite, Midianite, and Philistine ...Under David the situation was temporarily reversed (cf 2 S 8) and the Israelite empire enjoyed a certain amount of prestige. But matters soon worsened. There was hostility and covetousness from small neighboring kingdoms; the powerful will of the international giants, Egypt, Assyria, and Babylon*...The age of kings is filled with these bloody struggles which now and then are seen in their true colors. Just as in the time of exile (Ex 5—14), the proud nations, adorers of false gods, wished to cope with the living God Himself (2 K 18,33ff; 19,1-7.12-19). The same attempt will recur again when Antiochus Epiphanes attempts to Hellenize Judea (1 M 1,29-42). Viewed in this light, the dealings of Israel with the nations can only be established on a hostile plane.

b) Religious seduction. To the people of God the nations also represent paganism, sometimes seductive, at other times tyrannical. Sprung from idolatrous ancestors (Js 24,2), Israel is only too inclined to imitate them. In the time of the judges, Israel turned to Canaanite idolatry (Jn 2,11ff). Solomon, builder of the temple, set up sanctuaries for the gods of neighboring countries (1 K 11,5-8). During the succeeding centuries the cults of Assyria, the

ruling power, were added to those of Canaan (2 K 16,10-18; 21,3-7; Ez 8). In the time of the Maccabees, the Israelites were tempted by Greek paganism which carried with it cultural prestige, and which Antiochus Epiphanes tried to impose on them (1 M 1,43-61). In such circumstances, the severe prescriptions of Deuteronomy are explained: Israel must separate itself completely from foreign nations lest it be contaminated by their paganism (Dt 7,1-8).

2. *The nations in the plan of God.* We should err, however, were we to reduce the OT teaching on the nations to that attitude of opposition and separation. Yahweh is a universal God on whom all nations depend. Already their firstfruits have been incorporated into Israel in order to render Him genuine worship.

a) The nations before Yahweh. Yahweh oversees all the nations. He it is who makes the Philistines of Caphtor and the Aramaeans of Kir rise to prominence, just as He brought Israel out of Egypt (Am 9,7). This is an important truth which forbids any religious nationalism. But, in return, the nations must realize that they, like Israel, are subject to the judgment* of the one God (Am 1,3—2,3). In this twofold manner, the OT already affirms the universalism of the plan of salvation. Nevertheless, the role of the nations remains episodic in its unfolding. At one time they chastise Israel as instruments of the divine wrath* (Is 8,6f; 10,5; Jr 27); at another, like Cyrus, they are charged with a salvific mission (Is 41,1-5; 45,1-6). On the other hand, the human values which they bring should not be despised: in themselves they are gifts of God. Israel certainly turned them to their profit: the Hebrew in flight despoiled the Egyptians (Ex 12,35f); as invaders they profited from the Canaanite civilization (Dt 6,10f); each succeeding epoch borrowed some new features from international culture (cf 1 K 5,9-14; 7,13f).

b) The first-fruits of the nations. This cooperation with the divine plan occurred despite all extrinsic factors. The nations did not benefit as much as Israel from divine privileges. However, there were exceptions. In fact, certain members of the pagan nations did offer a homage to God which He accepted: Melchizedek (Gn 14,18ff), Jethro (Ex 18,12), Naaman (2 K 5,17)...Some were incorporated into the covenant people: Tamar (Gn 38), Rahab (Js 6,25), and Ruth (Rt 1,16), ancestors of Jesus (Mt 1,2-5); the clan of the Gibeonites (Js 9,19-27); the resident strangers* who underwent circumcision (Ex 12,48f; Nm 15,15f). All were prophetic of the universalism to which God would finally bring His people.

III. ISRAEL AND THE NATIONS IN PROPHECIES

The aspect of prophecy considered here is no longer that of experience; it is rather the ideal realization of the plan of God at the end of time* and of which the prophets caught but a glimpse. In the scheme of values represented by this aspect of prophecy, the nations play an important role, whether it be by subjection to God's judgment* or by benefiting from His salvation*.

1. *Judgment of the nations.* The oracles against the nations are standard in all the prophets (Is 13—21; Jr 46—51; Ez 25—32). They take on a particular significance in the abject periods, when the crushing of pagan oppressors seemed to be a necessary condition of Israel's liberation. When His day* comes, God will shatter Gog, king of Magog, a type of the bloody tyrant (Ez 38—39). He will cope with all enemy powers (Jl 4,9-14; Ze 14,1-6.12ff), He will destroy their cities (Is 24,7-13) and judge their kings (Is 24,21f). The story of Judith is exemplary; for together with the apocalypse of Daniel, it is constructed on this theme (cf Dn 7; 11,21-45) to which the persecution of Antiochus gave tragic actuality.

2. *Salvation of the nations.* But there is another side to the story. In fact, final salvation will not be the exclusive lot of Israel. If sin has from the beginning destroyed the unity of the human race, the final conversion of the nations must allow for its restoration. Those who come to Jerusalem do so to learn the Law of God; it is the return of universal peace* (Is 2,2ff). They are turning to the living God (Is 45,14-17.20-25) and participating in His cult (Is 60,1-16; 25,6; Ze 14,16). Egypt and Assyria are converted and Israel serves them as the unifying link (Is 19,16-25). Putting an end to the dispersion of Babel*, Yahweh reunites about Himself all nations and all tongues* (Is 66,18-21). All peoples acknowledge Him as king*, all are reunited with the people of Abraham (Ps 47), all give Zion the title of mother* (Ps 87). The Servant* of Yahweh plays the role of mediator* for them as He does for Israel (Is 42,4.6). And so, on the final day, a single people of God must be formed again which will recover once more the primitive universalism. Though the Law does give Israel an apparent exclusiveness, one sees in the prophets a reunion of the very large perspectives of the original mystery.

IV. ANTICIPATIONS

Postexilic Judaism, heir alike to the Law and the prophets, oscillates between these two tendencies which correspond to contrary necessities.

1. *Jewish exclusiveness.* The first need is to be shut off from paganism. Has not the contagion of pagan mentality and cults been the cause of all past evils? The Jewish restoration at the time of Nehemiah and Ezra was effected in a climate of intensified particularism (Ezr 9—10; Ne 10; 13). If this spirit broadened a little with time, the Maccabean crisis provoked a return to religious nationalism which will again crop up a few generations later among the Pharisees and Essenes.

2. *Jewish proselytism.* But in this same epoch, through a paradox explained by complementary exigencies of the Jewish faith, the community of Israel was opening to pagans of good will more so than it ever had before. The religious chauvinism, ironically caricatured by the author of Jonah, is rightly censured. An official statute is given to proselytes who wish to join themselves to Israel (Is 56,1-8), and it is pleasing to recount past instances where they were made: Ruth, the Moabite (Rt 1,16), Achior, the Ammonite (Jdt 5,5—6,20)...Alexandrine Judaism is distinguished by its initiative on this point. There the Bible was translated into Greek, an apologetic was drafted, specimens of which are to be found in the Book of Baruch (Ba 6) and Wisdom (Ws 13—15). Israel has here become conscious of its vocation as a witness and a missionary people.

NT

I. JESUS AND THE NATIONS

With Jesus, the final times are inaugurated (Mk 1,15). One would expect to see Him, at the beginning of His public life, enter on the path of universalism which the prophetic oracles laid open for Him. But things are, in reality, more complex than this.

1. *Words and attitudes contrasted.*

a) *Particularistic behavior.* Even while He was sojourning in foreign lands, Jesus did not go beyond the pale of Judaism to preach the gospel and work miracles: "I am sent only to the lost sheep of the house of Israel" (Mt 15, 24); "it is not right to take the bread of the children and throw it to the dogs" (Mk 7,27). To the twelve, when sending them on a mission, He gave the same recommendation: "do not go among the heathens" (Mt 10,5f).

b) *Universalist perspectives.* On the other hand, while He clashed with the ill will of those "lost sheep," He was not sparing in His admiration of the foreigners who believed in Him: the centurion of Capernaum (Mt 8,10 p), the Samaritan leper (Lk 17,17ff), the Canaanite woman (Mt 15,28)...In the kingdom* of God, these are the first-fruits of the nations. But the future development of the kingdom will see the number grow. They will come from all quarters to the eschatological banquet, while the Israelites, native subjects of the kingdom, will be excluded (Lk 13,28f p)...An astonishing perspective wherein the ancient situation of the Jews and the nations is reversed with relation to the covenant privileges: the vineyard of God will be taken away from Israel and entrusted to other vine-dressers (Mt 21,43).

2. *Solution of the antinomy.* There is no contradiction between the particularism and the universalism of Jesus. Rather is it an adaptation to successive phases of an evolving situation. At the beginning, He sought to convert Israel in order to make of it the missionary of the kingdom, in a perspective of total universalism. For this reason He did not go outside His own people. But the hardening of heart* of the Jews opposed this plan. God will certainly adapt the course of His plan of salvation: rejected by His people, Jesus will shed His blood "for many, unto the remission of sin" (Mt 26,28), and this sacrifice will open the kingdom to all men by setting the seal on the eschatological covenant*. Then the human race will be able to recover its internal unity* since it will again be united with God. For this reason, once He has consummated the sacrifice by His glorious resurrection, Jesus will give a universal mission* to the twelve: to preach the gospel to every creature (Mk 16,15), to make disciples of all nations (Mt 28,19), to be witnesses to the very ends of the earth (Ac 1,8). In the light of the resurrection, Jewish particularism becomes definitively superseded.

II. THE EVANGELIZATION OF THE NATIONS

1. *The primitive community and the pagans.*

a) *Progressive growth of the Church.* Despite the universalist significance of Pentecost*, when the praises of God were proclaimed "in all tongues" (Ac 2,8-11), the primitive community limited itself at first to the evangelization of Israel. It is from there that salvation should begin to be extended throughout the whole world. But little by little, under the impulse of the Spirit, the Church moved beyond this limited circle: Philip evangelizes Samaria (Ac 8); Peter baptizes the centurion Cornelius, a proselyte who had not yet been incorporated into Israel through the rite of circumcision (Ac 10); finally in Antioch, the Lord Jesus is preached to the Greeks who are converted in large numbers (Ac 11,20f). The call of Paul, moreover, gave to the Church the chosen instrument she needed to evangelize the nations (Ac 9,15; 22,15.21; 26,17) according to the prophecies (Ac 13,47; cf Is 49,6).

b) *The council of Jerusalem.* This growth of the Church posed a fundamental question: must the pagans who acceded to the faith obey the Law*? At the council of Jerusalem, Paul held out for the position that such a yoke ought not to be imposed (Ac 15,1-5; G 2); Peter seconded him and James proclaimed that the conversion of the pagans was conformable to the Scriptures (Ac 15,7-19). Thus were finally drawn into the light of experience the logical consequences implied in the cross and the resurrection of Jesus. In the Church, the new people* of God, the nations attain a stature equal to Israel's, and Paul sees his particular vocation confirmed as apostle to the pagans (G 2,7ff).

2. *Paul, apostle of the nations.* Paul's apostolate, nevertheless, does respect the order which flowed from the ancient covenant. He always announces the gospel to the Jews first, and only goes to the pagans after being rebuffed by their refusal (Ac 13,45ff; 18,5f; 19,8ff; cf R 1,16; 2,10). But elsewhere he clearly explains the situation of the nations relative to the gospel*.

a) *The nations confronted with the gospel.* Men descended from the pagan nations are, like the Jews, under the shadow of God's wrath* (R 1,18). God revealed Himself to them through His creation (1,19f; Ac 14,17), and they did not recognize Him (R 1,21f); He made known His Law to them through conscience (2,14f), but they gave themselves over to their unruly passions as a consequence of their idolatry (1,24-32). But today God wills to show them His mercy*, as He does to the Jews, if only they will believe in the gospel (1,16; 3,21-31; 10,12). For both, faith* brings justification. Following the witness of Scripture, the true sons of Abraham*, heirs of the blessing promised to him, are those who are reclaimed by faith (G 3,6-9). The people who now benefit from this promise* comprise together the circumcised, and thus Abraham becomes the father of a multitude of nations (R 4).

b) *The Jews and the nations in the Church.* In Jesus Christ the unity of mankind is indeed restored. There is no longer Jew nor Greek (G 3,28). Jews and pagans were reconciled once the wall of hatred which separated them fell. They form a single new humanity, a single construction with Christ as the cornerstone, a single body* of which He is the head (E 2,11-22). This mystery of unity* is now being realized in the Church, while it awaits its heavenly consummation. The ancient division of humanity into two segments, however, will always bespeak the dialectic of sacred history. At an earlier date, God passed over a hardened Israel, except for a remnant*. This was done in order to procure the salvation of the pagan nations by engrafting them onto the stock of Israel (R 11, 1-24), and to arouse Israel's jealousy that they might repent (11,11). At a later time, when all the nations will have entered the Church, all Israel will be saved (11,25-29). The ways of God end with the final salvation of all nations united to Israel. Together they will form the people of God (15,7-12).

III. CHRISTIAN REFLECTION

1. *The gospels.*

a) *The synoptics.* By gathering together recollections of Jesus' sojourn here on earth, the first three evangelists show, each in his own way, their interest in the salvation of the nations. In Mark, the entire account converges toward the act of faith of the pagan centurion

at the foot of the cross: "Truly this man was the son of God" (Mk 15,39). Matthew draws our attention to the fact that pagan women were included in the genealogy of Christ (Mt 1,2-6). From His childhood, we see Jesus as the king of nations (2;1-11). He starts off His ministry in "heathen Galilee" (4,15f) and His final words are a command to preach the gospel to all nations (28,19). In Luke, Christ's genealogy goes back to Adam, the father of the human race which Jesus has come to save (Lk 3,23-38). This is why Simeon recognizes in Him "the light which will be a revelation to the gentiles and the glory of His people, Israel" (2,32). Finally, the combination of the gospels and Acts shows that the salvation which Jesus gained in Jerusalem* by His sacrifice has spread from there "to the ends of the earth" (Ac 1,8).

b) *St. John* did not insist so much on this aspect because he was thinking rather of the fate of the unbelieving Jews* (Jn 12,37-43). Although they had been the people of God, the hardness* of their hearts had made them a nation like any other (11,48ff; 18,35). On the other hand, even during Jesus' lifetime, we see Him approached by men of faith, men who were the first-fruits of the gentiles (4,53; 12,20-32). Finally, His death brought about universal reconciliation* since He died not only for His nation but in order to unify all the dispersed sons of God (11,50ff).

2. *The Apocalypse.* The Apocalypse is a Christian prophecy; but like the OT prophecies, there are two situations of the gentiles' relation to God to which it is attentive.

a) *Judgment of the hostile nations.* The new people of God, like Israel, found itself confronted by hostile pagan nations (cf Ap 11,2). This is what is meant by the beasts* who make men adore them (13) and by the blaspheming prostitute, Babylon, drunk with the blood of the martyrs 17)...These forces carry on an eschatological war* against Christ (17,13f; 19,19; 20, 7ff) because they are vested with the power of Satan*. For this reason they will be judged and destroyed (14,6-11; 18); they will fall in their sruggle against Christ (17,14; 19,15.20f).

b) *The salvation of the converted nations.* But drawn up opposite this sinful humanity which rushes to its ruin, there is the new humanity which has been saved by the blood of the Lamb. It is a crowd drawn from all nations, races, peoples, and languages (7,9-17) which praises God as the king* of the nations (15,3f) and which will forever inhabit the new Jerusalem* (21,24ff). The NT ends on this prophetic note of hope since the redeemed human race will have finally achieved unity : *O Rex gentium et desideratus earum, lapisque angularis, qui facis utraque unum: veni, et salva hominem quem de limo formasti!* "King of the nations, object of their desire! Cornerstone, thanks to which everything is joined together! Come and save man, whom you have molded from the clay" (Antophon from December 22).

→Apostles II 2—Circumcision NT 1—Dispersion—Egypt—Exile II 2—Faith OT III 3, IV 2; NT III o—Fathers & Father II 2.3—Israel—Jew I—King OT I 4—Law *A* 2; *C* II 2—Mission—Pentecost II 1. 2 c d—People—Repentance/Conversion OT II 5; NT III 2—Stranger—Unity—Visitation OT 1—Worship OT II, III.

JP & PG tms

NEIGHBOR

OT

The word *neighbor*, which renders the Greek word *plēsion* exactly enough, corresponds only imperfectly to the Hebrew word *rēa'* which underlies it. It must not be confused with the word *brother*, although it often comes to mean that. Etymologically, it expresses the idea of being associated with someone, of entering into his company. Unlike a brother*, to whom a man is bound by a natural relationship, the neighbor does not belong to the father's house; if my brother is another I, my neighbor is other than I, another who for me can remain an "outsider," but who can also become a brother. A bond can thus be created between two beings, be it of a passing nature (Lv 19,13.16.18) or of a durable and personal nature, in virtue of friendship (Dt 13,7) or of love (Jr 3,1.20; Ct 1,9.15) or of comradeship (Jb 30,29).

In the ancient codes, it was not a question of "brothers" but of "those near" (vg Ex 20, 16f): despite this virtual universalism, the horizons of the Law hardly extended beyond the people of Israel. Hence, with their more vibrant realization of being chosen, Deuteronomy and the Law of holiness confuse *the other* and *brother* (Lv 19,16ff), looking thereby to the Israelites only (17,3). This does not mean a

restriction of love of "neighbor" to love of "brothers" only; on the contrary it is the intention of these passages to extend the commandment of love* by including in the Israelite circle the resident stranger* (17,8.10.13; 19,34).

After the exile, a double tendency appears. On the one hand the circle of *those near* is restricted; the duty of loving has only the Israelite or circumcized proselyte in view. But, on the other hand, when the Septuagint translates the Hebrew *rēa'* by the Greek *plēsion*, it removes *others* from *brother*. The neighbor whom one must love is the other, whether he be a brother or not. From the time two men meet, they are for each other neighbors, independently of their parental relationship or of what they think of each other.

NT

When the scribe asked Jesus: "Who is my neighbor?" (Lk 10,29), probably he still associated this neighbor with his brother, a member of the people of Israel. Jesus is going definitively to transform the notion of neighbor.

First of all, He consecrates the commandment of love: "You shall love your neighbor as yourself." Not only does He sum up all the other commandments in this one, but He binds it indissolubly to the command to love God (Mt 22,34-40 p). In accord with Jesus, Paul solemnly declares that this commandment "fulfills all the Law" (G 5,14), that it is the "summation" of the others (R 13,8ff); and James qualifies it as "the royal law" (Jm 2,8).

Next, Jesus universalizes this commandment: we must love our enemies, not only our friends (Mt 5,43-48). This supposes that we have destroyed all barriers in our hearts, so well that love can touch the enemy* himself.

Finally, in the parable of the good Samaritan, Jesus comes to practical applications of this command (Lk 10,29-37). It is not for me to decide who is my neighbor. The man in difficulty, though he has been my enemy, invites me to become his neighbor. Thus universal love keeps its concrete character: it will manifest itself in every man God puts in my path.

→Almsgiving NT 3 a—Brother—Friend—Hospitality—Love II—Mercy—Vengeance 2 a.

XLD jjk

NEW

The idea of newness is expressed in Greek by two different terms: *neos*, new in time, new, young (whence also, without maturity); *kainos*, new in nature, thus qualitatively better. The two words are applied in the Bible to the realities of salvation: the first underlines their character of recent presence with regard to the past; the second, much more frequent, describes them as wholly other realities, marvelous, divine; for man and the earth are growing old like a garment (Si 14,17; Is 50,9; 51,6), but in God nothing is old, all is new.

I. NEWNESS AND HOLINESS

Since all of creation belongs to God, new things not as yet profaned by use have a sacred character: the first-fruits* of the harvest and the newborn are reserved to God (Dt 26,1-11; Ex 13,11ff); certain sacrifices* are made with animals which have not yet borne the yoke (Nm 19,2; Dt 21,3); the ark* must be carried on a new chariot with animals which have not yet worked (1 S 6,7; 2 S 6,3); and to symbolize that he is going to purify unhealthy waters, Elisha makes use of a new vase filled with salt (2 K 2,20). The same reverence toward the sacred brings into use, for the burial of Jesus, a new tomb "where no one had yet been laid" (Mt 27,60; Jn 19,41).

II. THE EXPECTATION OF NEW TIMES

The Israelites admired the seasonal renewal of creation and attributed it to the breath of God (Ps 104,30). For the Messianic and eschatological times*, they expected likewise a universal renewal.

1. *A new exodus.* The Book of Consolation opposes to the prodigies of old those which are going to be produced on the return from the exile* (Is 42,9); the miracles of the departure from Egypt are going to be surpassed by those of the new exodus*: God is going "to make anew...to trace a route through the desert, paths in the wilderness" (43,19). By these prodigies, Yahweh will guide Israel into Palestine (40,3ff), there to reveal His glory and to establish henceforth His sovereignty over all peoples (45,14-17.20-25). These new realities must be celebrated with a new song (42,10; Ps 149,1), which all the earth should take up (Ps 96,1).

2. The power which God employs causes the Messianic salvation* to be considered as *a new creation** (Is 41,20; 45,8; 48,6f); the liberator of Israel is its Creator (43,1.15; 54,5), the first and the last (41,4; 44,6; 48,12). The Palestine of the future will be as the Garden of Eden (51,3; Ez 36,35) which the prophets described with paradisaic* colors (Is 11,6-9; 65,25; Ez 47,7-12). After the exile, there is to be expected even "new heavens and a new earth" (Is 65,17; 66,22).

3. *A new covenant.* Several of the great realities of the ancient covenant take on a figurative value and announce for future times a renewal and perfecting of the covenant*. The prophets await a new David* (Ez 34,23f), a new temple* (40—43), a new holy land (47,13—48,29), a new Jerusalem*, whose characteristic will be the eternal love of Yahweh (Is 54,11-17) and His presence* among the people (Ez 48,35). Zion will be called by a new name* (Is 62,2; 65,15): she will no longer be named *abandoned* but *espoused* (Is 62,4). Yahweh and Israel will resume their relations of love (54,4-10); "Yahweh creates anew upon the earth: the woman (Israel) seeks her husband (Yahweh)" (Jr 31,22). This covenant will be eternal (Is 55,3; 61,8).

But this will be at the same time a new covenant (Jr 31,31-34), different from that of Sinai. It will be characterized by purification from sins and by the interiority of the Law* (Ez 36, 26f). Such a covenant will be possible because God will give man a new heart* and a new spirit* (11,19; 18,31; 32,26). Finally it is divine Wisdom* which works the renewal of all things; it spreads into holy souls* to make of them friends of God (Ws 7,27).

III. THE NEW MESSIANIC COVENANT

1. *A new teaching.* From the beginning of Jesus' preaching, His hearers were struck by the newness of His teaching* (Mk 1,27); He comes to perfect the Law* and the prophets* (Mt 5,17); He opposes the teaching of the ancients to His own (Mt 5,21-48), as a used garment to a new cloak, as old bottles to new wine* (*neos,* Mt 9,16f p). The essentials of the Law remain intact, but it must be renewed by the perfecting of the gospel* and the new spirit of the kingdom*; the disciples are like a householder "who brings forth from his storeroom things new and old" (Mt 13,52).

The commandment of charity is at the same

time old and new (1 Jn 2,7f; 2 Jn 5): it is old, not because formulated in the Law (Lv 19,18), but because believers possess it from the times of their conversion. Jesus had called it "His precept" (Jn 15,12): for this reason it is a new commandment (13,34); for this charity must henceforth imitate that of Christ, who delivered Himself for us (13,1.34; 15,12f) and in whom is revealed the love* of the Father (3,16; 1 Jn 4,9); it is a love among brethren, a sharing in the love of communion* of Father and Son (Jn 15,9f; 17,26; 1 Jn 4,16).

2. *The new covenant.* At the last supper, Jesus declares: "This chalice is the new covenant in my blood which will be poured out for you" (Lk 22,20 p; 1 Co 11,25). The covenant of Sinai had already been sealed with the blood of its victims (Ex 24,3-8). The new covenant, which fulfills and perfects the old (He 8,1—10,18), was sealed on the cross* by the blood* of Jesus, perfect victim, perfect high priest, mediator* of the new covenant (He 9,15; 12,24). The remission of sins, announced by the prophets, is realized in the sacrifice of Christ (He 10,11-18). The blood of the new covenant is given in the eucharist*; but the eucharistic wine is of itself only an anticipation of the new wine which will be drunk in heaven at the eschatological banquet (Mt 26,29 p).

Another characteristic of the new covenant, prepared in the old (the law in the heart, Dt 30, 14), is that it is no longer written on tablets of stone, but in hearts* of flesh* (2 Co 3,3; cf Jr 31,33; Ez 36,26f). Paul underlines the antithesis: the Mosaic Law is "the Old Testament" (2 Co 3,14); he opposes the law which kills to the Spirit* which vivifies (3,6), the oldness of the letter to the newness of the Spirit (R 7,6). The new covenant is the covenant of the Spirit. Those who will be possessed by the Spirit will speak in new tongues* (Mk 16,17; Ac 2,4), that is to say, a heavenly language inspired by the Spirit.

3. *The new man.* The whole work of the redemption* is a great renewal. But the new creation of which the prophets spoke is made precise: it is basically a renovation of man*, and through him will the universe be renewed.

a) Christ, the new Adam, gives life to all (1 Co 15,22.44-49). Through Adam*, head of fallen humanity, the old man was a slave* to sin (R 6,6.17; E 4,22); the new man, after the redemption, is *humanity* renewed in Christ. In His own flesh, Christ has created pagans and Jews into a single new man (E 2,15). In imitation of Adam, this new man is re-created in the justice* and holiness of truth* (E 4,24). Henceforth, all are one in Christ (Col 3,11).

b) Because of his regeneration *each Christian* himself also can be called "the work of God" (E 2,10). "If anyone is in Christ, he is a new creation; the old creature has disappeared, a new creation is here" (2 Co 5,17; G 6,15). The new birth is accomplished through baptism (Jn 3,5; Tt 3,5), but also by the word* of truth (Jm 1,18; 1 P 1,23); that is to say, through faith*, gift of the Spirit (Jn 3,5; 1 Jn 5,1.4).

Paul speaks especially of renewal by way of the progressive sanctification of believers: "the inner man in us is being renewed day by day" (2 Co 4,16). The baptized must purify themselves from the old leaven in order to be a fresh and new dough (*neos*, 1 Co 5,7); they must put off the old man, put on the new man (Col 3,10; E 4,22ff), and live a new life* (R 6,4). The example* to imitate is Christ, the image* of God (R 8,29; 2 Co 3,18; 4,4; Col 1,15). To restore in us the image of the Creator (Col 3,10; Gn 1,27) is to put on Christ (R 13,14).

This transformation is above all the work of the Spirit (R 7,6; 8,1-16; G 5,16-25). It is not only the bath of regeneration which is necessary for salvation, but also the birth according to the Spirit (Jn 3,5.8), the work of renovation of the Spirit (Tt 3,5). The means of this renovation is the milk* of the Word of God (1 P 2,2), the truth which works in us justice and holiness (E 4,24), faith (G 5,5f). Thus the believer journeys toward this knowledge which gradually renews in him the image of Him who created him (Col 3,10).

c) Through the Christian, the work of renewal must extend itself to the entire *universe.* Christ has reconciled all things with God (Col 1,20; E 1,10); all creation* awaits redemption (R 8, 19-23). But this universal re-establishment will be realized only at the end of time, in "the new heavens and the new earth, where justice will dwell" (2 P 3,13).

IV.   THE NEW JERUSALEM

By His ascension*, Christ has inaugurated in His person a new and living way, that which gives access to the celestial sanctuary (He 10, 19f). The Apocalypse describes this final phase of the eschatological renovation. The city of God is the "new Jerusalem*" (Ap 3,12; 21,2), filled with the presence* of God (Ez 48,35). Adorned as a spouse*, dwelling place of God with men, she is the supreme realization of the covenant: "God will live among them" (Ap 21,3). All creation will have part in it, for it is now that there appears "a new heaven* and a new earth*: the first heaven and the first earth have disappeared" (21,1).

The great prophetic texts on the future renovation reappear here, charged with all their meaning. As of old, the Hebrews returning from the exile (Is 42,10), the aged and the elect intone a new song to celebrate the redemption at last accomplished (Ap 5,9; 14,3). Like the inhabitants of the Messianic Zion (Is 62,2; 65,15), Christian conquerors receive "a white pebble carrying a new name" (Ap 2,17); this name will have this time a specifically Christian character: this will be the name of God (3,12), that of the Lamb*, and that of the Father, which the elect will wear on their foreheads (14,1; 22,3f), as a sign of their belonging to God and to Christ. The Apocalypse ends in a final vision where God proclaims: "Behold I make all things new. I am the Alpha and the Omega, the beginning and the end" (21,5f). This last page of revelation says it with a perfect clarity: the basis of all newness is God* Himself.

The great work of the renovation of creatures is the work of salvation accomplished by Christ: "Christ has brought all newness in bringing Himself" (Irenaeus); thus, it is during Easter week, when she celebrates our redemption, that the Church invites us to pray that "purified of all that is old, we may be able to become new creatures."

→Adam II—Baptism IV 1.3.4—Covenant OT III 2; NT—Creation OT III 2; NT II—Earth OT II 4; NT III—Eucharist V—Exodus OT 2—Fatherland—Figure OT II 2.3—First Fruits—Flood 3—Fulfill—Heart II—Heaven VI—Image IV—Israel OT 3; NT 2.3—Jerusalem OT III; NT II 1.3—Know NT 3—Law *B* IV; *C*—Man III 2.3—Name NT 4—New Birth—Old Age 2—People *B*; *C*—Promises II 5—Prophet OT IV 3—Resurrection NT II 2—Spirit NT 2 —Spirit of God NT V 3—Teach NT I 2.3, II 2 —Temple NT I, II 2—Time OT III 2; NT III 1—Wine II 2 b—World OT III 2.3; NT II 2, III 3—Worship NT II.

IdlP phmcn

NEW BIRTH

The symbolism of the new birth is a common enough theme in the religions of humanity. Hence the widespread practices among primitive peoples by which the child is made an adult and the profane an initiate frequently consist in rites which make the "newborn" pass again through the stages of his first infancy. In like manner, royal enthronement can seem like a new birth (Ps 2,7; 110,3 LXX). But in the Judaeo-Christian revelation, the symbolism expresses realities of a unique order. "What is born of the flesh is flesh, what is born of the spirit is spirit" (Jn 3,6). To the natural birth of man the NT opposes a supernatural birth whose principle is either the Word* or the Spirit* of God, and is realized by faith* and baptism*.

1. *The preparations.* The OT never speaks of a new birth for man: for by his natural birth the Israelite possesses all the rights of one belonging to the people of God; he has no need of a new birth. Nevertheless, this theme is deeply rooted in the OT.

The establishment of Israel as God's people* is often represented in the OT as a true childbirth. Israel is the "first-born" of God (Ex 4, 22; Ws 18,13). God begot him when He brought him out of Egypt (Dt 32,6.18f), and the life in the desert* was like his early infancy (Dt 1,31; 31,10; Ho 11,1-5). Jewish tradition has especially associated this birth of Israel with the giving of the Law*: "Why does a man call Sinai 'the house of my mother?' Because there the Israelites became 'newborn infants' " (Midrash on Ct 8,2).

In the new covenant* foretold by the prophets, God will not be content to give His Law to His people; He will engrave it in the heart* of every man (Jr 31,31-34; Dt 30,10-14). Moreover it is the Spirit who must come to renew the heart of man (Ez 36,26f). Again, a new birth and a source of unheard of joy which will "open the womb" of Jerusalem and cause her to abound in children (Is 66,7-14).

In the first age of our era, *Judaism* was not unacquainted with the theme of a new birth. When a pagan was converted and received the baptism* of the proselytes, all his former ties were considered broken. To signify this break with the past, he was said to be like a newborn babe. This was only a metaphor, intended mainly to be on the juridical level. It would become a reality in the NT.

2. *The words of Jesus.* In the synoptics, Christ does not speak of a new birth. On one occasion, using Jr 31 and Dt 30 as starting points, He compares the Word of God to a seed* planted in the heart of man in order there to become the principle of a new moral life (Mt 13,18-23 p). Further, He teaches the necessity of "returning to the condition of children*" in order to enter the kingdom of heaven (Mt 18,3). Like a child, man must be willing to receive all from God. This truth is made explicit in the fourth gospel: "A man must be born anew in order to enter the kingdom of heaven" (Jn 3,3.5).

3. *Apostolic reflection.*

a) *The divine principle.* Every birth is effected from a germ of life which determines the nature of the being generated. To be reborn supernaturally, then, man must receive in himself the principle of life coming "from on high," from God. Apostolic tradition identified this with the Word or the Spirit of God.

The Word. According to Jm 1,18.21, God "has brought us forth by the word of His truth," which it is necessary "to receive" in order to be saved. In a Judaeo-Christian perspective, the Word* again is identified with the Mosaic Law (1,22-25) and it is difficult to determine whether this "bringing forth" concerns the establishment of God's holy people or the new birth of the Christian. According to 1 P 1,22-25, God regenerated us by His Word (the preaching of the gospel), which He planted in us like a "seed" of life, and which we must submit to. "Like newborn infants" (cf Introit of the Mass for the Sunday after Easter), we desire the milk* of the Word which should make us grow* unto salvation (1 P 2,2). In like manner, for John, our new birth is the effect of a seed of God, planted in us (1 Jn 3,9); Christ, the Word of God (2,14; 5,18) whom we must "receive" by faith (Jn 1,1.12f).

The Spirit. In Jn 3,3ff, it is no longer the Word, but the Spirit who is given as the principle of our new birth together with the water of baptism, as in Tt 3,5. For Paul it is the Spirit who makes of us "children of God" (R 8,15f; G 4,6). Birth is through the Word which one receives, thanks to faith, or through the Spirit who is given to us through baptism. These are two complementary aspects of one and the same reality, since the Word and the Spirit are inseparable. The Spirit gives effectiveness to the Word. As with creation (Gn 1,2f; Ps 33,6), the work of our regeneration cannot be conceived without the cooperation of the Word and the Spirit.

b) *New life.* In the NT, the "new birth" is no longer a metaphor, but a profound reality. Re-created by Word and Spirit, man has become a new* being (Tt 3,5) whose moral behavior is radically transformed. He has abandoned evil (1 P 2,1; Jm 1,21), he no longer follows his passions (1 P 1,14), but rather obeys the Word who enjoins him to love* his brethren (1,22f). He can no longer sin against the demands of fraternal love (1 Jn 3,9f). Henceforth he lives under the sway of the Spirit (R 8,14), engrafted onto the very life of Christ (R 6,5).

c) *Eschatological fruits.* Having become a son*, he must lay claim to the inheritance of the kingdom (Jn 3,5; 1 P 1,3ff; R 8,17; G 4,7). The seed planted in us is a germ of incorruptibility, since it is the Word "who lives for all eternity" (1 P 1,23ff). In order to mount up to heaven, it is necessary to have descended from there (Jn 3,13). This principle, valid in the first leader, the Son of Man, has a universal application; only he can mount to heaven who has received in himself that principle "coming from on high" (Jn 3,3; Jm 1,17): the Spirit of God (Jn 3,5), the pledge of our glorious resurrection (R 8, 10-23).

→Baptism IV—Child III—Grace V—Kingdom NT II 3—Life IV 4—Son of God NT II.

NIGHT

The event of the paschal night is at the center of the symbolism of night in Scripture. Of course, one also finds there the fundamental human experience which is common to the majority of religions: night is an ambivalent reality, fearful as death, and indispensable as the time when worlds come into being. When the light* of day disappears, then come malevolent beasts (Ps 104,20), dark plague (Ps 91,6), men who hate the light—adulterers, thieves, or assassins (Jb 24,13-17); thus one must beg Him who created the night (Gn 1,5) to protect men against nocturnal terrors (Ps 91,5). One must also pray to Him when night comes (Ps 134,2), the night that, like the day, celebrates His praise (19,3). However, if night is fearful because the day dies with it, it must in turn give way to the day which follows: so is the faithful one who relies on his Lord like the watcher who awaits the dawn (Ps 130,6). These rich symbols, mortal darkness and hope of day, nevertheless find their full meaning only in being rooted in a privileged experience: night is the time when the history of salvation is achieved in a unique fashion.

OT

1. *The night of deliverance.* According to the different traditions of the exodus, it is "toward the middle of the night" that Yahweh puts into execution the plan which He had formed to liberate His people from bondage (Ex 11,4; 12, 12.29); a memorable night, recalled each year by a night of vigil, in memory of the fact that Yahweh Himself had watched* over His people (12,42); a night which was prolonged until the column of cloud* illuminated the march of the fugitives (13,21f). Already there is manifested here the ambivalence of night: for the Egyptians the cloud becomes dense, like that night which once came down upon them, while light illuminated the Hebrews (10,21ff). "For your holy ones," comments Wisdom, "it was a full light" (Ws 18,1). Again, describing the unique night: "For when peaceful silence enveloped everything and the night in its rapid course was half spent, your all-powerful Word leaped down from the royal throne" (18,14f). Is it necessary to relate this nocturnal event to the prayer of the psalmist who arises at midnight to render thanks to God for His just ordinances (Ps 119, 62)? At any rate, night appears at the outset as a time of trial*, but of a trial from which one is freed by the judgment of God.

2. *Day and night.* Without ceasing, Israel dreamed of the day* on which Yahweh would deliver her again from the oppression in which she found herself. This hope was legitimate, but unfaithful conduct did not warrant it. The prophets also took up a position against it: "Woe to those who sigh after the day of Yahweh! What will it be for you? Darkness and not light" (Am 5,18), obscurity and thick darkness (Zp 1,15; Jl 2,2). Ambivalence still, but inherent this time in the day of Yahweh: for some, it will be a night; but it will be a blazing light for the remnant* of Israel who, meanwhile, feel their way through the darkness of the night (Is 8,22—9,1), but still hope (cf Is 60,1).

3. *In the night of trial.* Sages and psalmists transferred to individual life the experience of divine judgment which is effected in and through the night. If you practice justice*, "your light shall break forth like the dawn" (Is 58,8; Ps 112,4). Job curses the day of his birth and would have preferred to remain buried in the night of the maternal womb (Jb 3,3-10). But the psalmist returns to his bed at darkest night to call upon the Lord: the night belongs to God (Ps 74,16), who can therefore liberate man from it as of old in the time of the exodus (Ps 63,7; 77,3; 119,55). "My soul yearns for you in the night, that you might exercise judgment" (Is 26,9; cf Ps 42,2). In extending this recall of salvation as a liberation* from nocturnal trial, the apocalypses describe the resurrection* as an awakening after the sleep* of death (Is 26,19; Dn 12,2), a return to the light after the plunge into the total night of Sheol.

NT

The psalmist could say to God: "The darkness is not dark before you, and night is light as the day" (Ps 139,12). This saying was to be accomplished in a marvelous fashion, like a new* creation* worked out by Him who said, "From darkness let the light shine forth!" (2 Co 4,6): with the resurrection* of Christ, the light has shone forth from the night forever.

1. *The night and the day of Easter.* As long as it was day, Jesus made the light to shine forth from His works (Jn 9,4). When the hour* came, He delivered Himself to the snares of the night (11,10), of that night into which the traitor Judas buried himself (13,30), when His disciples will be scandalized* (Mt 26,31 p): He wanted to confront that "hour and the powers of darkness" (Lk 22,53). The primitive liturgy preserves its memory forever: it is on the "night that He was betrayed" that He instituted the eucharist (1 Co 11,23). And the day of His death became itself darkness over the land (Mt 27,45 p; cf Ac 2,20=Jl 3,4).

But "towards the beginning of the first day of the week" behold the lightning of the angels (Mt 28,3), announcing the triumph of life and of light over the darkness of night. This dawn the disciples had already known when Jesus had rejoined them, walking over the raging waters, "at the fourth watch of the night" (Mt 14,25 p). The night of deliverance the apostles would recognize again when they were miraculously freed from their prison in the dead of night (Ac 5,19; 12,6f; 16,25f). Paul, whose eyes were plunged into darkness, knew the night of light which awakened him to the brilliant light* of faith (Ac 9,3.8.18).

2. *"We are no longer of the night"* (1 Th 5,5). Henceforth the life of the believer assumes a meaning in relation to Easter day which knows no waning. This day shines forth in the depth of his heart: he is a "child of the day" (ib.; cf E 5,8), since, arisen from the dead, Christ has shone upon him (E 5,14). He has been "snatched from the power of darkness" (Col 1,13); he no longer has "darkened thoughts" (E 4,18), but reflects on his countenance the very glory* of Christ (2 Co 3,18). To guard against the prince of darkness (E 6,12), he must put on Christ and His armor of light, put off the "works* of darkness" (R 13,12ff; 1 Jn 2,8f). For him, it is now no longer night; for his night is luminous as the day.

3. *The day in the middle of the night.* Since the Christian has been "led from darkness into the marvelous light" (Ac 26,18; 1 P 2,9), he cannot be surprised by the day* of the Lord, which comes like a thief in the night (1 Th 5, 2.4). Of course, for the present he finds himself still "in the night," but this night "is advancing" toward the proximate day which will put an end to it (R 13,12). If he wants to avoid stumbling "on the darkened mountains" (Jr 13,16), in that night "when no one can work" (Jn 9,4), he should listen to the call of Christ to become a "son of light" (12,36). With Peter, illumined in the course of the night when, according to Luke, Christ was transfigured* (Lk 9,32.37), he finds in the Scriptures a light like a lamp* burning in a dark place, until the day begins to dawn and the morning star rises in his heart (2 P 1,19). Jesus has not revealed the exact moment of day which is to come (Mk 13,35), but there will be an identity between "that day" and "that night" (Lk 17,31.34). The Christ-spouse will come in the middle of the night (Mt 25,6); like the wise virgins with lamps aglow, the spouse says, "I sleep, but my heart watches" (Ct 5,2). During his wait, he forces himself to be attentive day and night, imitating the living creatures (Ap 4,8) and the elect of heaven (7,15) who, day and night, proclaim the divine praises. It is in the same spirit that the apostle, day and night, works (1 Th 2,9; 2 Th 3,8), exhorts (Ac 20,31), and prays (1 Th 3,10). Even on earth, the servants of Christ thus anticipate in some way the day without end when "there will be no more night" (Ap 21,25; 22,5).

→Cloud o.2—Day of the Lord NT III 1—Light & Dark—Passover I 1.6 c, III 2—Shadow O, I —Sleep—Watch I, III.

RF & XLD pmcm

NOAH

The picture of Noah, whatever may be its ultimate origin, represents at the different levels of scripture the type of the just man, who escapes punishment* and is blessed with salvation*. In the midst of the iniquity that is destroying the world, he appears as the source of a new humanity and so becomes a type of Christ.

1. *The Genesis traditions.* If the popular explanation associates the name of Noah with the verb *naham* (to console), this is perhaps an allusion to the vinedresser Noah (Gn 9,20), whose wine* consoles men in the midst of their toil and labor (5,29). In fact, Noah's consolation results from the words in which God undertakes never again to curse the earth after the Flood* (8,21). In spite of the divine good-will man can fall again, like the drunken Noah, father of Ham, the man with the evil habits (9,20-25). In Ham it is Canaan that is condemned: its licentious cult, associated with drunkenness, is contrasted with the vigilance of which Noah is supposed to be the model.

As the hero of the Flood, Noah is seen as the just man *par excellence*. His justice* earns him escape from the ruin of a condemned world and the task of reconciling the earth and its inhabitants with God. The priestly tradition saw in this reconciliation a covenant* of universal extent, offered to all the descendants of Noah (cf Gn 9,1; 10,32).

2. *The prophets and the wise men* stress in their different ways the exemplary value of Noah. If he is seen as evidence of a strictly personal responsibility* before the judgment-seat (Ez 14,13), his covenant with God still remains the pledge of mercy and patience (Is 54,9f). Although there may be temporary judgments, there will always be a remnant spared in order to ensure the continuation of the plan of salvation. Noah is the type of this Remnant* (Si 44,17), which is made up of the just people and will eventually be represented in the person of the Messiah alone. The Just One will save the world as Noah once saved it at the time of

the Flood, when "the hope of the world took refuge on a raft and. . .preserved the germ of a new generation for the ages to come" (Ws 14,6; cf 10,4f).

3. *In the New Testament*, the Gospel shows Noah as a model of watchfulness*; unlike his thoughtless contemporaries he lived in expectation of God's judgment (Mt 24,37ff p). More clearly still the Epistle to the Hebrews holds him up as the example of faith in the midst of unbelief; the just man who believed in the guarantee of God's word alone (He 11,7). In the epistles of Peter Noah is seen from a different angle. He is not only just in himself; he is also the herald of the divine justice, announcing to men the imminent judgment (2 P 2,5; cf 3,5). This judgment only falls on the evil world*. Noah emerges from it all as the type of the man saved in Christ, since the salvation granted to him foreshadows the salvation* through the waters of baptism* (1 P 3,20f).

→Animals I 2, II 3—Church II 1—Covenant OT II 3—Dove 3—Election OT I 3 a—Flood—Law *A* 1; *B* I 1—Remnant OT o—Salvation OT I 1—Vine 1—Wine I 1—Water II 2.

LS ems

NOURISHMENT

As all living beings, man is obliged to nourish himself in order to subsist; and this dependence on the material world is an essential sign of his impermanence. But it is also an appeal to be nourished by God, who alone is permanent. To teach man what his true nourishment is, as that of the Lord, the will of His Father (Jn 4,34), the Bible presents him with signs of nourishment on three different levels, that of creation and of obedience, of the covenant and of faith, that of the gospel and of charity.

I. GOD PROVIDES FOR THE NOURISHMENT OF HIS CREATURES

"I give you all the seed-bearing plants. . .and all trees which have fruit. . .To all the wild beasts, I give the green plants for food" (Gn 1,29f). Having created man and made him lord of creation*, God gives him nourishment, just as to all the animal world. In that golden age of universal peace, no animal* eats the flesh of

another; but when, after the flood, God "delivers into the hands of man" all living beasts to be his food, he employs the same language: "I give you all this by the same title as the green plants" (9,2f). In this language appears at once the dependence of man in relation to nature, without which he cannot live, and his autonomy. The animal feeds itself from the plant which it finds or from the quarry it pursues; man nourishes himself from the fruits and plants which he cultivates, from the beasts which belong to him and which he breeds: he feeds himself from the products of his cultivation and his labor (3,19), from "the work of his hands" (Dt 14,29).

There is, however, the risk of making excessive use of this nourishment and falling into gluttony or drunkenness*, which could lead to misery (Pr 23,20f; 21,17). On the other hand, man can make selfish use of it and so fall into luxury (Am 6,4), even going so far as to exploit the poor (Pr 11,26), forgetting that all nourishment is a gift* of God. If a solid wisdom tradition is capable of maintaining balance (Si 31, 12.31; 37,27-31), of recognizing simultaneously that "eating and drinking and satisfaction in work" form a large part of human happiness (Qo 2,24; 3,13 etc.), and that nevertheless, "better a dish of herbs with love than a fatted ox with hatred" (Pr 15,17; cf 17,1), it is because this tradition never, even in the sceptical and distrusting Qoheleth, forgot that "all this comes from the hand of God" (Qo 2,24). According to the Gospel the golden rule is to depend on Providence* to provide nourishment (Mt 6,25-33; Lk 12,22-31). Thus, it is necessary to ask the heavenly Father for it each day in prayer (Mt 6,11; Lk 11,3).

To sustain the living consciousness of being thus nourished at the hands of God, sacrifices* and offerings on the one hand, forbidden foods on the other, played a leading role. Good meals* and festal meals were celebrated once one had gone up to the sanctuary to immolate an animal, to offer the first ears of corn and the most beautiful fruits* of the harvest (Dt 16,1-17). The prohibition of impure animals (Lv 11), based on the principle, "to a holy people, holy food" (cf Dt 14,21), maintained, in an area as important for human existence as nourishment, respect for the sovereign will of God.

II. GOD NOURISHES HIS PEOPLE BY HIS WORD

Through the covenant* God assumes charge of the existence of His people. The manna* coming "from heaven" (Ex 16,4), a food procured directly by God (16,15), and in which the work* and the calculations of man have no part (16,4f), is the sign of this new condition. But this condition supposes faith*: the manna* is made to nourish the body and to nourish faith, to teach Israel to look for their subsistence and their survival from the word "which comes from the mouth of Yahweh" (Dt 8,3; Ws 16,26; cf Mt 4,4) and brings gladness (Jr 15,16). His commandments are sweeter than honey (Ps 19, 10f). It is no longer a matter of feeding on different sorts of fruit but on the word of the Lord (Ws 16,26). The prophet Ezechiel (Ez 2,5; 3,3) and the Apostle John (Ap 10,8), before delivering their message, both feed on this divine word under the symbol of a scroll that they have to swallow. Under the new Covenant Christians will continue to feed on God's oracles (He 5,12ff; cf 1 Co 3,1f; 1 P 2,2), to eat spiritual food and to drink from a spiritual rock, which is Christ (1 Co 10,3f).

III. GOD, NOURISHMENT OF HIS CHILDREN

Because he is a child* of God, man can at the same time dispense with all the foods of this world and utilize them all. "Kill and eat!" the voice from heaven said to Peter (Ac 10,13): the Christian no longer knows the distinction between pure* animals and impure ones; he is no longer "in bondage to the elements of this world," he has filial adoption (G 4,3f), and everything in the universe belongs to him (1 Co 3,22), even foods offered to idols* (8,4; 10,26), on condition that he remembers that he himself belongs to Christ, as Christ to God (3,23). Now, whatever he eats or drinks, all is for him a source of thanksgiving* (10,30f; 1 Tm 4,3f).

Christ, in order to show that God suffices for Him and that His food is the will* of His Father (Jn 4,34), fasts* forty days and forty nights (Mt 4,1-4). It is not that He despises food: He eats with His disciples (Jn 4,31), He receives and accepts invitations to meals* (Mt 11,19), He recommends to His disciples to take all that is offered them (Lk 10,8), He multiplies bread to prevent the people from suffering hunger* (Mt 15,32 p). By this miracle, Christ shows that the Father, protector of the birds of the air (Mt 6, 26), cares still more for His children, but He wishes above all to teach that He is, Himself, "the bread of God, which comes down from Heaven and gives life to the world" (Jn 6,32f). In the same way, in the sermon on the mount, He urged "not to be anxious about food" (Mt 6,25) and to "seek first the kingdom of God" (Mt 6,33); likewise He invites us to seek* something other than "the food which perishes" (Jn 6,27; cf R 14,17); and He Himself offers His flesh as real food and His blood as real drink (Jn 6,55). The eucharist*, in which the bread* of earth becomes the body of Christ, renders man, made a child of God, capable of nourishing himself, in all circumstances, with Jesus Christ; His words, His deeds, His life.

→Bread—Desert OT I 3—Eucharist III 1.2—Hunger & Thirst—Fasting—Manna—Meal—Milk—Oil—Providence I—Pure OT I 1; NT II 1—Salt 2.3—Taste o—Tree 1—Work I 2, IV 1.

PMG & JG phmcn

NUMBERS

On encountering numerical indications in the Sacred Scriptures, one must first of all verify whether or not they have been transmitted exactly. Since numbers were formerly written in letters, the text could have been altered or mutilated. Thus in 2 S 24,13, certain readings have read z (=7) while 1 Ch 21,12, a parallel text, has g (=3). Once the text is assured, it is still necessary to ask whether, in the intention of the author, the number in question was to be understood according to its exact arithmetical value, or as an approximation, or further, according to its symbolic meaning. It is certain, as a matter of fact, that the ancient Semitic civilizations had little concern for mathematical exactitude in the way our civilization takes it; on the other hand, they multiplied conventional and symbolic usages of numbers.

I. CONVENTIONAL ESTIMATES AND MEANINGS

1. From "round numbers" or "approximations," one passes easily in the Bible to conventional usages, which it would be erroneous to understand literally; the number 2 can mean

"some" (Nm 9,22), double, a superabundance (Jr 16,18; Is 40,2; 61,7; Ze 9,12; Ap 18,6). The number *3* is an approximation of the number π (1 K 7,23); in addition, the triple repetition of a gesture (1 K 17,21) or of a word (Jr 7,4) indicates emphasis, insistence, the "superlative of the superlative" (Is 6,3). The number *4* indicates the totality of the geographic horizon (before, behind, right, and left): the four winds (Ez 37,9; Is 11,12), the four rivers of Paradise (Gn 2,10). The number *5* has a mnemotechnic value (the fingers of one hand) which could be at the origin of certain ritual prescriptions (Nm 7,17.23.29); but it is purely approximative in Gn 43,34 (the portion of Benjamin is "5 times as large"), Lk 12,6 ("5 sparrows for 2 farthings"; Mt 10,29 has "2 sparrows for 1 farthing"), 1 Co 14,19 ("rather 5 words which instruct, than 10,000 in tongues"). The number *7* suggests a considerable number: Cain will be avenged 7 times (Gn 4,15), the just man falls 7 times a day (Pr 24,16), Peter wishes to pardon 7 times (Mt 18,21), and Jesus casts out 7 demons from Magdalen (Mk 16,9). But this number has a superlative: Lamech will be avenged 77 times (Gn 4,24) and Peter will have to pardon 77 times or 70 times 7 times (Mt 18,22). The number *10* has a mnemotechnic value (the 10 fingers), whence its usage for the 10 commandments (Ex 34,28; Dt 4,13) or the 10 plagues of Egypt (Ex 7,14—12,29); from this springs the idea of a quite sizable quantity: Laban changed 10 times the wages of Jacob (Gn 31,7), and Job was insulted 10 times by his friends (Jb 19,3). The number *12* is the number of the lunar phases of the year and suggests thereby the idea of a complete yearly cycle: the 12 prefectures of Solomon assure, in turn, the provisioning of the palace during a month (1 K 4,7—5,5); it has been supposed that the number of the 12 tribes of Israel was in relation to the cultural service in the common sanctuary during the 12 months of the year. The number *40* designates conventionally the years of one generation: 40 years of dwelling in the desert (Nm 14,34), 40 years of tranquility in Israel after each deliverance accomplished by the judges (Jg 3,11.30; 5,31, etc.), 40 years of kingship for David (2 S 5,4)...Thus comes the idea of a period quite long whose exact duration is not known: 40 days and 40 nights for the flood (Gn 7,4), the stay of Moses upon Mt. Sinai (Ex 24,18); but the 40 days' journey of Elijah (1 K 19,8) and of the fast of Christ (Mk 1,13 p) repeat symbolically the 40 years of Israel in the desert. Some similar usages are to be mentioned for *60*

and *80* (Ct 6,8), *100* (Lv 26,8; Qo 6,3; the hundredfold of Mt 19,29), whereas the 70 ancients of Nm 11,16.24 refer to the conventional use of 7 (cf Lk 10,1). At the same time, certain uses of the number *70* (10 times 7) relate to the symbolism of the week* and of the Sabbath* (Jr 25,11; 2 Ch 36,21; Dn 9,2). The number *1000* calls to mind a considerable quantity: God is kind to 1000 generations (Ex 20,6; Jr 32,18); for Him, 1000 years are as a day (Ps 90,4); and a day in His service is worth more than 1000 others (Ps 84,11). But the same number also serves to designate the interior divisions of the tribes; and the "thousand" is subdivided itself conventionally into hundreds, fifties, and tens (Ex 18,21). Further on, the myriad (10,000) designates a fabulous quantity (Lv 26,8). At any rate, these large numbers have a hyperbolic value, evident in some passages such as Gn 24, 60 or 1 S 18,7.

2. An original procedure for denoting emphasis consists in raising the value of a number by having it followed with the number which is higher: "Once has God spoken, twice have I understood" (Ps 62,12). The following occur also: *1+2* (Jr 3,14; Jb 40,5); *2+3* (Ho 6,2; Jb 33,29; Si 23,16) *3+4* (Am 1—2; Pr 30,15-33; Si 26,5; cf the *ter quaterque beati* of Virgil); *4+5* (Is 17,6); *5+6* (2 K 13,19); *6+7* (Pr 6,16; Jb 5,19); *7+8* (Mi 5,4; Qo 11,2); *9+10* (Si 25,7). Clearly the procedure is frequent among the wisdom authors, more often under the form of the numerical *māšāl*, a vivid account, which makes systematic use of this form of expression.

II. SYMBOLIC MEANINGS

The ancient East prized highly the symbolism of numbers. In Mesopotamia, where mathematics was relatively developed, certain sacred numbers were attributed to the gods. According to Pythagorean speculations, *1* and *2* were masculine, *3* and *4* feminine, *7* virginal, etc. These conceptions are sometimes found among the Jewish writings and among the fathers, but they are foreign to the Bible, where no number is sacred *per se*. On the other hand, stemming from certain conventional usages, or by the lateral influence of surrounding civilizations, there are found in great number certain symbolic usages or even some "gematria."

1. *Symbolic usages.* The number *4*, representing cosmic totality (which is also in the back-

ground of the "four living creatures" in Ez 1, 5…Ap 4,6), comes to mean everything which has a character of plenitude: 4 scourges in Ez 14,21; 4 beatitudes in Lk 6,20ff (and 8 in Mt 5, 1-10).

The number 7 designates traditionally a complete series: 7 aspersions with blood (Lv 4,6.17; 8,11; 14,7; Nm 19,4; 2 K 5,10), immolation of 7 animals (Nm 28,11; Ez 45,23; Jb 42,8; 2 Ch 29,21). It freely attaches itself to certain sacrosanct objects: the 7 angels of Tb 12,15; the 7 eyes on the rock in Ze 3,9. It is above all the number of days of the week* and characterizes the Sabbath*, the holy day *par excellence* (Gn 2,2). Thence come the apocalyptic speculations of Dn 9,2.24, where the 70 weeks of years (10 jubilees of 7 times 7 years) lead to the day* of salvation, independently of any real chronology. A number of perfection divisible into 3+4, the number 7 figures by this title in the prophetic visions (Is 30,26; Ze 4,2) and especially the apocalypses (Ap 1,12.16; 3,1; 4,5; 5,1.6; 8,2; 10,3; 15,1; 17,9), but its half is also mentioned, 3 1/2 (Dn 7,25; 8,14; 9,27; 12,8.11f; Ap 11,2f.9ff; 12,6.4; 13,5). Inversely, *6* (7 minus 1) is the type of a lack of perfection (Ap 13,18 : 666).

The number *12*, insofar as it is the number of the 12 tribes, is also a perfect number, which is applied symbolically to the people of God. Thence comes its significant usage for the 12 apostles* of Jesus, who will reign over the 12 tribes of the new Israel (Mt 19,28 p). Likewise, the new Jerusalem* of the Apocalypse has 12 gates on which are engraved the names of the 12 tribes (Ap 21,12), and 12 foundation stones which bear the names of the 12 apostles (21,14). In the same way, the people saved is to the number of 144,000, 12 thousand per tribe of Israel (7,4-8). But the 12 stars which crown the woman* (another symbol of the new humanity) may contain an allusion to the 12 zodiacal constellations (12,1).

2. *Gematria. Gematria* (corruption of the gr. *geōmetria*) refers to a procedure cherished by the ancients, according to which a given number designates a man or an object because the numerical value of the letters which constitute the name corresponds to the number in question. The Bible offers a few certain examples of this.

The 318 partisans of Abraham (Gn 14,14) probably correspond to the number of the name of Eliezer, Abraham's steward: '+L+Y+'+ Z + R = 1 + 30 + 10 + 70 + 7 + 200=318. The proposal has also been made to see in the

3 × 14 generations which compose the genealogy of Jesus (Mt 1) a gematria of the name of David (DWD), superimposed on the symbolic usage of the number 7: Jesus would thus be designated as a "triple David" (eminently David and Messiah). The case is a sure one for the number of the beast (666) in the Ap 13,18, even if the basis of the computation is open to discussion. St. Irenaeus had already proposed the name *Lateinos* (30 + 1 + 300 + 5 + 10 + 50 + 70 + 200) designating the Roman Empire. Today, it is more often thought to be a question of Nero Caesar, based upon his Hebrew name NRWN QSR (50+200+6+100+60+200). In any case, the symbolism of 6 is superimposed on the cryptic designation.

III. CONCLUSION

A certain number of biblical digits must be explained by the double procedure of symbolic values and gematria; but more often the key to this is lost for us, and it is extremely difficult to recover. Thus, the storied ages of the antediluvian patriarchs (otherwise modest alongside of those which figure in the Mesopotamian legends) probably have a meaning; but it hardly appears at all, except for Enoch, the only just man of the series, who lived 365 years, the perfect number of the solar year. Perhaps it is the same for the ages of the ancestors of Israel, the total of those counted in Nm 1,46, the 38 years of Jn 5,5, the 153 large fish of Jn 21, 11, etc.

However that may be, it remains certain that the numbers cited in the Sacred Scriptures ought not always be taken literally. To grasp their significance, the intention of the narrators must always be taken into account: is it a question of their furnishing exact numbers, or approximations whose eventual exaggeration has hyperbolic value, or symbols which result from pure arithmetic? In the historical books, the number of the combatants or prisoners is very often exaggerated (cf Ex 12,37); but it is a stylistic convention, and the affirmation of the hagiographer is to be understood in this light, beyond its more or less conventional arithmetical purport. In the same way, if symbolism intrudes, it is to the meaning of the symbols that the authors essentially apply themselves.

It is necessary, then, to see what is dealt with in each particular case, in order to avoid either involving oneself in an unbalanced symbolic interpretation, or fixing certain statements which should be understood in a flexible way, or, finally, draining the content of certain textual data. It must be remembered that alongside of the numerical value, numbers often enough represent notions of an entirely different order which, more than once, escape today's readers.

→Mystery OT 2 a—Time OT II 1, III 3—Week 1.

JdF & PG phmcn

O

OATH

In most religions men have recourse to the godhead as a solemn guarantee of the value of their word: whether it is a question of a promise, which they wish to ensure will be honored, or of a statement, which they wish to claim to be true.

OT

1. Throughout the OT *men* exchange oaths, whether to form alliances (Gn 21,22-32; 31,44-54) or to guarantee the irrevocability of their promises* (24,2-4; 47,29) or of their decisions (1 S 14,44; 25,22). Oaths also ensure the truth of a statement in everyday dealings (Jg 8,19; 1 S 20,3), judicial enquiries (Ex 22,7-10) and the predictions of the prophets (1 K 17,1; cf Dn 12, 7). This recourse to the divine guarantee often takes the form of an appeal to a sanction in the case of perjury: "may Yahweh do this to me..." (above all in the very early days: Gn 24,37-41; Jg 11,10; 1 S 14,24.48).

2. It is understandable that Israel often attributed oaths to *Yahweh* Himself: to conclude His covenant (Dt 4,31; 7,8), to guarantee its promises (Gn 22,16; 26,3), to announce His judgments (Nb 14,21; Am 4,2; 6,8) and to mark the authority of His word (Ez 20,3; 33,11). And then His usual formula is: "I am living." The only possible guarantee of God's word is Himself.

3. Despite the value lent to an oath by the presence and authority of the just judge, there are still cases of *perjury*. The Ten Commandments condemn it (Ex 20,7), and the prophets will never cease to denounce it (Ho 4,2; Jr 5,2; 7,9; Ez 17,13-19; Ml 3,5).

After the Exile there is a growing awareness of another abuse: the frequency of oaths that make use of God in the service of the most sordid interests and which increase the risks of perjury (Qo 5,1; Si 23,9-11; Qumran). The warning of the wise men does not amount to a rejection of oaths, but it is a sign of a better understanding of their value and an invitation to reserve them for solemn occasions.

NT

1. In the thought of *Jesus* there appear to be subtle distinctions. He never resorts to an oath to confirm the authority of His teaching; he confines Himself to introducing His most solemn statements with His usual formula: "Amen* I say to you." Elsewhere, in the Sermon on the Mount, He orders His followers to refrain from oaths (Mt 5,33-37): men should not be able to swear by what belongs to God, since they are not masters of this thing. The word of the disciples does not have to look for any further guarantee than their fraternal sincerity.

However, Jesus does attack vigorously the laxist casuistry of the scribes, who propose all sorts of expedients to water down the demands of oaths (Mt 23,16-22); when He is brought before the Sanhedrin, He accepts the challenge of the High Priest who adjures Him, that is puts Him on oath (Mt 26,63). On this solemn occasion, then, when He is announcing His mission in front of the legitimate authorities, Jesus gives implicit recognition to the value of oaths.

2. *Paul* condemns perjurers (1 Tm 1,10) and never uses the formulas condemned by Jesus nor those in use among the Jews. However, he frequently has recourse to the divine guarantee in the statements that are most important to him. He calls God to witness his lack of self-

interest (1 Th 2,5.10; 2 Co 1,23), his sincerity (G 1,20) and his love for his faithful (2 Co 11, 11; Ph 1,8; R 1,9). It seems that in Paul the instructions of Jesus on the subject of oaths are already exercising a corrective influence on Jewish habits.

3. *The other authors* of the NT show the same discretion as Jesus. The epistle of James (Jm 5,12) interprets Jesus' teaching in Mt 5,33-37 in its own way; but the epistle to the Hebrews (He 6,16) recognizes the value of oaths. As for the oaths attributed to God, they are recalled in the NT on several occasions (Ac 2,30; He 3,11ff; 6,13ff; 7,20ff), above all when it is a question of oaths concerning the Messiah.

To sum up, the NT hands on the thought of Jesus about the sincerity that must exist between men, about the respect owed to the honor of God and about the need to reserve oaths for serious cases.

→Amen 1 — Anathema NT — Covenant — Human Speech 1—Lie—Promises I—Truth— Witness.

AG ems

OBEDIENCE

Obedience is far from being an endured constraint and a passive compliance; it is, rather, the free adherence to the plan* of God still enclosed in mystery* but proposed by the Word* of faith*; and this obedience permits man to make of his life a service* of God and an entrance into His joy.

I. CREATION OBEYS GOD

We see in creation* itself, outside of man, a sort of presentiment of this obedience and joy*. The fact that the Lord put a hook into Leviathan (Jb 40,24) or crushes Rahab (Ps 89,11) is proof of His sovereign mastery. Jesus calming the storm or casting out demons is proof that, just as the demons, "the winds and the sea obey Him" (Mt 8,27 p; Mk 1,27), and these acts of power evoke a religious fear*. But more than the silence* of the universe acknowledging its master, what the Bible wonders at and expresses in outbursts of thanksgiving* is the joyous enthusiasm of creatures responding in haste to the voice of God: "The stars* shine... in joy;

He calls them and they say: 'Here we are!' and they shine with joy for Him who has created them" (Ba 3,34f; cf Ps 104,4; Si 42,23; 43,13-26). Before this ardor of the most beautiful creatures to fulfill the mission which God has assigned them in His universe, mankind, "enclosed in disobedience" (R 11,32), brings to mind unwittingly and sorrowfully what should have been his obedience, and God makes him glimpse and hope for what can be the spontaneous and unanimous obedience of creation freed by the obedience of His Son (R 8,19-22).

II. THE DRAMA OF DISOBEDIENCE

1. *From the very beginning, Adam* disobeys God, involving all his descendants in his rebellion (R 5,19) and subjecting creation to vanity (8,20). The revolt of Adam shows, by contrast, what obedience is and what God expects from it. It is the submission of man to the will* of God, the execution of a commandment whose meaning and value we do not see, but whose character we perceive as a divine imperative. If God demands our obedience, it is because He has a plan to fulfill, a universe to construct; and needs our collaboration, our adherence in faith. Faith* is not obedience, but it is its secret; obedience is the sign and the fruit of faith. If Adam disobeyed, it is because he forgot the Word* of God, and he listened to the voice of Eve and that of the tempter (Gn 3, 4ff).

2. To save mankind, God stirs up the faith of Abraham*; and to assure Himself of that faith, He makes it pass through obedience: "Leave your country" (Gn 12,1), "Walk in my presence and be perfect" (17,1), "Take your son ...offer him as a holocaust" (22,2). The whole existence of Abraham rests on the Word of God, but this Word constantly forces him to go forward blindly and perform acts whose meaning escapes him. Thus obedience is for him a test, a trial* from God (22,1), and for God a priceless witness: "You have not refused me your son, your only son" (22,16).

3. *The covenant* supposes exactly the same procedure: "All that Yahweh has spoken, we will heed and do," responds Israel in adhering to the pact which God proposes to it (Ex 24,7). The covenant* brings with it a charter, the Law*, a series of commandments and institutions framing the existence of Israel and in-

tended to make it live as the people* of God. Several of these arrangements impose duties of obedience on men—toward parents (Dt 21,18-21), the kings, prophets, priests (17,14—18,22). Often these duties are already inscribed in the nature of man, but the Word of God, by incorporating them into His covenant, makes of man's submission an obedience in faith. Since fidelity to the Law is genuine only in adherence to the Word and covenant of God, obedience to its precepts is not the submission of a slave, but an attitude of love*. Already the first Decalogue makes the connection: "...those who love me and keep my commandments" (Ex 20,6); Deuteronomy repeats and develops the idea (Dt 11,13.22); the psalms celebrate the Law as the great gift of God's love to men and the source of an obedience of love (Ps 19,8-11; 119).

III. CHRIST, OUR OBEDIENCE

1. But who obeys God? Israel is "a rebellious house" (Ez 2,5), "sons in revolt" (Is 1, 2); "glorying in the Law, it dishonors God in transgressing it" (R 2,23). It cannot take pride in any superiority over the pagan, for it is with him "enclosed in disobedience" (3,10; 11,32). Slave* of sin*, man, who nevertheless aspires to obedience in his depths, is incapable of obeying God (7,14). To arrive at this point, to find "the Law at the heart of his being" (Jr 31,33), it is necessary that God send His Servant*, that "every morning he opens his ears" (Is 50,4), that he might be able to say: "Behold, I come ...to do your will" (Ps 40,7ff).

"For just as by the disobedience of the one man the many were constituted sinners, so also by the obedience of the one the many will be constituted just" (R 5,19). The obedience of Jesus Christ is our salvation and enables us once again to discover obedience to God. The life of Jesus Christ was, from "His entrance into the world" (He 10,5) and "until His death on the cross" (Ph 2,8), obedience; that is to say, adherence to God through a series of intermediaries: persons, events, institutions, writings of His people, human authorities. Come "not to do His own will, but the will of Him who sent (Him)" (Jn 6,38; cf Mt 26,39), He spends His entire life in the normal duties of obedience to His parents (Lk 2,51), to legitimate authorities (Mt 17,27). In His passion*, He pushes obedience to its limit, delivering Himself without resistance to inhuman and unjust powers, "achieving through all His sufferings the ex-

perience of obedience" (He 5,8), making of His death the most precious sacrifice* to God, that of obedience (10,5-10; cf 1 S 15,22).

IV. THE OBEDIENCE OF THE CHRISTIAN

Having become through His obedience "the Lord*" (Ph 2,11) and clothed with "all power in heaven and on earth" (Mt 28,18), Jesus Christ has a right to the obedience of every creature. It is through Him, through obedience to His gospel and to the word of His Church* (2 Th 3,14; Mt 10,40 p) that man attains God in faith (Ac 6,7; R 1,5; 10,3; 2 Th 1,8), that he escapes from primordial disobedience and enters into the mystery* of salvation: Jesus Christ is the unique law* of the Christian (1 Co 9,21). This law embraces also obedience to legitimate human authorities—parents (Col 3,20), masters (3,22), husbands (3,18), public powers, recognizing everywhere "the authority of God" (R 13,1-7). But since he never obeys unless to serve God, the Christian is capable, if necessary, of defying an unjust order and of "obeying God rather than men" (Ac 4,19).

→Abraham I 2, II 3—Authority—Calling—Captivity—Covenant OT II 2—Faith—Faithfulness—Follow 1—Law—Listen 1—Piety OT 2—Plan of God—Servant of God III 2—Serve II 2—Sin I 1, IV 3—Virtues & Vices 1—Will of God.

CA & JG pmcm

OIL

1. *Oil as a gift of God.* Along with wheat and wine*, oil is one of the essential foods with which God has filled His faithful people (Dt 11, 14) in the land which is rich in olive trees (Dt 6,11; 8,8) where He has established His people gratuitously. It appears as a divine blessing* (Dt 7,13f; Jr 31,12). Its privation is a punishment for infidelity (Mi 6,15; Ha 3,17). Its abundance is a sign of salvation (Jl 2,19) and a symbol of eschatological happiness (Ho 2, 24). Besides, oil is not only an indispensable food even in needy times (1 K 17,14f; 2 K 4, 1-7), but it is also an ointment which perfumes the body (Am 6,6; Es 2,12), strengthens the limbs (Ez 16,9), and soothes wounds (Is 1,6; Lk 10,34). Finally, the oil in lamps is a source of light (Ex 27,20f; Mt 25,3-8).

This oil is not to be used to give worship to the Baals as if the earth's fertility came from them. It is not to be used to make treaties with pagan powers as if the people's salvation from God did not depend solely on its fidelity to the covenant (Ho 2,7.10; 12,2). To be faithful to the covenant it is not sufficient to reserve the best oil for the priests (Nm 18,12), nor to mix some oil with the oblations according to the ritual (Lv 2,1...; Nm 15,4; 28—29), nor even to pour out generous libations of oil. Such observances are agreeable to God only if the person walks with God in the way* of justice and love (Mi 6,7f).

2. *The symbolism of oil.* If oil is a sign of the divine blessing, the flourishing olive tree is a symbol of the just man* blessed by God (Ps 52, 10; 128,3; cf Si 50,10) and of divine Wisdom which reveals in the Law the path of justice and happiness (Si 24,14.19-23). The two olive trees which supply the oil for the seven lamps on the lampstand (Ze 4,11-14) represent the two "sons of oil," the two anointed ones of God, the king and the high priest whose mission is to enlighten the people and to lead them in the way of salvation.

Furthermore, if we compare oil to what is like it in its insinuating and elusive character (Pr 5,3; Ps 109,18; Pr 27,16), we can see clearly in it an ointment with a perfume that charms and gives joy, a beautiful symbol of love (Ct 1, 3) and friendship (Pr 27,9), and the happiness of fraternal union (Ps 133,2). Oil is also a symbol of joy* because it makes the face shine (Ps 104,15). To pour oil on someone's head (Ps 23,5; 92,11; Lk 7,46; Mt 26,7) is to wish him joy and happiness and to pay him a sign of friendship and honor.

The oil used for anointing the king deserves above all the name of the "oil of joy" (Ps 45, 8). It is an outward sign of divine election* and it is accompanied by the coming of the Spirit* to take possession of the chosen one (Is 10,1-6; 16,13). This connection between anointing and the Spirit is at the origin of the fundamental symbolism of oil in the Christian sacraments, especially in the anointing of the sick, which is mentioned in the epistle of St. James (Jm 5,14; cf Mk 6,13). The holy oils give the Christian the multiform grace of the Holy Spirit—the same Spirit who made Jesus* the unique anointed one *par excellence* and the Son of God (He 1,9 which applies Ps 45,8 to Christ to proclaim His divinity).

→Anointing—Messiah—Perfume.

CL & MFL jrs

OLD AGE

To live for a long time is the wish of anyone who is living happily amongst his own people; but, although old age can be rich in experience and wisdom, it can also weigh heavily on the unfortunate person who is worn out by age and at the end of his patience (Si 41,1f). Thus, old age has a different meaning, according to whether it is seen as the path of decline toward death or as the path of progress toward eternal happiness.

1. *Long life and the approach of death.* Even though threatened by death*, life* is a gift from God. Thus a long life is to be desired; it is promised to those who honor their parents (Ex 20,12) and it is a crown for the just man (Pr 10,27; 16,31), who has in this way the joy of seeing his children's children (Pr 17,6). Like Abraham full of days (Gn 25,8), the just man can die in peace after a happy and flourishing old age (Ps 92,15), conscious that his life has been a full one (Gn 15,15; Tb 14,1; Si 44,14). But it can also happen that death is seen as a deliverance (Si 41,2), when the old person feels his strength declining (Ps 71,9; Qo 12,5) and nothing has any interest for him any more (2 S 19,36).

2. *Experience of years and advance in wisdom.* All peoples have associated authority* with age and the experience that it brings. In the Bible too, the ancients are at the head of the communities (Ex 3,16; 18,12; 2 S 5,3; Es 6,7; Ac 11,30; 15,4). And although some old men may lead lives of scandalous corruption and injustice (Si 25,2; Dn 13,5), white hairs deserve respect (Lv 19,32; 1 Tm 5,1f), and children ought to come to the aid of their parents in their old age (Si 3,12). Because of his wisdom* (25,4f) and as a witness of tradition*, the old man can speak with authority: he ought, however, to do this with discretion (32,3; 42,8). There is in fact one danger that threatens the ancients: the danger that they will shut their minds to anything new instead of remaining open to the truth; it was this false fidelity to tradition (Mt 15,2-6) that led the elders of the people to take their place among the enemies of Christ, who insult Him as He hangs on the cross (27,

1.41). Length of years, then, is not enough to make the old man worthy of the honor that is paid him; in fact, wisdom can be the lot of the young person (Ps 119,100; Ws 4,8f.16), and, in order to be able to enter the Kingdom of heaven, everyone must receive it like a little child (Mk 10,15). Therefore, let aged Christians follow the advice of old Paul (Phm 9) and shine by their virtues* (Tt 2,2-5).

Finally, old age is the symbol of eternity. The Eternal appears to Daniel in the guise of an old man (Dn 7,9) and, in the Apocalypse, the twenty-four Elders stand for the court of God, which is eternally singing His glory (Ap 4,4; 5,14. . .).

→Child O—Death—Friend 1—Life II 1—Man III 3—New III 3 b—Sickness/Healing OT I 1 —Tradition OT II; NT I 1—Wisdom OT II 1.2.

MFL ems

P

PARABLE

From the time of the early Church, a story told by Jesus to illustrate His teaching was called a parable. At the base of the Greek word *parabolē* lies the idea of comparison. And of course the eastern mind does love to speak and instruct with the help of comparisons; it also makes use of enigmas, and the point of these is to arouse curiosity and encourage further enquiry. This inclination can be seen in the books of the Bible, especially in the sayings of the wise men (Pr 10,26; 12,4; Jg 14,14). However, this is not the real explanation for the use of the parabolic genre: the parable must be understood as the dramatic use of symbols, that is of images drawn from earthly realities in order to signify* the realities revealed by God (sacred history, the Kingdom...), a procedure that more often than not calls for an explanation in depth.

1. SYMBOLS IN SACRED HISTORY

1. *The extension of the procedure.* From the beginning of its history, Israel was faced with the challenge of speaking concretely of the transcendent God who admitted no sensible representation (Ex 20,4). They had, therefore, unceasingly to describe divine life by beginning with earthly realities, which take on the value of signs*. Anthropomorphisms, so numerous in the ancient texts, are so many symbols which contain in germ real parables (Gn 2,7f.19.21...).

They will be rarer afterwards, but the need for evocative description will only be stronger (Ez 1,26ff). The life of man itself, in its moral and religious aspect, had need of these associations. The prophets made use of them abundantly, both in their invectives (Am 4,1; Ho 4,16; Is 5,18...) and in order to express the divine promises (Ho 2,20f; Is 11,6-9; Jr 31,21...). At the same time, they are fond of symbolic actions, that is to say, their preaching acted out (Is 20,2; Jr 19,10; Ez 4—5). Some genuine parables are also found in the historical books to illustrate some important event of sacred history (Jg 9,8-15; 2 S 12,1-4; 14,5ff). The procedure is broadened in late Judaism to the point of becoming, with the rabbis, a real pedagogical method. The constructed image or history of the past came to the support of scripture teaching, introduced by the phrase: "To what shall this be likened?" Jesus placed Himself within this movement, frequently announcing the symbols that were the bearers of His message with similar introductions: "To what shall I compare it?" (Mk 4,30; Lk 13,18). "The kingdom of heaven is like..." (Mt 13,24.31).

2. *The religious import of the parables.* Using the concrete realities of everyday life to illustrate their teaching on the meaning of sacred history, the prophets make themes out of them: shepherd*, marriage*, the vine, are found in the gospel parables. The gratuitous and benevolent love of God, the reluctance of the people in their response, form the fabric of these portraits (vg Is 5,1-7; Ho 2; Ez 16), although more pre-

cise allusions to a certain attitude of moral life (Pr 4,18f; 6,6-11; 15,4) can also be found in them, or even to a certain determinate social situation (Jg 9,8-15) In the gospels the perspective is centered on the final realization of the kingdom of God in the person of Jesus. Hence the important group of parables of the kingdom (especially Mt 13,1-50 p; 20,1-16; 21, 33—22,14 p; 24,45—25,30).

3. *Parable and allegory.* It sometimes happens that the symbolic story does not only provide a general lesson, but that all the details have a particular meaning and require a special interpretation. The parable then becomes allegory. This is the case in certain passages of the OT (vg Ez 17), and one comes across this procedure in the fourth gospel (Jn 10,1-16; 15,1-6). In fact, the parables frequently include at least some allegorical traits, as when Jesus speaks of God and of Israel under the aspect of the master of the vineyard (Mt 21,33 p). The evangelists accentuate this characteristic in suggesting an interpretation. Thus Matthew allegorizes the "master of the house" of whom Jesus spoke in a parable into "your Master" (Mt 24,42; Mk 13,35), and Luke reports the parable of the good Samaritan in terms which make one think of Christ (Lk 10,33.35).

II. APOCALYPTIC PRESENTATION

1. *In OT prophecy.* Much more than to the sages' enigmas (1 K 10,1-3; Si 39,3), it is to the intentionally mysterious presentation of the late writings that we must turn in order to explain the enigmatic character of certain gospel parables. With Ezekiel, the prophetic announcement of the future shades off little by little into an apocalypse; i.e., it deliberately enfolds the content of the revelation in a series of images which need explanation in order to be understood. The presence of an "angel-interpreter" generally throws into relief the depth and difficulty of the message. Thus the allegory of the eagle, in Ez 17,3-10, called *enigma* and *parable* (*māšāl*), is afterwards explained by the prophet (17,12-21). The visions of Zechariah include an angel-interpreter (Ze 1,9ff; 4,5f...); so too the great apocalyptic visions of Daniel, in which the seer is always supposed not to understand (Dn 7,15f; 8,15f; 9,22). And so we have a three-part arrangement: symbol—request for explanation—application of the symbol to the reality signified.

2. *In the gospels.* The mystery of the kingdom and of Jesus' person is so new that He Himself can manifest it only gradually, in conformity with the diverse receptivity of His hearers. This is why Jesus, in the first part of His public life, enjoins for His own reasons the "Messianic secret," so strongly placed in relief by Mark (Mk 1,34.44; 3,12; 5,43...). This is also why He is fond of speaking in parables which, while giving an idea of His teaching, oblige one to reflect, and require an explanation to be perfectly grasped. Thus we have a method of teaching in two stages, which is well brought out by Mk 4,33-34: the use of classical themes (king, feast, vine, shepherd, sowing...sets the whole audience on the right path; but the disciples have a right to have the teaching developed at a deeper level, and this is what Jesus does. Their questions, then, are reminiscent of the interventions of the seers in the apocalypses (cf Dn 2,18f; 7,16; Mt 13,10-13. 34f.36.51; 15,15). In this way the parables are seen as a necessary means of opening up the mind to faith. The more the believer penetrates the revealed mystery*, the more he will understand the parables; and, conversely, the more a man refuses Jesus' message, the more difficult he will find it to understand the parables of the kingdom. The evangelists underline this fact, when, struck by the hardness of heart* shown by so many Jews toward the Gospel, they have Jesus answer His disciples with a quotation from Isaiah: the parables show clearly the blindness of those who deliberately refuse to open themselves to Christ's message (Mt 13,10-15 p). Nonetheless, alongside these parables rooted in the apocalypses, there are clearer ones aiming at moral teachings accessible to all (thus Lk 8,16ff; 10,30-37; 11,5-8).

III. THE INTERPRETATION OF THE PARABLES

By placing oneself back into this biblical and oriental context in which Jesus spoke, and keeping in mind His intent of progressive teaching, it becomes easier to interpret the parables. Their matter is the humble facts of daily life, but also, and perhaps above all, the great events of sacred history. Their classical themes, easily discovered, are already charged with meaning through their OT background at the moment Jesus makes use of them. No improbability should surprise one in these accounts freely composed and wholly orientated to teaching;

and the reader should not take offense at the attitude of certain characters who are presented to illustrate an *a fortiori* or *a contrario* argument (vg Lk 16,1-8; 18,1-5). At any rate, we must first bring to light the theocentric aspect, and more precisely, the Christocentric aspect, of the majority of the parables. Whatever be the exact degree of allegory, it is, after all, the heavenly Father (Mt 21,28; Lk 15,11), or Christ Himself—whether in His historic mission (the "sower" of Mt 13,3.24.31 p), or in His future glory (the "thief" of Mt 24,43; the "master" of Mt 25,14; the "spouse" of Mt 25, 1)—that the central character is most frequently to bring to mind; and when there are two characters, they are the Father and the Son (Mt 20,1-16; 21,33.37; 22,2). This is so true that the love of the Father, witnessed by men through the sending of His Son, is the great revelation brought by Jesus. This is the function of the parables, which show the perfect completion the new kingdom* confers on the plan of God for the world.

→Mystery NT I—Revelation NT I 1 b—Wisdom NT I 1—Word of God.

DS phmcn

PARACLETE

The word *paraclete* (gr. *paraklētos*) is an expression of Johannine literature. It designates the function of something rather than its nature: one who is "called to the side of" (*para-kaleō*; *ad-vocatus*), plays the active role of assistant, advocate, supporter (the sense of *consoler*, derived from a false etymology, is not attested in the NT). This function is held also by Jesus Christ who in heaven is "our advocate with the Father," interceding on behalf of sinners (1 Jn 2,1); and by the Holy Spirit, who actualizes the presence of Jesus, since, here below, He is, for believers, the revealer and the defender of Jesus (Jn 14,16f.26f; 15,26f; 16,7-11.13ff).

1. *The Holy Spirit, the presence of Jesus.* The coming of the Paraclete is linked to the departure of Jesus (Jn 16,7), who marks a new stage in the history of God's presence among men. In the discourse after the supper, Jesus announces that He will come again, not only at the end of time (14,3), but at the time of the Easter appearances (14,18ff; 16,16-19). The sight of the risen one will overwhelm the disciples

with joy* (16,22). Nevertheless His presence among His followers will no longer be of a sensible nature, but rather "spiritual." Up to that time, He "dwelt among" His followers (14,25). Now, in His name* (14,26), at His prayer, the Father will give them "another Paraclete" (14,16) whom Jesus Himself will send (15,26; 16,7). While being "other than" Jesus, the Spirit brings the presence of Jesus to its perfection. Like Jesus, He is "in" them (14,17; 17,23); like Jesus He dwells "with" the believers (14,17.25); but this is "forever" (14,16; cf Mt 28,20), for He anticipates the places which Jesus has gone to prepare in the mansion of the Father (14,2f). He is the Spirit of truth (14,17; 16,13), of the truth which Jesus is (14,6) by opposition to the father of lies* (8,44), of the truth which henceforth characterizes adoration* of the Father (4,23f). He is the Holy* Spirit (14,26) whom Jesus the holy one (6,69) has, by His consecration (17,19), merited to give them (20,22; 7,39); He "consecrates" them (17, 17), making them no longer of the world* (17, 16). Just as Jesus does not manifest Himself to the world (14,21f) which hates Him (7,7; 15,18f), so, too, the Spirit is not welcomed by the world (14,17).

2. *The Spirit of truth, living memory of the Church.* The Paraclete has an active presence in the community of the disciples; He should glorify Jesus (16,14), first of all in actualizing His teaching*: "He will teach you all things and bring to your minds whatever I have said to you" (14,26). This teaching and this reminding are done in close conjunction with Jesus, just as Jesus had carried out His mission, always united to His Father. As Jesus disposes of the gifts of the Father (16,15; 17,10), so the Spirit "will receive of what is mine and declare it to you" (16,14f). He will recall to mind what Jesus has said, for "He will not speak of Himself; but everything that He shall hear, He will speak." Thus Jesus drew everything from his Father (5,30; 8,40; 15,15) and His teaching was not "His own" (8,28; 12,49f; 14,10). Just as in seeing* Jesus, one saw the Father (14,9), so the anointing* (*chrisma*) teaches about all things (1 Jn 2,27), that is, the Spirit "leads to all truth" (Jn 16,13): He "re-presents" past events in the light of Easter (cf 2,22; 7,39; 11,51f; 12,16; 13,7). By this He bears testimony to Christ (15, 26) and enables the disciples to testify with Him and through Him (15,27).

3. *The Spirit of truth, defender of Jesus.* The

Paraclete reveals not only a truth which is opposed to error, but He justifies truth against the lie* of the world. He is the "Spirit of truth" and bears witness to Christ in the proceedings which the world* institutes against Jesus in the midst of His disciples. Whereas in the synoptic tradition the Spirit defended the disciples cited before the tribunal of kings (Mk 13,11 p), He is the defender of Jesus in John. Accused though they are, the disciples become judges of their judges, as Jesus had been in His earthly life (Jn 5,19-47). The Paraclete condemns the world on three counts (16,8-11): sin*, for sin is unbelief* with regard to Jesus; justice*, for justice is on the side of Jesus who has been glorified in the service of His Father; judgment*, for the verdict of condemnation is already pronounced against the prince of this world. Thus, thanks to the Paraclete whom the believer receives and listens to, a conviction dwells in his heart: it is not the world, it is Jesus who is right; he, too, then, is right in believing, in suffering for the cause of his master. Together with Him, he is already conqueror of the world and the devil (16,33).

→Mission NT III—Presence of God NT II—Spirit of God NT II—Teach NT II—Trial III 3 —World NT III 2.

XLD phmcn

PARADISE

The Greek word *paradeisos* is traced to an ancient Persian word, from which the Hebrew *pardēs*, which means "garden." The Septuagint uses this term in its literal sense (Qo 2,5; Ct 4,12) and in its religious sense. Only the latter use of the term will be considered here.

1. *God's garden.* In the religions of the Middle East, the portrayal of the life of the gods borrows its images from the lives of the powerful and wealthy here below: the gods revel in palaces surrounded by gardens where the "water* of life" flows and where, among other marvelous trees*, the "tree of life" flourishes. The immortals are nourished by the fruit* from the "tree of life." Here below, the temples* of the gods with their surrounding sacred gardens imitate this prototype. These portrayals of the gods, once they are purified of their polytheism, are introduced into the Bible; and according to the conventions of anthropomorphism, there is no hesitation to present God

"taking a walk in His garden for the day's air" (Gn 3,8); the garden and its trees are even cited proverbially (Gn 13,10; Ez 31,8f.16ff).

2. *From paradise lost to paradise regained.*

a) *Paradise lost.* The same imagery is introduced in relating sacred history to recall the state in which God created man and the purpose for which He placed him in this world. God planted a garden for him in Eden (Gn 2,8ff; cf Ez 28,13). Man's life in this garden included labor (Gn 2,15), but at the same time it had the character of ideal happiness. In more than one respect this is reminiscent of the classical descriptions of the golden age; familiarity with God, free use of the fruits of the garden, mastery over the animals* (2,19f), harmonious union of the primitive couple (2,18.23f), moral innocence that is signified by the absence of shame* (Gn 2,25), and the absence of death* which will only come into the world as a result of sin* (cf 3,19). Nevertheless, the trial* of man also occupies an essential place in this primitive paradise. God placed the tree of knowledge there, and the serpent will come there to tempt Eve. Still, the happiness of Eden is brought out by its contrast with the wretchedness and adversity of our present condition. This condition, the result of human sin*, is united to the theme of paradise lost (3,23).

b) *Promise of paradise.* The hope that man has within him is not false. It corresponds to his original calling*. This hope would remain forever unrealizable (cf Gn 3,23) if, through the disposition of Providence, all sacred history did not have for its purpose and meaning man's reinstatement. Thus, from the OT to the NT the theme of paradise regained, with all its various nuances, penetrates the eschatological oracles, mixing with those of the new holy land and new creation. Sins of the people of God have turned their earthly abode into a place of desolation (Jr 4,23), but in the last days God will transform it into a Garden of Eden (Ez 36,35; Is 51,3). In this new paradise, living waters* shall gush forth from the temple* where God shall dwell. On the banks wonderful trees* shall grow. These trees shall provide food and medicine for God's people* (Ez 47,12). The way of the tree of life shall be opened once again to man (Ap 2,7; 22,2 in contrast with Gn 3,24). The paradisaical life restored at the end of sacred history shall show forth characteristics equivalent to those of the primitive

Eden, and in several aspects shall surpass them. There shall be marvelous fertility in nature (Ho 2,23f; Am 9,13; Jr 31,23-26; Jl 4,18); universal peace*, not only of men among themselves (Is 2,4), but also with nature and animals (Ho 2,20; Is 11,6-9; 65,25); unmixed joy* (Jr 31,13; Is 35,10; 65,18. . .); suppression of all suffering*, even death* (Is 35,5f; 65,19. . .; 25,7ff; Ap 20, 14; 21,4); conquest of the serpent of old (Ap 20,2f.10); entrance into an eternal life* (Dn 12,2; Ws 5,15; Ap 2,11; 3,5). The reality that these images bring out, in contrast with the condition to which man is reduced by sin, recaptures the characteristics of his original state while eliminating any idea of trial or possibility of fall.

c) *Anticipations of paradise regained.* Paradise regained is an eschatological reality. The people of God knew only fleeting shadows of it in their historical experience. An example of this is the possession of a land "flowing with milk and honey" (Ex 3,17; Dt 6,3; etc.). Their spiritual experience, however, has given them an anticipation of another order; for God gave them His law which is the source of all wisdom (Dt 4,5f). But "wisdom is a tree of life" that insures happiness (Pr 3,18; cf Si 24,12-21). The law, in the man who observes it, causes wisdom to abound "like a river of paradise" (Si 24, 25ff; cf Gn 2,10. . .); the wise man who teaches it to others is "like a stream of water leading to paradise" (Si 24,30); grace and the fear of the Lord are a paradise of blessing (40,17.27). By wisdom, then, God restores to man a foretaste of the joy of paradise.

The NT reveals the ultimate secret of the divine plan*. Christ is the source of wisdom; He is wisdom itself (1 Co 1,30). He is also the new Adam* (R 5,14; 1 Co 15,45) through whom humanity approaches its eschatological state. At the time of His temptation He is victorious over the old serpent who is the devil and Satan* (cf Ap 20,2). At the time of His temptation He lives "with the wild beasts" in a sort of regained paradise (Mk 1,13; cf Gn 1,26; 2,19f). His miracles* show that henceforth death* and sickness* are conquered. The man who believes in Him has found the "food of life" (Jn 6,35), "the living water*" (4,14), "eternal life*" (5,24ff), and, in short, the gifts of the eschatological paradise that is now opened.

3. *Paradise, abode of the just.* In the biblical texts the description of the eschatological paradise remains restrained and is progressively purified. The apocrypha, however, exaggerate it a great deal and show a certain development in Jewish belief (vg in the Book of Enoch). In the last days*, before coming once again into the holy land, paradise is an intermediate abode where the just shall be gathered together by God to await judgment* day*, the resurrection*, and the future life*. This is the abode promised by Jesus to the good thief (Lk 23,43), but it has already been transformed by the presence of Him who is life: "You will be with me. . ." As for the beatitude* which is to be granted at the end of sacred history, Jesus is the first to enter it through His death in order to make it accessible to the sinners He has redeemed.

4. *Paradise and heaven.* As it is God's abode, paradise is located outside of this world. But biblical language also places the divine dwelling place in heaven*. Sometimes paradise is identified with the "highest of heavens," the one where God abides. That is where Paul was ravished in spirit to contemplate ineffable realities (2 Co 12,4). This is also the ordinary meaning of the word *paradise* in the language of of Christianity: *In Paradisum deducant te angeli. . .*"May the angels lead you into paradise. . ." (Funeral liturgy, ICEL translation). From now on, paradise is opened to all who die in the Lord.

→Adam I 2—Creation OT II 1—Desert OT II 3; NT I 1—Earth OT I 3, II 2.4—Fatherland OT 2—Heaven VI—Tree 1.

PG rco'c

PARDON

In the Bible, the sinner is a debtor for whom God remits the debt by His pardon (hb. *sālaḥ*: Nm 14,19). This remission is so effective that God no longer sees the sin which is, as it were, cast behind him (Is 38,17), taken away (hb. *nāsa'*; Ex 32,32), expiated, destroyed (hb. *kipper*; Is 6,7). Using this same vocabulary, Christ makes it emphatic that the remission is gratuitous and the debtor insolvent (Lk 7,42; Mt 18,25ff). The primitive preaching has for its object, simultaneously with the gift of the Spirit, the remission of sin which is its first effect and called *aphesis* (Lk 24,47; Ac 2,38; cf postcommunion for Pentecost Tuesday). Some other words are *purify*, *wash*, and *justify*. These appear in the apostolic writings that stress the positive aspects of pardon: reconciliation and union.

I. THE GOD OF PARDON

It is in a confrontation with sin that the jealous God (Ex 20,5) reveals Himself as the God of forgiveness. The apostasy that occasioned the covenant and merited the destruction of the people (Ex 32,30ff) is the occasion for God to proclaim Himself "God of love and pity, slow to anger, rich in grace and fidelity...who bears with faults, transgressions, and sin, but leaves nothing unpunished..." Thus, Moses can pray confidently: "We are a stiff-necked people. But pardon our faults and our sins, and possess us!" (Ex 34,6-9).

From a human and juridical point of view, the pardon is not justified. Should not the holy God reveal His holiness by His justice (Is 5,16) and strike those who scorn Him (5,24)? How could the unfaithful spouse of the covenant expect pardon: she who does not blush at her prostitution (Jr 3,1-5)? But God's heart is not like man's heart, and the holy one does not like to destroy (Ho 11,8f). Far from wishing the death of the sinner, He wishes his conversion (Ez 18,23) that He might lavish His pardon upon him; for "His ways are not our ways," and "His thoughts are exalted above our thoughts as the heavens are exalted above the earth" (Is 55,7ff).

The prayer of the psalmist is confident because God pardons the sinner who confesses his guilt (Ps 32,5; cf 2 S 12,13); God does not want him to be lost (Ps 78,38). Far from scorning him, He re-creates him, purifying and filling his contrite and humble heart with joy (Ps 51,10-14. 19; cf 32,1-11). God is an abundant source of redemption since He is a father who forgives all His children (Ps 103,3.8-14). After the exile, God is unceasingly invoked as the "God of forgiveness" (Ne 9,17) and "mercy" (Dn 9,9). He is always ready to repent of the evils with which He has threatened the sinner, if only the sinner will be converted (Jl 2,13). But Jonah, who is the representative type of the exclusiveness of Israel, is troubled to see this pardon offered to all men (Jon 3,10; 4,2). Contrary to Jonah, the Book of Wisdom sings praise to the God who loves all He has made, who has pity on all, who ignores men's sins that they might repent, who punishes them little by little and reminds them of how they sin in order that they

might believe in Him (Ws 11,23—12,2). In this way He shows that He is the almighty one whose characteristic is to pardon (Ws 11,23. 26; cf collect for the tenth Sunday after Pentecost and the prayer of the Litany of the Saints).

II. GOD'S PARDON THROUGH CHRIST

Like Israel (Lk 1,77), John the Baptist awaits the remission of sins, and he preaches a baptism that is the condition for this remission: do penance or He who is to come will baptize you in fire. For John this fire is the fire of anger and judgment that consumes the chaff, once the good grain has been separated from it (Mt 3, 1-12). The disciples of John who have followed Jesus keep this point of view; they want to have fire fall from the heavens on those who refuse to heed the preaching of the master (Lk 9,54). Even John the Baptist begins to wonder (cf Lk 7,19-23) about Jesus when he hears that Jesus not only invites sinners to be converted and believe (Mk 1,15), but also proclaims that He has come only to heal and to pardon.

1. *Message of pardon.* If, in fact, Jesus had come to cast fire upon the earth (Lk 12,49), He was not sent by His Father as a judge, but as a savior (Jn 3,17f; 12,47). He calls to conversion all those who have need of it (Lk 5,32 p) and He stirs up this conversion (Lk 19, 1-10) by revealing that God is a Father whose joy it is to pardon (Lk 15) and who wills that no man be lost (Mt 18,12ff). Jesus does not proclaim only that pardon to which humble faith is opened while pride refuses it (Lk 7,47-50; 18,9-14). He exercises the power of pardon, and His works witness that He has at His disposal a power belonging to God alone (Mk 2,5-11 p; cf Jn 5,21).

2. *Sacrifice for the remission of sins.* Christ crowns His work by obtaining the pardon of His Father for sinners. He prays (Lk 23,24) and sheds His blood (Mk 14,24) for the remission of sins (Mt 26,28). A true servant of God, He justifies the multitude by taking their sins upon Himself (1 P 2,24; cf Mk 10,45; Is 53,11f); for He is the Lamb who takes away the sins of the world (Jn 1,29) in saving the world. By His blood we are purified and cleansed from our faults (1 Jn 1,7; Ap 1,5).

3. *The communication of the power to pardon.* Having all power in heaven and on the

earth, the risen Christ communicates to the apostles the power to remit sins (Jn 20,22f; cf Mt 16,19; 18,18). The first remission of sin is to be granted at baptism to all those who shall be converted and believe in the name of Jesus (Mt 28,19; Mk 16,16; Ac 2,38; 3,19).

The apostles preach the remission of sin (Ac 2,38; 5,31; 10,43; 13,38; 26,18), but in their writings they insist less on the juridical aspect of pardon than on the divine love which, through Jesus, saves and sanctifies us (vg R 5,1-11). To be noted is the role of the Church's prayer and the mutual confession of sins as means in obtaining the pardon of one's sins (Jm 5,15f).

III. PARDON FOR OFFENSES

In the OT, already the Law not only puts a limit on vengeance by the rule of retaliation (Ex 21,23-25), but it also forbids hatred of one's brother and vengeance and rancor toward one's neighbor (Lv 19,17f). Ben Sira the sage meditated on these prescriptions and he discovered the bond that joins pardon granted by man to his fellow man to the pardon that he asks from God: "Pardon your neighbor his wrongs; then, at your prayer your own sins will be forgiven. If a man bears a grudge against another, how can he ask forgiveness from God? Being without compassion for his fellow man, does he still make entreaty for his own sins?" (Si 27,30 —28,7). The Book of Wisdom completes this lesson by reminding the just that in their judgments they must take the mercy of God as their example (Ws 12,19.22). Jesus will take this twofold lesson and transform it. Like the writer of Ecclesiastes, He teaches that God cannot pardon one who does not pardon his brother. The parable of the unmerciful debtor forcefully inculcates this truth (Mt 18,23-35) that Christ insists upon (Mt 6,14f) and prevents us from forgetting by having us repeat it daily in the Our Father. We must be able to say that we forgive. This statement is bound up with our request: in one place by the word *for* which makes forgiveness the condition of divine pardon (Lk 11,4) and in another place by the word *as* which establishes the measure (Mt 6,12).

Jesus goes further: similar to the Book of Wisdom, He makes God the model of mercy (Lk 6,35f) for those whose Father He is, and who must imitate Him to be His true children (Mt 5,43ff.48). Pardon is not only a prelimi-

nary condition of new life: it is one of its essential elements. Therefore, Jesus stipulates to Peter that he must not tire in forgiving. This is the very opposite of the sinner who insists on his full measure of revenge (Mt 18,21f; cf Gn 4,24). In imitation of our Lord (Lk 23,34). Stephen died while forgiving those who were stoning him (Ac 7,60). To be like Stephen and Jesus, and to conquer evil by good (R 12,21; cf 1 P 3,9), the Christian must always forgive, and forgive out of love; like Christ (Col 3,13), like His Father (E 4,32).

→Abel 2—Confession OT 2; NT 2—Curse V —Enemy II 3, III 1—Expiation 3—Justice *B* II OT—Love I OT 2; II NT 2—Memory 2— Mercy—Patience I 1, II 2—Repentance/Conversion OT I 2; NT III 1—Reward—Sin III 3, IV 1 c d—Tenderness—Vengeance 2 a. 4— Violence IV 3.

JGi & MFL rco'c

PASSOVER

In Jesus' time, the Jewish Passover brought the faithful of Moses together to Jerusalem for the purpose of offering and consuming the paschal lamb*. This commemorated the exodus* which liberated the Hebrews from Egyptian slavery. Today the Christian Passover unites Christ's disciples in communion with their Lord, the true Lamb of God. It associates them with His death* and resurrection* which have freed them from sin* and death. There is an obvious continuity from one festival to the other, but the perspective has been changed in passing from the old to the new covenant through the intermediary of Jesus' Passover.

I. THE ISRAELITE PASSOVER

1. *The early Passover, nomadic and domestic.* At the outset, the Passover was a family festival. It was celebrated at night*, at the full moon of the vernal equinox, the 14th of the month of Abib or of the corn (called Nisan after the exile). A young animal, born that year, was offered to Yahweh in order to draw down divine blessings upon the flocks. The victim was a lamb or kid, male, without blemish (Ex 12, 3-6); not a bone of him must be broken (12,46; Nm 9,12). His blood* was placed, as a sign of preservation, on the entrance of each dwelling

(Ex 12,7.22). His flesh was eaten during the course of a rapid meal*, taken in the manner of guests about to go on a journey (12,8-11). These nomadic and domestic traits suggest a very ancient origin for the Passover: it could have been the sacrifice which the Israelites asked of Pharaoh to celebrate in the desert (3,18; 5,1ff). It thus goes back beyond Moses and the departure from Egypt. But it is the exodus which gave it its definitive meaning.

2. *Passover and exodus.* The great springtime of Israel occurred when God liberated His people from the Egyptian yoke by a series of providential interventions, the most striking of which is expressed in the tenth plague: the killing of the first-born of the Egyptians (Ex 11,5; 12,12.29f). To this event, tradition later joined the offering of the first-born of the flock and the redeeming of the first-born Israelite (13,1f.11-15; Nm 3,13; 8,17). But this parallel comparison remains secondary. What matters is that the Passover coincides with the deliverance of the Israelites: it became the memorial of the exodus*, the greatest event of their history. It recalled that God had struck Egypt and *spared* His faithful (12,26f; 13,8ff). From now on such will be the meaning of the Passover and the new meaning of its name.

Pasch is the equivalent of the Greek *pascha*, derived from the Aramaic *pasḥā* and the Hebrew *pesaḥ*. The origin of this name is disputed. Some give it a foreign etymology, Assyrian (*pasahu*, to appease) or Egyptian (*pa-sh*, the remembrance; *pē-sah*, the blow); but none of these hypotheses is compelling. The Bible associates *pesaḥ* with the verb *pāsaḥ*, which means either to limp, or perform a ritual dance around a sacrifice (1 K 18,21.26), or figuratively, "to jump," "to pass," "to spare." The Passover is the *Passage* of Yahweh who *passed over* the Israelite houses while He struck those of the Egyptians (Ex 12,13.23.27; cf Is 31,5).

3. *Passover and unleavened bread.* In time, another feast was fused with the Passover. This feast of the Unleavened Bread was originally distinct but became associated because of its springtime date (Ex 12,15-20). The Passover was celebrated on the 14th of the month; the Unleavened Bread was finally fixed from the 15th to the 21st. These unleavened loaves accompanied the offering of the first-fruits of the harvest* (Lv 23,5-14; Dt 26,1). The removal of the old leaven was a rite of purity and of annual renewal, whose origin is thought to be either nomadic or agricultural. Whatever it may be, Israelite tradition also associated this rite with the departure from Egypt (Ex 23,15; 34, 18). It recalled the haste of the departure, so swift that the Israelites had to carry off their dough before it was leavened (Ex 12,34.39). In the liturgical calendars, the feasts of the Passover and Unleavened Bread are sometimes distinguished (Lv 23,5-8; cf Ezr 6,19-22; 2 Ch 35,17) and sometimes confused (Dt 16,1-8; 2 Ch 30,1-13).

At any rate, it is the deliverance of the exodus which is made present in the annual Passovers, and this profound meaning of the festival is felt with more intensity at the important stages of Israelite history: that of Sinai (Nm 9) and of the entrance into Canaan (Js 5); that of the reforms of Hezekiah around 716 (2 Ch 30), and of Josiah around 622 (2 K 23,21ff); that of the postexilic re-establishment in 515 (Ezr 6,19-22).

4. *Passover and the repetitions of the exodus.* The liberation from the Egyptian yoke is recalled on each occasion that Israel undergoes another enslavement:

Under the Assyrian yoke, toward 710, Isaiah hails deliverance as a passover night (30,29), when God will spare (*pasah*) Jerusalem (31,5; cf 10,26). One hundred years later Jeremiah celebrates the liberations of the exiles of 721 as a new exodus (Jr 31,2-21) and, according to the Greek of the LXX, as the exact anniversary of the first: "See, I will bring back the children of Israel, says God, on the feast of the Passover!" (Jr 31,8=Greek 38,8).

Under the babylonian yoke Jeremiah says that the return of the deported people of 597 will occupy the place of the Exodus in the memory of Israel (23,7f); and the Second Isaiah foretells the end of the exile* (587-538) as the decisive Exodus, which will eclipse the earlier one (Is 40,3-5; 41,17-20; 43,16-21; 49,9-11; 55, 12-13; cf 63,7—64,11). The gathering together of the dispersed (49,6) will be the work of the Lamb-Servant* (53,7), who will also become the light of the nations and who, together with the paschal lamb, will serve as a type of the Savior to come.

5. *The Passover, festival of the temple.* Thus, the Passover has evolved through the centuries. Some qualifications, some modifications took place. The most important was the innovation of Deuteronomy which transformed the old family celebration into a feast of the temple* (Dt 16,1-8). Perhaps this legislation saw a begin-

ning of realization under Hezekiah (2 Ch 30; cf Is 30,29). In any case, it is established as a fact under Josiah (2 K 23,21ff; 2 Ch 35). The Passover thus takes its place within the general centralization of worship*. Its rite is adapted: blood is poured out over the altar (2 Ch 35,11) and priests and Levites are the principal ministers in the ceremony.

After the exile, the Passover became the festival *par excellence*; its omission entailed a veritable excommunication for the Jews (Nm 9,13). All the circumcised, and they alone, must take part in it (Ex 12,43-49); in case of necessity, it can be put off for a month (Nm 9,9-13; cf 2 Ch 30,2ff). These qualifications of priestly legislation fixed a jurisprudence henceforth unchangeable. Outside the holy city, the Passover was doubtless celebrated here and there in family style, as was certainly the case with the Jewish colony at Elephantine in Egypt, according to a document of the year 419. But the sacrificing of the lamb was progressively eliminated from these private celebrations, which from now on were eclipsed by the solemnity in Jerusalem.

6. *Passover, the time of God's great works.* Thus, the Passover became one of the great pilgrimages* of the liturgical year. In Judaism it takes on a very rich meaning, developed by the Targum of Ex 12,42: Israel saved from bondage suggests the world drawn out of chaos, Isaac saved from death and mankind rescued from its misery by the longed for Messiah. These ideas find much support in the Bible:

a) *Passover and creation*: creation and redemption are in fact often linked together, especially in the great paschal Hallel: Ps 136, 4-15; cf Ho 13,4 (Greek); Jr 32,17-21; Is 51,9f; Ne 9; Ps 33,6f; 74,13-17; 77,17-21; 95,5-9; 100, 3; 124,4-8; 135,6-9; Ws 19. If God is able to divide the Red Sea (Ex 14,21), it is because He first divided the ocean at the beginning of time (Gn 1,6).

b) *Passover and Isaac*: similarly, if God can save the sons of Jacob, it is because He first saved their ancestors. It is suggested that Abraham is looking forward to the Exodus (Gn 15,13f), and for him the guarantee of this is the safety of Isaac (Gn 22). But Isaac is supposed to have been offered up on Zion (2 Ch 3,1), as the paschal lamb was to be later on (Dt 16), and also saved from the sword (Gn 22,12) like Israel later on (Ex 12,23; cf 1 Ch 21,15). Isaac is saved by the ram and Israel by the lamb. At his circumcision* Isaac sheds blood that is already rich in expiatory* value (Ex 4,24-26), as the blood of the paschal victims will be later on (Ez 45,18-24). But above all Isaac is ready to shed all his blood, thus deserving to foreshadow *the* paschal lamb: Jesus Christ (He 11,17-19).

c) *Passover and messianic era*: all God's interventions in the past give rise to the hope of a decisive intervention in the future. The final salvation (=eschatological) is seen as a new creation (Is 65,17), an irreversible exodus (65, 22f), a total victory* over evil, and paradise* regained (65,25). The envoy to whom God gives the task of setting this transformation in motion is none other than the Messiah* (11,1-9); so strong is this idea that the Jews look for his arrival on each paschal night. And since some continue to see the Messiah as a warrior, there is here a danger of a re-awakening of nationalism: and it is often at the time of the Passover that political movements appear (Lk 13,1ff) or that religious feelings are aroused (Ac 12,1-4). And during the Roman occupation the authorities are on the alert to preserve order during the paschal festivities and every year at this time the procurator goes up to Jerusalem. But religious faith can also see beyond this excitement and keep free from compromise: it leaves it to God to fix the time and the manner of the intervention of the Messiah whom He is to send.

II. THE PASSOVER OF JESUS

Indeed the Messiah did come. To begin with, Jesus took part in the Jewish Passover; His aim was to perfect it. He would finally supplant and fulfill it.

At the time of the Passover, Jesus uttered words and performed actions which little by little changed its meaning. Thus we have the Passover of the only *Son**, who stays behind close to the Holy of Holies because He knows that there He is close to His Father (Lk 2,41-51); the Passover of the new *temple**, where Jesus purified the temporary sanctuary and announced the definitive sanctuary, His risen body (Jn 2,13-23; cf 1,14.51; 4,21-24); the Passover of the multiplied *bread**, which will be His body* offered in sacrifice (Jn 6); finally and above all the Passover of the new *Lamb*, in which Jesus takes the place of the paschal victim, institutes the new paschal meal, and effects His own exodus, the "passage" from this sinful world to the kingdom* of the Father (Jn 13,1).

The evangelists understood well Jesus' intentions and, with various nuances, cast light upon them. The synoptics describe the last meal* of Jesus (even if it was consumed on the eve of the Passover) as a paschal meal: the supper is taken within the walls of Jerusalem and it is set in a liturgy which includes, among other things, the recitation of the Hallel (Mk 14,26 p). But it is the meal of a new Passover: onto the ritual blessings intended for bread* and wine*, Jesus grafts the institution of the eucharist*. In giving His body* to eat and His blood* poured out to drink, He describes His death as the sacrifice of the Passover of which He is the new Lamb (Mk 14,22-24 p). John prefers to emphasize this fact by inserting several allusions to Jesus the Lamb into his gospel (Jn 1,29.36), and in making coincide, on the afternoon of the 14th Nisan, the sacrificing of the lamb (18,28; 19,14.31.42) and the death on the cross of the true paschal victim (19,36).

III. THE CHRISTIAN PASSOVER

1. *The Sunday Passover.* Crucified on the eve of a Sabbath* day (Mk 15,42 p; Jn 19,31), Jesus arose on the day after this same Sabbath; the first day of the week* (Mk 16,2 p). It is also on the first day that the apostles find their risen Lord: He appears to them in the course of a meal which is a new version of the supper (Lk 24,30.42f; Mk 16,14; Jn 20,19-26; 21,1-14 [?]; Ac 1,4). And so, on the first day of the week the assembled Christians are going to join together for the breaking of the bread (Ac 20,7; 1 Co 16,2). This day would soon receive a new name: the day* of the Lord, *dies Domini*, Sunday (Ap 1,10). It recalls to Christians the resurrection* of Christ, unites them to Him in His eucharist, turns them toward the hope of His parousia (1 Co 11,26).

2. *The annual Passover.* Besides the Sunday Pasch, there is also a new content: the Jews celebrated their deliverance from a foreign yoke, and awaited a national Messiah-liberator while Christians celebrate their liberation* from sin* and death*, uniting themselves to Christ crucified and risen by sharing life eternal with Him, and turn their hope toward His glorious parousia.

On that night* which shines like the day, to prepare for their encounter in the holy supper with the Lamb of God who bears and carries away the sins of the world, they come together for a vigil where the account of the exodus is read to them with a new depth (1 P 1,13-21); baptized, they constitute the people* of God in exile (17), they go forward with loins* girded (13), delivered from evil, toward the promised land of the kingdom* of heaven. Since Christ, their paschal victim, has been sacrificed, they ought to celebrate the festival not with the old leaven of wicked conduct, but with the unleavened bread of purity and truth* (1 Co 5, 6ff). With Christ, they have personally lived the mystery of Easter by dying to sin and rising to a new life* (R 6,3-11; Col 2,12). This is why the feast of the resurrection* very soon became the privileged moment of baptism*, the resurrection of Christians in whom the paschal mystery is relived. The controversy of the 2nd century over the date of Easter left intact this profound meaning which underlines the final passing of the Jewish feast.

3. *The eschatological Passover.* The paschal mystery will be achieved by Christians through death, resurrection, encounter with the Lord. The earthly Passover prepares them for this last "passage," that Passover of the hereafter. In fact, the word *Passover* designates not only the mystery of the death and resurrection of Christ, nor the weekly or annual eucharistic rite, but it indicates also the heavenly banquet toward which we are all journeying. The Apocalypse lifts our eyes toward the Lamb still marked by His torments, but living and standing upright. Invested with glory, He draws His martyrs* to Himself (Ap 5,6-12; 12,11). According to His own words, Jesus has truly fulfilled the Passover by the eucharistic oblation of His death, by His resurrection, by the permanent sacrament of His sacrifice, and finally by His parousia (Lk 22,16), which is to unite us in the joy of the final banquet in the kingdom of His Father (Mt 26, 29).

→Apparitions of Christ—Baptism IV 1.4—Blood OT 3 b—Bread II 3—Calamity 1—Church IV 1—Day of the Lord NT III 3—Eucharist II 1—Exodus—Feasts—First Fruits I 1, II—Lamb of God 2—Meal II—Memory—Night—Pentecost I, II 2 b—Pilgrimage OT 2; NT—Preach I 2.3.4—Redemption—Resurrection NT—Sacrifice NT I, II 1.

PEB phmcn

PATIENCE

In dealing with His "stiff-necked" people, just as in dealing with sinful nations, God revealed His patience; for He loved them and wished to save them. This divine patience of which Jesus is the supreme revelation and for which He is the perfect model should be imitated by men (E 5,1; Mt 5,45). Following the example of his master, the disciple will have to face persecution and trials* with constant and joyful fidelity while filled with hope*. More humbly, then, he should bear daily the faults of his neighbor in all meekness and charity.

I. GOD'S PATIENCE

OT

"God affirms His justice* while not taking into account the sins committed during the time of divine patience" (R 3,25f). The OT is conceived by St. Paul as a time* when God was putting up with the sins of His people and other nations, with the intention of manifesting His salvific justice "in the present time" (cf 1 P 3,20; R 9,22ff). During its history, the chosen people realized more and more deeply this patience of God. At the time of the revelation made to Moses, Yahweh proclaimed: "God of tender love and pity, slow to anger, rich in grace* and fidelity, who is all merciful, bears with iniquity, wickedness, and sin"; but He is also the one who allows nothing to go unpunished, who chastises the iniquities of the fathers on their children and their children's children unto the third and fourth generation (Ex 34,6f; cf Nm 14,18). Subsequent revelations shall insist more and more on the patience, the merciful love of the Father who "knows of what we are made; slow to anger and full of love, He deals with us not according to our iniquities" (Ps 103, 8; cf Si 18,8-14). Although the themes of anger and judgment never disappear, the prophets put more emphasis upon divine pardon*. Certain texts show God always ready to repent of His threats (Jl 2,13f; Jon 4,2). But God's patience is never weakness; it calls to conversion: "Return to Yahweh your God, for He is loving and merciful, slow to anger, rich in mercy..." (Jl 2,13; cf Is 55,6). Israel gradually understands that it is not the only beneficiary of this patience; the nations are also loved by Yahweh. The story of Jonah is a reminder that the mercy of God is available to all men who are repentant.

NT

1. *Jesus*, by His attitude toward sinners and His teaching, illustrates and makes incarnate the divine patience. He reproaches His impatient and vindictive disciples (Lk 9,55). The parables of the barren fig tree (13,6-9), the prodigal son (15), and the unmerciful servant (Mt 18,23-35) are just revelations of the patience of God who wishes that sinners be saved, as the lessons of patience and love employed with His disciples. Jesus' courage in His passion, which is given special emphasis by Luke, will become the model of all patience for men subjected to persecution* but who begin to understand only now the meaning and the redemptive value of their sufferings.

2. The *apostles* see in the apparent delay of Jesus' return a manifestation of divine long-suffering: "The Lord does not delay accomplishing what He has promised, but He is patient toward you, wishing that no one perish, but that all repent" (2 P 3,9.15). But if man scorns this "treasure of goodness, of patience, of God's long-suffering," he amasses against himself, by his hard and unrepentant heart, a treasure of anger in the day of wrath* when the just judgment of God will be revealed (R 2,5). This is why, today, as long as God's daily patience and His call to repentance endure, the elect must hear His Word* and endeavor to enter into God's peace* (He 3,7—4,11).

II. MAN'S PATIENCE

Man must be inspired by God's patience and by Jesus' patience. In the suffering and persecution that God allows, man must draw his strength* from God who offers hope* and salvation*. In daily life, a man's patience with his brethren will be one of the signs of his love for them.

1. *Before God* who tests by sufferings or permits persecution, the man who gradually discovers the meaning of these sufferings learns to relate himself with regard to them with a patience that "bears fruit in him."

Job understood that suffering is not necessarily a chastisement for sin*, and in the face of it shows his patience. It is really a testing of his faith*. Faced with the mystery he submits humbly, but still without perceiving the meaning or the value of his trial. This was the patience of the persecuted Jewish people who steadfastly bore trials, all destined for the establishment of the Messianic kingdom* (1 and 2 M; Dn 12,12). Must not the just who are oppressed trust with persevering constancy in the Word and in the love of Yahweh (Ps 130,5; 25,3.5.21; Si 2)?

The Christian who knows that "Christ ought to have suffered in order to enter into His glory*" must, after His example, faithfully submit to trials and persecutions*. He bears them with hope of salvation in the time of Jesus' glorious second coming, and he knows that he cooperates, through his sufferings and patience, with the Savior; he "shares in the sufferings of Christ in order to be glorified with Him" (Ph 3,10; R 8,17). In adversity, he will take "the prophets who have spoken in the name of the Lord as models of suffering and patience" (Jm 5,10), and in general, all the great servants of God in the OT (He 6,12; 11), particularly Abraham (He 6,15) and Job (Jm 5,11). But, above all, he will imitate Jesus' patience (Ac 8,32; He 12,2f; 2 Th 3,5), and with eyes fixed on Him he "will run steadfastly in the trial that is set before him" (He 12,1f). This patience, just like love, is a "fruit of the spirit" (G 5,22; cf 1 Co 10,13; Col 1,11); ripened by trial (R 5,3ff; Jm 1,2ff), constancy produces in its turn the hope which does not deceive (R 5,5).

Strengthened in this way by God and consoled by the Scriptures (R 15,4), the Christian can remain faithful* in bearing trials endured for the name of Jesus (Ap 2,10; 3,21). Thus, he obtains the beatitude* promised to those who persevere until the end (Mt 10,22; cf Mt 5,11f; Jm 1,12; 5,11; cf Dn 12,12), and this will avail especially at the time of the great final tribulations (Mk 13,13; Lk 21,19). As for the apostles*, they are called to a union that is still closer with the passion and the patience of Christ. It is by their "constancy in tribulations, in distress, in anguish" that they proclaim themselves in all things the ministers of Christ (2 Co 6,4; 12,12; 1 Tm 6,11; 2 Tm 2,10; 3,10); and it is by their suffering and their patience that the Christ life is manifested in their bodies. Since death does its work in them, life can do its work in Christians (2 Co 4,10-12).

2. *Before his neighbor* who angers him, the wise man will remind himself that "a patient man is worth more than a hero, a man who is master of himself is worth more than a warrior who takes villages" (Pr 16,32; cf 25,15; Qo 7,8). Above all, he will imitate Jesus' patience toward His apostles and toward sinners. Far from being

without mercy (Mt 18,23-35), he will be tolerant (5,45); his daily patience will reveal his love* (1 Co 13,4). In order to live in accordance with his vocation, he "will support others with charity, in all humility, meekness, and patience" (E 4,2; Col 3,12f; 1 Th 5,14). This is the way he will be a true son of the patient God who loves, who pardons, and who wishes to save; and a disciple of Jesus, meek and humble of heart (Mt 11,29).

→Education—Faithfulness—Hardness of Heart I 2 b—Hope—Meekness—Mercy OT I 2 a—Persecution II 1.2—Poor NT III 3—Silence 1 Suffering—Trial/Temptation NT II—Watch—Wrath *A* 2; *B* OT III 1.

RD rco'c

PEACE

Man desires peace from the very depths of his being. But he is frequently ignorant of the nature of the benefit for which he intensely aspires; and the paths he follows in order to obtain it are not always the ways of God. So he must learn from sacred history in what the quest for true peace consists and he must hear God proclaiming the gift of this peace in Jesus Christ.

I. PEACE, PERFECT HAPPINESS

To appreciate at its full value the reality concealed beneath this word, one must sense the earthly flavor which subsists in the Semitic expression even in its most spiritual conception. We find it this way in the Bible right up through the last book of the NT.

1. *Peace and well-being.* The Hebrew word *šālōm* is derived from a root which, according to its usages, designates the fact of being intact, complete (Jb 9,4); e.g., to complete a house (1 K 9,25), or the action of re-establishing things to their former state, their integriy; e.g., "to appease" a creditor (Ex 21,34), to fulfill a vow (Ps 50,14). Biblical peace, then, is not only the "pact" which permits a tranquil life, nor the "time of peace" in opposition to "the time of war*" (Qo 3,8; Ap 6,4). It also indicates the well-being of daily existence, the state of the man who lives in harmony with nature, with himself, with God. Concretely, it is blessing*, rest*, glory*, riches, salvation*, life*.

2. *Peace and happiness.* "To be in good health" and "to be in peace" are two parallel expressions (Ps 38,4). To ask how someone is getting along, to inquire if all is going well, one says: "Is he in peace?" (2 S 18,32; Gn 43,27). Abraham who died in an old age happy and full of days (Gn 25,8), went away in peace (Gn 15, 15; cf Lk 2,29). In a broader sense, peace is security. Gideon need no longer fear* death before the heavenly apparition (Jg 6,23; cf Dn 10,19); Israel has no longer to dread its enemies*, thanks to Joshua the conqueror (Js 21, 44; 23,1), to David (2 S 7,1), to Solomon (1 K 5,4; 1 Ch 22,9; Si 47,13). Finally, peace is concord in a life of fraternity: my closest companion, my friend, is "the man of my peace" (Ps 41,10; Jr 20,10). It is mutual confidence which frequently sanctions a covenant* (Nm 25, 12; Si 45,24) or a treaty among good neighbors (Js 9,15; Jg 4,17; 1 K 5,26; Lk 14,32; Ac 12,20).

3. *Peace and salvation.* All these goods, material and spiritual, are contained in the greeting, in the wish for peace (in Arabic, the *salaam*) in which, in the OT and the NT, one says "good day" and "goodbye," whether in conversation (Gn 26,29; 2 S 18,29) or in writing (e.g., Dn 3, 98; Phm 3). Now, if it is fitting to wish peace or to ask about the peaceful disposition of the visitor (2 K 9,18), it is because peace is a state of conquering or defending; it is victory* over some enemy. Gideon and Ahab hope to return in peace, that is, as victors in war (Jg 8,9; 1 K 22,27f). In the same way, the success of an exploration is wished for (Jg 18,5f), the end of Hannah's sterility (1 S 1,17), the healing of wounds (Jr 6,14; Is 57,18f). Finally, one offers "peace sacrifices*" (*salutaris hostia*) which signify communion* between God and man (Lv 3,1).

4. *Peace and justice.* Peace, then, is what is good in opposition to what is bad (Pr 12,20; Ps 28,3; cf Ps 34,15). "No peace for the wicked" (Is 48,22); on the contrary, "behold the just man: there is a posterity for the man of peace" (Ps 37,37); "the humble will possess the land and will taste the delights of an unfathomable peace" (Ps 37,11; cf Pr 3,2). Peace is the sum of the benefits granted to justice*: to have a fruitful land, to eat to fullness, to dwell in security, to sleep without fear, to triumph over one's enemies, to be multiplied; and all this, in a word, because God is with us (Lv 26,1-13). Peace, then, far from being only an absence of war, is the fullness of happiness.

II. PEACE, GIFT OF GOD

If peace is the fruit and sign of justice*, how then can godless men be in peace (Ps 73,3)? The answer to this agonizing question will be given all through sacred history: conceived at first as an earthly happiness, peace appears increasingly as a spiritual good by reason of its heavenly source.

1. *The God of peace.* At the outset of biblical history, Gideon is seen building an altar to "Yahweh Shalom" (Jg 6,24). God who rules over heaven (Jb 25,2) can indeed create peace (Is 45,7). It is from Him, therefore, that this benefit is expected. "Yahweh is great, wishing peace for His servant" (Ps 35,27). He blesses Israel (Nm 6,26), His people (Ps 29,11), the house of David (1 K 2,33), the priesthood (Ml 2,5). From that time on, whoever places confidence* in Him can lie down to sleep in peace (Ps 4,9; cf Is 26,3). "Pray for peace over Jerusalem! May those who love you be in security!" (Ps 112,6; cf Ps 125,5; 128,6).

2. *Give peace, O Lord!* Man obtains this divine gift through confident prayer, but also through an "activity of justice," for according to God's own plan he ought to cooperate in the establishment of peace on earth; this cooperation shows itself ambiguous because of ever-present sin*. The history of the time of the judges is that of God raising up liberators entrusted with regaining peace which Israel has lost through its transgressions. David thinks he has accomplished his task when he has delivered the land from its enemies (2 S 7,1). Solomon is called the ideal king, the peaceful king (1 Ch 22,9), under whose reign the two peoples* of the North and South are fraternally united (1 K 5).

3. *The struggle for peace.*

a) The prophetic combat. This ideal very quickly becomes corrupted and the kings seek to procure peace for themselves not as the fruit of divine justice, but by means of political alliance, frequently godless. This is illusory conduct seemingly authorized by the apparently prophetic word of certain men, less anxious to hear God than "to have something to bite" (Mi 3,5): in a complete state of sin, they dare to proclaim a lasting peace (Jr 14,13). Toward the year 850, Micaiah, son of Imlah, undertakes to dispute with these false prophets about the word and the reality of peace (1 K 22,13-28).

The struggle becomes very sharp on the occasion of the siege of Jerusalem (cf Jr 23,9-40). The gift of peace requires the suppression of sin, and then a preliminary chastisement. Jeremiah makes the accusation: "They would repair on the surface the injury to my people in saying: Peace! Peace! And yet there is no peace" (Jr 6,14). Ezekiel cries out: "Enough whitewashings! The wall must fall" (Ez 13,15f). But when the wall is pulled down, those who were prophesying disaster, sure from then on that illusion was no longer possible, proclaimed peace again. To the exiles, God announces: "I myself know the plan I have for you, a plan of peace and not of woe: to give you a future full of hope" (Jr 29,11; cf 33,9). A covenant of peace will be concluded, taming wild beasts, assuring security, blessing (Ez 34,25-30); for, says God, "I will be with them" (Ez 37,26).

b) *Eschatological peace.* This controversy over peace underlies the prophetic message in its overall make-up. When it becomes an essential element in eschatological preaching, true peace is disengaged from its earthly limitations and from its sinful counterfeits. Threatening oracles of the prophets ordinarily close with an announcement of abundant restoration (Ho 2, 20...; Am 9,13...; etc). Isaiah dreams of the "prince of peace" (Is 9,5; cf Ze 9,9f) who will give a "peace without end" (Is 9,6) and open a new paradise*, for "it is He who will be the peace" (Mi 5,4). Nature will be submissive to man, the two separated kingdoms will be reconciled, the nations* will live in peace (Is 2, 2...; 11,1...; 32,15-20; cf 65,25), "the just man will flourish" (Ps 72,7). This gospel* of peace (Na 2,1), the deliverance from Babylon (Is 52, 7; 55,12), is accomplished by the suffering Servant* (53,5), who announces by His sacrifice what the price of peace will be. From then on, "peace to the far and the near! Wounds will be healed" (57,19). The governors of the people will be peace and justice (60,17). "I am coming to make peace spread over (Jerusalem) like a river, and the glory* of the nations as an overflowing torrent" (66,12; cf 48,18; Ze 8,12).

c) *Finally the wisdom reflection* takes up the question of true peace. Faith affirms: "Those who love you have great peace, and for them there is no scandal" (Ps 119,165); but events seem to contradict this (Ps 73,3), raising the problem of retribution. This will be fully resolved (Si 44,14) only by belief in perfect and personal survival: "The souls of the just are in the hand of God...in the view of the foolish they seem dead...but they are in peace" (Ws 3,1ff); that is, in the fullness of good things and communion with the One who gives them, beatitude*.

III. THE PEACE OF CHRIST

The hope of the prophets and sages becomes a reality granted in Jesus Christ, for sin has been conquered in Him and by Him. But so long as sin is not dead in every man, as long as the Lord has not come on the last day*, peace remains a future benefit. The prophetic message retains, then, its value: "the fruit of justice is sown in peace by those who practice peace" (Jm 3,18; cf Is 32,17). Such is the message which the NT proclaims, from Luke to John, passing through Paul.

1. *Luke*, in his Gospel, sketches in a special way the portrait of the peaceful king. At His birth, angels announced peace to men whom God loves (Lk 2,14). This message is repeated by the joyful disciples escorting the king* as He enters the city (19,38); but Jerusalem* has no wish to accept Him (19,42). In the mouth of the peaceful king, the prayer of earthly peace becomes the announcement of a salvation*. As a good Jew, Jesus says: "Go in peace!"; but with this expression He restores health to the hemorrhagic woman (8,48 p), forgives the sins of the repentant sinful woman (7,50), thus indicating His victory* over the power of sickness* and of sin*. Like Jesus, the disciples offer salvation in Jesus (10,5-9) to the towns, with their greeting of peace. But this salvation comes to overturn the peace of this world*: "Do you think that I have come to bring peace on earth? No, I tell you, but division" (12,51). Nor is Jesus content with uttering the same threats as the prophets against all false security (17,26-36; cf 1 Th 5,3). He separates the members of the same family. Following the expression of a Christian poet, it is not war which He came to destroy, but rather peace which He came to add —that peace of Easter which follows final victory (Lk 24,36). The disciples go out to radiate to the ends of the world the *pax israelitica* (cf Ac 7,26; 9,31; 15,33) which is, on the religious level, like a transfiguration of the *pax romana* (cf 24,2); for God has announced peace through Jesus Christ in showing Himself "the Lord of all" (10,36).

2. *Paul*, in the greetings of his letters, ordinarily joins grace* to peace, thus affirming its origin and stability. He shows above all the link which it has with the redemption*. Being "our peace," Christ has made peace; He has reconciled the two peoples, uniting them into one sole body (E 2,14-22). He has "reconciled all creatures through Him, whether on the earth or in the heavens, making peace through the blood* of His cross*'" (Col 1,20). It is, then, because "we are gathered together in one same body" that "the peace of Christ reigns in our hearts" (Col 3,15), thanks to the Spirit* who weaves between us as one solid bond (E 4,3). Every believer, once justified, is in peace through Jesus Christ with God (R 5,1), the God of love and peace (2 Co 13,11), who sanctifies him "completely" (1 Th 5,23). Like charity and joy*, peace is the fruit* of the Spirit (G 5,22; R 14,17). It is eternal life anticipated here below (cf 8,6); it surpasses all understanding (Ph 4,7), endures in tribulation (R 5,1-5), shines forth in our relations with men (1 Co 7,15; R 12,18; 2 Tm 2,22), until the day* when the God of peace who has raised up Jesus (He 13,20), having destroyed Satan (R 16,20), will restore all things in their original integrity.

3. *John* makes the revelation still more explicit. For him as for Paul, peace is the fruit of the sacrifice* of Jesus (Jn 16,33). As in the synoptic tradition, peace has nothing to do with the peace of this world.

Following the OT which saw the supreme benefit of peace in the presence* of God among His people (e.g., Lv 26,12; Ez 37,26), John shows the source and reality of peace in the presence of Jesus. Here lies one of the characteristic traits of his perspective. When sadness comes over the disciples who are going to be separated from their master, Jesus reassures them: "My peace I leave you, my peace I give unto you" (Jn 14,27). This peace is no longer linked to His presence on earth, but to His victory* over the world*. Victorious also over death*, Jesus gives, with His peace, the Holy Spirit and power over sin (20,19-23).

4. *"Blessed vision of peace."* Unshaken in the hope which causes him to contemplate the heavenly Jerusalem* (Ap 21,2), the Christian earnestly hopes to realize happiness: "Blessed are the peacemakers!" (Mt 5,9), for this is to live as God and to be a son* of God in the only Son, Jesus. He strives, then, with all his strength, to establish concord and tranquility here below.

Now this Christian policy of earthly peace shows itself the more effective to the extent it is free from illusion. Three principles guide its indefatigable pursuit.

Only the universal acknowledgment of the lordship* of Christ by the entire universe at the last coming will establish definitive and universal peace. Only the Church, which transcends distinction of race, class, and sex (G 3,28; Col 3, 11), is the locus, the sign, and the source on earth of peace among peoples; for she is the body of Christ and the giver of the Spirit. Finally, only justice* before God and among men is the foundation of peace; for it is justice which eliminates sin, the source of all division. The Christian will sustain his peacemaking effort by listening to God who alone gives peace, speaking through the following psalm, in which are gathered together the attributes of the God of history: "What God proclaims is peace for His people...Truth shall spring from the earth, and justice shall look down from heaven. Yahweh Himself will give His benefits, and our land shall yield its increase. Justice shall walk before Him and peace along the path of His steps" (Ps 85,9-14).

→Beatitude—Blessing II 1, IV 3—Cares 2— Jerusalem OT III 3—Reconciliation—Rest— Salvation OT I 2—Violence IV 3—War.

XLD phmcn

PENTECOST

The word *Pentecost* indicates that the feast celebrated on that day takes place fifty days after the Passover. The object of this feast has evolved. At first it was an agrarian feast, but later it became a feast commemorating the historic fact of the covenant. Finally, it became the feast of the gift of the Holy Spirit, the commencement of the new covenant on earth.

I. OT AND JUDAISM

Pentecost, together with the Passover and Tabernacles, was one of the three feasts* when Israel had to present itself before Yahweh in the place chosen by Him in order to make a dwelling for His name (Dt 16,16).

1. In the beginning. it was the *feast of Harvest**, a day of joy and thanksgiving (Ex 23,16;

Nm 28,26; Lv 23,16ff). The first-fruits that the land had produced were to be offered at that time (Ex 34,22 where the feast is referred to as the feast of Weeks, a name which places it seven weeks after the Passover and the offering of the first sheaf: cf Lv 23,15).

2. Later, the feast was an anniversary. The covenant* had been concluded fifty days (Ex 19, 1-16) after the departure from Egypt which was celebrated by the Passover. Pentecost naturally became the *anniversary of the covenant*, no doubt, in the second century before the birth of Christ. It appears to be considered as such most generally in the beginning of the present era, according to the rabbinic writings and the Qumrân manuscripts.

II. CHRISTIAN PENTECOST

1. *The theophany.* The gift of the Spirit, together with the signs that accompany it, the wind and the fire*, are similar in character to the theophanies of the OT. A double miracle emphasizes the meaning of the Christian Pentecost: first of all, the apostles, to praise the wonders of God, expressed themselves in "tongues" (Ac 2,3). Speaking in tongues* is a charismatic* form of prayer that was found in the early Christian communities. Then, although unintelligible in itself (cf 1 Co 14,1-25), this speaking in tongues was understood by all present. The miracle of hearing these tongues is a sign of the universal vocation of the Church, for the audience had come from the most diverse regions of the earth (Ac 2,5-11).

2. *The meaning of the event.*

a) Eschatological outpouring of the Spirit. In quoting the prophet Joel (Jl 3,1-5), Peter showed that Pentecost fulfilled God's promises* because in the fullness of time* the Spirit was to be given to all (cf Ez 36,27). The precursor had announced the presence of the One who would baptize in the Holy Spirit (Mk 1,8). And Jesus, after His resurrection, had confirmed those promises: "within a few days you will be baptized in the Holy Spirit" (Ac 1,5).

b) The crowning of Christ's Passover. According to the primitive catechesis, Christ, dead, risen, and exalted at the right hand of the Father, completed His work by sending the Holy Spirit on the apostolic community (Ac 2,

23-33). Pentecost is the fullness of Easter.

c) The gathering together of the Messianic community. The prophets preached that the dispersed would be gathered together on the mountain of Zion and in this way the assembly of Israel would be united around Yahweh. Pentecost made the spiritual unity of the Jews and the proselytes of all nations a reality at Jerusalem. They were docile to the teaching of the apostles and they communicated in fraternal love* at the eucharistic* table (Ac 2,42ff).

d) A community opened to all people. The Spirit was given in view of a witness to be borne to the ends of the earth (Ac 1,8); the miracle of hearing the tongues emphasizes the fact that the first Messianic community was extended to all people (Ac 2,5-11). The "Pentecost of the pagans" (Ac 10,44ff) culminated in making this seen. The division made at Babel* (Gn 11,1-9) finds here its antithesis and its end.

e) Beginning of the mission. The Pentecost that gathered together the Messianic community was also the beginning of its mission. Peter's discourse "standing up with the Eleven" (Ac 2, 14) was the first act in the mission* given to them by Jesus: "You will receive a power, the Holy Spirit...You will then be my witnesses at Jerusalem, in all Judea, and Samaria, and as far as the ends of the earth" (1,8).

The fathers have compared this "baptism in the Holy Spirit," a sort of apostolic investiture in the Church, with the baptism of Jesus, the solemn theophany at the beginning of Jesus' public ministry. They indicate that in Pentecost there is the gift of the new Law* to the Church (cf Jr 31,33; Ez 36,27) and the new creation* (cf Gn 1,2). These themes are not expressed in Ac 2, but they depend on reality (the interior action of the Spirit and the re-creation that it effects).

3. *Pentecost, mystery of salvation.* If the exterior aspect of the theophany was passing, the gift* to the Church was definitive. Pentecost inaugurated the time when the Church, in its journey to the meeting with the Lord, receives constantly from Him the Spirit which gathers it in faith and charity, sanctifies it, and sends it on its mission. The Acts, "gospel of the Holy Spirit," reveal the permanence of this gift, the most excellent charism; both by the place of the Spirit in the direction and missionary activity of the Church (Ac 4,8; 13,2; 15,28; 16,6),

and by its more visible manifestations (4,31; 10,44ff). The gift of the Spirit qualifies "the fullness of time*" as the period which began at the ascension* and will find its completion in the last day* when the Lord will return.

→Charisms I 1—Church IV 1—Dispersion 2— Drunkenness 3—Feasts QT II 1—Fire NT II 2 —First Fruits I 1—Harvest I, III 2 c—Holy NT O—Mission NT III 2—Nations NT II 1 a— Sign NT II 1—Spirit of God NT III, IV— Tongue 2—Week 1.

PdS rco'c

PEOPLE

The theme of the people of God, in which are gathered together in one synthesis all the aspects of the life of Israel*, is as central in the OT as the theme of the Church*, the new people of God but also the body* of Christ, will be in the NT. The prophetic eschatology acts as a relay between the two: in the framework of the ancient covenant*, it announces in advance and describes ahead of time the people of the new covenant, expected at the "end of time."

A. THE PEOPLE OF THE OLD COVENANT

To designate human groups of a certain size, the Hebrew words *'am* and *goy* originally stressed two of the constituent elements: the community of blood and the stable sociological structure. But gradually they became specialized in the language of the OT: *'am* (in the singular) preferably designated Israel, the people of God; but *goyim* (in the plural) was reserved for foreign nations*, for the pagans (already in Nm 23,9). However, this usage admitted some exceptions. In the Greek Bible, *laos* in parallel fashion designated the people of God (more rarely *dēmos* when one would insist on the political organization), while *ethnē* (in the plural) is applied to pagan nations; but again there are exceptions. This linguistic fact shows that people felt the need of a special word to express the nature of Israel, a people so different from others because of the mystery of its calling that its national experience acquired a religious meaning, and an essential aspect of the plan of salvation began to reveal itself there.

I. THE TRANSCENDENCE OF THE PEOPLE OF GOD

1. *Election*, calling*, covenant**. Israel, as all other nations, belongs to human history; but from its beginnings, revelation presents it as passing beyond the historical order. If it exists, it is because God chose it (Dt 7,7; Is 41,8) and called it (Is 48,12), not for its population, nor its strength, nor its merits (Dt 7,7; 8,17; 9,4), but because of love* (Dt 7,8; Ho 11,1). Having thus distinguished it from others, He ransomed and delivered Israel in the exodus (Dt 6,12; 7,8; 8,14...; 9,26). Setting it up as an independent nation, He in a certain sense created it (cf Is 48,15), formed as an infant in its mother's womb (Is 44,2.24). The living consciousness of a nation totally dependent in regard to God accompanied then in Israel the awareness of its being a nation as such. Thereupon came the covenant*; and this foundation act emphasized that henceforth, for Israel, all will be settled in a twofold plan: that of history and that of faith. A sacred pact in which the twelve tribes are contracting parties is sealed in the blood* of a sacrifice* (Ex 24,8); Yahweh thereby becomes the God of Israel—and Israel, the people of Yahweh (cf Dt 29,12; Lv 26,12; Jr 7,23 etc.; Ez 11,20 etc.). In this manner a unique bond was forged between God and a human community. Whoever through circumcision* will join this community will also share in this bond (cf Gn 17,10...).

2. *Titles and functions of the people of God*. Israel is the holy* people consecrated to Yahweh, put aside for Him (Dt 7,6; 14,2), His own possession (Ex 19,5; Jr 2,3), His inheritance* (Dt 9,26). It is His flock (Ps 80,2; 94,7), His vine* (Is 5,1; Ps 80,9), His son* (Ex 4,22; Ho 11, 1), His spouse* (Ho 2,4; Jr 2,2; Ez 16,8). It is a "kingdom* of priests" (Ex 19,6), in which God rules over subjects vowed to His service. This finality of worship contained in the covenant shows at the same time what function Israel fulfills in regard to other nations: witness* of God exceeding all others (Is 44,8), it is the mediating people through whom the bond is again fashioned between God and the totality of humanity, in the sense that the praise of all the earth (Is 45,14f.23f) ascends toward God and all nations have a part in the blessing* of God (Gn 12,3; Jr 4,2; Si 44,21).

II. THE RELIGIOUS SIGNIFICANCE OF A NATIONAL EXPERIENCE

In virtue of the covenant, Israel then fulfills a paradox at the heart of human history. A specifically religious community, transcendent by its very nature, the people of God is at the same time a reality belonging to this world, assuming all the temporal elements which compose the life of peoples here below. As a consequence, its national experience, in which all others can recognize themselves, is going to take on a religious meaning which will shed light on faith.

1. *A community of race.* The people of Israel represents to itself its own internal unity as deriving from its unity of origin. The Hebrew* patriarchs are the fathers* of the race, and the memories of history anterior to the exodus are crystalized in the framework of a genealogy which, from Abraham*, leads through Isaac to Jacob-Israel, father of twelve sons who give their names to the twelve tribes. It is true that in the course of ages the race has assimilated a number of heterogeneous elements: from the departure of Egypt (Ex 12,38), to the desert (Nm 11,4; Jg 4,11), after the conquest of Canaan (Js 9; Jg 3,1...). But in later periods, one sees rather an increase of concern over the purity of Jewish blood: they prohibit foreign marriages, to protect the "holy race" (Ezr 9,2) against the pagan peoples who have idolatry in their blood. They idealize the past in numbering in the patriarchal genealogy certain strangers long before assimilated to Israel, such as the Calebite clans (1 Ch 2,18; cf Nm 32,12 and Gn 15,19). This is because the election of Israel has passed through its fathers: does one not see, at each step of their genealogies, the neighboring peoples separated in their ancestry from the plan of salvation (Gn 19,30; 21,8...; 25,1...; 36)? In order to participate in the promises and divine covenant, it is therefore necessary to be of the race of Abraham, the friend of God (Is 41,8; 51,2; cf 63,16; Jr 33,26; Ps 105,6; 2 Ch 20,7). A certain universalism stands on the horizon of thought, because Abraham was to become the "father of numerous peoples" (Gn 17,5f). But in practice, the strangers* who are converted to Judaism, the proselytes (Is 56,8), in fact are gathered into the chosen race to participate in its religious privileges. The common faith does not yet suffice to constitute the people of God; it has for a concrete foundation an ethnic branch chosen by God in the midst of others.

2. *A community of institutions.* The race of patriarchs is not a shapeless mass but an organized society. Its fundamental cells, the family and the clan (*mišpāhāh*), in which is found community of blood, continued through the centuries and survived even to the uprooting of the dispersion (Ezr 2; Ne 7). But in economic matters they control the ownership of flocks, of land, of the rights to pasture; they govern the customs such as the vengeance* of blood (Nm 35,19), the Levirate (Dt 25,5...), the right of ransom (Rt 4,3). It is through them that each individual becomes aware of a social belonging which protects and at the same time obliges him. The clans themselves group again into tribes, at root political unities; and the first form that the organized nation takes is that of a confederation of twelve tribes, bound together by the pact of the covenant (Ex 24,4; Js 24). When the Israelite state will take on a greater consistency, the centralized monarchy will be superimposed upon it, without, however, doing away with it (2 S 2,4; 5,3); so that after the fall of the monarchical edifice, when the nation will be dispersed, the confederation of tribes will remain the ideal of the Jewish restorers (cf Ez 48). Now, if this evolution of institutions is dictated by diverse historical factors, it depends above all upon a principle which exceeds the pressure of facts: the Law*, the essential foundations of which Moses secured and which in its development assures, through the course of the centuries, the permanence of the same spirit in ways and customs (cf Ne 8). Through it, all the institutions of Israel take on a meaning and a value in the functioning of the plan of God: it is the providential "pedagogue" for the people of the covenant (G 3,24).

3. *A community of destiny.* Parallel to the institutions which structure the nation, the community of destiny gives to its members a common soul: the experience of nomadic life, of oppression and deliverance, of wanderings in the desert, of battles for the possession of a fatherland, of the national unity dearly paid for and of the imperial zenith, of the political division preluding the destruction of two sections of the state, of disaster and dispersion...But these experiences have a religious significance: they are, in their own way, a concrete experience of the ways of God. Their luminous appearance clearly shows the gifts* of God to His people and makes them foresee His secret intentions; their somber side lets them feel the divine wrath* which is manifested in exemplary judg-

ments*. Thereafter, history becomes revelation*. From its secular experiences, the people of God draw fundamental patterns of thought in which the experiences which follow them are molded (cf 1 M 2,51...; 2 M 8,19). It finds in its past terms of reference to represent to itself its own future and to express the object of its hopes (cf Is 63,8...).

4. *Taking roots in a fatherland.* From the desert, its primitive habitat, the people of God was led into Canaan. This is the land where its fathers lived and where they have their tombs (Gn 23; 25,9; etc.); it is the promised land (Gn 12,7; 13,15), later given by God as an inheritance* (Ex 23,27...; Dt 9,1...; Jr 2,7; Ps 78,54f). It is the land conquered in the course of a human enterprise which fulfilled the plan of God (Js 1,13...; 24,11...). This is no longer, then, Canaan, a pagan land; it is the land of Israel, the holy land where God Himself, present in the midst of His people, has taken up His residence (1 K 8,15). Jerusalem*, dwelling of Yahweh and the political capital, is a visible sign of national and religious unity all together (Ps 122). Thus the dispersion* which follows upon the national catastrophe only strengthens the attachment of the people of God to its land. The Zionist mystique is born from the time of the decree of Cyrus (Ezr 1,2) and remains vivid in the succeeding centuries (Ezr 7). Even when they dwell in the midst of strangers, the Jews never feel totally uprooted, because in that land they still have a fatherland* where the tombs of their fathers are (Ne 2,3), and toward which they turn to pray (Dn 6,11).

5. *The community of language.* In conquering the holy land, Israel made from the "language of Canaan" (Is 19,18) its own language. In a people, language is one factor of unity, it assures a common way of thinking, it conveys a culture and a conception of the world; it is a true spiritual fatherland. But, in Israel, it is the divine revelation itself which is expressed in Hebrew, joining itself to the categories of thought forged by the Semitic culture and benefiting from the concrete and dynamic character of Hebrew. From century to century, a true national culture takes shape, in which one recognizes quite different human contributions (Canaanite, Assyro-Babylonian, Iranian, even Greek); but always revelation effects a filtering in it, eliminating that element which cannot be assimilated, giving new content to words and conceptions of the mind in relation to the plan

of God. Finally, when the Jews speak Aramaic or Greek, Hebrew nevertheless remains the "holy language." However, the practice of the Targums and the translation of the Septuagint then permit Aramaic and Greek tongues to convey in their turn the doctrine which has been revealed, and to do so without corruption. Thus the cultural evolution of Israel is dominated by the Word of God, fixed in the sacred Scriptures; but to make itself intelligible, the Word of God is poured into a Jewish mold.

6. *The community of worship.* In the societies of the ancient Orient, worship was an essential aspect of the life of the city. In Israel, the worship* of the one God is, from the time of the covenant, the supreme function of the nation. The Hebrew language has technical terms to describe the people as assembled in this function of worship. It forms a community (*'ēdāh*), a holy gathering (*miqrā'*), an assembly (*qāhāl*); and these terms transposed in Greek have given birth to the words *synagōgē* and *ekklēsia*. Searching for its ideal in the sacred community of the desert, such as the Pentateuch describes it, Judaism is certainly not yet a church* in the full sense of the term, for it remains tied to the temporal structures of a particular nation; but it already outlines in itself the traits of a church, since the specific characteristics of the people of Israel are pointed up with the utmost clarity in its quality of a worshiping community (*qāhāl*/*ekklēsia*).

III. THE OLD COVENANT: VALUE AND LIMITS

From the time of the old covenant, therefore, the social structure of the plan of God is already revealed: man will not be saved by God by extricating himself from history; he will not find God in the solitude of a life of religion cut off from the world. He will be united to God by participating in the life and destiny of the community chosen by God to be His people. This divine plan enjoys the beginning of its realization in Israel, for the members of the people of the covenant already possess in effect a life of faith*, which has for supports the institutions of the nation and the national history as well as the Word of God and the assemblies of worship. However, this is where the imperfect nature of this preparatory and provisional realization appears. The life of faith, as an experience of the relationship of the covenant with God, already constitutes here a positive reality containing within it the promise of final salvation. But it still remains tied to conditions that limit it from two points of view: it does not look beyond the order of earthly things nor the horizon of a single nation. And perhaps, through this very joining of a transcendent reality (the "people of God") with a national and temporal reality in which it finds a tangible support, something of a profound mystery has become intelligible to men: beginning from the experiences of Israel as a people of this world, the diverse aspects of the holy society in which the plan of salvation will be accomplished are little by little outlined under the veil of figures*.

B. THE PROMISE OF THE NEW PEOPLE

The economy founded on the old covenant had not only the limits of which we just spoke; it was incapable of "making anything perfect*" (He 7,19; 9,9; 10,1), incapable of realizing here below the "holy* people" which Israel had been called to become. The facts themselves have shown this, since the sins of Israel drew upon it the radical punishment* of exile* and dispersion*. The plan of God did not die for all that. The prophetic eschatology also announced for the "last times*" the coming of a new* economy in which God would find this perfect people of whom the ancient was a sketch.

I. THE PEOPLE
OF THE NEW COVENANT

1. *Superiority of the new covenant.* Like the Israel of old, the new people must be born from the initiative of God. But this time God will triumph over the sin* which had acted against His first plan: He will purify His people, change their heart*, send upon it His Spirit* (Ez 36, 26...). He will separate sinners from it so that He may preserve a humble and just remnant* (Is 10,20f; Zp 3,13; Jb 3,5). With this people "created" by Him (Is 65,18), He will conclude a new covenant* (Jr 31,31...; Ez 37,26). This people will be the "holy people" (Is 62,12), the flock (Jr 31,10), and the spouse* (Ho 2,21) of Yahweh. The interior justice thus described contrasts with the spiritual condition of Israel, a sinful people; it reminds one of the state of humanity anterior to the sin of its first father* (Gn 2).

2. *Universality of the new people.* At the same time, the limits of the plan of God are enlarged, for the nations* are going to join themselves to Israel (Is 2,2...). They will share with it the blessing* promised to Abraham (Jr 4,2; cf Gn 12,3) and the covenant, the mediator of which will be the mysterious Servant* of Yahweh (Is 42,6). The setting aside of Israel appears thus as a temporary stage in the unfolding of the divine plan. At the end of time, the primitive universalism will be taken up again.

II. THE SYMBOLIC IMAGE
OF THE NEW PEOPLE

In order to conjure up the new people in concrete fashion, the prophets have only to search the past experience of the people of Israel: if they remove the imperfections and shadows from it, it appears as in figure* in anticipation of the "last times."

1. *A new race.* Israel will enter into the new people because of its being the race of Abraham* (Is 41,8). But the nations* also will be joined to the people of the God of Abraham (Ps 47,10), so that they may become in their turn the spiritual posterity of the patriarch. To Zion, symbolic mother* of the holy people, all will say: "Mother!" (Ps 87). It is thus the whole human race which will find again its original unity* when the remnants of the nations, dispersed since the fate of Babel, will be gathered together (Is 66,18ff; cf Gn 10—11; Ze 14,17).

2. *Some new institutions.* To describe in advance the new people as an organized community, one still appeals to figurative institutions: The Law* written in the heart (Jr 31,33; Ez 36,27); reunion of the twelve tribes (Ez 48) and end of the bitterness between Israel and Juda (Ez 37,15...); royalty of the seed of David (Is 9; 11; Jr 23,5; Ez 34,23; Ze 9,9); etc. Here again universalism makes the boundaries of past institutions give way. The king*, son of David, rules over all the nations (cf Ps 2,72); especially, they all recognize the one God as their king (Ze 14,16; Ps 96,10); and His law is taught them to bring them to the light* (Is 2, 2...; 42,1.4). Thus, without losing their personalities, they are united to the people of God in an organic way.

3. *The events of salvation.* The historical experience of Israel likewise furnishes the means

of representing the events of salvation: a new exodus*, which will be like the first redemption* and deliverance (Jr 31,11; Is 43,16...; 44, 23); a new march across the desert*, renewing the prodigies of old (Ho 2,16; Jr 31,2; Is 40,3; 43,14; 48,21; 49,10); the return to the promised land (Ho 2,17; Jr 31,12; Ez 37,21), triumph of the king over the neighboring enemies in order to inaugurate a reign of peace (Is 9)...But once more the horizon is broadened: not only Samaria will share in the promised restoration, but even Sodom (Ez 16,53...), figure of the city of sin! The universal peace* thus re-established at the end of the history of salvation* (Is 2) will lead the human race to a state which it knew no more after the sin of Cain (cf Gn 4,8).

4. *The new holy land.* The holy land will naturally be the site of the assembling of the new Israel (Ez 34,14; Jr 31,10...). But it will then have a marvelous fecundity which will leave far behind it the most enthusiastic descriptions of Deuteronomy (Ez 47,12; Jl 4,18). Literally, this will be a paradise* gained (Ez 36,35; Is 51,3). Jerusalem*, its capital, will become the center of the entire world (Is 2). Thus, in a re-created universe (Is 65,17). God will forge the unity of all fatherlands* to assure to His elect a paradisiac peace and happiness (Ho 2,20; Is 65,17-25).

5. *The gathering of all tongues.* It is not in vain that God made the holy language out of the language of Canaan. When Egypt will be converted at the last times, it will invoke Yahweh in the holy language (Is 19,18...). But the prophetic eschatology goes much farther: God will make pure the lips* of all the peoples, so that each one can praise Him in his own tongue* (Zp 3,9). Thus in a worship* which has again become united, the assembling of the nations and tongues will be achieved (Is 66,18); this will put an end to the splintering of the human race and will be the sign of rediscovered spiritual unity, such as was at the beginnings of the plan of God (Gn 11,1).

6. *The new worship of God.* The eschatological worship* is clearly described in the characteristics of the Israelite worship (cf Ez 40—48). But it is remarkable that the universalism is their constantly affirmed. Through the common service* of the only God will humanity find its own unity (Is 2,2...; 55,6f; 66,20f). Its final mustering will take the form of pilgrimages in which the people of God will gather again

for the feast* of Tabernacles (Ze 14,16). The people will gather for meals* of worship through which it will enter into communion* with God (Is 25,6). Although the word does not appear in the text, one dreams of a new "holy assembly" analogous to the *qāhāl* (=*ekklēsia*) of the desert, in which the nations would rejoin the remnant of Israel.

III. THE ESCHATOLOGICAL PEOPLE AND THE ISRAEL OF HISTORY

The people of the new covenant is therefore imagined in advance to share in the historical experience of Israel, the worth of whose prefiguration we clearly see. The facts of the experience are however transcended on two points: the national framework is bypassed, and the new people is open to all humanity; humanity and the universe itself find again their original perfection, lost because of human sin.

But in this symbolic picture, there remain certain ambiguities for which the appeal to the experience of Israel is in part responsible. The restoration of the unity* of mankind around the people of the ancient covenant, around its king, its holy city, at times maintains a narrowness (cf Is 52,1), some nationalistic overtones (Is 60,12), even a warlike aspect (Ps 2; 72), which will tend to develop in the shape of the eschatological war* (Ez 38—39). And most of all, even if the happiness promised to the new people implies the removal of all moral and physical evil (suffering*: Is 65,19; death* itself: Is 25,8), the horizon most often remains temporal, riveted upon earthly joys*. Even the "people of the holy* ones of the most high" (Dn 7, 22.27), which tends to pass over these limits and takes on a transcendent appearance, seems to be given a dominion which resembles that of the powers of this world (Dn 7,27. cf 14).

To dissipate the ambiguity, it is necessary that with Christ and His Church the eschatological people enter in its turn into the field of human experience.

C. THE PEOPLE OF THE NEW COVENANT

In the Greek of the NT, rather than in the Septuagint, we find the specialized usage of the words *laos*, "people of God"; and *ethnē*; "pagan nations." But to define the community of salvation, bound to God by the new covenant, the idea of the *ekklēsia*, "assembly of worship," stands out before all others. However, the Church* of Christ, into which the people of the old covenant is invited to enter, followed by the other nations, remains truly a people, with all the connotations which this term implies. In fulfilling its foreshadowings, the eschatological reality does not abolish their meanings, but fulfills* them.

I. THE NEW PEOPLE

By the new covenant*, sealed in the blood of Jesus, God had, therefore, created a new people, for whom the word of Scripture is fulfilled in its plenitude: "You shall be my people and I will be your God" (2 Co 6,16; cf Lv 26,12; He 8,10; cf Jr 31,33; Ap 21,3). This is the people for whose sins Jesus atoned (He 2,17), the people He sanctified by His own blood* (13,12), the people of whom one becomes a member by faith* (G 3,7; R 4,3...). Thus the titles of Israel are now transferred to this new people: the special people of God (Tt 2,14; cf Dt 7,6), chosen race, holy nation, a purchased people (1 P 2,9; cf Ex 19,5 and Is 43,20f), flock (Ac 20, 28; 1 P 5,2; Jn 10,16), and bride of the Lord (E 5,25; Ap 19,7; 21,2). And because the people of the old covenant had experienced the ways of God in the events of its own history, the experience of salvation granted to the new people is allowed to take form in the categories of thought which recall these figurative events: the people must enter into the divine rest* which the promised land prefigures (He 4,9); it must leave Babylon*, the city of evil (Ap 18,4), to be gathered together in Jerusalem*, the abiding place of God (Ap 21,3).

But this time, the level of temporal life on which the nations* are moving is exceeded. The transcendence of the people of God is total: "priestly kingdom*" (1 P 2,9), it does not belong to this world* (Jn 18,36); its fatherland* is in heaven (He 11,13...), where its citizens have the right of citizenship (Ph 3,20); for they are the children of the Jerusalem* on high (G 4,26), the same which at the end of time will come down from heaven onto the earth (Ap 21,1ff). However, this people will still continue here below. Through it, the spiritual and eschatological are joined to the temporal and the historical. After the paradox of Israel, we have the paradox of the Church: in its earthly state, it remains a visible people called to develop itself in time.

II. ISRAEL AND THE NATIONS IN THE NEW PEOPLE

It is natural that Israel* be the first called to constitute a part of the new people; this was its calling from the first covenant. Jesus has been sent as "the prophet* resembling Moses*" (Ac 3,23) to "save His people" (Mt 1,21), to bring it the light* (Mt 4,15f), redemption* (Lk 1,68), knowledge of salvation* (Lk 1,77), joy* (Lk 2,10), glory* (Lk 2,32). He is the leader who will rule it (Mt 2,6), and finally He will die for it (Jn 11,50). But around Jesus, and later around the announcement of the gospel*, is renewed the drama of the "stiff-necked people" of whom the OT already furnished startling examples (Mt 13,15; 15,8; Ac 13,45; 28,26; R 10,21; 11,1f).

Thus, the plan of salvation will achieve its complete objective. Effectually, the death of Jesus, who bore in its fullness the sin of the people of the old covenant (Mt 23,32-36; cf Ac 7,51f), puts an end to this first economy. It breaks through the barrier which had placed Israel apart from other nations* (E 2,14): Jesus died "not only for His nation, but to gather together again into a unity* all the sons* of God dispersed in all directions" (Jn 11,52). Of the first people of God, a remnant* will be converted and will pass into the new people; but God has determined to "draw also from among the nations a people for His own name" (Ac 15, 14). Out of those who were not His He now wishes to make His own people (R 9,25f; 1 P 2, 10), "so that all may have a part of the inheritance with the sanctified" (Ac 26,18).

Through this union of Israel and the nations the eschatological reunion of the "new humanity" is therefore realized (E 2,15); the chosen race (1 P 2,9) is still spiritually the race of Abraham (R 4,11f), but in fact includes the whole human race, now that Christ, the new Adam, recapitulates in Himself all the offspring of the first Adam (1 Co 15,45; R 5,12...). The holy people is henceforth made up of men of "all tribes, peoples, nations, and tongues" (Ap 5, 9; 7,9; 11,9; 13,7; 14,6), the old Israel being included in this enumeration. Such is the eternal appearance of the Church, which the seer of the Apocalypse contemplates in heaven. Such also is the earthly reality, for no longer being either Greek or Jewish (G 3,28), it constitutes a *tertium genus*, as the Christians of the first centuries used to say.

III. THE NEW PEOPLE MOVING TOWARD ITS CONSUMMATION

The Church thus remains a "people" rooted in history. Like the sons of Israel, its members have a community of origin, of institutions, and of destiny, a community of fatherland toward which they travel (He 11,16), a community of language assured by the Word of God, a community of worship which is the supreme purpose of the *ekklēsia* (cf 1 P 2,9; Ap 5,10). The earthly destiny of this people set apart still presents some striking parallelisms with that of Israel: the same infidelities of its sinful members (cf He 3,7...); the same persecutions coming from earthly powers which incarnate the diabolical beast* (Ap 13,1-7; cf Dn 7); the same necessity to quit Babylon* to escape the destruction threatening it (Ap 18,4...; cf Is 48,20). Sacred history and the Scriptures of the OT thus remain charged with meaning for the new people, as long as they are on the way toward their heavenly consummation.

→Authority OT II—Brother—Build I—Church —Communion OT 5—Covenant OT I 1—Dispersion 1—Earth OT II—Election—Fatherland —Fathers & Father I II—Generation—Growth 2 b—Hebrew—Holy OT III 2—Israel OT 1— Jew—Nations—New Birth 1—Priesthood NT II —Schism OT 2—Servant of God I—Shepherd & Flock OT—Trial/Temptation OT I—Unity II—Visitation OT 1—Witness OT III—Word of God OT 1.2.

PG jjk

PERFECTION

A phrase of the gospel gives as the model of perfection the imitation of God Himself: "Be perfect as your heavenly Father is perfect" (Mt 5.48). This striking precept has in the NT the place which the Levitic command had in the OT: "Be holy, for I am holy" (Lv 11,45; 19,2). From one to the other a change of viewpoint is clearly manifested.

OT

1. *Holiness of God and perfection.* The OT speaks of sanctity more than of perfection. God is holy*: that is to say that He is of a completely other order than the beings of this world: He is great, powerful, terrible (Dt 10,17; Ps 76);

He is also shown as marvelously good and faithful (Ex 34; Ps 136); He intervenes in history with a sovereign justice (Ps 99). One does not qualify Him as "perfect"; in Hebrew, the word applies correctly only to certain limited beings. But one speaks of perfection in His works (Dt 32,4), His Law (Ps 19,8), His ways (2 S 22,31).

2. *Demand of perfection.* When the God of holiness chooses a people for Himself, this people becomes holy in its turn; that is to say, separated from the profane, and consecrated. At the same time, a demand for perfection is imposed on it. What is consecrated must be whole and without defect.

Physical integrity, first of all. It is required in the animals offered in sacrifice: "You will not offer to Yahweh any blind, crippled, mutilated animal..." (Lv 22,22). The same law holds good for priests (Lv 21,17-23) and to a certain degree for all the people, since the rules about pure* and impure specify the qualifications of the people (Lv 11—15).

When it is a question of persons, moral integrity must be added to physical integrity. Israel knows that Yahweh must be served "with a perfect heart*" in all sincerity and fidelity (1 K 8,61; cf Dt 6,5; 10,12), and that this service entails obedience to the commandments and the struggle against evil: "You will make evil disappear, the evil in the midst of you" (Dt 17, 7.12). Deviations in a religious sense were sharply fought against by the prophets (Am 4, 4...; Is 1,10-17; 29,13): we must search after true justice* while expelling violence and egoism, while living in faith in God, respect for right, and the doing of good (Is 58). God's injunction to Abraham: "Walk in my presence and be perfect" (Gn 17,1), repeated in Dt 18,13, manifested thus more and more the richness of its content.

3. *The practice of perfection.* Meditating upon the examples of their ancestors (Ws 10; Si 44— 49), the pious Jews sought after perfection in the observation of the Law*: "Happy, perfect in their way, are those who walk in the Law of Yahweh" (Ps 119). But their very attachment to the ideal pointed up certain problems. Job is a model of perfection, "a man whole and righteous, fearing God and far from evil" (Jb 1,1); why did misfortune not spare him? This mournful question kept souls open and in expectation.

NT

1. *Perfection of the Law.* The gospel pays homage to this perfection orientated toward expectation, such as that of the parents of John the Baptist, "irreproachable" in their fidelity to the Law (Lk 1,6), or that of Simeon and Anna. But if the practice of the Law seems to be contained complacently within itself, it is no more than a false perfection and arouses the uncompromising opposition of Jesus (vg Lk 18, 9-14; Jn 5,44), continued by that of Paul (cf R 10,3f; G 3,10).

2. *Jesus and perfection.* In a completely different way, in fact, the Law must find its fulfillment*. In revealing fully that the most holy God is a God of love, Jesus gives a new orientation to the demand for the perfection which relationship with God arouses. It is no longer a question of preserving an integrity, but of receiving and spreading abroad the gifts and the love of God.

Jesus does not align Himself with the "just" who flee from contact with sinners: it is for sinners that He has come (Mt 9,12f). Certainly, He is the "Lamb without defect" (1 P 1,19) prefigured by the prescriptions of Leviticus; but He takes upon Himself our sins, and for their remission He pours out His blood; thus it is that He becomes our "perfect" priest (He 5,9f; 7, 26ff), capable of perfecting us in our turn (He 10,14).

3. *Perfection in humility.* The person who wants to profit from the salvation* which Christ brings must, therefore, recognize himself as a sinner (1 Jn 1,8) and renounce the idea of excelling because of any personal advantage, so that he might entrust himself only to His grace* (Ph 3,7-11; 2 Co 12,9). Without humility* and detachment, one cannot follow* Jesus (Lk 9, 23 p; 22,26f). All are not called to the same forms of effective renouncement (cf Mt 19,11f; Ac 5,4), but whoever wants to advance toward perfection must walk generously along the path. The word addressed to the rich young man is noteworthy: "If you wish to be perfect, go, sell what you have...and come, follow me" (Mt 19,21; cf Ac 4,36f).

4. *Perfection of love.* The children of God are called to the perfection of love (Col 3,14; R 13,8-10). In the passage of Luke parallel to Mt 5.48, in place of *perfect* one reads *merciful* (Lk 6.36); and the context of Matthew speaks also of universal charity, of love* extended even to an enemy and a persecutor. The Christian should certainly keep himself from evil (Mt 5, 29f; 1 P 1,14ff); but, in order to resemble his Father* (Mt 5,45; E 5,1f), he should at the same time be anxious for the sinner (cf R 5,8), love him, and although it be costly for him "conquer evil by the strength of good" (R 12,21; 1 P 3,9).

5. *Perfection and progress.* This conquering generosity never judges itself satisfied because of the results obtained. The idea of progress is henceforth bound to that of perfection. The disciples of Christ always have to progress, to grow* in knowledge and in love (Ph 1,9), even when they make up part of the category of formed Christians (in Greek "the perfect"; 1 Co 2,6; 14,20; cf Ph 3,12.15).

6. *Perfection at the parousia.* They do not cease to prepare themselves for the advent of their Lord, hoping that God will grant that they be found without reproach on that day* (1 Th 3,12f). They have it in their hearts to respond to the desire of Christ which is that He be seen to present at that time a Church "all resplendent..." (E 5,27); forgetting what has already been realized, they therefore reach forward (cf Ph 3,13), until "all meet together...to make up this perfect man*, in the strength of the age, which realizes its fullness* in Christ" (E 4,13).

→Fulfill—Fullness—Growth 3—Holy—Justice O—Pure—Time OT III 1—Virtues & Vices.

AV jjk

PERFUME

Like all the people of the East, Israel made great use of perfumes: and the Bible mentions no less than thirty of them. The patriarchs offer them to Joseph (Gn 43,11); Solomon (1 K 10, 2.10; cf Gn 37,25) and Hezekiah (2 K 20,13) had a monopoly of the sale of perfumes. Perfume was as much part of life as eating and drinking. Its meaning is twofold: in social life, it is a sign of joy or an expression of the intimacy of the persons concerned; in the liturgy, it is a symbol of offering and praise.

1. *Perfume and social life.* To wear perfume is to express outwardly one's joy in living (Pr 27.9). It also means making oneself more beautiful than ever: the guests wear it at banquets (Am 6,6) and lovers too at the moment

of carnal union (Pr 7,17). To pour perfume on the head of one's guest is a sign of one's pleasure in welcoming him (Mt 26,7 p) and the neglect of this gesture is bad manners (Lk 7,46). On the other hand in times of mourning these signs of joy are suppressed (2 S 12,20; 14,2). Nevertheless, the disciples of Christ will continue to wear perfume when they fast, in order not to make a show of their penance (Mt 6,17) nor to spoil true Christian joy by sadness.

Sometimes perfume can play a still more intimate role: the role of conveying the physical presence of a person in a subtler and more penetrating way. It is that silent vibration which breathes the very essence of a person and gives a glimpse of the life hidden within him. This is why Esther (Es 2,12-17) and Judith (Jdt 10,3-4) anoint themselves with oil and myrrh in order to be better able to stir the feelings of those whom they want to seduce. The fragrance of the harvest coming from Jacob's clothes (Gn 27,27) is a sign that God's blessing rests on him; the spouse in the Canticle compares the presence of her beloved to "nard," to a "sachet of myrrh" (Ct 1,12) or to "perfume" (1,3), while her spouse calls her "my myrrh and my balsam" (5,1; cf 4,10).

2. *Perfume and liturgy.* In its worship the ancient world made great use of perfumes, as symbols of offering; and Israel adopted this custom. The Temple liturgy called for an "altar of perfume" (Ex 30,1-10), censors (1 K 7,50) and bowls of incense (Nm 7,86); a sacrifice of perfume was offered every morning and evening in joyful adoration (Ex 30,7f; Lk 1,9ff). The perfume of the incense rising in smoke was a sign of the praise offered to the godhead (Ws 18,21; Ps 141,2; Ap 8,2-5; 5,8); and the burning of incense meant adoring and appeasing God (1 K 22,44; 1 M 1,55).

But there can only be one cult: the cult of the true God. As a result, then, incense and its perfume come to symbolize the perfect worship, the unbloody sacrifice, which all the nations will offer to God in eschatological times (Ml 1,11; Is 60,6; cf Mt 2,11). This perfect worship has been realized by Christ: He offered Himself "as a fragrant offering and a sacrifice to God" (E 5,2; cf Ex 29,18; Ps 40,7). This means that His life was burnt up as an offering of love pleasing to God.

The Christian in his turn, anointed* with Christ at his baptism with the sign of chrism, a mixture of costly perfumes (Ex 30,22-25), must spread "the sweet smell of Christ" (2 Co 2,14-17) by taking care that the least of his actions is imbued (Ph 4,18) with this spirit of offering.

→Altar—Anointing I—Burial 2—Fasting 2—Joy—Oil—Praise III—Sacrifice OT II 1—Worship OT I.

GB ems

PERSECUTION

The people of God, all through their history, undergo the experience of persecution. This does not spare the Son of God, come to save the world, and hated by it (Jn 3,17; 15,18), but even culminates in His passion (Mt 23,31f); and it will finally be the lot of His disciples: "If they have persecuted me, they will persecute you" (Jn 15,20).

Although connected with this mystery of suffering*, persecution is distinct from it. Suffering is a problem because it affects all men, even the just. The problem is more pressing when persecution strikes the just precisely because they are just. Persecution is distinguished from other tribulations because of its origin. By means of suffering, God wishes to purify the sinner and test the just in a plan of love by means of persecution; an evil man tries to oppose this plan and to separate man from God. Still, like all suffering, persecution is utilized by God: "In crucifying the Lord of glory, the princes of this world" did not recognize the instruments of His wisdom (1 Co 2,6ff). And the persecuted just one (Ac 3,14) has forever conquered the world (Jn 16,33). Sure of being persecuted (2 Tm 3,12), His disciples rejoiced (Mt 5,11f); it is the sign that they do not belong to the persecuting world (Jn 15, 19), but that they are of the number of those in whom the Lord Jesus will be glorified on the day when He triumphs over all persecution (2 Th 1,4-12).

I. THE MYSTERY OF PERSECUTION

1. *In the OT*, not only did the entire sacred people undergo the violent opposition of the pagans—from the stay in Egypt (Ex 1,8-14) to the Roman domination, at the same time passing through various internal crises (cf Ps 44,10-17; 79,1-4; 80,5ff)—but the great personages—chiefs, kings, and especially prophets—are frequently persecuted because of their love of

Yahweh and their fidelity to His Word. Moses is rejected by his own (Ex 2,14; Ac 7,27.35) and constantly plagued by their complaints (Ex 5, 21; 14,11-12; 15,24; 16,3...; Ez 20,13.21; Ps 78,17-42); David is pursued (1 S 19—24), as well as Elijah (1 K 19), Amos (Am 7,10-17), Jeremiah (Jr 11,18—12,6; 26; 37—38), the Maccabean martyrs (2 M 6—7; 1 M 1,57-64; Dn 11,33-35), etc. These persecutions appeared to Jeremiah as inseparable from his mission*, and it is thanks to them that the Servant* accomplished the plan* of God (Is 53,10). Likewise, the Book of Daniel shows that the persecution of the just, along with their resistance and their fidelity, is preparing the day* of judgment* and the coming of the kingdom* (Dn 7,25ff; 8,24f; 11,32-35). Finally the Book of Wisdom brings to light the profound motive of all persecution: the godless* hates the just because he is, for him, a "living reproach" (Ws 2,12ff), while at the same time he is a witness* to God whom he despises (2,16-20). Since he belongs to the devil, the persecutor aims at God through His witness; and the salvation of the just on the last day will judge the unbelief* of the persecutor (3,7-10; 5,1-6).

2. The persecuted *Jesus* fills out and crowns this line of sufferers, unjustly oppressed by even those to whom they had been sent. In condemning Him, the leaders of Israel heaped high the measure of the crimes of their fathers and gave witness that they are indeed the sons of those who killed the prophets (Mt 23,31f). But this persecution, like all the sufferings* of Christ, is necessary for the fulfillment of His mission and the realization of the plan of salvation.

3. The *disciples* can pretend to no other treatment than that of their master. In line with His example, like Him, and because of Him, they are persecuted (Jn 15,20; 16,1ff); they must drink His cup* and be baptized with His baptism* (Mk 10,39 p); in them Jesus relives His persecution (Ac 9,4f; cf Col 1,24). It is for them a grace* (Ph 1,29) and therefore a source of joy (1 P 4,12ff).

First the Jews oppress them (Ac 4,1...; 5, 17...; 8,1...; 13,50), just as before "the child of the flesh persecuted the child of the spirit" (G 4,29). Like Jesus, betrayed by His own (Jn 13,18; 18,35; cf Jr 12,6), the disciples* are to be persecuted by their own families (Mt 10,34ff). This is more than a simple parallel of situations: "The Jews, who have sent to death the Lord Jesus and the prophets and have perse-

cuted us...thus heap up the measure of their sins unto all time" (1 Th 2,15f).

The *pagans* also pursue the disciples of Jesus. Rome, the new Babylon*, will in its turn "get drunk on the blood" of saints and the blood of the witnesses of Jesus" (Ap 17,6); so true is it that "all those who want to live piously in Christ will be persecuted" (2 Tm 3,12).

4. *The root of the problem.*

a) The persecution of the friends of God is only one aspect of the centuries-old war* which Satan* and the powers of evil wage against God and His servant, and which ends in the crushing of the serpent. From the appearance of sin (Gn 3) up until the final struggles described in the Apocalypse, the dragon "pursues" the woman* and her descendants (Ap 12; cf 17; 19). This battle is extended to all history, but is amplified as time goes on. It reaches its summit during the passion of Jesus. Then, there takes place at the same time the hour* of the prince of darkness and the hour of Jesus, that of His death and that of His glorification (Lk 22,53; Jn 12,23; 17,1). In the Church, persecutions are the sign and the condition of the definitive victory* of Christ and His own. They have in this regard an eschatological significance, for they are a preface to the judgment* (1 P 4, 17ff) and to the complete setting up of the kingdom*. They are connected with the "great tribulation" (Mk 13,9-13.14-20) and are the prelude to the end of the world* and condition the birth of a new era (Ap 7,13-17).

b) If the persecuted who have remained faithful in the test (Ap 7,14) are from that moment the vanquishers and "superabound in joy," their glorious lot should not cause them to forget the tragic aspect of the punishment* of the persecutors. The wrath of God, which reveals itself from now on against sinners (R 1,18), will fall at the end of time upon those who will be hardened sinners, in particular upon the persecutors (1 Th 2,16; 2 Th 1,5-8; Ap 6,9ff; 11, 17f; 16,5f; 19,2). Their lot was already announced in the tragic end of Antiochus Epiphanes (2 M 9; Dn 7,11; 8,25; 11,45), which was repeated in that of Herod Agrippa (Ac 12,21ff). This union of persecutions as eschatological punishments is emphasized in the parables of the vineyard murderers (Mt 21,33-46 p) and the nuptial feast (22,1-14). The *last* crime of the vineyard workers and the evil treatment undergone by the *last* servants culminated in a

series of outrages and unleashed the anger of
the master or king. "They spilt the blood of
the saints and the prophets, and blood is what
you have given them to drink; it is what they
deserve" (Ap 16,6; 19,2).

II. THE CHRISTIAN
IN THE FACE OF PERSECUTION

The believer whose faith* penetrates the
mystery of persecution finds in his hope* the
force to hold onto that faith with joy. Already
the OT offered him models of this attitude to
which Jesus gives His own perfection* by His
example* and His counsels.

1. *The models.* In the face of persecution the
just of the OT all adopted an attitude of
patience* and of courageous fidelity in hope*.
Jeremiah is the type of the persecuted just man,
faithful and prayerful. His "confessions" are
as much protestations of fidelity as mournful
plaints. He knows that, whatever happens,
Yahweh "is with him" to protect him and to
save him (vg Jr 1,8.19). The same is true of the
suffering Servant (Is 52—53) and of the persecuted psalmists: "Lord, save me from those
who persecute me" (Ps 7,2): this cry of anguish
and of confidence runs through the entire
Psalter. Often accompanied by imprecations
against the enemy* (Ps 35; 55; 69; 70; 109) or
appeals to the vengeance* of God (Jr 11,20;
15,15; 17,18), such prayer is based upon the certainty of salvation* which the faithful God
grants to His own (Ps 31,6; cf 23,4; 91,15).

The persecuted Jesus not only trusted in His
Father who is with Him (Mt 26,53; Jn 16,32),
but He prayed for His persecutors (Lk 23,34).
He also gave His disciples a supreme example*
of the charity which bears every persecution
(1 Co 13,7).

Exposed to persecutions, the *apostles* and the
first Christians pray to be bold and thus to be
able to announce the gospel* (Ac 4,29; cf 12,5);
and they show confidence* and assurance (Ac
4,13.31; 28,31; Ph 1,20). Like their master, they
show themselves patient in the midst of persecution (2 Th 1,4); and like Him they ask God to
pardon their tormentors (Ac 7,60).

2. *The counsels given by Jesus* correspond to
the attitude of which He Himself gave them the
example. Like Him, the disciple should pray
for those who persecute him (Mt 5,44 p; cf R 12,
14). He should face up to the persecution with

courage. Even if he should not be rash and
should know how to flee from a town in which
he is pursued (Mt 10,23; Ac 13,50f), he should
also expect to be imprisoned, beaten, and put to
death (Mt 10,16-39; Jn 16,1-4). But faced with
such prospects he should not fear: his master
has conquered the world* (Jn 16,33), and He
will finally win out over godless* persecutors
"with His own, the called, the chosen, the faithful" (Ap 17,14). The enemies* of the disciple
can do nothing to his soul (Mt 10,28-31). The
Spirit* of God will assist him when he is
dragged before the tribunals and he will not
have to be preoccupied with his defense during
the trial* (Mt 10,19f). Still it will always be
necessary to watch* and pray, for persecution is
a test, a temptation; and if the spirit is willing,
the flesh is weak (Mt 26,41 p).

Paul develops the instructions of Jesus. Nothing, he says, can separate us from the love of
Christ, not even persecution or the sword (R 8,
35). In summary, the disciple faces persecution
with a hope which makes him faithful, constant,
and joyous (R 12,12; 2 Th 1,4; cf Mt 13,21 p).
He knows in whom he has placed his trust
(2 Tm 1,12). Surrounded also by the innumerable martyrs* of the Old and New Testaments,
with his eyes fixed on Christ "who underwent
for the sake of sinners such an abuse against
His person," he runs to the finish, with endurance, without discouragement (He 11,1—12,3).

3. The *joy** of hope* (R 12,12) is the result of
the persecution thus endured: "Happy will you
be when they insult you, when they persecute
you...for my sake. Rejoice and be glad..."
(Mt 5,11f). This promise of Jesus is accomplished in the Christian who "is glorified in
tribulations, knowing that tribulation produces
constancy, constancy produces tested virtue,
tested virtue produces hope, and hope is not deceiving..." (R 5,3ff; cf Jm 1,2ff). He "super-
abounds with joy in tribulation" (2 Co 7,4;
12,10; Col 1,24; cf Ac 5,41; He 10,34). Consolation *in tribulation (2 Co 1,3-10) is a fruit of
the Spirit (1 Th 1,6; Ac 13,52; cf G 5,22), and
at the same time the sign of the presence of the
kingdom.

Written during a time of terrible testing, the
Apocalypse, mirror of the life of the Church,
feeds this joyous hope in the hearts of the persecuted by assuring them of the victory* of
Jesus and the founding of the kingdom. To
each of them, as to the whole Church, the risen
Lord always addresses these words: "Do not be
afraid of the sufferings which await you. The

devil will throw some of you into prison to test you and for ten days you will suffer cruelly. Remain faithful until death, and I will give you the crown of life" (Ap 2,10).

→Antichrist—Babel/Babylon 2—Beatitude NT II—Blasphemy NT 2—Cross II 3—Enemy—Hate I 2, III 2—Joy NT II 2—Martyr 2—Patience I NT 1; II 1—Run 2—Suffering III —Trial/Temptation NT II—Violence II, IV 2 —War OT IV 1—Witness NT III 2—World NT III 2.

RD jjk

PETER

1. *Calling.* According to the correct translation, the name of Cephas which Christ gave to Simon (Mt 16,18; Jn 1,42; cf 1 Co 1,12; 15,5; G 1,18) means "rock" rather than "stone*." By the grace of this new name*, which indicates the task that is from now on his, Simon Peter participates in the durable solidity and the unbreakable faithfulness of Yahweh and His Messiah. It is a way of pointing up his exceptional situation.

If Peter was chosen, this cannot be because of his personality, completely engaging as it might be, or because of some worthiness (even before his denial). This gratuitous election and the greatness that goes with it are the result of the mission which Christ entrusted to him and which he must fulfill in fidelity and love (Jn 21,15ff).

2. *Primacy.* Simon was one of the first to be called by Jesus to follow* Him (Jn 1,35-42). The tendency of the synoptics is even to transpose in time the primacy of Peter and to make him the first disciple called by Christ (Mt 4,18-22 p). However that may be, Peter has a pre-eminent place among the disciples, at the head of the lists of apostles (Mt 10,2), or of the three privileged ones (vg Mt 17,1 p). At Capernaum, it is in the house of Peter that Jesus ordinarily stayed (vg Mk 1,29); he is the one who speaks up in the name of the others (Mt 16,23; 18,21; 19,27), especially on that solemn occasion when he recognizes Jesus' messiahship (Mt 16,16 p; Jn 6,68); and the message confided by the angels of the resurrection to the holy women (Mk 16,7) contains a special mention of Peter; John allows him to enter into the tomb first (Jn 20,1-10). Finally, and above all, the risen Christ appears to Peter before manifesting Himself to the twelve (Lk 24,34; 1 Co 15,5). Everywhere in the NT this pre-eminence of Peter is underlined. However, this excludes neither laborious efforts to find out what God's plans are (cf Ac 10—15 and G 2 with regard to universalism), nor the collegial responsibility of the apostles, nor the initiative of a man like Paul. After his conversion the latter goes up to Jerusalem to get in touch with Peter (G 1,18), although he is quite conscious of his own special vocation (1,15f). And even in recalling the incident at Antioch (G 2,11-14), where Peter timidly hesitated over the position he should take on a particular case, Paul addresses himself to Peter as to the one whose authority carries the whole Church with him.

3. *Mission.* This primacy of Peter is founded on his mission*, which is expressed in many gospel texts.

a) Mt 16,13-23. A new Abraham*, a quarry from which living stones are hewn (cf Is 51,1ff and Mt 3,9), the foundation on which Christ builds His eschatological community, Peter received a mission which was to be for the good of the whole people. Against the forces of evil, which are the powers of death, the Church* builds on Peter and is assured of victory. Thus is confided to Peter, who recognized in Jesus the Son of the living God, the supreme mission of gathering men again into a community in which they may receive a blessed and eternal life. Just as in the body a vital function cannot cease, so in the Church, a living and lifegiving organism, Peter, in some way or other, has to himself be perpetually present to ceaselessly communicate the life of Christ to the faithful.

b) Lk 22,31f and Acts. Alluding undoubtedly to his name, Jesus announces to Peter that, after he has repudiated his denial, he must "bolster" his brethren; thanks to Christ's prayer his faith* will not fail. This is really then the mission of Peter, described by Luke in Acts: he finds himself at the head of the group gathered together in the Cenacle (Ac 1,13); he presides at the election of Matthias (1,15); he judges Ananias and Sapphira (5,1-11); in the name of the other apostles, who are with him, he proclaims to the crowds the Messianic glorification of the risen Christ and announces the gift of the Spirit (2,14-36); he invites all men to baptism (2,37-41), including the "pagans" (10,1—11,18); and inspects all the churches (9,

427

32). As signs of his power over life, in the name of Jesus he cures sicknesses (3,1-10) and raises a dead man to life (9,36-42).

The fact that Peter had to justify his conduct at the baptism of Cornelius (11,1-18 , the developments of the council of Jerusalem (15,1-35), as well as certain allusions of Paul (G 1,18—2,14), reveal that in the direction (which was in good part collegial) of the Church of Jerusalem, James had an important position and that his vote was very important. But these facts and their relation, far from causing an obstacle to the primacy and the mission of Peter, clarify the profound meaning of that mission and that primacy. The authority of James actually did not have the same roots nor the same expression as that of Peter: it is in virtue of a particular title that Peter has received, with all that it implies, the mission of transmitting a rule of faith without fault (cf G 1,18); and that he is the depository of the promises of life (Mt 16, 18f).

c) *Jn 21*. Under a solemn and perhaps juridical form, expressed three times, the risen Christ entrusted to Peter the care of the entire flock, lambs and sheep. It is in the light of the parable of the Good Shepherd (Jn 10,1-28) that we must understand this mission. The good shepherd* saves his sheep, gathered in one flock (10,16; 11,52), and they have life in abundance. He even gives up his own life for them (10, 11); so that Christ, in announcing to Peter his future martyrdom, adds: "Follow me." If he must walk in the steps of his master, it is not only in giving up his life, but it is in communicating eternal life to his sheep, so that they may never perish (10,28).

In "following" Christ, a rock, a living stone (1 P 2,4, a shepherd who has the power to admit into the Church, that is to say, to save the faithful from death and to communicate to them divine life, Peter, inaugurating an essential function for the Church, is truly the "vicar" of Christ. Therein lie his mission and his greatness.

→Apostles—Build III 1—Church III 2 c, IV 2, V 2—Follow 2 b—Rock 1—Shepherd & Flock NT 2.

PL jjk

PHARISEE

The Jewish sect of the Pharisees (hb. *perusim*: "the separated") at the time of Jesus comprised about six thousand members. Like that of the Essenes, it ordinarily was attached to the Hasidim (hb. *ḥasidim*: "the pious") who at the time of the Maccabees fought with stubbornness against the influence of paganism (1 M 2,42). It included the totality of the scribes and doctors of the Law, but also a certain number of priests. Organizing its members into religious brotherhoods, it sought to preserve them in their fervor and their fidelity to the Law.

1. *At the beginnings of the conflict with Jesus*. Historically, it seems that the responsibility for the death of Jesus falls first of all upon the priestly caste and the Sadducees, since the Pharisees are not named in passion narratives (except Jn 18,3), and many of them seem to have been amongst those who wanted to establish contact with Jesus by inviting Him to a meal (Lk 7,36; 11,37; 14,1). Indeed some took it upon themselves to defend Jesus (Lk 13,31; Jn 7,50) and the Christians openly (Ac 5,34; 23,9); many Pharisees saw in Jesus Christ the one who would fulfill* their Jewish faith (Ac 15,5). Such is the case with Paul, their most famous representative (Ac 26,5; Ph 3,5). It still remains true, however, that a great number were violently opposed to the teaching and person of Jesus. It is this opposition and not the opportunism of the high priests which is of interest to the evangelists, for it characterized the conflict between Judaism and Christianity.

So as not to judge pharisaically the Pharisees of times past, it is important to recognize the qualities which are at the basis of their excesses. Jesus admires their zeal* (Mt 23,15), their concern for perfection and purity (5,20). Paul emphasizes their willingness to practice the Law minutely. They are to be admired for their devotion to the living oral traditions. But, confident in their knowledge of the Law, some of them destroyed the precept of God beneath their human traditions* (Mt 15,1-20). They looked down upon the ignorant in the name of their own justice (Lk 18,11f), and they prevented all contact with sinners and publicans, thus limiting the love* of God according to their own limited perspective. They even thought that they had some rights over God, because of their practice (Mt 20,1-15; Lk 15,25-30). And, as, according to Paul (R 2,17-24), they could not put this ideal into practice, they conducted themselves as hypocrites*, "whitened sepulchers" (Mt 23, 27). This is the legalistic world described by the evangelists, but they have made a system out of what must have been the behavior of some of them. Already we can see that it is the intention of the authors not to dwell on individuals but to describe the attitude of those who are blind to all light coming from anywhere and who refuse to recognize Jesus as anyone but an imposter or an ally of the devil.

2. *Pharisaism.* This use of the word *Pharisees* in a polemical context has unfortunately led to an abuse of language that is anything but Christian. Nevertheless, if care is taken to use this term, not of the Jews, but of the behavior of any man with a closed mind, then pharisaism understood in this way has nothing to do with the sect of the Pharisees; it is a spirit, opposed to that of the gospel. The fourth gospel has preserved some scenes typical of the Pharisees' blindness (Jn 8,13; 9,13.40), but it ordinarily joins them to Jews*, thus pointing out that their conflict with Jesus has a trans-historical value. It is pharisaism when a man covers himself with a mask of justice* so as to dispense with an interior life or to dispense with acknowledging himself as a sinner* and hearing the call of God; when a man binds the love of God within the narrow circle of his religious knowledge. This mentality is found again in early Christianity, among the Judaeo-Christians whom Paul attacked (Ac 15,5). They wanted to submit the converts coming from paganism to Jewish practices, and thereby keep under the yoke of the Law* those who had been freed by the death of Christ from that yoke. Pharisaism is also found in the Christian who despises the Jew cut away from the tree (R 11, 18ff). Pharisaism threatens Christianity to the extent that the latter retreats to a stage of legal observance and fails to recognize the universality of grace*.

→Arrogance 1.3—Godless Man NT 1—Hypocrite—Jew—Law *B* III 5; *C* I 1—Reward III 2—Unbelief II 1—Zeal II 1.

JCan & XLD jjk

PIETY

Piety is, for our modern world, fidelity to religious duties, often reduced to the exercises of piety. In the Bible, piety radiates further: it embraces also the relations of a man with his fellow men.

OT

1. *Piety in human relations.* In Hebrew, piety (*hesed*) designates first of all the mutual relation which unites relatives (Gn 47,29), friends (1 S 20,8), allies (Gn 21,23). It is an attachment which implies efficacious and faithful help. The expression "to exercise *hesed*" indicates that piety is shown through acts. In the couplet *hesed*/*'emet*, "piety/fidelity" (Gn 24,49; Pr 20, 28; Ps 25,10), the two terms are compenetrating: the second points up an attitude of soul without which the goodness expressed by the first could not be perfect. For the Septuagint which translates *hesed* by *eleos* (=*piety*), the essential of piety seems to be compassionate goodness.

2. *Piety in the relations with God.* This human bond of piety (*hesed*), which is so strong, allows an understanding of what God, through the covenant, established between Himself and His people. To the piety of God, that is to say, to His own merciful love for Israel, His first-born (Ex 34,6; cf 4,22; Jr 31,3; Is 54,10) should answer with another piety, that is to say, the filial attachment which faithful obedience* and loving worship* provoke (cf Dt 10,12f). From this love exercised toward God should come a fraternal love among men, an imitation of the goodness of God and of His solicitude for the poor. Thus, to define true piety, Micah associates it with justice, love, and humility (Mi 6,8).

This definition is that of the prophets and the sapiential writers. For Hosea, piety is not in a ritual, but in the love which animates the ritual (Ho 6,6=Mt 9,13), inseparable from justice* (Ho 12,7) and from fidelity to the Law (Ho 2,21f; 4,1f). For Jeremiah, God gives Himself to us as a model of piety and justice (Jr 9, 23). Elsewhere we see that piety is compromised when the poor are oppressed and justice is violated (Mi 7,2; Is 57,1; Ps 12,2-6). In the psalms, the worship of the pious man (hb. *hasīd*; gr. *hosios* or *eusebēs*) is expressed in loving praise*, confident and joyous praise (Ps 31,24; 149), which magnifies the piety of God (Ps 103). However, this worship is acceptable only if it is united to fidelity (Ps 50). God grants wisdom (Si 43,33) to pious men who do not separate worship and charity (Si 35,1-10), and they draw profit from all the good things created by God (Si 39,27).

It is this integral piety which, in the time of the Maccabees, animated the Hasidim (from *hasīdīm*: "pious"; 1 M 2,42) who fought to the death for their faith. That piety which made them strong is sure of the resurrection (2 M 12, 45). Such also is "the piety which is more powerful than all else" of whose victory at the last judgment Wisdom sings (Ws 10,12; cf the opposition of just/impious in Ws 2—5). This piety will be given the Messiah who will establish here on earth the kingdom of God (Is 11, 2; LXX *eusebeia*).

NT

1. *The piety of Christ.* The expectation of those who desired "to serve God in piety (*hosiotēs*) and justice" is rewarded by the piety (*eleos*) of God who sends Christ (Lk 1,75.78). Christ is above all others "pious" (Ac 2,27; 13, 35: *hosios*=Ps 16,10: *hasīd*). His filial piety made Him fulfill completely the will* of God, His Father (Jn 8,29; 9,31). It led Him to offer a perfect act of worship* (He 10,5-10) and it inspired the ardent prayer of His agony and the offering of the painful sacrifice by which He sanctifies us (Mk 14,35f p). Since Christ is the pious high priest whom we need (He 7,26), He is heard by God "because of His piety" (5,7). That is why the mystery of Christ is called "the mystery of piety" (1 Tm 3,16: *eusebeia*): in Him the piety of God realizes His plan of salvation; in Him the piety of the Christian has its source and its model.

2. *The piety of the Christian.* God was already pleased with the men of every nation, who by their prayers and their almsgiving animated by the fear of God, participated in the Jewish piety in its two elements: divine worship and the exercise of justice. Such were the Jew Simeon (Lk 2,25), the men come to Jerusalem for Pentecost (Ac 2,5), the centurion Cornelius (Ac 10, 2.4.22.34f). This piety is renewed by Jesus and by the gift of the Spirit. In Acts we perceive some of these pious (*eulabēs*) men, such as Ananias (Ac 22,12) or the Christians who come to bury Stephen (Ac 8,2). According to Pauline language, their worship is now animated with a filial spirit in regard to God (cf 4,6), and their justice is that of faith* which operates through charity (G 5,6). Such is the piety (*hosiotēs*) of the new man*, the truly Christian piety (E 4,24) which Paul opposes to the empty practices of a false and utterly human piety (Col 2,16-23); by it, we offer to God an accept-able worship, with reverence (*eulabeia*) and fear* (He 12,28).

In the pastoral epistles and in 2 Peter, piety (*eusebeia*) is included in the number of fundamental virtues of the shepherd*, of the man of God (1 Tm 6,11; Tt 1,8). It is just as necessary for every Christian (Tt 2,12; 2 P 1,6f). Two of its characteristics are emphasized. First it frees from the love of money. In opposition to a false and profit-seeking piety, it is content with the necessary; and its profit is freedom itself (1 Tm 6,5-10). Next, it gives the strength to bear up under persecutions* which are the portion of those for whom the piety of Christ is the model (2 Tm 3,10ff). Without this detachment and this constancy, a person has only the appearances of piety (3,5). To true piety is promised the assistance of God in the trials* of this life, and later, life eternal (2 P 2,9; 1 Tm 4,7f).

Taken in this way, piety designates last of all the Christian life with all its demands (cf 1 Tm 6,3; Tt 1,1). To answer the love of Him who "alone is pious" (Ap 15,4: *hosios*), the Christian should imitate Him and in this way reveal to his brothers the image of their heavenly Father.

→Almsgiving OT 3; NT 1—Creation OT IV 1 —Faithfulness—Fasting 2—Fear of God IV— Godless Man—Justice *A* I OT 2, NT—Mercy —Poor OT III; NT II—Prayer—Worship— Zeal II 1.

MFL jjk

PILGRIMAGE

Pilgrimages, which have been a practise in most religions, are a custom that to a great extent preceded the editing of the Bible. A pilgrimage is a journey made by believers to a place consecrated by some manifestation of the divine or by the activity of some great religious figure, in order to offer their prayers there in particularly favorable surroundings. Usually the visit to the holy place, which is the objective of the pilgrimage, is prepared for by rites of purification and is concluded by an assembly, making the faithful aware of the religious community of which they are part. Thus, a pilgrimage is a quest for God and an encounter with Him in the context of worship.

OT

1. *To the ancient sanctuaries.* Before the deuteronomic reform of Josiah reduced the number of sanctuaries to one, there is evidence of the existence in Israel of many centers of pilgrimage, of sacred places associated with sacred History, to which the people came in search of their God.

The history of the patriarchs only tells of one real pilgrimage (Gn 35,1-7). But in telling of the theophanies granted to Abraham (12,6f at Shechem; 18,1 at Mamre), to Isaac (26,24 at Beersheba) and to Jacob (28,12; 35,9 at Bethel; 32,31 at Peniel), the narrators are seeking to legitimize the adoption of Canaanite sanctuaries by showing that they were used by their fore-fathers. They explain what these sanctuaries looked like: their altars* (12,7f; 13,4; 26,25; 33,20), their steles (28,18), and their sacred trees (12,6; 18,1; 21,33)...They laid the foundation of the rites carried out in these places by later pilgrims: the invocation of the Name* of Yahweh under different titles (12,8; 13,4; 21,33; 33,20), the anointings with oil (28,18; 35,14), the purifications (35,2ff) and the tithes (14,20; 28,22).

There is evidence that the religious assemblies*, and so pilgrimages, at sanctuaries of different importance continued for a long time after this: at Shechem (Js 24,25; Jg 9,6; 1 K 12,1-9), Bethel (1 S 10,3 shows that pilgrims came here; 1 K 12,29ff; Am 5,5; 7,13), and Beersheba (Am 5,5). The sanctuaries of Ophra (Jg 6,24) and Zorah (= Rock: 13,19f) also appear, where they celebrated the memory of the appar-itions of the Angel* of Yahweh. There is also the sanctuary of Shilo where the Ark was kept and where a feast was celebrated each year in honor of Yahweh (21,19); it was probably to this feast that Elkanah and his wives were "going up" (1 S 1,3). Ancient accounts speak of other assemblies at Mizpah (1 S 7,5f), at Gilgal (11, 15), at Gibeon (1 K 3,4) and at Dan (12,29). But from the time that the Ark was brought by David into Jerusalem (2 S 6) and the Temple of Solomon was built (1 K 5—8), pil-grimages to Jerusalem became the most important (12,27).

For a long time, then, the ancient codes of the covenant (jahwist: Ex 34,18-23; elohist: Ex 23,14-17) had prescribed that all the male population should present themselves before the Lord Yahweh three times a year. This obliga-tion was to be fulfilled in the various sanc-tuaries of the country on the occasion of the feasts*.

2. *To the unique sanctuary.* The reform of Josiah, outlined by Ezekiah (2 K 18,4.22; 2 Ch 29—31) abolished the local sanctuaries and fixed Jerusalem as the place for the celebration of the Pasch* (2 K 23; 2 Ch 35) and of the two other feasts*, of the Weeks and of the Tents (Dt 16,1-17). In this way it sought to gather together the people before their God and to guard them from the contamination of local idols. This reform was of course challenged at the death of Josiah, but on the return from exile the Temple of Jerusalem become the only sanctuary from then on. There the pilgrims came for the great feasts of the year from all over Palestine and also from the Dispersion, which was beginning to extend. The "psalms of ascents" (Ps 120—134) give an example of the prayers and mood of the pilgrims: their attachment to the house of the Lord and to the holy City*, their faith, their adoration and their joy in bringing about the deep fellowship of God's people through the liturgical assembly. This frequent experience in Israel provided a striking expression for the eschatological hope: the Day* of salvation is seen in terms of a pilgrimage, as the assembly of the people and of the pagans at last reunited (Is 2,2-5; 60; 66,18-21; Mi 7,12; Ze 14,16-19; Tb 13,11).

NT

At first sight the NT does not seem to have anything new to say on this point: Jesus "goes up" to Jerusalem with His parents when He is twelve years old in obedience to the Law (Lk 2,41f) and throughout His mission He continues to "go up" there for the various feasts (Jn 2,13; 5,1; 7,14; 10,22f; 12,12). More than twenty-five years after the crucifixion Paul him-self is determined to make the Pentecost pil-grimage (Ac 20,16; 24,11).

But Jesus foretells the ruin of the temple (Mk 13,2 p) and the refusal of Israel brings about the final break between the Church and Judaism. Moreover, Jesus' resurrection makes His glorified person the new temple*, from now onward the centre of worship for His faith-ful followers, and no longer any place on earth (Jn 2,19-21; 4,21-23). Frow now on it is the life of the people of God themselves that is regarded as the real eschatological pilgrimage (2 Co 5,6ff; He 13,14). This pilgrimage is also an Exodus* under the leadership of the Lord Jesus (Ac 3, 15; 5,31; He 2,10); as its goal it has spiritual realities: the mountain* of Zion, the heavenly Jerusalem, the assembly of the first-born whose names are written in the heavens (He 12,22ff) and a temple* that is "the Lord God almighty and the Lamb*" (Ap 21,22-26).

The Church is too attached to history to refuse any importance to pilgrimages to the scenes of Christ's life on earth or of His manifestation in the lives of the saints. In these gatherings at the scenes of Christ's action it sees an opportunity for the faithful to show their fellowship in faith and prayer; and above all it seizes this opportunity to remind them that they are on a journey toward their Lord, and under His leadership.

→Altar 1—Feasts II 2—Jerusalem OT III 3; NT I 4—Mountain III 1—Passover I 5.6—Presence of God OT III 1—Stranger II—Temple OT I 4—Way I 1.

AG ems

PLAN OF GOD

God, "the author of all that has occurred, that is now taking place, and that will be later" (Jdt 9,5f), acts "with number, weight, and measure" (Ws 11,20). That is to say, human history does not develop according to the impulses of blind destiny. The result of the will* of God, history is polarized from end to end by the goal toward which it moves. That terminal point is divinely fixed from all eternity and it has two essential aspects: it is salvation* in Christ and the salvation of all men. Such is "the mystery* of God's will, the loving plan that He had formed to be accomplished in Him when the time* would be fulfilled" (E 1,9f; cf 3,11). Hidden for long centuries, suggested in the revelation* of the OT, it was not fully manifested until the moment of Christ's earthly intrusion into human history (E 3,1-12). This plan, nonetheless, confers unity and intelligibility on all sacred history and on the Scriptures. If its technical enunciation in specialized terms is rare in the OT, the plan is nonetheless delicately laced into the whole OT fabric.

OT

The OT provides the first approximations, incomplete and provisional, of God's plan. In the various literary currents corresponding to the diverse postures of Israel's faith in the light of its sacred history are the preliminary presentations of God's plan.

I. RITUAL CONFESSIONS OF FAITH

The Deuteronomic literature has preserved various ritual texts—confessions of faith (Dt 26, 5-10), catechetical formulas (Ex 12,26f; Dt 6, 20...), outlines of priestly sermons (Js 24,2-15) —all are drawn after the same model. This shows the central place of the idea of God's plan in the faith of Israel. Israel there imbibed in broad outline a religious understanding of its own past as a nation. On the part of God there had been the election* of Israel's forefathers, the promise* of a posterity and a land, the fulfillment* of the promise by providential events; preeminently the exodus*, the covenant* on Sinai, the gift of the Law*, the conquest of Canaan. The future is open. But how can it be doubted that the consummation of the plan, incipiently present in deeds, will be brought by God to its term? The Israelite is aware that his life is entirely involved in a drama currently taking place. Yet the drama's end is only partially disclosed.

II. THE PROPHETIC UNDERSTANDING OF EVENTS

To this presupposition the prophets introduce new factors. The fact is that "God does nothing here below without revealing His secret (*sōd*) to His servants, the prophets" (Am 3,7). Before events occur, they are assuredly preceded by a divine purpose (Is 5,19; 14,26; 19,17; 28,29; 46, 10; Jr 23,18-22), a plan (Mi 4,12), a will* of good pleasure (Is 44,28; 46,10; 48,14; 53,10). Such is the mysterious truth the prophets impress on the people of God. They underscore its presence in the national past: since the exodus*, God wished to raise Israel to the rank of son (Jr 3,19f). Present behavior of this ungrateful people ought to be judged in the light of this fact which demands their genuine conversion. For the plan of God continues to govern present history: if Nebuchadnezzar forces his yoke on Israel and neighboring nations it is as God's servant (Jr 27,4-8), as the instrument of His wrath* against these sinful peoples (Jr 25,15...). If one or other pagan nation meets its doom, it is in virtue of divine decree and to make known divine judgment (Jr 49,20; 50,45). If Cyrus becomes master of the East, it is to fulfill the divine pleasure and to assure Israel's liberation (Is 44,28; 46,10; 48,14). Finally, in their eschatological oracles the prophets disclose the goal toward which God directs history: salvation*—a salvation in which all nations*, as well as Israel, would have a share (cf Is 2, 1-4, etc.). Past events give an idea of this salvation inasmuch as they prefigured it. But this salvation will surpass any temporal design, since it will call for the redemption* of sinners in accord with the plan of God (Is 53,10). The prophets etch a tableau comprehending the whole of this plan. It even happens that all its aspects are joined in a synthesis, as in the parable in which Ezekiel summons up successively Israel's past, present, and future (Ez 16).

III. HISTORICAL SYNTHESES

Confessions of faith and prophetic understanding of events furnish the thought structure which gives historical description its unique aspect. Although in the eyes of modern science the historical materials are of diverse provenance and value, their synthetic use gives the attempts a permanent value surpassing the method of simple documentary narrative. Faith* unifies history in bringing to light its continuity (this is already true in the collection of Yahwistic traditions). Faith points out providential laws explaining historical development (as in the synthesis of Jg 2,11-13). Considered thus, all events appear in the same plan of salvation. The universalist perspective remains present (cf Gn 9,12; 10; 12,3; 49,10), although only Israel's destiny is directly in question. As time slips by, new happenings divulge ever more clearly fundamental elements of the plan. Thus to the ancient collections of traditions, which the priestly historian would recognize in abridged form; the Deuteronomic chroniclers add a history of the conquest (Js), of the judges (Jg), and of the monarchy (S and K) up to the collapse of the national institutions. Usuing the same basic outline, the Chronicler will complete the account by the history of the Jewish restoration (Ch, Ezr, Ne). Here is evidence that there is a practical enforcement of God's eternal plan, one capable of thwarting human plans (Ps 33,10f). Indeed, these same historical syntheses pass directly into Israel's prayer (Ps 77; 78; 105; 106); faith is nourished in the knowledge of God's plan disclosed by the medium of historical occurrences.

IV. REFLECTIONS OF THE WISDOM TRADITION

For the same reason reflection of the sages, elsewhere free from temporal considerations, uses history to draw morals from it. The wisdom tradition ponders the ways of God, so different from the ways of men (Is 55,8), so incomprehensible to sinners (Ps 94,10). Into this harmony Qoheleth casts a discordant note when he denounces the perpetual cycle of earthly phenomena (Qo 1,4-11) or the incomprehensibility of time as a whole (Qo 3,1-11). Deeply imbued with the sense of the mystery, he is not easily satisfied with facile solutions! Elsewhere, however, the thought orientation is completely different. Ben Sira meditates on his ancestors' example (Si 44—50). The author of Wisdom discovers in the history of the patriarchs and the exodus fundamental laws of God's guidance which are continuously applied in achieving His plan on earth (Ws 10—19)—a very valuable lesson for men who know they are involved in this plan and are awaiting its supreme fulfillment.

V. APOCALYPTIC CONTRIBUTIONS

At the point where wisdom and prophecy meet, the apocalyptic current ultimately synthesizes the late Judaic concept of the plan of salvation in the light of the older books of Scriptures which were completed by divine revelation. Already Is 25,1 describes the fall of the city of evil as a consequence of God's plan. But Daniel especially presents one comprehensive view of the nation's past history, its present state of affairs, and the eschatological future toward which it tends. Kingdoms pass; but their continuous succession prepares for the coming of the reign of God, object of age-old promises (Dn 2; 7). Persecuting powers hatch plots against the people of God; but they are heading for disaster while Israel goes to her salvation (Dn 8,19-26; 10,20—12,4). This is the mystery* (Dn 2,22.27f). Its substance was already contained in scriptural cipher (Dn 9). The same community of spirits is found in the apocryphal apocalypses (Henoch); and characterizes Judaism of the NT period.

Thus the theme of the plan is fundamental in the whole OT: sacred history is its realization; the Word* of God discloses it in revelation*. Not that man might thus establish a kind of monopoly on the divine mysteries*; but in His love God grants man little by little the knowledge of His plan, illuminating at the same time the meaning of man's existence.

NT

The whole NT is drawn on the same canvas. It merely discloses the final and most important gift, since in the event of Jesus the plan of God is manifested in its fullness with the achievement of its purpose under an historical form.

I. JESUS IN THE PLAN OF GOD

1. *Jesus sees Himself at the center of God's plan*, at the climax of the preparatory period, at the fullness of time*. This awareness is evident in a variety of expressions: the sending of Jesus by the Father (Mt 15,24; Jn 6,57; 10,36); His coming into this world (Mt 5,17; Mk 10,45; Jn 9,39); the fulfillment of the Father's will (Jn 4, 34; 5,30; 6,38) and the fulfillment of the Scriptures (Lk 22,37; 24,7.26.44; Jn 13,18; 17,12); or simply the necessity of His passion ("The Son of Man must": Mk 8,31 p; Lk 17,25; Jn 3,14; 12,34) and the coming of His hour* (Jn 12,23). These expressions portray a critical state of affairs. Jesus' actions are consistently a consequence of this life situation. If He preaches the good news of the kingdom (Mt 4,17.23 p), if He heals the sick and casts out evil spirits, it is to show that He is the one who was to come (Mt 11,3ff) and that the kingdom* of God is at hand (Mt 12,28). In Him, therefore, the plan of God reaches its decisive turning point. In Him are being fulfilled the Scriptures that foreshadowed the culmination. The Scriptures clarify the significance of His earthly destiny who passes from the cross* to His glory. Inversely His earthly destiny throws light on Scriptures by showing how prophecies should be incorporated in the actual occurrences.

2. To this revelation in action *Jesus added more explicit verbal indications*. Through the parables* where the mysteries* of the kingdom* of God are revealed (Mt 13,11 p), He shows the paradoxical manner in which the plan of salvation will attain its goal. His own death is indeed the central point (Mt 21,38f) of the plan, so that "the stone* rejected becomes the cornerstone" (Mt 21,42). As a result, the vineyard of the kingdom will be taken from Israel and given to other vinedressers (Mt 21,43). The banquet celebrating the eschatological nuptials is turned down by chosen Israelites and will be opened to the poor and the sinful from outside (Mt 22,1-11 p). The earthly establishment of the kingdom* will, moreover, not take place by a sudden world transformation. The Word* sown by Jesus will germinate slowly in hearts, like the grain of seed in the earth. It will experience setbacks as well as brilliant successes (Mt 13,1-9.18-23 p). In spite of everything, the kingdom will eventually cover the earth, like the tree sprung from a lowly seed (Mt 13,31f p). It will transform the earth like the leaven in the dough (Mt 13,33 p). Much time will be required. Jesus, therefore, perceives several successive stages to come: His approaching passion, His resurrection on the third day, His return in glory as the Son of Man (Mt 24,30f). When He considers the establishment of the kingdom, He likewise distinguishes between the time of its founding and the time of its consummation (Mt 13,24-30.47ff p). Hence He introduces into prophetic eschatology a temporal perspective that nothing, not even the preaching of John the Baptist, had been hitherto able to notice there. The plan of God will admit a new period between the fullness of time* and the end of ages (Mt 28,20). Foreseeing this interim period, Jesus gives the kingdom the form of a visible institution by founding His Church (cf Mt 16, 18).

II. PREACHING THE PLAN OF SALVATION

The primitive community faithfully appropriated these lessons in their entirety. The gospel* it preaches to the world is not only that of the kingdom: it is that of salvation* that had come in Jesus, the Messiah and Son of God, a salvation henceforth within reach of all men who believe in His name* (Ac 2,36-39; 4,10ff; 10,36; 13,23). In thus revealing the ultimate secret of the divine plan, the apostolic Church in its preaching to the Jews felt nonetheless compelled to overcome the scandal* caused by the cross of Jesus: how can one understand that God could have permitted the death of His Messiah*? But this death* was precisely the outcome of a carefully determined plan and of divine foreknowledge (Ac 2,23; 4,28...), as the Scriptures make abundantly clear. It is not a question of apologetic only: Christian reflection on the paradox of the cross* goes directly to the heart of God's plan. "Christ died for our sins according to the Scriptures" (1 Co 15,3). It is no accident that Scripture foreshadows in various ways the portrait of the just one who suffers. Thus does Scripture indicate how the Son* of Man would bring about the redemption*.

III. PAUL,
THEOLOGIAN OF GOD'S PLAN

1. *A total view.* The entire theology of St. Paul is indeed nothing other than a heralding of God's plan in its entirety (Ac 20,27). This theme is everywhere the substructure of the epistles, since Paul takes up and then systematizes ideas of the primitive community, particularly the paradox of the cross* (1 Co 1,17-25; 2,1-5). In two instances this theme comes to the foreground of his thought and finds formal expression. The first is that of the syntheses where Paul presents in abridged form the total view of God's plan which culminates in Jesus Christ and in His Church*. For those whom God loves, this plan unfolds in tightly connected stages: predestination*, calling, justification, glorification (R 8,28ff). This outline is developed more fully in the hymn which opens the epistle to the Ephesians (E 1,3-14). There the "loving plan," formulated in advance and achieved in the fullness of time, is identified with the mystery of the divine will* (1,9f), the mystery which Christ illuminated fully and of which Paul was constituted minister (3,1-12).

2. *The destiny of Israel.* Within this total view Paul distinguishes one particular point where the plan of God is asserted in an especially paradoxical manner, the destiny of Israel* in the economy of redemption. It was already rather a strange procedure—to assure the salvation of all men by setting one people apart, by giving them exclusive privileges (R 9,4f), by apparently placing one people alone on the path of redemption*. But what can be said when his people, not content with rejecting Jesus, hardens its heart to the message of the gospel? Is not this procedure scandalous too? Would God, whose call and gifts are not subject to change (R 11, 29), have rejected Israel (R 11,1)? By no means. But this hardness* of heart itself was foreseen in Scripture (R 9,23...; 10,19—11,10) and becomes a part of the plan of salvation: God wished to include all men in the disobedience that all might be included in His mercy* (R 11, 30ff). He wished to prune the sterile olive branches as an interim measure in order to

graft in the pagans in their place (R 11,16-24). The privilege of Israel in the plan of salvation thus appears for what it is. Through Israel God resumed His relations with mankind; through Israel's sin He eventually brought about salvation. The time of exclusivity is over. God wishes to reunite all men in Christ by reconciling Jews and pagans in the one Church* (E 2,14-22). To this definitive arrangement only the remnant* of Israel responded (R 11,1-6); but the mass of people will themselves respond to it when all the heathen will have entered the Church (R 11,25ff). Thus the Church's history no longer eludes God's plan as Israel's history did of old: the history of the Church reveals God's ultimate provision.

IV. COMPLETION OF GOD'S PLAN
IN THE FUTURE

God's plan, as presented in the OT, was achieved in eschatology: the sacred texts foreshadowed the goal. The NT is conscious that this term is now attained, inaugurated, made present in the center of time. Nonetheless, it is not totally consummated. The time of the Church constitutes the final stage of God's plan; but the period of the Church also makes its way toward an end. There is, therefore, room for a Christian eschatology, one which calls to mind the consummation of all things and which includes in this perspective the history which prepares for the end. This is the import of that series of texts from the synoptic apocalypse (Mk 13 p), to the brief Pauline indications (1 Th 4, 13-17; 2 Th 2,1-12; 1 Co 15,20-28), to the entire Johannine Apocalypse. The latter, interpreting ancient Scriptual testimony in the light of Christ and of the Church's experience, examines the future resolutely and looks directly at the events which will lead the plan of God to term. Seductions of Antichrist*, persecutions*, preludes of final judgment* written in the evil turns of history, are not chance occurrences. God knows them in advance; and it is through them that He makes salvation here below move to the day on which the number of His elect will be complete (Ap 7,1-8). Then the Son will finally be able to return all things to His Father (1 Co 15,24) so that God may be all in all (15,28).

→Abraham I—Church II o.1—Covenant—Creation OT III; NT II 1—Cross I 2.3—Day of the Lord—Election—Figure OT II—Fulfill—God OT I—Hour—Mission OT I 2, II 1—

Mystery—Nations O; OT II 2, III; NT I 2, II —Obedience—People *A* III; *B*; *C* II—Predestine—Prophet OT I 2—Providence—Remnant NT—Revelation OT II 1; NT I 1 a b, II 1 a—Seek III—Servant of God O, II 2—Sin III 2 b, IV 3 d—Time—Truth OT 3—Will of God —Wisdom OT III 3—Word of God OT II 1 b c. 2 a—Works OT I; NT I.

AAV & PG jrc

POOR

The poor, although they are often forgotten in our classical literatures, play a large role in the Bible. The concrete Hebrew vocabulary of that time permits us to call forth the pitiful cortege of terms: next to *rāš*, "indigent," there is *dal*, "frugal" or "meager," *'ebyōn*, unfilled "mendicant," *'ānî* and *'ānaw* (in the plural *'anāwîm*), the "degraded" and afflicted man. But the poverty that the Bible speaks about is not only an economic and social condition, but it can also be an interior disposition, a spiritual attitude. The OT reveals to us the spiritual riches of poverty, and the NT sees the truly poor as the privileged heirs of the kingdom of God.

OT

I. THE SCANDAL OF POVERTY

Far from spontaneously considering poverty as a spiritual ideal, Israel saw it as a misfortune to be borne, and even a despicable state. This was the result of judging poverty according to a long-standing and imperfect notion of divine retribution that considered material riches as certain recompense for fidelity to God (cf Ps 1, 3; 112,1.3).

Of course the wise men are not unaware of the fact that honest poor men do exist (Pr 19,1.22; 28,6), but they know that poverty is often the result of laziness and lack of order (Pr 11,16; 13,4.18; 21,17) and they severely condemn the idleness that leads to misery (Pr 6,6-11; 10,4f; 20,4.13; 21,25; etc.). Apart from this, poverty can itself become an occasion of sin, and the ideal seems to be the happy mean: "neither poverty nor riches" (Pr 30,8f; cf Tb 5,18ff).

II. CONSIDERATION DUE TO THE POOR

Another no less evident fact asserts itself: many of the poor are really the victims of fate or man's injustice, like the rural proletariat whose frightful distress is described by Job (24, 2-12). These disinherited found their titled defenders in *the prophets*. Following Amos who "blushes" over the crimes of Israel (Am 2,6ff; 4,1; 5,11), the messengers of Yahweh denounce unceasingly "the violence and highway robbery" (Ez 22,29) that soils the country, shameless frauds in trading (Am 8,5f; Ho 12,8), land grasping (Mi 2,2; Is 5,8), enslavement of the little ones (Jr 34,8-22; cf Ne 5,1-13), the abuse of power, and the perversion of justice itself (Am 5,7; Is 10,1f; Jr 22,13-17). It will be one of the tasks of the Messiah to defend the rights* of the wretched and the poor (Is 11,4; Ps 72, 2ff.12ff).

In all of this the prophets were in agreement with the Law (cf Ex 20,15ff; 22,21-26; 23,6). Deuteronomy in particular prescribes a whole group of charitable attitudes and social measures to mitigate the sufferings of the needy (Dt 15,1-15; 24,10-15; 26,12). Nor do the wise men fail to recall the sacred rights of the poor (Pr 14,21; 17,5; 19,17), whose powerful defender is the Lord (Pr 22,22f; 23,10f). It is known that almsgiving is an essential element of true biblical piety (Tb 4,7-11; Si 3,30-4,6).

III. THE PRAYER AND THE SPIRIT OF "YAHWEH'S POOR"

"The cry of the poor" that reaches as far as the ears of God (cf Jb 34,28) often echoes through the *psalms*. It is true that we do not hear there only the pleas of the needy, but also the prayer of the persecuted, the unfortunate, and the afflicted; all these are still part of the poor, and the psalms reveal to us their common spirit (Ps 9—10; 22; 25; 69). They are moved violently to express their hopes for a better tomorrow when the situation will be reversed (54,7ff; 69,23-30); but they look for their salvation from Yahweh upon whom they depend, like the "poor" Jeremiah who entrusts his cause to Him (Jr 20,12f). Their enemies are God's enemies, the haughty (cf Ps 18,28) and the godless* (9,14-19). Their distress is a title to God's love (cf 10,14).

The poor man of the psalms appears as the friend and the servant* of Yahweh (cf 86,1f) in whom he confidently takes shelter and whom he fears* and seeks* (cf 34,5-11). As the Greek translators well knew, it is here not a question of material misery alone: to translate 'anaw, apart from ptochos, "indigent," or penes, poor "needy," they also use praüs, which brings out the idea of a "meek" man, "calm" even in trial. It is with good reason that we also can often translate 'anāwîm as "humble" (Ps 10,17; 18,28; 37,11; cf Is 26,5f). Their basic disposition is really humility*, that 'anāwāh which certains texts of the OT unite with justice (Zp 2,3), "fear of God" (Pr 15,33; 22,4), and faith or fidelity (Si 45,4 hb.; cf 1,27; Nm 12,3).

Those who suffer and pray with similar feelings truly merit the name of "Yahweh's poor" (cf Ps 74,19; 149,4). They are the object of His benevolent love (cf Is 49,13; 66,2) and constitute the first-fruits of the "humble and modest people" (Zp 3,12f), of the "Church of the poor" that the Messiah will gather together.

NT

I. THE MESSIAH OF THE POOR

By beginning His inaugural discourse with the beatitude* concerning the poor (Mt 5,3; Lk 6, 20), Jesus wants the poor to be recognized as the privileged *heirs* of the *kingdom* that He proclaims (cf Jm 2,5). As Mary sang, the humble handmaid of the Lord (Lk 1,46-55), the time has now come when the former promises are going to be fulfilled: "The poor shall eat and shall be filled" (Ps 22,27), they are gathered together at God's table (cf Lk 14,21). Thus, Jesus appears as the Messiah of the poor, consecrated with oil that He might bring to them the good news (Is 61,1=Lk 4,18; cf Mt 11,5). And in fact it is above all the humble who come to Jesus (Mt 11,25; Jn 7,48f).

Moreover the Messiah of the poor is Himself *a poor man*. Bethlehem (Lk 2,7), Nazareth (Mt 13,55), the public life (8,20), the cross (27,35), are so many varied forms of poverty espoused by Jesus, to the point of total destitution. He can invite all those who toil to come to Him for He is "meek and humble of heart" (Mt 11,29: praüs and tapeinos, cf 'ānaw and 'āni in the psalms). Even in His triumphant entry into Jerusalem amidst the waving of palm branches, He remains the "modest" king proclaimed by Ze 9,9 (=Mt 21,5). Especially in His passion, He takes on suffering and resumes the prayer of all Yahweh's poor (Ps 22; cf Mt 27,35.43.46).

II. SPIRITUAL POVERTY

If in the OT there already existed a religious elite that viewed poverty as a spiritual attitude, it is normal that poverty would be viewed in somewhat the same manner by the disciples of Jesus. Indeed, this is the view stressed by St. Matthew: "Blessed are the poor in spirit" (5,3), that is, "those who have poverty of spirit." Jesus demanded that His followers have interior detachment regarding temporal goods, whether they possessed these goods or not, so that they might be capable of desiring and of receiving true riches (cf Mt 6,24.33; 13,22). In times of economic prosperity there is a great danger of having illusions about one's spiritual indigence (Ap 3,17). In any case it is best to make use of this world* as if one really did not use it, for "the world as we know it is passing away" (1 C 7,31). Material possessions are, however, only one of the objects of total renouncement to which one must agree if he is to be the disciple of Jesus (cf Lk 14,26.33). But to outline the complete picture of "the poor in spirit," heirs of the 'anāwîm, it is necessary also to note the conviction they have concerning their personal wretchedness on the religious level with respect to their need for God's help. Far from showing the illusory self-sufficiency of the Pharisee*, confident in his own justice*, they share the humility* of the publican of the parable (Lk 18,9-14). Through their need and weakness they resemble children*; and like these latter, they possess the kingdom of God (cf Lk 18,15ff; Mt 19,13-24).

III. ACTUAL POVERTY

The emphasis that the gospel puts on poverty of spirit must not let us forget the religious value of effective poverty, to the extent that it is the sign and means of interior detachment. This material poverty is good when it is inspired by filial confidence in God, the desire to follow Jesus, and generosity toward our neighbor. It can allow a more free acceptance of God's gift and a more complete consecration to service in His kingdom. St. Luke in particular, among the writers of the NT, liked to recall the many motives for material poverty (vg Lk 12,32ff).

1. *Voluntary poverty.* If Jesus warns all His disciples against the dangers of riches (Mt 6, 19ff; Lk 8,14), He asks those who wish to follow Him more closely, especially His apostles,

to embrace actual poverty (Lk 12,33; Mt 19,21. 27 p). Nevertheless, if the missionaries of "the house of Israel" are not to provide themselves with "gold or silver, not even with a few coppers" (Mt 10,9; cf Ac 3,6), this is partly explained by the social conditions of Palestine, where hospitality is widely practiced. In the Greco-Roman world an instruction of this kind will no longer be able to be applied literally, and St. Paul will have a budget for missionary and charitable work (cf 2 Co 8,20; 11,8f; Ac 21, 24; 28,30). Even then, however, the apostle continues to preach the gospel without recompense (1 Co 9,18; cf Mt 10,8), and he is able to live in need (Ph 4,11f). The community of the first Christians that was gathered around the apostles at Jerusalem endeavoured to imitate their poverty, and the Church has always preserved a feeling of nostalgia for the practice of that *vita apostolica* wherein "no one said that what belonged to him was his own" (Ac 4,32; cf 2,44f).

2. *Patient acceptance of poverty.* Just like the voluntarily poor, those whose lot is actual poverty due to circumstances or persecution are blessed in the kingdom of God, if they at least remain generous in their need (cf Mk 12, 41-44) and if they accept their lot willingly, "looking forward to better and more stable riches" (He 10,34). From now on, in spite of their material poverty, they are in fact rich because of their faithfulness in the face of trial (Ap 2,9f). Luke points out the marvelous rewards God has prepared for them in the future life (Lk 6,20f); they will find with Him, like the poor Lazarus, an eternal consolation (16,19-25).

3. *Christian service of the poor.* Wretched circumstances are not any less an inhuman condition, and the gospel has the same requirements for social justice that the prophets had (cf Mt 23,23; Jm 5,4). Here below, the rich have an urgent duty toward the poor; and they will be associated with them in their eternal happiness on the condition that they receive them according to God's example (Lk 14,13.21), and make friends for themselves with the "mammon of iniquity" (16,9). Further, from this time on, service to the poor is an expression of our love for Jesus, since He is truly the one that we help in helping them, while awaiting His glorious return (Mt 25,34-46; 26,11). "If anyone...sees his brother* in necessity and closes up his bowels to him, how can the love of God dwell in him?" (1 Jn 3,17).

From the prophets to Jesus, the Bible has been interested in the sufferings of the poor and has revealed their meaning to us. There is a spiritual and blessed poverty that in confident faith and patient humility is open to the gift of God. Beyond this poverty of spirit, there is real poverty which remains a privileged path. But its principle and purpose is communion in the mystery of the "liberality of our Lord Jesus Christ": "Being rich, He became poor for you, so that He might enrich you by His poverty" (2 Co 8,9).

→Almsgiving—Beatitude NT II—Cupidity OT 1; NT—David 2—Faith—Humility II—Hunger & Thirst OT 2; NT 1.3—Remnant OT 4—Rights OT 3; NT—Solitude I 1—Wealth—Widows 1.

LR rco'c

POWER

In every religion, power is an essential attribute of divinity. The Christian faith formulates the first article of biblical revelation: "I believe in God, the Father almighty, creator of heaven and earth." This formula indicates three aspects of the omnipotence of the true God. It is universal, for God has created everything (Gn 1, 1; Jn 1,3). It is loving, for God is the Father who is in heaven (Mt 6,9); it is mysterious, for only faith can discern it in manifestations that are at times disconcerting, and open itself to its salvific action (1 Co 1,18; 2 Co 12,9f). For this power is employed in the context of salvation history.

I. THE POWER OF YAHWEH, THE GOD OF ISRAEL

1. God manifests His omnipotence by His interventions here below. In the accounts dealing with the life of the patriarchs, this omnipotence was overpowering: for God, nothing is impossible (Gn 18,14). In every situation He can protect His chosen ones and realize for their benefit what He has willed (Gn 12,2f; 28,13ff). With this omnipotent God, Jacob had to wrestle; and at the end of the contest, God blessed him and gave him the name of Israel* (Gn 32,27-30). This is the name* that will designate the chosen people and express their wish: "May God show Himself strong." The strength of

Israel resides therefore in the intercession and protection of the God who has chosen them (Ps 20,2.8ff); 44,5-9; 105,3f; 124,8), who is the "mighty one of Jacob" (Gn 49,24; Is 1,24;49.26; 60,16; Ps 132,2). This God, by His strong hand (Ex 3,19) and His outstretched arm* (Dt 4,34), liberates His people in the exodus* accomplishment. By this unprecedented deliverance, Yahweh, God of Israel, reveals Himself as being alone all-powerful in heaven and on earth (Dt 4,32-39).

Head of the armies of Israel (Ex 12,41), Yahweh is the warrior who secures victory* for His people. Such is the first significance of His name Sabaoth (Ps 24,8ff; Ex 15,2ff; 1 S 17, 45; S 5,10; Am 5,14f). By means of the ark* of the covenant, the almighty assures His people of His presence (2 S 6,2; Ps 132,8).

2. Sometimes Yahweh intervenes to strengthen His people (Dt 8,17f) and their leaders: judges like Gideon (Jg 6,12ff), kings like David (2 S 7, 9; 22,30ff; 1 S 2,10). The Maccabees rely on this strength which comes from God and makes them invincible (1 M 3,18f; 2 M 8,18). On other occasions, God, in answer to the prayer of the people, intervenes in such a striking way that the people have nothing to do themselves (2 K 19,35; 2 Ch 20,15ff.24). The two types of intervention are combined at the battle of Gibeon under the leadership of Joshua (Js 10,8-11).

Yet, in every situation, it is Yahweh who is the strength* of His people. The psalms sing of it in their songs of praise (Ps 144,1f; 28,7f; 46,2; 68,34ff) or in their appeals for assistance (Ps 29, 11). Israel cannot fail to be saved, for its strength is that of God who loves Israel (Ps 59, 17f; 86,15ff) and who "can do anything that He wills" (Ps 115,3; Is 46,10).

II. THE POWER OF THE CREATOR AND OF MAN, HIS IMAGE

1. If the God of Israel is all-powerful in heaven and on earth, it is because heaven and earth are His creation (Gn 2,4); nothing is impossible for Him (Jr 32,17). He arranges His handiwork as He wills (Jr 27,5), having created it by His word and the breath of His mouth (Ps 33,6.9; Gn 1). He gives to the universe its stability (Ps 119,90), and controls the forces which could rise up to disturb its order, such as a violent sea* (Ps 65,8; 89,10f). But if He has determined this order (Jb 28,25f; Pr 8,27ff; Si 43), He can change it at will. Thus by His power mountains* leap or melt away (Ps 114, 4; 144,5). He transforms a desert* place into an oasis and dries up the sea (Ps 107,33ff; Is 50,2). At His glance all things tremble (Si 16,18f).

2. The power of God is therefore manifest in His creation (Ps 19,2; 104; Ws 13,4; R 1,20). It is exercised on behalf of those who have perfect faith* in its omnipotence. Thus Abraham believed that He who called creation out of nothingness into existence could likewise raise the dead (R 4,16-21; He 11,19). That is why God granted him the fatherhood of a nation of believers without number (Gn 22,16ff). It was the same way with Judith, by whose hand the almighty revealed Himself as master of heaven and earth (Jdt 9,12ff; 16,1-17), because she had given to Israel an example of confidence and unquestioning trust (8,11-27; 13,19).

Why not entrust oneself to Him whose word can effect all things (Es 4,17; Ws 18,15), who can bend hearts to His will (Pr 21,1), and out of whose hand no one can escape (Tb 13,2; Ws 11, 17; 16,15)? This power is infinitely wise in its work of creation and its direction of the world (Ws 7,21.25; 8,1). But creation catches only a faint echo of this infinite wisdom* and of the thunder of its power (Jb 26,7-14). It is sufficiently evident, however, that the just man is not scandalized by even the most trying experiences, but entrusts himself to the almighty in silent adoration (Jb 38,1—42,6).

3. The man who has faith in God becomes a collaborator with the almighty, since he is not only His creature but also His image* (Gn 1, 26ff). He testifies to this collaboration especially in the domination which he exercises over land and beast (Si 17,2ff). Far from cringing before the forces of nature, man ought to master them, a task which he can accomplish if he remains submissive to his Creator in humble trust. Now, in aspiring to independence, Adam has committed the fatal sin and misunderstood the mystery of the loving omnipotence of God (Gn 2,17, 3,5; R 1,20f). In consequence, he has lost his own dominion over the world (Gn 3, 17f).

III. THE EVIL POWERS WHO ENSLAVE MAN

The beginning of Genesis brings to light the effects of the use of power which opposes man to God. Cain uses his physical strength to kill his brother, and Lamech avenges himself without restraint (Gn 4,8.23f). Violence fills the earth (6,11). The collective sin at Babel* is of the same character as that of Adam. Men wish to attain heaven by their own resources. God, not without irony, comments on their presumption, "Nothing will be impossible to them" (11,4ff). This presumption leads men to a double enslavement. The powerful enslave the weak, and they themselves become the slaves of evil powers, the demons.

1. The oppression of man by man appears in fact only after the powerful ones of the earth forget that their power comes from God (R 13,1; 1 P 2,13; Jn 19,11) and that they ought to respect in every man the image of the almighty (Gn 9,6). The Pharaoh who does not reverence Yahweh makes a show of holding God's people in bondage and of imposing on them more and more arduous toil (Ex 5,2;6-18). Tyrants who would place their throne in heaven and thus rival God likewise attempt to subjugate other nations (Is 14,12ff). The proud abuse their power in acts of violence which the prophets denounce, whether done in Israel or among the gentiles (Am 1,3—2,7). The fact that Yahweh makes use of pagan nations* to chastise His people does not lessen the injustice of their violence (Is 47,6). Even more culpable are those who exercise power in Israel and abuse it by putting pressure on the poor, refusing to deal with them justly (Is 3,14f; 10,1f; Mi 3,9ff; Ps 58,2f). The mighty ones of the earth should remember Him who will "judge them with severity." He is the Lord of all, and it is His wish that they should cherish justice* (Ws 1,1; 6,3-8).

2. Moreover, those who do not recognize the almighty who has created them honor gods of their own fashioning who can only be without power. The prophets and wise men vie with each other in railing at idols without authority (Is 44,17ff; Jr 10,3ff; Ps 115,4-7; Dn 14,3-27; Ws 13,10-19). In honoring the stars* or various other creatures, pagans seek to placate natural forces which they have divinized, and thus they fail to see nature's master who is its author (Ws 13,1-8). Therefore, behind these false gods of the gentiles, are concealed demoniac powers (Ps 106,36f; Dt 32,17; 1 Co 8,4; 10,19). The devil, after having enticed men to sin (Gn 3,5; Ws 2,24), seeks their adoration of himself under diverse forms. He seduces them with a display

of the power which God has permitted to him for a time (2 Th 2,9; Ap 12,2-8; cf Mt 4,8f). His power is active in those who resist God (E 2,2); it is a power of the dead, for it is by a fear of death that he keeps man enslaved to himself (He 2,14f).

In the face of false gods, the name of Yahweh Sabaoth takes on a new sense. The true God* is the God of hosts, that is, of all the powers of the universe; the vast array of stars (Is 40,26; Ps 147,4), the legion of angels* (Ps 103,20f; 148,2; Lk 2,13f). Yahweh will intervene to free men.

IV. THE POWERS OF THE SAVIOR AND HIS SERVANT

1. How the almighty puts an end to social servitude of the oppressed and the spiritual servitude of sinners is revealed as early as Exodus. The exodus liberation* is the type of all the others, of which the feast of the Pasch is a perpetual reminder in Israel (Ex 13,3). The resistance of the tyrannical Pharaoh is the occasion for Yahweh especially to exhibit His power over all creation by means of unusual prodigies (Ex 9,14f). The human instrument of these prodigies and of the liberation of Israel is a man conscious of his weakness, Moses*, the humblest of men (Ex 4,10-13; Nm 12,3). Yet God has made him a prophet without peer (Dt 34,10ff).

The liberated people themselves resist their deliverer. God chastises* those who have not believed in His power despite so many miracles. They will die in the desert after having wandered about for forty years (Nm 14,22f). But God, at the intercession of Moses, does not destroy completely this rebellious people, so that no pretext may be given to the pagans to doubt His ability to protect His people (Nm 14, 16) or at least the efficacy of the salvation which His power affords (Ex 32,12). Furthermore, He exercises His power in pardoning* (Nm 14,17ff; cf the collect for the Tenth Sunday after Pentecost).

2. The ways of God remain the same throughout the course of history. To accomplish His plan, He stirs up the mighty ones of the earth. When He wishes to chastise His people by means of exile, Nebuchadnezzar is His servant (Jr 25,9). When the period of trial is over, Cyrus receives from Yahweh the universal power to arrange the return to Zion (Is 44,28—45,4; 2

Ch 36,22f). This second exodus* is the work of the almighty who grants new strength to those who put their hopes in Him (Is 40,10f. 29ff).

By His Spirit*, the divine power which the prophets oppose to the weakness of man which is "the flesh*" (Is 31,3; Ze 4,6), and by His perpetually efficacious Word* (Is 55,11), God confirms the weak instruments which He has chosen. The shepherd lad David*, filled with the Spirit from the chrism of coronation (1 S 16, 13), delivers Israel from all its enemies (2 S 7, 8-11). From his stock will be born the Messiah* whose name will be "God the Mighty." On Him will repose the Spirit of God (Is 9,5f; 11, 1f), and He will have God for His Father (2 S 7,14; Ps 89,27ff). Jeremiah, otherwise unable to speak, proclaims with irresistible force the words which the hand of God had placed in his mouth (Jr 1,6-10.18f). The people of Israel themselves, for whom the exile was the occasion of losing all hope, will be revived by the Spirit of God (Ez 37,11-14). In rescuing this people who serve Him and rely on Him for their strength (Is 49,3-7), and in opposition to idols* which are powerless for salvation, Yahweh reveals Himself as the unique Savior, the almighty whom all the nations ought to adore (Is 45,14f.20-24).

3. It is from sin that God wishes to save all men. The power of Yahweh accomplishes this salvation plan through His mysterious Servant* : He dies, weighed down by suffering and abuse (Is 53). But by means of His death, divine power brings it about that life springs forth for the countless justified. It is indeed a power of resurrection. Since death* is a consequence of sin, God will deliver from death those whom He delivers from sin. The just man will rise unto eternal life. Such is the teaching of the sages for the hour when the just must die for the sake of their faith (Dn 12,2f). The hope of resurrection through the power of the Creator strengthens the persecuted (2 M 7,9.14.23). At a predetermined moment, the power of the oppressors will end and then the company of the saints will share the eternal dominion to be given to the Son* of Man coming on the clouds of heaven (Dn 7,12ff.18.27).

4. At the end of the old covenant, a sage meditating on the history of salvation thus traces the portrait of the almighty who has directed it: He loves everything He has created (Ws 11,24ff). Just and full of mercy, He acknow-

ledges repentance and even excites it in men's hearts (11,23; 12,2.10-18). He protects the just and will give them eternal life, for they are placed in His hand and He is their Father (2,16ff; 3,1; 5,15f; cf Mt 22,29-32). And yet He permits unbelievers to see them die and so tests their hope. This is so that their crown may be due recompense for their holocaust (Ws 3,2-9).

V. THE POWER OF THE SPIRIT IN THOSE WHO BELIEVE IN CHRIST

1. It is in fact a holocaust which will seal the new covenant, namely the holocaust of Jesus in which the almighty reveals Himself fully and by means of which He accomplishes His plan. Jesus* is the almighty Word who was made flesh in the womb of a humble virgin (Lk 1,27. 48f; Jn 1,14; He 1,2f). This coming is the work of the Holy Spirit, the power of the most high for whom nothing is impossible (Lk 1,35ff; Mt 1,20). As the Son of Man, Jesus is anointed* with the Spirit and power (Ac 10,38). The Spirit reposes on Him and is given to Him without measure (Lk 3,22 p; Jn 1,32ff; 3,34f; cf Is 11,2; 42,1; 61,1). Jesus shows His power by miracles* which certify His mission (Ac 2,22) and which prove not only that God is with Him (Jn 3,2; 9,33) and that He is sent by the Father (5,36), but in addition that He is Emmanuel, "God with us" (Mt 1,23).

2. Far from exercising His power for His own glory*, in line with the Jewish expectations of a temporal Messiah (Mt 4,3-7; Jn 8,50), Jesus seeks only the glory of His Father and the accomplishment of His will (Jn 5,30; 17,4). This humility* is the source of His power. Creation is submissive to Him (Mt 8,27 p; 14,19ff p). He cures diseases and raises the dead (Mt 4,23f p; 9,25 p). He forgives sins (Mt 9, 6ff p), and through the power of the Holy Spirit He expels demons (Mt 12,28 p). He affirms His power to lay down his life and take it up again (Jn 10,18), that is, to immolate Himself freely on the cross and to rise again in resurrection. Finally, He announces His coming on the last day to exercise His power as sovereign judge (Mk 13,26 p; Jn 5,21-29). "You will see the Son of Man sitting at the right hand of the power and coming on the clouds of heaven" (Mt 26,64 p). This promise is made before the Sanhedrin at the hour when the

powers of darkness seem to have prevailed (Lk 22,53).

But, as He had already said, once "lifted up" Jesus reveals His person (Jn 8,28) and His power. He dethrones the principalities (Col 2, 15) at the same time as the prince of this world*, and He draws all things to Himself (Jn 12,31f). For that purpose He sends out His disciples* to give testimony that He has all power in heaven and on earth, and to bring all nations to submission, in faith and obedience, to His spiritual kingdom (Mt 28,18ff). That they might accomplish this mission*, He not only confirms their preaching* by miracles (Mk 16,20), but He "will be with them all days even to the end of the world." He will be with them through His Spirit, the power from on high whom He has promised to send them (Lk 24, 49; Ac 1,8).

3. The Spirit which fills the apostles* from Pentecost on (Ac 2,4) is a gift which the risen Christ has presented to them and which manifests His power as Savior (Ac 2,32-36; 4,7-12). When their powerful preaching has converted the hearts of men (Ac 2,37.43; 4,4.33), the apostles then exercise the power to forgive sins (Jn 20,21ff) and to communicate the Spirit (Ac 8,17). The expansion of the Church confirms the promise of Jesus to His disciples: they will accomplish works* greater than His own, and they will obtain from the Father everything that they ask in the name* of His Son (Jn 14, 12ff; 16,23f). Faith therefore renders prayer* all powerful (Mk 9,23; 10,27; 11,22ff).

Paul echoes Jesus in teaching that by faith* man opens himself to the power of salvation in the gospel* (R 1,16). Faith wins "the knowledge of Christ, and the power of His resurrection, and the fellowship of His sufferings" (Ph 3,9f). Jesus crucified saves the believing faithful. For them He is the power of God (1 Co 1,18.23f). For the weakness of God is stronger than men, and His power manifests itself in the frailty of His witnesses (1 Co 1,25; 2 Co 12,9). When these latter are handed over to the executioners for the sake of Jesus, the life of Jesus is made evident in them (2 Co 4,10ff). For they have put their belief in the power of God who has raised Christ from the dead (Col 2,12; 2 Co 13,4). They are powerfully fortified by His Spirit (E 3,16) which makes their words the Word of God and communicates to them the power of the divine Word (1 Th 1,5; 2.13). In them acts the incomprehensible grandeur of the divine power which sur-

passes every thought and expectation (2 Co 4,7; E 1,19ff; 3,20).

4. This same power preserves them for the salvation which will be revealed in the last days (1 P 1,5). God preserves unshakable those who humble themselves under His all-powerful hand and who, in faith, resist the devil (1 P 5,5-10). The unbelievers, on the other hand, will be seduced by those whose power comes from the devil (2 Th 2,9-12; Ap 13,2-7). The Lord will destroy these latter with the breath of His mouth on the day* of His coming (2 Th 2,8). On that day death* will be destroyed, along with every hostile power (1 Co 15,24ff). God will resurrect by His power the bodies* of those in whom the Spirit dwells (1 Co 6,14; R 8,11). He will be all in all (1 Co 15,28). In the Apocalypse, the elect are heard chanting to the Lord God almighty (gr. *Pantocratôr*), whose throne the Lamb* shares. God will create a new universe "where there will be no more sadness*"; i.e., no further power of disorder (Ap 21,1.5): "Alleluia! The Lord our God, sovereign over all, has entered on His reign!" (Ap 19,6). It is a kingdom of love*, for this all-powerful is the Father of "Him who loved us and has freed us from our sins by His blood. To Him be glory and dominion forever and ever. Amen" (Ap 1,5f).

→Arm & Hand—Arrogance—Authority—Creation OT III; NT I, II—Gate OT I—Glory—Imposition of Hands O; NT 2—Jesus (Name of) IV—Life IV 1—Magic 1—Miracle—Mountain I 2—Name OT 1; NT 1—Resurrection NT II—Right Hand 1—Rock—Sea—Seal—Shadow II—Spirit of God—Strength—Victory—Violence—Will of God OT I 2 a—Word of God OT II 2; NT I 1, II 1.

MFL jab

PRAISE

A distinction is commonly made in prayer* between praise, petition, and thanksgiving*. In the Bible, praise and thanksgiving are frequently united in the same movement of the soul, and on the literary level, in the same texts. In fact, God is revealed as worthy of praise in all His benefactions toward man. As a result, praise quite naturally becomes thanks and blessing*, which are brought together in many passages (Ps 35,18; 69,31; 109,30; Ezr 3,11). Praise and thanksgiving evoke the same exterior manifestations of joy*, especially in the people's worship* of God; they both give glory* to God (Is 42,12; Ps 22,24; 50,23; 1 Ch 16,4; Lk 17,15-18; Ac 11, 18; Ph 1,11; E 1,6.12.14) by confessing His greatness.

To the extent that the texts and the words themselves allow of a distinction, it can be said that praise looks more to the person of God than to His gifts. Praise is more theocentric, more deeply lost in God, closer to adoration; and it is conducive to ecstasy. Hymns of praise are generally detached from a particular context; they sing of God simply because He is God.

I. THE GOD OF PRAISE

The songs of praise, bursting with enthusiasm, multiply words in an attempt to describe God and His grandeur. They sing of Yahweh's goodness, justice (Ps 145,6f), salvation (Ps 71,15), assistance (1 S 2,1), love and fidelity (Ps 89,2; 117,2), glory (Ex 15,21), might (Ps 29,4), wonderful plan (Is 25,1), judgments causing liberation (Ps 146,7); all these things shine forth in the wonders of Yahweh (Ps 96,3), in His mighty deeds (Ps 105,1ff; 106,2), in all His works* (Ps 92,5f); and they include the miracles of Christ (Lk 19,37).

From the works themselves we are brought back to their author. "Great is the Lord and highly to be praised!" (Ps 145,3). "O Lord, my God, thou art very great; thou are robed with majesty and honor!" (Ps 104,1; cf 2 S 7,22; Jdt 16,13). The hymns celebrate the great name* of God (Ps 34,4; 145,2; Is 25,1). To praise God is to exalt and magnify Him (Lk 1,46; Ac 10, 46); it is to acknowledge His unique superiority, since it is He who dwells in the highest of the heavens* since He (Lk 2,14) is the holy one. Praise bursts forth from the exultant awareness of God's sanctity (Ps 30,5=97,12; 99,5; 105,3; cf Is 6,3); and this pure, religious exultation effects a profound union with God.

II. THE COMPONENTS OF PRAISE

1. *Praise and confession.* Above all, praise is the confession* of the grandeurs of God. In many different ways, praise is almost always introduced by a formal proclamation (cf Is 12,

4f; Jr 31,7; Ps 89,2; 96,1ff; 105,1f; 145,6; cf 79,13).

This announcement presupposes an audience which is prepared to react in unison; i.e., the assembly of the just* (Ps 22,23.26; cf 33,1). It is the humble and the righteous who are able to understand God's greatness and to sound His praises (Ps 30,5; 34,3; 66,16f), not the senseless man (Ps 92,7).

Bursting forth into contact with the living God, praise arouses the whole man (Ps 57,8; 108,2-6) and sweeps him along in a renewal of life*. Man uses all his powers in praising God; and if it is true praise, it is unceasing (Ps 145,1f; 146,2; Ap 4,8). It is an explosion of life; it is not the dead who have already gone down to Sheol who have the power to praise God, but only the living (Ps 6,6; 30,10; 88,11ff; 115,17f; Is 38,18; Ba 2,17; Si 17,27f).

The NT gives the predominant role in praise to confession*. Praising God always consists first of all in solemnly proclaiming His greatness (Mt 9,31; Lk 2,38; R 15,9=Ps 18,50; He 13,15; cf Ph 2,11).

2. *Praise and song.* Praise is born of wonder and admiration in God's presence. It presupposes a soul that has expanded and been caught up. Praise can be expressed in a shout, an exclamation, a joyous ovation (Ps 47,2.6; 81,2; 89,16f; 95,1...; 98,4). Since it must be ordinarily intelligible to the community, it readily develops into chant or song, which is frequently accompanied by music and even dancing (Ps 33,2f; cf Ps 98,6; 1 Ch 23,5). An invitation to sing is frequently found at the beginning of praise (Ex 15,21; Is 42,10; Ps 105, 1...; cf Jr 20,13).

One of the most characteristic and richest words referring to praise is the Hebrew *hillel*, which is ordinarily translated "to praise," as in our *laudate* psalms (vg Ps 100,1; 113; 117; 135). More often than not the object or motive of praise is mentioned explicitly. But sometimes this is not the case and then it is a praise for the sake of praise, especially in the exclamation *Alleluia=Hallelu-Yah=Praise Yah (weh)*.

The NT uses several terms to express the idea of chanted praise, emphasizing at one time the singing (gr. *aidô*: Ap 5,9; 14,3; 15,3), another the content of the hymn (gr. *hymneô*: Mt 26,30; Ac 16,25), or again the musical accompaniment (gr. *psallô*: R 15,9=Ps 18,50; 1 Co 14,15). A text such as E 5,19, however, seems to put these different words to a parallel usage. Moreover, in the LXX, *hillel* is most frequently translated by *aineô* which is found in the NT, especially in Luke (Lk 2,13.20; 19,37; 24,53; Ac 2,47; 3,8f).

3. *Praise and eschatology.* The Bible assigns the duty of praise first of all to Israel, a consequence of the fact that the chosen people is the beneficiary of revelation* and that it alone acknowledges the true God. Little by little, praise becomes tinged with universalism. Since the pagans also observe the glory and power of Yahweh, they are invited to unite their voice to that of Israel (Ps 117,1). The "royal psalms" are examples of this (Ps 96,3.7f; 97,1; 98,3f). Not only are all peoples of the earth invited to acknowledge God's victories, such as the return from exile, but even nature itself joins in the concert of praise (Is 42,10; Ps 98,8; 148; Dn 3,51-90).

Universalism prepares the way for eschatology. The universal praise begun with the return from exile only inaugurates the great praise to come, which will extend "through the ages." The hymns of the OT prefigure the eternal hymn of the day* of Yahweh, which has already been intoned and which is ever awaited. The "new songs" of the Psalter must find their final echo in the "new song" of the Apocalypse (Ap 5,9; 14,3).

III. PRAISE AND WORSHIP

Israel's praise has always appeared in conjunction with its liturgy, but this relation becomes even more real when, upon the construction of the temple*, its cult receives a more definite structure. The participation of the people in the worship of the temple was vibrant and joyous. It is at the temple especially, on the occasion of the annual festivals or solemn hours in the life of the people (consecration of the king, celebration of a victory, dedication of the temple, etc.) that all the elements of praise are found—the assembly, the enthusiasm expressed in cries of "Amen!" "Alleluia!" (1 Ch 16,36; Ne 8,6; cf 5,13), in refrains such as "Eternal is His love!" (Ps 136,1...; Ezr 3,11), in music and chants. And so, without doubt, a number of psalms were composed to supply the needs of cultic praise. These songs were thereafter dispersed throughout our Psalter, but they can be found more or less distinctly in the three traditional groupings: the "Little Hallel" (Ps 113 to 118), the "Great Hallel" (Ps 136), and the "Final Hallel" (Ps 146 to 150). In the temple the singing of psalms especially accompanied the *tôdâh*, "sacrifice of praise" (cf Lv 7, 12...; 22,29f; 2 Ch 33,16), which was a peaceful sacrifice* followed by a joyful and sacred meal in the buildings adjoining the temple.

In their turn the Christians just as spontaneously associate praise with worship. There are indications of this in the liturgical assemblies described in Acts and the epistles (Ac 2,46f; 1 Co 14,26; E 5,19) as well as in the description in the Apocalypse of worship and praise in heaven.

IV. CHRISTIAN PRAISE

Praise is essentially the same in both Testaments, but from now on praise is something Christian, since it is a response to Christ's gift manifested in His redemptive power. The praise of the angels* and shepherds (Lk 2,13f.20) has this Christian meaning, as does that of the crowds after witnessing Christ's miracles (Mk 7, 36f; Lk 18,43; 19,37). This is even the basic meaning of the Hosanna on Palm Sunday (cf Mt 21,16=Ps 8,2f) and of the Canticle of the Lamb in the Apocalypse (cf Ap 15,3).

Some fragments of the primitive hymns, which have been preserved in the epistles, re-echo that Christian praise addressed to God the Father who has revealed the mystery* of piety* (1 Tm 3,16) and who will bring about the return of Christ (1 Tm 6,15f). This praise confesses the mystery of Christ (Ph 2,5...; Col 1,15...) or the mystery of salvation (2 Tm 2,11ff) and thus becomes on occasion the true confession* of the faith and Christian life (E 5,14).

The NT praise, based upon the gift of Christ, is Christian also in the sense that it ascends to God with Christ and in Him (cf E 3,21). It is filial praise in imitation of Christ's own prayer* (cf Mt 11,25); it is even addressed directly to the person of Christ (Mt 21,9; Ac 19,17; He 13,21; Ap 5,9). It is altogether proper to say that henceforward the Lord Jesus is our praise.

With Scripture as its point of departure, praise had to remain always a basic element in Christianity. It ought to give rhythm to liturgical prayer with its *Alleluia* and *Gloria Patri*; it ought to infuse life into souls in prayer to the point of overwhelming them and transforming them into a pure "Praise of Glory."

→Adoration—Blessing II 3, III 5—Blasphemy —Confession—Eucharist I 1.2—Glory V—Lips 2—Perfume 2—Piety OT 2—Prayer II 3, V 2

—Thanksgiving—Tongue 1—Works OT I—Worship.

AR mjm

PRAYER

I. PRAYER IN THE HISTORY OF ISRAEL

The most stable constant among the elements of the OT prayer is undoubtedly its relation to the salvific plan of God: one prays, beginning with what has happened or with what is happening, so that something may happen and thus the salvation of God may be granted to the earth. The content of the prayer of Israel therefore sets it in history. On its side, sacred history is marked by prayer: it is revealing to determine how many great moments of this history are punctuated by the prayer of the mediators and the entire people, who depend upon the knowledge of the plan* of God to obtain His intervention in the present moment. We will give only a few examples of this, with the expectation that the prayer of Christ and that of His spouse the Church will come to confirm them.

1. *Moses.* He predominates among all the figures of the OT men of prayer. His prayer, a type of the prayer of intercession, harbingers that of Jesus. It is out of consideration for him that God saved the people (Ex 33,17), from whom Moses stood out (32,10; 33,16). This prayer is dramatic (32,32) and its arguments follow the scheme of every supplication: call upon the love of God, "this nation is your people" (33,13; cf 32,11; Nm 11,12); appeal to His justice and fidelity, "that we may thank you, recall your actions of the past"; consideration of the glory of God, "what will others say if you abandon us." (Ex 32,11-14). From this prayer, also, a more contemplative prayer which transformed him for the good of those about him (34,29-35) flowed from the work of Moses the legislator. The period of Moses, finally, recalls the type of a perversion of prayer: "to tempt God." Prayer here follows the inclination of covetousness in opposition to the call of grace* to the divine plan. In the episode of Meribah and that of the quails, God is put to the test (Ex 16,7; Ps 78; 106,32). This comes to telling Him what one will believe, if He does our will (cf Jdt 8,11-17).

2. *Kings and prophets.* The Messianic announcement of the prophet Nathan excites in David a prayer whose essential part is: "Do as you have spoken" (2 S 7,25; cf 1 K 8,26). Similarly, Solomon, at the inauguration of the temple*, includes in his prayer all the future generations (Office of Dedication: 1 K 8,10-61). An element of contrition predominates (1 K 8, 47), which is found again after the destruction of the temple (Ba 2,1—3,8; Ne 9). Other royal prayers have been preserved for us (2 K 19, 15-19; 2 Ch 14,10; 20,6-12; 32,12.18). Prayer for the people undoubtedly would enter into the official functions of the king.

It is because of his intercessory power (Gn 18, 22-32) that Abraham deserves to be called a prophet (20,7). The prophets* were men of prayer (Elijah: 1 K 18,36f; cf Jm 5,17f); and, like Samuel (cf Jr 15,1), Amos (Am 7,1-6), but especially Jeremiah, they were intercessors. In the last mentioned, tradition will see "him who prayed much for the people" (2 M 15,14). The function of intercessor supposes a clear understanding both of the distinction and of the relation which are established between the individual and the community. It is this understanding (cf also Jr 45,1-5) which constitutes the richness of Jeremiah's prayer, parallel in many ways to that of Moses, but more abundantly illustrated. At times it is he who asks for the salvation of the people (10,23; 14,7ff.19-22; 37,3...) whose sorrows he makes his own (4,19; 8,18-23; 14,17f). At other times he complains of the people (15,10; 12,1-5) and even cries for vengeance* (15,15; 17,18; 18,19-23); again, he unbosoms himself on his own fate (29,7-18...). Numerous are the relationships in form and in essence between these prayers and the collection of the psalms.

Ezra and Nehemiah also pray at one and the same time for themselves and for others (Ezr 9, 6-15; Ne 1,4-11). Likewise, a little later, the Maccabees never go into battle without praying (1 M 5,33; 11,71; 2 M 8,29; 15,20-28). The importance of formulated personal prayer grew in the post-exilic books which bear such precious testimony in this regard (Jon 2,3-10; Tb 3,11-16; Jdt 9,2-14; Es 4,17). These prayers were written to be read in a story. Thereafter we can, and the Church encourages this, make them our own. But the intention of those who made a collection of the Psalms was that the Psalter be prayed: no prayer of Israel is comparable to the Psalter because of its universal character.

PRAYER

II. THE PSALMS, PRAYER OF THE ASSEMBLY

The wonders of Yahweh (Ps 104...), the commandments (Ps 15; 81...), prophecy (Ps 50...), wisdom (Ps 37...)—all the Bible ends by capillary attraction in the psalms and therein becomes prayer. The idea of the unity of the chosen people's prayer guided its elaboration, as well as its adoption by the Church. In giving us the Psalter, God puts into our mouths the words He wishes to hear, and indicates to us the dimensions of prayer.

1. *Community and personal prayer.* Often it is the nation which rejoices, remembers, or laments: "Recall to mind," "until when?" (Ps 44; 74; 77); or again the community of the pious (Ps 42,5; the songs of the ascent to Jerusalem ...). The temple, close by or far away, center of the resounding prayer of the assembly (Ps 5,8; 28,2; 48,10...), here is often called vividly to mind. One invokes the just as witnesses (Ps 119,63); they serve as the basis for an argument: they do not lose their faith in seeing us fall (Ps 69,7); when prayer has been answered the just will be informed (Ps 22,23=He 2,12).

Despite the frequent occurrence of these same expressions, the Psalter is not a simple formulary or book of ceremonies. Its spontaneous nature indicates the origin of the psalms in a personal experience. Besides the properly individual prayers, it is especially the emphasis on the king which makes clear the equal importance granted to the individual and to the community: the king* is pre-eminently a singular person, and at the same time the group finds in him its living symbol. The traditional assignment of the collection to David, who was the first psalmist, indicates its bond with the mediating prayer of Jesus, Son of David.

2. *Prayer of trial.* The prayer of the psalms starts from the diverse situations of life. One senses in them little of the sweet odor of solitude (Ps 55,7; 11,1) but one does hear quite a bit of the market place and of war (Ps 55; 59; 22, 13f.17), which makes for a text that is much more chaotic and fiery than some people would expect from a book of prayers. If one calls upon God with these cries, these loud appeals (Ps 69,4; 6,7; 22,2; 102,6), it is because everything is at stake; one needs Him with all one's being, body and soul (Ps 63,2). The body, with its trials and its joys, has in this prayer the place it holds in life (Ps 22; 38...). The psalm-

ist seeks after all goods*: the *tôb* (Ps 4)—and he expects them only from God.

From the fact that he refuses neither life with God nor the journey here below, he prepares himself for the crucible of trial*. Outside of this perspective—the experience of being led by God upon the ways of the man who walks—we cannot understand his prayer. The cries of supplication begin from the moments when the adherence to faith* is put to the test: is the plan* of God for the individual or the people hindered or not? All those around the suppliant man ignore prayer (Ps 53,5); they torment him: "Where is your God?" (Ps 42,4), and he begins to question (Ps 42—43; 73): his certitude does not stem from those things which life would ever be able to take away or bring forth. This enlightens the passages in which innocence is itself proclaimed, not because of pure self-complacence, but in face of danger and because the enemy*, forever present, denies it (Ps 7,4ff and 26, recited at Mass).

3. *Prayer of confidence.* The leitmotif of the prayer of the psalms is *bāṭaḥ*: to trust (Ps 25,2; 55,24...). This confidence*, which passes from laughter to tears and vice versa (Ps 116,10; 23,4; 119,143), is balanced between supplication and thanksgiving*. One thanks even before receiving (Ps 140,14; 22,25ff; cf Jn 11,41). The psalms which contain only praise* are an important part of the collection. The three young men praising together in the furnace make up a generic class for the psalmist.

4. *Prayer in quest of the true good.* In waiting for good from God, whatever it may be, man is called upon to go beyond himself by the discovery that it is God* Himself who is given with this good. One declares the joy* of living beneath the gaze of God, of being with Him, of living in His house* (Ps 16; 23; 25,14; 65,5; 91; 119,33ff). As for the hope that God would cause man to come nearer to His own life*, one cannot say that the prayer of the psalms is nourished on it, but this gratuitous gift* is anticipated (Ps 73,24ff; 16). Anyone who is formed by the prayer of the psalms is prepared to receive it, and he will find in them the way to express this experience.

5. *The Psalter, prayer of Jesus.* For the revelation of Christ will authorize a change and an enrichment of the hopes of the psalmist, but it will not suppress the root of them in our human condition. Besides, the application of

the psalms will be able to be made to Christ before any transposition to others: the psalms will be His prayer (cf Mt 26,30) and He will be formed by them, as will all those about Him. Could a piety* that was anxious to "learn from Christ" (E 4,20) neglect this fundamental document?

III. PRAYER AS JESUS TEACHES IT

By the incarnation, the Son of God is placed squarely in the midst of men's incessant petitioning. He nourishes hope by answering it. At the same time He praises, encourages, or leads to faith* (Lk 7,9; Mt 9,22.29; 15,28). Thus at life's very center, it is first the manner of praying that He teaches, with greater stress here than on the necessity of prayer: "when you pray, say..." (Lk 11,2).

1. *The synoptics*. The Father is the center of this teaching (Lk 11,2ff; Mt 6,9-13). From the appeal to God as Father*, which extends the intimacy of the psalms while elevating it as well (Ps 27,10; 103,13; cf Is 63,16; 64,7), flows the whole attitude of one who prays. This appeal is an act of faith and already a gift of oneself which puts one on the path of love. Hence it follows that right at the very center of biblical prayer, the man at prayer first of all starts considering the purposefulness of the plan* of God: His name*, His kingdom* (cf Mt 9,38), the carrying out of His will*. But he also asks for this bread* (which he offers in the eucharist); then he seeks pardon*, after being reconciled with the Son of that same Father; finally he pleads for the grace not to be overcome by the trials* of future times.

The other prescriptions enclose or complete the Our Father, and often name the Father. The predominant impression is that the certainty of being heard is the source and condition of the prayer (Mt 18,19; 21,22; Lk 8,50). Mark expresses this in the most direct way: "if a man does not hesitate in his heart, but believes that what he says will happen, that will be granted him" (Mk 11,23; cf 9,23 and especially Jm 1, 5-8). But if a man is certain, it is because he prays to the Father (Lk 11,13; Mt 7,11). This interiority is founded on the presence of the Father who sees what is hidden (Mt 6,6; cf 6,4. 18); not on the piling up of words or endless repetition of speeches (Mt 6,7) as if God were far from us, after the fashion of Baal mocked by Elijah (1 K 18,26ff), for He is our Father.

We are commanded to pardon (Mk 11,25 p; Mt 6,14), to pray in fraternal union (Mt 18,19), to recall our faults in a contrite prayer (Lk 18, 9-14).

We must pray without ceasing (Lk 18,1; cf 11, 5-8). Our perseverance must be proved, our vigilance of heart must be manifested. The absolute necessity of prayer is taught in the context of the final times (Lk 18,1-7), made proximate by the passion. Without this, one would be overcome by "all that which must happen" (Lk 21,36; cf 22,39-46); likewise the Our Father finishes up by imploring God against temptation.

2. *John* presents the pedagogy of prayer under a very penetrating light. It is the passage from the request to true prayer, and from the desire* for the gifts of God to the desire of the gift which brings God Himself, as we already read in the psalms. Thus the Samaritan woman is led from her own desires to the longing for the gift* of God (Jn 4,10), the crowd to "the nourishment* which remains in everlasting life" (Jn 6,27). This is why faith is not only the condition of prayer, but its effect as well: the desire is at one and the same time heard and purified (Jn 4,50.53; 11,25ff.45).

IV. THE PRAYER OF JESUS

1. *His prayer and His mission*. Nothing in the gospels reveals better the absolute necessity of prayer than the place it holds in the life of Jesus. He often prays on the mountain (Mt 14, 23), alone (*ibid.*), in seclusion (Lk 9,18), even when "all the world is searching for Him" (Mk 1,37). We would be mistaken to reduce this prayer to a simple desire for silent intimacy with the Father: it has to do with the mission* of Jesus, or the education* of the disciples. These two points are mentioned in four comments about prayer proper to Luke: at the baptism (3,21), before the choice of the twelve (6,12), during the transfiguration (9,29), before the teaching of the Our Father (11,1). His prayer is the secret which attracts His closest friends and into which He makes them enter more and more (9,18). It concerns them since He has prayed for the faith of His own. The bond between His prayer and His mission is clear in the forty days which began it in the desert; for these days brought to mind again the example of Moses, while at the same time surpassing that example. This prayer is a test:

Jesus will triumph better than Moses over the satanic effort to tempt God (Mt 4,7=Dt 6,16: Massah); and from the time before His passion He shows us what obstacles our own prayer will have to overcome.

2. *His prayer and His passion*. The decisive test is the one at the end, when Jesus prays and wants to make His disciples pray with Him on the Mount of Olives. This moment sums up all Christian prayer: filial, "Abba"; assured, "everything is possible"; trial of obedience in which the temptor is repelled, "not what I want, but what you want" (Mk 14,36). It is groping also, just like our prayers, in regard to its true object.

3. *His prayer and His resurrection*. Prayer is here answered finally beyond all expectation. The comforting of the angel (Lk 22,43) is the immediate response which the Father makes for the present moment, but the letter to the Hebrews shows us in a radical and fearless manner that it is the resurrection that fulfills this so truly human prayer of Christ: "in the days of His earthly life, having offered with loud cries and tears prayers and supplications to Him who could save Him from death, and He was heard because of His piety*" (He 5,7). The resurrection of Jesus, the central moment of the salvation of humanity, is a response to the prayer of the Man-God who answers all the human pleas in the history of salvation (Ps 2,8: "ask me").

4. *The night of the last supper*. Here Jesus, among other things, having told first of all how to pray, now prays Himself. His teaching is in accord with that of the synoptics as regards the certainty of being heard (*parrēsia* in 1 Jn 3,21; 5,14), but the condition "in my name" opens up new perspectives. It is a question of passing from the request more or less instinctive to true prayer. The "up till now you have asked nothing in my name" (Jn 16,24) can therefore be applied to many of the baptized. To pray "in the name*" of Christ supposes more than a formula, just as to do something in the name* of another person supposes a real relationship with that other person. Thus to pray does not at all mean to ask only for the things of heaven, but rather to want what Jesus wants. But His will is His mission*: that His unity* with the Father become the foundation of the unity among those who are called. "That all be one as you, Father, are in me, and I in you" (Jn 17,

22f). To be in His name and to want what He wants is thus to walk in His commandments, the first of which imposes this charity which one asks for. Therefore charity is all in prayer: prayer's condition and its end result. The Father gives all for the sake of this unity. Thus the constant affirmation of the synoptics, that every prayer is heard, is here confirmed for all renewed hearts: "without speaking in parables*" (Jn 16,29). Here we find a new situation, but one which fulfills the promises of the day* of Yahweh when "all those who will invoke the name of Yahweh will be saved" (Jl 3,5=R 10,13). The prayer of the last supper promulgates the desired age in which the benefits of heaven will correspond to the desires of earth (Ho 2,23-25; Is 30,19-23; Ze 8,12-15; Am 9-13). Such is the prayer of Jesus, which transcends our own. He rarely says "I pray," generally "I ask," and once "I want" (at the end: Jn 17,24). This prayer expresses His intercession (eternal according to He 7,25) and reveals the interior content of the passion as well as of the eucharistic supper. For the eucharist* is the pledge of the total presence* of God in His gift and the possibility of perfect exchange.

V. THE PRAYER OF THE CHURCH

1. *The community*. The life of the Church has its beginnings in the framework of the prayer of Israel. The gospel of Luke ends in the temple where the apostles were "continually... praising God" (Lk 24,53; Ac 5,12). Peter prays at the sixth hour (Ac 10,9); Peter and John go to pray at the ninth hour (3,1; cf Ps 55,18 and our office of sext and none). They raise their hands to heaven (1 Tm 2,8; cf 1 K 8,22; Is 1,15), standing and at times on their knees* (Ac 9,40; cf 1 K 8,54). They chant the psalms (E 5,19; Col 3,16). "All, with one heart, were assiduous in prayer" (Ac 1,14). This community prayer which prepared for Pentecost likewise prepares all the great moments of the Church's life throughout the Acts of the Apostles: the replacement of Judas (1,24-26), the institution of the seven deacons (6,6) who should precisely facilitate the prayer of the twelve (6,4). They pray for the liberation of Peter (4,24-30), for the baptized of Philip in Samaria (8,15). We see Peter praying (9,40; 10,9), and Paul (9,11; 13,3; 14,23; 20,36; 21,5...). The Apocalypse brings us the echoes of the sung prayer of the assembled (Ap 5,6-14...).

2. *St. Paul.*

a) Struggle. Paul adds to the words which define prayer by the mention of "unceasing," "at every moment" (R 1,10; E 6,18; 2 Th 1,3.11; 2,13; Phm 4; Col 1,9), or "night and day" (1 Th 3,10; 1 Tm 5,5). He conceives of prayer as a struggle: "struggle with me in the prayers which you address to God for me" (R 15,30; Col 4,12), a struggle which is confused with that of the ministry (Col 2,1). To "see the faces" of the Thessalonians he prays "very much" (1 Th 3,10), the same untranslatable superlative which he uses to define the way in which God hears us (E 3,20). "Three times I have supplicated the Lord," he says (2 Co 12,8), in order that the sting fixed in his flesh may be removed.

b) Apostolic prayer. The example just cited is unique. For in his prayer, indissolubly linked to the divine plan which is fulfilled in his mission, all his explicit pleas concern the advancement of the kingdom of God. This entails concrete desires: the quest of Jerusalem (R 15, 30f) to be won over, the end of tribulation (2 Co 1,11), his own freedom (Phm 22); for this and for other things (Ph 1,19; 1 Th 5,25), he asks the prayers of others just as he indicates to the Colossians (4,12) that Epaphras struggles in his prayer for them. Prayer in the writings of Paul clearly appears as the link to the interior of the body* of Christ in growth (see also 1 Jn 5,16).

c) Thanksgiving. We constantly note in St. Paul the traditional balance between supplication and praise*: "prayers and supplication, with thanksgiving" (Ph 4,6; cf 1 Th 5,17f; 1 Tm 2,1). He himself begins his letters (except G and 2 Co, for special reasons) by rendering thanks for the progress of their recipients and by telling of his prayers that God may bring His graces to completion (Ph 1,9). It seems that thanksgiving* attracts to itself all the other components of prayer: after what we have received once for all in Jesus Christ, we cannot pray any more without starting with this gift, and we ask to be able to return thanks for it (2 Co 9,11-15).

d) Prayer in the Spirit of the Son. Paul plays a piercing light upon the role of the Spirit* in the prayer which unites us to the holy Trinity. Just as we still do in the moments of liturgical prayer, he addresses his prayers, through Christ, to the Father. It is rare that he addresses himself to "the Lord," that is, to Jesus (2 Co 12,8; cf E 5,19; but Col 3,16, a parallel, speaks of "God" in place of the Lord). But what makes us pray through Christ (=in His name), is precisely the Spirit of adoption (R 8,15). Through Him, like Jesus, we say "Father" and this under the familiar form "Abba," a word which the Jews reserved for their earthly fathers and would never have used for the Father of heaven. This favor can come only from on high; "God has sent into our hearts the Spirit of His Son who cries: Abba, Father" (G 4,6; cf Mk 14,36).

Thus the need which humanity feels to justify its prayer, penetrated by divine initiative, is really satisfied. Much more profound than a filial attitude, sonship is at the heart of our prayer. Thus, throughout our gropings (R 8,26), the Spirit who prays in us gives to our prayer (He 4,14ff; Jm 4,3ff) the assurance of reaching the depths out of which God calls to us, which are those of love. We know how to name this gift, which is the beginning and end of prayer; it is the Spirit of love already received (R 5,5) and yet asked for (Lk 11,13). In Him we seek a new world* in which we are sure of being heard. Outside of it, we pray "like the pagans." In Him all prayer is the opposite of a flight: a call hurrying the meeting of heaven and earth: "The Spirit and the bride say: 'come'...'Yes, come, Lord Jesus!'" (Ap 22,17.20).

→Adoration—Amen o.1—Blessing I, III 5—Communion OT 4—Confidence 2—Desire III, IV—Elijah NT 3—Eucharist I 1—Expiation 2—Fasting o.1—Glory V—Knee 2—Listen 2—Messiah OT I 2—Pardon I—Pilgrimage—Poor OT III—Praise—Priesthood OT III 2—Providence 1—Salvation OT II—Seek I, II—Temple OT I 1; NT I 1, III 2—Thanksgiving—Trial/Temptation NT III 1—Watch II, III—Worship.

PBp jjk

PREACH

To preach in our day is to announce the event of salvation as well as to exhort* (*parakalein*) or teach* (*didaskein*). In the NT, however, the verbs *kēryssein* and *euangelizesthai* restrict preaching to the solemn proclamation (*kērygma*) of a fact: Jesus is Lord and Savior. This restriction nonetheless does not impoverish preaching taken in the wider sense, for it uncovers the source which inspires all teaching and exhortation: the Easter message. This proclamation has some roots in the OT, since the one who preached the Word of God then was the prophet*. Urged on by the Spirit of God, he announced the divine judgment to his contemporaries; and his word was the Word* of God. In the NT, the word of the preachers is still the Word of God; but since the time that it was incarnated in Jesus, it is Christ who judges their word and their life.

I. THE MESSAGE
OF CHRISTIAN PREACHING

Despite the diversity of time, place, and listeners, the preaching of John the Baptist, of Jesus, of Peter, and of Paul all offer an identical idea and an identical orientation: the call to conversion and the announcement of an event.

1. *Call to conversion.* The same word inaugurates the preaching of Jesus and that of John the Baptist, His precursor, and crowns that of the first apostolic sermons: "Repent!" (Mt 3, 2; 4,17; Ac 2,38; 3,19; 5,31; 10,43; 13,38f). The truth which has been announced has therefore nothing to do with a theory which one is free to agree with or not; it requires of the listener a commitment, for according to their biblical sense, *Word** and *truth** have the value of life. All preaching which does not open on a call to penance runs the risk of ceasing to be the gospel* and turning into a talk.

2. *Proclamation of an event.* If preaching asks for a conversion, it is not in virtue of a moralizing exhortation, but because it announces the event of salvation.

The evangelists, and more particularly Matthew, wanted to show how Jesus during His earthly life began the apostolic preaching. "The kingdom of heaven is at hand" (Mt 4,17), proclaimed Jesus, as He followed upon the precursor (3,2); and, as an echo, the disciples (10, 7) announced the same fact: the prophecies are fulfilled* John is the "voice which cries in the desert, according to the prophet Isaiah" (3,3). Jesus presents Himself as the Servant* who evangelizes the poor: "today is fulfilled that word which you have just heard" (Lk 4, 17-21; Is 61,1f).

On the day of the Passover, the kingdom* announced earlier is made manifest in the glory of the risen one. On the day of Pentecost, the gift of the Spirit* caused the Church* to be born, thus actualizing the kingdom on earth. Henceforth preaching no longer simply announced something that will happen in the near future, as in the time of Jesus; it proclaimed an actual fact which shows the Holy Spirit at work, a fact which looks back to a past event (the Passover of Christ) and to a future event (the parousia of the Lord). The summaries of the first sermons reveal the new nature of this Christian present.

Peter thus explains that if people hear him speaking in a strange tongue* on Pentecost day, it is because the Holy Spirit is being given (Ac 2,4.11.15ff). Be it a question of a miracle such as that of the cripple made well (3,1-10) or of an astonishing boldness on the part of these preachers (4,13; 5,28), the preaching always put the listeners in the presence of a fact which posed a question. It is accompanied "by power, by the Holy Spirit, and by conviction" (1 Th 1,5). This perpetual present, this renewed Pentecost (Ac 10,44-47), is justified in its turn only by reference to a past and a future both of which are concerned with Christ. Jesus is raised from the dead, He is living: that is what the Holy Spirit bear witness to through the miracle of Pentecost (2,22-36), that is what the healing of the cripple means (3,12-16). Jesus is Lord*, glorified in heaven (3,21), and He will return in triumph for the judgment* (1 Th 1,10; 2 Th 1,7). The preaching is essentially the paschal message, and thereby the revelation of the mystery of sacred history.

3. *Presentation of the event.* By itself, the kerygma is a solemn proclamation, the cry of the herald who officially announces a fact. And as this fact is the victory* of Christ over death*, the listener sees his present moment suddenly acquire a dimension of eternity. This could suffice. Still it is necessary that the listener, conditioned by his time and his milieu, be able to understand the message. When the Athenians heard Paul "announce Jesus and the resurrection," they thought of two new divinities and treated him as a spreader of stories (Ac 17,18). Thus Paul seeks to make himself understood, without wishing for all that to justify his message by human reason. The Corinthians believed that Apollos, "a man eloquent and versed in the Scriptures" (Ac 18,24), was in this regard the model preacher. Paul disabuses them: for fear of reducing to naught the cross* of Christ, he refuses the wisdom* of language (1 Co 1,17). All preaching therefore must signify the re-

demptive event, while at the same time being intelligible. Hence there are necessary variations in the presentation of the message.

a) The audience of the apostles, like that of Jesus, believed in God and in His plan of salvation. Preaching, therefore, began with Scripture in order to present the event of redemption. Like Jesus and John the Baptist, the disciples showed in it the fulfillment* of the prophecies. We are in "the last days" announced by Joel (Ac 2,17) and by all the prophets (3,24); the promise* made to the father* is fulfilled (13, 33). The scandalous cross* has been foreseen by God Himself (2,23); it is the "wood" of which the OT used to speak (5,30; 10,39; 13,29; cf Dt 21,23); the lot of Christ has been announced by the prophets (3,18; 13,27), more especially by the poem of the Servant (8,32f; 3,13.26), by the psalms (2,25-28.30.34f; 13,22.33.35), or Moses (3,22). The duty of conversion is itself prophesied (2,21.39). The preaching thus is essentially scriptural and the formula "according to the Scriptures" punctuates the most ancient Credo (1 Co 15,3f).

b) It is possible that Jesus' contemporaries did not know Him during His earthly existence. In this way, the paschal message blossoms into a simple presentation of the existence of Jesus. And so, before the centurion Cornelius (Ac 10, 37-42), Peter outlines the high points of the gospel of Jesus' life. Jesus Himself does in fact belong to the preaching, but in the light of the paschal message.

c) The audience finally is capable of not even believing in the true God and can have need of knowing the underlying facts of biblical faith. At Lystra, Paul reaches his audience by speaking of the "living God who has made heaven and earth...who gives from heaven the seasons and the rains" (Ac 14,15ff). At Athens, he shows how the resurrection of Christ is the end of an historical economy which had its beginning in creation and the human quest for God (17,22-31). As for the Thessalonians, they "have abandoned idols to be converted to God, to serve the living and true God, and to expect from the heavens His Son whom He raised from the dead, Jesus, who freed us from the wrath which was upon us" (1 Th 1,9f). In every way, direct or by a circuitous path, it is to Christ, Lord of history, that preaching should lead.

4. *From preaching to teaching.* Beginning with the paschal mystery which sums up the Credo received through Paul (1 Co 15,3ff), and which should be repeated unceasingly so that the faith may rest in its true focal point, preaching becomes teaching*. Jesus Himself thus proceeded when He "taught" on the mountain (Mt 5,2) or in the synagogues (9,35); the disciples did likewise, according to the command received from the risen Christ (28,20; Ac 4,2). Paul elaborated his own teaching starting with the paschal mystery, when for example he teaches the wisdom* of the cross* (1 Co 1,23) or baptism* as a participation in the death and resurrection of Jesus (R 6). The preacher becomes a catechist and theologian, but the theologian merits this title only if he unceasingly refers to the proclamation of the paschal gospel.

II. THE MYSTERY OF PREACHING

Preaching is a mystery because of the content of the message; it is that also because of the form in which it is announced: mystery of the spoken word*, mystery of the preacher who announces the Word.

1. *The mystery of the Word.* If preaching has the value of action and demands an act of conversion, it is because preaching itself is an act of God. In fact, Paul gives witness that it makes men present to the mystery which it announces. Thus the faith* can be born of preaching (R 10, 17). The listener is placed before the dead and risen Christ, become the Lord of history, distributing the gifts and the Spirit to those who receive the Word, threatening those who refuse it with His wrath* (1 Th 1,10). Like the announcing of the herald proclaiming and inaugurating the kingdom of God (Is 40,9), preaching is an act of God who begins the lordship of Christ over the world. It is not submitted to the scrutiny of its hearers, but requires the "obedience of faith" (R 1,5), even to the end of the world (Mt 24,14).

2. *Word of God and the human word.* To be saved, one must believe; to believe, one must hear preaching; and "how will anyone preach unless he be sent?" (R 10,15). The preacher has received from Jesus Christ through His Church both mission and authority.

*a) The mission** alone can transform a human word into the Word of God. Not merely as among the prophets*, through the invasion of the Spirit, but in virtue of an embassy entrusted by Christ: "it is as if God were exhorting through us" (2 Co 5,20) with the purpose of reconciliation with God. The preacher must, like a herald, faithfully announce the Word so that the Word would be effective, even if he were not disinterested (Ph 1,15-18). Christ is announced in every way. Of what importance, then, is the servant by whom the faith has been communicated! The essential, the fundamental factor, is Jesus Christ; the rest is added on and the fire of judgment will prove its worth (1 Co 3,5-15). The newborn Church showed herself solicitous about authorizing preaching. Sometimes she confirmed an initiative which she did not at first take (Ac 8,14-17; 11,22ff); at other times she imposed* hands on the missionaries (13,2f).

The authority of the envoy derives also from the testimony which he gives concerning the paschal mystery. It is the testimony of the apostles* in a wide sense, which is linked to the unique testimony of the twelve (Ac 2,32; 3,15; 5,32; 10,39.41; 13,31), delivered at the command of the risen one (1,8). Through the uninterrupted tradition* of faithful witnesses, the Christian preaching really makes the Word of God heard.

b) *The boldness* of the preacher derives from this apostolic investiture. He has full authority and speaks, like the first apostles, with assurance (Ac 2,29; 4,13.29.31). He must "proclaim the Word in season and out of season" (2 Tm 4,2). If he speaks with confidence* (1 Th 2,2; Ph 1,20), it is because he believes (2 Co 4,13), for he has been "made capable" of such a ministry (2,16f; 3,4ff). Otherwise it would be only a fraudulent trafficking in the Word (2,17; 1 Th 2,4). His ideal remains that of Paul speaking to the Thessalonians: "You have received the Word which we have caused to be heard, not like the word of men, but like that which it really is, the Word of God" (1 Th 2,13).

3. *Preaching and redemption.* The mystery of the preacher is, again, not expressed by the nobility of the mission he has received. The preacher is in effect a "co-worker with God" (1 Co 3,9); he is "sent by God in the victory of Christ," "through him is spread abroad in all places the sweet odor of his knowledge." Tragic the lot of the preacher who is the "good odor of Christ," giving life or death (2 Co 2, 14ff). First of all he risks being himself reproved (1 Co 9,27), but especially must he share

the fate of Him whose herald he is: God "has set forth His apostles as the least of men" (1 Co 4,9): the preachers of the cross belong to the living crucified (2 Co 4,7-15; 6,4-10). Could they still seek to win any vain thing (cf Ac 14, 12ff)? But they must be daring to be thus united with the redeemer, the expiatory victim (the probable meaning of 1 Co 4,13), and to realize that while they are in the process of dying, life has been born in those to whom they preach (2 Co 4,12). Thus it is not simply the word of the preacher which is the Word of God, but his very life is the paschal mystery being acted out.

→Apostles—Confidence—Exhort—Faith NT II 2—Gospel—Kingdom NT I—Mission NT II 1, III 2—Persecution—Plan of God NT II, III—Resurrection NT I 3—Teach—Witness III 1—Word of God NT II 1.

JA & XLD jjk

PREDESTINE

It is only in the NT that the word "predestine" (*prohorizo*) is to be found, once in the Acts (Ac 4,28) and five times in Paul (R 8,29. 30; 1 Co 2,7; E 1,5.11). The noun "predestination" is not used, but terms like "plan, design" (*boule, prothesis*), foreknowledge (*prognosis*), election (*ekloge*) are used. It is as if the only thing that is of importance in our case is the divine action and not any theory of our own. Strictly speaking it could be said that the Bible contains no reflex doctrine of predestination. However, Paul made this divine activity an important part of his understanding of the plan* of God. This is why we give an account of his thought, before trying to find its biblical presuppositions and its parallels in John.

1. *Predestined by love to be His adopted sons.* At the end of his prophetic explanation of God's plan (R 1—8) Paul wants to reassure the believers in their hope, by revealing to them "the hidden wisdom of God which we teach in our mysteries...the wisdom that God predestined to be for our glory before the ages began" (1 Co 2,7): "God makes everything work for the good of those who love Him, those who are called according to His plan. Those whom He 'foreknew,' He has also 'predestined' to be conformed to the image of His son, in order that He might be the first-born

of many brothers" (R 8,28f). In the plan of God seen as a whole Paul distinguishes two aspects: God *knows* beforehand and God *destines* beforehand. These two ideas should not be confused.

a) In the mind of the Bible knowledge* consists not in a speculative act but in the relationship between two beings. From before creation there exists in the divine mind a relationship of love between God and certain men: they are "known by Him" (1 Co 8,3; G 4,9; cf Mt 7,23). It can be established that this foreknowledge is the equivalent of election: there are those whom "God has chosen from the beginning" (2 Th 2,13), "the elect according to the foreknowledge of God the Father" (1 P 1,1f). Behind predestination, then, lies this foreknowledge, this election.

b) But now we come to the second aspect of God's plan. The choice is made with an end in view, a precise destination. This too was made from the beginning and can be called "predestination." But, as we go back in this way to the beginnings, we can only understand it because now we know the end of time: the redeeming sacrifice has won reconciliation* with God and the adoption as sons: "in His good will and benevolence God has predestined us to be his adopted sons through Jesus Christ" (E 1,5). This is the context in which Pauline theology is situated: benevolence (E 1,9), grace* (R 11,5; E 1,6f; 2,5ff), mercy* (R 11,30ff; Tt 3,5) and finally love* (1 Th 1,4; 2 Th 2,13; R 11,28; E 1,4). If, then, being predestined means being loved by God, then there is nothing frightening in this mystery; on the contrary man has the joy of knowing not only the beginning but also the end of God's plan. Religious history takes on a meaning: the elect "have been prepared for this glory long ago" (R 9,23).

2. *Predestined in freedom*. Paul next describes the two temporal stages of God's plan: "those whom He has predestined, He has also called; those whom He has called, He has also justified; and those whom He has justified He has also glorified" (R 8,30). As a continuation of the act of predestination, there are in the present time the concrete calling* and justification*, then in the time to come glorification. Established in God's mystery, Paul expresses his absolute certainty by using verbs in the past tense. Leaving aside the nuances that

distinguish these two activities, let us examine the situation in which Paul places us. Everything is altogether God's work: "it is in Christ that, predestined according to the plan (*prothesis*) of the one who has fulfilled everything according to the plan (*boule*) of His will, we have been chosen as His portion" (E 1,11).

But what becomes of man's liberty* in this plan? There seems to be no place for it, and Paul says elsewhere: "you will ask me, 'in that case how can God ever blame anyone, since no one can oppose His will?'" (R 9,19). It is true that Paul was faced with this problem with regard to the whole people of Israel who refused Christ, and not with regard to individuals. And he solved it finally by appealing to the mysterious and inscrutable wisdom* of God before which the believer must marvel and be silent. Nevertheless, if Paul does clearly distinguish two groups in mankind—the elect and the others—he does not set them in God's plan in the same way: while the elect are "prepared for this glory long ago" (9,23), the others are only found "ready for perdition" (9,32). God does not predestine to perdition.

So Paul sees things from a point of view that we find difficult: we think of individuals and he thinks of Israel. For him the characters of sacred history—Esau or Pharaoh (R 9,13.17) —are prototypes and their personal salvation is not the point at issue. Therefore, the problem of the relationship between the two activities, divine and human, is not resolved here. However, a suggestion of the solution can be found in the calm way in which Paul affirms both one and the other, without seeing any contradiction between them. For example, when he uses the indicative of the situation (by which he declares a state of fact) together with the imperative of conduct (by which he states the duty to act): "you are dead in Christ, so live!" In this we see a problem of language, but not so Paul, who can say: "work for your salvation* 'in fear and trembling.' It is God, for His own loving purpose, who puts both the will and the action into you" (Ph 2,12f). "We are His work, created in Christ Jesus in view of the good works that God has prepared in advance in order that we might put them into practise" (E 2,10). So everything takes place here below as if human freedom consisted in realizing in time what has been foreseen from all eternity by God. This is the apocalyptic framework of revelation*, which contemporary thought would not confuse with fatalism if it recognized the priority of love in God.

3. *The biblical sources of pauline thought.* The foundation of predestination is already stated in the OT, namely the activity of God who "fore-sees" everything and cooperates in everything. In fact everything comes from the Lord (Si 11,4), even misfortune (Am 3,6; Is 45, 7). God has always had a plan (Is 37,26), which He carries out in the course of history (14,24) at fixed times (Ac 17,26.31). In this last passage the simple verb *horizo* is used, a word found elsewhere to describe the act by which God has appointed Jesus Son of God (R 1,4) and sovereign Judge (Ac 10,42). Nothing happens without being foreseen or decided by God (Ac 4,28; cf Mt 25,41). God has arranged all things and prepared them for the benefit of His elect (Mt 20,23; 25,34). There is no matter of chance with God nor anything out of His control (Pr 16,33), for "Yahweh made everything for its own purpose" (16,4). But all that has been said concerns foreknowledge and providence*. To be able to speak of predestination more is needed.

There is one belief that comes closer to this idea: that of inscription in the Book of Life. Not the account book in which good works are listed with a view to the last judgment (Dn 7, 10; Ap 20,12), but the pre-existing book of which the psalmist speaks: "you had scrutinized my every action, all were recorded in your book, my days listed and determined, even before the first of them occurred" (Ps 139,16). It could be called "the Book of the pre-destined": "and the inhabitants of the earth, whose names were not written from the beginning of the world will marvel at the sight of the Beast" (Ap 17,8; cf 13,8; Dn 12,1). And Jesus shared this conviction: "Rejoice rather that your names* are written in heaven" (Lk 10,20).

When these ideas are compared with Paul's, one thing can be seen to be missing: salvation accomplished by Jesus. While opening the way to the end of the history of salvation, Jesus allows us to go back to its origin and to follow clearly the mind of God, who in His love pre-destines His elect to be conformed to the image of His Son.

4. *Parallels in John.* However, it would be surprising if there were no parallels to the thought of Paul in the Gospels, which could give it further support. We are not speaking of the biblical idea of terror in which Jesus' own thought is rooted: as when He recalls the Book of the predestined (Lk 10,20) or when He uses the word knowledge to signify election* (Mt 7, 23; 25,12). More explicitly, in John, it is the Father who gives* believers to the Son (Jn 10, 29; 17,2.6.9.24); "no one can come to me unless he is drawn by the Father who sent me" (6,44). Here we find the problem of predestination with regard to individuals and not only the people. The believer is placed in a world that surrounds him and hems him in on all sides. The only way to avoid the impression of fatalism is to recognize a universal love behind the divine conduct (3,17; 12,47).

5. *Language and interpretation.* But is this biblical language, coherent and comforting as it is, at all intelligible today? The modern believer finds it difficult to accept the lack of clarity in the biblical Hebrew, which does not distinguish clearly between purpose and consequence: when it says "God wishes," the Hebrew can be speaking not of willing but of permitting ("He allows it to happen"). But this grammatical observation opens the door to arbitrary interpretations, which may weaken the meaning of the doctrine. Besides this, two major difficulties must be mentioned. The first, which is extrinsic, arises from the fact that we can hardly think of the problem of predestination in terms primarily of the group rather than of individuals; this is why the hard words of Paul in the epistle to the Romans have given rise to so many errors and have sometimes caused despair, leading people to believe themselves "predestined to eternal damnation," in the unfortunate words of St. Augustine. At a deeper level we often forget that, in order to express a religious experience, the language of the Bible uses categories of space and time and in this way attributes human behavior to God. To make this language into a metaphysical doctrine would be to make something eternal out of what is essentially temporal.

To say: "God predestines the elect to be His adopted sons" means that we are using the language of anthropomorphism: it does not mean that we are saying that God is bound by the categories which are a part of the structure of human language and which are used in an attempt to express the forces of our freedom. Thus, seen in the light of our temporal condition, the divine predilection cannot fail to appear as a "predestination," implying even the rejection of and the refusal to recognize those who are not chosen: but this is only a manner of speaking, a transposition into space and time of something that is not subject to them.

In these conditions, the prefixes "pre-" or "fore-," with which the terms used in the discussion of this problem are often made up, (cf pre-destination, pre-science, fore-see, fore-know, pre-dilection. . .), are only signs of men's attempts to say that the initiative comes not from them but from God. Transposed in this way into personal terms, the language of time finds its real meaning, so well expressed by John: "We are to love, then, because he loved us first" (1 Jn 4,19).

→Book III — Calling — Election — Gift O — Grace II 3—Know OT 1—Liberation/Liberty I—Love—Plan of God NT III 1—Providence 1—Will of God—Wisdom OT III.

XLD ems

PRESENCE OF GOD

The God of the Bible is not only the most high; He is the all-near God as well (Ps 119, 151). He is not a supreme being isolated from the world by His perfection, but on the contrary a reality which could be joined with the world. He is God the Creator present to His work (Ws 11,25; R 1,20), God the Savior present to His people (Ex 19,4ff), God the Father present to His Son (Jn 8,29) and to all those whom the Spirit of His Son vivifies and who love Him as His sons (R 8,14,28). He is present at all times, for He dominates time*, He who is the First and the Last (Is 44,6; 48,12; Ap 1,8. 17; 22,13). The presence of God, in order to be real, is not material, however. If this presence manifests itself through sensible signs, it is still the presence of a spiritual being whose love envelops His creature (Ws 11,24; Ps 139) and vivifies it (Ac 17,25-28), whose love wishes to communicate itself to man and make of him a luminous witness of His presence (Jn 17,21).

OT

God who created man wishes to be present to him. If, through sin, man flees this presence, the divine call continues to pursue him through history: "Adam, where are you?" (Gn 3,8f).

I. THE PROMISE
OF THE PRESENCE OF GOD

God showed Himself first to the privileged souls whom He assured of His presence: to the fathers with whom He makes the covenant (Gn 17,7; 26,24; 28,15) and to Moses who has the commission to set his people free (Ex 3,12). To this people He reveals His name* and the meaning of that name, and He thus guarantees to the people that the God of their fathers will be with them, as He was with their fathers. God* in fact calls Himself Yahweh and so defines Himself: "I am who am"; that is, I am eternal, immutable, and faithful. Or again: "I am He who is"; who is there, always and everywhere, walking with His people (3,13ff; 33,16). The promise of this all-powerful presence, made from the time of the covenant (34,9f), is renewed to the envoys through whom God leads His people: Joshua and the judges (Js 1,5; Jg 6,16; 1 S 3,19), the kings and the prophets (2 S 7,9; 2 K 18,7; Jr 1,8.19). Equally significant is the name of the child whose birth Isaiah announces and on whom depends the salvation of the people: Emmanuel, that is to say, "God with us" (Is 7,14; cf Ps 46,8).

Even when God must punish His people by exile, He does not abandon them. Over this people who remains His servant and His witness (Is 41,8ff; 43,10ff), He remains the shepherd* (Ez 34,15f.31; Is 40,10f), the king* (Is 52,7), the bridegroom, and the redeemer (Is 54,5f; 60,16). He then announces that He is going to freely save this people through fidelity to His promises* (Is 52,3.6), that His glory* will return to the holy city whose name will henceforth be "Yahweh is there" (Ez 48,35); thus He will make clear His presence to all the nations* (Is 45,14f) and will gather them all to Jerusalem in His light (Is 60). Finally, on the last day, He will be present as universal judge* and king (Ml 3,1; Ze 14,5.9).

II. THE SIGNS
OF THE PRESENCE OF GOD

God manifests Himself through diverse signs. The theophany of Sinai stirred holy fear* by storm*, thunder, fire, and wind (Ex 20,18ff), which we discover in other divine interventions (Ps 29; 18,8-16; Is 66,15; Ac 2,1ff; 2 P 3,10; Ap 11,19). But God also appears in a totally different atmosphere, that of the peacefulness of Eden where light breezes blow (Gn 3,8) while He converses with His friends Abraham (Gn 18,23-33), Moses (Ex 33,11), and Elijah (1 K 19,11ff).

As luminous as the signs of the divine

presence may be, God is wrapped in mystery* (Ps 104,2); it is in a column of cloud* and fire* that He guides His people in the desert (Ex 13,21) and that He lives in their midst, filling with His glory* the tent wherein lies the ark of the covenant (Ex 40,34) and later the holy of holies (1 K 8,10ff).

III. THE CONDITIONS FOR THE PRESENCE OF GOD

To have access to this mysterious and holy presence, it is necessary to learn from God the required conditions.

1. *The quest for God*. Man must respond to the signs which God offers him. For this reason man renders worship* to God in the places to which is attached the memory of a divine manifestation, such as Beersheba or Bethel (Gn 26, 23ff; 28,16-19). But God is not bound to any place, to any material abode. His presence, of which the ark* of the covenant is the sign, accompanies the people whom it guides through the desert and among whom it wishes to make its own abode and holy dwelling (Ex 19,5; 2 S 7,5f.11-16). It is with the line of David, in David's house*, that God wishes to live. And if He agrees that Solomon should build Him a temple, it is with the understanding that this temple is powerless to contain Him (1 K 8,27; cf Is 66,1). He is found there, to the extent that one there calls upon His name* in truth* (1 K 8,29f.41ff; Ps 145,18); that is to say, to the extent that one will there search out His presence through true worship, that of a faithful heart.

It is with a view to obtaining such a worship, while eliminating that of the high places and their corruption, that the Deuteronomic reform prescribed the pilgrimage* to Jerusalem three times a year and forbade sacrifice to be offered anywhere else (Dt 12,5; 16,16). This does not mean to say that the ascent to Jerusalem sufficed to find the Lord; it was still necessary that the worship which the people celebrated there express the respect owed to God who sees us and the fidelity due to God who speaks to us (Ps 15; 24). Otherwise, one is far from Him in his heart (Jr 12,2); and God abandons the temple whose destruction He announces, because men have made of it a den of thieves (Jr 7,1-15; Ez 10—11).

On the other hand, God is near to those who walk with Him, like the patriarchs (Gn 5,22;

6,9; 48,15), and act before Him like Elijah (1 K 17,1); who live with confidence in His sight (Ps 16,8; 23,4; 119,168) and invoke Him in their trials (Ps 34,18ff); who seek* after the good (Am 5,4.14) with a humble and contrite heart (Is 57,15) and come to the aid of the unfortunate (Is 58,9). Such are the faithful who will live forever, incorruptible, in the presence of God (Ws 3,9; 6,19).

2. *The gift of God*. But is such fidelity in the power of man? In the presence of the holy* God, man becomes aware of his sin* (Is 6,1-5), of a corruption which God alone can heal (Jr 17,1.14). If only God would come to change the heart* of man, to imprint in it His law* and His Spirit* (Jr 31,33; Ez 36,26ff)! The prophets announce this renewal, the fruit of a new covenant* which will make of the sanctified people* the home of God (Ez 37,26ff). The writers of Wisdom themselves also announce that God will send His Wisdom and His holy Spirit to men so that they may know His will and become His friends by receiving within themselves this Wisdom whose joy it is to dwell among them (Pr 8,31; Ws 9,17ff; 7,27f).

NT

I. THE GIFT OF THE PRESENCE IN JESUS

By His descent upon the Virgin Mary, the Holy Spirit brought the gift* promised to Israel: the Lord is with her and God is with us (Lk 1,28.35; Mt 1,21ff). Actually, Jesus, the son of David, is also the Lord (Mt 22,43f p), the Son of the living God (Mt 16,16), whose presence is revealed to little ones (Mt 11,25ff); He is the Word of God, come in the flesh to live among us (Jn 1,14) and to make present the glory* of His Father, whose body* is the true temple (Jn 2,21). Like His Father, who is with Him always, He is called "I am" (Jn 8,28f; 16, 32) and gives His own fulfillment to the promise of presence implied by that name*. In Him, in effect, is the fullness* of the divinity (Col 2,9). When He has achieved His mission, He assures His disciples that He is staying with them in spite of His farewells* (Mt 28,20; cf Lk 22,30; 23,42f).

II. THE MYSTERY OF THE PRESENCE IN THE SPIRIT

If the risen Jesus appears* to His disciples, it is not to make His presence with them corporal, for it is a good thing that they are deprived of this from now on (Jn 16,7); but it is in order to encourage them to look for Him by faith in the place where He is living. He is living with His Father (20,17); He is also present in all those suffering, in whom He wants to be served (Mt 25,40); He is in those who bear His Word and in whom He wants to be heard (Lk 10,16); He is in the midst of those who unite to pray in His name (Mt 18,20).

But Christ is not only among the believing; He is in them, as He revealed to Paul at the same time as He revealed His glory to him: "I am Jesus whom you persecute" (Ac 9,5). In fact He lives in those who have received Him by faith (G 2,20; E 3,17) and whom He nourishes* with His body (1 Co 10,16f). His Spirit lives in them, animates them (R 8,9.14), and makes of them the temple* of God (1 Co 3,16f; 6,19; E 2,21f) and members of Christ (1 Co 12,12f.27).

By this same Spirit, Jesus lives in those who eat His flesh* and drink His blood* (Jn 6,56f. 63); He is in them, as His Father is in Him (Jn 14,19f). This communion* supposes that Jesus has returned to the Father and has sent His Spirit (Jn 16,28; 14,16ff). This is why it is better that He be absent corporally (Jn 16,7). This absence is the condition of an interior presence realized by the gift of the Spirit*. Thanks to this gift, the disciples have in themselves the love which unites the Father and the Son (Jn 17,26). For this reason God dwells in them (1 Jn 4,12).

III. THE PLENITUDE OF THE PRESENCE IN THE GLORY OF THE FATHER

This presence of the Lord which Paul wishes for us (2 Th 3,16; 2 Co 13,11) will not be perfect till we are freed from our mortal bodies (2 Co 5,8). Then, risen through the Spirit who is in us (R 8,11), we will see God who will be all in all men (1 Co 13,12; 15,28). Then, in the place which Jesus has prepared for us near Him, we will see His glory (Jn 14,2f; 17,24), light of the new Jerusalem, the dwelling place of God with men (Ap 21,2f.22f). Then will be perfect the presence in us of the Father and

the Son through the gift of the Spirit (1 Jn 1,3; 3,24).

Such is the presence which the Lord offers every believer. "I stand at the gate and knock" (Ap 3,20). This is not a presence accessible to the flesh* (Mt 16,17), nor reserved to a people (Col 3,11), nor bound to one place (Jn 4,21); it is the gift of the Spirit (R 5,5; Jn 6,63), offered to all in the body of Christ in which it has its fullness* (Col 2,9), and who exists within the believer who enters into this fullness (E 3,17ff). The Lord offers this gift to whoever answers Him, with the bride and through the Spirit: "Come!" (Ap 22,17).

→Abide II—Adoration O—Altar—Apparitions of Christ 4 c. 7—Ark of the Covenant—Cloud—Day of the Lord NT O, III 2—Face 3.4—Farewell Speeches NT 1—Fire OT I—God OT III 1; NT II 2—Glory III 2—Heaven III, V 1—Hope OT III—Lamp 1—Light & Dark OT I 2, II 2—Manna 1—Name OT 2.4—Paraclete 1—See—Shadow II 2.3—Spirit of God—Storm 2—Temple—Visitation—Worship OT I; NT III 2.

MFL jjk

PRIDE

To free themselves of the feeling of inferiority the Greeks frequently appealed to a wisdom that was altogether human. The Bible founds the pride of man on his condition as creature and son of God. Unless he be a slave* to sin*, man cannot feel shame* before God or before men. Genuine pride has nothing to do with haughtiness, which is a caricature of it. It is perfectly compatible with humility*. Thus the Virgin Mary* sang the Magnificat with full consciousness of her worth, a worth created by God alone; and she proclaimed it before all generations (Lk 1,46-50).

The Bible has no proper term for designating pride, but it characterizes it reckoning from two attitudes. The one, always noble, which Greek translators call *parrēsia*, is related to liberty*; the Hebrews expressed it with the help of a paraphrase: the fact of standing erect, of having an elevated countenance, of expressing oneself openly; it is self-respect shown by full liberty of language and of deportment. The other attitude is related to the confidence* of which it is the radiance. The Greek translators call it *kauchēsis*; it is the act of glorying in

457

anything, or of taking one's stand on it to put on a good countenance, to be able to face oneself, another, even God. This glorying* may be noble or vain, as it finds its support in God or in man.

OT

1. *Pride of the chosen people.* When Israel was rescued from slavery and made free, the bonds of her yoke having been broken, she was able to "walk with head high" (Lv 26,13), with *parrēsia* (LXX). Pride deriving from a definitive consecration, this nobility obliged the people to live in the very holiness* of God (Lv 19,2). Although it could easily degenerate into contempt (vg Si 50,25f), this feeling justified in Israel the care of keeping separate from idolatrous people (Dt 7,1-6). Pride survives even in humiliation, but then it becomes shame*, as when Israel has its "belly to the ground," because Yahweh hides His face* (Ps 44,26). But because Israel humbles itself it will again be able "to lift its face to God" (Jb 23, 26). In every way, whether crushed to the earth or with its gaze fixed on heaven, the people preserves in its heart the pride of its election* (Ba 4,2ff; cf 2,15; Ps 119,46).

2. *Pride and vanity.* It is only a step from pride to haughtiness (Dt 8,17); pride then becomes vanity, for its support is illusory. This process of degredation can also be seen among the nations*, which are creatures and should therefore give glory* to God alone and not take pride in their beauty, power or riches (Is 23; 47; Ez 26—32). Genuine pride on the contrary is the radiance of confidence in God alone, the blossoming of faithfulness to His covenant. The glory of possessing a Temple* in which God lives is an empty boast if the people take this as something dispensing them from spiritual worship* (Jr 7,4-11). "The wise man should not glory in his wisdom, and let not the strong man glory in his strength, and let not the rich man glory in his riches. But let him who wishes to glorify himself glory in this, that he understands and knows* me" (9,22f). The wise men finally frequently repeat that the only motive for pride is the fear* of God (Si 1,11; 9,16), and not wealth or poverty (10,22); true glory is to be sons of the Lord (Ws 2,13) to have God for father (2,16). Now the pride of the just man is not merely interior, and its effulgence condemns the godless*: the latter in turn persecutes* the just man. And the pride of

the just man who is oppressed expresses itself in the prayer he directs, as is his right, to Him who is the cause of his existence: "I shall not be confounded" (Ps 25,3; 40,15ff).

3. *The pride of the Servant of God.* The suppliants in the psalter are expecting an immediate intervention from Yahweh to put an end to their shame. They give thanks that their enemies have been confounded: "You lift me high above those who attack me" (Ps 18,48); "you, by your kindness, raise our fortunes" (Ps 89,17). But during the Exile Israel feels that the just man can be re-established in his pride by means of humiliation accepted on behalf of all. Of course God continues to uphold His Servant* and takes him by the hand (Is 42,1.6); though he is persecuted he knows that he will not be confounded (50,7f). However, the prophet announces that the multitudes have been horrified in His regard: He did not have the appearance of a man*; disfigured as He was (52,14), one turned one's face away in His presence because He Himself had become contemptible and despised (53,2f). But if the Servant has in the eyes of man lost countenance, God takes His cause in hand and justifies His interior and unshakable pride by glorifying Him before the peoples: "He shall be high, exalted; He shall be raised aloft: my Servant shall succeed" (52,13) and "shall share His trophies with the powerful" (53,12). In the footsteps of the Servant every just man will be able to appeal to the judgment* of God: when He has been held as a fool and miserable, behold on the last day, "the just man will stand up full of assurance" (Ws 5,1-5).

NT

1. *The pride of Christ.* Jesus, who knew whence He came and whither He was going, manifests His pride when He proclaims Himself Son* of God. The fourth gospel presents this behavior as a *parrēsia*. Not concerned with any honor for Himself but seeking only the glory of the Father (Jn 8,49f), Jesus spoke "openly" to the world (18.20f), so much so that the people asked whether the authorities had not recognized Him as the Christ (7,25f). But as this frank speaking had nothing to do with the noisy publicity of the world* (7,3-10), they did not understand and He had to desist (11,54). Jesus then yielded to the Paraclete* who in that day* will make everything clear (16,13.25). Although the term is found only

apropos of the announcement of the passion (Mk 8,32), the synoptics depict behavior of Jesus which expresses His *parrēsia*, as when He claims in the face of all authority the rights of the Son of God or of His Father; before His parents (Lk 2,49), in the face of ungodly abuse (Mt 21,12ff p), in the face of the established authorities (Mt 23), as when He is struck on the face at the court of Annas (Jn 18,23).

2. *Pride and liberty of the believer.* With his faith, the faithful follower of Christ has received an initial pride (He 3,14) which he should preserve to the end as a pride that is joyful in its hope (3,6). In fact, through the blood* of Jesus it is full of assurance (10,19f) and can advance toward the throne of grace* (4,16); it cannot lose this assurance, whether it be in persecution* (10,34f), under pain of seeing Jesus blush for him (Lk 9,26 p) on the day of judgment*. But he can reassure his heart if he has been faithful, for God is greater than our heart (1 Jn 4,17; 2,28; 3,20ff).

The pride of the Christian is manifested here on earth in the liberty with which he gives witness to the resurrected Christ. Thus, from the first days of the Church, the apostles, unlettered as they were (Ac 4,13), preached the Word without weakening (4,29.31; 9,27f; 18, 25f) before a public or contemptuous enemy. Paul characterizes this attitude as the barefaced utterance of the believer: it even reflects the glory* of the risen Lord (2 Co 3,11f). Such is the foundation of apostolic pride: "We believe and that is why we speak" (4,13).

3. *Pride and glory.* At once Jeremiah took away from every man the right of "boasting," unless in his knowledge of Yahweh, so also Paul (1 Co 1,31: *kauchesis*). But he knew the radical means chosen by God to free man of every temptation to conceit: faith*. Henceforth there is no longer a privilege on which one can rely; neither the name of Jew, nor the Law, nor circumcision (R 2,17-29). Abraham himself could not boast in any work* (4,2), how much less the sinners that we all are (3,19f.27). But, thanks to Jesus, who has won reconciliation for him, the faithful can boast in God (5,11) and in the hope* of glory (5,2), fruit of justification* by faith. All else is contemptible (Ph 3,3-9); only the cross* of Jesus is the source of glory (G 6, 14), but not the preachers of this cross (1 Co 3,21).

The Christian may, finally, be proud of his tribulations (R 5,3), and how much more so the Apostle through his weaknesses (1 C 4,13; 2 C 11,30; 12,9f)! The churches that he has founded are his crown of glory (1 Th 2,19; 2 Th 1,4); and he can be proud of his sheep, even through the difficulties which they occasion (2 Co 7,4.14; 8,24). The mystery of Christian and apostolic pride is the paschal mystery, that of the glory which pierces the darkness. The proud man is the one who looks death in the face and discovers life there.

→Arrogance — Confidence 3 — Deception/ Disappointment I 2—Flesh II 1—Glory IV 5 —Liberation/Liberty III 3 a—Preaching II 2 b—Shame—Strength.

MJL & XLD wjy

PRIESTHOOD

"Jesus, since He lives eternally, has an unchanged priesthood" (He 7,24). The epistle to the Hebrews, by defining the mediation* of Christ in this way, compares it with an office which existed in the OT as in all other neighboring religions: the office of priests. In order to understand the priesthood of Jesus, then, it is important to have a well-defined knowledge of the priesthood of the OT, which prepared for and prefigured His.

OT

I. HISTORY OF THE DEVELOPMENT OF THE PRIESTHOOD

1. Among the civilized people which encompass Israel, the priest's position is often given security by the king, notably in Mesopotamia and in Egypt; the king then is assisted by a hierarchical clergy which is most often hereditary and which constitutes a real caste. Under the patriarchs, there is nothing of the sort. At this point in their history they have neither temple nor special priests of the God of Abraham, Isaac, and Jacob. The traditions of Genesis show the patriarchs building altars in Canaan (Gn 12,7f; 13,18; 26,25) and offering sacrifices (Gn 22; 31,54; 46,1). They exercise the familial priesthood practiced among the majority of ancient peoples. The only priests who appear are strangers: the priest-king of Jerusalem, Melchizedek* (Gn 14,18ff), and priests of the Pharaoh (Gn 41,45; 47,22). The tribe of Levi is still just an unconsecrated tribe,

without sacred functions (Gn 34,25-31; 49,5ff).

2. It is with Moses, a Levite himself, that the specification of this tribe in the functions of worship apparently gets its start. The ancient account in Ex 32,25-29 expresses the essential character of its priesthood: it is chosen and consecrated by God Himself for His service. The blessing of Moses, in contrast to that of Jacob, gives the tribe the specific tasks of priests (Dt 33,8-11). It is true that this text reflects a later situation. By this time the Levites are the priests *par excellence* (Jg 17,7-13; 18,19), connected with the various sanctuaries of the country. But alongside the Levitic priesthood, the familial priesthood continues to be carried on (Jg 6,18-29; 13,19; 17,5; 1 S 7,1).

3. In the monarchy, the king* performs several priestly functions, as did the kings of neighboring peoples: he offers sacrifice, from Saul (1 S 13,9) and David (2 S 6,13.17; 24,22-25) down to Ahaz (2 K 16,13); he blesses the people (2 S 1,18; 1 K 8,14)...However, he receives the title of priest only in the ancient Ps 110,4, which compares him to Melchizedek. In fact, despite this allusion to the royal priesthood of Canaan, he is rather a patron of the priesthood than a member of the sacred caste.

This caste has now become an organized institution, notably in the sanctuary of Jerusalem, Israel's center of worship since David. At first two priests have a share in the service: Abiathar and Zadok. Abiathar, a descendant of Eli, the minister at Shiloh, is most probably a Levite (2 S 8,17); but his family will be banished by Solomon (1 K 2,26f). Zadok is of unknown origin; but it is his descendants who direct the priesthood in the temple until the second century. Later genealogies will connect him, and Abiathar as well, to the lineage of Aaron* (cf 1 Ch 5,27-34).

The priesthood at Jerusalem numbers various officials subordinate to the chief priest. And the personnel of the temple includes, even before the exile, some uncircumcised persons (Ez 44,7ff; cf Js 9.27). In the other sanctuaries, especially in Judah, the Levites must be numerous enough; it seems that David and Solomon had sought to apportion them throughout the country (cf Js 21; Jg 18,30). But several local sanctuaries have priests of different origin (1 K 12,31).

4. The reform of Josiah in 621, by suppressing the local sanctuaries, confirms the Levitic monopoly and the supremacy of the priesthood in Jerusalem. Going beyond the exigencies of Deuteronomy (18,6ff), it in effect reserves the exercise of priestly functions to the descendants of Zadok alone; thus it is a prelude for the later distinction between priests and Levites which becomes clearer in Ez 44,10-31.

The simultaneous ruin of the temple and of the monarchy (587) puts an end to the royal tutelage over the priesthood and gives the latter greater authority over the people. Freed from influences and temptations of political power which pagans exercise from this point on, the priesthood becomes the religious guide of the nation. The progressive disappearance of prophetism, starting with the fifth century, further accentuates its authority. From 573, the reformist projects of Ezekiel exclude the "prince" from the sanctuary (Ez 44,1ff; 46). The Levitic caste enjoys from then on an uncontested monopoly (the sole exception in Is 66,21 concerns only the "last times"). The sacerdotal sections of the Pentateuch (5th-4th centuries) and then the work of the Chronicler (3rd century) complete a detailed picture of the sacerdotal hierarchy.

This hierarchy is rigorous. At the top, the high priest, son of Zadok, is the successor of Aaron, the archetype of the priesthood. There had always been, in each sanctuary, a priest in charge; the title of high priest appeared at the time when, due to the absence of a king, the need of a leader for the theocracy was felt. The anointing which he receives, from the fourth century on (Lv 8,12; cf 4,3; 16,32; Dn 9,25), recalls the one by which the kings were consecrated in the past.

Below him are the priests, sons of Aaron. Finally, the Levites, a subordinate clergy, are grouped in three families, to which the chanters and gate-keepers are added (1 Ch 25—26). These three classes constitute the sacred tribe, the whole of which is vowed to the service of the Lord.

5. Hereafter the hierarchy will know no further variations, save for the designation of the high priest. In 172, the last high-priest descendant of Zadok, Onias III, was assassinated as a result of political intrigues. His successors were designated from outside his lineage by the kings of Syria. The Maccabean reaction results in the investiture of Jonathan, a descendant of a rather obscure sacerdotal family. His brother Simon, who succeeded him (143), was the first of the dynasty of the Hasmonaeans, priests and kings

(134-37). Political and military, rather than religious leaders, they aroused opposition from the Pharisees. From its side, the traditionalist clergy reproached them for their non-Zadokite origin, while the priestly sect of Qumrân even put itself in a state of schism. Finally, originating with Herod's reign (37), the high priests were appointed by political authority, which chose them from among the great sacerdotal families; these latter constituted the group of "chief priests," named occasionally in the NT.

II. THE PRIESTLY FUNCTIONS

In the ancient religions, the priests are the ministers of worship, the guardians of the sacred traditions, the spokesmen of the divinity in their capacity as divines. In Israel, despite the social evolution and the dogmatic development marked in the course of the centuries, the priest always exercises two basic ministries which are two forms of mediation: the office of worship and the service of the Word.

1. *The office of worship**. The priest is the man of the sanctuary. Guardian of the ark* in the early period (1 S 1—4; 2 S 15,24-29), he gathers the faithful into the house of Yahweh (1 S 1) and presides over the liturgies at the time of the feasts of the people (Lv 23,11.20). His essential act is sacrifice*; it is here that he appears in the fullness of his role as mediator: he presents to God the offering of His faithful; he transmits to the faithful the divine blessing*. Witness Moses at the sacrifice of the covenant of Sinai (Ex 24,4-8), and Levi, head of the whole line (Dt 33,10). After the exile, the priests perform this task each day in the perpetual sacrifice (Ex 29,38-42). Once a year, the high priest appears in his role of supreme mediator by officiating, on the Day of Atonement (Lv 16; Si 50, 5-21). In addition, the priest is also placed in charge of the rites of consecration and purification: the anointing of the king (1 K 1,39; 2 K 11,12), the purification of lepers (Lv 14) and of mothers after delivery (Lv 12,6ff).

2. *The service of the Word**. In Mesopotamia and Egypt, the priest exercised divination; in the name of his God, he answered to the consultations of the faithful. In ancient Israel, the priest discharged an analogous function through the use of the ephod (1 S 30,7f) and of the Urim and Thummim (1 S 14,36-42; Dt 33,

8); but there is no more mention of these procedures after David.

In Israel, the Word of God, adapted to the various circumstances of life, came to His people through another voice: that of the prophets*, prompted by the Spirit*. But there existed as well a traditional form of the Word, which had its origin in the great events of sacred history and in the words of the covenant* of Sinai. This sacred tradition became crystalized partly in the accounts which recalled the great memories of the past and partly in the Law* which finds its meaning in them. The priests are the ministers of this Word, like Aaron in Ex 4,14-16. In the liturgy of the feasts*, they recount to the faithful the narratives on which their faith is based (Ex 1—15, Js 2—6 are probably echoes of these celebrations). At the time of the renovations of the covenant, they proclaim the Torah (Ex 24,7; Dt 27; Ne 8); they are likewise its ordinary interpreters, responding through practical instructions to the consultations of the faithful (Dt 33,10; Jr 18,18; Ez 44,23; Hg 2,11ff) and exercising a judiciary role (Dt 17,8-13; Ez 44,23f). As an extension of these activities, they insure the written redaction of the Law in the various codes: Deuteronomy, the Law of Holiness (Lv 17—26), the Torah of Ezekiel (40—48), the sacerdotal legislation (Ex, Lv, Nm), the final compilation of the Pentateuch (cf Ezr 7,14-26; Ne 8). Thus it is clear why the priest, in the holy books, appears as the man of knowledge* (Ho 4,6; Ml 2,6f; Si 45,17); he is the mediator* of the Word of God, under its traditional form of history and codes.

In the last centuries of Judaism, however, the synagogues multiply and the priesthood concentrates on its ritual duties. At the same time, the authority of the lay scribes grows noticeably. Connected for the most part with the Pharisaic sect, they will be the principal masters in Israel at the time of Jesus.

III. TOWARD THE PERFECT PRIESTHOOD

The priesthood of the OT was, on the whole, faithful to its mission: through its liturgies, its teaching, and the codification of the holy books, it kept the tradition* of Moses, and the prophets alive in Israel, and the religious life of the people of God firm from age to age. But finally it had to be transcended.

PRIESTHOOD

1. *Criticism of the priesthood*. The sacerdotal mission carried with it very high demands; but there were always priests who were inferior to their office. The prophets have stigmatized their failings: contamination of the worship* of Yahweh by Canaanite practices in the local sanctuaries of Israel (Ho 4,4-11; 5,1-7; 6,9), pagan syncretism at Jerusalem (Jr 2,26ff; 23, 11; Ez 8), violations of the Torah (Zp 3,4; Jr 2, 8; Ez 22,26), opposition to the prophets* (Am 7, 10-17; Is 28,7-13; Jr 20,1-6; 23,33f; 26), personal interest (Mi 3,11; cf 1 S 2,12-17; 2 K 12,5-9), lack of zeal for the worship of the Lord (Ml 2, 1-9). It would be an oversimplification to see in these reproaches only the polemics of two opposed castes: prophets against priests. Jeremiah and Ezekiel are priests; the priests who committed Deuteronomy and the Law of Holiness to writing manifestly sought to reform their own caste; in the final centuries of Judaism, the community of Qumrân, which turned away from the temple in opposition to the "impious priest," is a priestly sect.

2. *The priestly ideal*. The main interest in these criticisms and plans of reform is that they are all inspired by a priestly ideal. The prophets remind contemporary priests of their obligations: from them they demand pure worship*, fidelity to the Torah. The sacerdotal lawyers define the purity*, the holiness* of priests (Ez 44,15-31; Lv 21; 10).

It is knows from experience, however, that man, left to himself, is incapable of this purity, of this holiness. Accordingly, it is from God Himself finally that the realization of the perfect priesthood is hoped for on the day* of the restoration (Ze 3) and of the judgment* (Ml 3, 1-4). The faithful priest is awaited at the side of the Messiah* son of David (Ze 4; 6,12f; Jr 33,17-22). This hope of the two Messiahs of Aaron and Israel appears several times in the writings of Qumrân and in an apocryphal text, the "Testaments of the Patriarchs." In these texts, as in several other aftertouches applied to the biblical texts (Ze 3,8; 6,11), the priestly Messiah takes precedence over the regal Messiah. This primacy of the priest is in harmony with an essential aspect of the doctrine of the covenant: Israel is the "priest-people" (Ex 19,6; Is 61,6; 2 M 2,17f), the only people in the world which insures the worship of the true God; in its definitive achievement, it will be Israel which renders perfect worship to the Lord (Ez 40—48; Is 60—62; 2,1-5). How could it without a priesthood at its head?

The OT knows other mediations between God and His people than that of the priest. The king* guides the people of God in history as its institutional, military, political, and religious leader. The prophet* is personally called to bring from God an original message that is adapted to a particular situation in which he is responsible for the salvation of his brothers. The priest has, as does the prophet, a mission that is strictly religious; but he exercises it within the framework of institutions; he is designated hereditarily, connected with the sanctuary and its ceremonies. He brings the Word of God to the people in the name of tradition*, not as their proper leader, he commemorates the great memories of sacred history and teaches the Law of Moses. He lifts to God the prayer of the people of the liturgy and responds to this prayer with the divine blessing. He insures in the chosen people continuity of religious life through sacred tradition.

NT

The values of the OT achieve their significance only in Jesus who fulfills* and surpasses them. This general law of revelation is especially applicable to the priesthood.

I. JESUS, THE UNIQUE PRIEST

1. *The synoptic gospels*. Jesus Himself never claims the title of priest. The reason is clear: in His milieu this title designates a definite function reserved to the members of the tribe of Levi. But Jesus sees His task as quite different from theirs, much fuller and more creative. He prefers to call Himself the Son* and the Son* of Man. Nevertheless He uses priestly terms in describing His mission. As is usual for Him, these expressions are implicit and figurative.

This becomes especially clear when Jesus speaks of His death*. For His enemies, it is the punishment for blasphemy*; for His disciples, a scandalous defeat. For Him, it is a *sacrifice** which He describes with figures from the OT: sometimes He compares it to the expiatory sacrifice of the Servant* of God (Mk 10,45; 14,24; cf Is 53), at other times to the sacrifice of the covenant* of Moses at the foot of Sinai (Mk 14,24; cf Ex 24,8); and the blood which He gives at the time of the Pasch recalls that of the paschal lamb (Mk 14,24; cf Ex 12,7.13.22f). He accepts this death which is inflicted on Him;

He Himself offers it as the priest offers the victim; and this is why He expects it to bring about the expiation of sins, the establishment of the new covenant, the salvation of His people. In short, He is the priest of His own sacrifice.

The second function of the priests of the OT was the service of the Torah. Now Jesus has a clear position in relation to *the Law** of Moses; He comes to fulfill it (Mt 5,17f). Without being bound to its letter, which He transcends (Mt 5, 20-48), He illuminates its deep richness and enfolds it in the first commandment and the second which is like the first (Mt 23,24-40). This aspect of His ministry gives continuity to that of the priests of the OT, but surpasses it in every way; for the word* of Jesus is the supreme revelation, the gospel* of salvation which definitively fulfills the Law.

2. *From Paul to John.* Paul, who recalls the death of Jesus so frequently, presents it—in his master's fashion—under the figures* of the sacrifice of the paschal lamb* (1 Co 5,7), of the humiliation of the Servant* (Ps 2,6-11), of the Day of Atonement (R 3,24f). This sacrificial interpretation reappears in the images of communion in the blood* of Christ (1 Co 10,16-22), of the redemption* by this blood (R 5,9; Col 1,20; E 1,7; 2,13). The death of Jesus is, for Paul, the supreme act of His liberty, the sacrifice *par excellence*, the act characteristically sacerdotal, which He Himself offered. But the apostle does not, any more than his master (and apparently for the same reasons), give Jesus the title of priest.

It is the same with all the other writings of the NT, except for the epistle to the Hebrews: they present the death of Jesus as the sacrifice of the Servant (Ac 3,13.26; 4,27.30; 8,32f; 1 P 2,22ff), of the lamb (1 P 1,19); and they appeal to His blood (1 P 1,2.19; 1 Jn 1,7). They do not call Him a priest. The Johannine writings are a little less reticent: they describe Jesus in pontifical robes (Jn 19,23; Ap 1,13); and the narration of the passion, a sacrificial act, opens with the "priestly prayer" (Jn 17): as the priest, Jesus "sanctifies Himself"; that is, He consecrates Himself by the sacrifice (Jn 17,19), and thus exercises an efficacious mediation to which the priesthood of antiquity vainly laid claim.

3. *The epistle to the Hebrews* alone makes free and explicit mention of the priesthood of Christ. It resumes the themes already encountered, presenting the cross* as the sacrifice of atonement (9,1-14; cf R 3,24f), of the cov-

enant (9,18-24), of the Servant (9,28). But it concentrates attention on the personal role of Christ in the offering of this sacrifice. Just as Aaron had been called long before, so too Jesus, though in an even higher way, is called by God to intervene in favor of men and to offer sacrifices for their sins (5,1-4). His priesthood was prefigured in that of Melchizedek (Gn 14, 18ff), in conformity with the oracle of Ps 110,4. To shed light on this point, the author gives a subtle interpretation of the texts of the OT: the silence of Genesis on the genealogy of the priest-king appears to him to be an indication of the eternity of the Son of God (7,3); the tithe which Abraham offers him marks the inferiority of the priesthood of Levi before that of Jesus (7,4-10); the oath of God in Ps 110,4 proclaims the immutable perfection of the definitive priest (7,20-25). Jesus is the unique holy priest (7,26ff); His priesthood puts an end to the ancient priesthood.

This priesthood is rooted in His very being, which fact makes Him the perfect mediator: at once true man (2,10-18; 5,7f), partaking of our poor condition even to experiencing temptation (2,18; 4,15), true Son of God, higher than the angels (1,1-13); He is the unique, eternal priest. He accomplished His sacrifice in time once for all (7,27; 9,12.25-28; 10,10-14). Afterwards He is forever the intercessor (7,24f), the mediator of the new covenant (8,6-13; 10,12-18).

4. No title by itself alone exhausts the mystery of Christ: as Son of God inseparable from the Father, and Son of Man assembling in Himself all humanity, Jesus is at once the high priest of the new covenant, the Messiah-King, and the Word of God. The OT had distinguished the mediations of the king and the priest (the temporal and the spiritual), of the priest and the prophet (institution and passing event): distinctions necessary for understanding the proper values of revelation. But because His transcendence places Him above the ambiguities of history, Jesus reunites these various types of mediation in His person: as Son of God, He is the eternal Word who accomplishes and surpasses the message of the prophets; as Son of Man, He assumes in Himself all humanity and is its king with an authority and love unknown until His time; as unique mediator between God and His people, He is the perfect priest through whom men are sanctified.

II. THE PRIESTLY PEOPLE

1. *Jesus* did not explicitly attribute the priesthood to His own people any more than to Himself. But He did not cease to act as a priest, and He appears to have conceived the people of the new covenant as a priestly people. Jesus reveals Himself as a priest by the offering of His sacrifice and by the service of the Word. And it is striking to note that He calls each of His own to take part in these two functions of the priesthood : every disciple* must take up His cross* (Mt 16,24 p) and drink His cup* (Mt 20,22; 26,27); each must carry His message (Lk 9,60; 10,1-16) and bear witness to it even to death (Mt 10,17-42). As He makes all men sharers of His titles of Son and Messiah-King, Jesus also makes them priests with Him.

2. The apostles continue this idea of Jesus by presenting the Christian life as a liturgy, a participation in the priesthood of the unique priest.

Paul considers the faith of the faithful as a "sacrifice and an oblation" (Ph 2,17); the financial aid which he receives from the church of Philippi is "a fragrant perfume, an acceptable sacrifice, agreeable to God" (Ph 4,18). For him, the entire life of the Christian is a priestly act; he invites them to offer their bodies "as a living victim, holy, agreeable to God : this is the spiritual worship* that you have to offer" (R 12,1; cf Ph 3,3; He 9,14; 12,28). This worship consists as much in praise of the Lord as in charitableness and in putting their goods in common (He 13,15f). The epistle of *James* enumerates in detail the concrete acts which constitute true worship* : control of the tongue, helping orphans and widows, abstention from the defilements of the world (Jm 1,26f).

The first epistle of Peter and the *Apocalypse* are explicit : they attribute to the Christian people the "royal priesthood" of Israel (1 P 2, 5.9; Ap 1,6; 5,10; 20,6; cf Ex 19,6). By this title the prophets of the OT declare that Israel must carry the Word of the true God into the midst of the pagan peoples and must firmly establish His worship. The Christian people henceforth assume that task. The people can do it, thanks to Jesus who makes them participants in His Messianic dignity of king and priest.

III. THE MINISTERS
OF THE PRIESTHOOD OF JESUS

No text of the NT gives the name of priest to any of those responsible for the Church. But Jesus' reserve in using the title is so great that His silence is scarcely conclusive. Jesus makes His people participants in His priesthood; but in the NT, as in the OT, this priesthood of the people of God can be exercised concretely only through the ministers called by God.

1. It is an established fact that *Jesus* called the twelve in order to entrust them with the responsibility of His Church. He prepared them for the service of the Word; He transmitted to them some of His powers (Mt 10,8.40; 18,18); and on the last evening He confided to them the eucharist* (Lk 22,19). These are specific participations in His priesthood.

2. *The apostles* understand this and in their turn establish a group of men responsible for continuing their action. Some of these bear the title of elders, which is the origin of the present name of priests (presbyters : Ac 14,23; 20,17; Tt 1,5). Paul's reflection upon the apostolate and charisms* is already directed toward the priesthood of the Church's ministers. To those responsible for communities he gives priestly titles : "keepers of the mysteries of God" (1 Co 4,1f), "ministers of the new covenant" (2 Co 3, 6); and he describes apostolic preaching* as a liturgical service (R 1,9; 15,15f). Here is the starting point for further explicitations of the tradition on the ministerial priesthood. This is not an established caste of privileged men. Nor does it detract either from the unique priesthood of Christ or from the priesthood of the faithful. But, in the service of both, it is one of the mediations* ensuring the service of the people of God.

→Aaron—Altar 2—Anointing III 3—Calling I —Election OT I 3 c—Eucharist IV 2, V 1— Expiation 2—Imposition of Hands NT 2—King OT I 2—Law *B* III 1.5—Mediator I 1—Melchizedek—Messiah OT II 2; NT II 2—Ministry II 4—Oil 2—Prophet OT I 3—Sacrifice—Worship OT I 2.

AG ecu

PROMISES

I. PROMISES AND FAITH

To promise is one of the key words of the language of love. To promise is to announce and at the same time guarantee a gift, to pledge one's word, to proclaim oneself as sure of the future and sure of oneself and at the same time to stir in one's partner the wholehearted adherence and the generosity of his faith*. In His own way of promising, in the certitude which He possesses of never deceiving, God reveals His own unique greatness: "God is not a man that He should break His word, nor a son of Adam that He should change His mind" (Nm 23,19). To promise, for Him, is already to give; but first of all it is the giving of faith, capable of waiting for His gift* to come. By this grace*, the receiver is capable of thanksgiving* (cf R 4,20) and of recognizing in the gift the heart of the giver.

In Israel the promises are the key to a history of salvation, which is the fulfillment of the prophecies and oaths* of God (Gn 22,16-18; Ps 110,4; Lk 1,73). These oaths make God's gifts irrevocable (R 11,29; He 6,13ff). The infidelities of Israel will on occasions lead to some restrictions of these promises, but the promises themselves will stand, thanks to a Remnant*, to a "Son of Man" (Dn 7).

Judaism will on the one hand stress confidence in the promises and on the other hand stress the aspect of reward that is in them: the promised inheritance has to be merited by obeying the commandments (4 Esd 7,1.19ff). Christianity on the contrary will see in them the pure initiative of God, the gifts promised to those who believe. But, in the same period, the Qumrân community wants to restrict the privilege of the promises to its practicing members.

This is why St. Paul, anxious to show that the Christian life is based on faith, sees the substance of Scripture and of God's plan in the promise made to Abraham and fulfilled in Jesus Christ (G 3,16-29). This is why the letter to the Hebrews, eager to bring to light a history of faith in the OT, at the same time brings to the fore a history of promises (He 11,9.13,17.33. 39). This is why, even previous to the thoughts of Paul, the discourse of St. Peter at Pentecost, clearly from its tone one of the earliest sermons, characterizes with an unerring perspicacity the gift of the Spirit and the appearance of the Church as the "promise" (Ac 2,39) and the fulfillment of the prophecies (2,16). For a Jew, the Scriptures are first of all the Law*, the will* of God to be observed no matter what the cost; for the Christian, they become first of all the book of promises. The Israelites were the depositories of the promises (cf R 9,4); the Christians are the inheritors of them (G 3,29).

The language of the NT hands down this discovery: while the Hebrew has not a particular word to designate the idea of promise, and presents it through a constellation of words: *speech, oath*, blessing*, inheritance*, promised land*; or in the formulas: "the God of Abraham, of Isaac and of Jacob," "the race of Abraham"; the NT on the contrary is familiar with the proper word for *promise*: gr. *epangelia*, which emphasizes the value of this "given word"; it is a "declaration," The word is moreover related to that of *gospel*: *euangelion*, the "good news."

II. ISRAEL, PEOPLE OF THE PROMISES

Christian intuitiveness, so strongly brought to light by the letter to the Galatians, draws out a fundamental structure of the OT: the existence of Israel has for its unique and indestructible foundation the promise of God.

1. *The promises to the patriarchs.* The different traditions combined in Genesis run together, making of the book a story of promises. Abraham* is the one who receives the promises (Gn 12,1.7; 13,15ff; 15; 17; Ps 105,8f). These always contain an heir and an inheritance, a glorious and numerous offspring, a fertile land (cf Gn 15,4-7; 17,16; 26,24; 28,13ff; 35,12). They are, also, always joined to the destiny of humanity. The Yahwistic tradition makes the blessing promised to Abraham (Gn 12,2) the divine reply to the impious enterprise of Babel which aspired to raise the name of humanity to the heavens (11,4); but is also sees it as making up for the curse* brought upon the earth by the sin* of man (3,17; 4,11) and the first concrete figure* of the victorious hope revealed by God after the first sin (3,15). Moreover, this promise aims to include "all the families of the earth" (12,3). The "sacerdotal" tradition explicitly relates the blessing* of Abraham to the first blessing of creation* (1,22.28; 17,6.20). Certainly, circumcision* seems to limit the scope of the promises. In reality Israel can, through this rite, gather to itself any race at all (34): and in this way the promise received by Abraham of being "the

PROMISES

father of a multitude of peoples" is fulfilled (Gn 17,5; Si 44,19-22). The blessing of the families of Sem and Abraham, by preparing "a kingdom of priests and a consecrated nation" (Ex 19,6), will make the privilege of the promise concrete, namely being "a people of God."

2. *The promises and the Law.* The promises addressed to the patriarchs, manifestations of the initiative and of the grace* of God, already entail demands. They are addressed to faith*; that is, they stir up a new existence, founded on the Word* of God: the departure of Abraham (Gn 12,1), his walking in the presence of God (17,1), his obedience (22,1f). The Law* extends this demand to the entire life of the people. The Law is the charter of the covenant* (Ex 19,5; 24,8; Js 24,25f); that is, the means for Israel to enter into a new* and holy* life, to live in the role of the people* of God, to abandon itself to His guidance. The Law supposes an earlier promise and sets down the precise conditions of that promise. The promises offered in return for obedience are not the reward for the justice* of Israel, but they express the generosity of a God forever intent on blessing His own, although He is pitiless in the face of sin and incapable of giving Himself to whoever does not believe in Him.

3. *The promises to David.* So that the entire life of Israel may rest on faith, all its institutions must find their firmness only in the Word* of God. The monarchical institution, the normal foundation of the nation-community and expression of its will to live, has in Israel a paradoxical aspect. It is simply tolerated by God, almost against His will, because there is a serious risk of damaging the exclusive confidence that Yahweh demands from His people (1 S 8,7ff); and at the same time it is raised to a greatness and a future beyond the dreams of this earth (2 S 7). A lad "taken from the pasture" will know "a name equal to that of the greatest men" (2 S 7,9); he will be the founder of a royal dynasty (7,11f), and will enjoy the favor of Yahweh, who will overwhelm him with blessings (Ps 89,21-30); his descendant, seated "at the right hand of God" (Ps 110,1), will inherit the nations (Ps 2,8). In the hour of its worst abasement and even in the days of Christ, these promises will still nourish the faith of Israel (Is 11,1; Jr 23,5; Ze 6,12; Lk 1,32.69).

For a long time the promises were of a worldly nature: a son, a land, a king, an abundance of prosperity. However in Deuteronomy they are already associated with the idea of happiness and satisfaction. With the prophets they become spiritual and interior: the essential thing becomes a new covenant*: "Deep within them I shall plant my Law, writing it in their hearts" (Jr 31,33). Together with intimate knowledge, this covenant includes God's pardon* and a new heart* (Ez 36,26f; Ps 51,12). It is precisely when Jerusalem has lost any political role that the prophets make her the most wonderful promises, the psalmists sing "Yahweh is my heritage" (Ps 16,5; 73,26) and promise the inheritance* of God and the beatitudes to the poor*, and the wise men announce to the just a "hope...rich with immortality" (Ws 3,1-5), while the martyrs look forward to the resurrection* (Dn 12,2f; 2 M 7).

4. *The messianic promises.* The promises made to the patriarchs and to David ensure the glorious and permanent future of their race and culminate in the expectation of "the One who is to come" (Is 26,20; Ha 2,3f LXX). The prophets give expression to promises of messianic hope, alongside their threats of punishment. Isaiah sees Emmanuel, born of a virgin, as a sign of blessing for the people (Is 7,14); he speaks of the future prerogatives of this child of the line of David, "Prince of peace" (9,5f), "just King" (11,11). According to Mt 2,6, Micah names the place where "the One who is to rule over Israel" and whose "origin goes back...to the days of old" is to be born (Mi 5,1-5). Jeremiah promises a "virtuous branch" (Jr 23,5f; 33,15f; cf Is 4,2; Za 3,8f; 6,12), which will be the glory of Israel and the restorer of the people. Ezekiel foretells the shepherd who will come to feed his sheep like a new David (Ez 34,23f; cf 37, 24f). Zechariah sees the joyful procession of the Messiah-king entering Jerusalem humbly, bringing peace (Ze 9,9f).

5. *The new promises.* At the hour when Israel will exist no more, having lost its king*, its capital, its temple*, its honor, God will awaken its faith by new* promises. He dares to found this upon "the ancient things" foretold to Israel —the threats of destruction which are verified with a terrifying exactness (Is 48,3ff; 43,18)— in order to promise Israel "new things, secret and unknown" (48,6; 42,9; 43,19), unimaginable marvels. Of these marvels, the most expressive synthesis is the new Jerusalem*, "house of prayer for all people" (Is 56,7), mother* of an unnumbered race (54,3; 60,4), joy and pride of God (60,15).

6. *The promises of Wisdom*. The place which they hold in the writings of Wisdom* proves to what extent the promises of God are the foundation for the entire life of Israel. It is true that all wisdom contains a promise because it begins by regathering and classifying experiences, in order to discern the fruits which one can expect. The originality of the wisdom of Israel is to substitute a hope for this expectancy which was founded on the calculations drawn from experience. This hope* has come from elsewhere, from the fidelity to the authentic spirit of Yahwism, "to the covenant of the all-high God and to the Law of Moses" (Si 24,23). The wisdom of Israel comes to it from on high (Pr 8,22-31; Si 24,2ff; Ws 9,4.10). This is why the beatitude* which it promises (Pr 8,32-36) suprasses human hopes (Ws 7,8-11) in order to aim for "the favor of Yahweh" (Pr 8,35), "the friendship of God" (Ws 7,14). Ps 119, which is the echo of these promises in a just heart, attests that they support the faith within Israel, the certitude that God suffices.

III. THE PROMISES OF JESUS CHRIST

1. *The synoptics*. Jesus, the promised Messiah in whom "all the promises of God have their fulfillment" (2 Co 1,20), Himself the object of the promises, is presented first as the bearer of new promises. He begins His preaching with the announcement of the kingdom* (Mt 4,23), which He promises, in the beatitudes*, to the poor and the persecuted (5,3.10; Lk 6,20.23). He takes the disciples as partners while promising them a miraculous catch of men (4,19), power over the twelve tribes of Israel (19,28). To Peter*, He promises to found His Church* on him and guarantees him victory over hell (16, 16ff). To whoever follows Him, He promises a hundredfold and life eternal (19,29); to whoever takes His part, He promises His help before God (10,32). He makes His own all the promises of the OT, promises of a people* and of a land, of a kingdom, of beatitude. They all depend on His mission and on His person. They are not yet fulfilled*, since His hour* has not yet come; and one can follow Jesus only in faith. But belief in Him is to sense their accomplishment, to have found them fulfilled already (Jn 1,41.45).

2. *The gospel of John*, as a matter of fact, shows to what extent Jesus, by His person and by His actions, is already in the world the living presence of the promises. He is all that man expects, all that God has promised to His people; truth*, life*, bread*, living water*, light*, resurrection*, the glory* of God. But He is all this in the flesh* and can give Himself only in faith*. He is more than a promise; He is already a gift, but "given" in faith, "so that every man who believes in Him...may have eternal life" (Jn 3,16).

3. *The promise of the Spirit*. "The promise of the Father" (Lk 24,49; Ac 1,4) is the Spirit. "Filling the universe and holding all things united" (Ws 1,7), He also contains all promises (G 3,14). In order also that He be given, Jesus must achieve His work on earth (Jn 17,4), must love His own to the end (13,1), must give His body and His blood (Lk 22,19f). Then all the treasures of God are open to Him and He can promise everything. One can "in His name... ask everything of God," and one is sure of receiving it (14,13f). This *everything* is "the Spirit of Truth, which the world cannot receive" (14,7) because it cannot believe, and which is the living richness of the Father and of the Son (16,15). When "all is fulfilled," Jesus expires and "renders up His spirit*" (19,30); He has kept all His promises. He can promise to His own to be with them "till the end of the world," from the moment when He gives them "the Father, the Son, and the Holy Spirit" (Mt 28,19f).

IV. CHRISTIANS, HEIRS OF THE PROMISES

Possessing the Spirit, Christians are in possession of all promises (Ac 2,38f). From the moment that "the pagans also have received the gift of the Holy Spirit" (10,45), they who were formerly "strangers to the covenants of the promise" (E 2,12) have become in Christ "participants in the promise" (E 3,6). Ever since, the promise has always been addressed to the faith (R 4,13); it is "assured to every descendant who lays claim to...the faith of Abraham, the father of all" (4,16), circumcised and uncircumcised (4,9).

"Filled with all riches," "not lacking any gift of grace" (1 Co 1,5.7), Christians have nothing else to desire, because the Spirit is a permanent and living possession in them, an anointing* and a seal*. Yet, He is only "the pledge of our inheritance" (E 1,14; cf 2 Co 1, 22; 5,5), "the first-fruits*...of our redemption"

(R 8,23); and His prayer in us remains "a groaning" and a hope* (8,23f). Christians are still the pilgrims "of a better fatherland*" (He 11,16) and are tending toward it following the example of Abraham, "by faith and perseverance" (6,12.15). Until the last day, the promise is the means by which one offers himself to faith for the love of God.

→Abraham—Amen—Blessing III—Covenant OT I 1; NT II 1—Earth OT II—Faith NT III 1—Faithfulness—Fulfill—Gift OT 1—Hope—Inheritance—King OT II—Justification II 1—Milk 2—Oath—Plan of God OT I—Remnant —Revelation OT II 1 c—Truth OT 1—Word of God OT II 1 c.

MLR & JG jjk

PROPHET

OT

I. DIVERSITY AND UNITY OF PROPHECY WITHIN ISRAEL

Everywhere in the ancient East could be found men who practiced divination (cf Nm 22,5f; Dn 2,2; 4,3f), and thus were judged fit to receive communications from superior beings. One approached them for advice occasionally before a major undertaking. It devolved upon the prophets of Israel to perform similar functions (1 K 22,1-29); but it is the consideration of the prophetic office as a whole that gives us the best idea of its nature.

1. *Origins*. Where does biblical prophecy begin? The title of prophet was given to Abraham, but this was done by a later transfer (Gn 20,7). As for Moses, the authentic representative of God (Ex 3—4), he is rather an originator of the prophetic office (Ex 7,1; Nm 11,17-25), more therefore than another prophet (Nm 12, 6-8). Deuteronomy is the only book which gives him this title (Dt 18,15), but not as one among many prophets: no one after him has equalled him (Dt 34,10). At the end of the period of judges certain groups arose, "sons of the prophets" (1 S 10,5f), whose erratic behavior (1 S 19,20-24) gave the impression of Canaanite influence. With these individuals the term *nābî'* ("one called") came into use. But along with it the older titles remained: "seer" (1 S 9,9) or "clairvoyant" (Am 7,12); "man of God" (1

S 9,7f), the principal title of Elijah and especially Elisha (2 K 4,9). The title of *nābî'* is not moreover reserved to the genuine prophets of Yahweh. In addition there were *nebi'îm* of Baal (1 K 18,22); there were also men who made a vocation of prophecy without thereby being inspired by God (1 K 22,5f...). The study of the various terms therefore shows that prophecy exhibits various aspects. Yet the underlying unity will become evident as the investigation continues.

2. *Continuity*. A real prophetic tradition came into existence thanks to the disciples* of the prophets. The Spirit, as in the case of Moses (Nm 11,17), is communicated, as from Elijah to Elisha (2 K 2). Isaiah mentions his disciples (Is 8,16), and Jeremiah is accompanied by Baruch. The servant of Yahweh, a type who even more than Moses transcends the prophetic office, assumes the attitude of a prophet who teaches what He has heard (Is 50,4f; 42,2ff). In this body of living tradition*, Scripture naturally plays a role (Is 8,16; Jr 36,4) which grows with time. Not just His words does Yahweh put into the mouth of Ezekiel, but also a book*. From the beginning of the exile especially, the consciousness of a prophetic tradition impressed itself retrospectively on Israel (Jr 7,25; cf 25,4; 29,19; 35,15; 44,4). The Book of Consolation (of the school of Isaiah) leans on this tradition when it recalls the ancient prophecies of Yahweh (Is 45,21; 48,5). But the prophetic tradition has a source of unity which is of a different order from these measurable factors. The prophets from the beginning are all animated by the same Spirit* of God (even if many do not name the Spirit as the origin of their prophecy; cf however 1 S 10,6; Mi 3,8 (hb.); Ho 9,7; Jl 3,1f; Ez 11,5). Whatever may be their mutual dependance, it is from God that they have the Word*. The prophetic charism* is a charism of revelation* (Am 3,7; Jr 23,18; 2 K 6,12), which makes known to man what he could not discover by his own efforts. Its object is at the same time multiple and unique: it is the plan* of salvation which will be concentrated and fulfilled in Jesus Christ (cf He 1,1f).

3. *The prophet in the community*. Thus constituting a tradition, the prophetic office has also a definite position in the community of Israel. It is an integral part of it, but it does not absorb the community. One perceives that the prophet with the priest plays a role in the coronation rite of the king* (1 K 1). King, priest, and pro-

phet are for a considerable period of history the three pillars of the society of Israel, sufficiently distinguished so as occasionally to be antagonistic to one another, but normally linked in a necessary interdependence. Wherever the State as an institution exists, there prophets are on hand to counsel the kings: Nathan, Gad, Elisha, Isaiah especially, and on occasion Jeremiah. It is their prerogative to declare whether the action undertaken is such as God wishes, whether such a policy clearly fits into salvation history. Nevertheless, the prophetical office in the strict sense of the word is not an institution like the kingship and the priesthood*. Israel on its own initiative can make a king (Dt 17,14f), but it cannot create a prophet. The latter is a pure gift of God, object indeed of promise (Dt 18,14-19), yet freely given. One senses this especially in the period when prophecy is interrupted (1 M 9,27; cf Ps 74,9). Israel lived then in the expectation of the prophet already promised (1 M 4,46; 14,41). It is easy to understand why, under these circumstances, the Jews responded so enthusiastically to the preaching of John* the Baptist (Mt 3,1-12).

II. PERSONAL DESTINY OF THE PROPHET

1. *The divine call* The prophet finds a place in the community, but it is the divine call which constitutes him a prophet. This is evident in the call of Moses*, Samuel, Amos, Isaiah, Ezekiel, to say nothing of the Servant* of Yahweh. The poetic self-revelations of Jeremiah deal with this theme. God has the entire initiative and He dominates the person of the prophet: "The Lord Yahweh speaks; who would not prophesy?" (Am 3,8; cf 7,14f). Jeremiah, consecrated to God from the womb of his mother (1,5; cf Is 49,1), speaks of a (divine) deception (20,7ff). Ezekiel feels the hand of God pressing firmly upon him (Ez 3,14). The call awakens in Jeremiah the realization of his own weakness (Jr 1,6); in Isaiah, the sense of sin (Is 6,5). It leads always to a mission*, the instrument of which is the mouth of the prophet, who will speak the Word of God (Jr 1,9; 15,19; Is 6,6f; cf Ez 3,1ff).

2. *The message of the prophet and his life.* Certain meaningful bodily movements (more than thirty) precede or accompany the revelations made by word of mouth (Jr 28,10; 51,63

...; Ez 3,24—5,4; Ze 11,15...). The revealed Word does not reduce itself to mere words but it is life. It is accompanied by a symbolic (not magical) participation in that action of Yahweh which accomplishes what it proclaims. Some of these symbolic acts have immediate effects: purchase of a field (Jr 32), illness and mental anguish (Ez 3,25f; 4,4-8; 12,18). It is especially noteworthy that in the greatest revelations, conjugal and familial life become vehicles of expression. Such is the case for the marriage of Hosea (1—3). Isaiah only mentions the "prophetess" (Is 8,3), but she and her children become a sign* for the populace (8,18). At the time of the exile these signs become negative: the celibacy of Jeremiah (Jr 16,1-9), the widower status of Ezekiel (Ez 24,15-27). These are so many symbols not imagined, but lived out, and thereby related to the truth. The message cannot be foreign to its bearers. It is not a concept which the prophet would have acquired, but the manifestation in oneself of the living God (Elijah), of the holy God (Isaiah).

3. *Trials.* Those who speak in their own name (Jr 14,14f; 23,16), without having been sent (Jr 27,15), following their own inspirations (Ez 13, 3), are false prophets. The real prophets are conscious that another has made them speak out, so much so that they feel an obligation to correct themselves when they have spoken strictly from their own experience (2 S 7). The presence of this other (Jr 20,7ff), the burden of the mission entrusted to them (Pr 4,19), often causes an interior struggle. The serenity of Isaiah allows only a glimpse of this: "I wait for Yahweh who hides His face" (Is 8,17)... But Moses (Nm 11,11-15) and Elijah (1 K 19,4) experience the crisis of depression. Jeremiah especially complains bitterly, and for a moment he seems to turn away from his vocation (Jr 15,18f; 20,14-18). Ezekiel is "filled with bitterness and anger," "stupified" (Ez 3,14f). The Servant of Yahweh goes through a phase of apparent ineptitude and disquiet (Is 49,4). Finally, God scarcely lets the prophets hope in the success of their mission (Is 6,9f; Jr 1,19; 7,27; Ez 3,6f). That of Isaiah will end in the hardening of the hearts of the people (Is 6,9f=Mt 3, 14f; cf Jn 15,22). Ezekiel will have to speak "whether men will listen or not" (Ez 2,5.7; 3,11.27); thus men "will know that I am Yahweh" (Ez 36,38, etc.). But this recognition of the Lord will come only afterwards. The prophetic word transcends in every way its immediate consequences, for its efficacy lies in the

eschatological order. The word ultimately concerns us (1 P 1,10ff).

4. *Death.* A mass murder of prophets took place under Ahab (1 K 18,4.13; 19,10.14), probably under Manasseh (2 K 21,16), and certainly under Jehoiakim (Jr 26,20-23). Jeremiah saw nothing exceptional in these massacres (Jr 2,30). In the time of Nehemiah, mention of them had become a commonplace (Ne 9,26); and Jesus could say: "Jerusalem, thou that killest the prophets" (Mt 23,37)...The idea that the death* of the prophets is the crowning point of all their prophecies as lived experiences revealed itself slowly in the light of this experience. The mission of the Servant of Yahweh, as the summing up of the prophetic line, starts with a show of discretion (Is 42,2) and is completed in the silence* of the Lamb who is slaughtered (Is 53, 7). Thus this fulfillment is a peak that is foreseen. Since the time of Moses the prophets interceded for the people (Is 37,4; Jr 7,17; 10, 23f; Ez 22,30). The Servant, while interceding for sinners, will deliver them by His death (Is 53,5.11f).

III.   THE PROPHET
AND CONTEMPORARY INSTITUTIONS

The dramatic encounter between the prophet and the people makes itself felt first of all on the level of the old covenant* with its corresponding institutions: the Law, social institutions, worship.

1. *The Law.* The prophetic office and the Law do not present two different options, two divergent tendencies. Rather there is question of distinct functions, of spheres of influence which are in no way impervious to one another in their internal relations within a greater totality. The Law declares what is of obligation for all times and all men. The prophet's first task is to denounce offences against the Law. What distinguishes him here from the representatives of the Law is that the prophet does not wait to be notified of a case before pronouncing judgment on it but exercises authority without proper jurisdiction or accreditation. From what God reveals to him at the present moment, he relates the Law to the existential situation. He makes accusations, saying to the sinner as Nathan said to David, "You are the man" (2 S 12,7). He seizes on facts (1 K 21,20), often by surprise (1 K 20,38-43). Hosea (4,2), Jeremiah

(7,9), make appeals to the Decalogue; Ezekiel (18,5-18), to laws and established customs. Nonpayment of wages (Jr 22,13; cf Ml 3,5), fraud (Am 8,5; Ho 12,8; Mi 6,10f), the venality of judges (Mi 3,11; Is 1,23; 5,23), the refusal to free slaves at the proper time (Jr 34,8-22), the inhumanity of money lenders (Am 2,8) and of those "who grind the faces of the poor" (Is 3, 15; cf Am 2,6-8; 4,1; 8,4ff)—all these are so many faults against the Law, against the covenant! The essence of the Law to which the prophets appeal is not reduced simply to the written text. In every case the text cannot accomplish what the prophet achieves with his hearers. With the power of his charism*, he awakens in each man that hidden moment when the light is accepted or rejected. Hence, in the factual situation in which the prophetic word arises, what is right is not only refused but perverted (Mi 3,9f; Jr 8,8; Ha 1,4), changed to bitterness (Am 5,7; 6,12). Good is called evil and vice versa (Is 5,20; 32,5); such is the deception tirelessly condemned by Jeremiah (Jr 6,6...). Shepherds* stir up the water of the sheep (Ez 34, 18f); the weak are led astray (Is 3,12-15; 9,15; Am 2,7). The people, although culpable, do not deserve any special handling (Ho 4,9; Jr 6,28; Is 9,16); but the prophets attack more violently the priests and all those responsible (Is 3,2; Jr 5,4f) who withhold norms (Ho 5,1; Is 10,1) and falsify them. Against such a situation, the Law is defenseless. Lacking proper norms, the individual must have recourse to the discernment of spirits, between God and the evil one. It is in this situation that one sees prophet oppose prophet (Jr 28).

2. *Traditions.* Not only sin is in question. Society has changed. The prophets are aware of novelties within the traditional morality of clothing (Is 3,16-23), music (Am 6,5); or social relations. With changes increased on all social levels, Israel now experiences the situation which Samuel had foreseen (1 S 8,10-18). The relation of master to slave has been, since the stay in Egypt, transferred to the heart of society. Despite certain anti-monarchical convictions (Ho 13,11), the prophets do not seek a return to a former condition of things. That is not their function. Rather they oppose nostalgic thinking by the Jewish people, a seeking of the common good in some blissful image of past achievement which is expected to carry them along in the present. Such is the euphoria of those who say, "Is not Yahweh dwelling in our midst?" (Mi 3,11), who call Yahweh "the dear com-

panion of their youth" (Jr 3,4; Ho 8,2); likewise of those who think that at a moment's notice "Yahweh will renew for them all His former wonders" (Jr 21,2). Finally, it is the euphoria of those who believe that nothing has changed, "tomorrow will be the same as today" (Is 56, 12; cf 47,7)... Such individuals find themselves soothed by the soft words of false prophets (Jr 23,17) and find it impossible to open their eyes to the reality of the present condition. Yet the prophets of God are not opposed to the past as such. Elijah returned to Horeb; Hosea (11, 1-5) and Jeremiah (2,2f) are fascinated by the memories of the desert*; Deutero-Isaiah, by those of the exodus* (Is 43,16-21). But they do not confuse the true past with its moribund relics. They use the past to put into focus again the true basis of the nation's religion.

3. *Cult.* The prophets have harsh words for sacrifices* (Jr 7,21f; Is 1,11ff; Am 5,21-25), the ark* (Jr 3,16), and the temple* (Jr 7,4; 26,1-15) —the same temple where Isaiah received his calling (Is 6) and where Jeremiah preached (Jr 7), as Amos had preached in the sanctuary at Bethel (Am 7,13). Their words take in the true situation: they condemn sacrifices insofar as they have become sacrilegious. They would be just as valid criticism of acts of Christian worship performed under similar conditions. Their words speak again of the relative value only of signs which have not always existed or will not always endure in their present state (Am 5,25; Jr 7,22), which are in themselves incapable of purifying or of saving (cf He 10,1). These sacrifices have no value except in relation to the unique sacrifice of Christ. The contemporary criticism of the prophets prepares the way for this final and decisive understanding of sacrifice given in revelation. For the rest, following upon the exile, cult and prophetic office merged in the person of Ezekiel (Ez 40—48; cf Is 58,13), Malachi, Haggai. The Jewish ritual of the later epoch is a purified ritual, due in large part to the influence of the prophets, who never imagined a religion without ritual any more than a society without law.

IV. THE PROPHET AND THE NEW DISPENSATION

The prophets have related the living God to His creatures in the singularity of the present moment. But just for that reason, their message looks toward the future. They see the future coming with its twin aspects of punishment* and salvation*.

1. *Punishment.* Isaiah, Jeremiah, Ezekiel, over and above the multiplicity of individual transgressions, see the continuity of the community's sin* (Mi 7,2; Jr 5,1), a harsh reality grounded in historical fact (Is 48,8; Ez 20; Is 64,5). This sin is engraved (Jr 17,1), clinging like rust or the pigmentation of the skin (Jr 13,23; Ez 24,6). The prophets express this situation in terms of the historical moment. They proclaim that sin at this moment has reached its climax. God allows them to see, as He allowed Abraham to see in the case of Sodom (cf Am 4,11; Is 1,10...). Thus, as an exhortation, their message will announce a condemnation, with or without specific temporal references, but nonetheless quite detailed. Israel has broken the covenant (Is 24,5; Jr 11,10); thence follow definite consequences for the prophets. The nation awaits the day* of Yahweh as a triumphal moment; the prophets announce it as coming under opposite circumstances (Am 5,18ff). The deceitful vineyard* will be destroyed by the vine-dresser (Is 5,1-7).

2. *Salvation.* Nevertheless, the problem, from the time of Amos, know that God cannot only punish. Then comes Jeremiah "to root up and to pull down, to lay waste and destroy, to build up and to plant" (Jr 1,10). Israel has broken the covenant, but that is not the end of the matter. Does Yahweh who is the author of the covenant likewise intend to break His promises? No sage would dare to answer that question; for in the past, Israel gambled on the fidelity of God in order to be unfaithful to Him, and thus became locked up in sin. But where the sage must be silent (Am 5,13), the prophet speaks up. He alone is able to say that after due punishment*, God will triumph in pardoning His people, not because He must (Ez 16,61), but for the sake of His glory* alone (Is 48,11). This insight is understood better beginning with Hosea, when the doctrine of the covenant was developed under the metaphor of a marriage, as the prophetic response to difficulties about the covenant. Marriage is indeed a contract, but it has no meaning apart from love*. Love, therefore, renders strict retribution impossible, and makes pardon* conceivable.

3. *The heralds of the new covenant.* The exile* and the dispersion which followed upon it have accomplished the condemnation. If the Law has made Israel feel its powerlessness (cf R 7), it is

because the prophets have opened the eyes of the community to this reality. Then follows the hour of mercy*. From the time of the exile, the prophets speak of mercy when they make promises for the future. What they promise is not the restoration (Jr 31,32) of the former moribund institutions, but there will be a new covenant. Jeremiah announces it (Jr 31,31-34) and it is taken up again by Ezekiel (Ez 36,16-38) and by Deutero-Isaiah (Is 55,3; 54,1-10). Within this new perspective, the Law is not suppressed, but assumes a new position. From being a condition of the promise, it becomes an object of the promise* (Jr 31,33; 32,39f; Ez 36, 27). It is a great innovation, but the prophets come up with many others, with respect to all the points of biblical revelation. Prophetic experience touches on all things in order to renovate all things. By their manner of life, as well as by their doctrine, the prophets are the leaders of that band of men whom Pascal has called "the Christians of the Old Law."

4. *The definitive "today."* This renovation of the conceptions of salvation is inseparable from the circumstances of the exile and of the return, for the prophet sees with a single sweep of the eye the eternal truths and the events in which these truths are manifested. Both realities are revealed to him in virtue of his charism. But among the forms of knowledge which man cannot attain by his own unaided powers, knowledge of the future constitutes a special privileged category. Prediction of the future can take on various forms. It sometimes concerns events near in time, whose significance is slight but whose occurrence is quite unexpected (Am 7,17; Jr 28,15f; 44,29f; 1 S 10,1f; cf Lk 22,10ff). Such predictions, once realized, are themselves signs pointing to a more distant event which alone is momentous. That distant future, the denouement of history, is the essential object which prophecy envisages. The circumstances in which the prophecy is made are always intertwined with the contemporary historical background of the Israel of the flesh, but a decisive and universal import is concomitantly conveyed. If the seers describe salvation in terms of the events which they experience, that is due to the limitations of their situation. However, it also indicates that the future is already at work in the present. The prophets relate the present to he future because the latter will be the "today" *par excellence*. The use of hyperbole demonstrates well that the future reality will surpass all the historical objectives seen in the present con-

text. Rather than making us admire its literary form, the prophetic manner of speaking seeks to orientate the hearer or reader to an event that is absolute. Apocalyptic literature is revelation* *par excellence*, since it is more detached from political options than the prophecies of the Old Law; and this is what it aims at directly in its structuring of time, its numbers*, and its imaginative representations (cf Dn). Over and above what present history records, it foreshadows this absolute event which will be the center and end of history.

NT

I. THE FULFILLMENT OF THE PROPHECIES

The NT is a conscious fulfillment* of the prophecies of the OT. The Book of Isaiah which is in itself a summation of prophetic utterance, and especially the Servant Songs within it, appear to be an indispensable link between these two Testaments. This is because they predict the mode of fulfillment as well as its coming actuality. The evangelists themselves employ these texts of Isaiah to describe the poor reception which the message of salvation receives (Is 6,9 is cited by Mt 13,14f, Jn 12,39f, and Ac 28, 26f; Is 53,1 by R 10,16 and Jn 12,38; Is 65,2 by R 10,21).

In fact, if the NT deliberately stresses those events in the life of Jesus which fulfill the Scriptures, one should not forget that all the prophets taken together (Ac 3,18-24; Lk 24,27) anticipate in their own way the essential mystery, which is the passion and resurrection. The passion alone is mentioned many times as the object of prophecy (Mt 26,54-56; Ac 3,18; 13, 27), but more often the two are taken together. Our Lord's lesson in exegesis on the road to Emmaus, which was applied in the editing of the gospels, reunites those expressions whose usage otherwise breaks up into categories the different books that treat of the mystery of Christ: "the prophets," "Moses and all the prophets," "all the Scriptures," "the law of Moses, the prophets, and the psalms" (Lk 24,25.27.44; compare Ac 2,30; 26,22; 28,23; R 1,2; 1 P 1,11; 2 P 3,2...). It is the whole of the OT, which thus becomes a prophecy of the NT, a "prophetic writing" (2 P 1,19f).

II. THE PROPHETIC OFFICE IN THE NEW DISPENSATION

1. *Jesus' milieu.* Jesus appears, so to speak, within a tissue of prophetic utterances, represented by Zechariah (Lk 1,67), Simeon (Lk 2, 25ff), the prophetess Anna (Lk 2,36), and above all, John* the Baptist. John's presence was required to make evident the difference between the prophetic office and its object, Christ. Everyone looks on John as a prophet. like the prophets of old, he in effect translates the Law into terms of lived experience (Mt 14,4; Lk 3,11-14). He announces the imminence of divine wrath* and of salvation (Mt 3,2.8). In particular, John perceives prophetically Him who is at hand without being recognized for what He is; and he points Him out (Jn 1,26.31). Through him speak all the prophets who have rendered testimony to Jesus: "all the prophets, as well as the Law, have prophesied to the time of John" (Mt 11,13; Lk 16,16).

2. *Jesus.* Although the conduct of Jesus* is clearly distinguished from that of John the Baptist (Mt 9,14), yet He retains a number of prophetic characteristics. He makes known the "signs of the times" (Mt 16,2f) and announces their fulfillment (Mt 24—25), His attitude in the face of accepted values is critical like that of the prophets: severity toward those who hold the keys of authority and use them to prevent others entering (Lk 11,52); anger against religious hypocrisy* (Mt 15,7; cf Is 29,13); issuing a challenge to the title "sons of Abraham*" of which the Jews were boastful (Jn 8,39; cf 9,28); clarification of the spiritual heritage intermixed therein, whose broad lines had become difficult to discern; purification of the temple (Mk 11, 15ff p; cf Is 56,7; Jr 7,11); and the proclamation of a perfect worship* after the destruction of the material, local sanctuary (Jn 2,16; cf Ze 14,21). Last of all, a trait which is applicable particularly to the earlier prophets, He sees His message refused (Mt 13,13ff p), rejected by the same Jerusalem which has killed the prophets (Mt 23,37f p; cf 1 Th 2,15). To the extent that this denouement approaches, i.e., His death, He announces it and explains its significance. Being His own prophet, He thereby shows that He remains master of His own destiny, that He accepts it to accomplish the plan of the Father, spelled out in the Scriptures.

In view of the above convictions, accompanied as they are by miraculous signs, it is little wonder that the crowds spontaneously gave to Jesus the title of prophet (Mt 16,14; Lk 7,16; Jn 4,19; 9,17), a title which in individual situations means the prophet *par excellence* foretold in the Scriptures (Jn 1,21; 6,14; 7,40). Jesus, however, accepts this designation only in a passing way (Mt 13,57 p), and the primitive Church made little use of the expressions (Ac 3,22f; cf Lk 24, 19). The personality of Jesus surpasses in every respect the tradition surrounding a prophet: He is the Messiah*, the Servant* of God, the Son* of Man. The authority which He holds from His Father is also entirely His own. It is that of the Son*, which places Him far above the level of a prophet (He 1,1ff). He receives His message indeed; but, as eventually John will say, He is the Word* of God made flesh (Jn 1,14). In effect, what prophet could ever have presented himself as the source of truth* and of life*? The prophets used to say, "oracle of Yahweh!" Jesus on the other hand says, "Amen, Amen I say to you. . ." His mission and His person are of a different order.

3. *The Church.* "Some day prophesying will come to an end," explains St. Paul (1 Co 13,8). But that will come at the end of time*. The coming of Christ into this world, far from eliminating the prophetic charism, has rather provoked its further extension as had been predicted. "That all the people might prophesy," was the wish of Moses (Nm 11,29). And Joel saw this wish realized in the "last days" (Jl 3,1-4). On Pentecost*, Peter declares this prophecy accomplished: the Spirit* of Jesus is communicated to all flesh. Vision and prophecy are ordinary occurrences in the new people of God. The charism* of prophecy is effectively frequent in the apostolic Church (cf Ac 11,27f; 13, 1; 21,10f). In the churches which he has founded, Paul wishes that the office be not undervalued (1 Th 5,20). He places it above the gift of tongues* (1 Co 14,1-5). Still, it is necessary that it be exercised within limits and for the good of the community (14,29-32).

The prophetic office of the NT, no more than that of the OT, has for its sole function the prediction of the future: it "builds up, exhorts, consoles" (14,3); functions which approximate the preaching* office. The prophetic author of the Apocalypse commences by revealing the true state to the seven churches (Ap 2—3) in a manner similar to that of the prophets (1 Co 14,32) and the directives of authority (14,37); the prophet does not pretend to gather the community under his wing or govern the Church (cf 12,4-11). Genuine prophecy will be discernible up to the end, thanks to the rules for the discernment of spirits. Even in the OT, did not the Deuteronomist see in the doctrine preached by the prophets the authentic sign of their divine mission (Dt 13,2-6)? Thus it remains today. For prophecy did not die out with the apostolic age. It would be difficult to understand the mission of many saints in the Church without reference to the charism of prophecy, which remains subject to the rules laid down by St. Paul.

→Anointing III 4—Blessing III 4—Book II—Charisms—Clothing I 2—Curse III 2—Dreams OT—Election OT I 3 c—Elijah—Exhort—Exile II 1—Faith OT II, III—Fulfill OT 2; NT—Jesus Christ II 1 c—John the Baptist—Lie II 3 a—Love I OT 2—Magic 2 b—Mediator I 1—Messiah OT II 1; NT II 2—Miracle I 2 a—Mission OT I 1—Moses—Persecution I 1. 2—Prayer I 2—Priesthood OT III 2—Repentance/Conversion OT II; NT I—Revelation OT I 2—Run—Servant of God I—Sign OT II 3.4.5—Sin III—Spirit of God OT II, IV—Teach OT I 3—Witness OT II 2, III—Word of God—Writing II.

PBp jab

PROVIDENCE

The picture of God that we find in the Bible is that of a father* watching over His creatures and providing for their needs: "you give to all their nourishment in due time" (Ps 145,15f; 104,27f), to animals* as well as to men* (Ps 36, 7; 147,9). It is this aspect of the picture of God that is suggested by the word providence, a word for which there is no Hebrew equivalent and of which the Greek equivalent *pronoia* is only used on two occasions with reference to divine providence (Ws 14,3; 17,2). However, the watchfulness and solicitude of the creator is mentioned in the Bible (Jb 10,12), and it is mainly in the course of history that it shows itself. But it is not to be understood as a fate, which would oppress men with a sense of fatalism, nor as if God were a sort of magician* ensuring believers against accidents, nor again as if He were an indulgent Father. If Providence does establish man in hope*, it also lays upon him the duty of collaboration.

1. *Providence, the basis of confidence* and assurance.* There is not the slightest doubt that

God's plan*, the plan of love (Ps 103,8ff), will be carried out (33,11); for this reason men should live in confidence*. God watches over the order of the world (Gn 8,22); He ensures the fruitfulness of the earth (Ac 14,17) by giving sun and rain to all, good and bad alike (Mt 5,45); and He arranges all things so that all may seek* Him (Ac 17,24-28).

a) Although God watches over all patriarchs (Gn 20,6f; 28,15), it is above all in the story of Joseph that His mysterious and sovereign action is brought out, even making use of evil in the service of His plan of salvation. "It was not you who sent me here, but God...The evil you planned to do me has by God's design been turned to good, that he might bring about... the deliverance of a numerous people" (Gn 45, 8; 50,20). Thus, the Chosen People are able to face the desert*; God will feed them there every day "according to their needs" (Ex 16,15-18). The prophets proclaim this control of God, who knows from eternity what is going to happen (Is 44,7), on whom happiness and unhappiness depend (Am 3,6; Is 45,7), and who arranges all things and gives power to whomsoever He wishes (Jr 27,5f). According to the wise men too, man proposes and God disposes (Pr 16,1.33; 19.21; 20,24); good and evil*, life* and death*, poverty* and wealth* all come from the Lord (Si 11,14) who governs the world and whose orders are always carried out (10,4; 39,31).

This conviction is an inspiration to prayer*: God, who controls His creation and makes it fruitful (Ps 65,7-14), guards His people* in all things and in all ways (Ps 121); without Him men's efforts and vigilance are in vain (126,1). Thanks to Him, the good shepherd*, His sheep journey toward happiness with assurance, even in the midst of darkness (23). In brief, "count on the Lord, and he will act" (37,5).

b) Jesus renews this teaching, when He shows men in what way God is their Father; they must pray to Him quite simply: "Our Father, give us today our daily bread*" (Mt 6,11), and they should not be anxious for tomorrow, nor fear for their lives; for "their Father knows" everything they need and everything that will happen to them (Mt 6,25-34; 10,28-31; Lk 6, 34; 12,22-32; 21,18). This is enough to confirm the believer in unshakable faith; for, as the apostle Paul says, "God will make all things cooperate for his good, and nothing will be able to separate him from the love* that God shows to him in Jesus Christ*" (R 8,28.31-39), not even the worst trials. Indeed, on the contrary, it is thanks to these trials that he will be able to reveal to his brethren what the providence of his Father really means.

2. *Providence demands constancy and faithfulness.* In fact, God does not invite man to be passive nor to give up his freedom; on the contrary, He wants to educate* him. By means of trials He calls on him to work together with Him by his free initiative, while by His promises He arouses his confidence and in this way frees him from the fears that might paralyze him in the face of the risks involved by such a collaboration. If He provides for the needs of those He calls to be His children, it is in order that they may be able to be faithful to their calling as witnesses of His love.

a) Already in the OT the friends of God realize that they must respond in perfect faithfulness* to the one who has chosen them and then surrounds them with His protection. Abraham is certain that "God will provide" (Gn 22, 8.13f) and does not hesitate to sacrifice his son in obedience to the Lord. Joseph, not wanting to sin against God, does not hesitate to bring upon himself the wrath of his master's wife (39,9f).

But the people of Israel, from their beginnings, prove themselves unfaithful, precisely because they have not full confidence in the God who has freed them and who feeds them in the desert; instead of expecting to receive their food from Him each day, they want to store up reserve supplies, in spite of the divine command (Ex 16,20).

The Book of Judith was written to remind Israel of the demands of their calling; Judith refuses to put providence to the test (Jdt 8,12-16), but she does not hesitate to make herself its instrument, while at the same time taking care to remain faithful to all the demands of the Law (9,9; 12,2; 13,8f). Such an example is echoed by the maxim of the wise psalmist: "count on the Lord, and do well" (Ps 37,3).

b) If Jesus reveals to men the infinite love of which providence is an expression, He also teaches them, as much by His example as by His words, how to respond to it. This response consists in seeking first the reign of this love, in refusing to be subject to any other master (Mt 6,33.24). It consists in asking the Father that His will may be done on earth as in heaven. It consists in expecting in addition one's daily bread and all that a child of God needs to carry out the will of his Father (Mt 6,10f).

Above all there is need of faithfulness in the midst of trial; even Jesus was not spared these by providence, and He knew what it meant to be abandoned by His Father (Mt 27,46), and, obedient unto death, he declared His filial confidence in His last words from the Cross: "Father, into your hands I commit my spirit" (Lk 23,46).

By means of this confidence and faithfulness the Good Shepherd has passed through death and given us the only light that enables us to pass through the night into which we are sometimes plunged by evil and misfortune. By imitating Christ the disciple will follow the mysterious ways of providence and will have the joy of being the witness and the faithful collaborator of the love in which he trusts.

→Cares 2—Confidence—Fathers & Father III 3, IV, VI—God—Nourishment—Plan of God —Prayer—Power II 1.2—Predestine 3—Visitation—Wisdom OT III 3.

MFL ems

PUNISHMENTS

The kingdom of God is under the sign of beatitude and here is the Bible speaking of divine punishments; the plan of God aims at reconciling* every creature with God and here is hell* which separates the creature from Him definitively. It is an intolerable scandal since the theological meaning of the three realities underlying punishment is lost: sin*, wrath*, and judgment*. But thanks to Him, the believer adores the mystery of divine love which by His patience and His mercy obtains conversion of the sinner.

Calamities*, flood*, dispersions*, enemies*, hell*, war*, death*, and suffering*—all these punishments reveal three things to man. a state of sin, a logic which leads from sin to punishment, a personal view of God who judges and saves.

1. *Punishment, the sign of sin.* Through punishment, which it bears painfully, the will of the sinful creature knows that it is separated from God. The whole of creation gives witness of this. The serpent, seducer and murderer (Gn 3,14f; Jn 8,44; Ap 20,9f); man, discovering that

"by a single man, sin* entered into the world, and by sin death*," suffering, painful work* (R 5,12; Gn 3,16-19); the cities punished for their unbelief*: Babel, Sodom, Capernaum, Jesusalem, Nineveh; the enemies of the people of God: Pharaoh, Egypt, the nations*, even if God uses them to chastise His people (Is 10,5); the people of God Himself, in whom the positive finality of punishment ought to be most apparent (Ba 2,6-10.27-35); the beast* and the adorers of his image (Ap 14,9ff; 19,20); and finally, material creation*, subjected to vanity following upon the sin of Adam (R 8,20).

2. *Punishment, the fruit of sin.* Three periods can be distinguished in the genesis of punishment. In the beginning there is present both the gift* of God (creation, election) and sin*. Then the call of God to conversion is refused by the sinner (He 12,25) who sees, however, many times through the call the announcement of punishment (Is 8,5-8; Ba 2,22ff). Against such obstinacy the judge decides to chastise: "So indeed..." (Ho 13,7; Is 1,5; Lk 13,34f).

The end of chastisement is twofold according to the docility of one's heart*: certain punishments are "closed" and condemn—Satan* (Ap 20,10), Babel* (Ap 18), Ananias and Sapphira (Ac 5,1-11)—others are "open" and call to conversion (1 Co 5,5; 2 Co 2,6). So punishment is a barrier opposed to sin: for some it is an impasse of condemnation; for others it is an invitation to "return" to God (Ho 2,8f; Lk 15,14-20). But even in this latter case it remains a condemnation of the past and an anticipation of definitive condemnation if the heart does not return to its God.

It is not punishment, then which separates from God, but the sin for which it is the payment. Punishment emphasizes the fact that sin is incompatible with divine holiness* (He 10, 29f). If Christ knew punishment, it is not because of sin which He committed but because of the sins of man which He bore and removed (1 P 2,24; 3,18; Is 53,4).

3. *Punishment, revelation of God.* In its internal logic, punishment reveals God: it is like a theophany adapted to the sinner. He who does not accept the grace* of the divine visit clashes with holiness and encounters God Himself (Lk 19,41-44). This is what the prophet repeats without ceasing: "Then you will know that I am Yahweh" (Ez 11,10; 15,7). Because punishment is revelation, it is the Word which executes it (Ws 18,14ff; Ap 19,11-16); and it is

in confrontation with the crucified that it assumes its true dimensions (Jn 8,28).

Since punishment is thus ordered to the recognition of Yahweh and of Jesus, it is so much the more terrible when the one whom it affects is closer to God (Lv 10,1ff; Ap 3,19). The same presence*, sweet to the pure heart, becomes painful to the hardened heart even though all suffering* is not punishment.

Still more, punishment reveals the depths of God's heart: His jealousy as soon as one entered into His covenant* (Ex 20,5; 34,7), His wrath* (Is 9,11ff), His vengeance* toward His enemies* (Is 10,12), His justice* (Ez 18), His readiness to pardon* (Ez 18,31), His mercy (Ho 11,9), and finally His pressing love*: "And you have not come back to me!" (Am 4,6-11; Is 9,12; Jr 5,3).

But there is a punishment at the very heart of our history where the tempter and sin have been struck dead—it is the cross* where the Wisdom* of God shines forth (1 Co 1,17—2,9). In the cross the "closed" condemnation of Satan, sin, and death, and the "open" suffering, the source of life, coincide (1 P 4,1; Ph 3,10).

This wisdom has made its way through every ancient covenant (Dt 8,5f; Ws 10—12; He 12,5-13); the education* of liberty was not able to be accomplished without "correction" (Jdt 8,27; 1 Co 11,32; G 3,23f). Punishment is connected with the Law*; historically, this age has passed, but psychologically many Christians delay there still: punishment is, then, one of the bonds which continues to unite the sinner to God. But the Christian who lives with the Spirit is free from punishment (R 8,1; 1 Jn 4, 18). If he recognizes this as coming from the love of the Father*, it is in view of conversion (1 Tm 1,20; 2 Tm 2,25). And, in our eschatological times, the true and only punishment is final obduracy (2 Th 2,10f; He 10,26-29).

This proximity of decisive judgment, already at work, confers on the punishment of "carnal" man the value of a sign: it anticipates the condemnation of everything that is not able to inherit the kingdom*. But for the "spiritual," the judgment is justification*: the punishment then becomes expiation* in Christ (R 3,25f; G 2, 19; 2 Co 5,14); voluntarily accepted, it makes the flesh die to live according to the Spirit* (R 8,13; Col 3,5).

→Babel/Babylon 2—Calamity—Captivity I—Curse—Death OT II 1.2; NT I, II 1.2—Earth OT II 3 c—Education—Egypt 2—Exile I—Expiation 1—Fear of God III—Fire—Flood—

Godless Man OT 3; NT 3—Hardness of Heart
II 1—Hell OT II; NT I o—Judgment OT I 2,
II 1—Justice A II OT—Leprosy 1—Mercy OT
1 2 b—Persecution I 4 b—Prophet OT IV 1—
Repentance/Conversion OT I 1, II 3—Responsi-
bility 4—Reward—Sadness OT 2—Salt 1—
Silence 1—Sickness/Healing OT I 2—Sin I 2
—Sterility II—Vintage 2—Visitation OT 1; NT
2—War OT III 2; NT III 2—Water II 1.2—
Will of God OT O, II—Wrath B.

JCo pjb

PURE

Purity, a common conception in ancient religions, is the required disposition for approaching sacred things. Although it can also acces-
sorily imply moral virtue as opposed to
lewdness, it is obtained not by moral acts, but
through ritual; and it is lost through material
contacts, regardless of any moral responsibility.
Under ordinary circumstances, this primitive
conception tends to deepen, but it does so differently in different contexts of thought. Religious belief founded on the Bible sees all
creation as good. And so the notion of purity
tends to become interior and moral, reaching a
culmination in Christ who reveals the unique
source of purity to consist in His Word and in
His sacrifice.

OT

1. PURITY OF CULT

1. *In the life of the sacred community.* Lacking
direct relation to moral conduct, purity guarantees the juridical ability to participate in the
cult or even the ordinary daily contacts within
the sacred community. This complex notion,
developed especially in Lv 11—16, appears
throughout the entire OT.

It includes *bodily cleanliness*: removal from
what is indecent (excrement Dt 23,13ff), sickly
(lepers Lv 13—14; 2 K 7,3), or fetid (corpses
Nm 19,11-14; 2 K 23,13f). However, the discrimination between clean and unclean animals
(Lv 11), often borrowed from primitive taboos,
cannot be explained on hygienic grounds alone.

Ritual purity constituted a *protection against
paganism*. Canaan was tainted by the presence
of pagans: the spoils of war were reserved for
destruction (Js 6,24ff). Even the fruits of the
land were interdicted during the first three years

of harvesting (Lv 19,23ff). Certain animals, like
swine, are considered unclean (Lv 11,7), undoubtedly because pagans associated these animals with their own cult practices (cf Is 66,3).

Cultural purity regulated the use of *everything held to be sacred*. Everything which
touched on cult had to be eminently pure and
could not be approached without permission
(Lv 21,22; 1 S 21,5). Apart from this, both
sacred and impure are equally untouchable,
as if they were endowed with some fearful and
contagious power (Ex 29,37; Nb 19). Since
the vital powers, as a source of blessing, were
considered sacred, certain impurities were contracted even by the morally acceptable use of
the sexual power (Lv 12 and 15).

2. *Purificatory rites.* The majority of impurities, when they did not disappear of their own
accord (Lv 11,24f), were removed by the washing of the body or of the clothes (Ex 19,10; Lv
17,15f); by expiatory sacrifices (Lv 12,6f); and
on the Day of Expiation*, the purificatory feast
par excellence, by the driving into the desert
of a male goat symbolically laden with the
defilements and even the sins of the entire
people (Lv 16).

3. *Respect for the holy community.* At the
base of this still quite materialistic notion of
purity appears the idea that man* is so composed that body* and soul* cannot be separated;
and that therefore his religious actions, spiritual
as they are, remain incarnated. In a community
consecrated to God and desirous to surpass the
natural state of its existence, one does not eat
just anything, nor touch everything, nor use the
generative faculties indiscriminately. These
multiple restrictions, arbitrary perhaps in the
beginning, had a double effect. They preserved
the faith in monotheism against all contamination by the surrounding pagan milieu. Furthermore, assumed in a spirit of obedience to God,
they constituted a true moral discipline. In this
way the real spiritual demands of God were
progressively revealed.

II. TOWARD THE CONCEPT OF MORAL PURITY

1. *The prophets* proclaimed constantly that
neither ablutions nor sacrifices* have any value
in themselves, if they do not betoken an interior
purification (Is 1,15ff; 29,13; cf Ho 6,6; Am 4,
1-5; Jr 7,21ff). The cult aspect does not corre-

spondingly disappear (Is 52,11), but the real uncleanliness which defiles a man is revealed at its very source, in sin*. The legal impurities are only the exterior aspect (Ex 36,17f). There is an essential defilement about man which God alone can cleanse (Is 6,5ff). The radical purification of the lips*, the heart*, the entire person, is made a part of the Messianic promises: "I will pour over you clear water and you will be cleansed from all your defilements" (Ez 36,25f; cf Zp 3,9; Is 35,8; 52,2).

2. *With the wisdom philosophers*, the condition required to please God is characterized by the purity of hands, of heart, of countenance, of prayer (Jb 11,4.14f; 16,17; 22,30), and thus by irreproachable moral conduct. The wisdom philosophers were conscious indeed of a radical impurity of man before God (Pr 20,9; Jb 9,30f); it is presumptuous to believe oneself pure (Jb 4, 17). Nevertheless the sage pushes himself to establish the moral basis of purity, and in the beginning it is the sexual side of purity which is emphasized. Sarah keeps herself pure (Tb 3, 14), while the pagans indulge in a degrading impurity (Ws 14,24).

3. *With the psalmists*, one notices in the cultural setting that care for moral purity is more and more emphasized. The love of God is turned toward the pure of heart (Ps 73,1). Access to the sanctuary is reserved to the man with undefiled hands, with a clean heart (Ps 24,4). God fills the unstained hands of him who practices justice* (Ps 18,21.25). But since He alone can give this purity, prayer for cleanness of heart is directed to God. The *Miserere* reveals the moral effect of the purification which the supplicant expects from God alone. "Wash me from every imperfection...wash me with hyssop. I will be pure." More, preserving the heritage of Ezekiel (36,25f) and crowning the tradition of the OT, the supplicant cries out, "O God, create in me a clean heart" (Ps 51,12), a prayer already so spiritual that the believer of the NT can use it just as it is.

NT

I. PURITY IN THE GOSPELS

1. Practices with regard to purity persist in the Judaism of Jesus' time and legal formalism went further than the Law by accentuating the material conditions for purity: repeated ablutions (Mk 7,3f), meticulous washings (Mt 23, 25), aloofness from sinners who spread impurity (Mk 2,15ff), and especially from graves so as to avoid infection by inadvertence (Mt 23,27).

2. Jesus is careful to observe certain rules of legal purity (Mk 1,43f), and He seems to condemn at first only excesses in observances added to the Law (Mk 7,6-13). In the end, however, He proclaims that *real purity* is interior (Mk 7, 14-23 p): "Nothing which enters from outside into a man can render him impure...for it is from inside, from the heart of man, that proceed evil designs." It is in this sense that the evil* spirits themselves can be called "unclean spirits" (Mk 1,23; Lk 9,42). The liberating doctrine of Jesus was so new that the disciples were very slow to understand it.

3. Jesus bestows His personal friendship on those who give themselves to Him in simplicity* of faith and love, to the "clean of heart" (Mt 5,8). To see* God, to present oneself to Him, no longer in His temple at Jerusalem but in His kingdom*, even moral purity is not sufficient. What is needed is the active presence of the Lord in human existence. Then alone is man radically pure. Thus Jesus speaks to His apostles: "Already you have been purified, thanks to the word which I have declared to you" (Jn 15,3). And still more clearly: "A man who has bathed has no further need of washing; he is altogether clean; you also, you are clean" (Jn 13,10).

II. THE APOSTOLIC TEACHING

1. *Beyond the division between pure and impure*. The Jewish-Christian communities continue to observe the practices of purity. It needs a divine intervention for Peter to draw the triple conclusion from the teaching of Christ: there is no more unclean food (Ac 10,15; 11,9); the uncircumcised themselves are no longer defiled (Ac 10,28); it is by faith* that God henceforth purifies the hearts of pagans (Ac 15,9). For his own part, Paul, relying on the teaching of Jesus (cf Mk 7), declares straightforwardly that for the Christian, "nothing is impure in itself" (R 14,14). The regime of the old Law having passed away, the observances over cleanliness become "mean and beggarly spirits of the elements" from which Christ has liberated us (G 4,3.9; Col 2,16-23). "The solid reality is Christ's body" (Col 2,17), for His risen body is the seed of the new universe.

2. In place of rites incapable of purifying the interior man, *Christ has substituted His sacrifice**, fully efficacious (He 9; 10). The blood of Jesus having purified us from sin (1 Jn 1, 7.9), we hope to take our place among those who "have washed their robes in the blood of the Lamb" (Ap 7,14). This radical purification is actualized by the rite of baptism* which draws its efficacy from the cross*: "Christ delivered Himself up for the Church, in order to sanctify it, cleansing it by water and word" (E 5,26). Since the old observances produce merely an exterior purification, the waters* of baptism* free us from every stain in associating us to Jesus Christ risen from the dead (1 P 3, 21f). We are indeed purified by our hope in God who, through Christ, has made us His children (1 Jn 3,3).

3. *The transposition from the ritual level to the level of interior salvation* is expressed notably in the first epistle to the Corinthians where Paul invites the Christians to expel from their lives the "old leaven" and to replace it by the "unleavened bread of purity and of truth" (1 Co 5,8; cf Jm 4,8). The Christian ought therefore to purify himself from every stain of soul and body, thus to achieve the work of his sanctification (2 Co 7,1). The moral aspect of this purity is more developed in the pastoral epistles. "Everything is pure for the pure" (Tt 1,15) for nothing counts before God except the unseen disposition of regenerated hearts (cf 1 Tm 4,4). Christian charity leaps forth from a pure heart, a good conscience, and a straightforward faith (1 Tm 1,5; cf 5,22). Paul himself gives thanks to the Lord for being able to serve Him with a pure intention (2 Tm 1,3), as he himself asks of his disciples a pure heart, from which springs forth justice, faith, charity, and peace (2 Tm 2,22; cf 1 Tm 3,9).

Finally, what permits a Christian to lead a morally irreproachable life is his consecration to the new worship in the Spirit. The opposite of impurity is holiness (1 Th 4,7f; R 6,19). Moral purity which the OT has already esteemed is always required (Ph 4,8), but its true value comes from the fact that it leads to the encounter with Christ on the last day at His return (Ph 1,10).

→Animals II 2—Baptism—Conscience 2 b. 3—Dove 1—Expiation 1—Fire—Heart II—Holy—Leprosy—Liberation/Liberty II 3—Mary II 2 — Nourishment I, III — Pardon — Perfection OT 2—Priesthood OT III 2—Remnant—Sacrifice OT II 2; NT II 2—Salt 2—Sexuality II—Simple 2—Sin III 3—Trial/Temptation OT I 2—Virginity OT 1—Water—White 2.

LS jab

R

RECONCILIATION

Already within the OT, God has prefigured the reconciliation of men with Himself, in not ceasing to offer to them His pardon*. He reveals Himself as "the God of tenderness and of pity" (Ex 34,6), who freely restrains "the ardor of His wrath*" (Ps 85,4; cf 103,8-12) and speaks of peace* to His people (cf Ps 85,9). Israel's sins break the Sinai covenant*; but, far from resigning Himself to this, God will Himself take the initiative of a new and eternal covenant (Jr 31,31ff; Ez 36,60-63). Thus it is indeed a reconciliation—even if the word is not used—which Yahweh proposes to His unfaithful spouse* (Ho 2,16-22), to His rebellious children (Ez 18,31f). And all the rites of expiation* in the Mosaic ritual, ordered to purification from all kinds of imperfections, look ultimately to the reconciliation of man with God. Nevertheless the time has not yet arrived for the complete remission of sins, and the faithful servants of the true God remain in expectation of something better (cf 2 M 1,5; 7,33; 8,29).

Perfect and definitive reconciliation has been accomplished by Jesus Christ, "the mediator* between God and men" (1 Tm 2,5). Reconciliation is only one aspect of Christ's work of redemption*. It is, however, legitimate to contemplate the mystery of salvation from this special point of view in the light of certain

RECONCILIATION

Pauline texts (R 5,10f; 2 Co 5,18ff; E 2,16f; Col 1,20ff). Such is the scope of these lines.

I. OUR RECONCILIATION WITH GOD THROUGH CHRIST

1. *The divine initiative.* By himself man is incapable of reconciling himself with the Creator whom he has offended by his sin*. The action of God here is primary and decisive: "everything comes from God who reconciles us to Himself through Christ" (2 Co 5,18). He already loved us when we were His "enemies" (R 5, 10), and it is then that His Son "has died for us" (5,8). The mystery of our reconciliation is linked with that of the cross* (cf E 2,16) and of the "great love" with which we have been loved (cf E 2,4).

2. *The effects of reconciliation.* God no longer takes account of the faults of men (cf 2 Co 5, 19). But far from that being a simple juridical fiction, the action of God is rather, in the words of Paul, like "a new creation*" (2 Co 5,17). Reconciliation implies a renewal, complete for those who benefit from it; it coincides with justification* (R 5,9f) and sanctification (Col 1, 21f). Up to that point enemies* of God by our evil conduct (R 1,30; 8,7), we are now able "to exult in God" (R 5,11), who wishes to present us before Himself as dedicated men, "without blemish and innocent in His sight" (Col 1,22). We have, "all of us, in the one spirit, access to the Father" (E 2,18).

3. *The ministry of reconciliation.* On God's part the entire work of salvation* is already accomplished; but from another point of view, it continues even up to the parousia. Thus Paul can define apostolic activity as "the ministry of reconciliation" (2 Co 5,18). As "ambassadors for Christ," the apostles are the messengers of "the word of reconciliation" (5,19f). An ancient papyrus speaks even here of "the gospel of reconciliation," and such is the tenor of their apostolic message (cf E 6,15: "the gospel of peace"). In their ministry, the ministers of the gospel* make an effort, after the example of Paul, to be on their part the architects of the peace which they announce (2 Co 6,4-13).

4. *The reception of the gift of God.* From the fact that God is the first and principal author of reconciliation, it does not follow that man maintains an attitude which is purely passive: he must receive the gift of God. The divine action is efficacious only for those who will it and consent to it in faith*. Hence the urgent cry of Paul: "We beseech you in the name of Christ to be reconciled with God" (2 Co 5,20).

II. UNIVERSAL RECONCILIATION

1. *Reconciled creation.* In speaking of the reconciliation of the world* (2 Co 5,19; R 11, 15), Paul has in mind up to this point sinful mankind, without, however, overlooking the fact that the material world itself is in solidarity with mankind and is to share in its liberation* (cf R 8,19-22). In the Captivity letters, in Col and Eph, the horizon of the Apostle widens to include the whole universe, "on earth" and "in heaven" (Col 1,20). Reconciled with God by the blood of the cross, men are also reconciled with the heavenly spirits; the hostile attitude that the angelic* powers were able to adopt toward us under the superseded regime of the Law (cf Col 2,15) has now come to an end.

2. *The reconciliation of Jews and pagans.* Paul crowns his teaching in E 2,11-22. The action of Christ, "our peace" (2,14), is there put in full light, especially the marvelous benefits which He has obtained for the pagans of former times: they are now incorporated into the chosen people in the same way as the Jews. The era of separation and of hatred is over. All men form only one body* in Christ (2,16), a single holy temple* (2,21). Of little significance for the apostle of the gentiles are the glorious sufferings* which the proclamation of this mystery* has carried for him (E 3,1-13).

Paul has been the inspired theologian and the untiring minister of reconciliation; but it is Jesus who by His sacrifice* has been its creator "in His body* of flesh" (Col 1,22). He was first to underline the profound exigencies of this reconciliation: the sinner reconciled by God cannot render to Him a pleasing worship* if he does not first of all reconcile himself with his brother (Mt 5,23f).

→Brother OT 3; NT 1—Enemy III—Jew I 2—Nations III 1 b—Pardon—Peace II 3 b, III 2 —Redemption—Sin I 2—Trial II—Violence IV 3.

LR jab

REDEMPTION

The notion of redemption (gr. *lytrōsis* or *apolytrōsis*), in virtue of which God "frees" or "ransoms" (gr. *lytrousthai*) His people, and the very similar one of "acquisition" (gr. *peripoiesis*), in virtue of which He "buys" them, are closely related in the Bible to the idea of salvation*. They designate the privileged means chosen by God to save Israel in freeing it from Egyptian servitude (Ex 12,27; 14,13; cf Is 63,9), and in constituting Israel as a "special people" (Ex 19,5; Dt 26,18). In the NT, a text like Tt 2,13f, an evident reflection of a primitive catechesis, clearly reveals the source to which the author refers in describing the work of Christ: Jesus is "Savior" insofar as He "sets us free from all iniquity" and "makes us a pure people marked out for His own." Thus the continuity of the salvific design appears, and what is new and unforeseeable in no way hinders the fulfillment of every true prophecy.

OT

1. *Exodus and covenant.* It is in connection with the exodus* that the OT speaks most often of redemption: the religious experience which Israel undergoes permits best of all an understanding of the content of this notion. For in the Jewish consciousness the exodus cannot be dissociated from the covenant*. God frees His people from slavery only to attach them to Himself: "I am Yahweh...I will free you from slavery...and I will deliver (ransom) you by mighty acts...I will adopt you for my people and I will be your God" (Ex 6,6f; cf 2 S 7,23f). In virtue of the covenant, Israel becomes a "holy" people, "consecrated to Yahweh," God's "very own people" (Ex 19,5f). A *holy people* and *ransomed by Yahweh* are equivalent terms (Is 62,11f); and Jeremiah thus dates the covenant from the day when "God has taken His people by the hand to lead them out of Egypt" (Jr 31,32).

Thus the notion of redemption is essentially positive: union with God is no less affirmed than freedom from the slavery of sin. Besides, this is the etymology of the Latin term *redemptio*: it designates first of all a purchase (*emere*) which delivers us only to gain us for God. As such it is quite similar to the English term *atonement*. The latter, frequently used to translate *redemptio*, has as its original meaning "reunion," "reconciliation" ("at-one-ment").

2. *Messianic redemption.* The prophets deliberately take up the same formulas apropos of the liberation from the exile*, and *the Redeemer* becomes accordingly one of the favorite titles of Yahweh, notably in Second Isaiah. It is no surprise then that the object of the great Messianic hope expresses itself in terms of redemption: "For with the Lord is kindness, and with Him is plenteous 'redemption,' for He will 're-deem' Israel from all its guilt" (Ps 130,7f). More than the others, Ezekiel underlines the absolute gratuity of such a redemption accorded to sinners (Ez 16,60-63; 36,21ff). Apart from this, he makes the nature of this "new covenant" clear; and while in Jr 31,33 Yahweh had said: "Deep within them I shall plant my law," in Ez 36,27 He says: "I shall put my spirit in you." Redemption will consist in the communication of Yahweh's own Spirit in place of Law (cf Jn 1,17.29.33; 7,37ff; R 8,2-4).

NT

1. *Continuity with the OT.* The reference to this Messianic context is sometimes explicit: Zechariah extols the God who "has redeemed His people"; and the prophetess Hannah speaks of the child in reference to "all those who are looking for the liberation of Jerusalem" (Lk 1, 68; 2,38). Like the majority also of Messianic terms derived from the OT, which can be applied either to the first or the second coming of Christ, the term *redemption* serves not only to designate the work performed by Christ on Calvary (R 3,24; Col 1,14; E 1,7); it equally applies to what He will accomplish at the end of time, therefore in consequence of the parousia and the glorious resurrection of the body (Lk 21,28; R 8,23; E 1,14; 4,30; prob. 1 Co 1,30). In both cases, there is question of a deliverance, a liberation, but even more of an acquisition, of a "taking possession by God," at first initial and then definitive. Then man, body and soul, and the universe with him will be "filled with the utter fullness of God" (E 3,19), and God will be "all in all" (1 C 15,28), indeed will "fill the whole creation" (E 1,23).

That is, moreover, why the NT has been able to express this same notion with the help of the verb *to purchase* (gr. *agorazein,* 1 Co 6,20; 7,23; cf G 3,13; 4,5). Not that the NT writer has wished to assimilate the redemption to a commercial transaction regulated by the law of equity or commutative justice, where the jailer will free his prisoner and the merchant sell his merchandise only on condition that he suffer no loss. It wishes to signify doubtless that we have become the property of God in virtue of a contract whose conditions have all been fulfilled. One condition in particular was invariably pointed out: the price has been met (1 Co 6,20; 7,23; cf 1 P 1,18). Yet is should be noted that the metaphor stops there. There is never question of a person who demands or receives the payment of a price. Thus in this point also the NT appears to embody the notion of a purchase with which the OT was familiar. The Apocalypse, at any rate, by the use of the same verb *to purchase* makes explicit reference to the Sinai covenant: in the blood* of the Lamb men of all nations have become the special property of God, just as formerly Israel became His possession in virtue of the covenant which was likewise sealed in blood (Ap 5,9). To recall the same reality, Ac 20,28 moreover keeps the term proper to the OT and speaks of "the Church of God, which He won for Himself by His own blood" (cf 1 P 2,9; Tt 2,14).

The interpretation is furthermore traceable to Christ in person: the paschal setting deliberately chosen and the explicit appeal to the blood of the covenant were sufficiently clear that no one could make a mistake (Mt 26,28 p; 1 Co 11,25).

2. *The voluntary death of Christ*. But the NT also clearly outlines the distance which separates the figure* and its fulfillment*. Like the old, the new covenant is sealed in blood, but this blood is that of the only Son of God (1 P 1,18f; He 9,12; cf Ac 20,28; R 3,25).

"Priceless" redemption: to the immolation of irrational animals succeeded the personal and voluntary sacrifice* of the Servant* of Yahweh who "has handed over His life unto death" (Is 53,12) and "eminently served the community" (Is 53,11 LXX). Jesus "has not come to be served, but to serve and to give His life in ransom" (Mt 20,28; Mk 10,45): His sacrifice will be the instrument of our deliverance (*lytron*). It is this voluntary character of the death of Christ which the Johannine account of the passion intends to highlight (vg Jn 18,4-8). More clearly still, if that is possible, in the synoptics' account of the eucharistic* supper, where Christ literally in advance dedicates Himself to His death, the same point of the voluntary suffering of Christ is accentuated.

3. *The victory of Christ over death*. For the disciples His death* had been a scandal*, the proof that Christ was not the expected re-

deemer (Lk 24,21). Their minds illumined by the Easter and Pentecostal experiences, and having become the witnesses of the resurrection* (Ac 1,8; 2,31f; etc), they understood that, far from being a setback to the salvific plan of God, the passion and death of their master fulfilled this plan "in accord with the Scriptures" (1 Co 15,4). The stone* rejected by the builders has become the cornerstone (Ac 4,11=Ps 118, 22; 1 P 2,7), the foundation of the new temple* (Mt 21,42). The Servant* has been truly "exalted" (Ac 2,33; 5,31) and "glorified" (3,13), in the words of the text of Is 52,13. Still more, He has become a servant "in order to deliver His soul* unto death" (Is 53,12; Ph 2,9). An apparent defeat, the death of Christ was in reality a victory* over death and Satan*, the author of death (Jn 12,31f; cf He 2,14).

4. *Death and resurrection*. In initial preaching of the redemptive mystery, the resurrection* played a subordinate role, such that it was sometimes only mentioned (vg 1 P 1,3) in connection with the parousia (1 Th 1,10). But, guided by the Holy Spirit, the apostles began to discern more and more clearly in the passion and death on the one hand, and the resurrection and ascension on the other, two groups of events not only ordered to one another (vg Ph 2,9) but so mutually compenetrating that they constituted two indissoluble aspects of a unique mystery of salvation*.

Thus Luke is careful to place within the perspective of the ascension* (Lk 9,51) the whole long account of Jesus' journey toward Jerusalem, and in complementary fashion when he describes the "glorious life" of Christ, to recall with deliberate insistence His passion and death (24,7.26.39.46; cf 9,31). Similarly Paul, even when he does not mention the death, does not refrain from dwelling on the resurrection. The life to which he so often makes allusion is always conceived as a participation in that of the risen Christ (vg G 2,20; 6,14f; R 6,4.11; 8,2.5). Finally, with John the unity of the mystery is so profound that the terms which designated in the primitive catechesis the resurrection of Jesus have likewise been applicable to both the passion and the glorification of Christ (Jn 12,23.32.34). In addition, the Lamb of the Apocalypse appears to the seer of Patmos as "alive" in testimony to the resurrection and yet as "slain" as a sign of the immolation (Ap 5,6).

5. *Mystery of love.*

a) St. John. For John the mystery of redemption is essentially a mystery of love and thus of divine life, since "God is love" (1 Jn 4, 8). It is certainly the love of the Father who has "so loved the world as to give His only Son" (Jn 3,16; 17,23; 1 Jn 4,9); but likewise the love of the Son for His Father (Jn 14,31) and for men (10,11; I Jn 3,16; Ap 1,5); a love which the Son receives from the Father on whom He depends for everything, and consequently an "obedient" love (Jn 14,31); a love, finally, than which there is none greater (15,13). For if the whole life of Christ was one of "love for His own," the passion is the moment when "He loved them unto the end," even to the "consummation" (gr. *telos*) of His love (13,1). In the concrete this means that He allowed Himself to be betrayed by one of the twelve (18,2f), denied by the head of the group (18,25ff), condemned as a blasphemer in the very name of the Law (19,7), and subjected to a most shameful death, that of the cross, like a criminal whose body hanging on a gibbet contaminates the soil of Israel (19,31). At this precise moment He can declare in all truth that "it is consummated" (19,30: gr. *tetelestai*). The love of the Father which was revealed in the Scriptures and incarnated in the human heart of Jesus—this has obtained its supreme "actuation." And if He dies out of love, it is to communicate that love to men, His brothers. From His "pierced" side (19,37; Ze 12,10), John saw spring forth "the font opened for the house of David and the inhabitants of Jerusalem for the cleansing of sin and uncleanness" (Ze 13,1; cf Ez 47,1ff), a prelude of the effusion of that Spirit* (Jn 20,22) which John the Baptist saw descending at the baptism* and hovering over the Messiah (1,32f).

b) St. Paul. This point of view is just as obvious in Paul. He also sees in the death of Christ first of all a mystery of love: love of the Father (R 5,5-8; 8,39; E 1,3-6; 2,4; cf Col 1,13), "while we were as yet sinners" (R 5,8), His "enemies" (5,10); the Son's love, on the one hand, for His Father, under the form of obedience*, thus repairing the disobedience of the first Adam (5,19; Ph 2,6), and likewise for men (R 5,7f; 8,34). In this regard, not only does Paul employ the formula of the primitive catechesis (cf Mk 10,45), inspired in all likelihood by Is 53,10.12, and thus declare that "Christ delivered Himself up for us" or "for our sins"

(G 1,4; 1 Tm 2,6; Tt 2,14). In addition, he further defines that Christ has done this "because He has loved us" (G 2,20; E 5,2.25).

Like John, Paul knows that there is no greater love than to die for those whom one loves (Jn 15,13). In other words, every human love is conditioned, mediated by the circumstances in which it is exercised. To extraordinary circumstances corresponds an extraordinary love. More precisely, in accepting this love from His Father, Christ has accepted it in its fullness because of the circumstances in which the Father has placed Him. Thus Paul sees in the statement "God did not spare His Son but delivered Him up for us all" (R 8,32), the outstanding proof of the charity of Christ (8,35), better, of the "charity of God in Christ our Lord" (8,39).

Among all the attendant circumstances, Paul, like John, appeals notably to the infamy of the cross as a shameful means of execution, the shame of which seems to have especially moved the first Christians (cf Ac 5,30; 10,39). Just as formerly, in the case of the Servant* whom "people looked on as one afflicted by God" (Is 53,4), He, the just one, accepted the role in the eyes of the world of "an accursed thing," a violator of the Law (G 3,13). One cannot imagine a more profound humiliation for Christ (Ph 2,8), nor for that same reason, a more sublime act of obedience and love, deliberately willed from the very moment that He accepted this kind of death. Thus did Christ "redeem" humanity, "acquire it for His Father."

6. *Victory over sin in the flesh.*

On the other hand, since this is an act performed by a member of our human family, who therefore shares fully in our mortal condition, even while transcending it by His divinity, humanity thus finds itself "redeemed," "acquired for God" by an interior transformation. According to John, on the cross "the prince of this world was condemned" (Jn 16,11); that is, "thrown down" (12,31; cf Ap 12,9f), deposed from his kingdom. His empire is humanity, beings of flesh become offspring of Sin*. But Paul says: "God has condemned Sin in the flesh" (Rm 8,3), that is: to save us. God sent his own Son made flesh like all men, and it is in Him and through Him that redemption is achieved. So it is that God is victorious precisely where Satan thought himself sovereign forever: that is, "in the flesh", the earthly human condition which had become a sinful condition. The redeeming Christ fully took on our carnal condition. Certainly Christ's flesh was not, as is ours, an "instrument of sin"; but like ours, it was exposed to the consequences of universal sin: suffering and death. How in real terms did God triumph? *By giving to such flesh the life of the Spirit.* Given first to Jesus' flesh: Christ by his death and resurrection has become "the spirit who gives life" (1 Co 15,45); given then to our flesh, for if we are united with Christ, we are no longer of the flesh (of sin), but "of the spirit" (Rm 8,9; cf 8,2,4). This vision of God's triumph over the power of Evil is already present in the Old Testament: Ez 38—39 foretells a sort of eschatological battle, the prelude to the dawn of the messianic age, and this is connected with the giving of the Spirit (Ez 39,29; cf 36,27). The "return to God" ("redemption") is accomplished, according to Paul, through Christ having passed over from the "carnal" to the "spiritual" state, and we with Him.

Elsewhere in a formula particularly daring, Paul declares that "God has made His Son sin for our sakes, in order that we might become the justice of God" (2 Co 5,21). These expressions, which have been often misinterpreted, seem rather to be capable of being interpreted in function of the same context: to the end that in Christ, we, through our solidarity with Him who has become one with us, should be subjected to the beneficent effects of this power of life which the Bible and Paul call the "justice of God," the Father has wished that His Son, through His solidarity with sinful men, be subjected to the evil effects of this power of death, which is sin*. These effects would then constitute the *conditio optima* of the greatest act of love and obedience conceivable.

Thus the pernicious work of sin is repaired, humanity restored, redeemed, reunited to God, once again in possession of divine life. According to the ancient prophecy (Ez 36,27), the very Spirit of Yahweh has been communicated to the flesh. But the prophecy has been fulfilled with an unsuspected grandeur, by the mediation of the only Son of God made man in a supreme act of love.

→Adam I 2 b—Animals II—Blood NT—Body II 2—Body of Christ I 2, III 3—Captivity II—Creation NT II 1—Cross—Exodus OT 2; NT o—Expiation—First Fruits II—Lamb of God 2—Liberation/Liberty II 1, III 1—Passover—Plan of God—Preach II 3—Reconciliation—Reward II 3 d—Sacrifice NT I—Salvation—Sickness/Healing NT II 2—Sin III 3, IV 3 e—Slave II—Suffering OT III.

SL jab

REMNANT

OT

God promised to Abraham a progeny "numerous as the stars of heaven" (Gn 15,5). But through the mouth of Amos He warned Israel: "Just as a shepherd rescues from the mouth of a lion two shank bones or a piece of an ear, so will the Israelites be rescued" (Am 3,12). God "wishes that all men be saved" (1 Tm 2,4); and He announces that at the time of the great tribulation, "unless, for the sake of the elect, the days of distress were cut short, no living thing could survive" (Mt 24,22). This remnant, spared in the passing of judgment*, is an essential element in the biblical concept of hope*. The idea is related to the experience of wars and their consequent massacres. The annihilation of the vanquished so often practiced (Assyrian documents, stele of Mesha). posed the problem of survival for Israel and hence of the validity of the divine promises*.

According to context, the word can characterize the full sweep of the catastrophe ("only a remnant will survive" Is 10,22—"not even a remnant" Jr 11,23); or it can evoke hope, arising from the very survival of a remnant (Jr 40,11). The theme makes its appearance with the misfortunes of the ninth century (cf 1 K 19,15-18), but it has a prehistory: Noah* (Gn 6,5ff.17f), described as a remnant figure in Si 44,17, and the chastisements of Israel in the desert which caused the extinction of a large part of the people (Ex 32,28; Nm 17,16; 21,6; 25,9).

1. *Before the exile.* According to Amos, just as previous trials had reduced the nation to the present survivors (Am 5,15), so future chastisements, seen in the perspective of the eschatological judgment, will reduce Israel to a mere handful (3,12; 5,3). As with a sieve, He will let sinners fall through to perdition and retain the just (9,8ff).

For *Isaiah*, the remnant will share in the holiness of Yahweh (Is 4,3; cf 6,3), a destructive fire for the ungodly; but for the others, a luminous (10,17) and purifying (1,25-28) flame. This remnant, the work of Yahweh (4,4), will rely on God alone (10,20) through faith, thus escaping the punishment (7,9; 28,16). It exists already in germ in the disciples of the prophets (8,16.18); it is made up especially, so it seems, of the "poor" (14,32), something which will be clearly affirmed in a later oracle in another age

(Zp 3,12f). The Messiah, the vicar of Yahweh, around whom this remnant will be grouped (10,21: God the mighty=the Messiah, cf 9,5), will be both their head and principal glory (4,2). In addition, He will represent them, for remnant and Messiah are described in the same terms (cf 6,13 and 11,1; 11,2 and 28,5f).

With *Micah*, the contemporary of Isaiah, the remnant is already a technical term designating the purified people of the Messianic age who have become a "powerful nation" (Mi 4,7). For the pagans, the remnant will be a source of destruction or a blessing, depending on their attitude toward it (5,6ff). It thus becomes the heir of the role assigned to Abraham and his descendants (Gn 12,3).

2. *The turning point at the exile. Jeremiah* brings to the doctrine of the remnant a decisive deepening. Like his predecessors, he continues to give the name of remnant to the small group of Jews who have escaped deportation and remain in the holy land (Jr 40,11; 42,15; 44,12; cf Am 5,15; Is 37,4; Zp 2,7; Jr 6,9; 15,9). But the heirs in whom the Messianic hopes are sustained are the deportees (24,1-10). They are not called the remnant and are even contrasted with it (24,8). In his speech Jeremiah remains faithful to the old customs. However, in speaking of the glorious future reserved for the exiles, the term reappears quite naturally (23,3; 31,7). This remnant is therefore dissociated from the temporal community, the Jewish state.

Still another deepening is furnished by *Ezekiel*. Before his time, the prophets did not seem to distinguish immediate trials from the eschatological judgment which was to reduce the nation to a remnant of just souls. After the catastrophe of 587, Ezekiel had to admit that those who survived fared no better than those who had perished (Ez 6,8f; 12,15f; 14,21ff). Therefore, in advance, he had predicted that the just alone would be spared these trials (9,4ff). The eschatological judgment which he foresaw is still yet to come (20,35-38; 34,17). It alone will definitively separate the unbelievers and the holy remnant (20,38; 34,20).

3. *The three classifications of remnant.* Two distinct meanings of the term *remnant* can be presented in this way: the group, reduced in numbers, which survives any given catastrophe, or the *historical remnant* (Am 5,15; Is 37,4; Jr 6,9; Ez 9,8; etc); and the community of those who, in the last days, will gain the benefit

of salvation, *the eschatological remnant* (Mi 5, 6ff; Zp 3,12; Is 4,4; 10,22; 28,5; Jr 23,3; 31,7; etc.). The latter alone is holy. The first group is destined for rejection.

From the time of the exile a third notion appeared, that of a religious elite within the mass of the people, the true heir and depository of the promises. They can be called the *faithful remnant*, although never in the OT are they given the name *remnant*. The title will be conferred in the NT (R 11,5) and in certain non-biblical writings (Damascus Document 1,4; 2, 11). The same basic concept is at work here, but it has been raised from the material to the spiritual plane. The faithful remnant is the minority of those leading religious lives in the eyes of God.

This faithful remnant appears under the name of "Israel, the servant of Yahweh," "Israel, through whom I will show forth my glory" (Is 49,3). The remnant is charged with a mission which affects the whole of Israel (49, 5). From within this religious elite emerges an individual figure who personifies and incarnates its destinies: the Servant*. He, and He alone, will accomplish by His redemptive death the mission confided to this remnant (52,13—53, 12). But starting with this individual figure, an opposite movement will take place; so that not only all Israel, but even all the pagans will be incorporated into the remnant, which had been reduced to the Messiah alone (49,6; 53,11).

4. *After the exile.* The little community of exiles who have returned to Zion profess to be the remnant (Hg 1,12; 2,2; Ze 8,6). In addition, certain prophecies allow them to believe that they are the holy remnant, and that the eschatological promises (Ho 2,23f; Ez 34,26f) will be realized in their favor (Ze 8,11f). But the restoration proves to be Messianic only in an inchoative and symbolic sense, and the historical remnant after the exile still requires purification (Ze 13,8f; 14,2). The idea of the faithful remnant becomes clearer and clearer. The people* of God are identified with the "poor of Yahweh" (Is 49,13; Ps 18,28; 149,4). Psalm 73,1 identifies Israel with the pure of heart. In 1 M 1,52f the "people," meaning the mass of Israelites, is contrasted with "Israel," which is the faithful Remnant. The prophetic texts after the exile still announce the eschatological remnant (Is 65,8-12; Ob 17=Jl 3,5), but they introduce the pagan nations into the group (Is 66,19; Ze 9,7).

NT

In the NT, reference is still made to the "faithful remnant," to that portion of the people of God who have believed in Christ (R 11,5). The theme of the faithful remnant, alone the true Israel*, underlies very many texts in the NT (Mt 3,9.12; 22,14; Lk 12,32; Jn 1,11f; 1,47; R 2,28; 1 Co 10,18; G 6,16). In every case, it no longer has an autonomous existence. The remnant is now the Church*.

The deep signification of this theme in the plan of God is given by Paul, who in the epistle to the Romans, develops a veritable theology of divine providence (R 9—11). Thanks to the remnant which has believed in Christ, the infidelity of Israel has not rendered the divine promises* void; and the divine constancy* has been vindicated (R 11,1-7). On the other hand, the existence of a remnant which is the sole heir of the promises reveals the absolute gratuity of the election* of individuals, even within the larger election of an entire people (9,6-18.25-29). Again, the election of a minority within the chosen people, a minority which ultimately is reduced to the person of the Messiah, is nonetheless ordained to the redemption* of all; not only all Israel (11,26), but also the pagans (11,25). Thus are reconciled the apparently opposed demands of divine justice*. On the one hand there is punishment of sin, and on the other fidelity to the promise*, which the sins of men cannot corrupt, but which remains forever a gratuitous gift.

→Church II 2—Election OT III 1—Fire OT II 2—Flood—Growth OT 2; NT 3—Hardness of Heart I 2 b—Holy OT IV 3—Hope OT II 2—Inheritance OT II; NT I 1—Israel NT 3—Mediator I 2, II 1—Noah 2—People *B* I 1; *C* II—Plan of God NT III 2—Repentance/Conversion OT II 1.2.5; NT III 1—Resurrection OT II—Salvation NT I 2 a, II 1—Servant of God II 2—Trial/Temptation OT I 3; NT I.

FD jab

REPENTANCE/CONVERSION

God calls men to enter into communion with Him. This call is to sinful men; sinners from birth (Ps 51,7). Through the fault of their first father, sin* entered into the world (R 5,12); and since that time it dwells most intimately in them (7,20). They are sinners through personal culpability, for each of them "sold over to the power of sin" (7,14), voluntarily accepted this yoke of sinful passions (cf 7,5). The response to the call of God, then, will demand a conversion of them from the very beginning, then a repentant attitude throughout their lifetime. That is the reason why conversion and repentance hold such an important place in biblical revelation.

The vocabulary that expresses these ideas, however, has only slowly acquired the fullness of its meaning, and in proportion as the notion of sin deepened. Certain ways of speaking bring out the attitude of man who deliberately orders himself to God: "to seek Yahweh" (Am 5,4; Ho 10,12), "to seek His face" (Ho 5,15; Ps 24, 6; 27,8), "to humble oneself before Him" (1 K 21,29; 2 K 22,19), "to fix his heart in Him" (1 S 7,3)...But the most common term, the verb *šūb*, translates the idea of changing route; to come again, to retrace one's steps. In a religious context, it means to be turned away from what is bad and to be turned toward God. That implies a change of conduct, a new orientation of the whole being, and essentially defines the idea of conversion. At a later period of time, more of a distinction was made between the interior aspect of repentance and the exterior acts that it commands. The Greek Bible also uses conjointly the verb *epistrephein*, which connotes a return to God, which results in a change in practical conduct, and the verb *metanoein*, which looks to the interior change (*metanoia*, that is, repentance). In analyzing the biblical texts these two distinct but strictly complementary aspects must be considered.

OT

I. THE BEGINNING OF THE LITURGIES OF REPENTANCE

1. From the earliest times, in the perspective of the doctrine of the covenant*, it was known that the bond of community with God could be broken through the fault of man, whether it be a question of collective sins or individual sins that in some way include the entire collectivity. Public evils were also the occasion of an examination of conscience regarding faults committed (Js 7; 1 S 5—6). It is true that the idea of sin was often crude, every material failure to fulfill a divine requirement being capable of angering Yahweh. To re-establish union with Him and to recover His favor, the community had first of all to chastise those who were res-

ponsible. This could go as far as the death penalty (Ex 32,25-28; Nm 25,7ff; Js 7,24ff); at the very least, there is no "redemption" of the culpable (1 S 14,36-45). The guilty person can give himself over to divine chastisement so that the community will be spared (2 S 24,17).

2. Further, as long as the scourge lasted (or rather, to stop it from striking), divine pardon was implored through ascetical practices and penitential prayers. There was fasting* (Jg 20, 26; 1 K 21,8ff), the clothing was torn and sack-cloth put on (1 K 20,31f; 2 K 6,30; 19,1f; Is 22, 12; cf Jon 3,5-8), the suppliant rolled in the ashes* (Is 58,5; cf 2 S 12,16). In the gatherings for worship, groans and cries of mourning were heard (Jg 2,4; Jl 1,13; 2,17). Formulas for lamentation were provided. Our Psalter still preserves more than one example (cf Ps 60; 74; 79; 83; Lm 5, etc.). Recourse was had to rites and expiatory* sacrifices (Nm 16,6-15). Above all, a collective confession* of sin was made (Jg 10,10; 1 S 7,6), and eventually recourse was had to the intercession of a leader or a prophet, such as Moses (Ex 32,30ff).

3. Examples of this kind of practice are found in all periods. The prophet Jeremiah was himself involved in a penitential liturgy in the role of intercessor (Jr 14,1—15,4). After the exile, a considerable development was made in these practices. The danger was that they can remain completely exterior, without man engaging in them with his whole heart, and as a result, fail to translate his repentance into his actions. Opposed to this peril of superficial ritualism was the prophet's message of conversion.

II. THE PROPHETS' MESSAGE OF CONVERSION

During David's rule, when Nathan intervened with the adulterous king, the prophetic doctrine of repentance was proclaimed. David was persuaded to confess his fault (2 S 12,13). Then he did penance according to the rules and finally accepted divine chastisement (12,14-23). But the prophets' message of conversion, especially from the beginning of the eighth century, was addressed to the entire people. Israel had violated the covenant, "abandoned Yahweh and scorned the holy one of Israel" (Is 1,4); Yahweh would have had every right to abandon them at least until they were converted. The call to repentance also became an

essential aspect of prophetic preaching (cf Jr 25,3-6).

1. *Amos*, the prophet of justice, was not content to denounce the sins of his contemporaries. When he said that they must "seek God" (Am 5,4.6), the formula was not only that of worship. It meant to seek good and not evil, to hate* evil and love good* (5,14f). It implied a correction in conduct and the loyal practice of justice. Only a return of this nature could lead God to "take pity on the remnant* of Joseph" (5,15). In like manner *Hosea* demanded a real detachment from iniquity, especially idolatry*. He promised that in return God would grant His favor and turn away His anger (Ho 14,2-9). Stigmatizing the superficial conversion that cannot bear any fruit, he insisted on the interior character of true conversion that is inspired by the love* (*ḥesed*) and the knowledge of God (6,1-6; cf 2,9).

2. *Isaiah* denounced every kind of sin in the Judeans: violations of justice, deviations in worship, recourse to human politics, etc. Only a true conversion could bring salvation*, for worship is nothing (Is 1,11-15; cf Am 5,21-25) when there is no practical submission to the divine will: "Wash yourselves! Purify yourselves! Take your wickedness away from my sight! Stop doing evil, learn to do good! Seek again the right way, help the oppressed, do justice toward the orphan! (Is 1,16f). Then your sins, though scarlet, shall be made white like snow—crimson, they shall become like wool" (1,18f). Unfortunately, Isaiah knew that his message would run up against the hardness* of their hearts (6,10): "Through conversion and calmness you would have been saved...but you have not wanted it!" (30,15). The drama of Israel makes its way toward a catastrophic outcome. Isaiah clings to the certitude that "a remnant will return...to the powerful God" (10,21; cf 7,3). Only those who are converted will receive the gift of salvation.

3. The insistence on the interior dispositions that it is fitting to have toward God rapidly becomes a commonplace in the prophetic preaching. "Justice*, piety*, and humility*," cried Micah (Mi 6,8); "Humility and sincerity," echoed back Zephaniah (Zp 2,3; 3,12f). But it is *Jeremiah*, following the line of thought begun by Hosea, who developed at great length the theme of conversion. If the prophet foretold the evils that menaced Judah, it was "in order

that everyone would return from his evil ways so that God might pardon" (Jr 36,3). Really, the calls to "return" blaze out throughout the book, but they always specify the conditions for this return. Israel, the rebel, must "acknowledge his fault" if he wishes that God no longer look severely on him (3,11f; 2,23). The rebel sons must not be satisfied with weeping and supplications when confessing their sins (3,21-25); they must change their conduct and circumcise* their hearts (4,1-4).

The practical consequences of a change of heart did not at all escape the notice of the prophet (cf 7,3-11). He thus begins to doubt that a real conversion was possible. Those whom he called to conversion preferred to follow the hardness of their evil hearts (18,11f; cf 2,23ff). Far from deploring their wickedness, they sank further into it (8,4-7). That is the reason the prophet could proclaim only chastisement for inconvertible Jerusalem (13,20-27). His perspective of the future, however, did not remain less charged with hope. The day would come when the beaten people would accept the chastisement and would implore conversion of heart as a grace: "Make me return, that I might return!" (31,18f). And Yahweh will answer this humble demand, for at the time of the new covenant* "He will write the Law in their hearts" (31,33): "I will give them a heart to know that I am Yahweh; they shall be my people and I will be their God, for they will come back to me with all their hearts" (24, 7).

4. Faithful to the same tradition, Ezekiel centered his message on the time when the threats of God will be carried out, on the necessary conversion: "Cast far from you the transgressions that you have committed and make yourself a new heart and a new spirit. Why do you prefer to die, house of Israel? I do not desire the death of anyone! Be converted and you shall live" (Ez 18,31f). When he specified the divine requirements, the prophet doubtless gave a larger place to the prescriptions of worship than his predecessors (22,1-31). But, more than they, he also insists on the strictly personal character of the conversion: each can answer only for himself, each will be rewarded according to his own conduct (3,16-21; 18; 33,10-20). And without a doubt Israel is a "race of rebels" (2,4-8). But to these hard-hearted men, God could give as a grace* what He demanded of them so imperatively. At the time of the new covenant He will give them a new heart* and

send His spirit* to them, to the extent that they will attach themselves to His law and regret their evil conduct (36,26-31; cf 11,19f).

5. From Amos to Ezekiel, the doctrine of conversion is thus constantly deepened, parallel to an understanding of sin. At the end of the exile, *the message of consolation* noted the effective conversion of Israel, or at least the remnant*. The salvation that it proclaimed was for "those who in seeking justice seek Yahweh" (Is 51,1), "have the law in their hearts" (51,7). The latter could be assured that the "drudgery is over and sin expiated" (40,2). Yahweh said to Israel His servant: "I have scattered your sins as a cloud...Return to me, for I have redeemed you" (44,22). In this new perspective which presupposed that the people of God were strong in fidelity, the prophet envisaged an unheard of enlargement of the promises of salvation. After Israel, the nations in their turn are going to be converted: they will leave their idols* and convert themselves to the living God (45,14f.23f; cf Jr 16,19ff).

The ideal will gain headway. Not only post-exile Judaism will be opened to the converted proselytes from paganism (Is 56,3.6), but the eschatological tableaux will not fail to mention this religious universalism (cf Ps 22,28). The Book of Jonah will even show the prophetic preaching addressed directly to the pagans "that they might be converted and live." At the end of such a doctrinal development, it is seen how the notion of repentance was deepened; how far it is from pure ritualism which still had to have a place in ancient Israel.

III. LITURGY OF REPENTANCE AND CONVERSION OF HEART

1. The national conversion of Israel had been the twofold fruit of prophetic preaching and the trial of exile. The exile had been the providential occasion of an awareness of sin and a sincere confession, as, in full agreement, the later texts of the deuteronomic literature (1 K 8,46-51) and the sacerdotal literature (Lv 26, 39f) point out. After the exile, the sense of repentance was so well anchored in the spirit of Israel that it colored the whole Jewish spirituality. The old penitential liturgies survived (cf Jl 1—2), but the prophetic doctrine had renewed their content. The books of the time conserve the stereotyped formulas in which the community is seen to confess all the national

sins committed since the beginning, and to implore, in return, God's pardon* and the advent of His salvation (Is 63,7—64,11; Ezr 9,5-15; Ne 9; Dn 9,4-19; Ba 1,15—3,8). The collective lamentations of the Psalter are constructed on this pattern (Ps 79; 106), and the recall of the unrepentant past is still more frequent (cf Ps 95,8-11). One feels that Israel was led into a great effort of profound conversion that was always renewed. It was the period when the liturgies of expiation* also became more widespread: the shame for sin was so great (Lv 4—5; 16).

2. On the individual level there was no less an effort because the lesson of Ezekiel had been heard. The psalms of sickness* and persecution* return more than once to the confession of sin (Ps 6,2; 32; 38; 103,3f; 143,1f), and the poet of Job shows a profound sense of man's radical impurity (Jb 9,30f; 14,4). The most perfect expression of these sentiments is the *Miserere* (Ps 51) where the prophetic teaching of conversion runs throughout as a prayer, in the form of a dialogue with God (cf v 6): an admission of faults (v 5ff), a demand for interior purification (v 3f.9), a plea for grace which alone can change the heart (v 12ff), an orientation toward a fervent life (v 15-19). The penitential liturgy had at its center the sacrifice of a "broken heart" (v 18f). It can be seen, then, that formed in a school with such a text, and heirs to all the preceding traditions, the Qumrân sects had dreamed of retiring into the desert to be sincerely converted to the law of God "to prepare the way" for Him. If their efforts remain marked by a certain legalism, it is not so very different from that which is going to be found in the NT.

NT

I. THE LAST OF THE PROPHETS

At the threshold of the NT, the prophets' message of conversion is found in all its purity in the preaching of John* the Baptist, the last of them. Luke summed up John's mission in this way: "He will lead back numerous sons of Israel to the Lord their God" (Lk 1,16f; cf Ml 2,6; 3,24). One phrase sums up his message: "Be converted, for the kingdom of heaven is at hand" (Mt 3,2). The coming of the kingdom opens up a perspective of hope, but John particularly stressed the judgment* that must precede it. No one will know how to escape the anger that will be manifested on the day* of Yahweh (Mt 3,7.10.12). Membership in the race of Abraham* will not be of any use (Mt 3,9). All men must acknowledge themselves as sinners, produce fruit* that is worthy of penance (Mt 3,8), and adopt a new way of life proper to their state (Lk 3,10-14). As a sign of this conversion, John gave a baptism* of water which was to prepare the penitents for the baptism of fire and of the Holy Spirit that the Messiah would give (Mt 3,11 p).

II. CONVERSION AND ENTRANCE INTO THE KINGDOM OF GOD

1. Jesus was not content merely to preach the kingdom of God, He began powerfully to make it a reality. With Him, the kingdom is inaugurated, although it be directed toward mysterious fulfillments. But the call to conversion preached by John the Baptist did not become less real because of this. Jesus took it up in His own terms at the beginning of His ministry (Mk 1,15; Mt 4,17). If He has come, it is to "call sinners to conversion" (Lk 5,32). This is an essential aspect of the gospel of the kingdom. The man who becomes aware of his sinful state can, nevertheless, now turn confidently to Jesus; for the "Son* of Man has the power to forgive sins" (Mt 9,6 p). But the message of conversion collided with human self-sufficiency in all its forms, from the attachment to riches (Mk 10,21-25) to the proud assurance of the Pharisees* (Lk 18,9). Jesus was lifted up as a "sign of Jonah" in the midst of an evil generation*, less well-disposed with respect to God than was Nineveh in times past (Lk 11,29-32 p). He drew up against that evil generation an indictment full of threats: the men of Nineveh shall condemn it at the time of judgment (Lk 11,32); Tyre and Sidon shall have a fate less painful than that of the cities around the Lake of Gennesaret (Lk 10,13ff p). The actual impenitence of Israel was, in fact, the sign of the hardness of its heart (Mt 13,15 p; cf Is 6,10). If they did not change their conduct, the impenitent hearers of Jesus were to perish (Lk 13,1-5) like the barren fig tree (Lk 13,6-9; cf Mt 21,18-22 p).

2. When He called for conversion, Jesus did not make any allusion to the penitential liturgies. He distrusted signs that were too showy (Mt 6,16ff). What really counted was the change of heart that makes one become as a little

child* (Mt 18,3 p). Afterwards, it is the continued effort to "seek the kingdom of God and His justice*" (Mt 6,33), which means regulating one's life according to the new Law. The act of conversion was clearly brought out in the parables. Though a will for moral change was implied, conversion in the parables was more of a humble appeal, an act of confidence: "My God have pity on me, a sinner" (Lk 18,13). Conversion is a grace* due to the ever-present divine initiative: it is the shepherd* who leaves the flock to go in search of the lost sheep (Lk 15,4ff; cf 15,8). The human response to this grace is concretely analyzed in the parable of the prodigal son, which puts into surprising relief the mercy* of the father (Lk 15,11-32). For the gospel contains that disconcerting revelation: "There is more joy in heaven over a sinner who is converted than over the ninety-nine just who have no need of repentance" (Lk 15,7.10). Jesus also manifested to sinners an attitude of welcome that scandalized the Pharisees (Mt 9,10-13 p; Lk 15,2), but effected conversions. Luke's gospel likes to report some of these conversions in detail. Examples are the account of the sinful woman (Lk 7,36-50) and the story of Zaccheus (19,5-9).

III. CONVERSION AND BAPTISM

During His lifetime, Jesus had sent His apostles* to preach conversion in announcing the gospel of the kingdom (Mk 6,12). After His resurrection, He renewed that mission* for them. They were to preach repentance in His name to all nations with a view to the remission of sins (Lk 24,47); for the sins of those whom they forgive will be forgiven them (Jn 20,23). The Acts and the epistles witness the fulfillment of this command. But conversion, however, takes a different turn, depending on whether it is a question of Jews or pagans.

1. What is required of the Jews is, first of all, the moral conversion to which Jesus already called them. To their repentance (metanoia), God will respond by granting them pardon for sins (Ac 2,38; 3,19; 5,31). The pardon will be sealed by the reception of baptism* and the gift of the Holy Spirit (Ac 2,38). Nevertheless, while conversion means a moral change, it must also include a positive act of faith* in Christ: the Jews will return (epistrephein) to the Lord (Ac 3,19; 9,35). Now, as St. Paul attests, such an adherence to Christ is the most

difficult thing to obtain: the Jews have a veil over their hearts. If they would be converted, the veil would fall (2 Co 3,16). But, according to the text of Isaiah (Is 6,9f), their hardness* of heart rivets them to their unbelief (Ac 28,24-27). Just as much sinners as the pagans, threatened as they were by the divine anger, they did not understand that God manifested patience in order to urge them to repentance (R 2,4). Only a remnant responded to the apostolic preaching (R 11,1-5).

2. The gospel received a better welcome among the pagan nations. When Cornelius was baptized, the Christians of Jewish origin noted with surprise that "repentance that leads to life was offered to the pagans as well as to them" (Ac 11,18; cf 17,30). In fact, the message was successfully preached at Antioch and elsewhere (Ac 11,21; 15,3.19); it is even the special object of St. Paul's mission (Ac 26,18.20). But, simultaneously with moral repentance (metanoia), conversion demands in this case that one be detached from idols* in order to turn (epistrephein) to the living God (Ac 14,15; 26,18; 1 Th 1,9), according to a type of conversion already envisaged by the Second Isaiah. Once the first step had been taken, the pagans, like the Jews, were led "to turn toward Christ, shepherd and guardians of their souls" (1 P 2,25).

IV. SIN AND REPENTANCE IN THE CHURCH

1. The act of conversion, sealed by baptism, was accomplished once and for always; it was impossible to renew the grace (He 6,6). But the baptized are capable of falling once again into sin. The apostolic community very soon had this experience. In this case repentance is still necessary if one wishes to share in salvation in spite of everything. Peter urged Simon the magician to repent (Ac 8,22). James urged the fervent Christians to lead back the stray sinners (Jm 5,19f). Paul rejoices that the Corinthians repented (2 Co 7,9f), still fearing that there were certain sinners who had not done so (12,21). He urges Timothy to correct the dissenters, hoping that God will grant them the grace to repent (2 Tm 2,25). Finally, in the messages to the seven churches that open the Apocalypse, there are read clear invitations to repentance, which presupposes the corresponding falls from their first fervor (Ap 2,5.16.21f; 3,3.19). Without speaking explicitly of the sacra-

ment of penance, these texts show that the virtue of penance must have its place in the Christian life in prolonging baptismal conversion.

2. Only repentance, in fact, prepares man to face the judgment of God (cf Ac 17,30f). At present, history is on the way toward this judgment. If its coming seems to be delayed, it is only because God "exercises patience, wishing that no one perish, and that all, if possible, attain repentance" (2 P 3,9). Just as Israel hardened itself in impenitence at the time of Christ, and when confronted with the apostolic preaching, so too, according to the Apocalypse, will men be obstinate in not understanding the meaning of the calamities that cross their history and proclaim the day* of wrath. They will also be obdurate in their unrepentant hearts (Ap 9,20f), blaspheming* the name of God instead of repenting and rendering Him glory (16,9.11). The members of the Church are not the cause of it, but only the pagans and renegades (cf 21,8). The judgment of God will draw down the curtain on this somber scene. It is just as urgent that, through repentance, the Christians "save themselves from this perverse generation" (Ac 2,40).

→Ashes—Baptism II, IV 3—Confession OT 2; NT 2—Death OT III 2—Desert OT II 1—Desire III—Fasting—Godless Man OT 3; NT —Hardness of Heart II 2—Heart I 3—John the Baptist 1—Mercy OT I 2 c—Pardon—Preach I 1—Punishment 2.3—Responsibility 5 —Sadness OT 3—Search I, II—Sin III 3, IV 1 a—Sleep III 1—Wrath B OT III 2.

JGi & PG rco'c

RESPONSIBILITY

The realization of his responsibilities by a man who has become an adult or by a mankind with a developing culture is a major human problem that is far from unknown to the Bible. But this can only be mentioned marginally in this article, which is concerned mainly with the responsibility of man before God, seen from certain main points of view.

1. *Through one man sin entered the world* (R 5,12). The story of the sin* of Adam* (Gn 2—3) is told in answer to a fundamental question: who is responsible for death and the fact that life is hard? Paul makes this reply: the one who is responsible is not God, but a human action that gave the superhuman power of sin free rein. This action is partly but really responsible for the presence of evil in the world.

But this answer is shocking and unheard of. For the great religions that surround Israel evil is as old as the gods; from the gods it has passed to men. Both men and gods, then, are at the same time responsible and not responsible. They are all what they are, a mixture with a different measure of good and evil*. On the other hand, when the Bible states that God is good, that creation is good and that evil comes after creation, it lays the responsibility for evil on created freedom.

This responsibility is of more than human proportions. The Bible account realizes this when it tells the story of the sin of the Tempter*. But it also knows that in his sinful condition, even if man is overwhelmed by his responsibility, he cannot for all that repudiate it. In these pages every sinner can see the fate that brings out of his sins an evil that he did not want and at the same time the accurate picture of his faults, a mixture of weakness (cf flesh*) and of malice. He can also see there his own share of responsibility for the evil in the world.

2. *I should not have known what sin was except for the Law* (R 7,7). For Israel the Law* was a "pedagogue" given by God (G 3,24). It created in Israel a deep sense of responsibility. When it said: "you shall do this...you shall not do that..." it brought each Israelite face to face with his responsibilities and proved to him that he was in a position to accept them. In allowing room for the difference of circumstances and the influence of intentions, the Law refined his conscience. In showing that God wants good and condemns evil, it gave his actions an infinite value. And in associating the Law with the covenant it made the whole of life into a choice for or against God. Of course even "without the Law" pagans are capable of recognizing their responsibilities "in their heart" (R 2,15). But the Law made Israel into a people "wise and intelligent amongst us" (Dt 4,6), conscious of the seriousness of men's actions.

3. *Acknowledge what you have done* (Jr 2,23). What the Law proclaimed in general, the prophets* were sent to put in concrete terms to some unscrupulous prince or to the people

suffering from illusions, and to make them conscious of their responsibilities. Almost always, from Samuel and Nathan (1 S 3,13f; 2 S 12,10ff) to the last of Isaiah's heirs (Is 59,8ff), it was on the occasion of misfortunes, either already present or foreseeable, that the prophets intervened: "because you have done such and such an evil thing, such and such an evil has struck you too..." Every national catastrophe is an occasion for them to take a closer look at the responsibilities of the people.

The supreme disaster, the exile, was a decisive discovery for Ezekiel. Israel had collapsed because it had failed in its responsibilities, but everything remained possible for each individual Israelite. It was up to each to accept his responsibilities and to choose between life and death: "to the upright man his integrity will be credited, to the wicked his wickedness" (Ez 18,20).

4. *I have sinned against you* (Ps 51,6). The confession* of sins, in the form it takes in the Bible, echoing the Law and the prophets, is a sign of the recognition of responsibility. It does not try to make a list of faults or enumerate the maximum number of sins, in order to be sure of omitting nothing. It brings God's justice and man's injustice face to face (Is 59, 9.14; Dn 3,27-31; Ps 51,6...). This it not only so that the punishment* received may be recognized as deserved, but, from a more profound point of view and one approaching thanksgiving, so that the burden of the fault may rest on the sinner and so that God may be exonerated: "yours, Lord, the justice, ours the shame" (Dn 9,7; Ba 1,15...). And so the prayer of repentance rediscovers the intuition evident in the original story: God is good and it is the sinner who is responsible for evil.

5. *The Gospel* is for St. Paul the decisive revelation of this justice of God and the responsibility of the sinner. The first three chapters of the epistle to the Romans show the grave destructive power of sin and the burden of the critical choices open to man, while at the same time giving an explanation of this destiny that is beyond man's capacity. If God's wrath* invests the actions of man with such importance and makes his responsibility exceed anything that he could of himself foresee or desire, this paradoxical destiny is the reverse side of a love that is as great as God, for "God has imprisoned all men in their own disobedience only to show mercy to all mankind" (R 11,32).

This plan is evident in the Passion of Christ. The various responsibilities that combined to bring about the death of the Son of God are not equal (cf Jn 19,11; Ac 3,13f), nor total (Ac 3,17), but they are real and taken together they produced this monstrous crime. And so the preaching of the Gospel in the infant Church always reminded Jerusalem, considered as a whole, of its responsibility: "*You* killed him" (Ac 2,23; 3,14; 4,10; 5,30...). The sinner can only achieve faith through repentance* and the realization of his responsibility.

→Cares 1—Conscience—Good and Evil I 3— Law *C* III 2—Liberation/Liberty I—Repentance/Conversion—Reward II 1.2—Sin—Sowing I 2 a—Trial/Temptation OT II 2.

JG ems

REST

Human existence is alternately trouble and calm, work and rest. A full life seems to demand the coexistence of contraries: chase and capture, search and embrace, desire and satisfaction. If man succeeds, it is only to strive again, insatiably. Ecclesiastes recognized this rhythm, but denounced this sort of coming and going as a vain pursuit of wind (Qo 1—2) and preferred to await death, which would put an end to vanity: "there is no rest for man neither by day nor by night; what good is it to seek* since one never finds?" (8,16f). It is sufficient to embrace under God's watchful eye the modest joys of the present moment (2,24; 9,7-10). Biblical tradition, taken as a whole, accepts the fact of change and discovers its meaning. What among men are advance and regression are joined together, purified and brought into harmony in God. True repose is not passivity, but the fulfillment of activity. This type of rest here below is a foretaste of heaven.

I. REST AND WORK

From its origins, Israel had to "sanctify the Sabbath*" (Ex 20,8), to consecrate a day of rest to the Lord even at harvest time and other periods of activity (34,21). Two principal reasons were given for this command.

1. *Rest, a symbol of liberation.* The Covenant Code specifies that animals and field laborers

must be allowed to rest (23,12). The motive behind this is natural kindness, but Deuteronomy adds another from history: Israel should thus remember its liberation from forced labor in Egypt (Dt 5,15). To be able to rest is a sign of liberty*.

2. *Rest as a participation in the repose of the Creator.* According to the priestly tradition, man in observing the Sabbath imitates God who, after He had created* heaven and earth, "stopped work and rested on the seventh day." The Sabbath observance unites Yahweh and His faithful (Ex 31,17; Gn 2,2f). If therefore the Sabbath is holy, it is God who makes it holy (cf Ez 20,12). To rest is to reveal the image* of God within; one is not only free, but a son* of God.

3. *Rest and celebrating.* The Sabbath does not consist simply in stopping work, but in turning one's energies to joyfully praising the creator and the redeemer. It can be called "delight" because he who takes the Sabbath seriously "will find in Yahweh his delight" (Is 58,13f). The Sabbath gives entry into the mystery of God; but to achieve an identification between the Sabbath rest and God Himself, Christ must make His appearance.

II. TOWARD THE DIVINE REPOSE

In still another way* Israel was led to discover the spiritual character of the rest imposed upon it. Other themes are going to be joined to the Sabbath motif: that of sleep, breathing, of respite after danger or labor. Israel will come to recognize that God alone grants repose after the disturbing experiences of wandering, war, and exile.

1. *The promised land, symbol of the divine repose.* Setting out from Egypt, the Hebrews fled from slavery toward the land of liberty*. This hoped for repose will be the fruit of a slow conquest (vg Jg 1,19.21; cf Js 21,43f), until the moment when King David will at last "be given rest from all his enemies" (2 S 7,1). Solomon can proclaim at the dedication of the temple: "Blessed be Yahweh who has given peace to His people Israel according to all His promises" (1 K 8,56). In the days of "the man of rest," God will give to Israel "peace and tranquility" (1 Ch 22,9). Henceforth a man can "live in safety, each one under his vine and

fig tree" (1 K 4,20; 5,5). It is a quite terrestrial repose, but a repose safeguarded by Yahweh who has Himself decided to take up His rest in the temple* (Ps 132,14). He has sought out those who have sought Him and granted them rest (2 Ch 14,6).

Therefore the nature and duration of repose on this earth is conditioned by fidelity to the covenant. But repose degenerates quickly into backsliding and revolt against God (Dt 32,15; Ne 9,25-28). While salvation takes place in an atmosphere of calm conversion (Is 30,15), Ahaz is afraid of the enemies of Yahweh (7,2.4) and "wearies" God by his lack of faith (7,13). Consequently, the threat of wandering about in exile presses on the people. But after the pains of chastisement, the people will understand better that they will be delivered by Yahweh in person (Jr 30,10f); Israel will once again make its way toward rest (31,2), toward carefree dancing, happiness, and the satiety of divine blessings (31,12f). The shepherd* leads his sheep into good pastures (Ez 34,12-16; Is 40,10f). In this perspective, God the giver leads the way to the land which is given and Israel is en route to the divine repose.

2. *Foretaste of the definitive rest.* Israel has not had to wait for the day* of Yahweh before discovering in various ways the joys of spiritual rest. In persecution (Ps 55,8), trial (66,12), or the experience of his own nothingness (39,14), the psalmist asks God to allow him "to breathe easily," or to find "security for his flesh" (16, 9). He surrenders himself to the shepherd who will lead him to the waters of repose (23,1ff). The Law* offers this internal peace, and to take the road toward good is "to find rest" (Jr 6, 16). The poor* will be able "to feed and lie down, with none to disturb them" (Zp 3,13). The evildoers, on the contrary, resemble a troubled sea which cannot be calmed (Is 57,20).

With the experience of love which is at one and the same time search and embrace, flight and pursuit, quest and joyful possession, the spouse of the Canticle dreams of the hour of midday, of the complete rest which puts an end to wandering (Ct 1,7). In fact, at one time she considers herself sick of love in the embrace of the beloved (2,5f), at another moment she pursues in desperate fashion him whom she thought she would never again lose (3,1f.4). In a very real sense she already tastes* the presence of the beloved, but she will not surmount this restless fluctuation until the beloved will have effected her passage through death (8,6).

RESURRECTION

Wisdom for its part promises rest to him who will look for it. It is the prize after the quest (Si 6,28); and if the wisdom philosopher maintains that "he has had few ill effects in obtaining a great deal of rest" (51,27), this is because Wisdom has taken the lead in choosing Israel for the place of her own repose, a repose which is sovereign activity (24,7-11).

Was this foretaste of the repose of God sufficient for Job to surmount his trials*? God did not permit him to "take a breath" (Jb 9,18). Why then should he not have wished for death* and its "restful sleep" (3,13)? But everything will change when the light of the resurrection penetrates the darkness of the tomb: "Go thy way, take your rest and you will be lifted up at the end of days" (Dn 12,13). For the believer therefore the sleep* of the dead is a foretaste of the divine repose.

III. JESUS CHRIST THE REPOSE OF SOULS

1. *Rest and redemption.* Against the Pharisees, Jesus restores the true meaning of the Sabbath: "the Sabbath is made for man and not man for the Sabbath" (Mk 2,27), and therefore it is made for the saving of life (3,4): rest ought to signify the liberation of man and exalt the glory* of the Creator. Jesus gives its true significance to this symbol by curing diseases on this day. He "frees" the woman "bound" for many years (Lk 13,16). Thus He shows Himself "Lord of the Sabbath" (Mt 12,8), for He achieves that which the Sabbath prefigures. Through Christ, repose signifies the liberation of the children of God. To merit this liberation and repose for us, the redeemer willed "not to have whereon to lay (*klinein*) His head" (Mt 8,20), as one would rest it on a "couch" (*klinē*); He will not recline (*klinein*) until the moment of His death (Jn 19,30) on the cross.

2. *Revelation of the divine rest.* To justify His activity on the Sabbath, the day of rest, Jesus said: "My Father has never yet ceased His work, and I am working too" (Jn 5,17). In God, work* and rest are not mutually exclusive, but rather express the transcendent character of the divine life*. Wisdom proclaims this mystery of rest while working (Si 24,11). The work of Christ and of the harvest laborers is to succor with joyful* spirit the sheep who are weary and distressed (Mt 9,36; cf Jn 4,36ff); for Jesus offers rest to the souls who come to Him (Mt 11,29).

3. *Heavenly repose.* The "divine repose," which the Hebrews believed awaited them in penetrating into the promised land, was reserved for "the people of God," for those who remained faithful* and obedient* to Jesus Christ. Such is the commentary on Psalm 95, made by the author of Hebrews (He 3,7—4,11). This repose is heaven* where those find their way "who die in the Lord; from henceforth, they may rest from their labors, for their works follow them" (Ap 14,13). To rest in heaven is, moreover, not to cut short, but to perfect their activity. The adorers of the Beast* have rest neither by day nor by night (14,11). The (four) living creatures never cease repeating day and night the praises of the thrice-holy God (4,8).

→Abide—Beatitude—Death NT III 4—Peace —Sabbath—Sleep I—Work.

XLD jab

RESURRECTION

The biblical idea of resurrection is in no way comparable with the Greek idea of immortality. According to the Greek concept, the soul of man which is incorruptible by nature enters into divine immortality after death has severed its bodily ties. According to the biblical mode of thinking, the human person, whole and entire, is destined in its present state to fall under the power of death*. The soul* will be imprisoned in Sheol, while the body* corrupts in the tomb. But this will be no more than a transitory state from which man will re-arise, living by divine grace, in much the same manner as one gets up from a reclining position or awakens from the sleep into which one had slipped. Already conceived in OT times, the idea becomes the center of faith and hope for Christians, in that Christ Himself has returned to life, in the role of "the first born from among the dead."

OT

I. THE LORD OF LIFE

The nature cults in the ancient Orient gave an important place to the myth of the god who died and rose again as a dramatic portrayal of a common human experience: that of the springtime resurgence of life after winter's torpor. Osiris in Egypt, Tammouz in Mesopotamia, Baal in Canaan (becomes Adonis in a

494

later age), were gods of this type. Their life history, enacted in a primordial era, was repeated indefinitely in the nature cycles. By dramatizing them in a sacred representation, the rites were thought to contribute to the efficacy of the cycle, so important for pastoral and agricultural peoples.

But from the very beginning, OT revelation broke completely with this mythology and its accompanying rites. The one God* is the sole master of life and death: "He slays and makes alive; He brings down to Sheol and raises up" (1 S 2,6; Dt 32,39). For He has power* over Sheol itself (Am 9,2; Ps 139,8). Thus, the springtime resurrection of nature is itself the effect of His Word* and of His Spirit* (cf Gn 1,11f.22. 28; 8,22; Ps 104,29f). A still greater proof exists for men, it is Yahweh who rescues their souls from the pit (Ps 103,4) and who gives them back their life (Ps 41,3; 80,19). He does not abandon the souls of His friends to Sheol nor does He allow them to see corruption (Ps 16, 10f).

These expressions are understood undoubtedly in a hyperbolic sense to signify a temporary preservation from death. But the resurrection-miracles worked by the prophets Elijah and Elisha (1 K 17,17-23; 2 K 4,33ff; 13,21) show that Yahweh can even raise the dead and recall them from Sheol to which they had descended. These returns to life have evidently nothing more in common with the mythical resurrection of dead deities than the spatial representation of an ascent upward from the infernal pit to the land of the living.

II. THE RESURRECTION OF THE PEOPLE OF GOD

In an initial series of texts, this image of resurrection is used to express the collective hope* of the people of Israel. Struck by the divine punishments*, Israel is comparable to a sick man whom death has taken by surprise (cf Is 1,5f), like a body become death's prey. But if he should be converted, will not Yahweh lead him back to life? "Come, let us return unto the Lord!...He will revive after two days; the third day He will raise us up that we may live before Him" (Ho 6,1f).

Nor is this a simple wish of men, for the prophetic promises expressly attest that it will come to pass. After the trial of the exile*, God will raise up His people as one would restore life to dry, dead bones (Ez 37,1-14). He will

reawaken Jerusalem* and raise it from the dust where it lay like one dead (Is 51,17; 60,1). He will revive the dead, raise up their bodies, reawaken those who are lying in the dust (Is 26,19). A metaphorical resurrection no doubt, but already it is a true deliverance from the power of Sheol: "Where are your plagues, O Death? Where is your contagion, O Sheol?" (Ho 13,14). God triumphs over death for the benefit of His people.

Even the faithful minority of Israel could fall for a time into the power of hell, as the Servant* of Yahweh died and was interred with evildoers (Is 53,8f.12). But the day will come when, again like the Servant, this just remnant* will have its days extended, will see the light*, and share the trophies of victory* (Is 53,10ff). This is the initial sketch, still mysterious, of a promise of resurrection, thanks to which the persecuted just will see their defender arise at last and take their cause in hand (cf Jb 19,25f, reinterpreted by the Vulgate).

III. THE RESURRECTION OF INDIVIDUALS

Revelation took another step during the Maccabean crisis. The persecution of Antiochus and the experience of martyrdom posed in an acute manner the problem of individual retribution. That one must await the kingdom of God and the final triumph of the assembled saints of the most high, announced long ago in prophetic oracles, is a fundamental certainty (Dn 7,13f.27; cf 2,44). But the saints who have died for their faith, what will become of them? The apocalypse of Daniel responds: "Many of those who sleep in the land of dust shall awake, some to everlasting life, others to everlasting reproach and horror" (Dn 12,2). The image of resurrection used by Ezekiel and Is 26 is therefore to be understood in a realistic manner: God will raise up the dead from Sheol to participate in the kingdom*. The new life*, however, into which they will enter will no more resemble the life of this present world; but it will be a transfigured existence (Dn 12,3). Such is the hope which sustains the martyrs* in the midst of their trial*. Men can cut short their mortal existence; the God who creates life is also He who restores it (2 M 7,9.11.22; 14,46). But on the other hand, there will be no resurrection to life for the wicked (2 M 7,14).

From this moment on, the doctrine of the resurrection becomes the common heritage of

Judaism. If the Sadducean sect, out of a scrupulous regard for ancient traditions, did not admit the doctrine (cf Ac 23,8) and even scorned it by posing ridiculous questions in connection with it (Mt 22,23-28 p), it was nevertheless professed by the Pharisees as well as by the sect which produced the Book of Henoch (probably the ancient Essenes). For while the book has been interpreted materialistically, it furnishes a very spiritual representation of the resurrection doctrine. When the souls* of the dead will rise from hell to return to life, they will enter into a transformed universe which God has planned for "the world to come." Such is also the conception which Jesus will set forth: "At the resurrection, they will be like the angels in heaven" (Mt 22,30 p).

NT

I. THE FIRST-BORN FROM AMONG THE DEAD

1. *Preludes.* Jesus does not simply believe in the resurrection of the just on the last day. He knows that the mystery of the resurrection is to be initiated by Him, to whom God has given the mastery over life* and death*. He gives evidence of that power* which He has received from the Father in bringing back to life several dead people on whose behalf His intercession was sought: the daughter of Jairus (Mk 5,21-42 p), the son of the widow of Nain (Lk 7,11-17), His personal friend Lazarus (Jn 11). These resurrections from the dead, which recall the miracles of the prophets, are already a veiled proclamation of His own, which will be of an entirely different order.

To these acts He joins some precise predictions: the Son of Man must die and rise on the third day (Mk 8,31; 9,31; 10,34 p). It is, according to Matthew, "the sign of Jonah": the Son of Man will be three days and three nights in the bosom of the earth (Mt 12,40). It is also the sign of the temple*: "Destroy this temple, and I will rebuild it in three days"...now "He was speaking of the temple of His body" (Jn 2, 19ff; cf Mt 26,6 p). This announcement of a resurrection from the dead remains incomprehensible even for the twelve themselves (cf Mk 9,10). All the more was it unintelligible to His enemies, who took the precaution of placing guards around His tomb (Mt 27,63f).

2. *The paschal experience.* The twelve therefore had not understood that the announcement

of the resurrection in the Scriptures concerned first of all Jesus Himself (Jn 20,9). That is why His death and burial had caused them to lose hope (cf Mt 16,14; Lk 24,21-24.37; Jn 20,19). To stimulate their faith, nothing less than the paschal experience was required. The discovery of the empty tomb was not sufficient to convince them, for this could be explained by a simple transfer of the body (Lk 24,11f; Jn 20,2). John alone believed immediately (Jn 20,8).

But then the resurrection apparitions* began. The list compiled by Paul (1 Co 15,5ff) and that of the evangelists do not coincide perfectly, but the exact number of apparitions is of little significance. Jesus appeared "over a period of many days" (Ac 13,31); elsewhere it is put more precisely: "for forty days" (1,3), up to the all-important scene of the ascension*. The accounts underline the concrete character of these manifestations: He who appears is truly Jesus of Nazareth; the apostles see and touch Him (Lk 24,36-40; Jn 20,19-29); they eat with Him (Lk 24,29f.41f; Jn 21,9-13; Ac 10,41). He is there, not as a phantom, but with His own body (Mt 28,9; Lk 24,37ff; Jn 20,20.27ff). However, this body* is independent of the normal conditions of earthly existence (Jn 20,19; cf 20, 17). Jesus repeats actions familiar to the apostles from the public life and that permits them to recognize Him (Lk 24,30f; Jn 21,6.12). But He is now in that state of glory* which the Jewish apocalypses described earlier.

The common people are not made witnesses of these apparitions as they were of the passion and death. Jesus reserves His appearances to His chosen witnesses* (Ac 2,32; 10,41; 13,31), the last of these being Paul on the road to Damascus (1 Co 15,8). Witnesses to Him are thus made apostles*. He shows Himself to them "and not to the world" (Jn 14,22), for the world* is impervious to faith. Even the guards of the sepulcher, terrorized by the mysterious theophany (Mt 28,4), do not see Christ Himself. Just as well, for the fact of the resurrection, the moment when Jesus rises from the dead, is impossible to describe. Matthew only tries to call it to mind in conventional language drawn from Scripture (Mt 28,2f): trembling of the earth, blinding light, the appearance of the angel* of the Lord...Here one enters into the domain of the transcendent, and the expressions taken from the OT can only give a rough idea of it, while the reality to which they are applied remains ineffable.

3. *The good news of the resurrection in the*

apostolic preaching. From Pentecost* day on, the resurrection becomes the center of the apostolic preaching*, because in it is revealed the fundamental object of the Christian faith (Ac 2, 22-35). This Easter gospel* is before all the testimony rendered to a fact: Jesus has been crucified and slain; but God has raised Him from the dead and through Him has brought salvation to men. Such is the catechesis of Peter to the Jews (3,14f) and the substance of his confession before the Sanhedrin (4,10), the teaching of Philip to the Ethiopian eunuch (8,35), Paul's preaching to the Jews (13,33; 17,3) and to the gentiles (17,31), and his confession before his judges (23,6...). All this is nothing else than the content of the paschal experience.

One important point is always noted in connection with this experience: its conformity with the Scriptures (cf 1 Co 15,3f). On the one hand, the resurrection of Jesus fulfills the prophetic promises; promise of the glorious exaltation of the Messiah* at the right hand of God (Ac 2,34; 13,32f), of the glorification of the Servant* of Yahweh (Ac 4,30; Ph 2,7ff), of the enthronement of the Son* of Man (Ac 7,56; cf Mt 26,64 p). On the other hand, to express this mystery which lies beyond the limits of the common experience of history, it is again the Scripture texts which furnish a series of expressions sketching its various aspects: Jesus is the holy* one whom God delivers from corruption in hell (Ac 2,25-32; 13,35ff; cf Ps 16,8-11); He is the new Adam* to whom God has given dominion over all things (1 Co 15,27; He 1,5-13; cf Ps 8); He is the stone* rejected by the builders and now becomes the cornerstone (Ac 4,11; cf Ps 118,22)...The glorified Christ thus revealed Himself as the key to the interpretation of the whole of Scripture, something which occupied His attention much earlier (cf Lk 24, 27.44ff).

4. *Significance and import of the resurrection.* To the extent that apostolic preaching achieved some rapport between the resurrection and the Scriptures, it also elaborated a theological interpretation of the fact. Being the glorification of the Son by the Father (Ac 2,22ff; Rm 8,11; cf Jn 17,1ff), the resurrection imposed the divine seal* on the act of redemption* inaugurated at the incarnation and accomplished on the cross*. Through the cross, Jesus is constituted: "Son of God in His might" (R 1,4; cf Ac 13,33; He 1,5; 5,5; Ps 2,7), "Lord and Christ" (Ac 2,36), "head and savior" (Ac 5,31), "judge and Lord of the living and the dead" (Ac 10,42; R 14,9; 2 Tm

4,1). Ascended to the Father (Jn 20,17), He can now give to men the promised Spirit* (Jn 20,22; Ac 2,33). Therein the full and profound significance of His earthly life is fully revealed. It was the manifestation of God here below, of His love and His grace (2 Tm 1,10; Tt 2, 11; 3,4)—a hidden manifestation, in which the glory* was perceptible only in symbol (Jn 1, 11), or during brief moments such as the transfiguration* (Lk 9,32.35 p; cf Jn 1,14). Now that Jesus has definitively entered into His glory, this manifestation continues in the Church, through miracles* (As 3,16) and the gift of the Spirit to those who believe (Ac 2,38f; 10,44f).

Thus Jesus, "the first-born from among the dead" (Ac 26,23; Col 1,18; Ap 1,5), is the first to enter the new* creation (cf Is 65,17...) which is the redeemed universe. Being the "Lord of glory" (1 Co 2,8; cf Jm 2,1; Ph 2,11), He is the author of man's salvation (Ac 3,6...). Source of divine power, He creates for Himself a holy people (1 P 2,9f) which He gathers in His wake.

II. THE POWER OF THE RESURRECTION

The resurrection of Jesus offers a solution to the problem of salvation which each one of us poses for himself. The primary object of our faith, it is also the foundation of our hope, determining its perspective. Jesus rose "as the first-fruits* of those who sleep" (1 Co 15,20); and that relates our treatment of the resurrection to the last day. Still more, Christ is in person "the resurrection and the life: he who believes in Him, even if he die, shall live" (Jn 11,25). This latter aspect grounds our confidence of participating even now in the mystery of the new life which Christ makes accessible to us through the medium of sacramental signs.

1. *The resurrection on the last day.* The Jewish faith in the resurrection of the body has been guaranteed by Jesus, with its perspectives of renewed bodily integrity (Lk 14,14) and of radical transformation (Mt 22,30ff p). That the picture is inferior to the tableau of the last day* sketched by the synoptic apocalypse (Mt 24 p) is of little importance. What is significant is that this faith did not attain its definitive meaning until after the personal resurrection of Jesus. The primitive community was conscious of remaining faithful on this point to the Jewish faith (Ac 23,6; 24,15; 26,6ff). But it is the resurrection of Jesus which henceforth gives this

faith an objective basis. We all will rise, because Jesus has risen: "He who has raised Christ Jesus from the dead will also give new life to your mortal bodies through His indwelling Spirit" (R 8,11; cf 1 Th 4,14; 1 Co 6,14; 15,12-22; 2 Co 4,14).

In *Matthew's gospel*, the account of the resurrection of Jesus underlines this point through a concrete picture: at the moment when Jesus, having descended to the lower regions, ascends again as conqueror, the just who are there awaiting entry into heavenly bliss awake to form a triumphant cortege for Him (Mt 27,52f). There is no question here of return to earthly existence, and the account speaks only of strange apparitions. But it is a symbolic anticipation of what will come to pass on the last day. Is not this also the significance of the miraculous resurrections performed by Jesus during His mortal life?

St. Paul develops at much greater length the scenario of the general resurrection: the sound of the angel's voice, the trumpet call to assemble the elect, clouds* of the parousia, the procession of the elect...(1 Th 4,15ff; 2 Th 1,7f; 1 Co 15, 52). This conventional backdrop is classic among the Jewish apocalypses, but the underlying reality is more important than its accidental modifications. In opposition to the Greek conception of the human soul, freed from the constraint of the body, arising alone toward immortality, the Christian perspective looks for a restoration of the whole person. It supposes a simultaneous, total transformation of the body*, now become spiritual, immortal, and incorruptible (1 Co 15,35-53). Within his self-imposed perspective, Paul does not go into the question of the resurrection of the wicked. His vision is only of the just, of participation in Jesus' entry into glory (cf 1 Co 15,12...). Waiting for this "resurrection of the body" (R 8,23) is such that to express its reality, Christian vocabulary clothes the resurrection with an air of perpetual imminence (cf 1 Th 4,17). In any case, the natural impatience arising from Christian hope* (cf 2 Co 5,1-10) ought not to proliferate in vain speculations about the date of the day* of the Lord.

The Apocalypse paints an attractive tableau on the theme of the resurrection of the dead (Ap 20,11-15). Death and Hades give up the dead who are in their keeping so that all, the wicked as well as the good, might appear before the judge. Although the wicked are engulfed in a "second death," the elect enter into a new life, surrounded by a transformed universe

which is identified with the primeval Paradise* and the heavenly Jerusalem* (Ap 21—22). How can there be expressed otherwise than under the form of symbols an unutterable reality which human experience cannot attain? This fresco is not taken up in the *fourth gospel*. But it does constitute the backdrop for two brief allusions which underlie the particular role assigned to the Son of Man: it is at His call that the dead will rise (Jn 5,28; 6,40.44), some to eternal life, the rest to damnation (Jn 5,29).

2. *The Christian life, an anticipated resurrection.* If John develops the tableau of the final resurrection so meagerly, it is because he sees it realized by anticipation in the present age. Lazarus going forth from the tomb represents concretely the faithful freed from death at the command of Jesus (cf Jn 11,25f). Likewise the discourse on the vivifying activity of the Son of Man contains some explicit affirmations: "The hour* is coming, and is now at hand, when the dead shall hear the voice of the Son of God, and all those who hear it shall live" (Jn 5,25). This clear declaration recapitulates the Christian experience such as it is expressed in the first epistle of John: "We know that we have passed from death to life..." (1 Jn 3,14). Whoever possesses this life shall never fall under the power of death (Jn 6,50; 11,26; cf R 5,8f). This certitude certainly does not suppress the expectation of the final resurrection; but it transfigures even now a life which is entered upon in reliance on Christ.

St. Paul previously made the same point in underlying the paschal character of the Christian life, a real participation in the life of the risen Christ. Buried with Him at the moment of baptism*, we are also risen with Him, because we have believed in the power of God who has raised Christ from the dead (Col 2,12; R 6,4ff). The new* life into which we have entered is therefore nothing else than His glorified life (E 2,5f). In fact, He has said to us at this moment: "Awake, sleeper! Rise from the dead, and Christ will shine upon you" (E 5,14). This fundamental conviction dominates the whole Christian existence. It superimposes itself upon morality which is in turn imposed upon the new man*, reborn in Christ: "having risen with Christ, aspire to the heavenly realm, where Christ is seated at the right hand of God" (Col 3,1ff). This conviction is also the source of his hope*. For, granting that the Christian awaits with impatience the final transformation of his body from present misery to a glorified state

(R 8,22f; Ph 3,10f.20f), he already possesses the pledge of that future state (R 8,23; 2 Co 5, 5). His final resurrection will only bring to light what is already present in the hidden reality of the mystery (Col 3,4).

→Apparitions of Christ—Ascension—Baptism IV 1.4—Body II 3—Body of Christ I 3, III 3—Burial 2—Clothing II 3.4—Day of the Lord NT I 1, III 2—Death OT 3; NT II 3, III 4—Exodus NT III—Faith NT II, 1 IV—Flesh o —Glory IV 2—Hope NT III, IV—Jesus Christ I 3, II 1 a—Joy NT I 2—Life III 3, IV—Miracle II 3 b, III 1—Night NT—Passover III—Prayer IV 3—Redemption NT 4—Reward II 4, III—Sign NT I, II 1—Sleep III—Son of God NT I 2—Soul II 2.3—Transfiguration—Victory NT 1.
JR & PG jab

REVELATION

The religion of the Bible is founded on an historical revelation. This puts it in a class apart from other religions. Some of these religions do not have recourse to any revelation. Buddhism has for its starting point the completely human intellectual experience of a philosopher. Other religions present their doctrine as a heavenly revelation, but attribute the transmission of this revelation to a legendary or mythical founder, such as Hermes Trismegistus for hermetic gnosticism. In the Bible, on the contrary, revelation is an historically ascertainable fact: its functionaries are known and their words are preserved, whether directly or through a solid tradition*. The Koran would be in this category. But apart from the signs which authenticate biblical revelation, it likewise does not rest on the teaching of a single founder. One can see it develop over fifteen or twenty centuries before it attains its fullness in the reality of Christ, the revealer *par excellence*. Belief for a Christian means acceptance of this revelation which has come down to men through history.

OT

But why such a revelation? The reason is that God is infinitely superior to the thoughts and speech of men (Jb 42,3). He is a hidden God (Is 45,15), made even more inaccessible by the fact that through sin man has lost his familiarity with Him. His plan is a mystery* (cf Am 3,

7). He directs man's steps without letting him see the road ahead (Pr 20,24). In conflict with the enigmas of his existence (cf Ps 73,21f), man by himself cannot discover the necessary clarifications. He must turn to Him "in whom are hidden all things" (Dt 29,28), in order to discover these secrets, otherwise impossible to perceive (cf Dn 2,17f), so as to "see His glory" (Ex 33,18). Thus even before man turns to Him, God takes the initiative and is the first to speak to him.

I. HOW GOD REVEALS

1. *Ancient techniques.* The Near East used certain techniques in seeking to discover the secrets of heaven: divination, omens, dreams, casting lots, astrology, etc. For a long time the OT kept a certain number of these techniques. While purifying them of their polytheistic or magical trappings (Lv 19,26; Dt 18,10f; 1 S 15, 23; 28,3), they still attributed a certain value to them. As a condescension to the imperfect understanding of His people, God in effect confided His revelation to these traditional channels. Priests consulted Him through the urim and thummin (Nm 27,21; Dt 33,8; 1 S 14,41; 23,10ff), and on that basis uttered oracles (Ex 18,15f; 33,7-11; Jg 18,5f). Joseph possessed a cup for divination (Gn 44,2.5) and he was an expert in the interpretation of dreams (Gn 40—41). The dreams were in effect considered as the bearers of celestial messages (Gn 20,3; 28, 12-15; 31,11ff; 37,5-10), and this even until a much later date (Jg 7,13f; 1 S 28,6; 1 K 3,5-14). But progressively, a distinction was made between dreams which God sends to authentic prophets (Nm 12,6; Dt 13,2) and those of professional diviners (Lv 19,26; Dt 18,10) against which the prophets were pitted (Is 28,7-13; Jr 23,25-32), and likewise the wisdom philosophers (Jo 5,2; Si 34,1-6).

2. *Prophetic revelation.* Such techniques are regularly surpassed by the prophets*. With them, the experience of revelation is transmitted in two ways: through visions and through the hearing of the divine Word* (cf Nm 23,3f.15f). Visions by themselves remain enigmatic: even a prophet would not have direct knowledge of divine realities or the future unfolding of history. What he sees remains enclosed in symbols, some of them already in common use in the religions of the East (vg 1 K 22,16; Is 6,1ff; Ez 1), while others are a new creation (vg Am

499

7,1-9; Jr 1,11ff; Ez 9). In every case, the Word of God must furnish the key to these symbolic visions (vg Jr 1,14ff; Dn 7,15-18; 8,15...). More often, the Word comes to the prophets without any accompanying vision, and even without their being able to say in what way it has come (vg Gn 12,1f; Jr 1,4f). Such is the fundamental experience which, in the OT, characterized revelation.

3. *Wisdom reflections.* Unlike the prophets, the wisdom philosophers did not present their doctrine as the result of direct revelation. Wisdom* makes appeal to human reflection, to the intelligence and understanding (Pr 2,1-5; 8,12. 14). It is, however, a gift of God (2,6), for it is a transcendent wisdom from which flows all knowledge (8,15-21.32-36; 9,1-6). More precisely, the data which is the subject matter for this divinely guided reflection is drawn exclusively from divine revelation: creation*, which in its own way manifests the Creator (cf Ps 19,1; Si 43); history, which makes known His ways (Si 44—50, not to mention the historical books); Scripture, which includes the divine Law* and the words of the prophets (Si 39,1ff). Such wisdom is not therefore of human invention, but rather it is a mode of revelation which complements prophetic revelation. For divine Wisdom, which is its guide, like the Spirit is a transcendent reality, "a reflection of the essence of God" (Ws 7,15-21). Thus, the light which it communicates to men is that of supernatural knowledge (Ws 7,25f; 8,4-8).

4. *Apocalyptic.* At the very end of the OT, prophecy and wisdom literature are blended with the apocalyptic literature. *Apocalyptic* by definition is the revelation of divine secrets. Such revelation pertains more to wisdom (Dn 2, 23; 5,11.14) than to the divine Spirit (Dn 4, 5f.15; 5,11.14). It can have for its sources dreams and visions; but it can also be prompted by a meditation on Scripture (Dn 9,1ff). In any case, it is the Word of God which, through supernatural illumination, gives the key to the interpretation of dreams, visions, and sacred texts.

II. WHAT GOD REVEALS

The object of divine revelation is always something in the sphere of religion. It does not burden itself with cosmological data or metaphysical speculation, with which the sacred books of the majority of ancient religions were surfeited (for example, the Vedas of India, gnostic works, or even certain Jewish apocrypha). God reveals His plans which trace the way of salvation for men. He reveals Himself so that man may be able to meet Him.

1. *God reveals His plans.*

a) Since he is born a member of a sinful race, man is not precisely certain what God expects of him. God therefore reveals the rules of conduct to him. His Word takes the form of instruction and of Law* (Ex 20,1...), and man thus possesses "revealed truths" which he must put into practice (Dt 29,28). The Law derives its value from this divine origin, and hence is elevated from a juridical reality to become the delight of the spiritual minded (cf Ps 119,24. 97...). Similarly, the institutions of the people of God are the object of revelation: social institutions (Nm 11,16f), political institutions (1 S 9,17), as well as cult prescriptions (Ex 25, 40). While maintaining a provisional character, just as the status of the entire people of God in the OT was provisional, these institutions had nonetheless a positive signification with reference to the fulfillment of salvation in the NT. They were its prophetic prototypes.

b) In the second place, God reveals to His people the meaning of the events which in His providence they have experienced. These events constitute the visible thread of the divine salvific design. They prepare for its final realization and already prefigure it. By this double title, they present a mysterious appearance which the human eye is unable to fathom. But God "does nothing, except He reveals His purpose to His servants the prophets" (Am 3,7). Historians, prophets, psalmists, wisdom philosophers, all emulate one another in seeking this religious interpretation of history, which is born of the encounter between the divine Word and the facts of history, willed and shaped by providence. The facts accredit the Word and lead men to faith*, for they have the value of signs* (Ex 14,30f). The Word illumines the facts insofar as it removes from them any banality arising from daily occurrence or any suspicion of chance (vg Jr 27,4-11; Is 45,1-6), so as to place them as moments within a fixed plan.

c) Finally, God reveals progressively the secret of "the last days." His Word is a promise*. In this respect it foresees, beyond the present or even the near future, the term of its salutary design. It reveals the future of David's lineage (2 S 7,4-16), the final glory of Jerusalem and the temple (Is 2,1-4; 60; Ez 40—48), the unsuspected role of the suffering Servant (Is 52, 13—53,12), etc. This aspect of prophetic revelation gives us a knowledge of the NT by anticipation, still enveloped in figures on the one hand, but already delineating the traits of the eschatological covenant.

2. *God reveals Himself also* through what He accomplishes here below. His creation* already reveals Him in His wisdom and sovereign power (Jb 25,7-14; Pr 8,23-31; Si 42,15—43,33). Creation is like a tissue of symbols which permit Him to be represented figuratively, veiled in a cloud* (Ex 13,21), burning like a fire* (Ex 3,2; Gn 15,17), thundering like a storm* (Ex 19,16), soft as a gentle breeze (1 K 19,12f). These signs recognized by the pagans were, however, often interpreted by them in a contrary sense (Ws 13,1f). Revelation now allows the people of God to contemplate the Creator by analogy with the grandeur and beauty of His creatures (Ws 13,3ff).

It is however in the history of Israel that God* reveals Himself everywhere in quite specific fashion. His acts reveal who He is: the awesome God who judges and makes war; the compassionate God who consoles (Is 40,1) and delivers; the mighty God who saves and who triumphs. The biblical definition of God (Ex 34, 6f) is not the consequence of philosophical speculation but the result of a lived experience. And this concrete understanding, gained in the course of centuries, dominates the attitude which men ought to take before Him: faith and confidence, fear and love. It is a complex attitude which rectifies and complements that which men of religious instincts would spontaneously assume. For God is creator and master, king and Lord. But toward Israel, He shows Himself likewise as father and spouse. Thus the religious awe which is due Him must be nuanced by a familiar piety* (Ho 6,6) which can lead to mystical intimacy.

Is one justified therefore in saying more, and did the OT God reveal Himself in the intimacy of His personal being? We enter here into the realm of the ineffable. The OT records some mysterious manifestations of the angel* of Yahweh, in which the invisible God in some fashion took on a sensible form (Gn 16,7; 21,17; 31,11; Jg 2,1). It records the visions of Abraham, Moses, Elijah, Micheas ben Yimla, Isaiah, Eze-

kiel, Zechariah...The divine glory*, however, always veiled itself under symbols: cosmic symbols of fire or of the storm, symbols expressive of the divine majesty (1 K 22,19; Is 6,1ff), symbols inspired by Babylonian art (Ez 1). In any case, Yahweh Himself is never described (cf Ez 1,27f) and His face* is never seen (Ex 33,20), even by Moses who spoke to Him "face to face" (Ex 33,11; Nm 12,8). Men instinctively veil their eyes so as not to look fixedly at Him (Ex 3,6; 1 K 19,9f). To Moses, He grants the supreme revelation, that of His name* (Ex 3,14). But this still leaves intact the mystery of His being; for His reply to Moses—"I am He who is" or "I am who am"—can be understood as the declaration of a mystery*. Israel will not possess the name of its God in such wise as to control Him, as the surrounding pagan peoples controlled their gods. Hence God remains in His absolute transcendence, even while according to men a certain concrete insight into His mystery. If they do not yet penetrate into the intimacy of His being, they already are illuminated by His Word*, by the action of His Wisdom*; they are sanctified by His Spirit*. In "the last days" He will do more. Then, "His glory* will be revealed and all flesh will see it" (Is 40,5; 52,8; 60,1). It will be the supreme revelation, the details of which are not given out in advance. The event itself will alone reveal how it will come to be.

NT

The revelation begun in the OT is fulfilled in the NT. But instead of being transmitted by many intermediaries, it is concentrated now in Jesus Christ who is at the same time its author and object. Three stages must be distinguished. In the first, the revelation is handed over by Jesus Himself to His apostles. In the second, it is communicated to men by the apostles, and later by the Church under the influence of the Holy Spirit. In the third stage, revelation will attain its final consummation, when the direct vision of the divine mystery will replace for men the knowledge of faith. To characterize these successive stages, the NT uses a varied vocabulary: reveal (*apokalyptô*), manifest (*phaneroô*), make known (*gnôrizô*), put in the light (*phôtizô*), explain (*exēgeomai*), show (*deiknuô/-mi*), or, quite simply, speak; the apostles proclaim (*kēryssô*), teach (*didaskô*), this revelation which now constitutes the Word*, the gospel*, the mystery* of faith. All these themes are found within the different texts of the NT writings.

REVELATION

I. THE SYNOPTICS AND ACTS

1. *The revelation of Jesus Christ.*

a) Revelation through events. Even in the OT, the knowledge of God's salvific will remained enveloped in shadows. Its final consummation, though promised, was called to mind only in symbols. What disperses the shadows now and dissipates the ambiguity of the promise is the event which is Christ. The historic destiny of Jesus, crowned by His death and resurrection, makes known the real content of this promise through its historical fulfillment.

b) Verbal revelation. Revelation through events would remain incomprehensible unless Jesus had communicated by speech the meaning of His actions and His whole life. In the parables* of the kingdom, He "utters things kept secret since the foundation of the world" (Mt 13,35). If He still veiled His teaching to the crowd under the form of symbols, He clearly expounds the mystery* of His kingdom to His disciples (Mk 4,11 p); the kingdom is the terminus of the salvific will. Likewise, He reveals the hidden meaning of the Scriptures to them, when He shows them that the Son of Man must suffer, be put to death, and rise on the third day (Mt 16,21 p). Through His revelation advances toward its plenitude: "Nothing hidden unless it is to be disclosed, and nothing put under cover unless it is to come into the open" (Mk 4,22 p).

c) Revelation through the person of Jesus. In and through the words of Jesus and the facts of His life, men may penetrate to the mysterious center of His being where they will at last find divine revelation. Not only does Jesus contain in His own person the kingdom and the salvation which He proclaims, but He is the living revelation of the Godhead. Being the Son of the living God (Mt 16,16), He alone knows the Father and has the power to reveal Him (Mt 11,27 p). On the other hand, the mystery of His person remains inaccessible to "flesh and blood": incapable of being perceived without a revelation from the Father (Mt 16,17), which is denied to the wise and the clever but granted to little ones (Mt 11,25 p). These intimate relations between Father and Son, of which the OT had no inkling, constitute the culmination of the revelation communicated by Jesus. Yet this mystery of (divine) filiation is hidden behind a humble exterior: Jesus reveals Himself as the Son* of Man destined to suffer (Mk 8,31ff p). Even after His resurrection, Jesus does not show Himself to the world in the fullness of His glory.

2. *Revelation as transmitted.*

a) Revelation in the Church. The actions and words of Jesus were known directly only by a small number of men. Still fewer were the number of those who believed in Him and became His disciples. Yet the revelation which He transmitted was destined for the entire world. That is why Jesus made it known to His apostles together with the commission to communicate it to other men (cf Mt 10,26f). They will go into the entire world to carry the gospel to all nations* (Mt 28,19f; Mk 16,15). Thus, He makes them witnesses, thanks to the apparitions* with which they have been blessed (Ac 1,8). They were witnesses, not only in the sense that having seen Him with their eyes and heard His words, they could now report exactly what He had said and done (cf Lk 1,2), but because Jesus Himself authenticated their testimony: "He who hears you hears me" (Lk 10,16). The Acts of the Apostles shows how, thanks to these witnesses, the revelation of Jesus Christ set foot in the stream of world history. In this account one sees the Word become diffused, from Jerusalem to the ends of the earth—a foreshadowing of the action of the Church*, prolonging the work of the apostles*, from Pentecost to the end of time.

b) Revelation and the action of the Holy Spirit. Moreover, Acts shows us the direct relation between the communication of revelation within the Church and the action of the Holy Spirit* here below. From the day of Pentecost on, the Spirit has been given. He it is who assures the accuracy of the apostolic testimony (Ac 1,8; 2,1-21). Through His illuminations, the apostles will discover the total meaning of Scripture and that of Christ's earthly existence. Under this double perspective they will present their testimony (cf 2,22-41). Revelation thus being made known to men, those among them who are docile to the Spirit will receive it with faith, and by their baptism* will enter upon the way of salvation* (2,41.47).

3. *Toward the full revelation.* The revelation initiated by Jesus and communicated by His apostles and the Church still remains imperfect, for the divine realities are hidden under symbols. But this revelation proclaims the fullness

of revelation which will come at the end of history. Then the Son of Man will reveal Himself in His glory (Lk 17,30; cf Mk 13,26 p), and men will pass from "the present world" into "the world to come."

II. THE APOSTOLIC LETTERS

1. *The revelation of Jesus Christ.*

a) Revelation of salvation. If allusions to the words of Jesus are rare in the apostolic epistles, on the other hand the fact of Christ, and notably His death and resurrection, occupy a central place. In this reality is revealed the salvation* promised formerly to Israel. Christ, the spotless Lamb* predestined from the foundation of the world, in this last period of time has been made manifest for our sake (1 P 1,20). He has appeared once and for all to abolish sin by the sacrifice of Himself (He 9,26). By this appearance of our savior Christ Jesus, the grace* of God has been brought fully into view (2 Tm 1,10). In Him has been revealed the salvific justice* of God, which had sustained the Law and the prophets (R 3,21; cf 1,17). In Him is uncovered the mystery* hidden to previous generations (R 16,26; Col 1,26; 1 Tm 3, 16). God has made known to us His hidden purpose (E 1,9), as He has also revealed it to the principalities and powers (3,10). This mystery is the ultimate secret of the salvific design.

b) Revelation of the mystery of God. Even beyond the mystery of salvation, it is the Godhead itself which is revealed to us in Christ. Creation has been an initial manifestation of His invisible perfections; this manifestation was, however, quickly effaced in the minds of sinful men (R 1,19ff). Then the OT brought a still partial revelation of His glory*. Finally, "God caused to shine on the face of Christ Jesus the revelation of His glory" (2 Co 4,6), fulfilling thereby the prophetic oracle of Is 40,5. Such is the profound meaning of Christ, in His actions and in His person.

2. *Revelation communicated.*

The apostles have not understood all this on their own, but thanks to an interior illumination, understanding has been given to them (cf Mt 16,17). Paul received his gospel as a revelation of Jesus Christ, when it pleased the Father to reveal His Son in him (G 1,12.16). The Spirit who explores everything even to the depths of the Godhead revealed to him the meaning of the cross* which is true wisdom (1 Co 2,10). By a revelation the secret of Christ was made known to him, as to all the apostles and prophets, in the Spirit (E 3,3ff).

Here is why the gospel of the apostle is no human invention (G 1,11): as an echo of the Word* of God itself, it is "the saving power of God for everyone who believes" (R 1,16). In making known the mystery of the gospel (E 6, 19), Paul brings to light before the eyes of all the hidden purpose of this mystery, formerly hidden but now revealed (3,9f). Such is the significance of the apostolic word: it communicates divine revelation to men to lead them to faith* which will guarantee their salvation.

3. *Toward complete revelation.*

The supremacy of faith, however, will last only for a time. It is based on "the manifestation of the love of God our Savior" in the earthly life of Jesus (Tt 3,4). It continues even though Jesus has already entered into His glory. It will come to an end "when the splendor of our great God and Savior Christ Jesus will appear" (Tt 2, 13; cf Lk 17,30). This final revelation of Jesus (1 P 1,7.13), this manifestation of the head shepherd (1 P 5,4), becomes the object of Christian hope* (2 Th 1,7; 1 Co 1,7; cf Tt 2,13). In effect, when Christ who is our life is manifested, then we too will be manifested with Him in glory (Col 3,4). All creation aspires with us for this eschatological revelation of the sons of God (R 8,19-23). It will be a mysterious event, impossible to describe, after which direct vision will be substituted for the rule of faith (1 Co 13,12; 2 Co 5,7).

III. ST. JOHN

In the Johannine vocabulary, the theme of revelation is expressed especially by the word *to manifest (phaneroô)*; but the concept of revelation is everywhere evident in the texts.

1. *The revelation of Jesus Christ.*

a) The visible manifestation of Jesus. In the center of revelation is located the person of Jesus*, Son* of God made man. John the Baptist had borne witness "that He might be revealed to Israel" (Jn 1,31). In effect, "He appeared" (1 Jn 3,5.8), that is, He became the object of sense experience. It was not a stunning manifestation in the eyes of the world, as

His brethren would have preferred (Jn 7,4), but a quasi-secret manifestation, quite paradoxical, which ended in the lifting up on the cross* (Jn 12,32). For it looked to the removal of sin and the destruction of the devil's handiwork (1 Jn 3,5.8). Only after His resurrection does Jesus show Himself in glory, and this only for the benefit of His disciples (Jn 21,1.14).

b) The manifestation of the Godhead in Jesus Christ. The sensible appearance of Jesus had a transcendent meaning: it was the supreme revelation of God* to men. There was revelation through the words of Jesus. He who as Son had seen God, explained the Godhead to men (Jn 1,18), at first in veiled terms, later, on the eve of His departure, clearly in non-symbolical language (16,29). There was revelation through His actions. His miracles* were signs by which He manifested His glory so that men might believe in Him (2,11). For this glory which He possessed was His as that of the only-begotten Son of the Father (1,14). In this double fashion, therefore, He made manifest the name* of God to men (17,6); that is, the mystery of His being, crowning thereby the whole revelation of the OT (cf 1,17). The evangelist who had seen, heard, touched the Word of life (1 Jn 1,1), summarizes thus the meaning of his experience: In Jesus is revealed life* (1,2); in Jesus is made manifest the love* of God for us (4,9).

2. *The revelation communicated.* The revelation of Jesus Christ has not been accepted by all men. This is so not only because only a small number of men have known Him, but especially because acceptance of Him presupposes an interior grace*: "No one comes to me unless he is drawn by the Father who sent me" (Jn 6,44). Therefore those "who are taught by the Father" (6,45) are not numerous. Very many others flee the light and prefer the darkness (3,19ff), because they belong to an evil generation*. Jesus therefore has not made known the name of the Father except to those whom the Father has drawn from the world to give to Him (17,6).

But to these latter, He has confided a mission* —that of witnessing* to Him (16,27). It is a difficult role, one which will demand a profound understanding of what Jesus has said and done. That is why after His departure He will send them the Holy Spirit who will lead them to a complete understanding of the truth (16,12ff). Thanks to the Spirit, the apostolic testimony

will make known to all men the revelation of Jesus Christ, that they may believe and have life within them: "Life is revealed, we have seen it with our own eyes, and it is of this that we speak" (1 Jn 1,2). "We have seen for ourselves, and we attest, that the Father sent the Son to be the savior of the world" (4,14). In accepting this testimony, everyone, like the first witnesses, will be able to "share in the common life with the Father and His Son, Jesus Christ" (1,3f).

3. *Toward the perfect revelation.* In and through the mystery of the Word made flesh, the divine glory is still contemplated only through faith. Man "abides* in God," but he has not reached his fulfillment. "As of now, we are children of God, but what we shall be has not yet been revealed." The day will come when Christ will reveal Himself in glory, at the time of His coming (cf 2,28). Then we also will be revealed with Him, and "we shall become like to God because we shall see Him as He is" (3,2). Such is the object of Christian hope*.

IV. THE APOCALYPSE

The Apocalypse of John is, by its definition, a revelation (Ap 1,1). It is no longer concerned with the earthly life of Jesus, but is orientated toward His final manifestation to which the history of the Church and of the entire world is a prelude. As a form of Christian prophecy (1,3), it takes for granted the knowledge of salvation through the cross and the resurrection of Christ. It is in their light that the seer rereads prophetic Scriptures of old (cf 5,1; 10,8ff). Possessing the key to their interpretation, he makes use of them to lay out the mystery of Christ, in all its grandeur, from His birth (12,5) and immolation on the cross (1,18; 5,6) to the moment of His coming in glory (19,11-16). The brunt of his testimony bears on this last event, the coming of Christ for which the Church yearns (22,17).

His book arises therefore from the concurrence of two divine revelations, equally certain: that which the Scriptures define and Christ's revelation which is their fulfillment. Using the one to shed light on the other, as two sources of the knowledge of faith, the prophet brings to them their final complement. Through his efforts, the Church can see clearly that in its historic destiny persecution* will be paradoxically the means of victory* for God's forces over the world and Satan. In the midst of their trial, Christians already see in faith the heavenly Jerusalem, while waiting for its full revelation to them (22,2)...). Thus the revelation of Jesus Christ, who is "the same, yesterday, today, and forever" (He 13,8), illumines the whole history of the world, from beginning to end.

→Apparitions of Christ 1—Dreams—Fire— Glory III—God—Image—Know—Light & Dark Listen 1—Mountain II 1—Mystery—Parable II 1, III—Plan of God—Prophet OT I 2— Punishment 3—See—Sign—Tradition OT I— Transfiguration—Truth—Wisdom OT II 3; NT III 1—Word of God OT II; NT I 1—Yahweh.

BRi & PG jab

REWARD

Man makes of reward a question of justice; every activity deserves its reward. But in the religious sphere, it seems on the contrary that disinterestedness ought to go so far as to set aside any thought of recompense. Christ, however, did not require such an illusory ideal in His followers, but on the other hand He did demand of the disciple a perfect purity of intention.

I. REWARD AND PAYMENT

The notion of reward is presupposed at the heart of the religious life. But to understand its exact significance, one must describe its genesis in conscience. Like many other conceptions, this notion is rooted in human experience—in this case, in the relation between master and servant. But the idea infinitely transcends this category, for God Himself establishes the relationship. It is characterized undoubtedly by the vocabulary which expresses the idea of "payment," but it cannot be reduced to that which we understand today by payment due for work. This comes at the completion of a contract, whereas reward in the religious sphere is the result of a visitation* by God who by His judgment approves the work of His servant*.

From the beginning, man has existed on the earth with the idea of working* for God (Gn 2, 15; cf Jb 14,6; Mt 20,1-15), and this work admits of a payment (Jb 7,1f). God in fact is an equitable master: He will not fail to give to

each what is due him if he accomplishes the work assigned to him. On the other hand, man is not a lordly figure with self-sufficient means of existence who can thus gratuitously offer to God a "disinterested" kind of assistance. Man before God is poor*, a beggar, a servant* if not a slave*, who has nothing other than what the master gives him from day to day. Reward therefore is not seen to be the term of the religious life, but the normal benefit of the service of God.

That is why, in the beginning of salvation history, God promises a reward to Abraham (Gn 15,1); and in the last lines of the Bible "recompense according to deeds" (Ap 22,12) is underscored. Between these two quotations, Scripture repeats untiringly that God rewards each man according to his works* (Pr 12,14; Jr 31,16; Ps 28,4; 2 Ch 15,7; Jb 34,11; Is 59,18; Si 51,30; Lk 10,7; Jn 4,36; R 2,6; 2 Tm 4,14), a payment that belongs to God alone (Dt 32,35; Pr 20,22; cf R 12,17-20). This doctrine is so important that it is considered characteristic of the ungodly* to deny the existence of rewards (Ws 2,22). Likewise, that faith in God who "rewards those who seek Him" is the indispensable complement of faith in His very existence (He 11,6).

Granting that the man who does his job can count on his reward, he who refuses to serve will see himself deprived of his reward, and ultimately of his right to exist before God. In addition, to be rewarded according to one's works* is to pass under the judgment* of God; it is to receive recompense or punishment according to what one has done; and these alternatives mean a choice between life and death. Finally, this judgment of God transcends the judgments of men, for God alone plumbs the loins and the heart. Man cannot penetrate the mystery of God, who is mercy* and wrath*, fidelity, justice*, and love*.

II. THE STAGES OF ITS REVELATION

If the fact of recompense is a fundamental certainty, its nature is nonetheless mysterious, and God has only gradually revealed it.

1. *Solidarity and responsibility.* From the beginning, the actions of men seem to depend upon each man's personal responsibility and yet possess a significance for the group. The individual's existence is inseparable from that of the family, the clan, the nation. In the

record of the earliest times, the providence and the judgment of God falls globally on "man" (Gn 6,5ff). The covenant and Yahweh's consequent fidelity concern first of all a people*. Although the group dimension dominates here, personal responsibility is not unknown and the very existence of a penal code is proof of it. The ancient practice of the ordeal, the "judgment of God" (cf Nm 5,11-30), the "inquest" conducted by God in the Paradise account (Gn 3,11ff); all this implies a desire to discover and punish the one responsible. The episode of Achan well illustrates the constant concern to eliminate neither personal responsibility nor collective guilt. By the divine decree the guilty one must be found, and his presence in the group is revealed by a setback dealt the entire people (Js 7,5-12). The personal punishment* which he undergoes is extended equally to his family and property (7,24; cf Gn 3,16-19). Similarly, the reward given to the just man touches his relations also. So it is for Noah (Gn 6,18; 7,1), Lot (19,12), and Obededom (2 S 6,12).

Punishment and forgiveness have their repercussions through space (the entire people involved in the action of one of its members) and time (whole generations affected by one of their forebears). Yet the balance tips clearly toward mercy* which lasts infinitely longer (Ex 20,5f; 34,7).

Looked at in this light, the religious interpretation of events seems simplified: a just God rules the world. If I am unhappy or burdened by difficulties, it is through my own fault or that of another with whom I am linked (cf Jn 9,2). Inversely, my salvation*, irrespective of my heinous crimes and their consequences, can be achieved through solidarity with some just person. If there had been ten just men in Sodom, the inhabitants would not have been punished for their sin (Gn 18,16-33; cf 19,20ff). At this period of history, a scheme like this would seem to account of every situation. It could not, however, endure indefinitely.

2. *Man responsible for his destiny.* In fact, under the pressure of misfortunes in exile, the people had drawn from this inflexible pattern a dictum: "The fathers have eaten sour grapes, and the children's teeth are set on edge" (Jr 31,29f). A scandalous deduction, which questions the justice* of God. This proverb should no longer be quoted, proclaimed Jeremiah (Jr 31,29f); and for Ezekiel it had no further significance (Ez 18,2-3). In accord with the tradition of Dt 7,9f which appealed to solidarity for reward and to personal retribution for sin, Ezekiel puts heavy stress on the doctrine of conversion in announcing that the just can only save themselves. Noah, who formerly had saved his sons (Gn 7,7), would no longer be able to save them since the divine plan has reached a new stage (Ez 14,12-20). Thereupon Ezekiel analyzes all possible situations (18): every man is responsible at every moment for his own destiny. He can always compromise or regain it. Yet God in this drama is by no means hostile nor even impartial: "I have no pleasure in the death of anyone who dies. Turn then, and live" (Ez 18,32).

3. *The mystery of the justice of God.* If man is fully responsible for his destiny, his life gains in seriousness. But another problem is then raised whose full solution will be given only with the revelation of the afterlife. If there is a place for reward here below, why is it not constant? The traditional observation that the just man is always happy (Ps 37; 91; 92; 112) is contradicted by experience.

In portraying this conscience struggle, the Bible reveals the heartfelt thoughts of all those who loyally try to reconcile their faith and personal experience. Jeremiah obtained no further response to his troubled state than encouragement to continue bravely in his present path (Jr 12,1-5); but Job, Ecclesiastes, and the psalmists met the problem head on and tried to resolve it.

a) For a long time some philosophers clung tenaciously to the traditional solution, albeit with modifications: retribution, so long deferred, would nonetheless be manifested in this life, all concentrated in the dramatic moment of death*. Death will be characterized by extraordinary happiness or suffering* (Ps 49,17f; Si 1,13; 7,26; 11,18-28). Unquestionably it was this flimsy hypothesis that the psalmist thus rejects: "For there is no trouble to their death" (Ps 73,4hb.).

b) Ecclesiastes, who "sought wisdom and substance" (Qo 7,25) without finding anything other than inconsistency which undermined traditional principles (8,12ff), preached tempered activity which seeks to draw from daily existence the most of what is best (9,9f). All this is accomplished in an atmosphere of confidence* in God which remains tranquil but draws back from a resolution of the problem.

c) For those who suffer for their faith and who unconditionally adhere to the Lord, a light is given. God is their "portion," their "light," their "rock" in the midst of all their trials (Ps 16,5f; 18,1ff; 27,1f; 73,26; 142,6; Lm 3,24). They have no other purpose, they wish no further reward than to do His will (Ps 119,57; Si 2,18; 51,20f). This presupposes a climate of intense faith*, that in which Job lived. He had "seen* God"; and this mysterious contact with His holiness* left Job humble and adoring, conscious of his sinfulness and strengthened by a new level of understanding of God (Jb 42,5f).

d) Others finally had a presentiment that to explain the suffering* of the just one had to enlarge the horizon and pass from the plane of reward to that of redemption*. Such is the significance of the last of the Servant* poems (Is 53,10; cf Ps 22). But, just as in the vision of the dry bones brought back to life (Ez 37), reward seems to involve again only the group purified by the sufferings of the exile.

4. *Personal reward*. In a final stage, it is faith in personal resurrection* at the end of time which gives the solution to the problem posed. According to certain texts, difficult to interpret, God owes it to Himself to satisfy man in his thirst for justice: He (God) cannot punish the just man even if He had to release him for a moment from Sheol by way of recompense (Jb 19,25ff). God, therefore, cannot leave unanswered the appeal of man for union with Him (cf Ps 16,9ff). If He has "taken to Himself" Elijah or Enoch, why is not the just man "taken" near to God also (Ps 49,16; 73,24)?

The persecution of Antiochus Epiphanes, with its consequent martyrdoms, led the faithful to the conviction of a recompense in the afterlife through resurrection (2 M 7; cf Dn 12, 1ff). This faith in the resurrection is implicit in the Book of Wisdom through belief in immortality (Ws 3,1; 4,1). Following the divine visitation* at the last day*, the just will live forever in the friendship of God; and this will be their "reward" (cf Wm 2,22; 5,15), a reward that is also a grace* (cf 3,9.14; 4,15), infinitely surpassing the value of the human effort.

III. CHRIST AND MERIT

With the coming of Christ, merit found its full meaning and purpose.

1. *Confirmation of individual merit*. Many in Israel (Mt 22,22; Ac 23,8), including some of Christ's disciples (1 Co 15,12), still doubted in the resurrection, eternal life*, the kingdom* without end, as the reward of the just. But Jesus and His apostles maintained stoutly the authentic tradition of Israel (Mt 22,31f; 25,31-46; 1 Co 15,13-19; Ac 24,14ff). The God of Jesus Christ raises up His Son and so shows that He is just* (Ac 3,14ff; Col 2,12f). Thus, the believer knows that he will receive a reward for his works* (cf Mt 16,27; Mk 9,41; 2 Tm 4,14; 2 Jn 8; 2 P 2,13; Ap 18,6) and that at the judgment the "King" will send men, according to what they have done, to life* or to punishment* (Mt 25,46), to heaven* or to hell*. From now on it is a case of fighting the fight with enthusiasm in order to win the prize (1 C 9,24-27; G 5,7; 2 Tm 4,7).

2. *The real reward*. If individual merit is a reality, then the risk of reverting to Pharisiasm revives; i.e., that conception according to which heavenly reward is measured by human observance. But the believer is continually put on his guard against such a deformation of the doctrine of merit.

First of all, man should not especially seek material advantages; glory, reputation, recognition, or interest. For he who does good for these motives has "already received his reward" (Mt 6,1-16; Lk 14,12ff; cf 1 Co 9,17f). But above all, what the Christian aims at in putting Christ at the center of everything is not his own wellbeing, even though spiritual and acquired by self-renunciation. Christ constitutes the Christian's goal (Ph 1,21-26). His reward is the divine heritage (Col 3,24), which makes him immediately a co-heir and brother of Christ (R 8,17). The apostle will receive the crown which he desires by the very fact of the coming of Christ, a coming which is awaited with love (2 Tm 4,8). In brief, what he wishes is to be "with Jesus" forever (1 Th 4,17; cf Ph 1,23; Lk 23,43; Ap 21,3f). Fidelity to his baptism becomes the constant effort of daily life. Thus identified with the death of Christ, he prepares himself for the resurrection with Him (R 6,5-8; Col 3,1-4). The salvation* which the justified await (R 5,9f) is nothing else than the love of God made manifest in the person of Christ (R 8,38f). John expresses the same idea in somewhat different language: to the hunger* and thirst of men, to their passionate desire* to triumph over death, Jesus responds by presenting His own person. He is the source of living water*, bread*, light*, life* (Jn 7,37f; 6,26-35;

8,12; 11,23ff). Through living in Christ Jesus are resolved all the antinomies which the doctrine of reward formerly presented. Given to man at the outset of his strivings, it is nonetheless absolutely gratuitous, infinitely surpassing all merit and aspiration. Awaited with joy and confidence*, it is already possessed by justification*. Though a tranquil certitude, this doctrine remains founded solely on the testimony of God received in the obscurity and trying circumstances of an act of faith*. Touching each man in the depths of his personality, it yet makes vital contact with man within the context of the body* of Christ. There exists no opposition between a "morality of reward" and a "morality of love," for love itself seeks recompense.

→Almsgiving OT 3; NT 2 a—Beatitude OT I 2—Education I 2 a—Godless Man OT 3—Harvest III—Heaven VI—Hell—Inheritance OT II 1—Justice O; A I OT 3; B II OT—Poor OT—Punishment 2—Responsibility—Resurrection OT III—Vengeance 3—Water II 1—Works OT II; NT II.

CW jab

RIGHT HAND

The right stands for the right hand, symbol of power, or the place on the right, symbol of favor.

1. *The right hand.* This is not only the more skilled of the two but also the stronger, the hand that wields the sword. It is, then, a symbol of the power* of God, who makes Himself known by the mighty deeds of His right hand, strikes the enemy with it, and delivers His people (Ex 15,6; Ps 20,7; 21,9). And so after His death Jesus was "raised to the heights by God's right hand" (Ac 2,33), as the psalmist had foretold (Ps 118,16).

2. *The place of right.* The right hand protects those who are in this place. The right hand of God is the place where His friends will taste eternal delights (Ps 16,11), the place where the Messiah will be enthroned near Him (Ps 110,1). And, according to another translation of Ac 2,33, Jesus has been "raised to the right hand of God." He becomes the instrument of God's mighty hand, the "son of the right hand" (Ps 80,16.18), like the king of Israel whom God

confirmed with His strength* (cf Gn 35,18; Benjamin = son of the right hand). Jesus confirms and brings to realization these promises of the old covenant. When He will come to judge the whole universe as king, the Son of Man will place at His right the blessed of His Father (Mt 25,31-34). He Himself affirms that He will be seen sitting at the right hand of the power, according to the words of Ps 110 (Mt 26,64); and, before the hour when His enemies will see Him appear in this place as judge, Stephen sees Him standing there as a witness* (Ac 7,55).

→Arm & Hand—Jesus Christ II 1 a—Power.

JBB jrc

RIGHTS/LAWS

Laws and rights represent two poles, one collective and the other individual. Laws represent the order that governs the whole of human relations within a community, and rights are the recognition assured to each individual of certain determined possibilities. Every community possesses its own laws, distinguished by the way in which it defines and guarantees the personal rights of its members. Not only did the community of Israel possess its own code of laws, but it was proud of it and considered it as one of the most precious favors received from God (Dt 4,6ff).

OT

While not corresponding exactly to all the meanings of our two words, the Hebrew *mišpat* does convey well enough the basic ideas.

1. *Laws imposed by authority*.* The *mišpat* is the decision promulgated by one having the power to pronounce judgment*, that is, the recognized upholder of authority. In the plural the word is frequently associated with all those who give the orders, commandments, prescriptions, decrees..., in a juridical language that is careful to distinguish the various forms of power. Naturally enough this vocabulary was taken over to describe the law* of God, from the time when the whole of Israel's existence became governed by the divine will* because of the covenant*. In practise, the *mišpatim* given by God to His people formed the Israelitic code of law. It could be called a sacred code,

because it expressed the will of the holy God, but in all sorts of ways it went beyond the sphere of the sacred, the sphere of what strictly concerned worship, and covered the whole of existence.

2. *Laws and justice**. This all-pervading presence of the divine will in Israel's code of laws did not appear exceptional in the ancient East. But what was the pride of the people and bore the mark of the true God was that none of the great nations that ruled the world had received from their gods a code of laws as just as that of Yahweh (Dt 4,6ff). Throughout the Bible, the association of justice and integrity, the link between laws and justice, is a sign of a permanent demand of conscience. It is the message of the prophets (Am 5,7.24; 6,12...; Is 5,7.16...; Jr 4,2; 9,23...); it is the teaching of the wise men (Pr 2,9); and it is one of the main characteristics of the messianic hope (Is 1,27; 11,5; 28,17...). But the first to put this ideal into practise was God Himself (Ps 19,10; 89, 15; 119,7...). "Will the judge of the whole earth not administer justice?" (Gn 18,25).

3. *The rights of the poor*. The association between laws and justice seems to us perfectly natural. What would a code of laws be that paid no attention to justice? And what would become of justice if it did not support the law? But the force and the originality of this association in the Bible comes from the concrete and personal form assumed by law and justice. Justice is not just a matter of respecting a norm, however perfect, nor even simply of ensuring equality of opportunity and of treating each according to his merits. It must find out the real needs of each person, the precise form of attention that he needs in order to find his place among men. This essential requirement, more essential even than bread, is the basis of law, and justice is not true to itself as long as it has not responded to this appeal. Seen in this light, then, law concerns in the first place those who are not in a position to get out of their difficulties, the poor*, the afflicted (Ex 23,6; Is 10,2; Jr 5,28; Jb 36,6.17). Even guilty Israel experiences, in the midst of misfortune, the rights of the unfortunate (Is 40,27; 49,4).

NT

The outlook of the NT is rather different. Although justice continues to occupy an im-

portant place, even the idea of law seems to disappear: perhaps because the people of God is no longer a political people, with the social structures of a nation. Even the Epistle of James, which has, nevertheless, an approach similar to that of the prophets and is concerned about the poor, does not mention their rights. The only NT passage to refer to the *mišpat* is a saying in which Christ defines in three words "the weightier matters of the law —justice (*krisis = mišpat*), mercy (*eleos*) and good faith (*pistis*)" (Mt 23,23; cf Mi 6,8). This shows that Jesus gives full weight to the insistence of the OT on the law, but also that the word belongs more to the OT than the NT.

This disappearance comes from the fact that problems of social justice are less acute in the early Church than in the time of the prophets; it also comes from the increased importance attached to interior dispositions, which are the origin of practical behavior; and above all it comes from the fact that law itself, although just as profoundly personal as that of the OT, is transformed by the Gospel. Its golden rule is in fact: "always treat others as you would like them to treat you" (Mt 7,12). And Jesus' own commandment is: "just as I have loved you, you must also love one another" (Jn 13, 34). There is nothing here to abolish or lessen the concern for the rights of each person shown by the OT. But there is a new inspiration, the call to identify oneself with the other person, a desire to share and a desire for communion, even going as far as the total sacrifice. In the last resort laws can only be based on love.

→Authority — Judgment — Justice — Justification — Law — Liberation/Liberty II 1.2 — Marriage OT II 4—Poor OT II—Trial.

JG ems

ROCK

When Paul identifies the Lord Jesus with the rock of the desert (1 Co 10,40), he unites two themes which up to that point had been distinct. God is the "rock of Israel" (2 S 23,3); out of the rock, the sign of dryness, God has made life-giving water flow.

1. *God, solid as the rock*. The solidity of the rock makes it a shelter that is as safe as a

mountain* for a fugitive. The hollow of the rock offers refuge and safety (Jr 48,28). God is called the rock of Israel because He assures them salvation. Other divine titles used in close connection with *rock* emphasize the same meaning: God is a citadel, refuge, rampart, shield, strong tower, harbor (2 S 22,2f; Ps 18,3. 32; 31,4; 61,4; 144,2); one must put his confidence* in Him, for He is the eternal (Is 26,4; 30,29) and only (44,8) rock. Firm shelter, the rock is also a solid foundation: God is the rock because of His faithfulness* (Dt 32,4; Ps 92,16). He who has faith* in Him will not stumble (Is 28,16); but he who refuses to build his foundation on this rock will crash into it and be broken to pieces against the stone of scandal* (Is 8,14).

In the NT, it is Christ who is the foundation stone* (R 9,33; 1 P 2,6ff); one who listens* to His word builds* on rock (Mt 7,24). And Peter*, the rock on whom the Church is founded, shares this stability (Mt 16,18).

2. *The rock in the hand of God.* The rock on which nothing grows is the symbol of sterility*. Abraham* was a rock, because he was alone before God had blessed and multiplied him (Is 51,1f; cf Mt 3,9). The existence of the people of Israel, formed from this rock, is a sign of the infinite power* of God. In His hand*, the rocks of Palestine produce food (Dt 32,13). Still more, in the desert* of dryness, God manifests before our eyes His dominion over creatures by causing water to flow from arid soil and from the rock of Meribah (Ex 17,6; Nm 20,10f).

In this work* of God, piety sees an anticipation of the eschatological wonders (Ps 78,15-20; 105,41; Is 43,20). In the time of salvation a river will spring from the Temple and transform the holy land into a Paradise (Ez 47,1-12; Ze 14,8). This miracle of grace is accomplished in the gospel: Jesus, on whom the Spirit rested, opens the source of living water* to His followers by giving them the Spirit* (Jn 7,37ff; 19,34); He is the rock of the new people marching toward deliverance. Even from OT times, says Paul, He was the rock from which the people drew the true blessings* in the desert (1 Co 10,4). And He continues to be the one through whom we are able to maintain our stand—not through any human assurance, but through the grace of a faithful God (10,12f).

→Altar 1—God OT IV—Peter—Scandal I 1— Shadow II 1—Stone—Strength I.

MP ecu

RUN

Apart from the literal sense—as when the runners of the royal guard (1 S 22,17) hasten to announce the news of the battle (2 S 18,19-27)—the Bible makes metaphorical use of the word "run" (in Greek: *trecho*; sometimes *dioko*: "to hasten toward," "to pursue" [one's course], and hence, to "persecute") to describe the dynamism of the Word* of God or of those who announce it. Later on, under the influence of the Greek world's sporting competitions, the term will also be used of the "course" of life, life moving toward an objective.

1. *The Word of God runs.* The Word of God is rapid, effective and dynamic: "Down from the heavens, from the royal throne, leapt your all powerful word" (Ws 18,15; cf 1 S 22,17). It bears down upon Job like a warrior (Jb 16,14), with the idea of leaping replacing that of a runner's swiftness: "God sends His word to us, and His word runs swiftly" (Ps 17,15; cf Is 55,11). Perhaps Paul has this passage in mind when he asks for prayer so that "the word of the Lord may finish its race" (2 Th 3,1). The prophets* too, like the king's runners (1 S 8, 11), run to proclaim the Word. "The hand of Yahweh was on Elijah, and tucking his cloak he ran in front of Ahab as far as the outskirts of Jezreel (1 K 18,46). Even the prophets not sent by God do the same: "I have not sent those prophets, yet they are running; I have not spoken to them, yet they are prophecying (Jr 23,21).

2. *Life is a race.* Human existence, which is often compared with a journey (Jn 8,12; 1 Jn 1,6-7), becomes a race, when eager obedience or an urgent mission is suggested. Sometimes it is still a question of the proclamation of the Word, as with John the Baptist, who has finished his course (Ac 13,24f), or with Paul, whose race concerns the proclamation of the Good News (20,24). But the word can also simply refer to the appearance of alacrity that is given by a just life, adding to the metaphor of walking in the ways of God a note of joy, of eagerness and of liveliness: "I ran the way of your commandments, since you have set me free" (Ps 119,32); "those who hope in Yahweh ...put out wings like eagles. They run and do not grow weary" (Is 40,31). In the language of the Songs of Songs, this zeal* of a whole life spent in the service of Yahweh becomes the

eagerness of the bride overwhelmed with joy at the sound of the bridegroom's voice: "draw me in your footsteps, let us run" (Ct 1,4). Is this not the sort of idea that is suggested by the race of Peter and John to the tomb of the Master (Jn 20,4)?

In Paul's writings this race becomes a sporting competition, demanding sacrifices if the victory is to be won (1 Co 9,24-27). The same image, but using a different verb, is used to describe the whole adventure of Paul's life. On the road to Damascus, while in pursuit (*dioko*: in the sense of persecuting*) of the Christians, he is joined by Christ; he does not imagine that by this he has achieved his objective: "I am still running (*dioko*), trying to capture the prize for which Christ Jesus captured me...I forget the past and I strain ahead for what is still to come; I am racing for the finish, for the prize to which God calls us upwards to receive in Christ Jesus" (Ph 3,12ff).

Far from allowing ourselves to be put off by the obstacles (G 5,7), "with so many witnesses (that is to say, spectators in the stadium, the past champions) in a great cloud on every side of us, we too, then, should...keep running (*trechomen*) steadily in the race we have started. Let us not lose sight of Jesus, who leads us in our faith" (He 12,1f), our forerunner (*prodromos*, from *edramon*, the aorist of *trecho*) (6, 20). Then the race will not be in vain (1 Co 9, 26; G 2,2; Ph 2,16), and we should be able to say with Paul: "I have fought the good fight to the end; I have run the race to the finish; I have kept the faith" (2 Tm 4,7). But in all this it must not be forgotten that everything comes from God alone: "That does not depend on what we want, nor on the one who runs, but on God who shows mercy" (R 9,16).

→Way—Word of God OT II 2—Zeal II 2.

XLD ems

S

SABBATH

OT

1. *The institution of the Sabbath.* The word *Sabbath* designates a cessation from work for religious intentions. Its practice appears from the earliest stages of the Law (Ex 20,8; 23,12; 34,21). It probably has a pre-Mosaic origin which remains obscure. In the Bible, it is linked with the sacred rhythm of the week*, which it closes with a day of rest, of rejoicing, and reunion in worship (Ho 2,13; 2 K 4,23; Is 1,13).

2. *Reasons for the Sabbath.* The Covenant Code emphasizes the humanitarian side of this rest which allows slaves a breather (Ex 23,12). This is also the viewpoint of Deuteronomy (Dt 5,12...). But the sacerdotal legislation gives it another meaning. By his work* man imitates the activity of God the creator. By abstaining from work on the seventh day, he imitates the sacred rest* of God (Ex 31,12...; Gn 2,2f). Thus God has given the Sabbath to Israel as a

sign*, so that they might know that He has sanctified them (Ez 20,12).

3. *The observance of the Sabbath.* The Sabbath rest was conceived in a very strict way by the Law: it was forbidden to light a fire (Ex 35,3), to gather wood (Nm 15,32...), or to prepare food (Ex 16,23...). According to the testimony of the prophets, its observation was a condition for realizing the eschatological promises (Jr 17,19-27; Is 58,13f). And so, we see Nehemiah holding firmly to its integral observance (Ne 13,15-22). In order to "make this day holy" (Dt 5,12), there is a "holy assembly" (Lv 23,3), offering of sacrifices (Nm 28,9f), and renewal of the loaves of proposition (Lv 24,8; 1 Ch 9,32). Outside of Jerusalem, these rites are replaced by an assembly in the synagogue, consecrated to common prayer and to interpreted reading of Holy Scripture. At the time of the Maccabees, fidelity to the Sabbath rest is such that the Hasidaeans let themselves be massacred rather than violate it by taking up arms (1 M 2,32-38). Toward the time of the NT, we know

that the Essenes observed it in all its rigor, while the Pharisees elaborated a minute casuistry on the subject.

NT

1. *Jesus* does not explicitly abrogate the law of the Sabbath: on this day He frequents the synagogue and takes advantage of it to preach the gospel (Lk 4,16...). But He removes the formalistic rigorism of the Pharisees: "The Sabbath was made for man, not man for the Sabbath" (Mk 2,27); and the duty of charity takes precedence over the material observance of the rest (Mt 12,5; Lk 13,10-16; 14,1-5). Beyond this, Jesus attributes to Himself power over the Sabbath: the Son of Man is master over it (Mk 2,28). Here we meet one of the complaints that the doctors raise against Him (cf Jn 5,9...). But by doing good on the Sabbath, does He not imitate His Father who, having once entered into His rest at the completion of creation, continues to rule the world and to give life to men (Jn 5,17)?

2. *The disciples of Jesus* continued at first to observe the Sabbath (Mt 28,1; Mk 15,42; 16,1; Jn 19,42). Even after the ascension, the reunions on the Sabbaths serve for preaching the gospel among the Jews (Ac 13,14; 16,13; 17,2; 18,4). But the first day of the week, the day of Jesus' resurrection, very soon becomes the day of the Church's worship, insofar as it is the Lord's day* (Ac 20,7; Ap 1,10). The practices, such as almsgiving (1 Co 16,2) and divine praise, which the Jews of their own accord attached to the Sabbath, are transferred to it. In this new perspective the ancient Sabbath of the Jews acquires a figurative* meaning, just as many other OT institutions. By their rest, men commemorated God's rest on the seventh day. Now Jesus has entered into this divine rest by His resurrection*, and we have been promised a similar entrance following in His footsteps (He 4,1-11). The true Sabbath will come when men rest from their labors in imitation of God who rests from His works (He 4,10; Ap 14,13).

→Feasts—Day of the Lord NT III 3—Numbers I 1, II 1—Rest—Week—Sign OT II 2; NT II 1 —-Time intro 2a, OT I 1—Work I 1, III.

CS & PG ecu

SACRIFICE

A rapid survey of the Bible informs us of the importance and universality of sacrifice. Sacrifice puts its mark on all of history: primitive humanity (Gn 8,20), patriarchal action (Gn 15, 9...), the Mosaic epoch (Ex 5,3), the period of the judges and the kings (Jg 20,26; 1 K 8,64), and the post-exilic age (Ezr 3,1-6). It gives rhythm to the existence of the individual and the community. The mysterious episode of Melchizedek (Gn 14,18), wherein tradition discerns a sacrificial meal, and the liturgical activity of Jethro (Ex 18,12) broadens the horizon even further. Outside of the chosen people (cf Jon 1,16), sacrifice expresses personal and collective piety. The prophets, in their visions of the future, are not oblivious of the offerings of the pagans (Is 56,7; 66,20; Ml 1,11). And so, when the OT writers sketch their fresco of history, they consider sacrifice an essential part of religious life. The NT will make this intuition precise and will consecrate it in a way that is original and definitive.

OT

I. DEVELOPMENT OF SACRIFICIAL RITES

1. *From the original simplicity*...In the earliest period disclosed to our view by biblical history, rites are characterized by a rudimentary sobriety and conform to the mores of nomads or semi-nomads: the erection of altars*, the invocation of the divine name*, the offering of animals or products of the soil (Gn 4,3; 12,7f). There is no fixed place: they sacrifice where God manifests Himself. The primitive altar of turf and the mobile tent (Ex 20,24; 23,15) bear witness, in their own way, to the occasional and provisory character of ancient places of worship*. Neither were there specified ministers: the head of the family or clan and (under the monarchy) the king immolated the victims. But, at an early date, men who were specially chosen assumed this office (Dt 33,8ff; Jg 17). Just as under Josiah the temple* became the only center for all sacrificial activity, so the priests reserved to themselves, with or without the assistance of the levites, the monopoly of sacrifices.

2. ...*to the complexity of rites*. This complexity results from enrichments introduced

through history. Actually, an evolution occurs in the sense of the multiplicity, variety, and specialization of sacrifices. Multiple causes explain this development: the transition from the nomadic and pastoral state to the settled and agricultural life, Canaanite influence, and the growing importance of the priesthood*. Israel assimilates elements borrowed from its neighbors: it filters, corrects, and spiritualizes. In spite of the abuses of popular religion (Mi 6,7; Jg 11,30f; 1 K 16,34), it rejects human victims (Dt 12,31; 18,10; 1 S 15,33 describes not a sacrifice, but the execution of an anathema). Israel was enriched by a cultural heritage from other peoples and thus exercised her function of mediatrix by reorientating toward the true God practises which had been perverted by pagan notions. Its rites became complete and complicated.

II.   THE VARIOUS ASPECTS OF SACRIFICE

1. *From the varied types presented by history* ...The Bible, from the beginning, attests to the coexistence of different types. The holocaust ('ôlah), which was unknown to the Mesopotamians and imported later into Egypt, already figured in the early traditions and the period of the judges (Gn 8,20; Jg 6,21; 11,31; 13,19). The entire victim (bull, lamb, kid, bird) was burnt, to signify that the gift was total and irrevocable. Another category of sacrifice, very widespread among the Semites, consisted essentially in a sacred meal* (*zebah šelamîm*): the faithful ate and drank "before Yahweh" (Dt 12,18; 14, 26). To be sure, every sacred banquet does not necessarily suppose a sacrifice; but in the OT, these communion* banquets do, in fact, imply it: one part of the victim (a large or small animal) was returned by right to God, the master of life (the spilt blood, the consumed fat —"nourishment of God," "food of Yahweh"); whereas the flesh serves to nourish the diners. Expiatory rites were practiced rather early (1 S 3,14; 26,19; 2 S 24,15...; cf Ho 4,8; Mi 6,7). According to an ancient formula (Gn 8,21), preserved and spiritualized (Lv 1,9; 3,16), God accepts the offerings "in the odor of sweetness."

2. *...to the synthesis of Leviticus.* In technical language Leviticus systematically spells out the "gifts" offered to God (Lv 1—7; 22,17-30), bloody or unbloody, (*minhah*): holocaust, food offerings, communion sacrifices (eucharistic*, votive, spontaneous), sacrifice for sin (*hatta't*), sacrifice of reparation (*ašam*). But the rubrics do not stifle the spirit: the minute gestures are charged with a sacred meaning. Thanksgiving* and desire for atonement (Lv 1,4; cf 2 K 12,16; Jb 1,5) inspire the holocaust. Behind a terminology that is at times forbidding, one discovers a refined sense of God's holiness*, obsession with sin*, and an unassuaged need for purification. In this ritual, the notion of sacrifice tends to concentrate on the idea of atonement. Blood* plays a large role in it, but its efficacy is ultimately derived from the divine will (Lv 17,11; cf Is 43,25) and supposes sentiments of repentance*. The reparation of ritual impurities and unconscious faults initiates the faithful practically to purification of heart, just as the laws on purity* and impurity orientate souls toward abstaining from evil. The banquet of the *šelamîm* expresses and realizes in joy* and spiritual well-being the social nature of communion among themselves and with God, for all share the same victim.

III.   FROM RITES TO SPIRITUAL SACRIFICE

1. *Rites as signs of "spiritual sacrifice."* The God of the Bible draws no profit from sacrifices: Yahweh is not considered as man's debtor, but rather, man as God's client. The rites serve to make interior sentiments visible: adoration* (holocaust), concern for intimacy with God (*šelamîm*), confession of sin and desire for pardon* (expiatory rites). Sacrifice appears in the ceremonies of the covenant* with the divinity (cf Gn 8,20ff; 15,9-21; Ex 24,4ff); it consecrates national, family, and individual life, especially on the occasion of pilgrimages and feasts* (1 S 1,3; 20,6; 2 K 16,15). Dialogues (Ex 12,26; 13,8; 24,4ff), profession of faith (Dt 26, 5-11), confession* of sins (1 S 7,6; cf Lv 5,5), and psalms (cf Ps 22,23-30; 27,6; 54,8) often make explicit the spiritual significance of the material act. After Gn 22 (which is possibly the charter of temple sacrifices), God refuses human victims and accepts the immolation of animals; but He accepts these gifts only if they are offered by a heart capable of sacrificing in a spirit of faith* (following the example of the patriarch Abraham*) that which he holds most precious.

2. *Primacy of interior religion.* The temptation

to become attached to the rite while neglecting the meaning persists; hence the warnings of the prophets*. Men are at times deceived with regard to their intentions. The prophets do not condemn the sacrifice as such, but its counterfeits; and, in particular, the Canaanite practices (Ho 2,5; 4,13). Of itself, the multiplicity of rites does not honor God. Formerly, that proliferation did not exist (Am 5,25; Is 43,23f; Jr 7,22ff). Without the proper disposition of the heart, the sacrifice is reduced to a vain and hypocritical gesture; with perverse sentiments, it displeases God (Am 4,4; Is 1,11-16). The prophets vigorously insist, according to the genius of their speech, upon the primacy of the soul* (Am 5,24; Ho 6,6; Mi 6,8). They do not make any innovations; they prolong an ancient (Ex 19,5; 24,7f) and continuous tradition (1 S 15,22; 1 Ch 29,17; Pr 15,8; 21,3.27; Ps 40,7ff; 50, 16-23; 69,31f; Si 34,18ff). The interior sacrifice is not a substitute, but the essential (Ps 51,18f); oftentimes, it takes the place of the rite (Si 35, 1-10; Dn 3,38ff). This spiritual undercurrent, which reappears at Qumrân, denounces piety that is superficial, selfish, or out of harmony with life; and finally questions the rites themselves. In this sense, the prophets anticipate the revelation of the NT regarding the nature of sacrifice.

3. *The summit of interior religion in the OT*. Alongside the legislative synthesis of Leviticus, the Bible offers another synthesis—this one living, for it is incarnate in a person. The Servant* of God, according to Is 53, will offer His death in expiatory sacrifice. The prophetic oracle shows a progress that considerably surpasses the notions of Lv 16. The scapegoat, on the great day of atonement, took away the people's sins; but despite the rite of the imposition* of hands, they were not identified with the sacrificial victim. The doctrine of vicarious penal substitution did not level things off in that liturgy. In contrast, the Servant freely substitutes Himself for sinners. His flawless oblation profits the "multitude" in accordance with God's design. Here the maximum of interiority is coupled to the highest possible gift with the greatest efficacy.

NT

Jesus takes up the prophetic idea of the primacy of the soul over the rite (Mt 5,23f; Mk 12,33). By recalling it, He prepares spirits to understand the meaning of His own sacrifice.

Between the two Testaments, there is a continuity and a transcendence: the continuity is manifested by the application of the OT sacrificial terminology to the death of Christ; the transcendence is manifested by the absolute originality of Jesus' offering. In fact, this transcendence introduces into the world an essentially new reality.

I. JESUS OFFERS HIMSELF IN SACRIFICE

Jesus announces His passion, using word for word the terms which characterized the expiatory sacrifice of the Servant of God: He comes to "serve*," "gives His life," dies "as a ransom" for the benefit of the "multitude" (Mk 10,45 p; Lk 22,37; Is 53,10ff). In addition, the Passover* setting of the farewell supper (Mt 26, 2; Jn 11,55ff; 12,1...; 13,1) establishes an intended and precise relation between the death of Christ and the sacrifice of the paschal Lamb*. Finally, Jesus expressly refers to Ex 24,8 when He appropriates to Himself Moses' formula, "the blood of the covenant" (Mk 14,24 p). The triple reference to the Lamb whose blood* delivers the Jewish people, to the victims of Sinai which seals the ancient covenant*, and to the expiatory death of the Servant demonstrates clearly the sacrificial character of Jesus' death: it obtains remission of sins for mankind, consecrates the permanent covenant and the birth of a new people*, and insures redemption*. These effects highlight the aspect of fecundity in the immolation of Calvary: death* is the source of life*. The pregnant formula of Jn 17,19 reiterates this theme: "For them I consecrate myself in order that they may also be consecrated in truth." The eucharist*, destined to make the unique oblation of the cross* present *in memoriam* (cf Lv 24,7) in the setting of a meal, connects the new rite of the Christians with the ancient sacrifices of communion. And so, Jesus' offering, in its bloody reality and in its sacramental expression, sums up and fulfills* the sacrificial economy of the OT: it is at once a holocaust, *minḥah*, expiatory offering, and sacrifice of communion*. The continuity of the two Testaments is undeniable. But the oblation of Christ, by its unicity, due to the dignity of the Son* of God and the perfection of His offering, and by its universal efficacy, surpasses the many and varied sacrifices of the OT. Old terminology, new content. The reality transcends the categories of thought which serve to express it.

II. THE CHURCH REFLECTS ON THE SACRIFICE OF JESUS

1. *From the sacrifice of Calvary to the eucharistic banquet*. The apostolic writings develop these fundamental ideas under various forms. Jesus becomes "our Passover*" (1 Co 5,7; Jn 19,36); the "immolated Lamb" (1 P 1,19; Ap 5,6) inaugurates the new covenant in His blood (1 Co 11,25), redeems the flock (Ac 20,28), and achieves atonement for sins (R 3,24f) and reconciliation* between God and men (2 Co 5, 19ff; Col 2,14). As in Leviticus, the role of blood* is stressed (R 5,9; Col 1,20; E 1,7; 2,13; 1 P 1,2.18f; 1 Jn 1,7; 5,6ff; Ap 1,5; 5,9). But here a Son's blood is shed at the instigation of His Father. And so, the apostles draw the relationship between the sacrifice of Isaac and that of Jesus. This parallel highlights the perfection of the oblation of Calvary: Christ, "the well-beloved" Son, *agapētos* (cf Mk 12,6; 1,11; 9,7), delivers Himself up to death; and the Father, through love of men, does not spare His own Son (R 8,32; Jn 3,16). And thus the cross* reveals the intimate nature of the sacrifice "of pleasing fragrance" (E 5,2): the sacrifice is, in its spiritual substance, an act of love*. From now on, death*, the destiny of sinful mankind, is placed in an absolutely original perspective (R 5).

In the temple, a table for the loaves of proposition is provided: a "table of the Lord" is also found in the Christian community. Paul expressly compares the eucharist* to the sacred banquets of Israel (1 Co 10,18). But what a difference! The Christians no longer participate only in "holy*" or "very holy" things; they commune with the very body and blood of Christ (1 Co 10,16), the source of eternal life (Jn 6,53-58). This participation signifies and produces the union of the faithful in a single body* (1 Co 10,17). And thus, the ideal sacrifice foretold by Malachi (1,11) becomes a reality valid for all men for all times.

2. *Figures and reality*. The multiple allusions which the gospels and apostolic writings make to the ritual vocabulary of the OT disclose the profound meaning of the ancient liturgy. This latter prepared for and prefigured the redemptory sacrifice. The epistle to the Hebrews makes this doctrine explicit by a systematic comparison of the two economies. Jesus, high priest and victim, founds a convenant between God and His people, just as Moses did on Sinai. Hereafter this covenant is perfect and permanent (He 8,6-13; 9,15—10,18). Furthermore, Christ as high priest on the day of atonement, accomplishes a purifying action. But this time, He abolishes sin by pouring out His own blood, which is more efficacious than that of the temple victims. The faithful no longer obtain only "purity* of the flesh*," but "purification of consciences" (9,12ff). The personality of the pontiff and the excellence of the sanctuary where the sacrifice is consumed—heaven*—guarantee the singular value and the absolute and universal efficacy of the sacrifice of Christ. This sacrifice, archetype of all the others which were only shadows of the reality, does not need to be repeated (10,1.10). The liturgy which according to the Apocalypse (Ap 5,6...) unfolds in heaven around the immolated Lamb is in harmony with the portrayal in the epistle to the Hebrews.

3. *From the sacrifice of the head to the "spiritual sacrifice" of the members*. The prophets insisted on the extension of ritual action into daily life; what is more, Ecclesiasticus likened virtuous conduct to sacrifice (Si 35,1ff). The same spiritual application to the Christian and apostolic life is found in the NT (R 12,1; 15, 16; Ph 2,17; 4,18; He 13,15). The faithful, stimulated by the Spirit who animates them, in vital communion with their Lord, form "a holy priesthood*, with a view to offering spiritual sacrifice, pleasing to God through Jesus Christ" (1 P 2,5).

→Abraham I 2—Altar—Almsgiving OT 3— Animals II 3—Blood OT 3 b; NT 1—Bread II 3, III—Communion OT—Covenant—Death —Eucharist IV 2, V—Expiation—Fire OT II 1 —First Fruits I 2 a, II—Gift OT 3; NT 2— Holy—Lamb of God—Martyr—Meal II— Nourishment I—Passover—Peace I 3—Perfume 2—Priesthood OT II 1; NT I 1.2—Redemption NT 2—Salt 2—Servant of God II 2, III— Temple NT III 1—Wine I 2—Worship.

CH ecu

SADNESS

Joy* is bound to salvation* and the presence* of God. Inversely, sadness is the bitter fruit of sin*, which separates from God. Its apparent causes are various: a trial* indicating that God is hiding His face* (Ps 13,2f), a deceptively wicked wife (Si 25,23), a badly reared son (30, 9f), a traitorous friend* (37,2), one's own folly* (22,10ff) or perversity (36,20), another's slander (Pr 25,23). The Bible does not simply relate man's continual disappointment—man doomed "to drink tears" (Ps 80,6) and not to find a comforter (Qo 4,1)—but discloses sin as the true cause of man's immense misery. A cure is found in the Savior, for sadness comes from sin, while joy is the product of salvation (Ps 51,14).

OT

1. *Good sense and sadness.* The first steps of revelation do not reach the elevated concepts mentioned above. There is first the commonplace reaction, a sort of Stoicism which runs from sadness, even in the knowledge that only fear* of the Lord can insure a joyful life (Si 1, 12f). Even more than sickness (Pr 18,14), sadness depresses the heart (12,25), breaks the spirit (15,13), dries up the bones (17,22). For this reason the sages council: "Do not give yourself over to black thoughts" (Si 30,21); "expel sorrow, which has destroyed many," and cares*, which make men old before their time (30,22). We must, indeed, "grieve with those who grieve" (Si 7,34; cf Pr 25,20); but we must not excessively lament the loss of a dear one: "Be consoled when his spirit has gone" (Si 38,16-23). Wine* is a source of consolation in many sorrows (Pr 31,6f; Qo 9,7; 10,19). If "all joy soon ends in sorrow" (Pr 14,13), do not forget that "there is a time for tears and a time for laughter" (Qo 3,4). However prosaic, these words of advice can help to unmask the guile which cunningly insinuates itself into sadness. These words prepare the way for a yet higher revelation.

2. *Sadness, a sign of sin.* Viewed from a certain angle, covenant history is the education* of Israel by the sadness caused by merited chastisements. This education implies an awareness of separation from God. As a sanction for the sin of idolatry at Sinai, Yahweh "will no longer personally accompany His people." Holiday garments should be cast off as a sign of mourning and separation (Ex 33,4ff). The same rhythmic pattern is felt at the entrance to the promised land (Js 7,6f.11f) and during the period of the judges (Jg 2): sin, remoteness from God, punishment which begets sadness. The

prophets are to reveal this sadness by denouncing the illusory peace* of a sinful people. This they do by first allowing themselves to plunge to the depths of sadness. Jeremiah is a model. His own sorrowful cries should be those of the people. Before approaching war (Jr 4, 19), before famine (8,18), before misfortune (9,1), he is the contrite conscience of a sinful people (9,18; 13,17; 14,17). He lives in banishment, a witness against the people (15,17f; 16, 8f). Ezekiel does the same, but in an opposite way: he is not to weep for his wife, "delight of his eyes," so hardened is the granite heart of Israel (Ex 24,15-24).

3. *A sadness agreeable to God.* The prophetic mission is also to assure true compunction. Sadness certainly expresses itself powerfully in cries and gestures: fasting* (Jg 20,26), rent garments (Jb 2,12), sackcloth and ashes (2 S 12, 16; 1 K 20,31f; Lm 2,10; Jl 1,13f; Ne 9,1; Dn 9,3), cries and lamentations (Is 22,12; Lm 2,18f; Ez 27,30ff; Es 4,3). But sometimes these penitential liturgies deserve to be stigmatized by the prophets (Ho 6,1-6; Jr 3,21—4,22). For, if one must weep, it is not so much for gifts lost as for the absent Lord (Ho 7,14). Tears are no substitute for fidelity to the Law (Ml 2,13). Acts of penitence should express genuine contrition: "Rend your hearts and not your garments" (Jl 2,12f). Under these conditions such demonstrations are worthwhile (Ne 9,6-37; Ezr 9,6-15; Dn 9,4-19; Ba 1,15—3,8; Is 63,7—64,11). Tears draw God's compassion (Lm 1,2; 2,11.18; Ps 6,7f); sadness is an acknowledgment of the sinner's state: "Lord, gather my tears in your bottle" (Ps 56,9).

4. *Sadness and hope.* Heartbreak does not kill hope*. On the contrary, it calls to the Savior who wills not the death but the life of a sinner (Ez 18,23). Throughout the exile, recognized as the outstanding example of chastisement for sins committed, Israel had a glimmering hope that one day sadness would forever cease. Rachel wept for her deported children and would not be consoled. But Yahweh intervenes: "Cease your weeping; dry your eyes!" (Jr 31, 15ff). The prophet of the Lamentations, changed to a messenger of consolation*, proclaims a hope: "They departed in tears; I will lead them back in consolation. I will change their mourning to gladness; I will console and gladden them after their misery" (31,12f). Then on the heart of a Zion that did not want to sing joyful songs in exile (Ps 137) will the Book of Consolation

pour its soothing balm (Is 40—55; 35,10; 57,18; 60,20; 61,2f; 65,14; 66,10.19). "Those who plant in tears reap in song" (Ps 126,5; cf Ba 4,23; Tb 13,14). Surely sin and sadness can return once more (Ezr 10,1). The hope is that thereby only the city of chaos will be submerged (Is 24, 7-11), while on the mountain of God "the Lord will wipe way the tears of every face" (25,8).

Such is not, however, the last word of the OT. This vision of heaven, appearing again in the Apocalypse (Ap 21,4), does not conceal the sorrowful reality of the path leading to an eternal joy. There must be one day mourning over the "one who has been pierced" in order that the inexhaustible source of joy be opened in the bosom of the city (Ze 12,10f).

NT

1. *The sadness of Jesus Christ.* He who took away the sin of the world had to be overwhelmed, though never absolutely crushed, by the boundless sadness of men. Like the prophets, He was deeply distressed by the hardhearted Pharisees (Mk 3,5). He lamented Jerusalem's unawareness of the hour of its visitation* (Lk 19,41). Besides His sadness for the chosen people, Jesus wept over death*, over Lazarus, His friend already several days dead (Jn 11,35). This is not simply a matter of purely human friendship as the Jews* thought (11,36f); for Jesus shuddered interiorly a second time (11, 38), doubtless because He loved Lazarus with a love that came from His Father (15,9). But He had already groaned a first time and was troubled (11,33.38) at the sobbing which gave shocking expression to the reality of death which He was about to confront at the tomb of an already decaying Lazarus.

Not only in the face of death, but by death itself did Jesus wish to undergo "sadness and anguish," "to be sad to the point of dying" (Mt 26,37f p), with a sadness really the same as death. Was not His will in conflict with God's, creating a chasm which only persistent prayer could fill? But, when He gathered into His prayer the cries and tears of all men who face death, He was heard (He 5,7). On the cross, when He will express the Father's abandonment in which He feels Himself dying, He uses the confident psalm of the persecuted just one (Mt 27,46 p). In Luke's interpretation, this will be handing Himself over to the one who seems to forsake Him (Lk 23,46). Sadness is then conquered by the sinless one who commits Himself to sadness.

2. *Blessed are they who weep* (Lk 6,21)! He who felt the depth of sadness could in advance beatify not sorrow as such but sadness joined to His redemptive joy. There are types of sadness. "The sadness that God approves results in repentance that leaves no regret. The world's sadness ends in death" (2 Co 7,10). This Pauline statement is illustrated by familiar examples. Consider, on the one hand, a young man who goes away sad because he prefers his wealth* to Jesus (Mt 19,22); this is a distant harbinger of James condemning the rich and promising them eternal death (Jm 5,1). Recall also the disciples in Gethsemani, weighed down by sleep* and by grief, ready to abandon their master (Lk 22,45). Then there is Judas. Treason severs him from Jesus, so he gives up hope (Mt 27,3ff). Such is the world's* sadness. Opposed to this is the sadness that God approves. Such sadness afflicts the disciples at the thought of the treason that threatens Jesus (Mt 26,22). Peter sadly weeps because he denied his Lord (26,75). The disciples from Emmaus trudge along sadly at the thought of Jesus who has left them (Lk 24,17). Mary sobs because someone has taken away her Lord (Jn 20,11ff). The principle distinguishing these two types of sadness is love of Jesus. The sinner must experience that sadness which sets him apart from the world to attach him to Jesus. And he who is devoted to Jesus knows no sadness other than separation from Him.

3. *Joy is born of sadness.* One beatitude promises consolation* to those who weep. Yet Jesus had said that there would be weeping when the bridegroom would be taken away (Mt 9,15). The discourse after the last supper reveals the profound meaning of sadness. Jesus had been the cause of Rachel's renewed weeping for the innocent children (Mt 2,18). Nor did He fear to sadden His mother by the demands of His Father's business (Lk 2,48f). Clearly, at the last supper, He does not deny that His leaving will be a source of sadness. Were this not the case, He would not be the one without whom life is death. He also knows that the world* will rejoice at His disappearance (Jn 16,20). Hence, by the comparison often used to describe the birth of a new world (Is 26,17; 66,7-14; R 8, 22), He alludes to the joy of a woman who has brought a man into the world after first enduring the pain of labor (Jn 16,21). Thus "your sadness will turn into joy" (16,20). Sadness is over; or rather, it has now become joy. An instance is found in the wounds forever marking the heavenly Lamb as slaughtered (Ap 5,6).

Henceforth sadness is turned into permanent joy (Jn 16,22); for it comes from Him who is standing erect beyond the gates of death. This joy springs from trouble and fear (14,27) and tribulations (16,33). Jesus' disciples are no longer sad; they are not in solitude*, as seemingly abandoned orphans (14,18), nor are they consigned to a persecuting world (16,2f). The person of the resurrected Christ confers on them His own delight (17,13; 20,20).

From now on, trials (He 12,5-11; 1 P 1,6ff; 2, 19), separation from deceased brethren (1 Th 4, 13), or even from non-believers (R 9,2)—nothing can liquidate the believer's joy or sever him from the love of God (R 8,39). Seemingly sad, yet really in a state of perpetual joy (2 Co 6,10), the Lord's disciple may tread somber paths. Yet he is acquainted with a heavenly joy that will perpetually permeate the chosen ones. God will remain with them forever to dry every tear (Ap 7,17; 21,4).

→Ashes 2—Cares 2—Consolation—Deception/ Disappointment—Joy—Suffering.

MP & XLD dfb

SALT

1. *Salt and the desert region.* The inhabitants of Palestine lived near the Dead Sea, called according to old texts "the Salt Sea" (Gn 14,3; Js 3,16; 12,3...), which stretched south through the Valley of Salt (2 S 8,13; 2 K 14,7). These salty lands were real uninhabited deserts (Jr 17,6; Ps 107,34; Jb 39,6); it is as if they have been the victim of punishment*, and salt the instrument of the punishment: thus, Lot's wife was turned into a pillar of salt (Gn 19,26); and we are told that salt was sown on the defeated city (Jg 9,45). A similar threat is made against the wicked (Zp 2,9), and "nothing will grow any more in those places" (Dt 29,22*). Nevertheless one day water* will triumph: while the marshes and lakes will be abandoned to the salt (Ez 47,11), the river flowing from the right hand side of the temple will make the Salt Sea wholesome (47,8), so much so that life will abound even in these places (47,8f).

2. *Rites and Purifications.* In the ancient sacrificial rites the offerings must all be salted (Lv 2, 13; Ez 43,24). Is the idea to give flavour to the "food of God" (Lv 21,6.8.17.22) or to confirm what is suggested by "the salt of the covenant of God" (2,13), that is, as is noted later on, a lasting covenant? It is difficult to say. But, as in the case of incense (Ex 30,35), it seems likely that salt has a purifying* function, as is suggested by Elisha making "foul water" wholesome (2 K 2,19-22). Perhaps we must also see in the custom of rubbing salt on the new-born (Ez 16,4) a ritual gesture similar to exorcism rather than any concern for hygiene. And this purifying function may be connected with the saying of Jesus: "everyone will be salted by fire" (Mk 9,49); for fire* tries and purifies (1 Co 3,13).

3. *Flavor and duration.* Salt is one of the most necessary commodities in the life of man (Si 39, 26); thus, to "eat the salt of the palace" (Esd 4,14) means to receive one's "salary" (cf lat. *sal*) from the king. Salt gives flavor to food (Jb 6,6). And since it also has the property of preserving food (Ba 6,27), it comes to signify the lasting quality of a contract: a "covenant* of salt" (Nm 18,19) is a perpetual pact like that of God with David (2 Ch 13,5).

Amongst the sayings of Jesus that still remain obscure, the ones concerning the metaphor of salt are notorious. "But if the salt loses its taste, how can it be seasoned again?" (Lk 14,34; Mk 9,50). One possible meaning of this could refer to the "salt of the covenant," and it would then mean that the covenant with the Lord cannot be renewed once it is broken. According to Matthew's interpretation, the believer must be "the salt of the earth" (Mt 5,13), that is to say he must preserve and give flavor to the world of men through his covenant with God. Otherwise he is good for nothing any more, and the disciples deserve to be thrown outside (Lk 14, 35). But "salt is a good thing...have salt in yourselves and be at peace with one another" (Mk 9,50) is a saying for which we may be able to find a commentary in Paul: "Let your language be always agreeable, seasoned with salt, so that you may be able to reply to each one as you should" (Col 4,6).

→Desert O—Fire NT II 2—Nourishment.

XLD ems

SALVATION

The notion of salvation (gr. *sôzô* and derivatives) is expressed in Hebrew by a whole collection of roots, which are all related to the same

SALVATION

fundamental experience: to be saved is to be taken out of a dangerous situation in which one risked perishing. According to the nature of the danger, the act of saving manifests itself in protection, liberation, ransom, cure and health, victory, life peace...Using such a human experience as a starting point, and borrowing the very terms in which it was expressed, revelation has explained one of the most essential aspects of God's action on earth: God saves men, Christ is our Savior (Lk 2,11), the gospel brings salvation to every believer (R 1,16). We have here, then, a key word in biblical language; but its final overtones must not make us forget its slow process of development.

OT

I. GOD'S SALVATION IN HISTORY AND ESCHATOLOGY

The notion of a God who saves His faithful is common to all religions. In the OT it is a recurrent and venerable theme; witness the proper names with the root *to save* in their composition: (Joshua*, Isaiah, Elisha, and Hosea, to cite only the principal root, *yāša'*). But the historical experience of God's people gives the word a special coloring which explains, in part, its use in prophetic eschatology.

1. *The historical experience.* When Israel found herself in a time of crisis from which God delivered her, whether by a providential conjunction of circumstances which might go so far as to be a miracle*, or by sending her a human leader to bring her to victory, she experienced "God's salvation." The siege of Jerusalem by Sennacherib is a classic example of such a situation: the king of Assyria dares Yahweh to save Israel (2 K 18,30-35); Isaiah promises salvation (2 K 19,34; 20,6); and God indeed saves His people. Sacred historians reveal many such experiences in ancient times. God saved David (i.e., gave him victory) everywhere he went (2 S 8,6.14; 23,10.12). Using David as a medium, He saved His people from the hands of their enemies (2 S 3,18), as He had already done with Saul (1 S 11,13), Samuel (1 S 7,8), Samson (Jg 13,5), Gideon (Jg 6,14), and all the judges (Jg 2,16.18). Especially at the time of the exodus God saved Israel, by ransoming and liberating* her (Ex 14,13; cf Is 63,8f; Ps 106,8.10.21). Going even farther back into the past than this dominant experience, we find God saving the sons of

Jacob through the medium of Joseph (Gn 45,5), saving the life of Lot (Ws 10,6), saving Noah* at the time of the flood* (Ws 10,4; cf Gn 7,23)... We understand, then, why in every time of impending disaster Israel turns to Yahweh "in order to be saved" (Jr 4,14) and complains if the anticipated salvation fails to come (Jr 8,20). She knows that besides her God there is no savior (Is 43,11; cf 47,15; Ho 13,4); and, thinking of past incidents of salvation, she is fond of calling on Him under this title (cf Is 63,8; 1 M 4,30). It is true that even in this history the outline of a providential law can be seen more than once, with consequences that will become clear in the context of eschatology: amid the dangers caused by human sin*, only a Remnant* is saved (like Noah at the time of the flood). Salvation does not take place without a divine judgment accompanying it and the just being set apart from the sinners.

2. *Eschatological promises.* It is at times of great national trial that Israel looks with most confidence to God who will save her (cf Mi 7, 7). His title "Savior" becomes a major theme of prophetic eschatology (Zp 3,17; Is 33,32; 43,3; 45,15.21; 60,16; Ba 4,22); prophecies concerned with "the last days" describe under various aspects the final salvation of Israel. Yahweh, says Jeremiah, will save His people by bringing them back to their land (Jr 31,7) and by sending them the Messiah-King* (Jr 23,6). Yahweh, says Ezekiel, will save His sheep by bringing them back to good pastures (Ex 34,22); He will save His people from all their impurities by giving them the gift of His Spirit* (Ez 36,29). The Message of Consolation and the literature of revelation constantly evoke the image of a God who comes to save His people (Is 35,4) and, beyond Israel, the whole earth (Is 45,22). Salvation is the essential act of His victorious justice* (cf 63,1); to achieve it He will send His Servant* (Is 49,6.8). Note also that the pair of words *justice* and *salvation* tends to become a technical designation for His eschatological task, promised and hailed beforehand with enthusiasm (Is 46,13; 52,7-10; 56,1; 59,17; 61,10; 62,1. But even more than in the history of Israel, the experience of this salvation will be reserved for a Remnant* (Am 3,12; 5,15; 9,8; Is 10,20f; 28,5): and before it comes, the judgment of God will take place here below.

The post-exilic descriptions of the day* of Yahweh will sing of the joy* of the salvation (Is 12,2; 25,9) given to all who call on the name* of the Lord (Jl 3,5), to all those who are written

519

down in His book* (Dn 12,1). Finally, the Alexandrine Wisdom will describe the salvation of the just on the last day (Ws 5,2). Thus, in this series of texts, the idea of salvation is filled out by a whole scale of harmonizing notes. Connected with the kingdom* of God, it is synonymous with peace* and happiness (Is 52,7), with purification* (Ez 36,29), and with liberation* (Jr 31,7). Its human artificer, the eschatological king, also merits the title of savior (Ze 9,9 LXX); for he will save the oppressed poor (Ps 72,4.13). All these elements of prophecy directly prepare for the NT.

II. GOD'S SALVATION IN THE PRAYER OF ISRAEL

With such a background of historical experience and of prophecy, Israel's prayer gives a very high place to the salvation theme.

1. *The certitudes of faith.* Salvation is a gift of God: it is the fundamental certitude, in support of which one can recall the experience of conquest (Ps 44,4.7f). It is useless to entertain a presumptuous confidence* in human strength* (Ps 33,16-19): the salvation of the just comes from Yahweh (Ps 37,39f); He Himself is salvation (Ps 27,1; 35,3; 62,7). This doctrine is confirmed by many experiences. How many men in danger were saved by God when they cried out to Him (Ps 107,13.19.28; cf 22,6)! Numerous prayers of thanksgiving testify to deeds of this kind (vg Ps 118,14): the prayers of people saved from danger (Ps 18,20), from trial (Si 51, 11), from imminent death (Ps 116,6). The later books are fond of recounting similar stories: the three children saved from the fire (Dn 3,28 =95), Daniel snatched from the lion pit (Dn 6,28); for God always saves the man who hopes in Him (Dn 13,60). He assures all His servants of this (Ps 91,14ff), just as He has promised it for His people (Ps 69,36) and for His anointed one (Ps 20,7). The psalms list all the clients of God, those whom He has the habit of saving when they call upon Him: the just* (34,16.19), the poor* (34,7; 109,31), the meek* (18,28; 76, 10; 149,4), the little ones (116,6), the persecuted* (55,17), the righteous (7,11), the downcast (34, 19), and, in general, all those who fear Him (145,19). Here is something to inspire confidence and move to prayer.

2. *Appeals to God the Savior.* Suppliants invoke God under the title of Savior (Si 51,1;

"Savior of those without hope" Jdt 9,11) or "God of salvation" (Ps 51,16; 79,9). The content of their prayer is, in a word: "Save, Yahweh!" (Ps 118,25); "Save me, and I will be saved" (Jr 17,14). The remainder usually deal with concrete circumstances like those in which everyone finds himself at some time or another: trial* and suffering (Ps 86,2), imminent and mortal danger (69,2.15), the persecution* of enemies (22,22; 31,12.16; 43,1; 59,2). Sometimes Yahweh Himself answers the prayer by a prophecy of salvation (Ps 12,2.6). Over and above individual requests, the Israelite soul also appeals in her prayers to the eschatological salvation promised by the prophets (cf Ps 14,7; 80,3f.8.20): "Save us, Yahweh our God, and bring us back together from the midst of the nations!" (Ps 106, 47). Here again Yahweh answers through a prophecy (Ps 85,5.8.10). The message of consolation has such great influence that certain psalms sing in advance of the manifestation of the salvation that the message predicted (Ps 96, 2; 98,1ff), while others express the hope of feeling the joy of this salvation (Ps 51,14). Throughout all these texts we see how the soul of Israel, on the threshhold of the NT, is reaching out toward the salvation which Christ is about to bring to the world.

NT

I. THE REVELATION OF SALVATION

1. *Jesus, Savior of men.*

a) It is primarily by significant acts that Jesus reveals Himself as Savior. He saves the sick* by curing them (Mt 9,21 p; Mk 3,4; 5,23; 6,56); He saves Peter walking on the water and the disciples caught in the storm (Mt 8,25; 14, 30). The essential thing is to have faith in Him: it is their faith* which saves the sick (Lk 8,48; 17,19; 18,42); the disciples find themselves reproached for having doubted (Mt 8,26; 14,31). These facts already reveal the plan of salvation; yet, we must look beyond mere physical salvation. Jesus brings to men a much more important kind of salvation: the sinful woman is saved because He remits her sins (Lk 7,48ff), and salvation enters the house of the penitent Zaccheus (Lk 19,9). To be saved, then, one must accept in faith the gospel of the kingdom (cf Lk 8,12). As for Jesus, salvation is His life's purpose: He has come to the earth to save that which was lost (Lk 9,56; 19,10), to save the world and not to condemn it (Jn 3,17; 12,47). If He speaks, it is to save men (Jn 5,34). He is the gate*: whoever enters by way of Him will be saved (Jn 10,9).

b) These words help us see that it is the salvation of men which is the essential problem. Sin puts them in danger of perdition. Satan* is close by, ready to try anything to destroy them, to prevent them from being saved (Lk 8,12). These are the lost sheep (Lk 15,4.7); but Jesus has been sent precisely for them (Mt 15,24): they will no longer be lost if they join His flock (Jn 10,28; cf 6,39; 17,12; 18,9). The salvation which He offers, however, has a reverse side: for one who does not take the opportunity for this salvation, the risk of perdition is imminent and irreparable. A man must do penance while he has time, if he does not wish to be lost (Lk 13,3.5). He must enter by the narrow gate if he wishes to be among the saved (Lk 13,23f). He must persevere on this path up to the very end (Mt 24,13). The demand for detachment is so great that the disciples ask among themselves "Who then will be saved?" Indeed, this would be impossible for men: an act of God's omnipotence is required (Mt 19,25f p). Finally, the salvation which Jesus offers is presented under the form of a paradox: he who wishes to save himself will lose himself; whoever accepts the loss of himself will save himself for life eternal (Mt 10,39; Lk 9,24; Jn 12,25). This is the law, and Jesus Himself submits to it: He who has saved others does not save Himself at the hour of the cross* (Mk 15,30f). The Father could certainly have saved Him from death (He 5,7); but it was for this hour* that He came (Jn 12, 27). Whoever seeks salvation through faith in Him must follow* Him even to this point.

2. *The gospel of salvation.*

a) After the resurrection and Pentecost, the message of the apostolic community has for its object salvation achieved in accordance with the Scriptures. By His resurrection* Jesus has been established by God as "prince and Savior" (Ac 5,31; cf 13,23). The miracles* performed by the apostles confirm their message: if the sick have been saved in virtue of the name* of Jesus, it is because there is no other name by which we can be saved (Ac 4,9-12; cf 14,3). The gospel defines itself as the "Word of salvation" (Ac 13, 26); cf 11,14), addressed first to the Jews (Ac 13, 26) and then to other nations (Ac 13,47; 28,28). Men are asked, in return, to have faith, that

they may "save themselves from this perverse generation*" (Ac 2,40). The condition for salvation is faith* in the Lord Jesus (Ac 16,30f; cf Mk 16,16) and the invocation of His name (Ac 2,21; cf Jl 3,5). In this regard, Jews and pagans are in the same position. They do not save themselves; it is the grace* of the Lord Jesus that saves them (Ac 15,11). The apostles, then, offer men the only "way of salvation" (Ac 16,17). The proselytes were so conscious of this fact that they regarded themselves as the remnant* which must be saved (Ac 2,47).

b) This importance of the salvation theme in early preaching explains why the evangelists Matthew and Luke wished to underline Jesus' role as Savior from His infancy. Matthew links this role with His name, which means "Yahweh saves" (Mt 1,21). Luke gives Him the title "Savior" (Lk 2,11). He makes Zechariah hail the coming dawn of salvation promised by the prophets (1,69.71.77); and Simeon hails the apparition here on earth of that salvation, in a completely cosmic perspective (2,30). Finally, the preaching of John the Baptist, following the Scriptures, makes ready the ways of the Lord so that "all flesh may see the salvation of God" (3,2-6; cf Is 40,3ff; 52,10). The memories preserved in the course of the gospels present in a concrete way that manifestation of salvation which will culminate in the cross and the resurrection.

II. A CHRISTIAN THEOLOGY OF SALVATION

Although the apostolic writings have recourse to a varied vocabulary in describing the redemptive* work of Jesus, we can still attempt to construct a synthesis of Christian doctrine around the idea of salvation.

1. *Meaning of the life of Christ.* "God desires the salvation of all men" (1 Tm 2,4; cf 4,10). For this reason He has sent His Son as Savior of the world* (1 Jn 4,14). When "our God and Savior" (Tt 2,13) who came to save sinners (1 Tm 1,15) appeared here on earth, the grace and love of God our Savior (Tt 2,11; 3,4) were made known; for Christ, through His death and resurrection, became for us the "principle of eternal salvation" (He 5,9), savior of the body* which is the Church* (E 5,23). The title of Savior thus suits equally well the Father (1 Tm 1,1; 2,3; 4,10; Tt 1,3; 2,10) and Jesus (Tt 1,4; 2,

13; 3,6; 2 P 1,11; 2,20; 3,2.18). This is why the gospel which reports these truths is an "instrument of God's power* for the salvation of every believer" (R 1,16). In preaching it, an apostle* has no other purpose but the salvation of men (1 Co 9,22; 10,33; 1 Tm 1,15), whether pagans (R 11,11) or Jews, of whom at least a remnant* has been saved (R 9,27; 11,14), while expecting that all Israel will finally be saved (R 11,26).

2. *Meaning of the Christian life.* Once the gospel is proposed to men by the preaching of the apostles, the former have a choice which will determine their lot: salvation or doom (2 Th 2,10; 2 Co 2,15), life* or death*. Those who believe and confess* their faith are saved (R 10, 9f.13); their faith* having been sealed, besides, by baptism*, an actual experience of salvation (1 P 3,21). God saves them purely out of mercy* without considering their works (2 Tm 1,9; Tt 3, 5), by means of grace* (E 2,5.8), giving them the Holy Spirit (2 Th 2,13; E 1,13; Tt 3,5f). From this moment, the Christian must guard faithfully the Word* which can save his soul* (Jm 1,21); he must nourish his faith through acquaintance with the Scriptures (2 Tm 3,15) and he must make it bear fruit in good works* (Jm 2,14); he must labor with fear* and trembling "to accomplish his salvation" (Ph 2,12). This supposes a constant exercise of salutary virtues (1 Th 5,8), thanks to which he will grow with regard to his salvation (1 P 2,2). No negligence is permitted; salvation offers itself at every moment of life (He 2,3); "now is the day* of salvation" (2 Co 6,2).

3. *Expectation of final salvation.* If we are heirs of salvation (He 1,14) and fully justified* (R 5,1), we are not yet, for all that, saved except in hope* (R 8,24). God has set us aside for salvation (1 Th 5,9), but ours is a heritage that will not be made manifest until the end of time* (1 P 1,5). The toil of Christian life imposes itself because each day that passes brings salvation closer to us (R 13,11). Salvation, then, in the strongest sense of the word, is to be considered eschatologically as the day* of the Lord (1 Co 3,1ff; 5,5). Already reconciled* with God by the death of His Son, and justified* by His blood*, we will then be saved by Him from the wrath* (R 5,9ff). Christ will come to present us with salvation (He 9,28). We also await this final manifestation of the Savior, who will complete His task in transforming our body* (Ph 3,20f); and it is in this respect that our salvation is an object of hope (R 8,23ff). Then

will we be delivered from sickness*, suffering*, and death*; all the evils from which the psalmists begged to be delivered and over which Jesus, while living on earth, triumphed through His miracles, will be definitively wiped out. The accomplishment of such a task will be the victory of God and of Christ. It is in this sense that the liturgical acclamations of the Apocalypse testify: "To our God, and to the Lamb, belongs all saving power" (Ap 7,10; 12,10; 19,1).

→Beatitude—Cup 3—Day of the Lord—Death OT III—Faith NT III—Flood—Gospel IV 2 a —Heaven IV—Hope OT III—Joshua—Joy NT I 1—Judgment—Justice O; *A* II NT; *B* I—Law *C* III 2—Liberation/Liberty—Mercy OT I 2— Miracle II 2—Pardon II 1.2—Peace I 3, III 1— Plan of God—Power IV—Predestine 2.3—Prophet OT IV 2—Reconciliation I 3—Redemption —Revelation NT II 1 a—Servant of God III 1.2 —Sickness/Healing OT II 2.3; NT II—Spirit of God OT I—Victory—Visitation—Will of God —Word of God NT II 1—Works OT I 1; NT I 2—World OT II 3, III 2—Worship NT III 1.

CL & PG ecu

SATAN

By the name of Satan (hb. *satan*, enemy, adversary) or the devil (gr. *diabolos*, the slanderer), names occurring with almost equal frequency in the NT, the Bible designates a personal being, invisible in himself, but whose action or influence reveals itself sometimes in the activity of other beings (demons or unclean spirits) and sometimes in temptation. On this point, furthermore, in contrast to later Judaism and to the majority of the literatures of the ancient Near East, the Bible makes use of an extreme restraint, limiting itself to informing us of the existence of this personage and of his wiles, and of the means to fortify ourselves against them.

I. THE OPPONENT OF GOD'S PLAN FOR HUMANITY

1. The OT speaks of Satan only very rarely and then in a form which, preserving the transcendence of the one God, carefully avoids everything that could incline Israel to a dualism to which it was only too prone. Rather than an opponent properly so called, Satan appears as

one of the angels of the court of Yahweh, filling at the celestial tribunal a function parallel to that of the public prosecutor, entrusted with insuring respect on the earth for the justice and the rights of God. Nonetheless, beneath this pretended service of God, there is already discernible in Jb 1—3 a will hostile, if not to God Himself, at least to man and to His justice*. He does not believe in disinterested love (Jb 1,9), but without being a "tempter" he waits for Job to succumb; and secretly he desires it so that one feels that he would rejoice in Job's fall. In Ze 3,1-5, the accuser transforms himself into a veritable foe of the loving designs of God for Israel. In order that Israel may be saved, the angel of Yahweh must first impose silence on him in the very name of God: "May the Lord command you!" (Jude 9: Vulg.).

2. But the reader of the Bible knows that a mysterious being has played a cardinal role since the origin of humanity. Genesis speaks only of the serpent. A creature of God "like all the rest" (Gn 3,1), this serpent is, however, endowed with a knowledge and a cleverness which surpass man's. Above all, since his entry onto the scene, he is present as the enemy of human nature. Envious of the happiness of man (cf Ws 2,24), he arrives at his end by using weapons which will always be his, cunning and deceit: "the most cunning of all the animals of the fields" (Gn 3,1), the "deceiver" (Gn 3,13; R 7,11; Ap 12,9; 20,8ff), "murderer and liar from the beginning" (Jn 8,44). The Book of Wisdom gives to this serpent its true name: it is the devil (Ws 2,24).

II. THE ENEMY OF CHRIST

Since the first episode of its history, humanity, though conquered, nonetheless envisions that one day it will triumph over its adversary (Gn 3,15). The victory* of man over Satan is itself in fact the end of the mission of Christ, who has come to "reduce to impotence him who held the rule of death, the devil" (He 2,14); to "destroy his works" (1 Jn 3,8). In other words, to substitute the reign of His Father for that of Satan (1 Co 15,24-28; Col 1,13f). Thus the gospels present His public life as a struggle against Satan. The struggle begins with the episode of the temptation, where for the first time since the scene in Paradise*, a man* representing humanity, "son of Adam" (Lk 3,38), finds Himself face to face with the devil. The struggle is in-tensified by the deliverance of possessed persons (cf evil* spirits), a proof that "the kingdom of God is come" (Mk 3,22ff p) and that that of Satan has come to its end (cf Lk 10,17-20). The struggle is even evident from the cures of persons who are merely ill (cf Ac 10,38). The battle also continues more artfully in the effrontery which opposes Christ to the unbelieving Jews, those true "sons of the devil" (Jn 8,44; cf Mt 13,38), the "broods of vipers" (Mt 3,7ff; 12,34; 23,23). It reaches its paroxysm at the hour of the passion. Luke consciously links the passion to the temptation (Lk 4,13; 22,53), and John underlines the role of Satan in it (Jn 13,2.27; 14,30; cf Lk 22,3.31) only to proclaim his final defeat. Satan seems to call the play; but in reality "he has no power over Christ." All is the work of the love and obedience of the Son (Jn 14,30; cf redemption*). At the very moment when he believes himself certain of victory, the "prince of this world" is "cast down" (Jn 12,31; cf 16,11; Ap 12,9-13). The kingdom of the world which he had once dared to offer to Jesus (Lk 4,6) henceforth belongs to the dead and glorified Christ (Mt 28,18; cf Ph 2,9).

III. THE ENEMY OF CHRISTIANS

If the resurrection of Christ marks the defeat of Satan, the struggle will only be concluded, according to Paul, with the last act of "the history of salvation" on the "day of the Lord*," when "the Son, having reduced to impotence every principality and every power and death itself, will render the kingdom to His Father, in order that God may be all in all" (1 Co 15, 24-28).

Like Christ, the Christian will run afoul of the adversary. It is he who prevents Paul from going to Thessalonica (1 Th 2,18); and "the sting planted in his flesh," an obstacle in his apostolate, is "a messenger of Satan" (2 Co 12, 7-10). The gospel had already identified Satan with the enemy* who sows the cockle in the field of the father of the household (Mt 13,39), or who snatches the seed of the Word of God from the heart of men, "for fear that they believe and be saved" (Mk 4,15 p). In his turn Peter represents him as a greedy lion who ceaselessly roams about among the faithful, seeking whom he may devour (1 P 5,8). As in Paradise* he plays essentially the role of a tempter, endeavoring to lead men to sin (1 Th 3,5; 1 Co 7,5) and thus to oppose them to God Himself (Ac 5,3). Even more, behind that personified

SCANDAL

power which he calls sin, Paul ordinarily seems to suppose the action of Satan, the father of sin (comp R 5,12 and Ws 2,24; R 7,7 and Gn 3,13). Finally, if it is true that Antichrist* is already at work here below, it is the power of Satan which hides itself beneath his evil action (2 Th 2,7ff).

Thus the Christian—and this is the tragedy of his destiny—must choose between God and Satan, between Christ and Belial (2 Co 6,14), between the "evil one" and the "true one" (1 Jn 5,18f). On the last day, he will be forever with one or the other.

A spirit who is formidable by reason of his "wiles," his "deceits," his "traps," his "maneuvers" (2 Co 2,11; E 6,11; 1 Tm 3,7; 6,9...), loving to "disguise himself as an angel of light" (2 Co 11,14), Satan, despite all this, remains an enemy already vanquished. United to Christ by faith (E 6,10) and by prayer (Mt 6,13; 26,41 p) —while the prayer of Jesus supports his own (Lk 22,32; cf R 8,34; He 7,25)—the Christian is certain of conquering: only he will be conquered who so consents (Jm 4,7; E 4,27).

At the end of revelation, the Apocalypse offers, notably from Chapter 12 on, a sort of synthesis of the biblical teaching on this adversary against whom mankind must struggle from the beginning (Ap 12,9) until the end of the history of salvation. Powerless before the woman and Him whom she brings to birth (12,5f), Satan has turned against "the remainder of her offspring" (12,17). But the apparent triumph which the deceptions of the Antichrist* win for him (13—17) will be terminated by the definitive victory of the Lamb* and of the Church, His bride (18—22). With the beast* and the false prophet, with death* and hell, with all the men who will have succumbed to his wiles, Satan "will be thrown into the lake of fire and sulphur," which is the "second death" (Ap 20,10. 14f).

→Angels OT 2—Antichrist—Arrogance 5—Babel/Babylon 6—Beast & Beasts—Blasphemy —Calamity 1—Captivity II—Curse I—Death OT II 1; NT I 1, II 3—Enemy III 2—Error NT —Evil Spirits—Good & Evil I 4—Hate I 1—Lie III—Light & Dark NT II 1—Miracle II 2 b—Persecution I 1.4 a—Power III 2—Sea 2.3—Sickness/Healing OT I 2; NT I 1—Sign NT 3—Sin—Spirit OT 4; NT 1—Stars 4—Trial/Temptation—Victory NT—War OT IV; NT—Watch II 2—Woman OT 1; NT 3—World NT I 2—Wrath B OT I 2; NT III 2.

SL jpl

SCANDAL

To scandalize means to cause to fall, to be an occasion of falling. Concretely, scandal is the trap which one sets on the path of his enemy in order to make him fall. In truth, there are many ways of "making someone fall" in the moral and religious domain: the tempting which Satan or man practices, the proof to which God puts His people or His child, are "scandals." But always there is question of faith in God.

I. CHRIST, SCANDAL FOR MAN

1. The OT shows that God can be a cause of scandal for Israel: "He is the stone of scandal and the rock* which causes the two houses of Israel to fall...many will fall there, they will fall and will dash themselves to pieces" (Is 8, 14f). God, by His manner of acting, puts the faith of His people to the test.

Jesus has likewise appeared to men as such a sign of contradiction. For if He has been sent for the salvation of all, He is in fact an occasion of hardening of the heart* for many: "This child is for the fall and for the rising of many in Israel; He will be a sign exposed to contradiction" (Lk 2,34). Everything in His person and in His life causes scandal. He is the son of the carpenter of Nazareth (Mt 13,57) and He wishes to save the world, not by some Messianic (11, 2-5; cf Jn 3,17) or political vengeance (Jn 6,15), but by the passion and the cross (Mt 16,21). The disciples themselves are opposed to this as is Satan (16,22f), and after they have been scandalized they abandon their master (Jn 6,66). But the risen Jesus reassembles them (Mt 26, 31f).

2. *John* underlines the scandalous character of the gospel: Jesus is in everything a man like to others (Jn 1,14), whose origin is commonly thought to be known (1,46; 6,42; 7,27) and whose redemptive design through the cross (6, 52) and the ascension (6,62) is incomprehensible. The listeners all stumble at the revelation of the triple mystery of the incarnation, the redemption, and the ascension. But some are lifted up by Jesus, while the others fall: their sin is inexcusable (15,22ff).

3. In presenting Himself to men, Jesus has put them under the necessity of choosing either for or against Him: "Happy is he for whom I am

524

not a scandal" (Mt 11,6 p). Thus *the apostolic community* has applied to Jesus in person the oracle of Isaiah 8,14 which speaks of God. He is "the rock of scandal" and at the same time "the cornerstone" (1 P 2,7f; R 9,32f; Mt 21,42). Christ is at once the source of life and the cause of death (cf 2 Co 2,16).

4. *Paul* had to face this scandal in the Greek world as well as in the Jewish world. Had he not himself had experience of it before his conversion? He discovered that Christ, or, if one prefers, the cross*, is "folly for those who are lost, but for those who are saved, the power of God" (1 Co 1,18). For Christ crucified is "scandal for the Jews and folly for the gentiles" (1 Co 1,23). Human wisdom cannot understand that God wishes to save the world by a humiliated, suffering, and crucified Christ. Only the Spirit of God gives to a man the grace to pass beyond the scandal of the cross or rather to recognize in it the supreme wisdom* (1 Co 1,25; 2,11-16).

5. The same scandal, the same testing of the faith continues also during the entire history of the Church. The *Church* is always a sign of contradiction in the world; and hate and persecution* are the occasion of a fall for many (Mt 13,21; 24,10); although Jesus has predicted these in order that His disciples may not succumb (Jn 16,1).

II. MAN, SCANDAL FOR MAN

Man is a scandal for his brother when he seeks to draw him far from faithfulness* to God. He who misuses the weakness of his brother or the power over him which he has received from God, in order to withdraw him from the covenant, is guilty both toward his brother and toward God. God holds in horror those princes who have turned the people from following Yahweh: Jeroboam (1 K 14,16; 15, 30.34), Ahab, or Jezebel (1 K 21,22.25), and also those who have desired to draw Israel onto the slope of Hellenization, outside of the true faith (2 M 4,7...). On the other hand, those who resist scandal in order to preserve fidelity to the covenant are worthy of praise (Jr 35).

Jesus in fulfilling God's covenant has concentrated the human power of scandal on Himself; it is then His disciples who must not be scandalized. "Woe to whoever scandalizes one of these little ones who believe in me. It is better for him that a millstone be hung around his neck and that he be drowned in the depths of the sea!" (Mt 18,6). But Jesus knows that these scandals are inevitable; false teachers (2 P 2.1) or seducers like Jezebel of old (Ap 2,20) are always at work.

Scandal can come even from the disciple himself. Jesus also demands vigorously and pitilessly the renunciation of all that can present an obstacle to the kingdom of God. "If your eye scandalize you, pluck it out and cast it far from you" (Mt 5,29f; 18,8f).

Following Jesus who did not wish to trouble simple souls (Mt 17,26), Paul desires that one avoid scandalizing weak and unformed consciences: "Take care lest the liberty you use become an occasion of scandal for the weak" (1 Co 8,9; R 14,13-15.20). Christian liberty is only authentic if it is filled with charity (G 5, 13); faith is only authentic if it sustains the faith of the brethren (R 14,1-23).

→Cross I 1.2—Rock 1—Stone 5—Suffering OT II—Unbelief II.

CA jpl

SCHISM

There is only a shade of difference between schism (tearing) and heresy*. Foreshadowed by those that existed in Israel and contradicted its nature as the "assembly of Yahweh" (1 Co 28, 8), these dissensions split the Church into rival groups and contradict its nature as the Body of Christ.

OT

1. *Sin turns natural divisions into schisms.* The division (distribution) of men into different peoples, languages and countries is a natural process (Gn 1,28; 9,1; 10) and is a preparation for the history of salvation (Dt 32,8f). But sin* turns it into a source of numerous conflicts. This is why words expressing division often take on the pejorative sense of a breakdown of unity (Ps 55,10; cf Gn 49,7; Lm 4,16) or of a dispersion* as a punishment for human pride (Gn 11,1-9).

With Abraham*, in whose posterity all nations will be blessed (12,7; 13,15; 22,17f; cf G 3,16), there begins the gathering together of believers (G 3,7ff) and the restoration of human unity. But what conflicts are still in store before the final gathering round the Lamb (Ap 7,9)!

2. *Schism threatens the faith-life of the chosen people and compromises their witness.* The unity of the chosen people*, precarious on the sociological level (2 S 5,5; 15,6.13; 19,41; 20,2), was based on a fellowship of faith: it was mainly the covenant* with Yahweh that bound together the federated tribes in the acceptance of the same law and the same worship (Ex 24,4-8; Js 24). The pilgrimages* and the periodic gatherings at a central sanctuary (Shechem, Shilo..., and later the temple at Jerusalem) preserved the tribal unity and maintained it on its religious basis. On the other hand, it was a sin for a tribe to refuse to take part in the holy war (Nm 32,23; Jg 5,23) or to build a place of worship in opposition to the central sanctuary (Js 22,29). The split into two distinct kingdoms is nowhere condemned as a political event, but is described as an initiative on the part of God (1 K 11,31-39; 12,24; 2 K 17,21), who in this way was punishing the sins of Solomon (1 K 11,33). So it is as a religious schism that the break is condemned. The sin of Jeroboam was to turn the Israelites away from the central sanctuary at Jerusalem by building rival sanctuaries (12,27f) and making the divine presence rest on a pedestal fashioned in the form of a bull, thus encouraging idolatrous confusion (12,28.32; 14,9; 16,26; 2 K 10,29; 17,16; Ho 8,5f), and by settling in Bethel priests who were not descendants of Levi (1 K 12,31; 13,33; cf 2 Ch 13,4-12).

Certain texts from the exile foretell the reunification of Israel and Judah and suggest that the schism is an obstacle not only to the faith-life of the holy people but also to the strength of their witness before the nations (Is 43,10ff; 44, 8). In order that the nations may be gathered together on Zion (Jr 3,17) it is essential that Judah should walk with Israel (3,18; cf Is 11, 12ff; Ez 37,11f.28). The unity of the holy people is seen as the reflection and the affirmation of the fact that their God is the only God.

NT

"Destined to be a sign* that is rejected" (Lk 2,34), Jesus brings division (12,51) even into families (vv 52f), between those who are for Him and those who are against Him (cf Jn 7,43; 9,16; 10,19). But by this He is only disturbing a peace* that is illusory or too natural, for He has come "to gather together in unity the scattered children of God" (Jn 11,52; cf 10,16), "to kill hatred," to break down barriers and to establish true peace amongst men by making them sons of the same Father, members of the same Body*, endowed with the same Spirit (E 2, 14-18). In this Body any possible division is seen as a monstrosity (1 Co 12,25); it is the fruit of the "flesh*" (G 5,20; cf 1 Co 3,3f), a source of sin.

1. *The schisms resulting from the charisms*.* It is mainly in Corinth that Paul encounters the evil of divisions among the faithful (1 Co 1,10; 11,18f; 12,25). But, he writes, "is Christ divided?" Is it not in His name alone that they have been baptized*; is it not He alone who has saved them by His death (1,13)? Those who encourage factions are not really "wise men" (2,6) nor "spiritual men" (3,1), and Paul condemns the dissensions that are provoked by an uncontrolled eagerness to possess the spectacular charisms. They are forgetting the one divine source of the various gifts and the edification desired by the Spirit who distributes them as He wills (12,11). Some, by their greediness and selfishness in the agape, make the scandal of division worse (11,22.27-32). And finally all of them are forgetting the greatest of the spiritual gifts (12,31), the only one that is indispensable (13,1ff); brotherly love*, which has union and edification as its direct result (8,1), thus excluding division.

2. *Schisms corrupt the Church's witness.* Thus, even if they spare the unity of faith (which, however, they threaten every time they follow or precede some piece of heretical propaganda), internal divisions contradict the nature of the Church and impair charity. John suggests an important consequence of this second effect: the witness that the Church ought to give Christ is obstructed, since it is the mutual love of Christians that makes them recognized as His disciples (Jn 13,35). The seamless tunic that is not "torn" (19,35f) is a sign perhaps that Jesus is the High Priest of His sacrifice and that His Church is undivided. In any case He sacrificed Himself (17,19) in order that His followers should be one and in this way show the world the fellowship of love founded by the One sent by the Father (17,21.23).

→Charisms II 1—Church IV 3—Dispersion—Heresy 1—Israel OT 2 a—Unity II, III.

PT ems

SEA

Unlike the Phoenicians and the Greeks, the

Israelites were not a seafaring people. The maritime enterprises of Solomon (1 K 9,26) and of Josaphat (22,49) were not followed up. The experience of the dispersion* was necessary if the "islands" were to come within the geographical horizon of Israel (Is 41,1; 49,1); and the Jews grew accustomed to long sea voyages (Jon 1,3). It was something done at the time of the NT (Mt 23,15); and Paul, a Jew of the dispersion, found it natural to sail the Mediterranean to preach the gospel. However, from the most distant times the sea figured in the biblical texts with a determined religious signification.

1. *From the mythical monster to the creature of God.* Before the sea every man has the feeling of a formidable power, impossible to tame, terrible when it is let loose, threatening for the sailors (Ps 107,23-30) as for the populations along its shores, whom it is likely to submerge at any time (cf Gn 7,11; 9,11.15). It is that sea, that cosmic ocean surrounding the continent, which the Mesopotamian mythology personified under the form of a monstrous beast*. Under the name of Tiamat the dragon represented the chaotic and devastating powers which Marduk, the god of order, has reduced to impotence in order to organize the cosmos. The mythology of Ugarit set up in the same way Yam, the sea god, against Baal in a struggle for the sovereignty of the divine world.

In the Bible, on the contrary, the sea is reduced to the rank of a simple creature. In the classical account of creation*, Yahweh divides into two parts the waters of the abyss (Tehom) as Marduk did for the body of Tiamat (Gn 1,6f). But the image is completely demythicized, for there is no longer any struggle between the all-powerful God and the watery chaos of the beginnings. In organizing the world, Yahweh imposed on the waters, once for all, a limit which they were not to pass without His order (Gn 1,9f; Ps 104,6-9; Pr 8,27ff). The books of wisdom are pleased to describe this order of the world in which the sea takes its place, making use for that purpose of the data of an elementary science: the earth rested on the waters of a lower abyss (Ps 24,2), which rose through it to feed the springs (Gn 7,11; 8,2; Jb 38,16; Dt 33, 13) which were in communication with those of the ocean. It is thus that the sea is put in its place among the creatures, and invited with all the others to praise its Creator (Ps 69,35; Dn 3,78).

2. *Religious symbolism of the sea.* In this very firm doctrinal perspective, the sacred authors were able without any danger to take up the old mythical images after they were drained of their poison. The sea of bronze (1 K 7,23ff) introduced perhaps into the worship of the temple the cosmic symbolism of the primordial ocean, if it is true that the sea of bronze is a representation of the ocean. But the Bible uses rather another category of symbols. The waters of the abyss furnish it with the most striking image of a mortal danger (Ps 69,3), for their bottom is thought to be neighboring on Sheol (Jon 2,6f). Finally, the nasty smell of an evil, disordered, proud force continued to float about the sea which the figure of the mythological beasts still represented occasionally. It symbolizes, therefore, the adverse powers which Yahweh must overcome if He is to make His plan triumph.

This epic imagery knew three applications. First of all, the creative activity of God is sometimes evoked poetically under the features of a primordial combat (Is 51,9; Jb 7,12; 38,8-11; cf beasts*). More often the symbol is made historical. Thus the historical experience of the exodus, in which Yahweh dries up the Red Sea to make a way for His people (Ex 14—15; Ps 77,17.20; 114,3.5) becomes a divine victory over the dragon of the great abyss (Is 51,10); likewise, the roaring of the pagan nations in revolt against God is likened to the roar of the sea (Is 5,30; 17,12). Finally in the later apocalypses, the Satanic powers, which God will face in a final combat, take on features similar to the Babylonian Tiamat: beasts rise from the great abyss (Dn 7,2-7). But the Creator, whose cosmic royalty has from the beginning known how to tame the pride of the sea (Ps 65,8; 89,10; 93,3f), possesses also the mastery of history in which all the forces of disorder bestir themselves in vain.

3. *Christ and the sea.* The religious symbolism of the sea is not lost to view in the NT. It is perceptible even in the gospels. The sea remains the demoniacal place into which the possessed swine rush to precipitate themselves (Mk 5,13 p). Let loose, it continues to strike fear into men: but Jesus shows against it the divine power which triumphs over the elements: He comes to His disciples walking on the sea (Mk 6,49f; Jn 6,19f); or again, He calms it with a word that exorcises it: "Peace. Be still!" (Mk 4,39f). And the disciples recognized by this sign that there was a superhuman power in Him (4,41).

Finally, the Apocalypse is not content with setting up a relation between the sea and the evil powers which Christ the Lord must confront in the course of history (Ap 13,1; 17,1). In describing the new creation where His royalty will be exercised in its fullness it evokes an extraordinary day, when the "sea shall be no more" (21,1). The sea will then disappear insofar as it is a satanic abyss and a force for disorder. But there shall subsist on high that sea of crystal (4,6) which extends beyond sight to the divine throne, symbol of a luminous peace in a renewed universe.

→Antichrist OT 1—Baptism I 1—Beasts & Beast 1—Fire NT I 3—Salt 1—Water IV 2.

Jdf & PG wjy

SEAL

1. *Meaning and use of the seal.* The seal is not only a skillfully engraved jewel (Si 32,5f), but it is a symbol of the person (Gn 38,18) and of his authority* (Gn 41,42; 1 M 6,15). It is also often set in a ring which is not removed except for a serious reason (Hg 2,23; cf Jr 22,24). The stamp to which a person places his seal attests that an object belongs to him (Dt 32,34), that an act proceeds from him (1 K 21,8), that admittance to one of his possessions is forbidden (Dn 14, 10). The stamp is then a signature since it guarantees the validity of a document (Jr 32,10) and also indicates its destination (cf R 15,28). Sometimes it gives it a secret character, as in the case of a sealed scroll which no one may read except the one who has the right to break the seal (Is 29,11).

2. *The seal of God.*

a) The seal of God is a poetic symbol of His mastery over His creatures and over history; He can seal the stars (Jb 9,7), and it is black night; He seals the book of His plans (Ap 5, 1—8,1), and no one deciphers its secret except the Lamb, who brings His designs to pass. God seals sins, in the sense that He sets a limit to them, in regard both to individual sins (Jb 14, 17) and to collective sins (Dn 9,24). In this last instance He also at the same time seals the "prophecy"; that is to say that He puts an end to it by fulfilling it (*ib.*).

b) The symbolism takes on a new value when Christ says that He is marked with the seal of God, His Father (Jn 6,27); for this seal of the Father on the Son of Man is not simply the power which He gives Him of accomplishing His work (cf Jn 5,32.36), it is also the consecration which makes of Him the Son of God (Jn 10,36). The Christian participates in this consecration when God marks him with His seal by giving him the Spirit* (2 Co 1,22; E 1,13f), a gift which demands fidelity to the Spirit (E 4, 30). This seal is the mark of the servants of God, and it is their safeguard at the time of the ultimate testing (Ap 7,2-4; 9,4). Thanks to it, they will be able to remain faithful to the divine words, words that Paul calls a seal; in fact it is by them that God states irrevocably the conditions on which salvation is achieved (2 Tm 2, 19).

→Anointing III 6—Baptism IV 4—Book IV.

CL & MFL jpl

SEE

While the idols* "have eyes and do not see" (Ps 135,16), God sees "all that is under the heavens" (Jb 28,24). Especially does He see "the sons of men" (Ps 33,13f) and "probes the depths of their hearts" (7,10). For man, however, He remains "a hidden God" (Is 45,15) "whom no one has seen nor is able to see" (I Tm 6,16; 1,17; 1 Jn 4,12). Yet God chose a people "to whom He becomes seen" (Nm 14,14), even to the extent of appearing to this people in the person of His only Son (Jn 1,18; 12,45), before ultimately leading them into heaven* to "see His face" (Ap 22,4).

OT

I. THE DESIRE TO SEE GOD

To see God "eye to eye" (Is 52,8) is the most intense desire* of the OT. The nostalgia for paradise* which permeates the Bible is first an awareness of having lost direct and intimate contact with God. While this wistfulness is an abiding fear* of His wrath* it is also a lingering hope* of coming upon His face* and of seeing His smile. Israel's two great religious experiences—the experience of the Word* of God through the prophets and the experience of His presence in their worship—tend to the ultimate privileged experience: seeing God.

1. *God's appearances to the prophets* are the highest points in the prophets' existence. The lives and missions of the prophets Moses* and Elijah* had this experience in its most lofty form. Yet, when Moses prays: "Let me see your glory* (Ex 33,18), God listens to his prayer but answers: "I shall cover you with my hand while I pass by...you shall see my back; but my face will not be seen (33,22f). Elijah "veils his face" when Yahweh approaches and only hears a voice (1 K 19,13; cf Dt 4,12). No one can see God, unless God makes Himself seen. Moses' privilege is something unique: "He looks on the image* of Yahweh" (Nm 12,8). On other quite inferior levels, the prophets "in dreams and visions" (12,6) see something not of this world (Nm 24,4.16; 2 Ch 18,18; Am 9,1; Ez 1—3; Dn 7,1; etc.). Abraham* and Jacob had comparable experiences (Gn 15,17; 17,1; 28,13), as did Gideon (Jg 6,11-24) and Manoah and his wife (13,2-23). Even the seventy elders of Israel share the privilege of Moses to a certain extent when, on the mountain, they "look upon the God of Israel" (Ex 24,10; but the LXX translates: "they saw the place where God was").

2. *Worship* in the places where God made Himself present (Ex 20,24) stimulates among the most virtuous the desire to see God, to "seek His face" (Ps 24,6), "to see His sweetness" (27,4), "His power and glory" (63,3), and even to look from afar toward the temple* (Jon 2,5). Isaiah's vision, so like the theophanies to Moses, effects a coincidence between the prophetic vision, which centers on a word* and a mission*, and the vision achieved in worship, which is centered on presence* (Is 6; cf 2 Ch 18,18; Ez 10—11).

II. SEEING AND BELIEVING

The desire to see God is only rarely and partially fulfilled because God is "a hidden God" (Is 45,15) who reveals Himself to faith*. To know* Him it is necessary to listen* to His Word and to see His works*, for "the invisible is seen" (R 1,20) in the marvels of His creation. The sight of the stars* gives some idea of His power (Is 40,25f), and to contemplate the world (Jb 38—41) is already to see God.

But the hidden God can be seen even better in history. In the wonders He worked for His people (Ex 14,13; Dt 10,21; Js 24,17)—signs* such as had never been seen before (Ex 34,10)—Israel saw His glory (Ex 16,7). To know God, therefore, is "to see His great deeds" and "to understand who He is" (Ps 46,9ff; cf Is 41,20; 42,18; 43,10), to see His feats and believe in Him (Ex 14,31; Ps 40,4; Jdt 14,10), for beside Him "there is no other god" (Dt 32,39).

But like the witless idols*, men are deaf and blind (Is 42,18). "They have eyes and they see nothing, ears and they hear nothing" (Jr 5,21; Ez 12,2). Even God's signs and gifts, destined to enlighten the people, can then harden* them in their blindness. The preaching of the prophets* terminates in "dulling the mind of this people and obstructing their vision, lest their eyes see...and their minds understand" (Is 6, 10).

NT

I. GOD VISIBLE IN JESUS CHRIST

1. *In Jesus Christ makes visible the unheard of wonders* promised by the prophets (Is 52,15; 64,3; 66,8), things "never before seen" (Mt 9,33). Simeon can go in peace for "(his) eyes have seen salvation" (Lk 2,30). "Blessed are the eyes that see" the actions of Jesus. They see "what many prophets and just men wished to see and did not see" (Mt 13,16f). They see too from very close what Abraham saw "at a distance" (He 11,13), and in which he already rejoiced, "the day*" of Jesus (Jn 8,56). The eyes that see Jesus are blessed if they are not scandalized* by Jesus but rather actually see what is transpiring: "The blind see...the gospel preached" (Mt 11,5f).

2. *Seeing and believing.* Already in the synoptic Gospels, but still more clearly in *John*, the sight of what Jesus does and of what God brings about in Him is a summons to believe, to approach the invisible side of salvation history through faith*.

The signs* performed by Jesus should lead to faith (Jn 2,23; 10,41; 11,45; cf Lk 17,15.19). If further signs are not granted to anyone asking for them, no doubt it is, partly at least, because they would not result in faith (Mt 12,38f p; cf Mk 15,32). Apart from that, perfect faith should do without signs (Jn 4,38), but the reality is far from this ideal. In fact many can neither believe (Jn 12,37) nor even in any way see (Mt 13,14f; Jn 12,40; cf Is 6,9f), in spite of so many signs worked before their eyes. For them the light* of the world (Jn 8,12; 9,5) becomes darkness, clarity of vision turns into blindness: "If you were blind you would be without sin. But you say 'We see.' Your sin remains" (Jn 9,39ff).

In the resurrection accounts the same themes

recur. The sight of the empty tomb (Jn 20,28), the apparitions in which Jesus "lets Himself be seen" (*ophthe*: Ac 13,31; 1 Co 15,5-8; Mt 28, 7.10 p) by chosen witnesses* (Ac 10,40f), should lead to faith (Jn 20,29; cf Mt 28,17). But it is still possible to see or to hear those who have seen and to remain in a state of unbelief* (Lk 24,12; 27,39ff; Mk 16,11-14), when here again the ideal of faith would have been to believe without seeing (Jn 20,29).

3. *In Jesus Christ God is visible.* If there is a seeing that precedes faith, faith itself leads to a knowledge* and a vision. In fact not only are the heavens* opened on the Son of Man (Jn 1, 51; cf Mt 3,16), God's mysteries* revealed, and life given to those who believe in Him (Jn 3, 21.36), but God's glory itself—the glory Moses looked upon in a fleeting, fragmentary fashion (Ex 33,22f; 2 Co 3,11)—unceasingly and directly radiates from the person of the Lord (2 Co 3,18). "We have seen His glory, the glory of the only-begotten Son" (Jn 1,14). To see Jesus is already to see the Word and "the life which was with the Father and has been made visible to us" (1 Jn 1,1-3). And since "I am in the Father and the Father is in me," "to have seen me is to have seen the Father" (Jn 14,9f; cf 1,18; 12,45).

II. SEEING GOD AS HE IS

Even the incarnation of the Son cannot, however, fulfill our desire to see God because Jesus, before His return to the Father (Jn 14,12.28), has not as yet revealed all the glory which is properly His (17,1.5). Jesus must vanish to return once again to the invisible world from which He came, the world "of realities which one does not see" and which are the source of those that are visible (He 11,1f), the world of God. This is why He must be seen no more (Jn 16,10-19), and men must seek* without finding Him (7,34; 8,21). When the disciples have "seen" Him for the last time at His ascension* (Ac 1,9ff), the time will begin when those "who have not seen Him" will have to love Him and be happy "without seeing Him again, but by believing" (1 P 1,8f).

A day will come when the Son of Man will be seen "seated at the right hand of the Power" (Mt 26,64 p) and "coming on the clouds of heaven" (24,30 p). Stephen already "sees" that day* of the Lord as a thing of the present (Ac 7,55f). The Apocalypse suggests that this coming can be seen already throughout history:

"it is He who is coming on the clouds; everyone will see Him, even those who pierced Him..." (Ap 1,7; cf Jn 19,37). But in reality "we see Him no more," except in faith, "until all is subject to Him" (He 2,8). Now is no longer the time to "look up to heaven," but to bear witness that He will be seen coming back as He went (Ac 1,11), and to live in this state of double expectation: to be always with the Lord (1 Th 4,17; Ph 1,23) and to "see God" (Mt 5,8), "to see His face" (Ap 22,4), "to see Him as He is" (1 Jn 3,2), in His inaccessible mystery, totally committed to His children.

→Apparitions of Christ—Face—Faith—Image —Predestine 3.5—Presence of God NT III— Pure NT I 3—Revelation—Sign NT I 2.

JDu & JG dfb

SEEK

"Man strives in his seeking, but never finds" (Qo 8,17); but Jesus announces that "He who seeks, will find" (Mt 7,8). Beneath all human restlessness is a seeking for God, but often this search fails and must be set right. Then man discovers that his search for God is rooted in the fact that God first seeks out man.

I. SEEKING GOD: FROM THE CULTIC TO THE INNER SEARCH

Originally, *seeking Yahweh* or *seeking His word** means to consult God. Before an important decision (1 K 22,5-8), in resolving litigation (Ex 18,15f), or for direction in a crisis (2 S 21,1; 2 K 3,11; 8,8; 22,18), a person goes to the Tent of Meeting (Ex 33,7) or to the temple* (Dt 12,5) and inquires of the Lord, usually through the mediation of a priest* (cf Nm 5,11) or a prophet* (Ex 18,15; 1 K 22,7; cf Nm 23,3).

Such a proceeding could be merely a superstitious precaution, a way of involving the Lord in one's affairs. But the language of the Bible shows that it could also be a disinterested expression of love* for God. The man who seeks God hopes "to dwell in the house* of the Lord all the days of his life"; that is, "to taste* the sweetness of the Lord" and "to seek His face*" (Ps 27,4.8). Undoubtedly there is a question of sharing in the liturgy of the sanctuary (Ps 24, 6; Ze 8,21). But in the splendor and emotion of worship*, the loyal Israelite seeks "to see* the bounty of the Lord" (Ps 27,13). This desire* to be in God's presence* brings the exiles back from Babylon (Jr 50,4) and leads them to rebuild the temple (1 Ch 22,19; 28,8f). Finally, seeking God is giving proper worship and destroying false gods (Dt 4,29), which will be the norm of the Chronicler in judging the kings of Israel (2 Ch 14,3; 31,21).

This rejection of false gods involves a conversion, as the prophets constantly proclaim. There is no genuine seeking of God without a careful search for uprightness and justice*. Amos makes this equation: "Seek me and you shall live; but seek not Bethel" (Am 5,4f); and again: "Seek good and not evil, that you may live...hate evil and love the good, and let justice prevail at the gate" (5,14f). Likewise, Hosea urges: "Sow the seed of justice...for it is time to seek the Lord" (Ho 10,12; cf Zp 2,3). If one is "to seek the Lord so that He will be found," it is necessary "that the wicked forsake their ways and the criminal his evil thoughts" (Is 55,6). One must seek the Lord "with his whole heart" (Dt 4,29; Jr 29,13). This Jesus does not change: "Seek first the kingdom of God and His justice" (Mt 6,33).

II. TRUE AND FALSE SEEKING

Even in Israel there were some deviations in the search for God. Some members of the chosen people turned to false gods (Baal; 2 K 1,2ff): others made use of forbidden intermediaries (magicians: Lv 19,31; the dead: Dt 18,11; necromancers: 1 S 28,7; ghosts: Is 8,19). Many did not have the elementary interior dispositions and were "like a nation that wants to act with integrity, but forgets the law" (Is 58,2). None of these was able to find God; they were all separated from him by their sins (Is 59,2).

The true search for God takes place in simplicity* (Ws 1,1), humility* and poverty (Zp 2, 3; Ps 22,27), in a contrite heart and humble spirit (Dn 3,39ff). Then God, who is "good to him who seeks" (Lm 3,25), lets Himself be found (Jr 29,14); and "the humble who seek God will rejoice" (Ps 69,33).

Jesus Christ, who uncovers the secret thoughts of hearts (Lk 2,35), establishes a division between the true and false search for God. The attitude that people adopt toward Him (Jn 8, 21) establishes the difference between the true and false search. From then on there is a parallel between seeking God and seeking Jesus. To "gain Christ" and "to capture him" (Ph 3, 8.12), it is necessary to give up looking for one's own justice* (R 10,3) and allow oneself to be captured by Him in faith* (Ph 3,12). The quest for Jesus should, then, continue even after His departure (Jn 13,33) in the quest for things from above (Col 3,1).

III. GOD IN QUEST OF MAN

To seek God is eventually to discover that He has first loved us (1 Jn 4,19) and has sought us out, that He attracts us to lead us to His Son (Jn 6,44). This initiative taken by the grace* of God is not a case of jealously guarded supreme right; for the whole Bible shows that the initiative is one of love*, that the quest for man is a movement rising from the depths of the divine heart. When Israel forgets Him and runs after other lovers, God plans to allure His unfaithful spouse and "to speak to her heart" (Ho 2,15f). When none of the shepherds* of Israel would seek out the scattered sheep (Ez 34,5f), then God Himself announces His plan to gather the flock together and to "seek out the lost sheep" (34,12.16). At the very time of unfaithfulness, the Song of Songs sings of God passionately involved in His search (Ct 3,1-4; 5,6; 6,3).

The Son of God has revealed the extent of that passion: "The Son of Man came into the world to seek out and to save what was lost" (Lk 19,10), to set off in search of the single lost sheep (Mt 18,12; cf Lk 15,4-10). When Jesus is leaving His own, He thinks of that moment when He will return to seek them out and take them with Him, "so that, where I am, there you also may be" (Jn 14,3).

→Cares 1—Desire—Face 3—Hunger & Thirst —Pilgrimage OT 1—Prayer—Presence of God OT III 1—Rest—Repentance/Conversion O; OT II 1; NT II 2—Virtues & Vices 1.

PMG & JG wjw

SERVANT OF GOD

The name *servant of God* is, in the Bible, a title of honor. Yahweh names him whom He calls to collaborate in His plan* "my servant."

In order to accomplish this plan He sends His Son, the Servant of God *par excellence.*

This title indeed expresses the most mysterious aspect of His redemptive mission: by His sacrifice Christ effectively expiates that refusal to serve which is sin, and He unites all men in the one service of God.

I. THE SERVANTS OF GOD AND THE PEOPLE OF THE COVENANT

The title of servant of God is given to those men whose mission concerns the chosen people. Often given to Moses, the mediator of the covenant (Ex 14,31; Nm 12,7; Dt 34,5; 1 K 8, 56), and to David, type of the Messianic king (2 S 7,8; 1 K 8,24f; Ps 78,70; Jr 33,26), it also designates the patriarchs Abraham (Gn 26,24), Isaac (Gn 24,14), and Jacob (Ex 32,13; Ez 37, 25), and then Joshua who leads the people into the land (Js 24,29). It is applied to the prophets who have the mission of maintaining the covenant (Elijah: 1 K 18,36; "my servants the prophets": Am 3,7; Jr 7,25; 2 K 17,23) as well as to the priests who conduct divine worship in the name of the priestly people (Ps 134,1; cf Ex 19,5f). The choice of all these servants is finally destined to render the people faithful to the service which God expects of them (cf Ps 105, 6ff.26.45), as the angels, the servants of the divine will, are faithful (Ps 103,20f).

II. FROM UNFAITHFUL SERVANTS TO THE FAITHFUL SERVANTS

But, from the earliest times, the chosen people was unfaithful to its vocation of servant and untractable toward the servants of God (Dt 9, 24; Jr 7,25); therefore, it is chastised by the exile through the agency of a pagan king, Nebuchadnezzar, who, in this sense, is a servant of God (Jr 27,6). But God, who wills not the death of the sinner but his life, chooses for Himself a remnant* which will become faithful under the reign of His Servant, the new David (Ez 34,23f; 37,24f). It is to this remnant that the oracles of the Book of Consolation (Is 40—55) are addressed.

1. *The unfaithful servant.* The prophet who develops in this book the theme of Israel, servant of God, interweaves with it the theme of Zion, spouse* of God. This spouse has only been abandoned because her sons have been unfaithful (Is 50,1). Israel, rebellious from its mother's womb (48,8) is, by its own fault, a slothful servant, deaf and blind (42,18f.24; 43,8. 22f; cf 30,9ff). Far from forgetting this chosen servant, however, God pardons him (44,21f) and proceeds freely to save him (41,8ff) by means of the pagan king Cyrus, who is His shepherd, His anointed, and His friend (44,28; 45,1; 48,14). It even seems that the king-deliverer is the servant who is praised in 42, 1-7. Reread without consideration of the context, this song has been applied to the servant Israel, whose vocation, mission, and sacrifice are the subject of three other songs (49,1-6; 50, 4-9; 52,13—53,12). This interpretation is that of the LXX and will be followed by Matthew (Mt 12,18-21). In any event, thanks to Cyrus, Israel, the unfaithful yet liberated servant, bears witness among the gentiles to the impotence of the idols of Babylon in the face of the only true God and Savior (43,10ff; 45).

2. *The faithful servant.* But God wishes to make of this passive witness a faithful servant who, by his testimony, may bring to the nations the light* of salvation*. The second half of the Book of Consolation (Is 49—55) is dominated by the mysterious figure of a prophet whom God calls His Servant (49,3.6; 52,13). Just as the patriarch Jacob is inseparable from the people that bears his name and in whom he continues to live, so this Servant, who has the traits, though purified, of Jeremiah (49,1; 50,7; 53,7; cf Jr 1,5; 15,20; 11,19), is inseparable from this "Israel" whose name He bears, from this remnant "in whom God will glorify Himself" (Is 49,3). Nonetheless He is distinct from this Israel to the extent that He has the mission of reassembling it (49,5f) and of teaching it (50, 4-10). His patience* (50,6) and His humility* (53,7) make Him capable of offering His life and of accomplishing by His suffering* Yahweh's plan (53,4ff.10) of justifying* the sinners of all nations (53,8.11ff). By this sacrifice Zion is consoled*, the sterile* wife is once again united to God by an eternal covenant and becomes the fruitful mother* of all the servants of God (Is 54,1—55,4).

Israel, on returning from the exil, seems to have forgotten the universalist perspectives of salvation which the Servant was to achieve by His sufferings. At this moment a new prophet appears: he announces to the exiles the glory of the new Jerusalem, but no longer alludes to the expiation of the Servant (Is 61,1ff). This title of "servant" is then given by God to Zerubbabel (Hg 2,23), the "seed" which He raises up in the line of David (Ze 3,8; cf Jr 23,

5). As regards the servants of God, the joy which they await (Is 65,13f.17f) will indeed be the end of their sufferings, but it is no longer presented as the fruit of an oblation which transforms death into sacrifice* and which makes life spring forth from this (cf 53,10f).

III. THE TRUE SERVANT, SAVIOR OF MEN

1. *Jesus* makes the mission of the Servant His own: a master meek and humble of heart (Mt 11,29), who announces salvation to the poor* (Lk 4,18f), He is in the midst of His disciples "as one who serves" (Lk 22,27), He, who is their Lord and their master (Jn 13,12-15); and He goes to the very limits of the demands of the love which inspires this service (Jn 13,1; 15,13) by giving His life for the redemption of the multitude of sinners (Mk 10,43ff; Mt 20,26ff). It is for this that, treated like a criminal (Lk 22,37), He dies on the cross (Mk 14,24; Mt 26,28), knowing that He will rise again, as it is written of the Son of Man (Mk 8,31 p; 9,31 p; Lk 18,3ff p; 24,44; cf 53,10ff). If then He is the expected Messiah, the Son of Man does not come to re-establish a temporal kingdom, but to enter into His glory and to lead His people there by passing through the death of the Servant.

2. *The apostolic preaching* has applied to Jesus the title of Servant in order to proclaim the mystery of His death (Ac 3,13f.18; 4,27f), the source of blessing and light for all the nations (Ac 3,25f; 26,23). A Lamb* unjustly slain like the Servant (Ac 8,32f), Jesus has saved His lost sheep; and the wounds of His body have healed the souls of sinners (1 P 2,21-25). For Matthew, Jesus is the Servant who announces justice to the nations and whose name* is their hope (Mt 12,18-21=Is 42,1-4). Finally, a hymn allows Paul to present the mystery of Christ and of His love in a powerful summary: it proclaims that Christ has entered into glory by taking the condition of Servant and by dying on the cross in order to obey God His Father (Ph 2,5-11); the prophecy of the Servant then announced the redeeming sacrifice* of the Son of God made man. It is for this reason that the name of the holy Servant of God, Jesus, crucified and risen, is the only source of salvation* (Ac 4, 10ff.29ff).

3. *The servants of God* are henceforth the servants of Christ (R 1,1; G 1,10; Ph 1,1; cf Tt 1,1). Just as the Lord has taken for His mother the woman who called herself His servant (Lk 1,38.43.48), so He makes of His servants His friends (Jn 15,15) and the sons of His Father (20,17). They must, moreover, like their master, pass through the same way of suffering* (15,20). It is by triumphing in the trial* that the servants of God will enter into the glory of the kingdom* (Ap 7,3.14f; 22,3ff).

→Covenant OT III 2; NT I—Election OT III 2; NT I—Eucharist IV 1—Expiation—Friend 2—Jesus Christ I 3, II 1 b—Justice *A* I OT 2—Lamb of God 1—Man II 2—Mediator I 2—Messiah OT II 3; NT I 2, II 2—Moses 1.3 —Obedience III—Pride OT 3—Prophet—Remnant OT 3—Sacrifice OT III 3; NT I—Service II, III—Son of Man NT I 1 b—Spirit of God OT III; NT I 2—Suffering OT III—Victory OT 3 a; NT 1—Violence I 2, III 3, IV 2.

CA & MFL jpl

SERVICE

The word *service* has two opposite meanings in the Bible, according to whether it refers to the submission of man to God or to the bondage of one man to another, that is, slavery. The history of salvation teaches that the liberation of man depends on his submission to God and that "to serve God is to reign" (Blessing of Palms).

I. SERVICE AND SLAVERY

Even in human relations the same word can refer to two profoundly different concrete situations: that of the slave* as it appeared in the pagan world, where the man in slavery is put on the level of animals and things; and that of the servant as it was defined by the Law of the people of God, in which the slave remains a man and has his place in the family, so that the true servant can become a man of trust and an inheritor (Gn 24,2; 15,3). The word itself thus remains ambiguous: *'ābad* (hb.) and *douleuein* (gr.) are used for both situations. There are also words which designate services of dependence of an honorary character; either the service of the king by his officials (hb. *šērat*), or official duties, in the first rank of which is the service of worship (gr. *leitourgein*).

II. RELIGIOUS SERVICE AND OBEDIENCE (OT)

To serve God is an honor for the people with whom He has made the covenant. But such honor has its obligations. Yahweh is a jealous God who cannot endure divided allegiance (Dt 6,15), as a biblical passage which Christ will quote says: "Thou shalt adore the Lord thy God and thou shalt serve Him alone" (Mt 4,10; cf Dt 6,13). This fidelity must reveal itself in worship and in behavior. This is the meaning of the commandment in which the synonyms for the service of God are listed: "You shall follow Yahweh, you shall fear Him, you shall keep His commandments, you shall obey Him, you shall serve Him, and you shall bind yourselves to Him" (Dt 13,5).

1. *Cultic service.* To serve God is in the first place to offer gifts and sacrifices and to assure the maintenance of His temple. In this sense, the priests and the Levites are "those who serve Yahweh" (Nm 18; 1 S 2,11.18; 3,1; Jr 33, 21f). The priest* in fact is defined as the keeper of the sanctuary, the servant of the God who dwells there, and the interpreter of the oracles which He gives (Jg 17,5f). In his turn, the believer who performs an act of worship "comes to serve Yahweh" (2 S 15,8). Finally, the expression designates the customary worship of God and almost becomes synonymous with adoration* (Js 24,22).

2. *Obedience.* The service which Yahweh demands is not limited to ritual worship; but through obedience to the commandments, it extends to all of life. This is what the prophets and Deuteronomy never cease to repeat: "Obedience is preferable to the best sacrifice" (1 S 15,22; cf Dt 5,29ff); and they reveal the demanding profundity of this obedience: "It is love which I desire and not sacrifices" (Ho 6,6; cf Jr 7).

III. SERVE GOD BY SERVING MAN (NT)

Jesus borrows the very words of the Law and the prophets (Mt 4,10; 9,13) to recall that the service of God excludes any other worship, and that it must be integral by reason of the love which inspires it. He specifies the name of the rival which can place obstacles in the way of this service: money, the service of which makes man unjust (Lk 16,9) and the love of which the apostle, echoing his master, will call an idolatrous* worship (E 5,5). It is necessary to choose: "No one can serve two masters...You cannot serve God and mammon" (Mt 6,24 p). If a man loves one, he will hate and despise the other. It is for this reason that the renunciation of riches is necessary for the person who wishes to follow* Jesus, the Servant* of God (Mt 19, 21).

1. *The service of Jesus.* Sent by God to crown the work of the servants of the OT (Mt 21, 33...p), the well-beloved Son comes to serve. From His childhood He affirms that He must be about His Father's business (Lk 2,49). The unfolding of His entire life is under the sign of an "I must" which expresses His inescapable dependence on the will* of the Father (Mt 16, 21 p; Lk 24,26). But behind this necessity of service which leads Him to the cross, Jesus reveals the love which alone gives it its dignity and value: "It is necessary that the world know that I love the Father and that I act as the Father has commanded me" (Jn 14,30).

In serving God, Jesus saves men, for whose refusal to serve He makes amends; and He reveals to them how the Father wishes to be served. He wants them to spend themselves in the service of their brothers as their Lord and master, Jesus, has done Himself. "The Son of Man is not come to be served, but to serve and to give His life" (Mk 10,45 p); "I have given you an example...The servant is not greater than the master" (Jn 13,15f); "I am in the midst of you as one who serves" (Lk 22,27).

2. *The greatness of Christian service.* The servants of Christ are first the servants of the Word* (Ac 6,4; Lk 1,2); those who announce the gospel* and thus accomplish a sacred service (R 15,16; Col 1,23; Ph 2,22) "in all humility," and, if necessary, "in tears and in the midst of tribulations" (Ac 20,19). For those who serve the community, as the deacons do (Ac 6,1-4), Paul teaches them the conditions which will make their service worthy of the Lord (R 12, 7.9-13). Besides, all Christians have, through baptism, passed from the service of sin and of the Law, which was a bondage, to the service of justice and of Christ, which is liberty (Jn 8, 31-36; R 6—7; cf 1 Co 7,22; E 6,6). They serve God as sons and not as slaves (G 4), for they serve Him in the newness of the Spirit (R 7,6). The grace which has made them pass from the condition of servants to that of friends* of

Christ (Jn 15,15) gives them the ability to serve their Lord so faithfully that they are certain of sharing in His joy (Mt 25,14-23; Jn 15,10f).

→Adoration I 3—Angels—Authority NT I 1, II 1 — Friend 2 — Hospitality 2 — Liberation/ Liberty III 3 c—Mary III 1—Meal V— Ministry I—Obedience—Poor NT III 3—Priesthood—Reward I—Servant of God—Slave— Word of God OT III 1; NT II 1—Worship.

CA & MFL jpl

SEXUALITY

Although a number of articles in this dictionary deal with sexuality in passing, it is useful to gather together in this article whatever the Bible has to say on this subject. The word itself does not appear in the Bible, but the difference between the sexes is frequently mentioned in order to shed light on the relationship between man and woman. While respecting the specific contributions of the OT and the NT, it seems preferable not to deal with them in their chronological order: there is much in the OT on this subject that only acquires its full meaning with the coming of Jesus Christ.

I. SEXUALITY AND THE HUMAN CONDITION

While Genesis says: "male and female he created them" (Gn 1,27), Paul says: "there are no more distinctions between...male and female, but all of you are one in Christ Jesus" (G 3,28). It is clear that there is a certain tension between these two statements, yet they do not contradict one another, but shed light on one another and condition one another mutually.

1. *"Male and female he created them"* (Gn 1,27). In the OT the difference between the sexes is connected in the first place with the conviction that man was created "in the image* of God." The immediate context of this passage, the work of the priestly editor (P), is only concerned with connecting the sexual difference between man and woman with the fruitfulness* of God, who gives life* and controls the universe (Gn 1,28). The yahwist point of view (J) is more complete. In his eyes the basis of the difference between the sexes is the necessity for

man to live in society: "it is not good that man should be alone. I will make him a helpmate" (Gn 2,18). To the idea of fruitfulness, which is not overlooked by this author (3,20), is joined the idea of the relationship of otherness of the sexes. By these two motivations the individual is set in a social context. Ideally, in the climate of paradise, the scene of the meeting of the two beings is one of simplicity: "both of them were naked...but they felt no shame in front of each other" (2,25). But sin, involving separation from God, introduces a feeling of distance and fear into this scene. From now on the sexual relationship is ambiguous. It does not cease to be fundamentally good, but it has fallen under the control of sin, which is a divisive force. In place of the joy at the irreducible difference of the other, the partners experience the desire* of selfish possession (3,16). The sexual drive, which is naturally extrovert, is disturbed by a movement of introversion: instead of turning toward the other, it turns in on itself.

The goodness and the value of the sexual relationship in marriage* have never been in doubt as far as the Bible is concerned. Not only in the Canticle of Canticles (Ct 4,1; 5,9; 6,4), but also in most of the other books, these two aspects of otherness and fruitfulness with regard to marriage are to be found: "find joy with the wife you married in your youth" (Pr 5,18; cf Ez 24,15; Si 26,16ff; Qo 9,9). What is the object of the unique creation formed by God from man and woman? "Godgiven posterity" (Ml 2,14ff). Jesus echoes the very words of Genesis and stresses the indissolubility of the couple thus formed: "they are no longer two, therefore, but one body" (Mt 19,4ff). And finally, Paul, who is sometimes wrongly described as an ascetic opposed to the sexual life, gives the spouses guidance, which is still valid for our contemporaries (1 Co 7,1-6). In contrast to the illusory desires for continence displayed by the Corinthians, he reminds them of the normal path of marriage, the duty of sexual relations: "do not refuse each other except by mutual consent ['symphonically'], then only for an agreed time, to leave yourselves free for prayer; then come together again" (7,5; cf 1 Tm 4,3; 5,14). The situation resulting from creation is thus maintained and even enhanced. The community of husband and wife enters into the privileged domain of prayer.

2. *"There are no more distinctions between... male and female,* but all of you are one in Christ

Jesus" (G 3,28). This statement does not deny
any of the preceding points of view, but the
coming of Jesus has brought about a change in
the respective situation of man and woman,
allowing the full dimension of the sexual condition to appear.

Jesus did not work out the theory of the
matter, but for Himself He adopted a special
way of life and addressed an appeal to men.
In fact Jesus did not live like the Jewish rabbis,
who were expected to be married. The probable
practise of celibacy amongst the Essenes (Qumrân) perhaps helped to avoid any possible surprise or scandal at this state of affairs. But in
the case of Jesus it is not a case of an asceticism
hostile to woman. The reasons behind this can
be understood from the following statement,
which is a veiled confidence: "there are eunuchs
who have made themselves that way for the
sake of the kingdom of heaven" (Mt 19,12).
These words are an invitation to "anyone who
can accept this"; and there is in Luke an equally
abrupt parallel: in order to be Jesus' disciple,
one must renounce one's own wife (Lk 18,29).
Such a way of life can only be understood in
terms of a new state of affairs, revealed with
the coming of Jesus: the coming of the Kingdom of God, which one enters by "following
him." Entry into this new order of things can
be an invitation to go beyond the commandment
of creation, since a meaning is given to voluntary continence.

In the footsteps of Jesus, Paul, who may
have been married, makes himself the advocate
of virginity*. There are two reasons for this
new way of life: the charism* of a special call,
like the one he heard (1 Co 7,7) and the situation created by the end of time inaugurated in
the person of Jesus. In fact, the result of living
in the "last times" is that a distinction must be
made between two new groups amongst men:
to the age-old opposition man/woman must be
added the opposition married/virgin. These two
types of men or women are necessary in order
to establish and express in a complementary
way the fullness of the kingdom of heaven.
Thus, it would be wrong to take account only
of the OT statements and say that men and
women can only find their true fulfillment in
the effective union with a sexual partner. In
fact, in the whole human community, which
Jesus Christ stands for, it is possible to enter
into communion with a You, while at the same
time refraining the carnal exercise of sexuality.

II. SEXUALITY, THE SPHERE OF THE SACRED AND HOLINESS

1. The religions of the peoples surrounding
Israel had made sexuality a part of the world
of the gods even. There we see a profusion of
mother gods and father gods, gods of love
marrying amongst themselves or married to
human beings, and the sacred prostitutes who
represented the divinity. Israel was familiar with
the Baals and Astartes, the stakes driven into
the ground to symbolize the union of heaven
and earth; they even had some dealings with
these false gods themselves and they made a
"golden calf" (Ex 32,4), the symbol of virility.
However, the struggle against these foreign
religions ended with a victory for yahwism, even
if there is evidence of the continued existence
of these sacred prostitutes in spite of the prohibition of Dt 23,18 (1 K 14,24; 15,12; 22,47;
2 K 23,7; Ho 4,4; Mi 1,7).

Even after the purification of these pagan
customs Israel continued to maintain a link
between the sexual and the sacred. But the
reasons behind this sacralization changed. It
was no longer a case of imitating the sexuality
of the gods, but of carrying out a function
that was inspired by the Word of God, by
sharing in God's own creative power. After
giving birth to a child, Eve declared: "I have
acquired a man with the help of Yahweh" (Gn
4,1). One of the first consequences of this new
form of sacralization can be seen in the use of
sexual symbolism (parental or conjugal) to express the relationship between Israel and their
God. And the custom of circumcision to signify
the covenant* with Yahweh can be connected
with this (Gn 17,9-14; Lv 12,3).

Another aspect of this sacralization of sexuality concerns the rites of the pure* and of the
impure, inherited by Israel from the ancient
rites of the East. At the birth of a child the
woman was declared unclean and was not able
to approach the sanctuary (Lv 12,6); it was
the same during the time of her periods (15,
19-30), or for a man on the occasion of a nocturnal pollution (15,1-17; Dt 23,11). Sexual relations themselves made people unfit to join in
worship (Lv 15,18; Ex 19,15; 1 S 21,5f; 2 S 11,
11), which was of special importance for the
priests (Ex 20,26; 28,42; Dt 23,2). These prescriptions were not the result of any contempt for
sexuality, but of its sacralization, or rather of the
ambiguity of the sacred in this sphere and of the
ambiguity of ritual purity. Finally, is there not
a conflict between an act that participates

physically in the creative power of God and a cultic act that mimes the relationship with the godhead?

2. All these taboos disappeared with the arrival of the Christian faith. Or rather a change took place from the ancient idea of sacralization to a new way of looking at holiness*. This is the explanation of certain statements of Paul: "the unbelieving husband is made one with the saints through his wife...if this were not so, your children would be unclean, whereas in fact they are holy" (1 Co 7,14). The cause of this objective state is no longer the sacred character of the sexual relationship, but the membership of a holy people and ultimately the presence of the Holy Spirit. Paul must have had this gift of the Spirit in mind when he made the recommendations, probably following the primitive catachesis, about the demands of sexual purity, which are a mark of the Christian life. "What God wants is for you all to be holy. He wants you to keep away from fornication, and each one of you to know how to use the body that belongs to him in a way that is holy and honorable, not giving way to selfish lust like the pagans who do not know God" (1 Th 4,3ff). From now on the body* is sanctified by the gift of the Spirit and "is not meant for fornication; it is for the Lord" (1 Co 6,13).

Sexual symbolism is now used with regard to Christ and the Church. "Husbands should love their wives just as Christ loved the Church" (E 5,25). And recalling the commandment of the Creator: "A man must...be joined to his wife and the two will become one body," Paul adds: "this mystery has many implications; but I am saying it applies to Christ and the Church" (E 5,31f). The same symbolism is used to express the relationship of love that unites the faithful to God. It is the Prostitute who rides the Beast* (Ap 17), while the real believers follow the Lamb because they are "virgins" (14,4).

III. THE PRACTICE AND THE INTENTION

1. Sexual morality is the subject of a number of rules *in the OT*. This was not the result of any desire to condemn sexuality nor of any excessive moral attention paid to this particular sphere, but of the sacralization, of which we have already spoken. Apart from this, there is here a defensive reaction against a perverted

world, which often veiled its eroticism beneath the cloak of religion. And finally, we must not forget the educating role of the Law, which was anxious about the hygiene of the people of God. It would be tiresome to make an exhaustive list of these rules. Let us note the catalogue of Lv 20,10-21, which condemns fornification (cf Dt 22,23-29), sexual relations with a woman during her periods, adultery* (cf Dt 5,18; 22,22; together with the mention of covetousness in Ex 20,17 and Pr 2,16; 6,25; 7,55ff; Si 9,9), incest (cf Dt 23,1), homosexuality (cf Gn 18,20; 19,5) and bestiality (cf Ex 22,18). On the other hand there is no basis for the condemnation of what we call onanism in the sin of Onan, which consisted in his refusal to raise up posterity for his dead brother (Gn 38,9f). Apart from these there were special rules for the priests: they were not allowed to marry a prostitute or a divorced woman (Lv 21,7.13f). And finally, let us note that apart from the case of sacred prostitution there was no special censure attached to prostitution (Gn 38,15-23; Jg 16,1...), although the Wisdom literature, showing a clear advance by comparison with the ancient accounts, warns against the dangers that it represented (Pr 23,27; Si 9,3f; 19,2).

2. *Jesus* has nothing to say about the preceding ritual rules. He does not spend time condemning the fault committed, for example the sin of the woman caught in the act of adultery (Jn 8,11), or when He states that because of their faith prostitutes will find it easier to enter the kingdom of heaven than the Pharisees (Mt 21,31f; cf He 11,31). However, He makes the OT rules more radical, by going straight to the sin that is at the root of those faults, in the desire and in the looks (Mt 5,28; 15,19 p).

Jesus lived amongst Jews, while Paul found himself in the dissolute environment of the great port of Corinth. And so he took a strong stand against all forms of evil: "people of immoral lives, idolators, adulterers, catamites, sodomites, thieves, usurers, drunkards, slanderers and swindlers will never inherit the Kingdom of God" (1 Co 6,9; cf R 1,24-27). He was constantly warning against prostitution (1 Co 6,13ff; 10,8; 2 Co 12,21; Col 3,5). Being a realist, he forbade any association with immoral brethren, but not with the immoral people of this world, otherwise "you would have to withdraw from the world altogether" (1 Co 5,10).

What is the reason for the forcefulness of this exhortation? To protect the Christians of non-Jewish origin from the deviations of the flesh, Paul did not have at his disposal the bulwark of the Jewish Law with its minute rules. Of course he was not afraid of saying "there are no forbidden things" (1 Co 6,12), for he knew that morality was not dependent on this or that written rule, which is always conditioned by the culture of the time; but it was much more closely dependent on the relationship that existed from now on between the body* and the Lord. The body is the temple of the Holy Spirit and a member of Christ; "do you think I can take parts of Christ's body and join them to the body of a prostitute? Never! As you know, the man who goes with a prostitute is one body with her" (1 Co 6,15f). "Forget about satisfying your bodies with all their cravings" (R 13,14; cf G 5,16-19).

Thus, with the coming of Jesus and the teaching of Paul, sexuality was progressively removed from the sphere of the sacred. This movement can and should be continued, on one condition: the preservation of the dimension of holiness, which transforms the corporal nature of man and puts it constantly in touch with a divine world surrounding it on all sides.

→Adultery 1—Body I—Clothing I 1, II 1—Cupidity NT 1—Desire II—Fasting o. 1—Flesh II—Fruitfulness I—Man I 1 c, III 2—Marriage—Pure OT I 1, II 2—Sin IV 3 a—Spouse OT o. 1—Sterility—Virginity OT 1; NT 3—Woman OT I; NT 2—Works OT II 2.

XLD ems

SHADOW

Like the night* or the cloud*, the shadow symbolizes a double experience, according as it affirms the absence or supposes the presence of light*. Man wants the full light of day and seeks out the shade; God is light and burning fire*, but also refreshing shade, and He determined to dwell in the dark cloud. The Bible plays upon this ambivalence of meaning.

I. ANNOUNCEMENT OF DEATH

1. *The shadow which flees.* As a creature who knows himself bound to disappear, man recognizes his destiny in the lengthening or the fleeting presence of the shadow: "the day declines, the shadows of evening are lengthening" (Jr 6,4); thus human life, whose degrees add

up inexorably on the sundial of time (2 K 20, 9ff). "A shadow which flees without stopping," such is man (Jb 14,2; cf 8,9); his days wane in the night* like the shadow (Ps 102,12; 144, 4), pass hopelessly to death (1 Ch 29,15; Ws 5,9). On the thread of a life of vanity (Qo 6,12) he travels, like a shadow (Ps 39,7); but within this irreversible development, while experiencing his own changefulness, he maintains faith in the "Father of lights, in whom exists neither change nor the shadow of alteration" (Jm 1,17).

2. *Darkness and the shadow of death.* The LXX reverts to an etymology which is debatable, but possesses a deep sense of reality; when it ordinarily translated the Hebrew word signifying *deep shadow* by *shadow of death* the evangelists agreed with it (Is 9,1; Mt 4,16; Lk 1,79). For the shadow is not simply a phenomenon which changes and flees; it is a void, a nothingness, a dark obscurity which Job wishes for in his misery (Jb 3,1-6). Sheol, without hope, land of death*, is the place of darkness and of shadow (10,21) where all brightness is only night. The trial*, even in this life, already deprives man of the light of the living: "on my eyelids is a shadow" (16,16).

3. *The master of the shadow.* Before the threatening shadow of death, God is the only refuge. He who changes into a shadow dims the artificial light which forms the hope of the sinner (Jr 13,16; cf Ps 44,20); He can also "lead into light the dark shadow" (Jb 12,22), "draw from the shadow and from darkness those who were their captives" (Ps 107,10.14). Thus, full of confidence*, the psalmist cries: "If I should pass through a valley full of shadow, I shall fear no evil, for you are with me" (Ps 23,4). This hope has become a reality since Christ fulfilled the prophecy of Isaiah: "upon those who dwell in the shadows of death, a light has arisen" (Mt 4,16; Is 9,1).

II. PROTECTIVE PRESENCE

Just as the cloud* was a menacing darkness for some, a light and protection for others, so the terrible shadow can be protective; through the protection which it assures, man discovers a presence.

1. *Earthly shadows.* In everyday life, particularly in the East, the shade is appreciated,

for it saves one from the heat of the sun. All creatures seek the shade: that of the lotus tree is sought by the fierce Leviathan (Jb 40,22)—birds, beasts, and men seek that of trees* (Ez 31,6). For this reason, the tree which gives shade symbolizes protective power*; as Daniel explains to Nebuchadnezzar: "the tree is you, O King" (Dn 4,17ff). Similarly, security is guaranteed in the shadow of the king* (Jg 9,15); the just prince is "like the shadow of a huge rock* over the parched land" (Is 32,2). But such a shadow, being ambiguous, can deceive: as easily that of the withered gourd plant over Jonah's head (Jon 4,5ff), as that of the king of Israel (Lm 4,20); how much more that of Egypt (Is 30,2), or of the "cedars of Lebanon," which can be uprooted in an instant and hurled into the pit with those who felt confident in their deceitful shade (Ez 31; Dn 4).

2. *The shadow of God.* Instead of a fragile protection, God alone gives a secure shade. One must leave behind the pleasant shading of the sacred trees (Ho 4,13) and find in Yahweh his shade at all times (Ps 121,5; Is 25,4f). The dream of the faithful man is to "dwell in the shadow of Shaddai" (Ps 91,1); to be, as the true Servant, in the shadow of His powerful hand (Is 49,2; 51,16) or of His wings (Ps 17,8; 57,2; 63,8).

Behind these metaphors, one encounters certain memories of the exodus. The LXX was conscious of this when it translated the verb *sakan* (to shelter, to dwell, to repose) by *skiazein, episkiazein* (to shelter with its shadow, to overshadow). The cloud* overshadowed the tent of God (Ex 40,35), thus determining the length of the encampments (Nm 9,18.22); it sheltered even the Israelites with its shadow (10,34), protecting them marvelously, as the Book of Wisdom says (Ws 19,7). This protection will be renewed in the last times. Upon a purified Zion will rest the glory of Yahweh, like "a canopy and a tent, to shade from the parching heat of day, and serve as a refuge and a cover against the rain and the storm" (Is 4,5f). And while Israel journeys beneath this divine glory, "the forests will provide shade for them" (Ba 5,7ff; cf 1,12).

At the time of the consecration of the temple*, the cloud spread over the holy of holies; and Solomon cried out, "Yahweh has determined to dwell in the dark cloud" (1 K 8, 12). To the idea of protection is added here that of the intimate presence* of God. It is in this sense that Jerusalem, like the spouse of the Canticle, can "be seated in her desired shade" (Ct 2,3). In Mary* the dream has become reality, when she was overshadowed by the power of God (Lk 1,35), conceiving Him upon whom would rest the cloud at the transfiguration (9, 34 p).

3. *The shadow of Israel.* The chosen people become in their turn a source of divine protection. Formerly, high above other kingdoms, the vineyard of Israel covered the mountains with its shadow (Ps 80,11). Cast down by divine judgment, Israel will finally become again a verdant tree* where the birds will come to nest (Ez 17,23; cf Dn 4,9), a visible figure of the kingdom* of God open to all the nations (Mt 13,32 p). In the same way, when Peter heals the sick by his shadow (Ac 5,15), he reveals the salvific presence of God in His Church.

→Cloud—Death—Figure—Hell OT I 1—Light & Dark—Night—Tree 2.

XLD phmcn

SHAME

I. SITUATIONS IN WHICH SHAME IS EXPERIENCED

The vocabulary of shame does not have exactly the same meaning in the Scriptures as it does for us. It comes very close to the notion of frustration and disappointment. To fall on the ground, to be naked, to shrink back, to be useless, are to everyone typical situations of shame; but in the Bible, this feeling is extended to every kind of suffering. Thus even the experience of a famine (Ez 36,30) will be formulated in terms of opprobrium. For the man in the Bible all suffering is experienced in the sight of another person, and draws from others a judgment* to which shame is attached. This is why the notions of shame and judgment are often linked together, judgment being the moment which both during this life and at its term reveals to everyone in the divine light the foolishness or the solidity of one's hope.

1. *Shame and defeat.* As everyone knows, we depend upon exterior help, some plan or some defense which fails or which turns out to be useless. In failing we lose face; we become the object of laughter*. The notion of shame then is linked antithetically to that of support (Ps 22,

4ff: hb. "to be proud"), of hope, of confident faith*. This explains its extension. It is known that the just man depends on God; if this turns out to be ineffective, there will be shame. This is the source of the oft repeated prayer: "Let me not be confounded nor put to shame" (Ps 25,2f; 22,6...; cf Is 49,23). Inversely, when false supports like the Pharaoh (Is 20,5; 30,3ff) or the idols have fallen and have exposed their nothingness by a judgment, the senseless will blush, disappointed and confounded (Is 1,29). They "will shrink back in shame" (Is 42,17; Ps 6,11; 70,4). Frequently their humiliation will be to see the triumph of the very ones whom they thought they saw humiliated (Ws 2,20; 5,1ff) or would some day see humiliated (Ps 35, 26).

2. *Shame and nakedness.* The shame of being without clothing* finds its place among the mysterious facts which the account of paradise shows as going back to the first sin. It is the leveling of the conscience by a solitude* resulting from disorder. Being stripped of one's clothes will be a shame inflicted to punish the daughters of Israel (Ez 23,29; Is 47,1ff).

3. *Shame and sterility.** Whoever does not justify his existence before others by some fruit* is in a situation of opprobrium. Above all this is the case of the woman without children (Lk 1,25; Gn 30,23) and of her who lives alone without a husband (Is 4,1).

4. *Shame and idolatry. Shame* is almost a proper name for an idol* (Baal: 2 S 2,8 hb.). The idol is fragile and illusory, a lie and barrenness (Ws 4,11; Is 41,23f; 44,19), whereas looking on the face* of Yahweh saves one from shame (Ps 34,6).

II. THE JUST MAN SAVED FROM SHAME

1. *By God and by Christ.* The just man is attacked by shame. People turn away from him (Is 53,3; Ws 5,4; Ps 69,8). They identify him with shame (Ps 22,7; 109,25). But he sets his face like a flint (Is 50,7). We often find in the NT the expression of its equivalents—"not to blush"—in a sense that implies an active will to believe, and then to act and to speak, without fearing shame. The believer is promised opprobrium (Mt 5,11f), but he ought not blush either because of Jesus or of His Word (Lk 9,26).

St. Paul (R 1,16; cf 2 Tm 1,8) does not blush for the gospel. Although he still waits for the judgment which will give full verification to his hope, he stands firm in this hope and both acts and speaks on the basis of it. This attitude is the *parrēsia* (gr.) or assurance (some translate it *pride**) of the language and action of a man freed from shame by faith. Shame is thrown off by faith in Jesus: "such is the expectancy of my burning hope; nothing will confound me, but I will rather hold on to my assurance and...Christ will be glorified in my body..." (Ph 1,20). Actually Jesus was the first one to despise shame (He 12,2).

2. *Through fraternal charity.* Paul's vocabulary of shame is strikingly rich and attests to its importance in the sensitiveness of the apostle. Like the men of the OT, Paul experiences the social aspect of his trials (1 Co 4,13); thanks to them, he will experience the charity of those who do not blush for him (G 4,14). The Church is a body in which no part should blush for another (1 Co 12,23). Paul carries the opprobrium of Christ (He 11,26) who has carried our opprobrium and who does not blush to call us brothers (2,11). This is the basis of this notion of charity. It will serve as the rule for those that one would be tempted to despise (R 14,10).

→Confidence—Deception/Disappointment I 2 —Drunkenness 1—Pride—Silence 2—Solitude I 1—Sterility I 1.

PBp jrs

SHEPHERD & FLOCK

Since the patriarchs of Israel were in the heart of a pastoral civilization (cf Gn 4,2) and deeply rooted in the tradition of the "nomadic Arameans" (Dt 26,5), the metaphor of the shepherd leading his flock admirably expresses two aspects, apparently opposed and usually distinct, of authority that is exercised over men. The shepherd is simultaneously a leader and a companion. He is a strong man who is capable of defending his flock against wild beasts (1 S 17,34-37; cf Mt 10,16; Ac 20,29). He is also gentle with his flock, knowing their condition (Pr 27,23), adapting himself to their needs (Gn 33,13f), bearing them in his arms (Is 40,11), cherishing each and every one of them "as his daughter" (2 S 12,3). His authority is not disputed; it is based on his devotion and love.

Apart from this, in the ancient East (Babylonia and Assyria), the kings like to consider themselves shepherds to whom the divinity had entrusted the duty of gathering together and caring for the sheep of the flock. Against this background, the Bible describes in detail the relations which unite Israel with God (the expected Messiah, and the work of salvation accomplished), through Christ and His representatives.

OT

1. *Yahweh, leader and father of the flock.* Contrary to what one might expect, Yahweh* hardly ever receives the title of shepherd. There are two ancient designations (Gn 49,24; 48,15) and two invocations in the psalms (Ps 23,1; 80,2). The title seems to be reserved for the one who is to come. On the other hand, although it is not transferred allegorically to Yahweh, a true parable* of the good shepherd can describe the relations between God and His people. At the time of the exodus, "He urged His people forward as sheep" (Ps 95,7), like "a flock in the desert" (Ps 78,52f); "as the shepherd who feeds his flocks gathers the lambs in his arms, puts them on his breast, and leads to repose those that are with young" (Is 40,11), Yahweh continues thus "to lead" His people (Ps 80,2). Certainly, Israel is more like a stubborn heifer than a lamb in a meadow (Ho 4,16); Israel will have to go off into captivity (Jr 13,17). Then once again Yahweh "will lead him to the fountains of waters" (Is 49,10) and gather together the dispersed (cf 56,8) "by whistling" for them (Ze 10,8). He shows the same solicitude toward each of the faithful who, under the staff of God, lack nothing and can fear nothing (Ps 23,1-4). Finally, His mercy extends to all flesh* (Si 18, 13).

2. *The flock and its shepherds.* The Lord entrusts to His servants the sheep that He Himself leads to pasture (Ps 100,3; 79,13; 74,1; Mi 7,14); He guides them "by the hand of Moses" (Ps 77,21) and, lest "the community of Yahweh be without a shepherd," He appoints Joshua as leader after Moses (Nm 27,15-20). He draws David from behind the sheepfold in order to have him graze His people (Ps 78,70ff; 2 S 7,8; cf 5,2; 24,17). While the Judges (7,7), the leaders of the people (Jr 2,8) and the princes of the nations (Jr 25,34ff; Na 3,18; Is 44,28) are given the title of shepherd, it is not explicitly used of the kings of Israel, as it is not used of Yahweh; nevertheless the role is attributed to them (1 K

22,17; Jr 23,1-2; Ez 34,1-10). In fact the title is reserved for the new David*: it is an element of eschatological hope. This is the message of Ezekiel that was prepared for by Jeremiah: Yahweh again takes over the direction of His flock and will entrust it to the Messiah.

The shepherds of Israel prove to be unfaithful to their mission*. They have not sought Yahweh (Jr 10,21), but revolted against Him (2,8); they have not concerned themselves with the care of the flock, but have pastured themselves (Ez 34,3), leaving the sheep to scatter and disperse (Jr 23,1f; 50,6; Ez 34,1-10). "All these shepherds, the wind will send to pasture" (Jr 22,22). According to the vow of the prophet (Mi 7,14f), Yahweh will take the flock in hand (Jr 23,3), gather it together (Mi 4,6), lead it (Jr 50,19), and finally keep it (Jr 31,10; Ez 34, 11-22). Then He will try to provide it with "shepherds according to His heart who will feed their flocks with understanding and wisdom" (Jr 3,15; 23,4). Ultimately, according to Ezekiel, there will be only a single shepherd, the new David, with Yahweh for God (Ez 34, 23f): this will be "the flock that I shall feed" (34,31), and which will multiply (36,37f). It will be ruled by that one shepherd; and under His rule the former enemies, Juda and Israel, will be made one (37,22.24; cf Mi 2,12f).

After the exile, however, the shepherds of the community do not come up to the expectations of Yahweh; and Zechariah resumes the polemic against them, announcing the type of shepherd to come. Yahweh is going to visit* these wicked shepherds in His anger (Ze 10,3; 11,4-17) and brandish the sword (13,7). In Israel, after this manner of purification there will survive a remnant* (13,8f). The context of the prophecy calls for one to see in the stricken shepherd (13,7) not the foolish shepherd (11,15ff), but the "pierced" shepherd (12,10) whose death was salutary (13,1-6). This shepherd is identified concretely with the Servant who, like a dumb sheep, must justify the dispersed sheep by His sacrifice (Is 53,6f.11f).

NT

In the time of Christ, the shepherds were judged differently. In the eyes of the Law*, which it was hardly possible for them to practise, they were ranked with the thieves and murderers. Nevertheless, the prophecy of the shepherd who was to come was kept in mind. Jesus fulfilled the prophecy. He even seems to have wanted to place the shepherds among the "little ones" who, like the publicans and prostitutes, eagerly receive the good news. The welcome that the shepherds gave to Jesus, probably born in their stable, can be interpreted in this sense (Lk 2,8-20). Faithful to the biblical tradition, Jesus depicts the merciful solicitude of God under the figure of the shepherd who goes to look for the lost sheep (Lk 15,4-7). However, it is in His person that He fulfills the expectant hope for the good shepherd, and He is the one who delegates to certain men a pastoral function in the Church.

1. *Jesus, the good shepherd. The synoptics* give numerous characteristics which herald the Johannine allegory. The birth of Jesus in Bethlehem fulfilled the prophecy of Micah (Mt 2,6 = Mi 5,1); His merciful approach proves Him to be the shepherd that Moses wanted (Nm 27,17), for He comes to the aid of the sheep who have no shepherd (Mt 9,36; Mk 6,34). And Jesus sees Himself as sent to the lost sheep of Israel (Mt 15,24; 10,6; Lk 19,10). The "little flock" of disciples that He has gathered together (Lk 12, 32) represents the eschatological community to which is promised the kingdom* of the blessed (cf Dn 7,27). The flock will be persecuted by the wolves from without (Mt 10,16; R 8,36) and from within by those disguised as sheep (Mt 7, 15). The flock will be dispersed; but according to the prophecy of Zechariah, the shepherd who shall have been struck shall gather it together in the Galilee of nations* (Mt 26,31f; cf Ze 13, 7). Finally, at the end of time, the Lord of the sheep shall separate the good from the wicked in the flock (Mt 25,31f).

In this spirit other NT writers present the "great shepherd of the sheep" (He 13,20), greater than Moses, the "prince of shepherds" (1 P 5,4), "the shepherd and the guardian" who has led back the stray souls and cured them by His own death (1 P 2,24f). Finally, in the Apocalypse, which seems to follow an apocryphal tradition about the Messiah, the Christ-Lamb* becomes the shepherd who leads unto the source of life (Ap 7,17) and strikes the pagans with a rod of iron (19,15; 12,5).

In the fourth gospel these scattered marks form a grandiose tableau that depicts the living Church under the staff of one shepherd (Jn 10). Nevertheless, there is a special nuance: it considers not so much the king, Lord of the flock; but rather the Son of God revealing to His own the love of the Father. Jesus' discourse resumes the former ideas and develops them. As in Ezekiel (Ez 34,17), it is a matter of judgment

(Jn 9,39). Israel is like harassed sheep (Ez 34, 3) given over to "thieves and brigands" (Jn 10,1.10), dispersed (Ez 34,5f.12; Jn 10,12). Jesus, like Yahweh, "frees them" and "leads them to good pasture" (Ez 34,10-14; Jn 10,11.3.9.16); then they will know the Lord (Ez 34,15.30; Jn 10,15) who has saved them (Ez 34,22; Jn 10,9). The "one shepherd" who was foretold (Ez 34, 23), Jesus says "It is I" (Jn 10,11).

Jesus is still more explicit. He is the one mediator, the doorway to the sheep (10,7) and to the pastures (10,9f). He alone delegates the pastoral power (cf 21,15ff); He alone gives life* in the full liberty of going and coming (cf Nm 27,17). A new existence is founded upon the mutual knowledge of the pastor and the sheep (10,3f.14f), a reciprocal love founded upon the love that unites the Father and the Son (14,20; 15,10; 17,8f.18-23). Finally, Jesus is the perfect shepherd because He gives His life for the sheep (10,15.17f). He is not only "struck" (Mt 26,31; Ze 13,7), but of Himself, He lays down His life (Jn 10,18). The dispersed sheep that He calls come from the fold of Israel and from other nations (10,16; 11,52). Finally, the flock that is thus called together is united forever, for it is the love of the Father almighty that maintains it and assures it eternal life (10,27-30).

2. *The Church and its shepherds.* According to John, the discourse of the good shepherd inaugurated the Church. Jesus received the man who was born blind (whom He cured) after He was driven from the synagogue by the evil leaders of Israel. Peter, after the resurrection, received the mission of feeding the entire Church (21,16). Other "shepherds" (E 4,11) are charged with watching* over the churches: the "elders" and the "bishops" (1 P 5,1ff; Ac 20, 28). Following the example of the Lord, they must seek* the stray sheep (Mt 18,12ff) and watch out for the devouring wolves that will not spare the flock, those false teachers who lead into heresy (Ac 20,28ff). The very title, shepherd, should call forth those qualities of the shepherds and the behavior of Yahweh in the OT. The NT recalls some of these traits: the shepherds must feed the Church of God eagerly and lovingly, without seeking themselves (cf Ez 34,2f), while becoming the models for the flock. Then "you will be rewarded by the prince of shepherds" (1 P 5,3f).

→Authority—Church II 2, V 2—David 1.3—Gate NT—God OT IV—Lamb of God 3—

Ministry II 3—Peter 3 c—Unity III—Visitation OT 1.

CL & XLD rco'c

SICKNESS/HEALING

Sickness with its accompanying suffering poses a problem for men of all times. Their response depends on the idea they have of the world where they live and of the forces which control them. In the ancient Near East they considered sickness as a scourge caused by the evil spirits or sent by the gods who have been angered by a cultic fault. To obtain a cure they practiced exorcisms intended to get rid of the evil* spirits and they implored the gods' pardon by supplications and sacrifices. Babylonian writings preserve formulas of both kinds. Medicine likewise was a function particular to priests. It remained in some ways close to magic. Man had to wait for the empirical spirit of the Greeks to see it developed independently as a positive science. Departing from this state of affairs, biblical revelation leaves aside the scientific aspect of the problem. It is concerned exclusively with the religious meaning of sickness and of healing in the plan of salvation. This is all the more true since in sickness the power of Death* over man is already evident (cf 1 C 11, 28-32); it must, then, have a similar meaning.

OT

I.   SICKNESS

1.   Health supposes a fullness of vital strength; sickness is conceived especially as a *state of weakness and feebleness* (Ps 38,11). Beyond this empirical verification, medical observations are very summary. They are limited to what one sees: diseases of the skin, wounds and fractures, fever and shaking (thus in the psalms of the sick: Ps 6; 32; 38; 39; 88; 102). The classification of various diseases remained vague (for example, leprosy*). The natural causes were not even looked for, with the exception of those which are obvious—wounds, a fall (2 S 4,4), old age. Qoheleth describes the decline of old age with somber humor (Qo 12,1-6; cf Gn 27,1; 1 K 1,1-4; and in contrast Dt 34,7). In fact, for the religious man the essential point is completely different. What is the meaning of sickness for the stricken person?

2.   In a world where everything depends on *divine causality*, sickness was no exception. It is impossible not to see in it a blow from God which strikes man (Ex 4,6; Jb 16,12ff; 19,21; Ps 39,11f). Equally in dependence upon God, beings superior to man can also be recognized as intervening, such as the destroying angel* (2 S 24,15ff; 2 K 19,35; cf Ex 12,23), personified plagues (Ps 91,5f), or Satan* (Jb 2,7). In post-exilic Judaism attention is turned more and more to the action of demons, evil* spirits. Sickness lets us catch a glimpse of their influence over the world where we live. But why this demoniac influence, this presence of evil in the world, if God is the absolute master?

3.   By a spontaneous movement, the religious intuition of men established a *connection between sickness and sin**. Biblical revelation does not contradict this, it merely clarifies the conditions under which this connection should be understood. God created man for happiness (cf Gn 2). Sickness, as all other human ills, is contrary to this basic intention. Sickness entered the world only as a consequence of sin (cf Gn 3,16-19). It is one of the signs of the wrath* of God against a sinful world (cf Ex 9,1-12). It carries this meaning especially in the scheme of the doctrine of the covenant*. It is one of the principal curses which will strike the unfaithful people of God (Dt 28,21f.27ff.35). The experience of sickness, then, should result in a sharpening of a man's awareness of sin. It can be effectively shown that this is the way it is in the psalms of supplication. The request for a cure is always joined with a confession of sins (Ps 38,2-6; 39,9-12; 107,17). The question comes up, however, of how to know whether all sickness is caused by the personal sins of the sick person. Here the teaching is less precise. Recourse to the principle of collective guilt gives an inadequate reply (cf Jn 9,2). The OT glimpses only two possible solutions. When sickness strikes the just man, like Job or Tobit, it can be a providential test to show his fidelity (Tb 12, 13). In the outstanding example of the suffering just one, the Servant* of Yahweh, it will have a value of atonement for the faults of sinners (Is 53,4f).

II.   HEALING

1.   The OT in no way forbids recourse to *medical practices*. Isaiah used them to cure Ezekiel (2 K 20,7), and Raphael used them to nurse

Tobit (Tb 11,8.11f). The use of certain simple remedies was current (cf Is 1,6; Jr 8,22; Ws 7, 20), and Ben Sira even gave fine praise to the medical profession (Si 38,1-8.12f). What were proscribed were the magical practices connected with the idolatrous cults (2 K 1,1-4) which often corrupted medicine itself (cf 2 Ch 16,12).

2. But *it is to God above all that one must have recourse*, since He is the master of life (Si 38, 9ff.14). He it is who smites and He who cures (Dt 32,39; cf Ho 6,1). He is *the* doctor of men (Ex 15,26): that is why the angel sent to cure Sara is called Raphael (="God heals") (Tb 3, 17). Thus, sick people address themselves to His representatives, the priests (Lv 13,49ff; 14, 2ff; cf Mt 8,4) and prophets (1 K 14,1-13; 2 K 4,21; 8,7ff). With a humble confession* of their sins, they implore the cure as a grace*. The Psalter shows them laying bare their misery, imploring God's help, entreating His omnipotence and mercy (Ps 6; 38; 41; 88; 102. . .). Because of their trust in Him they are ready to receive the favor they implore. This comes at times in the form of a miracle* (1 K 17,17-24; 2 K 4,18-37; 5). In any case, it has the meaning of a sign; God has stooped down to suffering human nature to ease its pains.

3. Sickness nevertheless, even if it has a meaning, remains an evil. This is why the eschatological promises of the prophets foresee its *suppression in the new* world* where God will place His own people at the end of time*. No more sick people (Is 35,5f), no more suffering or tears (25,8; 65,19). In a world freed from sin, the consequences of sin which weigh so heavily on our race should vanish. When the suffering just* one has taken upon Himself our ills, we will be cured, thanks to His bruises (53,4f).

NT

I. JESUS CONFRONTS SICKNESS

1. Throughout His whole ministry, *Jesus found sick people* wherever He went. Without interpreting sickness in too narrow a perspective of retribution (cf Jn 9,2f), He saw in it an evil from which men suffer, a consequence of sin, a sign of the power of Satan* over men (Lk 13, 16). He felt pity because of it (Mt 20,34), and this pity called forth His action. Without stopping to distinguish natural sickness from diabolic possession, "He casts out spirits and cures

those who are ill" (Mt 8,16 p). The two things go together. They equally manifest His power (cf Lk 6,19) and they ultimately have the same meaning. They signify the triumph of Jesus over Satan and the inauguration of the kingdom* of God here below according to the Scriptures (cf Mt 11,5 p). Not that sickness would henceforth disappear from the world; but the divine power which will finally conquer it is from this moment on at work here below. This is why, of all the sick people who express their confidence in Him (Mk 1,40; Mt 8,2-6 p), Jesus made clear but one demand, that they believe; for all things are possible to faith* (Mt 9,28; Mk 5,36 p; 9,23). Their faith in Him implied faith in the kingdom* of God, and this is the faith which saves (Mt 9,22p; 15,28; Mk 10,52 p).

2. The miracles* of healing, then, anticipate in some measure the state of perfection which human nature will at length recover in the kingdom of God, according to the prophecies. But they also have a *symbolic meaning* pertaining to actual time. Sickness is a symbol of the state in which sinful man finds himself; spiritually he is blind, deaf, paralyzed. . .The cure of the sick man is, therefore, also a symbol. It represents the spiritual cure which Jesus came to work in men. He forgave the sins of the paralytic, and to show that He had this power, He cured him (Mk 2,1-12 p). This aspect of miracles is revealed especially in the fourth gospel. The cure of the paralytic of Bethzatha signifies the life-giving work accomplished by Jesus (Jn 5,1-9.19-26), and the cure of the man born blind shows Jesus as the light* of the world (Jn 9). The acts of Jesus for the sick, therefore, serve as a prelude to the Christian sacraments. He has come to our world as a physician for sinners (Mk 2,17 p), a physician who to remove infirmities and sicknesses takes them upon Himself (Mt 8,17=Is 53,4). This is the meaning of the passion; Jesus will take part in the condition of suffering humanity in order to be able to triumph finally over its ills.

II. THE APOSTLES AND THE CHURCH CONFRONT SICKNESS

1. The sign of the kingdom of God constituted by *miraculous cures* did not remain confined to the earthly life of Jesus. He associated His apostles, from their first mission, with His power to cure the sick (Mt 10,1 p). At the time of

their definitive mission, He promised them a continued realization of this sign to accredit their preaching of the gospel (Mk 16,17f). The Acts note repeatedly the miraculous cures (Ac 3, 1ff; 8,7; 9,32ff; 14,8ff; 28,8f) which show the power of the name* of Jesus and the reality of His resurrection. Likewise Paul mentions among the charisms that of healing (1 Co 12,9.28.30). This permanent sign continues to give witness to the Church of Jesus, by showing that the Holy Spirit acts in it. Yet the grace of God ordinarily comes to the sick in a less spectacular way. Taking up an action of the apostles (Mk 6,13), the "presbyters" of the Church anointed* the sick with oil in the name of the Lord, while they prayed with faith and confessed their sins. This prayer saved them, for their sins were forgiven and they could hope that, God willing, they would be cured (Jm 5,14ff).

2. This cure, however, is not produced infallibly, as if it were a magic effect of the prayer of the rite. As long as the present world lasts, humanity must continue to bear the consequences of sin. But "by taking upon Himself our ills" during the passion, Jesus has given them a new meaning. Like all suffering, they henceforth have a redemptive* value. Paul, who experienced them on many occasions (G 4,13; 2 Co 1,8ff; 12,7-10), knows that they unite a person to the suffering Christ. "We bear in our body the sufferings of the death of Jesus, so that the life of Jesus also may be seen in our body" (2 Co 4,10). Whereas Job could not manage to understand the meaning of his trial, the Christian rejoices "to make up in his own flesh what is lacking in Christ's—suffering for His body, which is the Church" (Col 1,24). While awaiting the arrival of this return to paradise* where men will forever be cured by the fruits of the tree* of life (Ap 22,2; cf Ez 47,12), sickness itself is integrated, like suffering* and death*, into the order of salvation*. Not that it will be easy to bear. It remains a trial*, and it is charity to help the sick bear it by visiting them and comforting them. "Bear the ills of everyone," advises Ignatius of Antioch. But serving the sick is to serve Jesus Himself in His suffering members. "I was sick and you visited me," He will say on judgment day (Mt 25,36). The sick man in the Christian world is no longer the one accursed from whom people turn away (cf Ps 38,12; 41,6-10; 88,9). He is the image and sign of Jesus Christ.

→Anointing II 1—Calamity—Death OT I 5—Evil Spirits OT 1; NT I—Good & Evil I 1—Imposition of Hands NT—Leprosy—Life IV 1 —Miracle II 2 b—Oil—Old Age 1—Salvation —Suffering.

JGi & PG hjb

SIGN

By a sign we mean something that allows us to know the thought or the will of a person, the existence or the truth of a thing, and this may be a matter of a natural association or of convention. The Bible is familiar with many sorts of signs used in dealings between men: signals for the use of warriors (Js 2,18; Jg 20,38; Is 13, 2; 18,3), the liturgical signal of the trumpets (1 M 4,40), an agreed sign to disclose the identity of a person (Tb 5,2), some sort of mark (Ez 39,15), distinctive handwriting (2 Th 3,17) or an indication of virtue (Ws 5,11.13), etc.

Since God adapts Himself to our nature, He too gives men signs (hb. *ôtot*, gr. *semeia*) in order to save them. They are often called symbolic prodigies (hb. *môftim*, gr. *terata*) and wonders (hb. *niflaôt*, gr. *thaumasia*); for it is mainly by the transcendence of His saving action that God "signifies" His power and His love. This is why the miracles*, because they are effective and extraordinary, occupy a privileged place among the divine signs connected with the history of salvation (the only ones with which we are concerned here). Nevertheless, miracles are not the only divine signs, and the great sign will ultimately be Jesus Himself, giving us the supreme proof of the Father's love.

OT

God nourishes the faith of His people by the memory of past signs and the giving of signs in the present. And he encourages their faith by the prophecy of future signs.

I. PAST SIGNS

The wonders of the life of Moses (Ex 3,20; 15,11; 34,10; Jg 6,13; Ps 77,12.15; 78,11f.32; Jr 21,2; Ne 9,17) and of the history of Joshua (Js 3,5) up to the occupation of the Promised Land inclusively (vg Ps 78,4; 105,2.5) are considered in the OT as the great divine signs (*ôtot*: vg Ex 4,9.17.28.40; 10,1f; Nm 14,11.22; Js 24,17): Through the wonders that shook

Egypt (Ex 11,9) and the events that followed (Ps 105,5) God not only convinced the Israelites of the mission of the men He had sent (Ex 4, 1-9.29.31; 13,31), but gave outstanding proof of His power and love (Ps 86,10; 106,7; 107,8) by freeing His people.

Deuteronomy (4,34; 6,22; 7,19...) and other texts following it (Ex 7,3; Ps 78,43; 105,27; 135, 9; Jr 32,20f; Ne 9,10; Est 10,3f; Ba 2,11; Ws 10,16) are fond of the pleonastic expression "signs and wonders." Their readers were no longer the witnesses of these events; but, in order to remain faithful to the God of the covenant, they had constantly to remind themselves of them (Dt 4,9; 8,14ff; Ps 105,5): the *sign-events* of their origins had to remain present in the memory* of Israel.

II. PRESENT SIGNS

1. The memories on which Israel's faith was nourished were preserved by the *liturgy* in the celebration of the feasts, "the memorial of the marvels" of Yahweh (Ps 111,4), especially in certain rites (Ex 13,9.16; cf Dt 6,8; 11,18) and Certain objects (Nm 17,3.25; cf Js 4,6).

2. The memory of faith went back even further than Moses, to the call of Abraham and beyond that to the creation of the world, singling out things that the priestly tradition interpreted as the ever-present divine signs: the *sabbath** (Ex 31,16f; Ez 20,12), the *rainbow* (Gn 9,8-17), *circumcision** (17,9-13), all meant to remind them of the first covenants, with Adam, with Noah and with Abraham.

For the God who worked the wonders of the Exodus was the same who created the wonders of the universe (Ps 89,6; 136,4; Jb 37,14). And the heavenly signs, that is the *stars**, were a constant reminder of the creator as well as a means of dividing time, marked by the liturgical feasts commemorating the events of mosaic history (Gn 1,14; Ps 65,9; Jr 10,2; Si 42,18f; cf 43, 1-10).

3. On the other hand, sacred history did not come to an end with the entry into the Promised Land, and Yahweh continued to show His saving power there sometimes by *miraculous signs* (1 K 13,3.5; 2 K 19,29; 20,8f; the histories of Elijah, Elisha and Isaiah), which might be offered on His own initiative (Is 7,11) or granted in answer to men's prayers (Jg 6,17.37; 2 K 20, 8f; 2 Ch 32,24). It is true that, by means of

magic*, false prophets were also able to prophecy and work really prodigious signs, interpret real or pretended dreams* (cf Jr 23,26ff). That is why the only things that would be recognized as divine signs were the ones produced by men whose preaching was in conformity with the true yahwist faith (Dt 13,2-6).

4. Certain chance circumstances were interpreted as the expression of the divine will (1 S 14,10; cf Gn 24,12ff). More often it happened that a natural but unforeseeable event was foretold by a prophet as the work of God. Then, when it came about, it was seen as a sign that God was in fact giving the mission foretold in the past (1 S 10,1.7) or that He would intervene in a more decisive way in the future (2,34; Jr 44,29f; cf 20,6; 28,15ff); it encouraged the witnesses to have confidence (Ex 14,13; Is 7,1-9) or to be converted (2 S 12,13f; Jr 36,3f). Apart from this, the fulfillment of these *short-term prophecies* was one of the criteria by which false and true prophets were distinguished (Dt 18,22).

5. *The symbolic actions of the prophets*, which were a type of prophecy in act (Is 20,3; Ez 4,3; 12,6.11; 24,24.27; Ho 1—3), signify the future efficacity of the Word of which these men were bearers. The children of Hosea (Ho 1,4-8; 2, 1-3.25) and of Isaiah (Is 8,1-4.18) were also signs, because their origin and their symbolic *names* contained a prophecy of certain events to be brought about by God. In the case of the prophesied birth of Emmanuel (God-with-us), who was the heir to the dynasty, the sign in itself already had a salvific importance (Is 7,14).

6. Certain *external marks of protection* (Gn 4,15; Ex 12,13; Ez 9,4.6), which with the support of the word of Yahweh helped to proclaim and bring about His sovereign will, can be classed with these signs.

All these present signs also have as their object the revelation in one way or another of the love and transcendence of God. This is why they were given to men who were open to the Word of God (cf Ex 7,13; Is 7,10ff) in order to make them live from faith.

III. FUTURE SIGNS

The cessation of signs—miracles and prophetic announcements (Ps 74,9)—had reinforced the anguish at God's absence caused by the destruction of the Temple. But then a voice was heard in exile announcing "a sign for ever, ineffaceable" (Is 55,13): the coming return, described as a new exodus* (43,16-20). Later on, after the disappointment of this return, the hope of a more decisive intervention was nursed: "send new portents, do fresh wonders" (Si 36, 5f). Certain inspired writers also suggested that this intervention would not be reserved for Israel: according to Is 66,19 Yahweh, in taking His revenge on the nations, would perform a sign that would be the beginning of their conversion. By means of these prophecies and hopes the holy Remnant was prepared for the coming of the Savior.

NT

In NT times the Jews expected the messianic days to produce wonders at least equal to those of the exodus, and connected with dreams of victory over the pagans (cf 1 Co 1,22). Jesus disappointed this expectation from the earthly point of view. But He fulfilled it perfectly from the spiritual point of view, by inaugurating the true salvation through His miracles and bringing it about by His "exodus" (Lk 9,31), by the great sign (Jn 12,33) of His elevation on the cross and in glory. Although He was opposed by some, Jesus was, throughout His mission as the Servant taking upon Himself our sicknesses (Mt 8,17=Is 53,4), the efficacious Sign bringing relief to the multitude (Lk 2,34), the standard (Is 11,10ff; hb. *nes*, gr. *semeion*) raised up for the scattered people to gather round (Jn 11,52).

I. SIGNS IN THE LIFE OF JESUS

1. Faithful to the divine promise that the wonders of old would be repeated (Mt 11,4f=Is 35, 5f; 26,19), *Jesus* worked many miracles, which lent authority to His word and were of the nature of saving sign-events and at the same time of prophetic miming (cf Mk 8,23ff). It was these above all, together with His personal authority and the whole of His activity, that constituted "the signs of the times" (Mt 16,3), that is the signs of the arrival of the messianic era. But, unlike Israel in the desert (Ex 17,2.7; Nm 14,22). He refused to tempt* God by asking for signs on His own account (Mt 4,7=Dt 6,16), or to satisfy those who asked Him for a sign in order to tempt Him (Mt 16,1ff), looking for spectacular wonders. The *Synoptics* too, echoing His reserve, avoid using the word "signs"

of the miracles, as His adversaries did (12,38 p; Lk 23,8). Of course, God did give signs of the coming of salvation to the poor, like Mary Lk 1,36ff) or the shepherds (2,12). But He could not give the Jews the signs that they expected: this would have been contrary to His mission. The blind should have begun by paying attention to the "sign of Jonah" according to Lk 11, 29-32, that is to the preaching of repentance by Jesus. They would then have been capable of discerning the "signs of the times," without demanding others to suit themselves, and would have been prepared to accept the most decisive witness of them all, the "sign of Jonah" according to Mt 12,40, that is the resurrection of Christ.

2. Any reserve about the use of the word *semeion* disappears in John's account (except for Jn 4,48), as well as in the Acts and the epistles. For *John* the sight of the signs should have led Jesus' contemporaries to believe in Him (Jn 9,37-38...): these signs revealed His glory (2,11) to the men whom He had tested (6,6), as Yahweh had revealed His glory (Nm 14,22) when He put the people to the test in the desert (Dt 8,2). In this way they prepared them to see* (Jn 19,37=Ze 12,10) by faith the sign of the pierced side of the One raised up on the cross, the source of life (12,33), fulfilling the type of the healing serpent raised up by Moses on a "standard" (Nm 21,8: hb. *nes*, gr. *semeion*; Jn 3,14) for the salvation of the people at the time of the Exodus.

To the Christians who had been converted by seeing these things in the light of faith (cf Jn 20,29) and who were represented by the Greeks who asked to see Jesus (12,21.32f), the blood and water flowing out of the pierced side (19,34) were then seen as the symbols of the life of the Spirit and of the reality of the sacrifice that opened up for us the way to this life through the sacraments of baptism, penance and the Eucharist. And the previous signs of Jesus (5,14; 6; 9; 13,1-10) would themselves be seen as foreshadowing these saving actions of the Risen Christ, the true Temple from whose side springs the living water (2,19; 7,37ff; 19,34; cf Ze 14,8; Ez 47,1f).

II. SIGNS OF THE TIME OF THE CHURCH

1. *The signs inaugurating the last times*. Baptism* will apply to men the saving power of the

resurrection, thus making the sign of physical circumcision* null and void (Col 2,11ff), and Sunday, the day* of the Lord, will be its memorial, thus making the sign of the sabbath* null and void (He 4,1-11; Col 2,16). Thus, with the resurrection the world enters into the "last days" (Ac 2,17). These begin with the pouring out of the Spirit at Pentecost, which brought the Passover to an end and opened up the time of apostolic preaching. In this regard, St. Luke recalled the heavenly "prodigies" of the apocalypse of Joel (Jl 3,1-5), but at the same time mentioning the earthly "signs," in order to make this text fit the Pentecost events, which brought in the decisive stage of the history of salvation "here below" (Ac 2,19).

2. *The signs of the genuine apostle.* Pentecost was the prelude to a new series of "signs and wonders" (Ac 2,43; 4,30; 5,12; 6,8; 14,3; 15,12; He 2,4) which, like the miracles of Jesus (Ac 2,22), "accredit" the apostles by "confirming their word" (Mk 16,20). And so Paul, "by the power of signs and wonders, by the power of the Holy Spirit" (R 15,19), saw his word welcomed as the word of God (1 Th 2,13) and could produce in men's hearts a faith based on the power of God (1 Co 2,4f).

These apostolic signs are, then, quite different from the charism* or the gift of tongues granted to certain Christians and resembling the incomprehensible language once inflicted on the unbelievers (1 Co 14,21f; cf Is 28,11f).

On the other hand, the miracles would not be enough to distinguish the genuine apostle from his imitator, without those other victories of the Spirit, his "perfect constancy" (2 Co 12,12) and his selflessness (1 Th 2,2-12; cf 2 P 2,3.14; Tt 1, 11; 2 Tm 3,2), together with the orthodoxy of his message (cf G 1,8; 2 Co 11,13ff; 1 Jn 4,1-6; Ac 13,6ff), which remained the decisive criterion for the faithful.

3. *The sign of the woman clothed in the sun.* Behind the persecutions that raged against the faithful and the attempts made by the false messiahs and false prophets to lead them astray by misleading signs (Ap 13,13f; 16,14; 19,20), the driving force was Satan*. And to encourage those who were being put to the test, the author of the Apocalypse described in the heaven of his visions, in the midst of the signs of the stars, a symbolic figure, a "great sign" (Ap 12,1): a woman, who represented the Church, against whom a "second sign" (12,3), the Satan-Dragon, proved powerless in the end. As the successor to

the Daughter of Zion, who gave birth to the Messiah (12,5), the Church* like Israel was put to the test in the desert (12,6.14; cf Ex 19,4; Dt 32,11; Is 40,31), but she was fed with a manna accessible to faith alone (Ap 12,6; cf 2,17; Jn 6,34f.47-51). In this way she led men to the possession of the true life by adoring the one true God (Ap 22,1ff).

4. *The signs of the end of times.* Compared with the abundant apocalyptic literature produced in Judaism to satisfy curiosity about the end of time, the NT is remarkable for its sober approach. The common apocalyptic language is retained but subordinated to the final state of affairs introduced by the death and resurrection of Christ. It is true that it is prophesied that in these "last days" there will be "a deceptive show of signs and portents" (2 Th 2,9), worked by magicians* and false prophets who will imitate the real apostles (Mt 24,24 p). It is true that the eschatological discourse, which in Mt speaks of the "sign of the coming of Jesus and of the end of the world" (24,3), still describes these events in the language of cosmic signs (24,29f; Lk 21,25). But in the end all these signs will give way to the sign of the Son of Man (Mt 24,30), that is in all probability to the reality of His triumph.

→Calamity 2—Charisms I 1—Circumcision OT 1.2—Cross I 4—Dreams OT—Figure—Faith—Miracle—Mystery—Name OT 1—Parable I 1 Pentecost II 2—Presence of God OT II—Prophet OT II 2, IV 4—Resurrection NT I 1—Revelation OT II; NT I 3—Sabbath NT 2—See OT II; NT I 2—Sickness/Healing NT I 2, II 1—Stars 2—Temple—Woman NT 3—Worship OT II.

PT ems

SILENCE

Preceding, interrupting, or prolonging speech, silence enlightens in its own way the dialogue between God and man.

1. *The silence of God.* "In the beginning the Word was God" (Jn 1,1), but like a "mystery shrouded in silence from eternal ages" (R 16,25), until revealed to man. This secret ripening of the Word is expressed in time by the predestination of the elect*: even before speaking to them, God knows* them from their mothers' wombs

(Jr 1,5; cf R 8,29). But there is another silence of God, which does not seem any longer heavy with the mystery of love, but rather full of the divine anger. In order to unsettle His sinful people, God no longer speaks through His prophets (Ez 3,26). Why, after having spoken so often and so forcefully, does God remain silent before the triumph of impiety (Ha 1,13)? Why does He no longer reply to the prayer* of Job (Jb 30,20) or to that of the psalmists (Ps 83,2; 109,1)? For Israel which desires to hear its God, this silence is a punishment* (Is 64,11) since it signifies the departure of its Lord (Ps 35,22). This silence is eqivalent to a sentence of death (cf Ps 28,1) and it proclaims the "silence of Sheol, where God and man no longer speak to each other" (Ps 94,17; 115,17). Nonetheless the dialogue is not broken off definitively, for the silence of God can also be a reflection of His patience* during the days of the infidelity of men (Is 57,11).

2. *The silence of man.* "There is a time for silence and a time for speech" (Qo 3,7). This maxim can be understood in different degrees of depth. In the course of time silence can signify indecision (Gn 24,21), approval (Nm 30, 5-16), confusion (Ne 5,8), fear (Es 4,14). Man shows his liberty by restraining his tongue* in order to avoid sin (Pr 10,19), especially in the midst of gossip or rash judgments (Pr 11,12f; 17,28; cf Jn 8,6).

Over and above this wisdom which could remain purely human, it is God who establishes the times of silence and of speech for man. Silence before God expresses shame* after sin (Jb 40,4; 42,6; cf 6,24; R 3,19; Mt 22,12), or confidence* in salvation (Lm 3,26; Ex 14,14). It signifies that confronted by the injustice of men, Christ, as a faithful* Servant* (Is 53,7), has placed His cause before God (Mt 26,63 p; 27, 12.14 p). But in other circumstances, not to speak would be to fail in trust and not to confess God (Mt 26,64 p; Ac 18,9; 2 Co 4,13): a man cannot then be silent (Jr 4,19; 20,9; Is 62,6; Lk 19,40).

Finally, when God goes to visit* man, the earth keeps silence (Ha 2,20; Zp 1,7; Is 41,1; Ze 2,17; Ps 76,9; Ap 8,1); and when He has come, a silence of fear or of respect expresses the adoration* of man (Lm 2,10; Ex 15,16; Lk 9,36). For one who meditates in his heart (Lk 2,19.51) this humble silence is not only the path to rest (Ps 131,2) but also the way to the revelation* promised by the Lord to little ones (Mt 11,25).

→Human Speech—Lamb of God 1—Lips— Tongue 1—Word of God.

AR jpl

SIMPLICITY

The simplicity which characterizes the child (hb. *petî*; gr. *nēpios*; vg *parvulus, innocens*) has different aspects: lack of experience and prudence, docility, absence of calculation, presence of rightness of heart which includes sincerity of language and excludes ill will in outlook and in action. Thus it is opposed either to discretion or to duplicity.

1. *Simplicity and wisdom.* Simplicity then can be a defect; if it consists in an ignorance (Pr 14,18) which causes us to act imprudently (Pr 22,3), to believe the first comer (Pr 14,15), or to yield to the seductions of a wicked pleasure (Pr 7,7; 9,16; R 16,18). It is a fatal levity (Pr 1,32), unworthy of a Christian (1 Co 14,20). From this simplicity wisdom delivers those who hear its proverbs (Pr 1,4), when they call upon her Pr 1, 22; 8,5; 9,4ff). Wisdom makes them wise (Ps 19, 8), if they open themselves to the light of the Word of God (Ps 119,130f) with this simplicity which Eve lacked (2 Co 11,3) and which those who trust to their own wisdom also lack (Mt 11, 25). This humble faith*, condition of salvation (Mk 10,15; 1 P 2,2), is the first aspect of the simplicity of the children of God. This simplicity is not infantilism. On the contrary, it implies uprightness and integrity (Ph 2,15), of which Job remains the model (Jb 1,8; 2,3).

2. *Simplicity and uprightness.* He who seeks God must flee all double dealing (Ws 1,1). Let nothing divide his heart (Ps 119,113; Jm 4,8), corrupt its intention (1 K 9,4; Si 1,28ff), restrain a generosity extending even to the risk of one's life (1 Ch 29,17; 1 M 2.37.60), or make his confidence hesitate (Jm 1,8). Let there be no deviations in his conduct (Pr 10,9; 28,6; Si 2,12) or in his words (Si 5,9).

He receives the gifts of God with simplicity (Ac 2,46) and gives without calculating, with a sincere love (R 12,8f; 1 P 1,22). His outlook is simple; unpracticed in evil, he aims only at the will of God and of Christ when he owes obedience to men (Co 3,22f; E 6,5ff). This sole intention illuminates his life (Mt 6,22; Lk 11,34) and it makes him more prudent than the serpent.

This purity of intention is symbolized by the simplicity of the dove (Mt 10,16).

→Child II—Hypocrite 1.3—Lie—Pure NT I 3.
CS & MFL jpl

SIN

The Bible speaks often, almost on every page, of the reality that we commonly call *sin*. The terms the OT uses to designate it are numerous and ordinarily borrowed from human relations: *omission, iniquity, rebellion, injustice,* etc. Judaism will add the notion of debt, and this designation will also be used by the NT. It is still more common for the sinner to be represented as "the one who does evil in the eyes of God"; and the "just" (*saddiq*) is normally opposed to the "wicked" (*rāšā'*). But it is particularly through the whole sweep of Bible history that the true nature of sin appears with all its malice and in all its dimensions. Here we also learn that this revelation about man is at the same time a revelation about God; about His love* to which sin is opposed, about His mercy* which He exercises in regard to sin; for the history of salvation is nothing other than the tirelessly repeated attempts of God the Creator to draw man away from his sin.

I. ORIGINAL SIN

Among all the narratives of the OT, that of the fall which opens the history of humanity offers at the start a lesson of extraordinary richness. To understand what sin is, although the word is not used, it is there that we must begin.

1. *The sin of Adam* was manifested essentially as disobedience, an act by which man consciously and deliberately puts himself in opposition to God by violating one of His precepts (Gn 3,3); but beyond this exterior act of rebellion, Scripture *expressly* mentions an interior act which preceded the latter: Adam and Eve disobeyed because, giving in to the suggestion of the serpent, they wished "to be like gods knowing both good and evil" (3,5), which means, according to the most common interpretation, that they wanted to substitute themselves for God in deciding between good* and evil; in taking themselves as the measure, they claimed to be the only masters of their destiny, and

would dispose themselves as they wished. They refused to depend upon Him who created them, thus perverting the relationship which unites man to God.

Now, according to Gn 2, this relationship was not only one of dependence, but also one of friendship. Unlike the gods we meet in the ancient myths (e.g. Gilgamesh X,3), the God of the Bible had refused nothing to man who was "created in His image and likeness" (Gn 1,26f); He reserved nothing for Himself, not even life* (cf Ws 2,23). It is only through the suggestion of the serpent that Eve, then Adam, began to doubt God's infinite generosity: the precept given by God for man's good (cf R 7,10) would only be a device invented by God to safeguard His privileges, and the threat joined to the precept only a lie. "No, you will not die! But God knew that the day you would eat of this fruit, you would be like gods, knowing good and evil" (Gn 3,4f). Man defied a god who had become his rival. The very notion of God was perverted: for the notion of God who is supremely disinterested because He is supremely perfect, who can lack nothing and can only give, was substituted the idea of an indigent being who is interested and entirely concerned in protecting Himself against His creature. Before provoking man to act, sin corrupted his spirit; and as it affected him in his very relation to God of whom he is the image*, a more radical perversion is inconceivable; nor is it surprising that it entails such grave consequences.

2. *The consequences of sin.* Between man and God everything has changed: this is the verdict of conscience*. Even before the chastisement, strictly speaking (Gn 3,23), begins, Adam and Eve who until that time were enjoying divine familiarity (cf 2,25) "hide themselves among the trees from the face of God Yahweh" (3,8). The initiative came from man and the responsibility* for his fault rests with him; he is the one who wished no more of God and fled from Him. The expulsion from Paradise will ratify the wish of man. Then man will learn that the threat was not a lie at all. Far away from God, access to the tree* of life is not possible (3,22). There is only definitive death* left. Adam and Eve were cast out of Paradise. From this time there existed a rupture in the relations between God and man.

Sin also introduced a rupture in the relations between members of human society, a rupture that was at the heart of the first parents. Hardly was the sin committed when Adam withdrew;

and he accused the person whom God had given him as a companion (2,18), "bone of his bone and flesh of his flesh" (2,23). The chastisement ratified this rupture: "You shall be in your husband's power and he shall have dominion over you" (3,16). Afterwards, this rupture shall be extended to the children of Adam: there will be the murder of Abel (4,8), then the reign of violence and the law of the strongest that the wild song of Lamech praised (4,24).

That is not all. The mystery of sin goes beyond the human world. Between God and man a third person has entered upon the scene. The OT will hardly speak about him, no doubt to avoid making him a second God. The Book of Wisdom (Ws 2,24) will identify him as the devil or Satan, and he will reappear in the NT.

Finally, the narration of the first sin is not complete unless hope is offered to man. Without a doubt, the servitude to which he was condemned while thinking he would acquire independence is in itself definitive. Once sin has entered into the world, it can only proliferate; and to the degree that it increases, life will diminish almost to the point of ceasing completely at the deluge (Gn 6,13ff). Since the rupture was started by man, it is clear that the initiative for reconciliation can come only from God. Precisely at the time of this first narrative God gives a hint that one day He will take the initiative (3,15). The goodness of God that man has scorned shall finally prevail; it "shall conquer evil by good" (R 12,21). The Book of Wisdom specifies that Adam "was freed from his fault" (Ws 10,1). At any rate, Genesis already shows this goodness at work because it preserves Noah and his family from universal corruption and its punishment (Gn 6,5-8) in order to create with him, so to speak, a new universe (8,17.21f in comparison with 1,22.28; 3,17). This goodness is also seen at work when, "of one mind in their perversity, the nations had been confounded" (Ws 10,5), it chose Abraham and drew him away from the sinful world (Gn 12,1; cf Js 24,2f.14) in order that "through him all nations of the earth would be blessed" (Gn 12,2f, clearly corresponding to the curses of 3, 14ff).

II. THE SIN OF ISRAEL

Just as sin put a mark on the beginning of the history of mankind, it also put a mark on the history of Israel. From its birth, the latter relived the drama of Adam. In its turn, it learns through its own experience and teaches us what sin is. Two episodes seem particularly instructive.

1. *The adoration of the golden calf.* Like Adam, yet more gratuitously, if that were possible, Israel was filled to overflowing with God's favors. Without any merit on its part (Dt 7,7; 9,4ff; Ez 16,2-5), and only by virtue of God's love (Dt 7,8)—for Israel was neither more nor less a "sinner" than the other nations (cf Js 24, 2.14; Ez 20,7f.18)—it was chosen to be the special people*, privileged among all the peoples of the earth (Ex 19,5), constituted the "first-born son of God" (4,22). To free it from the servitude of Pharaoh and the land of sin (the land where one cannot serve* Yahweh, according to 5,1), God multiplied His marvels. But at the very moment when God "made a covenant" with His people, committing Himself to them, handing down to Moses "the tablets of witness" (31, 18), the people asked Aaron: "Make us a god who walks before us" (32,1). In spite of the proofs that God had given of His "fidelity," Israel found Him too far away, too "invisible," and did not have faith in Him. Israel preferred a god within reach, a god whose anger it could appease through sacrifices*; in any case a god that could be changed over to Israel's way of thinking, rather than Israel being obliged to follow Him and obey His commandments (cf 40, 36ff). Rather than "walk with God," Israel wanted God to walk with it.

The "original" sin of Israel was the refusal to obey, which more profoundly is a refusal to believe in God and abandon itself to Him. Dt 9,7 mentions the refusal to obey; and in fact, it will be renewed with each of those innumerable rebellions of the "stiff-necked people." Much later, when Israel will be tempted to offer worship to the "Baals" besides the worship it offered to Yahweh, it is to be noted that it is because Israel refuses to see in Yahweh the "one thing necessary," the God to whom it owes it existence, and its duty to serve only Him (Dt 6,13; cf Mt 4,10). Later, when St. Paul describes the proper malice of the sin of idolatry, he will not hesitate, even among the pagans, to refer to that first sin of Israel (R 1,23 =Ps 106,20).

2. *The sepulchers of lust.* Immediately after the episode of the golden calf, Dt 9,22 recalls another sin of Israel that Paul also uses, presenting it as a type for the "sins of the desert" (1 Co 10,6). The meaning of the episode is

clear enough. Israel preferred dishes of its own choosing to the food miraculously chosen and provided by God: "Who will give us meat to eat?...Now we waste away, deprived of everything: our eyes see nothing more than manna!" (Nm 11,4ff). Israel refused to be led by God, refused to trust in Him, to submit to what according to the mind of God should constitute the spiritual experience in the desert* (Dt 8,3; cf Mt 4,4). Israel's "lust" will be satisfied; but, like Adam, it will know what it costs man to substitute his ways for the ways of God (Nm 11,33).

III. THE TEACHING OF THE PROPHETS

This is precisely the lesson that God through His prophets will not cease to repeat to Israel. Thus, the man who thinks he can build by himself will only bring about his own ruin. And so the people of God are destroyed as soon as they go off the path that God has traced out for them. Sin, then, is seen as the obstacle *par excellence*, really the only one, to God's plan for Israel, to His rule, to His "glory" which is concretely identified with the glory of Israel, people of God. No doubt in this respect the sin of the leader, of the king, of the priest, is clothed with special responsibility. That is why it is mentioned in particular, though not exclusively. The sin of Akan had stopped the army of all Israel before Ai (Js 7). Very often, the sins of the people as a group are held responsible by the prophets for the misfortunes of the nation: "No, the hand of Yahweh is not too short to save, nor His ear too deaf to hear. But your iniquities have dug an abyss between you and your God" (Is 59,1f).

1. *The denunciation of sin.* The preaching of the prophets also consists to a great extent in the denunciation of sin; both the sin of the leaders (vg 1 S 3,11; 13,13f; 2 S 12,1-15; Jr 22, 13) and that of the people. Thus we have those enumerations of sins that are so frequent in the prophetic literature, ordinarily in reference, more or less directly, to the Decalogue. These enumerations are more numerous in the sapiential literature (vg Dt 27,15-26; Ez 18,5-9; 33,25f; Ps 15; Pr 6,16-19; 30,11-14). Sin becomes a concrete reality, and we learn the cause of Yahweh's withdrawal: violence, theft, iniquitous judgments, lies, adulteries, perjuries, homicides, usury, disregard for rights, and, in short, all the social disorders. The "confession" inserted in

Is 59 reveals in a concrete way what these "iniquities" are which "have dug an abyss between the people and God" (59,2): "Our sins are before us, and we know our wrongs: revolting against and disowning Yahweh, turning away from our God, speaking of oppression and revolt, and murmuring lying words in our hearts. Judgment is put aside and justice has stood far off, for good faith stumbles in the street, and right cannot enter" (59,12ff). A long time before this, Hosea spoke in the same manner: "There is neither sincerity, nor love, nor knowledge of God in the land; but perjury and lying, assassination and theft, adultery and violence, and murder upon murder" (Ho 4,2; cf Is 1,17; 5,8; 65,6f; Am 4,1; 5,7-15; Mi 2,1f).

The lesson is of primary importance: the man who thinks to build by himself, independently of God, shall do it in most cases at another's expense, principally the small and the weak. The psalmist proclaims: "The man who has not put his fortress in God" (Ps 52,9) "plans crime the whole day long" (v 4), while "the just man trusts in the love of God forever and ever" (v 10). Does not David's adultery already give a suggestion of this? (2 S 12). However, from that episode whose importance is known in the Jewish concept of sin (cf *Miserere*), another truth that is no less important is derived: man's sin does not only make an attack on God's rights; but it affects, so to speak, the heart.

2. *Sin as an offense against God.* Certainly, the sinner is not able to injure God Himself. The Bible has too much concern for the divine transcendence not to recall occasionally: "Libations are poured for strange gods in order to hurt me. Is it I indeed whom they hurt? Says Yahweh. Is it not, rather, themselves and to their own confusion?" (Jr 7,18f). "If you sin, in what way do you hurt Him? If you multiply your offenses, do you do some evil to Him?" (Jb 35,6). By sinning against God, man only ends in destroying himself. If God prescribes laws for us, it is not in His interest, but in ours, "in order that we all may be happy and that we might live" (Dt 6,24). But the God of the Bible is not Aristotle's god who is indifferent to man and to the world.

a) If sin does not wound God in Himself, it does wound Him to the extent that it hurts those whom God loves. Thus, in "striking Uriah the Hittite with the sword and taking his wife," David thought, no doubt, that he only injured a man, and a non-Israelite at that. He had forgotten that God made Himself the guarantor of all human rights. In the name of God, Nathan teaches David that he has "scorned Yahweh" Himself, and that he will be punished in consequence of this (2 S 12,9f).

b) Moreover, sin separates man from God, the unique source of life, and so affects God in His plan of love by that very fact: "My people have changed their glory* for idols! They have abandoned me, the source of life, in order to build broken cisterns that do not hold water" (Jr 2,11ff).

c) To the extent that biblical revelation will make known the depths of that love*, it will let it be understood in what real sense the sin of man can "offend" God: sin is the child's ingratitude toward a very loving father* (vg Is 64,7), and indeed, the child's ingratitude toward his mother who would not be able to "forget the fruit of her womb, even though mothers should forget" (Is 49,15); especially is sin the infidelity of the wife* who prostitutes herself to all comers, indifferent to the tirelessly faithful love of her spouse: "Have you seen what Israel has done, the rebel?...I thought: 'After having done all that, she would return to me'; but she does not return!...Return, rebel Israel! ...I shall no longer have a severe countenance toward you for I am merciful" (Jr 3,7.12; cf Ez 16; 23).

At this stage of revelation, sin appears essentially as the violation of personal relations; as the refusal of man to allow himself to be loved by a God who suffers from not being loved, whom love has, so to speak, rendered "vulnerable": a mystery of love which will be fully revealed only in the NT.

3. *The remedy for sin.* The prophets denounce and reveal the gravity of sin only to invite more effectually to conversion. For if man is unfaithful, God always remains faithful*; man refuses the love of God, but God does not cease to offer it to him. As long as man is capable of returning, God urges him to return. As in the parable of the prodigal son, everything is ordered to this desired return, even anticipated: "That is why I am going to close her road with thorns; I shall obstruct her route so that she will no longer find her paths; she shall pursue her lovers and not reach them, she shall search for them and not find them. Then she will say: I want to return to my first hus-

band, for I was happier before than I am today" (Ho 2,8f; cf Ez 14,11; etc.).

Actually, if sin consists in the refusal of love, it is clear that it will be effaced, removed, pardoned, only to the degree that man will agree to love anew. To imagine a "pardon*" that might dispense man from returning to God would at one and the same time be wanting man to love while dispensing him from loving! The love itself of God would then forbid Him from ever asking this return. If God proclaims Himself a "jealous God" (Ex 20,5; Dt 5,9; etc.), it is because His jealousy is an effect of His love (cf Is 63,15; Ze 1,14). If He intends to obtain, Himself alone, man's happiness (man who is created in His image), it is because He alone can do so. As for the conditions of this return, they are found indicated under the words *ashes*, *confession*, *expiation*, *faith*, *pardon*, *repentance-conversion*, and *redemption*.

Evidently, the first condition on man's part is that he renounce his own will to be independent, that he agree to submit to God, to permit himself to love; in other words, that he renounce what constitutes the very basis of his sin. Now, he realizes that this is precisely the thing that is beyond his power. For man to be pardoned, it is not sufficient that God agree not to repulse him; more is necessary: "Make us return and we will return!" (Lm 5,21). God Himself will go to seek the dispersed sheep (Ez 34) and He will give man a "new heart," a "new spirit" (Ez 36,26f). It will be "the new covenant" wherein the Law will no longer be inscribed upon tablets of stone, but in the heart* of man (Jr 31,31ff; cf 2 Co 3,3). God will not be content in offering His love, nor in demanding ours: "Yahweh your God will circumcise your heart and the hearts of your posterity, that you may love the Lord thy God with all thy heart and with all thy soul in order that you may live" (Dt 30,6). The psalmist, too, in confessing his sin, begs God to "wash" him, to "purify" him, "to create in him a clean heart" (Ps 51), persuaded that justification for sin demands an act that is strictly divine and analogous to the creative act. Finally, the OT proclaims that this interior transformation of man which rescues him from his sin is accomplished by the sacrificial oblation of the mysterious Servant whose identity, before the fulfillment of the prophecy, no one would have been able to guess.

IV. THE TEACHING OF THE NT

The NT reveals that this Servant who has come to deliver man from sin (Is 53,11) is none other than the very Son of God. It is not surprising, then, that sin does not occupy a lesser place here than in the OT, nor that the full revelation about what the love of God has done to overcome sin permits its true dimension to be revealed, and at the same time its role in the plan of divine wisdom.

1. *Jesus and sinners.*

a) From the beginning of the synoptic catechesis, we see *Jesus in the midst of sinners.* For He has come for them and not the just (Mk 2,17). Using the Jewish vocabulary of the time, He proclaims to them that their sins are "remitted." By this, it does not mean sin is to be considered like a debt, though the term is sometimes used in this sense (Mt 6,12; 18,23ff). Rather, it means to suggest that sin could be pardoned by an act of God which would not at all demand the transformation of man's spirit and heart. Like the prophets and John the Baptist (Mk 1,4), Jesus preaches conversion, a radical change of spirit which puts man in a disposition to receive divine favor, to permit God to act upon him: "The kingdom of God is at hand; repent and believe the good news" (Mk 1,15). On the other hand, before those who refuse the light (Mk 3,29 p) or imagine that they have no need of pardon, like the Pharisee in the parable (Lk 18,9ff), Jesus is powerless.

b) As a result, Jesus, like the prophets, denounces sin wherever it may be; even in those who think they are just because they follow the prescriptions of an exterior law. For sin is within the heart "from which come all perverse deeds: debaucheries, thefts, murders, adultery, lust, wickedness, deceit, immodesty, envy, calumny, pride, and folly; all things that come from within and render man impure" (Mk 7, 21ff p). Because He came to perfect the Law in all its fullness, not to abolish it (Mt 5,17), the disciple of Jesus cannot be satisfied with the "justice of the Pharisees" (5,20); the justice of Jesus doubtless is ultimately reduced to love* (7,12). But in seeing his master act, the disciple will learn gradually what "to love" means; and in relation to this, he will see that sin is the refusal of love.

c) He will learn it especially in listening to Jesus reveal to him the inconceivable *mercy* of God for the sinner.* The parable of the prodigal son, or rather of the merciful father (Lk 15,11ff), is much like the teaching of the OT. Few passages in the NT are better than this parable for teaching how sin is an offense against God and how absurd it would be to conceive of a pardon that would not also include the return of the sinner. Besides the act of disobedience that can be presupposed—although it is only the older brother who alludes to it in order to make a comparison with his own obedience (vv 29f)—what has saddened the heart of the father is the departure of his son who no longer desires to be his son, who no longer allows his father to love him effectively. The son offended the father by depriving him of his presence. How could he "repair" his offense, if not through his return and by consenting to be treated as a son once more? That is the reason why the parable emphasizes the father's joy. Without such a return, there would be no pardon conceivable. More precisely, the father had always forgiven him, but the pardon only efficaciously reaches the son's sin in and through the latter's return.

d) Jesus revealed God's attitude toward sin more *through His actions* than by His words. He not only received sinners with the same love and delicacy as the father in the parable (vg Lk 7,36ff; 19,5; Mk 2,15ff; Jn 8,10f), at the risk of scandalizing the witnesses of such mercy who who were as incapable of understanding it as the elder son had been (Lk 15,28ff); but He acted directly against sin. He Himself first of all triumphed over Satan* at the time of the temptation. During His public life He snatched men from the power of the evil and from sin that sickness* and possession incorporate (cf Mk 1,23), thus inaugurating the role of servant* (Mt 8,16f) while waiting to "give up His life as a ransom" (Mk 10,45) and "to shed His blood, the blood of the covenant, for a multitude in remission of sins" (Mt 26,28).

2. *The sins of the world.*

Rather than "remission of sins," although he knows the traditional expression (Jn 20,23; 1 Jn 2,12), St. John speaks of Christ who came "to take away the sin of the world" (Jn 1,29). John perceives behind the individual acts the mysterious reality that engendered them, a power of hostility toward God and toward His reign. This power confronted Christ.

a) This hostility was concretely shown first in the voluntary refusal of *the light**. Sin has the opacity of darkness. "The light has come into the world and men have loved the darkness better than the light because their works were evil" (Jn 3,19). The sinner is opposed to the light because he dreads it, "for fear that his works be made known." He hates it: "Whoever does evil hates the light" (3,20). Blindly voluntary, blindly loved, because it is not recognised as the evil it is: "If you were blind you would be without sin. But you say: 'We see.' Your sin remains" (9,40).

b) Such blindness is only explained by the perverse *influence of Satan**. In effect, sin is at the service of Satan: "Whoever commits sin is a slave" (Jn 8,34). As the Christian is the son of God, the sinner is the "son of the devil, a sinner from the beginning"; and "he does his works" (1 Jn 3,8-10). Now, among these works, St. John points out two: homicide and the lie*. "From the beginning he was a killer and he was not established in the truth because there was no truth in him. When he tells his lies, he draws them from his own substance because he is a liar and the father of lies" (Jn 8,44). He was a killer in inflicting death on man (cf Ws 2,24) and also by inspiring Cain to kill his brother (1 Jn 3,12-15). He is a killer today by inspiring the Jews to put to death the one who speaks the truth to them: "You want to kill me, I who speak the truth that I have heard from God. You do the works of your father and you wish to fulfill your father's desires" (Jn 8,40f.44).

c) In their turn, homicide and lies are explained only by *hate**. With respect to the devil, Scripture spoke of jealousy (Ws 2,24). John does not hesitate to say "hate." In like manner, the obstinate unbeliever "hates the light" (Jn 3,20), as the Jews hate Christ and God His Father (15,22f). *The Jews* means the world at the service of Satan, whoever refuses to recognize Christ. And this hate will actually end in the murder of the Son of God (8,37).

d) And so we see the nature of this sin of the world over which Jesus triumphs. He can do so because He Himself is without sin (Jn 8,46; cf 1 Jn 3,5), "one" with God His Father (Jn 10,30), pure "light" "in whom there is no darkness" (1,5; 8,12), truth without any trace of lying or falsehood (1,14; 8,40), lastly, and especially perhaps, love; for "God is love" (1

Jn 4,8). If during His life He did not cease to love, still His death will be an act of love so great that a greater is not conceivable; and His death will be the "consummation" of love (Jn 15,13; cf 13,1; 19,30). This death was also a victory* over the "prince of this world" who thinks he wins the contest. But he is powerless against Jesus (14,30) and it is he who is "cast down" (12,31). Jesus has conquered the world (Jn 16,33).

e) Proof of the above is not only the fact that Jesus can "take up again the life He has given" (Jn 10,17). More of a proof is the fact that His disciples are made sharers in His victory. Having become "a child of God" for having received Jesus (1,12), the Christian "does not commit sin because he is born of God" (1 Jn 3,9). Moreover, to the extent that the "divine seed" lives in him—which probably means, as St. Paul expresses it, "to the extent that he acts through the spirit of God" (R 8, 14; cf G 5,16)—he "cannot sin." In fact, Jesus "takes away the sin of the world" (Jn 1,29) by "baptizing in the Spirit" (v 33), that is *by communicating the Spirit* to it,* which is symbolized by the water* gushing forth from the pierced side of the crucified as from the source of which Zechariah spoke, the fountain "open to the house of David for washing away sin and impurity" (Jn 19,30-37; cf Ze 12,10; 13,1), and which Ezekiel saw coming "from under the Temple threshold" and transforming the banks of the Dead Sea into a new paradise* (Ez 47, 1-12; Ap 22,2). Certainly the Christian, though born of God, can fall again into sin (1 Jn 2,1); but "Jesus was made a propitiation for our sins" (1 Jn 2,2), and He has communicated the Spirit to the apostles so that rightly they might "remit sins" (Jn 20,22f).

3. *The theology of sin according to St. Paul.*

a) A richer vocabulary permits Paul to distinguish even more clearly sin (gr. *hamartia,* in the singular) from sinful acts, preferably called faults outside of the traditional formulas (lit. *falls;* gr. *paraptôma*) or transgressions (gr. *parabasis*), without, however, wishing to diminish in the least the gravity of these latter. Thus, the sin committed by Adam in Paradise, to which, as it is well known, St. Paul attaches so much importance, is successively called transgression, fault, and disobedience (R 5,14. 17.19).

At any rate, in Paul's morality the sinful act

does not occupy a less important place than it does with the synoptics, as the *lists of sins* so frequently found in his epistles indicate: 1 Co 5,10f; 6,9f; 2 Co 12,20; G 5,19-21; R 1,29-31; Col 3,5-8; E 5,3; 1 Tm 1,9; Tt 3,3; 2 Tm 3,2-5. All of these sins, as St. Paul sometimes expressly states, exclude from the kingdom of God (1 Co 6,9; G 5,21). Now, it is to be noted that in these, exactly as in the analogous lists in the OT, there is a grouping together of sexual disorders, idolatry*, and social injustices (cf R 1,21-32 and the lists in 1 Co, G, Col, E). To be noted also is the gravity Paul attributed to cupidity (gr. *pleonexia*), that sin which consists in "always desiring to possess more," the vice that the old Latins called *avaritia* and which resembles greatly what the Decalogue (Ex 20, 17) forbids under the title of covetousness (cf R 7,7). Paul is not content to compare this with the sin of idolatry; he identifies the two: "that cupidity which is idolatry" (Col 3,5; cf E 5,5).

b) Beyond these sinful acts, Paul returns to their principal cause. In man the sinner, they are the expression and exteriorization of that force which is hostile to God and to His kingdom. This is the same thing that St. John talked about. The single fact that Paul practically reserves the term *sin* (in the singular) for it lends it special importance. But especially, the apostle sets himself to describe it, whether its origin or its effects in us, with enough precision to offer the rough outline of a true *theology of sin*.

Presented as a power and personified to the point of almost being confused with the person of Satan* who is the "god of this world" (2 Co 4,4), sin, nevertheless, is a distinct reality; it belongs to sinful man, it is interior to him. It was introduced into the human race by Adam's disobedience (R 5,12-19)—and by a kind of repercussion into the material universe itself (R 8,20; cf Gn 3,17), sin has passed on to all men without exception, drawing them to death* and eternal separation from God such as the condemned suffer in hell*. Independent of the redemption*, all make up according to the words of St. Augustine, which are exact if they be properly understood, a *massa damnata*. Paul likes to describe at great length this condition of man "sold to the power of sin" (R 7, 14), still able to "sympathize" with the good (7,16.22), indeed, to "desire" it (7,15.21). This proves that all in man is not corrupt, but that he is incapable of "accomplishing" what is good (7,18); and, because he is necessarily vowed to

eternal death (7,24), he is unable to avoid the "wages" or, better still, the "result," the fulfillment* of sin (6,21-23).

c) As a result of the above statements, the apostle is sometimes accused of pessimism. Those who make the accusation forget that Paul abstracted from the grace of Christ when he made these affirmations. His very argumentation momentarily forces him to stress the universality of sin and its tyranny for the single purpose of establishing the powerlessness of the Law* and to exalt the absolute necessity of Christ's liberating work. Moreover, Paul recalls the solidarity of the entire human race with Adam*, only to reveal a superior solidarity of all humanity with Jesus Christ; in God's thought, Jesus Christ, the antitype, is first (R 5,14). This means that Adam's sin and its consequences are permitted only because Jesus Christ must triumph over it, and in such a superabundant manner that even before showing the likenesses between the role of the first Adam and that of the second (5,17ff), Paul insists on pointing out the differences (5,15f).

For the victory of Christ over sin is not less striking for Paul than it was for John. The Christian, justified* by faith* and baptism* (G 3, 26ff; cf R 3,21ff; 6,2ff), has totally broken away from sin (R 6,10f). Dead to sin, he has become with Christ dead and risen, a new being (6,5), a "new creature" (2 Co 5,17). He is no longer "in the flesh*," but "in the spirit" (R 7,5; 8,9); although, as long as he lives in a "mortal body," he may fall again into sin and "yield himself up to his lusts" (6,12), if he refuses to "walk according to the spirit" (8,4).

d) God does not only triumph over sin. His *wisdom*, "infinite in resources"* (E 3,10), obtains this victory while making use of sin. That which was a supreme obstacle to God's kingdom and to man's salvation plays a role in the history of this salvation. As a matter of fact, it is in reference to sin that Paul speaks of the "wisdom of God" (1 Co 1,21-24; R 11. 33). He does this especially while meditating on the sin that was for his heart, without a doubt, the most telling wound (R 9,2), and in any case a scandal for his spirit. This was the unbelief* of Israel. He understands that this infidelity, however partial and temporary (R 11, 25), entered into God's salvific plan* for the human race, and that "God has included all men in the disobedience only that He might show Himself merciful to all" (R 11,32; cf G 3,

22). Paul will also proclaim with grateful admiration: "O the depth of the richness, of the wisdom, and of the knowledge of God! How unfathomable are His decrees, and incomprehensible His ways!" (R 11,33).

e) But this mystery of divine wisdom which makes use even of sin for man's salvation is nowhere more clearly revealed than *in the passion of the Son of God*. In fact, if God the Father "delivered up His Son" to death (R 8, 32), it was to place Him in conditions where He could accomplish the greatest act of obedience and love that can be imagined, and in this way bring about our redemption by passing, Himself first of all, from the state of the flesh to the state of the spirit. The circumstances of this death, which were ordered to create the most favorable conditions for such an act, are all the effects of man's sin: the betrayal of Judas, the abandonment by His apostles, the weakness of Pilate, the hatred of the authorities of the Jewish nation, the cruelty of the executioners, and beyond the visible drama our own sins which He dies to expiate. In order to permit Him to love as no other man has ever loved. God willed that His Son be made vulnerable to man's sin, that He be subject to the evil effects of the power of death that is sin in order that we might be subject, thanks to that supreme act of love, to the beneficial effects of the power of life that is the justice of God (2 Co 5,21). So it is true that "God makes all things work for the good of those that love Him" (R 8,28), all things, even sin.

→Adam — Animals — Ashes 1 — Blasphemy —Body I 1.2, II 2—Calamity—Captivity II—Clothing II 1—Confession OT 2; NT 2—Conscience—Cupidity OT 2—Curse—Desire II—Earth OT I 3, II 3 b—Error—Exile I 2.3—Expiation—Fear of God III—Flesh II—Good & Evil I 4, III—Hardness of Heart—Hate I 1.3, II—Hell OT II—Idols II 2—Judgment—Justification I—Law C III 2—Leprosy I—Liberation/Liberty III 2 a—Lie—Man II 1 Mercy—Pardon—Prophet OT III 1, IV 1—Punishment—Pure OT II—Redemption—Repentance/Conversion — Responsibility — Sadness OT 2—Satan I, III—Scandal—Sickness/Healing—Slave II—Sleep II, III—Solitude I 2 —Suffering OT II—Trial I, II—Trial/Temptation—Unbelief—Virtues & Vices—Work I 1, II—World NT I 2, III o.1.

SL rco'c

SLAVE

Slavery was practiced in Israel. A good number of slaves were of foreign origin: prisoners of war reduced to slavery, according to the general custom of antiquity (Dt 21,10), or slaves bought from merchants who trafficked in them (Gn 17,12). Even some Hebrews were sold or sold themselves as slaves (Ex 21,1-11; 22,2; 2 K 4,1).

In Israel, however, slavery never reached the amplitude nor the form that it knew in classical antiquity. Israel, in fact, was always marked by her double initial experience: her distress in the country of servitude and the marvelous history of her liberation* by God (Dt 26,6ff; Ex 22,20). Hence, on the one hand, her particular way of envisaging the social problem of slavery and, on the other, the religious reflection aroused by this reality.

I. THE SOCIAL PROBLEM

It is useful to observe first that in the Bible the same word designates servant as well as slave. True, the Law* accepts slavery properly so called as an established custom (Ex 21,21); but it has always tended to reduce its severity, and, even if this is the expression of an ideal rather than a reality, it does reveal a true appreciation of man. Although he is the owner of his slave, the master does not have by that fact the right to maltreat him according to his fancy (Ex 21,20.26f). In the case of a Hebrew slave the Law shows itself even more confining. Except with the consent of the interested party, it forbids slavery for life. The Code of the Covenant prescribes enfranchisement after seven years (Ex 21,2). Later, Deuteronomy provides for brotherly attentions at this enfranchisement (Dt 15,13f). The Levitical legislation, on its part, will institute a general enfranchisement during the jubilee year, perhaps to supply for the non-application of the preceding measures (Lv 25,10; cf Jr 34,8). Finally, the Law wishes to make the Hebrew slave rise to the salaried status (Lv 25,39-55); for the children of Israel, redeemed by God from the slavery of Egypt, can no longer be slaves of a man.

The problem of slavery comes up again in the Christian communities of the Graeco-Roman world. Paul met it principally at Corinth. His answer is very firm: what is of importance from now on is not one or other social condition but the call of God (1 Co 7,17...). The slave will then fulfill his duty as Christian by serving his master "as Christ" (E 6,5-8). The Christian master will understand that the slave is his brother* in Christ; he will treat him like a brother (E 6,9) and perhaps even, in an exceptional case, will find a way of freeing him (Phm 14-21). In the new man*, indeed, the old antinomy, *slave/free man*, no longer exists; what alone is of importance "is to be a new creature" (G 3,28; 6,15).

II. THE RELIGIOUS THEME

Though freed by God from slavery, Israel fell back into it if she was unfaithful (Jg 3, 7f; Ne 9,35f). Thus did she learn that sin* and slavery go together and felt the need of being freed from her faults (Ps 130; Ps 141,3f). The NT reveals even more this rather profound distress. Since sin entered the world through Adam, all men have been interiorly subject to it and cringe in fear from the same blow of death, its inevitable recompense (R 5,12...; 7, 13-24; He 2,14f). The Law itself only reinforced this slavery.

Only Christ could break it, since He was the only one over whom the prince of this world had no hold (Jn 14,30). He has come to liberate sinners (Jn 8,36). To dissolve their slavery, He has accepted to take on Himself a condition of being a slave (Ph 2,7), of having a flesh like to that of sin (R 8,3), and of being obedient until the death of the cross (Ph 2,8). He made Himself the servant not only of God but of men whom He has thus redeemed (Mt 20,28 p; cf Jn 13,1-17).

More than the Hebrews who were redeemed from Egypt, the baptized have therefore become the freed men of the Lord, or, if one wishes, the slaves of God and of justice* (1 Co 7,22f; R 6,16-22; cf Lv 25,55). They are now freed from sin, from death, from the Law (R 6—8; G 5,1). From slaves they have become sons in the Son (Jn 8,32-36; G 4,4-7.21-31). But although in comparison to all they are free, they nevertheless make themselves the servants and slaves of all after the example of their Lord (1 Co 9,19; Mt 20,26-27 p; Jn 13,14ff). For, even if the service of man is accidental and the slavery of sin and of the flesh is abnormal, the service of God and of His brethren constitutes the very calling of the Christian.

→Authority NT II 2—Captivity—Liberation/ Liberty—Serve I—Work.

CA gsa

SLEEP

Sleep, a necessary and mysterious element in human life, has two aspects: it is the repose which regenerates man; it is immersion into the darkness of night. Both source of life and figure of death, it has, for this reason, different metaphorical meanings.

I. THE REST OF MAN

In virtue of the rhythm imposed by the Creator on his existence, man is subject to the alternation of day* and night*, of waking and repose.

1. *Sign of confidence and abandonment.* It is fitting to appreciate the sweetness of the sleep which gives rest to the worker* (Qo 5,11) and to lament for those whom the cares* of wealth, sickness, or an evil conscience make the prey of insomnia (Ps 32,4; Si 31,1f). It is especially necessary to maintain the bond between justice* and sleep. The just man indeed, who ponders on the Law during his vigils (Ps 1,2; Pr 6,22) and who impresses wisdom on his heart (Pr 3,24) "sleeps in peace as soon as he goes to bed" (Ps 3,6; 4,9). He has confidence* in the protection of God. For the idols* made in the likeness of man can sleep (1 K 18,27). But God, the guardian of Israel, "neither sleeps nor slumbers" (Ps 121,4); He works without ceasing for the benefit of His children (Ps 127,2; cf Mk 4,27). At the height of the storm Jesus is not "troubled" (Mk 4,40; cf Jn 14,27; 2 Tm 1, 7); His sleep is a sign of perfect confidence in God (Mk 4,38). In this line of thought, to begin with an image familiar to all mankind, death* is considered as the entry into the repose of sleep after a life filled with works and days: a man sleeps with his fathers (Gn 47,30; 2 S 7,12). So the cemetery suggests the "sleeping chamber," according to the Greek etymology, where the dead rest. The Christian who has "fallen asleep in Jesus" (1 Th 4,14), with hope in the resurrection, goes to sleep for the space of a night, dreaming with confidence of the day when he will rise, returned to life (cf Dn 12,13).

2. *Time of God's visitation.* For a reason difficult to determine, perhaps because the sleeping man is no longer master of himself and does not offer resistance, the time of sleep is regarded as favorable to the coming of God. Thus, as if in order to act more in accordance with His will, God causes a profound sleep (hb. *tardēmāh*), a sort of ecstasy, to fall on Adam, who finds himself alone, in order to "fashion" a woman for him (Gn 2,21); or to fall on the troubled Abraham in order to seal His covenant with him (Gn 15,2.12). Then in the darkness the divine fire* leaps up (15,17). God also visits His elect in dreams, revealing His mysterious presence to Jacob (Gn 28,11-19) and revealing His mysterious plans to the two Josephs (Gn 37,5ff.9; Mt 1,20-25; 2,13f.19-23). This manner of revelation* makes its beneficiaries like to the prophets (Nm 12,6; Dt 13,2; 1 S 28,6), and the apocalypses use it by preference (Dn 2,4). Was it not promised as a sign of the end of time (Jl 3,1; Ac 2,17f)? But it must be rigorously examined (Jr 23,25-28; 29,8) in order that it be not confounded with the "dreams of an expectant woman" (Si 34,1-8).

II. DARKNESS OVER MAN

Night, the child of God, is, however, also the time of nightmares, of alarms and of the evil powers. Sleep may be visited by nocturnal monsters and reveal a guilty heart.

He who has great plans in his heart does not give rest to his eyes (Ps 132,3ff; Pr 6,4). On the contrary the lazy man who does not suceed in rising from his bed is committed to poverty (Pr 6,6-11; 20,13; 26,14). More dangerous still is the sleep which results from drunkenness, for it leads to the placing of irresponsible acts (Gn 9,21-24; 19,31-38)—or that which results from the love of women: thus the strength of Samson is surrendered to Delilah (Jg 16,13-21).

Sleep can be still more than the result of a fault, since it can signify a culpable interior disposition. Such is the sleep of Jonah (Jon 1, 5). When the prophet Elijah goes to sleep under the broom tree, it is under the blows of discouragement (1 K 19,4-8). Sleep then expresses the fact that a man is abandoned to sin; he reels in drunkenness* after having emptied the cup* of the wrath* of Yahweh (Jr 25,16; Is 51,17). The sleep which lays the disciples low during the prayer of Jesus at Gethsemani (Mk 14,34.37.40 p) signifies that they do not understand the approaching hour and that they separate themselves from Jesus. Because of this Jesus realizes that He must be absolutely alone in the work of salvation; thus He allows sleep to those who wish to bury themselves in their sin.

III. RISING FROM THE SLEEP OF SIN AND OF DEATH

From here on sleep signifies the state of death to which sin leads. To rise from it will be the sign of conversion and of a return to life.

1. *"Arise!"* "Awake," says Jesus to His sleeping disciples. Long before Him, the prophet made it plain that no one among the people of Israel would keep awake in order to rely on God, for God had turned away His face* (Is 64,6). But divine grace is going to hasten the hour of awakening: "Awake! Rise up, Jerusalem!" (Is 51,17—52,1). It is the hour of rising from torpor; the cup* of wrath has been emptied even to the bottom; God Himself snatches His people from their daze. This awakening of the holy city is a veritable resurrection*, and those who lay in the dust arouse themselves (Is 26,19). In the apocalypse of Daniel this image will become a reality: "A great number of those who sleep in the earth shall arise" (Dn 12,2). The just man must not then fear to "fall asleep in death" (Ps 13,4), for God is the master of death*, and He will show this by raising up Jesus.

To prepare for this resurrection, however, it is first necessary to awaken the heart by a sincere conversion. It is this dialogue of conversion which can be read in the Canticle of Canticles, depicted through the metaphor of sleeping and waking. The awakening of the faithless bride must not be abrupt: "Do not awake love before the hour of her good pleasure!" (Ct 2,7; 3,5; 8,4). But this good pleasure gradually wins over the heart of the bride led away into the desert*: God has spoken to her (Ho 2,16; Is 40,2), so that thereafter she can say: "I sleep, but my heart watches" (Ct 5,2). Love is still not very strong. However, on her wakening, the bride troubles herself with useless things and allows the bridegroom who has come (5,3.6) to depart. She does well to watch*, but her watchfulness cannot hasten the hour of God (Is 26,9); it is the bridegroom who will finally awaken the bride (Ct 8,5). Conversion itself is the work of God.

2. *Wakened from their sleep.* Before rising from the tomb where He has freely gone to sleep, Jesus has expressed by signs His mastery over death and over sleep, which is its image. He has allowed the disciples to be troubled by His sleep during the storm (Mk 4,37-41), as if He wished to make them repeat the bold prayer of the psalmists: "Arouse thyself, Lord!" (Ps 44,24; 78,65; Is 51,9). In reality He has shown by this that He is capable of commanding the sea in the same way as He commands death. When He awakens the daughter of Jairus (Mt 9,24) and His friend Lazarus (Jn 11,11) from their sleep, He foreshadows His own resurrection, to which the baptized will be mystically united: "Arouse theyself, thou who sleepest, rise from among the dead and Christ will illumine you" (E 5,14). The believer is no longer a being of the night; "he sleeps no more" (1 Th 5,6f), for he does not have anything more to do with sin and with the vices of the night. He watches*, awaiting without sleeping the return of the master (Mk 13,36). And if when the bridegroom is slow to come, he goes to sleep like the wise virgins, he at least has his lamp filled with oil (Mt 25,1-13). The word of the bride of the Canticle then takes on a new meaning, for the day* has already shone in the depth of the night: "I sleep, but my heart watches."

→Death OT I 2—Dreams—Drunkenness 2—Night OT 3—Rest—Watch.

DS & XLD jpl

SOLITUDE

Created in the image* of God, who, Father, Son, and Spirit, is the superabundant fruitfulness* of love, man must live in communion* with God and with his fellows, and by this means bring forth fruit*. Solitude then, is in itself an evil which comes from sin. It can nonetheless become a source of communion and of fruitfulness, if it is united to the redemptive solitude of Jesus Christ.

I. THE SOLITUDE OF MAN

1. *"It is not good that man should be alone"* (Gn 2,18). According to God, solitude is an evil. It delivers the poor, the stranger, and the widow and the orphan to the mercy of the wicked (Is 1,17.23). God thus demands that these receive special protection (Ex 22,21ff); and He regards their protectors as His sons and cherishes them more than a mother (Si 4,10). In the absence of human supports, God will Himself become the avenger of these poor people* (Pr 23,10f; Ps 146,9). Solitude also delivers up to reproach the woman who remains sterile*: and while waiting to reveal the meaning of virginity*, God proposes to remedy this reproach by the law of Levirate (Dt 25,5-10). Sometimes He even intervenes in person in order to console the solitary woman (1 S 2,5; Ps 113,9; Is 51,2). The trial of solitude is a call for absolute confidence* in God (Es 4,17—LXX v 19).

2. *God wills that the sinner be alone.* Solitude also reveals to man his sinful state and it then becomes a call for conversion. This is what the experience of sickness*, of suffering*, and of premature death* can teach: set aside from the society of men (Jb 19,13-22), the unhappy man realizes that he is in a state of sin*. God also reveals in another way that He abandons the sinner to solitude. He abandons His unfaithful wife* (Ho 2,5; 3,3); the prophet Jeremiah must signify by his celibacy that Israel is sterile (Jr 16,2; 15,17). Finally the exile* makes it clear that God alone can save men from solitude by making it fruitful (Is 49,21; 54,1ff).

II. FROM SOLITUDE TO COMMUNION

1. *Solitude accepted by Jesus Christ.* God gave men His only Son (Jn 3,16), so that through Emmanuel (="God with us," Is 7,14) they might find communion with Him once again. But, in order to rescue humanity from the solitude of sin, Jesus took upon Himself that solitude and especially the solitude of sinful Israel. He went into the desert* to conquer the Adversary (Mt 4,1-11; cf 14,23); He prayed alone (Mk 1,35.45; Lk 9,18; cf 1 K 19,10). Finally in Gethsemane He had to put up with His disciples falling asleep* because they were not ready to share His prayer (Mk 14,32-41), and He faced the anguish* of death on His own. Even God seemed to abandon Him (Mt 27,46). In fact He was not alone and the Father was always with Him (Jn 8,16.29; 16,32); and, like the grain of wheat falling to the earth, He did not remain alone but bore fruit (Jn 12,24): He "gathers together in unity* the scattered children of God" (11,52) and "draws all men

to Himself" (12,32). This is the triumph of communion.

2. *Alone with Jesus Christ in order to be with all.* This gathering together of the messianic people was started by Jesus when He called His disciples "to be with Him" (Mk 3,14).

He had come to look for the lost and solitary sheep (Lk 15,4) and He restored the broken communion by entering into private conversations with His disciples (Mk 4,10; 6,2), with sinful women (Jn 4,27; 8,9). The love that He asks for is unique, superior to every other (Lk 14,26), like the love prescribed by Yahweh, the only God (Dt 6,4; Ne 9,6).

Like its Spouse and Lord, the Church finds itself alone in a world* to which it does not belong (17,16) and from which it must flee into the desert (Ap 12,6). But thereafter there is no longer any real solitude: Christ, by His Spirit, has not left His disciples "orphans" (Jn 14,18), as they wait for the day when, having triumphed over the solitude which the death of dear ones imposes on us, "We shall be reunited to them ...with the Lord forever" (1 Th 4,17).

→Desert—Mountain III 1—Sadness OT 2; NT 3—Sterility—Widows 1.

MP & XLD jpl

SON OF GOD

In Hebrew the word *son* does not express solely the relations of consanguinity in the direct line. It also signifies the belonging to a group: "sons of Israel," "sons of Babylon" (Ez 23,17), "sons of Zion" (Ps 149,2), "sons of the prophets" (2 K 2,5), "sons of man" (Ez 2,1 ...; Dn 8,17); or the possession of a quality: "sons of peace" (Lk 10,6), "sons of light" (Lk 16,8; Jn 12,36). Our concern here is the use of the word to translate the relations between men and God.

OT

In the OT the expression "sons of God" designated sporadically the angels* who form the divine court (Dt 32,8; Ps 29,1; 89,7; Jb 1,6). It is probable that this usage distantly reflects the mythology of Canaan where the expression was taken in its strict meaning. In the Bible, since Yahweh has no spouse, it has no more than an attenuated meaning: it merely empha-

sizes the participation of the angels in the heavenly life of God.

I. ISRAEL, SON OF GOD

Applied to Israel, the term translates in terms of human kinship the relations between Yahweh and His people. It is in the happenings of the exodus* that Israel has felt the reality of this adoptive filiation (Ex 4,22; Ho 11,1; Jr 3,19; Ws 18,13); Jeremiah recalls it when he foretells the eschatological deliverance as a new exodus (Jr 31,9.20). Beginning with this experience, the title of son can be attributed (in the plural) to all the members of the people of God; whether it is to insist on their religious consecration to Him who is their Father* (Dt 14, 1f; cf Ps 73,15), or to reproach them with greater vigor for their infidelity (Ho 2,1; Is 1,2; 30, 1.9; Jr 3,14). Finally, the consciousness of filial adoption becomes one of the essential elements of Jewish piety*. It gives a foundation to the hope of future restorations (Is 63,8; cf 63,16; 64,7), such as that of the reward beyond the tomb (Ws 2,13.18): the just, sons of God, will be forever associated with the angels, sons of God (Ws 5,5).

II. THE KING, SON OF GOD

When the ancient East celebrated the divine filiation of kings it was always in a mystical perspective where the person of the monarch was properly divinized. The OT excluded this possibility. The king* is no more than one man among others, subject to the same divine law, and answerable to the same judgment. However, David* and his race have been made the object of a special election* which associates them definitively with the destiny of the people of God. It is for the purpose of translating the relationship thus created between Yahweh and the royal line that God said by the prophet Nathan: "I will be a father to him, and he will be a son to me" (2 S 7,14; cf Ps 89,27f). Henceforth the title Son of Yahweh is a royal title which will become quite naturally a Messianic title (Ps 2,7) when prophetic eschatology envisages the future birth of the king* beyond all others (cf Is 7,14; 9,1...).

SON OF GOD

NT

I. JESUS, ONLY SON OF GOD

1. *In the synoptics*, the title Son of God, easily associated with that of Christ (Mt 16,16; Mk 14,61 p), appears at first to be a Messianic title. For that reason it is exposed to equivocations which Jesus will have to dissipate. From the beginning, the scene of the temptation shows the opposition between two interpretations. For Satan, to be Son of God is to be sure of a stupendous power* and an invulnerable protection (Mt 4,3.6); for Jesus, it is to find no food or support but in God's will* (Mt 4,4.7). By rejecting every suggestion of earthly Messianism, Jesus at once caused to appear the indissoluble bond that unites Him with the Father*. He acted in like manner before the declarations of possessed persons (Mk 3,11 p; 5,7 p). These persons manifest in the presence of the demons an involuntary recognition of His person (Mk 1,34). But they are ambiguous, and that is why Jesus imposes silence. Peter's confession of faith, "Thou are the Christ, the Son of the living God," comes from a genuine adherence of faith (Mt 16,16f); and the evangelist who reports it could give it its full Christian meaning without difficulty. Nevertheless, Jesus at once prevents any mistake! His title does not assure Him a future of earthly glory. The Son of Man will die in order to reach His glory (16,21).

When, finally, Caiaphas solemnly poses the essential question: "Art thou the Christ, the Son of the blessed one?" (Mt 26,63; Mk 14,61), Jesus felt that the expression could still be understood in the sense of a temporal Messianism. He answers indirectly by opening another perspective: He foretells His coming as sovereign judge under the characteristics of the Son of Man. To the titles of Messiah* and of Son* of Man He gives also a meaning that is properly divine, well emphasized in Luke's gospel: "Thou art, then, the Son of God? You say well, I am" (Lk 22,70). A paradoxical revelation. Stripped of everything, and apparently abandoned by God (cf Mt 27,46 p), Jesus keeps His claims intact. He will remain sure of His Father until death (Lk 23,46). This death succeeds moreover in dissipating all equivocation. In reporting the confession of the centurion (Mk 15,39 p) the evangelists emphasize the fact that the cross is at the origin of Christian faith.

It was then that more than one mysterious word of Jesus was clarified in retrospect, words in which Jesus had revealed the nature of His relations with God. With relation to God, He is "the Son" (Mt 11,27 p; 21,37 p; cf 24,36 p); this is a familiar formula which permits Him to address God by calling Him "Abba! Father!" (Mk 14,36; cf Lk 23,46). Between God and Him there reigned this profound intimacy which supposes a perfect mutual knowledge and sharing of all things (Mt 11,25ff p). Thus Jesus gives their full meaning to the divine declarations: "Thou art my Son" (Mk 1,11; 9,7 p).

2. It is in the resurrection* of Jesus that the apostles finally understood the mystery of the divine sonship. The resurrection fulfilled Ps 2,7 (cf Ac 13,33). It brought God's confirmation to the claims of Jesus before Caiaphas and on the cross. From the morrow of Pentecost, the apostolic witness* and confession of Christian faith have for their object "Jesus, Son of God" (Ac 8,37; 9,20). In presenting the childhood of Jesus, Matthew and Luke discreetly emphasize this theme (Mt 2,15; Lk 1,35). In Paul it becomes the starting point of a theological reflection that is much more extended. God has sent His Son to earth (G 4,4; R 8,3) for the purpose of reconciling us by His death (R 5,10). Now He has established Him in His power* (R 1,4), and He calls us to communion* with Him (1 Co 1,9); for He has transferred us into His kingdom (Col 1,13). The Christian life is a life "in the faith of the Son of God who loved us and delivered Himself for us" (G 2,20), and an awaiting for the day* when He will come again from the heavens to "deliver us from the wrath*" (1 Th 1,10). The same certainty runs through the epistle to the Hebrews (He 1,2.5.8; *passim*).

3. In St. John, the theology of the divine sonship becomes a dominant theme. A few confessions of faith of persons in the gospel might still imply a sense of restraint (Jn 1,34; 1,51; especially 11,27). But Jesus speaks clearly of the relations between the Son and the Father. There is between them a unity of operation and of glory (Jn 5,19.23; cf I Jn 2,22f); the Father communicates all to the Son because He loves Him (Jn 5,20); power to give life (5,21.25f) and power to judge (5,22.27); when Jesus returns to God, the Father glorifies the Son because the Son glorifies Him (Jn 17,1; cf 14,13). Thus preciseness is given to the doctrine of the incarnation; God has sent His only Son into the world to save the world (1 Jn 4,9f.14). This only Son is the revealer of God (Jn 1,18), and

He communicates to men the eternal life which comes from God (1 Jn 5,11f). The work* to be accomplished is belief in Him (Jn 6,29; 20,31; 1 Jn 3,23; 5,5.10). He who believes in the Son has life everlasting (Jn 6,40); he who does not believe is condemned (Jn 3,18).

II.   MEN, ADOPTED SONS OF GOD

1. *In the synoptics*, the adoptive sonship of which the OT had already spoken is frequently affirmed. Not only does Jesus teach His followers to call God "our Father"; but He gives the title of "sons of God" to the peacemakers (Mt 5,9), to the charitable (Lk 6,35), to the just who have risen (Lk 20,36).

2. The foundation of this title is made precise *in the Pauline theology*. The adoption as sons was already one of the privileges of Israel (R 9,4), but it is true in a much stronger sense that all Christians are now sons of God through their faith in Christ (G 3,26; E 1,5). They have in them the Spirit* which makes them adopted sons (G 4,5ff; R 8,14-17). They are called to reproduce in themselves the image* of the only Son (R 8,29). They are made co-heirs with Him (R 8,17). This supposes in them a true regeneration (Tt 3,5; cf 1 P 1,3; 2,2) which makes them participate in the life of the Son. Such is, in fact, the meaning of baptism*, which makes a man live a new life (R 6,4). Thus we are sons of adoption in the Son by nature; and God treats us as such, even when it happens that He sends us His corrections (He 12,5-12).

3. The teaching of the *Johannine writings* sounds exactly the same note. One must be reborn, says Jesus to Nicodemus (Jn 3,3.5), of water and the Spirit. To those who believe in Christ, God gives the power of becoming children of God (Jn 1,12). This life of a son of God is for us a present reality, even if the world is ignorant of it (1 Jn 3,1). The day will come when it will be openly manifest, and then we shall be like to God because we shall see* Him as He is (1 Jn 3,2). It is not, therefore, any longer a question only of a title which shows God's love for His creatures. Man participates in the nature of Him who has adopted him as His son (2 P 1,4).

→Baptism III 2, IV 2.4—Child—Disciple OT 1 —Education—Fathers & Father III, IV, V— God NT—Grace II 3—Holy NT I—Image IV —Inheritance OT—Jesus Christ I 2, II—Lord —Love I NT—Man I, III 4—Messiah NT II 2—New Birth—Revelation NT I 1 c, II 2.3, III—Slave II—Son of Man NT I—Spirit of God—Transfiguration 2.3.

HR & PG wjy

SON OF MAN

In the gospels, Jesus habitually designates Himself by the title of Son of Man, an enigmatic expression which, while veiling the most transcendent aspect of His person, at the same time suggested it. To understand its range, we must refer to its use in the OT and in Judaism.

I.   THE CURRENT LANGUAGE OF THE BIBLE

The Hebrew and Aramaic expression *son of man* (*ben-'ādām, bar-'enōš*) appears very frequently as a synonym of *man** (cf Ps 80,18). It designates a member of the human race (son* of humanity). Thinking of him who is the father of the whole race and bears its name, we might translate it "son of Adam*." The use of the expression emphasizes the precariousness of man (Is 51,12; Jb 25,6), his smallness before God (Ps 11,4), at times his sinful condition (Ps 14,2f; 31,20), doomed to death (Ps 89, 48; 90,3). When Ezekiel, a man of mute adoration prostrate before the glory of God, is called by Yahweh "son of man" (Ez 2,1.3 etc.), the term marks the distances, and reminds the prophet of his condition as a mortal. The goodness of God for the "sons of Adam" is all the more admirable: He multiplies His marvels for them (Ps 107,8) and His Wisdom* is pleased to dwell with them (Pr 8,31). One is astounded that a being so feeble has been crowned by Him as king of all creation: "Who is man that you are mindful of him, the son of man that you have a care for him?" (Ps 8,5; cf Gn 1). The whole of the religious anthropology of the OT is there. Before God man is nothing but a breath, and yet God has filled him with His gifts.

II.   THE LANGUAGE OF THE APOCALYPSES

1. *The Book of Daniel*. To represent concretely the succession of human empires which have crumbled and made way for the kingdom*

of God, the apocalypse of Daniel 7 makes use of an amazing imagery. The empires are beasts* which rise from the sea*. They are stripped of their power when they appear before the tribunal of God, who is represented under the guise of an old man. Then there arrives on (or with) the clouds* of heaven one "like the Son of Man." He advances as far as the tribunal of God, and receives universal royalty (7,13f). The origin of this idea is uncertain. The "son of man" in the psalms or Ezekiel is not enough to explain it. Some suggest the Iranian myth of the primordial man returning as a savior at the end of time. Perhaps we ought to look for an explanation in the traditions that lie behind the divine Wisdom* personified or the Adam* of Gn 1 and Ps 8, created in the likeness of God and "little less than" God. In Dn 7 Son of Man and beasts are opposed as the divine is to the satanic. In the interpretation which follows the vision, the royalty falls to the "people of the saints of the most high" (7,18.22.27); it is, therefore, apparently He whom the Son of Man represents, certainly not in His persecuted condition (7,25), but in His final glory. However, the beasts typify the empires as well as their chiefs. We cannot, then, exclude completely any allusion to the head of the holy people to whom the empire will be entrusted in participating in the kingdom of God. At any rate, the attributions of the Son of Man go beyond those of the Messiah*, the son of David: the entire context places Him in relation with the divine world and accentuates His transcendence.

2. *The Jewish tradition.* The Jewish apocalyptic later than the Book of Daniel has taken up the symbol of the Son of Man, but interprets it in a strictly individual way and with the stress on its transcendental attributes. In the parables of Henoch (the most recent part of the book) he is a mysterious being, living with God, possessing justice and revealing all the good things of salvation held in reserve for the end of time. Then he will sit upon his throne of glory; universal judge, savior, and avenger of the just who will live in his presence after the resurrection. He has some of the features of the royal Messiah* and of the Servant* of Yahweh (he is the elect of justice, cf Is 42,1); but there is no question of his suffering, and he has not an earthly origin. Although the date of the parables of Henoch is disputed, they represent a doctrinal development which should have been acquired in certain Jewish circles before the ministry of Jesus. The interpretation of Dn 7

has left traces elsewhere in the Fourth Book of Ezra and in the rabbinical literature. Belief in this heavenly savior ready to reveal himself prepares the way for the gospel use of the expression *Son of Man.*

NT

I. THE GOSPELS

In the gospels, the expression *Son of the Man* (a Greek equivalent of the Aramaic which should have been translated "Son of Man") is found 70 times. Sometimes it is simply the equivalent of the personal pronoun "I" (cf Mt 5,11 and Lk 6,22; Mt 16,13-21 and Mk 8,27-31). The cry of Stephen as he saw "the Son of Man standing at the right hand of God" (Ac 7,56) may be an indication that this idea was current in certain parts of the early Church. But their influence could not explain all the uses of the expression in the Gospels. The fact that it appears only on the lips of Jesus suggests that it was retained as one of His typical expressions, while the post-paschal faith preferred to designate Him by other titles. It happens that Jesus does not identify Himself explicitly with the Son of Man (Mt 6,27; 24,30 p); but elsewhere it is clear that He is speaking of Himself (Mt 8,20 p; 11,19; 16,13; Jn 3,13f; 12,34). It is possible that He had chosen the expression because of its ambiguity: susceptible as it was of a commonplace meaning ("the man that I am"), it contained also a clear allusion to the Jewish apocalyptic.

1. *The synoptics.*

a) The eschatological pictures of Jesus are related to the apocalyptic tradition: the Son of Man will come on the clouds of heaven (Mt 24, 30 p), He will sit upon His throne of glory (19, 28), He will judge all men (16,27 p). Now in the course of His trial when He was questioned by the high priest, who wanted to know whether He was the "Messiah*, Son* of the blessed one," Jesus answers the question indirectly by identifying Himself with the Son of Man sitting at the right hand of God (cf Ps 110,1) and coming on the clouds of heaven (cf Dn 7,13; Mt 26,64 p). This affirmation caused Him to be condemned for blasphemy. In fact, setting aside all earthly concepts of the Messiah*, Jesus let His transcendence appear. The title of Son of Man, after its antecedents, was qualified for this revelation.

b) On the other hand, Jesus had also attached to the title Son of Man a content which the apocalyptic tradition did not directly foresee. He came to fulfill in His earthly life the vocation of Servant* of Yahweh, rejected and put to death to be finally glorified and save the multitudes. Now it was in the quality of Son of Man that He should undergo this destiny (Mk 8,31 p; Mt 17,9 p.22f p; 20,18 p; 26,2.24 p.45 p). Before appearing in glory on the last day, the Son of Man will have led an earthly existence in which His glory was veiled in humiliation and suffering—the same as in the Book of Daniel where the glory of the saints of the most high presupposed their persecution. Likewise, to define His career as a whole, Jesus preferred the title of Son of Man to that of Messiah (cf Mk 8,29ff) which was too involved in the temporal perspectives of Jewish hopes.

c) In the abasement of this hidden condition (cf Mt 8,20 p; 11,19) which might excuse the blasphemies* uttered against Him (Mt 12,32 p), Jesus nevertheless began to exercise some of the powers of the Son of Man: the power to forgive sins* (Mt 9,6 p), dominion over the Sabbath* (Mt 12,8 p), preaching of the Word* (Mt 13,37). The manifestation of His secret dignity announced in some measure that of the last day.

2. *The fourth gospel.*

The Johannine texts on the Son of Man show in their own way all the aspects of the theme which we have noted in the synoptics. The glorious aspect: it is as Son of Man that the Son of God will on the last day exercise the power of judging (Jn 5,26-29). Then the angels will be seen ascending and descending on Him (1,51); and this final glorification will make known His heavenly origin (3,13), since "He will ascend up to where He was before" (6,62). But before that the Son of Man must pass through a state of humiliation in which men will have trouble in recognizing Him to believe in Him (9,35). In order for them to be able "to eat His flesh and drink His blood" (6,53), His flesh must be "given for the life of the world" in sacrifice (cf 6,51). However, in the Johannine perspective the cross is bound up with the return of the Son of Man to heaven to constitute His elevation. "The Son of Man must be raised on high" (3,14f; 12,34). This raising aloft is paradoxically His glorification (12,23; 13,31), and it is by means of it that the revelation of His mystery is completed: "then you shall know

that I am" (8,28). We understand that by the anticipation of this final glory, the Son of Man exercises even now some of His powers, notably that of judging and giving life to men (5,21f. 25ff) by the gift of His flesh (6,53); food which He alone can give, because the Father has marked Him with His seal (6,27).

II. APOSTOLIC WRITINGS

Recourse to the symbol of the Son of Man is very rare in the rest of the NT, with the exception of a few apocalyptic passages. Stephen sees Jesus in glory, at the right hand of God (cf Ps 110,1) in the capacity of the Son of Man (Ac 7,55f). So too, the seer of the Johannine Apocalypse (Ap 1,12-16) who contemplates in advance His parousia for the eschatological harvest* (Ap 14,14ff). Perhaps St. Paul also recalled the theme of the Son of Man when he describes Jesus as the heavenly Adam* whose image risen men will reveal (1 Co 15,45-49). Finally, in applying Ps 8,5ff to Jesus, the epistle to the Hebrews sees in Jesus "the man," "the Son of Man," abased before being called to glory (He 2,5-9). Arriving at this point, Christian reflection completes the bond between the "son of Adam" of the psalms, the Son of Man of the apocalypses, and the new Adam of St. Paul. As the son of Adam Jesus has shared our lot of humiliations and sufferings. The Son of Man, of heavenly origin, is called to return for the judgment*; His passion and His death led Him to the glory* of His resurrection, in the character of the new Adam, head of regenerated humanity. In Him the two contrasting figures of Adam that appear in Gn 1 and 3 are fulfilled. Likewise, when He shall be manifested at the last day, we shall be amazed to have met Him already, mysteriously hidden in the smallest of His needy brethren* (cf Mt 15,31ff).

→Adam I 2 b, II—Cloud 4—Day of the Lord NT I 1—Heaven V 2.4—Jesus Christ I 3; II 2 b—Judgment OT II 2; NT I—Kingdom OT III; NT III 1—Lord—Man—Mediator I 2—Messiah OT II 3; NT I 2, II 2—Plan of God NT I 2—Son of God O; NT I 1—Suffering NT II—Victory OT 3 a.

JDel wjy

SOUL

Far from being a "part" which joins with

the body* to form the human being, the soul denotes the entire man, insofar as he is animated by a spirit* of life. To speak properly, the soul does not live in the body, but expresses itself through the body, which itself, like the flesh*, denotes the entire man. If in virtue of its relation with the Spirit the soul indicates man's spiritual origin, this "spirituality" is deeply rooted in the concrete world, as is clear from the extensive meaning of the term as it is used.

I. THE SOUL
AND THE LIVING PERSON

In the biblical languages, the terms which designate the soul, *nepheš* (hb.), *psychē* (gr.), *anima* (lat.), are connected more or less directly with the idea of breath.

1. *The living man.* Breath or respiration is, above all, the sign of life. To be alive is still to have breath in oneself (2 S 1,9; Ac 20,10); when man dies, the soul leaves (Gn 35,18), is exhaled (Jr 15,9), or poured out like a liquid (Is 53,12); if he comes back to life, the soul returns to him (1 K 17,21).

Greeks or Semites would be able to express themselves in this way. But under this identity of expression is hidden a diversity of perspective. According to a fairly frequent view (clearly stated in some Greek philosophy), the soul tends to become a subsistent principle which exists independently of the body in which it is found and from which it departs: this is a "spiritualist" conception based, no doubt, on the quasi-immaterial character of the breath, as opposed to the material body. For the Semite, on the other hand, breath remains inseparable from the body which it animates; breath simply indicates the manner in which the concrete life is manifested in man, above all by the fact that breathing continues even when, apparently motionless, he sleeps. Would there not be here one of the profound reasons which have led to identifying soul and blood* (Ps 72,14)? The soul is in the blood (Lv 17,10f), it is the blood itself (Lv 17,14; Dt 12,23), it is the living man.

2. *Life.* From the meaning of *living*, the term passes easily to that of *life**, as the parallel uses of the two terms show: "Do not deliver over to the beast the soul of your turtle-dove, the life of your unhappy ones do not forget" (Ps 74,19); elsewhere in the law of retaliation, *soul for soul* can be translated *life for life* (Ex 21,23). Thus *life* and *soul* are often assimilated, although it is not a question of only the "spiritual " life, in opposition to the "corporal" life. But on the other hand this life, for a long time limited to an earthly horizon, finally is revealed as open to a heavenly, eternal life. It is therefore necessary each time to examine the context to know the exact meaning of the word.

In certain cases, the soul is considered as a principle of the *temporal life*. One fears to lose it (Js 9,24; Ac 27,22), or would like to preserve it from death (1 S 19,11; Ps 6,5), to place it in security (Lk 21,19) when one senses that it is threatened (R 11,3=1 K 19,10; Mt 2,20=Ex 4, 19; Ps 35,4; 38,13). Conversely, it is unnecessary to worry over it too much (Mt 6,25 p), but to risk it is necessary (Ph 2,30), to deliver it up for the sheep (1 Th 2,8). It is this which Jesus gives up (Mt 20,28 p; Jn 10,11.15.17) and which, after His example*, we are to sacrifice (Jn 13, 37f; 15,13; 1 Jn 3,16).

If such a sacrifice of life can be made, it is not simply because one knows that Yahweh can bring life back (Ps 34,23; 72,14); it is because Jesus has revealed, through the same word, the gift of *eternal life*. Thus He plays upon the different meanings of this word: "He who wishes to save his soul will lose it, but he who loses his soul for my sake will find it" (Mt 16, 25f p; cf Mt 10,39; Lk 14,26; 17,33; Jn 12,25). Under these conditions the "salvation of the soul" is ultimately the victory of eternal life lodged in the soul (Jm 1,21; 5,20; 1 P 1,9; He 10,39).

3. *The human person.* If life is certainly the most precious human commodity (1 S 26,24), to save his soul is to save himself: ultimately the soul designates the person.

First of all, objectively one calls every living being *soul*, even the animal (Gn 1,20f.24; 2,19); but most of the time it is a question of men; thus one speaks of "a community of seventy souls" (Gn 46,27=Ac 7,14; Dt 10,22; Ac 2,41; 27,37). A soul is a man, it is someone (Lv 5, 1...; 24,17; Mk 3,4; Ac 2,43; 1 P 3,20; Ap 8,9); vg, as opposed to the cargo of a ship (Ac 27,10). The height of objectifying is reached when a corpse can be designated, in memory of what it was, as a "dead soul" (Nm 6,6).

Subjectively, the soul corresponds to our *I*, just as the heart* or the flesh*, but with a nuance of interiority and living power: "As truly as my soul lives!" (Dt 32,40; Am 6,8; 2 Co 1,23) signifies the profound commitment of one who takes an oath. David loved Jonathan "as his own soul" (1 S 18,1.3). Finally, this I expresses itself in some activities which are not all "spiritual." Thus the rich man: "I will say to my soul: My soul, rest, eat, drink, make a feast! And God said to him: Fool, this very night your soul (=your life) will be asked of you" (Lk 12,19f). The mention of soul emphasizes the desire and will to live, recalling slightly the demanding character which thirst in a burning throat assumes (Ps 63,2). The thirsting and famished soul can be satiated (Ps 107,9; Jr 31, 14). Its feelings go from enjoyment (Ps 86,4) to trouble (Jn 12,27) and to sadness (Mt 26, 38=Ps 42,6), from comfort (Ph 2,19) to lassitude (He 12,3). It wishes to be fortified to be able to convey the paternal blessing (Gn 27,4) or to bear up under persecution (Ac 14,22). It is made to love (Gn 34,3) or to hate (Ps 11,5), to be pleased with someone (Mt 12,18=Is 42,2; He 10,38=Ha 2,4), to search for God without reserve (Mt 22,37 p=Dt 6,5; E 6,6; Col 3,23) and to bless the Lord forever (Ps 103,1).

It is with such fullness of meaning that certain formulas can recapture their original vigor: souls should be sanctified (1 P 1,22). For them Paul pours himself out (2 Co 12,15), over them spiritual leaders watch (He 13,17), Jesus promises them rest (Mt 11,29). These souls are beings of flesh, but in them has been placed a seed of life, a germ of eternity.

II. THE SOUL
AND THE SPIRIT OF LIFE

1. *The soul and the principle of life.* If the soul is the sign of life, it is not the source of it. And therein lies a second difference which separates profoundly two mentalities, the Semitic and the Platonic. For the latter the soul is identified with the spirit of which it is in some way an emanation, conferring on man a true autonomy. For the Semites, it is not the soul but God who by His Spirit* is the source of life: "God breathed in his nostril a breath (nešāmāh) of life, and man became a living soul (nepheš)" (Gn 2,7). In every living being there is a "breath of the spirit (=of breathing) of life" (Gn 7,22), without which it would die. This breath is lent throughout man's mortal life: "you withdraw the breath from them, they expire and to dust they return; you send your breath, they are created" (Ps 104,29f). The soul (psychē), principle of life, and the spirit (pneuma), source of life, are thus distinguished one from the other at the heart of the human

being where only the Word of God can have access (He 4,12). Transposed into the Christian order, the distinction permits one to speak of "psychic experiences devoid of spirit" (Jude 19) or to look into the "psychic experiences" of believers who have regressed from the "spiritual" stage to which baptism has led them, to the "earthly" state (1 Co 2,14; 15,44; Jm 3,15).

2. *The soul and survival.* From what has been said there is an immediate consequence. Different from the spirit of which it is never said that it dies, but of which one affirms that it returns to Yahweh (Jb 34,14f; Ps 31,6; Qo 12,7), the soul can die (Nm 23,10; Jg 16,30; Ez 13,19), can be delivered to death (Ps 78,50), just like bones (Ez 37,1-14) or flesh (Ps 63,2; 16,9f). The soul descends to Sheol to lead the impoverished existence of the shadows* and the dead*, far from the "land of the living" of which it no longer knows anything (Jb 14,21f; Qn 9,5.10), far also from God whom it can no longer praise (Ps 88,11ff); for the dead live in silence* (Ps 94,17; 115,17). Briefly, the soul "is no longer" (Jb 7,8.21; Ps 39,14).

Nevertheless, the omnipotence of God will grant this soul descended into the depths of the abyss (Ps 30,4; 49,16; Pr 23,14) to raise from there (2 M 7,9.14.23) and to reanimate the dispersed bones: faith is sure of it.

3. *The soul and the body.* If the souls go to Sheol, this does not mean that they "live" there without bodies: their "existence" is not a real existence precisely because they cannot express themselves without their bodies. The doctrine of the immortality of man therefore is not identified with the notion of the spirituality of the soul. Moreover it does not seem that the Book of Wisdom introduced it into the patrimony of biblical revelation. Imbued with Hellenism, given the opportunity, the author of the Book of Wisdom uses some terms taken from Greek anthropology; but his cast of mind is always different. Undoubtedly, "the corruptible body dulls the soul, and its earthly habitation weighs heavily upon the thoughtful spirit" (Ws 9,15); but there is here a question of the intelligence of man, not of the spirit of life; especially there is question of belittling neither matter (cf 13,3) nor the body: "Being good, I have come in a body without stain," says the author (8,19f). If there is a distinction between the body and the soul, it is not such to envisage a true existence for the separated soul; as in the Jewish apocalypses of the time, the souls go to Hades (Ws 16,

14). God, who has them in His hand (3,1; 4,14), can raise them up again because He has created man* incorruptible (2,23).

The Bible, which attributes to the total man what much later would be reserved for the soul as a consequence of the distinction between body and soul, does not for all that offer a belief devoid of immortality. The souls which wait beneath the altar (Ap 6,9; 20,4) for their recompense (Ws 2,22) exist there only as a call to the resurrection*, which is a work of the Spirit of life, not of an immanent force. In the soul God has placed a seed of eternity which comes to flower in its own time (Jm 1,21; 5,20; 1 P 1,9). The whole man* will again become a "living soul;" and, as Paul says, "a spiritual body:" he will arise again in his integrity (1 Co 15,45=Gn 2,7).

→Blood OT—Body—Death—Flesh—Life II 3 —Man—Resurrection—Spirit.

XLD jjk

SOWING

The process of nature, the history of human generations, the creative and redemptive act, all take place according to the same cycle: seed time, growth*, fruition*, finally harvest*. There is a perfect correspondence between the proper sense and the figurative sense of the word *sowing*.

I. EARTHLY SOWINGS

1. *The divine action.* On the day of creation, God gave to the earth the ability to bring forth a vegetative life capable of reproducing itself, of "sowing a seed" (Gn 1,11f.29). He who ceaselessly "provides seed for the worker will grant it to you also" (2 Co 9,10). Ruling the times of sowing and of reaping (Gn 8,22), He blesses the sowing of the just even to a hundredfold (Gn 26,12) or on the other hand defeats the expectation of the wicked (Is 5,10; Mi 6,15), who have "sown wheat" and "reap brambles" (Jr 12,13; cf Gn 3,18). But to the man who becomes converted, God "will give rain for the seed sown in the ground" (Is 30,23), and his lands will be capable of receiving seed (Ez 36,9). In the Bible the divine blessing, realized in the success of the sowing, is always connected with the people's faithfulness* to the covenant.

2. *The role of man.* Although God blesses the sowing, it is in fact up to man to do it.

a) His responsibility*. God has charged him with the duty of preserving every seed on the earth and of saving it from the deluge (Gn 7,3). He must, in case of famine, seek this seed (Gn 47,19) and protect it from any unclean contact (Lv 11,37f). "In the morning sow your grain; in the evening do not remain idle!" (Qo 11,6).

To man also falls the hard work, which according to Palestinian practice ordinarily takes place after the sowing. Is this not the way Wisdom must be cultivated: "You will toil some time to cultivate it, but soon you will eat of its fruits" (Si 6,19)?

In a metaphorical sense, this responsibility* extends to the choice of the seed and of the ground. For "man harvests what he has sown" (G 6,7). To sow strange shoots (idolatry) is to obtain a rapid flowering perhaps, but no harvest (Is 17,10f). For sowing injustice or iniquity, one can harvest seven times more misery (Pr 22,8; Jb 4,8; Si 7,3); "he who sows the wind reaps the tempest" (Ho 8,7). Experience must never be forgotten: "thin sowing means thin reaping: the more you sow, the more you reap" (2 Co 9,6). In place of sowing in the flesh, we must sow in the spirit (G 6,8)—not among thorns (Jr 4,3), but in peace (Jm 3,18) and justice (Ho 10,12; Pr 11,18).

b) *Act of hope.* If it is true that the laborer has a right to his part of the produce (1 Co 9,10) and that the ideal is to harvest what one has sown, the proverb often remains valid: "There is one who sows and another who reaps" (Jn 4,37). The sower then must have confidence in the fruitful earth and hope in the water of heaven without counting on subduing the elements. Let him then sow without watching the wind (Qo 11,4), otherwise he will accomplish nothing. The least of the seeds can become a great tree (Mk 4,31f) and the fertile grain yields as much as 100 per cent. Although he has an active part to play in the sowing, man should not forget that, once it has been thrown on the ground, "the seed sprouts and grows of its own accord (gr *automate*)" (Mk 4,27). The obligation of the sabbatical year, when the duty of sowing the fields ceased (Lv 25,4), called for an act of absolute confidence in God, who had given a double harvest in the preceding year. To teach His disciples total dependence on the heavenly Father's providence*, Jesus gives them the example of the birds of the air, which neither sow nor reap (Mt 6,26p).

This confidence encourages man to bury the seed in the earth and to let it die in order that it may bring forth fruit (Jn 12,24). If he who carries the seed "goes forth weeping," he knows that he "will sing while bringing back the sheaves" (Ps 126,5f). This image depicts service "for the benefit of the saints" (G 6,7-10; 2 Co 9,6-13) and apostolic work (Jn 4,38; 1 Co 3,8; 2 Co 9,10ff). Finally, if the grain must die in order to take up its life again (1 Co 15,36), it is the same for mortal man, who must rise again: "He who sows corruption will rise in incorruption; he who sows a natural body rises a spiritual body" (15,42ff). Entrusted to the earth, the body will rise in the glory of Christ.

II. DIVINE SOWINGS

However the creator, whose activity could be compared with that of a sower, is only pictured as the Sower in an eschatological context. Knowing that the Son is both the Word of God and the divine Seed, the Christian can see God as the One who sows His Word in men's hearts and the One who sows in each man His Seed, His real offspring.

1. *The divine seed.* God blesses Adam by making him fruitful*. The term *seed* (gr. *sperma*) serves to indicate posterity, offspring, lineage, and race. From the beginning the seed of man passed on over the generations is seen in contrast with the lineage that will triumph over the serpent (Gn 3,15). This victory will be realized in Jesus, the offspring that comes from the crossing of two lines: Son of God, Son of Adam, of Abraham and of David.

On the one hand, the blessing is assured to the descendants of Noah (Gn 9,9), of Abraham (Gn 12,7), of Isaac (26,4), of Jacob (32,13); who will be as numerous as the dust of the earth (13,15f), the sand by the sea (22,17), or the stars of heaven (15,5; 26,4). It is also assured to the royal line of David (2 S 7,12; 22,51). And this is so because of a covenant concluded not only with the ancestor but also with his "seed."

But, whether it is a question of the seed of Abraham or of David, the infidelity of the people and of their kings forces God to withdraw His blessing. The tree of Jesse must be cut down, but from its stump there will then blossom a "holy seed" (Is 6,13). For God will be once again a sower (Ho 2,25; Jr 31,27) who will repeople Judah, the evil people (Is 1,4),

which has been decimated by its punishment*. More precisely, this seed will be concentrated in one shoot, which becomes one of the names* of the Messiah*. "Behold a man whose name is a shoot; where he is, something will spring up; he will rebuild the sanctuary" (Ze 6,12f).

2. *The Word of God.* In an expressly metaphorical sense, the seed is the Word* of God. Already the consoler of Israel announces the efficacious action of the divine Word in comparing it to the rain which makes the seed fruitful (Is 55,10f). In telling the parable of the sower Jesus connects the duty of bearing fruit* not with the harvest* but with the sowing. In this way He looks back to the inauguration of the last times (cf Ho 2,25), which is taking place as He speaks. This is the story, as it is actually lived, of the eschatological meeting between the divine Seed and the people of God. If there must be good ground, it is because the sowing is made with the very word of Jesus. And what a magnificent result! Yet alongside the good seed sown by the Son of Man there is also the cockle sown by the devil (Mt 13, 24-30.36-43).

This Word is Christ Himself, who has willed to die in the earth in order to bring forth fruit (Jn 12,24.32). And the Church has recognized her own history as contained in the parables of Jesus. She has strengthened her faith by her presentiment of the final glory through the humble beginnings of the kingdom of heaven: the grain of mustard becomes a large tree (Mt 13,31f; cf Ez 17,23; Dn 4,7-19), in accordance with the promise made to Abraham of a "seed" innumerable as the stars of heaven. Finally, the Church, "seed" of Jesus (Ap 12,17), fights the dragon victoriously; for Christ remains in her (1 Jn 3,9).

→Fruit — Fruitfulness — Growth — Harvest II, III 2 a—New Birth—Word of God NT I 2.
XLD jpl

SPIRIT

In all the classical and biblical languages *spirit* is a word capable of many different meanings. Between the spirit of wine and the man of spirit, between "giving up the spirit" and "living according to the Spirit," there are many differences, but also real analogies. *Spirit* tends always to designate the essential, indiscernible element of a being, that which makes it live and that which emanates from it without its willing it, that which is most itself and yet over which one cannot make oneself master.

OT

1. *Wind.* Spirit (in Hebrew *rūaḥ*) is the breath, especially that of the wind. There is a mystery in the wind: sometimes of an irresistible violence, it strikes houses, cedar trees, ships of the high sea (Ez 13,13; 27,26); sometimes it insinuates itself in a murmur (1 K 19,12), sometimes it scorches the sterile earth with its hot breath (Ex 14,21; cf Is 30,27-33); sometimes it spreads over the fruitful water* enabling it to bring forth life (1 K 18,45).

2. *Respiration.* Like the wind over the great and lifeless earth, man's delicate, oscillating breathing is the power which stirs and animates the body and its bulk. Man is not master of this breathing, though he cannot do without it. He dies when his breathing stops. Like the wind, but in a way much more immediate, breathing, especially man's breathing, comes from God (Gn 2,7; 6,3; Jb 33,4) and returns to Him at death (Jb 34,14f; Qo 12,7; Ws 15,11).

3. *The spirit of man.* As long as remains in man, this divine breath really belongs to him. It makes his inert flesh* an active being, a living soul* (Gn 2,7). On the other hand, everything related to the soul, all its feelings and emotions, are expressed by man's breathing: fear (Gn 41,8), anger (Jg 8,3), a joy (Gn 45,27), and pride—all affect man's breathing. The word *rūaḥ* is, therefore, the expression both of human consciousness and of spirit. To give up this spirit into the hands of God (Ps 31,6=Lk 23,46) is to emit one's final breath and at the same time to surrender to God one's most individual riches, one's very being.

4. *The spirits in man.* The consciousness of man seems sometimes invaded by a strange power which is not properly his own. Another force dwells within him, one which can only be itself a spirit. This can be an evil force: jealousy (Nm 5,14-30), hatred (Jg 9,23), prostitution (Ho 4,12), or impurity (Ze 13,2). It can also be a beneficent spirit—of justice (Is 28,6), of supplication (Ze 12,10). Unable to probe the depths of Satan*, since the redemption is not yet accomplished, the OT is reluctant to attribute the perverse spirits to someone other than God

(cf Jg 9,23; 1 S 19,9; 1 K 22,23...); but it does affirm, however, that the good spirits always come directly from God. And the OT urges the existence of a holy* and sanctifying Spirit, unique source of all inner transformation (cf Is 11,2; Ez 36,26f).

NT

The same difference of meaning is still to be found in the NT as in the OT. But apart from that the gift of the Holy Spirit in Jesus Christ makes evident the true dimensions of the spirit of man and the spirits which can actuate him.

1. *Discernment of spirits.* In unmasking Satan* and exposing his ruses and their weaknesses, Jesus Christ reveals His power over the evil spirits. In the power of the Spirit, He expels demons who cannot resist His holiness (Mt 8, 16; 12,28; Mk 1,23-27; 9,29). To His disciples He gives the same power (Mk 6,7; 16,17).

Among the charisms* of the Holy Spirit, discernment of spirits (1 Co 12,10) has an important place; it seems in fact to be related to the precious gift of prophecy*; the characteristic of spiritual men "taught by the Spirit" is "to evaluate the gifts of God" (1 Co 2,11f) and to "seek the better things" (12,31; cf 14,12).

2. *The Spirit joins Himself to our spirit.* To recognize the Spirit of God is not to renounce one's own personality, but rather to bring it into submission. In line with the OT, the NT sees in man a complex being, at once body, soul, and spirit (cf 1 Th 5,23). And it sees in spirit a force inseparable from breath and life (Lk 8,55; 23,46), sensitive to every emotion (Lk 1,47; Jn 11,33; 13,21; 2 Co 2,13; 7,13), often in contrast to the flesh* (Mt 26,41; G 5,17). But the essential experience is that the spirit of the believer is inhabited by the Spirit of God which renews it (E 4,23) and which "joins itself to it" (R 8,16), to awaken in it a prayer and filial pleading (8,26), and "to unite it to the Lord to make with Him one spirit" (1 Co 6,17).

It frequently happens, especially in Paul, that it is impossible to decide whether the word *spirit* refers to the spirit of man or the Spirit of God; for example when he speaks of "the fervor of the spirit in the service of the Lord*" (R 12, 11) or when he puts together "a holy spirit, a charity without deceit" (2 Co 6,6...). This ambiguity, embarrassing for a translator, is a light for faith: it is the proof that the Spirit of

God, while it permeates the spirit of man and transforms him, leaves man his complete personality; it indicates that so to take possession of His creature in making him exist before Him, "God is spirit" (Jn 4,24).

Because God* is spirit, that which is born of God "being born of the Spirit, is spirit" (Jn 3,6); and is capable of adoring God "in spirit and in truth" (4,24), and of renouncing the flesh* and its "dead works" (He 6,1) in order to produce the fruit* of the Spirit (G 5,22) which gives life (Jn 6,63).

→Adoration II 3—Angels O—Evil Spirits—Flesh—Fruit IV—God NT V—Heart—Man—Soul—Spirit of God O—Writing IV, V.

JG afmcg

SPIRIT OF GOD

The Spirit of God cannot be separated from the Father and the Son. He reveals Himself with them in Jesus Christ, but He has His own way of revealing Himself as He has His own personality. The Son*, in His humanity identical with ours, reveals to us at the same time who He is and who it is that He never ceases to look upon: the Father*. We are able to delineate the features of the Son and the Father, but the Spirit has neither the countenance nor even a name apt for evoking a human appearance. In every language His name (hb. *rūaḥ*, gr. *pneuma*, lat. *spiritus*) is a common name, borrowed from the natural phenomena of wind and breath, such that the same text: "You will send forth your breath, they (animals) are created, and you will renew the face of the earth" (Ps 104,30) is able to call forth with equal appropriateness the cosmic image of the divine breath whose rhythm rules the changes of the seasons, and the pouring out of the Holy Spirit vivifying hearts.

It is impossible to lay hand on the Spirit. You "hear His voice" or recognize His passing by signs which are often remarkable, but you cannot know "from whence He comes or where He goes" (Jn 3,8). He always acts through another person, when He takes possession of him and transforms him. Without a doubt, He produces extraordinary manifestations which "renew the face of the earth" (Ps 104,30). But His action always proceeds from the interior and it is from the interior that you recognize Him: "You know Him because He dwells within you" (Jn 14,17). The great symbols of the Spirit (water*, fire*, air, and wind) pertain to the world of nature and do not carry with them distinct features. They evoke above all the invasion of a presence*, an irresistible, ever deepening expansion. The Spirit is neither more nor less mysterious than the Father or the Son, but He more powerfully reminds us that God is a mystery*. He keeps us from forgetting that "God is Spirit" (Jn 4,24) and that "the Lord is Spirit" (2 Co 3,17).

OT

The Spirit of God is not yet revealed here as a person, but as a divine force transforming human personalities in order to make them capable of exceptional deeds. These deeds are always intended to strengthen the people in their vocation, and to make them the servants and the cooperators of the holy* God. Having come from God and leading to God, the Spirit is a holy Spirit. Having come from the God of Israel and consecrating Israel to the God of the covenant, the Spirit is sanctifying. This action and this revelation are asserted especially by three ways: the Messianic way of salvation, the prophetic way of the Word and witness, and the sacrificial way of service and consecration. According to these three ways, the people of Israel are called to receive the Spirit completely.

I. SPIRIT AND SALVATION

1. *The judges.* The judges of Israel are raised up by the Spirit of God. Without expecting it, without in any way being predisposed, and without power of resistance, the simple sons of peasants, Samson, Gideon, and Saul, are abruptly and totally changed. They are not only rendered capable of heroic deeds of daring and strength, but are endowed with a new personality which allows Him to fulfill a special role and to accomplish a mission of freeing this people. Through their hands and by their spirit, the Spirit of God prolongs the epic of the exodus and the desert, assures the unity* and salvation* of Israel, and so He is found to be the source of the holy people*; His action is already interior, although still signified by images which emphasize a sudden and strange control: The Spirit "was" upon Othniel and Jephthah (Jg 3,10; 11, 29): He "swoops down" like a bird on its prey (Jg 14,6; 1 S 11,6); He "puts on" as one does armor (Jg 6,34).

2. *The kings.* The judges are only temporary liberators, and the Spirit leaves them once their mission is completed. They have as their heirs the kings* who are given a permanent function. The rite of anointing*, which consecrates them, manifests the indelible imprint of the Spirit and invests them with a sacred majesty (1 S 10,1; 16,13).

3. *The Messiah.* Ritual anointing is not sufficient to make the kings loyal servants of God, able to assure Israel of salvation, justice, and peace. To complete this role, a more penetrating action of the Spirit was needed, the direct anointing by God which will designate the Messiah*. Upon Him the Spirit will not only descend, but will remain (Is 11,2); in Him, the Spirit will display all His resources, "wisdom* and intelligence" as in Bezalel (Ex 35,31) or in Solomon, "prudence and strength*" as in David, "knowledge and fear* of God"—in short, the ideal of the great religious souls of Israel. These gifts* will open up for the land governed in this way an era of happiness and holiness (Is 11,9).

II.   SPIRIT AND WITNESS

1. *The nabī'īm.* These forerunners of the prophets, professionals in religious exaltation, did not always discriminate between the human practices which put them into a trance and the divine action. Nevertheless they are one of the living forces of Israel because they give testimony to the power* of Yahweh; one can recognize in the power which makes them speak in the name of the true God the presence of His Spirit (Ex 15,20; Nm 11,25ff; 1 S 10,6; 1 K 18, 22).

2. *The prophets.* If the great prophets*, at least the more ancient ones, do not refer to the Spirit, if they prefer frequently to call the force that seizes them the hand of God (Is 8,11; Jr 1,9; 15,17; Ez 3,14), it is not because they do not think they possess the Spirit, but because they are aware of possessing Him in a different way from that in which their predecessors, the nabim, possessed Him. They have a special calling and duty. They are fully conscious of this duty, often in revolt against their whole being, and of a sovereign pressure which constrains them to speak (Am 3,8; 7,14f; Jr 20,7ff). The word they proclaim comes from them, and they know at what cost; but it is not born within

them. It is the very word of the God who sends them. This is the way in which the connection between the Word* of God and His Spirit shows itself, a connection which appears as early as Elijah (1 K 19,12f) and which will not end. So the Spirit does not limit Himself to raising up a new personality for the service of His activity, but He gives the prophet access to the meaning and secret of this action. The Spirit is no longer only "intelligence and strength" but "knowledge of God" and of His ways (cf Is 11,3).

At the same time as He opens the prophets to the Word of God, to the point of revealing the divine glory (Ez 3,12; 8,3), the Spirit makes them "stand on their feet" (Ez 2,1; 3,24) to speak to the people (Ez 11,5) and to proclaim to them the judgment* which is coming. Thus He makes witnesses of them and in doing so Himself gives witness to God (Ne 9,30; cf Ze 7,12).

III.   SPIRIT AND CONSECRATION
THE SERVANT OF YAHWEH

The convergence of the Messianic and liberating role of the Spirit and the prophetic role of announcing the Word and the judgment, already evident in the Messiah of Isaiah, is fully affirmed in the Servant* of Yahweh. Because God "has sent His Spirit upon Him," the Servant "will proclaim justice to the nations" (Is 42,1; cf 61,1ff). It is the prophet who proclaims justice*, but the king who establishes it. But the Servant "through His sufferings will justify the multitudes" (53,11), that is, He will establish them in justice. So His mission includes something royal in it. The prophetic tasks and the Messianic tasks are united, achieved through the same Spirit. On the other hand, the Servant is He in whom "God takes pleasure" (42,1), the pleasure which He expects from the sacrifices* due to Him. The whole life and death of His Servant are holy to God, expiation* for sinners, salvation of the multitudes. The Holy Spirit is sanctifying.

IV.   THE SPIRIT UPON THE PEOPLE

The action of the Spirit in the prophets and servants of God is itself prophetic; it declares its outpouring on the whole people, like rain which brings life to a thirsting land (Is 32,15; 44,3; Ez 36,25; Jl 3,1f), or like the breath of life coming to animate dried bones (Ez 37). This pouring out of the Spirit is like a new* creation*, the coming of right and justice in a land renewed (Is 32,16), the coming into hearts* transformed of a sensitivity receptive to the voice of God, of a spontaneous faithfulness to His Word (Is 59,21; Ps 143,10) and to His covenant (Ez 36,27), of a sense of supplication (Ze 12,10), and of praise* (Ps 51,17). Regenerated by the Spirit, Israel will recognize her God and God will find again His people: "I will no longer hide my face* from them because I shall have poured out my spirit on the house of Israel" (Ez 39,29).

This vision is still only a hope. In the OT, the Spirit cannot remain, "He is not yet given" (Jn 7,39). Without a doubt one sees that, at the beginning, at the time of the Red Sea and the cloud*, the Holy Spirit worked in Moses and led Israel to the place of its rest* (Is 63,9-14). But one also notices that the people are always able to "sadden the Holy Spirit" (63,10) and to paralyze His action. So that the gift may be made total and final, God must give an unprecedented sign that He intervenes in person: "It is you, Yahweh, you are our father...Why, Yahweh, do you let us wander far from your ways?...Ah! If you would rend the heavens and descend..." (63,15-19). The heavens opened, a Father God, a God descending on the earth, hearts converted—such will be in fact the work of the Holy Spirit, His definitive manifestations in Jesus Christ.

V. CONCLUSION: SPIRIT AND WORD

From one end of the OT to the other, the Spirit and the Word* of God never cease to act together. If the Messiah can observe the Word of the Law* given by God to Moses and achieve its justice, it is because He has the Spirit. If the prophet gives testimony to the Word, it is because the Spirit took hold of him. If the Servant is able to bring to the nations the Word of Salvation, it is because the Spirit rests upon Him. If Israel one day is able to keep this Word in her heart, it will be only in the Spirit. Though inseparable these two powers have nevertheless very distinct characteristics. The Word penetrates from the outside, as a sword lays bare the flesh; the Spirit is fluid and infiltrates imperceptibly. The Word makes itself heard and known; the Spirit remains invisible. The Word is revelation; the Spirit, an interior transformation. The Word stands erect,

upright, holding forth; the Spirit falls, spreads itself, submerges. This division of roles and their necessary association are found in the NT: the Word of God made flesh through the operation of the Spirit does nothing without the Spirit, and the consummation of His work is the gift of the Spirit.

NT

I. THE SPIRIT IN JESUS

1. *The baptism of Jesus.* John the Baptist, awaiting the Messiah, at the same time awaited the Spirit in all His power. For the works of man, the Spirit would substitute the irresistible action of God: "I baptize you with water with a view to repentance...He will baptize you in the Holy Spirit and with fire*" (Mt 3,11). Of the traditional symbols, John retains the most inaccessible, fire. Jesus does not repudiate this proclamation, but He accomplishes it in a way which confuses John. He receives His baptism*, and the Spirit is manifested over Him under a form quite simple yet divine and associated with both wind and water, in the vision of the sky opening and a dove* descending. The baptism of water, which John believed abolished, becomes through Jesus' action baptism in the Spirit. In the man who mingles with sinners, the Spirit reveals the promised Messiah* (Lk 3,22; Ps 2,7), the Lamb* offered in sacrifice for the sin of the world (Jn 1,29), and the beloved Son (Mk 1,11). But He reveals this in His mysterious way, without seeming to act. The Son acts and has Himself baptized, the Father speaks to the Son, but the Spirit neither speaks nor acts. His presence is, however, necessary for dialogue between the Father and the Son. Though indispensable, the Spirit remains silent and seemingly inactive: He does not add His voice to that of the Father, nor add any act to that of Jesus! What does He do then? He causes the encounter to take place, He communicates to Jesus the word of approval, of pride and of love which comes to Him from the Father, and He puts Him in His posture as Son. The Holy Spirit makes the consecration of Christ rise to the Father, the first-fruits* of the sacrifice of His beloved Son.

2. *Jesus conceived of the Holy Spirit.* The presence of the Spirit in Jesus, made known only at the baptism, dates back to the very beginning of His being. The baptism of Jesus

is not the scene of a calling but the investiture of the Messiah and the presentation by God of His Son, the Servant whom He held in reserve as the prophetic "behold" proclaimed (Is 42,1; 52,13). Judges, prophets, kings, find themselves one day taken possession of by the Spirit. John the Baptist is seized by Him three months before his birth. But in Jesus, the Spirit does not bring about a new personality. From His first instant, the Spirit dwells in Him and causes Him to exist; right from the maternal womb, He constitutes Jesus the Son of God. Both gospels describing the infancy emphasize this initial action (Mt 1,20; Lk 1,35). Luke by way of comparing Mary's annunciation to previous annunciations, indicates clearly that this action is more than a consecration. Samson (Jg 13,5), Samuel (1 S 1,11), and John the Baptist (Lk 1,15) were all three consecrated to God from their conception in a manner more or less total and direct. But Jesus Himself, without the medium of any rite or the intervention of any man, but solely by the action of the Spirit in Mary*, is no longer only consecrated to God but "holy" by His very being (Lk 1,35).

3. *Jesus acts in the Spirit.* In all His dealings, Jesus manifests the action of the Spirit within Him (Lk 4,14). In the Spirit He confronts the devil* (Mt 4,1) and frees his victims (12,28). And He brings to the poor the good news and the Word of God (Lk 4,18). In the Spirit He has access to the Father (Lk 10,21). His miracles* which overcome evil and death, the power and truth of His word, His direct familiarity with God, are all proof that the "Spirit rests" upon Him (Is 61,1) and that He is at the same time the Messiah who saves, the awaited prophet, and the beloved Servant.

In the inspired men of Israel, the manifestations of the Spirit were always something momentary and temporary. In Jesus they are permanent. He does not receive the Word of God: He declares it and expresses it. He does not wait for the moment to work a miracle: the miracle comes from Him as a simple gesture comes from us. He does not receive divine secrets: He lives always in the presence of God in complete transparency. No one ever possessed the Spirit as He does, "beyond all measure" (Jn 3,34).

No one at any time ever possessed the Spirit as He did. The inspired men of the OT, even though they preserve their own self-possession, know themselves possessed by something stronger than themselves. In Jesus we find no

trace of constraint to call the inspiration to our attention. One would say that He has no need of the Spirit to perform the works of God. Not that He can do without the Spirit, any more than He can do without the Father. But just as the Father "is always with" Him (Jn 8,29), so the Spirit can never fail Him. The absence in Jesus of habitual repercussions of the Spirit is a sign of His divinity. He does not experience the Spirit as a force which invades from without; He is in the Spirit and the Spirit is in Him, it is His own Spirit (cf Jn 16,14f).

II. JESUS PROMISES THE SPIRIT

Filled with the Spirit and acting only through Him, Jesus nevertheless hardly speaks of Him. He manifests Him by all His actions, but He is not able to point to Him as distinct from Himself as long as He lives among us. In order that the Spirit may be poured out and recognized, Jesus must first go away (Jn 7,39; 16,7); then men will recognize that this is the Spirit and that He comes from Him. Besides, Jesus does not speak to His own of the Spirit except when He separates Himself from them perceptibly and temporarily (Mt 10,20) or definitively (Jn 14,16f.26; 13,13ff).

In the synoptics the Spirit seems to have to show Himself only in grave situations, in the midst of conquering adversaries or before the tribunals (Mk 13,11). But the confidences of the discourse after the last supper are more exact: the hostility of the world* for Jesus is not just an accidental thing; and if it does not express itself by violent persecutions*, still the disciples will daily sense the weight of its threat (Jn 15, 18-21). And that is why each day the Spirit will be with them (14,16f).

As Jesus confessed* His Father by His life (Jn 5,41; 8,50; 12,49) so the disciples will have to give witness* to the Lord (Mk 13,9; Jn 15, 27). As long as Jesus was living with them, they feared nothing. He was their Paraclete*, always there to defend them and to get them out of difficulties (Jn 17,12). After He departs the Spirit will take His place as their Paraclete (14,16; 16,7). Distinct from Jesus, He will not speak in His own name, but always of Jesus from whom He is inseparable and whom He will "glorify" (16,13f). He will recall to the disciples the works and words of the Lord and will give them an understanding of them (14, 26). He will give them the strength to confront the world in the name* of Jesus, to discover the meaning of His death*, and to give testimony to the divine mystery which has been fulfilled in this shocking event: the condemnation of sin, the defeat of Satan, and the triumph of the justice* of God (16,8-11).

III. JESUS SENDS THE SPIRIT

Having died and risen again, Jesus makes a gift of His Spirit to the Church. When a man dies, no matter how great his spirit was or how profound his growing influence, he is still condemned to become part of the past. His work can survive him but it no longer pertains to him. He can no longer do anything about it and must abandon it to the mercy of human caprice. But when Jesus dies and "gives up His Spirit" to God, He "hands on" His Spirit to the Church in the same act (Jn 19,30). Until Jesus' death the Spirit appeared circumscribed by the normal limits of Jesus' human individuality and His sphere of activity. Now that the Son* of Man is exalted to the right hand of the Father in glory (12,23), He draws together redeemed humanity (12,32) and pours out the Spirit upon it (7,39; 20,22f; Ac 2,33).

IV. THE CHURCH RECEIVES THE SPIRIT

The Church, a new creation, can only be born of the Spirit from whom all that is born of God originates (Jn 3,5f). The Acts are like a "gospel of the Spirit."

This action of the Spirit in Acts has two characteristics already seen from the OT. On the one hand, prodigies and extraordinary deeds, inspired men caught up in ecstasy (Ac 2,4.5.11), sick and possessed persons cured (3,7; 5,12.15...), heroic self-assurance of the disciples (4,13.31; 5,20; 10,20). On the other hand, these wonders, signs of definitive salvation certify that conversion is possible, that sins are forgiven, and that the hour has come when God pours out His Spirit in the Church (2,38; 3,26; 4,12; 5,32; 10,43).

This Spirit is the Spirit of Jesus. He causes the works of Jesus to be repeated, His word to be proclaimed (4,30; 5,42; 6,7; 9,20; 18,5; 19, 10.20), His prayer to be reiterated (Ac 7,59f = Lk 23,34.46; Ac 21,14 = Lk 22,42), and His thanksgiving to be perpetuated in the breaking of the bread. The Spirit sustains union among the brethren (Ac 2,42; 4,32), this union which grouped the disciples around Jesus. It is im-

possible to conceive of these attitudes obtained by contact with Christ, persisting by a deliberate will to reproduce His existence. While living with them, Jesus needed all the strength of His personality to keep them near Him. Now that they see Him no longer, and although they know by His example to what they are exposed, His disciples spontaneously follow in His footsteps: they have received the Spirit of Jesus.

The Holy Spirit is the strength* which propels this newly born Church "even to the ends of the earth" (1,8); soon He directly takes hold of the pagans (10,44), thus proving that He is "poured out on all mankind" (2,17). And presently He sends forth on His mission* those whom He chooses: Philip (8,26.29f), Peter (10, 20), Paul, and Barnabas (13,2.4). But He is not merely present at the start. He accompanies and guides the action of the apostles (16,6f), He gives His own authority to their decisions (15, 28). If the Word "is believed and continued to spread" (6,7; 12,24), the interior source of this forward thrust in gladness is the Spirit (13,52).

V. EXPERIENCE OF THE SPIRIT IN ST. PAUL

1. *The Spirit, glory of Christ in us.* "He who raised Jesus" (R 8,11) by the power of His Spirit of sanctity (R 1,4) and made Him a "living spirit" (1 Co 15,45), at the same time has made the Spirit the "glory of the Lord arisen" (2 Co 3,18). The gift of the Holy Spirit is the presence* in us of the glory* of the Lord which transforms us into His image*. So Paul does not separate Christ and the Spirit, or life "in Christ" and life "in the Spirit." "To live is Christ" (G 2,20), and it is also the Spirit (R 8,2.10). To be "in Christ Jesus" (R 8,1) is to live "in the Spirit" (8,5...).

2. *Signs of the Spirit.* Life in the Spirit is not yet an intuitive possession of the Spirit; it is a life in faith. But it is a real experience and concrete certitude because it is, through signs, the experience of a presence*. These signs vary considerably. But all of them, from the relatively external charisms*, the gift of tongues or of healing (1 Co 12,28f; 14,12), to the "higher gifts" (12,31) of faith, hope, and charity, are at the service of the gospel to which they witness (1 Th 1,5f; 1 Co 1,5f) and of the body* of Christ which they build* (1 Co 12,4-30).

All the signs also make us perceive, by the

575

actions and states of man, by "the gifts which God has made to us" (1 Co 2,12), a personal presence, someone who "dwells" (R 8,11) in us, who "witnesses" (8,16), who "intercedes" (8,26), who "joins Himself to our spirit*" (8, 16), and who "groans in our hearts" (G 4,6).

3. *The Spirit, source of new life.* Under forms quite different, the experience of the Spirit is basically always the same: life* has taken the place of an existence which had been condemned and already marked out for death*. The Law*, which held us prisoners in the decay of its letter, gives way to "newness of the Spirit" (R 7,6); and the blessing* of Abraham in the Spirit of the promise (G 3,13f) takes the place of the curse* of the Law. The covenant* of the letter which kills gives way to the covenant of the Spirit which brings life (2 Co 3,6). The law of the Spirit and of justice takes the place of the law of sin which imposed the law of the flesh* (R 7,18.25; 8,2.4). The fruits* of the Spirit take the place of the works of the flesh (G 5,19-23). The condemnation which the "tribulation and anguish" (R 2,9) of the divine wrath* made to weigh upon the sinner now yields to the peace* and joy* of the Spirit (1 Th 1,6; G 5,22...).

This life is given to us, and in the Spirit we lack no other gift (1 Co 1,7); but it is given to us in the struggle, because in this world we have up till now only "the pledges" (2 Co 1,22; 5,5; E 1,14) and the "first-fruits" (R 8,23) of the Spirit. The Spirit calls us to fight against the flesh; along with the indicatives which affirm His presence are constantly intermingled the imperatives which proclaim His demands: "Since the Spirit is our life, the Spirit makes us act also" (G 5,25; cf 6,9; R 8,9.13; E 4,30) and transforms the "beings of flesh, the small children* in Christ" into "spiritual men" (1 Co 3, 1).

4. *The Spirit and the Church.* The new creation born of the Spirit is the Church. Church and Spirit are inseparable: the experience of the Spirit takes place in the Church and gives access to the mystery of the Church. The charisms* are so much the more precious as they contribute more effectively to building the Church (1 Co 12,7; 14,4...) and to consecrating the temple* of God (1 Co 3,16; E 2,22). The Spirit endlessly renews His action and His gifts. He works constantly for the unity* of the body of Christ (1 Co 12,13). The Spirit of communion* (E 4,3; Ph 2,1) pours out the supreme

gift of charity into hearts (1 Co 13; 2 Co 6,6; G 5,22; R 5,5) and draws them all together into His own unity* (E 4,4).

5. *The Spirit of God.* "Only one body and one Spirit...one Lord...and one God" (E 4,4ff). The Spirit unites because He is the Spirit of God; the Spirit makes holy (2 Co 1,22) because He is the Spirit of the holy God. All activity of the Spirit is given us to help us draw close to God, to put us in living communication with God, to introduce us into the sacred depths, and to confide to us the "secrets of God" (1 Co 2,10f). It is in the Spirit that we know Christ and confess that "Jesus is Lord" (12,3), that we pray to God (R 8,26) and call Him by His name*: "Abba" Father (R 8,15; G 4,6). From the moment that we possess the Spirit, nothing in the world can destroy us, because God gives Himself to us, and we live in Him.

→Abide II 3—Anointing III 5.6—Baptism III, IV—Blasphemy NT—Blessing IV 3—Calling III—Charisms—Church IV 1.2—Cloud 5—Console 2—Desire III—Dove 3—Dreams—Drunkenness 3—Education III 1—Fire NT II 2—Flesh II 2—Fruit IV—Gift NT 1—God NT II 4, V—Grace V—Holy NT II, III—Imposition of Hands—Joy NT I 2, II 1—Know NT 3—Love I NT 3—Mission OT III 2; NT III—New Birth 3 a—Oil 2—Paraclete—Pentecost II—Power IV 2, V—Prayer V 2 d—Presence of God OT III 2; NT II, III—Promises III 3—Prophet OT I 2; NT II 3—Revelation NT I 2 b—Seal 2 b—Soul II 1—Spirit OT 4; NT—Teach NT II—Temple NT II 2—Tradition NT II 2 a b—Truth NT 3 b—Virtues & Vices 2—Water III 2, IV—Wisdom OT III 3; NT II 2—Word of God OT I 1—Worship NT II, III.

JG afmcg

SPOUSE

The name bridegroom is one of those which God gives Himself (Is 54,5) which expresses His love* for His creatures. It is under this aspect that we will speak of Him here. We shall leave to the article on marriage* that which pertains to the strictly human activity.

OT

God does not reveal Himself only in His

mysterious name* (Ex 3,14f); other names, taken from daily life experience, make Him known in His relations with His people. He is their shepherd* and father*, He is also their bridegroom.

There is no question here of a myth, as in the Canaanite religion, where the god-bridegroom fecundates the earth of which he is Baal (= master and husband: Ho 2,18; cf Jg 2,11f). Sexual* rites respond to this myth, notably sacred prostitution. These rites appear tied to idolatry*; therefore, to stigmatize this more, the jealous God who condemns it calls it a prostitution (cf Ex 34,15f; Is 1,21). The God of Israel is the bridegroom not of His earth but of His people. The love which unites them has a history. The gratuitous providence of God and the triumph of His mercy* over the infidelity of His people are prophetic themes. They appear first in Hosea who knew their symbolic value through his own conjugal experience.

1. *Hosea's experience: the beloved and unfaithful bride.* Hosea marries a woman whom he loves and who bears him children, but who leaves him to give herself to temple prostitution. But the prophet, however, buys her back and brings her home. A time of austerity and trial will prepare her to take her place again at the hearth (Ho 1—3). Such is the probable meaning of this dramatic account. In this conjugal experience the prophet discovers the mystery of the relations between the love of God who binds Himself to a people and the betrayal of the covenant by Israel. The covenant* takes on a nuptial character. Idolatry is not only a prostitution, it is adultery—that of a bride who has been loaded with favors but who forgets everything that she has received. The divine wrath* is that of a bridegroom who in punishing his unfaithful bride wishes to bring back the wanderer and make her again worthy of his love. This love will have the last word. Israel will again pass through the time of the desert* (2,16f). A new betrothal will prepare for the marriage that will be accomplished in justice and tenderness. The purified people will know* its bridegroom and His faithful love (2,20ff).

Heretofore the covenant was lived as a social pact; its breaking would bring down God's wrath. This wrath now appears as the effect of a bridegroom's jealousy, and the covenant as a conjugal union together with the giving it implies, which is as intimate as it is exclusive.

This mutual giving, as that of two spouses, will experience vicissitudes, which symbolize the changes that characterize the history of Israel from the time of the judges (vg Jg 2,11-19): sin, chastisement, repentance, pardon.

2. *The prophetic message: the loving and faithful bridegroom.* As the spiritual heir of Hosea, Jeremiah employs the nuptial symbolism in some expressive imagery to contrast the betrayal and corruption of Israel with the eternal love of God for His people: "Thus says Yahweh: I recall the affection of your youth, the love of your betrothal. You followed me in the desert" Jr 2,2); but "on every hill and under every green tree. you have lain down like a prostitute" (2,20); nevertheless, "with an eternal love have I loved you; thus have I kept my favor for you" (31,3), The imagery used by Ezekiel which is even more crude represents Jerusalem as a foundling child whom its savior marries after having raised her up and who then prostitutes herself. But, although she has broken the covenant which united her to her bridegroom, he will re-establish it (Ez 16,1-43. 59-63; cf 23).

Finally it is the Book of Consolation which finds the most moving tones to reveal to Jerusalem with what love she is loved: "Do not be ashamed! You will no longer have to blush...For your bridegroom is your Creator ...Is the woman repudiated from her youth? For a short time have I abandoned you...but with an eternal love I have pitied you" (Is 54, 4-8). Gratuitous and faithful, unfathomable and eternal, the love of the bridegroom will triumph and will transform the unfaithful into a chaste bride (61,10; 62,4f) with whom He will be united with an eternal covenant.

Is it in this prophetic perspective that the songs of the Canticle should be read? Are they not rather inspired by the love of a bridegroom and a bride on this earth? Whether they trace the history of Israel allegorically, or whether they sing this conjugal love which the prophets have made the type of bond of the covenant, they do not give the key to the symbols they use: never is Yahweh identified with the bridegroom. However legitimate an allegorical interpretation of the text could be, it requires such ingenuity that it seems preferable to take the Canticle as a parable*. It sings of a love strong as death, whose inextinguishable flame is the image of the jealous love of God for His people (Ct 8,6f; cf Dt 4,24). Psalm 45 was originally written for the wedding of a king of Israel, but it was then applied to the King-Messiah. The epistle to the Hebrews will exploit its elements which gave divine titles to the king and would be a prelude to the revelation of the divine sonship of Christ (Ps 45,7f; He 1,8).

3. *Wisdom and union with God.* The realism of the prophets has set in relief the ardor of divine love. The meditation of the wise men is going to emphasize the personal and interior character of the union realized by this love. God communicates to His faithful a Wisdom which is His daughter (Pr 8,22) and which shows herself to man as a mother and as a bride (Si 15,2). The Book of Wisdom takes up this image. To acquire Wisdom is the way to become God's friend (Ws 7,14). One must look for her, desire her, and live with her (7,28; 8, 2.9). As the bride whom God alone can give (8,21), she makes immortal him with whom she is united. Sent by God, like the Holy Spirit (9, 17), Wisdom is a spiritual gift. She is a worker who achieves the work of God in us and who engenders the virtues in us (8,6f). The conjugal symbolism is here completely spiritualized. Thus was prepared the revelation of the mystery of grace with which the union of man with God will be consummated: the incarnation of Him who is the Wisdom of God, and His marriage with the Church, His bride.

NT

1. *The Lamb, bridegroom of the new covenant.* Wisdom, which is born of God and which delights to be among men (Pr 8,22ff.31), is not only a spiritual gift. It appears in the flesh. It is Christ, the Wisdom of God (1 Co 1,24). And it is the mystery of the cross, the folly of God, that He brings about the revelation of God's love for His unfaithful bride, sanctifying her to dispose her to His covenant (E 5,25ff).

Thus is unveiled the mystery of the union symbolized in the OT by the names of bridegroom and bride. The point is for man to share in the trinitarian life, to unite himself with the Son of God to become a child of the heavenly Father. The bridegroom is Christ, and Christ crucified. It is in His blood that the new covenant is sealed (1 Co 11,25); and that is why the Apocalypse no longer calls Jerusalem the bride of God, but the bride of the Lamb* (Ap 21,9).

2. *The Church, bride of the new covenant.* What is this Jerusalem*, called to the covenant with the Son of God? It is no longer the ser-

vant which represents the people of the old covenant, but the free woman, the Jerusalem on high (G 4,22-27). After the coming of the bridegroom to whom the precursor, His friend, has given testimony (Jn 3,29), humanity is represented by two women*, symbol of the two spiritual cities: on the one hand, the "prostitute," type of idolatrous Babylon* (Ap 17,1.7; cf Is 47); on the other, the bride of the Lamb, a type of the beloved city (Ap 20,9), of the holy Jerusalem which comes from heaven; for it is from her bridegroom that she gets her sanctity (21,2.9f).

This woman is the mother of the children of God, of those whom the Lamb saves from the dragon by virtue of His blood (12,1f.11.17). It seems then that the bride of Christ is not only the assembly of the elect, but that she is their mother*, she by whom and in whom each of them is born. They are sanctified by the grace of Christ (Tt 3,5ff) and they become virginal* beings, worthy of Christ, their bridegroom (2 Co 11,2), united forever with the Lamb (Ap 14,4).

3. *The eternal marriage.* From the fact that the Church is at the same time the mother of the elect and the city which gathers them together, therefore the marriage of the Lamb and the bride proceeds through different stages.

a) The first stage of the marriage, the time of Christ's coming (Mt 9,15 p), is achieved at the time when on the cross of Christ the new Adam* sanctifies the new Eve. She comes from His side, symbolized by the water* and the blood* of the sacraments of the Church (Jn 19,34; cf 1 Jn 5,6). The love which the bridegroom shows His spouse is the model of Christian marriage (E 5,25-32).

b) To this marriage, Christ invites men, and first His people (Mt 22,1-10). But to take part in it one must not only answer the invitation, which many refuse, but also wear a marriage garment (22,11ff). This standing invitation is good as long as the Church lasts. But as the time for the celebration is uncertain for each one, it requires vigilance so that the bridegroom, when He comes, will find ready the virgins who have been invited to partake of the nuptial feast (25,1-13).

c) Finally, at the end of history, the nuptial robe of the bride will be finished, a robe of linen of shining whiteness*, woven by the works* of the faithful. These await with joy and praise this marriage of the Lamb to which they have the happiness to be invited (Ap 19, 7ff). At this time, when the prostitute will be judged (19,2), the bridegroom will finally answer the appeal which His Spirit inspires in His bride. He will sate the thirst of all those who, like her and in her, desire* this union with His love and His life, a fecund union of which that of spouses is one of the best symbols (22,17).

→Adultery 2—Church—Clothing II 2.4—Covenant OT II 2; NT II 3—Fathers & Father O, III 2—Friend 3—God OT III 2; NT II 3—Head 3.4—Jerusalem OT III 1; NT II 3—John the Baptist 2—Lamb of God 3—Love—Marriage NT I 2—Mary I 2, V 1—Servant of God II—Sexuality II—Unity I, III—Vine 2—Virginity—Woman.

MFL gsa

STARS

1. *Stars in ancient paganism.* The people of the ancient East were more conscious of the presence of the stars than we are. The sun, moon, planets, and stars suggested to ancient man a mysterious world completely different from ours: that world of heaven* which he imagined in the form of superposed demi-spheres where the stars inscribed their orbits. Their regular cycles permitted him to measure time* and to form his calendar; however they also suggested that the world is governed by the law of eternal return and that the stars from on high impose on earthly things certain sacred rhythms transcending the changing events of history. These luminous bodies appeared to him, therefore, as a manifestation of supernatural powers which dominate humanity and determine its destiny. To these powers he spontaneously gave worship so as to assure himself of their favor. The sun, the moon, the planet Venus, etc., were for him so many gods or goddesses; and the constellations themselves outlined enigmatic figures in the heavens to which he gave mythical names. This interest he manifested in the stars led him to methodical investigations: the Egyptians and the Mesopotamians were renowned for their knowledge of astronomy; but this embryonic science was closely connected with divinatory

and idolatrous practices. Thus the men of ancient times were, as it were, held in subjection by some formidable powers which weighed upon their destiny and hid the true God from them.

2. *The stars, servants of God.* Open up the Bible and the atmosphere changes completely. Assuredly the stars are poorly distinguished from the angels* who make up the court of God (Jb 38,7; Ps 148,2f): these "celestial armies" (Gn 2,1) are regarded as animated beings. But they are creatures like all the rest of the universe (Am 5,8; Gn 1.14ff; Ps 33,6; 136,7ff). It is at the call of Yahweh that they shine forth from their post (Ba 3,3ff), upon His order that they intervene so as to strengthen His people in battle (Js 10,12f; Jg 5,20). The stars, therefore, are not gods but the servants of the Yahweh Sabaoth*. If they regulate the seasons, if they preside over night and day, it is because God has assigned them these precise functions (Gn 1,15f). The radiance of the sun (Ps 19,5ff), the beauty of the moon (Ct 6,10), the perfect order of the celestial revolutions (Ws 7,18ff) can be admired; but all this sings the glory* of the one God (Ps 19,2) who has fixed the "laws of the heavens" (Jb 38,31ff). Thus the stars no longer hide their Creator, they reveal Him (Ws 13,5). Purified of their idolatrous* meaning, they now symbolize earthly realities which manifest the providence of God: the multitude of the children of Abraham (Gn 15,5), the coming of the Davidic king (Nm 24,17), the light of future salvation (Is 60,1ff; Ml 3,20), or the eternal glory of those reborn through grace (Dn 12,3).

3. *The influence of paganism.* In spite of the decisiveness of biblical revelation, Israel does not escape the temptation of astral religions. At the periods of religious regression, the sun, the moon, and the whole host of heaven retain or again find adorers (2 K 17,16; 21,3.5; Ez 8,16): because of an instinctive fear* of these cosmic powers, men seek to conciliate them. Offerings are made to the "queen of heaven," Ishtar, the planet Venus (Jr 7,18; 44,17ff); "the signs of heaven" (Jr 10,2) are watched so as to read destinies there (Is 47,13). But the voice of the prophets is raised against this repulsive return to paganism; Deuteronomy stigmatizes it (Dt 4,19; 17,3); the king Josiah intervenes brutally in order to wipe out the practices (2 K 23,4f.11); to star worshipers Jeremiah promises the worst of punishments (Jr 8,1f). But

it will take the trial of the dispersion and of the exile for a converted Israel to break away definitively from this form of idolatry (cf Jb 31, 26ff), the vanity of which the Alexandrine Wisdom will loudly proclaim (Ws 13,1-5).

4. *From the stars to the wicked angels.* This secular struggle against the star cults had some repercussions within the domain of belief. If the stars constitute a snare for men by turning them away from the true God, is not this the sign that they themselves are connected with evil powers, hostile to God? Among the angels* who form the hosts of heaven, are there not some of the fallen who try to attract men to their following, setting themselves up to be adored by men? The old mythical theme of the war* of the gods furnishes here a whole body of materials which permits the poetic representation of the fall of the celestial powers who revolted against God (Lucifer: Is 14,12-15). The figure of Satan* in the NT will be enriched by these symbolic elements (Ap 8,10; 9, 1; 12,3f.7ff). Consequently we should not be astonished to see judgment* proclaimed on the day* of the Lord against the hosts of heaven, punished along with their terrestrial worshipers (Is 24,21ff): the stars appear there in the place and position of the bad angels.

5. *Within the universe redeemed by Christ,* the stars reassume, however, their providential role. The cross has freed men from the cosmic anguish which terrorized the Colossians: they are no longer enslaved to the "elements of the world," now that Christ has "despoiled the principalities and powers" in order to "draw them within His triumphal procession" (Col 2, 8.15-18; G 4,3). No more astral determinism, no more destinies written in the heavens: Christ has put an end to pagan superstitions. A star is supposed to reveal His birth (Mt 2,2), designating Him the incomparable morning star (Ap 2,28; 22,16) we await to rise in our hearts (2 P 1,19; cf *Exultet* of Easter). He is the true sun that illumines the renewed world (Lk 1,78f). And if it is certain that the darkening of the stars will provide a sign of His glorious coming (Mt 24,29 p; Is 13,9f; 34,4; Jl 4,15) as it marked the moment of His death (Mt 27,45 p), it is because in the future world these created lights will become obsolete: the glory of God will illumine the new Jerusalem and the Lamb of God will be its lamp (Ap 21,23).

→Heaven I—Idols II 2—Light & Dark OT I—

Magic 1—Sign OT II 2—Time OT I 1—Wicked Spirits OT 3.

ADa & PG pjb

STERILITY

The people of God attach a double importance to the fertility of the womb: it answers the call made by the creator at the beginning of time, and it allows the posterity of Abraham to become innumerable according to the promise. Sterility contradicts this plan of God; it is an evil, against which Israel fights constantly and of which God slowly reveals the meaning.

I. THE STRUGGLE AGAINST STERILITY

1. *Sterility is an evil,* like suffering* and death. In fact it seems to go against the command of the Creator who desires fruitfulness and life. Not to have one's name* survive is a source of shame*. Hence, the complaints of Abraham: What does my adopted servant matter, if I perish without children? (Gn 15,2f). And Sarai, his wife, feels herself despised by the fruitful servant woman (16,4f). Rachel cries to her husband: "Give me children or I die!" (Gn 30,1) but Jacob rails against her: "Am I in the place of God who has denied you motherhood?" (Gn 30,2). God alone can open the sterile womb (29,31; 30,22).

2. *It is necessary to struggle against this evil.* What Rachel did, as her mother-in-law Sarai had done previously (Gn 16,2), was to avail herself of a custom deriving from the Code of Hammurabi and to give to her husband one of her servants that she might "bear children on her knees" (Gn 30,3-6). And it was the same with Leah, when she ceased for a while to give birth, after having four children (30,9-13). Thus, by an artifice, man overcomes the obstacle of sterility, conferring on his adopted sons the same rights as on the children who would have come forth from his own flesh.

3. *God, the conqueror of sterility.* But these are simply stratagems, legal or illegal, to overcome the blockage of the stream of life. It is reserved to God alone to conquer sterility, and He proves faithful to His promise (Ex 23,26; Dt 7,14) and in this way announces a greater mystery. The sacred writer has intentionally

underlined the fact that the wives of the three ancestors of the chosen people are sterile: Sarai (Gn 11,30; 16,1), Rebecca (Gn 25,21), Rachel (29,31), before offspring were granted to them (cf vg 13,2-5). The long account of the birth of Isaac intends to point out simultaneously the mystery of gratuitous election* and of fruitful grace*. As Paul interpreted it, a man must confess himself impotent and must confess with faith the power of God to raise up life in a desert land. Faith* triumphs over sterile death and raises up life (R 4,18-24). Hannah, the sterile woman, praises this gratuitous election (1 S 2,1-11): "The sterile woman bears seven times, but the mother of many children is blighted" (2,5; cf Ps 113,9).

II. STERILITY ACCEPTED

God indeed "visits" sterile women, showing that men are wrong to consider sterility simply as a punishment. Certainly it is in one sense, since God orders Jeremiah to preserve his celibacy in order to signify the sterility of the people in a state of sin (Jr 16). And when the abandoned bride will return the favor, the prophet will be able to console her: "Cry with joy, barren one, you who did not bring forth ...More numerous are the sons of the deserted woman than those of the bride" (Is 54,1). In confessing her sin, Jerusalem has recognized that her sterility signified her divorce from God, and she prepared herself for a new and more wonderful fruitfulness. Henceforth she counts the nations* among her children (cf G 4,27).

What has meaning on the level of the community can only be slowly understood on the level of the individual. The Law, even while it took up the defense of "the woman less loved" (Dt 21,15ff), forbade a eunuch to offer sacrifices (Lv 21,20), reducing him to the lot of bastards (Dt 23,3ff). He was literally cut off from the people (Dt 23,2). The disaster of the exile was necessary to break this exclusive esteem for physical fruitfulness, since on the return from Babylon a completely new doctrine was proclaimed: "Let the eunuch not proceed to say: I am only a dry tree. For thus speaks Yahweh: To the eunuchs who hold fast to my covenant, I will give a monument and a name better than that of sons and daughters, I will give them an eternal name* which shall never be blotted out" (Is 56,3ff). Thus man realized that physical fruitfulness was not necessary to his survival, at least in the memory of God.

There is the same development among the wise men. They continue to give evidence of rather commonplace religious feeling: "One child is worth more than a thousand, and it is better to die without children than with wicked children" (Si 16,1-4). But along with faith in a full and glorious afterlife, the believers discover and proclaim the existence of an authentic spiritual fruitfulness: "Happy is the woman who is barren but without blemish! Her fruitfulness will appear at the time of the testing of souls. Happy is the eunuch whose hand does no evil. It is better for him to have no children to his memory" (Ws 3,13f; 4,1). Thenceforth the vision of the believer is no longer stubbornly fixed on the fruitfulness of the earth, but he is ready to discern a meaning in the fruit* of the works* produced by virtue which make a man immortal. That this might come about, it was necessary that the evil which is sterility be accepted and transformed.

II. VOLUNTARY STERILITY

Whereas the daughter of Jephthah, condemned to die without children, weeps over her "virginity" (Jg 11,37f), Jeremiah welcomes his divine mission of remaining a celibate (Jr 16, 1f). In this way he still only symbolizes a negative aspect, the culpable sterility of the people (cf Lk 23,29). Nonetheless the OT proclaimed fruitful virginity* in type. The sign which Mary receives at the time of the annunciation (Lk 1,36f) is precisely the miraculous pregnancy of her cousin Elizabeth. She, who by her barrenness (1,7.25) recalls the long history of barren women rendered fertile by the visitation of God, signifies for Mary the virginal motherhood which has been announced. Then a new age is begun in the person of Mary, whose fruit is the very Son of God, the fullness of fruitfulness*.

In this new age, Jesus calls to follow Him the "eunuchs who make themselves such for the sake of the kingdom of heaven" (Mt 19,12). What had been undergone as a curse*, or was at most borne as an evil whose good fruit would ripen in heaven, becomes a charism* in the eyes of Paul (1 Co 7,7). While Genesis said: "It is not good that man be alone" (Gn 2,18), Paul dares to proclaim, with certain precautions, "It is good that a man remain so" (1 Co 7,26), that is to say unmarried and alone without children. When it has come to that point, voluntary sterility can fulfill itself in virginity.

→Fruit I—Fruitfulness—Marriage OT II 3—Milk 2—Mother I 1, II 2—Rock 2—Shame I 3—Solitude I—Virginity—Woman NT 1.

XLD jpl

STONE

Because of its unbelievable abundance in Palestine, stone is always found at hand and present to the mind of the Hebrews. Moreover, in the primitive mentality and in the symbolism of all men, solid, lasting, weighty stone is a sign of strength. These two facts taken together make us understand why the Bible uses images furnished by stones, under their diverse forms, to apply them to the Messiah.

1. *The sacred stones and the altar of Christ.* The worship of sacred stones, quite developed in primitive religions, was forbidden in Israel. Nevertheless, under the idolatrous influence of the neighboring peoples, it was easy to slip and therefore necessary to keep on one's guard (Lv 26,1; Dt 16,22; Is 57,6). Taken out of its idolatrous context, the use of sacred stones kept a meaning, no longer magical but rather symbolic, and received its efficacy from a transcendent God. Thus Jacob at Bethel raised up a sacred pillar (Gn 28,16ff), and thus stones were set up in the figure of the twelve tribes sanctified by the nearness of the altar (Ex 28, 10.21; 24,4). Thus the altars* were built with untrimmed stones, and by means of these altars God touches and sanctifies the earth (Ex 20,25; cf Mt 23,19).

But all these sacred stones, more or less efficacious signs of the presence of God, constitute a variety of figures* of Christ. In Him God is made present on earth. By allusion in the NT (cf He 13,10; 1 Co 10,18), more explicitly among the fathers of the Church and in the liturgy, Christ is found to be identified with the altar.

2. *The memorial stone and the perpetuity of the covenant.* Although the distinction between the sacred stone and the memorial* stone is not always very clear, the concepts of unchangeableness and durability are especially attached to stone monuments. This is not only to give witness to a treaty (Gn 31,45-52), or to perpetuate the memory of the dead (Js 8,29; 2 S 18,17). These stones above all recall the covenant fixed between God and His people (Js 4,7. 20-24; 24,26), the covenant whose Law is written on tablets of stone (Ex 24,12). But the sign of the perpetuation of the covenant is in some way degraded through contact with those Israelites whose hearts* are hard as stone (Ez 11,19), until it becomes a sign of this obduracy of heart and a cold exterior. In opposition to this state of affairs it is in the interior of the heart of flesh*, as Jeremiah and Ezekiel predicted (Jr 31,33; Ez 11,19; 36,26), that the new Law is inscribed by the Spirit (2 Co 3,3).

3. *The rock of the desert and Christ the Savior.* In the rock* of the desert out of which Moses made water flow, Paul saw a reference to Christ who made the living water of salvation to flow from Himself (1 Co 10,4). Paul thereby shows his agreement not only with the rabbinic interpretations which identified this rock with Yahweh accompanying His people, but he prolongs the whole OT tradition. Unceasingly, the authors of the OT were, in fact, pleased to recall this miracle of Moses (Ps 78, 15; 105,41; Ws 11,4; etc.), because they saw quite justly there at work the merciful power of Yahweh, capable of drawing from a dry, arid, lifeless rock the fruitful and lifegiving water; perhaps this rock would also be for them the image of Yahweh who spreads abroad His blessings (cf in the same sense Ez 47,1-12; Ze 14,8; Ap 22,1). The similarity between the water from the rock and the water* of salvation which springs from the side of the dead Christ has perhaps been suggested by St. John (Jn 19,34; cf 7,37). It has been explicitly proposed by a number of the fathers of the Church.

4. *Christ the cornerstone and Christians, the living stones.* The salvation brought by Christ should be operative through trials and apparent defeat "The rock rejected by the builders has become the head* of the corner," had already been announced by Ps 118,22. Rejected by His own, as He foretold in the parable of the murderous workers in the vineyard, Christ becomes the cornerstone, that is the foundation of the building, or more probably the principal stone of the summit (Mt 21,42 p; Ac 4,11; 1 P 2,4.7). In this way He ensures that the holy Temple* will hold together; it is in Him that God's dwelling-place is built* up and grows (E 2,20f).

According to another metaphor Christ is an unshakable stone (Is 28,16; R 9,33; 1 C 3,11; 1 P 2,6), on which one can rely with faith, in such a way that the faithful, like living stones, are made a part of the construction of the spiritual building (1 P 2,15; E 2,21).

5. *Christ, the rock of destruction, the stumbling stone.* By the revelation of God's love and holiness, Christ forces every man to choose either the light or the darkness. For the proud unbelievers He becomes a stumbling stone (Is 8,14; R 9,33; 1 P 2,8), a rock of scandal*. And the enemies of Christ are finally crushed; the image of the rejected rock become the cornerstone is actually prolonged by Luke: "Whoever will fall on this rock will be shattered and he upon whom it will fall will be crushed" (Lk 20,17f). Perhaps he was alluding here to the rock which Daniel sees as a symbol of the Messiah and of His kingdom which will triumph over the powers of this world: "All of a sudden, a stone will come loose, without a hand having touched it, and fall to strike the statue, its feet of iron and clay, breaking them into pieces...And the stone which struck the statue became a great mountain which filled all the earth" (Dn 2,34f).

6. *Precious stones and the new Jerusalem.* A striking sign of the glorious transformation which awaits the new Jerusalem: the holy city will be constructed of precious stones (Is 54, 11f; Tb 13,16f; Ap 21,10-21).

→Altar 1—Build II, III 1—Hardness of Heart —Head 1.4—Peter—Rock 1—Scandal I 1.3— Temple.

PL jjk

STORM

1. *Pagan interpretation.* In the ancient East, the storm was regarded as the manifestation of a god (Baal in Canaan). This manifestation presents three characteristics. As an exhibition of cosmic forces before which man can do nothing, the storm reveals the terrifying majesty of the god. As a phenomenon dangerous for man, it is, in this respect, a sign of anger: the god, hidden in the clouds, speaks out against his enemies (=thunder) and hurls his arrows against them (=lightning flashes) (cf Ps 18,6-16). Finally, bringing fruitful rain,

the storm shows in the god the source of fecundity.

2. *The storm as a sign of the divine majesty.* In biblical language, every polytheistic overtone is cleared away, especially that attached to the fertility rites; but the storm retains a meaning. It is one of the marvels which proclaims the grandeur of the Creator (Jr 51,16f; Ps 135, 7; Jb 38,34-38), a veiled manifestation of His fearful majesty (Jb 36,29—37,5): God is seated on a throne above it in His transcendence (Ps 29). It is permitted thus to represent the Lord in His glory* (Jb 38,1; Ez 1,13f; 10,5; Ap 4,5; 8,5ff; 10,3f). It is the setting of the classic theophany where are evoked the interventions of God here below: those of sacred history, at the time of the exodus (Ps 77,19ff), at Sinai (Ex 19,16-19), for the entry into Canaan (Jg 5,4f); those by which He rescues His anointed (Ps 18) or His people (Ha 3,3-16); that which inaugurates His definitive reign (Ps 97,1-6). Yet God is not only a majestic presence* which inspires a sacred terror. Already at Horeb Elijah is invited to pass beyond this partial sign in order to grasp a higher revelation: God is also an intimate presence who speaks to man with the mildness of a gentle breeze (1 K 19,11ff).

3. *The storm as a sign of the divine anger.* To manifest the dispositions of God with regard to men, the storm remains an ambiguous sign: a beneficent sign when God graciously grants fruitfulness* to a nature in drought (1 K 18); but also a terrible scourge which God reserves for His enemies as a mark of His wrath* (Ex 9,13-34). The theophany of the storm, then, particularly suits God when He judges and chastises (Is 30,27ff), especially at the time of the final judgment* when He shall launch His thunderbolts against Babylon (Ap 16,18; cf 11, 19). This is why, by way of anticipating this judgment, the divine voice makes itself heard as a clap of thunder when it proclaims the glorification of the Son at the moment when the prince of this world will be cast down below (Jn 12,28-32).

The prospect of judgment would cause one to tremble in terror if God had not assured His own that He will be their shelter against the storm: the sinful world alone is threatened by this eschatological scourge (Is 4,6). For God* is far from being a thundering Jupiter: Jesus makes the "sons of thunder" understand (Mk 3,17) that He takes no delight in throwing thunderbolts upon those who do not accept

Him (Lk 9,54f). The theophany of the storm is henceforth completed by the revelation of divine grace*, which is given us in the person of Jesus (cf Tt 2,11). "At trumpets and lightning flashes the earth trembles; but when you descend into the womb of a Virgin, your step makes not a sound" (Christian epigram on the Nativity of Christ).

→Calamity o—Cloud—Fire OT I 2—Glory III 1—Presence of God OT II.

PG phmcn

STRANGER

Among strangers, the Bible distinguishes carefully those who belong to other nations* and those who, up to the coming of Christ, are ordinarily enemies*. The transient foreigner (*nokri*) is considered as unable to be assimilated (so also the "foreign woman") and most especially the prostitute who is often involved in idolatry (Pr 5). The resident alien (*ger*) is not autochthonous but his life is more or less associated with the people of the country, as the aliens in Greek cities. This article is concerned exclusively with foreigners who are residents.

I. ISRAEL AND THE RESIDENT ALIENS

The progressive assimilation of the *gerim* by Israel contributed very much to breaking through the racial circle in which it spontaneously tended to seclude itself, and thus prepares the way for Christian universalism.

Remembering that it had once been the foreigner in Egypt (Ex 22,20; 23,9), Israel ought not be content to exercise toward the "residents" the hospitality* which it gave to the *nokrim* (Gn 18,2-9; Jg 19,20f; 2 K 4,8ff); but it must love them as itself (Lv 19,34), because God watches over the foreigner (Dt 10,18) just as He extends His protection over the poor and the needy (Lv 19,10; 23,22). He established for them a juridical position analogous to that of His own people (Dt 1,16; Lv 20,2). He authorizes most especially that those who were circumcised should participate in the Pasch (Ex 12,48f), observe the Sabbath (Ex 20,10), and fast on the Day of Expiation* (Lv 16,29). Hence they should not blaspheme* the name of Yahweh (Lv 24,16). Their assimilation is such

that, in the Israel of the end of time, Ezekiel gives them a share in the land together with the citizens by birth (Ez 47,22).

On the return from the exile, a movement of separation is felt. The *ger* is obliged to embrace Judaism under pain of being excluded from the community (Ne 10,31; Ezr 9—10). In reality the assimilation should be more and more limited. When a son of an alien adheres to Yahweh and faithfully observes His Law, God receives him in His temple and under the same title as the Israelites (Is 56,6f). In the dispersion*, in fact, the Jews seek to spread their faith, as the Greek translation of the Bible testifies. The translation renders *ger* by *proselyte*, a term designating every foreigner who adheres completely to Judaism; and it gives a universal import to certain texts (Gn 12,3; 49, 10; Am 9,12; Is 54,15). The missionary movement which such an adaptation of texts supposes is alluded to by Jesus: the Pharisees plough the seas to make a proselyte (Mt 23, 15).

On the day of Pentecost, proselytes are present (Ac 2,11); and a number of them embrace the faith in Christ (Ac 13,43; 6,5). But in the land chosen by Paul for his missionary activity, there were men "fearing God" (Ac 18,7), pagans sympathetic to the Jewish religion but who have not gone to the point of circumcision, men like Cornelius (Ac 10,2). All these distinctions quickly disappear with the suppression of the barrier between Jews and pagans by means of the Christian faith: all are brothers* in Christ.

II. ISRAEL, FOREIGNER ON EARTH

A transposition of the condition of the *ger* still survives, on the other hand, even in the Christian faith.

The land of Canaan had been promised to Abraham and his descendants (Gn 12,1.7), but God continued to be its true owner. Israel, the *ger* of God, is only a tenant (Lv 25,23). This idea contains in germ a spiritual attitude which is rediscovered in the psalms. The Israelite knows that he has no rights before God. He wants only to be His guest (Ps 15). He recognizes that he is a stranger with Him, a wayfarer just as all his forefathers were (Ps 39,13; 1 Ch 29,15). He is a wayfarer also in the sense that his life here below is short. So he asks God to help him without delay (Ps 119,19).

In the NT, this understanding of man's condition goes still deeper. The Christian here below has no lasting abode (2 Co 5,1f). He is a stranger on earth not only because it belongs to God alone, but because he is a citizen of a heavenly fatherland* where he is no longer a guest or a stranger but a fellow citizen of the saints (E 2,19; Col 1,21). Since he has not reached this goal, his life* is a traveler's life (1 P 2,11), in imitation of the life of the patriarchs (He 11,13), who formerly uprooted themselves from their surroundings in order to put themselves on the way* to a better land (He 11,16). John also stresses this contrast between the world* where he must live at present and the true life* to which we have now been introduced. Born from above (Jn 3,7), the Christian can only be a stranger or a pilgrim* on this earth, because between him and the world accord is impossible: the world, in fact, lies under the power of the evil one (1 Jn 5,19). But if he is no longer of this world, the Christian knows as did Christ where he comes from and where he is going. He follows after Christ who pitched His tent among us (Jn 1,14) and who, having returned to the Father (16,28), prepares a place for His own (14,2f), so that where He is His servant may also be (12,26), at home with the Father.

→Brother O—Dispersion 1—Enemy I 1—Fatherland OT 1; NT 2—Hospitality—Nations —Neighbor OT—People *A* II 1.

ADa afmcg

STRENGTH

The whole Bible speaks and dreams of strength at the same time that it foretells the fall of the violent and the promotion of the humble. The paradox is developed up to the preaching of the cross*, in which that which appears as the "weakness of God" is proclaimed stronger than man (1 Co 1,25). Thus the giant Goliath, "a man of war from his youth," armed with sword, lance, and javelin, was overcome by David, a fair young man armed with a sling and five pebbles but advancing in the name* of Yahweh (1 S 17,45). And Paul, characterizing God's method, says, "But the foolish things of the world hath God chosen, that He may confound the strong" (1 Co 1,27).

This was not a defense of weakness, but the glorification of the "strength of God for the salvation of the believer" (R 1,16). By these words, Paul does not wish, as did Islam later, to exalt a divine power* beyond the nothingness of mortals; he opposes the strength that man finds in God to the impotence in which he lives without God; with God he will fight victoriously against a thousand (Js 23,10; Lv 26,8); without God he will be reduced to flight at the sound of a dead leaf (Lv 26,36). "With God we shall do mightily," sings the psalmist (60,14). "I can do all things in Him who strengthens me," cries St. Paul (Ph 4,13).

I. THE STRENGTH OF THE ELECT OF GOD

1. *Strength which inspires respect.* The Israelite dreamed of strength, because he dreamed of commanding the attention of the world about him: "Become strong in Ephrath," they wished for Boaz; "make for thyself a name* in Bethlehem" (Rt 4,11). The strength which can be imposed is first of all the strength of the arms* (Ps 76,5f), and of the loins* (Ps 93,1), that of the knees* which do not bend, of the heart* which remains firm in the struggle (Ps 57,8); it is also the strength which represents the vital power of a being; his health, his fecundity (Gn 49,3), or even his economic power, that which Israel exhausts in paying tribute or in buying from its allies (Ho 7,9; Is 30,6). Finally, if the strength which the wicked draw from their riches is scandalous (Jb; Ps 49,73), virtue, on the contrary (vg that of the "strong woman," Pr 31, 10-31), is worthy of praise.

Since it is a matter of exterior assertion, *to be strong* means in fact "to be stronger than." The strong man opposes the enemy with the resistance of a rock*, of a diamond (Ez 3, 9), of bronze (Jb 6,12); the resistance of the rock* which stands unshaken by the furious assault of the waves (Ps 46,3f), the resistance of the impregnable citadel (Is 26,5), the den perched on the inaccessible heights (Ob 3). The strong man stands erect, while the weakling stumbles and falls, stretched out like dead: "Yahweh is my rock, my rampart...my fortress, my refuge...a God who circles me with strength ...and holds me erect upon the heights" (Ps 18; 62,3).

This challenging strength cannot remain purely defensive. In the struggle for life one either wins or loses: there is no intermediate solution. The anointed* of Yahweh, whom divine strength keeps erect in face of a united world, will end by seeing all his enemies subdued at his feet (Ps 18,48), with not one of them able to escape from him (Ps 21,9). To judge it by the insistence of the royal psalms the truth asserts itself: there is no peace* without total and definitive victory*.

2. *Strength in the service of God.* If Israel thus dreams of being strong, it is with the purpose of realizing God's plan. Otherwise would Joshua have been able to conquer the land of Canaan (Js 1,6), the chosen people draw near to salvation (Is 35,3f)?

There was no less need of strength, although on another level, to have part in the kingdom of the NT. "Animated with a powerful energy through the vigor of His glory, you will acquire perfect constancy and endurance" (Col 1,11). The strength necessary for the Christians appears also as a potential of life and a victorious challenge. Participation in the strength itself of Christ risen, who sits at the right* hand of the Father (E 1,19f) makes, in fact the Christian a conqueror of the world (1 Jn 5,5), giving him power over all the force of evil (Mk 15,17f), first in himself (1 Jn 2,14; 5,18) (the OT does not insist on this) and then about him. The Spirit* of the Lord is power of resurrection* for us also (Ph 3,10f); it strengthens the interior man in us (E 3,16), even to permitting us to enter because of our plenitude into the very fullness* of God (3,19).

II. STRENGTH IN WEAKNESS

Man does not in himself possess the strength that will bring him salvation*: "The king is not saved by a great army...Vain is the horse for safety" (Ps 33,16f). This admission of powerlessness is certainly a commonplace in all prayer*. Disarmed in the face of a world stronger than they, mortals seek to put the power* of gods on their side. But the Bible is careful of thus furnishing man with effective recipes to compensate for his natural powerlessness. It is God who engages us in His service. If He makes man strong it is to have him fulfill His will and accomplish His plan (Ps 41, 10; 2 Co 13,8).

Now, whether it works with the strength or the other gifts of Yahweh, Israel finally forgets their origin to appropriate them to itself and make itself independent of Him from whom it has received all: "Be careful of saying: it is my strength, it is the vigor of my arm, which has

gotten me this power" (Dt 8,17). To maintain the mistake would be to open the way for a denial. And so, to make it clearly understood that one is strong only by Him and in Him, Yahweh chooses for Himself men of modest appearance but whose heart* is steady (1 S 16,7) in preference to those who, like Saul, are head and shoulders over all others (1 S 10,23). He wishes to act with more and more humble human means: "the people who are with you are too numerous that I should deliver Midian into their hands. Israel might take glory from it at my expense and say: it is my own hand that has delivered me" (Jg 7,2; Is 30,15ff). Thus the Lord reveals to Paul: "My grace is sufficient for you: for my strength is shown in weakness" (2 Co 12,9).

In fact, His glory* could not shine otherwise. When man can do nothing more, God intervenes (Is 29,4) in such a way that it will be quite clear that He alone has acted. He takes no account of the order of greatness in natural realities: pouring His contempt on princes (Ps 107,40), He then makes the poor* man sit at His side, whom He has lifted up out of the dust (Ps 113,7). He finds His glory in the exaltation of His Servant who, rejected by society, refuses to defend Himself by His power, and expects salvation from God alone. He manifests it in its fullness in the resurrection* of Jesus crucified. The preaching of this mystery constitutes the very message of the power of God (1 Co 1,18).

Christian humility* is that of Mary in the Magnificat. She does not reduce herself to the feeling of the weakness of a creature, or a sinner. She is at the same time conscious of a strength which proceeds entirely from God: "But we have this treasure in earthen vessels, so that it is evident that this extraordinary power belongs to God and does not come from us" (2 Co 4,7).

→Bread I 2—Egypt 1—Evil Spirits NT 1— Loins 1—Power—Right Hand 1—Rock 1— Spirit of God—Violence—Woman OT 3.

EB wjy

SUFFERING

Paul dares to write to the converts of Corinth, "I delight...in my sorrows, in my agonies" (2 Co 12,10). The Christian is certainly not a Stoic in order to sing of "the majesty of human sufferings," but a disciple of the "head of our faith" who "in place of the joy which was set before Him suffered the cross" (He 12,2). The Christian views all suffering in relation to Jesus Christ. In the trials of Moses, "who esteemed the shame of Christ as a treasure superior to all treasures of Egypt" (He 11,26), the Christian sees the passion of the Lord.

But what meanings does suffering take on in Christ? How does suffering, so often a curse* in the OT, become a blessing in the NT? How can Paul "superabound with joy in all tribulations" (2 Co 7,4; cf 8,2)? Is faith insensitivity or an unhealthy exaltation?

OT

I. THE SERIOUSNESS OF SUFFERING

The Bible takes suffering seriously, it does not minimize it, it profoundly compassionates with the sufferer and sees suffering as an evil which ought not to be.

1. *The cries of suffering.* Woes, defeats, and disasters give rise to a great concept of cries and laments in Scripture. Weeping is so frequent there that it has given birth to a special literary form, the lamentation. Most often these cries mount up to God. To be sure, the people cry out before Pharaoh in order to obtain bread (Gn 41,55), and the prophets cry out against the tyrants. But the slaves of Egypt cry out to God (Ex 1,23f), the sons of Israel cry out to Yahweh (14,10; Jg 3,9), and the psalms are full of these cries of distress. This litany of suffering is prolonged until the "great cry and tears" of Christ before death (He 5,7).

2. *The judgment passed on suffering* corresponds to this revolt of sensibility: suffering is an evil which ought not to be. Assuredly, we know that it is universal: "Man born of woman has a short life but miseries in abundance" (Jb 14,1; cf Si 40,1-9); but no one is resigned to it. Men hold that wisdom and good health go together (Pr 3,8; 4,22; 14,30), that good health is a blessing from God (Si 34,20) for which man praises Him (Si 17,27) and for which man prays (Jb 5,8; 8,5ff; Ps 107,19). Many psalms are prayers of the sick* asking for their cure (Ps 6; 38; 41; 88). The Bible does not enjoy suffering; it praises the doctor (Si 38); it awaits the Messianic era as a time of healing (Is 33,24) and of resurrection (26,19; 29,18; 61,2). Healing is one of the works of Yahweh (19,22; 57,18) and of the Messiah (53,4f). Does not the brazen serpent (Nm 21,6-9) become a figure of the Messiah (Jn 3,14)? All misfortunes, whether public or private, such as drought, loss of property, bereavements, wars, enslavements, exiles, are felt as evils from which deliverance is expected in the days of the Messiah. The OT is not familiar with the idea of voluntary suffering in the ascetic and pauline sense.

II. THE SCANDAL OF SUFFERING

Profoundly sensitive to suffering, the Bible cannot, like so many of the neighboring religions, have recourse to quarrels between different gods or to dualist solutions in order to explain suffering. Certainly, the temptation was great for the exiles of Babylon, overwhelmed by their miseries "numberless as the sea" (Lm 2, 13), to believe that Yahweh had been conquered by one stronger than He. But the prophets, in order to defend the true God, do not think of excusing Him, but of arguing that suffering does not escape His notice: "I fashion the light and create the darkness, I make happiness and cause misery" (Is 45,7; cf 63,3-6). The Israelite tradition will never abandon the bold principle formulated by Amos: "Does a woe come into a city without Yahweh being its author?" (Am 3,6; cf Ex 8,12-28; Is 7,18). But this insistence opens the door to violent reactions. The wicked man when faced by the evil in the world concludes: "There is no God!" (Ps 10,4; 14,1) or else there is only a God "incapable of knowledge" (73,11). The wife of Job reasons: "Curse God!" (Jb 2,9).

Of course, they do take into account explanations of sufferings other than a direct intervention of God. Wounds can be produced by natural agents (Gn 34,25; Js 5,8; 2 S 4,4) and the infirmities of old age are normal (Gn 27,1; 48,10). There are evil powers in the universe hostile to man, those of the curse* and of Satan*. Sin* brings misery (Pr 13,8; Is 3,11; Si 7,1), and there is a tendency to look for a fault at the source of every woe (Gn 12,17f; 42,21; Js 7,6-13). This is the conviction of the friends of Job. At the source of the evil which weighs upon the world, there must be placed the first sin (Gn 3,14-19).

The caprice with which death* strikes people of all sorts and conditions unexpectedly is deeply felt (Jb 21,28-33; Pr 11,4; Am 5,19). But worse still is the scandal of the death of the just man and the long life of the godless man (Qo 7,15; Jr 12,1f). Justice is really turned upside down in this world (Ha 1,2-4; Ml 2,17; 3,15; Ps 37; 73).

It remains true that none of these agents, neither nature nor chance (Ex 21,13), nor the fatality of human life (Jb 4,1ff; cf 4,7), nor the fatal offspring of sin, nor the curse (Gn 3,14; 2 S 16,5), nor even Satan himself falls outside of God's power; so that God Himself must necessarily act as cause. The prophets cannot understand the prosperity of the wicked and the misery of the just (Jr 12,1-6; Ha 1,13; 3,14-18), and the just when persecuted believe that they must be forgotten (Ps 13,2; 31,13; 44,10-18). Job enters an accusation against God and summons Him to explain Himself (Jb 13,22; 23,7). A psalmist takes up the same accusation with some vigor, but this time because of the unjust misfortunes of the nation (Ps 44,10-27). And yet, in spite of the worst catastrophes, pessimism never triumphed in Israel. And it is very significant that the author of Job cannot end his book on a note of despair, any more than the melancholic Ecclesiastes, whose advice, in spite of everything, is that life is meant to be enjoyed (Qo 3,2.24; 9,7-10; 11,7-10), or even the gloomiest of the prophets, in whom there is always a source of hope and happiness to be found (Jr 9,16-23). Presentiments, as yet vague, of the triumphant resurrection* seem to run like a breath of air through the Bible (Gn 22; Ps 22; 49; 73; Is 53; R 4,18-21).

III. THE MYSTERY OF SUFFERING

Bruised by suffering but carried on by their faith, prophets and wise men gradually enter "into the mystery*" (Ps 73,17). They discover the purifying value of suffering, like that of the fire* which separates metal from its dross (Jr 9,6; Ps 65,10); its value, like that of fatherly correction (Dt 8,5; Pr 3,11f; 2 Ch 32,26.31); and finally they see in the swiftness of the punishment* an effect, so to speak, of the divine good will (2 M 6,12-17; 7,31-38). They learn to receive from suffering the revelation* of a divine plan* which confounds us (Jb 42,1-6; cf 38,2). Before Job, Joseph had borne witness to this before his brothers (Gn 50,20). A similar design can explain the premature death of the wise man*, preserved thus from sin (Ws 4,17-20). In this sense, the OT already recognized happiness in the sterile* woman and the eunuch

(Ws 3,13f). It was seen that suffering and persecution could be expiation* for sin (Is 40,2).

By faith in the plan* of God, suffering becomes a very high test, which God reserves to the servants* of whom He is proud—Abraham* (Gn 22), Job (1,11; 2,5), and Tobit (Tb 12,13)—in order to teach them what He is worth and what man can suffer for Him. Jeremiah also passes from revolt to a new conversion (Jr 15,10-19).

Finally, suffering has an intercessory and redemptive* value. This value appears in the figure of Moses*, in his sorrowful prayer (Ex 17, 11ff; Nm 11,1f) and in the sacrifice of his life, which He offers to save a guilty people (32, 30-33). Moses and those prophets who are the most tried by suffering, such as Jeremiah (Jr 8,18.21; 11,19; 15,18), are always but types of the Servant of Yahweh.

The Servant* knows suffering under its most redoubtable and most shocking forms. It has worked all its ravages on Him and has disfigured Him to such an extent that He no longer provokes compassion but horror and contempt (Is 52,14f; 53,3); in His case suffering is not an accident, a tragic moment, but rather His daily existence and His distinctive mark: "a man of sorrows" (53,3). Seemingly it can only be explained by a monstrous crime or by an exemplary punishment* of a holy* God (53,4). There is indeed a fault and one of unheard of extent, not one committed by Him, but rather by all of us (53,6). He is innocent, and this is the height of the scandal*.

But there is the mystery*, "the success of the plan of God" (53,10). Innocent, "He intercedes for sinners" (53,12) by offering to God not only the supplication of His heart but "His own life in expiation" (53,10), by allowing Himself to be confused with sinners (53,12) in order to take their sins on Himself. Thus the supreme scandal becomes the unheard of wonder, the "revelation of the arm* of Yahweh" (53,1). All the suffering and all the sin of the world have been concentrated on Him; and because He has borne them in obedience, He obtains peace* and health (53,5).

NT

I. JESUS AND THE SUFFERING OF MEN

Jesus, the Man of Sorrows, in whom the mysterious figure of the suffering servant becomes incarnate, shows Himself sensitive to every human suffering. He cannot witness suffering without being profoundly moved with a divine mercy (Mt 9,36; 14,14; 15,32). If He had been there Lazarus would not be dead, Martha and Mary repeat to Him (Jn 11,21.32); and He Himself had given the twelve to understand this (11,14). But then, before an emotion so evident—"How He loved him!"—how can one explain this scandal: "Could He not have done something to keep this man from dying?" (11,36f).

1. *Jesus Christ, conqueror of suffering.* The cures and the raisings from the dead are signs of His Messianic mission (Mt 11,4; cf Lk 4,18f), the preludes of the definitive victory*. In the miracles* wrought by the twelve, Jesus sees the defeat of Satan (Lk 10,19). He fulfills the prophecy of the Servant, "loaded with our iniquities" (Is 53,4), by curing all of them (Mt 8,17). To His disciples He gives the power to heal in His name* (Mk 15,17); and the healing of the sick man at the Beautiful Gate attests the assurance of the infant Church in this regard (Ac 3,1-10).

2. *Jesus Christ makes suffering blessed.* Nonetheless Jesus suppresses neither death*, which He has come to "reduce to impotence" (He 3, 14), nor suffering in the world. If He refuses to establish a systematic connection between sickness* or accident and sin* (Lk 13,2ff; Jn 9, 3), He allows the curse* of Eden to bear its fruit*. He does this because He can change this fruit to joy. He does not suppress suffering, He consoles* it (Mt 5,5); He does not abolish tears, He only dries some of them while passing by (Lk 7,13; 8,52) as a sign of the joy* that will unite God and His children on the day when "He will wipe away tears from all eyes" (Is 25,8; Ap 7,17; 21,4). Suffering can be a blessing*, for it prepares man to welcome the kingdom; it allows for "the revelation of the works of God" (Jn 9,3), "of the glory of God," and "of the glory of the Son of God" (11,4).

II. THE SUFFERINGS OF THE SON OF MAN

Jesus "knows suffering" (Is 53,3); He suffers from the "incredulous and perverse" crowd (Mt 17,17), which is like a "brood of vipers" (Mt 12,34; 23,33); and He suffers rejection by His own, who "did not know Him" (Jn 1,11). He weeps before Jerusalem* (Lk 19,41; cf Mt 23,

37); He is "troubled" at the thought of His passion (Jn 12,27). His suffering then becomes a mortal distress, an "agony," a combat in anguish and fear (Mk 14,33f; Lk 22,44). The passion concentrates all possible human suffering, from betrayal even to abandonment by God (Mt 27,46). This culmination coincides with the great redemptive offering of Christ, the expiatory gift of His life (Mt 20,28), for which He was sent into the world according to the eternal plan of the Father (Ac 3,18). And Jesus submits to it obediently (He 3,7-8) and lovingly (Jn 14,30; 15,13). "It must be," *dei*—this little word, always connected with suffering, sums up His life, and casts light on its mystery; it recurs like a *leitmotif* on Jesus' lips, when He foretells His passion without worrying about the scandal of Peter and the disciples (Lk 17,25; cf Mk 8,31-33; Mt 17,22-23; Lk 9,42-45). But the redemptive passion reveals the glory of the Son (Jn 17,1; 12,31f); it "gathers round Him in unity* the scattered sons of God" (11,52). The One who was able "to come to the aid of those who were troubled" (He 2,18) in the days of His life on earth will, on the day* of judgment when He comes again in glory, want to identify Himself with all the suffering people on earth (Mt 25,35-40).

III. THE SUFFERINGS OF THE DISCIPLES

After the victory of Easter, an illusion threatens Christians: death is no more, suffering is no more; and they run the risk of being shaken in their faith by the tragic realities of existence (cf 1 Th 4,13). The resurrection does not abolish the instructions of the gospel; it confirms them. The message of the beatitudes*, the insistence on the daily cross* (Lk 9,23) take on all their urgency in the light of the destiny of the Lord. If His own mother has not been separated from sorrow (Lk 2,35), if the master, "in order to enter into His glory" (Lk 24,26), has known tribulations and persecutions*, the disciples must follow the same way* (Jn 15,20; Mt 10,24). The Messianic era is a time of trials (Mt 24,8; Ac 14,22; 1 Tm 4,1).

1. *To suffer with Christ.* Just as, if the Christian lives, "it is no longer (he) who lives, but Christ who lives in (him)" (G 2,20), so the sufferings of the Christian are "the sufferings of Christ in him" (2 Co 1,5). The Christian belongs to Christ even through his body*, and

suffering conforms him to Christ (Ph 3,10). Just as Christ, "Son though He was, learned obedience from what He suffered" (He 5,8), so we must "run with constancy the test that is set before us, fixing our eyes on the head of our faith...who suffered the cross" (He 12,1f). Christ has united Himself with those who suffer. He leaves to His own the same law (1 Co 12,26; R 12,15; 2 Co 1,7).

2. *In order to be glorified with Christ.* If "we suffer with Him," it is "in order to be glorified with Him also" (R 8,17). If "we carry everywhere and always in our body the sufferings of the death of Jesus" it is "in order that the life* of Jesus may also be manifested in our body" (2 Co 4,10). "The grace of God which has been given to us is not only to believe in Christ, but to suffer for Him" (Ph 1,29; cf Ac 9,16; 2 Co 11,23-27). From suffering borne with Christ there comes not only "the eternal weight of glory* prepared beyond all measure" (2 Co 4,17; cf Ac 14,21) after death, but joy* even today (2 Co 7,4; cf 1.5-7). There is the joy of the apostles being tested for the first time in Jerusalem and discovering "the joy of being judged worthy to suffer insults for His name" (Ac 5,41). There is the call of Peter to the joy of "sharing in the sufferings of Christ" in order to know the presence of "the Spirit of God, the Spirit of glory" (I P 4,13f). There is the joy of Paul "in the sufferings which he endures" to be able to "fill up in his flesh what is wanting to the sufferings of Christ for His body, which is the Church" (Col 1,24).

→Calamity—Console—Cross II 2—Curse I—Death—Good & Evil I 1.4, II 3—Martyr 1—Patience II 1—Persecution—Poor—Punishment —Sadness—Servant of God II 2, III—Shame—Sickness/Healing — Trial/Temptation — Work II.

MLR & JG jpl

T

TASTE

To taste is sometimes to absorb nourishment (Jon 3,7; Col 2,21), but it is above all to appreciate the flavor of our experience on all levels (2 S 19,36). The Bible applies it to the discerning of moral values and to the savoring knowledge* of God and of Christ, the delights of our life here below and in heaven.

1. *Discernment.* Taste includes diverse forms of wisdom*: practical knowledge (1 S 25,33), tact (Pr 11,22), settled judgment (Pr 26,16). A gift of God (Ps 119,66) who can take it back (Jb 12,20), it is at the same time the fruit of age and experience (Jb 12,11f). It orientates the conduct of man in the most practical domains (Pr 31,18); and yet, its higher form, the discernment of good and evil, is not simply a moral value, but religious, at the very basis of faith (Ps 119,66); and it is perfected by its attraction to the Word* of God, which one finds sweet (Ez 3,3), and for His commandments (Ps 119, 16; R 7,22).

2. *Religious experience.* Beyond the discernment of wisdom, we find the lived experience of the love God bears us. Temporal blessings* are the delights of the just man* of the OT who obeys God's law (Ne 9,25; Is 55,2). He relishes the indefinitely varied delights of the manna* (Ws 16,20f), he experiences how the Lord is good (Ps 34,9), and he is attached to Him as to his only treasure (Jb 22,26).

In the NT the entire life of the baptized is a union with Christ risen, but the reception of baptism implies the tasteful experience of having definitively drawn close to the heavenly blessings of salvation: the participation in the Holy Spirit, the word of the gospel assimilated through faith, the manifestations of the power of God, who already creates the new world (He 6,4f). All this is the supereminent pledge of the goodness of God (1 P 2,3). This sweetness* comes to us from the bitterness of the death which Jesus has tasted (He 2,9) to spare us the taste of eternal death (Jn 8,52). It is a foretaste of beatitude* (Ap 2,17).

→Beatitude — Fruit III, IV — Joy — Know —
Manna—Meekness 1—Rest—Seek 1—Wisdom.
                                    PS wjy

TEACH

In the two Testaments, faith is founded on a divine revelation* of which the prophets (in the general sense of the word) are the bearers. But this revelation should come to men's knowledge* even in its details and in its practical consequences. Hence in the people of God the importance of the function of teaching, which transmits in the form of instruction the knowledge of divine things. In the first place this teaching takes the form of preaching* and announcing God's salvation* as it appears in history (this is the *kerygma*); then it provides a deeper understanding of it and shows how the covenant* situation created by God can be applied in practise to the living conditions of His people.

OT

In the OT this function is fulfilled in diverse ways, according to the character of those who fulfill it. But through all of them it is always God who teaches His people.

I. DIVERSE FORMS OF TEACHING

1. *The father of the family*, who is responsible for the education* of his children, should pass on to them the religious legacy of the national past by teaching it. There is no question of a profound preaching, but an elementary catechesis which includes the essential elements of the faith. There is required moral catechesis which refers to the commandments of the divine Law*: "These commandments which I give you shall repeat to your children..." (Dt 6,7; 11,19). There is liturgical and historical catechesis, which uses the opportunity of the solemnities of Israel to explain the significance and recall the great events they commemorate: the sacrifice of the Passover* (Ex 12,26) and the rite of the Azyme (Ex 13,8), etc. The questions asked by the children on the subject of customs and of rites would naturally lead the father to teach them the Israelite Credo (Dt 6,20-25). It is he who teaches them the old poems which form part of the tradition* (Dt 31,19.22; 2 S 1,18f).

Thus the religious teaching starts in the family circle.

2. *The priests* have a greater responsibility in this domain. By the fact that they are charged with the professional duty of worship* and of the Law*, they fill the role of teacher. On Sinai Moses received the Law with the mission of making it known to the people; thus he became the first teacher in Israel (Ex 24,3.12). This Law the Levites now have to teach and to interpret so that it could be observed in life (Dt 17,10f; 33,10; cf 2 Ch 15,3). A man like Samuel fulfilled this duty conscientiously (1 S 12,23). Other priests neglect it and therefore incur the reproaches of the prophets (Ho 4,6; 5,1; Jr 5,31; Ml 2,7). It is not difficult to imagine the concrete background of this teaching. It consists of the feasts which are celebrated in the sanctuaries, such as the renewal of the covenant at Shechem (Dt 27,9f; Js 24, 1-24), of which the promulgation of the Law by Ezra will be but a variant (Ne 8). The teaching which is given bears on the Law, which has to be reread and explained (Dt 31,9-13), and on the history of God's plan* (cf Js 24). Exhortation is naturally mingled with instruction to guide the people to life in faith and to put the Law into practice. An echo of this priestly preaching is found in Chap. 4—11 of Deuteronomy, where quite a vocabulary of teaching is seen: "Hear, Israel..." (Dt 4,1; 5,1); "Know that..." (4,39); "Ask..." (4,32); "Do not forget..." (4,9; 8,11f). In effect it means making the Word of God known so that Israel may have it constantly in mind (D 11,18-21).

3. *The prophets* have a different mission. The Word* of God which they pass on was not in tradition*, but they receive it directly from God. In proclaiming it they threaten, exhort*, promise, console*... All this does not have a direct bearing on teaching. But they constantly stress a catechesis which they suppose is known (comp Ho 4,1f and the Decalogue) and from which they take their essential themes. They are themselves disciples (Is 8,16; Jr 36,4) who spread their oracles about, and their message comes to be added to the traditional teaching to enrich its data. The prophetic teaching itself, then, adopts a traditional form. There is a continuity between one prophet and the next, which is expressly mentioned by Jeremiah (Jr 28,8). Tangible proof of this can be seen when a prophet uses expressions borrowed from his predecessor in order to deliver his message (this

TEACH

is what Ezekiel did for the book of Jeremiah), or when the deuteronomic scribes adopt the prophetic interpretation of history in their own theology.

4. *The wise men* are essentially teachers (Qo 12,9). With regard to their disciples* they carry out the same teaching function that every father does with regard to his sons (Si 30,3; cf Pr 3,21; 4,1-17.20. . .). Woe to the disciples who will not listen to them (Pr 5,12f)! If, up to the exile, the sapiential teaching seems founded on the experience of generations more than on the Word of God, afterwards it gradually assimilates the content of the Law and of the prophetic books, and it circulates it for the use of all. Thus filled with the traditional teaching, the master wishes to pass on to his "sons" the true wisdom* (Jb 33,33), the knowledge, and the fear* of Yahweh (Pr 2,5; Ps 34,12); in short, the religious knowledge which is the condition of the happy life. Is it not in teaching the ways of God to the godless that He will lead them to be converted (Ps 51,5)? The didactic endeavor undertaken in the environment of the scribes therefore takes the place of that of the priests as well as of the prophets. In the "schoolhouse" (Si 51,23), the doctors give all a solid instruction (Si 51,25f) which allows them to find God.

I. YAHWEH, SOVEREIGN MASTER

1. Besides all these human masters, it is important to discover *the only true master* from whom they get all their authority: Yahweh. Inspiring Moses and the prophets, His Word is the source of the tradition which parents, priests, and wise men all transmit. Through them it is, therefore, He who teaches men knowledge and wisdom in bringing them to know His ways and His Law (Ps 25,9; 94,10ff). His Wisdom* personified addresses itself to them to instruct them (Pr 8,1-11.32-36) as a prophet or a doctor would; through it all good things come to them (Ws 7,11ff). Thus every pious Jew had the sense of having been instructed by God from his youth (Ps 71,17). In return he continually begs Him to teach him His ways, His commandments, His wishes (Ps 25,4; 143,10; 119,7.12 and *passim*). The opening of the heart to the divine teaching goes far beyond the theoretical knowledge of the Law and of Scripture. It supposes a close adherence which permits a deep understanding of the message of God and its implementation in life.

2. It is known, however, that Israel's attitude toward God did not always involve this *docility of heart*. The members of the people of God often turned their backs on Him, not listening to His lessons when He kept on instructing them (Jr 32,33). Hence the typical chastisements God inflicted on His unfaithful disciples. To obviate this hardness of heart, God promises through His prophets that in the end He will reveal Himself to men as the teacher beyond compare (Is 30,20f). He will act in the inner parts of their being so that they will know* His Law without having to instruct one another (Jr 31,33f). Thus instructed by Him directly, they will find happiness (Is 54,13). Supreme grace will render efficacious every instructive effort made by His divine representatives. The prayer of the psalmists will thus be granted.

NT

Christ is the greatest teacher of all. But in entrusting His Word to His apostles, He gives them a mission of teaching which continues His own.

I. CHRIST THE TEACHER

1. During the public life of Jesus, teaching is *an essential aspect of His activity*. He teaches in the synagogues (Mt 4,23 p; Jn 6,59), in the temple (Mt 21,23 p; Jn 7,14), on the occasion of feasts (Jn 8,20), and even daily (Mt 26,55). The forms of His teaching do not differ from those used by the teachers in Israel with whom He mingled during His youth (Lk 2,46), whom He received on occasion (Jn 3,10), and who interrogate Him more than once (Mt 22,16f. 36 p). Thus is He given like them the title of rabbi, that is to say, master; and He accepts it (Jn 13,13) although He reproaches the scribes of His time for seeking it, as if for men there were not only one master, God (Mt 23,7f).

2. However, if He seems to the crowd to be a teacher among the others, He distinguishes Himself from them in diverse ways. At times He speaks and acts as a prophet*. Or again He gives Himself as the authorized interpreter of the Law which He is bringing to its perfection (Mt 5,17). In this regard He teaches with a singular authority (Mt 13,54 p), different from that of the scribes who are so ready to hide

behind the authority of the elders (Mt 7,29 p). Besides, His teaching has the ring of newness* which makes an impression on His hearers (Mk 1,27; 11,18), whether He deals with His announcement of the kingdom or with the rules of life He gives. Breaking with the questions of the school, object of a tradition* which He rejects (cf Mt 15,1-9 p), He wishes to make the genuine message of God known and to lead men to accept it.

3. The secret of this rather new attitude is that, unlike that of the officially accredited human teachers *His doctrine is not His own*, but that of Him who sent Him (Jn 7,16f); He says only that the Father teaches Him (Jn 8,28). To accept His teaching then is to be docile to God Himself. But to get to that point, one must have a certain disposition of heart which inclines one to carry out the divine will (Jn 7,17). On a still deeper level, he must have received that interior grace* which, according to the promise of the prophets, makes man docile to the teaching of God (Jn 6,44f). Here one touches on the mystery of human liberty at grips with grace: the word of Christ the teacher runs counter to the willfull blindness of those who pretend to see clearly (cf Jn 9,39ff).

II. THE APOSTOLIC TEACHING

1. During His public life Jesus confides to His disciples* *temporary* missions which concern more the proclamation of the gospel* than detailed teaching (Mt 10,7 p). It is only after His resurrection that they receive from Him a definite order making them at the same time "preachers, apostles and teachers" (cf 2 Tm 1,11): "Go, make disciples of all nations... teaching them to observe everything that I have commanded you" (Mt 28,19f). To accomplish this task of such large dimensions He promised them that in time He would send them the Holy Spirit who would teach them all things (Jn 14,26). Disciples of the Spirit* in order to become perfect disciples of Christ, they will then pass on to men a teaching which will come not from them but from God. It is for this that they will be able to speak with authority. The Lord will Himself be with them until the end of the world (Mt 28,20; Jn 14,18f).

2. After Pentecost, *the apostles* carry out this mission* of teaching, not in their own name, but "in the name of Jesus" (Ac 4,18; 5,28) whose deeds and words they relate, always covering themselves with His authority. Like Jesus they teach in the temple (Ac 5,21), in the synagogue (Ac 13,14...), in private homes (Ac 5,42). The object of this teaching is above all the proclamation of the message of salvation. Jesus, Messiah and Son of God, fulfills the expectation of Israel; His death and His resurrection fulfill the Scriptures. They must be converted and believe in Him in order to receive the promised Spirit and to escape judgment (cf the Discourses in Acts). An elementary catechesis which intends to lead men to faith (cf Ac 2,22-40), it is completed after baptism by a more profound teaching to which the first Christians show themselves attentive (Ac 2,42). Among the listeners from the outside, some are surprised at its novelty (cf Ac 17,19f); the Jewish authorities are moved especially by its success; and they try to prohibit it to men who have not yet received the ordinary formation of the scribes (Ac 4,13; cf 5,28). In vain. After being diffused in Judea, the teaching is brought to considerable crowds in the whole Greek world. It is identified as the Word* (Ac 18,11), the testimony, the gospel*. If it finds its way into hearts, it is because the force of the Spirit accompanies it (cf Ac 2,17ff), this Spirit whose anointing rests on the Christians and instructs them in everything (1 Jn 2,27).

3. Moreover, the same Spirit, by His charisms* (cf 1 Co 12,8.29), raises in the Church beside the apostles other teachers who aid them in their function of evangelization: the *didascaloi*, catechists charged with determining and developing for the young communities the content of the gospel (Ac 13,1; E 4,11). At the same time a body of doctrine is formed which is the rule of faith (cf R 6,17). By the time of the pastoral epistles it already had a traditional form (1 Tm 4,13.16; 5,17; 6,1ff). While the faith seems threatened by erroneous or frivolous teachings (R 16,17; E 4,3.14; 1 Tm 1,3; 6,3; Ap 2,14f.24) spread by false teachers (2 Tm 4,3; 2 P 2,1), the preservation and transmission of this authentic deposit is one of the primary concerns of pastors.

→Charisms II 2—Disciple—Education—Exhort —Know—Law—Milk 3—Mystery NT II 1— New III 1—Parable—Paraclete 2—Preach— Revelation — Tradition — Wisdom — Word of God.

AB & PG gsa

TEMPLE

In all religions, the temple is the sacred place where the divinity is thought to make itself present to men to receive their worship and to make them participate in its favors and in its life. Its ordinary residence doubtless does not belong to this world. Still, the temple is identified in some way with it, so that by means of the temple man enters into communication with the world of the gods. This fundamental symbolism is found in the OT, where the temple of Jerusalem is the sign* of the presence* of God among men. But here it is only a matter of a provisional sign for which there will be substituted in the NT a sign of another sort: the body of Christ and His Church.

OT

I. THE TEMPLE OF JERUSALEM

1. *The ancient sanctuary of Israel.* The Hebrews of the patriarchal period did not have a temple, although they had sacred places, where they "called upon the name of Yahweh," such as Bethel (=House of God: Gn 12,8; 28,17f), Beersheba (Gn 26,25; 45,1), Shechem (Gn 33, 18ff). Sinai of the exodus is another place of this type, consecrated by a theophany (Ex 3; 19, 20). But in the following period Israel possessed a portable sanctuary by means of which God could permanently reside in the midst of the people whom He led across the desert. The tabernacle, of which Ex 26—27 gives an idealized description and which was partially inspired by the future temple, is the place of the encounter of the people with God (Nm 1,1; 7,89...). God dwells there among the cherubim, above the mercy seat which covers the ark* of the covenant. There He gives His oracles, whence the name "Tent of Witness" was given to the tabernacle (Ex 25,22; 26,33; etc.). His presence there is at once sensible and hidden: behind the cloud* (Ex 33,7-11; 40,36ff) His luminous glory* hides itself (Nm 14,10; 16,19). Thus the recollection of the Sinaitic covenant is maintained in a central sanctuary for the whole of the Israelite confederation. After the establishment of the confederation in Canaan, the common sanctuary for the tribes is successively located at Gilgal, at Shechem (Js 8,30-35; 24,1-28), at Shiloh (1 S 1—4), preserving from its origin an archaic character which sharply distinguishes it from the Canaanite places of worship, which are generally marked by temples built in stone: the God of Sinai does not mix with the pagan civilization of Canaan.

2. *The project of David.* It is this sanctuary of the confederation which David places at Jerusalem* after having freed the ark from the hands of the Philistines (2 S 6). The political capital which he has just conquered will also be the religious center of the people of Yahweh. Then, just as he has undertaken to organize his monarchy in the manner of contemporary kingdoms without, however, losing sight of the special character of Israel, he thinks also of modernizing the traditional place of worship. After having built himself a palace, he thinks of building a temple to Yahweh (2 S 7,1-4). God is opposed to this: it is not David who will build a house* (i.e., a temple) for Yahweh, but Yahweh who will build a house (i.e., a dynasty) for him (2 S 7,5-17). This reaction is explained in two ways. For the people of the covenant, the ideal sanctuary remains the tabernacle of the past, which explicitly recalls the sojourn in the desert (2 S 7,6f). Furthermore, the authentic cult of the one God is not pleased with a slavish copy of pagan cults, whose temples pretend to lay hold in some way of the divinity (for instance, the Babylonian ziggurats, cf Gn 11,1-9) and are defiled by idolatrous, magical, and immoral practices.

3. *Accomplishment by Solomon.* Nonetheless, during the reign of Solomon, David's project is accomplished without any prophetic opposition revealing itself (1 K 5,15—7,51). The religion of Yahweh is sufficiently strong to enrich itself with the elements which Canaanite culture offers without being unfaithful to the tradition of Sinai. Besides, this tradition is strongly affirmed in the temple: the ark of the covenant is its center (8,1-9), and the sanctuary of Jerusalem thus continues the ancient place of central worship for the tribes. Further, by manifesting His glory* in the midst of the cloud* (in the temple) (8,10-13) God visibly indicates that He accepts this temple as the dwelling place where He "makes His name* to dwell" (7,16-21). Certainly He is not Himself bound to this sensible sign of His presence; if the heavens would not be able to contain Him, still less would an earthly house (8,27). But in order to permit His people to encounter Him in an assured manner, He has chosen this abode, of which He has said: "My name is here" (8,29).

4. *The role of the temple among the people of God.* Henceforth, though it does not make other sanctuaries obsolete, the temple of Jerusalem will be the center of the worship of Yahweh. People come there in pilgrimage* from every land "in order to look upon the face* of God" (Ps 42,3), and the faithful have for it a touching love (cf Ps 84; 122). Without doubt men know that God's dwelling is "in heaven*" (Ps 2,4; 103,19; 115,3; etc.); but the temple is like a replica of His heavenly palace (cf Ex 25,40), which He makes present here below. Thus the worship possesses an official value: by it the kings and people perform the service of the national God.

II. FROM THE TEMPLE OF STONE TO THE SPIRITUAL TEMPLE

1. *Ambiguity of the temple as sign.* In the period of the kingdom, while it plays this essential role in the worship of Israel, the temple as sign still has a certain ambiguity. For men with a superficial religious sense, the ceremonies publicly enacted there tend to become empty gestures. Furthermore, the attachment which they have to the temple risks becoming a superstitious confidence. Men say: "Temple of Yahweh! Temple of Yahweh!" (Jr 7,4), as if God owed it to Himself to defend it at any price, even if the people who frequent it do not practice the Law*. These deviations explain the reserved attitude of the prophets with regard to the temple. Surely it is there that Yahweh reveals Himself to Isaiah in his inaugural vision (Is 6); and the same prophet announces that this place cannot be destroyed by the impious Sennacherib (Is 37,16-20.33ff). But Isaiah, Jeremiah, and Ezekiel compete in denouncing the superficial character of the worship* enacted there (Is 1,11-17; Jr 6,20; 7,9ff), which even includes imported idolatrous practices (Ez 8,7-18). Finally they envisage Yahweh's abandonment of this chosen dwelling in punishment for the sin of the nation (Mi 3,12; Jr 7,12-15; Ez 9—10). The authentic character of the worship of Israel is in fact of more importance than the material sign to which Yahweh had for a time bound His presence.

2. *From the first to the second temple.* Actually the temple of Jerusalem shares in the vicissitudes of the national destiny. Some attempts at religious reform at first cause an increase in its importance: under Hezekiah (2 K 18,4; 2 Ch 29—31) and especially under Josiah, who brings about the unity of sanctuary to its advantage (2 K 23,4-27). But the prophetic threats are finally realized (25,8-17) and the glory of Yahweh has abandoned His desecrated abode (cf Ez 10,4.18). Is this the end of the sign of the temple? Not at all, for the eschatological oracles of the prophets have given it an important place in their pictures of the future. Isaiah has seen it as the future religious center of all humanity reconciled in the worship of the true God (Is 2,1-4). Ezekiel has foreseen in detail its reconstruction at the time of the national restoration (Ez 40—48). Thus the first concern of the repatriated Jews at the end of the exile is to rebuild the temple with the encouragement of the prophets Haggai and Zechariah (Ezr 3—6), and once again oracles sing its coming glory (Hg 2,1-9; Is 60,7-11). In this second temple worship is resumed as in the past, and the temple is the center of Judaism, returned now to the theocratic structure of its origins. It is once again the sign of the divine presence among men—where men go on pilgrimage, and the splendor of whose ceremonies the son of Sirach celebrates in enthusiastic tones (Si 50,5-21). Thus when King Antiochus profanes it and installs there a pagan shrine, the Jews rise up to defend it and the first goal of their holy war is to purify it in order to resume the traditional worship (1 M 4,36-43). Some decades later Herod the great will rebuild it with splendor. But more important than this external splendor is the sincere piety* which finds free expression in its ceremonies.

3. *Toward the spiritual temple.* Despite this attachment to the temple of stone, a new current of thought began to be affirmed after the end of the prophetic epoch. The threats of Jeremiah against the temple (Jr 7), then the destruction of the edifice, and above all the experience of the exile, have contributed to make clear the necessity of a more spiritual worship* corresponding to the demands of the "religion of the heart" preached by the Deuteronomist and Jeremiah (Dt 6,4ff; Jr 31,31...). In the land of exile it was better understood that God is present wherever He rules and especially wherever He is adored (Ez 11,16). Is not His glory manifested to Ezekiel in Babylon (Ez 1)? Thus, at the end of the exile one sees certain prophets putting the Jews on guard against an excessive attachment to the temple of stone (Is 66,1f) as if the spiritual worship demanded by God—that of poor* and contrite hearts (66,2)—was better adapted to a spiritual presence* of God,

separated from sensible signs. Yahweh dwells in heaven and hears from there the prayers of His faithful ones in whatever place they are uttered (cf Tb 3,16). The existence of such a current of thought explains why, a little before the coming of Christ, the Essene sect could break with the worship of a temple which it considered defiled by an illegitimate priesthood, and could consider itself as a spiritual temple where God received adoration worthy of Him. This is the era in which the apocryphal apocalypses describe the temple in heaven* which is not made by the hand of man: there it is that God resides. The temple here below is only the imperfect image of the heavenly temple (cf Ws 9,8), which will appear here below at the end of time in order to be the divine dwelling place in the "world* to come."

NT

I. JESUS CHRIST, THE NEW TEMPLE

1. *Jesus and the old temple.* Jesus, like the prophets, professes the most profound respect for the old temple. He is presented there by Mary (Lk 2,22-39), and He goes up there for the solemnities as to a place of encounter with His Father (Lk 2,41-50; Jn 2,14; etc.). He approves its liturgical practices, even while condemning the formalism which threatens to vitiate them (Mt 5,23f; 12,3-7 p; 23,16-22). The temple is for Him the house* of God, a house of prayer, and the house of His Father; He becomes angry when it is made into a place of trade. Thus in prophetic gesture He drives the sellers of doves* out of it in order to purify it (Mt 21,12-17 p; Jn 2,16ff; cf Is 56,7; Jr 7,11). But nonetheless He announces the ruin of the splendid edifice, of which there will not remain a stone upon a stone (Mt 23,38f; 24,2 p). In the course of His trial, He will even be reproached with having declared that He would destroy this sanctuary made by the hand of man and that in three days He would rebuild another not made by the hand of man (Mk 14,58 p). And the same complaint is taken up abusively again when He is in agony on the cross (Mt 27,39f p). But here it is a question of a mysterious word, the meaning of which the future alone will explain. In the meantime, at the moment of His last breath, the tearing of the veil of the holy of holies shows that the ancient sanctuary loses its sacred character: the Jewish temple has ceased to fulfill its function as a sign of the divine presence.

2. *The new temple.* In reality this function is filled thereafter by another sign, which is the very body* of Jesus. The gospel of St. John places the mysterious utterance on the sanctuary destroyed and rebuilt in three days in the context of the cleansing of the temple (Jn 2,19). But he adds: "He was speaking of the sanctuary of His own body," and His disciples understood Him after His resurrection (2,21f). This then is the new and definite temple, which is not built by the hands of men, the temple in which the Word of God establishes His dwelling place among men (1,14) as in earlier times He establishes it in the tabernacle of Israel. But in order that the temple of stone fall into disuse, it is necessary that Jesus Himself die and rise again: the temple of His body will be destroyed and rebuilt, that is the will of His Father (10, 17f; 17,14). After His resurrection*, this body, sign of the divine presence here below, will experience a new, transfigured state which will permit it to make itself present in all places and at all times in the eucharistic* celebration. Then the ancient temple will disappear, and the destruction of Jerusalem in 70 will come to signify in a decisive fashion that its role is thenceforth at an end.

II. THE CHURCH, SPIRITUAL TEMPLE

1. *Christians and the Jewish temple.* During the period of transition which follows Pentecost, the apostles and the faithful who believe in the Word continue to frequent the temple of Jerusalem (Ac 2,46; 3,1-11; 21,26). In fact, so long as Judaism in its leaders and in its body did not reject the gospel, the ancient place of worship did not lose all connection with the new worship inaugurated by Jesus; the Jewish people by being converted could play a role in the conversion of the entire world. Signs of rupture, however, are visible. Stephen, in his apology for spiritual worship, anticipated the downfall of the temple made by the hand of man (Ac 7, 48ff); and these words are regarded as a blasphemy which required that he be put to death. Several years later the ruin of Jerusalem will precipitate the hardening of Judaism and the Temple will be destroyed.

2. *The spiritual temple.* But before that the Christians will have become aware that they themselves constitute a new temple, the spiritual temple, a prolongation of the body of Christ. Such is the explicit teaching of St. Paul: the

Church is the temple of God, built on Christ, the foundation and the cornerstone (1 Co 3,10-17; 2 Co 6,16ff; E 2,20ff); a shining temple where without distinction both Jews and pagans have access to the Father in the one identical Spirit (E 2,14-19).

Every Christian is himself a temple of God insofar as he is a member of the Body of Christ (1 Co 6,15; 12,27), and his body is the temple of the Holy Spirit (1 Co 6,19; cf R 8,11). The two statements are connected: since the risen body of Jesus, in which the divinity dwells corporeally (Col 2,9), is the perfect temple of God, the Christian members of this body form with Him the spiritual temple; and they are to work together in faith and charity for its increase (E 4,1-16). Thus Christ is the living rock, rejected by men but chosen by God. The faithful, living stones themselves, constitute with Him one spiritual edifice, a holy priesthood*, for the purpose of offering spiritual sacrifices* (1 P 2,4f; cf R 12,1). Here is the definitive temple, which is not made by the hands of men; it is the Church, the body of Christ, the place of the encounter between God and man, the sign of the divine presence here below. The ancient sanctuary then was only a figure* of the temple, suggestive but imperfect, provisional, and finally superseded.

III. THE HEAVENLY TEMPLE

1. *The epistle to the Hebrews.* But the NT exploits the symbolism of the ancient temple in another direction. Judaism had already seen in the temple the human replica of the heavenly residence of God, of that dwelling place which the apocalypses take pleasure in describing in terms of the temple. It is within this framework that the epistle to the Hebrews describes the sacrifice* of Christ the priest, accomplished by His death, resurrection, and ascension. At the end of His earthly life He has penetrated into the sanctuary of heaven, not with the blood of animal victims as in the figurative worship, but with His own blood* (He 9,11-14.24). He has entered there as a precursor in order to give us access to the presence of God (4,16; 10,19f). United to this unique priest, we will then be able to enjoy the divine presence* in our turn in this holy of holies where God dwells and to which we already have access by faith (6,19f).

2. *The Apocalypse of St. John.* In the Apocalypse the image of the heavenly temple domi-

nates that of the earthly temple which is the Church. Here below there is a temple in which the faithful give worship to God: the pagans crowd its outer porches, an image of the persecution* which vents its fury against the Church (Ap 11,1f). But there is also in heaven a temple where the immolated Lamb* is enthroned and where a liturgy of prayer and of praise is celebrated (5,6-14; 7,15). Now, at the end of time, this duality will cease. In fact, when the heavenly Jerusalem will descend here below as the betrothed of the Lamb, adorned for the eternal nuptials, there will no longer be any need of a temple in it; its temple will be God Himself and the Lamb (21,22). The faithful will then attain God without having need of any sign. Or rather they will see Him face to face in order to share fully in His life.

→Abide II 1—Altar 2—Ark of the Covenant—Body of Christ 1 3, III 3—Build—Church II 2, V—Cloud 2—Covenant OT I 3, II 1—David 2.3—Dove 1—Expiation 2—Gate OT II—Head 1.4—Holy NT III—House—Jerusalem—Mediator II 1—Name OT 4—Pilgrimage—Praise III—Presence of God OT III 1; NT I, II—Priesthood OT I 3.4, III 1—Prophet NT II 2—Sacrifice OT I 1—Spirit of God NT V 4—Stone 4—Water III—Worship.

FA jpl

TENDERNESS

The Hebrew word *rahamim* (bowels), the intensive plural of *rehem*, the maternal womb, signifies *tenderness*: the tenderness felt by women for their offspring (1 K 3,26), that felt by all human beings for their children or those close to them (Gn 43,30) and above all that of God Himself toward His creatures.

1. *The tenderness of God.* God is in effect father* (Ps 103,13) and mother* (Is 49,14f; 66, 13). His tenderness transcends men's tenderness and results in the creation of children made in His own image (Gn 1,26; 5,1-3); it is gratuitous (Dn 9,18), always on the alert (Ho 11,8; Jr 31,20; Is 63,15), immense (Is 54,7; Ba 2,27; Si 51,3), inexhaustible (Ps 77,10; Ne 9,19. 27.31), renewed every morning (Lm 3,22f), unshakably faithful (Ps 25,6; Lk 1,50), shown to all without exception (Si 18,12; Ps 145,9), especially to the most deprived, to the orphans

(Ho 14,4), and capable of reuniting faithful believers even after death (2 M 7,29).

This love, which nothing can stop, shows itself in all sorts of blessings (Is 63,7), in the gift of Life (Ps 119,77.156), of salvation, of deliverance (Dt 30,3; Ze 1,16) and even in trials that teach a man something (Lm 3,32; Ws 11,9). But above all it is His readiness to *pardon** that reveals the infinite tenderness of the Lord, His mercy* (Is 55,7; Dn 9,9). Every sinner, whether it is a case of the sinful people as a whole (Ho 2,25) or the individual (Ps 51,3), can and should always count on His disconcerting goodness, not of course in order to sin again (Si 5,4-7) but in order to return to the Father who is waiting for him (Ps 79,8; Lk 15,20).

"A God of *tenderness* and compassion" is the first title that God claims and which, after Exodus (34,6), Deuteronomy (4,31), the Psalms (86,15; 103,8; 111,4; 145,8), the Prophets (Jl 2, 13; Jon 4,2), the historical books (2 Ch 30,9; Ne 17.31) and the Wisdom literature (Si 2,11; Ws 15,1) will give Him. Except for one occasion, when it is used of man (Ps 112,4), the adjective "tender" is reserved to God (cf Ps 78,38; 106, 5). Therefore, the faithful can rely on their Lord as a child on its mother (Ps 131), and this will be the filial attitude of Jesus, in whom and by whom the tenderness of God is fully revealed.

2. *The tenderness of God as it appears in and through Christ.* In Jesus the goodness of God has appeared (Lk 1,78; Tt 3,4-7); in Him the Father of compassion (2 Co 1,3; R 12,1) has revealed Himself, giving us the supreme proof of His tenderness in the Resurrection of His Son, the guarantee of ours (E 2,4-6; 1 P 1,3).

In fact, Jesus is not only the recipient of divine tenderness, but He makes it His own and extends it to us: like God confronted by His wretched flock (Ez 34,16), He is moved with pity when He sees the sheep starved of the Gospel (Mk 6,34) or of bread (8,2). He groans with compassion when He sees the most deprived of all people, the lepers (1,41), the blind (Mt 20,34) and bereaved mothers or sisters (Lk 7,13; Jn 11,33). As tireless as that of God, the tenderness of Jesus triumphs over sin and goes as far as to pardon the most wretched of all men: the sinners (Lk 23,34).

3. *The tenderness of God as it appears in and through the Christian.* God wants His tenderness to penetrate men's hearts (Ze 7,9; Ps 112, 1.4; Si 28,1-7). Since they are incapable of acquiring it for themselves, He gives it to them

(Ze 12,10) as a wedding-gift (Ho 2,21) in the new covenant that is ratified by Jesus. Once it has become the tenderness of the Son of God made man, the tenderness of God can now become that of men, born again as children of God in Jesus. Paul has only one wish: to make the sentiments of Christ his own (Ph 1,8; Phil 20). And so he can urge Christians to *"clothe themselves with the compassionate bowels"* of God and of His Son (Col 3,12; E 4,32; cf 1 P 3,8). The evangelists speak in the same way: to shut one's heart against one's brethren is to cut oneself off from the love of the Father (1 Jn 3,17); to refuse pardon to a person like oneself is to refuse God's pardon for oneself (Mt 18, 23-35). All the sons of God ought to follow the example of their Father (Lk 6,36) by having a heart like His, moved with compassion for their neighbors (Lk 15,20.31), that is for all men without exception, after the pattern of the exemplary love of the Good Samaritan, which was not only affective but also effective (Lk 10,33). In this way they enter into the movement of divine tenderness, which comes to them from the Father, through Jesus, thanks to the Spirit of love (Ph 2,1), and which carries them toward the happiness that has no end, beyond sin and death, according to the hope expressed in the first Eucharistic Prayer of the Roman Missal: "Though we are sinners, we trust in your mercy and love (in your tenderness)..."

→Child I—Consolation—Fathers & Father III 3 —Grace—Love—Mercy—Milk 1—Mother II 1 —Pardon.

PEB ems

THANKSGIVING

The first reality of biblical history is the gift* of God, gratuitous, superabundant, without return. The encounter with God does not put man simply in the presence of the absolute; it completes him and transforms his life. Thanksgiving appears as the response to this progressive and continual grace* which one day should blossom *in Christo.* At the same time there is an intense awareness of the gifts of God, a spirit of soul permeated with wonder because of God's generosity, a joyous recognition before the divine greatness; thus thanksgiving is essential in the Bible because it is a fundamental religious reaction of the creature when he discovers, in a tremor of joy* and veneration, something of

God*, of His greatness and of His glory*. The capital sin of pagans, according to Paul, is "not to have rendered to God either glory or thanksgiving" (R 1,21). And, in fact, in the mass of hymns created by the piety of Mesopotamia, the sentiment of thanksgiving is rare; while it is very frequent in the Bible and brings out powerful outpourings of the soul.

OT

1. *From the first to the second covenant.* The thanksgiving of the OT announces that of the NT in the measure in which it is always, at the same time as gratitude, a tension toward the future and toward a higher grace. On the other hand, at the time of the new covenant, thanksgiving truly breaks forth, becoming present everywhere in the prayer and the life of the Christians as it had never existed before among the just of the past. Biblical thanksgiving is truly and essentially Christian. It is not exclusively Christian, however, to the extent that, as was written in the OT, "Israelites praise without giving thanks." If the OT does not yet know the fullness of thanksgiving, it is because it has not yet tasted the fullness of grace. If praise*, more spontaneous, more exteriorized, holds therein perhaps a greater place than thanksgiving properly so called, more reflective, more attentive to the actions of God, to His revelation*, it is because the most holy God reveals Himself only progressively, unveiling little by little the amplitude of His action and the depth of His gifts.

2. *Terminology.* To discover thanksgiving in the Bible is at the same time to find joy (Ps 33, 1-3.21), praise and exaltation (Ezr 3,11; Ps 69, 31), glorification of God (Ps 50,23; 86,12). More precisely, thanksgiving is a public confession* of definite divine actions. To praise God is to publicize His magnificence; to thank Him is to proclaim the wonders He performs and to offer witness to His works. Thanksgiving keeps step with revelation*; it is like an echo of revelation in one's heart. Thus it often implies mention of the assembly of the just or of the people gathered to hear it (Ps 35,18; 57,10; 109,30), an invitation to join it (Ps 92,2ff; 105,1f).

In hb. it is especially *tôdah* which expresses this nuance of admiring and grateful confession which English often translates by a word which is much less expressive and not too exact, acknowledge, to thank someone for something. The word which seems to crystallize thanks-

giving in the OT and to translate most exactly the religious attitude aimed at is that of blessing* (hb. *bārak*), which expresses "essential exchange" between God and man. To the blessing of God, who gives life and health to His creature (Dt 30,19; Ps 28,9), responds the blessing by which man, raised by that power and that generosity, thanks his Creator (Dn 3,90; cf Ps 68,20.27; Ne 9,5...; 1 Ch 29,10...).

3. *History of thanksgiving.* There exists a classical literary outline of thanksgiving, to be seen particularly in the psalms, which manifests well the character of thanksgiving as the reaction to an action of God. The confession of gratitude for salvation* obtained develops normally in a "narrative" in three parts; description of the danger experienced (Ps 116,3), anguished prayer (Ps 116,4), remembrance of the wonderful intervention of God (Ps 116,6; cf Ps 30; 40; 124). This literary style is found to be identical throughout the whole Bible, and obeys the same tradition of vocabulary, persisting through the psalms, the canticles, and the prophetic hymns.

If thanksgiving is one, it is because it responds to the unique work* of God. More or less confusedly, every particular kindness of Yahweh is always felt as one moment of a grand history in the process of realization. Thanksgiving carries biblical history and prolongs it in eschatological hope* (cf Ex 15,18; Dt 32,43; Ps 66,8; 96).

Not only does thanskgiving inspire certain very old literary pieces, which summarized the total faith of Israel—the canticle of Moses (Ex 15,1-21) or that of Deborah (Jg 5)—but it is very possible that at the root of the first traditions and even of the whole history of Israel there has been a cultic confession of faith* proclaiming in thanksgiving the great deeds of Yahweh for His people. Thus, from the very beginning, the true faith is a confession in thanksgiving. This tradition constantly expands in the measure in which Israel takes further cognizance of the generosity of God, and the tradition goes on to express itself in all areas: in prophetic literature (Is 12; 25; 42,10...; 63,7...; Jr 20,13) and priestly literature (1 Ch 16,8...; 29,10-19; Ne 9,5-37), in the monumental compositions of the later writings of the OT (Tb 13, 1-8; Jdt 16,1-17; Si 51,1-12; Dn 3,26-45.51-90).

NT

Because it is the revelation and the gift of perfect grace (cf Jn 1,17), the NT, in the person of the Lord, is also the revelation of the perfect thanksgiving rendered to the Father in the Holy Spirit.

1. *The Christian vocabulary.* Christian terminology inherits the tradition of the OT through the LXX. Thanksgiving is inseparable from confession* (gr. *homologeô*: Mt 11,25; Lk 2,38; He 13,15), from praise (gr. *aineô*: Lk 2,13.20; R 15, 11), from glorification (gr. *doxazô*: Mt 5,16; 9, 8), and always, in singular fashion, from blessing (gr. eulogeô: Lk 1,64.68; 2,28; 1 Co 14,16; Jm 3,9). But a new expression, practically unknown in the OT (gr. *eucharisteô, eucharistia*), enters the NT (more than sixty times), showing the originality and the importance of Christian thanksgiving, a response to the grace* (*charis*) given by God in Jesus Christ. Christian thanksgiving is eucharist*; and its perfect expression is the sacramental eucharist, the thanksgiving of the Lord given by Him to His Church.

2. *The Thanksgiving of the Lord.* The supreme act of the Lord is thanksgiving; the sacrifice* which Jesus made of His life in consecrating it to the Father in order that He might sanctify His own (Jn 17,19) is our eucharist. At the last supper and on the cross, Jesus reveals the drive of all His life and that of His death: thanksgiving from the heart of the Son*. The passion and death of Jesus were necessary that He might fully glorify the Father (Jn 17,1), but all His life was an incessant thanksgiving, which sometimes was made explicit and solemn, to draw men to believe and return thanks to God with Him (cf Jn 11,42). The essential object of this thanksgiving is the work of God, the Messianic realization, notably manifested by miracles (cf Jn 6,11; 11,41ff), the gift of His Word which God has made to men (Mt 11,25ff).

3. *The thanksgiving of the disciples.* The gift of the eucharist to the Church expresses an essential truth: only Jesus Christ is our thanksgiving, just as He alone is our praise. It is He first of all who gives thanks to the Father, and Christians afterwards and in Him: *per Ipsum et cum Ipso et in Ipso.* In Christian thanksgiving, Christ is sole model and sole mediator* (cf R 1,8; 7,25; 1 Th 5,18; E 5,20; Col 3,17).

Conscious of the gift they have received, and won over by the example of the master, the first Christians made thanksgiving the warp and woof of their new-found life. The abundance of such manifestations is surprising. There are the canticles of Lk 1 and 2, provoked, like certain canticles of the OT, by lingering and religious meditation upon events. There are the "reflexes" of thanksgiving of the apostles and the first communities (Ac 28,15; cf 5,41; 21,20; R 7,25; 2 Co 1,11; E 5,20; Col 3,17; 1 Th 5,18). There are also the great texts of Paul, so reminiscent of his own "continual" thanksgiving (1 Co 1,4; Ph 1,3; Col 1,3; 1 Th 1,2; 2,13; 2 Th 1,3), taking at times the solemn form of blessing (2 Co 1,3; E 1,3). The whole Christian life, the whole Church life, is for Paul carried along and wrapped in a constant combination of supplication and thanksgiving (1 Th 3,9f; 5,17f; R 1,8ff). The object of thanksgiving through all sorts of happenings and signs remains the same —that which fills the great thanksgiving of the epistle to the Ephesians: the kingdom* of God, the advent of the gospel*, the mystery* of Christ, fruit of the redemption, spread throughout the Church* (E 1,3-14).

The Apocalypse enlarges this thanksgiving to the dimensions of eternal life. In the heavenly Jerusalem*, with the Messianic work fulfilled, thanksgiving becomes pure praise of glory, dazzling contemplation of God and of His eternal marvels (cf Ap 4,9ff; 11,16f; 15,3f; 19,1-8).

→Blessing—Confession—Eucharist I—Grace I —Joy NT II 1—Praise—Prayer II 3, V 2 c.
AR & JG jjk

TIME

The Bible, revelation of the transcendent God, begins and ends with reference to time: "In the beginning God created heaven and earth" (Gn 1,1), and "surely, I come quickly" (Ap 22,20). Thus God is not understood in an abstract manner in the Bible, in His eternal essence, as is the case with Plato and Aristotle, but in His interventions here below which make the history of the world a sacred history. It is because of this that the biblical revelation can answer the religious questions which human consciousness, marked by becoming, asks itself about time; because this revelation is itself historical in its structure.

INTRODUCTION

1. *"In the beginning."* For its beginning Genesis evokes the creative act of God. This act marks an absolute beginning, in such a way that beginning from it duration belongs to the order of created things. This manner of think-

ing breaks completely with the concept of beginning which is found in neighboring paganisms. For example, in the Babylonian poem of the creation, the god Marduk establishes the framework of human and of cosmic time: stars, constellations, cycles of nature; then astronomical, measurable time begins. But before that, in a primordial time which is the model of cosmic time, the gods already had a history in the order of myth, the only sacred history known to Babylonian thought. From a primitive divine couple, Apsu and Tiamat, successive generations had come forth; a struggle had caused the gods to come to blows, and the appearance of the world and of men was the final result of this struggle. Thus the gods are included in one beginning with the entire cosmos as if they were themselves only imperfectly withdrawn from the category of time.

On the contrary, in the biblical Genesis, the transcendence of God is affirmed in a radical fashion: "In the beginning God created..." (Gn 1,1); "on the day when Yahweh God made heaven and earth..." (2,5). There is no primordial time in which a divine history could unroll, for the great scenes of the cosmic battle, in which God faces the forces of chaos (Ps 74,13f; 89,11) do not suggest any history of God Himself, but the history of the world, which God sets in order. The creative act marks the absolute beginning of our time, which is good like the rest of creation: but at this time God already existed. What unrolls in time is His plan for it, which first orders all creation with regard to man and then directs the destiny of man with regard to a mysterious end.

2. *Time and eternity.*

a) Time. Time, the work of God, then serves as framework for a history which concerns us. This is clearly marked in the biblical account of creation*. The seven days of Genesis doubtless have a pedagogical justification: they inculcate the sanctification of the Sabbath*. But they also furnish a religious view of the duration during which the universe was gradually completed. God progressively places His creatures in time. The frame which will finally receive man is gradually filled and man's appearance will give a meaning to all of what had preceded him. From this it can be seen that time is not an empy form, a pure succession of juxtaposed instants. It is the measure of terrestrial duration, and as such it presents itself concretely; first a cosmic duration, polarized by the coming

of man; then a historical duration, marked by the rhythm of generations*, in which man will journey toward his goal.

b) Eternity. God remains transcendent with regard to this twofold duration. Man lives in time; God lives in eternity. The Hebrew word 'ôlam, which is translated in various ways (age, eternity, world...), designates a duration which surpasses human measurement: God lives "forever" "in ages of ages." To make the nature of this duration of which we have no experience understood, the Bible opposes it to the transitory character of cosmic time ("In your eyes a thousand years are like yesterday that has slipped away, like a watch of the night," Ps 90, 4) and of human time ("My days are like the declining shadow...but you, Yahweh, are in glory for eternity," Ps 102,12f). A consideration of this type accents the significance of the divine transcendence which can be seen distinctly expressed in late texts. While Genesis regarded God "at the beginning," in His creative act, Proverbs contemplates Him before time, "from eternity," when there was nothing before Him but Wisdom (Pr 8,22ff). This eternity confuses Job (Jb 38,4); and the psalmist proclaims: "From eternity to eternity you are God" (Ps 90,2). The Bible, then, succeeds in reconciling its idea of the transcendence of God with the certainty of His intervention in history. It thus escapes a double temptation: either divinizing time (the god Chronos of the Greek pantheon), or like Islam, refusing it any significance before God.

OT

In human experience two aspects of time are superimposed one over the other: that over which the cycles of nature rule (cosmic time) and that which unfolds itself in the course of events (historical time). God governs them equally and orientates them together toward the same goal.

I. COSMIC TIME

1. *Measures of time.* God the Creator has established the rhythms which nature obeys: the alternation of day and night (Gn 1,5), the movement of the stars* which command one another (1,14), and the recurrence of the seasons (8,22). The fact that these cycles recur at regular intervals is a sign of the order which

He has put in His creation (cf Si 43). All peoples have taken these cycles as a basis for the measurement of time. From this point of view, the Jewish calendar has no originality except the use of the week* with its final Sabbath*. For the rest it is composed of borrowed elements and appears to have varied widely in the course of the ages. In the OT it oscillates between the solar reckoning and the lunar. The divisions of the year into twelve months correspond to the solar cycle. But the month, by its name and its divisions, follows the lunar cycle since it begins by the new moon (Si 43, 6ff). The Israelite year began at first in the autumn in Tishri (Ex 23,16; 34,22), then in the spring, in Nisan (Ex 12,2). At first years were counted according to determining events: reigns (Is 6,1) or natural happenings (Am 1,1). It is at a late epoch that the idea of an era is adopted: the era of the Seleucids (1 M 1,10; 14,1; 16,14), then in the time of the rabbis, the Jewish year, which begins from the creation of the world.

2. *Sacralization of time.* Cosmic time measured by the calendar is not a purely profane thing. All the ancient religions made it sacred. They recognized a sacred significance in the cycles of nature because they thought divine powers ruled them and revealed themselves through them. This mythical sacralization dictates the establishment of the calendar of feasts* which follows the rhythm of the seasons and of the months. Such a concept of sacred times constituted a permanent temptation for Israel which the prophets denounced (Ho 2,13). But in eliminating all references to polytheistic myths from its religious calendar, the OT has not thereby rejected the natural sacredness of the cosmic cycles.

It has preserved the celebration of the new moon (1 S 20,5; Am 8,5; Is 1,13) and the Pasch of the nomads in the springtime (Ex 12). It has respected the agrarian usages of the Canaanite calendar: the feasts of Azymes in the spring, at the beginning of the barley harvest (Ex 23, 15; cf Dt 16,8); offering of first-fruits* (Dt 26,1) and of the first sheaf (Lv 23,10f); the feast of the harvest, called the feast of Weeks or of Pentecost (Ex 23,16; 34,22; Lv 23,16); the feast of the harvest in the autumn with its rejoicings at the end of the season (Ex 23,16; Dt 16,13; Lv 23,34-43). But revelation has gradually given to these traditional celebrations a new content, which transformed their sacred character. It has made them the memorials of the great acts of God in history. The Pasch and the Azymes

recall the departure from Egypt (Ex 12,17.26f) and the arrival in Canaan (Js 5,10ff); Pentecost*, the covenant on Sinai; the autumn festival, the sojourn in the desert (Lv 23,43). Then new feasts have come to recall other events of sacred history (vg the Dedication: 1 M 4,36-59).

Beyond the year, other longer cycles occur: triennial tithes (Dt 14,28f), sabbatical and jubilee years (Lv 25). The regular cycle of weeks goes on from one feast to another. Finally the religious consecration of time penetrates into the daily cycle where the rituals envisage sacrifices, offerings, and prayers at fixed hours (2 K 16,15; Ez 46,13f; Nm 28,3-8). The entire existence of man is thus enclosed in a network of rites which sanctify it. The place of the sacred calendar in the life of Israel is so important that in offending against it, the persecuting king Antiochus Epiphanes will raise himself up against God Himself (Dn 7,25; 1 M 1,39.43.55), since he will desire to substitute a pagan sacralization for the sacralization of time sanctioned by revelation.

II. HISTORICAL TIME

1. *Cosmic cycles and historical time.* Cosmic time is of a cyclic nature. Oriental or Greek thought was so struck by the insertion of human life in these cycles of the cosmos that they made the eternal return of things the fundamental law of time. Without going all the way to this metaphysical conclusion, Qoheleth was vividly impressed by the same fact: human life is dominated by inescapable times ("a time to give birth and a time to die," Qo 3,1-8), by an incessant repetition of the same events ("That which was will be, that which has occurred will return," 1,9; 3,15). Thus the limits of human effort and even the difficulty of perceiving the action of the divine government in the perpetual return of things are pointed out. But this pessimism is the exception, for the Bible is dominated by another concept of time, which corresponds to its representation of history.

History does not obey the law of the eternal return. It is fundamentally oriented by the design of God which is unveiled and manifested in it. It is marked out by events which have a unique character and which are not repeated and are deposited in the memories of men. Thus gradually enriched by its experience of duration, mankind becomes capable of progress. In this way historical time is qualitatively different from cosmic time, which it assumes and transfigures in the image of man. It has its own measures of important events which are related to human life. In primitive times Israel had a familial notion of duration which was counted by generations* (the very word *tôledôth* practically designates history, Gn 2,4; 5,1; etc.). Beginning with the monarchy, time was reckoned in reigns; eras were to come later. In these historical calculations a certain interest in numbers appears more than once. Because of the lack of reliable data, however, the figures cited do not always correspond with what we now expect from history. Some of them are approximate and schematic (the 400 years of Gn 15,13); others have a symbolic value (the 365 years of the life of Enoch, Gn 5,23). But they show nonetheless the care which the sacred authors had to show revelation as inserted into time.

2. *Sacralization of historical time.* In the pagan religions historical time only possessed sacredness in the measure that a particular event, like the cycles of nature, reproduced the primordial history of the gods as do the cycles of nature. It is a matter of mythical sacredness. On this point biblical revelation makes a radical innovation. God manifests Himself in revelation actually by means of sacred history, and the events from which sacred history is woven are His acts here below. For this reason the time in which these events are recorded has a sacred value by itself not in the fact that it repeats primordial time, when God created the world once for all, but in the fact that it brings novelty to the extent that the steps of God's plan succeed one another, each having its own significance. What confers meaning on these points of time is not however the network of historical factors which are intertwined. Indeed, the Bible is quite unconcerned about this aspect of things, since it is exclusively the divine intention which orients them to a mysterious end, in which time will reach at once its end and its fulfillment.

III. THE END OF TIME

1. *The beginning and the end.* Sacred history, which includes the whole destiny of the people of God, is written between two correlative terms: a beginning and an end. Ancient thought, when it represented human perfection, generally placed it in the beginning as a golden age followed by a progressive deterioration in time. It sometimes envisioned a revival of this golden age with the return of the great year (Vergil's

Fourth Eclogue), which was still bound up with a cyclic conception of time.

The Bible also places a primitive perfection at man's origin (Gn 2). But for the Bible the loss of this initial state is not at all the result of a natural process of cosmic evolution; it is the sin* of man which has caused the entire drama. Thenceforward history is worked out by two contrary movements. On one side there is observed a progressive development of evil, a spiritual decadence, which infallibly provokes the judgment* of God. Thus it was in prehistory, that is, from the beginning to the deluge which is a type of judgment; thus it is in the course of the centuries so that the apocalypses can extend this catastrophic interpretation of time to the present and to the future (Dn 2; 7). But on the other hand, there is a progress toward the good, which infallibly prepares the salvation* of man. Thus was the case in prehistory when God chose Noah to save him and to make a covenant with him. Thus it will be in the end when the primitive perfection will return here below at the end of sacred history, assuredly not through an automatic process of return to the beginnings, but by a sovereign act of God, who will simultaneously accomplish the judgment of the sinful world and the salvation of the just. To snatch Israel from the attraction of paganism and from its concept of human duration, the prophets are going to insist on this end of time and on the moral preparations which it requires.

2. *What the end will be.* The day* of Yahweh, the first clearly expressed eschatological notion (Am 5,18; Is 2,12), appears at first as a constantly imminent threat suspended above the sinful world. Its date, however, though fixed in the secrets of God, remains unknown. In order to designate it, the prophets speak simply of "the end of days" (Is 2,2); or else they oppose to the "first time" the past, a "last time" which will form a contrast to it (Is 8,23). The present period of time, the period of the sinful world, will be ended by a definitive judgment*. Then a new age will begin, of which the texts give us some enchanting descriptions: an age of justice and happiness which will restore here below the perfection of paradise* (Ho 2,20ff; Is 11,1-9). The future will no longer be commensurable with the present. Nonetheless, in the beginning, the prophets did not establish any radical discontinuity between the two: the new times of unlimited duration (Is 9,6) will crown history without leaving the level on which his-

tory presently unfolds. After the exile the difference between the "age (or the world*) to come" and the "present world" was progressively accentuated; the world to come will be inaugurated by the creation* of "new heavens" and of a "new earth" (Is 65,17). In other words, it will be located on a radically new* plane, that of the divine mysteries*, the revelation* of which constitutes the proper object of the apocalypses.

3. *When the end will come.* The apocalypses look indeed with longing toward this end (Dn 9,2), this "time of the end" (11,40), which the hope* of the Jews awaits with impatience. They always perceive it in the near future, succeeding the burning present without transition. But the "times and seasons" fixed by God remain His secret (cf Ac 1,7). The numerical speculations which are proposed in this connection belong to the order of symbolism; for example, the seventy years of Jeremiah (Jr 29,10) and the seventy weeks of years of Daniel (Dn 9), periods whose significance is parallel to that of the sabbatical* year and of the jubilee year (cf Is 61,2; Lv 25,10). By this means the biblical proclamation of the last times is completely set off from the eschatological speculations for which troubled times have always provided occasion. What the OT provides is not a mathematical determination of the date of the birth of Jesus Christ or of the end of the world; it is a vision in depth of the whole of time; past, present, and future, which uncovers its secret orientation and thus reveals its meaning. Man will not be able to draw from it any satisfaction for his restless curiosity, but only an awareness of the spiritual demands required by the time in which he lives.

NT

I. JESUS AND TIME

1. *Jesus lives in historical time.* With Jesus there has come the end toward which the times of preparation were oriented. This ultimate act of God is placed in historical duration in a precise manner: Jesus is born "in the days of king Herod" (Mt 2,1); the preaching of John begins in "the fifteenth year of the reign of Tiberius Caesar" (Lk 3,1); Jesus "gives His testimony under Pontius Pilate" (1 Tm 6,13). Since this last deed is the principal event of sacred history, which has occurred "once for all" (R 6,10; He 9,12), all the confessions of the

Christian faith mention the moment when it took place in human time. Jesus further accepted during His life here below the normal delays which all human maturation demands (Lk 2,40.52). He has fully participated in our experience of time. Only His prophetic consciousness made Him master of the course of events so that He lived with His eyes fixed on the death which it "was necessary" for Him to undergo in order to rise afterwards (Mk 8,31; 9,31; 10,33f p). This is His hour* (Jn 17,1), which obedience to the Father forbids Him to anticipate (Jn 2,4).

2. *The time of Jesus, the fullness of time.* It is essential to grasp the significance of this time of Jesus. From the onset of His preaching He proclaims it with particular clarity: "The times are accomplished and the kingdom of God is at hand" (Mk 1,15; cf Lk 4,21). All during His ministry He urges His listeners to understand the signs of the time in which they live (Mt 16,1ff). Finally He will weep over Jerusalem which has not known the time of God's visitation* (Lk 19,44). Jesus then crowns the waiting of the Jews. With Him there has come "the fullness* of times" (G 4,4; E 1,10). He has introduced into the history of Israel the definitive element which the preaching of the gospel will put clearly in the light: "*Now,* without the Law, the justice of God witnessed by the Law and the prophets has manifested itself" (R 3,21). In the unrolling of the plan of God there has come an event in relation to which everything is defined as "before" or "after": "*Formerly* you were without Christ, strangers to the covenants of the promise" (E 2,12); "*Now* He has reconciled you in His body of flesh" (Col 1,22). The time of Jesus is then not only in the middle of earthly duration; bringing time to its accomplishment, it completely dominates it.

II. THE TIME OF THE CHURCH

1. *Prolongation of eschatology.* In the view of the OT, the end was envisaged in a lump fashion: the plan of God would reach its conclusion by instituting both judgment and salvation here below at the same time. The NT introduces a complexity into the midst of this end. The decisive event of time has come in Jesus; nevertheless it has not yet borne all its fruits. The last times have only been begun, and from the resurrection onward they are expanded in a way which the prophets and the apocalypses

had not explicitly foreseen. In the parables Jesus has already opened to view the journeying of the kingdom* to a future plenitude, a journeying which implied a certain lapse of time (Mt 13,30 p; Mk 4,26-29). After the resurrection the mission which He gives to the apostles presupposes the same prolongation of eschatological time (Mt 28,19f; Ac 1,6ff). Finally the scene of the ascension* sharply distinguishes the moment when Jesus takes His place "at the right hand of God" from the moment when He will again be in glory and consummate the realization of the prophetic promises* (Ac 1,11). Between these two there will be placed an intermediate time, qualitatively different both from the "time of ignorance" in which the pagans were sunk (Ac 17,30) and from the time of tutelage in which the people of Israel had lived up to that point (G 3,23ff; 4,1ff). This is the time of the Church.

2. *Significance of the time of the Church.* This time of the Church is a privileged epoch. It is the time of the Spirit (Jn 16,5-15; R 8,15ff), the time in which the gospel is proclaimed to all men, Jews and pagans, in order that all may benefit from salvation. This is a truly paradoxical situation. On the one hand, this time belongs to the definitive order of things which the Scriptures foretold. For us who have entered into this time by baptism, the "end of time" has arrived (1 Co 10,11). But, on the other hand, it coexists with the "present age" (Tt 2,12), which must pass away as the figure of this world will pass away (1 Co 7,29ff). Conversion to the gospel of Jesus Christ represents for every man a change of era since it is a passage from the "present world" to the "world to come," from the old time which hastened toward its ruin to the new time which journeys to its full expansion. The importance of the time of the Church comes from the fact that it makes this passage possible. It is "the acceptable time, the day of salvation," which is henceforth put within the reach of all (2 Co 6,1f). It is the "today" of God, during which each man is called to conversion and when it is important to make oneself attentive to the divine voice (He 3,7—4,11).

And just as in the OT the plan of salvation unrolled in accordance with the mysterious will of God, so the time of the Church also obeys a certain plan, the ordering of which can be glimpsed from some texts. First there will be "time of the pagans," which will include two aspects. On the one hand, "Jerusalem (symbol of all the ancient Israel) will be trampled upon by the feet of the pagans" (Lk 21,24); and on the other, these same pagans will gradually be converted to the gospel (R 11,25). Finally there will come the time of Israel*: then in its turn "all Israel will be saved" (R 11,26), and then will come the end. Such, in its complete unfolding, is the mystery of time which covers all human history. Jesus, who dominates it, is alone capable of opening the book with the seven seals in which the destinies of the world have been written (Ap 5).

3. *Sacralization of the time of the Church.* The time of the Church is of itself sacred from the very fact that it belongs to the "future world." Nonetheless it is clear that in order to be effective the sacralization of time by men must be marked by visible signs, the "sacred times" and the religious feasts*, whose annual return espouses the rhythms of cosmic time. Already the OT had sought a new source of sacredness for these signs in the commemoration of the great deeds of sacred history. Since the coming of Jesus here below, these deeds themselves no longer have a merely figurative* value, since the event of salvation has been placed in historical time. It is this unique event then which the Church actualizes now in the cycles of its liturgical calendar in order to sanctify human time. Each Sunday, the day* of the Lord (Ap 1,10; Ac 20,7; 1 Co 16,2) becomes within the framework of the week* a celebration of the resurrection of Jesus. The celebration takes on a more solemn character when the date of the Pasch, the feast *par excellence* (1 Co 5,8) and anniversary of the death and resurrection of the Lord, makes its annual return (cf 5,7). Thus one finds in the NT the first lineaments of the Christian liturgical cycles which will be developed in the Church. All of human life will, by this means, be placed in connection with the mystery of salvation which has come in history, the true exemplary time which will finally be substituted for the "primordial time" of pagan myths.

III. THE CONSUMMATION OF THE AGES

1. *Christian eschatology.* The time of the Church is not however sufficient in itself. In comparison with the OT, it already forms part of the "last times"; but it is extended in like manner toward a fulfillment which is to come

and is oriented toward an end which is the day* of the Lord. Now that the Spirit* has been given to men, all of creation longs for the final revelation of the sons of God and for the redemption* of their bodies (R 8,18-24). Only then will the work of Christ be accomplished by Him, who is the Alpha and the Omega, "He who is, who was, and who will be" (Ap 1,8). On that day the "present age" and the time of the Church will end together. The first will end by foundering in a definitive catastrophe when the seventh angel pours out his cup and a voice will cry: "It is finished" (16,17). The second will end by arriving at its total transfiguration when the new heavens and the new earth will appear (21,1). Then there will be neither sun nor moon to mark the time as in the old world (21,23), since men will have entered into the eternity of God.

2. *When will the end come?* Jesus has not made known the date when this consummation of the ages, this end of the world, is to come. It is a secret of the Father alone (Mk 13,32 p), and it does not belong to men to know the times and the seasons which He has fixed by His own authority (Ac 1,7). The infant Church, in its ardent hope for the parousia of the Lord, lived in the continual impression of its proximity: "The time is short" (1 Co 7,9); "Salvation is now nearer to us than when we came to the faith, the night* is advanced, the day* is near" (R 13,11f). This impression was so strong that, even while employing this language, St. Paul was obliged to put the Thessalonians on guard against any precise reckoning of the prophetic day (2 Th 2,1ff). Gradually, under the pressure of experience, men became aware of the lengthening of the "last times." But the imminence of the return of the Lord has remained an essential component in the psychology of hope*, since the Son of Man comes like a thief in the night (Mt 24,43; 1 Th 5,2; Ap 3,3). The time of the Church, which unfolds under our eyes, is itself marked by signs foreshadowing the end (2 Th 2,3-12; Ap 6—19). Thus the NT completes the prophetic vision of human history which the OT had sketched out.

→Day of the Lord—Feasts OT I; NT II—Figure OT II 1—Fulfill OT 3; NT 3—Fullness 1—Generation—Hour — Memory — New II — Plan of God—Stars 1.2—Tradition—Week—Word of God OT II 1 c. 2 c—World OT I—Worship NT III.

MJL & PG jpl

TONGUE

Man uses his tongue to communicate with his fellow men and to express to God the sentiments of his heart*. The loss of the use of one's tongue can be a divine punishment (Lk 1,20; Ps 137,6); restoring speech to the mute is a Messianic work (Is 35,6; Mk 7,33-37), whereby they can sing the praises of God (Lk 1,64).

1. *Good and evil use of the tongue.* "Death and life are in the power of the tongue" (Pr 18, 21). This ancient theme is re-echoed by the sages (Pr; Ps; Si) even to the time of James: "We use the tongue to bless our Lord and Father, and we use it to invoke curses upon our fellow men who are made in God's likeness" (Jm 3,2-12). From an evil tongue come lies*, fraud, duplicity, slander, and calumny (Ps 10,7; Si 51,2-6). It is a serpent (Ps 140,4), a sharpened razor (Ps 52,4), a keen sword (Ps 57,5), a deadly arrow (Jr 9,7; 18,18). To the realistic question "Who has never sinned by the tongue?" (Si 19, 16), there is the hoped for response, "Happy is he who has never sinned by his tongue!" (25,8). Moreover, the hope is expressed that on the day* of Yahweh "a deceitful tongue" will no longer be found among the remnant* of the elect (Zp 3,13).

This hope is not in vain. From now on the tongue of the just man can be described as pure silver (Pr 10,20); it extols justice and praises* God (Ps 35,28; 45,2); it announces His almighty power (Is 45,24). As do the lips*, the tongue reveals the heart of man, and his works* ought to correspond to his words*; "Let us not love in words and with the tongue, but truly and in deed" (1 Jn 3,18; cf Jm 1,26).

2. *Diversity of tongues.* The peoples of the world are of "every tongue." This concrete expression of the Bible designates the diversity of cultures. It is not simply an expression of the intellectual riches of mankind; it is a principle of incomprehension among men, an aspect of the mystery of sin*. The tower of Babel* (Gn 11) suggests a religious significance in the diversity of tongues; i.e., that the sacrilegious pride* of men in constructing their city without God resulted in this confusion of languages. Pentecost* overcomes the division of men (Ac 2, 1-13); the Holy Spirit* appears upon the apostles in tongues of fire so that the gospel will be understood in the tongues of all the nations. Thus men will be reconciled by the sole tongue of the Spirit, which is charity. The charismatic*

gift of tongues among the apostles is both an ecstatic prayer* in praise of God (Ac 2,4; 10,46) and a form of prophecy* announcing to men the wonderful things of God (Ac 2,6.11; 19,6). In order to regulate the use of this charism in the Church, Paul, while praising ecstatic prayer, expresses his preference for prophecy because of its greater usefulness (1 Co 14,5). The manifestations of Pentecost show that from its very inception the Church is catholic, addressing itself to men of all tongues and uniting them in one praise of the wonders of God (cf Is 66,18; Ap 5,9; 7,9...). Thus "every tongue will confess that Jesus is Lord, to the glory of God the Father" (Ph 2,11).

→Babel/Babylon 1 — Charisms — Hebrew — Human Speech—Lie—Lips—Nations OT I 2, III 2; NT II 1a—Pentecost II 1.2 d—People *A* II 5; *B* II 5; *C* II—Silence 2.

PdS mjm

TRADITION

Existence of tradition is a fact common to all human societies. Their spiritual continuity is assured by the fact that ideas, customs, etc., are consistently transmitted (*tradition = transmission*) from one generation to another. From a religious point of view in particular, beliefs, rites, formularies of prayer and song, etc., are transmitted with singular care. Religious tradition, furthermore, in the societies which surround the biblical world, is integrated with the entire set of human traditions which constitute civilization.

Modern vocabulary uses the word *tradition* in two different senses. It designates by this term a content transmitted from age to age (for example, the cultic tradition of Egypt). It also designates a method of transmission, characterized by its quite thorough stability. Writing plays only a secondary role, sometimes no role at all, in this method. (Hence Sumerian civilization and even more so, the purely oral civilizations, can be classed as traditional.) With regard to this general fact, the tradition proper to biblical revelation presents both resemblances and original peculiarities.

OT

I. TRANSMISSION OF A SACRED DEPOSIT

There is no doubt that a transmission of a sacred deposit, hence a tradition, takes place in Israel under the old Law. In conformity with the ordained individuality of the people of God*, this deposit embraces all aspects of life: historical recollections as well as beliefs rooted therein, forms of prayer as well as a wisdom to govern daily life, cultic rites and gestures as well as customs and law. It is the transmission of this deposit which gives Israel its characteristic features and assures its spiritual continuity from the age of the patriarchs even to the threshold of the NT.

If this deposit is sacred, this is not merely because it is a legacy of past generations, as in all human traditions. It is above all because of its divine origin. At the foundation of beliefs, there is a revelation* given to Israel through God's messengers. At the foundation of law and customs regulated by law, there are positive prescriptions announced in God's name by the trustees of His will. These positive elements deriving from revelation obviously do not exclude certain more ancient elements borrowed from the oriental milieu and taken on by revelation itself. But revelation alone is the foundation of the sacred character of the tradition dependent on it.

Defined thus in its connection with the revelation which constitutes its originality, the tradition of the people of God combines two complementary characteristics. There is stability. Its fundamental elements are fixed: matters of beliefs, of law, and of worship* (monotheism, the doctrine of the covenant*, customs coming from the patriarchs and Mosaic law, etc.). And there is progress. Revelation itself develops in proportion as new divine messengers complete the work of their predecessors in relation to the concrete needs of their times. This progress follows naturally the stride of history. But it is not submissive to the mere chance of cultural evolution, as is the case in other religious traditions, in which syncretism is the rule. Here again the tradition of Israel affirms its originality.

II. METHOD OF TRANSMISSION

1. *Literary forms and life milieux.* In order to transmit itself, this sacred deposit necessarily

takes a literary form. Accounts, laws, maxims, hymns, rituals, etc., are the means of expression. But such forms are themselves determined by usage, and by virtue of this they are traditional. They correspond in large part to the literary forms used in the cultures of neighboring peoples (Canaan, Mesopotamia, Egypt). Yet the individuality of Israel's doctrinal tradition shows itself here. Biblical tradition has its own way of treating certain common types, such as laws* or prophetic oracles. It has its own original store of expressions and set phrases, to which all its authors have recourse to a greater or lesser extent. It has its favorite forms, suited to the message it must transmit. A study of these forms is, therefore, indispensable to an understanding of the tradition itself. For this allows one to grasp the lived history of its formulation.

This study also allows one to see by what channels the tradition transmits itself through the years. Indeed, the forms which the tradition takes correspond directly both to the functions it fulfills in the life of God's people and to the milieux which carry the tradition. These functions are the teaching of the priests*, guardians of the Law and of worship; the preaching of the prophets*; and the practical wisdom* of the scribes. As regards the various milieux, each of them has its own traditions and preferred forms. Yet one also notices frequent interference due to contacts among diverse milieux and to the foundational unity of the Israelite tradition itself.

In the beginning, the traditional material is transmitted orally under forms suited to this method of transmission. Such methods are: religious accounts connected with sanctuaries or feasts; juridical formularies; rituals, hymns, prayer formularies; priestly or prophetic discourses; wise maxims, etc. Finally the written texts are born in the framework of this oral tradition and are nourished largely from it. Thus the biblical tradition slowly crystallizes into sacred writings*. With time these latter assume increasing importance. Composed under the influence of the Holy Spirit*, they furnish God's people a divine rule of their faith and life

2. *Writing and tradition.* In Judaism near the time of Christ, the legacy of the ancient tradition is essentially conserved under the written form. Yet the people* of God is not merely an aggregate of believers grouped about a book*. It is an organized institution. For this reason

there subsists within it, and parallel to Scripture, a living tradition. In its own way, this tradition continues that of past ages, though it has no just claim to the same normative authority as the Scriptures possess. We find this tradition among the priestly milieu, among the doctors, and indeed in the midst of those sects into which Judaism split. It is made the object of a true technique of transmission, based essentially on personal contact between the master and his disciples*. The master transmits, delivers (*māsar*). The disciple receives (aram. *qabbel*) that which he should in turn repeat (hb. *šānāh*; aram. *tenah*). This is tradition strictly so called (hb. *qabbala*; gr. *paradosis*). It is known in the NT. Mark cites the "tradition of the elders" (Mk 7,5.13 p). Paul cites the "tradition of my fathers*" (G 1,14). This legacy joins with Scripture to form "the traditions which Moses left" (Ac 6,14). For the scribes set the origin of these traditions far in the past in order to strengthen their authority. Moreover, their oral transmission cradles a new literature, which develops about the Bible, from the translations of the Bible in Greek (Septuagint) and Aramaic (Targums) up to the rabbinic writings, passing through the apocryphal books and the literary productions of the sects (vg Qumrân). But the late tradition to which these books witness must not be confused with the primitive oral tradition from which the canonical writings were nourished.

NT

I. TRADITION AT THE ORIGINS OF CHRISTIANITY

1. *Jesus and the "tradition of the elders."* From the start, Jesus serves notice of His independence with regard to Jewish tradition of His time. No essential of the traditional legacy conserved in the Scriptures is in question: the Law and the prophets are not to be abolished, but fulfilled (Mt 5,17). But the "tradition of the elders" does not enjoy the same privilege. This tradition is a thoroughly human thing, which even threatens to annul the Law (Mk 7, 8-13). Jesus therefore allows His disciples to shake it off. And He proclaims its decadence.

Yet at the same time, Jesus Himself acts as a master, not repeating a received tradition as the scribes do, but teaching* as one who has authority (cf Mk 1,22.27). And His disciples* receive a mission to repeat His teachings (Mt 28,19f).

Moreover, He is an innovator even in His actions. He pardons sins (Mt 9,1-8). He communicates the grace of salvation to men. He inaugurates new signs, and ordains that they be repeated after Him (1 Co 11,23ff). He is thus, by His words and actions, the origin of a new tradition which supplants that of the ancients as a basis of interpretation of the Scriptures.

2. *The apostolic tradition.* It is actually within the Church that we verify the existence of this tradition expressed in a vocabulary borrowed from Judaism. This fact is especially notable in Paul, whose first normal training was in the techniques of Jewish pedagogy. To the Thessalonians, he has "given instruction" in the name of the Lord Jesus (1 Th 4,2) and they have "received his teaching" (1 Th 4,1). He adjures them to "hold fast to the traditions (*paradoseis*) which they have received from him, whether by letter or by word of mouth" (2 Th 2,15). Paul says to the Philippians: "What you have grasped, received, and heard from me and seen verified in me, this is what you should practice" (Ph 4,9). He speaks precisely to the Corinthians: "I have transmitted to you from the very first that which I myself received" (1 Co 15, 3). "I received from the Lord that which I in turn transmitted to you" (11,23). The first statement pertains to a doctrinal summary regarding the death and resurrection of Christ. The second pertains to a liturgical account of the Supper. The object of the apostolic tradition consists, therefore, in actions as well as words.

Such facts allow the thought that, both before Paul and then in the framework of his teaching, the essential materials of this tradition were submitted to a transmission technique analogous to that of the Jewish tradition. But these materials constitute the very substance of the life of the Church, the stuff of the gospel*, the rule of Christian faith and conduct. Thus Luke is able to write in the preface of his work that "many have undertaken to compose an account of the (gospel) events, just as those who were witnesses and servants of the Word from the beginning have transmitted them" (Lk 1,2). The gospel collections, therefore, do no more than record in writing an already existent tradition. Parallel to these collections, the life of the Church preserves the actions and practices bequeathed by Christ and utilized by the apostles.

3. *From tradition to Scripture.* Apostolic tradition has its organs of transmission. Foremost of these are the apostles*, who "received" the tradition from Christ Himself. Paul is among these, thanks to the revelation on the road to Damascus (G 1,1.16). Then there are the masters whom the apostles commission and to whom they entrust the authority in the Christian communities (1 Tm 1,3ff; 4,11; 2 Tm 4,2; Tt 1,9; 2,1; 3,1.8). This tradition goes along in forms congruent with its nature and with the various roles it plays in the Christian communities. It ranges from accounts concerning Jesus to professions of faith (1 Co 15,1ff), from liturgical formulas (1 Co 11,23ff; Mt 28,19) to common prayers (Mt 6,9-13) and hymns about Christ (Ph 2,6-11; E 5,14; 1 Tm 3,16; Ap 7,12; etc.), from rules of life coming from Jesus to outlines of baptismal homilies (1 P 1,13...), and so on. Study of the apostolic tradition thus requires a constant attention to the literary forms evidenced in the NT. In effect, this Testament, in its diversity, is an occasional formulation of that tradition, brought about in a definitive way under the charism* of inspiration. As in the OT, the tradition issued from Christ and passed on by the apostles finally results in Scripture.

II. CHARACTER OF CHRISTIAN TRADITION

1. *Its source: the authority of Christ.* In the OT, the tradition finally crystallized in Scripture was founded on the authority of God's messengers. Tradition in the NT is distinguished from the "tradition of the ancients" (Mt 15,2) and from all "human tradition" (Col 2,8) by the fact that it is founded on Christ's authority. Christ has spoken and acted (Ac 1,1). He has given His disciples a normative interpretation of the ancient Scriptures (Mt 5,20-48). He has instructed them in what they will have to teach in His name* (28,20), giving them a living example* of what they must do (Jn 13,15; Ph 2, 5; 1 Co 11,1). The doctrine preached by Him was not His own, but His who sent Him (Jn 7, 16). In like manner, the apostolic tradition always keeps in itself this mark of Christ the Savior, whose spirit, prescriptions, and manner of acting it exactly conserves. But if, for want of a precise statement from Christ (cf 1 Co 7,25), an apostle gives out some personal advice to solve a practical problem in Christian life, he does this with the same authority. For has he not the "thought of Christ" (1 Co 2,16)? The Spirit* of the risen Christ effectively lives on in His own to teach them all things (Jn 14,26) and

to guide them in complete truth (Jn 16,13). There is, then, no difference between the authority of the apostles and that of their master. "Who hears you hears me; who rejects you rejects me, and rejects Him who sent me" (Lk 10,16).

2. *Apostolic tradition and the tradition of the Church.* The apostolic tradition thus enjoys a unique authority, which reaches by the same sweep to the Scriptures in which this tradition is crystallized. Yet it must not be opposed to the authority of the Church in such a way as to make the latter an entirely human tradition, analogous to that Judaic tradition which Christ abolished. There is real continuity from apostolic tradition to Church tradition.

a) *Continuity in the object transmitted.* Though not, properly speaking, creative, the tradition of the apostolic age still constituted a milieu in which revelation was progressing, insofar as the apostles explained the meaning of Jesus' words and actions. The ecclesiastic tradition is solely conservative; its norm is already fixed in the NT: "Keep the deposit" (1 Tm 6, 20; 2 Tm 1,12,14). This deposit is the apostolic tradition. It can no longer receive truly new elements. Revelation* is closed. Its development in the history of the Church is of another order. This development does no more than explicate what is virtually contained in the apostolic deposit. Naturally, Scripture, the inspired witness to the apostolic tradition, enjoys a capital role in the faithful conservation of that deposit. Scripture is the essential touchstone. Yet we have no assurance that all the elements of the original deposit are explicitly recorded therein. Moreover, the living tradition alone preserves one thing which Scripture cannot deliver: profound understanding of the inspired texts. This is the work of the spirit, acting in the Church. Thanks to this, the Word* fixed in Scripture remains the ever living Word of Christ the Lord.

b) *Continuity in the organs of transmission.* The tradition of the Church is transmitted not in an anonymous collectivity, but in a hierarchically structured society. This society is no mere human organization, but the very body* of Christ, governed by the Spirit, in which the functions of government perpetuate over the centuries those of the apostles, exercising their authority. Here again the pastoral epistles establish norms (vg 1 Tm 4,6f.16; 5,17ff; 6,2-14; 2 Tm 1,13f; 2,14ff; 3,14—4,5; Tt 1,9ff; 2,1,7f).

These texts show that the criterion of authentic apostolic deposit preserved in Church tradition is not the Scripture alone, but, conjointly, the guaranty of those who have received a commission to watch over it and grace to fulfill this role. The same Spirit which inspired the Scriptures continues to assist these men (1 Tm 4, 14; 2 Tm 1,6).

c) *Continuity in the fundamental and fixed literary forms of the tradition.* This permanence of forms sensibly translates the permanence of functions and atmosphere of life in the Church. No doubt literary forms in ecclesiastical literature will evolve with times and cultures. But, beyond this evolution, the most diverse works will remain deeply stamped with the forms of the apostolic tradition fixed in the NT. And certain very ancient documents, though not enjoying an authority identical with that of Scripture, can yet most directly echo the apostolic tradition itself (creedal and liturgical formulas of the post-apostolic age).

This said, it is important to make two remarks: 1) Ecclesiastical tradition must evolve in its contingent forms in order to preserve the apostolic deposit by adapting its presentation to the historical times and mentalities of the men to whom the deposit is transmitted; 2) It is important not to attribute to Church tradition in the strict sense all the contingent forms used and every tradition which was able to arise in later days—such traditions have strongly varied worth. But it is evident that we must not seek from the NT a direct solution of all the theological problems posed by this ecclesiastic tradition. For, by definition, this tradition emerged only after the Canon of inspired books was closed.

→Disciple—Law *B* III 5; *C* I 1—Memory 4—Old Age 2—Pharisees 1—Priesthood OT III o—Prophet OT I 2, III 2—Revelation—Teach —Writing.

PG dfb

TRANSFIGURATION

1. *The situation.* In the gospels, the transfiguration of Christ is situated at the decisive moment when Jesus, recognized by His disciples as Messiah*, reveals to them how He is going to fulfill His work. His glorification will be a resurrection. Hence it implies passing through

suffering and death (Mt 17,1-9 p; cf 16,13-28 p). This context gives the transfiguration scene its significance in Christ's life and its fruitfulness for the life of the Christian. Jesus appears here as fulfilling the Scriptures (cf Lk 24,44ff) in their prophecies about the Messiah. He is the Servant of God and the Son of Man.

2. *The mystery.* To witness this event Jesus chooses those who will witness His agony: Peter (cf 2 P 1,16ff), James, and John (Mk 14, 33 p; cf 5,37). This scene recalls the theophanies which Moses* and Elijah* witnessed on the mountain* of God (Sinai-Horeb, cf Ex 19,9; 24,15-18; 1 K 19,8-18). Not only does God manifest His presence, speaking in the midst of the cloud* and the fire* (Dt 5,2-5). Jesus also appears to His disciples, in the presence of Moses and Elijah, transfigured by the glory* of God.

This glory frightens them with that religious fear which arises in the presence of the divine (cf Lk 1,29f). But it also elicits a suggestive reflection from Peter, who expresses joy in the presence of His glory whose Messiahship he has confessed. God comes to dwell with His own, as the prophets of Messianic times had foretold. Yet the glory is not that of the last day*. It only illumines Jesus' garments and face*, as once it irradiated the countenance of Moses* (Ex 34,29f.35). It is the very glory of Christ (Lk 9,32), who is the well-beloved Son*, as the voice from the cloud proclaims. At the same time this voice ratifies the revelation Jesus has made to His disciples and which is the object of His conversation with Moses and Elijah: the "exodus" for which Jerusalem will be the point of departure (Lk 9,31), the passage through death*, necessary to His entrance into glory (cf Lk 24,25ff). For the divine voice commands them to listen* to Him who is the Son, the elect of God (Lk 9,35).

The Word resounding on the new Sinai reveals that a new Law* is going to replace the Law given of old. The Word recalls three prophecies of the OT. One concerns the Messiah* and His divine sonship (Ps 2,7). A second refers to the Servant* of God, His elect* (Is 42,1). The third announces a new Moses* (Dt 18,15; cf Jn 1,17f): "Your God Yahweh will raise up...a prophet* like me; to Him you will listen." To listen is, in effect, to listen to the Word made flesh. In Him the believer sees the glory of God (cf Jn 1,14).

3. *Aim and result of the event.* The transfigu-

ration confirms the confession of Caesarea (Mk 8,29) and consecrates the revelation of Jesus as the suffering and glorious Son of Man whose death and resurrection will fulfill the Scriptures. It reveals the person of Jesus, the beloved and transcendent Son, who possesses the very glory of God. It manifests Jesus and His Word* as a new Law. It anticipates and prefigures that paschal event, which, through the way of the cross, will usher Christ into the full flowering of His glory and filial dignity. This anticipated experience of Christ's glory is designed to support the disciples in their sharing in the mystery of the cross*.

By baptism Christians are made sharers in the resurrection mystery prefigured by the transfiguration. They are called, even here below, to be ever more thoroughly transfigured by the Lord's action (2 Co 3,18), while awaiting total bodily* transfiguration at the final coming (Ph 3,21). During their earthly participation in Christ's sufferings*, every authentic encounter with the Lord Jesus plays the same role in support of their faith* as did the transfiguration in support of the disciples' faith.

→Apparitions of Christ 1—Clothing II 3—Cloud 4—Elijah NT 3—Glory IV 3—Light & Dark NT I 3—Moses 3—Mountain III 1—White 2.

PdS dfb

TREE

In the eyes of man the tree is the tangible sign of that vital force which the Creator has spread throughout nature (cf Gn 1,11f). Every springtime, the tree announces the rebirth of nature (Mt 24,32). Cut down, it shoots up again (Jb 14,7ff). In the arid desert, it marks the places where water* allows life (Ex 15,27; Is 41, 19). It nourishes man with its fruits (cf Dn 4, 9). There is sufficient similarity here for one to liken persons to a verdant tree, whether the just man whom God has blessed (Ps 1,3; Jr 17, 7f), or the people upon whom He has heaped His favors (Ho 14,6f). It is true that here are good and bad trees, which one recognizes by their fruits*; the bad only deserve to be cut down and thrown into the fire; likewise with men, at the time of God's judgment* (Mt 7,16-20 p; cf 3,10 p; Lk 23,31). Apart from this general meaning, the symbolism of the tree develops in the Bible in three directions.

1. *The tree of life.* Using a symbol current in Mesopotamian mythology, Genesis places in the ancient Paradise* a tree of life* whose fruit communicates immortality (Gn 2,9; 3,22). In connection with this first symbol, the false wisdom which man usurped in attributing to himself the "knowledge of good and evil" is also represented as a tree whose fruit is forbidden (Gn 2,16f). Led astray by the deceiving appearance of this tree, man ate some of its fruit (Gn 3,2-6). As a consequence, the path to the tree of life is now cut off for him (Gn 3,22ff). But the whole unraveling of the scroll of sacred history will show how God has restored to man access to the tree. In prophetic eschatology, the holy land is described, in the last times, as a paradise regained; its marvelous trees will furnish men with nourishment and restorative power (Ez 47,12). From now on, wisdom*, for the man who grasps it, is a tree of life which gives him happiness (Pr 3,18; 11,30; cf Si 24,12-22). And finally, in the NT, Christ promises that those who remain faithful to Him will eat of the tree of life which is in the paradise of God (Ap 2,7).

2. *The tree of the kingdom of God.* The oriental mythologies were acquainted with the symbol of the cosmic tree, a figurative representation of the universe. This symbol is not taken over into the Bible. But it consciously likens human empires, which hold so many peoples under their shadow*, to an extraordinary tree: it rises up to the sky and descends to the lowest depths, it shelters all the birds and the beasts (Ez 31,1-9; Dn 4,7ff). This is an artificial grandeur, for it is founded on pride*. The judgment of God will strike this tree (Ez 31,10-18; Dn 4,10-14). But the kingdom* of God, born of humble seed, will itself become a great tree in which all the birds will come to nest (Mt 13,31f p).

3. *The tree of the cross.* The tree can become a sign of a curse when one uses it as a gibbet for those condemned to death (Gn 40,19; Js 8,29; 10,26; Es 2,23; 5,14): the weight which it supports defiles the sacred earth, for it is a curse from God (Dt 21,22f). Now Jesus wanted to take upon Himself precisely this curse (G 3, 13). He bore our sins in His body upon the wood of the cross* (1 P 2,24)—there He has nailed the sentence of death which was passed against us (Col 2,14). At the same time, the tree of the cross became the "wood which saves" (cf Ws 14,7): the way is open which

leads to paradise regained where the tree of life will bear fruit for us (Ap 22,2.14). The ancient sign of a curse has become itself this tree of life: *Crux fidelis, inter omnes Arbor una nobilis; nulla silva talem profert, Fronde, flore, germine* (liturgy of Good Friday).

→Cross I 3.4—Fruit—Kingdom NT II 1—Life III 1—Paradise— Shadow II--Wisdom OT III 3.

PEB & PG jjk

TRIAL

If trials hold an important position in the Bible, and if God often figures in them under the diverse roles of accused, judge, plaintiff, and lawyer, it is not because Israel was more inclined than others to wrangling and juridical proceedings. It is because the God of the Bible wishes justice* and reasonableness. In creating man* to His image*, He expected from him an acknowledgement in thanksgiving*, an adherence in freedom, a communion* in truth. Even after man had sinned, God did not despair in His heart for His creature and his intelligence. After having been led to reject him, God will first stir Himself to pursue man; and if God must condemn him it will not be without listening to him, but after having convinced him that he is in the wrong and that God is in the right. If God triumphs, it will be by the sole strength of the truth*. A trial supposes a disagreement, a litigation between the parties. It also supposes a minimum of agreement on some fundamental principles. And as long as the trial is still under way and the sentence has not yet been rendered, the hope remains of a reconciliation*; even with the verdict already pronounced, the light from earlier discussion persists and, reducing "every tongue to silence" (R 3,19), makes the justice* of God flash forth.

As a charter and statement of the covenant*, the OT is completely occupied with the debate which goes on between God and His people. The coming of Jesus closes the debate by an unheard of undertaking on God's part: confounding sin, He offers to sinners the opportunity of justifying* themselves by simply adhering to His Son by faith*. This sudden turn of events gives rise to a new phase: henceforth, it is about the trial of Jesus and according to the role which He takes in it that the trial of man before God will be played out.

I. GOD AND HIS PEOPLE ON TRIAL IN THE OT

1. *The sinner on trial with God.* To enter into a trial with God, to suspect Him of lying and wickedness, is the fundamental temptation, the one which the serpent slipped into the heart of Eve: "Not at all! You will not die." God is playing with you (Gn 3,3ff); it is the first reaction of Adam the sinner: "The woman whom you gave me as companion...," all the evil comes from you (3,12); it is the undying sin* of Israel in the desert, forgetting that its God saved it from Egypt and throwing doubt upon His power and His faithfulness. The episode of Meribah, on leaving the Red Sea (Ex 17,7; the proper name brings to mind the root *rîb*, which means trial), announces all the failings of the "perverse generation" (Dt 32,20) and all the trials brought against Yahweh by His people (Jr 2,29). It is always a question of faith*: to refuse to believe is to give oneself reasons against God, to put Him in question, to tempt Him.

2. *God on trial with His people.* God cannot suffer this questioning of Him, an insult to His love. In His turn He "enters into trial" with Israel (Ho 4,1; 12,3; Is 3,13; Mi 6,2; Jr 2,9). The trial supposes, according to the prophetic tradition, the covenant* and the signs which it offers to faith: God enters into a trial procedure with His chosen people. However, to the extent that the covenant is revealed to be at the center of the universe, the trial expands to become "the trial of the nations*" (Jr 25,31), then that of all false Gods (Is 41,21-24; 43, 8-13; 44,6ff).

The trial is a public explanation in the most grandiose and most vast background possible: "the mountains, the hills, the foundations of the earth" (Mi 6,1f; cf Ps 50,4). The entire world is called to testify: Kedar, and the islands of Cyprus (Jr 2,10) as well as the first passer-by come from Jerusalem or Judah (Is 5,3).

God presents Himself here, accompanied by His witnesses* (Is 43,10; 44,8), in the role of accuser (Ps 50,7.21; Ho 4,1-5), but also as victim at the end of His resources, having exhausted all other means (Mi 6,3f; Jr 2,9...; Is 43,22-25). He invites Israel to produce its arguments (Is 1,18; 43,26; Mi 6,3) and gets only deceitful denials (Jr 2,35). No one can answer Him, "no living thing can justify itself" before Him (Ps 143,2). It remains for Him only to pronounce sentence which should only be condemnation (Ho 2,4; 4,1f; Jr 2,9.29), which makes it evident that He alone can speak and that right is on His side (Is 41,24; 43,12f; 44,7; Ps 50,7.21; 51,6). Yet, at the very heart of the condemnation another recourse is had, an appeal implying a radical readjustment: "Come, and let us discuss: even though your sins were like scarlet, they will become white as snow" (Is 1,18; cf Ho 2,16-25).

3. *Job on trial with God.* If to put God under accusation is the capital sin*, it must be admitted that it is nevertheless a frequent temptation. And if not justified, it can be at least fatal because of God's disconcerting ways. Do not suffering* and the evil of the world put God on the defensive? Job is the exemplary case of the temptation pushed to paroxysm, and the whole poem seems to be nothing but a trial arranged against God. Because it is from God Himself that all the evil of Job's suffering comes (Jb 6, 4; 10,2; 16,12; 19,21), is it not for God to justify Himself? Job knows full well that it is absurd to imagine he has the right on his side against God (9,1-13), but if he could "plead his case" (9,14), "justify his conduct before Him" (13, 1f), simply appear before Him, he knows that his cause would triumph (23,3-7) and that his "vindicator...will defend him" (19,25ff). We have here the language used in trials, but in reality Job is stopped at the precise moment when his complaint would become a trial, where his question would become an accusation. He cannot understand God, he does not yield to the temptation to accuse Him. He maintains that God is on his side and that he remains His servant*.

It is normal for man to put formidable questions to God (cf Jr 12,1), and Job did not sin in raising them. However, it is necessary that he learn to let his questions drop. God Himself intervenes, man understands his blindness (38, 1f) and withdraws all his questions (42,6). Without needing to formulate a sentence, God's presence is sufficient to explain everything.

II. IN JESUS CHRIST, GOD CONCLUDES THE TRIAL

The trial brought into existence by the sin of man and pursued by the justice* of God finds its final point in Jesus Christ. The divine solution is a marvel of boldness; but it rigorously respects the demands of reason and of law, without which the trial would be meaningless. Sin* is here condemned without recourse and without compromise. Under all its forms and under any regime, that of paganism or of Judaism, it appears, in the meeting with Christ, as the supreme evil, the radical ingratitude to God, and the irreparable corruption of man (R 1,18—3,20). The holiness* manifested through the gospels of Jesus Christ lays bare the lie* hidden in every heart (3,4), reduces every tongue to silence* (3,19), and causes the victory of the truthful God to blaze forth (3,4).

But this triumph is at the same time the salvation* of man. Losing his own trial, the sinner who accepts his defeat and renounces the defense of his own personal justice* (Ph 3,9) in order to believe in the pardon, the grace*, and the justice* of God in Jesus Christ thereby gains his justification* (R 3,21-26), his price, and his worth before God. Belief in Jesus Christ and in the redemptive power of His death* is in fact at one and the same time disavowal of one's own sins, responsible for this death, and recognition of oneself as the object of the incomprehensible love* of a God capable of handing over His only Son for the sake of His enemies (R 5,6-10; 8,32). Man renounces any defense or accusation against God by abandoning himself to love and thanksgiving*. The trial is ended by a complete reconciliation*.

III.   THE TRIAL OF JESUS

This reconciliation takes place only in faith*, and the object of this faith is Christ in His death* and His resurrection*. To overcome the spontaneous movement which makes us accusers of God, we must recognize in Jesus the well-beloved Son delivered over by His Father. But the reaction of the sinner is to refuse the generosity of God, to reject Him whom He sends, to see blasphemies* in the miracles which He brings forth as proof of His mission. The trial directed by Caiaphas and pursued before all the tribunals of Jerusalem* is the perfect type of the trial aimed by man against God since the time of the first sin. Unable to entrust himself to God, man turns against Him all the testimonies which he receives from His love.

1.   *The gospel accounts* of the passion all place at the center of the trial the decisive question: is Jesus the Christ, the envoy of God charged with the salvation of the world (Mt 26,63 p; 27, 11 p; Jn 19,7)? They all strive to underline the certainty that Jesus is held to God by a bond which no force, that of men or that of death, is

able to break: among His adversaries the presence of a conscious refusal of the truth*, in the false testimonies of the Jewish trial (Mt 26,59), in the cowardice of Pilate (27,18.24), in the vanity of Herod (Lk 23,8-11), in the preference given to Barabbas (Lk 23,25), but also the excuse (Lk 23,34; Ac 3,24) for a situation in which God deliberately delivers up His Son and abandons Him (Ac 2,23; Mt 27,46) to the power of sin (Lk 22,53; Jn 14,30f; 2 Co 5,21).

2.   *The gospel of John* marks even more clearly the exemplary character of the trial of Jesus. This story is unfolded throughout His whole public life: after the first miracle at Jerusalem, "the Jews seek a quarrel with Jesus" (Jn 5,16) and they already foresee His death (5,18; cf Mk 3,6). All the discussions which are carried on between the Jews and Him are like the drawing up of a trial in which Jesus presents His proofs; that of John (5,33), His own signs and works, all finally constituting the unique testimony He is eager to reveal, that of God (5,31-37; 8,13-18). In this trial, the same thing is at stake as for the synoptics: the personality, divine and Messianic, of Jesus, His title of Son* of God (5,18; 8,25ff; 10,22-38; 19,7).

3.   *The reconsideration of the trial of Jesus* is the first public act of the Church, and that review remains her permanent mission. In raising Jesus from the dead, God has solemnly demonstrated the justice of His case and has confounded His adversaries. He has made "Lord and Christ" (Ac 2,36) Him whom they had condemned to death. Yet, in place of a demonstration of force, God, by making this resurrection an appeal to faith* and conversion, shows that His victory is one of His forgiveness. This double message, the triumph of God over sinners and the salvation which this victory brings to sinners, is the essential theme of the preaching of the newborn Church (Ac 2,36.38; 3,13.19; 4,10.12; 5,30f; 10,39f.43). It coincides exactly with the explicit theology of Paul in the epistle to the Romans.

Such is the testimony which the Christian bears to the world*. Like the apostles in Jerusalem, his mission is to show to the world the injustice of the trial which it does not cease to try against God and Christ. It is normal that the Christian be handed over to tribunals, accused and delivered by his neighbors (Mk 13, 9,13 p); it is fated that the world hate* and persecute* the disciples of Christ (Jn 15,18ff) and that their existence be exposed to the world's unpitying gaze (1 Co 4,9). It is necessary that they be "always ready with their defense whenever they are called to account for the hope* that is in them" (1 P 3,15). But this trial is not theirs, it is that of Christ who is pursued and to whom they should bear witness. Their testimony, therefore, is not their own, but that of the Holy Spirit* (Mk 13,11). Like an invincible advocate, the Paraclete*, through their lips and their life, "will confound the world", by making the injustice of their cause and the justice of Jesus Christ obvious to believers (Jn 16,8-11).

→Judgment—Justification—Lie I 1—Paraclete 3—Persecution—Witness—Wrath B OT II 2.

JG jjk

TRIAL/TEMPTATION

The word *trial* calls to mind two series of realities. One is geared toward action: an examination, a competition. The other is a certain recoil in affliction: a sickness, a bereavement, a failure. And if the word has passed from the first meaning to the second, it is doubtless because, according to a wisdom already religious, suffering is felt to be a test that reveals man.

The active sense is primary in the Bible: *nsh, bhn, hqr, peirazein, diakrinein*, to stay with the principal roots, mean "to put to the test," to try to know the reality hidden under uncertain appearances. Like an alloy, like an adolescent, man has "to undergo his tests." In itself, it contains no sense of affliction.

There are three actors who can take the initiative in any trial. *God* tests man to know the depths of his heart (Dt 8,2) and to give him life (Jm 1,12). *Man* also tries to prove to himself that he is "like God," but his efforts are the result of seduction and end in death (Gn 3; R 7,11). It is at this point that the trial becomes temptation and a third character intervenes: the *Tempter*. Thus trial is meant to lead to life (Gn 2,17; Jm 1,1-12), while temptation's "child is death" (Gn 3; Jm 1,13ff; a trial is a gift of grace and temptation is an invitation to sin.

The experience of the trial-temptation is not simply of the moral order. It is inserted into a religious and historical drama. It makes our liberty* act in time in the presence of God and Satan*. In the different stages of God's plan*, man is interrogated. In the first place this experience is lived out by the people of God: then

the reflection of the wise men discovers its meaning for every human condition: and finally Christ will resolve the drama. Similarly trial/temptation is seen first as the work of God; then, toward the end of the OT, Satan is seen as the personal author of the first temptation; but the meaning of this drama is not fully revealed until the single combat between Christ and the Tempter.

OT

I. THE TRIAL OF GOD'S PEOPLE

In Israel's consciousness, the drama begins with her election, in the promise that she will become the people of God through the covenant. But the hope thus raised will have to be purified.

1. At first, man is called to return the promise*. It is *the trial of his faith*. Such is the trial of Abraham, Joseph, Moses, Joshua (He 11,1-40; Si 44,20; 1 M 2,52). The typical event is doubtless the sacrifice of Isaac (Gn 22). For God to fulfill His promise, man's faith must freely accept to submit himself in the obedience that adjusts two wills.

After leaving Egypt Israel experiences the temptation to unbelief*. They doubt (Meriba) the saving presence of God in the trial (Massa) in the desert* (Ex 17,7). This refusal to believe leads to a judgment*; and the Passover is accomplished only for the faithful generation*, which alone inherits the promised land.

The experience in the desert also allows us to give its theological value to the expression *to tempt God*. Either man wants to get out of the trial, calling upon God to put an end to it (cf the antithesis Ex 15,25 and 17,1-7); or he puts himself in a situation from which there is no way "of seeing if" God is capable of taking him out of it; or again, he persists in spite of evident signs in demanding other "proofs" of the divine power (Ps 95,9; Mk 8,11ff).

2. With the assembly from which He has taken a people, God concludes a covenant*. In this second period, the trial bears on faithfulness* to the covenant. It can be called *the trial of love*. The people did well in choosing to serve their God (Js 24,18), but their heart is deceitful. The trial obliges love to declare and prove itself. It purifies the heart*. It is a work of long duration to which God puts a hand (the image of fire* and smelter: Is 1,25f). Slowly the codes

are elaborated (Covenant, Holiness, Priestly) in which is heard the call to holiness* which God gives to His people (Lv *passim*). A new judgment corresponds to this new trial. The exile* and the return to the desert punish the idolatry* which is an adultery (Ho 2).

3. Only a small remnant* will come out of captivity* after the trial. The divine action is the same in Israel's ordeal before Yahweh (1 K 19,18) and before Jesus (R 11,1-5). In all these cases, if the trial comes to a stop, it is solely by grace*. The captivity and the long period which follows it show how the promise is humanly unrealizable. Interminable delays, contradictions, persecutions, even weakness of the people call into question less their faith in Yahweh's word or their fidelity to His covenant than the very fulfillment of His promise. Thus from the exile to the coming of the Messiah the trial of the small remnant is principally a *trial of hope**. The kingdom seems to extend indefinitely in time. The temptation is of the present moment, of "this age," the temptation of the world*. The people of God, in danger of being secularized, are more aware of the action of Satan*, the "prince of this world" (Jb 1—2). This probation of hope is the most intimate, the most purifying. The nearer God is, the more He tests (Jdt 8,25ff). The testing will end in a last judgment: the coming of the kingdom*, the entry of the age to come into this world.

II. THE TRIAL EMANATING FROM THE HUMAN CONDITION

The OT has again a double message to give us.

1. *The personal trial.* The reflection of the sages, in transferring the trials of the people to the personal level, insists on another aspect of trial: suffering*, particularly of the just. Here trial is most acute—and God's presence is at its closest—for man is confronted no longer with the impossible but with the absurd. At this degree of sharpness the temptation is no longer to doubt God's power, to be unfaithful to Him, or to prefer the world to Him; it is that of insult, that of blasphemy*, which is Satan's way of giving testimony to God.

The Book of Job opens and ends the discussion in the mystery of God's wisdom, not as an alibi, but in a confused acknowledgment that trial gradually adjusts man to the mystery of God (cf Gn 22). Some rather clear lines of response are presented in the poem of the Servant* (Is 52,13—53,12), and above all in the book coming from the great tribulation (Dn 9,24-27; 12,1-4; Ws *passim*). The trial seems insoluble on the individual level; its source is outside of man (Ws 1,13; 2,24), for it is a natural fact pertaining to the whole human race. But only a person will make it issue in life; someone over whom Satan has no hold and who will be united to the "multitude" by substituting himself for it. The judgment will take place at the coming of the Servant.

2. *The trial of mankind.* These conclusions, in which the imprint of the sacerdotal reflection is felt, reflect those which, in the accounts of Genesis describing the beginnings, make us penetrate the depth of the human condition. Election* is finally the most expressive revelation of God's gratuitous love, of His liberty. Thus it evokes in man the greatest liberty in his response.

Trial is justly the field left to test this response. Gn 2 shows in a picturesque way this gratuitous solicitude for the king of creation who is man. Such a love of election is not imposed, it is chosen; hence the trial through the tree* of knowledge (Gn 2,17). The fundamental human condition is thus revealed: man is fully responsible* in this way only by the constant possibility of his choosing God, whose "image" he is by vocation.

Now Adam chooses himself as god (Gn 3,5). It is because between the trial and the choice the crisis has intervened, the temptation, of which the ultimate personal cause is Satan* (Gn 3; cf Jb 1—2). It is evident that temptation is more than trial; it is sin that "took the advantage" and led to death (R 7,9ff). New elements have made their entrance: the evil one, who is also the liar, appears as seducer. Man chooses his solitude* only because he believes he will there find life. If he finds only nudity and death, it is because he has been deceived. His ordeal is fundamentally therefore a fight against the lie*, a battle to choose according to truth* where only the sensation of liberty* is felt (Jn 8,32-44). This is the last answer in the reflection of the wise men.

Humanity is engaged in a trial which is too much for it and which it will overcome only by the effect of a promise which is grace (Gn 3,15), by the coming of "the" offspring that will bring the trial to its victorious conclusion.

NT

I. THE TRIAL OF CHRIST

Christ was put by Satan in the situations in which Adam and the people had succumbed and in which the poor* seemed crushed. In Him trial and temptation coincide and are overcome, for in undergoing them Jesus brings to successful issue the love of election which brought about trial and temptation.

Christ is "the" lineage according to the promise, the first-born of the new people. In the *desert** (Lk 4,1f), Jesus triumphs over the tempter on his own ground (Lk 11,24). He is the man* who is at last nourished substantially by the Word* of God as well as "Yahweh the Savior" whom His people continue to tempt (Mt 16,1; 19,3; 22,18).

Jesus is the faithful king, the good shepherd who loves His own until the end. The *cross** is the great trial (Jn 12,27f) where God "gives proof" of His love (3,14ff).

Jesus is the small remnant, the one in whom the Father concentrates His love of election. It is in this filial assurance that He is the enemy of the *world** as well as its vanquisher (Jn 15,18; 16,33).

Jesus is the Servant, the Lamb of God. By bearing men's sin on the cross, He transforms the temptation of blasphemy into a filial plea and the absurd death into *resurrection** (Mt 27,46; Lk 23,46; Ph 2,8f).

As the new Adam and image of the Father, He is tempted as the head. The temptation comes between the theophany and the exercise of His mission (Mk 1,11-14). All throughout He will meet temptation in counterpoint to the Father's will: His parents (Mk 3,33ff), Peter (Mk 8,33), spectacular signs (Mk 8,12), the temporal Messianism (Jn 6,15). Finally, the last stage of His mission will have to be inaugurated with the ultimate temptation, that of the agony (Lk 22,40.46). Thus vanquishing the tempter from the beginning to the end of His trial (Lk 4,13), Christ finally puts the new humanity in its true condition: the filial vocation (He 2,10-18).

II. THE TRIAL OF THE CHURCH

From Christ's trial the Church comes forth as the multitude justified by the Servant (Is 53,11). And her mission follows the same course as that of Christ (2 Tm 2,9ff; Lk 22,28ff). Baptism, by which the Passover of Christ becomes that of the Church, is a trial (Mk 10,38f), and gives notice of trials to come after it (He 10,32-39).

Here the terminology for *trial* is mingled with that of *suffering** (*thlipsis*-tribulation, *diôgmos*-persecution*) and of *patience** (especially *hypomonē*-constancy). Its tone in the NT is first eschatological before being psychological. The proximity of the Lord's return brings to paroxysm the contrast of light and darkness. The Church is the place of trial, the place where persecution should strengthen fidelity (Lk 8,13ff; 21,12-19; Mt 24,9-13) and where man comes out of tribulation "tried."

This trial of the Church is apocalyptic; it reveals the realities hidden from the carnal man, and the degree of responsibility entrusted to each one in the great mission which comes from the Father: Christ (He 2,14-18), Peter (Lk 22,31f), the disciples (Lk 21,12f), the whole faithful Church (Ap 2,10). In this sense trial and mission culminate in martyrdom*. But the great eschatological combat, which is the trial proper to the Church, reveals also the true author of temptation: God tries His own, only Satan tempts them (Lk 22,31; Ap 2,10; 12,9f). The Church after her trial unmasks the seducer, the accuser, by testifying through her Paraclete*, the victorious Spirit who leads her to the end of the Passover (Ap 2—3; Lk 12,11f; Jn 16,1-15). That is why she appears, in the apocalyptic literature, simultaneously persecuted and saved (Dn 12,1; Ap 3,10; 2 P 2,9). Trial is therefore the condition of the Church, which is still to be tested, although she is already pure; still to be reformed, although she is already glorious. The temptations which are properly the Church's come most often from the neglect of one of these two components.

III. THE TRIAL OF THE CHRISTIAN

1. The preaching of the gospel is part of the eschatological tribulation (Mt 24,14). Trial is therefore particularly necessary for those who receive the ministry of the Word (1 Th 2,4; 2 Tm 2,15); otherwise they are hawkers (2 Co 2,17). Trial is the sign of mission (1 Tm 3,10; Ph 2,22). Hence the discernment of false ambassadors (Ap 2,2; 1 Jn 4,1).

On the psychological level, God sounds the hearts and puts them on trial (1 Th 2,4). He merely permits temptation (1 Co 10,13). This comes from the tempter (Ac 5,3; 1 Co 7,5; 1 Th 3,5) through the world* (1 Jn 5,19) and, above all, through money (1 Tm 6,9). That is why we must pray that we may not "enter" into temptation (Mt 6,13; 26,41), for it leads to death (Jm 1,14f). This attitude of filial prayer is diametrically opposed to that of tempting God (Lk 11,1-11).

Trial—and temptation in which one does not succumb in a trial—is ordered to life. It is a gift of life in Jesus Christ: "Yes, all who wish to live piously in Christ will be persecuted" (2 Tm 3,12). It is an indispensable condition for growth (cf Lk 8,13ff), for sturdiness (1 P 1, 6f in view of the judgment), for the manifestation of truth (1 Co 11,19: the reason for the Christian divisions), for humility (1 Co 10,12); in a word, it is the very way of the interior Passover, that of hopeful love (R 5,3ff).

Hence to be a "tried" Christian or to experience the Spirit is one and the same. Trial disposes to a greater gift of the Spirit, for He now achieves by trial His work of liberation. Thus freed, the tried Christian knows how to discern, verify, "try" everything (R 12,2; E 5,10). This new sense of discernment is the Spirit (1 Jn 2,20.27). Here is the theological source of the examination of conscience, which is not spiritual arithmetic but dynamic discernment by which each one is tried in the light of the Spirit (2 Co 13,5; G 6,1).

2. The Bible attempts to give to trial a theological meaning. The trial is passage "to God" through His plan. The diverse aspects of the trial (faith, fidelity, hope, liberty) converge in Christ's great trial, which is continued in the Church and in every Christian and terminates in a cosmic childbirth (R 8,18-25). The affliction of the trial takes its meaning in the eschatological conflict.

In the plan of God who aims to divinize man in Christ, trial and its satanic exploitation, temptation, are inevitable. They lead from liberty offered to liberty lived, from the election to the covenant. Trial adjusts man to the mystery of God, and to man wounded; the nearness of God is the more painful in proportion to its intimacy. The Spirit makes one discern in the mystery of the cross the passage from the first to the second creation, the passage from egoism to love. The trial is paschal.

JCo gsa

TRUTH

Today's language calls a thought or word true when it conforms to the real. Something which has reality is itself called true when it reveals itself, when it is clear and evident to the intellect (true, *a-lēthēs*=not hidden). This strictly intellectual Greek approach is ordinarily operative among us. But the Bible conceived truth differently. The biblical notion of truth is founded on the religious experience of encounter with God. This concept of truth has, nevertheless, gone through a considerable evolution. Truth in the OT is primarily fidelity to the covenant; but in the NT truth will be the fullness of revelation hovering about the point of concentration, the person of Christ.

OT

'emet (truth) is formed from the word *'āman* (cf the liturgical Amen*, vg 2 Co 1,20). The basic meaning of *'āman* is to be reliable, certain, worthy of confidence. Truth then, is the quality of something stable and proven, something reliable. A true peace (Jr 14,13) is a secure, lasting peace. A true road (Gn 24,48) will surely lead to a determined objective. The phrase "in truth" sometimes (Is 16,5) means unalterable or perpetual. When truth is applied to God or man, it will often be best translated as trustworthiness; for it is a person's trustworthiness that elicits our confidence.

1. God's *'emet* is linked with His historical intervention on behalf of His people. Yahweh is the trustworthy *God* (Dt 7,9; 32,4; Ps 31,6; Is 49,7). The importance of this attribute comes clear only in the context of the covenant and the promises*. "Yahweh your God is God, the God worthy of trust who keeps His covenant of love forever with those who love Him" (Dt 7, 9). The entire eighty-ninth psalm, apropos of the Davidic covenant, is devoted to the praise of

God's trustworthiness. The basic sense of this work is most apparent in Ps 132,11 ("Yahweh swore *'emet* to David; He will not depart from it"). The oath*, called *'emet*, is hereby qualified as inviolable.

'emet is often associated with *ḥesed* (vg Ps 89; 138,2) to indicate God's basic covenant attitude. It is a gracious covenant in which God was never wanting (Ex 34,6f; cf Gn 24,27; 2 S 2,6; 15,20). Elsewhere faithfulness is joined to justice (Ho 2,21f; Ne 9,33; Ze 8,8) or to sanctify (Ps 71,22). In these cases there is a more general meaning, without precise reference to the covenant. In many psalms, the divine steadfastness is presented as a source of protection, a refuge for the just man seeking divine aid; hence the images of rampart, armor, and breastplate (Ps 91), which attract attention to the firmness and solidity of the divine assistance (cf Ps 40, 12; 43,2f; 54,7; 61,8).

'emet is also a characteristic of *God's Word* and *His Law*. Because the divine promises guarantee the perpetuity of David's house, David says to Yahweh: "Your words are truth" (2 S 7,28). The psalms praise the truth of divine law (Ps 19,10; 111,7f; 119,86.138.142.151.160). The last verse indicates that truth is all that is essential and basic in the Word of God; namely, that God's Word is irrevocable and everlasting.

2. *Man's 'emet*. Here also a fundamental attitude of faithfulness (cf Ho 4,2) is at issue. "Men of truth" (Ex 18,21; Ne 7,2) are men of trust; but the two texts add *fearing God*, and therefore place this moral evaluation in a religious and Yahwistic context. Ordinarily *truth* used of men applies directly to their *faithfulness to the covenant* and to divine law. Truth thus describes the entire moral posture of the just. Hence the parallelism with perfection (Js 24,14), with an undivided heart (2 K 20,3), the good and the right (2 Ch 31,20), right and justice (Is 59,14; cf Ps 45,5), and holiness (Ze 8,3). "To do the truth" (2 Ch 31,20; Ex 8,9), "to walk in truth" (1 K 2,4; 3,6; 2 K 20,3; Is 38,3) is to observe faithfully the Lord's law (cf Tb 3,5).

"To deal kindly and truly" (Gn 47.29; Js 2, 14) is an expression used for personal, human dealings. It means to act with good will, loyalty, and with consistent kindness. *'emet* is also to exercise equity together with Justice* (Pr 29, 14; Ez 18,8; Ze 7,9) and to be completely honest in speech. But here again the basic meaning of *'emet* appears: a sincere tongue* "endure forever" (Pr 12,19).

3. *Revealed truth*. The sapiential and apocalyptic traditions add a partially new dimension to the notion of truth, that of wisdom; i.e. revealed truth—ideas that will turn up in the NT. Some psalms (25,5; 26,3; 86,11) use the expression "to walk in God's truth"—an indication that the truth in question is not merely the framework of moral behavior, but the Law* itself, which God informs us is to be obeyed. Priests must transmit "true teaching" (Ml 2,6), the teaching* that comes from God. *Truth* becomes synonymous with *wisdom*: "Acquire truth and do not sell it. Get wisdom and instruction and understanding" (Pr 23,23; cf 8,7; 22,21; Qo 12,10). "Fight for the truth to the death" (Si 4,28 LXX).

Because *truth* denotes the plan and will of God, the word verges on the secret or mysterious* (Tb 12,11; Wm 6,22). At judgment time, the just "will understand the truth" (Wm 3,9). This is not in the sense of experiencing directly God's faithfulness to His promises, nor of seeing the person of God Himself, but rather of grasping in some fashion God's providential plan* for men. Daniel's "Book of Truth" (Dn 10,21) is where God's plan is registered; God's truth is His plan revealed (9,13); a heavenly vision or its explanation (8,26; 10,1; 11,2), the true faith, the religion of Israel (8,12).

Judaic apocalyptic and wisdom traditions continued the use of the term *truth* in the same sense. For the Qumrân community "understanding the truth of God" is an understanding of mysteries (Hymns of Qumrân: 1QH 7,26f), a knowledge that derives from correctly interpreting the law. Conversion to truth (*Manual of Discipline*: 1 QS 6,15) is "conversion to the law of Moses" (5,8). Truth is a revealed teaching with moral implications. Therefore truth is opposed to any form of iniquity. The "sons of truth" (4,5) follow "the ways of truth" (4, 17). Truth for Qumrân is the totality of religious ideas involved in being sons of the covenant.

NT

1. *Biblical heritage*. Much more than is the case elsewhere in the NT does Paul's notion of truth (*alētheia*) resemble the LXX meaning. For Paul uses truth in the sense of sincerity (2 Co 7,14; 11,10; Ph 1,18; 1 Co 5,8) or in the phrase "to tell the truth" (R 9,1; 2 Co 12,6; E 4,25; 1 Tm 2,7). The formula "God's truthfulness," that is, God's faithfulness to His promises, is profoundly biblical (R 3,7; cf 3,3;

15,8; 2 Co 1,18ff: the promises* of our faithful God have their "yes" in Christ). *Alētheia* is likewise used in the sense of moral truth, rectitude of life: it is opposed to injustice (1 Co 13, 6), it is synonymous with justice* (E 5,9; 6,14), it denotes the type of character Paul expects to find among his Christians (Col 1,6; 2 Co 13,8). For Paul, even the judgment* of God will bear the imprint of truth and justice (R 2,2).

The antithesis between "the truth of God" and the falsity of idols* (R 1,25; cf 1 Th 1,9) is inspired by the Jewish polemic against pagan idolatry (Jr 10,14; 13,25; Ba 6,7.47.50), for the true God is the living, reliable God; who both hears His people and saves them.

2. *The truth of the gospel.* The concept of Christian truth appears in the gospel where it reflects both the sapiential and apocalyptic ideas of revealed truth. The Jews prided themselves on possessing the explicit formulation of this truth in their Law (R 2,20) where they found the entire will* of God recorded (2,18). For the Jewish expression *the truth of the Law*, Paul substitutes *the truth of the gospel** (G 2,5.14) or *the word of truth* (Col 1,5; E 1,13; 2 Tm 2,15). Truth is the Word* of God preached* by the apostle (2 Co 4,2.5); and it is as much the object of revelation* (2 Co 4,2) as is God's mystery* (R 16,26; Col 1,26; 4,3).

a) *Truth and faith.* The gospel message is directed to men who must hear the Word (E 1, 13; R 10,14) and repent to arrive at knowledge* of the truth (2 Tm 2,25). While faith* is acceptance of the truth of the gospel (2 Th 2,13; Tt 1,1; cf 2 Th 2,12; G 5,7; R 2,8), love* of the truth (2 Th 2,10) is also required. "Arriving at knowledge of truth" in later texts (1 Tm 2,4; 2 Tm 3,7; cf He 10,26) becomes a stereotyped expression for adhering to the gospel, embracing Christianity; since believers are precisely those who know the truth (1 Tm 4,3), the Christian faith (Tt 1,1).

b) *Truth and Christian life.* The Catholic epistles describe believers as born to new life through the word of truth (Jm 1,18; 1 P 1,23), because they have sanctified their souls* (1 P 1,22) through obedience* to truth at time of baptism*. They must not, therefore, stray from this truth once they accept it (Jm 5,19); but with an eye to the final coming of Christ they must consolidate the truth they now possess (2 P 1,12). They must permanently desire the milk* of the word to grow up to salvation* (1 P 2,2).

Thus, Paul adds, a Christian clothes* himself with the new* man and achieves the holiness* demanded by truth (E 4,24).

c) *Sound teaching and error.* Polemic against heretics in the pastoral epistles gives a new twist to the concept of truth by making it mean *sound doctrine* (1 Tm 1,10; 4,6; 2 Tm 4,3; Tt 1,9; 2, 1) in opposition to the fiction (1 Tm 1,4; 4,7; 2 Tm 4,4; Tt 1,14) of teachers of lies* (1 Tm 4,2). Such teachers have turned their backs on truth (Tt 1,14; cf 1 Tm 6,5; 2 Tm 2,18; 4,4); they even stand up against it (2 Tm 3,8). But the Church of the living God remains "the pillar and foundation of truth" (1 Tm 3,15).

d) There is a close connection between the *truth and Christ.* The apostle does not preach an abstract doctrine, but rather the person of Christ Himself (2 Co 4,5; cf G 1,16; 1 Co 1,23; 2 Co 1,19; 11,4; E 4,20; Ph 1,15); Christ "manifest in the flesh...proclaimed to the pagans, believed throughout the world." Christ is the truth of which the Church is the custodian: He is the mystery* of piety* (1 Tm 3,16). Christ, the truth the gospel preaches, is not, then, a celestial being in a gnostic sense, but the Jesus of history, dead and risen for us. "Truth is in Jesus" (E 4,21).

3. *St. John.* John's theology is above all a theology of revelation*; hence the prominence of truth. Johannine *alētheia* is frequently interpreted in the Platonic or gnostic sense, as if it meant the very being of God, the divine revealing itself to man. John, however, never calls God Himself truth, a usage which would be essential in the preceding systems. Actually all John does is develop the apocalyptic and wisdom traditions of a revealed truth, a theme taken up elsewhere in the NT; Johannine emphasis, however, is much more on the revealed character and the interior power of truth.

a) *The Father's Word and Christ, the truth.* For John truth is not the being of God itself, but the Father's Word* (Jn 17,17; cf 1 Jn 1,8: "Truth is not in you"; and 1,10: "His Word is not in you"). The Word which Christ heard from the Father (Jn 8,26.40; cf 3,33) is the truth He comes to "proclaim" (8,40.45f) and for which He comes to "give testimony" (18,37; cf 5,33). Truth is both the Word Christ Himself addresses to us and that Word which should lead us to believe in Him (8,31f.45f). The difference of revelation here and in the OT is conspicuous:

"The Law was given through Moses. The Grace*
of the truth has come to us through Jesus Christ."
(1,17), because with Him and in Him is revelation* complete and final. While the devil is the
father of lies* (8,44) Christ Himself declares
the truth (8,45); He is "full of the grace of the
truth" (1,14). The great Christian innovation
is the fact that Christ is Himself the truth (14,6);
not insofar as He is God, but because, as Word
made flesh, He has in Himself the fullness of
revelation, letting us know the Father (1,18).
Jesus explains the meaning of this title when
He puts it between two others: He is "the Way,
the Truth and the Life." He is the Way* that
leads to the Father, precisely because He, the
man Jesus, as Truth, passes on to us in Himself
the revelation of the Father (17,8.14.17) and
because in this way He communicates divine
Life* to us (1,4; 3,16; 6,40.47.63; 17,2; 1 Jn
5,11ff). Indirectly this title also reveals the
divine person of Christ: if, alone among men,
Jesus can be the Truth for us, it is because He
is at the same time the Word, "the Word who
is nearest the Father's heart" (Jn 1,18), the only
Son.

b) The Spirit of truth. Once His revelation
to the world has ended (Jn 12,50), Jesus announces to His disciples the coming of the Paraclete*, the Spirit of truth (14,17; 15,26; 16,13).
For John the fundamental office of the Spirit is
to bear testimony to Christ (15,26; 1 Jn 5,6),
to lead the disciples to truth in its entirety (16,
13), to recall to their memory* all that Christ
said; that is, to make them grasp its true meaning (14,26). Since the Paraclete's role is to make
men comprehend Christ's truth in faith, the
Spirit is Himself called "truth" (1 Jn 5,6): He, as
witness to Christ, makes truth present in the
Church; for her the Spirit is "the doctor of truth"
(Tertullian).

c) Truth and holiness. John forcefully emphasizes the part that truth should play in the
life of the believer. The Christian ought to
strive to "be of the truth" (Jn 18,37; 1 Jn 3,19).
Having arrived once and for all by faith at the
new life* (cf Jm 1,18; 1 P 1,22f), he ought to
try to be habitually under the influence of the
truth dwelling in him (2 Jn 4), in order to become a man born of the Spirit (Jn 3,5.8). Only

the man who thus abides* in the Word* of Jesus
will come to a genuine knowledge of the truth
and to an internal freedom from sin which is
the product of this truth (Jn 8,31f). For faith
is a purifying agent (Ac 15,9), as is the Word of
Christ (Jn 15,3). Faith brings victory over the
evil one (1 Jn 2,14). When the believer lets the
seed of the Word "abide" actively in him, he
cannot sin (1 Jn 3,9). He is made holy* in the
truth (Jn 17,17.19).

Thus John sees in *alētheia* the interior principle of a virtuous life. He goes back to old
biblical phrases, such as, "to do the truth" (3,
21; 1 Jn 1,6), "to walk in the truth" (2 Jn 4;
3 Jn 3f); but he endows them with the fullness
of Christian meaning by making the expressions
mean "to observe the commands of Christ"
(2 Jn 6), "to allow all one's actions to be guided
by truth and faith." Loving one's brothers "in
truth" (2 Jn 1; 3 Jn 1) is loving them by the
power of the truth which abides in us (2 Jn 1ff;
cf 1 Jn 3,18). Adoration "in the Spirit and
in the Truth" (Jn 4,23f) is adoration* which
springs from within but does not thereby exclude exterior worship; it is worship* inspired
by the Spirit and by the truth of Jesus, worship
which the Spirit of truth activates in those He
has regenerated. Jesus-Truth thus becomes the
New Temple where the distinctive worship of
messianic times is to be celebrated. Finally, truth
has apostolic implications for the believer who
should cooperate with the truth (3 Jn 8) and apply
himself with the Church to the work of the internal
expansive force of the gospel message.

The Christian meaning of *truth* therefore, is
not the boundless area of being which we must
conquer by the powers of the mind. It is the
truth of the Gospel, the revealing Word of the
Father, present in Jesus Christ and illuminated
by the Spirit, which we must welcome in faith,
so that it may transform our lives. This truth
shines out for us in the person of Christ who is at
once the mediator and the fullness of revelation;
and it is in the sacred books that this truth of salvation is passed on to us authentically.

→Adoration II 3—Amen 2—Error—Faith—
Faithfulness—Heresy—Know—Lie—Light &
Dark NT III 1—Lips 1—Oath—Paraclete—
Witness—Word of God.

IdlP dfb

U

UNBELIEF

Unbelief concerns the people of God and so is different from idolatry* which characterizes pagan nations* and demands a conversion to faith* in God. The existence of unbelievers among the people of God has always been a scandal* for men of faith. The unbelief of an Israel confronted with Jesus Christ should cause "incessant sorrow" (R 9,2) in the heart of every Christian.

Unbelief is not simply the denial of God's existence or the rejection of Christ's divinity. It also includes failure to recognize the signs and witnesses of the divine Word*, and a refusal to obey it. Not to believe, according to the etymology of the Hebrew word *to believe*, is not to say "Amen" to God. It is a refusal of the relation which God wants to establish and maintain with man. This refusal expresses itself in various ways. The godless* man calls God's existence into question (Ps 14,1); the mocker questions His active presence in the course of history (Is 5,19); the weak-hearted questions His love* and His power; the rebel questions His sovereignty and His will*, etc. Unbelief is quite different from idolatry, which is essentially radical, and admits of degrees and can coexist along with a certain amount of faith. The line of demarcation between faith incredulity is discernible not so much between different men, but rather within the heart of each man (Mk 9,24).

I. UNBELIEF IN ISRAEL

To avoid relating the entire history of faith* whose obscure opposite is unbelief, it will be sufficient to set forth two major situations of the chosen people which are characteristic of the twofold way in which incredulity can take place: in the desert* where they lack the goods of faith—and in the promised land where they already possess the prefiguration of these goods.

1. *The murmuring of the Hebrews.* The historians use various expressions to designate the incredulity of the people in the desert: "rebels" (Nm 20,10; Dt 9,24) who balk and are recalcitrant (Nm 14,9; Dt 32,15); a "stiff-necked people" (Ex 32,9; 33,3; Dt 9,13; cf Jr 7,26; Is 48,4); and especially "murmurers." John takes up this last expression to characterize the Jews and disciples who refuse to believe in Jesus (Jn 6,41.43.61). Two passages treat of this principality: Ex 15—17 and Nm 14—17. In this inhospitable desert the people are afraid of dying of hunger* (Ex 16,2; Nm 11,4f) and thirst (Ex 15,24; 17,3; Nm 20,2f), and they miss the good fleshpots which they ate in Egypt. Or else they are sickened by the manna* and they become impatient (Nm 21,4f). Or again they fear the enemies who bar their entry into the promised land (Nm 14,1; cf Ex 14, 11). They forget the miraculous signs they had witnessed (Ps 78; 106). They murmur against Moses and Aaron, but actually against God Himself (Ex 16,7f; Nm 14,27; 16,11), whose goodness and power they question (cf Dt 8,2). Incredulity, a type of fear, consists in demanding from God an immediate realization of His promises. It is a type of blackmailing against God who made the covenant. It is "to scorn Yahweh," "not to believe" in Him (Nm 14,11), "not to obey His voice" (14,22), "to tempt Him and quarrel with Him" (Ex 17,7).

Another way to murmur against Yahweh is to make an image of Him with "a golden calf" (Ex 32; Dt 9,12-21). The Hebrews thus counted on putting the mastery over Him who did not wish to descend to their level and to be at their mercy. The same sin of unbelief characterizes the northern kingdom, "the sin of Jeroboam" (1 K 12,28ff; 16,26.31). Because they wanted to know the mystery of Yahweh they practiced divination, magic, and sorcery which lasted until the exile (1 S 18,3-25; 2 K 9,22; 17,17; cf Ex 22,17; Is 2,6; Mi 3,7; Jr 27,9; Ez 12,24; Dt 18,10ff); and this is also why they had recourse to false prophets (cf Jr 4,10).

2. *Israel with a divided heart.* Actually, when the people settled in Palestine, unbelief took another form, not less culpable—making agreements with the gods of the land or with the neighboring nations*. But Yahweh tolerates no

division. As Elijah proclaimed: "How long are you going to limp on both legs? If the Lord be God, follow Him, but if Baal, follow him" (1 K 18,21). In the same way, the prophets fought against the "double heart," the divided heart (Ho 10,2) which looks to the gentiles for the support that only Yahweh can give (Ho 7,11f). Instead of seeing the harvests and flocks as the gifts of their Master and Spouse, Israel goes in search of the goods of the covenant among their lovers, the Canaanite gods, in the fertility rites (2,7-15). Unbelief is the prostitution of the consecrated bride (2,1-6; Jr 2—4; Ex 16) who ought to have a perfectly faithful heart (Dt 18,13; Ps 18,24), "totally" for God (1 K 8, 23, 11,4), following* Yahweh without failing Dt 1,36; Nm 14,24; 32,11).

This ideal remains even though it cannot be realized by human forces. Isaiah shows the people clearly that "if you do not believe, you will not subsist" (Is 7,9). Faith is the only existence possible for God's people and it excludes every other recourse (28,14f; 30,15f). For Jeremiah unbelief consists in "relying on," "putting one's confidence" in creatures (Jr 5,17; 7,4; 8,14; 17,5; 46,25; 49,4). Ezekiel points out the consequence of incredulity: "You will know that I am Yahweh when you die" (Ez 6,7; 7,4; 11,10). Unbelief becomes the hardness* of heart which Isaiah prophesied (Is 6,9f): exiled, the people became deaf and blind (Is 42,19; 43,8). But Yahweh must raise up a Servant* whose "ear He wakens each morning" (50,4f). Through Him the great hope of the prophets will be realized. Unbelief will stop the day that "all are taught by Yahweh" (Jr 31,33f; Is 54, 13; Jn 6,45). Then all will recognize that Yahweh is the only God (Is 43,10).

II. UNBELIEF WHEN CONFRONTED BY JESUS CHRIST

Nevertheless Jesus should already have fulfilled the prophecies concerning Him that dealt with the Servant: "who has believed our report?" (Is 53,1; cf Jn 12,38; R 10,16). Unbelief seemingly triumphs in hearts that refuse to accept the incarnation of the Son of God and His redemptive work.

1. *Confronted by Jesus of Nazareth.* Formerly the prophets* spoke in the name of Yahweh and were to be believed. Jesus places His own Word* on the same level as the Word of God. Not to put His Word into practice is the same

as building upon sand, thus lacking all support (Mt 7,24-27). Such a claim seems too much: "Blessed the man for whom I will not be an occasion of scandal*!" (Mt 11,6). Actually, the only reply to His teaching and miracles is the hypocrisy* of the Pharisees* (15,7; 23,13...) and the unbelief of the lakeside towns (11,20-24), of Jerusalem (23,37f), of all the Jews (8,10ff). Jesus' power is even tied down by this unbelief (13,58) to the point that Jesus is astonished at their lack of faith (Mk 6,6). This lack, however, can be overcome by the Father who is the source of faith. He keeps the mystery of Jesus hidden from the eyes of the wise (Mt 11,25f), but gives it to the little ones who do His will and who make up the remnant* of Israel, the family of Jesus (12,46-50).

Among the believers, however, unbelief finds a place in different degrees. Some are "of little faith." This is when the disciples fear the storm (8,26) or the rising waves (14,31); when they cannot work a miracle though they have received the power to do so (17,17.20; cf 10,8). So too when they are anxious for the bread they lack (16,8; cf 6,24). Prayer can remedy these failures (Mk 9,24), and in this way Jesus guarantees Peter's faith (Lk 22,32).

2. *In the presence of the paschal mystery.* Unbelief reaches its peak when the mind must give way to divine wisdom which chooses the cross* as the road to glory (1 Co 1,21-24). When Jesus' lot is announced, Peter ceases to follow* his master so as to become a "scandal*" to Jesus (Mt 16,23). And when the hour comes, Peter is scandalized and denies Jesus just as Jesus had told him he would (26,31-35.69-75). Still, the disciple must carry this same cross (16,24), if he wants to be a witness* of Jesus before the tribunals (10,32f). His testimony actually refers to the resurrection, something scarcely believable (Ac 26,8) which the disciples themselves were so slow to believe on the occasion of the apparitions*, so great is unbelief rooted in man's heart (Lk 24,25.37.41; Mt 28,17; Mk 16,11.13.14).

III. THE UNBELIEF OF ISRAEL

Jesus had announced that the builders would reject the cornerstone (Mt 21,42). The early Church recalls this with force (Ac 4,33; 1 P 2, 4.7), attributing the refusal by Israel now to ignorance (Ac 3,17; 13,27f), now to culpability (2,23; 3,13; 10,39). She rapidly becomes aware that her preaching, far from converting Israel, is not even received by the majority of the Jews. This new situation is mysterious, and the theologians Paul and John will try to justify it.

1. *St. Paul and the unbelieving people.* At the beginning of his ministry, as the heir of the fiery Stephen (Ac 7,51f), Paul turns the unbelieving and persecuting Jews over to the divine wrath* (1 Th 2,16). He no longer considers them as the faithful remnant*. Later, when the conflict subsides and the gentiles enter the faith *en masse*, Paul examines the mystery of his people's unbelief. It makes him suffer profoundly (R 9,2; 11,13f). Especially this global refusal of the chosen people seems to place God and His promises in question (3,3), and to endanger the faith. He resolves the problem in R 9—11 not at the human level, but by plunging into the mystery of divine wisdom. God has not rejected His people but He remains faithful to His promises (9,6-29). God has not ceased to "hold out His hands to this rebellious people" (10,21), through the expedient of the apostolic preaching*. They are the Jews who rebelled and tried to seek justice in the law (9,30—10,21). But God will have the final word because Israel's hardening of heart* will one day cease. In this way disobedience will have manifested to all the infinite mercy* of God (11,1-32).

2. *St. John and the unbelieving Jew.* Already Paul and the whole Church quickly gave the name of "unbelievers" or "unfaithful" not just to the pagans but probably also to the Jews who did not share the faith in Jesus (1 Co 6,6; 7,12f; 10,27; 14,22f). Those are the ones that the god of this world* has blinded (2 Co 4,4), with whom no relation is possible (6,14f). Still they existed as living witnesses to what a Christian might become if he denied his faith: "worse than an infidel" (1 Tm 5,8). Whereas Paul would show the unbelieving Israel as a witness to God's severity (R 11,21f) and of a first election (11,16), John will present in the Jew* who rejects Jesus the type of the unbeliever, the precursor of the evil world*. The sin of unbelief is to not confess* that Jesus is the Christ (1 Jn 2,22f; 4,2f; 5,1-5); it is to make a liar of God (5,10). The fourth gospel centers unbelief in the refusal to accept in Jesus of Nazareth the Word incarnate (Jn 1,11; 6,36) and the redeemer of men (6,53). Not to believe is to be judged (3,18), to give oneself to lying and homicide (8,44), to be doomed to

death (8,24). In this way the unbeliever flees from the light* because his works are evil (3,20); and he plunges into the darkness, and gives himself up to Satan. A kind of determinism leads to hardness of heart, and he "*is no longer able* to hear the Word" of Jesus; he belongs to the race of the evil one (8.43f). On the other hand, compensating for this apparent fatality of unbelief, Jesus reveals the mystery of the Father's attraction (6,44). It will be exercised successfully by Him who "being lifted up from the earth, will draw all men to Himself" (12,32). As for Paul, unbelief will one day be dominated: "If we are unfaithful, God remains faithful" (2 Tm 2,13). Christian existence is an ever new discovery of the mystery of the risen Jesus: "Do not be unbelieving, but believing" (Jn 20,27).

→Adultery 2—Apparitions of Christ 4 b.7—Faith—Hardness of Heart—Hypocrite 3—Jew II—Laughter o.1.

XLD jrs

UNITY

Faith's acknowledgment of the one God—Father, Son and Holy Spirit—opens man to the love which united the Father and Son, the love the Holy Spirit communicates to the believer (Jn 15,9; 17,26; R 5,5). By uniting man to the one God, this charity makes man God's witness in the world, a cooperator in God's plan to unite all men and the entire universe in the one Son (R 8,29; E 1,5.10).

I. THE SOURCE OF UNITY
AND ITS BREACH THROUGH SIN

The variegated universe is the creation of God whose plan* is manifested in His command to man and woman: "Be fruitful, multiply, fill and subdue the earth" (Gn 1,28). There is an evident alliance of unity and diversity in the divine work. That creation* be unified under man's dominion, man must multiply; that man be fruitful*, his own unity is achieved by a loving union with his wife (Gn 2,23f). Realization of this plan, however, demands that man remain united to God and that he acknowledge dependence by a trusting faithfulness*.

Refusal of this faithfulness is the fundamental sin*. Man commits this sin in order to become equal to God—really a denial that God is one. There is a break, therefore, from the source of unity, God who is love (1 Jn 4,16). This initial rupture generates the divisions which are going to shatter the unity of marriage* by divorce and polygamy (Gn 4,19; Dt 24,1), the unity of brothers* by a deadly jealousy (Gn 4,6ff.24), the unity of society by misunderstanding vividly symbolized in diversity of language (11,9).

II. THE SEARCH FOR UNITY THROUGH THE COVENANT

As a remedy, God chooses men and offers them His covenant* ratified in faith (Ho 2,22). Faith* is actually the condition of union with God and of collaboration in His work of unifying, a work He unceasingly renews by calling new chosen individuals: Noah, Abraham (cf Is 51,2), Moses, David, the Servant. He gives His people the Law*, He chooses a king* from the house of David. He dwells with His people in the temple* at Jerusalem. He gives the Servant* as a model of faithfulness. All this God does to bring about a unified Israel. Then can Israel fulfill its mission as a priestly people* (Ex 19,6) and as a witness* (Is 43, 10ff).

When God makes Israel a people apart, it is to manifest Himself through her to the nations* and to reunite them in the unity of worship*. Even the dispersion punishing Israel's infidelity ultimately serves to acquaint the pagans with the one God, Creator and Savior (Is 45). Nevertheless, to fulfill the mission of the chosen people, to restore her unity shattered by the schism following Solomon's infidelity to the one God (1 K 11,31ff), and to gather the nations with Israel in the same worship (Is 56,6ff), He must come who will be the Servant*, the new David*, the Son* of Man. The one to come will be the Servant appointed to unite Israel and to save the multitude of sinners by His death (Is 42,1; 49,6; 53,10ff); He will be the new David to shepherd the Lord's flock united under His kingship (Ez 34,23f; 37,21-24); He will be the Son* of Man, head of the holy people, whose dominion will be everlasting and universal (Dn 7,13f.27). Because of the one to come, Zion, the sole spouse* of Yahweh's everlasting love, will become the common mother* of all nations (Ps 87,5; Is 54,1-10; 53,3ff). Of these nations Yahweh alone will be king (Ze 14,9).

III. UNITY ACHIEVED IN THE CHURCH

This chosen one of God is His only Son Jesus the Christ (Lk 9,35). He unites those who love Him and believe in Him by giving them His Spirit and His mother (R 5,5; Jn 19, 27) and by nourishing* them on one bread* alone, His body sacrificed on the cross (1 Co 10,16f). Thereby He makes all peoples one body* (E 2,14-18). He makes believers organisms of this body. For He endows the members with one or other charism* destined for the total good of His body, the Church* (1 Co 12, 4-27; E 1,22f). Jesus places believers as living stones in the one temple* of God (E 2,19-22; 1 P 2,4f). As the one and only shepherd*, Jesus knows His sheep in all their diversity (Jn 10,3). It is His desire to give His life and thus gather into His flock God's scattered children (Jn 10,14ff; 11,51f).

Christ restores unity on all levels—man's* interior unity, torn by his passions (R 7,14f; 8,2.9); conjugal unity, the model of which is the union of Christ and Church (E 5,25-32); the unity of all men, now made children of the same Father* by the Spirit (R 8,14ff; E 4,4ff). These children have but one heart* and one soul* (Ac 4,32); they praise their Father with one voice (R 15,5f; cf Ac 2,4.11).

Promotion of this unity, vulnerable to schism (1 Co 1,10), yet based on a single faith in a single Lord (E 4,5.13; cf Mt 16,16ff), depends upon individuals. The mark of the one Church, which has been committed to the love of Peter (Jn 21,15ff), is its unity. This unity is achieved by men living in the love of Christ and observing faithfully His great commandment: "Love one another as I have loved you" (13,34f). Fidelity and spiritual growth are measured by union with Christ, a union comparable to that of branches and vine (15,5-10). Christian unity is a requisite to manifest to men God's love in giving His only Son (3,16) and to achieve unity in Christ (E 4,13). When this occurs, Jesus' supreme desire will be fulfilled: "Father, that all may be one, as we are one!" (Jn 17,21ff).

MFL dfb

V

VENGEANCE

In current usage, to avenge is to punish an offense by returning evil for evil. In biblical language, vengeance primarily means a reestablishing of justice*, a victory over evil. It is always forbidden to avenge oneself through hate for an offender, but it is a duty to avenge a violated right. The execution of this obligation evolved in the course of history. Taken from the individual, it was conferred on society. Gradually, God indicates that He alone is the legitimate avenger of the order of justice.

1. *The avenger of blood.* In Israel's early nomadic society members of the clan had to supply mutual protection and defense. In case of murder, a *gŏ'ēl*, "an avenger of blood" (Nm 35,21), used to take vengeance for the clan by killing the assassin. To the idea of clan solidarity was added the conviction that, as in the case of Abel*, bloodshed cries for vengeance (cf Gn 4,10; Jb 16,18), for this blood profanes the land where Yahweh dwells (Nm 35,33f). Therefore, it was an obligation to safeguard justice.

When Israel finally stayed in one place, she retained this custom (cf 2 S 3,22-27). But though her laws (Ex 21,12; Lv 24,17) continued to consider the avenger of blood as an agent of justice (Nm 35,12.19), there was a concern to regulate the exercise of his right to avoid the excesses of anger (Dt 19,6). Henceforth, it is only the deliberate homicide (Dt 24,16) who is subject to the avenger of blood. And there must be a prior trial in the city of refuge to which the assassin has fled (Nm 35,24.30; Dt 19). Gradually, therefore, the right of vengeance passes from the individual to society.

2. *Personal vengeance.* With the law of talion (Ex 21,23ff; Lv 24,19; Dt 19,21), Israelite legislation curbs human emotions always eager to render evil for evil. It forbids the unlimited vendetta of barbarian times (cf Gn 4,15.24). Finally, Israelite law softens even the law of talion by granting pecuniary compensation in certain cases, a principle admitted by other oriental codes (Ex 21,18f.26f). Yet with the law of talion there was the risk of hindering a progressive growth of moral awareness. Even when codified by social justice, the desire for vengeance can remain in the soul. Man's sense of moral awareness, therefore, had to be educated*.

a) *Revenge forbidden.* The Law of Holiness goes to the root of revenge: "You shall not have hate for your brother in your heart...You shall not avenge yourself and you shall not harbor rancor against members of your own race. You shall love your neighbor as yourself" (Lv 19,17f). Certain examples of pardon* are famous: Joseph, who interprets the persecution he suffered as a plan of God who knows how to draw good from evil (Gn 45,3f.7; 50, 19); David, who does not avenge himself against Saul (1 S 24,4f; 26,5-12) lest he lay a hand on Yahweh's anointed. Yet this same David posthumously takes vengeance on Shimei and Joab (1 K 2,6-46). At any rate, the duty of pardon is limited to brothers* of the one race. Thus the Book of Judges in no way criticizes Samson for personally avenging himself against the Philistines (Jg 15,3.7). In the sapiential books this duty will tend to deepen and universalize pardon: "The avenger will experience the Lord's vengeance...Keep no rancor toward your neighbor*" (Si 28,1.7). The principle seems to exclude no one.

b) *The appeal to divine vengeance.* Confidence* in God motivates the just man to forego vengeance entirely: "Do not say: I will return the evil. Have confidence in Yahweh and He will deliver you" (Pr 20,22). The just man does not take vengeance, but leaves to God the concern for just vengeance: "Vengeance is mine, says the Lord" (Dt 32,35). Thus the persecuted Jeremiah acts when he "confides his cause to God" (Jr 20,12). He certainly wishes "to see God's vengeance" (11,20), but because he has identified his cause with God's cause (15,15). He desires not evil but justice*. This can be restored only by God.

The psalmist likewise, in a turgid Semitic

phrase, wishes "to wash his feet in the blood of his enemies" (Ps 58,11), to which he adds terrible curses (Ps 5,11; 137,7f). Yet he is animated by a desire of justice. He may deceive himself about the authenticity of the feeling, but the religious import of his attitude is undeniable. 'I know that my vindicator (*gōē'l*) lives; and that he, as the nearest relative, will rise on the earth" and restore justice (Jb 19,25).

3. *God the avenger.* The hope of Job, and of Jeremiah too, is not in vain: God is the judge* outstanding in every way; He probes the deepest recess of the heart and rewards everyone according to his works*; He is the *gō'ēl* of Israel (Is 41,14). The Day* of the Lord can be called a "day of vengeance" (Jr 46,10) because God will then avenge justice* and his honor. In this sense it can be said that only God can avenge "Himself." Justice, salvation, and vengeance therefore will accompany the day of the Lord (Is 59, 17f). Insofar as Israel is faithful to the covenant, she can then appeal from the injustice of human judges to her *gō'ēl*, to the "God of vengeances," that He come to judge the earth (Ps 94). If this is not quite Christian forgiveness, it is a humble submission to the Lord in awaiting the day of His visitation*.

4. *Christ and vengeance.* The time finally arrived when Jesus shed His blood*. Then the heights of human injustice showed the infinite justice* of God. Henceforth the believer's patterns of action will be staggered by the example* of Christ, who "was insulted and did not return insult" (1 P 2,23). Not only does Jesus inaugurate a new Law* which fulfills the principle of the talion law, but He goes further and commands us not to resist an evildoer (Mt 5,38-42). He does not condemn the justice of human tribunals, which Paul will say are responsible for the exercise of divine justice (R 13,4). But He demands that His disciples forgive offenses and love their enemies*. Above all, He suggests that only he who can bear injustice to himself will pardon the injustice of another. Recourse to divine vengeance is now not enough, for one must "conquer evil with good" (R 12,21). Thus one "heaps burning coals on the head of his enemy" and places himself in a situation where he must turn his hate* to love.

Although all justice is fulfilled in the blood of Christ, the fact is that the last day has not yet come. On earth charity suffers its reverses. Christians die, as did Jesus, victims of unjust

violence. Though they pardon their executioners (Ac 7,60), the blood of the victims cries nonetheless to God: "How long, holy and true master, will you hesitate to do justice and avenge our blood on the inhabitants of the earth?" (Ap 6,10; cf 16,6; 19,2). Deferred until the judgment of history, the vengeance of God will reestablish justice in the eternal kingdom, where there will never again be any curse (22,3).

→Abel 2—Blood OT 1; NT 4—Curse IV—Day of the Lord OT II—Enemy II 3—Hate I 3 —Judgment OT I 1; NT II 1—Liberation/ Liberty II 2—Mercy OT II—Pardon III—Violence I 1, III 2, IV 3—Wrath—Zeal I 2.

ADa & XLD dfb

VICTORY

Victory supposes combat and the risk of defeat. As a matter of fact, the drama of humanity in the Bible opens with a defeat where man is conquered by Satan*, sin*, and death*. But in the defeat itself there is hint of a promise of a coming victory over evil (Gn 3,15). Salvation* history is the story of progress toward this definitive victory.

OT

God's people first experience victory and defeat in their own worldly history. But this experience results in turning their faith ultimately toward expectation of another victory to be won on another level.

1. *The victories of God's people.* Originally the Israelites measure the strength* of their God by a rather imperfect standard, their own military success. They confuse God's triumph over evil with their own victories over their enemy*. In war are they not "the armies of Yahweh" (Ex 12,41; Jg 5,13; 1 S 17,26)? Therefore He fights for them and guarantees success: under Moses (Ex 14,14; 15,1-21; 17,8-16), under Joshua (Js 6,16; 10,10), under the judges (Jg 7,15), under the kings (1 S 14,6; 2 Ch 14,10f; 20,15,29). Fighting is necessary, but so also is recognition of the victory coming from God as a grace* and gift* (Ps 18,32-49; 20,7-10; 118,10-27). Subsequently the Maccabees will not hesitate to attribute the success of their armies to God (1 M 3,19; 2 M 10,38; 13, 15; 15,8-24).

627

Thus God appears as an unconquerable ally (Jdt 16,13; Dt 32,22-43; Is 30,27-33; Na 1,2-8; Ha 3; 1 Ch 29,11f). Just as originally He mastered the forces of chaos (Gn 1,2), personified by the monstrous beasts* (Ps 74,13), so too in history He continues to triumph over the pagan peoples, who are the historical embodiment of the powers of chaos and oppose His salvific plan*. For this reason the Israelites can prevail over their enemies. This experience has an undeniable religious content but a certain ambiguity, too. Will they not be tempted to think that God's victory necessarily coincides with their earthly power? A counterbalance will preserve them from this error.

2. *The defeats of God's people*. Even in the moment of success, the prophets remind the Israelites that the victory given by God is not necessarily a reward for good conduct (Dt 9, 4ff). But reversals are needed to make them truly aware of their spiritual misery. The trials of the exodus (Nm 14,42f; Dt 8,19f), delays in the conquest of Canaan (Js 7,1-12; Jg 2,10-23), failures undergone by the monarchy (2 Ch 21, 14; 24,20; 25,8-20), and especially the disaster of the exile (Jr 15,1-9; 27,6; Ez 22) show them that God does not hesitate to fight against them when they betray Him. These defeats are a chastisement for faithlessness (Ps 78; 106). Far from signifying a defeat of God, the master of empires, reversals show that God's victory is of a type different from earthly success. So misfortunes lead Israel to understand and to prepare the one true victory.

3. *Toward another victory*. The prophetic oracles state that in the "last times" there will be a divine victory which will surpass past triumphs in every way. And the sages conspicuously make the point of a spiritual victory in no way the result of arms.

a) *Eschatalogical victory*. The post-exilic prophets are fond of portraying the ultimate phase of history as a gigantic war* in which God will confront all His enemies* joined together. He will certainly crush them (cf Is 63, 1-6) as He crushed the primordial monsters (Is 27,1). This victory will preface His final reign (Ze 14; cf Ez 38—39). Other texts introduce the man through whom the ultimate victory will be won. Sometimes he has traits of a kingly Messiah* (Ps 2,1-9; 110,5ff); or he is personified by a transcendent Son* of Man before whom God reduces the beasts* to

nothingness (Dn 7). The victory of the Servant* of Yahweh is more paradoxical, for He triumphs by His own sacrifice (Is 52,13ff; 53, 11f) and He brings God's plan* to fulfillment. If the Son of Man's victory had more than earthly dimensions because it transcended history, the Servant's victory is immediately located on the spiritual plane, the only one of ultimate importance.

b) *Victory of the just*. The victory mentioned above is already won by the just who overcome sin, an idea in the background of all wisdom teaching. Toward the end of the OT, in the books of Wisdom, the concept becomes clearer. Because the just have conquered and been undefiled in battle, the just will wear the crown of conquerors in eternity (Ws 4,1f); the Lord will give them this deserved reward at the same moment He launches one last assault against the wicked (Ws 5,15-23). Such is also the victory Christ will win—and all Christians likewise.

NT

1. *Christ's victory*. Christ definitively transcends the mentality of merely earthly warfare because He introduces a struggle of quite another order. From the beginning of His public life He asserts Himself as the "stronger one" who defeats the strong one (Lk 11,14-22), that is, Satan*, prince of this world. On the eve of His death He warns His own not to fear the evil world* which will persecute them out of hatred: "Have confidence! It is the world that I have conquered" (Jn 16,33). This victory assumes and literally fulfills the paradoxical traits found in the Servant of Yahweh's victory. But it is by the resurrection that this victory is a concrete, definitive reality; for here Christ has triumphed over sin and death and He has dragged the defeated powers* behind His victorious chariot (Col 2,15). This lion of Judah (Ap 5,5) exceeded all the victories of Israel's kings of old, for the immolated Lamb* (5,12) has become master of human history. His victory will finally shine forth when He prevails over all opposing forces (17,14; 19,11-21) and conquers forever the last enemy, death* (1 Co 15,24ff). Apparently defeat, the cross has insured victory of the holy one over sin, victory of the living one over death.

2. *Victory of the new people*. Such is Christ's victory, such also is the victory of the new

people who follow in His wake. Nor is this any longer a victory on earth where apparent defeats take place. Thus the martyrs* were crushed by the beast (Ap 11,7; 13,7; cf 6,2), yet they have already conquered it, thanks to the blood* of the Lamb (12,10f; 15,2). Thus also the apostles who are part of Christ's triumph (2 Co 2,14), yet can be crushed by the demands of the apostolate (4,10). So also all Christians. In acknowledging their Father and in being nourished by His Word*, they have conquered the evil one (1 Jn 2,13f). Born of God, they have conquered the world* (5,4). Their victory is their faith* in the Son of God (5,5) in whom they overcome men inspired by the Antichrist (4,4). It remains to consolidate this victory by spiritual combat in which the Christian is not conquered by evil but must overcome evil with good (R 12,21). The Christian knows that from now on he can overcome all obstacles by the Spirit*. Nothing will ever again separate them from Christ's love (8,35ff).

The Christian shares the victory of his leader and will also share His glory*. The NT uses various figures of speech to describe the reward of the victorious. It is a crown prepared from on high: a crown of life (Jm 1,12; Ap 2,10), a crown of glory (1 P 5,4), a crown of justice (2 Tm 4,8); unlike earthly crowns (1 Co 9,25) it is imperishable, for it is a living crown composed of men the apostles brought to the faith (Ph 4,1; 1 Th 2,19). The Apocalypse, with its emphasis on Christians at war* against the beast, is especially descriptive about the lot of the conquerors. They will be sons* of God (Ap 21,7), they will sit on Christ's throne (3, 21), and with Him will rule the nations* (2,26). They will receive a new name* (2,17), will eat of the tree* of life (2,7), will become pillars in the temple* of their God (3,12). Once they have entered eternal life*, they will no longer have to fear a second death* (2,11), a state far different from that of the defeated, the cowards, the reprobate (21,8).

The NT concludes on this note of dazzling victory. The original promise of Genesis thus becomes a reality beyond all expectations. For man who was once conquered by Satan, by sin, and by death, has triumphed over all of them through Jesus Christ.

→Ascension II 2—Beasts & Beast 3—Captivity II—Creation OT II 2—Day of the Lord—Death NT II 3—Enemy II 2, III 2—Evil Spirits NT—Good & Evil III—Flesh II 2 c—Lamb of God 3 — Liberation/Liberty — Peace —
Revelation NT 3.6—Salvation—Sin IV 2 d e—Strength—Trial III 3—Visitation OT 1—War —World NT II 1.

PEB dfb

VINE

Few cultivated crops or plants are so completely dependent on both the careful, skilled work of man and the rhythm of the seasons as the vine. Palestine, land of vineyards, teaches Israel to relish products of the earth, to work wholeheartedly at a task rich in prospect, and yet to look forward to results as a gift of the divine liberality. At the same time, the highly esteemed vine is touched with mystery. It is worth nothing except in its fruit*. While the wood of the vine is worthless (Ez 15,2-5) and the barren branches good only for the fire (Jn 15,6), the fruit of the vine makes "gods and men" (Jg 9,13) happy. The mysterious element is that if the vine does bring joy to the human heart (Ps 104,15), then the product of the vine is a joy* from God.

1. *The vine, delight of man.* The just Noah* plants the vine in an earth which God has promised not to curse again (Gn 8,21; 9,20). Vineyards on the land are a sign that God's blessing* was not totally destroyed by Adam's sin (Gn 5,29). God promises and gives His people a land rich in vines (Nm 13,23f; Dt 8,8). But oppressors of the poor (Am 5,11) or those unfaithful to Yahweh (Zp 1,13) will not drink the wine* from their vines (Dt 28,30.39). For the vine will be devoured by locusts (Jl 1,7) or killed by briers (Is 7,23).

The king who seizes the vines of his subjects is guilty of a grave injustice. Ahab is guilty of this abuse (1 K 21,1-16) predicted by Samuel (1 S 8,14f). Under a good king, however, each man lives in peace* beneath his vine and his fig tree (1 K 5,5; 1 M 14,12), an ideal that will be achieved in Messianic times (Mi 4,4; Ze 3,10) when the vine will be extremely prolific (Am 9,14; Ze 8,12). The bourgeoning vine is an image of wisdom* (Si 24,17), of the just man's fruitful wife (Ps 128,3), and a symbol for the spouses singing love's mystery in the Canticle (Ct 6,11; 7,13; 2,13.15; cf 1,14).

2. *Israel, a vine unfaithful to God.* The God of Israel is spouse and vinedresser of the vine which is His people*. For Hosea, Israel is a

fruitful plant which gives thanks for its fruitfulness* to others than the God who is her spouse* by the covenant (Ho 10,1; 3,1). Isaiah says that God loves His vine and He has done everything for it. But instead of the anticipated fruit* of justice, His vine-harvest* has been poured-out blood; therefore He will hand over His vine to despoilers (Is 5,1-7). For Jeremiah, Israel is a chosen plant become degenerate and barren (Jr 2,21; 8,13), to be uprooted and trampled (Jr 5,10; 12,10). Finally, Ezekiel uses the comparison of a fertile vine which dries up and is burned and applies this to an Israel unfaithful to God (Ez 19,10-14; 15,6ff) and to a king unfaithful to a sworn covenant (Ez 17,5-19).

A day will come when the vine will flourish under God's watchful care (Is 27,2f). To this Israel calls on God's faithful* love asking that He save the vine He transplanted from Egypt to His land, the vine He had to leave to destruction and fire! Henceforth this vine will be faithful to Him (Ps 80,9-17). But it is not Israel who will keep that promise. Going back to the parable of Isaiah, Jesus summarizes the history of the chosen people by saying God still awaits fruit from His vine; but rather than listen to the prophets God sent, the vinedressers mistreated them (Mk 12,1-5). As the greatest manifestation of love, God now sends His beloved Son (12,6). In response to this love the leaders of the people will climax their faithlessness by killing the Son whose inheritance is the vine. Therefore the guilty will be punished, while the Son's death shall open a new chapter in God's plan*. Now the vine is given to conscientious vine-dressers and will finally bear its fruit (12, 7ff; Mt 21,41ff).

Who are these conscientious vine-dressers? Here idle protestations are worthless; the sole criterion is positive and fruitful work* (Mt 21, 28-32). To gather the vine-harvest* God will collect all His workers. Whether they labor from morning or are hired at the last moment, all shall receive the same reward. Not rights that man can claim, the call to work and the offer of a wage are gratuitous gifts, entirely the result of grace (Mt 20,1-15).

3. *The true vine, God's glory and joy.* What Israel was incapable of giving to God, Christ actually does give Him. Christ is the vine that produces, the authentic vine-stock worthy of its name. He is the true Israel; planted by His Father, surrounded with care, and pruned to bear abundant fruit (Jn 15,1f; Mt 15,13). He bears fruit by giving His life, by shedding His blood as the greatest proof of love (Jn 15,9.13; cf 10,10f.17). And wine*, the product of the vine, in the eucharistic mystery will sacramentally symbolize that blood* shed to seal the new covenant. Wine will be the means of sharing in the love of Jesus and of abiding* in Him (Mt 26,27ff p; cf Jn 6,56; 15,4.9f).

Christ is the vine and we the branches as He is the body* and we the members. The true vine is Christ; but it is also His Church*, whose members are in union with Him. Without that communion*, we can do nothing. Only Jesus, the true vine-stock, can bear fruit which glorifies His Father, the vine-dresser. Without this union with Him, we are branches cut off from the vine-stock, deprived of sap, barren, fit for the fire (Jn 15,4ff). All men are called to this union by the love of the Father and the Son—a gratuitous call, for it is Jesus who chooses His branches, His disciples*, not they who choose Him (15,16). By this union man becomes a branch of the true vine-stock, is given life by the love that unites Jesus and His Father, bears fruit which gives glory to the Father. Thus the disciple participates in the joy of the Son, which is to glorify His Father (15,8-11). The mystery of the true vine, that is, of Christ and His Church, is to express a union which is productive and a joy which is permanent, perfect, and everlasting (cf 17,23).

→Church II 2, V 2—Fruit—Vintage—Wine.

MFL dfb

VINTAGE

Formerly semi-nomads, in the promised land the Israelites became workers of the land, cultivating grain and the vine. Like the harvest*, the grape-gathering is a sign and source of joy*, though also a symbol of misfortune.

1. *Divine blessing.* The harvest feast (Ex 23, 16; 34,22) becomes the feast of Tabernacles (Dt 16,13). This is "the feast" *par exellence* (1 K 8,2.65), probably because of its popularity. It has no connection with the worship of Bacchus, but probably originates from the Canaanite vintage feast (Jg 9,27). Israel recognizes God's blessing in the harvest of grapes and gives thanks to God by the then ordinary forms of rejoicing: in dancing (Jg 21,19ff), in shouting of the workers in and out of the

vines* and at the wine press (Is 16,10; Jr 48,33), in the joy that new wine* brings (Ps 4,8), and perhaps even in drunkenness* (1 S 1,14f). All of these good things are for those faithful to the covenant*. But for those not faithful, a curse*: the vine is laid waste (Ho 2,14; Is 7,23) and there is no harvest (Dt 28,39); the vine "languishes" (Is 24,7); in place of dancing and drinking, lamentation (Is 32,10-13; Jl 1,5); no more merriment and joyous shouting in proud Moab (Is 16,9f; Jr 48,32f). But, when the people have expiated their faults, the locust shall no longer make the vine sterile* (Ml 3, 11). Flourishing vineyards (Jr 31,12; Hg 2,19) will once more produce a wine of superior quality (Ho 14,8). In brief, the vine-harvest is a superb expression of joy in the Messianic era (Am 9,13; Ez 28,26; Jl 2,24; Is 25,6).

2. *Symbol of divine chastisement.* A harvest* presupposes threshing and winnowing and symbolizes the chastisement of the hardened sinner. The figure of the vine-harvest is therefore applied to the faithless. First comes the stripping of the vine-branches, then the crushing of the grapes in the wine press. To punish the people who denied Him, God invites the invader to glean as a vine the remnant of Israel (Jr 6,9). He Himself treads, as in a wine press, the virgin daughter of Judah (Lm 1,15). Gathering the grapes, sorting the clusters, the grapes crushed in the vat—these images illustrate the chastisement of the nations, especially of Edom which did not help Judah during the capture of Jerusalem. The grape-gatherers will come and leave nothing in Edom to glean (Jr 49,9; Ob 5f). Yahweh will tread down Edom as in a wine press, and the blood* spurting out will stain His garments with purple (Is 63,1-6). The image of the vine-harvest, then, aptly symbolizes God's judgment*. To their misfortune, Yahweh will make the nations* drink their intoxicating cup* (Jr 25,15-30). Or, according to the Apocalypse, an angel armed with a sickle will gather the bunches of grapes and fling the whole into the great wine press of God's wrath* (Ap 14,17ff; 19,15).

→Feasts OT I—Harvest—Judgment OT II 2— Vine—Wine—Wrath.

ADa dfb

VIOLENCE

Although at first sight we see in violence nothing but brutal destruction, rape or violation, we must also recognize the vital force behind it, which strives to maintain itself as such and thus tends to destroy life itself. The term used for it comes, like the word for vital force itself, from an indo-european root meaning life (*bios-biazomai, vivo-vis*). And the Bible has no illusions when it describes the violent state in which mankind finds itself: the vital forces and the powers of death remain in a state of provisional equilibrium, of which the apparent order is often no more than a caricature. It also and above all reveals that, in Jesus Christ, the eschatological ideal of a time when life will flourish without violence (cf Is 11,6-9; Ap 21,4) can become reality. To guide us in this discussion, there are two terms that come close enough to the idea of violence; the Hebrew (*hms*) does so precisely, and the Greek (*biazomai*) with a simple nuance of constraint (to force, to insist on).

I. DESCRIPTION

1. The idea of the *transgression* of a norm allows us to describe a particular act as violent; this was how the Greek translators of the OT understood it, and in general they rendered *hms* by a word cognate with *adikia*, meaning injustice. According to the customs of the time, no doubt Simeon and Levi were obliged to avenge their sister Dina, who had been violated (Gn 34,2), but, because they went too far in their vengeance*, the knives they used to punish the oppressors were called by their father "instruments of violence" (49,5). The people and the priests violated the Law (Ez 22, 26; Zp 3,4); social justice is violated by fraud (Zp 1,9) and rights are violated (Ez 45,9). Normally violence is accompanied by some sort of premeditation or by the violation of the laws of language: snares and ambushes (Ps 140,5), pits dug out in the path of a neighbor (Ps 7, 15), guile (72,14), slander (140,11), cheating (Ml 2,16), but above all false witness (Ex 23,1; Dt 19,16; Ps 27,12; 35,11), from which the just* man whose prayer is undefiled, keeps himself free (Jb 16,17).

2. Violence is also understood in terms of its principal effect, the *destruction* of physical or social life; in this case the term is often asso-

ciated with another, signifying exploitation, oppression, devastation or ruin. The prophets lament over the state of violence into which the people have fallen (Am 3,10; Jr 6,7; 20,8; Is 60,18) and they appeal to Yahweh who alone can remedy this unjust state of affairs (Ha 1,3). In fact, God has a horror of violent men (Ps 11, 5; Ml 2,16): did He not cause the flood because "the earth grew corrupt...and filled with violence" (Gn 6,11.13)? And there is the ceaseless cry of the oppressed, praying to be delivered from violent men (2 S 22,3.49; Ps 18,49; 140, 2.5). The victims put their trust in a reply of the same kind: "may evil hound the man of violence to death" (Ps 140,11). In spite of all this, an ideal of perfect submission is offered in the picture of the Servant* of God, who is buried with the wicked, "though he has done no violence or deceit" (Is 53,9).

3. This rapid survey of the different uses of the word *hms* allows us to make a few remarks. Violence is not to be identified with force, nor with vengeance, nor anger, nor zeal. It is true that these various expressions of the vital force do sometimes lead to the destruction of life; but they do not necessarily imply the thing that in the eyes of the OT is the mark of violence, namely the transgression of a norm. However, it must be noted that this norm is not determined by some imperishable "natural order," as in Greek thought. It is defined according to a given age by justice*, that is by the God of the covenant, who is the end and the judge of every action. It is in such a context, temporal and theological, that the idea of violence in the OT must be judged.

II. SITUATIONS

With the help of the preceding criteria it is possible to decide the situations in the descriptions of which *hms* is at fault. By killing Abel*, Cain was guilty of an act of violence: "Listen to the sound of your brother's blood, crying out to me from the ground" (Gn 4,10), said God. Without any sense of proportion, Lamech "killed a man for wounding" him (4,23). Israel was oppressed ('*innah*, from '*anah*, the same root as '*anawim*, the poor*) in Egypt (Ex 1,12; Dt 26,6; cf 2 S 7,10). In condemning the rape of a woman, an act that destroys social relationships by neglecting the consent of the partner, the law condemned an unjustifiable violence (Dt 22,24.29; cf Gn 34,2; Jg 19,24; 20,5;

2 S 13,12.14; Lm 5,11; in Greek, *tapeinoo*). David had Uriah, the husband of Bathsheba, killed, by the trick of making use of the holy war* (2 S 11,15). On the other hand, in spite of the curse of Simei (16,7f; 19,19-24), he did not behave like a man of blood in his dealings with the house of Saul, for on two occasions he spared Saul's life (1 S 24; 26), who still kept on laying traps for him (18,10f; 19,9-17). There was another case of violence when Ahab seized the vineyard of Naboth, for the latter was stoned because of false witness plotted by Jezabel (1 K 21,8-16). And finally, mention must be made of the countless situations of cupidity* or persecution*, massacres and riots, that make the Bible story one long history of the violence of men up to the time of Jesus (Lk 13,1; Mk 15,7; cf Mt 2,16).

III. YAHWEH AND VIOLENCE

The behavior of God seems to be ambiguous: of course He rejects every violation of justice; but sometimes He seems to tolerate, approve, indeed perform acts that we should call violent. What are we to say about that?

1. There is no doubt that *God condemns* every violent injustice. But He does it progressively, taking into account the age in which His people are living. Thus, He gives His blessing to the law of retaliation (Ex 21,24), which represents a considerable advance when compared with the time of Lamech (Gn 4,15.24): He condemns crimes, which ought not to be committed, like the ones described by Amos according to the norms of his day and which are unjustifiable acts of violence: the deportation of entire populations without regard to blood-relationship, the disembowelling of pregnant women, the burning of corpses, the rejection of the Law and the crushing of the ordinary people (Am 1,1-2,8).

Yahweh *took the side of Israel* when they were oppressed in Egypt (Ex 3,9), and He expects of them a similar behavior toward the weak: "You must not oppress the stranger. You know how a stranger feels, for you lived as strangers in the land of Egypt" (23,9). Thus God makes Himself the defender of the victims of the injustice of men, especially the orphan, the widow* and the poor* (21—23; Dt 24,20).

2. On the other hand, as He is educating*

Israel in the midst of the idolatrous nations up to the birth of the Messiah, the God of the covenant takes seriously the conditions in which His people are living, and, even in the name of the covenant, reveals Himself as a God to be feared, a *warrior-God*. He exterminates the first-born of Egypt (Ex 12); He insists on the anathema* (Js 7) and puts Himself at their head in battle (cf 2 S 5,24). He approves of the vengeful and destructive strength* of Samson (Jg 15—16) and of the zeal* that goes as far as killing the one who transgresses the covenant (Nm 15,11).

In doing this, God is not considered by the Bible to be violent, for He is not transgressing the covenant of which He is the author and the guarantee. But He is showing that a greater good can involve the destruction of earthly life*. Apart from this, He is signifying the eschatological war* and the extermination of the evil that is in the world. However, it is not possible to cite this attitude as an example in dealing with contemporary political situations, for that would be a naive misunderstanding of the circumstances in which God has revealed Himself.

3. The paradoxical aspect of the behaviour of Yahweh is reflected in the *presentation of the living God*, which becomes more and more refined in the course of biblical revelation. At first God* manifests His presence by violating what we call the normal course of creation, on Sinai for example (Ex 19). Later on, Elijah comes to understand that God does not act like the storm or the hurricane or the earthquake, but like a gentle murmur (1 K 19,11f). The Messiah*, depicted at first as the warrior-king breaking the heads of the rebels (Ps 110,5f; cf Jr 17,25; 22,4), will come as a "king...humble and peaceful, riding on a donkey" (Ze 9,9; cf Gn 49,11; Jg 5,10). And finally the Servant* of God, in whom the Christians will see a prophetic figure* of Jesus, has absolute confidence* in God and triumphs over violence by submitting to it voluntarily. He does not resist the wicked (Is 50,5f) and commits neither deceit nor violence (53,9).

IV. JESUS AND VIOLENCE

When Jesus came, He astonished His contemporaries by the complexity of His behavior. Thus, if we are going to interpret His words

and His actions correctly, we must avoid making arbitrary choices, based on completely subjective preferences, between some and others. We must adopt the position that Jesus Himself took.

1. *The kingdom of God* came suddenly into the world and, contrary to the expectations of the Jews, it met with violence. "Since John the Baptist came, up to this present time, the kingdom of heaven has been subjected to violence (*biazetai*), and the violent (*biastai*) are taking it by storm" (Mt 11,12). According to the most probable interpretation (*biastai* always refers to the attackers, the enemy), Jesus is thinking of the opponents who prevent people from entering the kingdom. But the saying has been interpreted by Luke in the sense of Lk 13,24, where the disciple is urged to "try your best (*agonizesthe*) to enter by the narrow door": "up to the time of John it was the Law and the Prophets; since then the kingdom of God has been preached, and by violence everyone is getting in (*biazetai*)" (16,16). By its arrival, the kingdom of God unleashed the sort of violence that is difficult to describe since there are no proper terms for it, but which Jesus did not conceal.

2. *Confronted by an unjust order*, which was an obstacle to the kingdom of God insofar as it did not welcome it, Jesus followed the example of the prophets* and made His protest in words and actions that the upholders of this established order must have found violent. They were upset by them not because they were excessive but because they appeared to violate the Law. Thus, Jesus introduced the ambiguous situation of Christian resignation in the face of injustice and pointed out the demands of charity. He drove the sellers from the Temple (Mt 21,12f p; Jn 2,13-22). He flouted the conventions of religion, of society and of language. He showed Himself master of the sabbath* (Mk 2,28). He had come not to bring the spurious peace that the prophets had already condemned (cf Jr 6,14), but the sword (Mt 10,34; cf Lk 12,51); He brought dissension even into the most sacred institution, the family, dividing parents and children, brothers and sisters, because of the challenge that He issued (Mt 10,35ff). Brusquely He rejected the sacred duty of respect toward parents: "Leave the dead to bury their dead" (Lk 9,60 p). He turned upside down the normal care for bodily integrity: Pluck out your eye

and cut off your hand if they scandalize you! (Mt 5,29f p). In all these things order was violated because it was unjust, not in itself but in reference to something that Jesus considered to be superior, the kingdom of God. As for the upholders of this order, they were called hypocrites and whited sepulchres (23, 13-36).

In the eyes of the supporters of an established order, which refused to give way before something of a higher value, Jesus appeared, like Elijah* before Him (1 K 19,17f), as a violent trouble-maker, a revolutionary turning the people away from the path that had been traced out by the masters of this order (Lk 23,2). On the other hand, in the eyes of God, Jesus was a dynamic force restoring the real values that the institution had ended by stifling. According to the point of view from which things are seen, it would be possible, with the Apocalypse, to depict Jesus as a man of violence (Ap 6,4-8; 8,5...), who in the end brought peace (21,4). One could also keep to the portrait that Jesus drew of Himself and see in Him the Master meek and humble of heart, who put up with violence, triumphed over it (1 P 2,21-24) and offered the rest* that overcomes injustice (Mt 11,29). With this living ideal before his eyes, the Christian strives to bring his way of life into line with it (1 P 2,18-21; 3,14; Lk 5,9f; Ap 14,12). On the level of social structures the Gospel means revolution insofar as these paralyze justice and charity, without which no son of God can live. "Set your heart on the kingdom of God and its justice!" (Mt 6,33).

3. *Confronted by the violence* that reigned in the world, Jesus showed Himself more radical than the OT. The law of retaliation required that there should be a sense of proportion in the vengeance by which the damage to justice was put right; Jesus insisted on pardon* (Mt 6,12.14f; Mk 11,25), as often as seventy-seven times (Mt 18,22). To all He gave the command: "Love your enemies and pray for those who persecute you" (5,44; Lk 6,27). Each disciple He told: "Offer the wicked man no resistance" (nor the "evil" that is in the world) (Mt 5,39). In the three examples that He gave to illustrate His instructions (5,39-41), Jesus was not making any judgment on the act of social violence (striking, taking the tunic, requisitioning), for which there may have been good cause, any more than He was suggesting that we should imitate the unjust steward (Lk 16,1-8) or the unjust judge (18,1-5). He was looking at things from the point of view of the injured party and saying that one must learn how to suffer violence.

Jesus was the first to do so. He stood firm against the temptation to set up the kingdom of God by violent *means*: he was not prepared to turn the stones into bread by magic*, even in order to satisfy the hunger of the world (Mt 4,3ff). Nor was He ready to dominate men by force* (4,8ff). And He refused to be a revolutionary politician (Jn 6,15) and to win glory without undergoing the sacrifice of the cross* (Mt 16,22f). Finally, after sweating blood in the Garden of Olives, He would not accept the struggle that His companions were engaging in to defend Him by violence: "Leave off!... That will do!" And He even cured one of His enemies (Lk 22,49ff; cf 22,36ff). Jesus did not shed men's blood: He shed His own.

Why, then, should we offer no resistance to the wicked man? Not because of some tactic of non-violence, but in a spirit of love and of sacrifice, the only way of *obtaining reconciliation* between the violent man and his victim (cf Gn 33; 45; 1 S 26). The kingdom of God was not established by brutality, but by the power of God, which showed itself capable of triumphing over death by raising Jesus to life. From then on, "all who draw the sword will die by the sword" (Mt 26,52). The very opposite of the spirit of Jesus is the spirit that wanted to retaliate against the inhospitable Samaritans by calling down fire from heaven (Lk 9,54). It is the meek* who will inherit the earth* (Mt 5,4). Unlike "the rulers of the nations who want to make their power and control over them felt," the disciple of Jesus ought "to make himself the servant" of the others (Mt 20,25f). When Jesus retreated, like the Servant* of God, in the face of the wickedness of His enemies (Mt 12,15.18-21; 14,13; 16,4), He put Himself in God's hands and made the beatitude of the persecuted come true (Mt 5,10ff), the beatitude that had been prophesied in the Servant songs (Is 50,5; 53,9). But, when He pardoned those who crucified Him unjustly (Lk 23,34; 1 P 2,23f), when He told His disciple to turn the other cheek, Jesus surpassed the ideal of the OT. He was not content with any passive abandonment of oneself into the hands of God, the defender of the oppressed: He offered violence to the violent, for the aim of this confrontation is reconciliation, which can be obtained already here on earth.

→Anathema OT—Blood OT 1—Cupidity OT 1—Hate—Justice *A* I OT 1, NT 1—Persecu-

tion—Power II o. 1—War—Wrath *A* 1—Zeal.
XLD ems

VIRGINITY

In many ancient religions virginity had a sacred import. Some goddesses (Anat, Artemis, Athena) were called virgins to accentuate their eternal youthfulness, their thriving vitality, their incorruptibility. Christian revelation alone was to show the full religious significance of virginity, somewhat outlined in the OT, as faithfulness to a love given exclusively to God.

OT

1. *Sterility and virginity.* In the view of God's people, in their orientation toward their own increase, virginity was equivalent to sterility*, which was a humiliation, a matter for shame (Gn 30,23; 1 S 1,11; Lk 1,25). Jephthah's daughter, when condemned to die without offspring, bewails her "virginity" for two months (Jg 11,37); for she will not share the reward (Ps 127,3), the blessing* (Ps 128,3-6) which is the fruit of the womb. However, virginity before marriage was highly regarded (Gn 24,16; Jg 19,24). One sees for example that the High Priest (Lv 21,13f) and even the simple priest (Ez 44,22; cf Lv 21,7) could only marry a virgin. At the same time it must be noted that this was still only a concern for ritual purity* in the sphere of sexuality* (cf Lv 12; 15) and not any real regard for virginity in itself.

The real preparation for Christian virginity is found in the context of the promises and the covenant. By the mysterious economy of sterile women whom He makes fertile, God wishes to point out that the bearers of the promises* have not been raised up by the normal procedure of fruitfulness*, but by His infinitely powerful intervention. The gratuity of His choice is revealed in this discreet preference accorded the sterile.

2. *Voluntary continence.* Besides this main current of thought, there are isolated instances of voluntary continence. At Yahweh's command Jeremiah must renounce marriage (Jr 16,2); but this is merely a symbolic act to declare the imminence of Israel's chastisement, in which women and children will be slaughtered (16,3ff.10-13). The Essenes live in continence but they appear to be motivated primarily by a concern for legal purity.

Other examples have a more religious significance: Judith, by her voluntary widowhood and penitential life (Jdt 8,4ff; 16,22), deserves to be, as Deborah once was (Jg 5,7), the mother of her people (Jdt 16,4.11.17). Her manner of life prepares the ordinary respect for widowhood and virginity found in the NT where Hannah refuses remarriage in order to adhere more closely to the Lord (Lk 2,37); and John the Baptist prepares for the Messiah's coming by an ascetical life and dares to call himself the friend of the bridegroom (Jn 3,29).

3. *The espousals between God and His people.* The precursor is thus shown as the inheritor of the prophetic tradition of the nuptials between Yahweh and His people, which was really a preparation for Christian virginity. More than once the prophets give the name of virgin to a conquered nation (Is 23,12; 47,1; Jr 46,11), and to Israel in particular (Am 5,2; Is 37,23; Jr 14, 17; Lm 1,15; 2,13); this is to bewail the loss of her territorial integrity. Likewise, however, when Israel violates the covenant Jeremiah calls her "the virgin Israel" (Jr 18,13) as a reminder of what her faithfulness* should have been. The same title recurs in the context of the restoration when Yahweh and His people shall renew relations of love and faithfulness (Jr 31,4.21). For Isaiah (62,5) the marriage of a young man and a virgin symbolizes the Messianic nuptials of Yahweh and Israel. By exclusive claims, God was preparing His faithful to reserve their entire love for Him.

NT

From the time of Christ, the virgin Israel is called the Church*. Believers who wish to remain virgins share in the virginity of the Church. Virginity is an essentially eschatological reality and assumes its full meaning only in the final fulfillment of the Messianic nuptials.

1. *The virgin Church, spouse of Christ.* As in the OT, the motif of virginity, paradoxically enough, goes back to the idea of espousal; for the union of Christ and the Church is a virginal union though symbolized by marriage*. "Christ loved the Church and delivered Himself for her" (E 5,25). The Church of Corinth was engaged to Christ so Paul wishes to present her to Him as an immaculately pure virgin (2 Co 11,2; cf E 5,27). As the apostle feels God's own jealousy for her (2 Co 11,2) he

wants no slur to be cast on the perfection of her faith.

2. *Mary's virginity.* The virginity of the Church begins to materialize at the point of fusion between the two covenants, that is in Mary*, the daughter of Zion. Jesus' mother is the only woman in the NT to whom the name of virgin is applied, practically as a title (Lk 1,27; cf Mt 1,23). Out of a wish to preserve her virginity (cf Lk 1,34), she assumed the lot of women who remain childless. But what was once a humiliation was destined to become for her a blessing (Lk 1,48). Before the coming of the angel, Mary wished to belong entirely to God. By her *fiat* at the annunciation (1,38) she is vowed totally and undividedly to God's Son. Virginity, as prepared for over a long period of time in the OT, is fulfilled in the virginity of the woman who becomes God's mother. So too is the desire of fruitfulness* and the prayer of sterile* women therein answered by God.

3. *Virginity of Christians.* Remaining a virgin, as had John the Baptist and Mary, it is Jesus who revealed the true meaning and supernatural character of virginity. Virginity is not a command (1 Co 7.25) but a personal call from God, a *charism** (7,7). "Besides eunuchs from birth and those who were made so by man's action, there are also those who have made themselves so for the sake of the kingdom* of heaven" (Mt 19,12). Only the kingdom of heaven justifies Christian virginity, and only those with the special gift understand these words (19,11).

For Paul, virginity is superior to marriage* because it is an undivided attachment to the Lord (1 Co 7,32-35). Whereas a married man is divided, those who are virgins have undivided hearts, are dedicated entirely to Christ, are concerned with the works of the Lord, and do not tolerate distraction from this persistent concern.

Christ's phrase in Mt 19,12 ("for the sake of the kingdom of heaven") gives virginity its real eschatological dimension. Paul considers virginity suitable "because of the present distress" (1 Co 7.26) and because of the time which is running short (7,29). The married state is essentially bound up with the present time, but the shape of this world is passing (7,31). Virgins are detached from this age. As in the parable (Mt 25,1.6), they await the bridegroom and the kingdom of heaven. As a constant manifestation of the Church's virginity, the lives of these virgins also testify that Christians do not belong to this world. Virginity is a permanent "sign" of the Church's eschatological tension, an anticipation of the resurrection in which those judged worthy to share the future world will be like angels and sons of God (Lk 20,34ff p).

The state of virginity, therefore, is an indication of what the Church really is. As the wise virgins, Christians go to meet Christ, their bridegroom, to share with Him in the wedding feast (Mt 25,1-13). In the heavenly Jerusalem, all the chosen ones are called virgins (Ap 14, 4) because of their refusal to submit to the harlotry of idolatry* and because of the more basic fact that they are now totally given to Christ. With a docility that is complete "they follow the Lamb* wherever He goes" (cf Jn 10,4.27). Henceforth they belong to the heavenly city and are the brides of the Lamb (Ap 19,7.9; 21,9).

→Fruitfulness III 2—Marriage NT II—Mary II—Mother II 2—Sexuality I 2—Spouse—Sterility—Widows 2—Woman NT.

IdlP dfb

VIRTUES & VICES

The Bible names many virtues and vices, that is, habits acquired by man, by which he is perfected or degraded. However, its vocabulary is poor when it comes to speaking of virtue or vice in general. In fact, unlike Greek humanism, it is less concerned with the point of view of man and his perfection than with the point of view of God and His plans for man. God wants to unite men with Himself and between themselves, and this communion demands their moral advancement.

1. *The nature of virtue and of vice.* The perfect man is not the one who tries to become perfect, he is the one who seeks* God and who finds Him by following the way* that God points out to him and which is also the only way in which he will find his own personal fulfillment. This basic attitude is expressed in the formula: "to walk with God" (Gn 5,22. 24; 6,9). It is this attitude that makes Noah* a just man, unlike the godless men about him in whose hearts there is nothing but evil (6,5). Virtue consists in a living relationship with God, in conformity with His words, in obedience* to His will, in a profound and lasting

turning toward Him. It is this relationship that makes a man just; this faithfulness* in following the Lord's way is the fundamental virtue, which Abraham* must teach his sons (18,19), and which must be practised as the condition of the Covenant (Ex 19,5.8). On the other hand, the fundamental vice is to follow some god other than the one true God (Dt 6,14; cf 4,35); it is to be unfaithful to the Covenant by departing from God's way (Ex 32,8).

But this conformity with the divine order of things, which constitutes virtue and which the Bible most frequently calls justice*, is not acquired simply by performing the acts required by God; these acts must manifest a docility and a fidelity coming from the heart* and which are the expression of love*. This is the fundamental law of the covenant (Dt 6,5f; 10,16; 11,1; 30,20). It is in the heart that virtue or vice has its root. It is there that the words of God must be set, or rather engraved, in order to be the source of the love and fidelity which are the soul of every virtue. David is so great in spite of his faults and Josaphat advances in the ways of the Lord (1 K 15,3; 2 Ch 17,6), because their hearts are entirely God's. And if Ezekiah does what is good, just and loyal in the sight of God, it is because he is seeking Him with all his heart (2 Ch 31,20f).

The wisdom of the psalmists describes the virtuous man by saying that his heart is full of the law of God and takes pleasure in it (Ps 1,2; 37,31), while the evil man has a heart that is empty of God and considers Him as non-existent (14,1). The man formed by Wisdom in all the virtues useful to man: temperance and prudence, justice and strength of mind, is the one who loves justice (Ws 8,7, where justice is taken in one case in its Hebrew sense of the fundamental virtue and in the other in its Greek sense of the special virtue of social relationship).

Finally, the perfect justice preached by Jesus (Mt 5,20) and described in the Sermon on the Mount is that of a heart free from every evil desire* and full of a merciful love extending even to enemies (5,7f.28.44). It is the vices that come from his heart that make a man unclean (15,18f).

2. *The source of virtue and of vice.* There is no need to look outside man himself for the source of vice. By separating himself through sin from God he has become incapable of controlling his evil desires and of remaining master of himself; instead of perfecting the world, he

has corrupted it (1 Jn 2,16f). From now on he cannot find in himself the strength to resist the weight of his passions (Si 1,22; 18,30) and to become clean again. It is the strength* of the Lord that will be the source of his strength (Dt 8,17f; E 6,10); without it he will remain faint-hearted and listless (Si 2,12f). For his heart to become pure, it is necessary that he should be recreated by God and have put into him a new spirit, making him strong (Ps 51,12ff). This is the gift announced by the prophets and which will be fulfilled in the new covenant; then a new heart will be given to men and the law of God will be written on it; they will receive the Spirit* of God Himself and He will make them faithful (Jr 31,33; Ez 36,26f). This is the Spirit that will fill the Messiah and give him all the virtues he needs for his royal mission: wisdom to govern, strength to free men from their enemies, piety to remain united with the God whom He represents (Is 11,2-5).

Christ reveals to His disciples the role of this Spirit as the master of the interior life (Jn 14,26; 16,13). It is He who will give them the wisdom and strength they need to be invincible witnesses (Mt 10,20 p; Lk 21,14f; 24,48f; Ac 1,8). It is He who will free the believer from all the earthly desires that make a man vicious (G 5,19ff), by putting in his heart the divine charity and making him bear the fruit* that is all the virtues animated by this charity (R 5,5; G 5,22); in this way this Spirit strengthens man in his very depths (E 3,16).

3. *Connection between the virtues and catalogs of vices.* The Bible is not content with pointing out the path the virtuous man ought to follow and threatening the godless man with the judgment of God (Ps 1). Like the pagan moralists, it takes the trouble to make instructive lists of the chief characteristics of both vices and virtues.

The lists of vices are given by the prophets (Ho 4,1f; Jr 7,9), the wise men (Pr 6,16-19; Si 25,2; 26,5f), Christ (Mk 7,21f p) and His apostles (1 Co 6,9f; R 1,29ff; Col 3,5-9; 1 Tm 1,9f; 2 Tm 3,1-5; 1 P 2,1; 4,3). Paul especially stresses that the real cause of vice is the refusal to recognize the true God and the preference for idols. Sometimes vices have the effect of dividing men; sometimes too they are opposed to one another.

Such an opposition does not exist between the virtues, for they, on the contrary, complete one another, and the lists of them show why the just man is unified within himself and the source of unity*. Take for example the summary of the prophet Micah: "To act justly, to love tenderly and to walk humbly with your God" (Mi 6,8). As for Jesus, He stands out by His humility* and meekness* (Mt 11,29), of which He gives the example (Jn 13,15), and in the love that makes Him offer up His life (15, 13), a love that should be the model of the disciples' love for one another (13,34; 15,17), a love that will be their distinguishing mark (13,35). And Paul, who admits the Greek idea of virtue, when he recommends that we should do all that deserves praise (Ph 4,8), often insists on the "three that remain:" faith, hope and charity (1 Th 1,3; R 5,1-5; Col 1,4f...), and he declares that the greatest virtue is charity (1 Co 13,13). Other virtues are of course, recommended (1 Th 5,14-18; R 12,9-21; E 4,2; I Tm 4,12; 6,11; 1 P 3,8; 2 P 1,5ff); but charity is the bond of perfection; it establishes the reign of the peace* of Christ, in whom all men are one single Body (Col 3,12-15).

→Arrogance — Conscience — Cupidity — Desire II, III—Faithfulness OT 2, NT 2—Fear of God IV—Flesh II 2—Good & Evil I—Hardness of Heart—Heart—Humility—Idols II 3—Justice—Love II—Meekness 2.3—Obedience II 3, IV—Perfection—Piety—Pure OT II; NT I, II 3—Seek I—Sexuality III 1—Sin—Spirit of God NT V 3—Strength II—Way II—Wisdom OT III 4; NT III 2.

MFL ems

VISITATION

Salvation* history is often presented in the Bible as a series of "visitations" of Yahweh to His people or to some privileged persons. God, who took the initiative in the covenant* and who is in a secret fashion present in the evolution of His plan*, often intervenes in an extraordinary way in the life of His people either to bless or punish, but always to save. This masterly attention, these visible, personal interventions are signs of God's presence* and action, of the continuity of His saving plan, and of His demands throughout the volatile history of His people. Divine interventions are a preparation and announcement of the day which will be preeminently the day* of the Lord, the coming of God Himself in Jesus and His glorious return at the last judgment* in the ultimate act of salvation.

OT

1. "God shall visit you to take you out of this country to the land He promised by oath to Abraham, Isaac, and Jacob" (Gn 50,24f). The God who called Abraham to make him father of a great multitude and who, for this purpose, "visited" Sarah and made her fruitful (21,1f), intervenes in a unique manner by delivering His people from Egypt. The visitations of a God who loves and saves His people will be recreated throughout the course of Israel's history. They are the warp and woof of Yahweh's faithfulness* to His promises*. For the Israelites unfaithful to the covenant, the intervention of a jealous God takes the form of chastisement; but the intervention is still directed to the salvation of the people. All the prophets, and especially Jeremiah, make use of Yahweh's interventions in various modulations and frequencies. Victories* are visitations of God blessing His faithful (Zp 2,7). Misfortunes are likewise visitations of God who corrects the Israelites and their leaders to lead them back to Him. "Of all the families of the earth, I have known only you. So I will visit you for all your iniquities" (Am 3,2; Ho 4,9; Is 10,3; Jr 6,15; 23,2.34). Ezekiel describes this visitation as a shepherd's inspection of his flock passing in review (Ez 34). Therefore, the visitation always proceeds from God's love and is directed to the people's salvation. Neighboring nations*—Moab, Egypt, and especially Babylon—who oppose the divine plan of salvation will themselves be "visited" by God as a judge who will punish (Jr 46,21...; 48,44; 50,18.27.31) but finally save them (Jr 12, 14-17; 16,19ff). The return from exile, like the deliverance from Egypt, is a work of Yahweh: "When the seventy years allotted to Babylon have terminated, only then shall I visit you to fulfill my promise to lead you back here" (Jr 29,10; cf 32,5; Ps 80,15; Ze 10,3).

2. *Each Jew* shall then be more aware that he is the object of God's particular personal attention. "Lord, remember me for love of your people. Visit me with your salvation, that I may see the happiness of your elect" (Ps 106,4). Individual visitations are not limited to the realm of worship, for God enlightens the mind of the wise by examining their conduct (Jb 7, 18; Ps 17,3) or by sending them dreams (Si 34,6; cf the phenomenon as early as Gn 20,3).

Most especially after the exile the very onward thrust of revelation opens the mind to the *announcing of a definitive visitation*. God will come to judge* the people and the nations. That day* of Yahweh, already announced by the prophets before the exile, will be the triumphal day of the elect saved by the coming, the visitation, the reign of God. It shall extend by right to all peoples. "On the day of His visitation the just* shall shine...and the Lord shall reign over them forever" (Ws 3,7; Si 2,14). On this hope Jews of the first century will live (vg Qumrân). When Jesus comes and preaches the kingdom, the promised and hoped for divine visitation is going to become a reality.

NT

1. "Blessed be the Lord, the God of Israel, because He has visited and delivered His people" (Lk 1,68). God is moved by love (1,78) and a desire to fulfill His promises*, and He comes in the person of Jesus to save men; thus does God fulfill man's hopes and answer his prayers. The foregoing is the theme permeating the entire gospel. The precursor appears in the light of the prophecies as the one who came to prepare hearts for the arrival and manifestation of God in Jesus. John preaches an eschatological judgment and proclaims the arrival of the kingdom*. Jesus Himself will insist primarily on the salvific character and the universal aspect of His visitation. It is a visitation offered to all flesh* (Lk 3,6; cf 1 P 2,12), but destined to be received only by those pure hearts* capable of recognizing it: "A great prophet has arisen among us and God has visited His people" (Lk 7,16). But this will not be a universal interpretation; for, in spite of miracles*, God's visitation in Jesus is not like an overwhelming flash of lightning. One can decline to accept the visitation.

This dramatic aspect of God's visitation is emphasized by the evangelists, especially St. John: "He came among His own and His own received Him not" (Jn 1,11). This culpable refusal to acknowledge Jesus will turn grace to a threat of chastisement. Woe to those who cannot recognize the "time of visitation"! "Woe to Jerusalem!" (Lk 19,43f). Woe to the lakeside towns! This Jewish rejection, in striking contrast to the pagan attitude (Mt 8,10ff), is presented as the ultimate tragedy in a long series of refusals and disregard for Yahweh's visitations throughout the OT. Chastisement will be terrible for those who do not receive the king's son, sent by his father to "collect the fruits" of the vine (Mt 21,33-46). The destruction of Jerusalem—that is, the end of the Jewish world, a striking indication, as well as a perceptible prologue, of God's judgment*—is the awful visitation of the Son of Man who speaks of His final coming in glory (cf Mt 25,31-46).

2. Before that ultimate visitation which is anticipated by the "joyful entry" of Jesus over palm branches, the activity of Jesus goes on in the Church through the mission* of the apostles and the sending of the Spirit (*"mentes tuorum visita"*). The Lord Himself is a perpetual mediator in the life of the Church; as is shown, for example, in the Apocalypse where He is prepared to punish the Asian communities if they do not change their ways (Ap 2—3). Though we must go as a group before the Christ "who comes" (1 Th 4,17; cf Mt 25,6), each follower of Christ is personally invited to welcome Jesus' visitation: "Behold I stand at the door and knock..." (Ap 3,20). The follower of Christ must therefore watch* (Mt 24,42ff; 25,1-13) and pray*, until that day*, unknown to all, when Jesus "will appear a second time to those who are waiting for Him, to give them salvation" (He 9,28).

→Calamity 2—Day of the Lord—Hope NT II —Hour 1 — Judgment — Providence — Punishments 3—Reward I—Salvation—Sleep I 2— Sterility II, III—Watch I—Wrath *B* OT III 3; NT III 2.

RD dfb

W

WAR

War is not only a human fact which poses moral problems. Its presence in the world of the Bible allows revelation to express, beginning from a common experience, an essential aspect of the drama in which humanity is engaged and of which salvation is the stake—the spiritual combat between God and Satan. It is true that God's plan has peace* for its end; but this peace itself supposes a victory* won at the price of combat.

OT

I. WARS OF MAN AND COMBATS OF GOD

1. War at all times is an important element of the human condition. In the ancient East it was endemic. At the return of each year, the kings "took the field" (2 S 11,1). In vain did the empires in the periods of high culture sign treaties of "perpetual peace": the evolution of facts quickly broke these fragile contracts. Inserted in this framework the history of Israel is going to invoke an experience, sometimes elevating, sometimes cruel, of human combats. Introduced into the perspective of God's plan* this experience therein acquires a scope that is specifically religious: war will there be revealed at once as a permanent reality of this world and as an evil.

2. However, transferring to the religious domain the results of its social experience, the ancient East did not omit to introduce war also into its representation of the divine world. It frequently imagined at the beginning of time a war of gods, of which all of man's wars were like prolongations and earthly imitations. Israel, while cutting polytheism short, a polytheism supported by such images, preserves however that of a combatant God. But it transforms the imagery to adapt it to its monotheism and to give it a place in the earthly realization of God's plan*.

II. ISRAEL AT THE SERVICE OF THE WARS OF YAHWEH

1. The dimensions opened by the Sinaitic covenant are not those of peace, but of combat: God gives a fatherland* to His people, but the people must conquer it (Ex 23,27-33). This is an offensive war, which is sacred and which is justified in the viewpoint of the OT. Canaan, with its corrupted civilization made worse by a worship of the forces of nature, constitutes a snare for Israel (Dt 7,3f). Hence God sanctions its extermination (Dt 7,1f). The national wars of Israel will then be the "wars of Yahweh." Even more, in bringing Israel to birth in history, it is His own reign that God sets up here below, thanks to a people who worship Him and observe His law. In defending its independence against foreign aggressors, Israel at the same time defends God's cause: every defensive battle is still a "war of Yahweh."

2. It is thus that in the course of the centuries Israel has the experience of a life of combat, in which the national dynamism is placed at the service of a religious cause. Offensive wars against Sihon and Og (Nm 21,21-35; Dt 2,26—3,17), then the conquest of Canaan by Joshua* (Js 6—12); defensive wars against Midian (Nm 31) and against the oppressors of the period of the judges (Jg 3—12); the war of national liberation, with Saul and David (1 S 11-17; 28—30; 2 S 5; 8; 10): in this totality of events, Israel appears as the herald of God on earth; its king is Yahweh's lieutenant in history. The ardor of faith requires deeds of military prowess, which sustain the certitude of divine help and the hope of a victory* at once political and religious (cf Ps 2; 45,4ff; 60,7-14; 110). But the temptation to confuse God's cause with the earthly prosperity of Israel will be great.

III. THE COMBATS OF YAHWEH IN HISTORY

1. *Yahweh fights for His people.* The wars of Yahweh waged by Israel are, however, only one

aspect of the combats waged by God in human history. From the beginning He is personally struggling against the evil forces opposed to His designs. The fact is brought out in the history of His people, when different enemies* try to block their start. Then, asserting His control of events, God intervenes by His sovereign action; and Israel goes through the experience of wonderful deliverances. At the time of the exodus Yahweh fights against Egypt, striking it with prodigies of every kind (Ex 3,20), striking their first-born (Ex 11,4...), their head (Ex 14, 18...): in Canaan, He supports the armies of Israel (Jg 5,4.20; Js 5,13f; 10,10-14; 2 S 5,24); in the course of the ages, He helps the kings (Ps 20; 21) and delivers His holy city (Ps 48,4-8; 2 K 19,32-36)...All these facts show that human struggles do not attain their end except with His help. Men fight but God alone gives the victory* (Ps 118,10-14; 121,2; 124).

2. *God fights against sinners.* The combats of God here below do not have as their last end the temporal triumph of Israel. God's glory* is of another nature; His kingdom of another order. What He wishes is the establishment of a kingdom* of prosperity and justice, such as His Law* defines it. Israel has the mission to effect this; but if it fails, God must fight His sinful people for the same reason that He combats the pagan powers. That is why, as a reward for its infidelities, Israel also goes through the experience of military reverses: at the time in the desert (Nm 14,39-44), of Joshua (Js 7,2...), the judges (1 S 4), of Saul (1 S 31). During the time of the kings, the fact recurred periodically; and, after the ravages of a number of invasions, Israel and Judah will end in complete national ruin. In the eyes of the prophets these are the results of God's judgments*: Yahweh strikes His sinful people (Is 1,4-9); it is He who dispatches the invaders with the charge of punishing* it (Jr 4,5—5,17; 6; 5,26-30). The armies of Babylon* are under His orders (Jr 25,14-38) and Nebuchadnezzar is His servant(Jr 27,6ff).

Through these terrible events Israel understood that war is fundamentally an evil. It is the result of fratricidal hatred* among men (cf Gn 4), it is bound to the destiny of a sinful race. As a scourge of God it will not, therefore, disappear radically from here below until sin* itself shall have disappeared (Ps 46,10; Ez 39, 9f). That is why the eschatological promises of the prophets are all fulfilled by a marvelous vision of universal peace* (Is 2,4; 11,6-9, etc.). Such is the genuine salvation* to which Israel

should aspire rather than to holy wars of conquest and destruction.

IV. ESCHATOLOGICAL COMBATS

1. *The assault of enemy forces.* This salvation will not come, however, without combat. But this time the essentially religious character of the struggle will be much better distinguished from temporal incidents than it was in the past. Doubtless its expected meaning will still have something of the appearance of a military assault by pagans against Jerusalem (Ez 38; Ze 14,1-3; Jdt 1—7). But in the apocalypse of Daniel, written during the bloody persecution unleashed by the emperor Antiochus, it is clear that the enemy power represented under the features of monstrous beasts* has for its first purpose "to make war on the saints" and to attack God Himself (Dn 7,19-25; 11,40-45; cf Jdt 3,8). Behind the political combat can also be discerned the spiritual combat of Satan* and his allies against God.

2. *God's answer.* In the presence of this assault which a pagan totalitarian power was launching against its faith, Judaism could well react still by a military revolt which it renews with the traditions of the holy war (1 M 2—4; 2 M 8—10). In fact Israel knew itself to be engaged in a higher struggle for which it must first of all count on help from God (cf 2 M 15,22ff; Jdt 9). It is Yahweh who at the decreed time will determine the death of the beast* (Dn 7, 11.26) and break its power (Dn 8,25; 11,45). This perspective goes beyond the plan of temporal wars. It ends in a celestial combat by means of which God will crown all those whom He has already sustained in history (cf Is 59,15-20; 63, 1-6), all those whom He is actually sustaining in the defense of the just against their enemies* (Ps 35,1ff). This combat will have the final judgment* for its setting. It will put an end to all iniquity here below(Ws 5,17-23) and will be the direct prelude to the reign of God on earth. That is why it will be followed by an eternal peace*, in which all the just will have part (Dn 12,1ff; Ws 4,7ff; 5,15f).

NT

The NT fulfills these promises. The eschatological war is there waged on three levels; that of the earthly life of Jesus, that of the history of His Church, that of the final consummation.

I. JESUS

In Jesus is fully revealed the profound nature of the eschatological conflict. It is not a temporal conflict for a kingdom of this world (Lk 22,50f; Jn 18,38); and Jesus refuses the use of any human violence to defend Himself (Mt 26, 52; Jn 18,11). It is a spiritual conflict against Satan*, against the world*, against evil. Jesus is the strong one who comes to overthrow the prince of this world (Mt 4,1-11 p; 12,27ff p; Lk 11,18ff). Indeed, this latter reacts by trying a final assault against Him. Putting Jesus to death is his last attempt (Lk 22,3; Jn 13,2.27; 14,30). It is he who excites the activity of the earthly powers leagued against the anointed of the Lord (Ac 4,25-28; cf Ps 2). But in doing this he precipitates his own defeat. In fact, paradoxically, the cross* of Jesus assures His victory* (Jn 12,31). On His resurrection, the hostile evil powers*, despoiled of their authority, appear in His triumphal cortege (Col 2,15). Conqueror of the world by His death (Jn 16,33), He possesses henceforth the regency of history (Ap 5); but the conflict which He has personally waged will be prolonged through the centuries in the life of His Church.

II. THE CHURCH OF JESUS

1. *The Church militant.* The Church* is not a grandeur of the temporal order as was still the ancient people* of Israel. The wars of men are therefore none of her business. But on her own level she is in a state of militancy as long as the history of the present world lasts. What Jesus brings to men through her is peace* with God and peace among themselves (Lk 2,14; Jn 14,27; 16,33). But such a peace is not of this world. Thus men who believe in Him will be always exposed to the hatred of the world (Jn 15,18-21). On the temporal level Jesus has never brought them peace, but the sword (Mt 10,34 p); for the kingdom of God is exposed to violence (Mt 11,12 p). Individually, each Christian will have to wage a combat, not against adversaries of flesh and blood, but against Satan and his allies (E 6,10ff; 1 P 5,8f). Collectively, the Church will be delivered to the assaults of the powers of this world, which will become allies of Satan—such as imperial Rome, that new Babylon* (Ap 12,17—13,10; 17).

2. *Christian weapons.* In the conflict the Church and its members use no temporal arms, but those which Jesus has bequeathed them. The Christian virtues are the weapons of light worn by the soldier of Christ (1 Th 5,8; E 6,11. 13-17). It is faith* in Christ which overcomes the evil one and the world (1 Jn 2,14; 4,4; 5,4f). Apparently the world* can triumph over Christians when it persecutes* them and kills them (Ap 11,7-10); a precarious victory, it is a prelude to a reversal just as the cross of Christ prepared for His resurrection in glory (Ap 11,11.15-18). The Lamb* by His death vanquished the devil; in the same way His companions will triumph over their foe by their martyrdom* (Ap 12,11; 14,1-5). The heroism of such combats surpasses by far that of the ancient wars of Yahweh, and demands no less valor.

III. THE FINAL COMBAT

1. *Preliminary symptoms.* The "last times" inaugurated by Jesus thus take on the appearance of a war to the death between two camps; that of Christ and that of Antichrist*. There is no doubt that the struggle must increase in subtlety, in brutality, in intensity in the measure that history approaches its consummation. But the evil world, the world of sin, is under the certainty of a divine condemnation, the mark of which its destiny will henceforth bear. It is here that the wars of men reveal the fullness of their meaning. At the heart of the temporal experience of man, there are written the signs of the judgment* to come (Mt 24,6 p; Ap 6,1-4; 9, 1-11). They reveal the interior oppositions to which sinful humanity is doomed in the measure in which it refuses to accept the peace of Christ.

2. *Images of the last combat.* For time is infallibly running to its end. If, on the one hand, Christ gathers all the dispersed sons of God into His Church little by little (Jn 11,52); on the other, Satan who apes Him tries also to unite in one army all those whom he has seduced. At the end of the centuries, the Apocalypse represents them to us as reunited under his leadership, to open their last conflict (Ap 19,19; 20,7ff). But this time, Christ the victor will make His lordship* visibly flash forth, Word of God appearing in glory and exercising the office of exterminator (Ap 19,11-16.21; cf Mt 24,30 p). The temporal view of what is to come hides itself from us behind this supernatural picture, which ends with the end of time with the everlasting chastisement of Satan and his supporters (Ap 19,20; 20,10). After that,

all contradiction being overcome, whether between God and man, or between the different groups of men, the perfect peace* of the new Jerusalem will reintroduce saved humanity into paradise* (Ap 21). A vision of the final victory* which is the foundation of the constancy and the confidence of the saints (Ap 12,10), for then the Church militant shall die forever in the Church triumphant, united about Christ the victor (Ap 3,21f; 7).

→Anathema OT—Antichrist—Ark of the Covenant I — Babel/Babylon — Beasts & Beast — Calamity—Day of the Lord OT—Enemy—Evil Spirits—Hate I 3—Joshua 1—King NT II 2—Peace—Persecution I 4 a—Punishments—Satan —Victory—Violence III 2.

HC & PG wjy

WATCH

In its proper sense, *to watch* means to give up a night's sleep*. This may be done to allow more time for work (Ws 6,15) or to avoid being taken unawares by an enemy (Ps 127,1f). Hence, in a metaphorical sense, to watch is to be vigilant, to fight torpor and carelessness to reach a desired goal (Pr 8,34). The believer's objective is a state of preparation to receive the Lord when the Day* comes (Is 21,11-12; 52,8). The believer watches and is alert so that he can live in darkness in the night without being a part of the darkness.

I. TO WATCH:
TO BE READY FOR THE LORD'S RETURN

1. *In the synoptic gospels* the exhortation to vigilance is the main piece of advice Jesus gives His disciples at the conclusion of His discourse on the last things and the coming of the Son of Man (Mk 13,33-37). "Watch, then, for you do not know on what day your master will come" (Mt 24,42). To point out that His return is unforeseeable, Jesus uses various comparisons and parables which are the source of current usage of the word *to watch* (to abstain from sleep). The coming of the Son of Man will be as unexpected as that of a thief in the night (Mt 24,32f), or of a master returning in the late hours without warning his servants (Mk 13,35f). Just as the prudent father of a family or the good servant, a Christian should not be over-

come by sleep*. He must watch, be on guard, be ready to receive the Lord. Watchfulness thus characterizes the attitude of the disciple who hopefully* awaits the return of Jesus. This vigilance is primarily a state of alertness and therefore demands detachment from earthly pleasures and goods (Lk 21,34ff). Because the hour of the parousia cannot be foreseen, one must dispose oneself for the event of its imminence. This is the teaching of the parable of the virgins (Mt 25,1-13)

2. *The early Pauline epistles* manifest a concern with eschatological expectations and reflect gospel warnings of vigilance, especially 1 Th 5, 1-7. "We are not part of the darkness or of night. So let us not sleep as other men, but let us rather watch and be sober" (5,5f). Because he has turned to God, the Christian is a "child of light*." For this reason he should actively and consistently resist darkness, the symbol of evil; otherwise Christ's coming will take him by surprise. Watchfulness demands a certain sobriety, that is, renunciation of excesses associated with "the night" and of any other factor calculated to distract one from the Lord's coming. At the same time watchfulness demands that one shoulder spiritual weapons. "Let us wear faith and love as a coat of mail and hope of salvation as a helmet" (5,8). In a later letter, St. Paul, out of a fear that the Christians may lose their first fervor, urges them to stir themselves up a bit, to wake from their sleep*, to prepare for the salvation now at hand (R 13,11-14).

3. In the *Apocalypse*, the message which the judge at the end of time addresses to the community at Sardis is an urgent exhortation to watchfulness (3,1ff). That Church forgets that Christ will return. If it does not wake up, He will surprise it, like a thief. But blessed is "he who watches and has his clothes in readiness" (16,15); thus will he be able to join the triumphal procession of the Lord.

II. TO WATCH: TO BE ON GUARD
AGAINST DAILY TEMPTATION

This watchfulness, this persevering expectation of Jesus' return, should be a permanent part of Christian life and should manifest itself in the battle against the daily temptations which are the prologue of the great eschatological combat.

1. At the moment of accomplishing the Father's salvific will* Jesus must undergo a tormenting combat (*agônia*) in Gethsemani; it is a prelude of the struggle at the end of time. The synoptics present Jesus as a model of watchfulness in temptation, a model who stands out the more because the disciples, heedless of the master's warning, have fallen. "Watch and pray so that you do not invite temptation" (Mt 26,41), a word of Christian address transcending Gethsemani. The last petition of the Our Father is close to the preceeding, for it asks God's help not only at the eschatological moment but all the way along the battle of Christian life.

2. The command of watchfulness, because of the dangers inherent in the present life, recurs in the Pauline letters (1 Co 16,13; Col 4,2; E 6, 10-20). The exhortation is formulated in a particularly vivid manner in a passage read each evening at Compline: "Be sober and watch! Your adversary the devil, as a roaring lion, goes about looking for someone to devour" (1 P 5, 8). Here, as in E 6,10ff, the enemy is clearly described. With implacable hatred, Satan* and his helpers are continually spying on the Christian to effect some denial of Christ. May the Christian be always on his guard! May he pray with faith and by self-denial avoid the enemy's snares! This watchfulness is particularly recommended to leaders in the community; they are to defend the community against the "savage wolves" (Ac 20,28-31).

III. TO WATCH: TO PASS THE NIGHT IN PRAYER

In E 6,18 and Col 4,2, St. Paul very likely alludes to a practice of the early communities, that of prayer vigils. "Always make use of prayers and entreaties in the Spirit. To this end use your vigils with unfailing perseverance" (E 6,18). The vigil is a concrete instance of Christian vigilance and an imitation of Jesus' actions (Lk 6,12; Mk 14,38).

Conclusion. Watchfulness is a characteristic of the Christian, who hopes for and expects the glorious manifestation of the Lord Jesus. It consists in being ready to welcome the One who is coming (Ap 22,17.20) and to resist the apostasy of the last days. Since the temptations of this present life are an anticipation of the eschatological tribulation, Christian watchfulness must be exercised from day to day in the struggle against the Evil One; it demands constant prayer and sobriety from the disciple.

→Angels—Cares I—Day of the Lord NT II—Drunkenness 2—Hope NT III—Lamp 2—Ministry II 3—Night NT 2.3—Noah 3—Providence—Shepherd & Flock—Sleep—Visitation NT 2.

MD dfb

WATER

Water is first of all the source and strength of life: without it the earth is nothing but an arid desert*, a land of hunger and thirst, where men and beasts are doomed to death. But there are also waters of death*: the destructive flood that overruns the earth and swallows up the living. Finally, in the cultic ablutions, which take over a custom of domestic life, water purifies* persons and things from the stains incurred in the course of everyday life. Thus water, whether vivifying or menacing, always cleansing, is most closely intermingled with human life and the history of the people of the covenant.

I. CREATURE OF GOD

God, the master of the universe, dispenses water according to His will and therefore holds the destinies of mankind in His hand. The Israelites, maintaining the picture of the ancient Babylonian cosmogony, divide the waters into two distinct aggregates. The "waters from on high" were held back by the firmament, thought of as a solid surface (Gn 1,7; Ps 148,4; Dn 3,60; cf Ap 4,6). When the sluices are opened the water is permitted to fall to earth as rain (Gn 7,11; 8,2; Is 24,18; Ml 3,10) or as dew which is spread during the night over the grass (Jb 29, 19; Ct 5,2; Ex 16,13). Springs and rivers, however, flow not from rain but from an immense reservoir of water on which the earth rests: the "waters from below," the abyss (Gn 7,11; Dt 8,7; 33,13; Ez 31,4).

God, the founder of this order, is the master of the waters. He holds them back or releases them at His pleasure, those from on high as those from below; and thus He causes either aridity or flood (Jb 12,15). "He pours out the rain upon the land" (Jb 5,10; Ps 104,10-16), this rain that comes from God and not from men (Mi 5,6; cf Jb 38,22-28). He has "set laws" to it (Jb 28,26). He watches to see that it falls regularly, "in time" (Lv 26,4; Dt 28,12): if it comes too late (in January), the sowing time would be put off, just as the harvest if it stops too soon, "three months to harvest" (Am 4,7). On the other hand, when God deigns to grant to men the rains of autumn and spring (Dt 11,14; Jr 5,24), they insure the prosperity of the country (Is 30,23ff).

God likewise governs the abyss according to His will (Ps 135,6; Pr 3,19f). If He drains it, He dries up the springs and rivers (Am 7,4; Is 44,27; Ez 31,15) and calls forth desolation. If He opens the "floodgates" of the abyss, the rivers flow and cause the vegetation on their banks to flourish (Nm 24,6; Ps 1,3; Ez 19,10), especially when rain is scarce (Ez 17,8). In desert regions the springs and wells are the only sources of water that allows men and beasts to slake their thirst (Gn 16,14; Ex 15,23.27). They represent the reserves of life that are bitterly fought over (Gn 21,25; 26,20f; Js 15,19).

Psalm 104 sums up the admirable mastery of God over the waters; it is He who has created the waters on high (Ps 104,3) as well as those of the abyss (v 6); it is He who rules the extent of their course (v 7f), who holds them back lest they submerge the earth (v 9), who causes the springs to leap up (v 10) and the rain to fall (v 13), thanks to which prosperity is spread over the earth and the heart of man is gladdened (vv 11-18).

II. THE WATERS IN THE HISTORY OF THE PEOPLE OF GOD

1. *Waters and temporal retribution.* If God grants or denies the waters according to His good pleasure, He nevertheless does not do it arbitrarily but according to the conduct of His people. According as they remain faithful or not to the covenant, God grants or denies water. If the Israelites live according to the divine Law and obey the voice of God, God opens the heavens to bestow rain in good season (Lv 26, 3ff.10; Dt 28,1.12). Water is, then, the effect and the sign of the blessing* of God toward those who serve Him faithfully (Gn 27,28; Ps 133,3). On the other hand, if Israel is unfaithful, God punishes* her by making "a sky of iron and an earth of bronze" (Lv 26,19; Dt 28,23), that she might understand and be converted (Am 4,7). Dryness is, therefore, an effect of the divine curse* toward the godless* (Is 5,13; 19,5ff; Ez 4,16f; 31,15), like that which laid waste the

country under Ahab when Israel had "abandoned God to follow Baal" (1 K 18,18).

2. *Terrifying waters.* Water is not merely a power of life. Waters from the sea* reflect demoniacal restlessness by their perpetual agitation and the desolation of Sheol by their bitterness. The sudden swelling of the west wind, blowing away the earth and living things during a storm* (Jb 12,15; 40,23), symbolizes the misfortune that is prepared to fall upon man unexpectedly (Ps 124), the plots that the just man's enemies* weave against him (Ps 18,5f.17; 42, 8; 71,20; 144,7); by their machinations they attempt to drag him to the very bottom of the abyss (Ps 32,25; 69,2f). Now, if God knows how to protect the just man from these destructive tides (Ps 32,6; cf Ct 8,6f), He can just as easily permit them to break over the godless— just punishment* for conduct contrary to the love of one's neighbor (Jb 22,11). For the prophets, the destructive overflowing of the great rivers symbolizes the power* of the kingdoms that go to submerge and destroy small nations; the power of Assyria compared to the Euphrates (Is 8,7) or of Egypt likened to the Nile (Jr 46, 7f). These are the rivers that God is going to send to punish His people who are guilty of a lack of trust in Him (Is 8,6ff), as well as the traditional enemies of Israel (Jr 47,1f).

In the hands of the Creator, however, this brutal scourge is not blind; though it swallows up the godless world (2 P 2,5), the flood* allows Noah*, the just man, to survive (Ws 10,4). The waters of the Red Sea likewise made a distinction between the people of God and those of the idols (Ws 10,18f). The terrifying waters, then, anticipate the final judgment* by fire (2 P 3,5ff; cf Ps 29,10; Lk 3,16f); they leave a new earth after their passage (Gn 8,11).

3. *Purifying waters.* The theme of the waters of anger is joined with another aspect of beneficent water: this is not only the power of life but also that which bathes and washes away stains (cf Ez 16,4-9; 23,40). One of the elementary rites of hospitality* was to wash the feet of a guest in order to wipe away the dust of the journey (Gn 18,4; 19,2; cf Lk 7,44; 1 Tm 5,10); and on the eve of His death Jesus wished to perform this duty of a servant Himself as an exemplary sign of humility and Christian love (Jn 13,2-15).

A means of physical cleanliness, water is often the symbol of moral purity. People wash their hands to show that they are innocent and have not done the evil (Ps 26,6; cf Mt 27,24). The sinner who leaves off sinning and is converted is like a soiled man who bathes (Is 1,16). Likewise God "washes" the sinner whose sins He forgives (Ps 51,4). By means of the flood God "cleansed" the earth when He brought death to the godless (cf 1 P 3,20f).

The Jewish ritual provided for numerous purifications* by water: the high priest was to bathe to be prepared for his investiture (Ex 29,4; 40, 12) or for the great Day of Atonement (Lv 16, 4.24); ablutions with water were prescribed for one who had touched a dead body (Lv 11,40; 17,15f), to be cleansed from leprosy* (Lv 14,8f) or from any sexual impurity (Lv 15). These different bodily purifications were to signify interior purification of the heart*, essential to one who wished to draw near to the thrice-holy* God. But they were powerless to bring about effectively purity of soul. In the new covenant, Christ instituted a new mode of purification; at the wedding at Cana He foretold it in symbolic manner when He changed water destined for ritual cleansings (Jn 2,6) into wine*, which symbolizes both Spirit and the purifying Word (Jn 15,3; cf 13,10).

III. ESCHATOLOGICAL WATERS

1. The theme of water, finally, holds an important place *in the perspective of restoration* of the people of God. After the gathering together of all the dispersed*, God will distribute in abundance the purifying waters which will cleanse the heart of man and thus enable him to fulfill faithfully and completely the Law of Yahweh (Ez 36,24-27). There will be, then, an end to curses and aridity: God "will grant rain in good season" (Ez 34,26), the pledge of prosperity (Ez 36,29f). The seeds will bud, insuring a rich harvest; the meadows will be verdant (Is 30,23f). The people of God will be guided to the bubbling springs; hunger* and thirst will disappear forever (Jr 31,9; Is 49,10).

At the end of the Babylonian exile the memory of the exodus is frequently mingled with this thought of restoration. The return will be indeed a new exodus*, accompanied by even more striking wonders. God had formerly, by the hand of Moses, caused water to spring from the rock to quench the thirst of His people (Ex 17,1-7; Nm 20,1-13; Ps 78,16.20; 114.8; Is 48. 21). Henceforth God would renew this marvel (Is 43,20), and with such magnificence that the desert* would be changed into a fruitful orchard

(Is 41,17-20), the land of thirsts into springs (Is 35,6f).

Jerusalem*, the term of the pilgrimage, will have an inexhaustible spring. A river will rise from the temple* and flow to the Dead Sea; it will spread life and health throughout its way, and the trees* will put forth their buds, endowed with wonderful fruitfulness: it will be the return of the happiness of Paradise* (Ez 47,1-12; cf Gn 2,10-14). The people of God will find in these waters purity (Ze 13,1), life (Jl 4,18; Ze 14,8), and holiness (Ps 46,5).

2. In these eschatological perspectives water ordinarily takes on a *symbolic value*. Israel indeed does not fix its gaze on material possessions, and the good fortune that it glimpses is nothing but earthly prosperity. The water that Ezekiel sees rising from the temple symbolizes the life-giving power of God, which is going to spill over in the Messianic age and enable men to bring forth fruit in abundance (Ez 47, 12); Jr 17,8; Ps 1,3; Ez 19,10f). In Is 44,3ff water is the symbol of the Spirit* of God that can transform the desert into a flowering orchard and the unfaithful people into a true "Israel." Elsewhere the Word* of God is compared to the rain that comes to make the earth fruitful (Is 55,10f; cf Am 8,11f); and the teaching that Wisdom* inculcates is a life-giving water (Is 55, 1; Si 15,3; 24.25-31). In short, God is the source of life for man and grants him the strength to expand in love and faithfulness (Jr 2,13; 17,8). Far from God, man is only a dry and waterless land, doomed to death (Ps 143,6); he therefore longs for God as the deer pants for running water (Ps 42,2f). But if God is with him, he becomes like a garden that has in Him the very source of its life (Is 58,11).

IV. THE NEW TESTAMENT

1. *Life-giving waters*. Christ came to bring the life-giving waters promised by the prophets. He is the rock* which when struck (cf Jn 19,34) yields from His side waters enabling men to quench their thirst on the way to the true promised land (1 Co 10,4; Jn 7.38; cf Ex 17.1-7). He is likewise the temple* (cf Jn 2,19ff) from which springs up the river that will irrigate and vivify the new Jerusalem* (Jn 7.37f; Ap 22,1. 17; Ez 47,1-12), the new Paradise*. These waters are nothing other than the Holy Spirit*, the life-giving power of God the Creator (Jn 7. 39). In Jn 4,10-14, however, water seems rather

to symbolize the life-giving teaching brought by Christ-Wisdom (cf 4,25). At any rate, on the consummation of all things, living water will be the symbol of the endless happiness of the elect, guided to the plentiful meadows by the Lamb* (Ap 7,17; 21,6; cf Is 25,8; 49,10).

2. *Baptismal waters*. The symbolism of water finds its complete meaning in Christian baptism*. From its start, water was used at baptism because of its cleansing value. John baptized with water "for the remission of sins" (Mt 3, 11 p), using for this purpose the water of the Jordan which had formerly cleansed Naaman from his leprosy (2 K 5,10-14). But baptism brings about not the cleansing of the body but of the soul, of "conscience" (1 P 3,21). It is a bath that cleanses us from our sins (1 Co 6,11; E 5,26; He 10,22; Ac 22,16), applying to us the redemptive power of the blood* of Christ (He 9,13f; Ap 7,14; 22,14).

To this basic symbolism of baptismal water Paul adds another: the immersion and emerging of the neophyte symbolizes his burial with Christ and his spiritual resurrection (R 6,3-11). Perhaps Paul here envisioned, in the water of baptism, an image of the sea*, dwelling place of malevolent powers and symbol of death, overcome by Christ just as formerly the Red Sea was overcome by Yahweh (1 Co 10ff; cf Is 51, 10). Finally, by communicating to us the Spirit of God, baptism is also a principle of new life*. It is possible that Christ wished to allude to this by performing several cures by means of water (Jn 9,6f; cf 5,1-8). Baptism is thought of, then, as a "bath of rebirth and renewal of the Holy Spirit" (Tt 3,5; cf Jn 3,5).

→Baptism—Blessing II 1, III, 4, IV 3—Blood NT 4 — Death OT I 5 — Flood — Fruit II — Hunger & Thirst—Pure—Rock 2—Salt 1—Sea —Spirit of God O—Stone 3.

MEB jrc

WAY

The ancient Semite was a nomad. Consequently, an essential part of his life is the way, the route, or the path. He naturally uses this same vocabulary in speaking of the religious and moral life. Such usage is a common feature of the Hebrew language.

I. THE WAYS OF GOD

Abraham had set out at the call of God (Gn 12,1-5); and thus begins a vast religious adventure. The problem is always to recognize and to follow* the ways of God. These are often baffling: "My ways are not your ways," said the Lord (Is 55,8); but they lead to a marvelous fulfillment.

1. *The exodus** is the outstanding example of this religious adventure. The people experience what it is "to walk with their God" (Mi 6,8) and to enter into covenant* with Him. God goes ahead of them to mark out the route, with the cloud* and the column of fire* (Ex 13, 21f) making His presence visible. Even the sea does not halt Him: "Your way was on the sea and your path on the great waters" (Ps 77,20); with the result that Israel escapes from the Egyptians into freedom. Then follows the journey in the desert (Ps 68,8). There God fights for His people and carries them "as a father his little boy." He supplies food and drink, and "searches out a place for the camp." Under His care, nothing is lacking (Dt 1,30-33).

But God also takes action to punish Israel's lack of faith. Thus the journey with God has its difficulties. This desert* period can be seen as a time of trial*, when Yahweh sounds out His people to the depths of their hearts and seeks to correct them (Dt 8,2-6). Hence, the way of God is long and devious (Dt 2,1f). But it did have a term, for God was leading His people to rest* in a pleasant land where a satisfied Israel will bless Yahweh (Dt 8,7-10). It becomes clear that "the paths of the Lord are kindness and truth" (Ps 25,10; cf Ps 136), and that "all His ways are just" (Dt 32,4).

The memory of the exodus, recalled each year during the Passover and the feast of Tabernacles, impressed itself deeply on the Jewish mind. Pilgrimages*, made to Shechem, Shiloh, and later to Jerusalem, fix deeply the idea of the holy way leading to the rest given by God. When idolatry threatens to supplant Yahwism, Elijah* sets out on the way to Horeb. Later, the prophets idealize the time when Yahweh journeyed with His child (Ho 11,1ff).

2. *The Law**. After arriving in the promised land, Israel has no less obligations to continue "journeying in the ways of the Lord" (Ps 128, 1). Israel's knowledge* of these ways was its singular privilege (cf Ps 147,19f). God had revealed to His people "all the ways of un-

derstanding"; "this is the book of the precepts of God, the Law that endures forever" (Ba 3, 37; 4,1). One must, therefore, "walk in the Law of the Lord" (Ps 119,1), in order to continue in the covenant and to progress toward light, peace, and life (Ba 3,13f). The Law is the true way of man because it is the way of God.

To disobey the Law is to turn off (Dt 31,17) toward destruction. The final sanction will be exile* (Lv 26,41), a way reversing the exodus (Ho 11,5). But God cannot allow the final defeat of His people (Lv 26,44f); it is again necessary to "prepare in the desert a way for Yahweh" (Is 40,3). He Himself will "mark out a path through the wilderness" (Is 43,19) and "cut a road through all the mountains" (Is 49,11) for a triumphant return.

II. THE TWO WAYS

In the period of Judaism the doctrine of the "two ways" sums up the moral conduct of men. There are two kinds of conduct, two ways: the good way and the evil way (Ps 1,6; Pr 4,18f; 12,28). The good way is straight and perfect (1 S 12,23; 1 K 8,36; Ps 101,2.6; 1 Co 12,31); consisting in the practice of justice* (Pr 8,20; 12,28), in fidelity to the truth* (Ps 119,30; Tb 1,3), in seeking peace* (Is 59,8; Lk 1,79). Sapiential writings teach the way of life* (Pr 2,19; 5,6; 6,23; 15,24), a way that leads to a long and prosperous earthly existence.

The evil way is crooked (Pr 21,8); leading fools (Pr 12,15), sinners (Ps 1,1; Si 21,10), and the wicked (Ps 1,6; Pr 4.14.19; Jr 12,1) to disaster (Ps 1,6) and to death (Pr 12,28). Faced with the two ways, man is free to choose and is responsible for his choice (Dt 30,15-20; Si 15,12).

The Gospel points out the narrowness of the way leading to life and the small number of those taking it: while the large number take the broad path leading to death (Mt 7,13f).

III. CHRIST, THE LIVING WAY

The return from exile was only an image of the final reality of liberation. This was announced by John the Baptist in the very terms used by Second Isaiah for the new exodus: "Make ready the way of the Lord" (Lk 3,4=Is 40,3). A new exodus, in the Messianic age, leads effectively to the rest given by God (He 4,8f). Jesus, the new Moses*, is guide, escort, and leader (Lk 24,15; He 2,10f; 12,2ff). He calls men to follow* Him (Mt 4,19; Lk 9,57-62; Jn 12, 35f). As a foretaste of the future glorious kingdom*, the transfiguration* momentarily lights up the path; but the prediction of the passion recalls that it is necessary to stop first at Calvary. The only way to glory is that of the cross* (Mt 16,23; Lk 24,26; 9,23; Jn 16,28). Jesus sets out resolutely for Jerusalem* on a trip that ends with His sacrifice (Lk 9,51; 22,22.33). In contrast with ancient sacrifices, His reaches to heaven* itself (He 9,24) and at the same time marks out a way for us to follow. By the blood* of Jesus, we now have access to the true sanctuary. In His flesh, Jesus opened for us a new living way (He 10,19ff).

In the Acts of the Apostles, Christianity is first called simply "the way" (Ac 9,2; 18,25; 24,22). Indeed Christians are conscious of having found the true way, now revealed for the first time (He 9,8). This way is no longer a law, but a person, Jesus* (Jn 14,6). In Him occurs the Passover and exodus of the Christian. In Him, one must walk (Col 2,6), following the way of love (E 5,2; 1 Co 12,31); since in Him Jew and Greek alike have access to the Father in the one Spirit (E 2,18).

→Death OT II 2—Desert OT I 1—Example—Exile II 24—Exodus—Follow—Pilgrimage—Plan of God OT IV—Rest II—Run—Virtues & Vices 1.3.

ADa wjw

WEALTH

Concerning wealth and poverty, the views found in the OT and in the NT appear radically opposed. In fact, it is precisely when Christ reveals the kingdom of heaven as the priceless treasure worth the sacrifice of all one's goods (Mt 13,44) that He shows the inconsistency of all human wealth, however elevated. Still, He continues the theme of the OT, according to which any wealth not received as a gift from God is vain and dangerous; and He fulfills and does not destroy the ancient promises according to which God enriches His elect. If riches are perilous, and if evangelical perfection consists in sacrificing them, it is not that riches are evil, but that God alone is "good" (Mt 19,17) and is Himself our wealth.

I. GOD ENRICHES HIS ELECT

1. *Wealth is a good.* Even in the most recent texts, the OT delights in extolling the wealth of holy personages in the history of Israel: that of Job after his trials; that of the holy kings: David, Jehoshaphat, Hezekiah (2 Ch 32,27ff). As in Homeric Greece, so too in Israel wealth seems to be a claim to nobility, and God enriches those He loves: Abraham (Gn 13,2), Isaac (26,12f), Jacob (30,43); and the tribes counted on prosperity. Ephraim receives blessings from the skies (rain), from the depth (springs), and from the breast and womb (49, 25). Judah can be proud: "his eyes are darker than wine, his teeth, more white than milk" (49,12). In the land which Yahweh promises to His people, nothing shall be lacking (Dt 8, 7-10; 28,1-12).

Even the most material wealth is a good; it assures in particular a precious independence, it prevents having to beg (Pr 18,23) and being a slave of one's creditor (22,7), it procures useful friendships (Si 13,21ff). Its acquisition normally supposes meritorious human qualities: diligence (Pr 10,4; 20,13), wisdom (24,4), realism (12,11), courage (11,16), temperance (21, 17).

2. *A relative and secondary good.* Wealth can be a good, but it is never presented as the best of goods; preferable to it are, for example, peace* of soul (Pr 15,16), good reputation (22, 1), health (Si 30,14ff), justice* (Pr 16,8). Quickly enough do we see wealth's limits; there are many things which cannot be purchased; exemption from death (Ps 49,8), love (Ct 8,7). Wealth is a cause of useless cares*: men exhaust themselves feeding parasitic friends (Qo 5,10) and have strangers fall heir to their wealth (6,2). It is always necessary to prefer wisdom*, its source, to wealth (1 K 3,11ff; Jb 28,15-19; Ws 7,8-11); this is the treasure, the precious pearl which merits every concern (Pr 2,4; 3,15; 8,11).

3. *A gift of God.* Wealth is a sign of the divine generosity; it is one of the elements of the fullness of life which God never stops promising to His elect. Does not prosperity consecrate the result of effort? Thus it is a sign of accomplishment and glory (Ps 37,19), whereas destitution is a sign of failure and shame (Jr 12,13). Together with long years, health, and the esteem of men, wealth forms part of the peace and fullness of life. If God takes charge of someone, it is to fulfill him entirely; a person under His care lacks nothing (Ps 23,1; 34,10). In the desert He fed His people to contentment (Ex 16,8-15; Ps 78,24-29), and even more so in the promised land (Lv 26,5; 25,19; Dt 11,15; Ne 9,25). When He receives men in His dwelling, the temple, He fills them to inebriation (Ps 23,5; 36,9); and, in the fullness of joy which the presence of His face* gives (Ps 16, 11), if there is anything to be seen besides the abundance of a festive meal*, it is the acknowledgment of a people believing in the generosity of God and seeing signs of it in His gifts (Dt 16,14f). The commandment of almsgiving* is based on this imitation of the divine generosity: "Be like a father to orphans...And you will be like a son to the Most High" (Si 4,10; cf Jb 31,18).

4. *God fills with His wealth.* The wealth with which God fills us in His Son is that "of eloquence and knowledge" (1 Co 1,5), that "of His grace and goodness" (E 2,7). This is a wealth different from the riches of this world, none of which can satisfy our hunger (Jn 6,35) and our thirst (4,14). This wealth comes, nevertheless, from the divine generosity. Therefore, Paul invites Christians to give generously of their material wealth, because they have been supplied with spiritual gifts (2 Co 8,7). And, apart from this, when he promises them that God will repay them by "every kind of blessing" (9,8), he does not exclude material wealth which will allow them "to have always all that is necessary in every situation" and "to be enriched in every way" (9,8.11).

After the multiplication of the loaves it is no accident that the gospels stress the baskets filled with the remaining loaves (Mt 14,20; 15,37; 16, 9f); this is typical of God's gifts. The idea of satiety is deeply Christian: the person who comes to Christ will no longer hunger (Jn 6,35) or thirst (4,14). God more than provides for His chosen ones; He leaves them no room for regret or envy. Evangelical poverty removes any inferiority complex, any secret resentment. Even in his poverty, the Christian is richer than the world. Paul observes that he possesses all, even when others think that he is destitute (2 Co 6,10). Woe to the lukewarm person who believes himself rich, when he is lacking the only real treasure (Ap 3,16ff); and happy the poor and persecuted: such people are rich (2,9).

II. ILLUSIONS AND DANGERS OF WEALTH

If God enriches His friends, it does not follow that all wealth is consequence of His blessing*. Ancient folklore is acquainted with ill-gotten wealth; but unjustly acquired goods are of no profit (Pr 21,6; 23,4f; cf Ho 12,9). The wicked amass fortunes only to have the just man ultimately inherit them (Pr 28,8). Wealth is ill-acquired if it tends to exclude the majority from earthly goods and to reserve them for the privileged few. "Cursed are those who add house to house and join field to field, till they snatch up the whole area and become the sole inhabitants of the land" (Is 5,8); "their homes are filled with plunder: this is how they have become great and rich, fat and heavy" (Jr 5,27f).

The rich who think they can dispense with God are evil. They pride themselves on material goods and make them their fortress (Pr 10, 15), forgetting that God alone is the only fortress that can prevail (Ps 52,9). A land "full of silver and gold...of horses and chariots without number" is soon "a land full of idols" (Is 2, 7f). "He who relies on wealth will fall" (Pr 11,28; cf Jr 9,22). Instead of strengthening the covenant, divine gifts can be the occasion of denying it: "Having eaten their fill, their hearts became puffed with pride, and as a result they have forgotten me!" (Ho 13,6; cf Dt 8, 12ff). Israel constantly forgets the source of her abundant blessings (Ho 2). She soon prostitutes herself with the very adornments she owes to the love of her God (Ez 16). It is difficult to remain faithful in prosperity, because easy living closes the heart* (Dt 31,20; 32,15; Jb 15.27; Ps 73,4-9). Furthermore, even a king would be wise to distrust silver and gold (Dt 17,17) and to repeat the prayer in which Agur, before God, sums up his experience: "Give me neither poverty nor wealth, let me taste only the food I need; for fear that, having become sated, I should turn away and say: 'Who is Yahweh?' or for fear that, being in need, I should steal and profane the name of my God" (Pr 30,8f).

The NT in its turn draws freely from the reserves of the OT with regard to wealth. James's invectives against the satiated wealthy and their rotted wealth equal those of the most vehement prophets (Jm 5.1-5). "Those who are rich in this present world" are warned "not to think highly of themselves, not to put their hopes in wealth that may fail, but in God, who

supplies us liberally with everything we could need" (1 Tm 6,17). "The pride of wealth" is equivalent to the world; one cannot love both God and the world (1 Jn 2,15f).

III. GOD OR MONEY

1. *This change in the gospels* in relation to wealth is brutal. The phrase, "Cursed are you rich; for you already have your comfort" (Lk 6, 24), has the ring of an irreversible condemnation. This is thrown into full relief when the beatitudes and curses* of the Sermon on the Mount are compared with the blessings and curses promised by Deuteronomy (in the magnificent scene at Shechem) according to Israel's faithfulness or unfaithfulness to the Law (Dt 28). The difference between the OT and the NT is nowhere more striking than here.

In fact the gospel of the kingdom proclaims the total gift of God, the perfect communion, the entrance into the home of the Father; to receive all, a person must give all. To acquire the precious pearl, the peerless treasure, it is necessary to sell all (Mt 13,45f); for one cannot serve two masters (Mt 6,24). And money is an unmerciful master: it stifles the word of the gospel (Mt 13,22); it causes people to forget the essential, God's sovereignty (Lk 12,15-21); on the road to perfection it blocks even the best disposed heart (Mt 19,21f). The demand to sacrifice all is an absolute law and appears to brook neither exception nor mitigation: "It is impossible for anyone among you who does not renounce all his possessions to be my disciple" (Lk 14,33; cf 12,33). The rich man who has "his goods" (Lk 16,25) and "his comfort" (6, 24) in this world cannot enter into the kingdom; it would be "easier for a camel to pass through the eye of a needle" (Mt 19,23f p). Only the poor are capable of receiving the good news (Is 61,1=Lk 4,18; Lk 1,53). By making Himself poor for us our Lord was able to enrich us (2 Co 8,9) with His "unfathomable riches" (E 3,8).

2. *Give to the poor.* To renounce wealth does not necessarily mean to abdicate proprietorship. Even in Jesus' entourage, there are some well-to-do persons. It is a rich man of Arimathea who received the body of the Lord in his tomb (Mt 27,57). The gospel does not want a person to get rid of his wealth as if it were a hindrance; the demand is for distribution among the poor (Mt 19,21 p; Lk 12,33; 19,8). If a rich

man thus makes friends with "base wealth" —for what fortune on earth is not tainted by some injustice?—he can expect God to open for him the difficult road to salvation (Lk 16,9). The scandal is not that there was a rich man and a poor Lazarus, but that Lazarus "wanted to eat the crumbs which fell from the table of the rich man" (Lk 16,21) and that he did not receive a particle of them. The rich man has a responsibility toward the poor. The one who serves God gives his money to the poor, while the one who serves mammon keeps it and relies upon it.

Ultimately true wealth is not what one possesses, but what one gives. This giving calls down the generosity of God. It unites the donor and the recipient in thanksgiving (2 Co 9,11). Such giving allows the rich man himself to experience that it is "more blessed to give than to receive" (Ac 20,35).

→Almsgiving—Beatitude OT III 1—Blessing II 1—Cupidity—Fullness—Gift NT 3—Glory I— Grace IV —Milk 2—Poor—Sadness NT 2— Service III o.

EB & JG ecu

WEEK

1. *The week in social life and in the liturgy.* The problem of the *origin* of the week is difficult. Closely connected with the Sabbath* and perhaps with the lunar cycle, it has, from the beginning, taken from this fact a specifically religious character which sharply distinguishes it from the periods of seven days attested elsewhere in the Middle East (cf Gn 8,10 and the Babylonian poem of Gilgamesh; Gn 29,27; Jg 14.12; 2 K 3.9). Probably antedating the Mosaic legislation. the week figures prominently in the most ancient texts (Ex 20,8ff; 23,12; 34,21). Thus God gives to His people the rhythm of their work* and of their rest*.

The week plays an important role in the customs and religious practices of the OT. The feasts* of Azymes and of Tabernacles last a week (Dt 16,4; Lv 23,8.34). Pentecost*, or the feast of Weeks, takes place seven weeks after the Sabbath of the Pasch (Ex 34,22; Lv 23,15). Furthermore, after the exile, priests and Levites took turns of a week at a time to accomplish their ritual service. Alongside of the calendar which became official and which was preserved by the Christians, an archaic priestly calendar

harmonized the solar year of 364 days with a complete cycle of 52 weeks.

Each *week of years* ended with a sabbatical year, in which it was obligatory to set the slaves and debtors free and to let the earth lie fallow (Ex 21,2; 23,10ff; Dt 15,1ff; Lv 25,3f). At the end of seven weeks of years there was provision for a jubilee year, the year of liberation (Lv 25,8...). The prophecy of seventy weeks (Dn 9,24), which announces the final liberation of Israel, is built on the conventional number of ten jubilee periods; while the text of Jeremiah which is its starting point (Jr 25,11f) places salvation at the end of ten sabbatical periods.

2. *Theological significance.* According to the priestly theology, the week which regulates the activity of man has as its prototype the creative activity of God Himself (Gn 1,1—2,3; Ex 20,9ff; 31,17). The law of the week is thus considered as a divine institution of universal value.

In the NT the week acquires a new religious significance. Henceforth it begins on Sunday, the day of the Lord, the weekly celebration of His victory. The work* which the Christian achieves is thus carried on under the influence of Christ the redeemer who rules time. But it continues to move toward an eighth day* which, beyond the cycle of weeks, will introduce the people of God into the great divine rest* (He 4,1-11). The rest of Sunday already announces its coming.

→Creation OT II 2—Feasts—Numbers I 1, II 1—Pentecost I 1—Sabbath—Time OT I 1; NT II 3.

CT jpl

WHITE

In the world of the Bible, white accompanies the feasts and joyous expressions of man. It recalls innocence, joy*, purity; it arouses wonder. As a color of light* and life*, it is opposed to black, the color of darkness and mourning. The Bible makes use of these various meanings (Qo 9.8; Si 43,18) but gives them a new dimension, the eschatological: white is the mark of those who are associated with the glory* of God—heavenly or transfigured beings.

1. *Heavenly beings.* The Book of the Apocalypse in describing the heavenly world uses the

color white with more emphasis, thus underscoring its eschatological meaning: pebble (Ap 2,17), cloud (14,14), horse (19,11), throne (20, 11). But the whole Bible, both OT and NT, makes brightness—the whiteness of beings from heaven—stand out: whether it is a question of the man dressed in white in Ez 9,2 or of the angels, God's messengers, with their "dazzling garment" (Lk 24,4 p; Ac 10,30), of the twenty-four ancients of the heavenly court (Ap 4,4) or of the "Son of Man" (Ap 1,13f), of Christ Himself, announced by the Ancient of Days whose "clothing was white as snow and the hair of his head like pure wool" (Dn 7,9).

2. *Transfigured beings.* White, the celestial color of Christ, does not appear in His earthly life except at the special moment of the transfiguration* when His very clothes* "became shining with such a whiteness that no fuller can equal" (Mk 9,3 p). In the same manner, white is the color of transfigured beings, of saints who, purified of their sins (Is 1,18; Ps 51,9) and made white in the blood of the Lamb (Ap 7,14), share in the glorious being of God (7,9-13). They form the "white escort" of the conqueror (3,4f), a huge crowd shouting triumphantly with joy in an unending feast of light: the Lamb unites Himself to the bride dressed "in linen of brilliant whiteness" (19, 1-14).

The liturgy has always adopted white linen as a vestment (Lv 6,3) and lays a white covering on the newly baptized who through grace shares in the glory of the heavenly state with the innocence and the joy that it entails.

→Clothing II 4—Glory—Joy—Light & Dark—Pure.

GB pjb

WIDOWS

In her loneliness (Ba 4,12-16), the widow is a typical case of misfortune (Is 47,9). Her costume (Gn 38,14; Jdt 10,3) is a sign of a double mourning: barring a new marriage*, she has lost the hope of fruitfulness*; she is defenseless.

1. *Assistance for widows.* Like the orphan and the stranger, she is the object of special protection from the Law (Ex 22,20-23; Dt 14, 28-29; 24,17-22) and from God (Dt 10,17f), who listens to her complaints (Si 35,14f), makes Himself her defender and her avenger (Ps 94, 6-10). Woe to those who take advantage of her weakness (Is 10,2; Mk 12,40 p)! Like Elijah, Jesus gives back to a widow her only son (Lk 7,11-15; 1 K 17,17-24), and he entrusts Mary to the care of the beloved disciple (Jn 19,26f). In the daily service of the primitive Church care is taken to provide for the needs of widows (Ac 6,1). If they no longer have any relatives (1 Tm 5,16; cf Ac 9,36-39), the community ought to take them into its care, as true piety* demands (Jm 1,27; cf Dt 26,12f; Jb 31,16).

2. *The value of widowhood recognized.* Already toward the end of the OT a special esteem for the definitive widowhood of Judith begins to appear (Jdt 8,4-8; 16,22) and for that of Anne, the prophetess, (Lk 2,36f), consecrated to God in prayer and penance. The contrast between natural weakness and the strength* drawn from God stands out in the case of Judith.

In the same way, although Paul tolerates remarriage (1 Co 7,9.39) and even encourages it in the case of young widows (1 Tm 5,13-15) in order to avoid the dangers of misconduct, he still considers widowhood better (1 Co 7,8), seeing it as a providential sign that one should forgo marriage (7,17.24). In fact, like virginity*, widowhood is a spiritual ideal opening people to the influence of God and freeing them for His service (7,34).

3. *The institution of widowhood.* In the Church all widows should be beyond reproach (1 Tm 5,7.14). Some, who are truly on their own and free from any family obligation and ready to renounce all dissipation, will give themselves to prayer (5,5f). There also exists an official undertaking to remain in the permanent state of widowhood (5,12). Widows who have only been married once and have reached the age of sixty are admitted into this group (5,9). It is probable that they carry out charitable tasks, for in the past they are supposed to have given guarantees of devotion to this sort of work (5,10).

Thus, the ideal put before widows in the last stage of their lives can be summed up as prayer, chastity and charity.

→Fasting 1—Fruitfulness II 2—Marriage OT II 1; NT II—Solitude I 1—Virginity OT 2—Woman OT 3; NT 1.3.

PS ems

WILL OF GOD

The essential subject matter of God's will and plan* coincide. St. Paul summarizes all the prophecies and the message of Jesus by saying: "God wills that all men be saved" (1 Tm 2,4). All the historical manifestations of the divine will are, then, coordinated according to one total design in a plan of wisdom. Nevertheless, each individual historical manifestation of the total plan concerns a particular event; it is to accept God's mastery of that event that man prays: "May your will be done!" Thus history that has already expired reveals the plan of God, who has predestined* all things before the beginning of time. At the same time, by submission to God's will, man faces the future with confidence because he is already aware that God directs the future.

The will of God for man assumes a special form because of man's obligation to internal conformity and voluntary execution. God's will as presented to men is not inevitable fate, but rather a call, a command, a demand made upon man. The Law* puts together into one clearly expressed whole what God wants. Insofar as the Law is an institution, it is static. An effort is required to find in the Law that personal will which is perpetually a present event, which stimulates man's response, initiates a dialogue. Seen in this light, the will of God is quite similar to His Word*, which is both deed and statement. The will of God is first an action which discloses His good pleasure. In this sense it is not solely identified with His plan, which sums up God's will in one total plan, nor with His Law, the practical interpretation of God's will.

Rather than go into details here about the different manifestations of the divine will: predestination*, election*, calling*, liberation*, promises*, punishments*, salvation*, we must show that it must be accomplished here on earth at the same time as it is being accomplished in heaven (Mt 6,10). God's salvific will is efficacious in itself; it encounters the will of man not to supplant but rather to perfect it. To attain this, God must get the better of man's wickedness and bring about a mutual sharing of wills.

OT

From the very beginning the Creator's will appears to Adam* under two aspects. First, it is an open-handed blessing* accompanied by power over the animals and the presence of the perfect companion. Secondly, it is a limit to human liberty: "You shall not eat..." (Gn 2, 17). Then the drama begins. Instead of recognizing the prohibition as an educating* trial* designed to support the dependence which is the core of his real freedom, Adam attributes the prohibition to a will jealous of his supremacy; so he disobeys (3,5ff). When God again initiates dialogue (3,9), the divine will has become a curse for the serpent (3,14); for the man and woman it is an announcement of chastisement*, illuminated somewhat by the prospect of final victory* (3,15-19). Such is the basis of the problem of the will of God in the OT.

I. GOD DISCLOSES HIS WILL

At this point God's will is no longer revealed directly and universally to sinful humanity. There is a particular communication of God's will to an elect people through intrusions of God into history and by the bestowal of the Law.

1. *In history.* Israel first comes to know* the merciful and loving will of Yahweh through His great deeds. Yahweh has decided to free Israel from its slavery in Egypt (Ex 3,8), to raise her on eagles' wings (Ex 19,4), because it was His pleasure to make Israel his own people (1 S 12,22). After the trying time of exile, God wishes to reconstruct Jerusalem and rebuild the temple, even with heathen assistance (Is 44, 28). From this Israel should realize that God wills not death but life* (Ez 18,32), not misfortune but peace* (Jr 29,11). A will that finds such expression indicates love*.

The bestowal of the Law* is likewise a sign of love, for the Law allows Israel to understand that the Word, the expression of God's will, is constantly "very near you, in your mouth and in your heart, that you may put it in practice" (Dt 30,14). The psalmists put into song the experience of this contact with the divine will, the source of incomparable delight (Ps 1,2). In post-exilic literature Tobias appears as one who had been blessed by "God's will" (Tb 12, 18). And there is the fervent prayer: "Teach me to do your will" (Ps 143,10).

2. *In inspired reflection.* Prophets, sages, and psalmists feel the transcendence of the divine will; each stresses one or other aspect in order better to venerate this divine disposition.

a) Its sovereign independence. "God decides; who shall make Him change? What He has proposed, that He accomplishes" (Jb 23,13). The Word* He dispatches to earth "does all He wishes" (Is 55,11), even if there is a question of destruction (Is 10,23). God follows His own will and no human suggestion (Is 40,13). Such affirmations occur constantly in the Bible both as expressions of God's omnipotence and His total independence. As Creator He has all power in heaven and on earth; the forces of nature are at His disposition (Ps 135,6; Jb 37, 12; Si 43,13-17). Master of His work*, He guides even the beat of the human heart (Pr 21,1) and bestows kingdoms at will (Dn 4, 14,22.29). He exalts or humbles as He wishes (Tb 4,19). Confronted with the sovereign independence of a will which occasionally seems arbitrary (Ez 18,25), man could be tempted to revolt, as Adam. Scripture then reminds man of his radical dependence as a creature by using the traditional example of a potter who disposes of his clay according to his wish. "Who resists God's will? Who are you, my good man, to dispute with God?" (R 9,19ff; cf Jr 18,1-6; Is 29,16; 45,9; Si 33,13; Ws 12,12). A creature should humbly adore* any and every manifestation of the will of his Creator.

b) Wisdom of the divine will. To stand in adoration of a mystery is not to forfeit understanding but to rely on a rich faith* in the justice* of God, on a knowledge* of the purpose, the plan*, and the wisdom* governing the execution of His will. No merely human understanding can grasp God's will (Ws 9,13); but the gift of wisdom grants insight to him who prays for it (9,17). Then one sees that "God's plan and the thoughts of His heart remain forever" (Ps 33,11) quite different from those of man (Pr 19,21).

c) The benevolent will. God's will is here expressed in terms of benevolence, of good pleasure, of kindness, of graciousness. "To will someone" means to love him, in Hebrew as in other languages (vg in Italian). In this sense God "wills" His Servant (Is 42,1), His people (Ps 44,4), the just (Ps 22,9). And in His chosen ones, God loves—that is, He wills—mercy, pardon and goodness (Ho 6,6; Mi 6,8; Jr 9,23; Is 58,5ff).

II. IN CONFLICT WITH MAN'S REFUSAL

The loving will of God collides with the sinful will of man. The history of Adam is always current. Listen, for example, to the prophet Amos. For unfaithful Israel the will to bless becomes a will to punish* (vg Am 1,3. 6...); this is the price of being a select one (3,2). If man no longer recognizes his Lord (4,6-11), let him be prepared for a final punishment (4,12). The threat of hardness* of heart will weigh on man. But God's will for punishment is not callous because He is always ready "to turn" from His decision, to change His will (Jr 18,1-12; Ez 18; cf Ex 32,14; Jon 3,9f), as when He says that at least a remnant* will survive (Is 6,13; 10,21). He takes pleasure at the sight of "the sinner turning away from his way to live" (Ez 18,23).

This will would be an inefficacious intention unless God Himself takes the sinner's cause in hand. His procedure is to exert internal attraction on the will of His unfaithful spouse (Ho 2, 16) and, by giving her a new heart, to make Israel follow His will (Ez 36,26f; cf Jr 31,33). To this end, He raises up a Servant* whose ear He awakens each morning (Is 50,5) to make Him capable of obeying His will (Ps 40,8f). Because of the Servant, "the good pleasure of Yahweh will be fulfilled" (Is 53,10). Nevertheless, the will of God does not use constraint but only love. The beloved does not awaken his bride before she wishes it (Ct 2,7; 3,5; 8,4). But when she wishes to return to her spouse (Ho 2,17f) she will deserve to be called by God Himself; "my delight is in her" (Is 62,4).

NT

At the very beginning of the NT, Mary, the handmaid of the Lord and full of grace, welcomes the divine will in humility and obedience (Lk 1,28.38). And Jesus, pre-eminently the just one, comes into the world "to do your will, O God" (He 10,7.9). More than David is He "a man according to the heart of God, who will accomplish His will in its entirety" (Ac 13, 22).

I. CHRIST AND THE WILL OF GOD

1. *Jesus discloses preferences of the Father.* Against the annoying attitudes of the Pharisees* who wanted to constrict the heart of God, Jesus

declared that God is absolutely free in conferring His benefits. This liberty, governed by love, appears in the parable of the employer and the vineyard. "I will give this last as much as you. Am I not allowed to do what I will with what is mine? Or must you be envious because I am good?" (Mt 20,14f). So too it is God's good pleasure to reserve the Messianic revelation for children (11,25), to grant the gift of the kingdom to His little flock (Lk 12,32). Into this kingdom only those who do His will shall enter (Mt 7,21) because they alone are members of His family (12,50).

2. *Jesus fulfills the will of His Father.* In the fourth gospel, Jesus speaks not of the will of His Father (as in Mt), but of the will "of Him who sent me," a will of God which constitutes a mission*. Jesus is nourished by this will (Jn 4, 34); its fulfillment is His only desire (5,30); for He does everything that pleases the one who sent Him (8,29). The will of the Father is that Christ give resurrection and eternal life to all who come to Him (6,38ff). While this will appears to Jesus as a "command" (10,18), He sees in it a sign that "the Father loves Him" (10,17) so that the Son's obedience* is a participation of His will with the will of the Father (15,10).

The perfect adherence of Jesus to the divine will does not suppress but rather makes intelligible the painful acceptance that, according to the Synoptics, is to be seen in the passion. In Gethsemani, Jesus sees successively "what I will" and "what you will" seemingly opposed (Mk 14,36). His insistent prayer to His Father, "Not my will but yours be done!" dissolves the conflict (Lk 22,42). From that moment, even when He is apparently abandoned by the Father, Christ continues to feel Himself "the loved one" (Mt 27,43=Ps 22,9). During His earthly life Jesus did not achieve His desire to gather together again the children of Jerusalem (23,37); but by His will to sacrifice Himself He enkindled fire* on the earth (Lk 12,49).

II. "YOUR WILL BE DONE"

Since in Jesus the will of God is accomplished on earth as in heaven, the Christian can be sure of being heard in the Lord's Prayer (Mt 6,10). The genuine follower of Christ must recognize and execute that will.

1. *Discerning God's will.* Discernment and practice of the divine will are mutual conditions. Appreciation of Jesus' doctrine demands fulfillment of God's will (Jn 7,17); but, on the other hand, it is necessary to recognize in Jesus and His commands the very precepts of God Himself (14,23f). Here is the mystery of an encounter between two wills, the will of sinful man and the will of God. To come to Jesus one must be "drawn" by the Father (6,44), an attraction, according to the Greek word, which is both constraint and delight (the basis of St. Augustine's expression: "God who is closer to me than I myself"). To recognize the will of God, it is not sufficient to know the letter of the Law (R 2,18). Adherence to a person is necessary, though possible only through the Holy Spirit given by Jesus (Jn 14,26).

Once man's power of discrimination is verified by the Holy Spirit, he is able "to discern what is God's will, what is good, what pleases God and is perfect" (R 12,2). This power of discernment affects more than daily life; for it opens out into "full knowledge of His will, wisdom, and spiritual understanding" (Col 1,9). Such a state institutes a life pleasing to the Lord (1,10; cf E 5,17). Every prayer turns out to be a prayer "according to His will" (1 Jn 5,14) so that the common expression "if God wills it" assumes an entirely new dimension (Ac 18, 21; 1 Co 4,19; Jm 4,15) because it supposes an atmosphere of consistent reference to "the mystery of God's will" (E 1,3-14).

2. *Practicing God's will.* What good is it to know what the master wishes if one does not put it into practice (Lk 12,47; Mt 7,21; 21,31)? This "practice" really constitutes Christian life (He 13,21) as opposed to life guided by human passion (1 P 4,2; E 6,6). More exactly, God's will for us is holiness (1 Th 4,3), gratitude (5,18), patience (1 P 3,17), a good life (2,15). Doing God's will is possible, for "God is there who works in us both the wish and the accomplishment designed to advance His benevolent plan" (Ph 2,13). In this case there is unity of wills, an accord of grace and freedom.

→Authority OT I—Calling—Conscience 2 c—Election—God—Good & Evil I 3.4—Hardness of Heart I 2 a—Law—Liberation/Liberty I—Obedience — Plan of God — Predestine — Promises II 2—Way I—Works OT II 1.

EJ & XLD dfb

WINE

In the holy land wine, wheat, and oil* are staples of the everyday diet (Dt 8,8; 11,14; 1 Ch 12,41). Wine has the peculiar property of "making the heart of man glad" (Ps 104,15; Jg 9,13). Therefore, it is one of the elements of the Messianic banquet. It is also a primary element in the eucharistic meal, where the believer goes to the source of joy*, the charity of Christ.

I. WINE IN DAILY LIFE

1. *In profane life.* The Yahwistic tradition attributes the discovery of the culture of the vine to Noah*, then shows him surprised by the effects of wine (Gn 9,20f). Thus does the tradition simultaneously indicate the benefits and dangers of wine. A sign of prosperity (Gn 49,11f; Pr 3,10), wine is an asset capable of making life pleasant (Si 32,6; 40,20) if used with discretion, which is part of the sense of balance constantly praised in Wisdom literature. The clearest illustration (cf 2 M 15,39) is Ben Sira's axiom: "Wine is life for man when he drinks it with moderation" (Si 31,27). Counsels to moderation abound in the pastoral epistles (1 Tm 3,3.8; Tt 2,3), where a discreet use of wine is also recommended (1 Tm 5,23). Jesus Himself drank wine even at the risk of appearing in a bad light (Mt 11,19 p). The man who swerves from moderation is open to a variety of dangers. The prophets violently inveigh against leaders who are overly fond of drinking because these individuals forget God and their real responsibilities to a people both exploited and seduced to evil (Am 2,8; Ho 7,5; Is 5,11f; 28,1; 56,12). The sages focus more on the personal consequences of excessive drinking. Here the drinker is destined for poverty (Pr 21,17), to violence (Si 31,30f), to debauchery (19,2), to distortion in speech (Pr 22,30-35). St. Paul emphasizes that drunkenness* leads to dissolute living and injures the life of the Spirit in a Christian (E 5,18).

2. *In the life of worship.* Wine has a place in sacrifice because, like all products of the earth, it comes from God. At the old sanctuary of Shiloh, offerings of wine are brought (1 S 1, 24) which could serve for pouring the libations prescribed at the time of sacrifice (Ho 9,4; Ex 29,40; Nm 15,5.10). Wine is also part of the first-fruits given over to the priests (Dt 18,4; Nm 18,12; 2 Ch 31,5) and will ultimately have a role in the new covenant sacrifice which will put an end to the earlier rite of the first-fruits.

On the other hand, religious motivation causes some to abstain from wine. Priests are to abstain during the exercise of their office because these priestly functions require full self-mastery, especially for teaching and rendering judgment (Ez 42,21ff; Lv 10,9f). Abstinence from wine can also be a reminder of the desert period when Israel had no wine and drew near to its God in austerity (Dt 29,5). Long after the settlement in Canaan, the clan of the Rechabites wished to preserve the custom of their nomad days by not drinking wine (Jr 35,6-11). In the same spirit was the ascetical practice of abstaining from all fruit of the vine as a sign of consecration to God, a practice of the Nazirites (cf Am 2,12). Before his birth Samson was thus consecrated at the order of the Lord (Jg 13, 4f); the instances of Samuel (1 S 1,11) and John the Baptist (Lk 1,15; cf 7,33) are analogous. As codified in the priestly law, one could be a Nazirite also by a temporary vow (Nm 6,3-20)—a practice still observed in the Judaeo-Christian community (cf Ac 21,23f). The faithful too were often urged to renounce wine to avoid any danger of compromise with paganism as appears in post-exilic Judaism (Dn 1,8; cf Jdt 10,5). The self-imposed privation of certain Christians seems rather due to a concern for asceticism (1 Tm 5,23) which Paul recalls must be regulated by prudence and charity (R 14,21; cf 1 Co 10,31).

II. THE SYMBOLISM OF WINE

1. From the profane standpoint, wine is the symbol of everything that is pleasant in life: friendship (Si 9,10), human love (Ct 1,4; 4,10), and, in general, all joy* one experiences on earth, with all that is included therein (Qo 10, 19; Ze 10,7; Jdt 12; 13; Jb 1,18). Wine can also call to mind the unwholesome drunkenness* of idolatrous* cults (Jr 51,7; Ap 18,3) as well as the happiness of Wisdom's disciple (Pr 9,2).

2. From a religious point of view, the symbolism of wine appears in an eschatological context.

a) In the OT, God announces the great punishments against this recalcitrant people by speaking of the privation of wine (Am 5,11; Mi

6,15; Zp 1,13; Dt 28,39). At that time the only wine to drink is the wine of divine wrath*, a stunning cup (Is 51,17; cf Ap 14,8; 16,19). At the same time, the happiness God promises to His faithful ones is often expressed under the form of a great abundance of wine, as is seen in the prophets' consolation oracles (Am 9,14; Ho 2,24; Jr 31,12; Is 25,6; Jl 2,19; Ze 9,17).

b) In the NT, the "new wine" is the symbol of Messianic times. Jesus declares that the new covenant established in His person is a new wine that burst the old wine skins (Mk 2,22 p). The same idea appears in the Johannine account of the miracle at Cana: the nuptial wine, the good wine awaited "until now," is the gift of Christ's charity, the sign of the joy become a reality by the Messiah's advent (Jn 2,10; cf 4, 23; 5,25). The term *new wine* is found again in Mt 26,29 as a reminder of the eschatological banquet Jesus destines for His faithful in the kingdom of his Father. This will be the fulfillment of the Messianic times. This mention of wine is not merely symbolic because it is in the context of the account of the institution of the eucharist*. Before drinking new wine in the kingdom of the Father, a Christian will, all his life, drink the wine turned into the blood* shed by the Lord (cf 1 Co 10,16).

For the Christian, therefore, the use of wine is not only a reason for giving thanks (Col 3, 17; cf 2,20ff) but also an opportunity to recall to mind the sacrifice which is the source of salvation and of eternal joy (1 Co 11,25f).

→Cup — Drunkenness — Eucharist — Hunger & Thirst OT 1 c—Joy OT I—Meal—Noah 1— Vine—Vintage—Wrath *B* OT I 1; NT I 1, III 2.
DS dfb

WISDOM

The search for wisdom is common to all cultures in the ancient Orient. Collections of sapiential literature have been bequeathed to us by Egypt as well as by Mesopotamia, and in ancient Greece the seven sages were legendary. This wisdom has a practical aim: it concerns man's conducting himself with prudence and ability in order to succeed in life. That implies a certain reflection on the world; it is also conducive to the elaboration of an ethic from which the religious reference is not absent (notably in Egypt). In sixth-century Greece, the reflection will take a more speculative turn,

and wisdom will develop into philosophy. Alongside an embryonic science and developing crafts, wisdom then constitutes an important element of civilization. This is the humanism of antiquity.

In biblical revelation, the Word of God also takes the form of wisdom. An important fact— but it must be interpreted correctly. It does not mean that revelation, at a certain stage of its development, was transformed into humanism. Inspired wisdom, even when it integrates the best of human wisdom, is of a different nature. Perceptible even in the OT, this becomes clear in the NT.

OT

I. HUMAN WISDOM AND WISDOM ACCORDING TO GOD

1. *The planting of wisdom in Israel.* Except for Joseph (Gn 41,39f) and Moses (Ex 2,10; cf Ac 7,21f), Israel had no contact with the wisdom of the Orient before settling in Canaan; and it is necessary to wait until the time of the kings to see it open itself fully to the humanism of the times. Solomon is the initiator here: "Solomon's wisdom was greater than that of all the orientals and greater than that of Egypt" (1 K 5,9-14; cf 10,6f.23f). The statement refers both to his personal culture and to his art of good government. Now, for men of faith, this royal wisdom is not a problem: it is a gift of God that Solomon obtained by his prayer (1 K 3,6-14). This is an optimistic appreciation, echoes of which one finds elsewhere: whereas the writers at the court cultivate the sapiential genres (cf the old elements of Pr 10—22 and 25—29), the sacred historians eulogize Joseph, the wise administrator who had his wisdom from God (Gn 41; 47).

2. *The wisdom in question.* But there is wisdom and wisdom. True wisdom comes from God; it is He who gives to man "a heart* capable of discerning good from evil" (1 K 3,9). But all men are tempted, as their first father, to usurp this divine privilege, to acquire by their own powers "the knowledge* of good and evil" (Gn 3,5f). Fallacious wisdom, to which the serpent's ruse attracts (Gn 3,1). Such is the wisdom of the scribes who judge everything according to human views and "change the Law of Yahweh into a lie" (Jr 8,8); such is the wisdom of the royal counselors who work out a totally human policy (cf Is 29,15ff). The pro-

phets rise up against that wisdom: "Woe to those who are wise in their own eyes, prudent according to their own understanding" (Is 5,21). God will bring it about that their wisdom is cut short (Is 29,14). They will be ensnared for scorning the Word of Yahweh (Jr 8,9). For that Word* is the sole source of authentic wisdom. It is that wisdom that the spirits who have erred will apprehend after chastisement (Is 29,24). The king, son of David, who will rule "in the last times" will possess it in fullness, but he will have it from the Spirit* of Yahweh (Is 11,2). Thus the prophetic teaching thrusts aside the temptation of a humanism which pretends to be self-sufficient: man's salvation comes from God alone.

3. *Toward true wisdom.* The destruction of Jerusalem confirms the prophets' warnings: the royal counselors' false wisdom has led the country to catastrophe! With the mistake thus dissipated, true wisdom will now be able to expand freely in Israel. Its foundation will be the divine Law* which makes Israel the only wise and intelligent people (Dt 4,6). The fear* of Yahweh will be its beginning and its crowning (Pr 9,10; Si 1,14-18; 19,20). Without ever abandoning the perspectives of this religious wisdom, the inspired writers will henceforth integrate therein all the good that human reflection can offer them. The sapiential literature edited or composed after the exile is the fruit of this effort. Cured of its proud pretensions, humanism blossoms in the light of faith*.

II. ASPECTS OF WISDOM

1. *An art of living well.* The sage of the Bible is curious about the things of nature (1 K 5,13). He admires them, and his faith teaches him to see there the powerful hand of God (Jb 36,22—37,18; 38—41; Si 42,15—43,33). But he is preoccupied before all else with knowing how to conduct his life to obtain true happiness. Every expert in his profession merits by that fact the name of sage (Is 40,20; Jr 9,16; 1 Ch 22,15); the wise man *par excellence* is the expert in the art of good living. Over the world which surrounds him, he casts a penetrating glance that is without illusion; he knows its defects, which does not mean that he approves of them (vg Pr 13,7; Si 13,21ff). A psychologist, he knows what is hidden in the human heart, what is joyful or painful for him (vg Pr 13,12; 14,13; Qo 7,2-6).

But he does not isolate himself in this role of observer. A born educator*, he maps out rules for his disciples*: prudence, moderation in desires, work, humility, level-headedness, discretion, loyalty in speech, etc. . . . The entire ethic of the Decalogue passes in review under his practical advice. The social sense of Deuteronomy and of the prophets inspires in him exhortations to almsgiving (Si 7,32ff; Tb 4,7-11), respect for justice (Pr 11,1; 17,15), love of the poor (Pr 14,31; 17,5; Si 4,1-10). To support his counsels, he appeals to experience as often as possible; but his profound inspiration comes from a source much higher than experience. Once he has acquired wisdom at the price of a stumbling effort, he desires nothing so much as to transmit it to others (Si 51,13-20), and he invites his disciples to undergo courageously wisdom's difficult apprenticeship (Si 6,18-37).

2. *Reflection on existence.* We must not expect from the master of Israelite wisdom a metaphysical sort of reflection upon man; his nature, his powers, etc. On the other hand, he does have an acute sense of his situation in existence and he attentively scrutinizes his destiny. The prophets* concern themselves primarily with the lot of God's people as such, though the texts of Ezekiel on individual responsibility give the appearance of exceptions (Ez 14,12-20; 18; 33, 10,20). In contrast, the sages, without ceasing to be attentive to the global destiny of the people of the covenant (Si 44—50; 36,1-17; Ws 10—12; 15—19), are primarily interested in the life of the individual. They sense man's grandeur (Si 16,24—17,14) as well as his wretchedness (Si 40,1-11), his solitude (Jb 6,11-30; 19,13-22), his anguish in the face of suffering (Jb 7; 16) and death (Qo 3; Si 41,1-4), the impression of nothingness which his life gives him (Jb 14,1-12; 17; Qo 1,4-8; Si 18,8-14), and his uneasiness before God who appears to him incomprehensible (Jb 10) or absent (23; 30,20-23). In this perspective, the problem of reward* cannot help being broached; for otherwise the traditional conceptions would end in the denial of justice (Jb 9,22-24; 21,7-26; Qo 7,15; 8,14; 9,2f). But prolonged efforts will be necessary in order that, beyond the earthly reward that is so deceptive, the problem be resolved by faith in the resurrection* (Dn 12,2f) and in eternal life* (Ws 5,15).

3. *Wisdom and revelation*.* The teaching of the sages, which accords so large a place to

human experience and reflection, is evidently of another type than the prophetic Word*, the issue of a divine inspiration of which the prophet himself is conscious. But that does not prevent him from advancing doctrine also, by projecting upon problems the light gained through prolonged meditation on the Scriptures (cf Si 39,1ff). At an early epoch, prophecy and wisdom were joined in the apocalyptic genre to reveal the secrets of the future. If Daniel "reveals divine mysteries*" (Dn 2,28ff.47), it is not at all because of human wisdom (2,30), but because the divine Spirit, who dwells in him, gives him a higher wisdom (5,11.14). The religious wisdom of the OT here dons a characteristic form already significantly exemplified in ancient Israelite tradition (cf Gn 41,38f). Here the wise man as inspired by God appears the equal of the prophet.

III. THE WISDOM OF GOD

1. *Personified wisdom.* Among the post-exilic writers the cult of wisdom is such that they delight in personifying it in order to give it greater relief (Pr 14,1). She is a well-beloved who is eagerly pursued (Si 14,22ff), a protecting mother (14,26f) and nursing wife (15,2f), a hospitable hostess inviting to her banquet (Pr 9,1-6) as opposed to Dame Folly* whose house is the vestibule of death (9,13-18).

2. *Divine wisdom.* Now this feminine representation ought not to be understood simply as a figure of speech. The wisdom of man has a divine source. God can communicate it to whom He wishes because He is Himself the sage *par excellence*. And so, the sacred authors contemplate in God that wisdom from which their own flows. It is a divine reality which exists from eternity and for eternity (Pr 8,22-26; Si 24,9). Proceeding from the mouth of the most high as His breath or His Word* (Si 24,3), it is "the blast of divine power*, an effusion of the glory* of the all-powerful, a reflection of the eternal light*, a mirror of God's activity, an image* of His excellence" (Ws 7,25f). It dwells in heaven (Si 24,4), shares the throne of God (Ws 9,4), lives in His intimacy (8,3).

3. *The activity of wisdom.* This wisdom is not an inert principle. It is associated with all that God does in the world. Present from creation, it was playing at His side (Pr 8,27-31; cf 3,19f; Si 24,5), and continues to govern the universe (Ws 8,1). Throughout the history of salvation, God has sent it on missions here below. It settled in Israel, at Jerusalem, as a tree* of life (Si 24,7-19), manifesting itself under the concrete form of the Law* (Si 24,23-34). Since then, it resides familiarly with men (Pr 8,31; Ba 3,37f). It is the providence which directs history (Ws 10,1—11,4), and is what assures men salvation (9,18). It plays a role analogous to that of the prophets, addressing its reproaches to the heedless whose judgment it proclaims (Pr 1,20-33), and inviting the docile to benefit from all its goods (Pr 8,1-21.32-36), to sit at its table (Pr 9,4ff; Si 24,19-22). God acts through it as He acts through His Spirit* (cf Ws 9,17); it is therefore one and the same thing to receive it and to be docile to the Spirit. If these texts do not yet make wisdom a divine person in the NT sense, they at least scrutinize to the depths the mystery of the unique God and prepare for a more precise revelation of Him.

4. *The gifts of wisdom.* It is not astonishing that this wisdom should be for men a treasure superior to all else (Ws 7,7-14). Itself a gift of God (8,21), it is the distributor of all goods (Pr 8,21; Ws 7,11): life and happiness (Pr 3,13-18; 8,32-36; Si 14,25-27), security (Pr 3,21-26), grace and glory (4,8f), wealth and justice (8,18ff), and all the virtues (Ws 8,7f). How has man resisted taking her for a spouse (8,2)? It is she in fact that makes men friends of God (7,27f). Intimacy with her is not distinguished from intimacy with God Himself. When the NT identifies wisdom with Christ, Son and Word of God, it will find in this doctrine the exact preparation for a full revelation: united to Christ, man participates in divine wisdom and sees himself introduced into the intimacy of God.

NT

I. JESUS AND WISDOM

1. *Jesus, master of wisdom.* Jesus presents Himself to His contemporaries under a complex exterior: prophet* of penitence, but more than a prophet (Mt 12,41); Messiah*, but one who must pass through the suffering of the Servant* of Yahweh before knowing the glory of the Son* of Man (Mk 8,29ff); teacher, but not in the manner of the scribes (Mk 1,21f). What best recalls His manner of teaching* is that of the masters of wisdom in the OT: He commonly takes up their genres (proverbs, par-

ables*) and gives, as they did, rules for life (cf Mt 5—7). In this, those spectators are not deceived who are astounded at this wisdom which is both unequaled and also accredited by miraculous works (Mk 6,2); Luke notes it even from His infancy (Lk 2,40.52). Jesus Himself lets it be understood that it poses a problem: the queen of the south rose up to hear Solomon's wisdom, but here there is one greater than Solomon (Mt 12,42 p).

2. *Jesus, the wisdom of God.* Effectively, it is in His own name that Jesus promises to His own the gift of wisdom (Lk 21,15). Misunderstood by His incredulous generation*, but received by hearts docile to God, He concludes mysteriously: "Wisdom has been justified by her children" (Lk 7,35; or "by her works" Mt 11,19). His secret pierces deeper when He fashions His words after those which the OT attributed to divine wisdom: "Come to me..." (Mt 11,28ff; cf Si 24,19); "He who comes to me will hunger no more, he who believes in me will thirst no more" (Jn 6,35; cf 4,14; 7,37; Is 55, 1ff; Pr 9,1.6; Si 24,19-22). These appeals go beyond what a person would expect from one wise man among others; they offer a glimpse into the mysterious personality of the Son* (cf Mt 11,25ff p). The lesson was harvested in the apostolic writings. If they call Jesus "the wisdom of God" (1 Co 1,24.30), it is not only because He communicates wisdom to men; it is because He Himself is wisdom. Thus, in order to speak of His pre-existence with the Father, the same words are used which described the divine wisdom long before: He is the first-born before any creature and the artisan of creation* (Col 1,15ff; cf Pr 8,22-31), the resplendence of God's glory* and the image of His substance (He 1,3; cf Ws 7,25f). The Son is the wisdom of the Father as He is also His Word* (Jn 1,1ff). Of old, this personal wisdom had been hidden in God, although it governed the universe, guided history, and manifested itself indirectly in the Law and in the teaching of the sages. Now, it is revealed in Jesus Christ. Thus all the sapiential texts of the OT find in Him their definitive meaning.

II. THE WORLD'S WISDOM AND CHRISTIAN WISDOM

1. *The world's wisdom condemned.* At the time of this supreme revelation of wisdom, the drama that the prophets had already set before men's eyes was renewed. Having grown foolish from the time it failed to recognize the living God (R 1,21f; 1 Co 1,21), the wisdom of this world crowned its folly* when men "crucified the Lord of glory" (1 Co 2,8). Therefore God condemned this wisdom of the sages (1,19f; 3, 19f), which is "earthly, animal, demoniacal" (Jm 3,15); in order to turn the trick on the world, God decided to save it by the folly of the cross* (1 Co 1,17-25). Thus, when the gospel* of salvation* is announced, men can set aside all that arises from human wisdom, culture, and fine speech (1 Co 1,17; 2,1-5): one does not play tricks with the folly of the cross.

2. *True wisdom.* And so, the revelation of true wisdom is made in a paradoxical manner. It is not to the wise and prudent that it is accorded, but to the little ones (Mt 11,25); in order to confound the proud sages, God chose what was foolish in the eyes of the world (1 Co 1,27) in order to make it wise according to God (3,18). For Christian wisdom is not acquired by human effort at all, but through the Father's revelation (Mt 11,25ff). In itself it is a divine thing, mysterious and hidden, impossible for human intelligence to fathom (1 Co 2,7ff; R 11,33ff; Col 2,3). Though made manifest by the historical accomplishment of salvation (E 3,10), it cannot be communicated except by the Spirit of God to those who are docile to Him (1 Co 2,10-16; 12,8; E 1,17).

III. ASPECTS OF CHRISTIAN WISDOM

1. *Wisdom and revelation.* Christian wisdom, such as it has just been described, presents some clear affinities with the Jewish revelations: it is primarily not a rule of life, but a revelation* of the mystery* of God (1 Co 2,6ff), the summit of religious knowledge* which Paul asks of God for the faithful (Col 1,9) and which they can teach each other (3,16) "in words taught by the Spirit" (1 Co 2,13).

2. *Wisdom and moral life.* Still, the moral aspect of wisdom is not, by that fact, eliminated. On the contrary, all the rules of conduct connected in the OT with wisdom according to God attain the fullness of their meaning in the light of the revelation of Christ, the wisdom of God—not only the fruit arising from the apostle's work (1 Co 3,10; 2 P 3,15); but also matters of daily Christian life (E 5,15; Col 4,5), in which the conduct of the prudent, and not

the foolish, virgins must be imitated (Mt 25,1-12). The teaching of the ancient sages now gives place to the counsels of practical ethics enunciated by St. Paul in his last letters. The fact is more evident still with regard to the epistle of James, which on this precise point opposes false wisdom with the "wisdom from above" (Jm 3,13-17). This last implies a perfect moral rectitude. One must force oneself to conform one's acts to it, all the while asking for it as a gift from God (Jm 1,5).

Such is the only perspective in which the acquisitions of humanism can be integrated with Christian life and thought. Sinful man must permit himself to be crucified with his proud wisdom if he wishes to be reborn in Christ. If he does that, his whole human effort will take on a new meaning, for he will fulfill himself under the tenure of the Spirit.

→Creation OT II 3; NT I 2—Disciple OT 2—Education—Fear of God IV—Folly—Fullness 2—Image III—Jesus Christ II 1 d—Justice *A* I OT 4—Know OT 4—Law *B* III 4—Light & Dark OT I 3—Milk 3—Mother II 1—Mystery OT 2 b; NT II 1—Old Age 2—Paradise 2 c —Plan of God OT IV—Predestine 2—Promise II 6—Revelation OT I 3—Simple 1—Sin IV 3 d—Son of Man OT II 1—Spouse OT 3; NT 1—Taste 1—Teach OT I 4, II 1—Truth OT 3—Will of God OT I 2 b—Woman OT 3—Word of God OT I 1, IV—Works OT I 3; NT I 1.

AB & PG ecu

WITNESS

OT

I. THE WITNESS OF MEN

To bear witness is to attest the reality of an event by giving to the affirmation of it all the solemnity which the circumstances require. A trial or legal action is the natural setting for witness. Certain objects can fill this role by virtue of a convention: thus the cairn of Galaad for the treaty between Jacob and Laban (Gn 31, 45-52), and the pledges received by Tamar when she was accused of misconduct (38,25). But it is especially the witness of men with which the Bible concerns itself by underlining its seriousness. The Law regulates its use: there is no condemnation possible without the evidence of

witness (Nm 5,13); to prevent error or ill will, there must be at least two of them (Nm 35,30; Dt 17,6; 19,15; cf Mt 18,16); and in capital cases, involving the responsibility for condemnation, they must be the first to execute the sentence (Dt 17,7; cf Ac 7,58). But a lie* can slip into that act by which a man pledges his word*: the psalmists complain of false witnesses who overwhelm them (Ps 27,12; 35,11), and there are instances of tragic trials where they have played an essential part (1 K 21,10-13; Dn 13,34-41). From the time of the Decalogue, false witness is strictly forbidden (Dt 19,16f; Dt 5,20); Deuteronomy punishes it according to the law of talion (Dt 19,18f); the teaching of the wise men condemns it (Pr 14,5.25; 19,5.9; 21,28; 24, 28; 25,18), for it is a thing which God abominates (Pr 6,19).

II. THE WITNESS OF GOD

1. *God is witness.* Beyond the witness of men, there is that of God, which no one can contradict. At the time of marriage He is a witness between a man and the woman of his youth (Ml 2,14). In the same way, He is the guarantor of human contracts made before Him (Gn 31,53f; Jr 42,5). He can be taken as a witness in a solemn affirmation (1 S 12,5; 20,12). He is the supreme witness to whom appeal can be made to refute the false testimony of men (Jb 16,7f.19).

2. *The witness of God in the Law and by the prophets.* However, the witness of God can be understood in another meaning, closely connected with the doctrine of the Word*. In the first place God bears witness to Himself, when He reveals to Moses the meaning of His Name* (Ex 3,14) or when He declares that He is the only God (20,2f). This witness is made under oath* (Is 45,21-24) and forms the basis of the monotheism of Israel. But God also gives witness through the commandments contained in the Law* (2 K 17,13; Ps 19,8; 78,5.56; 119, *passim*). For this reason the tables of the Law have been called the witness (Ex 25,16...; 31, 18). Placed in the ark of the covenant, they make it the ark of witness (25,22; 40,3.5.21f), and the tabernacle becomes the dwelling of witness (38, 21; Nm 1,50-53). There is finally a divine witness which the prophets bear. This is a matter of a solemn affirmation (cf Jr 42,18) set in the context of the legal action brought by God against His unfaithful people (cf Ps 50,7). A

witness whom nothing can escape, God denounces all the sins of Israel (Jr 29,23); He becomes an accusing witness (Mi 1,2; Am 3,13; Ml 3,5) in order to obtain the conversion of sinners.

III. THE WITNESSES OF GOD

As in human agreements, the commitments of Israel to God are attested by object-signs, which bear witness against the people in case of infidelity; as, for instance, the book of the Law (Dt 31,26) and the canticle of Moses (Dt 31, 19ff). Even heaven and earth could bear this testimony (Dt 4,26; 31,28). However there is one function of witness which only men can fill, for God must still call them to it. It is the mission of the prophets. The mission of David, whom God established as a faithful witness* (Ps 89,37f; cf 1 S 12,5), a witness for the nations*, is similar (Is 55,4); as is the mission of the entire people of Israel, which is charged here below with bearing witness for God before other nations and with affirming that He alone is God (Is 43,10ff; 44,8), as opposed to the idols which cannot produce witnesses in their own behalf (43,9). The infidelities of Israel to this vocation of witness-people do not prevent them from forming the reason for Israel's separation from others and do not prevent Israel from finding in her vocation a source of confidence (44,8).

NT

I. FROM THE WITNESS OF MEN TO THE WITNESS OF GOD

Like the OT, the NT condemns false witness, of which examples are still found in the trial of Jesus (Mt 26,59-65 p) and of Stephen (Ac 6,11ff). The Christian community takes up again for its interior discipline the rule of two or three witnesses formulated by the Deuteronomist (Mt 18,16; 2 Co 13,1; 1 Tm 5,19). But the notion of witness is enlarged in a less juridical direction: those who know a good man render favorable witness to him. Thus the Jews bear witness in regard to Christ (Lk 4,22), to Cornelius (Ac 10, 22), and to Ananias (22,12). The Christian community bears this favorable witness to the first deacons (6,3), to Timothy (16,2), to Demetrius (3 Jn 12; cf 3.6), to Paul himself (1 Th 2,10); and Paul for his part does the same for the

churches of Corinth (2 Co 8,3) and of Galatia (G 4,15). Here witness takes on a distinctly religious value. Our Christian life does not make us isolated individuals but it unfolds in the presence of a multitude of witnesses who encourage us to fervor, not only the living (1 Tm 6,12), but also those who have preceded us in the faith (He 12,1ff). God Himself is the first of these witnesses. He accords favorable witness to the saints of the OT (Ac 13,22; He 11,2.4f.39) as well as to the converts recently come from paganism (Ac 15,8).

II. THE WITNESS OF JESUS

The problem of witness in the sense which it had in the Law and in the preaching of the prophets centers now around Jesus, who is the faithful witness *par excellence* (Ap 1,5; 3,14). He has come into the world to bear witness to the truth (Jn 18,37). He bears witness of what He has seen and heard in the presence of the Father (3,11.32f). He bears witness against the evil world* (7,7), and He bears witness of what He Himself is (8,13f). His confession* before Pilate is a supreme testimony (1 Tm 6,13) which makes plain the divine plan of salvation (2,6). Now this testimony, though contested by the unbelieving world* (Jn 3,11; 8,13), possesses juridically an incontestable value because other evidences support it: the witness of John the Baptist, which summarizes his whole mission (1,6ff.15.19; 3,26ff; 5,33-36); the witness of the works* accomplished by Jesus at the command of the Father (5,36; 10,25); witness of the Father Himself (5,31f.37f; 8,16ff); which is clearly manifested by the witness of the Scriptures (5, 39; cf He 7,8.17; Ac 10,43; 1 P 1,11), and which ought to be received if one does not wish to make God a liar (1 Jn 5,9ff). To all this there is added in Christian experience the witness of the baptismal water* and of the blood* of the eucharist, which attest in their symbolic language the same thing which the Holy Spirit attests in us (1 Jn 5,6ff). For the Spirit which is given to us gives witness to Jesus (Jn 15,26), and He witnesses also that we are sons of God (R 8,6). Such is the cluster of witnesses which strengthen the witness of Jesus. In accepting them a man becomes docile to the witness of Jesus and enters into the life of faith.

III.   THE WITNESSES OF JESUS

1. *The apostolic witness.* In order to reach men, witness must take a concrete form: the preaching* of the gospel* (Mt 24,14). It is in order to carry the gospel into the entire world that the apostles* are constituted witnesses of Jesus (Ac 1,8); they are to attest solemnly before men to all the events occurring from the baptism of John until the ascension of Jesus, especially the resurrection*, which has consecrated His lordship (1,22; 2,32; etc.). The mission of Paul is defined in the same terms: on the road to Damascus, he has been constituted a witness of Christ before all men (22,15; 26,16); in a pagan land he attests especially to the resurrection of Jesus (1 Co 15,15), and the faith is born in the communities by the acceptance of this witness (2 Th 1,10; 1 Co 1,6). There is the same identification of the gospel and of witness in the Johannine writings. The evangelist's narrative is an attestation by an eyewitness (Jn 19,35; 21,24); but, inspired by the Spirit (Jn 16,13), the witness belongs also to the mystery* which the events conceal: the mystery of the Word of life come in the flesh (1 Jn 1,2; 4,14). The believers who have accepted this apostolic witness already possess in themselves the very testimony of Jesus, which is the prophecy of the new times (Ap 12,17; 19,21). It is for this reason that the witnesses charged with transmitting the testimony take on once more the traits of the prophets of old (11,3-7).

2. *From witness to martyrdom.* The role of the witnesses of Jesus is made still more evident when they have to bear witness before the authorities and the tribunals, in line with the perspective which Jesus had already opened before the twelve (Mk 13,9; Mt 10,18; Lk 21,13f). Then the attestation takes a solemn turn, and it often preludes suffering*. If in fact the believers are persecuted, it is "because of their witness of Jesus" (Ap 1,9). Stephen was the first to seal his witness with the pouring out of his blood (Ac 22,20). The same fate awaits here below the witnesses of the gospel (Ap 11,7). How many will be slain "for the witness of Jesus and the Word of God" (6,9; 17,6)! Babylon*, the hostile power aroused against the heavenly city, will glut itself with the blood of these witnesses, of these martyrs (17,6). But she will only have an apparent victory. Really it is they who, with Christ, will have conquered the devil "by the blood of the Lamb and the word of their testimony" (12,11). Martyrdom* is witness to

the faith consecrated by the testimony of blood.

→Altar 1—Amen—Apostles—Apparitions of Christ 7—Ark of the Covenant II—Book II—Confession O; OT 1; NT 1—Example—John the Baptist—Lie I 1—Martyr—Mission—Oath —Paraclete 2—Persecution—Preach II 2 a—Schism OT 2; NT 2—Spirit of God OT II—Trial—World NT III 2.

MP& PG jpl

WOMAN

In the Israelitic codes of law, as in those of the rest of the ancient Middle East, the status of woman was still that of a minor; her influence remained restricted to her function as mother. But Israel did stand out by reason of their faith in God the creator, who insisted on the fundamental equality of the two sexes. Still the true position of woman was only revealed with the coming of Christ. For if, according to the order of creation, woman finds fulfillment in becoming a wife and mother, she now also can find fulfillment, in the order of this new creation, through virginity.

OT

WIFE AND MOTHER

1. *In the earthly Paradise.* The sexes are a fundamental fact of human nature: man* was created "male and female" (Gn 1,27). This brief statement by the priestly compiler presupposes the Yahwistic account where the double role of the woman in respect to man is explained.

Woman was taken from an intimate part of Adam himself; and so, unlike the animals, she has the very same nature as Adam. Such is the position of man before the creature whom God places before him. Not only this, but Adam responds to the divine plan of giving him "a helper who is like him" (2,18), and he recognizes himself in her. In naming her, he gives himself a name*: before her, he is not just Adam, he becomes *iš*, and she is *iššah*. Following the plan of creation*, woman completes man in having him become her spouse. This relation should have remained perfectly equal in their difference, but sin perverted this by subjecting the wife to her husband (3,16).

Woman not only gives human society its initial life, but she is the mother* of all the living. Where numerous religions freely compare woman to the earth*, the Bible rather identifies her with life*. She is, by her natural name, Eve, "the living one" (3,20). If, because of sin, she transmits life only at the cost of suffering* (3, 16), she nevertheless triumphs over death by insuring the continuation of the race. And to sustain herself in this hope, she knows that one day her descendants will crush the head of the serpent, their hereditary enemy (3,15).

2. *In sacred history*. While awaiting this blessed day, the role of woman remains limited. Certainly her rights at home appear equal to her husband's, at least in regard to the children whom she educates*. But the Law* considers her as second in rank. A woman takes no official part in worship*. She may rejoice publicly during the feasts (Ex 15,20f; Dt 12,12; Jg 21,21; 2 S 6), but she does not exercise any sacerdotal office, and only the men were bound by the obligatory pilgrimages* (Ex 23,17). The wife is not even listed among those strictly bound to observe the sabbath (20,10). Outside of worship, the Law is very careful to protect the woman, especially in her own proper domain, life itself. Is she not the very presence here below of the fruitful* life (vg Dt 25,5-10)? Man must respect her in her own rhythm of existence (Lv 20,18). He respects her to such an extent that he demands of her an ideal of fidelity in marriage* to which he does not oblige himself.

In the course of the history of the covenant, certain women played important roles, either for good or evil. Foreign women turned the heart of Solomon toward their gods (1 K 11,1-8; cf Qo 7,26; Si 47,19). Jezebel demonstrates the power of a woman on the religion and morals of her husband (1 K 18,13; 19,1f; 21,25f); and there are even cases of children familiar with their mother's language but unable to "speak the language of Judah" (Ne 13,23f). Woman appears to influence as she pleases the religious life which she does not officially exercise in worship. But in contrast with these examples we find the wives of the patriarchs who show a praiseworthy enthusiasm for fecundity. Here are heroines. Though access to worship is forbidden them, the Spirit of Yahweh makes use of certain women, transforming them, just as He would with men, into prophetesses, thus showing that their sex is not an obstacle to the intrusion of the Spirit. For example: Miriam (Ex 15,20f), Deborah and Jael (Jg 4,4—5,31),

Huldah (2 K 22,14-20).

3. *In the thought of the sages.* Infrequent, and not even there tender, are the maxims attributed to women about women (Pr 31,1-9). The biblical portrait of woman bears man's signature. If the portrait is not always flattering, that does not prove that the authors were misogynists. The harshness of man regarding women is the ransom for the need man has of them. So man describes his dream: "to find a wife is to find happiness" (Pr 18,22; cf 5,15-18), it is to have "a helper like himself," a solid support, an enclosure for his own domain, a nest against the call to wander (Si 36,24-27). To find a woman is to find beauty personified (Pr 11,16), an addition to his own masculine power which gives him confidence. What are we to say if this woman is brave (Pr 12,4; 31,10-31)! It is enough to recall the description of the wife in the Song of Songs (Ct 4,1-5; 7,2-10).

But the man who has had some experience fears the essential weakness of his companion. Beauty does not suffice (Pr 11,22). In fact it is quite dangerous when it is united in a Delilah with trickery (Jg 14,15ff; 16,4-21), or when it seduces a plain man (Si 9,1-9; cf Gn 3,6). Young girls are a cause of worry to their parents (Si 42,9ff); and the man who allows himself liberties away from the wife of his youth (cf Pr 5, 15-20) fears the inconstancy of woman and her inclination to adultery* (Si 25,13—26,18). He deplores it when she manifests vanity (Is 3,16-24) or shows herself a "fool" (Pr 9,13-18; 19,14; 11,22); quarrelsome, peevish, and vexatious (Pr 19,13; 21,9.19; 27,15f).

The understanding of women which these sages had should not be limited to these descriptions of morals and manners. For woman is, in fact, a figure* of divine wisdom* (Pr 8,22-31). She manifests the power* of God who uses weak instruments to procure His glory. Hannah glorified the Lord of the humble (1 S 2); Judith shows, as a prophetess in action, that all can count on the protection of God. Her beauty, her prudence, her capability, her courage, and her chastity in widowhood make her a perfect type of woman according to the plan of God in the OT.

NT

VIRGIN, WIFE, AND MOTHER

Beautiful as it may be, this portrait still does not confer on woman her sovereign dignity.

The daily prayer of the Jew even in our present day candidly proclaims this fact: "Blessed may you be, O God, for not having made me a gentile, nor a woman, nor an ignoramus!" while the woman is content to say: "Praised be you, Lord, who created me according to your will." Christ alone consecrates woman with full dignity.

1. *Dawn of redemption.* This consecration took place on the day of the annunciation. The Lord willed to be born of a woman (G 4,4). Mary*, virgin and mother, fulfills in herself the feminine hope of fruitfulness*. At the same time she reveals and sanctifies a desire suppressed until now, the desire of virginity*, which before had been compared to shameful sterility*. In Mary the ideal of womanhood becomes incarnate, for she gave birth to the prince of life. But, while a woman here below runs the risk of restricting her admiration to the physical life which she gave to the most beautiful of the children of men, Jesus revealed that there is a spiritual maternity, fruit born through the virginity of faith (Lk 11,28f). Through Mary, woman can become the symbol of the believing soul. From this we can understand Jesus' acceptance in letting Himself be followed* by holy women (Lk 8,1ff), his taking faithful virgins as an example (Mt 25,1-13), or entrusting women with a mission* (Jn 20,17). And so the infant Church draws attention to the position occupied by numerous women and the role they play (Ac 1,14; 9,36-41; 12,12; 16,14f), who from now on are called upon to collaborate in the work of the Church.

2. *In Christ Jesus.* This participation presupposes the discovery of a new dimension in woman: virginity*. So Paul worked out a theology of woman, showing in what sense the division of sexes* has been overcome and consecrated. "There is neither male nor female: you are all one in Christ Jesus" (G 3,28). In a certain sense the distinction between the sexes is overcome, as are the divisions in the racial and social order. Existence in heaven can be anticipated in this angelic life of which Jesus spoke (Mt 22,30). But faith alone can justify it. If Paul maintains wisely that "it is better to marry than to burn" (1 Co 7,9), he is exalting the charism* of virginity. He dares even to contradict Genesis which said, "it is not good for man to be alone" (Gn 2,18; 1 Co 7,26). All persons, young men or women, can, if they are called, remain virgins. And so a new distinction between the married and virgins is added to the first distinction between man and woman. Faith and the life of heaven find in a life of virginity a concrete example in which the soul attaches itself without vexation to its Lord (7,35). In order to fulfill her vocation a woman need not become a wife and mother; she can remain a virgin in heart and body.

This ideal of virginity which woman can now decide upon and realize does not suppress the normal condition of marriage* (1 Tm 2,15). It carries with it a compensatory value, just as heaven* balances and situates the earth. Finally, and most profoundly, the natural relation of man and woman is founded on the relation of Christ to the Church. Woman stands now face to face not simply with Adam but with Christ, and she now represents the Church* (E 5,22ff).

3. *Woman and the Church.* Although the division of the sexes had been transcended by faith, it came to life again in the course of time and imposed itself on the concrete life of the Church. From the order which exists in creation, Paul deduces two aspects of woman's behavior. A woman should wear a veil to the assembly for worship. She expresses by this symbol that her Christian dignity does not exempt her from dependence on her husband (1 Co 11,2-16), nor from being second in rank, the place which she still occupies in the official teaching. She should also not "speak" in Church; that is, she is not able to teach* (1 Co 14,34; cf 1 Tm 2,12). That is the "commandment of the Lord" which Paul received (1 Co 14,37). But Paul does not deny a woman the possibility of prophesying* (11,5), because, just as in the OT, the Spirit does not recognize the distinction between the sexes. Though she is veiled and silent at worship, so that "order" might be kept, the woman is encouraged on the other hand to give witness* at home by a "chaste and fully submissive life" (1 P 3,1f; 1 Tm 2,9f). And when as a widow she has attained an advanced age which keeps her from her earlier function, she plays an important role in the Christian community (1 Tm 5,9).

And finally, the Apocalypse does not lose sight of the typical role played by Jezebel (Ap 2,20) nor the crimes of the famous prostitute (17,1.1ff; 18,3.9; 19,2). But above all it glorifies "the Woman," crowned with stars who gives birth to a male child and who is pursued into the desert by the dragon, but who must triumph over him through her offspring (Ap 12). This woman is first of all the Church, the new Eve who gives birth to the body* of Christ. Then, according to the traditional interpretation, she is Mary* herself. We can see in her the proto- type of the woman, whom each woman longs in her heart to become.

→Adultery—Clothing—Flesh I 2—Fruitfulness —Joy OT I—Man—Marriage—Mary—Mother —Sexuality I—Sign NT II 3—Spouse—Sterility —Virginity—Widows.

XLD afmcg

WORD OF GOD

"They have mouths and they do not speak" (Ps 115,5; Ba 6,7). This satire of the "mute idols" (1 Co 12,2) emphasizes one of the most characteristic traits of the living God* in biblical revelation. God speaks to man, and the im- portance of His Word in the OT is only to prepare for the central fact of the NT wherein that Word—the Logos—becomes flesh.

OT

I. GOD SPEAKS TO MAN

In the OT the theme of the divine Word is not an object of abstract speculation, as is the case in other currents of thought (cf the *logos* of the Alexandrian philosophers). It is prin- cipally a fact of experience. God speaks directly to some privileged men, and through them to His people and to all men.

1. Prophecy is one of the basic elements of the OT; at all times God speaks to some chosen men who have the mission to transmit His Word. In the broad sense of the term, these men are prophets*. The manner in which God addresses Himself to them can vary: to some He speaks in "visions and in dreams" (Nm 12, 6; cf 1 K 22,13-17), to others, by a less definable interior inspiration (2 K 3,15...; Jr 1,4, etc.), while to Moses, He speaks "mouth to mouth" (Nm 12,8). Very often the mode of expression of His Word is not even precise (vg Gn 12,1). That, however, is not the essential thing. All these prophets are clearly aware that God speaks to them, that His Word enters them somehow, almost to the point of doing them violence (Am 7,15; cf 3,8; Jr 20,7ff). For them, the Word of God is the main thing that deter- mines the direction of their lives. The extra-

ordinary way the Word surges up in them causes them to attribute its origin to the action of the Spirit* of God. However, in other cases, the Word can also come in more secret ways that are apparently more in harmony with normal psychology. These would be the ways which divine Wisdom borrows in order to address the hearts of men (Pr 8,1-21.32-36; Ws 7—8), whether it be to teach men how to live their lives or to reveal divine secrets to them (Dn 5, 11f; cf Gn 41,39). In any case, it is not a ques- tion of a man's word that is subject to change or error. Prophets and sages are in direct com- munication with the living God.

2. But the divine Word is not given to the heavenly privileged as an esoteric teaching that they must hide from common mortals. It is a message to be transmitted, not to a small circle, but to the entire people of God with whom God wishes to communicate through the human in- strument of His spokesman. Thus, the experi- ence of the Word of God is not merely the act of a small number of mystics, since all Israel is called to acknowledge that God has spoken to them through the mouths of His messengers. If, at first, it should happen that the divine Word is misunderstood and scorned (vg Jr 36), unmistakable signs would always end up im- posing the evidence. At the time of the NT, all Judaism shall profess that "God spoke to our fathers at many times and in a multiplicity of ways" (He 1,1).

II. ASPECTS OF THE WORD

The Word of God can be considered under two inseparable but distinct aspects; it reveals and it acts.

1. *By speaking, God reveals.* In order to put the thought of man in communication with His own thought, God speaks. His Word is, in turn: law and rule of life, revelation of the meaning of things and events, and promise and fore- telling of the future.

a) The conception of the Word as *law* and *rule of life* goes back to the very beginnings of Israel. At the time of the covenant on Sinai, Moses gave to the people, on behalf of God, a moral and religious charter that was summed up in ten "words," the Decalogue (Ex 20,1-17; Dt 5,6-22; cf Ex 34,28; Dt 4,13; 10,4). This statement of the one God, together with the revelation of His essential demands, was one of the first things that allowed Israel to realize that "God speaks." Some biblical accounts have emphasized this by building up the scene on Sinai and by showing God speaking directly to the people of Israel from the center of the cloud (cf Ex 20,1...; Dt 4,12). At any rate, it is in the name of the divine Word that the Law is imposed. For this reason the sages and the psalmists saw the Law as a source of happiness (Pr 18,13; 16,20; Ps 119).

b) From the beginning, however, there is found united to the divine Law a *revelation** *of God and His activity here below:* "I am Yahweh, your God, who has brought you out of the land of Egypt" (Ex 20,2). This is the essential truth that establishes the authority of the Law itself. If Israel is a monotheistic people, it is not at all because of human reason, but because Yahweh has spoken to their fathers, then to Moses, in order to make Himself known as the "only God" (Ex 3,13-15; cf Dt 6,4). Moreover, as sacred history gradually unfolds, it is the Word of its God that enlightens Israel concerning the hidden meaning of that history. In each of the great national trials, the Word reveals God's hidden purposes (Js 24,2-13). This recognition of God's plan in the events of this world is no longer of human origin. It rises out of prophetic knowledge that has been deepened by sapiential reflection (cf Ws 10—19). In short, it flows from the Word of God.

c) Finally, the Word of God is able to go beyond the limits of time and to uncover the future. Step by step it enlightens Israel about the next stage in God's plan (Gn 15,13-16; Ex 3,7-10; Js 1,1-5, etc.). In addition to an immediate future, which is painted in sombre colors, the Word of God reveals what is to come "in the last days" when God will carry out His plan in all its fullness. It is the whole object of prophetic eschatology. Law, revelation, and promises: these three aspects of the divine Word accompany and mutually condition each other throughout the entire OT. They call for a response on the part of man, but we will return later to a consideration of that subject.

2. *In speaking, God acts.* The Word of God, however, is not only an intelligible message directed to men. It is a dynamic reality; a power that infallibly brings about the effects at which God aims (Js 21,45; 23,14; 1 K 8,56). God sends it as a living messenger (Is 9,7; Ps 107,20; 147,15), and it takes hold in some way upon men (Ze 1,6). God watches over it to see that it is fulfilled (Jr 1,12); and, in fact, it always produces what it proclaims (Nm 23,19; Is 55,10f), whether it concerns historical events, cosmic realities, or the end of the plan of salvation.

a) This dynamic concept of the Word was not unknown in the ancient East where it was considered as something quasi-magical. In the OT, at first it was applied to the prophetic word: when God reveals His plans in advance, it is certain that afterwards He will realize them. History is a fulfillment of His promises (cf Dt 9,5; 1 K 2,4; Jr 11,5). Things happen when He speaks (Is 44,7f). At the time of the exodus, "He speaks and the insects go away" (Ps 105, 31.34). At the end of the Babylonian captivity, "He says of Jerusalem: 'Let it be inhabited,' and He says of Cyrus: 'My shepherd...'" (Is 44,26.28).

b) If all this is historically true, how can there be any doubt that the whole of creation obeys the Word of God? In fact, it is under the form of a word that it was fitting for the original act of the Creator* to be represented: "He spoke and it was" (Ps 33,6-9; cf Gn 1; Lm 3,37; Jdt 16,14; Ws 9,1; Si 42,15). Ever since that time, the very same Word remains active in the universe, ruling the stars (Is 40,26), the waters of the deep (Is 44,27), and the totality of natural phenomena (Ps 107,25; 147,15-18; Jb 37, 5-13; Si 39,17.31). More than the food from the earth it is this Word, which like a heavenly manna* conserves in being those who believe in God (Ws 16,26; cf Dt 8,3 LXX).

c) An effectiveness such as this, verifiable in creation as in history, cannot be lacking in the oracles of salvation which concern the "last days*"; in fact, "the Word of God lives forever" (Is 40,8). For this reason, from one century to another, the people of God piously gather together all those words which foretell their future. No event is without meaning for them as long as the "last days" have not come (cf Dn 9).

III. MAN BEFORE GOD WHO SPEAKS

The Word of God, then, is a fact that confronts man and will not permit him to remain passive. The bearer of the Word exercises a ministry that has very heavy responsibilities. The hearer of the Word realizes that he is called upon to take a position that involves his destiny.

1. *The minister of the Word* is not presented in the OT as a source of mystical joy. On the contrary, every prophet* is exposed to contradiction and even persecution*. Certainly, in putting into His prophet's mouth His own words, God gives him sufficient power to transmit fearlessly the message entrusted to him (Jr 1,6-10). In return, however, the prophet is responsible before God for this mission* upon which the fate of man depends (Ez 3,16-21; 33,1-9). In fact, if he tries to escape his duty, God can draw him back by force, as can be understood in the story of Jonah (Jon 1; 3). More often, the prophets acquit themselves of their mission at the risk of their peace, indeed, of their lives; and this heroic fidelity is a cause of suffering for them (Jr 15,16ff), a difficult task for which they do not immediately receive payment (1 K 19,14).

2. *Acceptance of the Word.* As for the hearers of the Word, they must prepare a confident and docile reception for it in their hearts. Insofar as it is a revelation and rule of life, the Word is a light* for them (Ps 119,105). Insofar as it is a promise, it gives assurance for the future. Whoever may be the one who transmits the revelation, Moses or a prophet, it is fitting to hear him (Dt 6,3; Is 1,10; Jr 11,3.6), whether it be for "having it in his heart" (Dt 6,6; 30,14) and putting it into practice (Dt 6,3; Ps 119,9.17. 101), or of counting on it and hoping in it (Ps 119,42.74.81, etc. 130,5). The human response to the Word of God constitutes a complex interior attitude which bears all the marks of theological life: faith, since the Word is the revelation of the living God and of His plans; hope, since it is a promise of an entry; love, since it is a rule of life (cf Dt 6,4ff).

IV. PERSONIFICATION OF THE WORD OF GOD

The divine Word is not just one element among others in the economy of the OT but it dominates it entirely, giving meaning to history insofar as it is creative of it. In men, it gives rise to a life of faith insofar as it is addressed to them as a message. Thus, it is not so surprising to see this importance sometimes translated into a personification of the Word, parallel to that of Wisdom* and the Spirit* of God. This

is the case for the revealing Word (Ps 119,89) and, especially, for the acting Word who is the executor of the divine commands (Ps 147,15; 107,20; Is 55,11; Ws 18,14ff). In the fibre of these texts is already discovered the action of the Word of God here below, even before the NT revealed it to men in its fullness.

NT

Some passages of the NT take up again the doctrine of the Word of God in a sense that is identical to that of the OT (cf Mt 15,6). Mary* believes in the Word that is delivered to her by the angel (Lk 1,37f.45), and the Word is addressed to John the Baptist as to the prophets of old (Lk 3,2). But, from this time on, the mystery of the Word usually has the person of Jesus for its center of focus.

I. THE WORD OF GOD AND THE WORD OF JESUS

1. *The Word effects and reveals.* Nowhere is it said that the Word of God was addressed to Jesus as it was formerly said of the prophets. However, in St. John's gospel, as in the synoptics, the Word of God is presented exactly as the Word of God in the OT—power which effects, and light which reveals.

Power* which effects: by a word, Jesus accomplishes the miracles that are the signs of the kingdom of God (Mt 8,8.16; Jn 4,50-53). Moreover, by a word, He brings about spiritual effects in hearts for which these miracles are the symbols, as when He forgives sins (Mt 9,1-7 p). By a word, He gives His powers to the twelve (Mt 18,18; Jn 20,23) and institutes the signs of the new covenant (Mt 26,26-29 p). In Him and through Him, the creative Word is at work effecting salvation here below.

Light* which reveals: Jesus proclaims the gospel* of the kingdom; He "proclaims the Word" (Mk 4,33), making known through parables* the mysteries* of the kingdom of God (Mt 13,11 p). In appearance, He is a prophet* (Jn 6,14) or a doctor who teaches* in God's name (Mt 22,16 p). In reality, He speaks "with authority" (Mk 1,22 p), as on His own authority and with the certitude that "His words will not pass away" (Mt 24,35 p). This attitude lets us glimpse into a mystery that the fourth gospel is fond of considering. Jesus "speaks God's words" (Jn 3,34). He says "what the Father has taught Him" (8,28). For that reason "His words have spirit and life" (6,63). More than once, the evangelist uses the word "to speak" (*lalein*) to emphasize the importance of this characteristic about Jesus (vg 3,11; 8,25-40; 15, 11; 16,4...); for Jesus "does not speak concerning Himself" (12,49f; 14,10), but "as the Father has first spoken to Him" (12,50). The mystery of the prophetic Word inaugurated in the OT attains its perfect fulfillment in Him.

2. *Man in confrontation with the Word.* From the above we can see that men are called to take positions when confronted by this Word that puts them in contact with God Himself. The synoptics report remarks made by Jesus that clearly show the stakes involved in the choice of positions. In the parable of the sower*, the Word—which is the gospel of the kingdom— is received differently by various listeners. All "hear," but only those who "understand it" (Mt 13,23) or "accept it" (Mk 4,20) or "keep it" (Lk 8,15) see its fruit* in them. At the conclusion of the Sermon on the Mount where He has just proclaimed the new Law*, Jesus contrasts the condition of those who "understand His words and put it into practice" with that of those who "understand it, but do not put it into practice" (Mt 7,24.26; Lk 6,47.49). The one is a house built on rock; the other, a house built on sand. These metaphors introduce a perspective of judgment*. Each will be judged according to his attitude toward the Word: "Whoever shall be ashamed of me and my words, the Son of Man shall also be ashamed of him when He comes into the glory of the Father" (Mk 8,38 p).

The fourth gospel goes on to consider these same ideas, but with a special stress. It shows that among Jesus' listeners a division is brought about by His words (Jn 10,19). On the one hand, there are those who believe (Jn 2,22; 4, 39.41.50), who hear His Word (5,24), who keep it (8,51f; 14,23f; 15,20), who dwell in it (8,31), and in whom it dwells (5,38; 15,7). These have eternal life (5,24) and they shall never see death (8,51). On the other hand, there are those who find this Word too hard (6,60), who "cannot hear it" (8,43), and who, by this fact, refuse it and reject Christ. These will be judged by the very Word of Jesus on the last day (12,48) because it is not His Word, but that of the Father (12,49; 17,14) who is truth* (17,17). It is, therefore, one and the same thing to take a position regarding the Word of Jesus, regarding His person, and regarding God. After the decision has been made, man sees himself introduced into a life of the theological virtues of faith, hope, and charity, or the opposite: cast into the darkness of the evil world.

II. THE WORD IN THE CHURCH

1. *The action of the Word of God.* The Acts and the apostolic epistles show us the Word of God pursuing here below the work of salvation that was begun by Jesus. This Word, however, is less a series of "words of the master" gathered together and repeated by the disciples (cf Mt 10, 14; 1 Co 7,10.12.25), than the very message of the "gospel" that was proclaimed in the early Christian preaching. The apostolic minister is essentially a service of the Word (Ac 4,29ff; 6,2.4) that must be preached so that it be heard throughout the entire world (8,4.25; 13,5; 18,9f; 1 Th 1,8), a sincere service which must not falsify the message (2 Co 2,17; 4,2), a courageous service which boldly proclaims that message (Ac 4,31; Ph 1,14).

This Word is in itself a power of salvation*. The growth* of the Church is identified with its growth (Ac 6,7; 12,24; 19,20), and even the bonds that bind the apostle do not succeed in binding it (2 Tm 2,9). It is the "Word of salvation" (Ac 13,26), the "Word of life" (Ph 2,16), the unfailing Word (1 Tm 1,15; 2 Tm 2,11; Tt 3,8), the living and efficacious Word (He 4,12); so many expressions that stress its action in the hearts of believers. Moreover, it is the Word to which they owe their regeneration, since they believed in it at the time of their baptism* (1 P 1,23; Jm 1,18; cf E 5,26). The same effectiveness of the Word is seen in the work of salvation as was observed in the OT within the framework of creation and the unfolding of history, which the gospels attributed to the Word of Jesus. But, really, is the Word proclaimed by the apostles something different from the Word of Jesus, exalted at the right hand of God, speaking through His apostles, and confirming their Word by miracles (Mk 16,20)?

2. *Men before God's Word.* Consequently, the same division takes place in confrontation with the apostolic Word as was already seen with respect to Jesus: rejection by some (Ac 13,46; 1 P 2,8; 3,1); acceptance by others (1 Th 1,6) who receive the Word (1 Th 2,13), hear it (Col 1,5; E 1,13), docilely acknowledge it that they might put it into practice (Jm 1,21ff), keep it in order to be saved (1 Co 15,2; cf Ap 3,8), and glorify it (Ac 13,48) so that it dwells in them (Col 3,16; 1 Jn 1,10; 2,14). If necessary, these

latter will undergo trials and martyrdom* for its sake (Ap 1,9f; 6,9; 20,4) and with its help they defeat the powers of evil (Ap 12,11). Thus the action of the divine Word extends into history and, in men, gives birth to faith, hope, and charity.

III. THE MYSTERY OF GOD'S WORD

1. *The Word made flesh.* Regarding this mystery of the divine Word, John gives us the deepest insight by comparing it in the strictest manner with the very mystery of Jesus, the Son of God. Insofar as He is Son, Jesus is the subsistent Word, the Word of God. It is from Him that ultimately is derived every manifestation of the divine Word in creation, in history, in the final work of salvation. This is understood from the manner of speaking in the epistle to the Hebrews: "After having spoken to our fathers through the prophets, God speaks to us through His Son" (He 1,1f).

As Word, Jesus was existing from the beginning in God, and He was God (Jn 1,1f). He was the creative Word by whom all things had been made (1,3; cf He 1,2; Ps 33,6ff), that illuminative Word which enlightened the darkness of the world in order to bring the revelation of God to men (Jn 1,4f.9). In OT times, He was already manifesting Himself secretly under the guise of the acting and revealing Word. Finally, in the fullness of time, this Word entered openly into history by being made flesh (1,14). He then became the object of a concrete experience for men (1 Jn 1,1ff) in such a way that "we have seen His glory" (Jn 1,14).

By this means He perfected His twofold activity as revealer and author of salvation: as only Son, He has made the Father known to men (1,18); in order to save men, He has brought grace* and truth* into the world (1,14. 16f). Henceforth the Word, manifested to the world, is at the very heart of human history: before His coming, history looked toward His incarnation; after His coming, it looks to His final triumph. For He is the one who will yet manifest Himself in a final battle, end the workings of the evil powers, and assure the definitive victory of God here below (Ap 19,13).

2. *Men before the Word made flesh.* Since Christ the subsistent Word "was made flesh," it is clear that the attitude men take toward His Word and His person determines their attitude at the same time toward God. His coming here below has brought about an effective division among men. On the one hand, the darkness has not received Him (Jn 1,5), the evil world* has not known Him (1,10), His own—His own people—have not received Him (1,11). And so, the whole gospel story ends in the passion. But on the other hand, there are those who have "believed in His name" (1,12); these have "received from His fullness* grace upon grace" (1,16), and He gave them power to become the children of God (1,12), He who is the Son by nature (1,14.18).

Thus, around the incarnate Word, a lasting drama has crystallized. It began when God first spoke to man through His prophets. And when the prophets proclaimed the Word of God, was it not the Word Himself who expressed Himself through their mouths; the same Word who was to become flesh in the fullness of time in order to address Himself directly to men when the Father would send Him into this world personally? A direct and visible presence would be substituted for this hidden and preparatory activity. Yet, for men, the vital problem posed by the Word of God has not changed: he who believes in the Word, who acknowledges and receives the Word, enters through Him into the life of the theological virtues of the child of God (Jn 1,12). He who rejects the Word or scorns it remains in the darkness of the world and is judged thereby (cf 3,17ff). Everyone must face this formidable prospect: openly, if he is brought into contact with the gospel of Jesus Christ; secretly, if the divine Word is attained only under imperfect forms. To every man the Word speaks; He awaits an answer from every man, and man's eternal destiny depends upon his answer.

→Amen 2—Ark of the Covenant II—Blessing—Book III—Bread III—Creation NT I 2—Disciple OT 1.2; NT 3—Dreams—Faith NT II 2—Fulfill OT 1.2—God OT III—Gospel—Growth 2 c—Human Speech 2—Hunger & Thirst—Jesus Christ II 2 d—Judgment OT I 1—Kingdom NT II 1—Lamp 1—Law—Listen—Manna 1.3—Memory 1 b—Milk 3—Miracle II 2 a—Mystery OT 1; NT II 1—New Birth 3 a—Nourishment II—Oath OT 2—Parable—Plan of God—Preach II—Priesthood OT II 2—Prophet OT I 2, II 1—Revelation—Run 1—Silence 1—Sowing II 2—Spirit of God—Teach—Truth—Will of God—Wisdom—Writing II—Yahweh 2.

AF & PG rco'c

WORK

Everywhere in the Bible man is at work. Yet, because the work of an artisan or small farmer is so different from the intensive and highly organized work we see today, we are led to believe that Scripture is uninformed or ill-informed on work. Further, because Scripture seldom admits a formulation of basic principles on the value and meaning of work, we are sometimes tempted arbitrarily to remove one or other random statement from its context to advance personal preconceptions. The Bible does not answer all our questions. Yet, taken in its entirety, it introduces us to the reality of work, its value, its affliction, and its redemption.

I. THE VALUE OF WORK

1. *The Creator's command.* In spite of a current presumption, work does not come from sin* : before the fall, "The Lord God took man and put him in the Garden of Eden to till it and look after it" (Gn 2,15). If the Decalogue prescribes a Sabbath*, this is at the end of six days of work (Ex 20,8ff). The vivid presentation of creation in six days underlines the fact that man's work corresponds to the divine will and shows it as a reflection of the action of the Creator. The story tells us that, in forming man "in the image of Himself" (Gn 1,27), God wanted to take him in as a partner in His plan. Then, having once set the universe in place, God entrusted it to the hands of man, with the power to fill and subdue the earth* (Gn 1,28). Not all who work "are eminent in instruction or judgment"; yet each individual, by his occupation, "contributes to the support of the world" (Si 38, 34). It is, therefore, not in the least astonishing that the Creator's action is easily described by the actions of a worker; fashioning man (Gn 2,7), forging heaven "by His fingers," and setting the stars in their place (Ps 8,4). In return, the great hymn which God the creator sings depicts man going out in the morning "to his job, to do his work until evening" (Ps 104,23; cf Si 7,15). This work of man is the flowering of God's creation. It is the fulfillment of His will*.

2. *Natural value of work.* This authentic will of God is not even partly expressed in the commandments of the covenant, nor in those of the Decalogue or the gospel. This is not surprising. The omission is quite normal, for work is a law of the human condition (cf Dt 5,13) imposed on every man, even before he knows he is called to God's salvation*. It follows that, in the Bible, many reactions to work are simply judgments of a sound and right conscience. These reactions will obviously appear in the writing of the sages, men intentionally careful to make Israel's religion profit to the utmost from mankind's normal moral experience.

Thus the Bible is severe on idleness for the simple reason that the sluggard has nothing to eat (Pr 13,4) and risks death from hunger (21, 25). Nor does hunger stimulate the lazy man to work (16,26). St. Paul does not hesitate to use this argument to show the aberration of those who refuse to work: "let them no longer eat" (2 Th 3,10). Furthermore, idleness is a type of decay. We admire the woman who is always wide awake. She "does not eat the bread of idleness" (Pr 31,27). Humor is directed to the lazy individual. "As the door turns on its hinges, so a sluggard turns on his bed" (26,14). He is "a spattered rock" rather than a man, "a handful of dung" (Si 22,1f), which one shakes out of his hand with disgust.

The Bible, furthermore, is capable of appreciation for the job well done, the skillful touch, the total preoccupation of the ploughman, the smith, and the potter (Si 38,26.28.30). The Bible is full of admiration for artistic success—Solomon's palace (1 K 7,1-12) and throne, "unrivaled in any realm" (10,20); and, above all, for the temple of Yahweh and its magnificent details (1 K 6; 7,13-50). Relentlessly against the blindness of the one who fashions idols*, the Bible respects his skill, though indignant that so much effort is expended uselessly, for "nothing" (Is 40,19f; 41,6f).

3. *Social value of work.* This esteem of work does not arise merely from admiration for artistic success, but comes from a penetrating insight into the place of work in social life and in the economic structure. Without farm laborers and artisans "no city can be built" (Si 38,32). Three factors are at the beginning of the sea voyage: "thirst for gain...the craftsman's wisdom...the guidance of providence" (Ws 14,2f). The respective roles of these three elements in this realistically balanced concept can explain possible aberrations in the project as well as the wonders the work may achieve. Thus is explained, for example, how the seafarer "dare trust his life to the smallest plank" and how he thus perfects God's creation by preventing "the works of (His) wisdom from remaining sterile" (Ws 14,5).

II. THE AFFLICTION OF WORK

But since work is a fundamental fact of human existence, it is directly and deeply affected by sin*. "In the sweat of your brow you shall make your living" (Gn 3,19). The divine curse* is not directed any more to work than it is to childbirth. As childbirth is the painful victory* of life over death, so the daily affliction of the man at work marks the exercise of his God-given power over creation. The power continues to exist, but the cursed soil fights back and has to be subdued (3,17f). The worst part of the suffering* involved in the struggle, which frequently enough ends in spectacular success—for example, the great works of Solomon—is that death* comes to make the struggle useless. "What does a man have from toil. . .? And the days of sorrow, and the anxiety of business, and the restless nights? This too is vanity" (Qo 2,22f).

Sorrowful, often sterile, work is one field of human endeavor where sin makes its largest and strongest inroads. Caprice, violence, injustice, greed, constantly make work not simply a crushing burden but also a source of hatred and divisions. Workers deprived of their pay (Jr 22, 12; Jm 5,4), peasants despoiled by taxes (Am 5, 11), whole peoples subjected to forced labor by an enemy government (2 S 12,31) and even by their own king (1 S 8,10-18; 1 K 5,27; 12,1-14), slaves* condemned to work and blows (Si 33, 25-29). There is not always personal guilt in this sinister picture; we have here simply the routine world of work among the sons of Adam. Israel knew this world and knew it in its most unfeeling form in Egypt: forced labor, at an exhausting pace, under pitiless surveillance, among a hostile people, to profit an enemy government—work systematically organized to reduce a people to nothing and to make them incapable of resisting (Ex 1,8-14; 2,11-15; 5,6-18). This is already the world of the concentration camp and of forced labor.

III. THE REDEMPTION OF WORK

Now Yahweh has freed His people from this inhuman world of work which is the result of sin. His covenant with Israel includes a series of clauses designed to save work, if not from every troublesome aspect, at least from the more grisly forms imposed by human malice. The Sabbath* is made to introduce a note of relief into the depressing sequence of work days (Ex 20,9ff), to assure man and beast alike a time of rest* (Ex 23,12; Dt 5,14). This is in imitation of a God revealed as a God who works, rests, and frees from servitude (Dt 5,15). Several articles of the Law mean to protect the slave* or the hired man. The hired laborer should be paid the same day (Lv 19,13) and must not be exploited (Dt 24,14f).

The prophets will recall these demands (Jr 22,13). Faithfulness to the covenant will not dispense Israel from work but rather render the work profitable, for "God will bless* her enterprises" (Dt 14,29; 16,15; 28,12; Ps 128,2). Effort will produce its normal fruit*. The vine-planter will taste its fruit; the builder will dwell in the house he constructed (Am 9,14; Is 62,8f; cf Dt 28,30).

IV. CHRIST AND WORK

The coming of Jesus Christ casts the paradoxes and enlightenment of the gospel on work. In the NT work is sometimes praised, sometimes appears to be unknown or just touched on as a detail of minor importance. Work is extolled by the fact that Jesus is a worker (Mk 6,3) and the son of a laboring man (Mt 13,55); by the example of Paul, who works with his hands (Ac 18,3) and is proud of it (Ac 20,34; 1 Co 4,12). And yet the gospels are astonishingly silent about work. Their acquaintance with the word itself seems confined to duties of obligation, that is, works of God (Jn 5,17; 6,28), or to the use of examples: the birds of heaven "who neither sow nor reap" (Mt 6,26), the lilies of the field which "neither toil nor spin" (6,28). This lack of importance on the one hand and on the other the importance attached to work are not contradictory; they are the two poles of an essential Christian attitude.

1. *Work that perishes.* "Work not for perishable nourishment*, but for that which endures for eternal life" (Jn 6,27). Jesus Christ comes to bring the kingdom* of God. He has no other mission and speaks of nothing else because this kingdom transcends all else (Mt 6,33). Other things—eating, drinking, clothing* oneself—are not unimportant. But preoccupation with them to the point of missing the kingdom, even gaining the world, is a total loss (Lk 9,25). Before the absolute, the possession of God, all else is eclipsed. In this world, whose "present form is passing" (1 Co 7,31), the only matter of importance is "total attachment to the Lord" (7,35).

2. *Positive value of work.* To put work in its place, distinct from God, is in no way a devaluation, but a recognition of its true worth in the scheme of creation*, a worth that is lofty indeed. Like Yahweh in the OT, Jesus borrows titles and comparisons from the world of work: shepherd, vine-dresser, doctor, sower (Jn 10,1ff; 15,1; Mk 2,17; 4,3), but without a shadow of Sirach's typically intellectualist condescension toward manual work, its necessity and limits (Si 38,32ff). Christ presents the apostolate as a work, the work of harvesting* (Mt 9,37; Jn 4,38) or fishing (Mt 4,19). He is aware of the occupation of those He chooses (Mt 4,18). But more than all this, His total behavior presumes a world at work: the farmer in his field (Lk 9,62), the housewife cleaning the house (15,8). He finds it abnormal to let a talent lie without producing (Mt 25,14-30). If he happens to multiply loaves—loaves baked in our ovens— He is anxious to point out that this is an exception; He leaves it up to man to make and bake his own bread. In the same spirit of faithful commitment to the human condition, Paul will tell us "to keep away from any brother who lives in idleness" under the pretext that the final coming is near (2 Th 3,6).

3. *Christian value of work.* Christ, the new Adam*, permits humanity to perform the task of subduing the world (He 2,5ff; E 1,9ff). For by saving man, Christ gives work its full value. The need to work becomes more urgent because it is based on the concrete demands of supernatural love*. In revealing man's call to divine sonship, Christ highlights the dignity of man* and of the work at hand. He establishes a value hierarchy for man's judgment and conduct at work. By inaugurating the kingdom* not of this world*, but rather the world's leaven, He confers the same spiritual quality on the worker; in addition Christ installs the dimensions of charity in work, and bases work in all its implications on the new principle of brotherhood in Christ (Phm). Because of His law of love (Jn 13,34), there is an obligation to act against egoism and to do everything to lessen the troubles of men at work. And yet, by introducing the Christian to the mystery of His suffering* and death*, He gives a new value to inevitable affliction.

4. *Work and the new world.* Ultimately at the final coming of the Lord, His risen glory* will clothe His elect. Then man's subjection of the entire world will be fully realized, through Him and in Him, unfettered from sin, death, and suffering. Even before the last day, insofar as work is done in Christ, it shares in creation's* return to God. The slave* who endures his rank in Christ is already "a freedman of the Lord" (1 Co 7,22); he prepares "creation itself for freedom from its bondage to decay and for entrance into the glorious liberty of God's children" (R 8,21). Beyond this, will there be a permanence of work accomplished? Scripture does not encourage any temporal Messianism: "the shape of this world is passing away" (1 Co 7,31). And the break between the present and future state of the world allows no place for a simple and direct transition to the world to come. Nevertheless, there is, though indefinable, a certain permanence to man's work. At least this seems to fit Pauline statements about the dominion and recapitulation of the world by Christ (R 8,19ff; E 1,10; Col 1,16.20). Though no single text satisfies an inevitably naive and necessarily limited inquisitiveness, the total sweep of Scripture invites the hope that a redeemed and freed creation will forever remain the world of God's children gathered together in Christ.

→Cares 1—Earth OT I 2, II 3 a; NT II 3— Man I 1 b, III 4—Nourishment I, II—Rest— Reward—Sowing I 2 a—Week—Works OT II 2.

PdS & JG dfb

WORKS

The words *works* can assume any number of meanings. It may designate action, labors, various things produced, and more especially "the work of the flesh," consisting in generation. Applied to God, it indicates as well all the aspects of His external activity. In each case, the work can be understood only if referred back to the worker who produced it. And behind every human work, there is question of discovering the first-born of creation: God's own Son, to whom the work is related and whom it wishes to express in its own way.

OT

I. THE WORK OF GOD

Before anything further is said, it must be noted that the works of God* (*ma'aseh yahweh*) do not fit inside the framework of history, but constitute history in its truth. In the OT, revelation pursues a particular direction: Israel recognizes God at work in its history before becoming interested in His creative work.

1. *The work of God in history.* The divine work begins to show itself through "actions and mighty deeds which nothing can equal" (Dt 3, 24): the liberation of Israel, the marvelous episodes in the desert where the people "saw the works" of Yahweh (Ps 95,9), the settlement in the promised land (Dt 11,2-7; Js 24,31). Thoughts of this past arouse enthusiasm: "Come and see the works of God!" (Ps 66,3-6). But it is not enough to recall the past (Ps 77,12f); attention must be paid to the present work of God (Is 5,12; Ps 28,5), who fashions everything without ceasing (Is 22,11). It is necessary to have a foreboding of His work to come on His day* (Is 28,21), whether it is a question of the deportation to Babylon (Ha 1,5) or of liberation from the exile (Is 45,11); working by the intermediary of the nations* (Jr 51,10) or of the liberator Cyrus (Is 45,1-6), God will accomplish His "work of salvation*" (41,4) in favor of Israel, His chosen people (43,1; 44,2).

The divine work, then, looks above all to Israel, considered collectively. It is not for that reason uninterested in individuals: it is interested not only in those whom God has raised up for His people, such as Moses and Aaron (1 S 12,6), David and the prophets*; but further, in each man in particular, about whom God is concerned even in daily life, as the Book of Tobit shows in detail. Such is "the work of His hands," perfect (Dt 32,4), faithful and true (Ps 33,4), profound (Ps 92,5f), full of goodness and love (Ps 145,9.17; 138,8), which ought to arouse an overflowing joy in the heart of man (Ps 107,22; Tb 12,21).

2. *The work of God in creation.* From the beginning, Israel had to admire "Him who made heaven and earth" (Gn 14,19), "the Pleiades and Orion..., who formed the mountains and the wind" (Am 5,8; 4,13). But it is only with the exile that creation* becomes a motive of confidence in the Lord of history: is not this stable, majestic, and powerful work surely the guarantee of the power and faithfulness of God (Is 40, 12ff)? He is praised for everything which is "the work of His hands": the heavens (Ps 19,2) and the earth (102,26), man who is placed over all creation (8,4-7). Thanks must be rendered Him for His works (145,10), the admirable

beauty of which is acknowledged (Jb 36,24f). Conscious of being the work of God, man ought to draw a genuine boldness from this certitude of faith, for God cannot "spurn His work" (Jb 10,3); but likewise must man have a profound humility, for can "a product say to its maker: I am not your work?" (Is 29,16; 45,9; Ws 12,12; R 9,20f).

3. *Wisdom, the divine artisan.* The movement which leads from the God of history to God the Creator terminates in a final effort to foresee in God the creative Word*, the Spirit* who directs the progress of the world. Ecclesiasticus meditates on the work of God in creation (Si 42,15—43,33), and in time (44,1—50,29); the Book of Wisdom attempts a theology of history (Ws 10—19). What both recognize is the divine Wisdom* at work here below. Presented as "the craftsman" of creation (Pr 8,30), this royal Wisdom was produced by God at the outset of His designs, before His oldest works (8,22). She chose to dwell most especially in Israel (Si 24, 3-8); but she existed well before (24,9), for she was "the craftsman of all things" (Ws 7,21): she it is who enables men to recognize through her work the Lord of nature and of history.

II. THE WORKS OF MAN

In the likeness of God, His creator, man himself must also be ceaselessly at work.

1. *The origin of human works.* It is not simply an interior need which impels man to act, but the will* of God. From the time of Paradise, this has been manifested to him in the form of a commandment which corresponds to the plan* of Yahweh (Gn 2,15f). The works of man thus appear as the overflow of the divine work. They demand, notwithstanding, a personal effort on his part, an engagement, a choice. For to human liberty*, the will of God presents itself concretely under the form of a Law* exterior to him, a law which he must obey.

2. *The major works of man.* Before the commandments of the Law are even enumerated, the account of creation manifests the two principal tasks that man will have to fulfill: fruitfulness and toil.

Man has a duty of fruitfulness*: in order to populate the earth (Gn 1,28), he will procreate sons in his image (5,1ff), which itself reproduces the image of God. It is in virtue of this duty that the race of patriarchs will give birth to the people of Israel—a people mediating* on behalf of all the families of the earth—from whom the Christ will finally be born. The "work of the flesh" thus takes on a meaning by the twofold reasons of creation and the history of salvation. Man must also labor* to dominate the earth and subdue it (Gn 1,28), even if the soil is cursed (3,17ff) because of his sin. This labor allows him to subsist (3,19), but it is in worship that labor attains its full religious significance: the masterpiece of Israel is the temple*, constructed to the glory of God.

It is true that men thus risk deviating from their purpose their two essential tasks, whether in profaning procreation (R 1,26f), or in adoring the works of their hands in making dumb idols* (1 Co 12,2). The commandments of the Law seek to prevent such a degradation of human works. The Law also prescribes a large number of other works, among which late Judaism will single out those especially which concern the neighbor*: to give alms*, to visit the sick, to bury the dead. The latter are the primary "good works."

3. *The purpose of works.* Judaism never lost sight of the fact that works prescribed by the Law were directed to the kingdom* of God. Nevertheless, casuistry often masked the true meaning of the works to be fulfilled, in focusing the effort of man on the letter of the Law. Above, all, a misunderstanding of the covenant* tended to transform it into a contract and to give to its "practitioners" an excessive confidence* in their human possibilities, as if the works accomplished accorded man a claim upon God and sufficed to confer interior justice* upon him. Jesus will address Himself to this degraded conception of religion in recalling the unique meaning of human works: to manifest the glory* of God which alone is at work through man.

NT

I. THE WORK OF JESUS CHRIST

"My Father is unceasingly at work, and I myself, too, am at work" (Jn 5,17). In these words Jesus underlines the identity of operation of Son and Father, the work of the Father fully expressing itself through that of the Son.

1. *Jesus Christ, masterpiece of God.* Visible image of the Father, Jesus is the Wisdom* spoken of in the OT. Through Him all was made in the beginning, and by Him the work of salvation is accomplished in history. He is also seen to make creation come to life in His parables, revealing, for example, the kinship of the laws of growth* of wheat and of sacrifice* (Jn 12,24). He rescues human works from the danger threatening them when He shows the hidden significance of carnal fruitfulness* (Lk 11,27f), the profound meaning of the temple* and of worship* (Jn 4,21-24). He concentrates in His person the expectation of the kingdom and obedience* to the Law. If it is true that the work of man must be accomplished in the image of that of God, henceforth it is enough to see Jesus acting to know how to act according to the will* of the Father.

2. *Jesus and the works of the Father.* The synoptics speak only rarely of the works of Jesus (Mt 11,2), although they pause to recount His miracles* and all the acts which prepare for the coming of His Church*. On the contrary, John shows that Christ accomplished the works which the Father had given Him (Jn 5,36). These works attest that He is not only the Messiah, but also the Son* of God; for they are identically the works of the Father*, without confusion of the persons acting. The Father did not give the Son works wholly accomplished, as if He were the sole author of them (14,10; 9,31; 11,22.41f); nor, further, did He give works simply to be performed as He might give commands to be carried out (4,34; 15,10). The Son's mission* is to glorify the Father in bringing to completion the unique work which God wishes achieved here below—the salvation* of men. And this completion is the cross* (17, 4). All the works of Christ are related to it. They are not only a seal* upon the mission of Jesus (6,27); they reveal the Father through the Son (14,9f). The Son shows Himself to be as active as the Father, but in His position as Son, in the love which unites Him indissolubly to the Father.

3. *Christ, revealer of human works.* Coming into a sinful world*, Jesus also reveals human works; and this revelation* is both a choice and a judgment*. "Now this is the judgment: The light* has come into the world, yet men have loved the darkness rather than the light, for their works were evil. In fact, everyone who does evil hates the light and does not come to the light, that his deeds may not be exposed;

but he who does the truth comes to the light that his deeds may be made manifest, for they have been performed in God" (Jn 3,19ff). Appearing among men, Christ thus reveals to them their state. Before this encounter, they lived, in some way, in the darkness (1,5), which was not precisely a state of sin (cf 9,41; 15,24). When Jesus comes, then is revealed the depth of their being, until then semi-conscious of its goodness or evil. The decision which they make with regard to the Son of Man, based on their previous conduct, makes a synthesis of their past and reveals it for what it is. Not that "good works" merit final adherence to Christ; but this adherence manifests the goodness of the works (cf E 5,6-14).

II. THE WORKS OF THE CHRISTIAN

The believer endows his actions with full meaning in modeling it on that of Jesus Christ; through the Holy Spirit, he is enabled to fulfill the new law of charity and to cooperate in building up the body of Christ.

1. *Faith, the unique work.* According to the synoptics, Jesus requires the practice of "good works" in purity of intention (Mt 5,16). In the two primary commandments (Mt 22,36-40 p), Jesus shows the unity of the commandments of the Law*. In this way He effects a simplification and a purification indispensable in the innumerable works which Jewish tradition* imposed. With the fourth gospel, this simplification appears still more clearly: to the Jews* who ask what they must do to "perform the works of God," Jesus replies: "This is the work of God, that you believe in Him whom He has sent" (Jn 6,28f). The will* of God is summarized by faith* in Jesus who does the works of the Father.

As a vigorous polemicist, St. Paul says the same thing when he rejects justification* by the works of the Law*: it is not the Law, it is not works as such which are the source of salvation*. It is the cross*, it is grace* accepted through faith*. This critique of salvation through works must not be reduced to a critique of Jewish law alone; it is valid for all religious practice which boasts of leading by itself to salvation.

2. *Charity, work of faith.* But if works are not the source of salvation, they remain the necessary expression of faith. James has emphasized this (Jm 2,14-26); Paul also (cf E 2,10). There are some "works of faith" which are the fruit of the Spirit (G 5,22f). The faith which Christ demands is that which "works through charity" (G 5,6). Contrary to evil works, which are multiple (G 5,19ff), the works of faith are summed up in the practice of the precept which contains the whole Law (G 5,14). Such is "the work of faith, the labor of charity" (1 Th 1,3). Jesus taught, moreover, that in awaiting His return, one must keep his lamp* lit (Mt 25,1-13), employ his talents profitably (25,14-30), love his brethren (25,31-46). The commandment of love* is His own testament (Jn 13,34). The apostles thus accept this teaching and draw its consequences.

3. *The building up of the Church, body of Christ.* The work of charity does not find its completion in comfort brought to certain individuals. Beyond this objective, charity cooperates in the great work of Christ, foreseen from all eternity: the building* up of His body* which is the Church. For "His workmanship we are, created in Christ Jesus in view of the good works which God has made ready beforehand that we may practice them" (E 2,10). Here is the mystery of the cooperation of man with the work of God who does everything in all, conferring on man's action its dignity and eternal import (cf 1 Co 1,9; 15,58; R 14,20; Ph 1,6). In this new perspective, heavenly reward can be attached to the works which man has done here below. "Blessed are those who are dead in the Lord, for their works follow them" (Ap 14,13).

→Abraham II 3—Build—Creation—Faith III 2 —Fruit—Fruitfulness III 3—Fulfill NT 2— Grace V—Justice—Law *B* III 5; *C* III 1— Miracle I 2 b c, III 2 b—Reward I, III 1—Will of God NT I 2, II 2—Work.

FA & XLD phmcn

WORLD

OT

The common designation of the world is the expression "heavens and earth" (Gn 1,1); the word *tēbēl* applies only to the terrestrial world (vg Jr 51,15); works of the Greek period speak of the *kosmos* (Ws 11,17; 2 M 7,9.23), including in this term a specifically biblical content. For the Greeks, the *kosmos*, with its laws, beauty, perpetuity, and eternally cyclic processes, effectively expresses the ideal of an order closed in upon itself, including all men and encompassing even the gods themselves. The elements of the world are poorly distinguished in this virtual or avowed pantheism. The biblical conception is quite different, for there the cosmological and cosmogonic representations only constitute a secondary material placed at the service of an essentially religious affirmation: as a creature of God the world has meaning only through its function in the plan of salvation, and it is in the framework of this plan also that the world finds its final destiny.

I.   ORIGIN OF THE WORLD

Contrary to the mythologies of Mesopotamia, Egypt, Canaan, etc., the biblical representation of the origin of the world is remarkably sober. It is no longer on the plane of myth, of a pretemporal divine history. On the contrary, it inaugurates time*. Between God* and the world there is an abyss expressed by the word *create* (Gn 1,1). If Genesis and other corroboratory texts (Ps 8; 104; Pr 8,22-31; Jb 38f) evoke a creative activity of God, this is solely in order to underline certain points of faith: the distinction between the world and the one God; the dependence of the world in relation to a sovereign God who "speaks and things are" (Ps 33,6-9), who governs the laws of nature (Gn 8,22), and through His providence integrates the universe into the plan of salvation* which has man* at its center. This sacred cosmology, as foreign to scientific problems as it is to philosophical speculation, thus places the world in relation to man: man emerges from it to dominate the world (Gn 1,28) and, for this reason, involves it in his own destiny.

II.   SIGNIFICANCE OF THE WORLD

The actual significance of the world for man's religious conscience is also twofold.

1.   Coming as it does from God's hand, the world is a continual manifestation of the *goodness of God*. In His wisdom*, God has organized it in unity and harmony as a true work of art (Pr 8,22-31; Jb 28,25ff). His power* and divinity in some fashion (Ws 13,3ff) are made so manifest through sensible creation that man, looking upon the universe, is at a loss to express his admiration (Ps 8; 19,1-7; 104).

2.   But for the sinner, a pawn in his own tragedy, the world also signifies *the wrath of God*, for which it becomes the instrument (Gn 3,17f): He who made all things for man's good* and enjoyment also makes use of them to chastise him. This end is achieved by calamities* of all sorts where an ungrateful nature arrays itself against humanity, from the deluge to the plagues of Egypt and the curses* which await a faithless Israel (Dt 28,15-46).

3.   In this twofold manner the world is actively involved in the *history of salvation*, and in this function it receives its truly religious significance. Every creature comprising the world possesses a certain ambivalence which is set in relief in the Book of Wisdom. The same water* brings death to the Egyptians and salvation to Israel (Ws 11,5-14). Though it is true this principle cannot be applied mechanically, since just men and sinners live here below in a solidarity of destiny, there still remains the apparent but mysterious bond between the world and man. Over and above the cyclic phenomena which for us constitute the actual face of the world, there is another history of the world which began before man but has its ending in him (Gn 1,1—2,4); this history now parallels human history in order to be consummated with it at the same final point.

III.   THE FINAL DESTINY OF THE WORLD

As the bearer of a humanity that derived its corporeal existence (Gn 2,7; 3,19) from it, the world is effectively incomplete: it is man's task to perfect it by his labor, subduing it (1,28) and leaving his mark on it. But of what value is this humanizing of the world if sinful man involves it in his sin? This is why the eschatology of the prophets is less concerned with what becomes of the world under man's governance than with the term—of necessity ambiguous— toward which it leads.

1.   *At the final judgment** which awaits all humanity, all the elements of the world will be associated, as if the order of things created in the beginning were to see a total reversal through a sudden return to chaos (Jr 4,23-26). Hence the images of a cracking earth (Is 24,19f), of dimming stars (Is 13,10; Jl 2,10; 4,15); the

aging universe will be drawn into the cataclysm which overshadows guilty humanity...

2. But in the same way as pure divine grace is preparing salvation for man after the judgment, so also a *profound renovation* is being prepared for the world, which the sacred text refers to as a new creation*: God will create "a new heaven and a new earth" (Is 65,17; 66,22); and the description of this renovated world is given in terms used once for the primitive paradise*.

3. *The present world and the world to come.* In a prolongation of these mysterious prophecies the Jewish contemporaries of the NT represented the end of human history as the passage of the present world (or age) into the world (or age) to come. The present world is the one we inhabit since that time when death entered upon the scene (Ws 2,24) through the envy of the devil (and man's sin). The world to come will appear when God comes to establish His kingdom*. Then will the realities of the present world, purified together with mankind itself, recover their primitive perfection: they will be truly transfigured like the image of heavenly realities.

NT

The NT makes frequent use of the Greek word *kosmos*. But the meaning that it gives it is the result of all the elaboration done in the OT and already adopted in its Greek translation.

I. AMBIGUITY OF THE WORLD

1. It is true that the world, so designated, remains fundamentally the *excellent creature* which God made in the beginning (Ac 17,24) by the agency of His Word (Jn 1,3.10; cf He 1,2; Col 1,16). This world continues to bear witness to God (Ac 14,17; R 1,19f). Moreover, it would be wrong to prize the world too highly, for man far surpasses it in real worth: what will it profit him to gain the whole world if he loses his own soul (Mt 16,26)?

2. But there is more yet: in its present state, this world, closely linked as it is with sinful man's condition, is, in fact, *under the power of Satan**. Sin* entered the world at the beginning of history, and with sin, death (R 5,12). Hence,

it has become a debtor to divine justice (3,19), for it is intimately bound up with the mystery of evil which is at work here below. Its most apparent element is made up of those rebellious men who set their will in opposition to God and to His Christ (Jn 3,18f; 7,7; 15,18f; 17,9.14...). Behind them stands the invisible leader, Satan, prince of this world (12,31; 14,30; 16,11), the god of the present age (2 Co 4,4). Established as chief of this world by his creator's will, Adam* has given to Satan's hands his person and his dominion; since then the world has lain in the power of the evil one (1 Jn 5,19), who communicates power and glory to whomever he will (Lk 4,6).

This world of darkness is ruled by evil spirits (E 6,12); it is a deceiving world whose constitutive elements weigh man down and enslave him, even in the ancient economy itself (G 4, 3.9; Col 2,8.10). The spirit of this world, since it is incapable of tasting the secrets and gifts of God (1 Co 2,12), is opposed to the Spirit of God, just as is the spirit of Antichrist which is at work in the world (1 Jn 4,3). The wisdom* of this world, because it relies on the speculations of human thought cut off from God, is convicted of folly* by God (1 Co 1,20). The peace* which this world gives, comprised as it is of material prosperity and false security, is only a shadow of the true peace which only Christ can give (Jn 14,27): the final effect of this false peace is a sadness* which brings death (2 Co 7,10).

Through all this is revealed the sin* of the world (Jn 1,29), a mass of hatred and incredulity accumulated from the beginning, a stumbling block for those who would enter the kingdom of God. Woe to the world because of scandals (Mt 18,7)! This is why the world can offer man no sure value: its image passes away (1 Co 7,31) as do also its lusts (1 Jn 2,16). The tragic element of our destiny comes from the fact that by birth we belong to this world.

II. JESUS AND THE WORLD

For "God so loved the world that He gave His only-begotten Son" (Jn 3,16). Such is the paradox by which a new history enters the world which has two complementary aspects: the victory of Jesus over the evil world ruled by Satan, and the inauguration in Him of the renovated world foretold by the prophetic promises.

1. *Jesus, conqueror of the world.* The first point is set in full relief by the fourth gospel: "He was in the world, and the world was made by Him, and the world knew Him not" (Jn 1,10). Such is the résumé of Jesus' earthly career. Jesus is not of this world (8,23; 17,14), nor is His Kingdom (18,36). It is from God (Mt 28,18) and not from the prince of this world that He holds His power* (Lk 4,5-8), for Satan has no power over Him (Jn 14,31). Because of this the world hates Him (15,18), and all the more so as He is its light (9,5), since He brings it life (6,33), since He comes to save it (12,47). Blind hatred seems to dominate the gospel drama. It finally provokes Jesus' condemnation to death (cf 1 Co 2,7f). But in that very moment the situation is reversed: the judgment* of the world then occurs, along with the fall of its prince (Jn 12,31). This is Christ's victory* over the evil world (16,33). For by accepting in a supreme act of love the mysterious will* of the Father (14,30), Jesus leaves this world (16, 28) in order to return to the Father, where He henceforth will sit in glory (17,1.5) and from where He will direct the course of history (Ap 5,9).

2. *The world renewed.* By this same deed, Jesus realized the end for which He had come into this world: by His death He "took away the sin of the world" (Jn 1,29), He gave His flesh "for the life of the world" (6,51). And the world, God's creature which had fallen under the yoke of Satan, was redeemed from its slavery*. It was washed in the blood* of Jesus: *Terra, pontus, astra, mundus, quo lavantur flumine!* "In this stream the whole world, earth, sky and sea are purified!" (Hymn from Passiontide). He in whom all things were created (Col 1,16) is established as the chief of a new creation* by His resurrection. God places all at His feet (E 1,20ff), reconciling all creation in Him and restoring unity to a divided universe (Col 1,20). Throughout this new world light* and life flow abundantly: they are given to all who have faith* in Jesus.

Nevertheless it remains true that this present world has not yet attained its end. The grace of redemption* is at work in a suffering universe. The victory of Christ will only be complete on the day of His manifestation in glory*, when He shall return all things to His Father (1 Co 15,25,28). Until that time the universe remains in the expectation of a painful childbirth (R 8,19...): that of the new man* in his full stature (E 4,13), that of the new world definitively succeeding the old (Ap 21,4f).

III. THE CHRISTIAN AND THE WORLD

By their relation to the world Christians find themselves in the same complex situation in which Christ was while on earth. They are not of the world (Jn 15,19; 17,16); nevertheless, they are in the world (11,11), and Jesus does not pray His Father to withdraw them from the world, but only to guard them from the evil one (17,15). Their separation from a wicked world leaves intact their positive duty to redeem the world (cf 1 Co 5,10).

1. *Separation from the world.* First, separation: the Christian must guard himself from the contamination of the world (Jm 1,27). He must not love the world (1 Jn 2,15), for friendship with the world is enmity toward God (Jm 4,4) and leads to the worst kind of destitution (2 Tm 4,10). By endeavoring not to model himself after the present age (R 12,2), He will definitively renounce the lusts which define its spirit (1 Jn 2,16). In a word, the world will be crucified to him, and he to the world (G 6,14). He will use it as if he used it not (1 Co 7,29ff). Profound detachment, which evidently does not exclude use of the world's goods, is conformed to the exigencies of fraternal charity (1 Jn 3, 17): such is the sanctity required of Christians.

2. *A witness to Christ before the world.* On the other hand, there is the positive mission of the Christian living in a world currently captivated by sin. Just as Christ came down to bear witness to the truth (Jn 18,37), so is the Christian sent into the world (17,18) to bear this very same witness (1 Jn 4,17). Christian living, which is wholly contrary to the spectacular manifestations which Christ Himself refused to engage in (Jn 7,3f; 14,22; cf Mt 4,5ff), will reveal to men the true notion of God (cf Jn 17,21.23). He thus joins himself to the witness of the Word. For the preachers* of the gospel received a commission to preach to the entire world (Mk 14,9; 16,15): in so doing they shall shine like luminous stars (Ph 2,15).

But the world will oppose them just as it formerly opposed Christ (Jn 15,18), trying in any way possible to win back those who have fled its corrupting influence (2 P 2,19f). The weapon for the struggle and victory in this inevitable warfare* will be faith* (1 Jn 5,4f): our faith will condemn the world (He 11,7; Jn 15,22). The Christian should by no means be astonished if he is hated* and misunderstood (1 Jn 3,13; Mt 10,14 p), even persecuted by the world (Jn 15,18ff); he shall be comforted by the Paraclete*, the Spirit of truth, sent here below to confound the world. The Spirit testifies to the believing heart that the world sins in its refusal to believe in Jesus, that Jesus' cause is just since He is with the Father, and that the prince of this world is already condemned (16, 8-11). Although the world can neither see nor understand Him, (14,17), the Spirit will abide in the faithful and make them triumph over the Antichrists* (1 Jn 4,4ff). And little by little, thanks to this witness, those men whose destiny is not irrevocably bound up with the world will take their places in the redeemed universe which has Christ for its head.

3. *While awaiting the last day.* So long as this present age lasts, one ought not to hope that this tension between the world and Christians will disappear. Until the day* of the final judgment, the subjects of the kingdom and the slaves of evil will live intermingled like the wheat and the cockle in the field of God, which is the world (Mt 13,38ff). But even now the judgment* begins to take place in the secrecy of man's heart (Jn 3,18-21); on that day when God will judge the world (R 3,6) the only difference will be that then the judgment will be publicly rendered when He associates His faithful with His judgment (1 Co 6,2). At that time the present world will finally disappear, as foretold by the prophets, in order that regenerated humanity may find their joy* in a universe completely renewed (cf Ap 21).

→Cares — Creation — Earth — Generation 2 —Hate I 1; III 1.2—Heaven I—Jesus Christ II 1 d—Jew II—Man I 1 b—Mission—Persecution —Poor NT II—Reconciliation II 1—Sin IV 2 —Stars—Time OT I—Trial/Temptation OT I 3; NT I—Victory NT.

CL & PG tms

WORSHIP

In all religions the form of worship institutes the relations between man and God. According to the Bible, the initiative for these relations springs from the living God who reveals Himself. In answer, man adores* God in worship which takes a communal form. This worship not only expresses the need a man has of a Creator upon whom he entirely depends, but it also fulfills a duty: God indeed has chosen a people who are to "serve" Him and by doing so become His witness. The chosen people, therefore, is to perform its mission by worshiping God. (In Hebrew, the word *worship* is a derivation from the root '*ābad,* which means "to serve.")

OT

I. THE WORSHIP OF THE TRUE GOD IN HISTORY

Biblical worship has evolved, and in the course of its history there appear elements common to all forms of worship: sacred places, objects, and persons (sanctuaries, the ark*, altars*, priests*); sacred times (feasts*, the Sabbath*); acts of worship (purifications, consecrations, circumcision*, sacrifices*, prayer* in all its forms); religious prescriptions (fasting*, prohibitions...).

Before sin, the relations of man with God are uncomplicated. On condition of not violating the prohibition concerning the tree* of the knowledge of good and evil, and of thus showing his dependence, man can eat of the tree of life (Gn 2,9; 3,22). By a kind of act pertaining to worship he would thus be able to communicate with God. The same tree of life is in the heavenly Jerusalem where worship no longer serves as intermediary between God and His servants (Ap 22,2f).

After the first sin, sacrifice appears in worship. The patriarchs invoke Yahweh and erect altars* to Him (Gn 4,26; 8,20; 12,8). But God does not approve just any kind of worship. He not only considers the interior dispositions of the one offering (Gn 4,3ff), but He excludes certain exterior forms such as human sacrifice (Gn 22; 2 K 16,3; Lv 20,2f) or ritual prostitution (1 K 22,47; Dt 23,18) and even the making of images* to symbolize the invisible God (Dt 4,15-18; cf Ex 32,4f). When the covenant had made Israel the people of God, its worship was submitted to ever more exact and demanding legislation.

The focus of this worship is the ark, symbol of the presence* of God among His people. At first movable, the ark rested in various sanctuaries (vg Shiloh: Js 18,1). David finally installed it at Jerusalem (2 S 6) where Solomon built the temple* (1 K 6). After the Deuteronomic reform it would become the sole place for sacrificial worship.

After the exile the worship of the second temple was governed by the ritual prescriptions that were traced back to Moses, just as the priestly genealogy was traced back to Aaron, in order to highlight the tie-up of the cult with the covenant that established it. The sage Ben Sira would underline this bond shortly before the struggle led by the Maccabees that the people might be able to remain faithful to the Law and to the worship of the one true God (1 M 1,41-64). The liturgy of the synagogue, composed of songs and prayers and destined after the exile to maintain the life of communal prayer among the Jews of the dispersion, completes the liturgy of the temple. It does not, however, take from the one temple its privilege; and if a sect, such as that of Qumrân, breaks off from the priesthood of Jerusalem, that is because it aspires to a purified worship in a renovated temple.

II. THE RITES OF WORSHIP
AND THE EDUCATION
OF THE PEOPLE OF GOD

The people of God borrowed from neighboring rituals elements that reflected the life of nomadic shepherds or of settled farmers. But they bestow on the rites they adopt a new meaning by linking them with the chronicle of the covenant* (vg Dt 16,1-8 for the Pasch; Lv 23,43 for Tabernacles) and with the sacrifice which ratified it (Ex 5,1ff; 19,6; Ps 50,5). The form of worship thus becomes an enduring instruction that gives to the religious life of Israel its three historical dimensions and its momentum.

The cult recalls first of all the events of the past whose celebration it renewed. At the same time it gives them present reality and thus revives the faith of the people in a God who is as present and as powerful as of old (Ps 81; 106; discourse of Dt 1—11; renewal of the covenant: (Js 24). Finally it stimulates the hope of the people and their expectancy of the day when God would inaugurate His kingdom and when the nations* would be joined to a liberated Israel in the worship of the true God.

This forward look takes on its total fullness only little by little, thanks to the prophets who foretell the new covenant (Jr 31,31ff). It is especially in the Book of Consolation (Is 45) and in the post-exilic prophecies (Is 66,18-23; Ze 14,16-21) that the one God reveals His plan*: He wishes to be made known to all peoples in order to receive from them the worship which is due Him as universal Creator and Savior. The prophets*, witnesses of this plan, proclaim at the same time the demands of the God of the covenant who does not accept lifeless worship. They thus attack at one and the same time national particularism and ritual formalism so that Israel's worship should become more and more spiritual and thus be the efficacious testimony that God expects of His people.

III. THE SOUL OF TRUE WORSHIP:
FAITHFULNESS TO THE COVENANT

Israel's worship will become spiritual insofar as the people listen to the prophets and recognize the interior nature of the covenant demands. It is this interior loyalty that is the condition of an authentic worship and the proof that Israel has no other God* but Yahweh (Ex 20,2f p). The saving God of the exodus and Decalogue is holy* and demands that the people whom He would mold into a priestly* nation* be holy (Lv 19,2). In recalling this the prophets do not reject the rites but demand that they be given their true meaning. The gifts of our sacrifices are to express our thanksgiving* to God, the source of every gift* (Ps 50).

Samuel had already affirmed that God rejects the worship of whose who are disobedient (1 S 15,22). Amos and Isaiah repeat this vigorously (Am 5,21-26; Is 1,11-20; 29,13). And Jeremiah proclaims in the temple itself the emptiness of the cult there offered and denounces the wickedness of their hearts (Jr 7,4-15.21ff). Ezekiel, the prophet-priest, while heralding the ruin of the temple that had been sullied by idolatry, describes the new temple of the new covenant (Ez 37,26ff), which will be the center of worship for the faithful people (Ez 40—48). The prophet of the return points out the condition on which God would approve the worship of His people: they must be a genuinely fraternal community (Is 58,6f.9f.13; 66,1f).

This community opens its arms to pagans who fear God and observe the Law (Is 56,1-8). Moreover, universal worship will become decentralized (Ml 1,11). If Ben Sira was overwhelmed by such expectations, he nonetheless shows himself the heir to the prophetic tradition, uniting very closely faithfulness to the Law and ritual worship (Si 34,18ff; 35,1-16). And in a particularist and formalistic Israel that would shut itself off from His message, Christ would find poor* hearts in whom the psalms will have linked both the meaning of true justice (the condition of genuine worship: Lk 1,74f) and hope for the Messiah who will institute the perfect form of worship (Ml 3,1-4).

NT

I. THE END OF THE OLD CULT

1. *Jesus* puts an end to the old cult by fulfilling it. At first He renews it by conforming to its rites and quickening them with His spirit of filial prayer. At His birth He is presented in the temple (Lk 2,22ff). All His life He visits the temple for the feasts (Lk 2,41; Jn 2,13; 10, 22). And He preaches often in the place where people gather to worship (Mk 14,49; Jn 18,20). Like the prophets He demands faithfulness to the spirit of worship (Mt 23,16-23): without purity of heart ritual cleansings were useless (Mt 23,25f; 5,8.23f).

But He surpasses the old cult with His sacrifice*. And if He affirms His respect for the old temple by cleansing it (Jn 2,14ff), He predicts at the same time that this temple, destroyed through the fault of the Jews, would be followed by a new one, His resurrected body (2,19ff). Then the cult of Jerusalem will cease (Jn 4,21).

2. *The early Church* breaks with the figurative* worship of the temple only by transcending it. Like Jesus, the apostles pray and teach in the temple (Ac 2,46; 5,20). But as Stephen declares, the true temple is that in which God dwells and over which Jesus rules (Ac 6,13f; 7,48ff.55f). Therefore, Paul, out of respect for converted Jews, permits participation in the religious practices to which they are faithful (Ac 21,24.26; cf 1 Co 10,32f); yet he preaches always that circumcision* is valueless and that the Christian is no longer bound by the old observance. Christian worship is new (G 5,1.6).

II. ORIGINS OF THE NEW WORSHIP

1. *Jesus* defines the new cult He preaches. True worship is spiritual. It is not necessarily without rites, but is impossible without the Holy Spirit*, who makes those led by Him capable of worship (Jn 4,23f; cf 7,37ff; 4,10.14). The sacrifice of Jesus, who ratifies the new covenant (Mk 10,45; 14,22ff), gives their full meaning to formulas inspired by the earlier worship (He 10, 1-18; cf Ps 40,7ff). He also establishes the new cult because He had truly made expiation* for the sins of the world and communicates eternal life to those who partake of the flesh* and blood* of Christ (Jn 1,29; 6,51). At the last supper He Himself initiated the sacrificial banquet and commanded them to renew it (Lk 22, 19f).

2. *The Church* has obeyed. In their gatherings for worship the first disciples climax their prayers and their dinner with the "breaking of bread" (Ac 2,42; 20,7.11), the eucharistic rite whose traditional meaning and requirements were recalled by Paul to those who had forgotten them (1 Co 10,16; 11,24).

To share in the eucharist*, one must have been joined to the Church by the rite of baptism*, prescribed by Jesus (Mt 28,19) as the condition of the new life (Mk 16,16; Jn 3,5) and performed by the apostles from the day of Pentecost (Ac 2,3-41). Finally by the act of imposing* hands the apostles give the Spirit to the baptized (Ac 8,15ff).

To these three fundamental rites of the Christian worship are added traditional practices of unequal importance: celebration of Sunday, "the first day of the week*" (Ac 20,7; 1 Co 16,2), "the day* of the Lord" (Ap 1,10); disciplinary rules, such as wearing the veil by women*, their silence in the religious gatherings; rules instituted for peace and good order (1 Co 11,5-16; 14,34.40).

III. THE STRUCTURE AND TRIPLE ASPECT OF CHRISTIAN WORSHIP

The worship of the Church, like that of Israel, has a triple aspect: it commemorates a past divine work, it makes this activity present, and it makes it real; it thus permits the Christian to live in hope of the day when the glory of God will be made manifest completely in Christ. But despite the fact that it has borrowed certain rites from the prior cult, Christian worship is not a simple figure* of the worship to come—it is its image*. The novelty of Christian worship derives from its basis which is the perfect and definitive sacrifice* of Christ, the Son of God (He 1,2f). Through Him the Father is perfectly glorified. Through Him all who hope in Him are cleansed of their sins and are able to be united in the filial worship which Christ offers

His Father in heaven, the realization of which is life eternal (He 7,26; 8,1f; 9,14.26).

1. *The past action* which Christian worship commemorates is the offering of Christ for our salvation, an offering whose fruits are the resurrection and the gift of the Spirit. This action puts an end to the old worship which was destined to express and support the humble and confident expectation of salvation* which is henceforth consummated (He 7,18-28). Christ gives us the means to receive the benefit of the sacrifice He offered on the altar of the cross*, that is, by sharing in the eucharist (He 13,10).

2. *Now* indeed is realized a communion* which prepares us for the everlasting communion of heaven. The eucharist* rite, center of the new worship and channel of the new life, is its sign and means. By this rite the glorified Christ mysteriously makes Himself present that we may join ourselves to the body and blood He has offered and that thus we may all be one body*, glorifying the Father by and with Christ through the impulse of the Holy Spirit (1 Co 10,16f; 11,24ff; Ph 3,3).

By this fact we have access to the heavenly sanctuary (He 10,19ff) where Christ, the eternal priest (He 7,24f; 9,11f.24), dwells. There is celebrated the adoration* of the Father in spirit and truth, the only worship worthy of the living God (Jn 4,23f; He 9,14). It is celebrated by the Lamb* immolated before the throne of God in heaven. Here is the true temple of God where the real ark* of the covenant is (Ap 5,6; 11,19). The elect who glorify God by the *Sanctus* whose echo Isaiah heard (Ap 4,2-11; Is 6,1ff) also glorify the Lamb who is the Son (Ap 14,1) and who has made of them a kingdom of priests to unite them to His perfect worship (Ap 5,9-13).

Now the rites which join us to Christ and to His heavenly worship imply certain moral demands. By baptism* we have died to sin* to live by the holy life of the risen Christ (R 6,1-11; Col 3,1-10; 1 P 1,14f). To sin, therefore, is to make oneself unworthy to share in the body and blood of the Lord, to sentence oneself if one does partake (1 Co 11,27ff). On the other hand, to follow* Christ, to unite oneself to the love* which inspired His sacrifice with a steadfast faithfulness, is to be a living victim whom God accepts (E 5,1f; R 12,1f; 1 P 2,5; He 12,28). Our liturgical worship, then, with its songs of praise*, expresses the spiritual worship of perpetual thanksgiving* to the Father through His

Son, the Lord Jesus (Col 3,12-17).

3. *The last day* terminates those rites which presage it—rites we celebrate "until the Lamb comes," in answer to the call of His spouse (*Marana tha*=Come, Lord!) to consummate the nuptials with her (1 Co 11,26; 16,22; Ap 19,7; 22,17). Then the temple will no longer symbolize the presence of God. In the heavenly Jerusalem the glory* of the Lord will no longer show itself through signs (Ap 21,22). Because in the holy city of eternity, the servants of God who will worship Him no longer will be sinners but sons*—sons in the universe that has been renewed and brightened by the glory of God and of the Lamb. They will see their Father face to face and will drink at the source of the living water* of the Spirit* (Ap 21,1-7.23; 22, 1-5).

→Adoration—Altar—Animals II 3—Blessing III 3—Blood OT 3—Bread II—Burial 1—Communion OT 1—Conscience 3—Covenant OT I 3, II 1—Day of the Lord O; OT I; NT III 3—Death OT I 3—Eucharist—Exile II 2—Fasting 2—Feasts—Figure OT II 4—Fire OT II 1; NT II 2—Holy OT II; NT IV—Idols I—Joy OT II 1—Law *A* 1; *B* 2; *C* IV 1—Magic 2 c—Memory 1 b. 4 b—Mountain II 2—Oil 1—Passover I 5, III 1—People *A* II 6; *B* II 6—Perfume 2—Piety OT 2; NT—Praise III, IV—Prayer—Presence of God OT III 1; NT II—Priesthood—Prophet OT III 3—Pure OT I—Repentance/Conversion OT I 2, III 1—Sabbath—Sacrifice—See OT I 2—Seek I—Service II 1—Sign OT II 1—Stars 1.3—Temple—Thanksgiving—Wine I 2.

MFL jrc

WRATH

It would be offensive to speak of God's wrath if we did not also know of His holiness* and love*. But, just as man must repent his sins to enter into God's grace, so the believer must approach the mystery of God's anger if he will rightly approach God's love. To wish to reduce the mystery of divine wrath to a mythical expression of human experience is to mistake the seriousness of sin and to forget the tragic side of God's love. There is a fundamental incompatibility between holiness and sin. Admittedly, it is human anger that allows us to express the mysterious reality that is God's wrath; but our experience of the mystery is primarily in relation to language and of quite another origin.

A. THE ANGER OF MAN

1. *Anger condemned.* God condemns the violent reaction of rage against others, as in Cain's jealousy (Gn 4,5), Esau's fury (Gn 27,44f), and in the excessive revenge taken by Simeon and Levi after the rape of their sister (Gn 49,5ff; cf 34,7-26; Jdt 9,2). Such anger normally leads to murder. In their time, the wisdom writers condemn the foolishness of the quick-tempered person (Pr 29,11) who cannot, according to the original figure of speech, control "the breath of his nostrils." They admiringly commend the wise man of self-control ("of long breath") in contrast with the hothead ("the man of short breaths") (Pr 14,29; 15,18) whose anger gives rise to injustice (Pr 14,17; 29,22; cf Jm 1,19f). Jesus went to the extent of putting anger on the same level with its ordinary effect, murder (Mt 5,22). Paul judges anger incompatible with charity (1 Co 13,5) and calls it evil pure and simple (Col 3,8). A person must avoid giving way to anger, especially because of the nearness of God (1 Tm 2,8; Tt 1,7).

2. *Holy anger.* In contrast with the stoic reprobation of all emotional arousal as against their ideal of *apatheia*, the Bible portrays examples of "holy anger" which give visible expression to God's reaction to man's rebellion. Thus Moses rages against the Israelites for their lack of faith (Ex 16,20), for the apostasy at Horeb (Ex 32,19.22), the neglect of the liturgy (Lv 10,16), and for their failure to observe the stipulation against booty (Nm 31,14). So also Phinehas whose zeal* God praises (Nm 25,11), and Elijah who massacred false prophets (1 K 18,40) and brought fire from heaven on the legates of the king (2 K 1,10.12). Finally, we have Paul's animus at Athenian idolatry (Ac 17,16). These men of God were, like Jeremiah, "filled with God's wrath" (Jr 6,11; 15,17) in the face of idols and sin. Thus they imperfectly prefigure the wrath of Jesus (Mk 3,5).

But God alone can without paradox react in anger. In the OT the terms connected with anger and rage occur five times as often for God as they do for man. Paul, who more than once was inflamed to anger (Ac 15,39), has this wise advice: "Do not take revenge yourself, but leave place for God's wrath; for it is written, 'I will bring about justice, I will give due rewards, says the Lord'" (R 12,19). Thus wrath is God's business, not man's.

B. THE WRATH OF GOD

OT

I. IMAGES AND REALITY

1. *It is a fact.* God reacts in anger. Isaiah collects all sorts of inspired images by which God's wrath is expressed: "His wrath blazes, with lips spouting fury, and His tongue like a consuming fire. His breath is like a raging torrent rising up to the neck...and His arm falls in the heat of His anger with consuming fire, with the thunder-clap, storm, and hail...The breath of the Lord is like streams of brimstone coming to ignite the straw and logs of the pyre for Topheth" (Is 30,27-33). As fire*, breath, storm, and torrent, His anger sets afire, it flows (Ez 20,33). It must be drunk from a cup* (Is 51,17) like an intoxicating wine* (Jr 25,15-38).

This wrath brings as its result death* and all that goes with death. David must choose between famine, flight, or pestilence (2 S 24,13ff). In other cases God's wrath brings plagues (Nm 17,11), leprosy* (Nm 12,9f), or death (1 S 6,19). His wrath falls on hardened sinners; first of all on Israel since it is so near to the all-holy God (Ex 19; 32; Dt 1,34; Nm 25,7-13). It strikes the community (2 K 23,26; Jr 21,5) or individuals, and finally whole nations* (1 S 6,9); since Yahweh is God of all the earth (Jr 10,10). There is hardly a document or book of the Bible that fails to express this conviction.

2. But in the face of a God described as having violent feeling, *reason rebels* and tries to purify the divinity of sentiments that are judged unworthy. Thus, one peripheral tendency of the Bible makes Satan* the agent of God's wrath (comp 1 Ch 21 and 2 S 24). This is more common in other religions, as in the Erinyes of the Greeks. In any case, the religious sense of the Bible did not allow its grasp of the mystery of God's wrath to be biased in the direction of demythologizing and attribution of divine wrath to other subjects.

Revelation does come to us through poetic images, but these are not simply metaphors. God appears as stirred by real "passion" that He turns loose, not suppressing (Is 9,11) or turning it back (Jr 4,8). But He can and does restrain His wrath (Ho 14,5; Jr 18,20) as He "returns" to those who come back to Him

(2 Ch 30,6; cf Ex 34,6; Is 63,17). In God the "emotions" of anger and mercy* strain against each other (cf Is 54,8ff; Ps 30,6). But both express God's ardent attachment to man, each in its own way. His wrath is now held back until the last day* when it will be identified with hell*. His merciful love rules forever in heaven*, but now it works here below in the chastisements that call the sinner to conversion. This is the mystery of God's wrath that Israel gradually and in a variety of ways has brought out.

II. WRATH AND HOLINESS

1. *Toward adoration of God most holy.* A first set of the oldest texts reveals the irrational character of this. Death threatens anyone who rashly approaches near to the holiness* of Yahweh (Ex 19,9-25; 20,18-21; 33,20; Jg 13,22). Uzzah was struck down by lightning as he reached out to hold up the ark (2 S 6,7). It was in this light the psalmists will understand calamities*, sickness*, premature death*, and the victory of enemies* (Ps 88,16; 90,7-10; 102, 9-12; Jb). Such an attitude is penetrating in that it sees evil for what it is. But it is also naive in attributing unexplained evil to a wrath of God, a wrath conceived as the vengeance of a taboo. Yet beneath such thinking lay a profound faith in God's presence* in all happenings and a proper sense of reverential fear* before the holiness of God (Is 6,5).

2. *Wrath and sin.* In later texts, the believer does not remain content with fearful adoration* of the divine power that intervenes to call in question his very existence. Rather, he goes on to seek out the meaning of God's wrath. Israel does not attribute it to some malicious hatred*, as in the Greek *mēnis*. Nor is it capricious, like the jealous Babylonian god *Enlil*. Such a concept would transfer one's own guilt to another. Rather, Israel acknowledges her own sin. Frequently God Himself indicates the guilty ones when He punishes those who complain (Nm 11, 1), or Miriam of the wicked tongue (Nm 12,1-10). At times the community draws down divine wrath (Ex 32). In the case of Achan (Js 7), lots were cast to discover the guilty one. If there is a wrath of God it is because there had been a sin* of man. Such a conviction guides the editor of the Book of Judges as he portrays the rhythm of Israel's history in the three stages of popular apostasy, wrath of God, and conversion of Israel.

Thus God is the one who is justified in the proceedings brought against Him by the sinner (Ps 51,6). The sinner comes to discover that a basic meaning of divine wrath is the jealousy of a holy love. The prophets explain past punishments* by the people's unfaithfulness to the covenant* (Ho 5,10; Is 9,11; Ez 5,13...). The fearful images of Hosea—moth, decay, lion, hunter, bear (Ho 5,12.14; 7,12; 13,8)—strive to show how serious is God's love. The holy one of Israel cannot allow sin in His chosen people. Wrath falls on the nations* according to the extent of their arrogance*, which makes them exceed the mission* given to them (Is 10,5-15; Ez 25,15ff). If the wrath of God hovers over the world, it is because this is a sinful world*. This threatening wrath strikes man with terror and man turns to confess* his sin and hope for grace* (Mi 7,9; Ps 90,7f).

III. THE PERIOD OF WRATH

The development of the religious sense is not yet complete. After passing from blind adoration to confession of sin and on to grasping the holiness that strikes down the sinner, man must further advance to acknowledge the love* that brings the sinner back to life.

1. *Wrath and love.* In the manifestations of His wrath, God does not conduct Himself like a weak man. He masters His feelings. At times the wrath strikes the Hebrews immediately, "while the meat was still between their teeth" (Nm 11,33), and similarly in the case of Miriam (Nm 12,9). But this is not impatience, for God is also "slow to anger" (Ex 34,6; Is 48,9; Ps 103,8), and His mercy is always close at hand (Jr 3,12). Even in Hosea, the prophet of violent images, we read: "I will not vent my blazing anger, I will not destroy Ephraim again. For I am God, I am, and not man" (Ho 11,9). Gradually man realizes that God is not a god of wrath but the God of mercy*. After the symbolic chastisement of the exile*, God speaks to His spouse: "only for a moment have I forsaken you. But then my great pity moved me to bring you back. In an outburst of anger, I hid my face from you for a moment. But then my everlasting love brought me to pity you" (Is 54,7f). And the triumph of pity supposes the suffering of the faithful Servant* who was struck down to death for the sins of the people,

changing that very injustice into justice* (Is 53,4.8).

2. *To be freed from wrath.* God reveals to man the teaching* scope of the chastisements brought on by His wrath (Am 4,6-11). For God punishes in His own time and not under the influence of impetuosity. God's wrath reveals itself as part of a larger plan of mercy; and so it is not a fatal specter to paralyze man, but a call for him to be converted to God's love (Jr 4,4).

Since God's purpose is one of heartfelt love, Israel can beg to be freed from His wrath. Her sacrifices* proceed from faith in the divine justice, and not from the wish to charm divine power through magic. Prayers* of intercession also express the conviction that God can call back His wrath. Moses intercedes for the unfaithful people (Ex 32,11.31f; Nm 11,1f; 14, 11f...), or for an individual sinner (Nm 12,13; Dt 9,20). Likewise Amos intercedes for Israel (Am 7,2.5), Jeremiah for Judah (Jr 14,7ff; 18, 20), Job for his friends (Jb 42,7f). As a result, the effects of divine wrath are lessened (Nm 14; Dt 9) and even suppressed (Nm 11; 2 S 24). The grounds on which the requests are based show that the bond between Israel and God has not been broken (Ex 32,12; Nm 14,15f; Ps 74, 2). In the dialogue, the intercessors plead their own weakness (Am 7,2.5; Ps 79,8) and recall to God that He is above all merciful* and faithful* (Nm 14,18).

3. *Wrath and chastisement.* As she advances from emphasis on the wrath striking down the hardened sinner to stress chastisement undergone for the correction and conversion of the sinner, Israel does not completely reject the earlier concept of wrath in the strict sense. Rather, she located it more precisely in its exact place; that is, on the last day*. The day of darkness mentioned by Amos (Am 5,18ff) becomes the "day of wrath" (*Dies irae*, Zp 1,15—2,3) that no one can escape but the religious man whose sin has been forgiven (Ps 30,6; 65,3f; 103,3). It is a day of wrath for pagans (Ps 9,17f; 56,8; 79,6ff), and even for sinners in the community of Israel (Ps 7,7; 11,5f; 28,4; 94,2).

Thus two kinds of wrath came to be distinguished. Through the course of history, divine chastisements are not strictly the wrath of God that strikes down forever, but are figures* that anticipate the final wrath. Through them the wrath to fall at the end of time does a salutary work now in revealing one aspect of the love of the all-holy God. God's visitations* upon His sinful people can and should be understood in terms of this final wrath. He comes now in acts of forebearance that put off the operation of His final wrath (cf 2 M 6,12-17). The writers of the apocalypses saw clearly that a period of wrath had to precede the final period of grace: "Go in, my people, enter your rooms and close the doors behind you. Hide for a short while, until the time of wrath goes by" (Is 26,20; cf Dn 8,19; 11,36).

NT

From the preaching of the precursor (Mt 3, 7 p) to the last pages of the NT (Ap 14,10), the gospel of grace* retains the wrath of God as a basic element of its message. To eliminate it would be to revive the heresy of Marcion who saw God's wrath as foreign to the proper notion of "the good God." But the coming of Christ did transform basic elements of the OT in the process of fulfilling them.

I. IMAGES AND REALITY

1. *Divine "emotion" and the effects of wrath.* Though the OT images continue, there is an change of meaning. Fire* (Mt 5,22; 1 Co 3,13. 15), exterminating breath (2 Th 1,8; 2,8), wine*, cup*, winepress, trumpets of wrath (Ap 14,10.8; 16,1ff)—all are used, but not so much to give the psychology of God's reaction as to describe the effects of this reaction. We have entered into the final times*. John the Baptist proclaims a fire of judgment* (Mt 3,12) and Jesus echoes his words in the parable of the wedding feast (Mt 22,7). For Jesus as well, the enemy and the infidel are to be destroyed (Lk 19,27; 12,46) and cast into everlasting fire (Mt 13,42; 25,41).

2. *Jesus' wrath.* The NT goes beyond the terror of the inspired words, and beyond the tragedy of the prophets who were overwhelmed between the all-holy God and His sinful people. For more terrible and more tragic than both is the reaction of a man who is God Himself. In Jesus, the wrath of God is revealed. Jesus' conduct is not that of a stoic who is never stirred (Jn 11,33), for He forcefully commands Satan (Mt 4,10; 16,23) and levels threats against the demons (Mk 1,25). He is beside Himself at the diabolical cunning of men (Jn 8,44), especially that of the Pharisees* (Mt 12,34). His anger rises against those who had killed the prophets (Mt 23,33) and against the hypocrites* (Mt 15,7).

Just as Yahweh, so Jesus directs His wrath to anyone who rises up to oppose God.

Jesus sharply rebukes the disobedient (Mk 1, 43; Mt 9,30) and even His disciples for their lack of faith (Mt 17,17). Most of all His wrath stirs against those who would not show themselves merciful (Mk 3,5), like the older brother of the prodigal son who had been taken back by the father of mercies (Lk 15,28). Finally, Jesus shows the wrath of a judge, much like the lord who gave the banquet (Lk 14,21) or the master of the unpitying servant (Mt 18,34). So He condemns the unrepentant towns (Mt 11, 20f), drives the sellers from the temple (Mt 21, 12f), and curses the barren fig tree (Mk 11,21). As with the wrath of God, so the wrath of the Lamb is not an empty word (Ap 6,16; He 10, 31).

II. THE PERIOD OF WRATH

1. *Justice and wrath.* By His coming on earth, our Lord made a division of salvation history into two eras. This is the new message of which Paul is the theologian. Christ has revealed the justice* of God for the benefit of all who believe, and at the same time the wrath of God on the unbeliever. This wrath, like the concrete chastisements stressed in the OT, anticipates the final wrath of God. In the view of John the Baptist, the earthly coming of the Messiah fused with His coming at the end of time, so that Jesus' ministry should have been the final judgment* of men. But Paul teaches that Jesus began an interim period in which the justice and wrath of God are both fully revealed as two dimensions of divine activity. Paul retains some OT views, such as the concept of the civil power as an instrument of God, "as God's agent of punishment for retribution on the offender" (R 13,4). But Paul's main work is to describe the new situation of man before God.

2. *From wrath to mercy.* From the beginning, man is a sinner (R 1,18-32) and deserves death (3,20). He is rightly a target of the divine wrath, "a vessel of wrath" on the brink of destruction (9,22; E 2,3). John transposes this as he writes that "the wrath of God rests upon the non-believer" (Jn 3,36). Since man is congenitally a sinner, he can turn to evil even the most holy of divine institutions. So the holy Law* "brings wrath" (R 4,15). But God's plan* is one of mercy*, and the vessels of wrath can choose conversion and become "vessels of mercy", which He has prepared in advance for glory (R 9,23). Any man can do this, whether he be pagan or Jew, "for God has enclosed all men in disobedience so as to work His mercy on all" (11,32). Just as in the OT, God does not give free rein to His wrath, but manifests both His power, tolerating the sinner, and His goodness, by calling the sinner to conversion.

II. FREED FROM WRATH

1. *Jesus and the wrath of God.* The radical change with the coming of Christ is that it is now Jesus Himself and no longer the Law (1 Th 1,10) that frees us from the "wrath to come" (Mt 3,7). God has no longer "destined us for wrath, but for salvation*" (1 Th 5,9). He assures us that "being justified, we are saved from the wrath" (R 5,9); and further, that it is our faith that joins us to those who are "saved" (1 Co 1,18). Jesus has "taken away the sin of the world" (Jn 1,29), becoming "sin*" so that we might become the justice of God through Him (2 Co 5,21). Dying on the cross* He became "accursed" that we might be blessed* (G 3,13). The power of love and holiness so met in Jesus that when the wrath fell on the one "made sin," it was love that won the victory. This long journey of man searching after the love* behind wrath is completed and summed up in the moment of Jesus' death. It is a moment that anticipates the final wrath so that whoever believes in Him may be free from wrath forever.

2. *In expectation of the day of wrath.* Wholly freed from the divine wrath, the Church continues to be the place of the battle with Satan*. For "the devil, quivering with wrath, has come among us" (Ap 12,12). He comes to battle with the woman* and her posterity and to intoxicate the nations* with the fierce wine of divine wrath (14,8ff). But the Church has no fear of this parody on the wrath of God; she is certain that the new Babylon* will fall. For the king of kings will come "treading in the press the wine* of God's burning wrath" (19,15). Thus, she is assured of the victory* of God on the last day.

→Cup 2—Curse V—Day of the Lord OT II; NT 0—Fear of God III—Fire OT II 2, III—Godless Man NT 3—Hardness of Heart I 2—Judgment—Mercy OT I 2 b—Pardon—Patience — Punishment — Silence 1 — Storm 3 — Vengeance 1—Vintage 2—Wine II 2 a—Zeal.

XLD wjw

WRITING

I. THE COST OF WRITING

In Babylon or in Egypt, where writing material was expensive and bulky, where the system of writing was extremely complicated, the science of writing was the privilege of a caste, that of the scribes, and passed as an invention of the gods Nebo and Thout. To be initiated into its secret was to be admitted into the mysterious zone where the destinies of the world are determined. Certain kings of Assyria would bring themselves glory by having access to it. Even in our time the child, and especially the adult, steps into a new world when he learns to write.

In Palestine, between Sinai and Phoenicia, precisely at the place where the genius of man invented the alphabet, Israel found from its birth a writing available for all, which made it take a decisive step forward in comparison with the ancient cultures of Egypt and Mesopotamia, prisoners of their archaic writing. In the time of Gideon, long before David, a young man of Succoth was able to furnish in writing a list of the elders of his village (Jg 8,14). From the earliest times writing is, if not widespread, at least known in Israel and becomes an essential tool of its religion. Well before Samuel consigned to writing "the nature of the kingship" (1 S 10,25), it is not anachronistic that Joshua was able to put into writing the clauses of the treaty with Shechem (Js 24,26), or Moses the laws of Sinai (Ex 24,4) and the recollection of the victory over Amalek (17,14).

II. THE WEIGHT OF WRITING

"What I have written is written" (Jn 19,22), answers Pilate to the high priests who came to complain of the inscription affixed to the cross of Jesus. The Roman, the Jews, and the evangelist agree in finding in that inscription a sign: there is something irrevocable about a thing written down; it is a solemn and definitive expression of the word*, and therefore it naturally is made use of to express the infallible and intangible character of the divine Word, which remains forever (Ps 119,89). Evil fortune to him who alters it (Ap 22,18f)! He is a fool,

who thinks to make it vain by destroying it (cf Jr 36,23).

If the rite of the "bitter waters" (Nm 5,23), in spite of the progress that it manifests by comparison with primitive ordeals, yet presupposes an archaic thought, then the inscribing of the divine words enjoined to be written on the lintel of the doors of every house (Dt 6,9; 11, 20), on the copy of laws given to the king at his enthronement (17,18), on the diadem of the high priest (Ex 39,30), expresses in a very pure manner the sovereignty over Israel of the Word of Yahweh, the irrevocable demand of His will*.

It is entirely natural that the prophets* should entrust to writing the text of their oracles. The solemn and irrevocable form of the word *writing* is used constantly in the East by those who claim to fix destiny. Even though they are aware of receiving the Word from Yahweh, the prophets of Israel attest that if they entrust it to writing it is at the divine order (Is 8,1; Jr 36, 1-4; Ha 2,2; Ap 14,13; 19,9); in order that this publicly ratified testimony (Is 8,16) might attest, when the events occur, that only Yahweh had already revealed them (Is 41,26). Writing thus bears witness to the faithfulness* of God.

III. SACRED WRITINGS

As the permanent and official expression of the operation of God, of His demands and His promises, the transcription of the divine Word is therefore sacred: the writings of Israel are "holy writings." The word is not again found in the OT, but already the tablets of stone containing the essentials of the Law (Ex 24,12) are thought of as "writings of the finger of God" (31,18), imbued with His holiness*.

The NT uses at times the rabbinic term, "sacred writings" (R 1,2; cf "the Sacred Letters," 2 Tm 3,15); but generally it speaks of "the writings" or again of "writing" in the singular, whether to designate a precise text (Mk 12,10; Lk 4,21) or even the entire OT (Jn 2,22; 10,35; Ac 8,32; G 3,22). Thus was expressed the vital awareness of the profound unity in the different writings of the OT that the traditional Christian name of Bible would pass on, in an even more suggestive manner, to indicate the collection of sacred books*. But the most frequently occurring formula is the simple "It is written," where the passive designates God without naming Him, and which thus affirms at one and the same time the unapproachable holiness of God, the infallible certainty of His gaze, and the unbreakable faithfulness of His promises*.

IV. FULFILLMENT OF THE SCRIPTURES

"All that is written of me must be fulfilled*" (Lk 24,44); the Scriptures must be fulfilled (cf Mt 26,54). God does not speak vainly (Ez 6,10) and His writing "cannot be abolished" (Jn 10, 35). Jesus, who was seen actually writing only once—in the sand (Jn 8,6)—left no writing whatsoever; but He solemnly ratified the value of the written Scripture even to the slightest punctuation mark, "one jot" (Mt 5,18), and defined its meaning: it cannot pass away; it remains.

But it can only remain by being fulfilled; there is in Scripture the living permanence of the eternal Word of God, but there can also be there the survival of former conditions destined to pass away. There is a Spirit* that gives life and a letter that kills (2 Co 3,6). Christ made the transit from letter to Spirit (3,14). When one recognizes Christ throughout the Scriptures of Israel, one lays hold of eternal life (Jn 5,39); and those that refuse to believe in the words of Jesus show by that action that if they put their hope in Moses and their trust in his writings they do not believe him or take him seriously (5,45ff).

V. THE LAW WRITTEN IN HEARTS

The new covenant is no longer that of the letter, but of the Spirit (2 Co 3,6); the new Law* is "written in the hearts" of the new people (Jr 31,33), who no longer need to be taught by a text imposed from outside (Ez 36, 27; Is 54,13; Jn 6,45). Nevertheless, the NT again allows writings in which the Church quickly recognized the same authority and gave the same name as the Scriptures (cf 2 P 3,16) and found in them the same Word of God (cf Lk 1,2) and the same Spirit. In fact, these writings are not only in the same tradition of the Scriptures of Israel, but they clarify its meaning and import. Without them the writings of the NT would be unintelligible, they would speak a language to which none would have the key; but without the NT the Jewish books would contain nothing but myths: a divine law become a dead letter; a promise unable to answer the hope that it excited; an adventure lacking results.

There are still writings in the new covenant: in fact, the time is not yet wiped away, it is necessary to fix in the memory of future generations the recollection of what Jesus Christ is and what He does. But the Scriptures are no longer for the Christian a book that one deciphers page by page; they are a book* entirely opened, all its pages encompassed at one glance and yielding their mystery: Christ, the Alpha and Omega, the beginning and end of all writing.

→Book I—Fulfill—Gospel IV 2 b—Memory 1 b —Prophet NT I—Revelation OT I 3—Tradition.

MLR & JG jrc

Y

YAHWEH

Yahweh is the name that God* gave Himself. Not that it was the only way He had of revealing Himself; for, even outside Israel, man was capable of coming to know the true God. For example He allowed Himself to be known under a name like *El 'Elyon*, a name that was actually in use among the neighboring religions. But, by using the name of Yahweh, God did more than make Himself known: He was the first to pronounce, and in His own way, the name that was adopted by His people in their prayer and worship, and He Himself gave its meaning (Ex 3,13-15; 34,6f). And He did so in a context and at a time that show both the mysterious depth of this name and the salvation* that it brought. While the manifestations of El to the patriarchs took place in a familiar land and in simple and homely forms, Yahweh revealed Himself to Moses* in the wild terrain of the desert and under the frightening form of fire*. But this was precisely the God who saw and heard the wretchedness of His people at the height of their misfortune and sinfulness (3,7) and pardoned their faults and transgressions, for He was "the God of tenderness and compassion" (34,6f).

1. *The name and its origins.* As far as the Bible itself is concerned, the origins of the divine name presuppose, apart from the outline presentation of Ex 3, a complex process. A number of passages show Yahweh carrying out His plans from the very beginnings of humanity and revealing Himself more and more clearly through the long line of patriarchs. This is the point of view of the yahwist historian (Gn 4,26; 9,26; 12,8...), a point of view that is rearranged and completed by the priestly history (Ex 6,3). Another point of view sees the time of Moses as the time when Israel's religion took its final shape and makes this coincide with the revelation of the name of Yahweh. This is the approach that governs the priestly tradition (6,2-8); it is based on the elohist account (3,13-15) and is confirmed in its own way by the yahwist account (33,19).

Naturally enough modern historians have looked for the prehistory of this name, for it cannot have established itself all at once and without reference to any previous experience. And in fact the genealogy of Moses attributes to his mother a theophoric name, *Yokebed*, where *Yo* could well be the equivalent of *Yau* and stand for the divine name, linked with the root KBD, which suggests glory*. In Babylon, and quite evidently at the time of the patriarchs, the same form *Yau*, which is used in the proper names that are equally theophoric, indicates the god invoked by the bearer of this name. But it is certain that *yau* comes from a pronominal form and means "mine." "Mine" is the name given by the believer to the god whose protection he claims. While the mystery of this god is respected, the bond attaching him to his servant is clearly stated. This god is indeed in the line of Abraham's God and already has some of the characteristics of Yahweh. And the continuity between *Yau* and *Yahu*, an abbreviated and current form of the divine name (Jeremiah = *Yirmeyahu* = God

builds), is quite normal.

2. *The meaning of the name.* The scene in which the name is revealed to Moses suggests at least a reinterpretation of the old word and probably a material transformation. It established a connection between the name *Yahweh* and the first person of the verb *hawah/hayah*: *ehyeh*, "I am." To God's "I am" man relies: "He is" or "He brings into being." It is hard to say whether *yahweh* represents the causative form, which would be grammatically more usual, or a simple archaic form, which would correspond better with the whole tenor of the passage. In any case it is certain that the divine name is no longer a pronoun, by which a man points to his god, nor a noun setting him among other beings nor an adjective describing him by some characteristic. It is understood as a verb and is the echo on the lips of man of the Word* by which God defines Himself.

This Word is at once a refusal and a gift. It is a refusal to allow Himself to be contained in man's categories: *ehyeh ašer ehyeh*, "I am who I am" (Ex 3,14); and it is the gift of His presence*: *ehyeh 'immak*, "I am with you" (3, 12). For the verb *hayah* has a dynamic sense: it means more than the neutral fact of existence, it means an event, an ever-present and effective existence, an *adesse* more than a simple *esse*.

3. *Later history.* The word *Sabaoth* is frequently associated with the name *Yahweh*. This title does not seem to be a primitive one and appears to go back to the sanctuary of Shilo (cf 1 S 1,3) and to be attached especially to the ark* (cf 1 S 4,4). The meaning of *Sabaoth* is not certain: perhaps it refers to the armies of Israel; but more likely to the world of the heavens* and of the stars*. For the ancients this was a world of living beings, and for the pagan religions a world of gods. For Israel the one God has control of all the powers of the universe; and, if the causative sense of *yahweh* is understood, He gives them existence. But it is also possible that *Sabaoth* is a singular title, with an ending analogous to that of Accadian words in *-atu* and meaning a function: Yahweh—The Warrior* (?).

Between the time of the exile and Christ the Jews ceased to pronounce the name of Yahweh, out of a more formalistic respect than that of the old Israelites but also in an effort to avoid pagan profanations. However, they continued to write the four consonants of the sacred tetragram YHWH, while interposing the vowels of the name that they pronounced instead of Yahweh, *Adonai*, the Lord*. These vowels a-o-a (written as e-o-a) gave rise to the purely artificial form *Yehowah*, from which came the Jehovah of the old English translations. The LXX translation, *Kyrios*, is the equivalent of the word *Adonai* that was used. If, through all these equivalents and translations, the actual name *Yahweh* disappeared, His personality was too real and independent of all possible names to be affected by this. And in Jesus Christ*,

God no longer allows Himself to be known through a name, but through the One who is above all names (Ph 2,9).

→Creation OT I—Fathers & Father III 3—Glory III—God OT—Jesus (Name of) IV—Lord OT—Moses 1—Name OT—Power I, III 2—Presence of God OT I—Revelation OT II 2—War OT II, III—Word of God OT II 1 b.
JG ems

Z

ZEAL

The Greek word *zēlos* comes from a root which means that something is hot or at the boiling point. The Greek translates adequately the Hebrew word *qin'ah*, whose root designates the flush that comes to the face of a man involved in a strong emotion. This emotional state, quite often similar to anger (Dt 29,19), is reminiscent of fire* (Zp 1,18; Is 26,11). The emotion can come from various sentiments, ranging from disinterested love to sordid envy. Loves, hates, jealousies (Qo 9,6), fury, trouble (Si 40,4), worry (30,24), zeal for the people's welfare (2 S 21,2) or for God's honor (Nm 25, 11): all these feelings can overrun the human heart and turn into anger (Pr 27,4) or lead to death (Gn 4,5.8; Nm 25,7f). The force here involved is not necessarily blameworthy in itself; the principle of judging depends upon whether the emotion is an asset or a liability, whether or not the driving power at work is unselfishness. Obviously there is such a thing as selfish motivation. With the sages it must be acknowledged that envy devastates the heart like "decay in the bone marrow" (Pr 14,30). Envy rises up between brothers (Gn 4,5-11; 37,11), women (30,1), spouses (Pr 6,24; Nm 5), races (Gn 26,14; Is 11,13), even between the just and the sinner (Ps 37,1; 73,3; Pr 3,31; 23, 17). Envy divides the Christian community by quarrels (R 13,13), arguments (1 Co 3,3; 2 Co 12,20), bitterness, and wrangling (Jm 3,14.16). From this summary it must not be concluded, as *Ecclesiastes*, that every human effort and

emotion comes from jealousy (Qo 4,4). Even though a well-intentioned zeal is sometimes the excuse of a narrow mind (Nm 11,29), there is also the streak of a very pure love (Ct 8,6) which one must acknowledge, especially in the seeming jealousy of God.

I. THE JEALOUS GOD

1. *The jealousy of the one God*. In most mythologies the gods believed in by men share their feelings. Gods are jealous of human happiness, careful to defend their privileges. Men try to appease the gods by according each some form of the adoration they demand. Israel herself knew this simple form of syncretism (2 K 23,4-14), even though she was supposed to belong totally to Yahweh (Dt 18,13).

The jealousy of Yahweh has nothing in common with any type of human pettiness. God is not jealous of some "other" who might be His equal; but He does want exclusive adoration from man whom He created in His own image* In anthropomorphic terms, this divine attitude is expressed as jealousy of "other gods." So the oldest texts vindicate the first commandment of the Decalogue: "You shall not bow down before another god, for God is called the 'jealous one'; He is a jealous God" (Ex 20,5; 34,14; Dt 6,14f). This intransigence is unparalleled in pagan religions and is found in early and later texts. For example, the divine attitude is equivalent to "devouring fire" (Dt 4,24); God becomes jealous of idols* (Ps 78,58;

Dt 32,16.21; 1 K 14,22), which are frequently called "idols of jealousy" (Ez 8,3.5; 2 K 21,7). Ultimately, if God is jealous, it is because He is holy* and cannot tolerate any slur cast on His honor (Js 24,19f).

2. *The zeal of the Lord of hosts.* The sentiment of jealousy is the foundation for the divine reactions in covenant history when an ardent zeal defends the oppressed and punishes the wicked. It is interesting to observe that the prophets Hosea and Jeremiah, who presented the covenant* as an espousal, do not use the word *jealousy,* but employ the term *anger* to express the intensity of God's love. From the earliest texts (Ex 20,3-6; 34,14) and up to the time of the exile (Dt 6,15; 29,19; Ez 5,13; 16, 38.42; 23,25), the jealousy of God is exclusively concerned with the relationship of God and Israel. It is seen as a reaction of the offended holiness of God (Js 24,19; Dt 4,23f) and puts all the violence of which it is capable at the service of this holiness (Ez 16,38.42; 23,25). But in exile the humiliation of Israel, the people of God and the bearer of the divine Name in the eyes of the nations, involves the humiliation of the divine Name itself (39,25; cf 36,23). To avenge the honor of His holiness, God's jealousy then turns against the pagans, who are responsible for this profanation (35,11; 36, 3-6). At the same time it brings about the salvation of Israel and works toward the redemption that Yahweh undertakes in favor of His people in His capacity as *goel,* avenging warrior (Is 42,13; 59,17; 26,11). And if Israel cries impatiently to God, appealing to His pity and fatherly feelings, in the name of His powerful jealousy (63,15), God promises them that this jealousy will hasten the arrival of the messianic times (9,6). It then appears that the passion burning in the heart of the holy God living in the midst of His people (Dt 6,15) was only a sign of the uncompromising nature of His love. This passion is now identified with the tenderness* of God (Jl 2,18; cf Ze 1,14f; 8,2) and with the love that brings Yahweh and Israel together in a fullness and a security that are unshakable (Ct 8,6).

II. THE ZEAL OF GOD

1. *Zealots of Yahweh.* Yahweh has many ways of arousing in Israel a zeal comparable to His own. For example, He excites the jealousy of His own people by benevolence to the nations* (Dt 32,21). Ordinarily He communicates His own fervor to one or other chosen individual. Thus Phinehas "has the same jealousy as I" (Nm 25,11) and the Lord is pacified by this. So the prophet Elijah, though under a real illusion when he says he alone is left, feels himself on fire with the divine zeal (1 K 19,14; Si 48,2). And the psalmist can proclaim: "The zeal of your house devours me" (Ps 69,10; 119,139). Mattathias the Maccabean consciously follows the example of those who preceded him on the ways of God's zeal (1 M 2,54.58). Seeing God's honor scoffed at by idolaters, his heart shuddered (2,24.27).

Reacting against pagan practices which lead to idolatrous surrender of principle (2 M 4,14), the pious* (1 M 2,42), from whom the pharisees* originate, are "zealous for good" (Si 51, 18) and seek* it eagerly. Others, called "zealots," consider it necessary to preach revolt against the pagan ruler (Ac 5,35ff) and violence against those such as Paul, whom they consider heretical (23,12ff).

2. *Christian zeal.* The followers of Jesus are going to find themselves as objects of a Jewish zeal that seeks to wipe out the Christians (Ac 5,17; 13,45; 17,5). Precisely this genuinely religious jealousy, though unenlightened (R 10, 2), inspired Saul to persecute the Church of God (Ph 3,6; G 1,14; Ac 22,3). Christians are not to be contaminated by that zeal even though its spirit can survive in some "zealous defenders of the Law" (Ac 21,20).

Jesus, however, had no trace of the zealot. He refuses to justify revolt against Caesar (Mt 22,15-21). Although He does have Simon the zealot among His disciples (Mk 3,18), He condemns the attitudes of the "sons of thunder" (3,17; Lk 9,54) though He accepts their protestations of martyrdom (Mt 20,22). From the moment of His arrest, He refuses to resist by taking up the arms at hand (Mt 26,51ff); for He has nothing in Him of the "gangster" or of the "gang leader" (26,55).

In His complete rejection of the zealot spirit, Jesus maintains a passion for the kingdom of heaven which "suffers violence" (Mt 11,12). Anyone wanting to follow* Him must sacrifice everything, even his life (16,24f). In the expulsion of the sellers from the temple, the disciples see the action of the just one whose zeal will lead Him to death (Jn 2,17).

There is, then, a Christian zeal. It is manifested by Paul for the Churches entrusted to him as the friend of the bridegroom (2 Co

11,2). The purity that He defends for all of them is the preservation from all false teaching, as in the OT jealousy was directed against idolatry. With regard to the Jewish people Paul's zeal is an echo of the zeal of Yahweh who aroused jealousy in His people by giving His grace to the nations* (R 11,11.14; 10,19).

It is possible to manifest zeal in various ways, as, for example, fund raising (2 Co 9,2). Zeal should always consist in seeking gifts of the highest order (1 Co 12,31; 14,1.12.39) because salvation given in Christ has aroused a "people zealous for good" (Tt 2,14; cf 1 P 3,13).

→Elijah OT 2—Fire OT I 3, II 2—God OT III 3—Jesus (Name of) IV—Law *B* III 5; *C* II——Love I OT 2—Pharisees 1—Run—Violence III 2—Wrath *A* 2; *B* II 2.

BRe & XLD dfb

ANALYTIC TABLE

A

AARON

Abandon→Confidence — Deception / Disappointment III—Faith—Providence—Sadness NT 1—Sleep I 1

Abba→Adoration II 3—Fathers & Father V 1, VI—God NT IV—Grace V—Heart II 2 b—Mission NT III 2—Prayer IV 2, V 2 d—Son of God NT I 1—Spirit of God NT V 5

ABEL

ABIDE

Abnegation→Cross II—Death NT III

ABRAHAM

Absence→Farewell Speeches—Hell NT III—Presence of God—Silence 1

Abstinence→Fasting—Wine I 2

Abundance→Blessing—Fullness—Wealth

Abyss→Beasts & Beast 3 a—Creation OT II 2 —Hell—Sea—Water I, II 2

Acclamation→Amen 1—Blessing II 3—Confession NT 1—Praise

Accomplish→Fulfill

Accuse→Satan—Trial

Actions→Arm & Hand—Fruit—Grace V—Heart I 1—Work—Works

ADAM

Admiration→Adoration—Blessing I, II 3, III 5 —Eucharist IV 2—Miracle—Praise II 2—Thanksgiving—Works OT I 1.2

Adonai→Lord OT—Name OT 4—Yahweh 3

Adoption→Child III—Fathers & Father III 3. 4, V 2, VI—Fruitfulness II 3—Son of God I; NT II—Sterility

ADORATION

ADULTERY

Advent→Day of the Lord—Fulfill NT 1—Visitation—Watch I

Adversary→Antichrist—Satan

Advice→Plan of God—Wisdom

Affliction→Console—Joy NT I 2, II 2—Persecution — Poor — Sadness — Suffering — Widows o

Afterlife→Death—Resurrection—Soul II 2.3

Agape→Eucharist II 3—Love O—Meal III

Age→Time OT III 2; NT II 2, III 1—World NT

Agony→Anguish—Death NT II 1—Sadness NT 1—Suffering NT II—Watch II 1

Agriculture→Earth OT I, II 3—Fruit—Harvest —Sowing I—Vine—Vintage—Work

Aid→Grace V—Providence 1—Salvation—Strength II—Woman OT 1

Alien→Stranger

Allegory→Figure NT III—Parable I 3

Alleluia→Praise II 2

Alliance→Covenant

ALMSGIVING

Alone→Solitude

Alpha & Omega→New IV—Time NT III 1—Writing V

ALTAR

AMEN

ANATHEMA

ANGELS

Ancestors→Adam I 3—Fathers & Father I 2, II —Fruitfulness III 1—Generation 1—Man I 1

Anger→Wrath

ANGUISH

ANIMALS

Announce→Figure—Gospel—Preach—Word of God

ANOINTING

Anthropomorphisms→God OT III 5—Idols I—Image I—Parables I 1

ANTICHRIST

Anxious→Cares

Apocalypse→Apparitions of Christ 3—Day of the Lord O, I 1—Mystery—Parable II—Revelation OT I 4; NT O, IV

Apostasy→Antichrist NT—Cross II 3—Heresy 1—Hypocrite 3—Idols—Watch III

APOSTLES

APPARITIONS OF CHRIST

ARK OF THE COVENANT

ARM & HAND

Arms→War

Arrhes→First Fruits I 2 b—Promises IV—Spirit of God NT V 3

ARROGANCE

Ascend→Ascension—Jerusalem OT III 3; NT I 1.4—Mountain—Pilgrimage—Way

ASCENSION

Ascetics→Abnegation—Death NT III 3—Fasting—Repentance/Conversion OT I 2—Watch I 2, II 2—Wine I 2—World NT III 1
ASHES
Assembly→Church—Faith OT IV—Heresy 2—People *A* II 6; *B* II 6; *C* O—Pilgrimage OT —Prayer II—Sabbath OT 3—Schism O—Worship
Assurance→Anguish 1—Confidence 3—Faith O —Liberation/Liberty III 3 a—Miracle III 3 a —Pride
Atonement→Expiation
AUTHORITY
Avarice→Arrogance 3—Cupidity—Sin IV 3 a—Wealth II, III
Avenge→Vengeance
Awake→Night OT 3—Resurrection—Sleep III —Watch I 2
Awe→Fear of God
Azymes→Bread II 3—Feasts OT I—Passover I 3, III 2—Pure NT II 3

B

Baal→Fathers & Father I 1, III 2—Idols II 1—Lord OT—Marriage OT II 1—Oil 1—Shame I 4—Spouse OT o
BABEL/BABYLON
Banquet→Joy OT; NT III—Meal—Wine 2 b
BAPTISM
Barren→Sterility
BEASTS & BEAST
BEATITUDE
Beauty→Glory I—Good & Evil I 1—Grace I—Perfume I—Woman OT 3
Beelzebul→Evil Spirits NT 1
Being→Creation—God OT II 2, III 1—Life—Name OT 2—Presence of God—Yahweh 2
Beget→Fathers & Father — Fruitfulness — Mother—New Birth—Sterility
Belial→Satan III
Believe→Faith
Benediction→Blessing
Betrothal→Marriage—Spouse
Bible→Book—Writing III
Bind/Unbind→Authority NT II 1—Church III 2 c—Pardon II 3
Birth→New Birth
Bishop→Church III 2 c—Ministry II 3.4
BLASPHEMY
BLESSING
Blind→Hardness of Heart—Hypocrite—Light & Dark—See OT II; NT I 1.2—Sin IV 2 a
BLOOD
Blush→Shame
BODY

BODY OF CHRIST
Boldness→Confidence—Liberation/Liberty III 3 a—Pride
BOOK
Bounty→Blessing—Gift—Good & Evil—Justice *A* I OT 4—Love—Meekness 3—Mercy—Tenderness
BREAD
Breaking of Bread→Bread I 1—Communion NT 1—Eucharist II 3—Meal III—Passover III 1.
Breath→Life II 2—Man—Soul I 1, II 1—Spirit OT 2.3—Spirit of God O
Bride(groom)→Spouse
BROTHER
Brow→Face
BUILD
BURIAL

C

Caesar→Antichrist NT 3—Authority NT I 2, II 3—Babel/Babylon 6—King NT I—Numbers II 2
Cain→Abel—Brother OT 1—Hate I 1.2
CALAMITY
Calendar→Day of the Lord NT III 3—Sabbath —Time intr.; OT I, NT II 3—Week
CALLING
Calumny→Human Speech 1—Lie I—Satan O
Canaan→City OT 1—Earth OT II—Inheritance OT—Joshua 1
Canticle→Blessing III 5—Glory V—Praise—Thanksgiving
CAPTIVITY
CARES
Carmel (mount)→Elijah OT 2—Mountain II 1
Catechesis→Disciple—Preach I 4—Teach OT I; NT II—Tradition
Celibacy→Charisms 2—Marriage NT II—Sexuality I 2—Sterility—Virginity—Woman NT 2
Cemetery→Burial—Death OT I 2.3—Hell OT I—Sleep I 1
Chaos→Clothing I—Creation OT II 2.3—Desert O—Sea 1
CHARISMS
Charity→Almsgiving—Charisms II 2.3—Communion—Conscience 2—Gift—Humility III —Hunger & Thirst OT 2; NT 3—Love—Prayer IV 4—Unity—Widows 3—Works NT II 2
Chastity→Marriage NT II—Sexuality—Sterility III—Virginity—Widows 3—Woman NT 2
Cherubim→Angels OT 1—Ark of the Covenant O
Chief→Authority—Body of Christ III 2—

Church V 1—Head—King—Shepherd & Flock
CHILD
Choice→Election—Good & Evil—Heresy 1—Liberation/Liberty I—Way II
Christ→Anointing III 5—Jesus Christ II—Messiah—Mystery NT II
Christian→Calling III—Church—Disciple NT—Holy NT II, IV—Image V—New III 3 b
CHURCH
CIRCUMCISION
Citadel→City—Rock 1—Strength I 1
CLOTHING
CLOUD
Collection→Almsgiving NT 3 b—Church IV 3, V 1
Combat→Enemy—Faithfulness NT 2—Prayer V 2 a—Run—Trial/Temptation
Coming of the Lord→Cloud 3.4—Day of the Lord—Mission NT I—Visitation
COMMUNION
Community→ Brother — Church — Circumcision OT 1—Communion—Meal—People—Prophet OT I 3—Unity
Comparison→Figure—Image—Parable
Compassion→Console—Mercy—Tenderness
Complaint→Prayer I 2, II 2—Repentance/Conversion OT I 2—Suffering OT I 1—Widows 1
Concupiscence→Cupidity—Desire II
Condemnation→Curse V—Judgment—Punishments 2—Trial
CONFESSION
CONFIDENCE
Confirm→Amen—Anointing III 6—Strength
Confusion→Arrogance 4—Deception/Disappointment I 2—Pride—Shame
Conquest→Wrath OT II 2—Joshua 1—Plan of God OT I—Victory—War OT II 2
CONSCIENCE
Consecrate→Anathema—Anointing III—Blessing II 2—Blood OT 3 d—First Fruits—Holy Imposition of Hands OT; NT 2—Priesthood OT II 1—Sacrifice—Seal 2 b—Spirit of God OT III; NT I 1.2, V 5
CONSOLE
Constancy→Hope—Patience—Persecution II—Trial/Temptation
Contemplate→Face—Glory III 2, IV o—Presence of God NT III—See
Continence→Sexuality I—Virginity
Contrition→Confession NT II—Humility II, IV Repentance/Conversion—Sadness OT 3
Conversion→Repentance/Conversion
Correction→Education O, I 2 b, III 2—Punishments

Courage→Persecution II—Pride—Strength
Counsel→Plan of God—Wisdom
COVENANT
Covetousness→Cupidity—Desire II, III—Flesh II 2 b—Good & Evil I 4, III 1.4—Sin II 2, IV 3 a
Crib→Shepherd & Flock
CREATION
CROSS
Crown→Reward III 2—Victory NT 2
Cry—Joy O—Prayer—Suffering OT I 1
CUP
CUPIDITY
CURSE

D

Danger→Fear of God II—Salvation
DAVID
Day→Day of the Lord—Light & Dark—Night—Stars 1.2—Time OT I
DAY OF THE LORD
Deacon→Ministry—Service III 2
DEATH
Debt→Pardon—Reward—Sin IV 1 a
Decalogue→Law—Word of God II 1 a
Deceive→Error NT—Hypocrite—Lie—Satan
DECEPTION/DISAPPOINTMENT
Dedication→Feasts OT I; NT I—Holy OT III 1—Temple OT
Defeat→Enemy II 2—Shame I 1—Victory OT 2—War OT III 2
Deliverance→Captivity—Death OT III—Exodus—Justice A II OT; B II OT, NT 2—Liberation/Liberty II, III—Night OT 1; NT 1—Redemption OT 1; NT 1—War OT III 1
Depart→Ascension II 4—Calling I—Exodus—Farewell Speeches—Mission OT I; NT II—Way
Deportation→Captivity I—Exile
Deposit→Tradition
Descent→Fathers & Father I 2, III 2—Fruitfulness—Generation—House I
Descend→Ascension I, II 1—Heaven IV—Hell
DESERT
DESIRE
Desolation→Calamity — Console — Sadness — Solitude
Destiny→Plan of God—Predestine 1 b—Responsibility—Reward II 2
Destroy→Anathema OT—Build I 2—Temple OT I 1.2.3; NT I
Devil→Satan
Dew→Heaven IV—Water I
Dialogue→Communion — Love — Silence — Solitude II 1—Word of God
Diaspora→Dispersion

ANALYTIC TABLE

Didascalia→Teach NT II 3
Discernment→Conscience—Evil Spirits NT 2—
Prophet OT III 1—Sign—Simple 1—Spirit
NT 1—Taste 1—Trial/Temptation NT III—
Will of God NT II 1.
DISCIPLE
Disinterestedness→Almsgiving NT 1—Gift NT
3—Grace IV—Love—Reward
Disobedience→Listen 1—Obedience II—Sin I 1
—Unbelief
DISPERSION
Dissension→Heresy—Schism—Unity
Divination→Magic
Division→Dispersion—Heresy—Man II 1 a—
Schism—Unity
Divorce→Adultery 1—Marriage OT II 3; NT
I 1
Docility→Child—Disciple—Hardness of Heart
—Listen—Simple 2
Doctor of Law→Disciple OT 3—Law B; C I 2
—Pharisees—Teach NT I
Doctrine→Gospel — Preach — Teach — Tradi-
tion—Truth NT 2—Wisdom—Word of God
Doubt→Confidence—Sin I 1—Unbelief
DOVE
Doxology→Blessing III 5, IV o 1—Confession
OT 1; NT 1—Glory V—Praise
Dragon→Animals—Beasts & Beast—Persecu-
tion I 4 a—Satan—Sea 2
DREAMS
Drink→Blood OT 2—Cup—Hunger & Thirst—
Milk—Nourishment—Water—Wine
DRUNKENNESS
Duplicity→Heart I—Hypocrite—Lie—Lips 1—
Simple 2
Dust→Adam I 1—Ashes—Death OT I 2
Duty→Conscience—Good & Evil—Law—Obe-
dience II 3—Service II, III—Will of God NT
II

E

EARTH
Eat→Bread — Hunger & Thirst — Meal —
Nourishment—Tree 1
Eden→Creation OT II 1—Paradise
EDUCATION
Egoism→Cupidity—Earth OT II 3 b—Love I
OT 2; NT 2—Reward III 2—Shame—Sin I 1,
III 1—Wealth III 2
EGYPT
ELECTION
Elders→Ministry II 1.3.4—Old Age 2—Priest-
hood NT III 2—Shepherd & Flock NT 2—
Tradition OT II 2; NT I 1
ELIJAH

Elohim (El)→Creation OT I—Fathers & Father
III 2—God OT II, IV—Name OT 4—Yah-
weh o.
Emmanuel→Abide II 2—Jesus (Name of) II—
Presence of God OT I—Solitude II 1
Encounter→Communion — Face 3.4 — Gate—
Presence of God—See—Seek—Visitation
End of the world→Day of the Lord—Time OT
III; NT III—World OT III; NT III 3
ENEMY
Enfranchise→Liberation/Liberty II, III—Slave
Engagement→Amen—Faith O—Faithfulness—
Oath—Promises
Entrails→Mercy—Mother I 1, II 1—Tenderness
Envy→Death OT II 1—Hate—Satan I—Zeal O
Epiphany→Apparitions of Christ 1—Day of the
Lord NT O—Glory III 2—Revelation NT O,
III
Episcopos→Hospitality 2—Ministry II 3—Shep-
herd & Flock NT 2
Err→Error—Seek—Way
ERROR
Eschatology→City NT 2—Creation OT III 2;
NT II 3—Day of the Lord—Earth OT II 4—
Election NT III—Figure OT II 3—Glory IV
1—Hope NT IV—Hour 1—Inheritance OT
II 1—Jerusalem OT III 3; NT II 3—Jesus
Christ I 1, II 1 a—Kingdom OT III; NT III
3—Light & Dark OT II 3; NT II 4—Meal IV
—New IV—Paradise 2 b. 3—Passover III 3
—Peace II 3 b—Plan of God OT II; NT IV
—People B; C III—Praise II 3—Salvation OT
I 2—Time OT III; NT II 1, III—Virginity
NT 3—Visitation OT 3; NT—Wine II 2
Eternal→God OT V; NT II 2
Eternity→Abide I 2—Heaven VI—Hope NT
IV—Mountain I 1—Old Age 2—Plan of God
OT III—Time intr. 2 b
EUCHARIST
Eunuch→Sexuality I 2—Sterility—Virginity
Eve→Adam I 2 o, II 2—Church IV 1—Desire II
—Fruitfulness I 1—Mary V—Mother—Wo-
man OT 1
Event→Miracle—Sign OT II 4—Time OT II
Evil→Good & Evil
EVIL SPIRITS
Exaltation of Christ→Ascension—Glory—Hu-
mility IV—Jesus Christ II 1 a—Pride—
Strength II
Examination→Conscience — Judgment—Trial/
Temptation
EXAMPLE
Excommunication→Anathema NT
EXHORT
EXILE
EXODUS

Exorcism→Anointing II 2—Evil Spirits NT—Miracle II 2 b—Satan II, III—Sickness/Healing O

Experience→Know—Old Age 2—Presence of God OT II, III—Taste 2—Wisdom

EXPIATION

Extreme Unction Anointing II 1—Oil 2—Sickness/Healing NT II 1

Eye→Light & Dark OT II 1.2; NT II 3—Scandal II—See—Simple 2

F

Fables→Error NT—Heresy 3—Teach NT II 3—Truth NT 2 c

FACE

FAITH

Faithful→Apostles II 2—Disciples NT—Faithfulness NT 2

FAITHFULNESS

Family→Authority OT I 1.2; NT II 2—Brother—Build I 1—Child—Education—Fathers & Father—Generation—House—Man I 1 c, II 1 a—Marriage—Mother—People A II 1—Priesthood OT 1 1—Teach OT I 1—Woman OT 2; NT 3

Famine→Calamity 1—Hunger & Thirst

FAREWELL SPEECHES

FASTING

Fatality→Liberation/Liberty I—Predestine

FATHERLAND

FATHERS & FATHER

Fatigue→Rest—Work

FEAR OF GOD

Fear→Anglish—Confidence 3—Fear of God I—Unbelief I 1

FEASTS

Feast→Joy OT; NT III—Meal—Wine II 2 b

FIGURE

FIRE

Firmness→Confidence—Faith O—Faithfulness—Truth OT 1.2

Finger of God→Arms & Hand 1—Writing III

First→Adam—First Fruits—God OT I—Head—New II 2—Resurrection NT I 4, II o—Seek III—Time OT III 1

First-born→First-Fruits—Jesus Christ II 1 d—New Birth 1—Passover I 2—Resurrection NT I

FIRST-FRUITS

Flavor→Salt 2.3—Taste

FLESH

Flight→Desert—Egypt 1—Exodus

Flock→Shepherd & Flock

FLOOD

FOLLOW

Food→Animals II 2—Bread—Eucharist II 3, III — Manna — Meal — Milk — Nourishment—Oil 1—Pure OT I 3; NT II 1—Salt 2.3—Tree 1

Formalism→Hypocrite—Pharisee—Pure NT I 1

Forty→Ascension II 3—Numbers I 1

Foundations→Apostles I 1—Build II, III 2—Church III 2—Rock 1

FRIEND

FRUIT

FRUITFULNESS

FULFILL

FULLNESS

Future→Feasts OT II 2—Hope—Time—Worship OT II; NT III o.3

G

Galilee→Apparitions of Christ 3—City NT 1—Jerusalem NT I 1.2

GATE

Gather→Body of Christ III—Church I, II 1—Communion OT 5; NT—Dispersion—Meal—Pentecost II 1 c—Unity

Gehenna→Fire OT III; NT I 1—Hell OT II

Genealogy→Fruitfulness—Generation

GENERATION

Generosity→Almsgiving—Blessing I, II 1—Gift—Grace—Love—Wealth

Gentiles→Apostles II 2—Nations

GIFT

GLORY

Gluttony→Desire II—Hunger & Thirst OT 1a

Gnosis→Know NT 3—Jesus Christ II 2—Mystery O—Revelation O

GOD

GODLESS MEN

Goel→Blood OT 1—Liberation/Liberty I 2—Vengeance 1.3

GOOD & EVIL

GOSPEL

Govern→Authority—King—Ministry II

GRACE

Grain→Fruit II—Harvest—Martyr 2—Sowing

Gratuity→Abraham I 1, II 3—Election—Grace—Predestine—Reward III 2

Greatness→Glory—God III 5—Holy OT I 1—Power—Strength

Greek→Church IV 2—Heresy 3—Jew—Nations NT—Wisdom O

GROWTH

Guide→Ark of the Covenant I—Cloud 1—Example—Follow—Way I, III

H

Hades→Hell

Hand→Arm & Hand

Happiness→Beatitude—Good & Evil II 1.3—Heaven VI—Paradise—Peace

HARDNESS OF HEART

HARVEST

HATE

HEAD

Healing→Sickness/Healing

Health→Peace I 2—Sickness/Healing

Hear→Apparitions of Christ 4 c—Faith NT I 2—Listen—Preach—Word of God NT I 2

HEART

HEAVEN

Heavenly Armies→Angel—Power III 2—Stars—Yahweh 3

HEBREW

Height→Ascension—Heaven—Mountain

HELL

HERESY

Hide→Mystery—Revelation—See

Hierarchy→Charisms II 4—Ministry II—Priesthood OT I 4.5

High Places→Altar 1—Mountain II 2—Pilgrimage—Presence of God OT III 1

HOLY

Holocaust→Fire OT II 1—Sacrifice OT II; Nt I

Homicide→Blood OT 1—Hate—Lie III—Satan I—Sin IV 2 b—Vengeance 1—Violence II—Wrath A

Homage→Adoration—Obedience—Praise

Honey→Earth OT II 1—Meekness 1—Milk 2

Honour→Anointing I 2—Glory IV 5—Pride

HOPE

Horeb (Mount)→Covenant OT I 1—Elijah OT 1—Fire OT I 1—Mountain II 1—Name OT 2

Hosannah→Praise IV

HOSPITALITY

HOUR

HOUSE

HUMAN SPEECH

Humiliation→Humility—Shame I 1

HUMILITY

HUNGER & THIRST

HYPOCRITE

I

IDOLS

IMAGE

Imitate→Disciple NT 2—Example—Fathers & Father IV—Figure—Follow

Immolation→Death—Sacrifice

Immortality→Death—Image II OT—Life IV 5—Resurrection—Soul II

IMPOSITION OF HANDS

Imprecation→Curse O—Prayer II 2—Vengeance 2 b

Incarnation→Ascension II 1—Body II 2—Body of Christ I—Fathers & Father V 3—Flesh I 3 b, II 2 c—Jesus Christ—Mediator II 1—Presence of God NT I—Son of God NT I 3—Visitation NT 1

Incense→Perfume 2

Infidelity→Adultery—Faithfulness—Spouse OT 1

Inhabit→Abide—Earth OT II—Fullness 2—House

INHERITANCE

Initiative of God→Abraham I 1, II 3—Apparitions of Christ 4 a—Calling—Election—Grace—Know OT 1—Predestine

Innocent→Blood OT 1—Child—Pure OT II; NT—Simple—White

Inspiration→Spirit of God OT II—Word of God OT I 1; NT I 1—Writing III, V

Instinct→Education—Teach—Wisdom

Insult→Blasphemy—Curse

Integrity→Justice O; A I—Perfection—Pure—Rights/Laws—Simple

Intelligence→Know—Revelation—Wisdom

Intercession→Abraham I 3—Expiation 2—Mediator—Moses 3—Paraclete o—Prayer

Interpretation→ Dreams OT — Jesus Christ concl.—Parable III

Invite→Calling—Exhort

Isaac→Abraham I 2, II 1—Passover I 6 b

ISRAEL

J

Jacob→Abraham II 1—Brother OT 2—Earth OT II 1—Election OT I 3 b—Enemy I 1—Fathers & Father I 2, II—House II 1—Imposition of Hands OT—Israel OT o—Lie I 1—Name OT 1—People A II 1—Power I 1—Wealth I 1

Jealousy→Fire OT I 3—God OT III 3.4—Hate—Love I—Sin III 3—Spouse OT 1—Zeal

Jehovah→Yahweh 3

Jeremiah→Persecution I 1—Prophet—Repentance/Conversion OT II 3—Servant of God II 2

JERUSALEM

JESUS (NAME OF)

JESUS CHRIST

JEW

JOHN THE BAPTIST

Jordan→Baptism II, III 1—Water IV 2
Joseph→David—Mary O, II 4, III 2
JOSHUA
Journey→Pilgrimage—Stranger II—Way
JOY
Jubilee→Week 1
Judah→Israel OT 2—Jerusalem OT II 1—Jew
I 1—King OT I 1.3
Judaism→Authority OT II 2—Israel OT 2 b—
Jew—Nations OT IV—People *A* II 1—Tra-
dition OT II 2; NT I 2—Works OT II 3
Judaizers→Circumcision NT 1—Heresy 2.3—
Law *C* III—Pharisees 2
JUDGMENT
Jurisdiction→Apostles II 1—Authority NT II
1.3—Church III 2 c—Ministry II
Just→Abel—Beatitude OT I 2, II—Godless
Man OT 2; NT 1,2—Hell OT II—Jesus Christ
II 1 b—Justice—Justification—Noah—Per-
secution
JUSTICE
JUSTIFICATION

K

Kerygma→Confession NT 1—Gospel III 1—
Preach I 2.3—Teach O; NT II 1.2
Key→Gate
KING
KINGDOM
KNEE
KNOW
Kyrios→God—Jesus Christ II 1 a—Lord—
Name OT 4; NT 3—Yahweh 3

L

LAMB OF GOD
Lamentation→Death OT I 3—Prayer II 2—Re-
pentance/Conversion OT I, III—Sadness OT
3.4; NT 1—Suffering OT I 1
LAMP
Language→People *C* II—Salt 3—Tongue 2—
Writing V
Largesse→ Almsgiving — Blessing — Gift —
Grace—Wealth I 3.4
Last→Adam II 2—Day of the Lord OT II; NT
—Fulfill—God OT I 1; NT IV—New—Time
OT III; NT III
LAUGHTER
LAW
Laziness→Sleep II—Watch O, I—Work I 2
Leaven→Bread II 3—Passover I 3, III 2
Legalism→Law—Pharisees—Pure NT I 1.2
LEPROSY
Letter & Spirit→Covenant NT II 1—Law—
Writing IV, V

Leviathan→Beasts & Beast
Levite→Aaron—Election OT I 3 c—First Fruits
II—Priesthood OT I—Teach OT I 2
Libation→Bread II 1—Sacrifice—Wine I 2
LIBERATION/LIBERTY
LIE
LIFE
LIGHT & DARK
LIPS
LISTEN
Liturgy→Almsgiving OT 3—Altar—Amen 1—
Blessing—Confession—Covenant OT I 3.4, II
1—Day of the Lord III 3—Feasts—Memory
4 b—Perfume 2—Pilgrimage—Praise II, III,
IV—Prayer II, V—Repentance/Conversion
OT I, III—Sacrifice—Temple—Thanksgiving
—Time NT II 3—Worship
Logos→Word of God
LOINS
LORD
LOVE
Loyalty→Lie—Lips 1—Truth OT 2; NT 1

M

MAGIC
Mammon→Cupidity NT 2—Service III o—
Wealth III 2
MAN
Manifestation→Apparitions of Christ 1—Day
of the Lord—Fire OT I—Glory III—Light
& Dark OT I 2, II 2; NT I 3—Presence of
God OT II—Resurrection NT I 1.2—Revela-
tion—Sign—Storm—Transfiguration
MANNA
Marana Tha→Hope NT IV—Jesus Christ II 1 a
—Lord NT—Worship NT III 3
MARRIAGE
MARTYR
Marvels→Desert OT II 2—Miracle—Sign
MARY
Master→ Authority — Disciple — Education —
Fathers & Father I 1—Lord—Marriage OT
II 1—Obedience—Reward I—Service—Slave
—Teach
MEDIATOR
MEEKNESS
Meet→ Communion — Face 3.4 — Gate — Pre-
sence of God—See—Seek—Visitation
MELCHIZEDEK
MEMORY
MERCY
Merit→Grace IV—Justice—Justification II—
Reward
Message→Angels—Faith NT II 2—Gospel—

Mission—Preach—Prophet OT II 2.3—Repentance/Conversion OT II; NT I—Word of God OT I 2, III 1

MESSIAH

MILK

MINISTRY

MIRACLE

Mirror→Face—Image—Wisdom OT III 2

Misery→Hunger & Thirst—Mercy—Poor

Misfortune→ Ashes 2 — Calamity — Curse — Drunkenness 1—Good & Evil II 2.3—Shame —Suffering—Water II 2

Mislead→Antichrist NT—Error—Heresy—Hypocrite—Lie II 3—Satan—Shepherd & Flock

MISSION

Mock→Godless Man—Laughter

Moderation→Drunkenness 2—Virtues & Vices —Watch—Wine I

Modesty→Humility

Money→Arrogance 3—Cupidity—Poor NT III —Service III—Wealth

Moon→Stars—Time OT I—Week 1

Morals→Flesh II—Good & Evil—Justice—Reward III 2—Virtues & Vices

Mortification→Cross II—Death III 3

MOSES

MOTHER

MOUNTAIN

Mourning→Ashes 2—Burial—Console—Death —Fasting—Sadness—Widows

Mouth→ Human Speech — Lips — Tongue — Word of God

Murder→Abel—Blood OT 1; NT 1—Hate I 1 —Heart II 2 a—Vengeance 1—Violence II

Murmuring→Desert OT I 2—Unbelief

MYSTERY

Myth→Apparitions of Christ 6—Creation OT I —Figure OT II 1.4—King O—Resurrection OT I—Time intr. 1

N

NAME

NATIONS

Nebuchadnezzar→Arrogance 2—Babel/Babylon 2.5—Power IV 2—War OT III 2

Need→Desire—Hunger & Thirst

NEIGHBOR

NEW

NEW BIRTH

NIGHT

Niniveh→Babel/Babylon 2.3—City OT 2—Repentance/Conversion NT II

NOAH

Nomad→Abide—City OT 1—Shepherd & Flock O—Stranger II—Way—Wine I 2

Nothingness→Ashes—Creation OT II 3—Death OT I 2.4—Deception/Disappointment I 1—Idols II 2—Lie II 1

NOURISHMENT

Nudity→Clothing II—Sexuality I 1—Shame I 2

NUMBERS

O

OATH

OBEDIENCE

Oblivion→Drunkenness 2—Memory 2.3

Odour→Perfume

Offence→Pardon—Sin III 2—Vengeance

Offering→Altar—Bread II—Eucharist IV 2, V —Gift OT 2; NT 2—First-Fruits—Perfume 2—Sacrifice—Wine I 2—Worship

OIL

OLD AGE

Olives (Mount of)→Ascension II 3.4—Mountain III 1

Open→Book III, IV—Faith NT II 2—Gate—Heaven V 4—Hospitality 2—Lips 2—Listen 1

Oppression→Arrogance 2.3—Enemy II 2—Humility II—Persecution—Power III 1—Violence I 1.2

Oracle→Ark of the Covenant II—Priesthood OT II 2—Revelation OT I 1—Seek I

Orphan→Console 2—Poor—Widows 1

P

Pagan→Anathema OT—Apostles II 2—Heresy 2.3—Idols—Jew I—Nations—People C II

Pain→ Console — Punishments — Sadness — Suffering—Trial/Temptation—Work II

PARABLE

PARACLETE

PARADISE

PARDON

Parents→Child—Education O, I 1—Fathers & Father—Mother

Parousia→ Antichrist NT — Apparitions of Christ 1—Ascension III—Day of the Lord NT—Farewell Speeches NT 1—Glory IV 1, V—Hope NT II, IV—Jesus Christ II 1 a—Judgment O; NT—King NT II 2—Kingdom NT III 3—Passover III 1.3—Parience I NT 2 —Perfection NT 6—Plan of God NT IV—Spouse NT 3 b c—Time NT III—Victory OT 3 a—Visitation NT—War NT III—Watch I

Parresia→Confidence 3 — Liberation/Liberty III 3 a—Prayer IV 4—Preach II 2 b—Pride —Shame II 1—Spirit of God NT IV

Passage→Abide—Death—Passover—Time NT

II 2—Trial/Temptation NT III 2—Visitation —World OT III 3

Passion→Desire—Love O; I OT 2—Seek— Wrath—Zeal

Passion of Christ→Cross—Death NT II—Glory IV 3—Hour 2—Jesus Christ I 3, II 1 b—King NT I 2—Patience I NT 1—Prayer IV 2—Redemption NT 2.4—Sacrifice NT—Sadness NT 1—Servant of God III 1.2—Sin IV 1 d. 3 c—Suffering NT II

PASSOVER

PATIENCE

Patriarchs→Abraham—Election OT I 3 b— Fatherland OT—Fathers & Father I 2, II

Paul→Apostles II—Apparitions of Christ 5— Faith III—Gospel IV—Law C III—Mission NT II 2—Nations NT II 2

PEACE

Pedagogy→Education—Law C III 2

PENTECOST

PEOPLE

Perdition→Babel/Babylon 5.6—Death—Godless Man OT 3; NT 3—Hardness of Heart— Hell O; OT II; NT I, III—Salvation NT I 1 b—Seek III—Sin—Way II

PERFECTION

Perseverance→Confidence 3 — Faithfulness — Patience II.

PERSECUTION

Person→Body O, I 1—Clothing I 1—Face— Heart O—Jesus (Name of) I—Name—Soul I 3—Visitation OT 2

Perversion→Desire II—Good & Evil I 4—Sin— Virtues & Vices 2

PETER

Pharaoh→Arrogance 2—Egypt—Hardness of Heart I 1, II 1.2—King O—Miracle I 3— Moses 1.2—Power III 1—Punishments 1

Philanthropy→Almsgiving OT 3; NT 2 c— Friend—Love II

PIETY

PILGRIMAGE

Pity→Mercy—Miracle II 2 b—Pardon—Sickness/Healing NT I 1—Tenderness

Plague→Calamity—Leprosy—Miracle I 1— Passover I 2—Punishments—Sickness/Healing OT—Wrath B OT I 1

PLAN OF GOD

Plant→Build I 2, III 2.3—Harvest II—Sowing —Vine

Pleroma→Church V 1—Fullness

Polygamy→Adultery 1—Marriage OT II 2.3

POOR

Possession (diabolical)→Evil Spirits NT— Miracle II 2 b—Satan II—Sickness/Healing

Posterity→Abraham I 3, II—Beatitude OT II 1

—Fathers & Father I, II—Fruitfulness—Inheritance NT I—Woman OT 1

POWER

Powerlessness→Flesh I 3 b—Power IV 1.2, V 3

Powers (heavenly)→Angels—Ascension II 2— Heaven—Power III 2—Reconciliation II 1— Stars

PRAISE

PRAYER

PREACH

PREDESTINE

Preexistence→Ascension II 1—Jesus Christ II 1 d. 2 d

Presbyterate→Ministry II—Priesthood NT III 2

PRESENCE OF GOD

PRIDE

Priest→Aaron—Anointing III 3—Election OT I 3 c—Law B III 1—Melchizedek 2.3—Messiah OT II 2—Ministry II 4—Priesthood— Teach OT I 2

PRIESTHOOD

Primacy→Authority—Head—King—Peter 2

Prison→Captivity

Privation→Fasting—Poor NT III 1—Wine I 2

Prize→Justice A I OT 3; B II OT—Redemption NT 1—Reward—Run 2

Proclaim→Gospel III 1—Plan of God NT II— Preach I 2—Teach NT II

Prodigy→Magic—Miracle—Sign—Works OT I

Profane→Holy O

Profession of Faith→Confession O; OT 1; NT 1—Faith

Progress→ Build — Education — Growth — Perfection NT 5—Run 2—Time OT III 1— Way

PROMISES

Proof→Sign—Trial/Temptation—Witness

Property→Earth OT I 1, II 2; NT II 3—Inheritance OT I 1.3—Wealth

PROPHET

Propitiatory→Ark of the Covenant—Blood NT 2—Expiation 2—Temple OT I 1

Proselyte→Baptism I 2—Dispersion 1—Fruitfulness II 3—Mission OT II 2—Nations OT IV 2; NT—Stranger I

Prostitution→Adultery 1—Babel/Babylon 6— Marriage OT II 3—Sexuality II, III—Spouse

Protect→Arm & Hand—Mountain—Providence —Salvation—Shadow II

PROVIDENCE

Prudence→Simple 2—Virtues & Vices 1—Wisdom

Psalms→Blessing III 5—David 3—Praise— Prayer II—Thanksgiving OT 3

PUNISHMENTS

PURE

Q

Queen→Mother I 3

R

Rabbi→Jesus Christ II 1 a—Jesus (Name of) III—Teach NT I 1

Race→Fathers & Father I, II—Fruitfulness—Generation—Nations—People

Rahab→Beasts & Beast 1.2

Rain→Desert O—Flood—Fruit II—Heaven I—Storm 1—Water

Ransom→Liberation/Liberty II 1—Redemption

Ready→Watch

Recognition→Eucharist I 1—Thanksgiving

RECONCILIATION

Red Sea→Exodus OT 2; NT 1—Sea 2

REDEMPTION

Refuge→City OT 2.3—Confidence—Egypt 1—Mountain—Rock—Salvation—Shadow II

Refusal→Hardness of Heart—Unbelief—Visitation NT 1—Will of God OT II

Regeneration→Baptism IV—New III 3—New Birth 3

Reign→King—Kingdom

Reject→Curse—Election OT III 1; NT III

Religion→Almsgiving OT 3; NT 1—Fear of God IV—Piety—Sacrifice OT III—Temple OT II 3—Worship

REMNANT

Renunciation→Cross II—Death NT III 3—Follow 2 a—Good & Evil III 3—Perfection NT 3—Poor NT II, III—Wealth III—Wine I 2

Renew→Covenant OT II 1—New

Repent→Baptism I 3, III 2—Confession NT 2—Pardon—Repentance/Conversion

REPENTANCE/CONVERSION

Reprove→Curse—Hardness of Heart I 2 a—Hell OT II; NT I—Wrath B

RESPONSIBILITY

REST

RESURRECTION

Return→Exile II 3—Repentance/Conversion O—Watch I

REVELATION

Revolt→Authority OT II 2; NT II 3—Obedience II 1, IV—Sin—Zeal II

REWARD

RIGHT HAND

RIGHTS/LAWS

Righteousness→Justice—Simple 2—Truth OT 1.2; NT 1

Rites→Altar 2—Piety OT 2—Priesthood OT II 1—Time OT I 2—Worship

Road→Way

ROCK

Rome→Babel/Babylon 6

Royalty→King—Kingdom

RUN

S

Sabaoth→Ark of the Covenant I—Power I 1, III 2—Stars 2—Yahweh 3—Zeal I 2

SABBATH

Sacrament→Sign NT I 2

Sacred→Anathema OT—Fear of God I—Holy—Meal II—Pure OT I 1—Sacrifice—Sexuality II 1

SACRIFICE

SADNESS

Saducees→King OT II 3—Law B III 5—Pharisees 1—Resurrection OT III

Salary→Grace IV—Justice—Kingdom NT II 3—Reward—Work II, III

SALT

SALVATION

Salvation History→Antichrist—Covenant OT II 3—Creation OT III 1—Day of the Lord—Feasts—Figure OT II—Fulfill NT 1—Generation—Hour—Israel—Jesus Christ II 1 a d; concl.—Judgment OT I 2—Law B III 3—Memory—Mystery NT II—People—Plan of God—Prayer I—Providence o—Remnant—Revelation OT I 3, II; NT IV—Sign OT I Time OT II—War OT III—Will of God OT I 1—Word of God OT II 1 b. 2 a—Works OT I 1—World OT II 3

Sanctuary→Ark of the Covenant—Pilgrimage OT 1—Temple—Worship

SATAN

Satisfy→Abraham I 3—Fruit—Joy—Harvest I—Meal—Wealth I 3.4

Savior→Jesus Christ II 1 b. 2 c—Joshua 2—Salvation

SCANDAL

SCHISM

Science→Conscience—God NT II 2—Know—Wisdom

Scorn→Arrogance 1—Pride OT 3; NT 2

Scourge→Beasts & Beast 3 a—Calamity

Scribe→Law C I—Priesthood OT II 2—Teach OT I 4; NT I, II 2—Tradition OT II; NT I 1

SEA

SEAL

Secret→God NT II 3.4—Mystery—Plan of God OT II; NT II—Revelation—Seal

Sects→Heresies—John the Baptist—Law B III 5—Pharisees—Priesthood OT III 1—Tradition OT II 2—Zeal II

Security→Faith O—Gate OT I—Peace
Seduce→ Antichrist — Error — Heresy — Satan —Trial/Temptation
Seed→King OT II 1.2—Promises II 4—Servant of God II 2—Sowing II 1
SEE
SEEK
Send→Apostles—Mediator—Mission
Sentiments→Heart O—Loins 2
Separation→ Anathema — Dispersion — Holy —Schism—Solitude—Unity
Seraphim→Angels NT 1
Serpent→Animals—Antichrist OT 1—Beasts & Beast—Cross I 4—Desert OT I 3—Mary V 2—Satan I—Sign NT I 2—Simple 2
SERVANT OF GOD
SERVICE
Seven→Apostles I 2—Ministry II 2—Numbers
SEXUALITY
Shaddai→God OT II 1—Mountain O—Name OT 2
SHADOW
SHAME
Share→Almsgiving—Bread I 1—Communion OT 5; NT—Love II
Sheep→Animals—Lamb of God—Shepherd & Flock
Sheol→Death—Hell—Light & Dark OT II 3—Resurrection OT—Sea 2—Shadow I 2—Soul II 2
Shelter→Confidence—House Mountain—Rock I—Shadow II
SHEPHERD & FLOCK
Shut→Gate—Seal
SICKNESS/HEALING
SIGN
SILENCE
SIMPLICITY
SIN
Sinai→Cloud 2—Covenant OT I—Fire OT I—Law B I 1, II 2—Mountain II 1.3, III 2—Transfiguration 2
Sincere→Human Speech — Hypocrite — Lie—Lips 1—Oath—Simplicity 2—Tongue 1—Truth OT 2; NT 1
Slander→Human Speech 1—Lips 1—Tongue 1
SLAVE
SLEEP
Small→Child—Humility—Poor
Sobriety→Drunkenness—Watch I 2, II 2—Wine I
Society→Authority OT II—Brother—Church—City—Clothing I 1—Covenant OT O—Generation—Justice A 1—Liberation/Liberty II 4, III 2 o—Man I 1 c. 2 c—Marriage OT II 1—People—Rights/Laws—Sexuality I 1—

Slave I—Unity I—Woman OT 1—Work I 3
Sodom & Gomorrha→City OT 2—Fire OT III—Hell OT II—Punishments 1
Solidarity→Adam—Fathers & Father I 2, II—Generation—Man I 1 o—Responsibility 1—Reward II 1.2—Suffering NT III 1
Solidity→Amen—Faithfulness—Rock 2—Stone—Truth OT
SOLITUDE
Solomon→Peace II 2—Temple OT I 3—Wisdom OT I 1; NT I 1
Son of David→David 3—Messiah OT I 1
SON OF GOD
SON OF MAN
Song→Blessing III 5—Joy—Praise II, III—Prayer V 1—Thanksgiving
Sonship→Fathers & Father—Son of God
Sorrow→Console—Sadness—Suffering
SOUL
SOWING
SPIRIT
SPIRIT OF GOD
Spring→Life III 2, IV 2—Rock 2—Water
SPOUSE
Stability→Abide—Faithfulness—Mountain I 1—Truth
STARS
State (political)→Authority—Nations—People
Stele→Altar—Covenant OT I 3—Pilgrimage OT 1—Witness OT I
STERILITY
STONE
STORM
STRANGER
Struggle→Enemy—Faithfulness NT 2—Prayer V 2 a—Run 2—Trial/Temptation—War
Succour→ Almsgiving — Gift — Grace — Salvation
SUFFERING
Sun→Light & Dark OT II 1.3; NT I 1—Stars—Time OT I 1—Week 1
Sunday→Day of the Lord NT III 3—Feasts NT II—Passover III 1—Sabbath NT 2—Time NT II 3—Week 2
Supper→Covenant NT I—Eucharist—Meal III—Passover II
Supplication→Knee 2—Prayer II 3, V 2 a c
Support→Confidence—Pride—Rock 1
Swear→Human Speech 1—Oath
Symbol→Angels OT 2—Animals O—Antichrist OT 1—Figure—Mystery—Numbers—Parable I 1—Revelation OT I 2, II 2—Sign
Synagogue→Church I—Jew II

T

Tablets of the Law→Ark of the Covenant O, II—Book II—Covenant OT I 3—Law *B*—Witness OT II 2

Tabor→Mountain I

Talion→Enemy II 3—Pardon III—Vengeance 2.4—Villence III 1, IV 3

TASTE

TEACH

Tears→Book III—Death OT I 1.3—Laughter 2—Repentance/Conversion OT I 2, II 3, III 1—Sadness—Suffering

Temperance→Drunkenness—Wine

TEMPLE

Temptation→Trial/Temptation

Tempter→Adam II 1—Satan

TENDERNESS

Tent→Abide—Ark of the Covenant—Feasts—House II 1—Temple OT I 1—Witness OT II 2

Testament→Covenant NT—Farewell Speeches—Inheritance

THANKSGIVING

Theophany→Apparitions of Christ 1—Ascension II 4—Day of the Lord OT; NT I—Fire OT I—Glory III 2—Light & Dark OT I 2, II 2; NT I 3—Pentecost II 1—Presence of God OT II—Resurrection NT I 2—Revelation—See OT I 1—Storm—Transfiguration

Thirst→Hunger & Thirst

Thoughts→Heart O—Loins 2—Plan of God OT IV—Will of God OT I 2 b

Throne→Ark of the Covenant O, III—David—King

TIME

Tithe→Almsgiving OT 2; NT 1—First-Fruits I 3—Gift OT 2

Tomb→Burial—Resurrection NT I 1.2

TONGUE

Torah→Law

Town→City

TRADITION

TRANSFIGURATION

Treason→ Deception/Disappointment III —Friend 1—Meal I—Sadness NT 2

TREE

TRIAL

TRIAL/TEMPTATION

Tribe→Fathers & Father I 2—Israel OT 1 b—King OT O—People

Tribulation→Calamity — Persecution — Suffering—Trial/Temptation

Trinity→Baptism IV 2—God NT IV—Love I NT 4

TRUTH

Twelve→Apostles I—Church III 2—Election NT II 1—Israel OT 1 b—Numbers I 1, II 1

Type→Figure

Tyrant→ Arrogance — Babel/Babylon 5.6 — Power III 1

Tyre & Sidon→City OT 2—Repentance/Conversion NT II

U

UNBELIEF

UNITY

Universe→Ascension II 2—Creation—Head 2.4—Heaven I, II—New III 3 b—Sea 1—Stars Water I—World

Universalism→Abraham II 4—Brother—Mission OT II 2—Nations—Neighbor—Pentecost II—People *B* I 2—Plan of God—Praise II 3

V

Vanity→Arrogance—Creation NT II 3—Deception/Disappointment I 1—Flesh I 3 b—Glory II—Humility—Idols—Lie II 1—Pride OT 2—Shadow I 1

Veil→Clothing I 1, II 4—Moses 5—Woman NT 3

VENGEANCE

Vices→Virtues & Vices

Victim→Altar—Blood OT 3—Eucharist IV—Lamb of God—Redemption NT 2—Sacrifice

VICTORY

Vigilance→Watch

VINE

VINTAGE

Violation→Adultery—Covenant OT III 1—Oath OT 3—Sin III 2 c—Spouse OT 1—Violence I

VIOLENCE

VIRGINITY

VIRTUES & VICES

Visions→Charisms I—Dreams—Prophet OT I 1—Revelation OT I 2—See OT I

VISITATION

W

Waiting→Calamity 2—Day of the Lord OT II; NT II—Desire—Heaven VI—Hope—Kingdom OT III—Memory 3—Messiah OT; NT I—Patience—Salvation NT II 3—Watch I

Walk→Abide O—Follow—Run—Virtues & Vices 1—Way

WAR

Wash→Baptism—Blood NT 4—Pardon O—Pure—Water

WATCH
WATER
WAY
Ways of God→Law *B* I 4—Way—Will of God
Weakness→Child—Flesh I 3 b—Poor—Power
IV, V 3—Responsibility 1—Sickness/healing
Strength—Widows 1—Woman OT 3
WEALTH
Wedding→Lamb of God 3—Marriage—Meal
III—Spouse
Wedding Garment→Clothing II 4—Kingdom
NT II 3—Meal IV—Spouse NT 3 b c—
White 2
WEEK
Weep→Console—Death OT I 1.3—Repent-
ance/Conversion OT I 2—Sadness—Suffer-
ing
Welcome→Calling—Child II—Confession O—
Disciple—Faith OT I; NT I 1.2, II 2—Gate
—Gift—Hardness of Heart II 1—Heart II
2 a—Hospitality—Listen—Reconciliation I 4
—Salvation NT I 1 a—Simple 2—Teach OT
II 2; NT I 3—Visitation NT 1—Watch I—
Will of God—Word of God OT III 2; NT I
2, II 2, III 2
WHITE
WIDOWS
WILL OF GOD
Wind→Pentecost I 1—Presence of God OT II
—Spirit OT 1—Spirit of God O
WINE
Wings→Shadow II 2

WISDOM
Wish→Amen o—Blessing II 3—Curse IV—
Desire
WITNESS
WOMAN
Wood→Cross I, II 3—Tree 3
WORD OF GOD
WORK
Worker→Harvest III 2 b—Work—Works
WORKS
WORLD
WRATH
WRITING

Y

YAHWEH
Year→Feasts OT I; NT II—Time OT I—Week
1
Yes→Amen—Beatitude NT I 1—Fulfill NT 1
—Promises III 1—Truth NT 1
Yoke→Law *C* I 2, II 2, III 2
Youth→New—Old Age

Z

ZEAL
Zealots→Zeal II
Zion→Fatherland OT 2—Jerusalem—Mary I
2, III 4, V 2—Mother II 3—Mountain O, II
2.3, III—Servant of God II 1—Unity II

INDEX

This index makes no more claim than does the *Dictionary* itself to present a synthesis of biblical theology. Other presentations could have been chosen; we offer this one simply as guidance to the reader who would like to study the Bible from various specific aspects. It would have been possible to make the Index more detailed, or to organize it differently, since the same article could be mentioned several times under various headings; but we have avoided multiplying entries, in the interests of conciseness. The section titles and subtitles present the overall structure that justifies our linking of ideas, which may at first seem strange. The words italicised are those which seem most suitable to read first, as a beginning.

A. GOD, FATHER AND CREATOR. HIS PLAN

I. THE LIVING GOD
—*God*—holy—life—love
—name—(fathers &) Father—Yahweh

II. THE WORD OF GOD, creative and revealing
Word of God—*plan of God*—will of God

A) GOD CREATES THE UNIVERSE

1. Creation
creation—*power*—*good & evil*

2. Creatures
world—paradise
heaven—*angels*—stars—white
earth—sea—water—fire—storm—mountain—rock—stone
tree—animals—dove

3. Man
• his make-up
Adam—*man*—*woman*—sexuality
spirit—*flesh*—soul—body
conscience—responsibility—desire—hunger & thirst—freedom
heart—loins—face—lips—tongue—arm & hand—right hand

• his nourishment
nourishment—meal—bread—wine—cup—milk—oil—salt

• his activity and his goods
work—rest—sleep
wealth—clothing—lamp—seal
farewell speeches—burial

• his means of expression
human speech—oath—silence & laughter

• his fruitfulness
marriage—virginity—widows
fruitfulness—sterility—fathers (& Father)—mother—generation

B. THE LORD JESUS, SAVIOR

I. HIS PERSON

II. HIS MISSION

INDEX

D) Its Life